Jordan

P9-DCV-280

Webster's Everyday Spanish-English Dictionary

Created in Cooperation with
the Editors of
MERRIAM-WEBSTER

FEDERAL
STREET
PRESS

A Division of Merriam-Webster, Incorporated
Springfield, Massachusetts

Copyright © by Merriam-Webster, Incorporated

Federal Street Press is a trademark of
Federal Street Press,
a division of Merriam-Webster, Incorporated

All rights reserved. No part of this book covered by
the copyrights hereon may be reproduced or copied
in any form or by any means—graphic, electronic,
or mechanical, including photocopying, taping, or
information storage and retrieval systems—without
written permission of the publisher.

This 2011 edition published by Federal Street Press,
a division of Merriam-Webster, Incorporated
P.O. Box 281
Springfield, MA 01102

Federal Street Press books are available for bulk
purchase for sales promotion and premium use. For
details write the manager of special sales, Federal
Street Press, P.O. Box 281, Springfield, MA 01102

ISBN 978-1-59695-117-4

Printed in the United States of America

3rd Printing Craftline Graphics, Inc. Fort Wayne IN 05/2015 NK

Contents

Preface 4a

Conjugation of Spanish Verbs 6a

Irregular English Verbs 18a

Abbreviations Used in This Work 23a

Pronunciation Symbols 24a

Spanish-English Dictionary 1

English-Spanish Dictionary 187

Common Spanish Abbreviations 417

Spanish Numbers 422

English Numbers 424

Preface

This Spanish-English Dictionary is a concise reference to the core vocabulary of Spanish and English. Its 40,000 entries and over 50,000 translations provide up-to-date coverage of the basic vocabulary and idioms in both languages. In addition, the book includes many specifically Latin-American words and phrases.

IPA (International Phonetic Alphabet) pronunciations are given for all English words. Included as well are tables of irregular verbs in both languages and the most common Spanish and English abbreviations.

This book shares many details of presentation with larger Spanish-English Dictionaries, but for reasons of conciseness it also has a number of features uniquely its own. Users need to be familiar with the following major features of this dictionary.

Main entries follow one another in strict alphabetical order, without regard to intervening spaces or hyphens. The Spanish letter combinations *ch* and *ll* are alphabetized within the letters *C* and *L*; however, the Spanish letter *ñ* is alphabetized separately between *N* and *O*.

Homographs (words spelled the same but having different meanings or parts of speech) are run on at a single main entry if they are closely related. Run-on homograph entries are replaced in the text by a boldfaced swung dash (as **haber** . . . *v aux* . . . — ∼ *nm* . . .). Homographs of distinctly different origin (as **date¹** and **date²**) are given separate entries.

Run-on entries for related words that are not homographs may also follow the main entry. Thus we have the main entry **calcular** *vt* followed by run-on entries for — **calculador, -dora** *adj* . . . — **calculadora** *nf* . . . and — **cálculo** *nm*. However, if a related word falls later in the alphabet than a following unrelated main entry, it will be entered at its own place; **ear** and its run-on — **eardrum** precede the main entry **earl** which is followed by the main entry **earlobe**.

Variant spellings appear at the main entry separated by *or* (as **judgment** *or* **judgement, paralyze** *or Brit* **paralyse,** and **cacahuate** *or* **cacahuete**).

Inflected forms of English verbs, adjectives, adverbs, and nouns are shown when they are irregular (as **wage** . . . **waged; waging; ride** . . . **rode; ridden; good** . . . **better, best;** and **fly** . . . *n, pl* **flies**) or when there might be doubt about their spelling (as **ego** . . . *n, pl* **egos**). Inflected forms of Spanish irregular verbs are shown in the section Conjugation of Spanish Verbs on page 6a; numerical references to this table are included at the main entry (as **poseer** {20} *vt*). Irregular plurals of Spanish nouns or adjectives are shown at the main entry (as **ladrón, -drona** *n, mpl* **-drones**).

Cross-references are provided to lead the user to the appropriate main entry (as **mice** → **mouse** and **sobrestimar** → **sobreestimar**).

Pronunciation information is either given explicitly or implied for all English words. Pronunciation of Spanish words is assumed to be regular and is generally omitted; it is included, however, for certain foreign borrowings (as **pizza** ['pitsa, 'pisa]). A full list of the pronunciation symbols used appears on page 24a.

The grammatical function of entry words is indicated by an italic **functional label** (as *vt, adj,* and *nm*). Italic **usage labels** may be added at the entry or sense as well (as **timbre** *nm* . . . 4 *Lat* : postage stamp, **center** *or Brit* **centre** . . . *n* . . ., or **garra** *nf* . . . 2 *fam* : hand, paw). These labels are also included in the translations (**bag** *n* . . . 2 HANDBAG : bolso *m,* cartera *f Lat*).

Usage notes are occasionally placed before a translation to clarify meaning or use (as **que** *conj* . . . 2 (*in comparisons*) : than).

Synonyms may appear before the translation word(s) in order to provide context for the meaning of an entry word or sense (as **sitio** *nm* . . . 2 ESPACIO : room, space; or **meet** . . . *vt* . . . 2 SATISFY : satisfacer).

Bold notes are sometimes used before a translation to introduce a plural sense or a common phrase using the main entry word (as **mueble** *nm* . . . 2 ~s *nmpl* : furniture, furnishings, or **call** . . . vt . . . 2 ~ **off** : cancelar). Note that when an entry word is repeated in a bold note, it is replaced by a swung dash.

Conjugation of Spanish Verbs

Simple Tenses

Tense	Regular Verbs Ending in -AR hablar	
PRESENT INDICATIVE	hablo	hablamos
	hablas	habláis
	habla	hablan
PRESENT SUBJUNCTIVE	hable	hablemos
	hables	habléis
	hable	hablen
PRETERIT INDICATIVE	hablé	hablamos
	hablaste	hablasteis
	habló	hablaron
IMPERFECT INDICATIVE	hablaba	hablábamos
	hablabas	hablabais
	hablaba	hablaban
IMPERFECT SUBJUNCTIVE	hablara	habláramos
	hablaras	hablarais
	hablara	hablaran
	or	
	hablase	hablásemos
	hablases	hablaseis
	hablase	hablasen
FUTURE INDICATIVE	hablaré	hablaremos
	hablarás	hablaréis
	hablará	hablarán
FUTURE SUBJUNCTIVE	hablare	habláremos
	hablares	hablareis
	hablare	hablaren
CONDITIONAL	hablaría	hablaríamos
	hablarías	hablaríais
	hablaría	hablarían
IMPERATIVE		hablemos
	habla	hablad
	hable	hablen
PRESENT PARTICIPLE (GERUND)	hablando	
PAST PARTICIPLE	hablado	

Regular Verbs Ending in -ER		**Regular Verbs Ending in -IR**	
comer		vivir	
como	comemos	vivo	vivimos
comes	coméis	vives	vivís
come	comen	vive	viven
coma	comamos	viva	vivamos
comas	comáis	vivas	viváis
coma	coman	viva	vivan
comí	comimos	viví	vivimos
comiste	comisteis	viviste	vivisteis
comió	comieron	vivió	vivieron
comía	comíamos	vivía	vivíamos
comías	comíais	vivías	vivíais
comía	comían	vivía	vivían
comiera	comiéramos	viviera	viviéramos
comieras	comierais	vivieras	vivierais
comiera	comieran	viviera	vivieran
or		*or*	
comiese	comiésemos	viviese	viviésemos
comieses	comieseis	vivieses	vivieseis
comiese	comiesen	viviese	viviesen
comeré	comeremos	viviré	viviremos
comerás	comeréis	vivirás	viviréis
comerá	comerán	vivirá	vivirán
comiere	comiéremos	viviere	viviéremos
comieres	comiereis	vivieres	viviereis
comiere	comieren	viviere	vivieren
comería	comeríamos	viviría	viviríamos
comerías	comeríais	vivirías	viviríais
comería	comerían	viviría	vivirían
	comamos		vivamos
come	comed	vive	vivid
coma	coman	viva	vivan
comiendo		viviendo	
comido		vivido	

Compound Tenses

1. Perfect Tenses

The perfect tenses are formed with *haber* and the past participle:

PRESENT PERFECT
> he hablado, etc. (*indicative*);
> haya hablado, etc. (*subjunctive*)

PAST PERFECT
> había hablado, etc. (*indicative*);
> hubiera hablado, etc. (*subjunctive*)
> *or*
> hubiese hablado, etc. (*subjunctive*)

PRETERIT PERFECT
> hube hablado, etc. (*indicative*)

FUTURE PERFECT
> habré hablado, etc. (*indicative*)

CONDITIONAL PERFECT
> habría hablado, etc. (*indicative*)

2. Progressive Tenses

The progressive tenses are formed with *estar* and the present participle:

PRESENT PROGRESSIVE
> estoy llamando, etc. (*indicative*);
> esté llamando, etc. (*subjunctive*)

IMPERFECT PROGRESSIVE
> estaba llamando, etc. (*indicative*);
> estuviera llamando, etc. (*subjunctive*)
> *or*
> estuviese llamando, etc. (*subjunctive*)

PRETERIT PROGRESSIVE
> estuve llamando, etc. (*indicative*)

FUTURE PROGRESSIVE
> estaré llamando, etc. (*indicative*)

CONDITIONAL PROGRESSIVE
     estaría llamando, etc. (*indicative*)

PRESENT PERFECT PROGRESSIVE
     he estado llamando, etc. (*indicative*);
     haya estado llamando, etc. (*subjunctive*)

PAST PERFECT PROGRESSIVE
     había estado llamando, etc. (*indicative*);
     hubiera estado llamando, etc. (*subjunctive*)
     or
     hubiese estado llamando, etc. (*subjunctive*)

Irregular Verbs

The *imperfect subjunctive*, the *future subjunctive*, the *conditional*, and most forms of the *imperative* are not included in the model conjugations, but can be derived as follows:

The *imperfect subjunctive* and the *future subjunctive* are formed from the third person plural form of the preterit tense by removing the last syllable (*-ron*) and adding the appropriate suffix:

PRETERIT INDICATIVE, THIRD PERSON PLURAL (querer)	quisieron
IMPERFECT SUBJUNCTIVE (querer)	quisiera, quisieras, etc. *or* quisiese, quisieses, etc.
FUTURE SUBJUNCTIVE (querer)	quisiere, quisieres, etc.

The conditional uses the same stem as the future indicative:

FUTURE INDICATIVE (poner)	pondré, pondrás, etc.
CONDITIONAL (poner)	pondría, pondrías, etc.

The third person singular, first person plural, and third person plural forms of the *imperative* are the same as the corresponding forms of the present subjunctive.

The second person singular form of the *imperative* is generally the same as the third person singular of the present indicative. Exceptions are noted in the model conjugations list.

The second person plural *(vosotros)* form of the *imperative* is formed by removing the final *-r* of the infinitive form and adding a *-d* (ex.: *oír* → *oíd*).

Model Conjugations of Irregular Verbs

The model conjugations below include the following simple tenses: the *present indicative* (*IND*), the *present subjunctive* (*SUBJ*), the *preterit indicative* (*PRET*), the *imperfect indicative* (*IMPF*), the *future indicative* (*FUT*), the second person singular form of the *imperative* (*IMPER*) when it differs from the third person singular of the present indicative, the *gerund* or *present participle* (*PRP*), and the *past participle* (*PP*). Each set of conjugations is preceded by the corresponding infinitive form of the verb, shown in bold type. Only tenses containing irregularities are listed, and the irregular verb forms within each tense are displayed in bold type.

Each irregular verb entry in the Spanish-English section of this dictionary is cross-referenced by number to one of the following model conjugations. These cross-reference numbers are shown in curly braces { } immediately following the entry's functional label.

1 **abolir** *(defective verb)* : *IND* abolimos, abolís *(other forms not used); SUBJ (not used); IMPER (only second person plural is used)*

2 **abrir** : *PP* abierto

3 **actuar** : *IND* **actúo, actúas, actúa**, actuamos, actuáis, **actúan**; *SUBJ* **actúe, actúes, actúe**, actuemos, actuéis, **actúen**; *IMPER* **actúa**

4 **adquirir** : *IND* **adquiero, adquieres, adquiere**, adquirimos, adquirís, **adquieren**; *SUBJ* **adquiera, adquieras, adquiera**, adquiramos, adquiráis, **adquieran**; *IMPER* **adquiere**

5 **airar** : *IND* **aíro, aíras, aíra**, airamos, airáis, **aíran**; *SUBJ* **aíre, aíres, aíre**, airemos, airéis, **aíren**; *IMPER* **aíra**

6 **andar** : *PRET* **anduve, anduviste, anduvo, anduvimos, anduvisteis, anduvieron**

7 **asir** : *IND* **asgo**, ases, ase, asimos, asís, asen; *SUBJ* **asga, asgas, asga, asgamos, asgáis, asgan**

8 **aunar** : *IND* **aúno, aúnas, aúna**, aunamos, aunáis, **aúnan**; *SUBJ* **aúne, aúnes, aúne**, aunemos, aunéis, **aúnen**; *IMPER* **aúna**

9 **avergonzar** : *IND* **avergüenzo, avergüenzas, avergüenza**, avergonzamos, avergonzáis, **avergüenzan**; *SUBJ* **avergüence, avergüences, avergüence**, avergoncemos, avergoncéis, **avergüencen**; *PRET* **avergoncé**; *IMPER* **avergüenza**

10 **averiguar** : *SUBJ* **averigüe, averigües, averigüe, averigüemos, averigüéis, averigüen;** *PRET* **averigüé,** averiguaste, averiguó, averiguamos, averiguasteis, averiguaron

11 **bendecir** : *IND* **bendigo, bendices, bendice,** bendecimos, bendecís, **bendicen;** *SUBJ* **bendiga, bendigas, bendiga, bendigamos, bendigáis, bendigan;** *PRET* **bendije, bendijiste, bendijo, bendijimos, bendijisteis, bendijeron;** *IMPER* **bendice**

12 **caber** : *IND* **quepo,** cabes, cabe, cabemos, cabéis, caben; *SUBJ* **quepa, quepas, quepa, quepamos, quepáis, quepan;** *PRET* **cupe, cupiste, cupo, cupimos, cupisteis, cupieron;** *FUT* **cabré, cabrás, cabrá, cabremos, cabréis, cabrán**

13 **caer** : *IND* **caigo,** caes, cae, caemos, caéis, caen; *SUBJ* **caiga, caigas, caiga, caigamos, caigáis, caigan;** *PRET* caí, **caíste, cayó, caímos, caísteis, cayeron;** *PRP* **cayendo;** *PP* **caído**

14 **cocer** : *IND* **cuezo, cueces, cuece,** cocemos, cocéis, **cuecen;** *SUBJ* **cueza, cuezas, cueza, cozamos, cozáis, cuezan;** *IMPER* **cuece**

15 **coger** : *IND* **cojo,** coges, coge, cogemos, cogéis, cogen; *SUBJ* **coja, cojas, coja, cojamos, cojáis, cojan**

16 **colgar** : *IND* **cuelgo, cuelgas, cuelga,** colgamos, colgáis, **cuelgan;** *SUBJ* **cuelgue, cuelgues, cuelgue, colguemos, colguéis, cuelguen;** *PRET* **colgué,** colgaste, colgó, colgamos, colgasteis, colgaron; *IMPER* **cuelga**

17 **concernir** *(defective verb; used only in the third person singular and plural of the present indicative, present subjunctive, and imperfect subjunctive) see* 25 **discernir**

18 **conocer** : *IND* **conozco,** conoces, conoce, conocemos, conocéis, conocen; *SUBJ* **conozca, conozcas, conozca, conozcamos, conozcáis, conozcan**

19 **contar** : *IND* **cuento, cuentas, cuenta,** contamos, contáis, **cuentan;** *SUBJ* **cuente, cuentes, cuente,** contemos, contéis, **cuenten;** *IMPER* **cuenta**

20 **creer** : *PRET* creí, **creíste, creyó, creímos, creísteis, creyeron;** *PRP* **creyendo;** *PP* **creído**

21 **cruzar** : *SUBJ* **cruce, cruces, cruce, crucemos, crucéis, crucen;** *PRET* **crucé,** cruzaste, cruzó, cruzamos, cruzasteis, cruzaron

22 **dar** : *IND* **doy,** das, da, damos, **dais,** dan; *SUBJ* **dé,** des, **dé,** demos, **deis,** den; *PRET* **di, diste, dio, dimos, disteis, dieron**

23 **decir** : *IND* **digo, dices, dice,** decimos, decís, **dicen;** *SUBJ* **diga, digas, diga, digamos, digáis, digan;** *PRET* **dije, dijiste, dijo,** dijimos, dijisteis, dijeron; *FUT* **diré, dirás, dirá, diremos, diréis, dirán;** *IMPER* **di;** *PRP* **diciendo;** *PP* **dicho**

24 **delinquir** : *IND* **delinco,** delinques, delinque, delinquimos, delinquís, delinquen; *SUBJ* **delinca, delincas, delinca, delincamos, delincáis, delincan**

25 **discernir** : *IND* **discierno, disciernes, discierne,** discernimos, discernís, **disciernen;** *SUBJ* **discierna, disciernas, discierna,** discernamos, discernáis, **disciernan;** *IMPER* **discierne**

26 **distinguir** : *IND* **distingo,** distingues, distingue, distinguimos, distinguís, distinguen; *SUBJ* **distinga, distingas, distinga, distingamos, distingáis, distingan**

27 **dormir** : *IND* **duermo, duermes, duerme,** dormimos, dormís, **duermen;** *SUBJ* **duerma, duermas, duerma, durmamos, durmáis, duerman;** *PRET* dormí, dormiste, **durmió,** dormimos, dormisteis, **durmieron;** *IMPER* **duerme;** *PRP* **durmiendo**

28 **elegir** : *IND* **elijo, eliges, elige,** elegimos, elegís, **eligen;** *SUBJ* **elija, elijas, elija, elijamos, elijáis, elijan;** *PRET* elegí, elegiste, **eligió,** elegimos, elegisteis, **eligieron;** *IMPER* **elige;** *PRP* **eligiendo**

29 **empezar** : *IND* **empiezo, empiezas, empieza,** empezamos, empezáis, **empiezan;** *SUBJ* **empiece, empieces, empiece, empecemos, empecéis, empiecen;** *PRET* **empecé,** empezaste, empezó, empezamos, empezasteis, empezaron; *IMPER* **empieza**

30 **enraizar** : *IND* **enraízo, enraízas, enraíza,** enraizamos, enraizáis, **enraízan;** *SUBJ* **enraíce, enraíces, enraíce, enraicemos, enraicéis, enraícen;** *PRET* **enraicé,** enraizaste, enraizó, enraizamos, enraizasteis, enraizaron; *IMPER* **enraíza**

31 **erguir** : *IND* **irgo** *or* **yergo, irgues** *or* **yergues, irgue** *or* **yergue,** erguimos, erguís, **irguen** *or* **yerguen;** *SUBJ* **irga** *or* **yerga, irgas** *or* **yergas, irga** *or* **yerga, irgamos, irgáis, irgan** *or* **yergan;** *PRET* erguí, erguiste, **irguió,** erguimos, erguisteis, **irguieron;** *IMPER* **irgue** *or* **yergue;** *PRP* **irguiendo**

32 **errar** : *IND* **yerro, yerras, yerra,** erramos, erráis, **yerran;** *SUBJ* **yerre, yerres, yerre,** erremos, erréis, **yerren;** *IMPER* **yerra**

33 **escribir** : *PP* **escrito**

34 **estar** : *IND* **estoy, estás, está,** estamos, estáis, **están;** *SUBJ* **esté, estés, esté,** estemos, estéis, **estén;** *PRET* **estuve, estuviste, estuvo, estuvimos, estuvisteis, estuvieron;** *IMPER* **está**

35 **exigir** : *IND* **exijo,** exiges, exige, exigimos, exigís, exigen; *SUBJ* **exija, exijas, exija, exijamos, exijáis, exijan**

36 **forzar** : *IND* **fuerzo, fuerzas, fuerza,** forzamos, forzáis, **fuerzan;** *SUBJ* **fuerce, fuerces, fuerce, forcemos, forcéis, fuercen;** *PRET* **forcé,** forzaste, forzó, forzamos, forzasteis, forzaron; *IMPER* **fuerza**

37 **freír** : *IND* **frío, fríes, fríe, freímos,** freís, **fríen;** *SUBJ* **fría, frías, fría, friamos, friáis, frían;** *PRET* **freí, freíste, frió, freímos, freísteis, frieron;** *IMPER* **fríe;** *PRP* **friendo;** *PP* **frito**

38 **gruñir** : *PRET* **gruñí,** gruñiste, **gruñó,** gruñimos, gruñisteis, **gruñeron;** *PRP* **gruñendo**

39 **haber** : *IND* **he, has, ha, hemos,** habéis, **han;** *SUBJ* **haya, hayas, haya, hayamos, hayáis, hayan;** *PRET* **hube, hubiste, hubo, hubimos, hubisteis, hubieron;** *FUT* **habré, habrás, habrá, habremos, habréis, habrán;** *IMPER* **he**

40 **hacer** : *IND* **hago,** haces, hace, hacemos, hacéis, hacen; *SUBJ* **haga, hagas, haga, hagamos, hagáis, hagan;** *PRET* **hice, hiciste, hizo, hicimos, hicisteis, hicieron;** *FUT* **haré, harás, hará, haremos, haréis, harán;** *IMPER* **haz;** *PP* **hecho**

41 **huir** : *IND* **huyo, huyes, huye,** huimos, huís, **huyen;** *SUBJ* **huya, huyas, huya, huyamos, huyáis, huyan;** *PRET* **huí,** huiste, **huyó,** huimos, huisteis, **huyeron;** *IMPER* **huye;** *PRP* **huyendo**

42 **imprimir** : *PP* **impreso**

43 **ir** : *IND* **voy, vas, va, vamos, vais, van;** *SUBJ* **vaya, vayas, vaya, vayamos, vayáis, vayan;** *PRET* **fui, fuiste, fue, fuimos, fuisteis, fueron;** *IMPF* **iba, ibas, iba, íbamos, ibais, iban;** *IMPER* **ve;** *PRP* **yendo;** *PP* **ido**

44 **jugar** : *IND* **juego, juegas, juega,** jugamos, jugáis, **juegan;** *SUBJ* **juegue, juegues, juegue, juguemos, juguéis, jueguen;** *PRET* **jugué,** jugaste, jugó, jugamos, jugasteis, jugaron; *IMPER* **juega**

45 **lucir** : *IND* **luzco,** luces, luce, lucimos, lucís, lucen; *SUBJ* **luzca, luzcas, luzca, luzcamos, luzcáis, luzcan**

46 **morir** : *IND* **muero, mueres, muere,** morimos, morís,

mueren; *SUBJ* **muera, mueras, muera, muramos, muráis, mueran;** *PRET* morí, moriste, **murió,** morimos, moristeis, **murieron;** *IMPER* **muere;** *PRP* **muriendo;** *PP* **muerto**

47 **mover** : *IND* **muevo, mueves, mueve,** movemos, movéis, **mueven;** *SUBJ* **mueva, muevas, mueva,** movamos, mováis, **muevan;** *IMPER* **mueve**

48 **nacer** : *IND* **nazco,** naces, nace, nacemos, nacéis, nacen; *SUBJ* **nazca, nazcas, nazca, nazcamos, nazcáis, nazcan**

49 **negar** : *IND* **niego, niegas, niega,** negamos, negáis, **niegan;** *SUBJ* **niegue, niegues, niegue, neguemos, neguéis, nieguen;** *PRET* **negué,** negaste, negó, negamos, negasteis, negaron; *IMPER* **niega**

50 **oír** : *IND* **oigo, oyes, oye, oímos,** oís, **oyen;** *SUBJ* **oiga, oigas, oiga, oigamos, oigáis, oigan;** *PRET* **oí, oíste, oyó, oímos, oísteis, oyeron;** *IMPER* **oye;** *PRP* **oyendo;** *PP* **oído**

51 **oler** : *IND* **huelo, hueles, huele,** olemos, oléis, **huelen;** *SUBJ* **huela, huelas, huela,** olamos, oláis, **huelan;** *IMPER* **huele**

52 **pagar** : *SUBJ* **pague, pagues, pague, paguemos, paguéis, paguen;** *PRET* **pagué,** pagaste, pagó, pagamos, pagasteis, pagaron

53 **parecer** : *IND* **parezco,** pareces, parece, parecemos, parecéis, parecen; *SUBJ* **parezca, parezcas, parezca, parezcamos, parezcáis, parezcan**

54 **pedir** : *IND* **pido, pides, pide,** pedimos, pedís, **piden;** *SUBJ* **pida, pidas, pida, pidamos, pidáis, pidan;** *PRET* pedí, pediste, **pidió,** pedimos, pedisteis, **pidieron;** *IMPER* **pide;** *PRP* **pidiendo**

55 **pensar** : *IND* **pienso, piensas, piensa,** pensamos, pensáis, **piensan;** *SUBJ* **piense, pienses, piense,** pensemos, penséis, **piensen;** *IMPER* **piensa**

56 **perder** : *IND* **pierdo, pierdes, pierde,** perdemos, perdéis, **pierden;** *SUBJ* **pierda, pierdas, pierda,** perdamos, perdáis, **pierdan;** *IMPER* **pierde**

57 **placer** : *IND* **plazco,** places, place, placemos, placéis, placen; *SUBJ* **plazca, plazcas, plazca, plazcamos, plazcáis, plazcan;** *PRET* plací, placiste, plació *or* **plugo,** placimos, placisteis, placieron *or* **pluguieron**

58 **poder** : *IND* **puedo, puedes, puede,** podemos, podéis, **pueden;** *SUBJ* **pueda, puedas, pueda,** podamos, podáis, **puedan;** *PRET*

pude, pudiste, pudo, pudimos, pudisteis, pudieron; *FUT* **podré, podrás, podrá, podremos, podréis, podrán;** *IMPER* **puede;** *PRP* **pudiendo**

59 **podrir** *or* **pudrir** : *PP* **podrido** (*all other forms based on* **pudrir**)

60 **poner** : *IND* **pongo,** pones, pone, ponemos, ponéis, ponen; *SUBJ* **ponga, pongas, ponga, pongamos, pongáis, pongan;** *PRET* **puse, pusiste, puso, pusimos, pusisteis, pusieron;** *FUT* **pondré, pondrás, pondrá, pondremos, pondréis, pondrán;** *IMPER* **pon;** *PP* **puesto**

61 **producir** : *IND* **produzco,** produces, produce, producimos, producís, producen; *SUBJ* **produzca, produzcas, produzca, produzcamos, produzcáis, produzcan;** *PRET* **produje, produjiste, produjo, produjimos, produjisteis, produjeron**

62 **prohibir** : *IND* **prohíbo, prohíbes, prohíbe,** prohibimos, prohibís, **prohíben;** *SUBJ* **prohíba, prohíbas, prohíba,** prohibamos, prohibáis, **prohíban;** *IMPER* **prohíbe**

63 **proveer** : *PRET* **proveí, proveíste, proveyó, proveímos, proveísteis, proveyeron;** *PRP* **proveyendo;** *PP* **provisto**

64 **querer** : *IND* **quiero, quieres, quiere,** queremos, queréis, **quieren;** *SUBJ* **quiera, quieras, quiera,** queramos, queráis, **quieran;** *PRET* **quise, quisiste, quiso, quisimos, quisisteis, quisieron;** *FUT* **querré, querrás, querrá, querremos, querréis, querrán;** *IMPER* **quiere**

65 **raer** : *IND* **rao** *or* **raigo** *or* **rayo,** raes, rae, raemos, raéis, raen; *SUBJ* **raiga** *or* **raya, raigas** *or* **rayas, raiga** *or* **raya, raigamos** *or* **rayamos, raigáis** *or* **rayáis, raigan** *or* **rayan;** *PRET* **raí, raíste, rayó, raímos, raísteis, rayeron;** *PRP* **rayendo;** *PP* **raído**

66 **reír** : *IND* **río, ríes, ríe, reímos,** reís, **ríen;** *SUBJ* **ría, rías, ría, riamos, riáis, rían;** *PRET* **reí, reíste, rió, reímos, reísteis, rieron;** *IMPER* **ríe;** *PRP* **riendo;** *PP* **reído**

67 **reñir** : *IND* **riño, riñes, riñe,** reñimos, reñís, **riñen;** *SUBJ* **riña, riñas, riña, riñamos, riñáis, riñan;** *PRET* **reñí,** reñiste, **riñó,** reñimos, reñisteis, **riñeron;** *PRP* **riñendo**

68 **reunir** : *IND* **reúno, reúnes, reúne,** reunimos, reunís, **reúnen;** *SUBJ* **reúna, reúnas, reúna,** reunamos, reunáis, **reúnan;** *IMPER* **reúne**

69 **roer** : *IND* **roo** *or* **roigo** *or* **royo,** roes, roe, roemos, roéis, roen;

SUBJ roa *or* **roiga** *or* **roya**, roas *or* **roigas** *or* **royas**, roa *or* **roiga** *or* **roya**, roamos *or* **roigamos** *or* **royamos**, roáis *or* **roigáis** *or* **royáis**, roan *or* **roigan** *or* **royan**; *PRET* roí, **roíste**, royó, roímos, **roísteis, royeron**; *PRP* **royendo**; *PP* **roído**

70 **romper** : *PP* **roto**

71 **saber** : *IND* **sé**, sabes, sabe, sabemos, sabéis, saben; *SUBJ* **sepa, sepas, sepa, sepamos, sepáis, sepan**; *PRET* **supe, supiste, supo, supimos, supisteis, supieron**; *FUT* **sabré, sabrás, sabrá, sabremos, sabréis, sabrán**

72 **sacar** : *SUBJ* **saque, saques, saque, saquemos, saquéis, saquen**; *PRET* **saqué**, sacaste, sacó, sacamos, sacasteis, sacaron

73 **salir** : *IND* **salgo**, sales, sale, salimos, salís, salen; *SUBJ* **salga, salgas, salga, salgamos, salgáis, salgan**; *FUT* **saldré, saldrás, saldrá, saldremos, saldréis, saldrán**; *IMPER* **sal**

74 **satisfacer** : *IND* **satisfago**, satisfaces, satisface, satisfacemos, satisfacéis, satisfacen; *SUBJ* **satisfaga, satisfagas, satisfaga, satisfagamos, satisfagáis, satisfagan**; *PRET* **satisfice, satisficiste, satisfizo, satisficimos, satificisteis, satisficieron**; *FUT* **satisfaré, satisfarás, satisfará, satisfaremos, satisfaréis, satisfarán**; *IMPER* **satisfaz** *or* **satisface**; *PP* **satisfecho**

75 **seguir** : *IND* **sigo, sigues, sigue**, seguimos, seguís, **siguen**; *SUBJ* **siga, sigas, siga, sigamos, sigáis, sigan**; *PRET* seguí, seguiste, **siguió**, seguimos, seguisteis, **siguieron**; *IMPER* **sigue**; *PRP* **siguiendo**

76 **sentir** : *IND* **siento, sientes, siente**, sentimos, sentís, **sienten**; *SUBJ* **sienta, sientas, sienta, sintamos, sintáis, sientan**; *PRET* sentí, sentiste, **sintió**, sentimos, sentisteis, **sintieron**; *IMPER* **siente**; *PRP* **sintiendo**

77 **ser** : *IND* **soy, eres, es, somos, sois, son**; *SUBJ* **sea, seas, sea, seamos, seáis, sean**; *PRET* **fui, fuiste, fue, fuimos, fuisteis, fueron**; *IMPF* **era, eras, era, éramos, erais, eran**; *IMPER* **sé**; *PRP* **siendo**; *PP* **sido**

78 **soler** (*defective verb; used only in the present, preterit, and imperfect indicative, and the present and imperfect subjunctive*) *see* 47 **mover**

79 **tañer** : *PRET* tañí, tañiste, **tañó**, tañimos, tañisteis, **tañeron**; *PRP* **tañendo**

80 **tener** : *IND* **tengo, tienes, tiene**, tenemos, tenéis, **tienen**; *SUBJ* **tenga, tengas, tenga, tengamos, tengáis, tengan**; *PRET* **tuve**,

tuviste, tuvo, tuvimos, tuvisteis, tuvieron; *FUT* tendré, ten-
drás, tendrá, tendremos, tendréis, tendrán; *IMPER* ten

81 traer : *IND* traigo, traes, trae, traemos, traéis, traen; *SUBJ*
    traiga, traigas, traiga, traigamos, traigáis, traigan; *PRET*
    traje, trajiste, trajo, trajimos, trajisteis, trajeron; *PRP*
    trayendo; *PP* traído

82 trocar : *IND* trueco, truecas, trueca, trocamos, trocáis, true-
    can; *SUBJ* trueque, trueques, trueque, troquemos, troquéis,
    truequen; *PRET* troqué, trocaste, trocó, trocamos, trocasteis,
    trocaron; *IMPER* trueca

83 uncir : *IND* unzo, unces, unce, uncimos, uncís, uncen; *SUBJ*
    unza, unzas, unza, unzamos, unzáis, unzan

84 valer : *IND* valgo, vales, vale, valemos, valéis, valen; *SUBJ*
    valga, valgas, valga, valgamos, valgáis, valgan; *FUT* valdré,
    valdrás, valdrá, valdremos, valdréis, valdrán

85 variar : *IND* varío, varías, varía, variamos, variáis, varían;
    SUBJ varíe, varíes, varíe, variemos, variéis, varíen; *IMPER*
    varía

86 vencer : *IND* venzo, vences, vence, vencemos, vencéis, vencen;
    SUBJ venza, venzas, venza, venzamos, venzáis, venzan

87 venir : *IND* vengo, vienes, viene, venimos, venís, vienen; *SUBJ*
    venga, vengas, venga, vengamos, vengáis, vengan; *PRET*
    vine, viniste, vino, vinimos, vinisteis, vinieron; *FUT* vendré,
    vendrás, vendrá, vendremos, vendréis, vendrán; *IMPER* ven;
    PRP viniendo

88 ver : *IND* veo, ves, ve, vemos, veis, ven; *PRET* vi, viste, vio,
    vimos, visteis, vieron; *IMPER* ve; *PRP* viendo; *PP* visto

89 volver : *IND* vuelvo, vuelves, vuelve, volvemos, volvéis, vuel-
    ven; *SUBJ* vuelva, vuelvas, vuelva, volvamos, volváis, vuel-
    van; *IMPER* vuelve; *PP* vuelto

90 yacer : *IND* yazco *or* yazgo *or* yago, yaces, yace, yacemos,
    yacéis, yacen; *SUBJ* yazca *or* yazga *or* yaga, yazcas *or* yazgas
    or yagas, yazca *or* yazga *or* yaga, yazcamos *or* yazgamos *or*
    yagamos, yazcáis *or* yazgáis *or* yagáis, yazcan *or* yazgan *or*
    yagan; *IMPER* yace *or* yaz

Irregular English Verbs

INFINITIVE	PAST	PAST PARTICIPLE
arise	arose	arisen
awake	awoke	awoken *or* awaked
be	was, were	been
bear	bore	borne
beat	beat	beaten *or* beat
become	became	become
befall	befell	befallen
begin	began	begun
behold	beheld	beheld
bend	bent	bent
beseech	beseeched *or* besought	beseeched *or* besought
beset	beset	beset
bet	bet	bet
bid	bade *or* bid	bidden *or* bid
bind	bound	bound
bite	bit	bitten
bleed	bled	bled
blow	blew	blown
break	broke	broken
breed	bred	bred
bring	brought	brought
build	built	built
burn	burned *or* burnt	burned *or* burnt
burst	burst	burst
buy	bought	bought
can	could	—
cast	cast	cast
catch	caught	caught
choose	chose	chosen
cling	clung	clung
come	came	come
cost	cost	cost
creep	crept	crept
cut	cut	cut
deal	dealt	dealt
dig	dug	dug
do	did	done
draw	drew	drawn

INFINITIVE	PAST	PAST PARTICIPLE
dream	dreamed *or* dreamt	dreamed *or* dreamt
drink	drank	drunk *or* drank
drive	drove	driven
dwell	dwelled *or* dwelt	dwelled *or* dwelt
eat	ate	eaten
fall	fell	fallen
feed	fed	fed
feel	felt	felt
fight	fought	fought
find	found	found
flee	fled	fled
fling	flung	flung
fly	flew	flown
forbid	forbade	forbidden
forecast	forecast	forecast
forego	forewent	foregone
foresee	foresaw	foreseen
foretell	foretold	foretold
forget	forgot	forgotten *or* forgot
forgive	forgave	forgiven
forsake	forsook	forsaken
freeze	froze	frozen
get	got	got *or* gotten
give	gave	given
go	went	gone
grind	ground	ground
grow	grew	grown
hang	hung	hung
have	had	had
hear	heard	heard
hide	hid	hidden *or* hid
hit	hit	hit
hold	held	held
hurt	hurt	hurt
keep	kept	kept
kneel	knelt *or* kneeled	knelt *or* kneeled
know	knew	known
lay	laid	laid
lead	led	led
lean	leaned	leaned
leap	leaped *or* leapt	leaped *or* leapt
learn	learned	learned

INFINITIVE	PAST	PAST PARTICIPLE
leave	left	left
lend	lent	lent
let	let	let
lie	lay	lain
light	lit *or* lighted	lit *or* lighted
lose	lost	lost
make	made	made
may	might	—
mean	meant	meant
meet	met	met
mow	mowed	mowed *or* mown
pay	paid	paid
put	put	put
quit	quit	quit
read	read	read
rend	rent	rent
rid	rid	rid
ride	rode	ridden
ring	rang	rung
rise	rose	risen
run	ran	run
saw	sawed	sawed *or* sawn
say	said	said
see	saw	seen
seek	sought	sought
sell	sold	sold
send	sent	sent
set	set	set
shake	shook	shaken
shall	should	—
shear	sheared	sheared *or* shorn
shed	shed	shed
shine	shone *or* shined	shone *or* shined
shoot	shot	shot
show	showed	shown *or* showed
shrink	shrank *or* shrunk	shrunk *or* shrunken
shut	shut	shut
sing	sang *or* sung	sung
sink	sank *or* sunk	sunk
sit	sat	sat
slay	slew	slain
sleep	slept	slept

INFINITIVE	PAST	PAST PARTICIPLE
slide	slid	slid
sling	slung	slung
smell	smelled *or* smelt	smelled *or* smelt
sow	sowed	sown *or* sowed
speak	spoke	spoken
speed	sped *or* speeded	sped *or* speeded
spell	spelled	spelled
spend	spent	spent
spill	spilled	spilled
spin	spun	spun
spit	spit *or* spat	spit *or* spat
split	split	split
spoil	spoiled	spoiled
spread	spread	spread
spring	sprang *or* sprung	sprung
stand	stood	stood
steal	stole	stolen
stick	stuck	stuck
sting	stung	stung
stink	stank *or* stunk	stunk
stride	strode	stridden
strike	struck	struck
swear	swore	sworn
sweep	swept	swept
swell	swelled	swelled *or* swollen
swim	swam	swum
swing	swung	swung
take	took	taken
teach	taught	taught
tear	tore	torn
tell	told	told
think	thought	thought
throw	threw	thrown
thrust	thrust	thrust
tread	trod	trodden *or* trod
wake	woke	woken *or* waked
waylay	waylaid	waylaid
wear	wore	worn
weave	wove *or* weaved	woven *or* weaved
wed	wedded	wedded
weep	wept	wept
will	would	—

INFINITIVE	PAST	PAST PARTICIPLE
win	won	won
wind	wound	wound
withdraw	withdrew	withdrawn
withhold	withheld	withheld
withstand	withstood	withstood
wring	wrung	wrung
write	wrote	written

Abbreviations in this Work

adj	adjective	*nmf*	masculine or feminine noun
adv	adverb		
adv	adverbial phrase	*nmfpl*	plural noun invariable for gender
algn	alguien (someone)	*nmfs & pl*	noun invariable for both gender and number
art	article		
Brit	Great Britain	*nmpl*	masculine plural noun
conj	conjunction	*nms & pl*	invariable singular or plural masculine noun
conj phr	conjunctive phrase		
esp	especially	*npl*	plural noun
etc	et cetera	*ns & pl*	noun invariable for plural
f	feminine		
fam	familiar or colloquial	*pl*	plural
fpl	feminine plural	*pp*	past participle
interj	interjection	*prep*	preposition
Lat	Latin America	*prep phr*	prepositional phrase
m	masculine	*pron*	pronoun
mf	masculine or feminine	*s.o.*	someone
mpl	masculine plural	*sth*	something
n	noun	*usu*	usually
nf	feminine noun	*v*	verb
nfpl	feminine plural noun	*v aux*	auxiliary verb
nfs & pl	invariable singular or plural feminine noun	*vi*	intransitive verb
		v impers	impersonal verb
nm	masculine noun	*vr*	reflexive verb
		vt	transitive verb

Pronunciation Symbols

VOWELS

æ	ask, bat, glad
ɑ	cot, bomb
a	*New England* **aunt**, *British* ask, glass, *Spanish* **casa**
ɛ	egg, bet, fed
ə	about, javelin, Alabama
ə	when italicized as in əl, əm, ən, indicates a syllabic pronunciation of the consonant as in bottle, prism, button
i	very, any, thirty, *Spanish* piña
i:	eat, bead, bee
ɪ	id, bid, pit
o	Ohio, yellower, potato, *Spanish* óvalo
o:	oats, own, zone, blow
ɔ	awl, maul, caught, paw
ʊ	sure, should, could
u:	boot, few, coo
ʌ	under, putt, bud
eɪ	eight, wade, bay
aɪ	ice, bite, tie
aʊ	out, gown, plow
ɔɪ	oyster, coil, boy
:	indicates that the preceding vowel is long. Long vowels are almost always diphthongs in English, but not in Spanish.

STRESS MARKS

'	high stress	**pen**manship
ˌ	low stress	penman**ship**

CONSONANTS

b	baby, labor, cab
d	day, ready, kid
dʒ	just, badger, fudge
ð	then, either, bathe
f	foe, tough, buff
g	go, bigger, bag
h	hot, aha
j	yes, vineyard
k	cat, keep, lacquer, flock
l	law, hollow, boil
m	mat, hemp, hammer, rim
n	new, tent, tenor, run
ŋ	rung, hang, swinger
p	pay, lapse, top
r	rope, burn, tar
s	sad, mist, kiss
ʃ	shoe, mission, slush
t	toe, button, mat
t̬	indicates that some speakers of English pronounce this sound as a voiced alveolar flap [ɾ], as in later, catty, battle
tʃ	choose, batch
θ	thin, ether, bath
v	vat, never, cave
w	wet, software
z	zoo, easy, buzz
ʒ	azure, beige
h, k, *p, t*	when italicized indicate sounds which are present in the pronunciation of some speakers of English but absent in the pronunciation of others, so that *whence* ['hwɛnts] can be pronounced as ['hwɛns], ['hwɛnts], ['wɛnts], or ['wɛns]

Spanish-English
Dictionary

A

¹ *nf* : a, first letter of the Spanish alphabet

² *prep* **1** : to **2 ~ las dos** : at two o'clock **3 al día siguiente** : (on) the following day **4 ~ pied** : on foot **5 de lunes ~ viernes** : from Monday until Friday **6 tres veces ~ la semana** : three times per week **7 ~ la** : in the manner of, like

badía *nf* : abbey

bajo *adv* **1** : down, below, downstairs **2 ~ de** *Lat* : under, beneath **3 de ~** : (at the) bottom **4 hacia ~** : downwards

balanzarse {21} *vr* : hurl oneself, rush

bandonar *vt* **1** : abandon, leave **2** RENUNCIAR A : give up — **abandonarse** *vr* **1** : neglect oneself **2 ~ a** : give oneself over to — **abandonado, -da** *adj* **1** : abandoned, deserted **3** DESCUIDADO : neglected **3** DESALIÑADO : slovenly — **abandono** *nm* **1** : abandonment, neglect **2 por ~** : by default

banico *nm* : fan — **abanicar** {72} *vt* : fan

baratar *vt* : lower the price of — **abaratarse** *vr* : become cheaper

barcar {72} *vt* **1** : cover, embrace **2** *Lat* : monopolize

barrotar *vt* : pack, cram — **abarrotes** *nmpl Lat* **1** : groceries **2 tienda de ~** : grocery store

bastecer {53} *vt* : supply, stock — **abastecimiento** *nm* : supply, provisions — **abasto** *nm* **1** : supply **2 no dar ~ a** : be unable to cope with

batir *vt* **1** : knock down, shoot down **2** DEPRIMIR : depress — **abatirse** *vr* **1** : get depressed **2 ~ sobre** : swoop down on — **abatido, -da** *adj* : dejected, depressed — **abatimiento** *nm* : depression, dejection

bdicar {72} *v* : abdicate — **abdicación** *nf, pl* **-ciones** : abdication

bdomen *nm, pl* **-dómenes** : abdomen — **abdominal** *adj* : abdominal

becé *nm* : ABC — **abecedario** *nm* : alphabet

bedul *nm* : birch

beja *nf* : bee — **abejorro** *nm* : bumblebee

berración *nf, pl* **-ciones** : aberration

abertura *nf* : opening

abeto *nm* : fir (tree)

abierto, -ta *adj* : open

abigarrado, -da *adj* : multicolored

abismo *nm* : abyss, chasm — **abismal** *adj* : vast, enormous

abjurar *vi* **~ de** : abjure

ablandar *vt* : soften (up) — **ablandarse** *vr* : soften

abnegarse {49} *vr* : deny oneself — **abnegado, -da** *adj* : self-sacrificing — **abnegación** *nf, pl* **-ciones** : self-denial

abochornar *vt* : embarrass — **abochornarse** *vr* : get embarrassed

abofetear *vt* : slap

abogado, -da *n* : lawyer — **abogacía** *nf* : legal profession — **abogar** {52} *vi* **~ por** : plead for, defend

abolengo *nm* : lineage

abolir {1} *vt* : abolish — **abolición** *nf, pl* **-ciones** : abolition

abollar *vt* : dent — **abolladura** *nf* : dent

abominar *vt* : abominate — **abominable** *adj* : abominable — **abominación** *nf, pl* **-ciones** : abomination

abonar *vt* **1** : pay (a bill, etc.) **2** : fertilize (the soil) — **abonarse** *vr* : subscribe — **abonado, -da** *n* : subscriber — **abono** *nm* **1** : payment, installment **2** FERTILIZANTE : fertilizer **3** : season ticket (to the theater, etc.)

abordar *vt* **1** : tackle (a problem) **2** : accost, approach (a person) **3** *Lat* : board — **abordaje** *nm* : boarding

aborigen *nmf, pl* **-rígenes** : aborigine — **~** *adj* : aboriginal, native

aborrecer {53} *vt* : abhor, detest — **aborrecible** *adj* : hateful — **aborrecimiento** *nm* : loathing

abortar *vi* : have a miscarriage — *vt* : abort — **aborto** *nm* : abortion, miscarriage

abotonar *vt* : button — **abotonarse** *vr* : button up

abovedado, -da *adj* : vaulted

abrasar *vt* : burn, scorch — **abrasarse** *vr* : burn up — **abrasador, -dora** *adj* : burning

abrasivo, -va *adj* : abrasive — **abrasivo** *nm* : abrasive

abrazar {21} *vt* : hug, embrace — **abrazarse** *vr* : embrace — **abraza-**

dera *nf* : clamp — **abrazo** *nm* : hug, embrace

abrebotellas *nms & pl* : bottle opener — **abrelatas** *nms & pl* : can opener

abrevadero *nm* : watering trough

abreviar *vt* **1** : shorten, abridge **2** : abbreviate (a word) — **abreviación** *nf*, *pl* **-ciones** : shortening — **abreviatura** *nf* : abbreviation

abridor *nm* : bottle opener, can opener

abrigar {52} *vt* **1** : wrap up (in clothing) **2** ALBERGAR : cherish, harbor — **abrigarse** *vr* : dress warmly — **abrigado, -da** *adj* **1** : sheltered **2** : warm, wrapped up (of persons) — **abrigo** *nm* **1** : coat, overcoat **2** REFUGIO : shelter, refuge

abril *nm* : April

abrillantar *vt* : polish, shine

abrir {2} *vt* **1** : open **2** : unlock, undo — *vi* : open up — **abrirse** *vr* **1** : open up **2** : clear up (of weather)

abrochar *vt* : button, fasten — **abrocharse** *vr* : fasten, do up

abrogar {52} *vt* : annul, repeal

abrumar *vt* : overwhelm — **abrumador, -dora** *adj* : overwhelming, oppressive

abrupto, -ta *adj* **1** ESCARPADO : steep **2** ÁSPERO : rugged, harsh **3** REPENTINO : abrupt

absceso *nm* : abscess

absolución *nf*, *pl* **-ciones** **1** : absolution **2** : acquittal (in law)

absoluto, -ta *adj* **1** : absolute, unconditional **2 en absoluto** : not at all — **absolutamente** *adv* : absolutely

absolver {89} *vt* **1** : absolve **2** : acquit (in law)

absorber *vt* **1** : absorb **2** : take up (time, energy, etc.) — **absorbente** *adj* **1** : absorbent **2** INTERESANTE : absorbing — **absorción** *nf*, *pl* **-ciones** : absorption — **absorto, -ta** *adj* : absorbed, engrossed

abstemio, -mia *adj* : abstemious — ~ *n* : teetotaler

abstenerse {80} *vr* : abstain, refrain — **abstención** *nf*, *pl* **-ciones** : abstention — **abstinencia** *nf* : abstinence

abstracción *nf*, *pl* **-ciones** : abstraction — **abstracto, -ta** *adj* : abstract — **abstraer** {81} *vt* : abstract — **abstraerse** *vr* : lose oneself in thought — **abstraído, -da** *adj* : preoccupied

absurdo, -da *adj* : absurd, ridiculous — **absurdo** *nm* : absurdity

abuchear *vt* : boo, jeer — **abucheo** *nm* : booing

abuelo, -la *n* **1** : grandfather, grandmother **2 abuelos** *nmpl* : grandparents

abulia *nf* : apathy, lethargy

abultar *vi* : bulge, be bulky — *vt* : enlarge, expand — **abultado, -da** *adj* : bulky

abundar *vi* : abound, be plentiful — **abundancia** *nf* : abundance — **abundante** *adj* : abundant

aburrir *vt* : bore — **aburrirse** *vr* : get bored — **aburrido, -da** *adj* **1** : bored **2** TEDIOSO : boring — **aburrimiento** *nm* : boredom

abusar *vi* **1** : go too far **2** ~ **de** : abuse — **abusivo, -va** *adj* : outrageous, excessive — **abuso** *nm* : abuse

abyecto, -ta *adj* : abject, wretched

acá *adv* : here, over here

acabar *vi* **1** : finish, end **2** ~ **de** : have just (done something) **3** ~ **con** : put an end to **4** ~ **por** : end up (doing sth) — *vt* : finish — **acabarse** *vr* : come to an end — **acabado, -da** *adj* **1** : finished, perfect **2** AGOTADO : old, worn-out — **acabado** *nm* : finish

academia *nf* : academy — **académico, -ca** *adj* : academic

acaecer {53} *vi* : happen, occur

acallar *vt* : quiet, silence

acalorar *vt* : stir up, excite — **acalorarse** *vr* : get worked up — **acalorado, -da** *adj* : emotional, heated

acampar *vi* : camp — **acampada** *nf* **ir de** ~ : go camping

acanalado, -da *adj* **1** : grooved **2** : corrugated (of iron, etc.)

acantilado *nm* : cliff

acaparar *vt* **1** : hoard **2** MONOPOLIZAR : monopolize

acápite *nm Lat* : paragraph

acariciar *vt* **1** : caress **2** : cherish (hopes, ideas, etc.)

ácaro *nm* : mite

acarrear *vt* **1** : haul, carry **2** OCASIONAR : give rise to — **acarreo** *nm* : transport

acaso *adv* **1** : perhaps, maybe **2 por si** ~ : just in case

acatar *vt* : comply with, respect — **acatamiento** *nm* : compliance, respect

acatarrarse *vr* : catch a cold

acaudalado, -da *adj* : wealthy, rich

acaudillar *vt* : lead

acceder *vi* **1** : agree **2** ~ **a** : gain access to, enter

acceso *nm* **1** : access **2** ENTRADA : entrance **3** : attack, bout (of an illness) — **accesible** *adj* : accessible

accesorio *nm* : accessory — **accesorio, -ria** *adj* : incidental

accidentado, -da *adj* **1** : eventful, turbulent **2** : rough, uneven (of land, etc.) **3** HERIDO : injured — **～** *n* : accident victim

accidental *adj* : accidental — **accidentarse** *vi* : have an accident — **accidente** *nm* **1** : accident **2** : unevenness (of land)

acción *nf, pl* **-ciones 1** : action **2** ACTO : act, deed **3** : share, stock (in finance) — **accionar** *vt* : activate — *vi* : gesticulate — **accionista** *nmf* : stockholder

acebo *nm* : holly

acechar *vt* : watch, stalk — **acecho** *nm* **estar al ～ por** : be on the lookout for

aceite *nm* : oil — **aceitar** *vt* : oil — **aceitera** *nf* **1** : oilcan **2** : cruet (in cookery) **3** *Lat* : oil refinery — **aceitoso, -sa** *adj* : oily

aceituna *nf* : olive

acelerar *v* : accelerate — **acelerarse** *vr* : hurry up — **aceleración** *nf, pl* **-ciones** : acceleration — **acelerador** *nm* : accelerator

acelga *nf* : (Swiss) chard

acentuar {3} *vt* **1** : accent **2** ENFATIZAR : emphasize, stress — **acentuarse** *vr* : stand out — **acento** *nm* **1** : accent **2** ÉNFASIS : stress, emphasis

acepción *nf, pl* **-ciones** : sense, meaning

aceptar *vt* : accept — **aceptable** *adj* : acceptable — **aceptación** *nf, pl* **-ciones 1** : acceptance **2** ÉXITO : success

acequia *nf* : irrigation ditch

acera *nf* : sidewalk

acerbo, -ba *adj* : harsh, caustic

acerca *prep* **～ de** : about, concerning

acercar {72} *vt* : bring near or closer — **acercarse** *vr* : approach, draw near

acero *nm* **1** : steel **2** **～ inoxidable** : stainless steel

acérrimo, -ma *adj* **1** : staunch, steadfast **2** : bitter (of an enemy)

acertar {55} *vt* : guess correctly — *vi* **1** ATINAR : be accurate **2** **～ a** : manage to — **acertado, -da** *adj* : correct, accurate

acertijo *nm* : riddle

acervo *nm* : heritage

acetona *nf* : acetone, nail-polish remover

achacar {72} *vt* : attribute, impute

achacoso, -sa *adj* : sickly

achaparrado, -da *adj* : squat, stocky

achaque *nm* : aches and pains

achatar *vt* : flatten

achicar {72} *vt* **1** : make smaller **2** ACOBARDAR : intimidate **3** : bail out

(water) — **achicarse** *vr* : become intimidated

achicharrar *vt* : scorch, burn to a crisp

achicoria *nf* : chicory

aciago, -ga *adj* : fateful, unlucky

acicalar *vt* : dress up, adorn — **acicalarse** *vr* : get dressed up

acicate *nm* **1** : spur **2** INCENTIVO : incentive

ácido, -da *adj* : acid, sour — **acidez** *nf, pl* **-deces** : acidity — **ácido** *nm* : acid

acierto *nm* **1** : correct answer **2** HABILIDAD : skill, sound judgment

aclamar *vt* : acclaim — **aclamación** *nf, pl* **-ciones** : acclaim, applause

aclarar *vt* **1** CLARIFICAR : clarify, explain **2** : rinse (clothing) **3** **～ la voz** : clear one's throat — *vi* : clear up — **aclararse** *vr* : become clear — **aclaración** *nf, pl* **-ciones** : explanation — **aclaratorio, -ria** *adj* : explanatory

aclimatar *vt* : acclimatize — **aclimatarse** *vr* **～ a** : get used to — **aclimatación** *nf, pl* **-ciones** : acclimatization

acné *nm* : acne

acobardar *vt* : intimidate — **acobardarse** *vr* : become frightened

acodarse *vr* **～ en** : lean (one's elbows) on

acoger {15} *vt* **1** REFUGIAR : shelter **2** RECIBIR : receive, welcome — **acogerse** *vr* **1** : take refuge **2** **～ a** : resort to — **acogedor, -dora** *adj* : cozy, welcoming — **acogida** *nf* **1** : welcome **2** REFUGIO : refuge

acolchar *vt* : pad

acólito *nm* MONAGUILLO : altar boy

acometer *vt* **1** : attack **2** EMPRENDER : undertake — *vi* **～ contra** : rush against — **acometida** *nf* : attack, assault

acomodar *vt* **1** ADAPTAR : adjust **2** COLOCAR : put, make a place for — **acomodarse** *vr* **1** : settle in **2** **～ a** : adapt to — **acomodado, -da** *adj* : well-to-do — **acomodaticio, -cia** *adj* : accommodating, obliging — **acomodo** *nm* : job, position

acompañar *vt* **1** : accompany **2** ADJUNTAR : enclose — **acompañamiento** *nm* : accompaniment — **acompañante** *nmf* **1** COMPAÑERO : companion **2** : accompanist (in music)

acompasado, -da *adj* : rhythmic, measured

acondicionar *vt* : fit out, equip — **acondicionado, -da** *adj* : equipped

acongojar *vt* : distress, upset — **acongojarse** *vr* : get upset

aconsejar *vt* : advise — **aconsejable** *adj* : advisable

acontecer {53} *vi* : occur, happen — **acontecimiento** *nm* : event

acopiar *vt* : gather, collect — **acopio** *nm* : collection, stock

acoplar *vt* : couple, connect — **acoplarse** *vr* : fit together — **acoplamiento** *nm* : connection, coupling

acorazado, -da *adj* : armored — **acorazado** *nm* : battleship

acordar {19} *vt* 1 : agree (on) 2 *Lat* : award — **acordarse** *vr* : remember

acorde *adj* 1 : in agreement 2 ~ **con** : in keeping with — ~ *nm* : chord (in music)

acordeón *nm, pl* **-deones** : accordion

acordonar *vt* 1 : cordon off 2 : lace up (shoes)

acorralar *vt* : corner, corral

acortar *vt* : shorten, cut short — **acortarse** *vr* : get shorter

acosar *vt* : hound, harass — **acoso** *nm* : harassment

acostar {19} *vt* : put to bed — **acostarse** *vr* 1 : go to bed 2 TUMBARSE : lie down

acostumbrar *vt* : accustom — *vi* ~ **a** : be in the habit of — **acostumbrarse** *vr* ~ **a** : get used to — **acostumbrado, -da** *adj* HABITUADO : accustomed 2 HABITUAL : usual

acotar *vt* 1 ANOTAR : annotate 2 DELIMITAR : mark off (land) — **acotación** *nf, pl* **-ciones** : marginal note — **acotado, -da** *adj* : enclosed

acre *adj* 1 : pungent 2 MORDAZ : harsh, biting

acrecentar {55} *vt* : increase — **acrecentamiento** *nm* : growth, increase

acreditar *vt* 1 : accredit, authorize 2 PROBAR : prove — **acreditarse** *vr* : prove oneself — **acreditado, -da** *adj* 1 : reputable 2 : accredited (in politics, etc.)

acreedor, -dora *adj* : worthy — ~ *n* : creditor

acribillar *vt* 1 : riddle, pepper 2 ~ **a** : harass with

acrílico *nm* : acrylic

acrimonia *nf or* **acritud** *nf* 1 : pungency 2 RESENTIMIENTO : bitterness, acrimony

acrobacia *nf* : acrobatics — **acróbata** *nmf* : acrobat — **acrobático, -ca** *adj* : acrobatic

acta *nf* 1 : certificate 2 : minutes *pl* (of a meeting)

actitud *nf* 1 : attitude 2 POSTURA : posture, position

activar *vt* 1 : activate 2 ESTIMULAR : stimulate, speed up — **actividad** *nf* : activity — **activo, -va** *adj* : active — **activo** *nm* : assets *pl*

acto *nm* 1 ACCIÓN : act, deed 2 : act (in theater) 3 **en el** ~ : right away

actor *nm* : actor — **actriz** *nf, pl* **-trices** : actress

actual *adj* : present, current — **actualidad** *nf* 1 : present time 2 ~**es** *nfpl* : current affairs — **actualizar** {21} *vt* : modernize — **actualización** *nf, pl* **-ciones** : modernization — **actualmente** *adv* : at present, nowadays

actuar {3} *vi* 1 : act, perform 2 ~ **de** : act as

acuarela *nf* : watercolor

acuario *nm* : aquarium

acuartelar *vt* : quarter (troops)

acuático, -ca *adj* : aquatic, water

acuchillar *vt* : knife, stab

acudir *vi* 1 : go, come 2 ~ **a** : be present at, attend 3 ~ **a** : turn to

acueducto *nm* : aqueduct

acuerdo *nm* 1 : agreement 2 **de** ~ : OK, all right 3 **de** ~ **con** : in accordance with 4 **estar de** ~ : agree

acumular *vt* : accumulate — **acumularse** *vr* : pile up — **acumulación** *nf, pl* **-ciones** : accumulation — **acumulador** *nm* : storage battery — **acumulativo, -va** *adj* : cumulative

acunar *vt* : rock

acuñar *vt* 1 : mint (money) 2 : coin (a word)

acuoso, -sa *adj* : watery

acupuntura *nf* : acupuncture

acurrucarse {72} *vr* : curl up, nestle

acusar *vt* 1 : accuse 2 MOSTRAR : reveal, show — **acusación** *nf, pl* **-ciones** : accusation, charge — **acusado, -da** *adj* : prominent, marked — ~ *n* : defendant

acuse *nm* ~ **de recibo** : acknowledgment of receipt

acústica *nf* : acoustics — **acústico, -ca** *adj* : acoustic

adagio *nm* 1 REFRÁN : adage, proverb 2 : adagio (in music)

adaptar *vt* 1 : adapt 2 AJUSTAR : adjust, fit — **adaptarse** *vr* ~ **a** : adapt to — **adaptable** *adj* : adaptable — **adaptación** *nf, pl* **-ciones** : adaptation — **adaptador** *nm* : adapter (in electricity)

adecuar {8} *vt* : adapt, make suitable — **adecuarse** *vr* ~ **a** : be appropriate for — **adecuado, -da** *adj* : suitable, appropriate

adelantar *vt* **1** : advance, move forward **2** PASAR : overtake **3** : pay in advance — **adelantarse** *vr* **1** : move forward, get ahead **2** : be fast (of a clock) — **adelantado, -da** *adj* **1** : advanced, ahead **2** : fast (of a clock) **3 por ~** : in advance — **adelante** *adv* **1** : ahead, forward **2 ¡~!** : come in! **3 más ~** : later on, further on — **adelanto** *nm* **1** : advance **2 or ~ de dinero** : advance payment

adelgazar {21} *vt* : make thin — *vi* : lose weight

ademán *nm, pl* **-manes 1** GESTO : gesture **2 ~es** *nmpl* : manners **3 en ~ de** : as if to

además *adv* **1** : besides, furthermore **2 ~ de** : in addition to, as well as

adentro *adv* : inside, within — **adentrarse** *vr* **~ en** : go into, get inside of

adepto, -ta *n* : follower, supporter

aderezar {21} *vt* : season, dress — **aderezo** *nm* : dressing, seasoning

adeudar *vt* **1** : debit **2** DEBER : owe — **adeudo** *nm* **1** DÉBITO : debit **2** *Lat* : debt

adherirse {76} *vr* : adhere, stick — **adherencia** *nf* : adherence — **adhesión** *nf, pl* **-siones 1** : adhesion **2** APOYO : support — **adhesivo, -va** *adj* : adhesive — **adhesivo** *nm* : adhesive

adición *nf, pl* **-ciones** : addition — **adicional** *adj* : additional

adicto, -ta *adj* : addicted — **~** *n* : addict

adiestrar *vt* : train

adinerado, -da *adj* : wealthy

adiós *nm, pl* **adioses 1** : farewell **2 ¡~!** : good-bye!

aditamento *nm* : attachment, accessory

aditivo *nm* : additive

adivinar *vt* **1** : guess **2** PREDECIR : foretell — **adivinación** *nf, pl* **-ciones** : guessing, prediction — **adivinanza** *nf* : riddle — **adivino, -na** *n* : fortune-teller

adjetivo *nm* : adjective

adjudicar {72} *vt* : award — **adjudicarse** *vr* : appropriate — **adjudicación** *nf, pl* **-ciones** : awarding

adjuntar *vt* : enclose (with a letter, etc.) — **adjunto, -ta** *adj* : enclosed, attached — **~** *n* : assistant

administración *nf, pl* **-ciones 1** : administration **2** : administering (of a drug, etc.) **3** DIRECCIÓN : management — **administrador, -dora** *n* : administrator, manager — **administrar** *vt* **1** : manage, run **2** : administer (a drug, etc.) — **administrativo, -va** *adj* : administrative

admirar *vt* : admire — **admirarse** *vr* : be amazed — **admirable** *adj* : admirable — **admiración** *nf, pl* **-ciones 1** : admiration **2** ASOMBRO : amazement — **admirador, -dora** *n* : admirer

admitir *vt* **1** : admit **2** ACEPTAR : accept — **admisible** *adj* : admissible, acceptable — **admisión** *nf, pl* **-siones 1** : admission **2** ACEPTACIÓN : acceptance

ADN *nm* : DNA

adobe *nm* : adobe

adobo *nm* : marinade

adoctrinar *vt* : indoctrinate — **adoctrinamiento** *nm* : indoctrination

adolecer {53} *vi* **~ de** : suffer from

adolescente *adj & nmf* : adolescent — **adolescencia** *nf* : adolescence

adonde *conj* : where

adónde *adv* : where

adoptar *vt* : adopt (a child), take (a decision) — **adopción** *nf, pl* **-ciones** : adoption — **adoptivo, -va** *adj* : adopted, adoptive

adoquín *nm, pl* **-quines** : cobblestone

adorar *vt* : adore, worship — **adorable** *adj* : adorable — **adoración** *nf, pl* **-ciones** : adoration, worship

adormecer {53} *vt* **1** : make sleepy **2** ENTUMECER : numb — **adormecerse** *vr* : doze off — **adormecimiento** *nm* : drowsiness — **adormilarse** *vr* : doze

adornar *vt* : decorate, adorn — **adorno** *nm* : ornament, decoration

adquirir {4} *vt* **1** : acquire **2** COMPRAR : purchase — **adquisición** *nf, pl* **-ciones 1** : acquisition **2** COMPRA : purchase

adrede *adv* : intentionally, on purpose

adscribir {33} *vt* : assign, appoint

aduana *nf* : customs (office) — **aduanero, -ra** *adj* : customs — **~** *n* : customs officer

aducir {61} *vt* : cite, put forward

adueñarse *vr* **~ de** : take possession of

adular *vt* : flatter — **adulación** *nf, pl* **-ciones** : adulation, flattery — **adulador, -dora** *adj* : flattering — **~** *n* : flatterer

adulterar *vt* : adulterate

adulterio *nm* : adultery — **adúltero, -ra** *n* : adulterer

adulto, -ta *adj & n* : adult

adusto, -ta *adj* : stern, severe

advenedizo, -za *n* : upstart

advenimiento *nm* : advent, arrival

adverbio *nm* : adverb — **adverbial** *adj* : adverbial

adversario, -ria *n* : adversary, opponent — **adverso, -sa** *adj* : adverse — **adversidad** *nf* : adversity

advertir {76} *vt* **1** AVISAR : warn **2** NOTAR : notice — **advertencia** *nf* : warning

adviento *nm* : Advent

adyacente *adj* : adjacent

aéreo, -rea *adj* : aerial, air

aerobic *nm* : aerobics *pl*

aerodinámico, -ca *adj* : aerodynamic

aeródromo *nm* : airfield

aerolínea *nf* : airline

aeromozo, -za *n* : flight attendant, steward *m*, stewardess *f*

aeronave *nf* : aircraft

aeropuerto *nm* : airport

aerosol *nm* : aerosol, spray

afable *adj* : affable — **afabilidad** *nf* : affability

afán *nm, pl* **afanes 1** ANHELO : eagerness **2** EMPEÑO : effort, hard work — **afanarse** *vr* : toil — **afanosamente** *adv* : industriously, busily — **afanoso, -sa** *adj* **1** : eager **2** TRABAJOSO : arduous

afear *vt* : make ugly, disfigure

afección *nf, pl* **-ciones** : ailment, complaint

afectar *vt* : affect — **afectación** *nf, pl* **-ciones** : affectation — **afectado, -da** *adj* : affected

afectivo, -va *adj* : emotional

afecto *nm* : affection — **afecto, -ta** *adj* ~ **a** : fond of — **afectuoso, -sa** *adj* : affectionate, caring

afeitar *vt* : shave — **afeitarse** *vr* : shave — **afeitada** *nf* : shave

afeminado, -da *adj* : effeminate

aferrarse {55} *vr* : cling, hold on

afianzar {21} *vt* : secure, strengthen — **afianzarse** *vr* : become established

afiche *nm Lat* : poster

afición *nf, pl* **-ciones 1** : penchant, fondness **2** PASATIEMPO : hobby — **aficionado, -da** *n* **1** ENTUSIASTA : enthusiast, fan **2** AMATEUR : amateur — **aficionarse** *vr* ~ **a** : become interested in

afilar *vt* : sharpen — **afilado, -da** *adj* : sharp — **afilador** *nm* : sharpener

afiliarse *vr* ~ **a** : join, become a member of — **afiliación** *nf, pl* **-ciones** : affiliation — **afiliado, -da** *adj* : affiliated

afín *adj, pl* **afines** : related, similar — **afinidad** *nf* : affinity, similarity

afinar *vt* **1** : tune **2** PULIR : perfect, refine

afirmar *vt* **1** : state, affirm **2** REFORZAR : strengthen — **afirmación** *nf, pl* **-ciones** : statement, affirmation — **afirmativo, -va** *adj* : affirmative

afligir {35} *vt* **1** : afflict **2** APENAR : distress — **afligirse** *vr* : grieve — **aflic-ción** *nf, pl* **-ciones** : grief, sorrow — **afligido -da** *adj* : sorrowful, distressed

aflojar *vt* : loosen, slacken — *vi* : ease up — **aflojarse** *vr* : become loose, slacken

aflorar *vi* : come to the surface, emerge — **afloramiento** *nm* : outcrop

afluencia *nf* : influx — **afluente** *nm* : tributary

afortunado, -da *adj* : fortunate, lucky — **afortunadamente** *adv* : fortunately

afrentar *vt* : insult — **afrenta** *nf* : affront, insult

africano, -na *adj* : African

afrontar *vt* : confront, face

afuera *adv* **1** : out **2** : outside, outdoors — **afueras** *nfpl* : outskirts

agachar *vt* : lower — **agacharse** *vr* : crouch, stoop

agalla *nf* **1** BRANQUIA : gill **2** **tener** ~**s** *fam* : have guts

agarrar *vt* **1** ASIR : grasp **2** *Lat* : catch — **agarrarse** *vr* : hold on, cling — **agarradera** *nf Lat* : handle — **agarrado, -da** *adj fam* : stingy — **agarre** *nm* : grip, grasp — **agarrón** *nm, pl* **-rones** : tug, pull

agasajar *vt* : fête, wine and dine — **agasajo** *nm* : lavish attention

agave *nm* : agave

agazaparse *vr* : crouch down

agencia *nf* : agency, office — **agente** *nmf* : agent, officer

agenda *nf* **1** : agenda **2** LIBRETA : notebook

ágil *adj* : agile — **agilidad** *nf* : agility

agitar *vt* **1** : agitate, shake **2** : wave, flap (wings, etc.) **3** PERTURBAR : stir up — **agitarse** *vr* **1** : toss about **2** INQUIETARSE : get upset — **agitación** *nf, pl* **-ciones 1** : agitation, shaking **2** INTRANQUILIDAD : restlessness — **agitado, -da** *adj* **1** : agitated, excited **2** : choppy, rough (of the sea)

aglomerar *vt* : amass — **aglomerarse** *vr* : crowd together

agnóstico, -ca *adj & n* : agnostic

agobiar *vt* **1** : oppress **2** ABRUMAR : overwhelm — **agobiado, -da** *adj* : weary, weighed down — **agobiante** *adj* : oppressing, oppressive

agonizar {21} *vi* : be dying — **agonía** *nf* **1** : death throes **2** PENA : agony — **agonizante** *adj* : dying

agorero, -ra *adj* : ominous

agostar *vt* : wither

agosto *nm* : August

agotar *vt* **1** : deplete, use up **2** CANSAR : exhaust, weary — **agotarse** *vr* **1**

: run out, give out **2 CANSARSE** : get
tired — **agotado, -da** *adj* **1 CANSADO**
: exhausted **2** : sold out — **agotador,
-dora** *adj* : exhausting — **agotamiento** *nm* : exhaustion
agraciado, -da *adj* **1** : attractive **2 AFOR-
TUNADO** : fortunate
agradar *vi* : be pleasing — **agradable**
adj : pleasant, agreeable — **agrado**
nm **1** : taste, liking **2 con ~** : with
pleasure
agradecer {53} *vt* : be grateful for,
thank — **agradecido, -da** *adj* : grateful — **agradecimiento** *nm* : gratitude
agrandar *vt* : enlarge — **agrandarse** *vr*
: grow larger
agrario, -ria *adj* : agrarian, agricultural
agravar *vt* **1** : make heavier **2 EMPEORAR**
: aggravate, worsen — **agravarse** *vr*
: get worse
agraviar *vt* : insult — **agravio** *nm* : insult
agredir {1} *vt* : attack
agregar {52} *vt* : add, attach — **agregado, -da** *n* : attaché — **agregado** *nm*
: aggregate
agresión *nf, pl* **-siones** : aggression,
attack — **agresividad** *nf* : aggressive-
ness — **agresivo, -va** *adj* : aggressive
— **agresor, -sora** *n* : aggressor, attacker
agreste *adj* : rugged, wild
agriar *vt* : sour — **agriarse** *vr* **1** : turn
sour (of milk, etc.) **2** : become embittered
agrícola *adj* : agricultural — **agricultura** *nf* : agriculture, farming —
agricultor, -tora *n* : farmer
agridulce *adj* **1** : bittersweet **2** : sweet-
and-sour (in cooking)
agrietar *vt* : crack — **agrietarse** *vr* **1**
: crack **2** : chap
agrimensor, -sora *n* : surveyor
agrio, agria *adj* : sour
agrupar *vt* : group together — **agruparse** *vr* : form a group — **agru-
pación** *nf, pl* **-ciones** : group, association — **agrupamiento** *nm* : grouping
agua *nf* **1** : water **2 ~ oxigenada** : hydrogen peroxide **3 ~s negras** *or* **~s
residuales** : sewage
aguacate *nm* : avocado
aguacero *nm* : downpour
aguado, -da *adj* **1** : watery **2** *Lat fam*
: soft, flabby — **aguar** {10} *vt* **1**
: water down, dilute **2 ~ la fiesta** *fam*
: spoil the party
aguafuerte *nm* : etching
aguanieve *nf* : sleet
aguantar *vt* **1 SOPORTAR** : bear, with-

stand **2 SOSTENER** : hold — *vi* : hold
out, last — **aguantarse** *vr* **1** : resign
oneself **2 CONTENERSE** : restrain oneself — **aguante** *nm* **1** : patience **2 RE-
SISTENCIA** : endurance
aguardar *vt* : await
aguardiente *nm* : clear brandy
aguarrás *nm* : turpentine
agudo, -da *adj* **1** : acute, sharp **2** : shrill,
high-pitched (in music) — **agudeza**
nf **1** : sharpness **2** : witticism
agüero *nm* : augury, omen
aguijón *nm, pl* **-jones 1** : stinger (of an
insect) **2 ESTÍMULO** : goad, stimulus —
aguijonear *vt* : goad
águila *nf* : eagle
aguja *nf* **1** : needle **2** : hand (of a clock)
3 : spire (of a church)
agujero *nm* : hole
agujeta *nf* **1** *Lat* : shoelace **2 ~s** *nfpl*
: (muscular) stiffness
aguzar {21} *vt* **1** : sharpen **2 ~ el oído**
: prick up one's ears
ahí *adv* **1** : there **2 por ~** : somewhere,
thereabouts
ahijado, -da *n* : godchild, godson *m*,
goddaughter *f*
ahínco *nm* : eagerness, zeal
ahogar {52} *vt* **1** : drown **2 ASFIXIAR**
: smother — **ahogarse** *vr* : drown —
ahogo *nm* : breathlessness
ahondar *vt* : deepen — *vi* : elaborate,
go into detail
ahora *adv* **1** : now **2 ~ mismo** : right
now
ahorcar {72} *vt* : hang, kill by hanging
— **ahorcarse** *vr* : hang oneself
ahorita *adv* *Lat fam* : right now
ahorrar *vt* : save, spare — *vi* : save up
— **ahorrarse** *vr* : spare oneself —
ahorro *nm* : saving
ahuecar {72} *vt* **1** : hollow out **2** : cup
(one's hands)
ahumar {8} *vt* : smoke, cure — **ahu-
mado, -da** *adj* : smoked
ahuyentar *vt* : scare away, chase away
airado, -da *adj* : irate, angry
aire *nm* **1** : air **2 ~ acondicionado**
: air-conditioning **3 al ~ libre** : in the
open air, outdoors — **airear** *vt* : air, air
out
aislar {5} *vt* **1** : isolate **2** : insulate (in
electricity) — **aislamiento** *nm* **1** : isolation **2** : (electrical) insulation
ajar *vt* **1** : crumple, wrinkle **2 ESTRO-
PEAR** : spoil
ajedrez *nm* : chess
ajeno, -na *adj* **1** : someone else's **2 EX-
TRAÑO** : alien **3 ~ a** : foreign to
ajetreado, -da *adj* : hectic, busy —

ajetrearse *vr* : bustle about — **ajetreo** *nm* : hustle and bustle

ají *nm, pl* **ajíes** *Lat* : chili pepper

ajo *nm* : garlic

ajustar *vt* 1 : adjust, adapt 2 ACORDAR : agree on 3 SALDAR : settle — **ajustarse** *vr* : fit, conform — **ajustable** *adj* : adjustable — **ajustado, -da** *adj* 1 : close, tight 2 CEÑIDO : tight-fitting — **ajuste** *nm* : adjustment

ajusticiar *vt* : execute, put to death

al (*contraction of a and* el) → **a²**

ala *nf* 1 : wing 2 : brim (of a hat)

alabanza *nf* : praise — **alabar** *vt* : praise

alacena *nf* : cupboard, larder

alacrán *nm, pl* **-cranes** : scorpion

alado, -da *adj* : winged

alambre *nm* : wire

alameda *nf* 1 : poplar grove 2 : tree-lined avenue — **álamo** *nm* : poplar

alarde *nm* : show, display — **alardear** *vi* : boast

alargar {52} *vt* 1 : extend, lengthen 2 PROLONGAR : prolong — **alargarse** *vr* : become longer — **alargador** *nm* : extension cord

alarido *nm* : howl, shriek

alarmar *vt* : alarm — **alarma** *nf* : alarm — **alarmante** *adj* : alarming

alba *nf* : dawn

albahaca *nf* : basil

albañil *nm* : bricklayer, mason

albaricoque *nm* : apricot

albedrío *nm* libre ~ : free will

alberca *nf* 1 : reservoir, tank 2 *Lat* : swimming pool

albergar {52} *vt* : house, lodge — **albergue** *nm* 1 : lodging 2 REFUGIO : shelter 3 ~ juvenil : youth hostel

albóndiga *nf* : meatball

alborear *v impers* : dawn — **albor** *nm* : dawning — **alborada** *nf* : dawn

alborotar *vt* : excite, stir up — *vi* : make a racket — **alborotarse** *vr* : get excited — **alborotado, -da** *adj* : excited, agitated — **alborotador, -dora** *n* : agitator, rioter — **alboroto** *nm* : ruckus

alborozar {21} *vt* : gladden — **alborozo** *nm* : joy

álbum *nm* : album

alcachofa *nf* : artichoke

alcalde, -desa *n* : mayor

alcance *nm* 1 : reach 2 ÁMBITO : range, scope

alcancía *nf* : money box

alcantarilla *nf* : sewer, drain

alcanzar {21} *vt* 1 : reach 2 LLEGAR A : catch up with 3 LOGRAR : achieve, attain — *vi* 1 : suffice, be enough 2 ~ a : manage to

alcaparra *nf* : caper

alcázar *nm* : fortress, castle

alce *nm* : moose, European elk

alcoba *nf* : bedroom

alcohol *nm* : alcohol — **alcohólico, -ca** *adj & n* : alcoholic — **alcoholismo** *nm* : alcoholism

aldaba *nf* : door knocker

aldea *nf* : village — **aldeano, -na** *n* : villager

aleación *nf, pl* **-ciones** : alloy

aleatorio, -ria *adj* : random

aleccionar *vt* : instruct, teach

aledaño, -ña *adj* : bordering — **aledaños** *nmpl* : outskirts

alegar {52} *vt* 1 : assert, allege — *vi Lat* : argue — **alegato** *nm* 1 : allegation (in law) 2 *Lat* : argument

alegoría *nf* : allegory — **alegórico, -ca** *adj* : allegorical

alegrar *vt* : make happy, cheer up — **alegrarse** *vr* : be glad — **alegre** *adj* 1 CONTENTO : glad, happy 2 : colorful, bright — **alegremente** *adv* : happily — **alegría** *nf* : joy, cheer

alejar *vt* 1 : remove, move away 2 ENAJENAR : estrange — **alejarse** *vr* : move away, drift apart — **alejado, -da** *adj* : remote — **alejamiento** *nm* 1 : removal 2 : estrangement (of persons)

alemán, -mana *adj, mpl* **-manes** : German — **alemán** *nm* : German (language)

alentar {55} *vt* : encourage — **alentador, -dora** *adj* : encouraging

alergia *nf* : allergy — **alérgico, -ca** *adj* : allergic

alero *nm* : eaves *pl*

alertar *vt* : alert — **alerta** *adv* : on the alert — **alerta** *adj & nf* : alert

aleta *nf* 1 : fin, flipper 2 : small wing

alevosía *nf* : treachery — **alevoso, -sa** *adj* : treacherous

alfabeto *nm* : alphabet — **alfabético, -ca** *adj* : alphabetical — **alfabetismo** *nm* : literacy — **alfabetizar** {21} *vt* 1 : teach literacy 2 : alphabetize

alfalfa *nf* : alfalfa

alfarería *nf* : pottery

alféizar *nm* : sill, windowsill

alfil *nm* : bishop (in chess)

alfiler *nm* 1 : pin 2 BROCHE : brooch — **alfiletero** *nm* : pincushion

alfombra *nf* : carpet, rug — **alfombrilla** *nf* : small rug, mat

alga *nf* : seaweed

álgebra *nf* : algebra

algo *pron* 1 : something 2 ~ **de** : some, a little — ~ *adv* : somewhat, rather
algodón *nm, pl* **-dones** : cotton
alguacil *nm* : constable, bailiff
alguien *pron* : somebody, someone
alguno, -na *adj* (**algún** *before masculine singular nouns*) 1 : some, any 2 (*in negative constructions*) : not any, not at all 3 **algunas veces** : sometimes — ~ *pron* 1 : one, someone, somebody 2 **algunos, -nas** *pron pl* : some, a few
alhaja *nf* : jewel
alharaca *nf* : fuss
aliado, -da *n* : ally — ~ *adj* : allied — **alianza** *nf* : alliance — **aliarse** {85} *vr* : form an alliance
alias *adv & nm* : alias
alicaído, -da *adj* : depressed
alicates *nmpl* : pliers
aliciente *nm* 1 : incentive 2 : attraction (to a place)
alienar *vt* : alienate — **alienación** *nf, pl* **-ciones** : alienation
aliento *nm* 1 : breath 2 ÁNIMO : encouragement, strength
aligerar *vt* 1 : lighten 2 APRESURAR : hasten, quicken
alimaña *nf* : pest, vermin
alimentar *vt* : feed, nourish — **alimentarse** *vr* ~ **con** : live on — **alimentación** *nf, pl* **-ciones** 1 : feeding 2 NUTRICIÓN : nourishment — **alimenticio, -cia** *adj* : nourishing — **alimento** *nm* : food, nourishment
alinear *vt* : align, line up — **alinearse** *vr* ~ **con** : align oneself with — **alineación** *nf, pl* **-ciones** 1 : alignment 2 : lineup (in sports)
aliño *nm* : dressing, seasoning — **aliñar** *vt* : season, dress
alisar *vt* : smooth
alistarse *vr* : join up, enlist — **alistamiento** *nm* : enlistment
aliviar *vt* : relieve, soothe — **aliviarse** *vr* : recover, get better — **alivio** *nm* : relief
aljibe *nm* : cistern, tank
allá *adv* 1 : there, over there 2 **más** ~ : farther away 3 **más** ~ **de** : beyond
allanar *vt* 1 : smooth, level out 2 *Spain* : break into (a house) 3 *Lat* : raid — **allanamiento** *nm* 1 *Spain* : breaking and entering 2 *Lat* : raid
allegado, -da *n* : close friend, relation
allí *adv* : there, over there
alma *nf* : soul
almacén *nm, pl* **-cenes** 1 : warehouse 2 *Lat* : shop, store 3 **grandes almacenes** : department store — **alma-**

cenamiento *or* **almacenaje** *nm* : storage — **almacenar** *vt* : store
almádena *nf* : sledgehammer
almanaque *nm* : almanac
almeja *nf* : clam
almendra *nf* 1 : almond 2 : kernel (of nuts, fruit, etc.)
almiar *nm* : haystack
almíbar *nm* : syrup
almidón *nm, pl* **-dones** : starch — **almidonar** *vt* : starch
almirante *nm* : admiral
almohada *nf* : pillow — **almohadilla** *nf* : small pillow, pad — **almohadón** *nm, pl* **-dones** : bolster, large cushion
almorranas *nfpl* : hemorrhoids, piles
almorzar {36} *vi* : have lunch — *vt* : have for lunch — **almuerzo** *nm* : lunch
alocado, -da *adj* : crazy, wild
áloe *or* **aloe** *nm* : aloe
alojar *vt* : house, lodge — **alojarse** *vr* : lodge, room — **alojamiento** *nm* : lodging, accommodations *pl*
alondra *nf* : lark
alpaca *nf* : alpaca
alpinismo *nm* : mountain climbing — **alpinista** *nmf* : mountain climber
alpiste *nm* : birdseed
alquilar *vt* : rent, lease — **alquilarse** *vr* : be for rent — **alquiler** *nm* : rent, rental
alquitrán *nm, pl* **-tranes** : tar
alrededor *adv* 1 : around, about 2 ~ **de** : approximately — **alrededor de** *prep phr* : around — **alrededores** *nmpl* : outskirts
alta *nf* : discharge (of a patient)
altanería *nf* : haughtiness — **altanero, -ra** *adj* : haughty
altar *nm* : altar
altavoz *nm, pl* **-voces** : loudspeaker
alterar *vt* 1 : alter, modify 2 PERTURBAR : disturb — **alterarse** *vr* : get upset — **alteración** *nf, pl* **-ciones** 1 : alteration 2 ALBOROTO : disturbance — **alterado, -da** *adj* : upset
altercado *nm* : altercation, argument
alternar *vi* 1 : alternate 2 ~ **con** : socialize with — *vt* : alternate — **alternarse** *vr* : take turns — **alternativa** *nf* : alternative — **alternativo, -va** *adj* : alternating, alternative — **alterno, -na** *adj* : alternate
Alteza *nf* : Highness
altiplano *nm* : high plateau
altitud *nf* : altitude
altivez *nf, pl* **-veces** : haughtiness — **altivo, -va** *adj* : haughty
alto, -ta *adj* 1 : tall, high 2 RUIDOSO

: loud — **alto** *adv* 1 ARRIBA : high 2
: loud, loudly — **~** *nm* 1 ALTURA
: height, elevation 2 : stop, halt — **~**
interj : halt!, stop! — **altoparlante** *nm*
Lat : loudspeaker
altruista *adj* : altruistic — **altruismo**
nm : altruism
altura *nf* 1 : height 2 ALTITUD : altitude
3 **a la ~ de** : near, up by
alubia *nf* : kidney bean
alucinar *vi* : hallucinate — **alucinación**
nf, pl -**ciones** : hallucination
alud *nm* : avalanche
aludir *vi* : allude, refer — **aludido, -da**
adj **darse por ~** : take it personally
alumbrar *vt* 1 : light, illuminate 2 PARIR
: give birth to — **alumbrado** *nm*
: (electric) lighting — **alumbramiento** *nm* : childbirth
aluminio *nm* : aluminum
alumno, -na *n* : pupil, student
alusión *nf, pl* -**siones** : allusion
aluvión *nm, pl* -**viones** : flood, barrage
alzar {21} *vt* : lift, raise — **alzarse** *vr*
: rise (up) — **alza** *nf* : rise — **alza-
miento** *nm* : uprising
ama → **amo**
amabilidad *nf* : kindness — **amable**
adj : kind, nice
amaestrar *vt* : train
amagar {52} *vt* 1 : show signs of 2
AMENAZAR : threaten — *vi* : be imminent — **amago** *nm* 1 INDICIO : sign 2
AMENAZA : threat
amainar *vi* : abate
amamantar *v* : breast-feed, nurse
amanecer {53} *v impers* : dawn — *vi*
: wake up — **~** *nm* : dawn, daybreak
amanerado *adj* : affected, mannered
amansar *vt* 1 : tame 2 APACIGUAR
: soothe — **amansarse** *vr* : calm down
amante *adj* **~ de** : fond of — **~** *nmf*
: lover
amañar *vt* : rig, tamper with
amapola *nf* : poppy
amar *vt* : love
amargar {52} *vt* : make bitter — **amar-
gado, -da** *adj* : embittered — **amargo, -ga** *adj* : bitter — **amargo** *nm*
: bitterness — **amargura** *nf* : bitterness, grief
amarillo, -lla *adj* : yellow — **amarillo**
nm : yellow
amarrar *vt* 1 : moor 2 ATAR : tie up
amasar *vt* 1 : knead 2 : amass (a fortune, etc.)
amateur *adj & nmf* : amateur
amatista *nf* : amethyst
ambages *nmpl* **sin ~** : without hesitation, straight to the point

ámbar *nm* : amber
ambición *nf, pl* -**ciones** : ambition —
ambicionar *vt* : aspire to — **ambicioso, -sa** *adj* : ambitious
ambiente *nm* 1 AIRE : atmosphere 2
MEDIO : environment, surroundings *pl*
— **ambiental** *adj* : environmental
ambigüedad *nf* : ambiguity — **ambiguo, -gua** *adj* : ambiguous
ámbito *nm* : domain, sphere
ambos, -bas *adj & pron* : both
ambulancia *nf* : ambulance
ambulante *adj* : traveling, itinerant
ameba *nf* : amoeba
amedrentar *vt* : intimidate
amén *nm* 1 : amen 2 **~ de** : in addition
to
amenazar {21} *vt* : threaten — **amenaza** *nf* : threat, menace
amenizar {21} *vt* : make pleasant, enliven — **ameno, -na** *adj* : pleasant
americano, -na *adj* : American
ameritar *vt Lat* : deserve
ametralladora *nf* : machine gun
amianto *nm* : asbestos
amiba → **ameba**
amígdala *nf* : tonsil — **amigdalitis** *nf*
: tonsilitis
amigo, -ga *adj* : friendly, close — **~** *n*
: friend — **amigable** *adj* : friendly
amilanar *vt* : daunt — **amilanarse** *vr*
: lose heart
aminorar *vt* : diminish
amistad *nf* : friendship — **amistoso,
-sa** *adj* : friendly
amnesia *nf* : amnesia
amnistía *nf* : amnesty
amo, ama *n* 1 : master *m,* mistress *f* 2
ama de casa : homemaker, housewife 3 **ama de llaves** : housekeeper
amodorrado, -da *adj* : drowsy
amolar {19} *vt* 1 : grind, sharpen 2 MO-
LESTAR : annoy
amoldar *vt* : adapt, adjust —
amoldarse *vr* **~ a** : adapt to
amonestar *vt* : admonish, warn —
amonestación *nf, pl* -**ciones** : admo-
nition, warning
amoníaco *or* **amoniaco** *nm* : ammonia
amontonar *vt* : pile up — **amontonarse** *vr* : pile up (of things), form a
crowd (of persons)
amor *nm* : love
amordazar {21} *vt* : gag
amorío *nm* : love affair — **amoroso,
-sa** *adj* 1 : loving 2 *Lat* : sweet, lovable
amoratado, -da *adj* : black-and-blue
amortiguar {10} *vt* : muffle, soften,
tone down — **amortiguador** *nm*
: shock absorber

amortizar {21} *vt* : pay off — **amortización** *nf* : repayment

amotinar *vt* : incite (to riot) — **amotinarse** *vr* : riot, rebel

amparar *vt* : shelter, protect — **ampararse** *vr* 1 ~ **de** : take shelter from 2 ~ **en** : have recourse to — **amparo** *nm* : refuge, protection

ampliar {85} *vt* 1 : expand 2 : enlarge (a photograph) — **ampliación** *nf, pl* **-ciones** 1 : expansion, enlargement 2 : extension (of a building)

amplificar {72} *vt* : amplify — **amplificador** *nm* : amplifier

amplio, -plia *adj* : broad, wide, ample — **amplitud** *nf* 1 : breadth, extent 2 ESPACIOSIDAD : spaciousness

ampolla *nf* 1 : blister 2 : vial, ampoule — **ampollarse** *vr* : blister

ampuloso, -sa *adj* : pompous

amputar *vt* : amputate — **amputación** *nf, pl* **-ciones** : amputation

amueblar *vt* : furnish (a house, etc.)

amurallar *vt* : wall in

anacardo *nm* : cashew nut

anaconda *nf* : anaconda

anacrónico, -ca *adj* : anachronistic — **anacronismo** *nm* : anachronism

ánade *nmf* : duck

anagrama *nm* : anagram

anales *nmpl* : annals

analfabeto, -ta *adj & n* : illiterate — **analfabetismo** *nm* : illiteracy

analgésico *nm* : painkiller, analgesic

analizar {21} *vt* : analyze — **análisis** *nm* : analysis — **analítico, -ca** *adj* : analytical, analytic

analogía *nf* : analogy — **análogo, -ga** *adj* : analogous

ananá *or* **ananás** *nm, pl* **-nás** : pineapple

anaquel *nm* : shelf

anaranjado, -da *adj* : orange-colored

anarquía *nf* : anarchy — **anarquista** *adj & nmf* : anarchist

anatomía *nf* : anatomy — **anatómico, -ca** *adj* : anatomic, anatomical

anca *nf* 1 : haunch 2 ~**s de rana** : frogs' legs

ancestral *adj* : ancestral

ancho, -cha *adj* : wide, broad, ample — **ancho** *nm* : width

anchoa *nf* : anchovy

anchura *nf* : width, breadth

anciano, -na *adj* : aged, elderly — ~ *n* : elderly person

ancla *nf* : anchor — **anclar** *v* : anchor

andadas *nfpl* 1 : tracks 2 **volver a las** ~ : go back to one's old ways

andadura *nf* : walking, journey

andaluz, -luza *adj & n, mpl* **-luces** : Andalusian

andamio *nm* : scaffold

andanada *nf* 1 : volley 2 **soltar una** ~ : reprimand

andanzas *nfpl* : adventures

andar {6} *vi* 1 CAMINAR : walk 2 IR : go, travel 3 FUNCIONAR : run, work 4 ~ **en** : rummage around in 5 ~ **por** : be approximately — *vt* : cover, travel — ~ *nm* : gait, walk

andén *nm, pl* **-denes** 1 : (train) platform 2 *Lat* : sidewalk

andino, -na *adj* : Andean

andorrano, -na *adj* : Andorran

andrajos *nmpl* : tatters — **andrajoso, -sa** *adj* : ragged

anécdota *nf* : anecdote

anegar {52} *vt* : flood — **anegarse** *vr* 1 : be flooded 2 AHOGARSE : drown

anemia *nf* : anemia — **anémico, -ca** *adj* : anemic

anestesia *nf* : anesthesia — **anestésico, -ca** *adj* : anesthetic — **anestésico** *nm* : anesthetic

anexar *vt* : annex, attach — **anexo, -xa** *adj* : attached — **anexo** *nm* : annex

anfibio, -bia *adj* : amphibious — **anfibio** *nm* : amphibian

anfiteatro *nm* : amphitheater

anfitrión, -triona *n, mpl* **-triones** : host, hostess *f*

ángel *nm* : angel — **angelical** *adj* : angelic, angelical

angloparlante *adj* : English-speaking

anglosajón, -jona *adj, mpl* **-jones** : Anglo-Saxon

angosto, -ta *adj* : narrow

anguila *nf* : eel

ángulo *nm* 1 : angle 2 ESQUINA : corner — **angular** *adj* : angular — **anguloso, -sa** *adj* : angular

angustiar *vt* 1 : anguish, distress 2 INQUIETAR : worry — **angustiarse** *vr* : get upset — **angustia** *nf* 1 : anguish 2 INQUIETUD : worry — **angustioso, -sa** *adj* 1 : anguished 2 INQUIETANTE : distressing

anhelar *vt* : yearn for, crave — **anhelante** *adj* : yearning, longing — **anhelo** *nm* : longing

anidar *vi* : nest

anillo *nm* : ring

ánima *n* : soul

animación *nf, pl* **-ciones** 1 VIVEZA : liveliness 2 BULLICIO : hustle and bustle — **animado, -da** *adj* : cheerful, animated — **animador, -dora** *n* 1 : (television) host 2 : cheerleader

animadversión *nf, pl* **-siones** : animosity

animal *nm* : animal — ~ *nmf* : brute, beast — ~ *adj* : brutish

animar *vt* **1** ALENTAR : encourage **2** ALEGAR : cheer up — **animarse** *vr* **1** : liven up **2** ~ **a** : get up the nerve to

ánimo *nm* **1** : spirit, soul **2** HUMOR : mood, spirits *pl* **3** ALIENTO : encouragement

animosidad *nf* : animosity, ill will

animoso, -sa *adj* : spirited, brave

aniquilar *vt* : annihilate — **aniquilación** *n, pl* **-ciones** : annihilation

anís *nm* : anise

aniversario *nm* : anniversary

ano *nm* : anus

anoche *adv* : last night

anochecer {53} *vi* : get dark — ~ *nm* : dusk, nightfall

anodino, -na *adj* : insipid, dull

anomalía *nf* : anomaly

anonadado, -da *adj* : dumbfounded

anónimo, -ma *adj* : anonymous — **anonimato** *nm* : anonymity

anorexia *nf* : anorexia

anormal *adj* : abnormal — **anormalidad** *nf* : abnormality

anotar *vt* **1** : annotate **2** APUNTAR : jot down — **anotación** *nf, pl* **-ciones** : annotation, note

anquilosarse *vr* **1** : become paralyzed **2** ESTANCARSE : stagnate — **anquilosamiento** *nm* **1** : paralysis **2** ESTANCAMIENTO : stagnation

ansiar {85} *vt* : long for — **ansia** *nf* **1** INQUIETUD : uneasiness **2** ANGUSTIA : anguish **3** ANHELO : longing — **ansiedad** *nf* : anxiety — **ansioso, -sa** *adj* **1** : anxious **2** DESEOSO : eager

antagónico, -ca *adj* : antagonistic — **antagonismo** *nm* : antagonism — **antagonista** *nmf* : antagonist

antaño *adv* : yesteryear, long ago

antártico, -ca *adj* : antarctic

ante[1] *nm* **1** : elk, moose **2** GAMUZA : suede

ante[2] *prep* **1** : before, in front of **2** : in view of **3** ~ **todo** : above all

anteanoche *adv* : the night before last

anteayer *adv* : the day before yesterday

antebrazo *nm* : forearm

anteceder *vt* : precede — **antecedente** *adj* : previous, prior — ~ *nm* : precedent — **antecesor, -sora** *n* **1** : ancestor **2** PREDECESOR : predecessor

antedicho, -cha *adj* : aforesaid

antelación *nf, pl* **-ciones** **1** : advance notice **2 con** ~ : in advance

antemano *adv* **de** ~ : beforehand

antena *nf* : antenna

antenoche → **anteanoche**

anteojos *nmpl* **1** : glasses, eyeglasses **2** ~ **bifocales** : bifocals

antepasado, -da *n* : ancestor

antepecho *nm* : ledge

antepenúltimo, -ma *adj* : third from last

anteponer {60} *vt* **1** : place before **2** PREFERIR : prefer

anterior *adj* **1** : previous, earlier **2** DELANTERO : front — **anterioridad** *nf* **con** ~ : beforehand, in advance — **anteriormente** *adv* : previously

antes *adv* **1** : before, earlier **2** ANTERIORMENTE : previously **3** PRIMERO : first **4** MEJOR : rather **5** ~ **de** : before, previous to **6** ~ **que** : before

antesala *nf* : waiting room

antiaéreo, -rea *adj* : antiaircraft

antibiótico *nm* : antibiotic

anticipar *vt* **1** : move up (a date, etc.) **2** : pay in advance — **anticiparse** *vr* **1** : be early **2** ADELANTARSE : get ahead — **anticipación** *nf, pl* **-ciones** **1** : anticipation **2 con** ~ : in advance — **anticipado, -da** *adj* **1** : advance, early **2 por** ~ : in advance — **anticipo** *nm* **1** : advance (payment) **2** : foretaste

anticoncepción *nf, pl* **-ciones** : contraception — **anticonceptivo, -va** *adj* : contraceptive — **anticonceptivo** *nm* : contraceptive

anticongelante *nm* : antifreeze

anticuado, -da *adj* : antiquated, outdated

anticuario, -ria *n* : antique dealer — **anticuario** *nm* : antique shop

anticuerpo *nm* : antibody

antídoto *nm* : antidote

antier → **anteayer**

antiestético, -ca *adj* : unsightly

antifaz *nm, pl* **-faces** : mask

antífona *nf* : anthem

antigualla *nf* : relic, old thing

antiguo, -gua *adj* **1** : ancient, old **2** ANTERIOR : former **3** ANTICUADO : old-fashioned **4 muebles antiguos** : antique furniture — **antiguamente** *adv* **1** : long ago **2** ANTES : formerly — **antigüedad** *nf* **1** : antiquity **2** : seniority (in the workplace) **3** ~**es** *nfpl* : antiques

antihigiénico, -ca *adj* : unsanitary

antihistamínico *nm* : antihistamine

antiinflamatorio, -ria *adj* : anti-inflammatory

antílope *nm* : antelope

antinatural *adj* : unnatural

antipatía *nf* : aversion, dislike — **antipático, -ca** *adj* : unpleasant
antirreglamentario, -ria *adj* : unlawful
antirrobo, -ba *adj* : antitheft
antisemita *adj* : anti-Semitic — **antisemitismo** *nm* : anti-Semitism
antiséptico, -ca *adj* : antiseptic — **antiséptico** *nm* : antiseptic
antisocial *adj* : antisocial
antítesis *nf* : antithesis
antojarse *vr* **1** APETECER : crave **2** PARECER : seem, appear — **antojadizo, -za** *adj* : capricious — **antojo** *nm* : whim, craving
antología *nf* : anthology
antorcha *nf* : torch
antro *nm* : dive, den
antropófago, -ga *nmf* : cannibal
antropología *nf* : anthropology
anual *adj* : annual, yearly — **anualidad** *nf* : annuity — **anuario** *nm* : yearbook, annual
anudar *vt* : knot — **anudarse** *vr* : tie, knot
anular *vt* : annul, cancel — **anulación** *nf, pl* **-ciones** : annulment, cancellation
anunciar *vt* **1** : announce **2** : advertise (products) — **anunciante** *nmf* : advertiser — **anuncio** *nm* **1** : announcement **2** *or* — **publicitario** : advertisement
anzuelo *nm* **1** : fishhook **2 morder el ~** : take the bait
añadir *vt* : add — **añadidura** *nf* **1** : additive, addition **2 por ~** : in addition, furthermore
añejo, -ja *adj* : aged, vintage
añicos *nmpl* **hacer(se) ~** : smash to pieces
añil *adj & nm* : indigo (color)
año *nm* **1** : year **2 Año Nuevo** : New Year
añorar *vt* : long for, miss — **añoranza** *nf* : nostalgia
añoso, -sa *adj* : aged, old
aorta *nf* : aorta
apabullar *vt* : overwhelm
apacentar {55} *vt* : pasture, graze
apachurrar *vt Lat* : crush
apacible *adj* : gentle, mild
apaciguar {10} *vt* : appease, pacify — **apaciguarse** *vr* : calm down
apadrinar *vt* **1** : be a godparent to **2** : sponsor (an artist, etc.)
apagar {52} *vt* **1** : turn or switch off **2** EXTINGUIR : extinguish, put out — **apagarse** *vr* EXTINGUIRSE : go out **2** : die down — **apagado, -da** *adj* **1** : off, out **2** : dull, subdued (of colors, sounds, etc.) — **apagador** *nm Lat*

: (light) switch — **apagón** *nm, pl* **-gones** : blackout
apalancar {72} *vt* **1** LEVANTAR : jack up **2** ABRIR : pry open — **apalancamiento** *nm* : leverage
apalear *vt* : beat up, thrash
aparador *nm* **1** : sideboard **2** *Lat* : shop window
aparato *nm* **1** : machine, appliance, apparatus **2** : system (in anatomy) **3** OSTENTACIÓN : ostentation — **aparatoso, -sa** *adj* **1** : ostentatious **2** ESPECTACULAR : spectacular
aparcar {72} *v Spain* : park — **aparcamiento** *nm Spain* **1** : parking **2** : parking lot
aparcero, -ra *n* : sharecropper
aparear *vt* : mate, pair up — **aparearse** *vr* : mate
aparecer {53} *vi* **1** : appear **2** PRESENTARSE : show up — **aparecerse** *vr* : appear
aparejar *vt* **1** : rig (a ship) **2** : harness (an animal) — **aparejado, -da** *adj* **llevar ~** : entail — **aparejo** *nm* **1** : equipment, gear **2** : harness (for an animal) **3** : rigging (for a ship)
aparentar *vt* **1** : seem **2** FINGIR : feign — **aparente** *adj* : apparent, seeming
aparición *nf, pl* **-ciones 1** : appearance **2** FANTASMA : apparition — **apariencia** *nf* **1** : appearance, look **2 en ~** : apparently
apartado *nm* **1** : section, paragraph **2 ~ postal** : post office box
apartamento *nm* : apartment
apartar *vt* **1** ALEJAR : move away **2** SEPARAR : set aside, separate — **apartarse** *vr* **1** : move away **2** DESVIARSE : stray — **aparte** *adv* **1** : apart, separately **2** ADEMÁS : besides
apasionar *vt* : excite, fascinate — **apasionarse** *vr* : get excited — **apasionado, -da** *adj* : passionate, excited — **apasionante** *adj* : exciting
apatía *nf* : apathy — **apático, -ca** *adj* : apathetic
apearse *vr* **1** : dismount **2** : get out of or off (a vehicle)
apedrear *vt* : stone
apegarse {52} *vr* **~ a** : become attached to, grow fond of — **apegado, -da** *adj* : devoted — **apego** *nm* : fondness
apelar *vi* **1** : appeal **2 ~ a** : resort to — **apelación** *nf, pl* **-ciones** : appeal
apellido *nm* : last name, surname — **apellidarse** *vr* : have for a last name
apenar *vt* : sadden — **apenarse** *vr* **1** : grieve **2** *Lat* : become embarrassed

apenas *adv* : hardly, scarcely — ~ *conj* : as soon as
apéndice *nm* : appendix — **apendicitis** *nf* : appendicitis
apercibir *vt* **1** : warn **2** *Lat* : notice — **apercibirse** *vr* ~ **de** : notice — **apercibimiento** *nm* : warning
aperitivo *nm* **1** : appetizer **2** : aperitif
apero *nm* : tool, implement
apertura *nf* : opening
apesadumbrar *vt* : sadden — **apesadumbrarse** *vr* : be weighed down
apestar *vi* : stink — **apestoso, -sa** *adj* : stinking, foul
apetecer {53} *vt* : crave, long for — **apetecible** *adj* : appealing
apetito *nm* : appetite — **apetitoso, -sa** *adj* : appetizing
ápice *nm* **1** : apex, summit **2** PIZCA : bit, smidgen
apilar *vt* : pile up — **apilarse** *vr* : pile up
apiñar *vt* : pack, cram — **apiñarse** *vr* : crowd together
apio *nm* : celery
apisonadora *nf* : steamroller
aplacar {72} *vt* : appease, placate — **aplacarse** *vr* : calm down
aplanar *vt* : flatten, level
aplastar *vt* : crush — **aplastante** *adj* : overwhelming
aplaudir *v* : applaud — **aplauso** *nm* **1** : applause **2** : acclaim
aplazar {21} *vt* : postpone, defer — **aplazamiento** *nm* : postponement
aplicar {72} *vt* : apply — **aplicarse** *vr* : apply oneself — **aplicable** *adj* : applicable — **aplicación** *nf, pl* -ciones : application — **aplicado, -da** *adj* : diligent
aplomo *nm* : aplomb
apocarse {72} *vr* : belittle oneself — **apocado, -da** *adj* : timid — **apocamiento** *nm* : timidity
apodar *vt* : nickname
apoderar *vt* : empower — **apoderarse** *vr* ~ **de** : seize — **apoderado, -da** *n* : agent, proxy
apodo *nm* : nickname
apogeo *nm* : peak, height
apología *nf* : defense, apology
apoplejía *nf* : stroke, apoplexy
aporrear *vt* : bang on, beat
aportar *vt* : contribute — **aportación** *nf, pl* -ciones : contribution
apostar[1] {19} *v* : bet, wager
apostar[2] *vt* : station, post
apostillar *vt* : annotate — **apostilla** *nf* : note
apóstol *nm* : apostle

apóstrofo *nm* : apostrophe
apostura *nf* : elegance, grace
apoyar *vt* **1** : support **2** INCLINAR : lean, rest — **apoyarse** *vr* ~ **en** : lean on, rest on — **apoyo** *nm* : support
apreciar *vt* **1** ESTIMAR : appreciate **2** EVALUAR : appraise — **apreciable** *adj* : considerable — **apreciación** *nf, pl* -ciones **1** : appreciation **2** VALORACIÓN : appraisal — **aprecio** *nm* **1** : appraisal **2** ESTIMA : esteem
aprehender *vt* : apprehend — **aprehensión** *nf, pl* -siones : apprehension, capture
apremiar *vt* : urge — *vi* : be urgent — **apremiante** *adj* : pressing, urgent — **apremio** *nm* : urgency
aprender *v* : learn — **aprenderse** *vr* : memorize
aprendiz, -diza *n, mpl* -dices : apprentice, trainee — **aprendizaje** *nm* : apprenticeship
aprensión *nf, pl* -siones : apprehension, dread — **aprensivo, -va** *adj* : apprehensive
apresar *vt* : capture, seize — **apresamiento** *nm* : seizure, capture
aprestar *vt* : make ready — **aprestarse** *vr* : get ready
apresurar *vt* : speed up — **apresurarse** *vr* : hurry — **apresuradamente** *adv* : hurriedly, hastily — **apresurado, -da** *adj* : in a rush
apretar {55} *vt* **1** : press, push (a button) **2** : tighten (a knot, etc.) **3** ESTRECHAR : squeeze — *vi* **1** : press (down) **2** : fit too tightly — **apretón** *nm, pl* -tones **1** : squeeze **2** ~ **de manos** : handshake — **apretado, -da** *adj* **1** : tight **2** *fam* : tightfisted
aprieto *nm* : predicament, jam
aprisa *adv* : quickly
aprisionar *vt* : imprison
aprobar {19} *vt* **1** : approve of **2** : pass (an exam, etc.) — *vi* : pass — **aprobación** *nf, pl* -ciones : approval
apropiarse *vr* ~ **de** : take possession of, appropriate — **apropiación** *nf, pl* -ciones : appropriation — **apropiado, -da** *adj* : appropriate
aprovechar *vt* : take advantage of, make good use of — *vi* : be of use — **aprovecharse** *vr* ~ **de** : take advantage of — **aprovechado, -da** *adj* **1** : diligent **2** OPORTUNISTA : opportunistic
aproximar *vt* : bring closer — **aproximarse** *vr* : approach — **aproximación** *nf, pl* -ciones : approximation — **aproximadamente** *adv*

: approximately — **aproximado, -da**
adj : approximate

apto, -ta *adj* 1 : suitable 2 CAPAZ : capable — **aptitud** *nf* : aptitude, capability

apuesta *nf* : bet, wager

apuesto, -ta *adj* : elegant, good-looking

apuntalar *vt* : prop up, shore up

apuntar *vt* 1 : aim, point 2 ANOTAR : jot down 3 SEÑALAR : point at 4 : prompt (in theater) — **apuntarse** *vr* 1 : sign up 2 : score, chalk up (a victory, etc.) — **apunte** *nm* : note

apuñalar *vt* : stab

apurar *vt* 1 : hurry, rush 2 AGOTAR : use up 3 PREOCUPAR : trouble — **apurarse** *vr* 1 : worry 2 *Lat* : hurry up — **apuradamente** *adv* : with difficulty — **apurado, -da** *adj* 1 : needy 2 DIFÍCIL : difficult 3 *Lat* : rushed — **apuro** *nm* 1 : predicament, jam 2 *Lat* : hurry

aquejar *vt* : afflict

aquel, aquella *adj, mpl* **aquellos** : that, those

aquél, aquélla *pron, mpl* **aquéllos** 1 : that (one), those (ones) 2 : the former

aquello *pron* : that, that matter

aquí *adv* 1 : here 2 AHORA : now 3 por ~ : hereabouts

aquietar *vt* : calm — **aquietarse** *vr* : calm down

ara *nf* 1 : altar 2 en ~s de : for the sake of

árabe *adj* : Arab, Arabic — ~ *nm* : Arabic (language)

arado *nm* : plow

arancel *nm* : tariff

arándano *nm* : blueberry

araña *nf* 1 : spider 2 LÁMPARA : chandelier

arañar *v* : scratch, claw — **arañazo** *nm* : scratch

arar *v* : plow

arbitrar *v* 1 : arbitrate 2 : referee, umpire (in sports) — **arbitraje** *nm* : arbitration — **arbitrario, -ria** *adj* : arbitrary — **arbitrio** *nm* 1 : (free) will 2 JUICIO : judgment — **árbitro, -tra** *n* 1 : arbitrator 2 : referee, umpire (in sports)

árbol *nm* : tree — **arboleda** *nf* : grove

arbusto *nm* : shrub, bush

arca *nf* 1 : ark 2 COFRE : chest

arcada *nf* 1 : arcade 2 ~s *nfpl* : retching

arcaico, -ca *adj* : archaic

arcano, -na *adj* : arcane, secret

arce *nm* : maple tree

archipiélago *nm* : archipelago

archivar *vt* : file — **archivador** *nm* : filing cabinet — **archivo** *nm* 1 : file 2 : archives *pl*

arcilla *nf* : clay

arco *nm* 1 : arch 2 : bow (in sports, music, etc.) 3 : arc (in geometry) 4 ~ **iris** : rainbow

arder *vi* : burn

ardid *nm* : scheme, ruse

ardiente *adj* 1 : burning 2 FOGOSO : ardent

ardilla *nf* 1 : squirrel 2 ~ **listada** : chipmunk

ardor *nm* 1 : burning 2 ENTUSIASMO : passion, ardor

arduo, -dua *adj* : arduous

área *nf* : area

arena *nf* 1 : sand 2 PALESTRA : arena — **arenoso, -sa** *adj* : sandy, gritty

arenque *nm* : herring

arete *nm* *Lat* : earring

argamasa *nf* : mortar

argentino, -na *adj* : Argentinian, Argentine

argolla *nf* : hoop, ring

argot *nm* : slang

argüir {41} *vt* 1 : argue 2 DEMOSTRAR : prove, show — *vi* : argue

argumentar *vt* : argue, contend — **argumentación** *nf, pl* **-ciones** : (line of) argument — **argumento** *nm* 1 : argument, reasoning 2 TRAMA : plot, story line

árido, -da *adj* : dry, arid — **aridez** *nf, pl* **-deces** : aridity

arisco, -ca *adj* : surly

aristocracia *nf* : aristocracy — **aristócrata** *nmf* : aristocrat — **aristocrático, -ca** *adj* : aristocratic

aritmética *nf* : arithmetic — **aritmético, -ca** *adj* : arithmetic, arithmetical

armar *vt* 1 : arm 2 MONTAR : assemble — **arma** *nf* 1 : arm, weapon 2 ~ **de fuego** : firearm — **armada** *nf* : navy — **armado, -da** *adj* : armed — **armadura** *nf* 1 : armor 2 ARMAZÓN : framework — **armamento** *nm* : armament, arms *pl*

armario *nm* 1 : (clothes) closet 2 : cupboard, cabinet

armazón *nmf, pl* **-zones** : frame, framework

armisticio *nm* : armistice

armonizar {21} *vt* 1 : harmonize 2 : reconcile (differences, etc.) — *vi* : harmonize, go together — **armonía** *nf* : harmony — **armónica** *nf* : harmonica — **armónico, -ca** *adj* : harmonic — **armonioso, -sa** *adj* : harmonious

arnés *nm, pl* **-neses** : harness

aro *nm* 1 : hoop, ring 2 *Lat* : earring
aroma *nm* : aroma, scent — **aromático, -ca** *adj* : aromatic
arpa *nf* : harp
arpón *nm, pl* **-pones** : harpoon
arquear *vt* : arch, bend — **arquearse** *vr* : bend, bow
arqueología *nf* : archaeology — **arqueológico, -ca** *adj* : archaeological — **arqueólogo, -ga** *n* : archaeologist
arquero, -ra *n* 1 : archer 2 PORTERO : goalkeeper, goalie
arquetipo *nm* : archetype
arquitectura *nf* : architecture — **arquitecto, -ta** *n* : architect — **arquitectónico, -ca** *adj* : architectural
arrabal *nm* 1 : slum 2 **~es** *nmpl* : outskirts
arracimarse *vr* : cluster together
arraigar {52} *vi* : take root, become established — **arraigarse** *vr* : settle down — **arraigado, -da** *adj* : deeply rooted, well established — **arraigo** *nm* : roots *pl*
arrancar {72} *vt* 1 : pull out, tear off 2 : start (an engine), boot (a computer) — *vi* 1 : start an engine 2 : get going — **arranque** *nm* 1 : starter (of a car) 2 ARREBATO : outburst 3 **punto de ~** : starting point
arrasar *vt* 1 : destroy, devastate 2 LLENAR : fill to the brim
arrastrar *vt* 1 : drag 2 ATRAER : draw, attract — *vi* : hang down, trail — **arrastrarse** *vr* 1 : crawl, creep 2 HUMILLARSE : grovel — **arrastre** *nm* 1 : dragging 2 : trawling (for fish)
arrear *vt* : urge on
arrebatar *vt* 1 : snatch, seize 2 CAUTIVAR : captivate — **arrebatarse** *vr* : get carried away — **arrebatado, -da** *adj* : hotheaded, rash — **arrebato** *nm* : outburst
arreciar *vi* : intensify, worsen
arrecife *nm* : reef
arreglar *vt* 1 COMPONER : fix 2 ORDENAR : tidy up 3 SOLUCIONAR : solve, work out — **arreglarse** *vr* 1 : get dressed (up) 2 **arreglárselas** *fam* : get by, manage — **arreglado, -da** *adj* 1 : fixed, repaired 2 ORDENADO : tidy 3 SOLUCIONADO : settled, sorted out 4 ATAVIADO : smart, dressed-up — **arreglo** *nm* 1 : arrangement 2 REPARACIÓN : repair 3 ACUERDO : agreement
arremangarse {52} *vr* : roll up one's sleeves
arremeter *vi* : attack, charge — **arremetida** *nf* : attack, onslaught

arremolinarse *vr* 1 : crowd around, mill about 2 : swirl (about)
arrendar {55} *vt* : rent, lease — **arrendador, -dora** *n* : landlord, landlady *f* — **arrendamiento** *nm* : rent, rental — **arrendatario, -ria** *n* : tenant, renter
arrepentirse {76} *vr* 1 : regret, be sorry 2 : repent (for one's sins) — **arrepentido, -da** *adj* : repentant — **arrepentimiento** *nm* : regret, repentance
arrestar *vt* : arrest, detain — **arresto** *nm* : arrest
arriar *vt* : lower
arriba *adv* 1 (*indicating position*) : above, overhead 2 (*indicating direction*) : up, upwards 3 : upstairs (of a house) 4 **~ de** : more than 5 **de ~ abajo** : from top to bottom
arribar *vi* 1 : arrive 2 : dock, put into port — **arribista** *nmf* : parvenu, upstart — **arribo** *nm* : arrival
arriendo → **arrendamiento**
arriesgar {52} *vt* : risk, venture — **arriesgarse** *vr* : take a chance — **arriesgado, -da** *adj* : risky
arrimar *vt* : bring closer, draw near — **arrimarse** *vr* : approach
arrinconar *vt* 1 : corner, box in 2 ABANDONAR : push aside
arrobar *vt* : entrance — **arrobarse** *vr* : be enraptured — **arrobamiento** *nm* : rapture, ecstasy
arrodillarse *vr* : kneel (down)
arrogancia *nf* : arrogance — **arrogante** *adj* : arrogant
arrojar *vt* 1 : hurl, cast 2 EMITIR : give off, spew out 3 PRODUCIR : yield — **arrojarse** *vr* : throw oneself — **arrojado, -da** *adj* : daring — **arrojo** *nm* : boldness, courage
arrollar *vt* 1 : sweep away 2 DERROTAR : crush, overwhelm 3 : run over (with a vehicle) — **arrollador, -dora** *adj* : overwhelming
arropar *vt* : clothe, cover (up) — **arroparse** *vr* : wrap oneself up
arroyo *nm* 1 RIACHUELO : stream 2 : gutter (in a street)
arroz *nm, pl* **arroces** : rice
arrugar {52} *vt* : wrinkle, crease — **arrugarse** *vr* : get wrinkled — **arruga** *nf* : wrinkle, crease
arruinar *vt* : ruin, wreck — **arruinarse** *vr* 1 : be ruined 2 EMPOBRECERSE : go bankrupt
arrullar *vt* : lull to sleep — *vi* : coo — **arrullo** *nm* 1 : lullaby 2 : cooing (of doves)
arrumbar *vt* : lay aside
arsenal *nm* : arsenal

arsénico *nm* : arsenic
arte *nmf (usually m in singular, f in plural)* **1** : art **2** HABILIDAD : skill **3** ASTUCIA : cunning, cleverness **4** → **bello**
artefacto *nm* : artifact, device
arteria *nf* : artery
artesanía *nf* **1** : craftsmanship **2** : handicrafts *pl* — **artesanal** *adj* : handmade — **artesano, -na** *n* : artisan, craftsman
ártico, -ca *adj* : arctic
articular *vt* : articulate — **articulación** *nf, pl* **-ciones 1** : articulation, pronunciation **2** COYUNTURA : joint
artículo *nm* **1** : article **2** **~s de primera necesidad** : essentials **3** **~s de tocador** : toiletries
artífice *nmf* : artisan, craftsman
artificial *adj* : artificial
artificio *nm* **1** HABILIDAD : skill **2** APARATO : device **3** ARDID : artifice, ruse — **artificioso, -sa** *adj* : cunning, deceptive
artillería *nf* : artillery
artilugio *nm* : gadget
artimaña *nf* : ruse, trick
artista *nmf* **1** : artist **2** ACTOR : actor, actress *f* — **artístico, -ca** *adj* : artistic
artritis *nms & pl* : arthritis — **artrítico, -ca** *adj* : arthritic
arveja *nf Lat* : pea
arzobispo *nm* : archbishop
as *nm* : ace
asa *nf* : handle
asado, -da *adj* : roasted, grilled — **asado** *nm* : roast — **asador** *nm* : spit — **asaduras** *nfpl* : offal, entrails
asalariado, -da *n* : wage earner — **~** *adj* : salaried
asaltar *vt* **1** : assault **2** ROBAR : mug, rob — **asaltante** *nmf* **1** : assailant **2** ATRACADOR : mugger, robber — **asalto** *nm* **1** : assault **2** ROBO : mugging, robbery
asamblea *nf* : assembly, meeting
asar *vt* : roast, grill — **asarse** *vr fam* : roast, feel the heat
asbesto *nm* : asbestos
ascender {56} *vi* **1** : ascend, rise up **2** : be promoted (in a job) **3** **~ a** : amount to — *vt* : promote — **ascendencia** *nf* : ancestry, descent — **ascendiente** *nmf* : ancestor — **~** *nm* : influence — **ascensión** *nf, pl* **-siones** : ascent — **ascenso** *nm* **1** : ascent, rise **2** : promotion (in a job) — **ascensor** *nm* : elevator
asco *nm* **1** : disgust **2 hacer ~s de** : turn up one's nose at **3 me da ~** : it makes me sick

ascua *nf* **1** : ember **2 estar en ~s** *fam* : be on edge
asear *vt* : clean, tidy up — **asearse** *vr* : get cleaned up — **aseado, -da** *adj* : clean, tidy
asediar *vt* **1** : besiege **2** ACOSAR : harass — **asedio** *nm* **1** : siege **2** ACOSO : harassment
asegurar *vt* **1** : assure **2** FIJAR : secure **3** : insure (a car, house, etc.) — **asegurarse** *vr* : make sure
asemejarse *vr* **1** : be similar **2** **~ a** : look like, resemble
asentar {55} *vt* **1** : set down **2** INSTALAR : set up, establish **3** *Lat* : state — **asentarse** *vr* **1** : settle **2** ESTABLECERSE : settle down — **asentado, -da** *adj* : settled, established
asentir {76} *vi* : assent, agree — **asentimiento** *nm* : assent
aseo *nm* : cleanliness
asequible *adj* : accessible, attainable
aserrar {55} *vt* : saw — **aserradero** *nm* : sawmill — **aserrín** *nm, pl* **-rrines** : sawdust
asesinar *vt* **1** : murder **2** : assassinate — **asesinato** *nm* **1** : murder **2** : assassination — **asesino, -na** *n* **1** : murderer, killer **2** : assassin
asesorar *vt* : advise, counsel — **asesorarse** *vr* **~ de** : consult — **asesor, -sora** *n* : advisor, consultant — **asesoramiento** *nm* : advice, counsel
asestar {55} *vt* **1** : aim (a weapon) **2** : deal (a blow)
aseverar *vt* : assert — **aseveración** *nf, pl* **-ciones** : assertion
asfalto *nm* : asphalt
asfixiar *vt* : asphyxiate, suffocate — **asfixiarse** *vr* : suffocate — **asfixia** *nf* : asphyxiation, suffocation
así *adv* **1** : like this, like that, thus **2** **~ de** : so, that (much) **3** **~ que** : so, therefore **4** **~ como** : as soon as **5** **~ como** : as well as — **~** *adj* : such, like that — **~** *conj* AUNQUE : even though
asiático, -ca *adj* : Asian, Asiatic
asidero *nm* : handle
asiduo, -dua *adj* : frequent, regular
asiento *nm* : seat
asignar *vt* **1** : assign, allocate **2** DESTINAR : appoint — **asignación** *nf, pl* **-ciones 1** : assignment **2** SUELDO : salary, pay — **asignatura** *nf* : subject, course
asilo *nm* **1** : asylum, home **2** REFUGIO : refuge, shelter — **asilado, -da** *n* : inmate
asimilar *vt* : assimilate — **asimilarse** *vr* **~ a** : resemble

asimismo *adv* 1 : similarly, likewise 2 TAMBIÉN : as well, also

asir {7} *vt* : seize, grasp — **asirse** *vr* ~ **a** : cling to

asistir *vi* ~ **a** : attend, be present at — *vt* : assist — **asistencia** *nf* 1 : attendance 2 AYUDA : assistance — **asistente** *nmf* 1 : assistant 2 los ~s : those present

asma *nf* : asthma — **asmático, -ca** *adj* : asthmatic

asno *nm* : ass, donkey

asociar *vt* : associate — **asociarse** *vr* 1 : form a partnership 2 ~ **a** : join, become a member of — **asociación** *nf, pl* **-ciones** : association — **asociado, -da** *adj* : associate, associated — ~ *n* : associate, partner

asolar {19} *vt* : devastate

asomar *vt* : show, stick out — *vi* : appear, show — **asomarse** *vr* 1 : appear 2 : stick one's head out (of a window)

asombrar *vt* : amaze, astonish — **asombrarse** *vr* : be amazed — **asombro** *nm* : amazement, astonishment — **asombroso, -sa** *adj* : amazing, astonishing

asomo *nm* 1 : hint, trace 2 ni por ~ : by no means

aspaviento *nm* : exaggerated gestures, fuss

aspecto *nm* 1 : aspect 2 APARIENCIA : appearance, look

áspero, -ra *adj* : rough, harsh — **aspereza** *nf* : roughness, harshness

aspersión *nf, pl* **-siones** : sprinkling — **aspersor** *nm* : sprinkler

aspiración *nf, pl* **-ciones** 1 : breathing in 2 ANHELO : aspiration

aspiradora *nf* : vacuum cleaner

aspirar *vi* ~ **a** : aspire to — *vt* : inhale, breathe in — **aspirante** *nmf* : applicant, candidate

aspirina *nf* : aspirin

asquear *vt* : sicken, disgust

asquerosidad *nf* : filth, foulness — **asqueroso, -sa** *adj* : disgusting, sickening

asta *nf* 1 : flagpole 2 CUERNO : antler, horn 3 : shaft (of a spear) — **astado, -da** *adj* : horned

asterisco *nm* : asterisk

asteroide *nm* : asteroid

astigmatismo *nm* : astigmatism

astillar *vt* : splinter — **astilla** *nf* : splinter, chip

astillero *nm* : shipyard

astral *adj* : astral

astringente *adj & nm* : astringent

astro *nm* 1 : heavenly body 2 : star (of movies, etc.)

astrología *nf* : astrology

astronauta *nmf* : astronaut — **astronáutica** *nf* : astronautics

astronave *nf* : spaceship

astronomía *nf* : astronomy — **astronómico, -ca** *adj* : astronomical — **astrónomo, -ma** *n* : astronomer

astucia *nf* 1 : astuteness 2 ARDID : cunning, guile — **astuto, -ta** *adj* 1 : astute 2 TAIMADO : crafty

asueto *nm* : time off, break

asumir *vt* : assume — **asunción** *nf, pl* **-ciones** : assumption

asunto *nm* 1 : matter, affair 2 NEGOCIO : business

asustar *vt* : scare, frighten — **asustarse** *vr* ~ **de** : be frightened of — **asustadizo, -za** *adj* : jumpy, skittish — **asustado, -da** *adj* : frightened, afraid

atacar {72} *v* : attack — **atacante** *nmf* : attacker

atado *nm* : bundle

atadura *nf* : tie, bond

atajar *vt* : block, cut off — *vi* ~ **por** : take a shortcut through — **atajo** *nm* : shortcut

atañer {79} *vi* ~ **a** : concern, have to do with

ataque *nm* 1 : attack, assault 2 ACCESO : fit 3 ~ **de nervios** : nervous breakdown

atar *vt* : tie up, tie down — **atarse** *vr* : tie (up)

atardecer {53} *v impers* : get dark — ~ *nm* : late afternoon, dusk

atareado, -da *adj* : busy

atascar {72} *vt* 1 : block, clog 2 ESTORBAR : hinder — **atascarse** *vr* 1 OBSTRUIRSE : become obstructed 2 : get bogged down — **atasco** *nm* 1 : blockage 2 EMBOTELLAMIENTO : traffic jam

ataúd *nm* : coffin

ataviar {85} *vt* : dress (up) — **ataviarse** *vr* : dress up — **atavío** *nm* : attire

atemorizar {21} *vt* : frighten — **atemorizarse** *vr* : get scared

atención *nf, pl* **-ciones** 1 : attention 2 **prestar** ~ : pay attention 3 **llamar la** ~ : attract attention — ~ *interj* : attention!, watch out!

atender {56} *vt* 1 : attend to 2 CUIDAR : look after 3 : heed (advice, etc.) — *vi* : pay attention

atenerse {80} *vr* ~ **a** : abide by

atentamente *adv* 1 : attentively 2 **le saluda** ~ : sincerely yours

atentar {55} *vi* ~ **contra** : make an attempt on — **atentado** *nm* : attack
atento, -ta *adj* **1** : attentive, mindful **2** CORTÉS : courteous
atenuar {3} *vt* **1** : dim (lights), tone down (colors, etc.) **2** DISMINUIR : lessen — **atenuante** *nmf* : extenuating circumstances
ateo, atea *adj* : atheistic — ~ *n* : atheist
aterciopelado, -da *adj* : velvety, downy
aterido, -da *adj* : frozen stiff
aterrar {55} *vt* : terrify — **aterrador, -dora** *adj* : terrifying
aterrizar {21} *vi* : land — **aterrizaje** *nm* : landing
aterrorizar {21} *vt* : terrify
atesorar *vt* : hoard, amass
atestar {55} *vt* **1** : crowd, pack **2** : testify to (in law) — **atestado, -da** *adj* : stuffed, packed
atestiguar {10} *vt* : testify to
atiborrar *vt* : stuff, cram — **atiborrarse** *vr* : stuff oneself
ático *nm* **1** : penthouse **2** DESVÁN : attic
atildado, -da *adj* : smart, neat
atinar *vi* : be on target
atípico, -ca *adj* : atypical
atirantar *vt* : tighten
atisbar *vt* **1** : spy on **2** VISLUMBRAR : catch a glimpse of — **atisbo** *nm* : sign, hint
atizar {21} *vt* **1** : poke (a fire) **2** : rouse, stir up (passions, etc.) — **atizador** *nm* : poker
atlántico, -ca *adj* : Atlantic
atlas *nm* : atlas
atleta *nmf* : athlete — **atlético, -ca** *adj* : athletic — **atletismo** *nm* : athletics
atmósfera *nf* : atmosphere — **atmosférico, -ca** *adj* : atmospheric
atolondrado, -da *adj* **1** : scatterbrained **2** ATURDIDO : bewildered, dazed
átomo *nm* : atom — **atómico, -ca** *adj* : atomic — **atomizador** *nm* : atomizer
atónito, -ta *adj* : astonished, amazed
atontar *vt* : stun, daze
atorar *vt* : block — **atorarse** *vr* : get stuck
atormentar *vt* : torment, torture — **atormentarse** *vr* : torment oneself, agonize — **atormentador, -dora** *n* : tormenter
atornillar *vt* : screw
atorrante *nmf Lat* : bum, loafer
atosigar {52} *vt* : harass, annoy
atracar {72} *vi* : dock, land — *vt* : hold up, mug — **atracarse** *vr fam* ~ **de** : gorge oneself with — **atracadero**

nm : dock, pier — **atracador, -dora** *n* : robber, mugger
atracción *nf, pl* **-ciones** : attraction
atraco *nm* : holdup, robbery
atractivo, -va *adj* : attractive — **atractivo** *nm* : attraction, appeal
atraer {81} *vt* : attract
atragantarse *vr* : choke
atrancar {72} *vt* **1** : block, bar — **atrancarse** *vr* : get blocked, get stuck
atrapar *vt* : trap, capture
atrás *adv* **1** DETRÁS : back, behind **2** ANTES : before, earlier **3 para** ~ *or* **hacia** ~ : backwards
atrasar *vt* **1** : put back (a clock) **2** DEMORAR : delay — *vi* : lose time — **atrasarse** *vr* : fall behind — **atrasado, -da** *adj* **1** : late, overdue **2** : backward (of countries, etc.) **3** : slow (of a clock) — **atraso** *nm* **1** RETRASO : delay **2** : backwardness **3** ~**s** *nmpl* : arrears
atravesar {55} *vt* **1** CRUZAR : cross **2** TRASPASAR : pierce **3** : lay across (a road, etc.) **4** : go through (a situation) — **atravesarse** *vr* : be in the way
atrayente *adj* : attractive
atreverse *vr* : dare — **atrevido, -da** *adj* **1** : bold **2** INSOLENTE : insolent — **atrevimiento** *nm* **1** : boldness **2** DESCARO : insolence
atribuir {41} *vt* **1** : attribute **2** : confer (powers, etc.) — **atribuirse** *vr* : take credit for
atribular *vt* : afflict, trouble
atributo *nm* : attribute
atrincherar *vt* : entrench — **atrincherarse** *vr* : dig oneself in
atrocidad *nf* : atrocity
atronador, -dora *adj* : thunderous
atropellar *vt* **1** : run over **2** : violate, abuse (a person) — **atropellarse** *vr* : rush — **atropellado, -da** *adj* : hasty — **atropello** *nm* : abuse, outrage
atroz *adj, pl* **atroces** : atrocious
atuendo *nm* : attire
atufar *vt* : vex — **atufarse** *vr* : get angry
atún *nm, pl* **atunes** : tuna
aturdir *vt* **1** : stun, shock **2** CONFUNDIR : bewilder — **aturdido, -da** *adj* : dazed, bewildered
audaz *adj, pl* **-daces** : bold, daring — **audacia** *nf* : boldness, audacity
audible *adj* : audible
audición *nf, pl* **-ciones** **1** : hearing **2** : audition (in theater, etc.)
audiencia *nf* : audience
audífono *nm* **1** : hearing aid **2** ~**s** *nmpl Lat* : headphones, earphones
audiovisual *adj* : audiovisual

auditar vt : audit — **auditor, -tora** n : auditor

auditorio nm 1 : auditorium 2 PÚBLICO : audience

auge nm 1 : peak 2 : (economic) boom

augurar vt : predict, foretell — **augurio** nm : omen

augusto, -ta adj : august

aula nf : classroom

aullar {8} vi : howl — **aullido** nm : howl

aumentar vt : increase, raise — vi : increase, grow — **aumento** nm : increase, rise

aun adv 1 : even 2 ~ **así** : even so

aún adv 1 : still, yet 2 **más** ~ : furthermore

aunar {8} vt : join, combine — **aunarse** vr : unite

aunque conj 1 : though, although, even if 2 ~ **sea** : at least

aureola nf 1 : halo 2 FAMA : aura

auricular nm 1 : telephone receiver 2 ~**s** nmpl : headphones

aurora nf : dawn

ausentarse vr : leave, go away — **ausencia** nf : absence — **ausente** adj : absent — ~ nmf 1 : absentee 2 : missing person (in law)

auspicios nmpl : sponsorship, auspices

austero, -ra adj : austere — **austeridad** nf : austerity

austral adj : southern

australiano, -na adj : Australian

austriaco or **austríaco, -ca** adj : Austrian

auténtico, -ca adj : authentic, genuine — **autenticidad** nf : authenticity

auto nm : auto, car

autoayuda nf : self-help

autobiografía nf : autobiography — **autobiográfico, -ca** adj : autobiographical

autobús nm, pl **-buses** : bus

autocompasión nf : self-pity

autocontrol nm : self-control

autocracia nf : autocracy

autóctono, -na adj : indigenous, native

autodefensa nf : self-defense

autodidacta adj : self-taught

autodisciplina nf : self-discipline

autoestop → **autostop**

autografiar vt : autograph — **autógrafo** nm : autograph

autómata nm : automaton

automático, -ca adj : automatic — **automatización** nf, pl **-ciones** : automation — **automatizar** {21} vt : automate

automotor, -triz adj, fpl **-trices** : self-propelled

automóvil nm : automobile — **automovilista** nmf : motorist — **automovilístico, -ca** adj : automobile, car

autonomía nf : autonomy — **autónomo, -ma** adj : autonomous

autopista nf : expressway, highway

autopropulsado, -da adj : self-propelled

autopsia nf : autopsy

autor, -tora n 1 : author 2 : perpetrator (of a crime)

autoridad nf : authority — **autoritario, -ria** adj : authoritarian

autorizar {21} vt : authorize, approve — **autorización** nf, pl **-ciones** : authorization — **autorizado, -da** adj 1 PERMITIDO : authorized 2 : authoritative

autorretrato nm : self-portrait

autoservicio nm 1 : self-service restaurant 2 SUPERMERCADO : supermarket

autostop nm 1 : hitchhiking 2 **hacer** ~ : hitchhike — **autostopista** nmf : hitchhiker

autosuficiente adj : self-sufficient

auxiliar vt : aid, assist — ~ adj : auxiliary — ~ nmf 1 : assistant, helper 2 ~ **de vuelo** : flight attendant — **auxilio** nm 1 : aid, assistance 2 **primeros** ~**s** : first aid

avalancha nf : avalanche

avalar vt : guarantee, endorse — **aval** nm : guarantee, endorsement

avanzar {21} v : advance, move forward — **avance** nm : advance — **avanzado, -da** adj : advanced

avaricia nf : greed, avarice — **avaricioso, -sa** adj : avaricious, greedy — **avaro, -ra** adj : miserly — ~ n : miser

avasallar vt : overpower, subjugate — **avasallador, -dora** adj : overwhelming

ave nf : bird

avecinarse vr : approach

avecindarse vr : settle, take up residence

avellana nf : hazelnut

avena nf 1 : oats pl 2 or **harina de** ~ : oatmeal

avenida nf : avenue

avenir {87} vt : reconcile, harmonize — **avenirse** vr : agree, come to terms

aventajar vt : be ahead of, surpass

aventar {55} vt 1 : fan 2 : winnow (grain) 3 Lat : throw, toss

aventurar vt : venture, risk — **aventurarse** vr : take a risk — **aventura** nf 1 : adventure 2 RIESGO : risk 3 AMORÍO : love affair — **aventurado, -da** adj

: risky — **aventurero, -ra** *adj* : adventurous — **~** *n* : adventurer

avergonzar {9} *vt* : shame, embarrass — **avergonzarse** *vr* : be ashamed, be embarrassed

averiar {85} *vt* : damage — **averiarse** *vr* : break down — **avería** *nf* 1 : damage 2 : breakdown (of an automobile) — **averiado, -da** *adj* 1 : damaged, faulty 2 : broken down (of an automobile)

averiguar {10} *vt* 1 : find out 2 INVESTIGAR : investigate — **averiguación** *nf, pl* **-ciones** : investigation, inquiry

aversión *nf, pl* **-siones** : aversion, dislike

avestruz *nm, pl* **-truces** : ostrich

aviación *nf, pl* **-ciones** : aviation — **aviador, -dora** *n* : aviator

aviar {85} *vt* : prepare, make ready

ávido, -da *adj* : eager, avid — **avidez** *nf, pl* **-deces** : eagerness

avío *nm* 1 : preparation, provision 2 **~s** *nmpl* : gear, equipment

avión *nm, pl* **aviones** : airplane — **avioneta** *nf* : light airplane

avisar *vt* 1 : notify 2 ADVERTIR : warn — **aviso** *nm* 1 : notice 2 ADVERTENCIA : warning 3 *Lat* : advertisement, ad 4 **estar sobre ~** : be on the alert

avispa *nf* : wasp — **avispón** *nm, pl* **-pones** : hornet

avispado, -da *adj fam* : clever, sharp

avistar *vt* : catch sight of

avivar *vt* 1 : enliven, brighten 2 : arouse (desire, etc.) 3 : intensify (pain)

axila *nf* : underarm, armpit

axioma *nm* : axiom

ay *interj* 1 : oh! 2 : ouch!, ow!

ayer *adv* : yesterday — **~** *nm* : yesteryear, days gone by

ayote *nm Lat* : pumpkin

ayudar *vt* : help, assist — **ayudarse** *vr* **~ de** : make use of — **ayuda** *nf* : help, assistance — **ayudante** *nmf* : helper, assistant

ayunar *vi* : fast — **ayunas** *nfpl* **en ~** : fasting — **ayuno** *nm* : fast

ayuntamiento *nm* 1 : town hall, city hall (building) 2 : town or city council

azabache *nm* : jet

azada *nf* : hoe — **azadonar** *vt* : hoe

azafata *nf* : stewardess *f*

azafrán *nm, pl* **-franes** : saffron

azalea *nf* : azalea

azar *nm* 1 : chance 2 **al ~** : at random — **azaroso, -sa** *adj* : hazardous (of a journey, etc.), eventful (of a life)

azorar *vt* 1 : alarm 2 DESCONCERTAR : embarrass — **azorarse** *vr* : get embarrassed

azotar *vt* : beat, whip — **azote** *nm* 1 LÁTIGO : whip, lash 2 CALAMIDAD : scourge

azotea *nf* : flat or terraced roof

azteca *adj* : Aztec

azúcar *nmf* : sugar — **azucarado, -da** *adj* : sugary — **azucarera** *nf* : sugar bowl — **azucarero, -ra** *adj* : sugar

azufre *nm* : sulphur

azul *adj & nm* : blue — **azulado, -da** *adj* : bluish

azulejo *nm* 1 : ceramic tile 2 *Lat* : bluebird

azur *n* : azure, sky blue

azuzar {21} *vt* : incite, urge on

B

b *nf* : b, second letter of the Spanish alphabet

babear *vi* : drool, slobber — **baba** *nf* : saliva, drool

babel *nmf* : bedlam

babero *nm* : bib

babor *nm* : port (side)

babosa *nf* : slug — **baboso, -sa** *adj* 1 : slimy 2 *Lat fam* : silly

babucha *nf* : slipper

babuino *nm* : baboon

bacalao *nm* : cod

bache *nm* 1 : pothole, rut 2 DIFICULTADES : bad time

bachiller *nmf* : high school graduate — **bachillerato** *nm* : high school diploma

bacon *nm Spain* : bacon

bacteria *nf* : bacterium

bagaje *nm* : baggage, luggage

bagatela *nf* : trinket

bagre *nm* : catfish

bahía *nf* : bay

bailar *v* : dance — **bailarín, -rina** *n, mpl* **-rines** : dancer — **baile** *nm* 1 : dance 2 FIESTA : dance party, ball

bajar *vt* 1 : bring down, lower 2 DESCENDER : go down, come down — *vi* : descend, drop — **bajarse** *vr* **~ de** : get out of, get off — **baja** *nf* 1 : fall, drop 2 CESE : dismissal 3 PERMISO : sick leave 4 : (military) casualty — **bajada** *nf* 1 : descent, drop 2 PENDIENTE : slope

bajeza *nf* : lowness, meanness

bajío *nm* : sandbank, shoal

bajo, -ja *adj* 1 : low, lower 2 : short (in stature) 3 : soft, faint (of sounds) 4 VIL : base, vile — **bajo** *adv* 1 : low 2 **habla más** ~ : speak more softly — ~ *nm* 1 : ground floor 2 DOBLADILLO : hem 3 : bass (in music) — ~ *prep* : under, below — **bajón** *nm, pl* **-jones** : sharp drop, slump

bala *nf* 1 : bullet 2 : bale (of cotton, etc.)

balada *nf* : ballad

balancear *vt* 1 : balance 2 : swing (one's arms, etc.), rock (a boat) — **balancearse** *vr* : swing, sway — **balance** *nm* 1 : balance 2 : balance sheet — **balanceo** *nm* : swaying, rocking

balancín *nm, pl* **-cines** 1 : seesaw 2 MECEDORA : rocking chair

balanza *nf* : scales *pl*, balance

balar *vi* : bleat

balaustrada *nf* : balustrade, banister

balazo *nm* 1 DISPARO : shot 2 : bullet wound

balbucear *vi* 1 : stammer, stutter 2 : babble (of a baby) — **balbuceo** *nm* : stammering, muttering, babbling

balcón *nm, pl* **-cones** : balcony

balde *nm* 1 : bucket, pail 2 **en** ~ : in vain

baldío, -día *adj* 1 : uncultivated 2 INÚTIL : useless — **baldío** *nm* : wasteland

baldosa *nf* : floor tile

balear *vt Lat* : shoot (at) — **baleo** *nm Lat* : shot, shooting

balido *nm* : bleat

balín *nm, pl* **-lines** : pellet

balística *nf* : ballistics — **balístico, -ca** *adj* : ballistic

baliza *nf* 1 : buoy 2 : beacon (for aircraft)

ballena *nf* : whale

ballesta *nf* 1 : crossbow 2 : spring (of an automobile)

ballet *nm* : ballet

balneario *nm* : spa

balompié *nm* : soccer

balón *nm, pl* **-lones** : ball — **baloncesto** *nm* : basketball — **balonvolea** *nm* : volleyball

balsa *nf* 1 : raft 2 ESTANQUE : pond, pool

bálsamo *nm* : balsam, balm — **balsámico, -ca** *adj* : soothing

baluarte *nm* : bulwark, bastion

bambolear *vi* : sway, swing — **bambolearse** *vr* : sway, rock

bambú *nm, pl* **-búes** *or* **-bús** : bamboo

banal *adj* : banal

banana *nf Lat* : banana — **banano** *nm Lat* : banana

banca *nf* 1 : banking 2 BANCO : bench — **bancario, -ria** *adj* : bank, banking

bancarrota *nf* : bankruptcy —

banco *nm* 1 : bank 2 BANCA : stool, bench, pew 3 : school (of fish)

banda *nf* 1 : band, strip 2 : band (in music) 3 PANDILLA : gang 4 : flock (of birds) 5 ~ **sonora** : sound track — **bandada** *nf* : flock (of birds), school (of fish)

bandazo *nm* : lurch

bandeja *nf* : tray, platter

bandera *nf* : flag, banner

banderilla *nf* : banderilla

banderín *nm, pl* **-rines** : pennant, small flag

bandido, -da *n* : bandit

bando *nm* 1 : proclamation, edict 2 PARTIDO : faction, side

bandolero, -ra *n* : bandit

banjo *nm* : banjo

banquero, -ra *n* : banker

banqueta *nf* 1 : stool, footstool 2 *Lat* : sidewalk

banquete *nm* : banquet

bañar *vt* 1 : bathe, wash 2 SUMERGIR : immerse 3 CUBRIR : coat, cover — **bañarse** *vr* 1 : take a bath 2 : go swimming — **bañera** *nf* : bathtub — **bañista** *nmf* : bather — **baño** *nm* 1 : bath, swim 2 BAÑERA : bathtub 3 **¿donde está el** ~? : where is the bathroom? 4 ~ **María** : double boiler

baqueta *nf* 1 : ramrod 2 ~**s** *nfpl* : drumsticks

bar *nm* : bar, tavern

barajar *vt* 1 : shuffle (cards) 2 CONSIDERAR : consider — **baraja** *nf* : deck of cards

baranda *nf* : rail, railing — **barandal** *nm* : handrail, banister

barato, -ta *adj* : cheap — **barato** *adv* : cheap, cheaply — **barata** *nf Lat* : sale, bargain — **baratija** *nf* : trinket — **baratillo** *nm* : secondhand store, flea market

barba *nf* 1 : beard, stubble 2 BARBILLA : chin

barbacoa *nf* : barbecue

barbaridad *nf* 1 : barbarity, cruelty 2 **¡qué** ~**!** : that's outrageous! — **barbarie** *nf* : barbarism, savagery — **bárbaro, -ra** *adj* : barbaric

barbecho *nm* : fallow land

barbero, -ra *n* : barber — **barbería** *nf* : barbershop

barbilla *nf* : chin

barbudo, -da *adj* : bearded

barca *nf* 1 : boat 2 ~ **de pasaje** : ferryboat — **barcaza** *nf* : barge — **barco** *nm* : boat, ship

barítono *nm* : baritone

barman *nm* : bartender
barnizar {21} *vt* **1** : varnish **2** : glaze (ceramics) — **barniz** *nm, pl* **-nices 1** : varnish **2** : glaze (on ceramics)
barómetro *nm* : barometer
barón *nm, pl* **-rones** : baron — **baronesa** *nf* : baroness
barquero *nm* : boatman
barquillo *nm* : wafer, cone
barra *nf* **1** : bar, rod, stick **2** : counter (of a bar, etc.)
barraca *nf* **1** : hut, cabin **2** CASETA : booth, stall
barranco *nm* *or* **barranca** *nf* : ravine, gorge, gully
barredera *nf* : street-sweeping machine
barrenar *vt* : drill — **barrena** *nf* : drill, auger
barrer *v* : sweep
barrera *nf* : barrier
barreta *nf* : crowbar
barriada *nf* : district, quarter
barrica *nf* : cask, keg
barricada *nf* : barricade
barrido *nm* : sweep, sweeping
barriga *nf* : belly
barril *nm* **1** : barrel, keg **2 de ~** : draft
barrio *nm* **1** : neighborhood **2 ~ bajo** : slums *pl*
barro *nm* **1** : mud **2** ARCILLA : clay **3** GRANO : pimple, blackhead — **barroso, -sa** *adj* : muddy
barrote *nm* : bar (on a window)
barrunto *nm* **1** : suspicion **2** INDICIO : sign, indication
bártulos *nmpl* : things, belongings
barullo *nm* : racket, ruckus
basa *nf* : base, pedestal — **basar** *vt* : base — **basarse** *vr* **~ en** : be based on
báscula *nf* : scales *pl*
base *nf* **1** : base **2** FUNDAMENTO : basis, foundation **3 ~ de datos** : database — **básico, -ca** *adj* : basic
basquetbol *or* **básquetbol** *nm* *Lat* : basketball
bastar *vi* : be enough, suffice — **bastante** *adv* **1** : fairly, rather **2** SUFICIENTE : enough — **~** *adj* : enough, sufficient — **~** *pron* : enough
bastardo, -da *adj* & *n* : bastard
bastidor *nm* **1** : frame **2** : wing (in theater) **3 entre ~es** : behind the scenes, backstage
bastilla *nf* : hem
bastión *nf, pl* **-tiones** : bastion, stronghold
basto, -ta *adj* : coarse, rough
bastón *nm, pl* **-tones 1** : cane, walking stick **2** : baton (in parades)

basura *nf* : garbage, rubbish — **basurero, -ra** *n* : garbage collector
bata *nf* **1** : bathrobe, housecoat **2** : smock (of a doctor, laboratory worker, etc.)
batallar *vi* : battle, fight — **batalla** *nf* **1** : battle, fight, struggle **2 de ~** : ordinary, everyday — **batallón** *nm, pl* **-llones** : battalion
batata *nf* : yam, sweet potato
batear *v* : bat, hit — **bate** *nm* : baseball bat — **bateador, -dora** *n* : batter, hitter
batería *nf* **1** : battery **2** : drums *pl* **3 ~ de cocina** : kitchen utensils *pl*
batir *vt* **1** : beat, whip **2** DERRIBAR : knock down — **batirse** *vr* : fight — **batido** *nm* : milk shake — **batidor** *nm* : eggbeater, whisk — **batidora** *nf* : electric mixer
batuta *nf* : baton
baúl *nm* : trunk, chest
bautismo *nm* : baptism — **bautismal** *adj* : baptismal — **bautizar** {21} *vt* : baptize — **bautizo** *nm* : baptism, christening
baya *nf* : berry
bayeta *nf* : cleaning cloth
bayoneta *nf* : bayonet
bazar *nm* : bazaar
bazo *nm* : spleen
bazofia *nf fam* : rubbish, hogwash
beato, -ta *adj* : blessed
bebé *nm* : baby
beber *v* : drink — **bebedero** *nm* : watering trough — **bebedor, -dora** *n* : (heavy) drinker — **bebida** *nf* : drink, beverage — **bebido, -da** *adj* : drunk
beca *nf* : grant, scholarship
becerro, -rra *n* : calf
befa *nf* : jeer, taunt
beige *adj* & *nm* : beige
beisbol *or* **béisbol** *nm* : baseball — **beisbolista** *nmf* : baseball player
beldad *nf* : beauty
belén *nf, pl* **-lenes** : Nativity scene
belga *adj* : Belgian
beliceño, -ña *adj* : Belizean
bélico, -ca *adj* : military, war — **belicoso, -sa** *adj* : warlike
beligerancia *nf* : belligerence — **beligerante** *adj* & *nmf* : belligerent
belleza *nf* : beauty — **bello, -lla** *adj* **1** : beautiful **2 bellas artes** : fine arts
bellota *nf* : acorn
bemol *adj* & *nm* : flat (in music)
bendecir {11} *vt* **1** : bless **2 ~ la mesa** : say grace — **bendición** *nf, pl* **-ciones** : benediction, blessing — **bendito, -ta** *adj* **1** : blessed, holy **2** DI-

CHOSO : fortunate **3 ¡bendito sea Dios!** : thank goodness!
benefactor, -tora *n* : benefactor
beneficiar *vt* : benefit, assist — **beneficiarse** *vr* : benefit, profit — **beneficiario, -ria** *n* : beneficiary — **beneficio** *nm* **1** BIEN : benefit — **beneficioso, -sa** *adj* : beneficial — **benéfico, -ca** *adj* : charitable
benemérito, -ta *adj* : worthy
beneplácito *nm* : approval, consent
benévolo, -la *adj* : benevolent, kind — **benevolencia** *nf* : benevolence, kindness
bengala *nf or* **luz de ~** : flare
benigno, -na *adj* **1** : mild **2** : benign (in medicine) — **benignidad** *nf* : mildness, kindness
benjamín, -mina *n, mpl* **-mines** : youngest child
beodo, -da *adj & n* : drunk
berenjena *nf* : eggplant
berrear *vi* **1** : bellow, low **2** : bawl, howl (of a person) — **berrido** *nm* **1** : bellowing **2** : howl, scream (of a person)
berro *nm* : watercress
berza *nf* : cabbage
besar *vt* : kiss — **besarse** *vr* : kiss (each other) — **beso** *nm* : kiss
bestia *nf* : beast, animal — **bestial** *adj* : bestial, brutal — **bestialidad** *nf* : brutality
betabel *nm Lat* : beet
betún *nm, pl* **-tunes** : shoe polish
bianual *adj* : biannual
biberón *nm, pl* **-rones** : baby's bottle
Biblia *nf* : Bible — **bíblico, -ca** *adj* : biblical
bibliografía *nf* : bibliography — **bibliográfico, -ca** *adj* : bibliographic, bibliographical
biblioteca *nf* : library — **bibliotecario, -ria** *n* : librarian
bicarbonato *nm* **~ de soda** : baking soda
bicentenario *nm* : bicentennial
bíceps *nms & pl* : biceps
bicho *nm* : small animal, bug
bicicleta *nf* : bicycle — **bici** *nf fam* : bike
bicolor *adj* : two-tone
bidón *nm, pl* **-dones** : large can, drum
bien *adv* **1** : well, good **2** CORRECTAMENTE : correctly, right **3** MUY : very, quite **4** DE BUENA GANA : willingly **5 ~ que** : although **6 más ~** : rather — **bien** *adj* **1** : all right, well **2** AGRADABLE : pleasant, nice **3** SATISFACTORIO : satisfactory **4** CORRECTO : correct, right — **bien** *nm* **1** : good **2 ~es** *nmpl* : property, goods

bienal *adj & nf* : biennial
bienaventurado, -da *adj* : blessed, fortunate
bienestar *nm* : welfare, well-being
bienhechor, -chora *n* : benefactor
bienintencionado, -da *adj* : well-meaning
bienvenido, -da *adj* : welcome — **bienvenida** *nf* **1** : welcome **2 dar la ~ a** : welcome (s.o.)
bife *nm Lat* : steak
bifocales *nmpl* : bifocals
bifurcarse {72} *vr* : fork — **bifurcación** *nf, pl* **-ciones** : fork, branch
bigamia *nf* : bigamy
bigote *nm* **1** : mustache **2 ~s** *nmpl* : whiskers (of an animal)
bikini *nm* : bikini
bilingüe *adj* : bilingual
bilis *nf* : bile
billar *nm* : pool, billiards
billete *nm* **1** : bill, banknote **2** BOLETO : ticket — **billetera** *nf* : billfold, wallet
billón *nm, pl* **-llones** : trillion
bimensual, -suale *adj* : twice a month — **bimestral** *adj* : bimonthly
binario, -ria *adj* : binary
bingo *nm* : bingo
binoculares *nmpl* : binoculars
biodegradable *adj* : biodegradable
biofísica *nf* : biophysics
biografía *nf* : biography — **biográfico, -ca** *adj* : biographical — **biógrafo, -fa** *n* : biographer
biología *nf* : biology — **biológico, -ca** *adj* : biological, biologic — **biólogo, -ga** *n* : biologist
biombo *nm* : folding screen
biomecánica *nf* : biomechanics
biopsia *nf* : biopsy
bioquímica *nf* : biochemistry — **bioquímico, -ca** *adj* : biochemical
biotecnología *nf* : biotechnology
bipartidista *adj* : bipartisan
bípedo *nm* : biped
biquini → bikini
birlar *vt fam* : swipe, pinch
bis *adv* **1** : twice (in music) **2** : A (in an address) — *nm* : encore
bisabuelo, -la *n* : great-grandfather *m*, great-grandmother *f*
bisagra *nf* : hinge
bisecar {72} *vt* : bisect
biselar *vt* : bevel
bisexual *adj* : bisexual
bisiesto *adj* **año ~** : leap year
bisnieto, -ta *n* : great-grandson *m*, great-granddaughter *f*
bisonte *nm* : bison, buffalo
bisoño, -ña *n* : novice

bistec *nm* : steak
bisturí *nm* : scalpel
bisutería *nf* : costume jewelry
bit *nm* : bit (unit of information)
bizco, -ca *adj* : cross-eyed
bizcocho *nm* : sponge cake
bizquear *vi* : squint — **bizquera** *nf* : squint
blanco, -ca *adj* : white — **blanco, -ca** *n* : white person — **blanco** *nm* 1 : white 2 DIANA : target, bull's-eye 3 : blank (space) — **blancura** *nf* : whiteness
blandir {1} *vt* : wave, brandish
blando, -da *adj* 1 : soft, tender 2 DÉBIL : weak-willed 3 INDULGENTE : lenient — **blandura** *nf* 1 : softness, tenderness 2 DEBILIDAD : weakness 3 INDULGENCIA : leniency
blanquear *vt* 1 : whiten, bleach 2 : launder (money) — *vi* : turn white — **blanqueador** *nm Lat* : bleach
blasfemar *vi* : blaspheme — **blasfemia** *nf* : blasphemy — **blasfemo, -ma** *adj* : blasphemous
bledo *nm* **no me importa un ~** *fam* : I couldn't care less
blindaje *nm* : armor, armor plating — **blindado, -da** *adj* : armored
bloc *nm, pl* **blocs** : (writing) pad
bloquear *vt* 1 OBSTRUIR : block, obstruct 2 : blockade — **bloque** *nm* 1 : block 2 : bloc (in politics) — **bloqueo** *nm* 1 OBSTRUCCIÓN : blockage 2 : blockade
blusa *nf* : blouse — **blusón** *nm, pl* **-sones** : smock
boato *nm* : showiness
bobina *nf* : bobbin, reel
bobo, -ba *adj* : silly, stupid — **~** *n* : fool, simpleton
boca *nf* 1 : mouth 2 ENTRADA : entrance 3 **~ arriba** : faceup 4 **~ abajo** : facedown, prone 5 **~ de riego** : hydrant
bocacalle *nf* : entrance (to a street)
bocado *nm* 1 : bite, mouthful 2 : bit (of a bridle) — **bocadillo** *nm Spain* : sandwich
bocajarro *nm* **a ~** : point-blank
bocallave *nf* : keyhole
bocanada *nf* 1 : swallow, swig 2 : puff, gust (of smoke, wine, etc.)
boceto *nm* : sketch, outline
bochorno *nm* 1 VERGÜENZA : embarrassment 2 : muggy weather — **bochornoso, -sa** *adj* 1 VERGONZOSO : embarrassing 2 : muggy, sultry
bocina *nf* 1 : horn 2 : mouthpiece (of a telephone) — **bocinazo** *nm* : honk, toot
boda *nf* : wedding
bodega *nf* 1 : wine cellar 2 : warehouse

3 : hold (of a ship or airplane) 4 *Lat* : grocery store
bofetear *vt* : slap — **bofetada** *nf or* **bofetón** *nm* : slap (in the face)
boga *nf* : fashion, vogue
bohemio, -mia *adj & n* : bohemian
boicotear *vt* : boycott — **boicot** *nm, pl* **-cots** : boycott
boina *nf* : beret
bola *nf* 1 : ball 2 *fam* : fib
bolera *nf* : bowling alley
boleta *nf Lat* : ticket — **boletería** *nf Lat* : ticket office
boletín *nm, pl* **-tines** 1 : bulletin 2 **~ de noticias** : news release
boleto *nm* : ticket
boliche *nm* 1 : bowling 2 BOLERA : bowling alley
bolígrafo *nm* : ballpoint pen
bolillo *nm* : bobbin
boliviano, -na *adj* : Bolivian
bollo *nm* : bun, sweet roll
bolo *nm* 1 : bowling pin 2 **~s** *nmpl* : bowling
bolsa *nf* 1 : bag 2 *Lat* : pocketbook, purse 3 **la Bolsa** : the stock market — **bolsillo** *nm* : pocket — **bolso** *nm Spain* : pocketbook, handbag
bomba *nf* 1 : bomb 2 **~ de gasolina** : gas pump
bombachos *nmpl* : baggy trousers
bombardear *vt* : bomb, bombard — **bombardeo** *nm* : bombing, bombardment — **bombardero** *nm* : bomber (airplane)
bombear *vt* : pump — **bombero, -ra** *n* : firefighter
bombilla *nf* : lightbulb — **bombillo** *nm Lat* : lightbulb
bombo *nm* 1 : bass drum 2 **a ~s y platillos** : with a great fanfare
bombón *nm, pl* **-bones** : candy, chocolate
bonachón, -chona *adj, mpl* **-chones** *fam* : good-natured
bonanza *nf* 1 : fair weather (at sea) 2 PROSPERIDAD : prosperity
bondad *nf* : goodness, kindness — **bondadoso, -sa** *adj* : kind, good
boniato *nm* : sweet potato
bonificación *nf, pl* **-ciones** 1 : bonus, extra 2 DESCUENTO : discount
bonito, -ta *adj* : pretty, lovely
bono *nm* 1 : bond 2 VALE : voucher
boquear *vi* : gasp — **boqueada** *nf* : gasp
boquerón *nm, pl* **-rones** : anchovy
boquete *nm* : gap, opening
boquiabierto, -ta *adj* : open-mouthed, speechless

boquilla *nf* : mouthpiece (of a musical instrument)

borbollar *vi* : bubble

borbotar *or* **borbotear** *vi* : boil, bubble, gurgle — **borbotón** *nm, pl* **-tones** 1 : spurt 2 **salir a borbotones** : gush out

bordar *v* : embroider — **bordado** *nm* : embroidery, needlework

borde *nm* 1 : border, edge 2 **al ~ de** : on the verge of — **bordear** *vt* : border — **bordillo** *nm* : curb

bordo *nm* **a ~** : aboard, on board

borla *nf* 1 : pom-pom, tassel 2 : powder puff

borracho, -cha *adj & n* : drunk — **borrachera** *nf* : drunkenness

borrar *vt* : erase, blot out — **borrador** *nm* 1 : rough draft 2 : eraser (for a blackboard)

borrascoso, -sa *adj* : stormy

borrego, -ga *n* : lamb, sheep — **borrego** *nm Lat* : false rumor, hoax

borrón *nm, pl* **-rrones** 1 : smudge, blot 2 **~ y cuenta nueva** : let's forget about it — **borroso, -sa** *adj* 1 : blurry, smudgy 2 INDISTINTO : vague, hazy

bosque *nm* : woods, forest — **boscoso, -sa** *adj* : wooded

bosquejar *vt* : sketch (out) — **bosquejo** *nm* : outline, sketch

bostezar {21} *vi* : yawn — **bostezo** *nm* : yawn

bota *nf* : boot

botánica *nf* : botany — **botánico, -ca** *adj* : botanical

botar *vt* 1 : throw, hurl 2 *Lat* : throw away 3 : launch (a ship) — *vi* : bounce

bote *nm* 1 : small boat 2 *Spain* : can 3 TARRO : jar 4 SALTO : bounce, jump

botella *nf* : bottle

botín *nm, pl* **-tines** 1 : ankle boot 2 DESPOJOS : booty, plunder

botiquín *nm, pl* **-quines** 1 : medicine cabinet 2 : first-aid kit

botón *nm, pl* **-tones** 1 : button 2 YEMA : bud — **botones** *nmfs & pl* : bellhop

botulismo *nm* : botulism

boutique *nf* : boutique

bóveda *nf* : vault

boxear *vi* : box — **boxeador, -dora** *n* : boxer — **boxeo** *nm* : boxing

boya *nf* : buoy — **boyante** *adj* 1 : buoyant 2 PRÓSPERO : prosperous, thriving

bozal *nm* 1 : muzzle 2 : halter (for a horse)

bracear *vi* 1 : wave one's arms 2 NADAR : swim, crawl

bracero, -ra *n* : day laborer

bragas *nf Spain* : panties

bragueta *nf* : fly, pants zipper

braille *adj & nm* : braille

bramante *nm* : twine, string

bramar *vi* 1 : bellow, roar 2 : howl (of the wind) — **bramido** *nm* : bellow, roar

brandy *nm* : brandy

branquia *nf* : gill

brasa *nf* : ember

brasier *nm Lat* : brassiere

brasileño, -ña *adj* : Brazilian

bravata *nf* 1 : boast, bravado 2 AMENAZO : threat

bravo, -va *adj* 1 : fierce, savage 2 : rough (of the sea) 3 *Lat* : angry — **~** *interj* : bravo!, well done! — **bravura** *nf* 1 FEROCIDAD : fierceness 2 VALENTÍA : bravery

braza *nf* 1 : breaststroke 2 : fathom (measurement) — **brazada** *nf* : stroke (in swimming)

brazalete *nm* 1 : bracelet 2 : (cloth) armband

brazo *nm* 1 : arm 2 : branch (of a river, etc.) 3 **~ derecho** : right-hand man 4 **~s** *nmpl* : hands, laborers

brea *nf* : tar

brebaje *nm* : concoction

brecha *nf* : breach, gap

brécol *nm* : broccoli

bregar {52} *vi* 1 LUCHAR : struggle 2 TRABAJAR : work hard — **brega** *nf* **andar a la ~** : struggle

breña *nf or* **breñal** *nm* : scrubland, brush

breve *adj* 1 : brief, short 2 **en ~** : shortly, in short — **brevedad** *nf* : brevity, shortness — **brevemente** *adv* : briefly

brezal *nm* : moor, heath — **brezo** *nm* : heather

bricolaje *or* **bricolage** *nm* : do-it-yourself

brida *nf* : bridle

brigada *nf* 1 : brigade 2 EQUIPO : gang, team, squad

brillar *vi* : shine, sparkle — **brillante** *adj* : brilliant, shiny — **~** *nm* : diamond — **brillantez** *nf* : brilliance — **brillo** *nm* 1 : luster, shine 2 ESPLENDOR : splendor — **brilloso, -sa** *adj* : shiny

brincar {72} *vi* : jump about, frolic — **brinco** *nm* : jump, skip

brindar *vi* : drink a toast — *vt* : offer, provide — **brindarse** *vr* : offer one's assistance — **brindis** *nm* : drink, toast

brío *nm* 1 : force, determination 2 ÁNIMO : spirit, verve — **brioso, -sa** *adj* : spirited, lively

brisa *nf* : breeze

británico, -ca *adj* : British

brizna *nf* **1** : strand, thread **2** : blade (of grass)

brocado *nm* : brocade

brocha *nf* : paintbrush

broche *nm* **1** : fastener, clasp **2** ALFILER : brooch

brocheta *nf* : skewer

brócoli *nm* : broccoli

bromear *vi* : joke, fool around — **broma** *nf* : joke, prank — **bromista** *adj* : fun-loving, joking — **~** *nmf* : joker, prankster

bronca *nf fam* : fight, row

bronce *nm* : bronze — **bronceado, -da** *adj* : suntanned — **bronceado** *nm* : tan — **broncearse** *vr* : get a suntan

bronco, -ca *adj* **1** : harsh, rough **2** : untamed, wild (of a horse)

bronquitis *nf* : bronchitis

broqueta *nf* : skewer

brotar *vi* **1** : bud, sprout **2** : stream, gush (of a river, tears, etc.) **3** : arise (of feelings, etc.) **4** : break out (in medicine) — **brote** *nm* **1** : outbreak **2** : sprout, bud, shoot (of plants)

brujería *nf* : witchcraft — **bruja** *nf* **1** : witch **2** *fam* : old hag — **brujo** *nm* : warlock, sorcerer — **brujo, -ja** *adj* : bewitching

brújula *nf* : compass

bruma *nf* : haze, mist — **brumoso, -sa** *adj* : hazy, misty

bruñir {38} *vt* : burnish, polish

brusco, -ca *adj* **1** SÚBITO : sudden, abrupt **2** TOSCO : brusque, rough — **brusquedad** *nf* : abruptness, brusqueness

brutal *adj* : brutal — **brutalidad** *nf* : brutality

bruto, -ta *adj* **1** : brutish, stupid **2** : crude (of petroleum, etc.), uncut (of diamonds) **3 peso ~** : gross weight — **~** *n* : brute

bucal *adj* : oral

bucear *vi* **1** : dive, swim underwater **2 ~ en** : delve into — **buceo** *nm* : (underwater) diving

bucle *nm* : curl

budín *nm, pl* **-dines** : pudding

budismo *nm* : Buddhism — **budista** *adj & nmf* : Buddhist

buenamente *adv* **1** : easily **2** VOLUNTARIAMENTE : willingly

buenaventura *nf* **1** : good luck **2 decir la ~ a uno** : tell s.o.'s fortune

bueno, -na *adj* (**buen** *before masculine singular nouns*) **1** : good **2** AMABLE : kind **3** APROPIADO : appropriate **4** SALUDABLE : well, healthy **5** : nice,

fine (of weather) **6 buenos días** : hello, good day **7 buenas noches** : good night **8 buenas tardes** : good afternoon, good evening — **bueno** *interj* : OK!, all right!

buey *nm* : ox, steer

búfalo *nm* : buffalo

bufanda *nf* : scarf

bufar *vi* : snort — **bufido** *nm* : snort

bufet *or* **bufé** *nm* : buffet-style meal

bufete *nm* **1** : law practice **2** MESA : writing desk

bufo, -fa *adj* : comic — **bufón, -fona** *n, mpl* **-fones** : buffoon, jester — **bufonada** *nf* : wisecrack

buhardilla *nf* : attic, garret

búho *nm* : owl

buitre *nm* : vulture

bujía *nf* : spark plug

bulbo *nm* : bulb (of a plant)

bulevar *nm* : boulevard

búlgaro, -ra *adj* : Bulgarian

bulla *nf* : uproar, racket

bulldozer *nm* : bulldozer

bullicio *nm* **1** : uproar **2** AJETREO : hustle and bustle — **bullicioso, -sa** *adj* : noisy, boisterous

bullir {38} *vi* **1** : boil **2** AJETREARSE : bustle, stir

bulto *nm* **1** : package, bundle **2** VOLUMEN : bulk, size **3** FORMA : form, shape **4** PROTUBERANCIA : lump, swelling

bumerán *nm, pl* **-ranes** : boomerang

buñuelo *nm* : fried pastry

buque *nm* : ship

burbujear *vi* : bubble — **burbuja** *nf* : bubble

burdel *nm* : brothel

burdo, -da *adj* : coarse, rough

burgués, -guesa *adj & n, mpl* **-gueses** : bourgeois — **burguesía** *nf* : bourgeoisie

burlar *vt* : trick, deceive — **burlarse** *vr* **~ de** : make fun of — **burla** *nf* **1** MOFA : mockery, ridicule **2** BROMA : joke, trick

burlesco, -ca *adj* : comic, funny

burlón, -lona *adj, mpl* **-lones** : mocking

burocracia *nf* : bureaucracy — **burócrata** *nmf* : bureaucrat — **burocrático, -ca** *adj* : bureaucratic

burro, -rra *n* **1** : donkey **2** *fam* : dunce — **~** *adj* : stupid — **burro** *nm* **1** : sawhorse **2** *Lat* : stepladder

bus *nm* : bus

buscar {72} *vt* **1** : look for, seek **2 ir a ~ a uno** : fetch s.o. — *vi* : search — **busca** *nf* : search — **búsqueda** *nf* : search

busto *nm* : bust (in sculpture)
butaca *nf* **1** : armchair **2** : (theater) seat
butano *nm* : butane

buzo *nm* : diver
buzón *nm, pl* **-zones** : mailbox
byte ['bait] *nm* : byte

C

c *nf* : c, third letter of the Spanish alphabet
cabal *adj* **1** : exact **2** COMPLETO : complete — **cabales** *nmpl* **no estar en sus ~** : not be in one's right mind
cabalgar {52} *vi* : ride — **cabalgata** *nf* : cavalcade
caballa *nf* : mackerel
caballería *nf* **1** : cavalry **2** CABALLO : horse, mount — **caballeriza** *nf* : stable
caballero *nm* **1** : gentleman **2** : knight (rank) — **caballerosidad** *nf* : chivalry — **caballeroso, -sa** *adj* : chivalrous
caballete *nm* **1** : ridge (of a roof) **2** : easel (for a canvas) **3** : bridge (of the nose)
caballito *nm* **1** : rocking horse **2 ~s** *nmpl* : merry-go-round
caballo *nm* **1** : horse **2** : knight (in chess) **3 ~ de fuerza** : horsepower
cabaña *nf* : cabin, hut
cabaret *nm, pl* **-rets** : nightclub, cabaret
cabecear *vi* **1** : shake one's head, nod **2** : pitch, lurch (of a boat)
cabecera *nf* **1** : head (of a bed, etc.) **2** : heading (in a text) **3 médico de ~** : family doctor
cabecilla *nmf* : ringleader
cabello *nm* : hair — **cabelludo, -da** *adj* : hairy
caber {12} *vi* **1** : fit, go (into) **2 no cabe duda** : there's no doubt
cabestro *nm* : halter
cabeza *nf* **1** : head **2 de ~** : head first — **cabezada** *nf* **1** : butt (of the head) **2 dar ~s** : nod off
cabezal *nm* : bolster, headrest
cabida *nf* **1** : room, capacity **2 dar ~ a** : accomodate, find room for
cabina *nf* **1** : booth **2** : cab (of a truck, etc.) **3** : cabin, cockpit (of an airplane)
cabizbajo, -ja *adj* : downcast
cable *nm* : cable
cabo *nm* **1** : end, stub **2** TROZO : bit **3** : corporal (in the military) **4** : cape (in geography) **5 al fin y al ~** : after all **6 llevar a ~** : carry out, do
cabra *nf* : goat

cabriola *nf* **1** : leap, skip **2 hacer ~s** : prance around
cabrito *nm* : kid (goat)
cacahuate *or* **cacahuete** *nm* : peanut
cacao *nm* **1** : cacao (tree) **2** : cocoa (drink)
cacarear *vi* : crow, cackle — *vt fam* : boast about
cacería *nf* : hunt
cacerola *nf* : pan, saucepan
cacharro *nm* **1** *fam* : thing, piece of junk **2** *fam* : jalopy **3 ~s** *nmpl* : pots and pans
cachear *vt* : search, frisk
cachemir *nm or* **cachemira** *nf* : cashmere
cachete *nm Lat* : cheek — **cachetada** *nf Lat* : slap
cacho *nm* **1** *fam* : piece, bit **2** *Lat* : horn
cachorro, -rra *n* **1** : cub **2** PERRITO : puppy
cactus *or* **cacto** *nm* : cactus
cada *adj* : each, every
cadalso *nm* : scaffold
cadáver *nm* : corpse
cadena *nf* **1** : chain **2** : (television) channel **3 ~ de montaje** : assembly line
cadencia *nf* : cadence
cadera *nf* : hip
cadete *nmf* : cadet
caducar {72} *vi* : expire — **caducidad** *nf* : expiration
caer {13} *vi* **1** : fall, drop **2 ~ bien a uno** : be to one's liking **3 dejar ~** : drop **4 me cae bien** : I like her, I like him — **caerse** *vr* : drop, fall (down)
café *nm* **1** : coffee **2** : café — *nm ~ adj Lat* : brown — **cafetera** *nf* : coffeepot — **cafetería** *nf* : coffee shop, cafeteria — **cafeína** *nf* : caffeine
caída *nf* **1** : fall, drop **2** PENDIENTE : slope
caimán *nm, pl* **-manes** : alligator
caja *nf* **1** : box, case **2** : checkout counter, cashier's desk (in a store) **3 ~ fuerte** : safe **4 ~ registradora** : cash register — **cajero, -ra** *n* **1** : cashier **2** : (bank) teller — **cajetilla** *nf* : pack (of cigarettes) — **cajón** *nm, pl* **-jones 1**

: drawer (in furniture) **2** : large box, crate

cajuela *nf Lat* : trunk (of a car)

cal *nf* : lime

cala *nf* : cove

calabaza *nf* **1** : pumpkin, squash, gourd **2 dar ~s a** *fam* : give the brush-off to — **calabacín** *nm, pl* **-cines** *or* **calabacita** *nf Lat* : zucchini

calabozo *nm* **1** : prison **2** CELDA : cell

calamar *nm* : squid

calambre *nm* **1** ESPASMO : cramp **2** : (electric) shock

calamidad *nf* : calamity

calar *vt* **1** : soak (through) **2** PERFORAR : pierce — **calarse** *vr* : get drenched

calavera *nf* : skull

calcar {72} *vt* **1** : trace **2** IMITAR : copy, imitate

calcetín *nm, pl* **-tines** : sock

calcinar *vt* : char

calcio *nm* : calcium

calcomanía *nf* : decal

calcular *vt* : calculate, estimate — **calculador, -dora** *adj* : calculating — **calculadora** *nf* : calculator — **cálculo** *nm* **1** : calculation **2** : calculus (in mathematics and medicine) **3 ~ biliar** : gallstone

caldera *nf* **1** : cauldron **2** : boiler (for heating, etc.) — **caldo** *nm* : broth, stock

calefacción *nf, pl* **-ciones** : heating, heat

calendario *nm* : calendar

calentar {55} *vt* : heat (up), warm (up) — **calentarse** *vr* : get warm, heat up — **calentador** *nm* : heater — **calentura** *nf* : temperature, fever

calibre *nm* **1** : caliber **2** DIÁMETRO : bore, diameter — **calibrar** *vt* : calibrate

calidad *nf* **1** : quality **2 en ~ de** : as, in the capacity of

cálido, -da *adj* : hot, warm

calidoscopio *nm* : kaleidoscope

caliente *adj* **1** : hot **2** ACALORADO : heated, fiery

calificar {72} *vt* **1** : qualify **2** EVALUAR : rate **3** : grade (an exam, etc.) — **calificación** *nf, pl* **-ciones** **1** : qualification **2** EVALUACIÓN : rating **3** NOTA : grade — **calificativo, -va** *adj* : qualifying — **calificativo** *nm* : qualifier, epithet

caligrafía *nf* : penmanship

calistenia *nf* : calisthenics

cáliz *nm, pl* **-lices** : chalice

caliza *nf* : limestone

callar *vi* : keep quiet, be silent — *vt* **1**

: silence, hush **2** OCULTAR : keep secret — **callarse** *vr* : remain silent — **callado, -da** *adj* : quiet, silent

calle *nf* : street, road — **callejear** *vi* : wander about the streets — **callejero, -ra** *adj* **1** : street **2 perro callejero** : stray dog — **callejón** *nm, pl* **-jones 1** : alley **2 ~ sin salida** : dead-end street

callo *nm* : callus, corn

calma *nf* : calm, quiet — **calmante** *adj* : soothing — **~** *nm* : tranquilizer — **calmar** *vt* : calm, soothe — **calmarse** *vr* : calm down — **calmo, -ma** *adj Lat* : calm — **calmoso, -sa** *adj* **1** : calm **2** LENTO : slow

calor *nm* **1** : heat, warmth **2 tener ~** : be hot — **caloría** *nf* : calorie

calumnia *nf* : slander, libel — **calumniar** *vt* : slander, libel

caluroso, -sa *adj* **1** : hot **2** : warm, enthusiastic (of applause, etc.)

calvo, -va *adj* : bald — **calvicie** *nf* : baldness

calza *nf* : wedge

calzada *nf* : roadway

calzado *nm* : footwear — **calzar** {21} *vt* **1** : wear (shoes) **2** : put shoes on (s.o.)

calzones *nmpl Lat* : panties — **calzoncillos** *nmpl* : underpants, briefs

cama *nf* : bed

camada *nf* : litter, brood

camafeo *nm* : cameo

cámara *nf* **1** : chamber **2** *or* **~ fotográfica** : camera **3** : house (in government)

camarada *nmf* : comrade — **camaradería** *nf* : camaraderie

camarero, -ra *n* **1** : waiter, waitress *f* **2** : steward *m*, stewardess *f* (on a ship, etc.) — **camarera** *nf* : chambermaid *f*

camarón *nm, pl* **-rones** : shrimp

camarote *nm* : cabin, stateroom

cambiar *vt* **1** : change **2** CANJEAR : exchange — *vi* **1** : change **2** : shift gears (of an automobile) — **cambiarse** *vr* **1** : change (clothing) **2** : move (to a new address) — **cambiable** *adj* : changeable — **cambio** *nm* **1** : change **2** CANJE : exchange **3 en ~** : on the other hand

camello *nm* : camel

camilla *nf* : stretcher — **camillero** *nm* : orderly (in a hospital)

caminar *vi* : walk — *vt* : cover (a distance) — **caminata** *nf* : hike

camino *nm* **1** : road, path **2** RUTA : way **3 a medio ~** : halfway (there) **4 ponerse en ~** : set out

camión *nm, pl* **-miones 1** : truck **2** *Lat*

: bus — **camionero, -ra** *n* **1** : truck driver **2** *Lat* : bus driver — **camioneta** *nm* : light truck, van

camisa *nf* **1** : shirt **2** ~ **de fuerza** : straitjacket — **camiseta** *nf* : T-shirt, undershirt — **camisón** *nm, pl* **-sones** : nightshirt, nightgown

camorra *nf fam* : fight, trouble

camote *nm Lat* : sweet potato

campamento *nm* : camp

campana *nf* : bell — **campanada** *nf* : stroke (of a bell), peal — **campanario** *nm* : bell tower — **campanilla** *nf* : (small) bell

campaña *nf* **1** : countryside **2** : (military or political) campaign

campeón, -peona *n, mpl* **-peones** : champion — **campeonato** *nm* : championship

campesino, -na *n* : peasant, farm laborer — **campestre** *adj* : rural, rustic

camping *nm* **1** : campsite **2 hacer** ~ : go camping

campiña *nf* : countryside

campo *nm* **1** : field **2** CAMPIÑA : countryside, country **3** CAMPAMENTO : camp

camuflaje *nm* : camouflage — **camuflar** *vt* : camouflage

cana *nf* : gray hair

canadiense *adj* : Canadian

canal *nm* **1** : canal **2** MEDIO : channel **3** : (radio or television) channel — **canalizar** {21} *vt* : channel

canalete *nm* : paddle (of a canoe)

canalla *nf* : rabble — ~ *nmf fam* : swine, bastard

canapé *nm* **1** : canapé **2** SOFÁ : sofa, couch

canario *nm* : canary

canasta *nf* : basket — **canasto** *nm* : large basket

cancelar *vt* **1** : cancel **2** : pay off, settle (a debt) — **cancelación** *nf, pl* **-ciones** **1** : cancellation **2** : payment in full (of a debt)

cáncer *nm* : cancer — **canceroso, -sa** *adj* : cancerous

cancha *nf* : court, field (for sports)

canciller *nm* : chancellor

canción *nf, pl* **-ciones** **1** : song **2** ~ **de cuna** : lullaby — **cancionero** *nm* : songbook

candado *nm* : padlock

candela *nf* : candle — **candelabro** *nm* : candelabra — **candelero** *nm* **1** : candlestick **2 estar en el** ~ : be in the limelight

candente *adj* : red-hot

candidato, -ta *n* : candidate — **candidatura** *nf* : candidacy

cándido, -da *adj* : naïve — **candidez** *nf* **1** : simplicity **2** INGENUIDAD : naïveté

candil *nm* : oil lamp — **candilejas** *nfpl* : footlights

candor *nm* : naïveté, innocence

canela *nf* : cinnamon

cangrejo *nm* : crab

canguro *nm* : kangaroo

caníbal *nmf* : cannibal — **canibalismo** *nm* : cannibalism

canicas *nfpl* : tire (game of) marbles

canino, -na *adj* : canine — **canino** *nm* : canine (tooth)

canjear *vt* : exchange — **canje** *nm* : exchange, trade

cano, -na *adj* : gray, gray-haired

canoa *nf* : canoe

canon *nm, pl* **cánones** : canon — **canonizar** {21} *vt* : canonize

canoso, -sa *adj* : gray, gray-haired

cansar *vt* : tire (out) — *vi* : be tiring — **cansarse** *vr* : get tired — **cansado, -da** *adj* **1** : tired **2** PESADO : tiresome — **cansancio** *nm* : fatigue, weariness

cantalupo *nm* : cantaloupe

cantar *v* : sing — ~ *nm* : song — **cantante** *nmf* : singer

cántaro *nm* **1** : pitcher, jug **2 llover a** ~ **s** *fam* : rain cats and dogs

cantera *nf* : quarry (excavation)

cantidad *nf* **1** : quantity, amount **2 una** ~ **de** : lots of

cantimplora *nf* : canteen, water bottle

cantina *nf* **1** : canteen, cafeteria **2** *Lat* : tavern, bar

canto *nm* **1** : singing, song **2** BORDE, LADO : edge **3 de** ~ : on end, sideways **4** ~ **rodado** : boulder — **cantor, -tora** *adj* **1** : singing **2 pájaro** ~ : songbird — ~ *n* : singer

caña *nf* **1** : cane, reed **2** ~ **de pescar** : fishing pole

cáñamo *nm* : hemp

cañería *nf* : pipes, piping — **caño** *nm* **1** : pipe **2** : spout (of a fountain) — **cañón** *nm, pl* **-ñones** **1** : cannon **2** : barrel (of a gun) **3** : canyon (in geography)

caoba *nf* : mahogany

caos *nm* : chaos — **caótico, -ca** *adj* : chaotic

capa *nf* **1** : cape, cloak **2** : coat (of paint, etc.), coating (in cooking) **3** ESTRATO : layer, stratum **4** : (social) class

capacidad *nf* **1** : capacity **2** APTITUD : ability

capacitar *vt* : train, qualify — **capacitación** *nf, pl* **-ciones** : training

caparazón nm, pl **-zones** : shell
capataz nmf, pl **-taces** : foreman
capaz adj, pl **-paces 1** : capable, able **2** ESPACIOSO : spacious
capellán nm, pl **-llanes** : chaplain
capilla nf : chapel
capital adj **1** : capital **2** PRINCIPAL : chief, principal — ~ nm : capital (assets) — ~ nf : capital (city) — **capitalismo** nm : capitalism — **capitalista** adj & nmf : capitalist, capitalistic — **capitalizar** {21} vt : capitalize
capitán, -tana n, mpl **-tanes** : captain
capitolio nm : capitol
capitular vi : capitulate, surrender — **capitulación** nf, pl **-ciones** : surrender
capítulo nm : chapter
capó nm : hood (of a car)
capote nm : cloak, cape
capricho nm : whim, caprice — **caprichoso, -sa** adj : whimsical, capricious
cápsula nf : capsule
captar vt **1** : grasp **2** ATRAER : gain, attract (interest, etc.) **3** : harness (waters)
capturar vt : capture, seize — **captura** nf : capture, seizure
capucha nf : hood (of clothing)
capullo nm **1** : cocoon **2** : (flower) bud
caqui adj & nm : khaki
cara nf **1** : face **2** ASPECTO : appearance **3** fam : nerve, gall **4** ~ **a** or **de** ~ **a** : facing
carabina nf : carbine
caracol nm **1** : snail **2** Lat : conch **3** RIZO : curl
carácter nm, pl **-racteres 1** : character **2** ÍNDOLE : nature — **característica** nf : characteristic — **característico, -ca** adj : characteristic — **caracterizar** {21} vt : characterize
caramba interj : oh my!, good grief!
carámbano nm : icicle
caramelo nm **1** : caramel **2** DULCE : candy
carátula nf **1** CARETA : mask **2** : jacket (of a record, etc.) **3** Lat : face (of a watch)
caravana nf **1** : caravan **2** REMOLQUE : trailer
caray → **caramba**
carbohidrato nm : carbohydrate
carbón nm, pl **-bones 1** : coal **2** : charcoal (for drawing) — **carboncillo** nm : charcoal — **carbonero, -ra** adj : coal — **carbonizar** {21} vt : char — **carbono** nm : carbon — **carburador** nm : carburetor — **carburante** nm : fuel
carcajada nf : loud laugh, guffaw

cárcel nf : jail, prison — **carcelero, -ra** n : jailer
carcinógeno nm : carcinogen
carcomer vt : eat away at — **carcomido, -da** adj : worm-eaten
cardenal nm **1** : cardinal **2** CONTUSIÓN : bruise
cardíaco or **cardiaco, -ca** adj : cardiac, heart
cárdigan nm, pl **-gans** : cardigan
cardinal adj : cardinal
cardiólogo, -ga n : cardiologist
cardo nm : thistle
carear vt : bring face-to-face
carecer {53} vi — **de** : lack — **carencia** nf : lack, want — **carente** adj ~ **de** : lacking (in)
carestía nf **1** : high cost **2** ESCASEZ : dearth, scarcity
careta nf : mask
cargar {52} vt **1** : load **2** : charge (a battery, a purchase, etc.) **3** LLEVAR : carry **4** ~ **de** : burden with — vi **1** : load **2** ~ **con** : pick up, carry away — **carga** nf **1** : load **2** CARGAMENTO : freight, cargo **3** RESPONSABILIDAD : burden **4** : charge (in electricity, etc.) — **cargado, -da** adj **1** : loaded, burdened **2** PESADO : heavy, stuffy **3** : charged (of a battery) **4** FUERTE : strong, concentrated — **cargamento** nm : cargo, load — **cargo** nm **1** : charge **2** PUESTO : position, office
cariarse vr : decay (of teeth)
caribe adj : Caribbean
caricatura nf **1** : caricature **2** : (political) cartoon — **caricaturizar** vt : caricature
caricia nf : caress
caridad nf **1** : charity **2** LIMOSNA : alms pl
caries nfs & pl : cavity (in a tooth)
cariño nm : affection, love — **cariñoso, -sa** adj : affectionate, loving
carisma nf : charisma — **carismático, -ca** adj : charismatic
caritativo, -va adj : charitable
cariz nm, pl **-rices** : appearance, aspect
carmesí adj & nm : crimson
carmín nm, pl **-mines** or ~ **de labios** : lipstick
carnada nf : bait
carnal adj **1** : carnal **2** **primo** ~ : first cousin
carnaval nm : carnival
carne nf **1** : meat **2** : flesh (of persons or fruits) **3** ~ **de cerdo** : pork **4** ~ **de gallina** : goose bumps **5** ~ **de ternera** : veal
carné nm → **carnet**

carnero *nm* **1** : ram, sheep **2** : mutton (in cooking)

carnet *nm* **1 ~ de conducir** : driver's license **2 ~ de identidad** : identification card, ID

carnicería *nf* **1** : butcher shop **2** MATANZA : slaughter — **carnicero, -ra** *n* : butcher

carnívoro, -ra *adj* : carnivorous — **carnívoro** *nm* : carnivore

carnoso, -sa *adj* : fleshy

caro, -ra *adj* **1** : expensive **2** QUERIDO : dear — **caro** *adv* : dearly

carpa *nf* **1** : carp **2** TIENDA : tent

carpeta *nf* : folder

carpintería *nf* : carpentry — **carpintero, -ra** *n* : carpenter

carraspear *vi* : clear one's throat — **carraspera** *nf* **1** : hoarseness **2 tener ~** : have a frog in one's throat

carrera *nf* **1** : running, run **2** COMPETICIÓN : race **3** : course (of studies) **4** PROFESIÓN : career, profession

carreta *nf* : cart, wagon

carrete *nm* : reel, spool

carretera *nf* : highway, road

carretilla *nf* : wheelbarrow

carril *nm* **1** : lane (of a road) **2** : rail (for a railroad)

carrillo *nm* : cheek

carrito *nm* : cart, trolley

carrizo *nm* : reed

carro *nm* **1** : wagon, cart **2** *Lat* : automobile, car — **carrocería** *nf* : body (of an automobile)

carroña *nf* : carrion

carroza *nf* **1** : carriage **2** : float (in a parade)

carruaje *nm* : carriage

carrusel *nm* : merry-go-round, carousel

carta *nf* **1** : letter **2** NAIPE : playing card **3** : charter (of an organization, etc.) **4** MENÚ : menu **5** MAPA : map, chart

cartel *nm* : poster, bill — **cartelera** *nf* : billboard

cartera *nf* **1** : briefcase **2** BILLETERA : wallet **3** *Lat* : pocketbook, handbag — **carterista** *nmf* : pickpocket

cartero, -ra *nm* : mail carrier, mailman *m*

cartílago *nm* : cartilage

cartilla *nf* **1** : primer, reader **2** : booklet, record (of a savings account, etc.)

cartón *nm*, *pl* **-tones 1** : cardboard **2** : carton (of cigarettes, etc.)

cartucho *nm* : cartridge

casa *nf* **1** : house **2** HOGAR : home **3** EMPRESA : company, firm **4 ~ flotante** : houseboat

casar *vt* : marry — *vi* : go together, match up — **casarse** *vr* **1** : get married **2 ~ con** : marry — **casado, -da** *adj* : married — **casamiento** *nm* **1** : marriage **2** BODA : wedding

cascabel *nm* : small bell

cascada *nf* : waterfall

cascanueces *nms & pl* : nutcracker

cascar {72} *vt* : crack (a shell, etc.) — **cascarse** *vr* : crack, chip — **cáscara** *nf* : skin, peel, shell — **cascarón** *nm*, *pl* **-rones** : eggshell

casco *nm* **1** : helmet **2** : hull (of a boat) **3** : hoof (of a horse) **4** : fragment (of ceramics, etc.) **5** : center (of a town) **6** ENVASE : empty bottle

caserío *nm* **1** *Spain* : country house **2** POBLADO : hamlet

casero, -ra *adj* **1** : homemade **2** DOMÉSTICO : domestic, household — **~** *n* : landlord, landlady *f*

caseta *nf* : booth, stall

casete → cassette

casi *adv* **1** : almost, nearly **2** (*in negative phrases*) : hardly

casilla *nf* **1** : compartment, pigeonhole **2** CASETA : booth **3** : box (on a form)

casino *nm* **1** : casino **2** : (social) club

caso *nm* **1** : case **2 en ~ de** : in the event of **3 hacer ~** : pay attention **4 no venir al ~** : be beside the point

caspa *nf* : dandruff

cassette *nmf* : cassette

casta *nf* **1** : lineage, descent **2** : breed (of animals) **3** : caste (in India)

castaña *nf* : chestnut

castañetear *vi* : chatter (of teeth)

castaño, -ña *adj* : chestnut (color)

castañuela *nf* : castanet

castellano *nm* : Spanish, Castilian (language)

castidad *nf* : chastity

castigar {52} *vt* **1** : punish **2** : penalize (in sports) — **castigo** *nm* **1** : punishment **2** : penalty (in sports)

castillo *nm* : castle

casto, -ta *adj* : chaste, pure — **castizo, -za** *adj* : pure, traditional (in style)

castor *nm* : beaver

castrar *vt* : castrate

castrense *adj* : military

casual *adj* : chance, accidental — **casualidad** *nf* **1** : coincidence **2 por ~** *or* **de ~** : by chance — **casualmente** *adv* : by chance

cataclismo *nm* : cataclysm

catalán, -lana *adj*, *mpl* **-lanes** : Catalan — **catalán** *nm* : Catalan (language)

catalizador *nm* : catalyst

catalogar {52} *vt* : catalog, classify — **catálogo** *nm* : catalog

catapulta *nf* : catapult

catar *vt* : taste, sample

catarata *nf* **1** : waterfall **2** : cataract (in medicine)

catarro *nm* RESFRIADO : cold

catástrofe *nf* : catastrophe, disaster — **catastrófico, -ca** *adj* : catastrophic, disastrous

catecismo *nm* : catechism

cátedra *nf* : chair (at a university)

catedral *nf* : cathedral

catedrático, -ca *n* : professor

categoría *nf* **1** : category **2** RANGO : rank **3 de ~** : first-rate — **categórico, -ca** *adj* : categorical

católico, -ca *adj* & *n* : Catholic — **catolicismo** *nm* : Catholicism

catorce *adj* & *nm* : fourteen — **catorceavo** *nm* : fourteenth

catre *nm* : cot

cauce *nm* **1** : riverbed **2** VÍA : channel, means *pl*

caucho *nm* : rubber

caución *nf*, *pl* **-ciones** : security, guarantee

caudal *nm* **1** : volume of water, flow **2** RIQUEZA : wealth

caudillo *nm* : leader, commander

causar *vt* : cause, provoke — **causa** *nf* **1** : cause **2** RAZÓN : reason **3** : case (in law) **4 a ~ de** : because of

cáustico, -ca *adj* : caustic

cautela *nf* : caution — **cauteloso, -sa** *adj* : cautious — **cautelosamente** *adv* : cautiously, warily

cautivar *vt* **1** : capture **2** ENCANTAR : captivate — **cautiverio** *nm* : captivity — **cautivo, -va** *adj* & *n* : captive

cauto, -ta *adj* : cautious

cavar *v* : dig

caverna *nf* : cavern, cave

cavidad *nf* : cavity

cavilar *vi* : ponder

cayado *nm* : crook, staff

cazar {21} *vt* **1** : hunt **2** ATRAPAR : catch, bag — *vi* : go hunting — **caza** *nf* **1** : hunt, hunting **2** : game (animals) — **cazador, -dora** *n* : hunter

cazo *nm* **1** : saucepan **2** CUCHARÓN : ladle — **cazuela** *nf* : casserole

CD *nm* : CD, compact disc

cebada *nf* : barley

cebar *vt* **1** : bait **2** : feed, fatten (animals) **3** : prime (a firearm, etc.) — **cebo** *nm* **1** CARNADA : bait **2** : charge (of a firearm)

cebolla *nf* : onion — **cebolleta** *nf* : scallion, green onion — **cebollino** *nm* : chive

cebra *nf* : zebra

cecear *vi* : lisp — **ceceo** *nm* : lisp

cedazo *nm* : sieve

ceder *vi* **1** : yield, give way **2** DISMINUIR : diminish, abate — *vt* : cede, hand over

cedro *nm* : cedar

cédula *nf* : document, certificate

cegar {49} *vt* **1** : blind **2** TAPAR : block, stop up — *vi* : be blinded, go blind — **ceguera** *nf* : blindness

ceja *nf* : eyebrow

cejar *vi* : give in, back down

celada *nf* : trap, ambush

celador, -dora *n* : guard, warden

celda *nf* : cell (of a jail)

celebrar *vt* **1** : celebrate **2** : hold (a meeting), say (Mass) **3** ALEGRARSE DE : be happy about — **celebrarse** *vr* : take place — **celebración** *nf*, *pl* **-ciones** : celebration — **célebre** *adj* : famous, celebrated — **celebridad** *nf* : celebrity

celeridad *nf* : swiftness, speed

celeste *adj* **1** : celestial, heavenly **2** *or* **azul ~** : sky blue — **celestial** *adj* : celestial, heavenly

celibato *nm* : celibacy — **célibe** *adj* : celibate

celo *nm* **1** : zeal **2 en ~** : in heat **3 ~s** *nmpl* : jealousy **4 tener ~s** : be jealous

celofán *nm*, *pl* **-fanes** : cellophane

celoso, -sa *adj* **1** : jealous **2** DILIGENTE : zealous

célula *nf* : cell — **celular** *adj* : cellular

celulosa *nf* : cellulose

cementerio *nm* : cemetery

cemento *nm* **1** : cement **2 ~ armado** : reinforced concrete

cena *nf* : supper, dinner

cenagal *nm* : bog, quagmire — **cenagoso** *adj* : swampy

cenar *vi* : have dinner, have supper — *vt* : have for dinner or supper

cenicero *nm* : ashtray

cenit *nm* : zenith

ceniza *nf* : ash

censo *nm* : census

censurar *vt* **1** : censor **2** REPROBAR : censure, criticize — **censura** *nf* **1** : censorship **2** REPROBACIÓN : censure, criticism

centavo *nm* **1** : cent **2** : centavo (unit of currency)

centellear *vi* : sparkle, twinkle — **centella** *nf* **1** : flash **2** CHISPA : spark — **centelleo** *nm* : twinkling, sparkle

centenar *nm* : hundred — **centenario** *nm* : centennial

centeno *nm* : rye

centésimo, -ma *adj* : hundredth
centígrado *adj* : centigrade, Celsius
centigramo *nm* : centigram
centímetro *nm* : centimeter
centinela *nmf* : sentinel, sentry
central *adj* : central — ~ *nf* : main office, headquarters — **centralita** *nf* : switchboard — **centralizar** {21} *vt* : centralize
centrar *vt* : center — **centrarse** *vr* ~ **en** : focus on — **céntrico, -ca** *adj* : central — **centro** *nm* **1** : center **2** : downtown (of a city) **3** ~ **de mesa** : centerpiece
centroamericano, -na *adj* : Central American
ceñir {67} *vt* **1** : encircle **2** : fit (s.o.) tightly — **ceñirse** *vr* ~ **a** : limit oneself to — **ceñido, -da** *adj* : tight
ceño *nm* **1** : frown **2 fruncir el** ~ : knit one's brow, frown
cepillo *nm* **1** : brush **2** : (carpenter's) plane **3** ~ **de dientes** : toothbrush — **cepillar** *vt* **1** : brush **2** : plane (wood)
cera *nf* **1** : wax, beeswax **2** : floor wax, furniture wax
cerámica *nf* **1** : ceramics *pl* **2** : (piece of) pottery
cerca[1] *nf* : fence — **cercado** *nm* : enclosure
cerca[2] *adv* **1** : close, near **2** ~ **de** : near, close to **3** ~ **de** : nearly, almost — **cercano, -na** *adj* : near, close — **cercanía** *nf* **1** : proximity **2** ~**s** *nfpl* : outskirts
cercar {72} *vt* **1** : fence in **2 RODEAR** : surround
cerciorarse *vr* ~ **de** : make sure of
cerco *nm* **1** : circle, ring **2 ASEDIO** : siege **3** *Lat* : fence
cerda *nf* : bristle
cerdo *nm* **1** : pig, hog **2** ~ **macho** : boar
cereal *adj & nm* : cereal
cerebro *nm* : brain — **cerebral** *adj* : cerebral
ceremonia *nf* : ceremony — **ceremonial** *adj* : ceremonial — **ceremonioso, -sa** *adj* : ceremonious
cereza *nf* : cherry
cerilla *nf* : match — **cerillo** *nm Lat* : match
cerner {56} *or* **cernir** *vt* : sift — **cernerse** *vr* **1** : hover **2** ~ **sobre** : loom over — **cernidor** *nm* : sieve
cero *nm* : zero
cerrar {55} *vt* **1** : close, shut **2** : turn off (a faucet, etc.) **3** : bring to an end — *vi* **1** : close up, lock up **2** : close down (a business, etc.) — **cerrarse** *vr* **1**

: close, shut **2 TERMINAR** : come to a close, end — **cerrado, -da** *adj* **1** : closed, shut, locked **2** : overcast (of weather) **3** : sharp (of a curve) **4** : thick, broad (of an accent) — **cerradura** *nf* : lock — **cerrajero, -ra** *n* : locksmith
cerro *nm* : hill
cerrojo *nm* : bolt, latch
certamen *nm, pl* **-támenes** : competition, contest
certero, -ra *adj* : accurate, precise
certeza *nf* : certainty — **certidumbre** *nf* : certainty
certificar {72} *vt* **1** : certify **2** : register (mail) — **certificado, -da** *adj* : certified, registered — **certificado** *nm* : certificate
cervato *nm* : fawn
cerveza *nf* **1** : beer **2** ~ **de barril** : draft beer — **cervecería** *nf* **1** : brewery **2 BAR** : beer hall, bar
cesar *vi* : cease, stop — *vt* : dismiss, lay off — **cesación** *nf, pl* **-ciones** : cessation, suspension — **cesante** *adj* **1** : laid off **2** *Lat* : unemployed — **cesantía** *nf Lat* : unemployment
cesárea *nf* : cesarean (section)
cese *nm* **1** : cessation, stop **2 DESTITUCIÓN** : dismissal
césped *nm* : lawn, grass
cesta *nf* : basket — **cesto** *nm* **1** : (large) basket **2** ~ **de basura** : wastebasket
cetro *nm* : scepter
chabacano *nm Lat* : apricot
chabola *nf Spain* : shack, shanty
chacal *nm* : jackal
cháchara *nf fam* : gabbing, chatter
chacra *nf Lat* : (small) farm
chafar *vt fam* : flatten, crush
chal *nm* : shawl
chaleco *nm* : vest
chalet *nm Spain* : house
chalupa *nf* **1** : small boat **2** *Lat* : small stuffed tortilla
chamarra *nf* : jacket
chamba *nf Lat fam* : job
champaña *or* **champán** *nm* : champagne
champiñón *nm, pl* **-ñones** : mushroom
champú *nm, pl* **-pús** *or* **-púes** : shampoo
chamuscar {72} *vt* : scorch
chance *nm Lat* : chance, opportunity
chancho *nm Lat* : pig
chanclos *nmpl* : galoshes
chantaje *nm* : blackmail — **chantajear** *vt* : blackmail
chanza *nf* : joke, jest
chapa *nf* **1** : sheet, plate **2 INSIGNIA** : badge — **chapado, -da** *adj* **1** : plated

2 chapado a la antigua : old-fashioned

chaparrón *nm, pl* **-rrones** : downpour

chapotear *vi* : splash

chapucero, -ra *adj* : shoddy, sloppy — **chapuza** *nf* : botched job

chapuzón *nm, pl* **-zones** : dip, short swim

chaqueta *nf* : jacket

charca *nf* : pond — **charco** *nm* : puddle

charlar *vi* : chat — **charla** *nf* : chat, talk — **charlatán, -tana** *adj, mpl* **-tanes** : talkative — ~ *n* 1 : chatterbox 2 FARSANTE : charlatan

charol *nm* 1 : patent leather 2 BARNIZ : varnish

chasco *nm* 1 : trick, joke 2 DECEPCIÓN : disappointment

chasis *nms & pl* : chassis

chasquear *vt* 1 : click (the tongue), snap (one's fingers) 2 : crack (a whip) — **chasquido** *nm* 1 : click, snap 2 : crack (of a whip)

chatarra *nf* : scrap (metal)

chato, -ta *adj* 1 : pug-nosed 2 APLANADO : flat

chauvinismo *nm* : chauvinism — **chauvinista** *adj* : chauvinist, chauvinistic

chaval, -vala *n fam* : kid, boy *m*, girl *f*

checo, -ca *adj* : Czech — **checo** *nm* : Czech (language)

chef *nm* : chef

cheque *nm* : check — **chequera** *nf* : checkbook

chequear *vt Lat* 1 : check, inspect, verify 2 : check in (baggage) — **chequeo** *nm* 1 : (medical) checkup 2 *Lat* : check, inspection

chica → **chico**

chicano, -na *adj* : Chicano, Mexican-American

chícharo *nm Lat* : pea

chicharrón *nm, pl* **-rrones** : pork rind

chichón *nm, pl* **-chones** : bump

chicle *nm* : chewing gum

chico, -ca *adj* : little, small — ~ *n* : child, boy *m*, girl *f*

chiflar *vt* : whistle at, boo — *vi Lat* : whistle — **chiflado, -da** *adj fam* : crazy, nuts — **chiflido** *nm* : whistling

chile *nm* : chili pepper

chileno, -na *adj* : Chilean

chillar *vi* 1 : shriek, scream 2 CHIRRIAR : screech, squeal — **chillido** *nm* 1 : scream 2 CHIRRIDO : screech, squeal — **chillón, -llona** *adj, mpl* **-llones** : shrill, loud

chimenea *nf* 1 : chimney 2 HOGAR : fireplace

chimpancé *nm* : chimpanzee

chinche *nf* : bedbug

chino, -na *adj* : Chinese — **chino** *nm* : Chinese (language)

chiquillo, -lla *n* : kid, child

chiquito, -ta *adj* : tiny — ~ *n* : little child, tot

chiribita *nf* : spark

chiripa *nf* 1 : fluke 2 **de** ~ : by sheer luck

chirivía *nf* : parsnip

chirriar {85} *vi* 1 : squeak, creak 2 : screech (of brakes, etc.) — **chirrido** *nm* 1 : squeak, creak 2 : screech (of brakes)

chisme *nm* : (piece of) gossip — **chismear** *vi* : gossip — **chismoso, -sa** *adj* : gossipy — ~ *n* : gossip

chispear *vi* : spark — **chispa** *nf* : spark

chisporrotear *vi* : crackle, sizzle — **chisporroteo** *nm* : crackle

chiste *nm* : joke, funny story — **chistoso, -sa** *adj* : funny, witty

chivo, -va *n* : kid, young goat

chocar {72} *vi* 1 : crash, collide 2 ENFRENTARSE : clash — **chocante** *adj* 1 : striking, shocking 2 *Lat* : unpleasant, rude

choclo *nm Lat* : ear of corn, corncob

chocolate *nm* : chocolate

chofer *or* **chófer** *nm* 1 : chauffeur 2 CONDUCTOR : driver

choque *nm* 1 : shock 2 : crash, collision (of vehicles) 3 CONFLICTO : clash

chorizo *nm* : chorizo, sausage

chorrear *vi* 1 : drip 2 BROTAR : pour out, gush — **chorro** *nm* 1 : stream, jet 2 HILO : trickle

chovinismo → **chauvinismo**

choza *nf* : hut, shack

chubasco *nm* : downpour, squall

chuchería *nf* 1 : knickknack, trinket 2 DULCE : sweet

chueco, -ca *adj Lat* : crooked

chuleta *nf* : cutlet, chop

chulo, -la *adj fam* : cute, pretty

chupar *vt* 1 : suck 2 ABSORBER : absorb 3 *fam* : guzzle — *vi* : suckle — **chupada** *nf* : suck, sucking — **chupete** *nm* 1 : pacifier 2 *Lat* : lollipop

churro *nm* 1 : fried dough 2 *fam* : botch, mess

chusco, -ca *adj* : funny

chusma *nf* : riffraff, rabble

chutar *vi* : shoot (in soccer)

cianuro *nm* : cyanide

cicatriz *nf, pl* **-trices** : scar — **cicatrizar** {21} *vi* : form a scar, heal

cíclico, -ca *adj* : cyclical

ciclismo *nm* : cycling — **ciclista** *nmf* : cyclist

ciclo *nm* : cycle

ciclón *nm, pl* **-clones** : cyclone

ciego, -ga *adj* : blind — **ciegamente**
adv : blindly

cielo *nm* 1 : sky 2 : heaven (in religion)

ciempiés *nms & pl* : centipede

cien *adj* : a hundred, hundred — ~ *nm*
: one hundred

ciénaga *nf* : swamp, bog

ciencia *nf* 1 : science 2 a ~ **cierta** : for
a fact

cieno *nm* : mire, mud, silt

científico, -ca *adj* : scientific — ~ *n*
: scientist

ciento *adj* (*used in compound numbers*)
: one hundred — ~ *nm* 1 : hundred,
group of a hundred 2 **por** ~ : percent

cierre *nm* 1 : closing, closure 2 BROCHE
: fastener, clasp

cierto, -ta *adj* 1 : true 2 SEGURO : certain
3 **por** ~ : as a matter of fact

ciervo, -va *n* : deer, stag *m*, hind *f*

cifra *nf* 1 : number, figure 2 : sum (of
money, etc.) 3 CLAVE : code, cipher —
cifrar *vt* 1 : write in code 2 ~ **la esperanza en** : pin all one's hopes on

cigarrillo *nm* : cigarrette — **cigarro** *nm*
1 : cigarette 2 PURO : cigar

cigüeña *nf* : stork

cilantro *nm* : cilantro, coriander

cilindro *nm* : cylinder — **cilíndrico, -ca**
adj : cylindrical

cima *nf* : peak, summit

címbalo *nm* : cymbal

cimbrar *or* **cimbrear** *vt* : shake, rock —
cimbrarse *or* **cimbrearse** *vr* : sway

cimentar {55} *vt* 1 : lay the foundation
of 2 : cement, strengthen (relations,
etc.) — **cimientos** *nmpl* : base, foun-
dation(s)

cinc *nm* : zinc

cincel *nm* : chisel — **cincelar** *vt* : chisel

cinco *adj & nm* : five

cincuenta *adj & nm* : fifty — **cincuentavo, -va** *adj* : fiftieth — **cincuentavo**
nm : fiftieth

cine *nm* : cinema, movies *pl* — **cine-
matográfico, -ca** *adj* : movie, film

cínico, -ca *adj* : cynical — ~ *n* : cynic
— **cinismo** *nm* : cynicism

cinta *nf* 1 : ribbon, band 2 ~ **adhesiva**
: adhesive tape 3 ~ **métrica** : tape
measure 4 ~ **magnetofónica** : magnetic tape

cinto *nm* : belt, girdle — **cintura** *nf*
: waist — **cinturón** *nm, pl* **-rones** 1
: belt 2 ~ **de seguridad** : seat belt

ciprés *nm, pl* **-preses** : cypress

circo *nm* : circus

circuito *nm* : circuit

circulación *nf, pl* **-ciones** 1 : circulation 2 TRÁFICO : traffic — **circular** *vi* 1
: circulate 2 : drive (a vehicle) — ~
adj : circular

círculo *nm* : circle

circuncidar *vt* : circumcise — **circuncisión** *nf, pl* **-siones** : circumcision

circundar *vt* : surround

circunferencia *nf* : circumference

circunscribir {33} *vt* : confine, limit —
circunscribirse *vr* ~ **a** : limit oneself to — **circunscripción** *nf, pl*
-ciones : district, constituency

circunspecto, -ta *adj* : circumspect,
cautious

circunstancia *nf* : circumstance — **cir-
cunstancial** *adj* : chance — **circun-
stante** *nmf* 1 : bystander 2 **los** ~**s**
: those present

circunvalación *nf, pl* **-ciones** 1 : encir-
cling 2 **carretera de** ~ : bypass

cirio *nm* : candle

ciruela *nf* 1 : plum 2 ~ **pasa** : prune

cirugía *nf* : surgery — **cirujano, -na** *n*
: surgeon

cisma *nf* : schism

cisne *nm* : swan

cisterna *nf* : cistern

cita *nf* 1 : appointment, date 2 REFEREN-
CIA : quote, quotation — **citación** *nf,
pl* **-ciones** : summons — **citar** *vt* 1
: quote, cite 2 CONVOCAR : make an appointment with 3 : summon (in law)
— **citarse** *vr* ~ **con** : arrange to meet

cítrico *nm* : citrus (fruit)

ciudad *nf* : city, town — **ciudadano,
-na** *n* 1 : citizen 2 HABITANTE : resident
— **ciudadanía** *nf* : citizenship

cívico, -ca *adj* : civic

civil *adj* : civil — ~ *nmf* : civilian —
civilidad *nf* : civility — **civilización**
nf, pl **-ciones** : civilization — **civilizar** {21} *vt* : civilize

cizaña *nf* : discord, rift

clamar *vi* : clamor, cry out — **clamor**
nm : clamor, outcry — **clamoroso,
-sa** *adj* : clamorous, loud

clan *nm* : clan

clandestino, -na *adj* : clandestine, secret

clara *nf* : egg white

claraboya *nf* : skylight

claramente *adv* : clearly

clarear *v impers* 1 : dawn 2 ACLARAR
: clear up — *vi* : be transparent

claridad *nf* 1 : clarity, clearness 2 LUZ
: light

clarificar {72} *vt* : clarify — **clarificación** *nf, pl* **-ciones** : clarification

clarín *nm, pl* **-rines** : bugle

clarinete *nm* : clarinet
clarividente *adj* **1** : clairvoyant **2** PERSPICAZ : perspicacious — **clarividencia** *nf* **1** : clairvoyance **2** PERSPICACIA : farsightedness
claro *adv* **1** : clearly **2** POR SUPUESTO : of course, surely — ~ *nm* **1** : clearing, glade **2** ~ **de luna** : moonlight — **claro, -ra** *adj* **1** : clear, bright **2** : light (of colors) **3** EVIDENTE : clear, evident
clase *nf* **1** : class **2** TIPO : sort, kind
clásico, -ca *adj* : classic, classical — **clásico** *nm* : classic
clasificar {72} *vt* **1** : classify, sort out **2** : rate, rank (a hotel, a team, etc.) — **clasificarse** *vr* : qualify (in competitions) — **clasificación** *nf, pl* **-ciones** **1** : classification **2** : league (in sports)
claudicar {72} *vi* : back down
claustro *nm* : cloister
claustrofobia *nf* : claustrophobia — **claustrofóbico, -ca** *adj* : claustrophobic
cláusula *nf* : clause
clausurar *vt* : close (down) — **clausura** *nf* : closure, closing
clavado *nm Lat* : dive
clavar *vt* **1** : nail, hammer **2** HINCAR : drive in, plunge
clave *nf* **1** CIFRA : code **2** SOLUCIÓN : key **3** : clef (in music) — ~ *adj* : key
clavel *nm* : carnation
clavicémbalo *nm* : harpsichord
clavícula *nf* : collarbone
clavija *nf* **1** : peg, pin **2** : (electric) plug
clavo *nm* **1** : nail **2** : clove (spice)
claxon *nm, pl* **cláxones** : horn (of an automobile)
clemencia *nf* : clemency, mercy — **clemente** *adj* : merciful
clerical *adj* : clerical — **clérigo, -ga** *n* : clergyman, cleric — **clero** *nm* : clergy
cliché *nm* **1** : cliché **2** : negative (of a photograph)
cliente, -ta *n* : customer, client — **clientela** *nf* : clientele, customers *pl*
clima *nm* **1** : climate **2** AMBIENTE : atmosphere — **climático, -ca** *adj* : climatic
climatizar {21} *vt* : air-condition — **climatizado, -da** *adj* : air-conditioned
clímax *nm* : climax
clínica *nf* : clinic — **clínico, -ca** *adj* : clinical
clip *nm, pl* **clips** : (paper) clip
cloaca *nf* : sewer
cloquear *vi* : cluck — **cloqueo** *nm* : cluck, clucking
cloro *nm* : chlorine

clóset *nm Lat, pl* **clósets** : (built-in) closet, cupboard
club *nm* : club
coacción *nf, pl* **-ciones** : coercion — **coaccionar** *vt* : coerce
coagular *v* : clot, coagulate — **coagularse** *vr* : coagulate — **coágulo** *nm* : clot
coalición *nf, pl* **-ciones** : coalition
coartada *nf* : alibi
coartar *vt* : restrict, limit
cobarde *nmf* : coward — ~ *adj* : cowardly — **cobardía** *nf* : cowardice
cobaya *nf* : guinea pig
cobertizo *nm* : shelter, shed
cobertor *nm* : bedspread
cobertura *nf* **1** : cover **2** : coverage (of news, etc.)
cobijar *vt* : shelter — **cobijarse** *vr* : take shelter — **cobija** *nf Lat* : blanket — **cobijo** *nm* : shelter
cobra *nf* : cobra
cobrar *vt* **1** : charge, collect **2** : earn (a salary, etc.) **3** ADQUIRIR : acquire, gain **4** : cash (a check) — *vi* : be paid — **cobrador, -dora** *n* **1** : collector **2** : conductor (of a bus, etc.)
cobre *nm* : copper
cobro *nm* : collection (of money), cashing (of a check)
cocaína *nf* : cocaine
cocción *nf, pl* **-ciones** : cooking
cocear *vi* : kick
cocer {14} *vt* **1** : cook **2** HERVIR : boil
coche *nm* **1** : car, automobile **2** : coach (of a train) **3** or ~ **de caballos** : carriage **4** ~ **fúnebre** : hearse — **cochecito** *nm* : baby carriage, stroller — **cochera** *nf* : garage, carport
cochino, -na *n* : pig, hog — ~ *adj fam* : dirty, filthy — **cochinada** *nf fam* : dirty thing — **cochinillo** *nm* : piglet
cocido, -da *adj* **1** : boiled, cooked **2** **bien** ~ : well-done — **cocido** *nm* : stew
cociente *nm* : quotient
cocina *nf* **1** : kitchen **2** : (kitchen) stove **3** : (art of) cooking, cuisine — **cocinar** *v* : cook — **cocinero, -ra** *n* : cook, chef
coco *nm* : coconut
cocodrilo *nm* : crocodile
coctel *or* **cóctel** *nm* **1** : cocktail **2** FIESTA : cocktail party
codazo *nm* **1** : nudge **2** **dar un** ~ **a** : elbow, nudge
codicia *nf* : greed — **codiciar** *vt* : covet — **codicioso, -sa** *adj* : covetous, greedy

código *nm* **1** : code **2** ~ **postal** : zip code **3** ~ **morse** : Morse code

codo *nm* : elbow

codorniz *nf, pl* **-nices** : quail

coexistir *vi* : coexist

cofre *nm* : chest, coffer

coger {15} *vt* **1** : take (hold of) **2** ATRA-PAR : catch **3** : pick up (from the ground) **4** : pick (fruit, etc.) — **cogerse** *vr* : hold on

cohechar *vt* : bribe — **cohecho** *nm* : bribe, bribery

coherencia *nf* : coherence — **coherente** *adj* : coherent — **cohesión** *nf, pl* **-siones** : cohesion

cohete *nm* : rocket

cohibir {62} *vt* **1** : restrict **2** : inhibit (a person) — **cohibirse** *vr* : feel inhibited — **cohibido, -da** *adj* : inhibited, shy

coincidir *vi* **1** : coincide **2** ~ **con** : agree with — **coincidencia** *nf* : coincidence

cojear *vi* **1** : limp **2** : wobble (of furniture, etc.) — **cojera** *nf* : limp

cojín *nm, pl* **-jines** : cushion — **cojinete** *nm* **1** : pad, cushion **2** : bearing (of a machine)

cojo, -ja *adj* **1** : lame **2** : wobbly (of furniture) — ~ *n* : lame person

col *nf* **1** : cabbage **2** ~ **de Bruselas** : Brussels sprout

cola *nf* **1** : tail **2** FILA : line (of people) **3** : end (of a line) **4** PEGAMENTO : glue **5** ~ **de caballo** : ponytail

colaborar *vi* : collaborate — **colaboración** *nf, pl* **-ciones** : collaboration — **colaborador, -dora** *n* **1** : collaborator **2** : contributor (to a periodical)

colada *nf Spain* **1** : laundry **2 hacer la** ~ : do the washing

colador *nm* : colander, strainer

colapso *nm* : collapse

colar {19} *vt* : strain, filter — **colarse** *vr* : sneak in, gate-crash

colcha *nf* : bedspread, quilt — **colchón** *nm, pl* **-chones** : mattress — **colchoneta** *nf* : mat

colear *vi* : wag its tail

colección *nf, pl* **-ciones** : collection — **coleccionar** *vt* : collect — **coleccionista** *nmf* : collector — **colecta** *nf* : collection (of donations)

colectividad *nf* : community — **colectivo, -va** *adj* : collective — **colectivo** *nm* **1** : collective **2** *Lat* : city bus

colector *nm* : sewer

colega *nmf* : colleague

colegio *nm* **1** : school **2** : (professional) college — **colegial, -giala** *n* : schoolboy *m*, schoolgirl *f*

colegir {28} *vt* : gather

cólera *nm* : cholera — ~ *nf* : anger, rage — **colérico, -ca** *adj* **1** : bad-tempered **2** FURIOSO : angry

colesterol *nm* : cholesterol

coleta *nf* : pigtail

colgar {16} *vt* **1** : hang **2** : hang up (a telephone) **3** : hang out (laundry) — *vi* : hang up — **colgante** *adj* : hanging — ~ *nm* : pendant

colibrí *nm* : hummingbird

cólico *nm* : colic

coliflor *nf* : cauliflower

colilla *nf* : (cigarette) butt

colina *nf* : hill

colindar *vi* ~ **con** : be adjacent to — **colindante** *adj* : adjacent

coliseo *nm* : coliseum

colisión *nf, pl* **-siones** : collision — **colisionar** *vi* ~ **contra** : collide with

collar *nm* **1** : necklace **2** : collar (for pets)

colmar *vt* **1** : fill to the brim **2** : fulfill (a wish, etc.) **3** ~ **de** : shower with — **colmado, -da** *adj* : heaping

colmena *nf* : beehive

colmillo *nm* **1** : canine (tooth) **2** : fang (of a dog, etc.), tusk (of an elephant)

colmo *nm* **1** : height, limit **2 ¡eso es el** ~ **!** : that's the last straw!

colocar {72} *vt* PONER : place, put **2** : find a job for — **colocarse** *vr* **1** SITU-ARSE : position oneself **2** : get a job — **colocación** *nf, pl* **-ciones** **1** : placement, placing **2** EMPLEO : position, job

colombiano, -na *adj* : Colombian

colon *nm* : (intestinal) colon

colonia *nf* **1** : colony **2** PERFUME : cologne **3** *Lat* : residential area — **colonial** *adj* : colonial — **colonizar** {21} *vt* : colonize — **colonización** *nf, pl* **-ciones** : colonization — **colono, -na** *n* : settler, colonist

coloquial *adj* : colloquial — **coloquio** *nm* **1** : talk, discussion **2** CONGRESO : conference

color *nm* : color — **colorado, -da** *adj* : red — **colorear** *vt* : color — **colorete** *nm* : rouge — **colorido** *nm* : colors *pl*, coloring

colosal *adj* : colossal

columna *nf* **1** : column **2** ~ **vertebral** : spine, backbone — **columnista** *nmf* : columnist

columpiar *vt* : push (on a swing) — **columpiarse** *vr* : swing — **columpio** *nm* : swing

coma¹ *nm* : coma

coma² *nf* : comma

comadre *nf* **1** : godmother of one's child, mother of one's godchild **2** *fam*

: (female) friend — **comadrear** *vi fam* : gossip

comadreja *nf* : weasel

comadrona *nf* : midwife

comandancia *nf* : command headquarters, command — **comandante** *nmf* 1 : commander 2 : major (in the military) — **comando** *nm* 1 : commando 2 *Lat* : command

comarca *nf* : region, area

combar *vt* : bend, curve

combatir *vt* : combat, fight against — *vi* : fight — **combate** *nm* 1 : combat 2 : fight (in boxing) — **combatiente** *nmf* : combatant, fighter

combinar *vt* 1 : combine 2 : put together, match (colors, etc.) — **combinarse** *vr* : get together — **combinación** *nf*, *pl* **-ciones** 1 : combination 2 : connection (in travel)

combustible *nm* : fuel — *adj* : combustible — **combustión** *nf*, *pl* **-tiones** : combustion

comedia *nf* : comedy

comedido, -da *adj* : moderate

comedor *nm* : dining room

comensal *nmf* : diner, dinner guest

comentar *vt* 1 : comment on, discuss 2 MENCIONAR : mention — **comentario** *nm* 1 : comment, remark 2 ANÁLISIS : commentary — **comentarista** *nmf* : commentator

comenzar {29} *v* : begin, start

comer *vt* 1 : eat 2 *fam* : eat up, eat into — *vi* 1 : eat 2 CENAR : have a meal 3 **dar de** ~ : feed — **comerse** *vr* : eat up

comercio *nm* 1 : commerce, trade 2 NEGOCIO : business — **comercial** *adj* : commercial — **comercializar** {21} *vt* : market — **comerciante** *nmf* : merchant, dealer — **comerciar** *vi* : do business, trade

comestible *adj* : edible — **comestibles** *nmpl* : groceries, food

cometa *nm* : comet — ~ *nf* : kite

cometer *vt* 1 : commit 2 ~ **un error** : make a mistake — **cometido** *nm* : assignment, task

comezón *nf*, *pl* **-zones** : itchiness, itching

comicios *nmpl* : elections

cómico, -ca *adj* : comic, comical — ~ *n* : comic, comedian

comida *nf* 1 ALIMENTO : food 2 *Spain* : lunch 3 *Lat* : dinner **4 tres** ~**s al día** : three meals a day

comienzo *nm* : beginning

comillas *nfpl* : quotation marks

comino *nm* : cumin

comisario, -ria *n* : commissioner — **comisaría** *nf* : police station

comisión *nf*, *pl* **-siones** 1 : commission 2 COMITÉ : committee

comité *nm* : committee

como *conj* 1 : as, since 2 SÍ : if — ~ *prep* 1 : like, as 2 **así** ~ : as well as — ~ *adv* 1 : as 2 APROXIMADAMENTE : around, about

cómo *adv* 1 : how 2 ~ **no** : by all means 3 ¿~ **te llamas?** : what's your name?

cómoda *nf* : chest of drawers

comodidad *nf* : comfort, convenience

comodín *nm*, *pl* **-dines** : joker (in playing cards)

cómodo, -da *adj* 1 : comfortable 2 ÚTIL : handy, convenient

comoquiera *adv* 1 : in any way 2 ~ **que** : however

compacto, -ta *adj* : compact

compadecer {53} *vt* : feel sorry for — **compadecerse** *vr* ~ **de** : take pity on

compadre *nm* 1 : godfather of one's child, father of one's godchild 2 *fam* : buddy

compañero, -ra *n* : companion, partner — **compañerismo** *nm* : companionship

compañía *nf* : company

comparar *vt* : compare — **comparable** *adj* : comparable — **comparación** *nf*, *pl* **-ciones** : comparison — **comparativo, -va** *adj* : comparative

comparecer *vt* : appear (before a court, etc.)

compartimento *or* **compartimiento** *nm* : compartment

compartir *vt* : share

compás *nm*, *pl* **-pases** 1 : compass 2 : rhythm, time (in music)

compasión *nf*, *pl* **-siones** : compassion, pity — **compasivo, -va** *adj* : compassionate

compatible *adj* : compatible — **compatibilidad** *nf* : compatibility

compatriota *nmf* : compatriot, fellow countryman

compeler *vt* : compel

compendiar *vt* : summarize — **compendio** *nm* : summary

compensar *vt* : compensate for — **compensación** *nf*, *pl* **-ciones** : compensation

competir {54} *vi* : compete — **competencia** *nf* 1 : competition, rivalry 2 CAPACIDAD : competence — **competente** *adj* : competent — **competición** *nf*, *pl* **-ciones** : competition — **competidor, -dora** *n* : competitor

compilar vt : compile
compinche nmf fam : friend, chum
complacer {57} vt : please — **complacerse** vr ~ en : take pleasure in — **complaciente** adj : obliging, helpful
complejidad nf : complexity — **complejo, -ja** adj : complex — **complejo** nm : complex
complementar vt : complement — **complementario, -ria** adj : complementary — **complemento** nm 1 : complement 2 : object (in grammar)
completar vt : complete — **completo, -ta** adj 1 : complete 2 PERFECTO : perfect 3 LLENO : full — **completamente** adv : completely
complexión nf, pl **-xiones** : constitution, build
complicar {72} vt 1 : complicate 2 IMPLICAR : involve — **complicación** nf, pl **-ciones** : complication — **complicado, -da** adj : complicated, complex
cómplice nmf : accomplice — ~ adj : conspiratorial, knowing
complot nm, pl **-plots** : conspiracy, plot
componer {60} vt 1 : make up, compose 2 : compose, write (a song) 3 ARREGLAR : fix, repair — **componerse** vr ~ de : consist of — **componente** adj & nm : component, constituent
comportarse vr : behave — **comportamiento** nm : behavior
composición nf, pl **-ciones** : composition — **compositor, -tora** n : composer, songwriter
compostura nf 1 : composure 2 REPARACIÓN : repair
comprar vt : buy, purchase — **compra** nf 1 : purchase 2 ir de ~s : go shopping — **comprador, -dora** n : buyer, shopper
comprender vt 1 : comprehend, understand 2 ABARCAR : cover, include — **comprensible** adj : understandable — **comprensión** nf, pl **-siones** : understanding — **comprensivo, -va** adj : understanding
compresa nf 1 : compress 2 or ~ higiénica : sanitary napkin
compresión nf, pl **-siones** : compression — **comprimido** nm : pill, tablet — **comprimir** vt : compress
comprobar {19} vt 1 VERIFICAR : check 2 DEMOSTRAR : prove — **comprobación** nf, pl **-ciones** : verification, check — **comprobante** nm 1 : proof 2 RECIBO : receipt, voucher
comprometer vt 1 : compromise 2 ARRIESGAR : jeopardize 3 OBLIGAR : commit, put under obligation — **comprometerse** vr 1 : commit oneself 2 ~ con : get engaged to — **comprometedor, -dora** adj : compromising — **comprometido, -da** adj 1 : compromising, awkward 2 : engaged (to be married) — **compromiso** nm 1 : obligation, commitment 2 : (marriage) engagement 3 ACUERDO : agreement 4 APURO : awkward situation
compuesto, -ta adj 1 : compound 2 ~ de : made up of, consisting of — **compuesto** nm : compound
compulsivo, -va adj : compelling, urgent
computar vt : compute, calculate — **computadora** nf or **computador** nm 1 : computer 2 ~ portátil : laptop computer — **cómputo** nm : calculation
comulgar {52} vi : receive Communion
común adj, pl **-munes** 1 : common 2 ~ y corriente : ordinary 3 por lo ~ : generally
comuna nf : commune — **comunal** adj : communal
comunicar {72} vt : communicate — **comunicarse** vr 1 : communicate 2 ~ con : get in touch with — **comunicación** nf, pl **-ciones** : communication — **comunicado** nm : communiqué — **comunicativo, -va** adj : communicative
comunidad nf : community
comunión nf, pl **-niones** : communion, Communion
comunismo nm : Communism — **comunista** adj & nmf : Communist
con prep 1 : with 2 A PESAR DE : in spite of 3 (before an infinitive) : by 4 ~ (tal) que : so long as
cóncavo, -va adj : concave
concebir {54} v : conceive — **concebible** adj : conceivable
conceder vt 1 : grant, bestow 2 ADMITIR : concede
concejal, -jala n : councilman, alderman
concentrar vt : concentrate — **concentrarse** vr : concentrate — **concentración** nf, pl **-ciones** : concentration
concepción nf, pl **-ciones** : conception — **concepto** nm 1 : concept 2 OPINIÓN : opinion
concernir {17} vi ~ a : concern — **concerniente** adj ~ a : concerning
concertar {55} vt 1 : arrange, coordinate 2 (used before an infinitive) : agree 3 : harmonize (in music) — vi : be in harmony

concesión *nf, pl* **-siones 1** : concession **2** : awarding (of prizes, etc.)

concha *nf* : shell

conciencia *nf* **1** : conscience **2** CONOCIMIENTO : consciousness, awareness — **concientizar** {21} *vt Lat* : make aware — **concientizarse** *vr Lat* — **de** : realize

concienzudo, -da *adj* : conscientious

concierto *nm* **1** : concert **2** : concerto (musical composition)

conciliar *vt* : reconcile — **conciliación** *nf, pl* **-ciones** : reconciliation

concilio *nm* : council

conciso, -sa *adj* : concise

conciudadano, -na *n* : fellow citizen

concluir {41} *vt* : conclude — *vi* : come to an end — **conclusión** *nf, pl* **-siones** : conclusion — **concluyente** *adj* : conclusive

concordar {19} *vi* : agree — *vt* : reconcile — **concordancia** *nf* : agreement — **concordia** *nf* : harmony, concord

concretar *vt* : make concrete, specify — **concretarse** *vr* : become definite, take shape — **concreto, -ta** *adj* **1** : concrete **2** DETERMINADO : specific **3** en ~ : specifically — **concreto** *nm Lat* : concrete

concurrir *vi* **1** : come together, meet **2** ~ a : take part in — **concurrencia** *nf* : audience, turnout — **concurrido, -da** *adj* : busy, crowded

concursar *vi* : compete, participate — **concursante** *nmf* : competitor — **concurso** *nm* **1** : competition **2** CONCURRENCIA : gathering **3** AYUDA : help, cooperation

condado *nm* : county

conde, -desa *n* : count *m*, countess *f*

condenar *vt* **1** : condemn, damn **2** : sentence (a criminal) — **condena** *nf* **1** : condemnation **2** SENTENCIA : sentence — **condenación** *nf, pl* **-ciones** : condemnation, damnation

condensar *vt* : condense — **condensación** *nf, pl* **-ciones** : condensation

condesa *nf* → **conde**

condescender {56} *vi* **1** : acquiesce, agree **2** ~ a : condescend to — **condescendiente** *adj* : condescending

condición *nf, pl* **-ciones 1** : condition, state **2** CALIDAD : capacity, position — **condicional** *adj* : conditional

condimento *nm* : condiment, seasoning

condolerse {47} *vr* : sympathize — **condolencia** *nf* : condolence

condominio *nm* **1** : joint ownership **2** *Lat* : condominium

condón *nm, pl* **-dones** : condom

conducir {61} *vt* **1** DIRIGIR : direct, lead **2** MANEJAR : drive — *vi* **1** : drive **2** ~ a : lead to — **conducirse** *vr* : behave

conducta *nf* : behavior, conduct

conducto *nm* : conduit, duct

conductor, -tora *n* : driver

conectar *vt* **1** : connect **2** ENCHUFAR : plug in — *vi* : connect

conejo, -ja *n* : rabbit — **conejera** *nf* : (rabbit) hutch

conexión *nf, pl* **-xiones** : connection — **conexo, -xa** *adj* : connected

confabularse *vr* : conspire, plot

confeccionar *vt* : make (up), prepare — **confección** *nf, pl* **-ciones 1** : making, preparation **2** : tailoring, dressmaking

confederación *nf, pl* **-ciones** : confederation

conferencia *nf* **1** : lecture **2** REUNIÓN : conference

conferir {76} *vt* : confer, bestow

confesar {55} *v* : confess — **confesarse** *vr* : go to confession — **confesión** *nf, pl* **-siones 1** : confession **2** CREDO : religion, creed

confeti *nm* : confetti

confiar {85} *vi* : trust — *vt* : entrust — **confiable** *adj* : trustworthy, reliable — **confiado, -da** *adj* **1** : confident **2** CRÉDULO : trusting — **confianza** *nf* **1** : trust **2** : confidence (in oneself)

confidencia *nf* : confidence, secret — **confidencial** *adj* : confidential — **confidencialidad** *nf* : confidentiality — **confidente** *nmf* **1** : confidant, confidante *f* **2** : (police) informer

configuración *nf, pl* **-ciones** : configuration, shape

confín *nm, pl* **-fines** : boundary, limit — **confinar** *vt* **1** : confine **2** DESTERRER : exile

confirmar *vt* : confirm — **confirmación** *nf, pl* **-ciones** : confirmation

confiscar {72} *vt* : confiscate

confitería *nm* : candy store

confitura *nf* : jam

conflagración *nf, pl* **-ciones 1** : war, conflict **2** INCENDIO : fire

conflicto *nm* : conflict

confluencia *nf* : junction, confluence

conformar *vt* : shape, make up — **conformarse** *vr* **1** RESIGNARSE : resign oneself **2** ~ con : content oneself with — **conforme** *adj* **1** : content, satisfied **2** ~ a : in accordance with — ~ *conj* : as — **conformidad** *nf* **1** : agreement **2** RESIGNACIÓN : resignation

confortar *vt* : comfort — **confortable** *adj* : comfortable

confrontar *vt* **1** : confront **2** COMPARAR : compare — *vi* : border — **confrontarse** *vr* ~ **con** : face up to — **confrontación** *nf, pl* **-ciones** : confrontation

confundir *vt* : confuse, mix up — **confundirse** *vr* : make a mistake, be confused — **confusión** *nf, pl* **-siones** : confusion — **confuso, -sa** *adj* **1** : confused **2** INDISTINTO : hazy, indistinct — **congelar** *vt* : freeze — **congelarse** *vr* : freeze — **congelación** *nf, pl* **-ciones** : freezing — **congelado, -da** *adj* : frozen — **congelador** *nm* : freezer

congeniar *vi* : get along

congestión *nf, pl* **-tiones** : congestion — **congestionado, -da** *adj* : congested

congoja *nf* : anguish, grief

congraciarse *vr* : ingratiate oneself

congratular *vt* : congratulate

congregar {52} *vt* : bring together — **congregarse** *vr* : congregate — **congregación** *nf, pl* **-ciones** : congregation, gathering

congreso *nm* : congress — **congresista** *nmf* : member of congress

conjeturar *vt* : guess, conjecture — **conjetura** *nf* : guess, conjecture

conjugar {52} *vt* : conjugate — **conjugación** *nf, pl* **-ciones** : conjugation

conjunción *nf, pl* **-ciones** : conjunction

conjunto, -ta *adj* : joint — **conjunto** *nm* **1** : collection **2** : outfit (of clothing) **3** GRUPO : band **4 en** ~ : as a whole

conjurar *vt* : ward off — *vi* : conspire, plot

conllevar *vt* : entail

conmemorar *vt* : commemorate — **conmemoración** *nf, pl* **-ciones** : commemoration — **conmemorativo, -va** *adj* : commemorative

conmigo *pron* : with me

conminar *vt* : threaten

conmiseración *nf, pl* **-ciones** : pity, commiseration

conmocionar *vt* : shock — **conmoción** *nf, pl* **-ciones** **1** : shock, upheaval **2** *or* ~ **cerebral** : concussion

conmover {47} *vt* **1** : move, touch **2** SACUDIR : shake (up) — **conmoverse** *vr* : be moved — **conmovedor, -dora** *adj* : moving, touching

conmutador *nm* **1** : (electric) switch **2** *Lat* : switchboard

cono *nm* : cone

conocer {18} *vt* **1** : know **2** : meet (a person), get to know (a city, etc.) **3** RECONOCER : recognize — **conocerse** *vr* **1** : meet, get to know each other **2** : know oneself — **conocedor, -dora** *adj* & *n* : expert — **conocido, -da** *adj* : well-known — ~ *n* : acquaintance — **conocimiento** *nm* **1** : knowledge **2** SENTIDO : consciousness

conque *conj* : so

conquistar *vt* : conquer — **conquista** *nf* : conquest — **conquistador, -dora** *adj* : conquering — **conquistador** *nm* : conqueror

consabido, -da *adj* **1** : well-known **2** HABITUEL : usual

consagrar *vt* **1** : consecrate **2** DEDICAR : devote — **consagración** *nf, pl* **-ciones** : consecration

consciencia *nf* → **conciencia** — **consciente** *adj* : conscious, aware

consecución *nf, pl* **-ciones** : attainment

consecuencia *nf* **1** : consequence **2 en** ~ : accordingly — **consecuente** *adj* : consistent

consecutivo, -va *adj* : consecutive

conseguir {75} *vt* **1** : get, obtain **2** ~ **hacer algo** : manage to do sth

consejo *nm* **1** : advice, counsel **2** : council (assembly) — **consejero, -ra** *n* : adviser, counselor

consenso *nm* : consensus

consentir {76} *vt* **1** : allow, permit **2** MIMAR : pamper, spoil — *vi* : consent — **consentimiento** *nm* : consent, permission

conserje *nmf* : caretaker, janitor

conservar *vt* **1** : preserve **2** GUARDAR : keep, conserve — **conservarse** *vr* : keep — **conserva** *nf* **1** : preserve(s) **2** ~**s** *nfpl* : canned goods — **conservación** *nf, pl* **-ciones** : conservation, preservation — **conservador, -dora** *adj* & *n* : conservative — **conservatorio** *nm* : conservatory

considerar *vt* **1** : consider **2** RESPETAR : respect — **considerable** *adj* : considerable — **consideración** *nf, pl* **-ciones** **1** : consideration **2** RESPETO : respect — **considerado, -da** *adj* **1** : considerate **2** RESPETADO : respected

consigna *nf* **1** ESLOGAN : slogan **2** ORDEN : orders **3** : checkroom (for baggage)

consigo *pron* : with her, with him, with you, with oneself

consiguiente *adj* **1** : consequent **2 por** ~ : consequently

consistir *vi* ~ **en 1** : consist of **2** : lie in, consist in — **consistencia** *nf* : consistency — **consistente** *adj* **1** : firm, solid **2** ~ **en** : consisting of

consolar {19} *vt* : console, comfort — **consolarse** *vr* : console oneself — **consolación** *nf, pl* **-ciones** : consolation

consolidar *vt* : consolidate — **consolidación** *nf, pl* **-ciones** : consolidation

consomé *nm* : consommé

consonante *adj* : consonant, harmonious — ~ *nf* : consonant

consorcio *nm* : consortium

conspirar *vi* : conspire, plot — **conspiración** *nf, pl* **-ciones** : conspiracy — **conspirador, -dora** *n* : conspirator

constancia *nf* **1** : record, evidence **2** PERSEVERANCIA : perseverance — **constante** *adj* : constant — **constantemente** *adv* : constantly, continually

constar *vi* **1** : be evident, be clear **2** ~ **de** : consist of

constatar *vt* **1** : verify **2** AFIRMAR : state, affirm

constelación *nf, pl* **-ciones** : constellation

consternación *nf, pl* **-ciones** : consternation

constipado, -da *adj* estar ~ : have a cold — **constipado** *nm* : cold — **constiparse** *vr* : catch a cold

constituir {41} *vt* **1** FORMAR : constitute, form **2** FUNDAR : establish, set up — **constituirse** *vr* ~ **en** : set oneself up as — **constitución** *nf, pl* **-ciones** : constitution — **constitucional** *adj* : constitutional — **constitutivo, -va** *adj* : constituent — **constituyente** *adj* & *nm* : constituent

constreñir {67} *vt* **1** : force, compel **2** RESTRINGIR : restrict, limit

construir {41} *vt* : build, construct — **construcción** *nf, pl* **-ciones** : construction, building — **constructivo, -va** *adj* : constructive — **constructor, -tora** *n* : builder

consuelo *nm* : consolation, comfort

consuetudinario, -ria *adj* : customary

cónsul *nmf* : consul — **consulado** *nm* : consulate

consultar *vt* : consult — **consulta** *nf* : consultation — **consultor, -tora** *n* : consultant — **consultorio** *nm* : office (of a doctor or dentist)

consumar *vt* **1** : consummate, complete **2** : commit (a crime)

consumir *vt* : consume — **consumirse** *vr* : waste away — **consumición** *nf, pl* **-ciones 1** : consumption **2** : drink

(in a restaurant) — **consumido, -da** *adj* : thin, emaciated — **consumidor, -dora** *n* : consumer — **consumo** *nm* : consumption

contabilidad *nf* **1** : accounting, bookkeeping **2** : accountancy (profession) — **contable** *nmf Spain* : accountant, bookkeeper

contactar *vi* ~ **con** : get in touch with, contact — **contacto** *nm* : contact

contado, -da *adj* : numbered, few — **contado** *nm* al ~ : (in) cash

contador, -dora *n Lat* : accountant — **contador** *nm* : meter

contagiar *vt* **1** : infect **2** : transmit (a disease) — **contagiarse** *vr* **1** : be contagious **2** : become infected (with a disease) — **contagio** *nm* : contagion, infection — **contagioso, -sa** *adj* : contagious, infectious

contaminar *vt* : contaminate, pollute — **contaminación** *nf, pl* **-ciones** : contamination, pollution

contar {19} *vt* **1** : count **2** NARRAR : tell — *vi* **1** : count **2** ~ **con** : rely on, count on

contemplar *vt* MIRAR : look at, behold **2** CONSIDERAR : contemplate — **contemplación** *nf, pl* **-ciones** : contemplation

contemporáneo, -nea *adj* & *n* : contemporary

contender {56} *vi* : contend, compete — **contendiente** *nmf* : competitor

contener {80} *vt* **1** : contain **2** RESTRINGIR : restrain, hold back — **contenerse** *vr* : restrain oneself — **contenedor** *nm* : container — **contenido, -da** *adj* : restrained — **contenido** *nm* : contents *pl*

contentar *vt* : please, make happy — **contentarse** *vr* ~ **con** : be satisfied with — **contento, -ta** *adj* : glad, happy, contented

contestar *vt* : answer — *vi* : reply, answer back — **contestación** *nf, pl* **-ciones** : answer, reply

contexto *nm* : context

contienda *nf* **1** COMBATE : dispute, fight **2** COMPETICIÓN : contest

contigo *pron* : with you

contiguo, -gua *adj* : adjacent

continente *nm* : continent — **continental** *adj* : continental

contingencia *nf* : contingency — **contingente** *adj* & *nm* : contingent

continuar {3} *v* : continue — **continuación** *nf, pl* **-ciones 1** : continuation **2 a** ~ : next, then — **continuidad** *nf* : continuity — **continuo, -nua** *adj* **1**

: continuous, steady **2** FRECUENTE
: continual

contorno *nm* **1** : outline **2** **~s** *nmpl*
: surrounding area

contorsión *nf, pl* **-siones** : contortion

contra *prep* **1** : against **2** **en ~** : against
— **~** *nm* **los pros y los ~s** : the pros
and cons

contraatacar {72} *v* : counterattack —
contraataque *nm* : counterattack

contrabajo *nm* : double bass

contrabalancear *vt* : counterbalance

contrabandista *nmf* : smuggler —
contrabando *nm* **1** : smuggling **2**
: contraband (goods)

contracción *nf, pl* **-ciones** : contraction

contrachapado *nm* : plywood

contradecir {11} *vt* : contradict —
contradicción *nf, pl* **-ciones** : contradiction — **contradictorio, -ria** *adj*
: contradictory

contraer {81} *vt* **1** : contract **2** **~ matrimonio** : get married — **contraerse**
vr : contract, tighten up

contrafuerte *nm* : buttress

contragolpe *nm* : backlash

contralto *nmf* : contralto

contrapartida *nf* : compensation

contrapelo: a ~ *adv phr* : the wrong
way

contrapeso *nm* : counterbalance

contraponer {60} *vt* **1** : counter, oppose **2** COMPARAR : compare

contraproducente *adj* : counterproductive

contrariar {85} *vt* **1** : oppose **2** MO-
LESTAR : vex, annoy — **contrariedad**
nf **1** : obstacle **2** DISGUSTO : annoyance
— **contrario, -ria** *adj* **1** OPUESTO : opposite **2 al contrario** : on the contrary
3 ser ~ a : be opposed to

contrarrestar *vt* : counteract

contrasentido *nm* : contradiction (in
terms)

contraseña *nf* : password

contrastar *vt* **1** : check, verify **2** RESIS-
TIR : resist — *vi* : contrast — **contraste** *nm* : contrast

contratar *vt* **1** : contract for **2** : hire, engage (workers)

contratiempo *nm* **1** : mishap **2** DIFICUL-
TAD : setback

contrato *nm* : contract — **contratista**
nmf : contractor

contraventana *nf* : shutter

contribuir {41} *vi* **1** : contribute **2** : pay
taxes — **contribución** *nf, pl* **-ciones 1**
: contribution **2** IMPUESTO : tax — **contribuyente** *nmf* **1** : contributor **2** : taxpayer

contrincante *nmf* : opponent

contrito, -ta *adj* : contrite

controlar *vt* **1** : control **2** COMPROBAR
: monitor, check — **control** *nm* **1**
: control **2** VERIFICACIÓN : inspection,
check — **controlador, -dora** *n* : con-
troller

controversia *nf* : controversy

contundente *adj* **1** : blunt **2** : forceful,
convincing (of arguments, etc.)

contusión *nf, pl* **-siones** : bruise

convalecencia *nf* : convalescence —
convaleciente *adj & nmf* : convalescent

convencer {86} *vt* : convince, persuade — **convencerse** *vr* : be convinced — **convencimiento** *nm* : conviction, belief

convención *nf, pl* **-ciones** : convention
— **convencional** *adj* : conventional

convenir {87} *vi* **1** : be suitable, be advisable **2 ~ en** : agree on — **conveniencia** *nf* **1** : convenience **2** : suitability (of an action, etc.) — **conveniente**
adj **1** : convenient **2** ACONSEJABLE
: suitable, advisable **3** PROVECHOSO
: useful — **convenio** *nm* : agreement,
pact

convento *nm* : convent, monastery

converger {15} *or* **convergir** *vi* : converge

conversar *vi* : converse, talk — **conversación** *nf, pl* **-ciones** : conversation

conversión *nf, pl* **-siones** : conversion
— **converso, -sa** *n* : convert

convertir {76} *vt* **1** : convert — **convertirse** *vr* **~ en** : turn into — **convertible** *adj & nm* : convertible

convexo, -xa *adj* : convex

convicción *nf, pl* **-ciones** : conviction
— **convicto, -ta** *adj* : convicted

convidar *vt* : invite — **convidado, -da**
n : guest

convincente *adj* : convincing

convite *nm* **1** : invitation **2** : banquet

convivir *vi* : live together — **convivencia** *nf* : coexistence, living together

convocar {72} *vt* : convoke, call together

convulsión *nf, pl* **-siones 1** : convulsion **2** TRASTORNO : upheaval — **convulsivo, -va** *adj* : convulsive

conyugal *adj* : conjugal — **cónyuge**
nmf : spouse, partner

coñac *nm* : cognac, brandy

cooperar *vi* : cooperate — **cooperación** *nf, pl* **-ciones** : cooperation
— **cooperativa** *nf* : cooperative, coop — **cooperativo, -va** *adj* : cooperative

coordenada *nf* : coordinate

coordinar *vt* : coordinate — **coordinación** *nf, pl* -**clones** : coordination — **coordinador, -dora** *n* : coordinator

copa *nf* **1** : glass, goblet **2** : cup (in sports) **3 tomar una ~** : have a drink

copia *nf* : copy — **copiar** *vt* : copy

copioso, -sa *adj* : copious, abundant

copla *nf* **1** : (popular) song **2** ESTROFA : verse, stanza

copo *nm* **1** : flake **2** *or* **~ de nieve** : snowflake

coquetear *vi* : flirt — **coqueteo** *nm* : flirting, flirtation — **coqueto, -ta** *adj* : flirtatious — **~** *n* : flirt

coraje *nm* **1** : valor, courage **2** IRA : anger

coral[1] *nm* : coral

coral[2] *adj* : choral — **~** *nf* : choir, chorale

Corán *nm* **el ~** : the Koran

coraza *nf* **1** : armor plating **2** : shell

corazón *nm, pl* -**zones 1** : heart **2** : core (of fruit) **3 mi ~** : my darling — **corazonada** *nf* **1** : hunch IMPULSO : impulse

corbata *nf* : tie, necktie

corchete *nm* **1** : hook and eye, clasp **2** : square bracket (punctuation mark)

corcho *nm* : cork

cordel *nm* : cord, string

cordero *nm* : lamb

cordial *adj* : cordial — **cordialidad** *nf* : cordiality

cordillera *nf* : mountain range

córdoba *nf* : córdoba (Nicaraguan unit of currency)

cordón *nm, pl* -**dones 1** : cord **2 ~ policial** : (police) cordon **3 cordones** *nmpl* : shoelaces

cordura *nf* : sanity

corear *vt* : chant

coreografía *nf* : choreography

cornamenta *nf* : antlers *pl*

corneta *nf* : bugle

coro *nm* **1** : chorus **2** : (church) choir

corona *nf* **1** : crown **2** : wreath, garland (of flowers) — **coronación** *nf, pl* -**clones** : coronation — **coronar** *vt* : crown

coronel *nm* : colonel

coronilla *nf* **1** : crown (of the head) **2 estar hasta la ~** : be fed up

corporación *nf, pl* -**clones** : corporation

corporal *adj* : corporal, bodily

corporativo, -va *adj* : corporate

corpulento, -ta *adj* : stout

corral *nm* **1** : farmyard **2** : pen, corral (for animals) **3** *or* **corralito** : playpen

correa *nf* **1** : strap, belt **2** : leash (for a dog, etc.)

corrección *nf, pl* -**clones 1** : correction **2** : correctness, propriety (of manners) — **correccional** *nm* : reformatory — **correctivo, -va** *adj* : corrective — **correcto, -ta** *adj* **1** : correct, right **2** CORTÉS : polite

corredizo, -za *adj* : sliding

corredor, -dora *n* **1** : runner, racer **2** AGENTE : agent, broker — **corredor** *nm* : corridor, hallway

corregir {28} *vt* : correct — **corregirse** *vr* : mend one's ways

correlación *nf, pl* -**clones** : correlation

correo *nm* **1** : mail **2 ~ aéreo** : airmail

correr *vi* **1** : run, race **2** : flow (of a river, etc.) **3** : pass (of time) — *vt* **1** : run **2** RECORRER : travel over, cover **3** : draw (curtains) — **correrse** *vr* **1** : move along **2** : run (of colors)

corresponder *vi* **1** : correspond **2** PERTENECER : belong **3** ENCAJAR : fit **4 ~ a** : reciprocate, repay — **corresponderse** *vr* : write to each other — **correspondencia** *nf* **1** : correspondence **2** : connection (of a train, etc.) — **correspondiente** *adj* : corresponding, respective — **corresponsal** *nmf* : correspondent

corretear *vi* : run about, scamper

corrida *nf* **1** : run **2** *or* **~ de toros** : bullfight — **corrido, -da** *adj* **1** : straight, continuous **2** *fam* : worldly

corriente *adj* **1** : current **2** NORMAL : common, ordinary **3** : running (of water, etc.) — **~** *nf* **1** : current (of water, electricity, etc.), draft (of air) **2** TENDENCIA : tendency, trend — **~** *nm* **al ~ 1** : up-to-date **2** ENTERADO : aware, informed

corrillo *nm* : clique, circle — **corro** *nm* : ring, circle (of people)

corroborar *vt* : corroborate

corroer {69} *vt* **1** : corrode (of metals) **2** : erode, wear away — **corroerse** *vr* : corrode

corromper *vt* **1** : corrupt **2** PUDRIR : rot — **corrompido, -da** *adj* : corrupt

corrosión *nf, pl* -**siones** : corrosion — **corrosivo, -va** *adj* : corrosive

corrupción *nf, pl* -**clones 1** : corruption **2** DESCOMPOSICIÓN : decay, rot — **corrupto, -ta** *adj* : corrupt

corsé *nm* : corset

cortar *vt* **1** : cut **2** RECORTAR : cut out **3** QUITAR : cut off — *vi* : cut — **cortarse** *vr* **1** : cut oneself **2** : be cut off (on the telephone) **3** : curdle (of milk) **4 ~ el pelo** : have one's hair cut — **cortada**

nf Lat : cut — **cortante** *adj* : cutting, sharp

cortauñas *nms & pl* : nail clippers

corte[1] *nm* **1** : cutting **2** ESTILO : cut, style **3** ~ **de pelo** : haircut

corte[2] *nf* **1** : court **2 hacer la** ~ **a** : court, woo — **cortejar** *vt* : court, woo

cortejo *nm* **1** : entourage **2** NOVIAZGO : courtship **3** ~ **fúnebre** : funeral procession

cortés *adj* : courteous, polite — **cortesía** *nf* : courtesy, politeness

corteza *nf* **1** : bark **2** : crust (of bread) **3** : rind, peel (of fruit)

cortina *nm* : curtain

corto, -ta *adj* **1** : short **2** ESCASO : scarce **3** *fam* : timid, shy **4** ~ **de vista** : nearsighted — **cortocircuito** *nm* : short circuit

corvo, -va *adj* : curved, bent

cosa *nf* **1** : thing **2** ASUNTO : matter, affair **3** ~ **de** : about **4 poca** ~ : nothing much

cosechar *v* : harvest, reap — **cosecha** *nf* **1** : harvest, crop **2** : vintage (of wine)

coser *v* : sew

cosmético, -ca *adj* : cosmetic — **cosmético** *nm* : cosmetic

cósmico, -ca *adj* : cosmic

cosmopolita *adj* : cosmopolitan

cosmos *nm* : cosmos

cosquillas *nfpl* **1** : tickling **2 hacer** ~ : tickle — **cosquilleo** *nm* : tickling sensation, tingle

costa *nf* **1** : coast, shore **2 a toda** ~ : at any cost

costado *nm* **1** : side **2 al** ~ : alongside

costar {19} *v* : cost

costarricense *or* **costarriqueño, -ña** *adj* : Costa Rican

coste *nm* → **costo** — **costear** *vt* : pay for

costero, -ra *adj* : coastal

costilla *nf* **1** : rib **2** CHULETA : chop, cutlet

costo *nm* : cost, price — **costoso, -sa** *adj* : costly

costra *nf* : scab

costumbre *nf* **1** : custom, habit **2 de** ~ : usual

costura *nf* **1** : sewing, dressmaking **2** PUNTADAS : seam — **costurera** *nf* : dressmaker

cotejar *vt* : compare

cotidiano, -na *adj* : daily

cotizar {21} *vt* : quote, set a price on — **cotización** *nf, pl* **-ciones** : quotation, price — **cotizado, -da** *adj* : in demand

coto *nm* : enclosure, reserve

cotorra *nf* **1** : small parrot **2** *fam* : chatterbox — **cotorrear** *vi fam* : chatter, gab

coyote *nm* : coyote

coyuntura *nf* **1** : joint **2** SITUACIÓN : situation, moment

coz *nm, pl* **coces** : kick (of an animal)

cráneo *nm* : cranium, skull

cráter *nm* : crater

crear *vt* : create — **creación** *nf, pl* **-ciones** : creation — **creativo, -va** *adj* : creative — **creador, -dora** *n* : creator

crecer {53} *vi* **1** : grow **2** AUMENTAR : increase — **crecido, -da** *adj* **1** : fullgrown **2** : large (of numbers) — **creciente** *adj* **1** : growing, increasing **2** : crescent (of the moon) — **crecimiento** *nm* **1** : growth **2** AUMENTO : increase

credenciales *nfpl* : credentials

credibilidad *nf* : credibility

crédito *nm* : credit

credo *nm* : creed

crédulo, -la *adj* : credulous, gullible

creer {20} *v* **1** : believe **2** SUPONER : suppose, think — **creerse** *vr* : regard oneself as — **creencia** *nf* : belief — **creíble** *adj* : believable, credible — **creído, -da** *adj fam* : conceited

crema *nf* : cream

cremación *nf, pl* **-ciones** : cremation

cremallera *nf* : zipper

cremoso, -sa *adj* : creamy

crepe *nmf* : crepe, pancake

crepitar *vi* : crackle

crepúsculo *nm* : twilight, dusk

crespo, -pa *adj* : curly, frizzy

crespón *nm, pl* **-pones** : crepe (fabric)

cresta *nf* **1** : crest **2** : comb (of a rooster)

cretino, -na *n* : cretin

creyente *nmf* : believer

criar {85} *vt* **1** : nurse (a baby) **2** EDUCAR : bring up, rear **3** : raise, breed (animals) — **cría** *nf* **1** : breeding, rearing **2** : young animal — **criadero** *nm* : farm, hatchery — **criado, -da** *n* : servant, maid *f* — **criador, -dora** *n* : breeder — **crianza** *nf* : upbringing, rearing

criatura *nf* **1** : creature **2** NIÑO : baby, child

crimen *nm, pl* **crímenes** : crime — **criminal** *adj & nmf* : criminal

críquet *nm* : cricket (game)

crin *nf* : mane

criollo, -lla *adj & n* : Creole

cripta *nf* : crypt

crisantemo *nm* : chrysanthemum

crisis *nf* **1** : crisis **2** ~ **nerviosa** : nervous breakdown

crispar *vt* **1** : tense (muscles), clench (one's fist) **2** IRRITAR : irritate, set on edge — **crisparse** *vr* : tense up

cristal *nm* **1** : crystal **2** VIDRIO : glass, piece of glass — **cristalería** *nf* : glassware — **cristalino, -na** *adj* : crystalline — **cristalino** *nm* : lens (of the eye) — **cristalizar** {21} *vi* : crystallize

cristiano, -na *adj & n* : Christian — **cristianismo** *nm* : Christianity — **Cristo** *nm* : Christ

criterio *nm* **1** : criterion **2** JUICIO : judgment, opinion

criticar {72} *vt* : criticize — **crítica** *nf* **1** : criticism **2** RESEÑA : review, critique — **crítico, -ca** *adj* : critical — ~ *n* : critic, reviewer

croar *vi* : croak

cromo *nm* : chromium, chrome

cromosoma *nm* : chromosome

crónica *nf* **1** : chronicle **2** : (news) report

crónico, -ca *adj* : chronic

cronista *nmf* : reporter, newscaster

cronología *nf* : chronology — **cronológico, -ca** *adj* : chronological

cronometrar *vt* : time, clock — **cronómetro** *nm* : chronometer, stopwatch

croqueta *nf* : croquette

croquis *nms & pl* : (rough) sketch

cruce *nm* **1** : crossing **2** : crossroads, intersection **3** ~ **peatonal** : crosswalk

crucero *nm* **1** : cruise **2** : cruiser (ship)

crucial *adj* : crucial

crucificar {72} *vt* : crucify — **crucifijo** *nm* : crucifix — **crucifixión** *nf, pl* **-fiones** : crucifixion

crucigrama *nm* : crossword puzzle

crudo, -da *adj* **1** : harsh, crude **2** : raw (of food) — **crudo** *nm* : crude oil

cruel *adj* : cruel — **crueldad** *nf* : cruelty

crujir *vi* : rustle, creak, crackle, crunch — **crujido** *nm* : rustle, creak, crackle, crunch — **crujiente** *adj* : crunchy, crisp

cruzar {21} *vt* **1** : cross **2** : exchange (words) — **cruzarse** *vr* **1** : intersect **2** : pass each other — **cruz** *nf, pl* **cruces** : cross — **cruzada** *nf* : crusade — **cruzado, -da** *adj* : crossed — **cruzado** *nm* : crusader

cuaderno *nm* : notebook

cuadra *nf* **1** : stable **2** *Lat* : (city) block

cuadrado, -da *adj* : square — **cuadrado** *nm* : square

cuadragésimo, -ma *adj* : fortieth, forty- — ~ *n* : fortieth, forty- (in a series)

cuadrar *vi* **1** : conform, agree **2** : add up, tally (numbers) — *vt* : square — **cuadrarse** *vr* : stand at attention

cuadrilátero *nm* **1** : quadrilateral **2** : ring (in sports)

cuadrilla *nf* : gang, group

cuadro *nm* **1** : square **2** PINTURA : painting **3** DESCRIPCIÓN : picture, description **4** : staff, management (of an organization) **5** CUADRADO : check, square **6** : (baseball) diamond

cuadrúpedo *nm* : quadruped

cuadruple *adj* : quadruple — **cuadruplicar** {72} *vt* : quadruple

cuajar *vi* **1** COAGULAR : clot, coagulate **2** : curdle **3** : set (of pudding, etc.) **4** AFIANZARSE : catch on — *vt* **1** : curdle **2** ~ **de** : fill with

cual *pron* **1** **el** ~, **la** ~, **los** ~**es**, **las** ~**es** : who, whom, which **2** **lo** ~ : which **3** **cada** ~ : everyone, everybody — ~ *prep* : like, as

cuál *pron* : which (one), what (one) — ~ *adj* : which, what

cualidad *nf* : quality, trait

cualquiera (**cualquier** *before nouns*) *adj, pl* **cualesquiera** : any, whatever — ~ *pron, pl* **cualesquiera** : anyone, whatever

cuán *adv* : how

cuando *conj* **1** : when **2** SI : since, if **3** ~ **más** : at the most **4** **de vez en** ~ : from time to time — ~ *prep* : during, at the time of

cuándo *adv* **1** : when **2** ¿**desde** ~? : since when?

cuantía *nf* **1** : quantity, extent **2** IMPORTANCIA : importance — **cuantioso, -sa** *adj* : abundant, considerable

cuanto *adv* **1** : as much as **2** ~ **antes** : as soon as possible **3** **en** ~ : as soon as **4** **en** ~ **a** : as for, as regards — **cuanto, -ta** *adj* : as many, whatever — ~ *pron* **1** : as much as, all that, everything **2** **unos cuantos, unas cuantas** : a few

cuánto *adv* : how much, how many — **cuánto, -ta** *adj* : how much, how many — ~ *pron* : how much, how many

cuarenta *adj & nm* : forty — **cuarentavo, -va** *adj* : fortieth — **cuarentavo** *nm* : fortieth

cuarentena *nf* : quarantine

Cuaresma *nf* : Lent

cuartear *vt* : quarter, divide up — **cuartearse** *vr* : crack, split

cuartel *nm* **1** : barracks *pl* **2** ~ **general** : headquarters **3** **no dar** ~ : show no mercy

cuarteto nm : quartet

cuarto, -ta adj : fourth — **~** n : fourth (in a series) — **cuarto** nm 1 : quarter, fourth 2 HABITACIÓN : room

cuarzo nm : quartz

cuatro adj & nm : four — **cuatrocientos, -tas** adj : four hundred — **cuatrocientos** nms & pl : four hundred

cuba nf : cask, barrel

cubano, -na adj : Cuban

cubeta nf 1 : keg, cask 2 Lat : pail, bucket

cúbico, -ca adj : cubic, cubed — **cubículo** nm : cubicle

cubierta nf 1 : cover, covering 2 : (automobile) tire 3 : deck (of a ship) — **cubierto** nm 1 : cutlery, place setting 2 a **~** : under cover

cubo nm 1 : cube 2 Spain : pail, bucket 3 : hub (of a wheel)

cubrecama nm : bedspread

cubrir {2} vt : cover — **cubrirse** vr 1 : cover oneself 2 : cloud over

cucaracha nf : cockroach

cuchara nf : spoon — **cucharada** nf : spoonful — **cucharilla** or **cucharita** nf : teaspoon — **cucharón** nm, pl **-rones** : ladle

cuchichear vi : whisper — **cuchicheo** nm : whisper

cuchilla nf 1 : (kitchen) knife 2 **~ de afeitar** : razor blade — **cuchillada** nf : stab, knife wound — **cuchillo** nm : knife

cuclillas nfpl **en ~** : squatting, crouching

cuco nm : cuckoo — **cuco, -ca** adj fam : pretty, cute

cucurucho nm : ice-cream cone

cuello nm 1 : neck 2 : collar (of clothing)

cuenca nf 1 : river basin 2 : (eye) socket — **cuenco** nm 1 : bowl 2 CONCAVIDAD : hollow

cuenta nf 1 : calculation, count 2 : (bank) account 3 FACTURA : check, bill 4 : bead (for a necklace, etc.) 5 **darse ~** : realize 6 **tener en ~** : bear in mind

cuento nm 1 : story, tale 2 **~ de hadas** : fairy tale

cuerda nf 1 : cord, rope, string 2 **~s vocales** : vocal cords 3 **dar ~ a** : wind up

cuerdo, -da adj : sane, sensible

cuerno nm 1 : horn 2 : antlers pl (of a deer)

cuero nm 1 : leather, hide 2 **~ cabelludo** : scalp

cuerpo nm 1 : body 2 : corps (in the military, etc.)

cuervo nm : crow

cuesta nf 1 : slope 2 a **~s** : on one's back 3 **~ abajo** : downhill 4 **~ arriba** : uphill

cuestión nf, pl **-tiones** : matter, affair — **cuestionar** vt : question — **cuestionario** nm 1 : questionnaire 2 : quiz (in school)

cueva nf : cave

cuidar vt 1 : take care of, look after 2 : pay attention to (details, etc.) — vi 1 **~ de** : look after 2 **~ de que** : make sure that — **cuidarse** vr : take care of oneself — **cuidado** nm 1 : care 2 PREOCUPACIÓN : worry, concern 3 **tener ~** : be careful 4 **¡cuidado!** : watch out!, careful! — **cuidadoso, -sa** adj : careful — **cuidadosamente** adv : carefully

culata nf : butt (of a gun) — **culatazo** nm : kick, recoil

culebra nf : snake

culinario, -ria adj : culinary

culminar vi : culminate — **culminación** nf, pl **-ciones** : culmination

culo nm fam : backside, bottom

culpa nf 1 : fault, blame 2 PECADO : sin 3 **echar la ~ a** : blame 4 **tener la ~** : be at fault — **culpabilidad** nf : guilt — **culpable** adj : guilty — **~** nmf : culprit, guilty party — **culpar** vt : blame

cultivar vt : cultivate — **cultivo** nm 1 : farming, cultivation 2 **~s** : crops

culto, -ta adj : cultured, educated — **culto** nm 1 : worship 2 : (religious) cult — **cultura** nf : culture — **cultural** adj : cultural

cumbre nf : summit, top

cumpleaños nms & pl : birthday

cumplido, -da adj 1 : complete, full 2 CORTÉS : courteous — **cumplido** nm : compliment, courtesy

cumplimentar vt 1 : congratulate 2 CUMPLIR : carry out — **cumplimiento** nm : carrying out, performance

cumplir vt 1 : accomplish, carry out 2 : keep (a promise), observe (a law, etc.) 3 : reach (a given age) — vi 1 : expire, fall due 2 **~ con el deber** : do one's duty — **cumplirse** vr 1 : expire 2 REALIZARSE : come true

cúmulo nm 1 : heap, pile 2 : cumulus (cloud)

cuna nf 1 : cradle 2 ORIGEN : birthplace

cundir vi 1 PROPAGARSE : spread, propagate 2 : go a long way

cuneta nf : ditch (in a road), gutter (in a street)

cuña nf : wedge

cuñado, -da *n* : brother-in-law *m*, sister-in-law *f*

cuota *nf* **1** : fee, dues **2** CUPO : quota **3** *Lat* : installment, payment

cupo *nm* **1** : quota, share **2** *Lat* : capacity, room

cupón *nm*, *pl* **-pones** : coupon

cúpula *nf* : dome, cupola

cura *nf* : cure, treatment — ~ *nm* : priest — **curación** *nf*, *pl* **-ciones** : healing — **curar** *vt* **1** : cure **2** : dress (a wound) **3** CURTIR : tan (hides) — **curarse** *vr* : get well

curiosear *vi* **1** : snoop, pry **2** : browse (in a store) — *vt* : look over — **curiosidad** *nf* : curiosity — **curioso, -sa** *adj* **1** : curious, inquisitive **2** RARO : unusual, strange

currículum *nm*, *pl* **-lums** *or* **currículo** *nm* : résumé, curriculum vitae

cursar *vt* **1** : take (a course), study **2** ENVIAR : send, pass on

cursi *adj fam* : affected, pretentious

cursiva *nf* : italics *pl*

curso *nm* **1** : course **2** : (school) year **3** **en ~** : under way **4 en ~** : current

curtir *vt* **1** : tan **2** : harden (skin, features, etc.) — **curtiduría** *nf* : tannery

curva *nf* **1** : curve, bend **2 ~ de nivel** : contour — **curvo, -va** *adj* : curved, bent

cúspide *nf* : apex, peak

custodia *nf* : custody — **custodiar** *vt* : guard, look after — **custodio, -dia** *n* : guardian

cutáneo, -nea *adj* : skin

cutícula *nf* : cuticle

cutis *nms & pl* : skin, complexion

cuyo, -ya *adj* **1** : whose, of whom, of which **2 en cuyo caso** : in which case

D

d *nf* : d, fourth letter of the Spanish alphabet

dádiva *nf* : gift, handout — **dadivoso, -sa** *adj* : generous

dado, -da *adj* **1** : given **2 dado que** : provided that, since — **dados** *nmpl* : dice

daga *nf* : dagger

daltónico, -ca *adj* : color-blind

dama *nf* **1** : lady **2 ~s** *nfpl* : checkers

damnificar {72} *vt* : damage, injure

danés, -nesa *adj* : Danish — **danés** *nm* : Danish (language)

danzar {21} *v* **1** : dance — **danza** *nf* : dance, dancing

dañar *vt* : damage, harm — **dañarse** *vr* **1** : be damaged **2** : hurt oneself — **dañino, -na** *adj* : harmful — **daño** *nm* **1** : damage, harm **2 ~s y perjuicios** : damages

dar {22} *vt* **1** : give **2** PRODUCIR : yield, produce **3** : strike (the hour) **4** MOSTRAR : show — *vi* **1 ~ como** : consider, regard as **2 ~ con** : run into, meet **3 ~ contra** : knock against **4 ~ para** : be enough for — **darse** *vr* **1** : happen **2 ~ contra** : bump into **3 ~ por** : consider oneself **4 dárselas de** : pose as

dardo *nm* : dart

dársena *nf* : dock

datar *vt* : date — *vi* **~ de** : date from

dátil *nm* : date (fruit)

dato *nm* **1** : fact **2 ~s** *nmpl* : data

de *prep* **1** : of **2 ~ Managua** : from Managua **3 ~ niño** : as a child **4 ~ noche** : at night **5 las tres ~ la mañana** : three o'clock in the morning **6 más ~ 10** : more than 10

deambular *vi* : wander about, stroll

debajo *adv* **1** : underneath **2 ~ de** : under, underneath **3 por ~** : below, beneath

debatir *vt* : debate — **debatirse** *vr* : struggle — **debate** *nm* : debate

deber *vt* : owe — *v aux* **1** : have to, should **2** (*expressing probability*) : must — **deberse** *vr* **~ a** : be due to — ~ *nm* **1** : duty **2 ~es** *nmpl* : homework — **debido, -da** *adj* **~ a** : due to, owing to

débil *adj* : weak, feeble — **debilidad** *nf* : weakness — **debilitar** *vt* : weaken — **debilitarse** *vr* : get weak — **débilmente** *adv* : weakly, faintly

débito *nm* **1** : debit **2** DEUDA : debt

debutar *vi* : debut — **debut** *nm*, *pl* **~s** : debut — **debutante** *nf* : debutante *f*

década *nf* : decade

decadencia *nf* : decadence — **decadente** *adj* : decadent

decaer {13} *vi* : decline, weaken

decano, -na *n* : dean

decapitar *vt* : behead

decena *nf* : ten, about ten

decencia *nf* : decency

decenio *nm* : decade

decente *adj* : decent

decepcionar *vt* : disappoint — **decepción** *nf, pl* **-ciones** : disappointment
decibelio *or* **decibel** *nm* : decibel
decidir *vt* : decide, determine — *vi* : decide — **decidirse** *vr* : make up one's mind — **decididamente** *adv* : definitely, decidedly — **decidido, -da** *adj* : determined, resolute
decimal *adj* : decimal
décimo, -ma *adj & n* : tenth
decimoctavo, -va *adj* : eighteenth — ∼ *n* : eighteenth (in a series)
decimocuarto, -ta *adj* : fourteenth — ∼ *n* : fourteenth (in a series)
decimonoveno, -na *or* **decimonono, -na** *adj* : nineteenth — ∼ *n* : nineteenth (in a series)
decimoquinto, -ta *adj* : fifteenth — ∼ *n* : fifteenth (in a series)
decimoséptimo, -ma *adj* : seventeenth — ∼ *n* : seventeenth (in a series)
decimosexto, -ta *adj* : sixteenth — ∼ *n* : sixteenth (in a series)
decimotercero, -ra *adj* : thirteenth — ∼ *n* : thirteenth (in a series)
decir {23} *vt* **1** : say **2** CONTAR : tell **3 es** ∼ : that is to say **4 querer** ∼ : mean — **decirse** *vr* **1** : tell oneself **2 ¿cómo se dice...en español?** : how do you say...in Spanish? — ∼ *nm* : saying, expression
decisión *nf, pl* **-siones** : decision — **decisivo, -va** *adj* : decisive
declarar *vt* : declare — *vi* : testify — **declararse** *vr* **1** : declare oneself **2** : break out (of a fire, an epidemic, etc.) — **declaración** *nf, pl* **-ciones** : statement
declinar *v* : decline
declive *nm* **1** : decline **2** PENDIENTE : slope
decolorar *vt* : bleach — **decolorarse** *vr* : fade
decoración *nf, pl* **-ciones** : decoration — **decorado** *nm* : stage set — **decorar** *vt* : decorate — **decorativo, -va** *adj* : decorative
decoro *nm* : decency, decorum — **decoroso, -sa** *adj* : decent, proper
decrecer {53} *vi* : decrease
decrépito, -ta *adj* : decrepit
decretar *vt* : decree — **decreto** *nm* : decree
dedal *nm* : thimble
dedicar {72} *vt* : dedicate — **dedicarse** *vr* ∼ **a** : devote oneself to — **dedicación** *nf, pl* **-ciones** : dedication — **dedicatoria** *nf* : dedication, inscription
dedo *nm* **1** : finger **2** ∼ **del pie** : toe

deducir {61} *vt* **1** INFERIR : deduce **2** DESCONTAR : deduct — **deducción** *nf, pl* **-ciones** : deduction
defecar {72} *vi* : defecate
defecto *nm* : defect — **defectuoso, -sa** *adj* : defective, faulty
defender {56} *vt* : defend — **defenderse** *vr* : defend oneself — **defensa** *nf* : defense — **defensiva** *nf* : defensive — **defensivo, -va** *adj* : defensive — **defensor, -sora** *n* **1** : defender **2** *or* **abogado defensor** : defense counsel
deferencia *nf* : deference — **deferente** *adj* : deferential
deficiencia *nf* : deficiency — **deficiente** *adj* : deficient
déficit *nm, pl* **-cits** : deficit
definir *vt* : define — **definición** *nf, pl* **-ciones** : definition — **definitivo, -va** *adj* **1** : definitive **2 en definitiva** : in short
deformar *vt* **1** : deform **2** : distort (the truth, etc.) — **deformación** *nf, pl* **-ciones** : distortion — **deforme** *adj* : deformed — **deformidad** *nf* : deformity
defraudar *vt* **1** : defraud **2** DECEPCIONAR : disappoint
degenerar *vi* : degenerate — **degenerado, -da** *adj* : degenerate
degradar *vt* **1** : degrade **2** : demote (in the military)
degustar *vt* : taste
dehesa *nf* : pasture
deidad *nf* : deity
dejar *vt* **1** : leave **2** ABANDONAR : abandon **3** PERMITIR : allow — *vi* ∼ **de** : quit — **dejado, -da** *adj* : slovenly, careless
dejo *nm* **1** : aftertaste **2** : (regional) accent
delantal *nm* : apron
delante *adv* **1** : ahead **2** ∼ **de** : in front of
delantera *nf* **1** : front **2 tomar la** ∼ : take the lead — **delantero, -ra** *adj* : front, forward — ∼ *n* : forward (in sports)
delatar *vt* : denounce, inform against
delegar {52} *vt* : delegate — **delegación** *nf, pl* **-ciones** : delegation — **delegado, -da** *n* : delegate, representative
deleitar *vt* : delight, please — **deleite** *nm* : delight
deletrear *vi* : spell (out)
delfín *nm, pl* **-fines** : dolphin
delgado, -da *adj* : thin
deliberar *vi* : deliberate — **deliberación** *nf, pl* **-ciones** : deliberation

— **deliberado, -da** *adj* : deliberate, intentional

delicadeza *nf* 1 : delicacy, daintiness 2 SUAVIDAD : gentleness 3 TACTO : tact — **delicado, -da** *adj* 1 : delicate 2 SENSIBLE : sensible 3 DISCRETO : tactful

delicia *nf* : delight — **delicioso, -sa** *adj* 1 : delightful 2 RICO : delicious

delictivo, -va *adj* : criminal

delimitar *vt* : define, set the boundaries of

delincuencia *nf* : delinquency, crime — **delincuente** *adj & nmf* : delinquent, criminal — **delinquir** {24} *vi* : break the law

delirante *adj* : delirious — **delirar** *vi* 1 : be delirious 2 ~ **por** *fam* : rave about — **delirio** *nm* 1 : delirium 2 ~ **de grandeza** : delusions of grandeur

delito *nm* : crime

delta *nm* : delta

demacrado, -da *adj* : emaciated

demandar *vt* 1 : sue 2 PEDIR : demand 3 *Lat* : require — **demanda** *nf* 1 : lawsuit 2 PETICIÓN : request 3 **la oferta y la** ~ : supply and demand — **demandante** *nmf* : plaintiff

demás *adj* : rest of the, other — ~ *pron* 1 **lo (la, los, las)** ~ : the rest, others 2 **por** ~ : extremely 3 **por lo** ~ : otherwise 4 **y** ~ : and so on

demasiado *adv* 1 : too 2 : too much — ~ *adj* : too much, too many

demencia *nf* : madness — **demente** *adj* : insane, mad

democracia *nf* : democracy — **demócrata** *nmf* : democrat — **democrático, -ca** *adj* : democratic

demoler {47} *vt* : demolish — **demolición** *nf, pl* **-ciones** : demolition

demonio *nm* : devil, demon

demorar *v* : delay — **demorarse** *vr* : take a long time — **demora** *nf* : delay

demostrar {19} *vt* : demonstrate 2 MOSTRAR : show — **demostración** *nf, pl* **-ciones** : demonstration

demudar *vt* : change, alter

denegar {49} *vt* : deny, refuse — **denegación** *nf, pl* **-ciones** : denial, refusal

denigrar *vt* 1 : denigrate 2 INJURIAR : insult

denominador *nm* : denominator

denotar *vt* : denote, show

densidad *nf* : density — **denso, -sa** *adj* : dense

dental *adj* : dental — **dentado, -da** *adj* : toothed, notched — **dentadura** *nf* ~ **postiza** : dentures *pl* — **dentífrico** *nm* : toothpaste — **dentista** *nmf* : dentist

dentro *adv* 1 : in, inside 2 ~ **de poco** : soon, shortly 3 **por** ~ : inside

denuedo *nm* : courage

denunciar *vt* 1 : denounce 2 : report (a crime) — **denuncia** *nf* 1 : accusation 2 : (police) report

departamento *nm* 1 : department 2 *Lat* : apartment

depender *vi* 1 : depend 2 ~ **de** : depend on — **dependencia** *nf* 1 : dependence, dependency 2 SUCURSAL : branch office — **dependiente** *adj* : dependent — **dependiente, -ta** *n* : clerk, salesperson

deplorar *vt* : deplore, regret

deponer {60} *vt* : remove from office, depose

deportar *vt* : deport — **deportación** *nf, pl* **-ciones** : deportation

deporte *nm* : sport, sports *pl* — **deportista** *nmf* : sportsman *m*, sportswoman *f* — **deportivo, -va** *adj* 1 : sporty 2 **artículos deportivos** : sporting goods

depositar *vt* 1 : put, place 2 : deposit (in a bank, etc.) — **depósito** *nm* 1 : deposit 2 ALMACÉN : warehouse

depravado, -da *adj* : depraved

depreciarse *vr* : depreciate — **depreciación** *nf* : depreciation

depredador *nm* : predator

deprimir *vt* : depress — **deprimirse** *vr* : get depressed — **depresión** *nf, pl* **-siones** : depression

derecha *nf* 1 : right side 2 : right wing (in politics) — **derechista** *adj* : rightwing — **derecho** *nm* 1 : right 2 LEY : law — ~ *adv* : straight — **derecho, -cha** *adj* 1 : right, right-hand 2 VERTICAL : upright 3 RECTO : straight

deriva *nf* 1 : drift 2 **a la** ~ : adrift — **derivación** *nf, pl* **-ciones** : derivation — **derivar** *vi* 1 : drift 2 ~ **de** : derive from

derramamiento *nm* ~ **de sangre** : bloodshed

derramar *vt* 1 : spill 2 : shed (tears, blood) — **derramarse** *vr* : overflow — **derrame** *nm* 1 : spilling 2 : discharge, hemorrhage

derrapar *vi* : skid — **derrape** *nm* : skid

derretir {54} *vt* : melt, thaw — **derretirse** *vr* 1 : melt, thaw 2 ~ **por** *fam* : be crazy about

derribar *vt* 1 : demolish 2 : bring down (a plane, a tree, etc.) 3 : overthrow (a government, etc.)

derrocar {72} *vt* : overthrow

derrochar *vt* : waste, squander — **der-**

rochador, -dora *n* : spendthrift — **derroche** *nm* : extravagance, waste
derrotar *vt* : defeat — **derrota** *nf* : defeat
derruir {41} *vt* : demolish, tear down
derrumbar *vt* : demolish, knock down — **derrumbarse** *vr* : collapse, break down — **derrumbamiento** *nm* : collapse — **derrumbe** *nm* : collapse
desabotonar *vt* : unbutton, undo
desabrido, -da *adj* : bland
desabrochar *vt* : unbutton, undo — **desabrocharse** *vr* : come undone
desacato *nm* **1** : disrespect **2** : contempt (of court) — **desacatar** *vt* : defy, disobey
desacertado, -da *adj* : mistaken, wrong — **desacertar** {55} *vi* : be mistaken — **desacierto** *nm* : mistake, error
desaconsejar *vt* : advise against — **desaconsejable** *adj* : inadvisable
desacreditar *vt* : discredit
desactivar *vt* : deactivate
desacuerdo *nm* : disagreement
desafiar {85} *vt* : defy, challenge — **desafiante** *adj* : defiant
desafilado, -da *adj* : blunt
desafinado, -da *adj* : out-of-tune, off-key
desafío *nm* : challenge, defiance
desafortunado, -da *adj* : unfortunate — **desafortunadamente** *adv* : unfortunately
desagradar *vt* : displease — **desagradable** *adj* : disagreeable, unpleasant
desagradecido, -da *adj* : ungrateful
desagrado *nm* **1** : displeasure **2 con ~** : reluctantly
desagravio *nm* : amends, reparation
desagregarse {52} *vr* : disintegrate
desaguar {10} *vi* : drain, empty — **desagüe** *nm* **1** : drainage **2** : drain (of a sink, etc.)
desahogar {52} *vt* **1** : relieve **2** : give vent to (anger, etc.) — **desahogarse** *vr* : let off steam, unburden oneself — **desahogado, -da** *adj* **1** : roomy **2** ADINERADO : comfortable, well-off — **desahogo** *nm* **1** : relief **2 con ~** : comfortably
desahuciar *vt* **1** : deprive of hope **2** DESALOJAR : evict — **desahucio** *nm* : eviction
desaire *nm* : snub, rebuff — **desairar** *vt* : snub, slight
desalentar {55} *vt* : discourage — **desaliento** *nm* : discouragement
desaliñado, -da *adj* : slovenly
desalmado, -da *adj* : heartless, cruel

desalojar *vt* **1** : evacuate **2** DESAHUCIAR : evict
desamparar *vt* : abandon — **desamparo** *nm* : abandonment, desertion
desamueblado, -da *adj* : unfurnished
desangrarse *vr* : lose blood, bleed to death
desanimar *vt* : discourage — **desanimarse** *vr* : get discouraged — **desanimado, -da** *adj* : downhearted, despondent — **desánimo** *nm* : discouragement
desanudar *vt* : untie
desaparecer {53} *vi* : disappear — **desaparecido, -da** *n* : missing person — **desaparición** *nf*, *pl* **-ciones** : disappearance
desapasionado, -da *adj* : dispassionate
desapego *nm* : indifference
desapercibido, -da *adj* : unnoticed
desaprobar {19} *vt* : disapprove of — **desaprobación** *nf*, *pl* **-ciones** : disapproval
desaprovechar *vt* : waste
desarmar *vt* **1** : disarm **2** DESMONTAR : dismantle, take apart — **desarme** *nm* : disarmament
desarraigar {52} *vt* : uproot, root out
desarreglar *vt* **1** : mess up **2** : disrupt (plans, etc.) — **desarreglado, -da** *adj* : disorganized — **desarreglo** *nm* : untidiness, disorder
desarrollar *vt* : develop — **desarrollarse** *vr* : take place — **desarrollo** *nm* : development
desarticular *vt* **1** : break up, dismantle **2** : dislocate (a bone)
desaseado, -da *adj* **1** : dirty **2** DESORDENADO : messy
desastre *nm* : disaster — **desastroso, -sa** *adj* : disastrous
desatar *vt* **1** : undo, untie **2** : unleash (passions) — **desatarse** *vr* **1** : come undone **2** DESENCADENARSE : break out, erupt
desatascar {72} *vt* : unclog
desatender {56} *vt* **1** : disregard **2** : neglect (an obligation, etc.) — **desatento, -ta** *adj* : inattentive
desatinado, -da *adj* : foolish, silly
desautorizado, -da *adj* : unauthorized
desavenencia *nf* : disagreement
desayunar *vi* : have breakfast — *vt* : have for breakfast — **desayuno** *nm* : breakfast
desbancar {72} *vt* : oust
desbarajuste *nm* : disorder, confusion
desbaratar *vt* : ruin, destroy — **desbaratarse** *vr* : fall apart

desbocarse {72} *vr* : run away, bolt
desbordar *vt* **1** : overflow **2** : exceed (limits) — **desbordarse** *vr* : overflow — **desbordamiento** *nm* : overflow
descabellado, -da *adj* : crazy
descafeinado, -da *adj* : decaffeinated
descalabrar *vt* : hit on the head — **descalabro** *nm* : misfortune, setback
descalificar {72} *vt* : disqualify — **descalificación** *nf, pl* **-ciones** : disqualification
descalzarse {21} *vr* : take off one's shoes — **descalzo, -za** *adj* : barefoot
descaminar *vt* : mislead, lead astray
descansar *v* : rest — **descanso** *nm* **1** : rest **2** : landing (of a staircase) **3** : intermission (in theater), halftime (in sports)
descapotable *adj & nm* : convertible
descarado, -da *adj* : insolent, shameless
descargar {52} *vt* **1** : unload **2** : discharge (a firearm, etc.) — **descarga** *nf* **1** : unloading **2** : discharge (of a firearm, of electricity, etc.) — **descargo** *nm* **1** : unloading **2** : discharge (of a duty, etc.) **3** : defense (in law)
descarnado, -da *adj* : scrawny, gaunt
descaro *nm* : insolence, nerve
descarrilar *vi* : derail — **descarrilarse** *vr* : be derailed
descartar *vt* : reject — **descartarse** *vr* : discard
descascarar *vt* : peel, shell, husk
descender {56} *vt* **1** : go down **2** BAJAR : lower — *vi* **1** : descend **2** ~ **de** : be descended from — **descendencia** *nf* **1** : descendants *pl* **2** LINAJE : lineage, descent — **descendiente** *nmf* : descendant — **descenso** *nm* **1** : descent **2** : drop, fall (in level, in temperature, etc.)
descifrar *vt* : decipher, decode
descolgar {16} *vt* **1** : take down **2** : pick up, answer (the telephone)
descolorarse *vr* : fade — **descolorido, -da** *adj* : faded, discolored
descomponer {60} *vt* : break down — **descomponerse** *vr* **1** : rot, decompose **2** *Lat* : break down — **descompuesto, -ta** *adj Lat* : out of order
descomunal *adj* : enormous
desconcertar {55} *vt* : disconcert, confuse — **desconcertante** *adj* : confusing — **desconcierto** *nm* : confusion, bewilderment
desconectar *vt* : disconnect
desconfiar {85} *vi* ~ **de** : distrust — **desconfiado, -da** *adj* : distrustful — **desconfianza** *nf* : distrust

descongelar *vt* **1** : thaw, defrost **2** : unfreeze (assets)
descongestionante *nm* : decongestant
desconocer {18} *vt* : not know, fail to recognize — **desconocido, -da** *adj* : unknown — ~ *n* : stranger
desconsiderado, -da *adj* : inconsiderate
desconsolar *vt* : distress — **desconsolado, -da** *adj* : heartbroken — **desconsuelo** *nm* : grief, sorrow
descontar {19} *vt* : discount
descontento, -ta *adj* : dissatisfied — **descontento** *nm* : discontent
descontinuar *vt* : discontinue
descorazonado, -da *adj* : discouraged
descorrer *vt* : draw back
descortés *adj, pl* **-teses** : rude — **descortesía** *nf* : discourtesy, rudeness
descoyuntar *vt* : dislocate
descrédito *nm* : discredit
descremado, -da *adj* : nonfat, skim
describir {33} *vt* : describe — **descripción** *nf, pl* **-ciones** : description — **descriptivo, -va** *adj* : descriptive
descubierto, -ta *adj* **1** : exposed, uncovered **2 al descubierto** : in the open — **descubierto** *nm* : deficit, overdraft
descubrir {2} *vt* **1** : discover **2** REVELAR : reveal — **descubrimiento** *nm* : discovery
descuento *nm* : discount
descuidar *vt* : neglect — **descuidarse** *vr* **1** : be careless **2** ABANDONARSE : let oneself go — **descuidado, -da** *adj* **1** : careless, sloppy **2** DESATENDIDO : neglected — **descuido** *nm* : neglect, carelessness
desde *prep* **1** : from (a place), since (a time) **2** ~ **luego** : of course
desdén *nm* : scorn, disdain — **desdeñar** *vt* : scorn — **desdeñoso, -sa** *adj* : disdainful
desdicha *nf* **1** : misery **2** DESGRACIA : misfortune — **desdichado, -da** *adj* : unfortunate, unhappy
desear *vt* : wish, want — **deseable** *adj* : desirable
desecar *vt* : dry up
desechar *vt* **1** : throw away **2** RECHAZAR : reject — **desechable** *adj* : disposable — **desechos** *nmpl* : rubbish
desembarazarse {21} *vr* ~ **de** : get rid of
desembarcar {72} *vi* : disembark — *vt* : unload — **desembarcadero** *nm* : jetty, landing pier — **desembarco** *nm* : landing
desembocar {72} *vi* ~ **en 1** : flow

into 2 : lead to (a result) — **desembocadura** nf 1 : mouth (of a river) 2 : opening, end (of a street)

desembolsar vt : pay out — **desembolso** nm : payment, outlay

desembragar vi : disengage the clutch

desempacar {72} v Lat : unpack

desempate nm : tiebreaker

desempeñar vt 1 : play (a role) 2 : redeem (from a pawnshop) — **desempeñarse** vr : get out of debt

desempleo nm : unemployment — **desempleado, -da** adj : unemployed

desempolvar vt : dust

desencadenar vt 1 : unchain 2 : trigger, unleash (protests, crises, etc.) — **desencadenarse** vr : break loose

desencajar vt 1 : dislocate 2 DESCONECTAR : disconnect

desencanto nm : disillusionment

desenchufar vt : disconnect, unplug

desenfadado, -da adj : carefree, confident — **desenfado** nm : confidence, ease

desenfrenado, -da adj : unrestrained — **desenfreno** nm : abandon, lack of restraint

desenganchar vt : unhook

desengañar vt : disillusion — **desengaño** nm : disappointment

desenlace nm : ending, outcome

desenmarañar vt : disentangle

desenmascarar vt : unmask

desenredar vt : untangle — **desenredarse** vr ~ **de** : extricate oneself from

desenrollar vt : unroll, unwind

desentenderse {56} vr ~ **de** : want nothing to do with

desenterrar {55} vt : dig up, disinter

desentonar vi 1 : be out of tune 2 : clash (of colors, etc.)

desenvoltura nf : confidence, ease

desenvolver {89} vt : unfold, unwrap — **desenvolverse** vr : unfold, develop

desenvuelto, -ta adj : confident, self-assured

deseo nm : desire — **deseoso, -sa** adj : eager, anxious

desequilibrar vt : throw off balance — **desequilibrado, -da** adj : unbalanced — **desequilibrio** nm : imbalance

desertar vt : desert — **deserción** nf, pl -**ciones** : desertion — **desertor, -tora** n : deserter

desesperar vt : exasperate — vi : despair — **desesperarse** vr : become exasperated — **desesperación** nf, pl -**ciones** : desperation, despair — de-

sesperado, -da adj : desperate, hopeless

desestimar vt : reject

desfalcar {72} vt : embezzle — **desfalco** nm : embezzlement

desfallecer {53} vi 1 : weaken 2 DESMAYARSE : faint

desfavorable adj : unfavorable

desfigurar vt 1 : disfigure, mar 2 : distort (the truth)

desfiladero nm : mountain pass, gorge

desfilar vi : march, parade — **desfile** nm : parade, procession

desfogar {52} vt : vent — **desfogarse** vr : let off steam

desgajar vt : tear off, break apart — **desgajarse** vr : come off

desgana nf 1 : lack of appetite 2 : lack of enthusiasm, reluctance

desgarbado, -da adj : gawky, ungainly

desgarrar vt : tear, rip — **desgarrador, -dora** adj : heartbreaking — **desgarro** nm : tear

desgastar vt : wear away, wear down — **desgaste** nm : deterioration, wear and tear

desgracia nf 1 : misfortune 2 **caer en** ~ : fall into disgrace 3 **por** ~ : unfortunately — **desgraciadamente** adv : unfortunately — **desgraciado, -da** adj : unfortunate

deshabitado, -da adj : uninhabited

deshacer {40} vt 1 : undo 2 DESTRUIR : destroy, ruin 3 DISOLVER : dissolve 4 : break (an agreement), cancel (plans, etc.) — **deshacerse** vr 1 : come undone 2 ~ **de** : get rid of 3 ~ **en** : lavish, heap (praise, etc.) — **deshecho, -cha** adj 1 : undone 2 DESTROZADO : destroyed, ruined

desheredar vt : disinherit

deshidratar vt : dehydrate

deshielo nm : thaw

deshilachar vt : unravel — **deshilacharse** vr : fray

deshonesto, -ta adj : dishonest

deshonrar vt : dishonor, disgrace — **deshonra** nf : dishonor — **deshonroso, -sa** adj : dishonorable

deshuesar vt 1 : pit (a fruit) 2 : bone, debone (meat)

desidia nf 1 : indolence 2 DESASEO : sloppiness

desierto, -ta adj : deserted, uninhabited — **desierto** nm : desert

designar vt : designate — **designación** nf, pl -**ciones** : appointment (to an office, etc.)

designio nm : plan

desigual adj 1 : unequal 2 DISPAREJO

: uneven — **desigualdad** *nf* : inequality

desilusionar *vt* : disappoint, disillusion — **desilusión** *nf, pl* **-siones** : disappointment, disillusionment

desinfectar *vt* : disinfect — **desinfectante** *adj & nm* : disinfectant

desinflar *vt* : deflate — **desinflarse** *vr* : deflate, go flat

desinhibido, -da *adj* : uninhibited

desintegrar *vt* : disintegrate — **desintegrarse** *vr* : disintegrate — **desintegración** *nf, pl* **-ciones** : disintegration

desinteresado, -da *adj* : unselfish, generous — **desinterés** *nm* : unselfishness

desistir *vi* ~ **de** : give up

desleal *adj* : disloyal — **deslealtad** *nf* : disloyalty

desleír {66} *vt* : dilute, dissolve

desligar {52} *vt* **1** : untie **2** SEPARAR : separate — **desligarse** *vr* : extricate oneself

desliz *nm, pl* **-lices** : slip, mistake — **deslizar** {21} *vt* : slide, slip — **deslizarse** *vr* : slide, glide

deslucido, -da *adj* : dingy, tarnished

deslumbrar *vt* : dazzle — **deslumbrante** *adj* : dazzling, blinding

deslustrar *vt* : tarnish, dull

desmán *nm, pl* **-manes** : outrage, excess

desmandarse *vr* : get out of hand

desmantelar *vt* : dismantle

desmañado, -da *adj* : clumsy

desmayar *vi* : lose heart — **desmayarse** *vr* : faint — **desmayo** *nm* : faint

desmedido, -da *adj* : excessive

desmejorar *vt* : impair — *vi* : deteriorate

desmemoriado, -da *adj* : forgetful

desmentir {76} *vt* : deny — **desmentido** *nm* : denial

desmenuzar {21} *vt* **1** : crumble **2** EXAMINAR : scrutinize — **desmenuzarse** *vr* : crumble

desmerecer {53} *vt* : be unworthy of — *vi* : decline in value

desmesurado, -da *adj* : excessive

desmigajar *vt* : crumble

desmontar *vt* **1** : dismantle, take apart **2** ALLANAR : level — *vi* : dismount

desmoralizar {21} *vt* : demoralize

desmoronarse *vr* : crumble

desnivel *nm* : unevenness

desnudar *vt* : undress, strip — **desnudarse** *vr* : get undressed — **desnudez** *nf, pl* **-deces** : nudity, nakedness — **desnudo, -da** *adj* : nude, naked — **desnudo** *nm* : nude

desnutrición *nf, pl* **-ciones** : malnutrition

desobedecer {53} *v* : disobey — **desobediencia** *nf* : disobedience — **desobediente** *adj* : disobedient

desocupar *vt* : empty, vacate — **desocupado, -da** *adj* **1** : vacant **2** DESEMPLEADO : unemployed

desodorante *adj & nm* : deodorant

desolado, -da *adj* **1** : desolate **2** DESCONSOLADO : devastated, distressed — **desolación** *nf, pl* **-ciones** : desolation

desorden *nm, pl* **desórdenes** : disorder, mess — **desordenado, -da** *adj* : untidy — **desordenadamente** *adv* : in a disorderly way

desorganizar {21} *vt* : disorganize — **desorganización** *nf, pl* **-ciones** : disorganization

desorientar *vt* : disorient, confuse — **desorientarse** *vr* : lose one's way

desovar *vi* : spawn

despachar *vt* **1** : deal with (a task, etc.) **2** ENVIAR : dispatch, send **3** : wait on, serve (customers) — **despacho** *nm* **1** : dispatch, shipment **2** OFICINA : office

despacio *adv* : slowly

desparramar *vt* : spill, scatter, spread

despavorido, -da *adj* : terrified

despecho *nm* **1** : spite **2 a** ~ **de** : despite, in spite of

despectivo, -va *adj* **1** : pejorative **2** DESPRECIATIVO : contemptuous

despedazar {21} *vt* : tear apart

despedir {54} *vt* **1** : see off **2** DESTITUIR : dismiss, fire **3** DESPRENDER : emit — **despedirse** *vr* : say good-bye — **despedida** *nf* : farewell, good-bye

despegar {52} *vt* : detach, unstick — *vi* : take off — **despegado, -da** *adj* : cold, distant — **despegue** *nm* : take-off

despeinar *vt* : ruffle (hair) — **despeinado, -da** *adj* : disheveled, unkempt

despejar *vt* : clear, free — *vi* : clear up — **despejado, -da** *adj* **1** : clear, fair **2** LÚCIDO : clear-headed

despellejar *vt* : skin (an animal)

despensa *nf* : pantry, larder

despeñadero *nm* : precipice

desperdiciar *vt* : waste — **desperdicio** *nm* **1** : waste **2** ~**s** *nmpl*: scraps

desperfecto *nm* : flaw, defect

despertar {55} *vi* : awaken, wake up — *vt* : wake, rouse — **despertador** *nm* : alarm clock

despiadado, -da *adj* : pitiless, merciless

despido nm : dismissal, layoff

despierto, -ta adj : awake

despilfarrar vt : squander — **despilfarrador, -dora** n : spendthrift — **despilfarro** nm : extravagance, wastefulness

despistar vt : throw off the track, confuse — **despistarse** vr : lose one's way — **despistado, -da** adj 1 : absentminded 2 DESORIENTADO : confused — **despiste** nm 1 : absentmindedness 2 ERROR : mistake

desplazar {21} vt : displace — **desplazarse** vr : travel

desplegar {49} vt : unfold, spread out — **despliegue** nm : display

desplomarse vr : collapse

desplumar vt 1 : pluck 2 fam : fleece

despoblado, -da adj : uninhabited, deserted — **despoblado** nm : deserted area

despojar vt : strip, deprive — **despojos** nmpl 1 : plunder 2 RESTOS : remains, scraps

desportillar vt : chip — **desportillarse** vr : chip — **desportilladura** nf : chip, nick

despota nmf : despot

despotricar vi : rant (and rave)

despreciar vi : despise, scorn — **despreciable** adj 1 : despicable 2 **una cantidad ~** : a negligible amount — **desprecio** nm : disdain, scorn

desprender vt 1 : detach, remove 2 EMITIR : give off — **desprenderse** vr 1 : come off 2 DEDUCIRSE : be inferred, follow — **desprendimiento** nm **~ de tierras** : landslide

despreocupado, -da adj : carefree, unconcerned

desprestigiar vt : discredit — **desprestigiarse** vr : lose face

desprevenido, -da adj : unprepared

desproporcionado, -da : out of proportion

despropósito nm : (piece of) nonsense, absurdity

desprovisto, -ta adj **~ de** : lacking in

después adv 1 : afterward 2 ENTONCES : then, next 3 **~ de** : after 4 **después (de) que** : after 5 **~ de todo** : after all

despuntado, -da adj : blunt, dull

desquiciar vt : drive crazy

desquitarse vr 1 : retaliate 2 **~ con** : take it out on, get back at — **desquite** nm : revenge

destacar {72} vt : emphasize — vi : stand out — **destacado, -da** adj : outstanding

destapar vt : open, uncover — **destapador** nm Lat : bottle opener

destartalado, -da adj : dilapidated

destellar vi : flash, sparkle — **destello** nm : sparkle, twinkle, flash

destemplado, -da adj 1 : out of tune 2 MAL : out of sorts 3 : unpleasant (of weather)

desteñir {67} vt : fade, bleach — vi : run, fade — **desteñirse** vr : fade

desterrar {55} vt : banish, exile — **desterrado, -da** n : exile

destetar vt : wean

destiempo adv **a ~** : at the wrong time

destierro nm : exile

destilar vt : distill — **destilería** nf : distillery

destinar vt 1 : assign, allocate 2 NOMBRAR : appoint — **destinado, -da** adj : destined — **destinatario, -ria** n : addressee — **destino** nm 1 : destiny 2 RUMBO : destination

destituir {41} vt : dismiss — **destitución** nf, pl **-ciones** : dismissal

destornillar vt : unscrew — **destornillador** nm : screwdriver

destreza nf : skill, dexterity

destrozar {21} vt : destroy, wreck — **destrozos** nmpl : damage, destruction

destrucción nf, pl **-ciones** : destruction — **destructivo, -va** adj : destructive — **destruir** {41} vt : destroy

desunir vt : split, divide

desusado, -da adj 1 : obsolete 2 INSÓLITO : unusual — **desuso** nm **caer en ~** : fall into disuse

desvaído, -da adj 1 : pale, washed-out 2 BORROSO : vague, blurred

desvalido, -da adj : destitute, needy

desvalijar vt : rob

desván nm, pl **-vanes** : attic

desvanecer {53} vt : make disappear — **desvanecerse** vr 1 : vanish 2 DESMAYARSE : faint

desvariar {85} vi : be delirious — **desvarío** nm : delirium

desvelar vt : keep awake — **desvelarse** vr : stay awake — **desvelo** nm 1 : sleeplessness 2 **~s** nmpl : efforts

desvencijado, -da adj : dilapidated, rickety

desventaja nf : disadvantage

desventura nf : misfortune

desvergonzado, -da adj : shameless — **desvergüenza** nf : shamelessness

desvestir {54} vt : undress — **desvestirse** vr : get undressed

desviación nf, pl **-ciones** 1 : deviation 2 : detour (in a road) — **desviar** {85} vt : divert, deflect — **desviarse** vr 1 : branch off 2 APARTARSE : stray — **desvío** nm : diversion, detour

detallar *vt* : detail — **detallado, -da** *adj* : detailed, thorough — **detalle** *nm* **1** : detail **2 al ~** : retail — **detallista** *adj* : retail — **~** *nmf* : retailer

detectar *vt* : detect — **detective** *nmf* : detective

detener {80} *vt* **1** : arrest, detain **2** PARAR : stop **3** RETRASAR : delay — **detenerse** *vr* **1** : stop **2** DEMORARSE : linger — **detención** *nf, pl* **-ciones** : arrest, detention

detergente *nm* : detergent

deteriorar *vt* : damage — **deteriorarse** *vr* : wear out, deteriorate — **deteriorado, -da** *adj* : damaged, worn — **deterioro** *nm* : deterioration, damage

determinar *vt* **1** : determine **2** MOTIVAR : bring about **3** DECIDIR : decide — **determinarse** *vr* : decide — **determinación** *nf, pl* **-ciones 1** : determination **2 tomar una ~** : make a decision — **determinado, -da** *adj* **1** : determined **2** ESPECÍFICO : specific

detestar *vt* : detest

detonar *vi* : explode, detonate — **detonación** *nf, pl* **-ciones** : detonation

detrás *adv* **1** : behind **2 ~ de** : in back of **3 por ~** : from behind

detrimento *nm* **en ~ de** : to the detriment of

deuda *nf* : debt — **deudor, -dora** *n* : debtor

devaluar {3} *vt* : devalue — **devaluarse** *vr* : depreciate

devastar *vt* : devastate — **devastador, -dora** *adj* : devastating

devenir {87} *vi* **1** : come about **2 ~ en** : become, turn into

devoción *nf, pl* **-ciones** : devotion

devolución *nf, pl* **-ciones** : return

devolver {89} *vt* **1** RESTITUIR : give back **2** : refund, pay back — *vi* : vomit — **devolverse** *vr Lat* : return, come back

devorar *vt* : devour

devoto, -ta *adj* : devout — **~** *n* : devotee

día *nm* **1** : day **2** : daytime **3 al ~** : up-to-date **4 en pleno ~** : in broad daylight

diabetes *nf* : diabetes — **diabético, -ca** *adj & n* : diabetic

diablo *nm* : devil — **diablillo** *nm* : imp, rascal — **diablura** *nf* : prank — **diabólico, -ca** *adj* : diabolic, diabolical

diafragma *nm* : diaphragm

diagnosticar {72} *vt* : diagnose — **diagnóstico, -ca** *adj* : diagnostic — **diagnóstico** *nm* : diagnosis

diagonal *adj & nf* : diagonal

diagrama *nm* : diagram

dial *nm* : dial (of a radio, etc.)

dialecto *nm* : dialect

dialogar {52} *vi* : have a talk — **diálogo** *nm* : dialogue

diamante *nm* : diamond

diámetro *nm* : diameter

diana *nf* **1** : reveille **2** BLANCO : target, bull's-eye

diario, -ria *adj* : daily — **diario** *nm* **1** : diary **2** PERIÓDICO : newspaper — **diariamente** *adv* : daily

diarrea *nf* : diarrhea

dibujar *vt* **1** : draw **2** DESCRIBIR : portray — **dibujante** *nmf* : draftsman *m*, draftswoman *f* — **dibujo** *nm* **1** : drawing **2 ~s animados** : (animated) cartoons

diccionario *nm* : dictionary

dicha *nf* **1** ALEGRÍA : happiness **2** SUERTE : good luck — **dicho** *nm* : saying, proverb — **dichoso, -sa** *adj* **1** : happy **2** AFORTUNADO : lucky

diciembre *nm* : December

dictar *vt* **1** : dictate **2** : pronounce (a sentence), deliver (a speech) — **dictado** *nm* : dictation — **dictador, -dora** *n* : dictator — **dictadura** *nf* : dictatorship

diecinueve *adj & nm* : nineteen — **diecinueveavo, -va** *adj* : nineteenth

dieciocho *adj & nm* : eighteen — **dieciochoavo, -va** *or* **dieciochavo, -va** *adj* : eighteenth

dieciséis *adj & nm* : sixteen — **dieciseisavo, -va** *adj* : sixteenth

diecisiete *adj & nm* : seventeen — **diecisieteavo, -va** *adj* : seventeenth

diente *nm* **1** : tooth **2** : prong, tine (of a fork, etc.) **3 ~ de ajo** : clove of garlic **4 ~ de león** : dandelion

diesel ['disel] *adj & nm* : diesel

diestra *nf* : right hand — **diestro, -tra** *adj* **1** : right **2** HÁBIL : skillful

dieta *nf* : diet — **dietético, -ca** *adj* : dietetic, dietary

diez *adj & nm, pl* **dieces** : ten

difamar *vt* : slander, libel — **difamación** *nf, pl* **-ciones** : slander, libel

diferencia *nf* : difference — **diferenciar** *vt* : distinguish between — **diferenciarse** *vr* : differ — **diferente** *adj* : different

diferir {76} *vt* : postpone — *vi* : differ

difícil *adj* : difficult — **dificultad** *nf* : difficulty — **dificultar** *vt* : hinder, obstruct

difteria *nf* : diphtheria

difundir *vt* **1** : spread (out) **2** : broadcast (television, etc.)

difunto, -ta *adj & n* : deceased
difusión *nf, pl* **-siones** : spreading
digerir {76} *vt* : digest — **digerible** *adj*
: digestible — **digestión** *nf, pl* **-tiones**
: digestion — **digestivo, -va** *adj* : digestive
dígito *nm* : digit — **digital** *adj* : digital
dignarse *vr* ~ **a** : deign to
dignatario, -ria *n* : dignitary — **dignidad** *nf* : dignity — **digno, -na** *adj*
: worthy
digresión *nf, pl* **-ciones** : digression
dilapidar *vt* : waste, squander
dilatar *vt* **1** : expand, dilate **2** PROLONGAR : prolong **3** POSPONER : postpone
dilema *nm* : dilemma
diligencia *nf* **1** : diligence **2** TRÁMITE
: procedure, task — **diligente** *adj*
: diligent
diluir {41} *vt* : dilute
diluvio *nm* **1** : flood **2** LLUVIA : downpour
dimensión *nf, pl* **-siones** : dimension
diminuto, -ta *adj* : minute, tiny
dimitir *vi* : resign — **dimisión** *nf, pl*
-siones : resignation
dinámico, -ca *adj* : dynamic
dinamita *nf* : dynamite
dínamo *or* **dinamo** *nmf* : dynamo
dinastía *nf* : dynasty
dineral *nm* : large sum, fortune
dinero *nm* : money
dinosaurio *nm* : dinosaur
diócesis *nfs & pl* : diocese
dios, diosa *n* : god, goddess *f* — **Dios**
nm : God
diploma *nm* : diploma — **diplomado, -da** *adj* : qualified, trained
diplomacia *nf* : diplomacy — **diplomático, -ca** *adj* : diplomatic — ~ *n* : diplomat
diputación *nf, pl* **-ciones** : delegation — **diputado, -da** *n* : delegate
dique *nm* : dike
dirección *nf, pl* **-ciones** **1** : address **2** SENTIDO : direction **3** GESTIÓN : management **4** : steering (of an automobile) — **direccional** *nf Lat* : turn signal, blinker — **directa** *nf* : high gear — **directiva** *nf* : board of directors — **directivo, -va** *adj* : managerial — ~ *n* : manager, director — **directo, -ta** *adj* **1** : direct **2** DERECHO : straight — **director, -tora** *n* **1** : director, manager **2** : conductor (of an orchestra) — **directorio** *nm* : directory — **directriz** *nf, pl* **-trices** : guideline
dirigencia *nf* : leaders *pl*, leadership — **dirigente** *nmf* : director, leader
dirigible *nm* : dirigible, blimp

dirigir {35} *vt* **1** : direct, lead **2** : address (a letter, etc.) **3** ENCAMINAR : aim **4** : conduct (music) — **dirigirse** *vr* **1** ~ **a** : go towards **2** ~ **a algn** : speak to s.o., write to s.o.
discernir {25} *vt* : discern, distinguish — **discernimiento** *nm* : discernment
disciplinar *vt* : discipline — **disciplina** *nf* : discipline
discípulo, -la *n* : disciple, follower
disco *nm* **1** : disc, disk **2** : discus (in sports) **3** ~ **compacto** : compact disc
discordante *adj* : discordant — **discordia** *nf* : discord
discoteca *nf* : disco, discotheque
discreción *nf, pl* **-ciones** : discretion
discrepancia *nf* **1** : discrepancy **2** DESACUERDO : disagreement — **discrepar** *vi* : differ, disagree
discreto, -ta *adj* : discreet
discriminar *vt* **1** : discriminate against **2** DISTINGUIR : distinguish — **discriminación** *nf, pl* **-ciones** : discrimination
disculpar *vt* : excuse, pardon — **disculparse** *vr* : apologize — **disculpa** *nf* **1** : apology **2** EXCUSA : excuse
discurrir *vi* **1** : pass, go by **2** REFLEXIONAR : ponder, reflect
discurso *nm* : speech, discourse
discutir *vt* **1** : discuss **2** CUESTIONAR : dispute — *vi* : argue — **discusión** *nf, pl* **-siones** **1** : discussion **2** DISPUTA : argument — **discutible** *adj* : debatable
disecar {72} *vt* : dissect — **disección** *nf, pl* **-ciones** : dissection
diseminar *vt* : disseminate, spread
disentería *nf* : dysentery
disentir {76} *vi* ~ **de** : disagree with — **disentimiento** *nm* : disagreement, dissent
diseñar *vt* : design — **diseñador, -dora** *n* : designer — **diseño** *nm* : design
disertación *nf, pl* **-ciones** **1** : lecture **2** : (written) dissertation
disfrazar {21} *vt* : disguise — **disfrazarse** *vr* ~ **de** : disguise oneself as — **disfraz** *nm, pl* **-fraces** **1** : disguise **2** : costume (for a party, etc.)
disfrutar *vt* : enjoy — *vi* : enjoy oneself
disgustar *vt* : upset, annoy — **disgustarse** *vr* **1** : get annoyed **2** ENEMISTARSE : fall out (with s.o.) — **disgusto** *nm* **1** : annoyance, displeasure **2** RIÑA : quarrel
disidente *adj & nmf* : dissident
disimular *vt* : conceal, hide — *vi* : pretend — **disimulo** *nm* : pretense
disipar *vt* **1** : dispel **2** DERROCHAR : squander

diskette [di'sket] *nm* : floppy disk, diskette

dislexia *nf* : dyslexia — **disléxico, -ca** *adj* : dyslexic

dislocar {72} *vt* : dislocate — **dislocarse** *vr* : become dislocated

disminuir {41} *vt* : reduce — *vi* : decrease, drop — **disminución** *nf, pl* **-ciones** : decrease

disociar *vt* : dissociate

disolver {89} *vt* : dissolve — **disolverse** *vr* : dissolve

disparar *vi* : shoot, fire — *vt* : shoot — **dispararse** *vr* : shoot up, skyrocket

disparatado, -da *adj* : absurd — **disparate** *nm* : nonsense, silly thing

disparejo, -ja *adj* : uneven — **disparidad** *nf* : difference, disparity

disparo *nm* : shot

dispensar *vt* **1** : dispense, distribute **2** DISCULPAR : excuse

dispersar *vt* : disperse, scatter — **dispersarse** *vr* : disperse — **dispersión** *nf, pl* **-siones** : scattering

disponer {60} *vt* **1** : arrange, lay out **2** ORDENAR : decide, stipulate — *vi* ~ **de** : have at one's disposal — **disponerse** *vr* ~ **a** : be ready to — **disponibilidad** *nf* : availability — **disponible** *adj* : available

disposición *nf, pl* **-ciones 1** : arrangement **2** APTITUD : aptitude **3** : order, provision (in law) **4 a** ~ **de** : at the disposal of

dispositivo *nm* : device, mechanism

dispuesto, -ta *adj* : prepared, ready

disputar *vi* **1** : argue **2** COMPETIR : compete — *vt* : dispute — **disputa** *nf* : dispute, argument

disquete → **diskette**

distanciar *vt* : space out — **distanciarse** *vr* : grow apart — **distancia** *nf* : distance — **distante** *adj* : distant

distinguir {26} *vt* : distinguish — **distinguirse** *vr* : distinguish oneself, stand out — **distinción** *nf, pl* **-ciones** : distinction — **distintivo, -va** *adj* : distinctive — **distinto, -ta** *adj* **1** : different **2** CLARO : distinct, clear

distorsión *nf, pl* **-siones** : distortion

distraer {81} *vt* **1** : distract **2** DIVERTIR : entertain — **distraerse** *vr* **1** : get distracted **2** ENTRETENERSE : amuse oneself — **distracción** *nf, pl* **-ciones 1** : amusement **2** DESPISTE : absentmindedness — **distraído, -da** *adj* : distracted, absentminded

distribuir {41} *vt* : distribute — **distribución** *nf, pl* **-ciones** : distribution — **distribuidor, -dora** *n* : distributor

distrito *nm* : district

disturbio *nm* : disturbance

disuadir *vt* : dissuade, discourage — **disuasivo, -va** *adj* : deterrent

diurno, -na *adj* : day, daytime

divagar {52} *vi* : digress

diván *nm, pl* **-vanes** : divan, couch

divergir {35} *vi* **1** : diverge **2** ~ **en** : differ on

diversidad *nf* : diversity

diversificar {72} *vt* : diversify

diversión *nf, pl* **-siones** : fun, entertainment

diverso, -sa *adj* : diverse

divertir {76} *vt* : entertain — **divertirse** *vr* : enjoy oneself, have fun — **divertido, -da** *adj* : entertaining

dividendo *nm* : dividend

dividir *vt* **1** : divide **2** REPARTIR : distribute

divinidad *nf* : divinity — **divino, -na** *adj* : divine

divisa *nf* **1** : currency **2** EMBLEMA : emblem

divisar *vt* : discern, make out

división *nf, pl* **-siones** : division — **divisor** *nm* : denominator

divorciar *vt* : divorce — **divorciarse** *vr* : get a divorce — **divorciado, -da** *n* : divorcé *m*, divorcée *f* — **divorcio** *nm* : divorce

divulgar {52} *vt* **1** : divulge, reveal **2** PROPAGAR : spread, circulate

dizque *adv Lat* : supposedly, apparently

doblar *vt* **1** : double **2** PLEGAR : fold **3** : turn (a corner) **4** : dub (a film) — *vi* **1** : turn — **doblarse** *vr* **1** : double over **2** ~ **a** : give in to — **dobladillo** *nm* : hem — **doble** *adj & nm* : double — ~ *nmf* : stand-in, double — **doblemente** *adv* : doubly — **doblegar** {52} *vt* : force to yield — **doblegarse** *vr* : give in — **doblez** *nm, pl* **-bleces** : fold, crease

doce *adj & nm* : twelve — **doceavo, -va** *adj* : twelfth — **docena** *nf* : dozen

docente *adj* : teaching

dócil *adj* : docile

doctor, -tora *n* : doctor — **doctorado** *nm* : doctorate

doctrina *nf* : doctrine

documentar *vt* : document — **documentación** *nf, pl* **-ciones** : documentation — **documental** *adj & nm* : documentary — **documento** *nm* : document

dogma *nm* : dogma — **dogmático, -ca** *adj* : dogmatic

dólar *nm* : dollar

doler {47} *vi* **1** : hurt **2 me duelen los pies** : my feet hurt — **dolerse** *vr* ~ **de** : complain about — **dolor** *nm* **1** : pain **2** PENA : grief **3** ~ **de cabeza** : headache **4** ~ **de estómago** : stomachache — **dolorido, -da 1** : sore **2** AFLIGIDO : hurt — **doloroso, -sa** *adj* : painful

domar *vt* : tame, break in

domesticar {72} *vt* : domesticate, tame — **doméstico, -ca** *adj* : domestic

domicilio *nm* : home, residence

dominar *vt* **1** : dominate, control **2** : master (a subject, a language, etc.) — **dominarse** *vr* : control oneself — **dominación** *nf, pl* **-ciones** : domination — **dominante** *adj* : dominant

domingo *nm* : Sunday — **dominical** *adj* **periódico** ~ : Sunday newspaper

dominio *nm* **1** : authority **2** : mastery (of a subject)

dominó *nm, pl* **-nós** : dominoes *pl* (game)

don[1] *nm* : courtesy title preceding a man's first name

don[2] *nm* **1** : gift **2** TALENTO : talent — **donación** *nf, pl* **-ciones** : donation — **donador, -dora** *n* : donor

donaire *nm* : grace, charm

donar *vt* : donate — **donante** *nmf* : donor — **donativo** *nm* : donation

donde *conj* : where — ~ *prep Lat* : over by

dónde *adv* **1** : where **2 ¿de ~ eres?** : where are you from? **3 ¿por ~?** : whereabouts?

dondequiera *adv* **1** : anywhere **2** ~ **que** : wherever, everywhere

doña *nf* : courtesy title preceding a woman's first name

doquier *adv* **por** ~ : everywhere

dorar *vt* **1** : gild **2** : brown (food) — **dorado, -da** *adj* : gold, golden

dormir {27} *vt* : put to sleep — *vi* : sleep — **dormirse** *vr* : fall asleep — **dormido, -da** *adj* **1** : asleep **2** ENTUMECIDO : numb — **dormilón, -lona** *n* : sleepyhead, late riser — **dormitar** *vi* : doze — **dormitorio** *nm* **1** : bedroom **2** : dormitory (in a college)

dorso *nm* : back

dos *adj & nm* : two — **doscientos, -tas** *adj* : two hundred — **doscientos** *nms & pl* : two hundred

dosel *nm* : canopy

dosis *nfs & pl* : dose, dosage

dotar *vt* **1** : provide, equip **2** ~ **de** : endow with — **dotación** *nf, pl* **-ciones 1** : endowment, funding **2** PERSONAL : personnel — **dote** *nf* **1** : dowry **2** ~**s** *nfpl* : gift, talent

dragar {52} *vt* : dredge — **draga** *nf* : dredge

dragón *nm, pl* **-gones** : dragon

drama *nm* : drama — **dramático, -ca** *adj* : dramatic — **dramatizar** {21} *vt* : dramatize — **dramaturgo, -ga** *n* : dramatist, playwright

drástico, -ca *adj* : drastic

drenar *vt* : drain — **drenaje** *nm* : drainage

droga *nf* : drug — **drogadicto, -ta** *n* : drug addict — **drogar** {52} *vt* : drug — **drogarse** *vr* : take drugs — **droguería** *nf* : drugstore

dromedario *nm* : dromedary

dual *adj* : dual

ducha *nf* : shower — **ducharse** *vr* : take a shower

ducho, -cha *adj* : experienced, skilled

duda *nf* : doubt — **dudar** *vt* : doubt — *vi* ~ **en** : hesitate to — **dudoso, -sa** *adj* **1** : doubtful **2** SOSPECHOSO : questionable

duelo *nm* **1** : duel **2** LUTO : mourning

duende *nm* : elf, imp

dueño, -na *n* **1** : owner **2** : landlord, landlady *f*

dulce *adj* **1** : sweet **2** : fresh (of water) **3** SUAVE : mild, gentle — ~ *nm* : candy, sweet — **dulzura** *nf* : sweetness

duna *nf* : dune

dúo *nm* : duo, duet

duodécimo, -ma *adj* : twelfth — ~ *n* : twelfth (in a series)

dúplex *nms & pl* : duplex (apartment)

duplicar {72} *vt* **1** : double **2** : duplicate, copy (a document, etc.) — **duplicado, -da** *adj* : duplicate — **duplicado** *nm* : copy

duque *nm* : duke — **duquesa** *nf* : duchess

durabilidad *nf* : durability

duración *nf, pl* **-ciones** : duration, length

duradero, -ra *adj* : durable, lasting

durante *prep* **1** : during **2** ~ **una hora** : for an hour

durar *vi* : endure, last

durazno *nm Lat* : peach

duro *adv* : hard — **duro, -ra** *adj* **1** : hard **2** SEVERO : harsh — **dureza** *nf* **1** : hardness **2** SEVERIDAD : harshness

E

e[1] *nf* : e, fifth letter of the Spanish alphabet

e[2] *conj (used instead of* **y** *before words beginning with* **i** *or* **hi***)* : and

ebanista *nmf* : cabinetmaker

ébano *nm* : ebony

ebrio, -bria *adj* : drunk

ebullición *nf, pl* **-ciones** : boiling

echar *vt* **1** : throw, cast **2** EXPULSAR : expel, dismiss **3** : give off, emit (smoke, sparks, etc.) **4** BROTAR : sprout **5** PONER : put (on) **6 ~ a perder** : spoil, ruin **7 ~ de menos** : miss — **echarse** *vr* **1** : throw oneself **2** ACOSTARSE : lie down **3 ~ a** : start (to)

eclesiástico, -ca *adj* : ecclesiastic — **~** *nm* : clergyman

eclipse *nm* : eclipse — **eclipsar** *vi* : eclipse

eco *nm* : echo

ecología *nf* : ecology — **ecológico, -ca** *adj* : ecological — **ecologista** *nmf* : ecologist

economía *nf* **1** : economy **2** : economics (science) — **económico, -ca** *adj* **1** : economic, economical **2** BARATO : inexpensive — **economista** *nmf* : economist — **economizar** {21} *v* : save

ecosistema *nm* : ecosystem

ecuación *nf, pl* **-ciones** : equation

ecuador *nm* : equator

ecuánime *adj* **1** : even-tempered **2** : impartial (in law)

ecuatoriano, -na *adj* : Ecuadorian, Ecuadorean, Ecuadoran

ecuestre *adj* : equestrian

edad *nf* **1** : age **2 Edad Media** : Middle Ages *pl* **3 ¿qué ~ tienes?** : how old are you?

edición *nf, pl* **-ciones 1** : publishing, publication **2** : edition (of a book, etc.)

edicto *nm* : edict

edificar {72} *vt* : build — **edificio** *nm* : building

editar *vt* **1** : publish **2** : edit (a film, a text, etc.) — **editor, -tora** *n* **1** : publisher **2** : editor — **editorial** *adj* : publishing — **~** *nm* : editorial — **~** *nf* : publishing house

edredón *nm, pl* **-dones** : (down) comforter, duvet

educar {72} *vt* **1** : educate **2** CRIAR : bring up, raise **3** : train (the body, the voice, etc.) — **educación** *nf, pl* **-ciones 1** : education **2** MODALES : (good) manners *pl* — **educado, -da** *adj* : polite — **educador, -dora** *n* : educator — **educativo, -va** *adj* : educational

efectivo, -va *adj* **1** : effective **2** REAL : real — **efectivo** *nm* : cash — **efectivamente** *adv* **1** : really **2** POR SUPUESTO : yes, indeed — **efecto** *nm* **1** : effect **2 en ~** : in fact **3 ~s** *nmpl* : goods, property — **efectuar** {3} *vt* : bring about, carry out

efervescente *adj* : effervescent — **efervescencia** *nf* : effervescence

eficaz *adj, pl* **-caces 1** : effective **2** EFICIENTE : efficient — **eficacia** *nf* **1** : effectiveness **2** EFICIENCIA : efficiency

eficiente *adj* : efficient — **eficiencia** *nf* : efficiency

efímero, -ra *adj* : ephemeral

efusivo, -va *adj* : effusive

egipcio, -cia *adj* : Egyptian

ego *nm* : ego — **egocéntrico, -ca** *adj* : egocentric — **egoísmo** *nm* : egoism — **egoísta** *adj* : egoistic — **~** *nmf* : egoist

egresar *vi* : graduate — **egresado, -da** *n* : graduate — **egreso** *nm* : graduation, commencement

eje *nm* **1** : axis **2** : axle (of a wheel, etc.)

ejecutar *vt* **1** : execute, put to death **2** REALIZAR : carry out — **ejecución** *nf, pl* **-ciones** : execution

ejecutivo, -va *adj & n* : executive

ejemplar *adj* : exemplary — **~** *nm* **1** : copy, issue **2** EJEMPLO : example — **ejemplificar** {72} *vt* : exemplify — **ejemplo** *nm* **1** : example **2 por ~** : for example

ejercer {86} *vt* **1** : practice (a profession) **2** : exercise (a right, etc.) — *vi* **~ de** : practice as, work as — **ejercicio** *nm* **1** : exercise **2** : practice (of a profession, etc.)

ejército *nm* : army

el, la *art, pl* **los, las** : the — **el** *pron (referring to masculine nouns)* **1** : the one **2 ~ que** : he who, whoever, the one that

él *pron* : he, him

elaborar *vt* **1** : manufacture, produce **2** : draw up (a plan, etc.)

elástico, -ca *adj* : elastic — **elástico** *nm* : elastic — **elasticidad** *nf* : elasticity

elección *nf, pl* **-ciones 1** : election **2** SELECCIÓN : choice — **elector, -tora** *n* : voter — **electorado** *nm* : electorate — **electoral** *adj* : electoral

electricidad *nf* : electricity — **eléctrico, -ca** *adj* : electric, electrical — **electricista** *nmf* : electrician — **electrificar** {72} *vt* : electrify — **electrizar** {21} *vt* : electrify, thrill — **electrocutar** *vt* : electrocute

electrodo *nm* : electrode

electrodoméstico *nm* : electric appliance

electromagnético, -ca *adj* : electromagnetic

electrón *nm, pl* **-trones** : electron — **electrónico, -ca** *adj* : electronic — **electrónica** *nf* : electronics

elefante, -ta *n* : elephant

elegante *adj* : elegant — **elegancia** *nf* : elegance

elegía *nf* : elegy

elegir {28} *vt* **1** : elect **2** ESCOGER : choose, select — **elegible** *adj* : eligible

elemento *nm* : element — **elemental** *adj* **1** : elementary, basic **2** ESENCIAL : fundamental

elenco *nm* : cast (of actors)

elevar *vt* **1** : raise, lift **2** ASCENDER : elevate (in a hierarchy), promote — **elevarse** *vr* : rise — **elevación** *nf, pl* **-ciones** : elevation — **elevador** *nm* **1** : hoist **2** *Lat* : elevator

eliminar *vt* : eliminate — **eliminación** *nf, pl* **-ciones** : elimination

elipse *nf* : ellipse — **elíptico, -ca** *adj* : elliptical, elliptic

elite *or* **élite** *nf* : elite

elixir *or* **elíxir** *nm* : elixir

ella *pron* : she, her — **ello** *pron* : it — **ellos, ellas** *pron pl* **1** : they, them **2 de ellos, de ellas** : theirs

elocuente *adj* : eloquent — **elocuencia** *nf* : eloquence

elogiar *vt* : praise — **elogio** *nm* : praise

eludir *vt* : avoid, elude

emanar *vi* **~ de** : emanate from

emancipar *vt* : emancipate — **emanciparse** *vr* : free oneself — **emancipación** *nf, pl* **-ciones** : emancipation

embadurnar *vt* : smear, daub

embajada *nf* : embassy — **embajador, -dora** *n* : ambassador

embalar *vt* : wrap up, pack — **embalaje** *nm* : packing

embaldosar *vt* : pave with tiles

embalsamar *vt* : embalm

embalse *nm* : dam, reservoir

embarazar {21} *vt* **1** : make pregnant **2** IMPEDIR : restrict, hamper — **embarazada** *adj* : pregnant — **embarazo** *nm* **1** : pregnancy **2** IMPEDIMENTO : hindrance, obstacle — **embarazoso, -sa** *adj* : embarrassing

embarcar {72} *vt* : load — **embarcarse** *vr* : embark, board — **embarcación** *nf, pl* **-ciones** : boat, craft — **embarcadero** *nm* : pier, jetty — **embarco** *nm* : embarkation

embargar {52} *vt* **1** : seize, impound **2** : overwhelm (with emotion, etc.) — **embargo** *nm* **1** : embargo **2** : seizure (in law) **3 sin ~** : nevertheless

embarque *nm* : loading (of goods), boarding (of passengers)

embarrancar {72} *vi* : run aground

embarullarse *vr fam* : get mixed up

embaucar {72} *vt* : trick, swindle — **embaucador, -dora** *n* : swindler

embeber *vt* : absorb — *vi* : shrink — **embeberse** *vr* : become absorbed

embelesar *vt* : enchant, delight — **embelesado, -da** *adj* : spellbound

embellecer {53} *vt* : embellish, beautify

embestir {54} *vt* : attack, charge at — *vi* : charge, attack — **embestida** *nf* **1** : attack **2** : charge (of a bull)

emblema *nm* : emblem

embobar *vt* : amaze, fascinate

embocadura *nf* **1** : mouth (of a river, etc.) **2** : mouthpiece (of an instrument)

émbolo *nm* : piston

embolsarse *vr* : put in one's pocket

emborracharse *vr* : get drunk

emborronar *vt* **1** : smudge, blot **2** GARABATEAR : scribble

emboscar {72} *vt* : ambush — **emboscada** *nf* : ambush

embotar *vt* : dull, blunt

embotellar *vt* : bottle (up) — **embotellamiento** *nm* : traffic jam

embrague *nm* : clutch — **embragar** {52} *vi* : engage the clutch

embriagarse {52} *vr* : get drunk — **embriagado, -da** *adj* : intoxicated, drunk — **embriagador, -dora** *adj* : intoxicating — **embriaguez** *nf* : drunkenness

embrión *nm, pl* **-briones** : embryo

embrollo *nm* : tangle, confusion

embrujar *vt* : bewitch — **embrujo** *nm* : spell, curse

embrutecer *vt* : brutalize

embudo *nm* : funnel

embuste *nm* : lie — **embustero, -ra** *adj* : lying — **~** *n* : liar, cheat

embutir *vt* : stuff — **embutido** *nm* : sausage, cold meat

emergencia *nf* : emergency

emerger {15} *vi* : emerge, appear

emigrar *vi* 1 : emigrate 2 : migrate (of animals) — **emigración** *nf, pl* **-ciones** 1 : emigration 2 : migration (of animals) — **emigrante** *adj & nmf* : emigrant

eminente *adj* : eminent — **eminencia** *nf* : eminence

emitir *vt* 1 : emit 2 EXPRESAR : express (an opinion, etc.) 3 : broadcast (on radio or television) 4 : issue (money, stamps, etc.) — **emisión** *nf, pl* **-siones** 1 : emission 2 : broadcast (on radio or television) 3 : issue (of money, etc.) — **emisora** *nf* : radio station

emoción *nf, pl* **-ciones** : emotion — **emocional** *adj* : emotional — **emocionante** *adj* 1 : moving, touching 2 APASIONANTE : exciting, thrilling — **emocionar** *vt* 1 : move, touch 2 APASIONAR : excite, thrill — **emocionarse** *vr* 1 : be moved 2 APASIONARSE : get excited — **emotivo, -va** *adj* 1 : emotional 2 CONMOVEDOR : moving

empacar {72} *vt Lat* : pack

empachar *vt* : give indigestion to — **empacharse** *vr* : get indigestion — **empacho** *nm* : indigestion

empadronarse *vr* : register to vote

empalagoso, -sa *adj* : excessively sweet, cloying

empalizada *nf* : palisade (fence)

empalmar *vt* : connect, link — *vi* : meet, converge — **empalme** *nm* 1 : connection, link 2 : junction (of a railroad, etc.)

empanada *nf* : pie, turnover — **empanadilla** *nf* : meat or seafood pie

empanar *vt* : bread (in cooking)

empantanar *vt* : flood — **empantanarse** *vr* 1 : become flooded 2 : get bogged down

empañar *vt* 1 : steam (up) 2 : tarnish (one's reputation, etc.) — **empañarse** *vr* : fog up

empapar *vt* : soak — **empaparse** *vr* : get soaking wet

empapelar *vt* : wallpaper

empaquetar *vt* : pack, package

emparedado, -da *adj* : walled in, confined — **emparedado** *nm* : sandwich

emparejar *vt* : match up, pair — **emparejarse** *vr* : pair off

emparentado, -da *adj* : related, kindred

empastar *vt* : fill (a tooth) — **empaste** *nm* : filling

empatar *vi* : result in a draw, be tied — **empate** *nm* : draw, tie

empedernido, -da *adj* : inveterate, hardened

empedrar {55} *vt* : pave (with stones) — **empedrado** *nm* : paving, pavement

empeine *nm* : instep

empeñar *vt* : pawn — **empeñarse** *vr* 1 : insist, persist 2 ENDEUDARSE : go into debt 3 **~ en** : make an effort to — **empeñado, -da** *adj* 1 : determined, committed 2 ENDEUDADO : in debt — **empeño** *nm* 1 : determination, effort 2 **casa de ~** : pawnshop

empeorar *vi* : get worse — *vt* : make worse

empequeñecer {53} *vt* : diminish, make smaller

emperador *nm* : emperor — **emperatriz** *nf, pl* **-trices** : empress

empezar {29} *v* : start, begin

empinar *vt* : raise — **empinarse** *vr* : stand on tiptoe — **empinado, -da** *adj* : steep

empírico, -ca *adj* : empirical

emplasto *nm* : poultice

emplazar {21} *vt* 1 : summon, subpoena 2 SITUAR : place, locate — **emplazamiento** *nm* 1 : location, site 2 CITACIÓN : summons, subpoena

emplear *vt* 1 : employ 2 USAR : use — **emplearse** *vr* 1 : get a job 2 USARSE : be used — **empleado, -da** *n* : employee — **empleador, -dora** *n* : employer — **empleo** *nm* 1 : occupation, job 2 USO : use

empobrecer {53} *vt* : impoverish — **empobrecerse** *vr* : become poor

empollar *vi* : brood (eggs) — *vt* : incubate

empolvarse *vr* : powder one's face

empotrar *vt* : fit, build into — **empotrado, -da** *adj* : built-in

emprender *vt* : undertake, begin — **emprendedor, -dora** *adj* : enterprising

empresa *nf* 1 COMPAÑIA : company, firm 2 TAREA : undertaking — **empresarial** *adj* : business, managerial — **empresario, -ria** *n* 1 : businessman *m*, businesswoman *f* 2 : impresario (in theater), promoter (in sports)

empujar *v* : push — **empuje** *nm* : impetus, drive — **empujón** *nm, pl* **-jones** : push, shove

empuñar *vt* : grasp, take hold of

emular *vt* : emulate

en *prep* 1 : in 2 DENTRO DE : into, inside

(of) **3** SOBRE : on **4** ~ **avión** : by plane **5** ~ **casa** : at home

enajenar *vt* : alienate — **enajenación** *nf, pl* **-ciones** : alienation

enagua *nf* : slip, petticoat

enaltecer {53} *vt* : praise, extol

enamorar *vt* : win the love of — **enamorarse** *vr* : fall in love — **enamorado, -da** *adj* : in love — ~ *n* : lover, sweetheart

enano, -na *adj & n* : dwarf

enarbolar *vt* **1** : hoist, raise **2** : brandish (arms, etc.)

enardecer {53} *vt* : stir up, excite

encabezar {21} *vt* **1** : head, lead **2** : put a heading on (an article, a list, etc.) — **encabezamiento** *nm* **1** : heading **2** : headline (in a newspaper)

encabritarse *vr* : rear up

encadenar *vt* **1** : chain, tie (up) **2** EN-LAZAR : connect, link

encajar *vt* : fit (together) — *vi* **1** : fit **2** CUADRAR : conform, tally — **encaje** *nm* : lace

encalar *vt* : whitewash

encallar *vi* : run aground

encaminar *vt* : direct, aim — **encaminarse** *vr* ~ **a** : head for — **encaminado, -da** *adj* ~ **a** : aimed at, designed to

encandilar *vt* : dazzle

encanecer {53} *vi* : turn gray

encantar *vt* : enchant, bewitch — *vi me* **encanta esta canción** : I love this song — **encantado, -da** *adj* **1** : delighted **2** HECHIZADO : bewitched — **encantador, -dora** *adj* : charming, delightful — **encantamiento** *nm* : enchantment, spell — **encanto** *nm* **1** : charm, fascination **2** HECHIZO : spell

encapotarse *vr* : cloud over — **encapotado, -da** *adj* : overcast

encapricharse *vr* ~ **con** : be infatuated with

encapuchado, -da *adj* : hooded

encaramar *vt* : lift up — **encaramarse** *vr* ~ **a** : climb up on

encarar *vt* : face, confront

encarcelar *vt* : imprison — **encarcelamiento** *nm* : imprisonment

encarecer {53} *vt* : increase, raise (price, value, etc.) — **encarecerse** *vr* : become more expensive

encargar {52} *vt* **1** : put in charge of **2** PEDIR : order — **encargarse** *vr* ~ **de** : take charge of — **encargado, -da** *adj* : in charge — ~ *n* : manager, person in charge — **encargo** *nm* **1** : errand **2** TAREA : assignment, task **3** PE-DIDO : order

encariñarse *vr* ~ **con** : become fond of

encarnar *vt* : embody — **encarnación** *nf, pl* **-ciones** : embodiment — **encarnado, -da** *adj* **1** : incarnate **2** ROJO : red

encarnizarse {21} *vr* ~ **con** : attack viciously — **encarnizado, -da** *adj* : bitter, bloody

encarrilar *vt* : put on the right track

encasillar *vt* : pigeonhole

encauzar {21} *vt* : channel

encender {56} *vt* **1** : light, set fire to **2** PRENDER : switch on, start **3** AVIVAR : arouse (passions, etc.) — **encenderse** *vr* **1** : get excited **2** RUBORIZARSE : blush — **encendedor** *nm* : lighter — **encendido, -da** *adj* : lit, on — **encendido** *nm* : ignition (switch)

encerar *vt* : wax, polish — **encerado, -da** *adj* : waxed — **encerado** *nm* : blackboard

encerrar {55} *vt* **1** : lock up, shut away **2** CONTENER : contain

encestar *vi* : score (in basketball)

enchilada *nf* : enchilada

enchufar *vt* : plug in, connect — **enchufe** *nm* : plug, socket

encía *nf* : gum (tissue)

encíclica *nf* : encyclical

enciclopedia *nf* : encyclopedia — **enciclopédico, -ca** *adj* : encyclopedic

encierro *nm* **1** : confinement **2** : sit-in (at a university, etc.)

encima *adv* **1** : on top **2** ADEMÁS : as well, besides **3** ~ **de** : on, over, on top of **4** **por** ~ **de** : above, beyond

encinta *adj* : pregnant

enclenque *adj* : weak, sickly

encoger {15} *v* : shrink — **encogerse** *vr* **1** : shrink **2** : cower, cringe **3** ~ **de hombros** : shrug (one's shoulders) — **encogido, -da** *adj* **1** : shrunken **2** TÍMIDO : shy

encolar *vt* : glue, stick

encolerizar {21} *vt* : enrage, infuriate — **encolerizarse** *vr* : get angry

encomendar {55} *vt* : entrust

encomienda *nf* **1** : charge, mission **2** *Lat* : parcel

encono *nm* : rancor, animosity

encontrar {19} *vt* **1** : find **2** : meet, encounter (difficulties, etc.) — **encontrarse** *vr* **1** : meet **2** HALLARSE : find oneself, be — **encontrado, -da** *adj* : contrary, opposing

encorvar *vt* : bend, curve — **encorvarse** *vr* : bend over, stoop

encrespar *vt* **1** : curl **2** IRRITAR : irritate — **encresparse** *vr* **1** : curl one's hair

2 IRRITARSE : get annoyed **3** : become choppy (of the sea)

encrucijada *nf* : crossroads

encuadernar *vt* : bind (a book) — **encuadernación** *nf, pl* **-ciones** : bookbinding

encuadrar *vt* **1** : frame **2** ENCAJAR : fit **3** COMPRENDER : contain, include

encubrir {2} *vt* : conceal, cover (up) — **encubierto, -ta** *adj* : covert — **encubrimiento** *nm* : cover-up

encuentro *nm* : meeting, encounter

encuestar *vt* : poll, take a survey of — **encuesta** *nf* **1** : investigation, inquiry **2** SONDEO : survey — **encuestador, -dora** *n* : pollster

encumbrado, -da *adj* : eminent, distinguished

encurtir *vt* : pickle

endeble *adj* : weak, feeble — **endeblez** *nf* : weakness, frailty

endemoniado, -da *adj* : wicked

enderezar {21} *vt* **1** : straighten (out) **2** : put upright, stand on end

endeudarse *vr* : go into debt — **endeudado, -da** *adj* : indebted, in debt — **endeudamiento** *nm* : debt

endiablado, -da *adj* **1** : wicked, diabolical **2** : complicated, difficult

endibia *or* **endivia** *nf* : endive

endosar *vt* : endorse — **endoso** *nm* : endorsement

endulzar {21} *vt* **1** : sweeten **2** : soften, mellow (a tone, a response, etc.) — **endulzante** *nm* : sweetener

endurecer {53} *vt* : harden — **endurecerse** *vr* : become hardened

enema *nm* : enema

enemigo, -ga *adj* : hostile — **~** *n* : enemy — **enemistad** *nf* : enmity — **enemistar** *vt* : make enemies of — **enemistarse** *vr* **~ con** : fall out with

energía *nf* : energy — **enérgico, -ca** *adj* : energetic, vigorous, forceful

enero *nm* : January

enervar *vt* **1** : enervate, weaken **2** *fam* : get on one's nerves

enésimo, -ma *adj* **por enésima vez** : for the umpteenth time

enfadar *vt* : annoy, make angry — **enfadarse** *vr* : get annoyed — **enfado** *nm* : anger, annoyance — **enfadoso, -sa** *adj* : annoying

enfatizar {21} *vt* : emphasize — **énfasis** *nms & pl* : emphasis — **enfático, -ca** *adj* : emphatic

enfermar *vt* : make sick — *vi* : get sick — **enfermedad** *nf* : sickness, disease — **enfermería** *nf* : infirmary — **enfermero, -ra** *n* : nurse — **enfermizo, -za**

adj : sickly — **enfermo, -ma** *adj* : sick — **~** *n* : sick person, patient

enflaquecer {53} *vi* : lose weight

enfocar {72} *vt* **1** : focus (on) **2** : consider (a problem, etc.) — **enfoque** *nm* : focus

enfrascarse {72} *vr* **~ en** : immerse oneself in, get caught up in

enfrentar *vt* **1** : confront, face **2** : bring face to face — **enfrentarse** *vr* **~ con** : confront, clash with — **enfrente** *adv* **1** : opposite **2 ~ de** : in front of

enfriar {85} *vt* : chill, cool — **enfriarse** *vr* **1** : get cold **2** RESFRIARSE : catch a cold — **enfriamiento** *nm* **1** : cooling off **2** CATARRO : cold

enfurecer {53} *vt* : infuriate — **enfurecerse** *vr* : fly into a rage

enfurruñarse *vr fam* : sulk

engalanar *vt* : decorate — **engalanarse** *vr* : dress up

enganchar *vt* : hook, snag, catch — **engancharse** *vr* **1** : get caught **2** ALISTARSE : enlist

engañar *vt* EMBAUCAR : trick, deceive **2** : cheat on, be unfaithful to — **engañarse** *vr* **1** : deceive oneself **2** EQUIVOCARSE : be mistaken — **engaño** *nm* : deception, deceit — **engañoso, -sa** *adj* : deceptive, deceitful

engatusar *vt* : coax, cajole

engendrar *vt* **1** : beget **2** : engender, give rise to (suspicions, etc.)

englobar *vt* : include, embrace

engomar *vt* : glue

engordar *vt* : fatten — *vi* : gain weight

engorroso, -sa *adj* : bothersome

engranar *v* : mesh, engage — **engranaje** *nm* : gears *pl*

engrandecer {53} *vt* **1** : enlarge **2** ENALTECER : exalt

engrapar *vt Lat* : staple — **engrapadora** *nf Lat* : stapler

engrasar *vt* : lubricate, grease — **engrase** *nm* : lubrication

engreído, -da *adj* : conceited

engrosar {19} *vt* : swell — *vi* : gain weight

engrudo *nm* : paste

engullir {38} *vt* : gulp down, gobble up

enhebrar *vt* : thread

enhorabuena *nf* : congratulations *pl*

enigma *nm* : enigma — **enigmático, -ca** *adj* : enigmatic

enjabonar *vt* : soap (up), lather

enjaezar {21} *vt* : harness

enjalbegar {52} *vt* : whitewash

enjambrar *vi* : swarm — **enjambre** *nm* : swarm

enjaular *vt* **1** : cage **2** *fam* : jail

enjuagar {52} vt : rinse — enjuague nm 1 : rinse 2 ~ bucal : mouthwash

enjugar {52} vt 1 : wipe away (tears) 2 : wipe out (debt)

enjuiciar vt 1 : prosecute 2 JUZGAR : try

enjuto, -ta adj : gaunt, lean

enlace nm 1 : bond, link 2 : junction (of a highway, etc.)

enlatar vt : can

enlazar {21} vt : join, link — vi ~ con : link up with

enlistarse vr Lat : enlist

enlodar vt : cover with mud

enloquecer {53} vt : drive crazy — enloquecerse vr : go crazy

enlosar vt : pave, tile

enlutarse vr : go into mourning

enmarañar vt 1 : tangle 2 COMPLICAR : complicate 3 CONFUNDIR : confuse — enmarañarse vr 1 : get tangled up 2 CONFUNDIRSE : become confused

enmarcar {72} vt : frame

enmascarar vt : mask

enmendar {55} vt 1 : amend 2 CORREGIR : emend, correct — enmendarse vr : mend one's ways — enmienda nf 1 : amendment 2 CORRECCIÓN : correction

enmohecerse {53} vr 1 : become moldy 2 OXIDARSE : rust

enmudecer {53} vt : silence — vi : fall silent

ennegrecer {53} vt : blacken

ennoblecer {53} vt : ennoble, dignify

enojar vt 1 : anger 2 MOLESTAR : annoy — enojarse vr ~ con : get upset with — enojo nm 1 : anger 2 MOLESTIA : annoyance — enojoso, -sa adj : annoying

enorgullecer {53} vt : make proud — enorgullecerse vr ~ de : pride oneself on

enorme adj : enormous — enormemente adv : enormously, extremely — enormidad nf : enormity

enraizar {30} vi : take root

enredadera nf : climbing plant, vine

enredar vt 1 : tangle up, entangle 2 CONFUNDIR : confuse 3 IMPLICAR : involve — enredarse vr 1 : become entangled 2 ~ en : get mixed up in — enredo nm 1 : tangle 2 EMBROLLO : confusion, mess — enredoso, -sa adj : tangled up, complicated

enrejado nm 1 : railing 2 REJILLA : grating, grille 3 : trellis (for plants)

enrevesado, -da adj : complicated

enriquecer {53} vt : enrich — enriquecerse vr : get rich

enrojecer {53} vt : redden — enrojecerse vr : blush

enrolar vt : enlist — enrolarse vr ~ en : enlist in

enrollar vt : roll up, coil

enroscar {72} vt 1 : roll up 2 ATORNILLAR : screw in

ensalada nf : salad

ensalzar {21} vt : praise

ensamblar vt : assemble, fit together

ensanchar vt 1 : widen 2 AMPLIAR : expand — ensanche nm 1 : widening 2 : (urban) expansion, development

ensangrentado, -da adj : bloody, bloodstained

ensañarse vr : act cruelly

ensartar vt : string, thread

ensayar vi : rehearse — vt : try out, test — ensayo nm 1 : essay 2 PRUEBA : trial, test 3 : rehearsal (in theater, etc.)

enseguida adv : right away, immediately

ensenada nf : inlet, cove

enseñar vt 1 : teach 2 MOSTRAR : show — enseñanza nf 1 EDUCACIÓN : education 2 INSTRUCCIÓN : teaching

enseres nmpl 1 : equipment 2 ~ domésticos : household goods

ensillar vt : saddle (up)

ensimismarse vr : lose oneself in thought

ensombrecer {53} vt : cast a shadow over, darken

ensoñación nf, pl -ciones : fantasy, daydream

ensordecer {53} vt : deafen — vi : go deaf — ensordecedor, -dora adj : deafening

ensortijar vt : curl

ensuciar vt : soil — ensuciarse vr : get dirty

ensueño nm : daydream, fantasy

entablar vt : initiate, start

entallar vt : tailor, fit (clothing) — vi : fit

entarimado nm : floorboards, flooring

ente nm 1 : being 2 ORGANISMO : body, organization

entender {56} vt 1 : understand 2 OPINAR : think, believe — vi 1 : understand 2 ~ de : know about, be good at — entenderse vr 1 : understand each other 2 LLEVARSE BIEN : get along well — ~ nm a mi ~ : in my opinion — entendido, -da adj 1 : understood 2 eso se da por ~ : that goes without saying 3 tener ~ : be under the impression — entendimiento nm 1 : understanding 2 INTELIGENCIA : intellect

enterar *vt* : inform — **enterarse** *vr* : find out, learn — **enterado, -da** *adj* : well-informed

entereza *nf* **1** HONRADEZ : integrity **2** FORTALEZA : fortitude **3** FIRMEZA : resolve

enternecer {53} *vt* : move, touch

entero, -ra *adj* **1** : whole **2** TOTAL : absolute, total **3** INTACTO : intact — **entero** *nm* : integer, whole number

enterrar {55} *vt* : bury

entibiar *vt* : cool (down) — **entibiarse** *vr* : become lukewarm

entidad *nf* **1** : entity **2** ORGANIZACIÓN : body, organization

entierro *nm* **1** : burial **2** : funeral (ceremony)

entomología *nf* : entomology — **entomólogo, -ga** *n* : entomologist

entonar *vt* : sing, intone — *vi* : be in tune

entonces *adv* **1** : then **2 desde ~** : since then

entornado, -da *adj* : half-closed, ajar

entorno *nm* : surroundings *pl*, environment

entorpecer {53} *vt* **1** : hinder, obstruct **2** : numb, dull (wits, reactions, etc.)

entrada *nf* **1** : entrance, entry **2** BILLETE : ticket **3** COMIENZO : beginning **4** : inning (in baseball) **5 ~s** *nfpl* : income **6 tener ~s** : have a receding hairline

entraña *nf* **1** : core, heart **2 ~s** *nfpl* VÍSCERAS : entrails, innards — **entrañable** *adj* : close, intimate — **entrañar** *vt* : involve

entrar *vi* **1** : enter **2** EMPEZAR : begin — *vt* : introduce, bring in

entre *prep* **1** : between **2** : among

entreabrir {2} *vt* : leave ajar — **entreabierto, -ta** *adj* : half-open, ajar

entreacto *nm* : intermission

entrecejo *nm* **fruncir el ~** : knit one's brows, frown

entrecortado, -da *adj* : faltering (of the voice), labored (of breathing)

entrecruzar {21} *vi* : intertwine

entredicho *nm* : doubt, question

entregar {52} *vt* : deliver, hand over — **entregarse** *vr* : surrender — **entrega** *nf* **1** : delivery **2** DEDICACIÓN : dedication, devotion **3 ~ inicial** : down payment

entrelazar {21} *vt* : intertwine — **entrelazarse** *vr* : become intertwined

entremés *nm, pl* **-meses 1** : hors d'oeuvre **2** : short play (in theater)

entremeterse → entrometerse

entremezclar *vt* : mix (up)

entrenar *vt* : train, drill — **entrenarse**

vr : train — **entrenador, -dora** *n* : trainer, coach — **entranamiento** *nm* : training

entrepierna *nf* : crotch

entresacar {72} *vt* : pick out, select

entresuelo *nm* : mezzanine

entretanto *adv* : meanwhile — **~** *nm* **en el ~** : in the meantime

entretener {80} *vt* **1** : entertain **2** DESPISTAR : distract **3** RETRASAR : delay, hold up — **entretenerse** *vr* **1** : amuse oneself **2** DEMORARSE : dawdle — **entretenido, -da** *adj* : entertaining — **entretenimiento** *nm* **1** : entertainment, amusement **2** PASATIEMPO : pastime

entrever {88} *vt* : catch a glimpse of, make out

entrevistar *vt* : interview — **entrevista** *nf* : interview — **entrevistador, -dora** *n* : interviewer

entristecer {53} *vt* : sadden

entrometerse *vr* : interfere — **entrometido, -da** *adj* : meddling, nosy — *n* : meddler

entroncar {72} *vi* : be related, be connected

entumecer {53} *vt* : make numb — **entumecerse** *vr* : go numb — **entumecido, -da** *adj* **1** : numb **2** : stiff (of muscles, etc.)

enturbiar *vt* : cloud — **enturbiarse** *vr* : become cloudy

entusiasmar *vt* : fill with enthusiasm — **entusiasmarse** *vr* : get excited — **entusiasmo** *nm* : enthusiasm — **entusiasta** *adj* : enthusiastic — **~** *nmf* : enthusiast

enumerar *vt* : enumerate, list — **enumeración** *nf, pl* **-ciones** : enumeration, count

enunciar *vt* : enunciate — **enunciación** *nf, pl* **-ciones** : enunciation

envalentonar *vt* : make bold, encourage — **envalentonarse** *vr* : be brave

envanecerse {53} *vr* : become vain

envasar *vt* **1** : package **2** : bottle, can — **envase** *nm* **1** : packaging **2** RECIPIENTE : container **3** : jar, bottle, can

envejecer {53} *v* : age — **envejecido, -da** *adj* : aged, old — **envejecimiento** *nm* : aging

envenenar *vt* : poison — **envenenamiento** *nm* : poisoning

envergadura *nf* **1** ALCANCE : scope **2** : span (of wings, etc.)

envés *nm, pl* **-veses** : reverse side

enviar {85} *vt* : send — **enviado, -da** *n* : envoy, correspondent

envidiar *vt* : envy — **envidia** *nf* : envy,

jealousy — **envidioso, -sa** *adj* : jealous, envious

envilecer {53} *vt* : degrade, debase — **envilecimiento** *nm* : degradation

envío *nm* **1** : sending, shipment **2** : remittance (of funds)

enviudar *vi* : be widowed

envolver {89} *vt* **1** : wrap **2** RODEAR : surround **3** IMPLICAR : involve — **envoltorio** *nm or* **envoltura** *nf* : wrapping, wrapper

enyesar *vt* **1** : plaster **2** ESCAYOLAR : put in a plaster cast

enzima *nf* : enzyme

épico, -ca *adj* : epic — **épica** *nf* : epic

epidemia *nf* : epidemic — **epidémico, -ca** *adj* : epidemic

epilepsia *nf* : epilepsy — **epiléptico, -ca** *adj & n* : epileptic

epílogo *nm* : epilogue

episodio *nm* : episode

epitafio *nm* : epitaph

epíteto *nm* : epithet

época *nf* **1** : epoch, period **2** ESTACIÓN : season

epopeya *nf* : epic poem

equidad *nf* : equity, justice

equilátero, -ra *adj* : equilateral

equilibrar *vt* : balance — **equilibrado, -da** *adj* : well-balanced — **equilibrio** *nm* **1** : balance, equilibrium **2** JUICIO : good sense

equinoccio *nm* : equinox

equipaje *nm* : baggage, luggage

equipar *vt* : equip

equiparar *vt* **1** IGUALAR : make equal **2** COMPARAR : compare — **equiparable** *adj* : comparable

equipo *nm* **1** : equipment **2** : team, crew (in sports, etc.)

equitación *nf, pl* **-ciones** : horseback riding

equitativo, -va *adj* : equitable, fair, just

equivaler {84} *vi* : be equivalent — **equivalencia** *nf* : equivalence — **equivalente** *adj & nm* : equivalent

equivocar {72} *vt* : mistake, confuse — **equivocarse** *vr* : make a mistake — **equivocación** *nf, pl* **-ciones** : error, mistake — **equivocado, -da** *adj* : mistaken, wrong

equívoco, -ca *adj* : ambiguous — **equívoco** *nm* : misunderstanding

era *nf* : era

erario *nm* : public treasury, funds *pl*

erección *nf, pl* **-ciones** : erection

erguir {31} *vt* : raise, lift — **erguirse** *vr* : rise (up) — **erguido, -da** *adj* : erect, upright

erigir {35} *vt* : build, erect — **erigirse** *vr* ~ **en** : set oneself up as

erizarse {21} *vr* : bristle, stand on end — **erizado, -da** *adj* : bristly

erizo *nm* **1** : hedgehog **2** ~ **de mar** : sea urchin

ermitaño, -ña *n* : hermit

erosionar *vt* : erode — **erosión** *nf, pl* **-siones** : erosion

erótico, -ca *adj* : erotic

erradicar {72} *vt* : eradicate

errar {32} *vt* : miss — *vi* **1** : be wrong, be mistaken **2** VAGAR : wander — **errado, -da** *adj Lat* : wrong, mistaken

errata *nf* : misprint

errático, -ca *adj* : erratic

error *nm* : error — **erróneo, -nea** *adj* : erroneous, mistaken

eructar *vi* : belch, burp — **eructo** *nm* : belch, burp

erudito, -ta *adj* : erudite, learned

erupción *nf, pl* **-ciones 1** : eruption **2** SARPULLIDO : rash

esa, ésa → **ese, ése**

esbelto, -ta *adj* : slender, slim

esbozar {21} *vt* : sketch, outline — **esbozo** *nm* : sketch, outline

escabechar *vt* : pickle — **escabeche** *nm* : brine (for pickling)

escabel *nm* : footstool

escabroso, -sa *adj* **1** : rugged, rough **2** ESPINOSO : thorny, difficult **3** ATREVIDO : shocking, risqué

escabullirse {38} *vr* : slip away, escape

escalar *vt* : climb, scale — *vi* : escalate — **escala** *nf* **1** : scale **2** ESCALERA : ladder **3** : stopover (of an airplane, etc.) — **escalada** *nf* : ascent, climb — **escalador, -dora** *n* ALPINISTA : mountain climber

escaldar *vt* : scald

escalera *nf* **1** : stairs *pl*, staircase **2** ESCALA : ladder **3** ~ **mecánica** : escalator

escalfar *vt* : poach

escalinata *nf* : flight of stairs

escalofrío *nm* : shiver, chill — **escalofriante** *adj* : chilling, horrifying

escalonar *vt* **1** : stagger, spread out **2** : terrace (land) — **escalón** *nm, pl* **-lones** : step, rung

escama *nf* **1** : scale (of fish or reptiles) **2** : flake (of skin) — **escamoso, -sa** *adj* : scaly

escamotear *vt* **1** : conceal **2** ~ **algo a algn** : rob s.o. of sth

escandalizar {21} *vt* : scandalize — **escandalizarse** *vr* : be shocked — **escándalo** *nm* **1** : scandal **2** ALBOROTO : scene, commotion — **escandaloso,**

-sa *adj* 1 : shocking, scandalous 2 RUI-
DOSO : noisy
escandinavo, -va *adj* : Scandinavian
escáner *nm* : scanner
escaño *nm* 1 : seat (in a legislative
body) 2 BANCO : bench
escapar *vi* : escape, run away — **escaparse** *vr* 1 : escape 2 : leak out (of
gas, water, etc.) — **escapada** *nf* : escape
escaparate *nm* : store window
escapatoria *nf* : loophole, way out
escape *nm* 1 : leak (of gas, water, etc.)
2 : exhaust (from a vehicle)
escarabajo *nm* : beetle
escarbar *vt* 1 : dig, scratch, poke 2 ~
en : pry into
escarcha *nf* : frost (on a surface)
escarlata *adj & nf* : scarlet — **escarlatina** *nf* : scarlet fever
escarmentar {55} *vi* : learn one's lesson — **escarmiento** *nm* : lesson, punishment
escarnecer {53} *vt* : ridicule, mock —
escarnio *nm* : ridicule, mockery
escarola *nf* : escarole, endive
escarpa *nf* : steep slope — **escarpado,
-da** *adj* : steep
escasear *vi* : be scarce — **escasez** *nf,
pl* **-seces** : shortage, scarcity — **escaso, -sa** *adj* 1 : scarce 2 ~ **de** : short of
escatimar *vt* : be sparing with, skimp
on
escayolar *vt* : put in a plaster cast —
escayola *nf* 1 : plaster (for casts) 2
: plaster cast
escena *nf* 1 : scene 2 ESCENARIO : stage
— **escenario** *nm* 1 : setting, scene 2
ESCENA : stage — **escénico, -ca** *adj*
: scenic
escepticismo *nm* : skepticism — **escéptico, -ca** *adj* : skeptical — ~ *n*
: skeptic
esclarecer {53} *vt* : shed light on, clarify
esclavo, -va *n* : slave — **esclavitud** *nf*
: slavery — **esclavizar** {21} *vt* : enslave
esclerosis *nf* ~ **múltiple** : multiple
sclerosis
esclusa *nf* : floodgate, lock (of a canal)
escoba *nf* : broom
escocer {14} *vi* : sting
escocés, -cesa *adj, mpl* **-ceses** 1
: Scottish 2 : tartan, plaid — **escocés**
nm, pl **-ceses** : Scotch (whiskey)
escoger {15} *vt* : choose — **escogido,
-da** *adj* : choice, select
escolar *adj* : school — ~ *nmf* : student, pupil

escolta *nmf* : escort — **escoltar** *vt* : escort, accompany
escombros *nmpl* : ruins, rubble
esconder *vt* : hide, conceal — **esconderse** *vr* : hide — **escondidas** *nfpl* 1
Lat : hide-and-seek 2 **a** ~ : secretly,
in secret — **escondite** *nm* 1 : hiding
place 2 : hide-and-seek (game) — **es-
condrijo** *nm* : hiding place
escopeta *nf* : shotgun
escoplo *nm* : chisel
escoria *nf* 1 : slag 2 : dregs *pl* (of society, etc.)
escorpión *nm, pl* **-piones** : scorpion
escote *nm* 1 : (low) neckline 2 **pagar a**
~ : go Dutch
escotilla *nf* : hatchway
escribir {33} *v* : write — **escribirse** *vr*
1 : write to one another, correspond 2
: be spelled — **escribiente** *nmf* : clerk
— **escrito, -ta** *adj* : written — **escritos** *nmpl* : writings — **escritor,
-tora** *n* : writer — **escritorio** *nm*
: desk — **escritura** *nf* 1 : handwriting
2 : deed (in law)
escroto *nm* : scrotum
escrúpulo *nm* : scruple — **escrupuloso, -sa** *adj* : scrupulous
escrutar *vt* 1 : scrutinize 2 : count
(votes) — **escrutinio** *nm* 1 : scrutiny 2
: count (of votes)
escuadra *nf* 1 : square (instrument) 2
: fleet (of ships), squad (in the military) — **escuadrón** *nm, pl* **-drones**
: squadron
escuálido, -da *adj* 1 : skinny 2 SUCIO
: squalid
escuchar *vt* 1 : listen to 2 *Lat* : hear —
vi : listen
escudo *nm* 1 : shield 2 *or* ~ **de armas**
: coat of arms
escudriñar *vt* : scrutinize, examine
escuela *nf* : school
escueto, -ta *adj* : plain, simple
esculpir *v* : sculpt — **escultor, -tora** *n*
: sculptor — **escultura** *nf* : sculpture
escupir *v* : spit
escurrir *vt* 1 : drain 2 : wring out
(clothes) — *vi* 1 : drain 2 : drip-dry (of
clothes) — **escurrirse** *vr* 1 : drain 2
fam : slip away — **escurridizo, -da**
adj : slippery, evasive — **escurridor**
nm 1 : dish drainer 2 COLADOR : colander
ese, esa *adj, mpl* **esos** : that, those
ése, ésa *pron, mpl* **ésos** : that one,
those ones *pl*
esencia *nf* : essence — **esencial** *adj*
: essential

esfera nf **1** : sphere **2** : dial (of a watch) — **esférico, -ca** adj : spherical

esfinge nf : sphinx

esforzar {36} vt **1** : strain — **esforzarse** vr : make an effort — **esfuerzo** nm : effort

esfumarse vr : fade away, vanish

esgrimir vt **1** : brandish, wield **2** : make use of (an argument, etc.) — **esgrima** nf **1** : fencing **2 hacer ~** : fence

esguince nm : sprain, strain

eslabonar vt : link, connect — **eslabón** nm, pl **-bones** : link

eslavo, -va adj : Slavic

eslogan nm, pl **-lóganes** : slogan

esmaltar vt : enamel — **esmalte** nm **1** : enamel **2 ~ de uñas** : nail polish

esmerado, -da adj : careful

esmeralda nf : emerald

esmerarse vr : take great care

esmeril nm : emery

esmoquin nm, pl **-móquines** : tuxedo

esnob nmf, pl **esnobs** : snob — **~** adj : snobbish

eso pron (neuter) **1** : that **2 ¡~ es!** : that's it!, that's right! **3 en ~** : at that point, then

esófago nm : esophagus

esos, ésos → ese, ése

espabilarse vr **1** : wake up **2 DARSE PRISA** : get moving — **espabilado, -da** adj **1** : awake **2 LISTO** : bright, clever

espaciar vt : space out, spread out — **espacial** adj : space — **espacio** nm **1** : space **2 ~ exterior** : outer space — **espacioso, -sa** adj : spacious

espada nf **1** : sword **2 ~s** nfpl : spades (in playing cards)

espagueti nm or **espaguetis** nmpl : spaghetti

espalda nf **1** : back **2 ~s** nfpl : shoulders, back

espantar vt : scare, frighten — **espantarse** vr : become frightened — **espantajo** nm or **espantapájaros** nms & pl : scarecrow — **espanto** nm **1** : fright, fear — **espantoso, -sa** adj **1** : frightening, horrific **2 TERRIBLE** : awful, terrible

español, -ñola adj : Spanish — **español** nm : Spanish (language)

esparadrapo nm : adhesive bandage

esparcir {83} vt : scatter, spread — **esparcirse** vr **1** : be scattered, spread out **2 DIVERTIRSE** : enjoy oneself

espárrago nm : asparagus

espasmo nm : spasm — **espasmódico, -ca** adj : spasmodic

espátula nf : spatula

especia nf : spice

especial adj & nm : special — **especialidad** nf : specialty — **especialista** nmf : specialist — **especializarse** {21} vr **~ en** : specialize in — **especialmente** adv : especially

especie nf **1** : species **2 CLASE** : type, kind

especificar {72} vt : specify — **especificación** nf, pl **-ciones** : specification — **específico, -ca** adj : specific

espécimen nm, pl **especímenes** : specimen

espectáculo nm **1** : show, performance **2 VISIÓN** : spectacle, view — **espectacular** adj : spectacular — **espectador, -dora** n : spectator

espectro nm **1** : spectrum **2 FANTASMA** : ghost

especulación nf, pl **-ciones** : speculation

espejo nm : mirror — **espejismo** nm **1** : mirage **2 ILUSIÓN** : illusion

espeluznante adj : terrifying, hairraising

esperar vt **1** : wait for **2 CONTAR CON** : expect **3 ~ que** : hope (that) — vi **1** : wait — **espera** nf : wait — **esperanza** nf : hope, expectation — **esperanzado, -da** adj : hopeful — **esperanzar** {21} vt : give hope to

esperma nmf **1** : sperm **2 ~ de ballena** : blubber

esperpento nm : (grotesque) sight, fright

espesar vt : thicken — **espesarse** vr : thicken — **espeso, -sa** adj : thick, heavy — **espesor** nm : thickness, density — **espesura** nf **1 ESPESOR** : thickness **2** : thicket

espetar vt : blurt (out)

espiar {85} vt : spy on — vi : spy — **espía** nmf : spy

espiga nf : ear (of wheat, etc.)

espina nf **1** : thorn **2** : (fish) bone **3 ~ dorsal** : spine, backbone

espinaca nf **1** : spinach (plant) **2 ~s** nfpl : spinach (food)

espinazo nm : spine, backbone

espinilla nf **1** : shin **2 GRANO** : blackhead, pimple

espinoso, -sa adj **1** : prickly **2** : bony (of fish) **3** : difficult, thorny (of problems, etc.)

espionaje nm : espionage

espiral adj & nf : spiral

espirar v : breathe out, exhale

espíritu nm **1** : spirit **2 Espíritu Santo** : Holy Spirit — **espiritual** adj : spiritual — **espiritualidad** nf : spirituality

espita nf : spigot, faucet

espléndido, -da adj **1** : splendid **2 GE-**

NEROSO : lavish — **esplendor** *nm*
: splendor
espliego *nm* : lavender
espolear *vt* : spur on
espoleta *nf* : fuse
espolvorear *vt* : sprinkle, dust
esponja *nf* 1 : sponge 2 **tirar la ~**
: throw in the towel — **esponjoso,
-sa** *adj* : spongy
espontaneidad *nf* : spontaneity —
espontáneo, -nea *adj* : spontaneous
espora *nf* : spore
esporádico, -ca *adj* : sporadic
esposo, -sa *n* : spouse, wife *f*, husband
m — **esposar** *vt* : handcuff — **esposas** *nfpl* : handcuffs
esprintar *vi* : sprint (in sports) — **esprint** *nm* : sprint
espuela *nf* : spur
espumar *vt* : skim — **espuma** *nf* 1
: foam, froth 2 : (soap) lather 3 : head
(on beer) — **espumoso, -sa** *adj* 1
: foamy, frothy 2 : sparkling (of wine)
esqueleto *nm* : skeleton
esquema *nf* : outline, sketch
esquí *nm* 1 : ski 2 : skiing (sport) 3 **~
acuático** : waterskiing — **esquiador,
-dora** *n* : skier — **esquiar** {85} *vi* : ski
esquilar *vt* : shear
esquimal *adj* : Eskimo
esquina *nf* : corner
esquirol *nm* : strikebreaker, scab
esquivar *vt* 1 : evade, dodge (a blow) 2
EVITAR : avoid — **esquivo, -va** *adj*
: shy, elusive
esquizofrenia *nf* : schizophrenia — **esquizofrénico, -ca** *adj & n* : schizophrenic
esta, ésta → este¹, éste
estable *adj* : stable — **estabilidad** *nf*
: stability — **estabilizar** {21} *vt* : stabilize
establecer {53} *vt* : establish — **establecerse** *vr* : establish oneself, settle —
establecimiento *nm* : establishment
establo *nm* : stable
estaca *nf* : stake — **estacada** *nf* 1
: (picket) fence 2 **dejar en la ~**
: leave in a lurch
estación *nf*, *pl* **-ciones** 1 : season 2 **~
de servicio** : gas station — **estacionar** *v* : park — **estacionamiento**
nm : parking — **estacionario, -ria** *adj*
: stationary
estadía *nf Lat* : stay
estadio *nm* 1 : stadium 2 FASE : phase,
stage
estadista *nmf* : statesman
estadística *nf* : statistics — **estadístico, -ca** *adj* : statistical

estado *nm* 1 : state 2 **~ civil** : marital
status
estadounidense *adj & nmf* : American
(from the United States)
estafar *vt* : swindle, defraud — **estafa**
nf : swindle, fraud — **estafador,
-dora** *n* : cheat, swindler
estallar *vi* 1 : explode 2 : break out (of
war, an epidemic, etc.) 3 **~ en llamas** : burst into flames — **estallido**
nm 1 : explosion 2 : report (of a gun) 3
: outbreak (of war, etc.)
estampar *vt* : stamp, print — **estampa**
nf 1 : print, illustration 2 ASPECTO : appearance — **estampado, -da** *adj*
: printed
estampida *nf* : stampede
estampilla *nf* : stamp
estancarse {72} *vr* 1 : stagnate 2
: come to a halt — **estancado, -da** *adj*
: stagnant
estancia *nf* 1 : stay 2 HABITACIÓN
: (large) room 3 *Lat* : (cattle) ranch
estanco, -ca *adj* : watertight
estándar *adj & nm* : standard — **estandarizar** {21} *vt* : standardize
estandarte *nm* : standard, banner
estanque *nm* 1 : pool, pond 2 : reservoir (for irrigation)
estante *nm* : shelf — **estantería** *nf*
: shelves *pl*, bookcase
estaño *nm* : tin
estar {34} *v aux* : be — *vi* 1 : be 2 : be
at home 3 QUEDARSE : stay, remain
4 **¿cómo estás?** : how are you? 5 **~
a** : cost 6 **~ bien (mal)** : be well
(sick) 7 **~ para** : be in the mood for 8
~ por : be in favor of 9 **~ por** : be
about to — **estarse** *vr* : stay, remain
estarcir {83} *vt* : stencil
estárter *nm* : choke (of an automobile)
estatal *adj* : state, national
estático, -ca *adj* 1 : static 2 INMÓVIL
: unmoving, still — **estática** *nf* : static
estatua *nf* : statue
estatura *nf* : height
estatus *nm* : status, prestige
estatuto *nm* : statute — **estatutario,
-ria** *adj* : statutory
este¹, esta *adj*, *mpl* **estos** : this, these
este² *adj* : eastern, east — **este** *nm* 1
: east 2 : east wind 3 **el Este** : the Orient
éste, ésta *pron*, *mpl* **éstos** 1 : this one,
these ones *pl* 2 : the latter
estela *nf* 1 : wake (of a ship) 2 : trail (of
smoke, etc.)
estera *nf* : mat
estéreo *adj & nm* : stereo — **estere-
ofónico, -ca** *adj* : stereophonic

estereotipo *nm* : stereotype

estéril *adj* 1 : sterile 2 : infertile — **esterilidad** *nf* 1 : sterility 2 : infertility — **esterilizar** {21} *vt* : sterilize

estética *nf* : aesthetics — **estético, -ca** *adj* : aesthetic

estiércol *nm* : dung, manure

estigma *nm* : stigma — **estigmatizar** {21} *vt* : stigmatize

estilarse {21} *vr* : be in fashion

estilo *nm* 1 : style 2 MANERA : fashion, manner — **estilista** *nmf* : stylist

estima *nf* : esteem, regard — **estimación** *nf, pl* **-ciones** 1 : esteem 2 VALORACIÓN : estimate — **estimado, -da** *adj* **Estimado señor** : Dear Sir — **estimar** *vt* 1 : esteem, respect 2 VALORAR : value, estimate 3 CONSIDERAR : consider

estimular *vt* 1 : stimulate 2 : encourage — **estimulante** *adj* : stimulating — ~ *nm* : stimulant — **estímulo** *nm* : stimulus

estío *nm* : summertime

estipular *vt* : stipulate

estirar *vt* : stretch (out), extend — **estirado, -da** *adj* 1 : stretched, extended 2 ALTANERO : stuck-up, haughty — **estiramiento** *nm* ~ **facial** : face-lift — **estirón** *nm, pl* **-rones** : pull, tug

estirpe *nf* : lineage, stock

estival *adj* : summer

esto *pron* (*neuter*) 1 : this 2 **en ~** : at this point 3 **por ~** : for this reason

estofa *nf* 1 : class, quality 2 **de baja ~** : low-class

estofar *vt* : stew — **estofado** *nm* : stew

estoicismo *nm* : stoicism — **estoico, -ca** *adj* : stoic, stoical — ~ *n* : stoic

estómago *nm* : stomach — **estomacal** *adj* : stomach

estorbar *vt* : obstruct — *vi* : get in the way — **estorbo** *nm* 1 : obstacle 2 MOLESTIA : nuisance

estornino *nm* : starling

estornudar *vi* : sneeze — **estornudo** *nm* : sneeze

estos, éstos → **este, éste**

estrabismo *nm* : squint

estrado *nm* : platform, stage

estrafalario, -ria *adj* : eccentric, bizarre

estragar {52} *vt* : devastate — **estragos** *nmpl* 1 : ravages 2 **hacer ~ en** *or* **causar ~ entre** : wreak havoc with

estragón *nm* : tarragon

estrangular *vt* : strangle — **estrangulación** *nf* : strangulation

estratagema *nf* : stratagem

estrategia *nf* : strategy — **estratégico, -ca** *adj* : strategic

estrato *nm* : stratum

estratosfera *nf* : stratosphere

estrechar *vt* 1 : narrow 2 : strengthen (a bond) 3 ABRAZAR : embrace 4 ~ **la mano a uno** : shake s.o.'s hand — **estrecharse** *vr* : narrow — **estrechez** *nf, pl* **-checes** 1 : narrowness 2 **estrecheces** *nfpl* : financial problems — **estrecho, -cha** *adj* 1 : tight, narrow 2 ÍNTIMO : close — **estrecho** *nm* : strait

estrella *nf* 1 : star 2 DESTINO : destiny 3 ~ **de mar** : starfish — **estrellado, -da** *adj* 1 : starry 2 : star-shaped

estrellar *v* : crash — **estrellarse** *vr* ~ **contre** : smash into

estremecer {53} *vt* : cause to shudder — *vi* : tremble, shake — **estremecerse** *vr* : shudder, shiver (with emotion) — **estremecimiento** *nm* : shaking, shivering

estrenar *vt* 1 : use for the first time 2 : premiere, open (a film, etc.) — **estrenarse** *vr* : make one's debut — **estreno** *nm* : debut, premiere

estreñirse {67} *vr* : be constipated — **estreñimiento** *nm* : constipation

estrépito *nm* : clamor, din — **estrepitoso, -sa** *adj* : noisy, clamorous

estrés *nm, pl* **estreses** : stress — **estresante** *adj* : stressful — **estresar** *vt* : stress (out)

estría *nf* : groove

estribaciones *nfpl* : foothills

estribar *vi* ~ **en** : stem from, lie in

estribillo *nm* : refrain, chorus

estribo *nm* 1 : stirrup 2 : running board (of a vehicle) 3 CONTRAFUERTE : buttress 4 **perder los ~s** : lose one's temper

estribor *nm* : starboard

estricto, -ta *adj* : strict

estridente *adj* : strident, shrill

estrofa *nf* : stanza, verse

estropajo *nm* : scouring pad

estropear *vt* 1 : ruin, spoil 2 DAÑAR : damage — **estropearse** *vr* 1 : go bad 2 AVERIARSE : break down — **estropicio** *nm* : damage, havoc

estructura *nf* : structure — **estructural** *adj* : structural

estruendo *nm* : din, roar — **estruendoso, -sa** *adj* : thunderous

estrujar *vt* : squeeze

estuario *nm* : estuary

estuche *nm* : kit, case

estuco *nm* : stucco

estudiar *v* : study — **estudiante** *nmf* : student — **estudiantil** *adj* : student — **estudio** *nm* 1 : study 2 OFICINA

: studio, office **3 ~s** *nmpl* : studies, education — **estudioso, -sa** *adj* : studious

estufa *nf* : stove, heater

estupefaciente *adj & nm* : narcotic — **estupefacto, -ta** *adj* : astonished

estupendo, -da *adj* : stupendous, marvelous

estúpido, -da *adj* : stupid — **estupidez** *nf, pl* **-deces** : stupidity

estupor *nm* **1** : stupor **2** ASOMBRO : amazement

etapa *nf* : stage, phase

etcétera : et cetera, and so on

éter *nm* : ether

etéreo, -rea *adj* : ethereal

eterno, -na *adj* : eternal — **eternidad** *nf* : eternity — **eternizarse** {21} *vr* : take forever

ética *nf* : ethics — **ético, -ca** *adj* : ethical

etimología *nf* : etymology

etíope *adj* : Ethiopian

etiqueta *nf* **1** : tag, label **2** PROTOCOLO : etiquette **3 de ~** : formal, dressy — **etiquetar** *vt* : label

étnico, -ca *adj* : ethnic

eucalipto *nm* : eucalyptus

Eucaristía *nf* : Eucharist, communion

eufemismo *nm* : euphemism — **eufemístico, -ca** *adj* : euphemistic

euforia *nf* : euphoria — **eufórico, -ca** *adj* : euphoric

europeo, -pea *adj* : European

eutanasia *nf* : euthanasia

evacuar *vt* : evacuate, vacate — *vi* : have a bowel movement — **evacuación** *nf, pl* **-ciones** : evacuation

evadir *vt* : evade, avoid — **evadirse** *vr* : escape

evaluar {3} *vt* : evaluate — **evaluación** *nf, pl* **-ciones** : evaluation

evangelio *nm* : gospel — **evangélico, -ca** *adj* : evangelical — **evangelismo** *nm* : evangelism

evaporar *vt* : evaporate — **evaporarse** *vr* : evaporate, disappear — **evaporación** *nf, pl* **-ciones** : evaporation

evasión *nf, pl* **-siones 1** : evasion **2** FUGA : escape — **evasiva** *nf* : excuse, pretext — **evasivo, -va** *adj* : evasive

evento *nm* : event

eventual *adj* **1** : temporary **2** POSIBLE : possible — **eventualidad** *nf* : possibility, eventuality

evidencia *nf* **1** : evidence, proof **2 poner en ~** : demonstrate — **evidenciar** *vt* : demonstrate, show — **evidente** *adj* : evident — **evidentemente** *adj* : evidently, apparently

evitar *vt* **1** : avoid **2** IMPEDIR : prevent — **evitable** *adj* : avoidable

evocar {72} *vt* : evoke

evolución *nf, pl* **-ciones** : evolution — **evolucionar** *vi* : evolve

exacerbar *vt* **1** : exacerbate **2** IRRITAR : irritate

exacto, -ta *adj* : precise, exact — **exactamente** *adv* : exactly — **exactitud** *nf* : precision, accuracy

exagerar *v* : exaggerate — **exageración** *nf, pl* **-ciones** : exaggeration — **exagerado, -da** *adj* : exaggerated

exaltar *vt* **1** : exalt, extol **2** EXCITAR : excite, arouse — **exaltarse** *vr* : get worked-up — **exaltado, -da** *adj* : worked up, hotheaded

examen *nm, pl* **exámenes 1** : examination, test **2** ANÁLISIS : investigation — **examinar** *vt* **1** : examine **2** ESTUDIAR : study, inspect — **examinarse** *vr* : take an exam

exánime *adj* : lifeless

exasperar *vt* : exasperate, irritate — **exasperación** *nf, pl* **-ciones** : exasperation

excavar *v* : excavate — **excavación** *nf, pl* **-ciones** : excavation

exceder *vt* : exceed, surpass — **excederse** *vr* : go too far — **excedente** *adj & nm* : surplus, excess

excelente *adj* : excellent — **excelencia** *nf* **1** : excellence **2 Su Excelencia** : His/Her Excellency

excéntrico, -ca *adj & n* : eccentric — **excentricidad** *nf* : eccentricity

excepción *nf, pl* **-ciones** : exception — **excepcional** *adj* : exceptional

excepto *prep* : except (for) — **exceptuar** {3} *vt* : exclude, except

exceso *nm* **1** : excess **2 ~ de velocidad** : speeding — **excesivo, -va** *adj* : excessive

excitar *vt* : excite, arouse — **excitarse** *vr* : get excited — **excitable** *adj* : excitable — **excitación** *nf, pl* **-ciones** : excitement, agitation, arousal — **excitante** *adj* : exciting

exclamar *v* : exclaim — **exclamación** *nf, pl* **-ciones** : exclamation

excluir {41} *vt* : exclude — **exclusión** *nf, pl* **-siones** : exclusion — **exclusivo, -va** *adj* : exclusive

excomulgar {52} *vt* : excommunicate — **excomunión** *nf, pl* **-niones** : excommunication

excremento *nm* : excrement

exculpar *vt* : exonerate

excursión *nf, pl* **-siones** : excursion —

excursionista *nmf* **1** : tourist, sight-seer **2** : hiker

excusar *vt* **1** : excuse **2** EXIMIR : exempt — **excusarse** *vr* : apologize — **excusa** *nf* **1** : excuse **2** DISCULPA : apology

exento, -ta *adj* : exempt

exequias *nfpl* : funeral rites

exhalar *vt* **1** : exhale **2** : give off (an odor, etc.)

exhaustivo, -va *adj* : exhaustive — **exhausto, -ta** *adj* : exhausted, worn-out

exhibir *vt* : exhibit, show — **exhibición** *nf, pl* **-ciones** : exhibition

exhortar *vt* : exhort, admonish

exigir {35} *vt* : demand, require — **exigencia** *nf* : demand, requirement — **exigente** *adj* : demanding

exiguo, -gua *adj* : meager

exiliar *vt* : exile — **exiliarse** *vr* : go into exile — **exiliado, -da** *adj* : exiled, in exile — ~ *n* : exile — **exilio** *nm* : exile

eximir *vt* : exempt

existir *vi* : exist — **existencia** *nf* **1** : existence **2** ~**s** *nfpl* MERCANCÍA : goods, stock — **existente** *adj* : existing

éxito *nm* **1** : success, hit **2** tener ~ : be successful — **exitoso, -sa** *adj* Lat : successful

éxodo *nm* : exodus

exorbitante *adj* : exorbitant

exorcizar {21} *vt* : exorcize — **exorcismo** *nm* : exorcism

exótico, -ca *adj* : exotic

expandir *vt* : expand — **expandirse** *vr* : spread — **expansión** *nf, pl* **-siones** : expansion — **expansivo, -va** *adj* : expansive

expatriarse {85} *vr* **1** : emigrate **2** EXILIARSE : go into exile — **expatriado, -da** *adj & n* : expatriate

expectativa *nf* **1** : expectation, hope **2** ~**s** *nfpl* : prospects

expedición *nf, pl* **-ciones** : expedition

expediente *nm* **1** : expedient **2** DOCUMENTOS : file, record **3** INVESTIGACIÓN : inquiry, proceedings

expedir {54} *vt* **1** : issue **2** ENVIAR : dispatch — **expedito, -ta** *adj* : free, clear

expeler *vt* : expel, eject

expendedor, -dora *n* : dealer, seller

expensas *nfpl* : expenses **2 a** ~ **de** : at the expense of

experiencia *nf* : experience

experimentar *vi* : experiment — *vt* **1** : experiment with, test out **2** SENTIR : experience, feel — **experimentado, -da** *adj* : experienced — **experimental** *adj* : experimental — **experimento** *nm* : experiment

experto, -ta *adj & n* : expert

expiar {85} *vt* : atone for

expirar *vi* **1** : expire **2** MORIR : die

explayar *vt* : extend — **explayarse** *vr* **1** : spread out **2** HABLAR : speak at length

explicar {72} *vt* **1** : explain — **explicarse** *vr* : understand — **explicación** *nf, pl* **-ciones** : explanation — **explicativo, -va** *adj* : explanatory

explícito, -ta *adj* : explicit

explorar *vt* : explore — **exploración** *nf, pl* **-ciones** : exploration — **explorador, -dora** *n* : explorer, scout — **exploratorio, -ria** *adj* : exploratory

explosión *nf, pl* **-siones** **1** : explosion **2** : outburst (of anger, laughter, etc.) — **explosivo, -va** *adj* : explosive — **explosivo** *nm* : explosive

explotar *vt* **1** : exploit **2** : operate, run (a factory, etc.), work (a mine) — *vi* : explode — **explotación** *nf, pl* **-ciones** **1** : exploitation **2** : running (of a business), working (of a mine)

exponer {60} *vt* **1** : expose **2** : explain, set out (ideas, theories, etc.) **3** EXHIBIR : exhibit, display — *vi* : exhibit — **exponerse** *vr* ~ **a** : expose oneself to

exportar *vt* : export — **exportaciones** *nfpl* : exports — **exportador, -dora** *n* : exporter

exposición *nf, pl* **-ciones** **1** : exposure **2** : exhibition (of objects, art, etc.) **3** : exposition, setting out (of ideas, etc.) — **expositor, -tora** *n* **1** : exhibitor **2** : exponent (of a theory, etc.)

exprés *nms & pl* **1** : express (train) **2** *or* **café** ~ : espresso

expresamente *adv* : expressly, on purpose

expresar *vt* : express — **expresarse** *vr* : express oneself — **expresión** *nf, pl* **-siones** : expression — **expresivo, -va** *adj* **1** : expressive **2** CARIÑOSO : affectionate

expreso, -sa *adj* : express — **expreso** *nm* : express train, express

exprimir *vt* **1** : squeeze **2** EXPLOTAR : exploit — **exprimidor** *nm* : squeezer, juicer

expuesto, -ta *adj* **1** : exposed **2** PELIGROSO : risky, dangerous

expulsar *vt* : expel, eject — **expulsión** *nf, pl* **-siones** : expulsion

exquisito, -ta *adj* **1** : exquisite **2** RICO : delicious — **exquisitez** *nf* **1** : exquisiteness **2** : delicacy, special dish

éxtasis *nms & pl* : ecstasy — **extático, -ta** *adj* : ecstatic

extender {56} *vt* **1** : spread out **2** : draw up (a document), write out (a check)

— **extenderse** *vr* 1 : extend, spread 2 DURAR : last — **extendido, -da** *adj* 1 : widespread 2 : outstretched (of arms, wings, etc.)
extensamente *adv* : extensively
extensión *nf, pl* **-siones** 1 : extension 2 AMPLITUD : expanse 3 ALCANCE : range, extent — **extenso, -sa** *adj* : extensive
extenuar {3} *vt* : exhaust, tire out
exterior *adj* 1 : exterior, external 2 EXTRANJERO : foreign — ~ *nm* 1 : outside 2 **en el** ~ : abroad — **exteriorizar** {21} *vt* : show, reveal — **exteriormente** *adv* : outwardly, externally
exterminar *vt* : exterminate — **exterminación** *nf, pl* **-ciones** : extermination — **exterminio** *nm* : extermination
externo, -na *adj* : external
extinguir {26} *vt* 1 : extinguish (a fire) 2 : put an end to, wipe out — **extinguirse** *vr* 1 : go out (of fire, light, etc.) 2 : become extinct — **extinción** *nf, pl* **-ciones** : extinction — **extinguidor** *nm Lat* : fire extinguisher — **extinto, -ta** *adj* : extinct — **extintor** *nm* : fire extinguisher
extirpar *vt* : remove, eradicate
extorsión *nf, pl* **-siones** 1 : extortion 2 MOLESTIA : trouble
extra *adv* : extra — ~ *adj* 1 ADICIONAL : additional 2 : top-quality — ~ *nmf* : extra (in movies) — ~ *nm* : extra (expense)
extraditar *vt* : extradite
extraer {81} *vt* : extract — **extracción** *nf, pl* **-ciones** : extraction — **extracto** *nm* 1 : extract 2 RESUMEN : abstract, summary

extranjero, -ra *adj* : foreign — ~ *n* : foreigner — **extranjero** *nm* : foreign countries *pl*
extrañar *vt* : miss (someone) — **extrañarse** *vr* : be surprised — **extrañeza** *nf* : surprise — **extraño, -ña** *adj* 1 : foreign 2 RARO : strange, odd — ~ *n* : stranger
extraoficial *adj* : unofficial
extraordinario, -ria *adj* : extraordinary
extrasensorial *adj* : extrasensory
extraterrestre *adj & nmf* : extraterrestrial
extravagante *adj* : extravagant, outrageous — **extravagancia** *nf* : extravagance, outlandishness
extraviar {85} *vt* : lose, misplace — **extraviarse** *vr* : get lost — **extravío** *nm* : loss
extremar *vt* : carry to extremes — **extremarse** *vr* : do one's utmost — **extremadamente** *adv* : extremely — **extremado, -da** *adj* : extreme — **extremidad** *nf* 1 : tip, end 2 **-es** *nfpl* : extremities — **extremista** *adj & nmf* : extremist — **extremo, -ma** *adj* 1 : extreme 2 **en caso** ~ : as a last resort — **extremo** *nm* 1 : end 2 **en** ~ : in the extreme, extremely 3 **en último** ~ : as a last resort
extrovertido -da *adj* : extroverted — ~ *n* : extrovert
exuberante *adj* : exuberant — **exuberancia** *nf* : exuberance
exudar *vt* : exude
eyacular *vi* : ejaculate — **eyaculación** *nf, pl* **-ciones** : ejaculation

F

f *nf* : f, sixth letter of the Spanish alphabet
fabricar {72} *vt* 1 : manufacture 2 CONSTRUIR : build, construct 3 INVENTAR : fabricate — **fábrica** *nf* : factory — **fabricación** *nf, pl* **-ciones** : manufacture — **fabricante** *nmf* : manufacturer
fábula *nf* 1 : fable 2 MENTIRA : story, lie
fabuloso, -sa *adj* : fabulous
facción *nf, pl* **-ciones** 1 : faction 2 **-es** *nfpl* RASGOS : features
faceta *nf* : facet
facha *nf* : appearance, look
fachada *nf* : façade
facial *adj* : facial
fácil *adj* 1 : easy 2 PROBABLE : likely — **fácilmente** *adv* : easily, readily —

facilidad *nf* 1 : facility, ease 2 **-es** *nfpl* : facilities, services — **facilitar** *vt* 1 : facilitate 2 PROPORCIONAR : provide, supply
facsímil *or* **facsímile** *nm* 1 COPIA : facsimile, copy 2 : fax
factible *adj* : feasible
factor *nm* : factor
factoría *nf* : factory
factura *nf* 1 : bill, invoice 2 HECHURA : making, manufacture — **facturar** *vt* 1 : bill for 2 : check in (baggage, etc.)
facultad *nf* 1 : faculty, ability 2 AUTORIDAD : authority 3 : school (of a university) — **facultativo, -va** *adj* : optional
faena *nf* 1 : task, job 2 **-s domésticas** : housework

fagot *nm* : bassoon

faisán *nm, pl* **-sanes** : pheasant

faja *nf* 1 : sash 2 : girdle, corset 3 : strip (of land)

fajo *nm* : bundle, sheaf

falda *nf* 1 : skirt 2 : side, slope (of a mountain)

falible *adj* : fallible

fálico, -ca *adj* : phallic

fallar *vi* : fail, go wrong — *vt* 1 : pronounce judgment on 2 ERRAR : miss — **falla** *nf* 1 : flaw, defect 2 : (geological) fault

fallecer {53} *vi* : pass away, die — **fallecimiento** *nm* : demise, death

fallido, -da *adj* : failed, unsuccessful

fallo *nm* 1 : error 2 SENTENCIA : sentence, verdict

falo *nm* : phallus, penis

falsear *vt* : falsify, distort — **falsedad** *nf* 1 : falseness 2 MENTIRA : falsehood, lie — **falsificación** *nf, pl* **-ciones** : forgery, fake — **falsificador, -dora** *n* : forger — **falsificar** {72} *vt* 1 : counterfeit, forge 2 ALTERAR : falsify — **falso, -sa** *adj* 1 : false, untrue 2 FALSIFICADO : counterfeit, forged

falta *nf* 1 CARENCIA : lack 2 DEFECTO : defect, fault, error 3 AUSENCIA : absence 4 : offense, misdemeanor (in law) 5 : foul (in sports) 6 hacer ~ : be lacking, be needed 7 sin ~ : without fail — **faltar** *vi* 1 : be lacking, be needed 2 : be missing 3 QUEDAR : remain, be left 4 ¡no faltaba más! : don't mention it! — **falto, -ta** *adj* ~ **de** : lacking (in)

fama *nf* 1 : fame 2 REPUTACIÓN : reputation

famélico, -ca *adj* : starving

familia *nf* : family — **familiar** *adj* 1 : familial, family 2 CONOCIDO : familiar 3 : informal (of language, etc.) — ~ *nmf* : relation, relative — **familiaridad** *nf* : familiarity — **familiarizarse** {21} *vr* ~ **con** : familiarize oneself with

famoso, -sa *adj* : famous

fanático, -ca *adj* : fanatic, fanatical — ~ *n* : fanatic — **fanatismo** *nm* : fanaticism

fanfarria *nf* : fanfare

fanfarrón, -rrona *adj, mpl* **-rrones** *fam* : boastful — ~ *n fam* : braggart — **fanfarronear** *vi* : boast, brag

fango *nm* : mud, mire — **fangoso, -sa** *adj* : muddy

fantasear *vi* : fantasize, daydream — **fantasía** *nf* 1 : fantasy 2 IMAGINACIÓN : imagination

fantasma *nm* : ghost, phantom — **fantasmal** *adj* : ghostly

fantástico, -ca *adj* : fantastic

fardo *nm* : bundle

farfullar *v* : jabber, gabble

farmacéutico, -ca *adj* : pharmaceutical — ~ *n* : pharmacist — **farmacia** *nf* : drugstore, pharmacy

faro *nm* 1 : lighthouse 2 : headlight (of an automobile) — **farol** *nm* 1 LINTERNA : lantern 2 FAROLA : streetlight — **farola** *nf* 1 : lamppost 2 FAROL : streetlight

farsa *nf* : farce — **farsante** *nmf* : charlatan, fraud

fascículo *nm* : installment, part (of a publication)

fascinar *vt* : fascinate — **fascinación** *nf, pl* **-ciones** : fascination — **fascinante** *adj* : fascinating

fascismo *nm* : fascism — **fascista** *adj & nmf* : fascist

fase *nf* : phase

fastidiar *vt* : annoy, bother — *vi* : be annoying or bothersome — **fastidio** *nm* : annoyance — **fastidioso, -sa** *adj* : annoying, bothersome

fatal *adj* 1 : fateful 2 MORTAL : fatal 3 *fam* : awful, terrible — **fatalidad** *nf* 1 : fate, destiny 2 DESGRACIA : misfortune

fatídico, -ca *adj* : fateful, momentous

fatiga *nf* : fatigue — **fatigado, -da** *adj* : weary, tired — **fatigar** {52} *vt* : tire — **fatigarse** *vr* : get tired — **fatigoso, -sa** *adj* : fatiguing, tiring

fatuo, -tua *adj* 1 : fatuous 2 PRESUMIDO : conceited

fauna *nf* : fauna

favor *nm* 1 : favor 2 a ~ **de** : in favor of 3 por ~ : please — **favorable** *adj* 1 : favorable 2 ser ~ **a** : be in favor of — **favorecedor, -dora** *adj* : flattering — **favorecer** {53} *vt* 1 AYUDAR : favor 2 : look well on, suit — **favoritismo** *nm* : favoritism — **favorito, -ta** *adj & n* : favorite

fax *nm* : fax — **faxear** *vt* : fax

faz *nf, pl* **faces** : face, countenance

fe *nf* 1 : faith 2 dar ~ **de** : bear witness to 3 de buena ~ : in good faith

fealdad *nf* : ugliness

febrero *nm* : February

febril *adj* : feverish

fecha *nf* 1 : date 2 ~ **de caducidad** *or* ~ **de vencimiento** : expiration date 3 ~ **límite** : deadline — **fechar** *vt* : date, put a date on

fechoría *nf* : misdeed

fécula *nf* : starch (in food)

fecundar *vt* 1 : fertilize (an egg) 2 : make fertile — **fecundo, -da** *adj* : fertile

federación *nf, pl* **-ciones** : federation — **federal** *adj* : federal

felicidad *nf* **1** : happiness **2** ¡**~es!** : best wishes!, congratulations!, happy birthday! — **felicitación** *nf, pl* **-ciones** : congratulation — **felicitar** *vt* : congratulate — **felicitarse** *vr* **~ de** : be glad about

feligrés, -gresa *n, mpl* **-greses** : parishioner

felino, -na *adj & n* : feline

feliz *adj, pl* **-lices 1** : happy **2** AFORTUNADO : fortunate **3 Feliz Navidad** : Merry Christmas

felpa *nf* **1** : plush **2** : terry cloth (for towels, etc.)

felpudo *nm* : doormat

femenino, -na *adj* **1** : feminine **2** : female (in biology) — **femenino** *nm* : feminine (in grammar) — **feminidad** *nf* : femininity — **feminismo** *nm* : feminism — **feminista** *adj & nmf* : feminist

fenómeno *nm* : phenomenon — **fenomenal** *adj* **1** : phenomenal **2** *fam* : fantastic, terrific

feo, fea *adj* **1** : ugly **2** DESAGRADABLE : unpleasant, nasty

féretro *nm* : coffin

feria *nf* **1** : fair, market **2** FIESTA : festival, holiday **3** *Lat fam* : small change — **feriado, -da** *adj* **día feriado** : public holiday

fermentar *v* : ferment — **fermentación** *nf, pl* **-ciones** : fermentation — **fermento** *nm* : ferment

feroz *adj, pl* **-roces** : ferocious, fierce — **ferocidad** *nf* : ferocity, fierceness

férreo, -rrea *adj* **1** : iron **2 vía férrea** : railroad track

ferretería *nf* : hardware store

ferrocarril *nm* : railroad, railway — **ferroviario, -ria** *adj* : rail, railroad

ferry *nm, pl* **ferrys** : ferry

fértil *adj* : fertile, fruitful — **fertilidad** *nf* : fertility — **fertilizante** *nm* : fertilizer — **fertilizar** *vt* : fertilize

fervor *nm* : fervor, zeal — **ferviente** *adj* : fervent

festejar *vt* **1** : celebrate **2** AGASAJAR : entertain, wine and dine — **festejo** *nm* : celebration, festivity

festín *nm, pl* **-tines** : banquet, feast

festival *nm* : festival — **festividad** *nf* : festivity — **festivo, -va** *adj* **1** : festive **2 día festivo** : holiday

fetiche *nm* : fetish

fétido, -da *adj* : foul-smelling, fetid

feto *nm* : fetus — **fetal** *adj* : fetal

feudal *adj* : feudal

fiable *adj* : reliable — **fiabilidad** *nf* : reliability

fiado, -da *adj* : on credit — **fiador, -dora** *n* : bondsman, guarantor

fiambres *nfpl* : cold cuts

fianza *nf* **1** : bail, bond **2 dar ~** : pay a deposit

fiar {85} *vt* **1** : guarantee **2** : sell on credit — *vi* **ser de ~** : be trustworthy — **fiarse** *vr* **~ de** : place trust in

fiasco *nm* : fiasco

fibra *nf* **1** : fiber **2 ~ de vidrio** : fiberglass

ficción *nf, pl* **-ciones** : fiction

ficha *nf* **1** : token **2** TARJETA : index card **3** : counter, chip (in games) — **fichar** *vt* : file, index — **fichero** *nm* **1** : card file **2** : filing cabinet

ficticio, -cia *adj* : fictitious

fidedigno, -na *adj* : reliable, trustworthy

fidelidad *nf* : fidelity, faithfulness

fideo *nm* : noodle

fiebre *nf* **1** : fever **2 ~ del heno** : hay fever **3 ~ palúdica** : malaria

fiel *adj* **1** : faithful, loyal **2** PRECISO : accurate, reliable — **~** *nm* **1** : pointer (of a scale) **2 los ~es** : the faithful — **fielmente** *adv* : faithfully

fieltro *nm* : felt

fiero, -ra *adj* : fierce, ferocious — **fiera** *nf* : wild animal, beast

fierro *nm Lat* : iron (bar)

fiesta *nf* **1** : party **2** DÍA FESTIVO : holiday, feast day

figura *nf* **1** : figure **2** FORMA : shape, form — **figurar** *vi* **1** : figure (in), be included (among) **2** DESTACAR : stand out — *vt* : represent — **figurarse** *vr* : imagine

fijar *vt* **1** : fasten, affix **2** CONCRETAR : set, fix — **fijarse** *vr* **1** : settle **2 ~ en** : notice, pay attention to — **fijo, -ja** *adj* **1** : fixed, firm **2** PERMANENTE : permanent

fila *nf* **1** : line, file, row **2 ponerse en ~** : line up

filantropía *nf* : philanthropy — **filantrópico, -ca** *adj* : philanthropic — **filántropo, -pa** *n* : philanthropist

filatelia *nf* : philately, stamp collecting

filete *nm* : fillet

filial *adj* : filial — **~** *nf* : affiliate, subsidiary

filigrana *nf* **1** : filigree **2** : watermark (on paper)

filipino, -na *adj* : Filipino

filmar *vt* : film, shoot — **filme** *or* **film** *nm* : film, movie

filo *nm* **1** : edge **2 dar ~ a** : sharpen

filón *nm, pl* **-lones 1** : vein (of minerals) **2** *fam* : gold mine

filoso, -sa *adj Lat* : sharp

filosofía *nf* : philosophy — **filosófico, -ca** *adj* : philosophical — **filósofo, -fa** *n* : philosopher

filtrar *v* : filter — **filtrarse** *vr* : leak out, seep through — **filtro** *nm* : filter

fin *nm* **1** : end **2** OBJETIVO : purpose, aim **3 en ~** : well, in short **4 ~ de semana** : weekend **5 por ~** : finally, at last

final *adj* : final — **~** *nm* : end, conclusion — **~** *nf* : final (in sports) — **finalidad** *nf* : purpose, aim — **finalista** *nmf* : finalist — **finalizar** {21} *v* : finish, end — **finalmente** *adv* : finally

financiar *vt* : finance, fund — **financiero, -ra** *adj* : financial — **~** *n* : financier — **finanzas** *nfpl* : finance

finca *nf* **1** : farm, ranch **2** *Lat* : country house

fingir {35} *v* : feign, pretend — **fingido, -da** *adj* : false, feigned

finito, -ta *adj* : finite

finlandés, -desa *adj* : Finnish

fino, -na *adj* **1** : fine **2** DELGADO : slender **3** REFINADO : refined **4** AGUDO : sharp, keen — **finura** *nf* **1** : fineness **2** REFINAMIENTO : refinement

firma *nf* **1** : signature **2** : (act of) signing **3** EMPRESA : firm, company

firmamento *nm* : firmament, sky

firmar *v* : sign

firme *adj* **1** : firm, resolute **2** ESTABLE : steady, stable — **firmeza** *nf* **1** : strength, resolve **2** ESTABILIDAD : firmness, stability

fiscal *adj* : fiscal — **~** *nmf* : district attorney — **fisco** *nm* : (national) treasury

fisgar {52} *vt* : pry into — *vi* : pry — **fisgón, -gona** *n, mpl* **-gones** : snoop, busybody

física *nf* : physics — **físico, -ca** *adj* : physical — **~** *n* : physicist — **físico** *nm* : physique

fisiología *nf* : physiology — **fisiológico, -ca** *adj* : physiological — **fisiólogo, -ga** *n* : physiologist

fisioterapia *nf* : physical therapy — **fisioterapeuta** *nmf* : physical therapist

fisonomía *nf* : features *pl*, appearance

fisura *nf* : fissure

fláccido, -da *or* **flácido, -da** *adj* : flaccid, flabby

flaco, -ca *adj* **1** : thin, skinny **2** DÉBIL : weak

flagrante *adj* : flagrant

flamante *adj* **1** : bright, brilliant **2** NUEVO : brand-new

flamenco, -ca *adj* **1** : flamenco (of music or dance) **2** : Flemish — **flamenco** *nm* **1** : flamingo **2** : flamenco (music or dance)

flaquear *vi* : weaken, flag — **flaqueza** *nf* **1** : thinness **2** DEBILIDAD : weakness

flash *nm* : flash

flatulencia *nf* : flatulence

flauta *nf* **1** : flute **2 ~ dulce** : recorder — **flautín** *nm, pl* **-tines** : piccolo — **flautista** *nmf* : flutist

flecha *nf* : arrow

fleco *nm* **1** : fringe **2** *Lat* : bangs *pl*

flema *nf* : phlegm — **flemático, -ca** *adj* : phlegmatic

flequillo *nm* : bangs *pl*

fletar *vt* **1** : charter, rent **2** *Lat* : transport — **flete** *nm* **1** : charter **2** : shipping (charges) **3** *Lat* : transport, freight

flexible *adj* : flexible — **flexibilidad** *nf* : flexibility

flirtear *vi* : flirt

flojo, -ja *adj* **1** SUELTO : loose, slack **2** DÉBIL : weak **3** PEREZOSO : lazy — **flojera** *nf fam* : lethargy

flor *nf* : flower — **flora** *nf* : flora — **floral** *adj* : floral — **floreado, -da** *adj* : flowered — **florear** *vi* *Lat* : flower, bloom — **florecer** {53} *vi* **1** : bloom, blossom **2** PROSPERAR : flourish — **floreciente** *adj* : flourishing — **florero** *nm* : vase — **florido, -da** *adj* : flowery — **florista** *nmf* : florist — **floritura** *nf* : frill, flourish

flota *nf* : fleet

flotar *vi* : float — **flotador** *nm* **1** : float **2** : life preserver (for a swimmer) — **flotante** *adj* : floating, buoyant — **flote: a ~** *adv phr* : afloat

flotilla *nf* : flotilla, fleet

fluctuar {3} *vi* : fluctuate — **fluctuación** *nf, pl* **-ciones** : fluctuation

fluir {41} *vi* : flow — **fluidez** *nf* **1** : fluidity **2** : fluency (of language, etc.) — **fluido, -da** *adj* **1** : fluid **2** : fluent (of language) — **fluido** *nm* : fluid — **flujo** *nm* : flow

fluorescente *adj* : fluorescent

fluoruro *nm* : fluoride

fluvial *adj* : river

fobia *nf* : phobia

foca *nf* : seal (animal)

foco *nm* **1** : focus **2** : spotlight, floodlight (in theater, etc.) **3** *Lat* : lightbulb

fofo, -fa *adj* : flabby

fogata *nf* : bonfire

fogón *nm, pl* **-gones** : burner

fogoso, -sa *adj* : ardent

folklore *nm* : folklore — **folklórico, -ca** *adj* : folk, traditional

follaje *nm* : foliage

folleto *nm* : pamphlet, leaflet

fomentar *vt* : promote, encourage — **fomento** *nm* : promotion, encouragement

fonda *nf* : boarding house

fondear *vt* : sound out, examine — *vi* : anchor

fondillos *nmpl* : seat (of pants, etc.)

fondo *nm* **1** : bottom **2** : rear, back, end **3** PROFUNDIDAD : depth **4** : background (of a painting, etc.) **5** *Lat* : slip, petticoat **6** ~**s** *nmpl* : funds, resources **7 a** ~ : thoroughly, in depth **8 en el** ~ : deep down

fonético, -ca *adj* : phonetic — **fonética** *nf* : phonetics

fontanería *nf Spain* : plumbing — **fontanero, -ra** *n Spain* : plumber

footing ['fu,tɪŋ] *nm* **1** : jogging **2 hacer** ~ : jog

forajido, -da *adj* : bandit, outlaw

foráneo, -nea *adj* : foreign, strange

forastero, -ra *n* : stranger, outsider

forcejear *vi* : struggle — **forcejeo** *nm* : struggle

forense *adj* : forensic

forja *nf* : forge — **forjar** *vt* **1** : forge **2** CREAR, FORMAR : build up, create

forma *nf* **1** : form, shape **2** MANERA : manner, way **3 en** ~ : fit, healthy **4** ~**s** *nfpl* : appearances, conventions — **formación** *nf, pl* **-ciones 1** : formation **2** EDUCACIÓN : training

formal *adj* **1** : formal **2** SERIO : serious **3** FIABLE : dependable, reliable — **formalidad** *nf* **1** : formality **2** SERIEDAD : seriousness **3** FIABILIDAD : reliability

formar *vt* **1** : form, shape **2** CONSTITUIR : constitute **3** EDUCAR : train, educate — **formarse** *vr* **1** DESARROLLARSE : develop, take shape **2** EDUCARSE : be educated

formato *nm* : format

formidable *adj* **1** : tremendous **2** *fam* : fantastic, terrific

fórmula *nf* : formula

formular *vt* **1** : formulate, draw up **2** : make, lodge (a complaint, etc.)

formulario *nm* : form

fornido, -da *adj* : well-built, burly

foro *nm* : forum

forraje *nm* : forage, fodder — **forrajear** *vi* : forage

forrar *vt* **1** : line (a garment) **2** : cover (a book) — **forro** *nm* **1** : lining **2** CUBIERTA : book cover

fortalecer {53} *vt* : strengthen — **fortaleza** *nf* **1** : fortress **2** FUERZA : strength **3** : (moral) fortitude

fortificar {72} *vt* : fortify — **fortificación** *nf, pl* **-ciones** : fortification

fortuito, -ta *adj* : fortuitous, chance

fortuna *nf* **1** SUERTE : fortune, luck **2** RIQUEZA : wealth, fortune **3 por** ~ : fortunately

forzar {36} *vt* **1** : force **2** : strain (one's eyes) — **forzosamente** *adv* : necessarily — **forzoso, -sa** *adj* : necessary, inevitable

fosa *nf* **1** : pit, ditch **2** TUMBA : grave **3** ~**s nasales** : nostrils

fósforo *nm* **1** : phosphorus **2** CERILLA : match — **fosforescente** *adj* : phosphorescent

fósil *nm* : fossil

foso *nm* **1** : ditch **2** : pit (of a theater) **3** : moat (of a castle)

foto *nf* : photo

fotocopia *nf* : photocopy — **fotocopiadora** *nf* : photocopier — **fotocopiar** *vt* : photocopy

fotogénico, -ca *adj* : photogenic

fotografía *nf* **1** : photography **2** : photograph, picture — **fotografiar** {85} *vt* : photograph — **fotográfico, -ca** *adj* : photographic — **fotógrafo, -fa** *n* : photographer

fotosíntesis *nf* : photosynthesis

fracasar *vi* : fail — **fracaso** *nm* : failure

fracción *nf, pl* **-ciones 1** : fraction **2** : faction (in politics) — **fraccionamiento** *nm Lat* : housing development

fractura *nf* : fracture — **fracturarse** *vr* : fracture, break (a bone)

fragancia *nf* : fragrance, scent — **fragante** *adj* : fragrant

fragata *nf* : frigate

frágil *adj* **1** : fragile **2** DÉBIL : frail, delicate — **fragilidad** *nf* **1** : fragility **2** DEBILIDAD : frailty

fragmento *nm* : fragment

fragor *nm* : clamor, din

fragoso, -sa *adj* : rough, rugged

fragua *nf* : forge — **fraguar** {10} *vt* **1** : forge **2** IDEAR : concoct — *vi* : harden, solidify

fraile *nm* : friar, monk

frambuesa *nf* : raspberry

francés, -cesa *adj, mpl* **-ceses** : French — **francés** *nm* : French (language)

franco, -ca *adj* **1** : frank, candid **2** : free (in commerce) — **franco** *nm* : franc

francotirador, -dora *n* : sniper

franela *nf* : flannel

franja *nf* **1** : stripe, band **2** FLECO : fringe

franquear *vt* **1** : clear (a path, etc.) **2** : cross over (a doorstep, etc.) **3** : pay postage on (mail) — **franqueo** *nm* : postage

franqueza *nf* : frankness

frasco *nm* : small bottle, vial, flask

frase *nf* 1 : phrase 2 ORACIÓN : sentence

fraternal *adj* : brotherly, fraternal — **fraternidad** *nf* : brotherhood, fraternity — **fraternizar** {21} *vi* : fraternize — **fraterno, -na** *adj* : brotherly, fraternal

fraude *nm* : fraud — **fraudulento, -ta** *adj* : fraudulent

fray *nm* (*used in titles*) : brother, friar

frazada *nf Lat* : blanket

frecuencia *nf* 1 : frequency 2 **con ~** : often, frequently — **frecuentar** *vt* : frequent, haunt — **frecuente** *adj* : frequent

fregadero *nm* : kitchen sink

fregar {49} *vt* 1 : scrub, wash 2 *Lat fam* : annoy — *vi Lat fam* : be a pest

freír {37} *vt* : fry

fregona *nf Spain* : mop

frenar *vt* 1 : brake 2 RESTRINGIR : curb, check

frenesí *nm* : frenzy — **frenético, -ca** *adj* : frantic, frenzied

freno *nm* 1 : brake 2 : bit (of a bridle) 3 CONTROL : check, restraint

frente *nm* 1 : front 2 : facade (of a building) 3 **al ~ de** : at the head of 4 **~ a** : opposite 5 **de ~** : (facing) forward 6 **hacer ~ a** : face up to, brave — **~** *nf* : forehead

fresa *nf* : strawberry

fresco, -ca *adj* 1 : fresh 2 FRÍO : cool 3 *fam* : insolent, nervy — **fresco** *nm* 1 : fresh air 2 FRESCOR : coolness 3 : fresco (art or painting) — **frescor** *nm* : coolness, cool air — **frescura** *nf* 1 : freshness 2 FRÍO : coolness 3 *fam* : nerve, insolence

fresno *nm* : ash (tree)

frialdad *nf* 1 : coldness 2 INDIFERENCIA : indifference

fricción *nf, pl* **-ciones** 1 : friction 2 MASAJE : rubbing, massage — **friccionar** *vt* : rub

frigidez *nf* : frigidity

frigorífico *nm Spain* : refrigerator

frijol *nm Lat* : bean

frío, fría *adj* 1 : cold 2 INDIFERENTE : cool, indifferent — **frío** *nm* 1 : cold 2 INDIFERENCIA : coldness, indifference 3 **hacer ~** : be cold (outside) 4 **tener ~** : be cold, feel cold

frito, -ta *adj* 1 : fried 2 *fam* : fed up

frívolo, -la *adj* : frivolous — **frivolidad** *nf* : frivolity

fronda *nf* 1 : frond 2 *or* **~s** *nfpl* : foliage — **frondoso, -sa** *adj* : leafy

frontera *nf* : border, frontier — **fronterizo, -za** *adj* : border, on the border — **frontero, -ra** *adj* : facing, opposite

frotar *vt* : rub — **frotarse** *vr* **~ las manos** : rub one's hands

fructífero, -ra *adj* : fruitful

frugal *adj* : frugal, thrifty — **frugalidad** *adj* : frugality

fruncir {83} *vt* 1 : gather (in pleats) 2 **~ el ceño** : frown 3 **~ la boca** : purse one's lips

frustrar *vt* : frustrate — **frustrarse** *vr* : fail — **frustración** *nf, pl* **-ciones** : frustration — **frustrado, -da** *adj* 1 : frustrated 2 FRACASADO : failed, unsuccessful — **frustrante** *adj* : frustrating

fruta *nf* : fruit — **frutilla** *nf Lat* : strawberry — **fruto** *nm* 1 : fruit 2 RESULTADO : result, consequence

fucsia *adj & nm* : fuchsia

fuego *nm* 1 : fire 2 : flame, burner (on a stove) 3 **~s artificiales** *nmpl* : fireworks 4 **¿tienes fuego?** : have you got a light?

fuelle *nm* : bellows

fuente *nf* 1 : fountain 2 MANANTIAL : spring 3 ORIGEN : source 4 PLATO : platter, serving dish

fuera *adv* 1 : outside, out 2 : abroad, away 3 **~ de** : outside of, beyond 4 **~ de** : aside from, in addition to

fuerte *adj* 1 : strong 2 : bright (of colors), loud (of sounds) 3 EXTREMO : intense 4 DURO : hard — **~** *adv* 1 : strongly, hard 2 : loudly 3 MUCHO : abundantly, a lot — **~** *nm* 1 : fort 2 ESPECIALIDAD : strong point

fuerza *nf* 1 : strength 2 VIOLENCIA : force 3 PODER : power, might 4 **~s armadas** *nfpl* : armed forces 5 **a ~ de** : by dint of 6 **a la ~** : necessarily

fuga *nf* 1 : flight, escape 2 : fugue (in music) 3 ESCAPE : leak — **fugarse** {52} *vr* : flee, run away — **fugaz** *adj, pl* **-gaces** : fleeting — **fugitivo, -va** *adj & n* : fugitive

fulano, -na *n* : so-and-so, what's-his-name, what's-her-name

fulgor *nm* : brilliance, splendor

fulminar *vt* 1 : strike with lightning 2 : strike down (with an illness, etc.) — **fulminante** *adj* : devastating

fumar *v* : smoke — **fumarse** *vr* 1 : smoke 2 *fam* : squander — **fumador, -dora** *n* : smoker

funámbulo, -la *n* : tightrope walker

función *nf, pl* **-ciones** 1 : function 2 TRABAJOS : duties *pl* 3 : performance, show (in theater) — **funcional** *adj* : functional — **funcionamiento** *nm* 1

: functioning **2 en ~** : in operation —
funcionar *vi* **1** : function, run, work
2 no funciona : out of order —
funcionario, -ria *n* : civil servant, official

funda *nf* **1** : cover, sheath **2** *or* **~ de almohada** : pillowcase

fundar *vt* **1** ESTABLECER : found, establish **2** BASAR : base — **fundarse** *vr* **~ en** : be based on — **fundación** *nf, pl* **-ciones** : foundation — **fundador, -dora** *n* : founder — **fundamental** *adj* : fundamental, basic — **fundamentalmente** *adv* : basically — **fundamentar** *vt* **1** : lay the foundations for **2** BASAR : base — **fundamento** *nm* **1** : foundation **2 ~s** *nmpl* : fundamentals

fundir *vt* **1** : melt down, smelt **2** FUSIONAR : fuse, merge — **fundirse** *vr* **1** : blend, merge **2** DERRETIRSE : melt **3** : burn out (of a lightbulb) — **fundición** *nf, pl* **-ciones 1** : smelting **2** : foundry

fúnebre *adj* **1** : funeral **2** LÚGUBRE : gloomy

funeral *adj* : funeral, funerary — **~** *nm* **1** : funeral **2 ~es** *nmpl* EXEQUIAS : funeral (rites) — **funeraria** *nf* : funeral home

funesto, ta *adj* : terrible, disastrous

fungir {35} *vi Lat* : act, function

furgón *nm, pl* **-gones 1** : van, truck **2** : freight car (of a train) **3 ~ de cola** : caboose — **furgoneta** *nf* : van

furia *nf* **1** CÓLERA : fury, rage **2** VIOLENCIA : violence — **furibundo, -da** *adj* : furious — **furioso, -sa** *adj* **1** : furious, irate **2** INTENSO : intense, violent — **furor** *nm* : fury

furtivo, -va *adj* : furtive

furúnculo *nm* : boil

fuselaje *nm* : fuselage

fusible *nm* : fuse

fusil *nm* : rifle — **fusilar** *vt* : shoot (by firing squad)

fusión *nf, pl* **-siones 1** : fusion **2** UNIÓN : union, merger — **fusionar** *vt* **1** : fuse **2** UNIR : merge — **fusionarse** *vr* : merge

futbol *or* **fútbol** *nm* **1** : soccer **2 ~ americano** : football — **futbolista** *nmf* : soccer player, football player

fútil *adj* : trifling, trivial

futuro, -ra *adj* : future — **futuro** *nm* : future

G

g *nf* : g, seventh letter of the Spanish alphabet

gabán *nm, pl* **-banes** : topcoat, overcoat

gabardina *nf* **1** : trench coat, raincoat **2** : gabardine (fabric)

gabinete *nm* **1** : cabinet (in government) **2** : (professional) office

gacela *nf* : gazelle

gaceta *nf* : gazette

gachas *nfpl* : porridge

gacho, -cha *adj* : drooping

gaélico, -ca *adj* : Gaelic

gafas *nfpl* **1** : eyeglasses **2 ~ de sol** : sunglasses

gaita *nf* : bagpipes *pl*

gajo *nm* : segment (of fruit)

gala *nf* **1** : gala **2 de ~** : formal **3 hacer ~ de** : display, show off **4 ~s** *nfpl* : finery

galáctico, -ca *adj* : galactic

galán *nm, pl* **-lanes 1** : leading man (in theater) **2** *fam* : boyfriend

galante *adj* : gallant — **galantear** *vt* : court, woo — **galantería** *nf* **1** : gallantry **2** CUMPLIDO : compliment

galápago *nm* : (aquatic) turtle

galardón *nm, pl* **-dones** : reward

galaxia *nf* : galaxy

galera *nf* : galley

galería *nf* **1** : corridor **2** : gallery, balcony (in a theater)

galés, -lesa *adj, mpl* **-leses** : Welsh

gaigo *nm* : greyhound

galimatías *nms & pl* : gibberish

gallardía *nf* **1** : bravery **2** ELEGANCIA : elegance — **gallardo, -da** *adj* **1** : brave **2** APUESTO : elegant, good-looking

gallego, -ga *adj* : Galician

galleta *nf* **1** : (sweet) cookie **2** : (salted) cracker

gallina *nf* **1** : hen **2 ~ de Guinea** : guinea fowl — **gallinero** *nm* : henhouse, (chicken) coop — **gallo** *nm* : rooster, cock

galón *nm, pl* **-lones 1** : gallon **2** : stripe (military insignia)

galopar *vi* : gallop — **galope** *nm* : gallop

galvanizar {21} *vt* : galvanize

gama *nf* **1** : range, spectrum **2** : scale (in music)

gamba *nf* : large shrimp, prawn

gamuza *nf* **1** : chamois (animal) **2** : chamois (leather), suede

gana *nf* **1** : desire, wish **2** APETITO : appetite **3 de buena ~** : willingly, heartily **4 de mala ~** : unwillingly **5 no me da la ~** : I don't feel like it **6 tener ~s de** : feel like, be in the mood for

ganado *nm* **1** : cattle *pl*, livestock **2 ~ ovino** : sheep *pl* **3 ~ porcino** : swine *pl* — **ganadería** *nf* **1** : cattle raising **2** GANADO : livestock

ganador, -dora *adj* : winning — **~** *n* : winner

ganancia *nf* : profit

ganar *vt* **1** : earn **2** : win (in games, etc.) **3** CONSEGUIR : gain **4** ADQUIRIR : get, obtain **5 ~ a algn** : win over s.o., beat s.o. — *vi* : win — **ganarse** *vr* **1** : win, gain **2 ~ la vida** : make a living

gancho *nm* **1** : hook **2** HORQUILLA : hairpin **3** *Lat* : (clothes) hanger

gandul, -dula *adj & n fam* : good-for-nothing — **gandul** *nm Lat* : pigeon pea

ganga *nf* : bargain

gangrena *nf* : gangrene

gángster *nmf* : gangster

ganso, -sa *n* : goose, gander *m* — **gansada** *nf* : silly thing, nonsense

gañir {38} *vi* : yelp — **gañido** *nm* : yelp

garabatear *v* : scribble — **garabato** *nm* : scribble

garaje *nm* : garage

garantizar {21} *vt* : guarantee — **garante** *nmf* : guarantor — **garantía** *nf* **1** : guarantee, warranty **2** FIANZA : surety

garapiñar *vt* : candy (fruits, etc.)

garbanzo *nm* : chickpea, garbanzo

garbo *nm* : grace, elegance — **garboso, -sa** *adj* : graceful, elegant

gardenia *nf* : gardenia

garfio *nm* : hook, gaff

garganta *nf* **1** : throat **2** CUELLO : neck **3** DESFILADERO : ravine, gorge — **gargantilla** *nf* : necklace

gárgara *nf* **1** : gargling, gargle **2 hacer ~s** : gargle

gárgola *nf* : gargoyle

garita *nf* **1** : sentry box **2** CABAÑA : cabin, hut

garito *nm* : gambling den

garra *nf* **1** : claw, talon **2** *fam* : hand, paw

garrafa *nf* : decanter, carafe — **garrafón** *nm, pl* **-fones** : large decanter or bottle

garrapata *nf* : tick

garrocha *nf* **1** : lance, pike **2** *Lat* : pole (in sports)

garrote *nm* : club, cudgel

garúa *nf Lat* : drizzle

garza *nf* : heron

gas *nm* **1** : gas **2 ~ lacrimógeno** : tear gas

gasa *nf* : gauze

gaseosa *nf* : soda, soft drink

gasolina *nf* : gasoline, gas — **gasoil** *or* **gasóleo** *nm* : diesel fuel — **gasolinera** *nf* : gas station, service station

gastar *vt* **1** : spend **2** CONSUMIR : consume, use up **3** DESPERDICIAR : squander, waste — **gastarse** *vr* **1** : spend **2** DETERIORARSE : wear out — **gastado, -da** *adj* **1** : spent **2** : worn-out (of clothing, etc.) — **gastador, -dora** *n* : spendthrift — **gasto** *nm* **1** : expense, expenditure **2 ~s generales** : overhead

gástrico, -ca *adj* : gastric

gastronomía *nf* : gastronomy — **gastrónomo, -ma** *n* : gourmet

gatas: a ~ *adv phr* : on all fours

gatear *vi* : crawl, creep

gatillo *nm* : trigger — **gatillero** *nm Mex* : gunman

gato, -ta *n* : cat — **gatito, -ta** *n* : kitten — **gato** *nm* : jack (for an automobile)

gaucho *nm* : gaucho

gaveta *nf* : drawer

gavilla *nf* **1** : sheaf **2** PANDILLA : gang

gaviota *nf* : gull, seagull

gay ['ge, 'gai] *adj* : gay (homosexual)

gaza *nf* : loop

gazpacho *nm* : gazpacho

géiser *nm* : geyser

gelatina *nf* : gelatin

gema *nf* : gem

gemelo, -la *adj & n* : twin — **gemelo** *nm* **1** : cuff link **2 ~s** *nmpl* : binoculars

gemir {54} *vi* : moan, groan, whine — **gemido** *nm* : moan, groan, whine

gen *or* **gene** *nm* : gene

genealogía *nf* : genealogy — **genealógico, -ca** *adj* : genealogical

generación *nf, pl* **-ciones** : generation

generador *nm* : generator

general *adj* **1** : general **2 en ~** *or* **por lo ~** : in general, generally — **~** *nmf* : general — **generalidad** *nf* **1** : generalization **2** MAYORÍA : majority — **generalizar** {21} *vi* : generalize — *vt* : spread (out) — **generalizarse** *vr* : become widespread — **generalmente** *adv* : usually, generally

generar *vt* : generate

género *nm* **1** : kind, sort **2** : gender (in

grammar) **3 ~ humano** : human race
— **genérico, -ca** *adj* : generic
generoso, -sa *adj* **1** : generous, unselfish **2** : ample (in quantity) — **generosidad** *nf* : generosity
génesis *nfs & pl* : genesis
genética *nf* : genetics — **genético, -ca**
adj : genetic
genial *adj* **1** : brilliant **2** ESTUPENDO
: great, terrific
genio *nm* **1** : genius **2** CARÁCTER : temper, disposition **3** : genie (in mythology)
genital *adj* : genital — **genitales** *nmpl*
: genitals
genocidio *nm* : genocide
gente *nf* **1** : people **2** *fam* : relatives *pl*,
folks *pl* **3 ser buena ~** : be nice, be
kind
gentil *adj* **1** AMABLE : kind **2** : gentile
(in religion) — **gentileza** *nf* : kindness, courtesy
gentío *nm* : crowd, mob
gentuza *nf* : riffraff, rabble
genuflexión *nf, pl* **-xiones** : genuflec-
tion
genuino, -na *adj* : genuine
geografía *nf* : geography — **geográfico, -ca** *adj* : geographic, geographical
geología *nf* : geology — **geológico,
-ca** *adj* : geologic, geological
geometría *nf* : geometry — **geométrico, -ca** *adj* : geometric, geometrical
geranio *nm* : geranium
gerencia *nf* : management — **gerente**
nmf : manager
geriatría *nf* : geriatrics — **geriátrico,
-ca** *adj* : geriatric
germen *nm, pl* **gérmenes** : germ
germinar *vi* : germinate, sprout
gestación *nf, pl* **-ciones** : gestation
gesticular *vi* : gesticulate, gesture —
gesticulación *nf, pl* **-ciones** : gestic-
ulation
gestión *nf, pl* **-tiones 1** : procedure, step
2 ADMINISTRACIÓN : management —
gestionar *vt* **1** : negotiate, work towards **2** ADMINISTRAR : manage, handle
gesto *nm* **1** : gesture **2** : (facial) expression **3** MUECA : grimace
gigante *adj & nm* : giant — **gigantesco, -ca** *adj* : gigantic
gimnasia *nf* : gymnastics — **gimnasio**
nm : gymnasium, gym — **gimnasta**
nmf : gymnast
gimotear *vi* : whine, whimper
ginebra *nf* : gin
ginecología *nf* : gynecology — **gine-
cólogo, -ga** *n* : gynecologist
gira *nf* : tour

girar *vi* : turn (around), revolve — *vt* **1**
: turn, twist, rotate **2** : draft (checks) **3**
: transfer (funds)
girasol *nm* : sunflower
giratorio, -ria *adj* : revolving
giro *nm* **1** : turn, rotation **2** LOCUCIÓN
: expression **3 ~ bancario** : bank
draft **4 ~ postal** : money order
giroscopio *nm* : gyroscope
gis *nm* *Lat* : chalk
gitano, -na *adj & n* : Gypsy
glaciar *nm* : glacier — **glacial** *adj* : glacial, icy
gladiador *nm* : gladiator
glándula *nf* : gland
glasear *vt* : glaze, ice (cake, etc.) —
glaseado *nm* : icing
glicerina *nf* : glycerin
globo *nm* **1** : globe **2** : balloon **3 ~ ocular** : eyeball — **global** *adj* **1** : global
2 TOTAL : total, overall
glóbulo *nm* : blood cell, corpuscle
gloria *nf* : glory
glorieta *nf* **1** : bower, arbor **2** *Spain* : rotary, traffic circle
glorificar {72} *vt* : glorify
glorioso, -sa *adj* : glorious
glosario *nm* : glossary
glotón, -tona *adj, mpl* **-tones** : gluttonous — **~** *n* : glutton — **glotonería** *nf*
: gluttony
glucosa *nf* : glucose
gnomo ['nomo] *nm* : gnome
gobernar {55} *v* **1** : govern, rule **2** DIRI-
GIR : direct, manage **3** : steer (a boat,
etc.) — **gobernación** *nf, pl* **-ciones**
: governing, government — **gobernador, -dora** *n* : governor — **gobernante** *adj* : ruling, governing — **~** *n*
: ruler, leader — **gobierno** *nm* : government
goce *nm* : enjoyment
gol *nm* : goal (in sports)
golf *nm* : golf — **golfista** *nmf* : golfer
golfo *nm* : gulf
golondrina *nf* **1** : swallow **2 ~ de mar**
: tern
golosina *nf* : sweet, candy — **goloso,
-sa** *adj* : fond of sweets
golpe *nm* **1** : blow **2** PUÑETAZO : punch
3 : knock (on a door, etc.) **4 de ~**
: suddenly **5 de un ~** : all at once **6
~ de estado** : coup d'etat — **gol-
pear** *vt* **1** : hit, punch **2** : slam, bang (a
door, etc.) — *vi* : knock (at a door)
goma *nf* **1** CAUCHO : rubber **2** PEGAMEN-
TO : glue **3** *or* **~ elástica** : rubber
band **4 ~ de mascar** : chewing gum
5 ~ de borrar : eraser
gong *nm* : gong

gordo, -da *adj* **1** : fat, plump **2** GRUESO
: thick **3** : fatty (of meat) **4** *fam* : big,
serious — ~ *n* : fat person — **gorda**
nf Lat : thick corn tortilla — **gordo** *nm*
1 GRASA : fat **2** : jackpot (in a lottery)
— **gordura** *nf* : fatness, flab

gorgotear *vi* : gurgle, bubble

gorila *nm* : gorilla

gorjear *vi* **1** : chirp, tweet **2** : gurgle (of
a baby) — **gorjeo** *nm* : chirping

gorra *nf* **1** : cap, bonnet **2 de ~** *fam*
: for free

gorrear *vt fam* : bum, scrounge

gorrión *nm, pl* **-rriones** : sparrow

gorro *nm* **1** : cap, bonnet **2 de ~** *fam*
: for free

gota *nf* **1** : drop **2** : gout (in medicine)
— **gotear** *vi* : drip, leak — **goteo** *nm*
: drip, dripping — **gotera** *nf* : leak

gótico, -ca *adj* : Gothic

gozar {21} *vi* **1** : enjoy oneself **2 ~ de**
algo : enjoy sth

gozne *nm* : hinge

gozo *nm* **1** : joy **2** PLACER : enjoyment,
pleasure — **gozoso, -sa** *adj* : joyful,
glad

grabar *vt* **1** : engrave **2** : record, tape —
grabación *nf, pl* **-ciones** : recording
— **grabado** *nm* : engraving — **grabadora** *nf* : tape recorder

gracia *nf* **1** : grace **2** FAVOR : favor, kindness **3** HUMOR : humor, wit **4 ~s** *nfpl*
: thanks **5 ¡(muchas) ~s!** : thank you
(very much)! — **gracioso, -sa** *adj*
: funny, amusing

grada *nf* **1** : step, stair **2** : row (in a theater, etc.) **3 ~s** *nfpl* : bleachers,
grandstand — **gradación** *nf, pl*
-ciones : gradation, scale — **gradería**
nf : rows *pl*, stands *pl* — **grado** *nm* **1**
: degree **2** : grade (in school) **3 de**
buen ~ : willingly

graduar {3} *vt* **1** : regulate, adjust **2**
MARCAR : calibrate **3** : confer a degree
on (in education) — **graduarse** *vr*
: graduate (from a school) — **graduación** *nf, pl* **-ciones 1** : graduation **2**
: alcohol content, proof — **graduado,
-da** *n* : graduate — **gradual** *adj* : gradual — **gradualmente** *adv* : little by
little, gradually

gráfico, -ca *adj* : graphic — **gráfica** *nf*
: graph — **gráfico** *nm* **1** : graph **2**
: graphic (in computers)

gragea *nf* : pill, tablet

grajo *nm* : rook (bird)

gramática *nf* : grammar — **gramatical**
adj : grammatical

gramo *nm* : gram

gran → *grande*

grana *nf* : scarlet

granada *nf* **1** : pomegranate **2** : grenade
(in the military)

granate *nm* : garnet

grande *adj* (**gran** *before singular
nouns*) **1** : large, big **2** ALTO : tall **3**
: great (in quality, intensity, etc.) **4** *Lat*
: grown-up — **grandeza** *nf* **1** : greatness **2** NOBLEZA : nobility — **grandiosidad** *nf* : grandeur — **grandioso, -sa**
adj : grand, magnificent

granel: a ~ *adv phr* **1** : in bulk **2** : in
abundance

granero *nm* : barn, granary

granito *nm* : granite

granizar {21} *v impers* : hail — **grani-
zada** *nf* : hailstorm — **granizado** *nm*
: iced drink — **granizo** *nm* : hail

granja *nf* : farm — **granjero, -ra** *n*
: farmer

grano *nm* **1** : grain **2** SEMILLA : seed **3**
: (coffee) bean **4** BARRO : pimple

granuja *nmf* : rascal

grapa *nf* : staple — **grapadora** *nf* : stapler — **grapar** *vt* : staple

grasa *nf* **1** : grease **2** : fat (in cooking,
etc.) — **grasiento, -ta** *adj* : greasy, oily
— **graso, -sa** *adj* : fatty, greasy, oily —
grasoso, -sa *adj Lat* : greasy, oily

gratificar {72} *vt* **1** : give a tip or bonus
to **2** SATISFACER : gratify, satisfy —
gratificación *nf, pl* **-ciones 1** : bonus,
tip, reward **2** SATISFACCIÓN : gratifica-
tion

gratis *adv & adj* : free

gratitud *nf* : gratitude

grato, -ta *adj* : pleasant, agreeable

gratuito, -ta *adj* **1** : gratuitous, unwarranted **2** GRATIS : free

grava *nf* : gravel

gravar *vt* **1** : tax **2** CARGAR : burden —
gravamen *nm, pl* **-vámenes 1** : burden, obligation **2** IMPUESTO : tax

grave *adj* **1** : grave, serious **2** : deep,
low (of a voice, etc.) — **gravedad** *nf*
: gravity

gravilla *nf* : gravel

gravitar *vi* **1** : gravitate **2 ~ sobre**
: weigh on — **gravitación** *nf, pl*
-ciones : gravitation

gravoso, -sa *adj* : costly, burdensome

graznar *vi* : caw, quack, honk —
graznido *nm* : caw, quack, honk

gregario, -ria *adj* : gregarious

gremio *nm* : guild, (trade) union

greñas *nfpl* : shaggy hair, mop

griego, -ga *adj* : Greek — **griego** *nm*
: Greek (language)

grieta *nf* : crack, crevice

grifo *nm Spain* : faucet, tap

grillete *nm* : shackle

grillo *nm* 1 : cricket 2 **~s** *nmpl* : fetters, shackles

grima *nf* **dar ~** : annoy, irritate

gringo, -ga *adj & n Lat fam* : Yankee, gringo

gripe *nf or* **gripa** *nf Lat* : flu, influenza

gris *adj & nm* : gray

gritar *v* : shout, scream, cry — **grito** *nm* 1 : shout, scream, cry 2 **dar ~s** : shout

grosella *nf* : currant

grosería *nf* 1 : vulgar remark 2 DESCORTESÍA : rudeness — **grosero, -ra** *adj* 1 : coarse, vulgar 2 DESCORTÉS : rude

grosor *nm* : thickness

grotesco, -ca *adj* : grotesque, hideous

grúa *nf* : crane, derrick

grueso, -sa *adj* 1 : thick 2 CORPULENTO : stout, heavy — **gruesa** *nf* : gross — **grueso** *nm* 1 GROSOR : thickness 2 : main body, mass 3 **en ~** : wholesale

grulla *nf* : crane (bird)

grumo *nm* : lump, clot — **grumoso, -sa** *adj* : lumpy

gruñir {38} *vi* 1 : growl, grunt 2 *fam* : grumble — **gruñido** *nm* 1 : growl, grunt 2 *fam* : grumble — **gruñón, -ñona** *adj, mpl* **-ñones** *fam* : grumpy, grouchy — **~** *n fam* : grouch

grupa *nf* : rump, hindquarters *pl*

grupo *nm* : group

gruta *nf* : grotto

guacamayo *nm or* **guacamaya** *nf Lat* : macaw

guacamole *nm* : guacamole

guadaña *nf* : scythe

guagua *nf Lat* 1 : baby 2 AUTOBÚS : bus

guajalote, -ta *or* **guajolote, -ta** *n Lat* : turkey

guante *nm* : glove

guapo, -pa *adj* : handsome, good-looking

guaraní *nm* : Guarani (language of Paraguay)

guarda *nmf* 1 : keeper, custodian 2 GUARDIÁN : security guard — **guardabarros** *nms & pl* : fender — **guardabosque** *nmf* : forest ranger — **guardacostas** *nmfs & pl* : coast guard vessel — **guardaespaldas** *nmfs & pl* : bodyguard — **guardameta** *nmf* : goalkeeper — **guardapolvo** *nm* : overalls *pl* — **guardar** *vt* 1 : keep 2 PROTEGER : guard, protect 3 RESERVAR : save — **guardarse** *vr* **~ de** 1 : refrain from 2 : guard against — **guardarropa** *nm* 1

: cloakroom, checkroom 2 ARMARIO : wardrobe

guardería *nf* : nursery, day-care center

guardia *nf* 1 : guard, vigilence 2 TURNO : duty, watch — **~** *nmf* 1 : guard 2 *or* **~ municipal** : police officer — **guardián, -diana** *n, mpl* **-dianes** 1 : guardian, keeper 2 GUARDA : security guard

guarecer {53} *vt* : shelter, protect — **guarecerse** *vr* : take shelter

guarida *nf* 1 : den, lair (of animals) 2 : hideout (of persons)

guarnecer {53} *vt* 1 : adorn, garnish 2 : garrison (an area) — **guarnición** *nf, pl* **-ciones** 1 : garnish, trimming 2 : (military) garrison

guasa *nf fam* 1 : joke 2 **de ~** : in jest — **guasón, -sona** *adj, mpl* **-sones** *fam* : joking, witty — **~** *n fam* : joker

guatemalteco, -ca *adj* : Guatemalan

guayaba *nf* : guava

gubernamental *or* **gubernativo, -va** *adj* : governmental

guepardo *nm* : cheetah

güero, -ra *adj Lat* : blond, fair

guerra *nf* 1 : war, warfare 2 LUCHA : conflict, struggle — **guerrear** *vi* : wage war — **guerrero, -ra** *adj* 1 : war, fighting 2 BELICOSO : warlike — **~** *n* : warrior — **guerrilla** *nf* : guerrilla warfare — **guerrillero, -ra** *adj & n* : guerrilla

gueto *nm* : ghetto

guiar {85} *vt* 1 : guide, lead 2 ACONSEJAR : advise — **guiarse** *vr* : be guided by, go by — **guía** *nf* 1 : guidebook 2 ORIENTACIÓN : guidance — **~** *nmf* : guide, leader

guijarro *nm* : pebble

guillotina *nf* : guillotine

guinda *nf* : morello (cherry)

guiñar *vi* : wink — **guiño** *nm* : wink

guión *nm, pl* **guiones** 1 : script, screenplay 2 : hyphen, dash (in punctuation) — **guionista** *nmf* : scriptwriter, screenwriter

guirnalda *nf* : garland

guisa *nf* 1 : manner, fashion 2 **a ~ de** : by way of 3 **de tal ~** : in such a way

guisado *nm* : stew

guisante *nm* : pea

guisar *vt* : cook — **guiso** *nm* : stew, casserole

guitarra *nf* : guitar — **guitarrista** *nmf* : guitarist

gula *nf* : gluttony

gusano *nm* 1 : worm 2 : maggot (larva)

gustar *vt* 1 : taste 2 *Lat* : like — *vi* 1 : be pleasing 2 **como guste** : as you like 3

me gustan los dulces : I like sweets
— **gusto** nm 1 : taste 2 PLACER : pleasure, liking 3 a ~ : comfortable, at ease 4 al ~ : to taste 5 mucho ~ : pleased to meet you — **gustoso, -sa** adj 1 : tasty 2 AGRADABLE : pleasant 3 hacer algo ~ : do sth willingly

gutural adj : guttural

H

h nf : h, eighth letter of the Spanish alphabet

haba nf : broad bean

habanero, -ra adj : Havanan — **habano** nm : Havana cigar

haber {39} v aux 1 : have, has 2 ~ de : must — v impers 1 **hay** : there is, there are 2 **hay que** : it is necessary (to) 3 ¿**qué hay?** or ¿**qué hubo?** : how's it going? — ~ nm 1 : assets pl 2 : credit side (in accounting) 3 ~**es** nmpl : income, earnings

habichuela nf 1 : bean 2 ~ **verde** : string bean

hábil adj 1 : able, skillful 2 LISTO : clever 3 **horas** ~**es** : business hours — **habilidad** nf : ability, skill

habilitar vt 1 : equip, furnish 2 AUTORIZAR : authorize

habitar vt : inhabit — vi : reside, dwell — **habitable** adj : habitable, inhabitable — **habitación** nf, pl **-ciones** 1 : room, bedroom 2 MORADA : dwelling, abode 3 : habitat (in biology) — **habitante** nmf : inhabitant, resident — **hábitat** nm : habitat

hábito nm : habit — **habitual** adj : habitual, usual — **habituar** {3} vt : accustom, habituate — **habituarse** vr ~ a : get used to

hablar vi 1 : speak, talk 2 ~ de : mention, talk about 3 ~ **con** : talk to, speak with — vt 1 : speak (a language) 2 DISCUTIR : discuss — **hablarse** vr 1 : speak to each other 2 **se habla inglés** : English spoken — **habla** nf 1 : speech 2 IDIOMA : language, dialect 3 **de** ~ **inglesa** : English-speaking — **hablador, -dora** adj : talkative — ~ n : chatterbox — **habladuría** nf 1 : rumor 2 ~**s** nfpl : gossip — **hablante** nmf : speaker

hacedor, -dora n : creator, maker

hacendado, -da n : landowner, rancher

hacer {40} vt 1 : do, perform 2 CONSTRUIR, CREAR : make 3 OBLIGAR : force, oblige — vi : act — v impers 1 ~ **calor/viento** : be hot/be windy 2 ~ **falta** : be necessary 3 **hace mucho tiempo** : a long time ago 4 **no lo hace** : it doesn't matter — **hacerse** vr 1 VOLVERSE : become 2 : pretend (to be) 3 ~ **a** : get used to 4 **se hace tarde** : it's getting late

hacha nf 1 : hatchet, ax 2 ANTORCHA : torch

hachís nm : hashish

hacia prep 1 : toward, towards 2 CERCA DE : near, around, about 3 ~ **abajo** : downward 4 ~ **adelante** : forward

hacienda nf 1 : estate, ranch 2 BIENES : property 3 Lat : livestock 4 **Hacienda** : department of revenue

hacinar vt : stack

hada nf : fairy

hado nm : fate

halagar {52} vt : flatter — **halagador, -dora** adj : flattering — **halago** nm : flattery — **halagüeño, -ña** adj 1 : flattering 2 PROMETEDOR : promising

halcón nm, pl **-cones** : hawk, falcon

halibut nm, pl **-buts** : halibut

hálito nm : breath

hallar vt 1 : find 2 DESCUBRIR : discover, find out — **hallarse** vr : be, find oneself — **hallazgo** nm : discovery, find

halo nm : halo

hamaca nf : hammock

hambre nf 1 : hunger 2 INANICIÓN : starvation, famine 3 **tener** ~ : be hungry — **hambriento, -ta** adj : hungry, starving — **hambruna** nf : famine

hamburguesa nf : hamburger

hampa nf : underworld — **hampón, -pona** n, mpl **-pones** : criminal, thug

hámster nm : hamster

hándicap nm : handicap (in sports)

hangar nm : hangar

haragán, -gana adj, mpl **-ganes** : lazy, idle — ~ n : slacker, idler — **haraganear** vi : be lazy, loaf

harapiento, -ta adj : ragged, in rags — **harapos** nmpl : rags, tatters

harina nf : flour

hartar vt 1 : glut, satiate 2 FASTIDIAR : annoy — **hartarse** vr 1 : gorge oneself 2 CANSARSE : get fed up — **harto, -ta** adj 1 : full, satiated 2 CANSADO : tired, fed up — **harto** adv : extremely, very — **hartura** nf 1 : surfeit 2 ABUNDANCIA : abundance, plenty

hasta prep 1 : until, up until (in time) 2

: as far as, up to (in space) **3 ¡~
luego!** : see you later! **4 ~ que** : until
— **~ adv** : even

hastiar {85} *vt* **1** : make weary, bore **2**
ASQUEAR : sicken — **hastiarse** *vr* **~
de** : get tired of — **hastío** *nm* **1** : weariness, tedium **2** REPUGNANCIA : disgust

hato *nm* **1** : flock, herd **2** : bundle (of
possessions)

haya *nf* : beech

haz *nm, pl* **haces 1** : bundle, sheaf **2**
: beam (of light)

hazaña *nf* : feat, exploit

hazmerreír *nm fam* : laughingstock

he {39} *v impers* **~ aquí** : here is, here
are, behold

hebilla *nf* : buckle

hebra *nf* : strand, thread

hebreo, -brea *adj* : Hebrew — **hebreo**
nm : Hebrew (language)

hecatombe *nm* : disaster

hechizo *nm* **1** : spell **2** ENCANTO : charm,
fascination — **hechicería** *nf* : sorcery,
witchcraft — **hechicero, -ra** *n* : sorcerer, sorceress *f* — **hechizar** {21} *vt* **1**
: bewitch **2** CAUTIVAR : charm

hecho, -cha *adj* **1** : made, done **2**
: ready-to-wear (of clothing) **3 ~ y
derecho** : full-fledged, mature —
hecho *nm* **1** : fact **2** SUCESO : event **3**
ACTO : act, deed **4 de ~** : in fact —
hechura *nf* **1** : making, creation **2**
FORMA : shape, form **3** : build (of the
body) **4** ARTESANÍA : workmanship

heder {56} *vi* : stink, reek — **hedion-
dez** *nf, pl* **-deces** : stench — **hedion-
do, -da** *adj* : stinking — **hedor** *nm*
: stench

helar {55} *v* : freeze — **helarse** *vr*
: freeze up, freeze over — **helado, -da**
adj **1** : freezing cold **2** CONGELADO
: frozen — **helada** *nf* : frost —
heladería *nf* : ice-cream parlor —
helado *nm* : ice cream — **heladora** *nf*
: freezer

helecho *nm* : fern

hélice *nf* **1** : propeller **2** ESPIRAL : spiral,
helix

helicóptero *nm* : helicopter

helio *nm* : helium

hembra *nf* **1** : female **2** MUJER : woman

hemisferio *nm* : hemisphere

hemorragia *nf* **1** : hemorrhage **2 ~
nasal** : nosebleed

hemorroides *nfpl* : hemorrhoids, piles

henchir {54} *vt* : stuff, fill

hender {56} *vt* : cleave, split — **hendidura** *nf* : crevice, fissure

henequén *nm, pl* **-quenes** : sisal

heno *nm* : hay

hepatitis *nf* : hepatitis

heraldo *nm* : herald

herbolario, -ria *n* : herbalist

heredar *vt* : inherit — **heredad** *nm*
: rural property, estate — **heredero,
-ra** *n* : heir, heiress *f* — **hereditario,
-ria** *adj* : hereditary

hereje *nmf* : heretic — **herejía** *nf*
: heresy

herencia *nf* **1** : inheritance **2** : heredity
(in biology)

herir {76} *vt* **1** : injure, wound **2** : hurt
(feelings, pride, etc.) — **herida** *nf* : injury, wound — **herido, -da** *adj* **1** : injured, wounded **2** : hurt (of feelings,
pride, etc.) — **~** *n* : injured person,
casualty

hermano, -na *n* : brother *m*, sister *f* —
hermanastro, -tra *n* : half brother *m*,
half sister *f* — **hermandad** *nf* : brotherhood

hermético, -ca *adj* : hermetic, watertight

hermoso, -sa *adj* : beautiful, lovely —
hermosura *nf* : beauty

hernia *nf* : hernia

héroe *nm* : hero — **heroico, -ca** *adj*
: heroic — **heroína** *nf* **1** : heroine **2**
: heroin (narcotic) — **heroísmo** *nm*
: heroism

herradura *nf* : horseshoe

herramienta *nf* : tool

herrero, -ra *n* : blacksmith

herrumbre *nf* : rust

hervir {76} *v* **1** : boil — **hervidero** *nm* **1**
: mass, swarm **2** : hotbed (of intrigue,
etc.) — **hervidor** *nm* : kettle — **fervor**
nm **1** : boiling **2** ENTUSIASMO : fervor,
ardor

heterogéneo, -nea *adj* : heterogeneous

heterosexual *adj & nmf* : heterosexual

hexágono *nm* : hexagon — **hexagonal**
adj : hexagonal

hez *nf, pl* **heces** : dregs *pl*, scum

hiato *nm* : hiatus

hibernar *vi* : hibernate — **hibernación**
nf, pl **-ciones** : hibernation

híbrido, -da *adj* : hybrid — **híbrido** *nm*
: hybrid

hidalgo, -ga *n* : nobleman *m*, noble-
woman *f*

hidratante *adj* : moisturizing

hidrato *nm* **~ de carbono** : carbohydrate

hidráulico, -ca *adj* : hydraulic

hidroavión *nm, pl* **-aviones** : seaplane

hidroeléctrico, -ca *adj* : hydroelectric

hidrofobia *nf* : rabies

hidrógeno *nm* : hydrogen

hidroplano *nm* : hydroplane

hiedra *nf* 1 : ivy 2 ~ **venenosa** : poison ivy

hiel *nm* 1 : bile 2 AMARGURA : bitterness

hielo *nm* 1 : ice 2 FRIALDAD : coldness 3 **romper el** ~ : break the ice

hiena *nf* : hyena

hierba *nf* 1 : herb 2 CÉSPED : grass 3 **mala** ~ : weed — **hierbabuena** *nf* : mint

hierro *nm* 1 : iron 2 ~ **fundido** : cast iron

hígado *nm* : liver

higiene *nf* : hygiene — **higiénico, -ca** *adj* : hygienic

higo *nm* : fig

hijo, -ja *n* 1 : son *m*, daughter *f* 2 **hijos** *nmpl* : children, offspring — **hijastro, -tra** *n* : stepson *m*, stepdaughter *f*

hilar *v* 1 : spin 2 ~ **delgado** : split hairs — **hilado** *nm* : yarn, thread

hilaridad *nf* : hilarity

hilera *nf* : file, row

hilo *nm* 1 : thread 2 LINO : linen 3 ALAMBRE : wire 4 : trickle (of water, etc.) 5 ~ **dental** : dental floss

hilvanar *vt* 1 : baste, tack 2 : put together (ideas, etc.)

himno *nm* 1 : hymn 2 ~ **nacional** : national anthem

hincapié *nm* **hacer** ~ **en** : emphasize, stress

hincar {72} *vt* : drive in, plunge — **hincarse** *vr* ~ **de rodillas** : kneel (down)

hinchar *vt Spain* : inflate, blow up — **hincharse** *vr* 1 : swell (up) 2 *Spain fam* : stuff oneself — **hinchado, -da** *adj* 1 : swollen 2 POMPOSO : pompous — **hinchazón** *nf, pl* **-zones** : swelling

hindú *adj & nmf* : Hindu — **hinduismo** *nm* : Hinduism

hinojo *nm* : fennel

hiperactivo, -va *adj* : hyperactive

hipersensible *adj* : oversensitive

hipertensión *nf, pl* **-siones** : hypertension, high blood pressure

hípico, -ca *adj* : equestrian, horse

hipil → **huipil**

hipnosis *nfs & pl* : hypnosis — **hipnótico, -ca** *adj* : hypnotic — **hipnotismo** *nm* : hypnotism — **hipnotizador, -dora** *n* : hypnotist — **hipnotizar** {21} *vt* : hypnotize

hipo *nm* 1 : hiccup, hiccups *pl* 2 **tener** ~ : have hiccups

hipocondríaco, -ca *adj* : hypochondriacal — ~ *n* : hypochondriac

hipocresía *nf* : hypocrisy — **hipócrita** *adj* : hypocritical — ~ *nmf* : hypocrite

hipodérmico, -ca *adj* : hypodermic

hipódromo *nm* : racetrack

hipopótamo *nm* : hippopotamus

hipoteca *nf* : mortgage — **hipotecar** {72} *vt* : mortgage

hipótesis *nfs & pl* : hypothesis — **hipotético, -ca** *adj* : hypothetical

hiriente *adj* : hurtful, offensive

hirsuto, -ta *adj* 1 : hairy 2 : bristly, wiry (of hair)

hirviente *adj* : boiling

hispano, -na *or* **hispánico, -ca** *adj & n* : Hispanic — **hispanoamericano, -na** *adj* : Latin-American — ~ *n* : Latin American — **hispanohablante** *or* **hispanoparlante** *adj* : Spanish-speaking

histeria *nf* : hysteria — **histérico, -ca** *adj* : hysterical — **histerismo** *nm* : hysteria

historia *nf* 1 : history 2 CUENTO : story — **historiador, -dora** *n* : historian — **historial** *nm* : record, background — **histórico, -ca** *adj* 1 : historical 2 IMPORTANTE : historic, important — **historieta** *nf* : comic strip

hito *nm* : milestone, landmark

hocico *nm* : snout, muzzle

hockey ['hɔke, -ki] *nm* : hockey

hogar *nm* 1 : home 2 CHIMENEA : hearth, fireplace — **hogareño, -ña** *adj* 1 : home-loving 2 DOMÉSTICO : home, domestic

hoguera *nf* : bonfire

hoja *nf* 1 : leaf 2 : sheet (of paper) 3 ~ **de afeitar** : razor blade — **hojalata** *nf* : tinplate — **hojaldre** *nm* : puff pastry — **hojear** *vt* : leaf through — **hojuela** *nf Lat* : flake

hola *interj* : hello!, hi!

holandés, -desa *adj, mpl* **-deses** : Dutch

holgado, -da *adj* 1 : loose, baggy 2 : comfortable (of an economic situation, a victory, etc.) — **holgazán, -zana** *adj, mpl* **-zanes** : lazy — ~ *n* : slacker, idler — **holgazanear** *vi* : laze about, loaf — **holgura** *nf* 1 : looseness 2 BIENESTAR : comfort, ease

hollín *nm, pl* **-llines** : soot

holocausto *nm* : holocaust

hombre *nm* 1 : man 2 **el** ~ : mankind 3 ~ **de estado** : statesman 4 ~ **de negocios** : businessman

hombrera *nf* 1 : shoulder pad 2 : epaulet (of a uniform)

hombría *nf* : manliness

hombro *nm* : shoulder

hombruno, -na *adj* : mannish

homenaje *nm* **1** : homage **2 rendir ~ a** : pay tribute to

homeopatía *nf* : homeopathy

homicidio *nm* : homicide, murder — **homicida** *adj* : homicidal, murderous — **~** *nmf* : murderer

homogéneo, -nea *adj* : homogeneous

homólogo, -ga *adj* : equivalent — **~** *n* : counterpart

homosexual *adj & nmf* : homosexual — **homosexualidad** *nf* : homosexuality

hondo, -da *adj* : deep — **hondo** *adv* : deeply — **hondonada** *nf* : hollow

hondura *nf* : depth

hondureño, -ña *adj* : Honduran

honesto, -ta *adj* : decent, honorable — **honestidad** *nf* : honesty, integrity

hongo *nm* **1** : mushroom **2** : fungus (in botany and medicine)

honor *nm* : honor — **honorable** *adj* : honorable — **honorario, -ria** *adj* : honorary — **honorarios** *nmpl* : payment, fee — **honra** *nf* : honor — **honradez** *nf, pl* **-deces** : honesty, integrity — **honrado, -da** *adj* : honest, upright — **honrar** *vt* : honor — **honrarse** *vr* : be honored — **honroso, -sa** *adj* : honorable

hora *nf* **1** : hour **2** : (specific) time **3** CITA : appointment **4 a la última ~** : at the last minute **5 ~ punta** : rush hour **6 media ~** : half an hour **7 ¿qué ~ es?** : what time is it? **8 ~s de oficina** : office hours **9 ~s extraordinarias** : overtime

horario *nm* : schedule, timetable

horca *nf* **1** : gallows *pl* **2** : pitchfork (in agriculture)

horcajadas: a ~ *adv phr* : astride

horda *nf* : horde

horizonte *nm* : horizon — **horizontal** *adj* : horizontal

horma *nf* **1** : form, mold, last **2** : shoe tree

hormiga *nf* : ant

hormigón *nm, pl* **-gones** : concrete

hormigueo *nm* : tingling, pins and needles

hormiguero *nm* **1** : anthill **2** : swarm (of people)

hormona *nf* : hormone

horno *nm* **1** : oven (for cooking) **2** : small furnace, kiln — **hornada** *nf* : batch — **hornear** *vt* : bake — **hornillo** *nf* : portable stove

horóscopo *nm* : horoscope

horquilla *nf* **1** : hairpin, bobby pin **2** HORCA : pitchfork

horrendo, -da *adj* : horrendous, awful

horrible *adj* : horrible — **horripilante** *adj* : horrifying — **horror** *nm* **1** : horror, dread **2** ATROCIDAD : atrocity — **horrorizar** {21} *vt* : horrify, terrify — **horrorizarse** *vr* : be horrified — **horroroso, -sa** *adj* : horrifying, dreadful

hortaliza *nf* : (garden) vegetable — **hortelano, -na** *n* : truck farmer — **horticultura** *nf* : horticulture

hosco, -ca *adj* : sullen, gloomy

hospedar *vt* : put up, lodge — **hospedarse** *vr* : stay, lodge — **hospedaje** *nm* : lodging

hospital *nm* : hospital — **hospitalario, -ria** *adj* : hospitable — **hospitalidad** *nf* : hospitality — **hospitalizar** {21} *vt* : hospitalize

hostería *nf* : small hotel, inn

hostia *nf* : host (in religion)

hostigar {52} *vt* **1** : whip **2** ACOSAR : harass, pester

hostil *adj* : hostile — **hostilidad** *nf* : hostility

hotel *nm* : hotel — **hotelero, -ra** *adj* : hotel — **~** *n* : hotel manager, hotelier

hoy *adv* **1** : today **2 de ~ en adelante** : from now on **3 ~ (en) día** : nowadays **4 ~ mismo** : this very day

hoyo *nm* : hole — **hoyuelo** *nm* : dimple

hoz *nf, pl* **hoces** : sickle

huarache *nm* : huarache (sandal)

hueco, -ca *adj* **1** : hollow, empty **2** ESPONJOSO : soft, spongy **3** RESONANTE : resonant — **hueco** *nm* **1** : hollow, cavity **2** : recess (in a wall, etc.) **3 ~ de escalera** : stairwell

huelga *nf* **1** : strike **2 declararse en ~** : go on strike — **huelguista** *nmf* : striker

huella *nf* **1** : footprint **2** VESTIGIO : track, mark **3 ~ digital** *or* **~ dactilar** : fingerprint

huérfano, -na *n* : orphan — **~** *adj* : orphaned

huerta *nf* : truck farm — **huerto** *nm* **1** : vegetable garden **2** : (fruit) orchard

hueso *nm* **1** : bone **2** : pit, stone (of a fruit)

huésped, -peda *n* : guest — **huésped** *nm* : host (organism)

huesudo, -da *adj* : bony

huevo *nm* **1** : egg **2 ~s estrellados** : fried eggs **3 ~s revueltos** : scrambled eggs — **hueva** *nf* : roe

huida *nf* : flight, escape — **huidizo, -za** *adj* **1** : shy **2** FUGAZ : fleeting

huipil *nm Lat* : traditional embroidered blouse or dress

huir {41} *vi* **1** : escape, flee **2** ~ **de** : shun, avoid

hule *nm* **1** : oilcloth **2** *Lat* : rubber

humano, -na *adj* **1** : human **2** COMPASIVO : humane — **humano** *nm* : human (being) — **humanidad** *nf* **1** : humanity, mankind **2** BENEVOLENCIA : humaneness **3** ~**es** *nfpl* : humanities — **humanismo** *nm* : humanism — **humanista** *nmf* : humanist — **humanitario, -ria** *adj & n* : humanitarian

humear *vi* : smoke, steam — **humareda** *nf* : cloud of smoke

humedad *nf* **1** : dampness **2** : humidity (in meteorology) — **humedecer** {53} *vt* : moisten, dampen — **humedecerse** *vr* : become moist — **húmedo, -da** *adj* **1** : moist, damp **2** : humid (in meteorology)

humildad *nf* : humility — **humilde** *adj* : humble — **humillación** *nf, pl* **-ciones** : humiliation — **humillante** *adj* : humiliating — **humillar** *vt* : humiliate — **humillarse** *vr* : humble oneself

humo *nm* **1** : smoke, steam, fumes **2** ~**s** *nmpl* : airs, conceit

humor *nm* **1** : mood, temper **2** GRACIA : humor **3 de buen** ~ : in a good mood — **humorismo** *nm* : humor, wit — **humorista** *nmf* : humorist, comedian — **humorístico, -ca** *adj* : humorous

hundir *vt* **1** : sink **2** : destroy, ruin (a building, plans, etc.) — **hundirse** *vr* **1** : sink **2** DERRUMBARSE : collapse — **hundido, -da** *adj* : sunken — **hundimiento** *nm* **1** : sinking **2** DERRUMBE : collapse

húngaro, -ra *adj* : Hungarian

huracán *nm, pl* **-canes** : hurricane

huraño, -ña *adj* : unsociable

hurgar {52} *vi* ~ **en** : rummage around in

hurón *nm, pl* **-rones** : ferret

hurra *interj* : hurrah!, hooray!

hurtadillas: a ~ *adv phr* : stealthily, on the sly

hurtar *vt* : steal — **hurto** *nm* **1** ROBO : theft **2** : stolen property

husmear *vt* : sniff out, pry into — *vi* : nose around

huy *interj* : ow!, ouch!

I

i *nf* **1** : i, ninth letter of the Spanish alphabet

ibérico, -ca *adj* : Iberian — **ibero, -ra** *or* **íbero, -ra** *adj* : Iberian

iceberg *nm, pl* **-bergs** : iceberg

icono *nm* : icon

ictericia *nf* : jaundice

ida *nf* **1** : outward journey **2** ~ **y vuelta** : round-trip **3** ~**s y venidas** : comings and goings

idea *nf* **1** : idea **2** OPINIÓN : opinion

ideal *adj & nm* : ideal — **idealismo** *nm* : idealism — **idealista** *adj* : idealistic — ~ *nmf* : idealist — **idealizar** {21} *vt* : idealize

idear *vt* : devise, think up

ídem *nm* : the same, ditto

identidad *nf* : identity — **idéntico, -ca** *adj* : identical — **identificar** {72} *vt* : identify — **identificarse** *vr* **1** : identify oneself **2** ~ **con** : identify with — **identificación** *nf, pl* **-ciones** : identification

ideología *nf* : ideology — **ideológico, -ca** *adj* : ideological

idílico, -ca *adj* : idyllic

idioma *nm* : language — **idiomático, -ca** *adj* : idiomatic

idiosincrasia *nf* : idiosyncrasy — **idiosincrásico, -ca** *adj* : idiosyncratic

idiota *adj* : idiotic — ~ *nmf* : idiot — **idiotez** *nf* : idiocy

ídolo *nm* : idol — **idolatrar** *vt* : idolize — **idolatría** *nf* : idolatry

idóneo, -nea *adj* : suitable, fitting — **idoneidad** *nf* : fitness, suitability

iglesia *nf* : church

iglú *nm* : igloo

ignición *nf, pl* **-ciones** : ignition

ignífugo, -ga *adj* : fire-resistant, fireproof

ignorar *vt* **1** : ignore **2** DESCONOCER : be unaware of — **ignorancia** *nf* : ignorance — **ignorante** *adj* : ignorant — ~ *nmf* : ignorant person

igual *adv* **1** : in the same way **2 por** ~ : equally — ~ *adj* **1** : equal **2** IDÉNTICO : the same **3** LISO : smooth, even **4** SEMEJANTE : similar — ~ *nmf* : equal, peer — **igualar** *vt* **1** : make equal **2** : be equal to **3** NIVELAR : level (off) — **igualdad** *nf* **1** : equality **2** UNIFORMI-

DAD : uniformity — **igualmente** *adv* : likewise

iguana *nf* : iguana

ijada *nf* : flank

ilegal *adj* : illegal

ilegible *adj* : illegible

ilegítimo, -ma *adj* : illegitimate — **ilegitimidad** *nf* : illegitimacy

ileso, -sa *adj* : unharmed

ilícito, -ta *adj* : illicit

ilimitado, -da *adj* : unlimited

ilógico, -ca *adj* : illogical

iluminar *vt* : illuminate — **iluminarse** *vr* : light up — **iluminación** *nf, pl* **-ciones** 1 : illumination 2 ALUMBRADO : lighting

ilusionar *vt* : excite — **ilusionarse** *vr* : get one's hopes up — **ilusión** *nf, pl* **-siones** 1 : illusion 2 ESPERANZA : hope — **ilusionado, -da** *adj* : excited

iluso -sa *adj* : naïve, gullible — **~** *n* : dreamer, visionary — **ilusorio, -ria** *adj* : illusory

ilustrar *vt* 1 : illustrate 2 ACLARAR : explain — **ilustración** *nf, pl* **-ciones** 1 : illustration 2 SABER : learning 3 **la Ilustración** : the Enlightenment — **ilustrado, -da** *adj* 1 : illustrated 2 ERUDITO : learned — **ilustrador, -dora** *n* : illustrator

ilustre *adj* : illustrious

imagen *nf, pl* **imágenes** : image, picture

imaginar *vt* : imagine — **imaginarse** *vr* : imagine — **imaginación** *nf, pl* **-ciones** : imagination — **imaginario, -ria** *adj* : imaginary — **imaginativo, -va** *adj* : imaginative

imán *nm, pl* **imanes** : magnet — **imantar** *vt* : magnetize

imbécil *adj* : stupid, idiotic — **~** *nmf* : idiot

imborrable *adj* : indelible

imbuir {41} *vt* **~ de** : imbue with

imitar *vt* 1 COPIAR : imitate, copy 2 : impersonate — **imitación** *nf, pl* **-ciones** 1 COPIA : imitation, copy 2 : impersonation — **imitador, -dora** *n* : impersonator

impaciencia *nf* : impatience — **impacientar** *vt* : make impatient, exasperate —**impacientarse** *vr* : grow impatient — **impaciente** *adj* : impatient

impacto *nm* : impact

impar *adj* : odd — **~** *nm* : odd number

imparcial *adj* : impartial — **imparcialidad** *nf* : impartiality

impartir *vt* : impart, give

impasible *adj* : impassive

impasse *nm* : impasse

impávido, -da *adj* : fearless

impecable *adj* : impeccable, spotless

impedir {54} *vt* 1 : prevent 2 DIFICULTAR : impede, hinder — **impedido, -da** *adj* : disabled — **impedimento** *nm* : obstacle, impediment

impeler *vt* : drive, propel

impenetrable *adj* : impenetrable

impenitente *adj* : unrepentant

impensable *adj* : unthinkable — **impensado, -da** *adj* : unexpected

imperar *vi* 1 : reign, rule 2 PREDOMINAR : prevail — **imperante** *adj* : prevailing

imperativo, -va *adj* : imperative — **imperativo** *nm* : imperative

imperceptible *adj* : imperceptible

imperdible *nm* : safety pin

imperdonable *adj* : unforgivable

imperfección *nf, pl* **-ciones** : imperfection — **imperfecto, -ta** *adj* : imperfect — **imperfecto** *nm* : imperfect (tense)

imperial *adj* : imperial — **imperialismo** *nm* : imperialism — **imperialista** *adj & nmf* : imperialist

impericia *nf* : lack of skill

imperio *nm* 1 : empire 2 DOMINIO : rule — **imperioso, -sa** *adj* 1 : imperious 2 URGENTE : pressing, urgent

impermeable *adj* 1 : waterproof 2 **~ a** : impervious to — **~** *nm* : raincoat

impersonal *adj* : impersonal

impertinente *adj* : impertinent — **impertinencia** *nf* : impertinence

ímpetu *nm* 1 : impetus 2 ENERGÍA : energy, vigor 3 VIOLENCIA : force — **impetuoso, -sa** *adj* : impetuous — **impetuosidad** *nf* : impetuosity

impío, -pía *adj* : impious, ungodly

implacable *adj* : implacable

implantar *vt* 1 : implant 2 ESTABLECER : establish, introduce

implemento *nm Lat* : implement, tool

implicar {72} *vt* 1 : involve, implicate 2 SIGNIFICAR : imply — **implicación** *nf, pl* **-ciones** : implication

implícito, -ta *adj* : implicit

implorar *vt* : implore

imponer {60} *vt* 1 : impose 2 : command (respect, etc.) — *vi* : be imposing — **imponerse** *vr* 1 : assert oneself, command respect 2 PREVALECER : prevail — **imponente** *adj* : imposing, impressive — **imponible** *adj* : taxable

impopular *adj* : unpopular — **impopularidad** *nf* : unpopularity

importación *nf, pl* **-ciones** 1 : importation 2 **importaciones** *nfpl* : imports — **importado, -da** *adj* : imported — **importador, -dora** *adj* : importing — **~** *n* : importer

importancia *nf* : importance — **importante** *adj* : important — **importar** *vi* 1 : matter, be important 2 **no me importa** : I don't care — *vt* 1 : import 2 ASCENDER A : amount to, cost

importe *nm* 1 : price 2 CANTIDAD : sum, amount

importunar *vt* : bother — **importuno, -na** *adj* 1 : inopportune 2 MOLESTO : bothersome

imposible *adj* : impossible — **imposibilidad** *nf* : impossibility

imposición *nf, pl* **-ciones** 1 : imposition 2 IMPUESTO : tax

impostor, -tora *n* : impostor

impotente *adj* : powerless, impotent — **impotencia** *nf* : impotence

impracticable *adj* 1 : impracticable 2 INTRANSITABLE : impassable

impreciso, -sa *adj* : vague, imprecise — **imprecisión** *nf, pl* **-siones** 1 : vagueness 2 ERROR : inaccuracy

impredecible *adj* : unpredictable

impregnar *vt* : impregnate

imprenta *nf* 1 : printing 2 : printing shop, press

imprescindible *adj* : essential, indispensable

impresión *nf, pl* **-siones** 1 : impression 2 IMPRENTA : printing — **impresionable** *adj* : impressionable — **impresionante** *adj* : impressive — **impresionar** *vt* 1 : impress 2 CONMOVER : affect, move — *vi* : make an impression — **impresionarse** *vr* 1 : be impressed 2 CONMOVERSE : be affected

impreso, -sa *adj* : printed — **impreso** *nm* 1 FORMULARIO : form 2 **~s** *nmpl* : printed matter — **impresor, -sora** *n* : printer — **impresora** *nf* : (computer) printer

imprevisible *adj* : unforeseeable — **imprevisto, -ta** *adj* : unexpected, unforeseen

imprimir {42} *vt* 1 : print 2 DAR : impart, give

improbable *adj* : improbable — **improbabilidad** *nf* : improbability

improcedente *adj* : inappropriate

improductivo, -va *adj* : unproductive

improperio *nm* : insult

impropio, -pia *adj* 1 : inappropriate 2 INCORRECTO : incorrect

improvisar *v* : improvise — **improvisado, -da** *adj* : improvised, impromptu — **improvisación** *nf, pl* **-ciones** : improvisation — **improviso: de ~** *adv phr* : suddenly

imprudente *adj* : imprudent, rash —

imprudencia *nf* : imprudence, carelessness

impúdico, -ca *adj* : shameless, indecent

impuesto *nm* 1 : tax 2 **~ sobre la renta** : income tax

impugnar *vt* : challenge, contest

impulsar *vt* : propel, drive — **impulsividad** *nf* : impulsiveness — **impulsivo, -va** *adj* : impulsive — **impulso** *nm* 1 : drive, thrust 2 MOTIVACIÓN : impulse

impune *adj* : unpunished — **impunidad** *nf* : impunity

impuro, -ra *adj* : impure — **impureza** *nf* : impurity

imputar *vt* : impute, attribute

inacabable *adj* : interminable, endless

inaccesible *adj* : inaccessible

inaceptable *adj* : unacceptable

inactivo, -va *adj* : inactive — **inactividad** *nf* : inactivity

inadaptado, -da *adj* : maladjusted — **~** *n* : misfit

inadecuado, -da *adj* 1 : inadequate 2 INAPROPIADO : inappropriate

inadmisible *adj* : inadmissible

inadvertido, -da *adj* 1 : unnoticed 2 DISTRAÍDO : distracted — **inadvertencia** *nf* : oversight

inagotable *adj* : inexhaustible

inaguantable *adj* : unbearable

inalámbrico, -ca *adj* : wireless, cordless

inalcanzable *adj* : unreachable, unattainable

inalterable *adj* 1 : unchangeable 2 : impassive (of character) 3 : fast (of colors)

inanición *nf, pl* **-ciones** : starvation, famine

inanimado, -da *adj* : inanimate

inaplicable *adj* : inapplicable

inapreciable *adj* : imperceptible

inapropiado, -da *adj* : inappropriate

inarticulado, -da *adj* : inarticulate

inasequible *adj* : unattainable

inaudito, -ta *adj* : unheard-of, unprecedented

inaugurar *vt* : inaugurate — **inauguración** *nf, pl* **-ciones** : inauguration — **inaugural** *adj* : inaugural

inca *adj* : Inca, Incan

incalculable *adj* : incalculable

incandescencia *nf* : incandescence — **incandescente** *adj* : incandescent

incansable *adj* : tireless

incapacitar *vt* : incapacitate, disable — **incapacidad** *nf* : incapacity, inability — **incapaz** *adj, pl* **-paces** : incapable

incautar *vt* : confiscate, seize

incendiar *vt* : set fire to, burn (down) — **incendiarse** *vr* : catch fire — **incendiario, -ria** *adj* : incendiary — ~ *n* : arsonist — **incendio** *nm* 1 : fire 2 ~ **premeditado** : arson

incentivo *nm* : incentive

incertidumbre *nf* : uncertainty

incesante *adj* : incessant

incesto *nm* : incest — **incestuoso, -sa** *adj* : incestuous

incidencia *nf* 1 : impact 2 SUCESO : incident — **incidental** *adj* : incidental — **incidente** *nm* : incident

incidir *vi* ~ **en** 1 : fall into (a habit, mistake, etc.) 2 INFLUIR EN : affect, influence

incienso *nm* : incense

incierto, -ta *adj* : uncertain

incinerar *vt* 1 : incinerate 2 : cremate (a corpse) — **incineración** *nf, pl* -**ciones** 1 : incineration 2 : cremation (of a corpse) — **incinerador** *nm* : incinerator

incipiente *adj* : incipient

incisión *nf, pl* -**siones** : incision

incisivo, -va *adj* : incisive — **incisivo** *nm* : incisor

incitar *vt* : incite, rouse

incivilizado, -da *adj* : uncivilized

inclinar *vt* : tilt, lean — **inclinarse** *vr* 1 : lean (over) 2 ~ **a** : be inclined to — **inclinación** *nf, pl* -**ciones** 1 : inclination 2 LADEAR : incline, tilt

incluir {41} *vt* 1 : include 2 ADJUNTAR : enclose — **inclusión** *nf, pl* -**siones** : inclusion — **inclusive** *adv* : up to and including — **inclusivo, -va** *adj* : inclusive — **incluso** *adv* : even, in fact — **incluso, -sa** *adj* : enclosed

incógnito, -ta *adj* 1 : unknown 2 **de** ~ : incognito

incoherente *adj* : incoherent — **incoherencia** *nf* : incoherence

incoloro, -ra *adj* : colorless

incombustible *adj* : fireproof

incomible *adj* : inedible

incomodar *vt* 1 : inconvenience 2 ENFADAR : bother, annoy — **incomodarse** *vr* 1 : take the trouble 2 ENFADARSE : get annoyed — **incomodidad** *nf* : discomfort — **incómodo, -da** *adj* 1 : uncomfortable 2 INCONVENIENTE : inconvenient, awkward

incomparable *adj* : incomparable

incompatible *adj* : incompatible — **incompatibilidad** *nf* : incompatibility

incompetente *adj* : incompetent — **incompetencia** *nf* : incompetence

incompleto, -ta *adj* : incomplete

incomprendido, -da *adj* : misunderstood — **incomprensible** *adj* : incomprehensible — **incomprensión** *nf, pl* -**siones** : lack of understanding

incomunicado, -da *adj* 1 : isolated 2 : in solitary confinement

inconcebible *adj* : inconceivable

inconcluso, -sa *adj* : unfinished

incondicional *adj* : unconditional

inconformista *adj & nmf* : nonconformist

inconfundible *adj* : unmistakable

incongruente *adj* : incongruous

inconmensurable *adj* : vast, immeasurable

inconsciente *adj* 1 : unconscious, unaware 2 IRREFLEXIVO : reckless — ~ *nm* **el** ~ : the unconscious — **inconsciencia** *nf* 1 : unconsciousness 2 INSENSATEZ : thoughtlessness

inconsecuente *adj* : inconsistent — **inconsecuencia** *nf* : inconsistency

inconsiderado, -da *adj* : inconsiderate

inconsistente *adj* 1 : flimsy 2 : watery (of a sauce, etc.) 3 : inconsistent (of an argument) — **inconsistencia** *nf* : inconsistency

inconsolable *adj* : inconsolable

inconstante *adj* : changeable, unreliable — **inconstancia** *nf* : inconstancy

inconstitucional *adj* : unconstitutional

incontable *adj* : countless

incontenible *adj* : irrepressible

incontestable *adj* : indisputable

incontinente *adj* : incontinent — **incontinencia** *nf* : incontinence

inconveniente *adj* 1 : inconvenient 2 INAPROPIADO : inappropriate — ~ *nm* : obstacle, problem — **inconveniencia** *nf* 1 : inconvenience 2 : tactless remark

incorporar *vt* 1 AGREGAR : incorporate, add 2 : mix (in cooking) — **incorporarse** *vr* 1 : sit up 2 ~ **a** : join — **incorporación** *nf, pl* -**ciones** : incorporation

incorrecto, -ta *adj* 1 : incorrect 2 DESCORTÉS : impolite

incorregible *adj* : incorrigible

incrédulo, -la *adj* : incredulous — **incredulidad** *nf* : incredulity, disbelief

increíble *adj* : incredible, unbelievable

incrementar *vt* : increase — **incremento** *nm* : increase

incriminar *vt* 1 : incriminate 2 ACUSAR : accuse

incrustar *vt* : set, inlay — **incrustarse** *vr* : become embedded

incubar *vt* : incubate — **incubadora** *nf* : incubator

incuestionable *adj* : unquestionable
inculcar {72} *vt* : instill
inculpar *vt* : accuse, charge
inculto, -ta *adj* 1 : uneducated 2 : uncultivated (of land)
incumplimiento *nm* 1 : noncompliance 2 ~ **de contrato** : breach of contract
incurable *adj* : incurable
incurrir *vi* ~ **en** 1 : incur (expenses, etc.) 2 : fall into, commit (crimes)
incursión *nf, pl* **-siones** : raid
indagar {52} *vt* : investigate — **indagación** *nf, pl* **-ciones** : investigation
indebido, -da *adj* : undue
indecente *adj* : indecent, obscene — **indecencia** *nf* : indecency, obscenity
indecible *adj* : inexpressible
indecisión *nf, pl* **-siones** : indecision — **indeciso, -sa** *adj* 1 : undecided 2 IRRESOLUTO : indecisive
indefenso, -sa *adj* : defenseless, helpless
indefinido, -da *adj* : indefinite — **indefinidamente** *adv* : indefinitely
indeleble *adj* : indelible
indemnizar {21} *vt* : indemnify, compensate — **indemnización** *nf, pl* **-ciones** : compensation
independiente *adj* : independent — **independencia** *nf* : independence — **independizarse** {21} *vr* : become independent
indescifrable *adj* : indecipherable
indescriptible *adj* : indescribable
indeseable *adj* : undesirable
indestructible *adj* : indestructible
indeterminado, -da *adj* : indeterminate
indicar {72} *vt* 1 : indicate 2 MOSTRAR : show — **indicación** *nf, pl* **-ciones** 1 : sign, indication 2 **indicaciones** *nfpl* : directions — **indicador** *nm* 1 : sign, signal 2 : gauge, dial, meter — **indicativo, -va** *adj* : indicative — **indicativo** *nm* : indicative (mood)
índice *nm* 1 : indication 2 : index (of a book, etc.) 3 : index finger 4 ~ **de natalidad** : birth rate
indicio *nm* : indication, sign
indiferente *adj* 1 : indifferent 2 **me es** ~ : it doesn't matter to me — **indiferencia** *nf* : indifference
indígena *adj* : indigenous, native — ~ *nmf* : native
indigente *adj & nmf* : indigent — **indigencia** *nf* : poverty
indigestión *nf, pl* **-tiones** : indigestion — **indigesto, -ta** *adj* : indigestible
indignar *vt* : outrage, infuriate — **indignarse** *vr* : become indignant — **indignación** *nf, pl* **-ciones** : indignation

— indignado, -da *adj* : indignant — **indignidad** *nf* : indignity — **indigno, -na** *adj* : unworthy
indio, -dia *adj* 1 : American Indian 2 : Indian (from India)
indirecta *nf* 1 : hint 2 **lanzar una** ~ : drop a hint — **indirecto, -ta** *adj* : indirect
indisciplina *nf* : lack of discipline — **indisciplinado, -da** *adj* : undisciplined
indiscreto, -ta *adj* : indiscreet — **indiscreción** *nf, pl* **-ciones** 1 : indiscretion 2 : tactless remark
indiscriminado, -da *adj* : indiscriminate
indiscutible *adj* : indisputable
indispensable *adj* : indispensable
indisponer {60} *vt* 1 : upset, make ill 2 ENEMISTAR : set against, set at odds — **indisponerse** *vr* 1 : become ill 2 ~ **con** : fall out with — **indisposición** *nf, pl* **-ciones** : indisposition, illness — **indispuesto, -ta** *adj* : unwell, indisposed
indistinto, -ta *adj* : indistinct
individual *adj* : individual — **individualidad** *nf* : individuality — **individualizar** {21} *vt* : individualize — **individuo** *nm* : individual
indivisible *adj* : indivisible
índole *nf* 1 : nature, character 2 TIPO : type, kind
indolente *adj* : indolent, lazy — **indolencia** *nf* : indolence, laziness
indoloro, -ra *adj* : painless
indómito, -ta *adj* : indomitable
indonesio, -sia *adj* : Indonesian
inducir {61} *vt* 1 : induce 2 DEDUCIR : infer
indudable *adj* : beyond doubt — **indudablemente** *adv* : undoubtedly
indulgente *adj* : indulgent — **indulgencia** *nf* : indulgence
indultar *vt* : pardon, reprieve — **indulto** *nm* : pardon, reprieve
industria *nf* : industry — **industrial** *adj* : industrial — ~ *nmf* : industrialist, manufacturer — **industrialización** *nf, pl* **-ciones** : industrialization — **industrializar** {21} *vt* : industrialize — **industrioso, -sa** *adj* : industrious
inédito, -ta *adj* : unpublished
inefable *adj* : inexpressible
ineficaz *adj, pl* **-caces** 1 : ineffective 2 INEFICIENTE : inefficient
ineficiente *adj* : inefficient — **ineficiencia** *nf* : inefficiency
inelegible *adj* : ineligible

ineludible *adj* : unavoidable, inescapable

inepto, -ta *adj* : inept — **ineptitud** *nf* : ineptitude

inequívoco, -ca *adj* : unequivocal

inercia *nf* : inertia

inerme *adj* : unarmed, defenseless

inerte *adj* : inert

inesperado, -da *adj* : unexpected

inestable *adj* : unstable — **inestabilidad** *nf* : instability

inevitable *adj* : inevitable

inexacto, -ta *adj* **1** : inexact **2** INCORRECTO : incorrect, wrong

inexistente *adj* : nonexistent

inexorable *adj* : inexorable

inexperiencia *nf* : inexperience — **inexperto, -ta** *adj* : inexperienced, unskilled

inexplicable *adj* : inexplicable

infalible *adj* : infallible

infame *adj* **1** : infamous, vile **2** *fam* : horrible — **infamia** *nf* : infamy, disgrace

infancia *nf* : infancy — **infanta** *nf* : infanta, princess — **infante** *nm* **1** : infante, prince **2** : infantryman (in the military) — **infantería** *nf* : infantry — **infantil** *adj* **1** : child's, children's **2** INMADURO : childish

infarto *nm* : heart attack

infatigable *adj* : tireless

infectar *vt* : infect — **infectarse** *vr* : become infected — **infección** *nf, pl* **-ciones** : infection — **infeccioso, -sa** *adj* : infectious — **infecto, -ta** *adj* **1** : infected **2** : foul, sickening

infecundo, -da *adj* : infertile

infeliz *adj, pl* **-lices** : unhappy — **infelicidad** *nf* : unhappiness

inferior *adj & nmf* : inferior — **inferioridad** *nf* : inferiority

inferir {76} *vt* **1** DEDUCIR : infer **2** : cause (harm or injury)

infernal *adj* : infernal, hellish

infestar *vt* : infest

infiel *adj* : unfaithful — **infidelidad** *nf* : infidelity

infierno *nm* **1** : hell **2 el quinto ~** *fam* : the middle of nowhere

infiltrar *vt* : infiltrate — **infiltrarse** *vr* : infiltrate

infinidad *nf* **1** : infinity **2 una ~ de** : countless — **infinitivo** *nm* : infinitive — **infinito, -ta** *adj* : infinite — **infinito** *nm* : infinity

inflación *nf, pl* **-ciones** : inflation — **inflacionario, -ria** *or* **inflacionista** *adj* : inflationary

inflamar *vt* : inflame — **inflamable** *adj* : flammable, inflammable — **inflamación** *nf, pl* **-ciones** : inflammation — **inflamatorio, -ria** *adj* : inflammatory

inflar *vt* **1** : inflate **2** EXAGERAR : exaggerate — **inflarse** *vr* **~ de** : swell (up) with

inflexible *adj* : inflexible — **inflexión** *nf, pl* **-xiones** : inflection

infligir {35} *vt* : inflict

influencia *nf* : influence — **influenciar** → **influir**

influenza *nf* : influenza

influir {41} *vt* : influence — *vi* **~ en** *or* **~ sobre** : have an influence on — **influjo** *nm* : influence — **influyente** *adj* : influential

información *nf, pl* **-ciones 1** : information **2** NOTICIAS : news **3** : directory assistance (on the telephone)

informal *adj* **1** : informal **2** IRRESPONSABLE : unreliable

informar *v* : inform — **informarse** *vr* : get information, find out — **informante** *nmf* : informant — **informática** *nf* : information technology — **informativo, -va** *adj* : informative — **informatizar** {21} *vt* : computerize

informe *adj* : shapeless — **~** *nm* **1** : report **2 ~s** *nmpl* : information, data **3 ~s** *nmpl* : references (for employment)

infortunado, -da *adj* : unfortunate — **infortunio** *nm* : misfortune

infracción *nf, pl* **-ciones** : violation, infraction

infraestructura *nf* : infrastructure

infrahumano, -na *adj* : subhuman

infranqueable *adj* **1** : impassable **2** INSUPERABLE : insurmountable

infrarrojo, -ja *adj* : infrared

infrecuente *adj* : infrequent

infringir {35} *vt* : infringe

infructuoso, -sa *adj* : fruitless

infundado, -da *adj* : unfounded, baseless

infundir *vt* : instill, infuse — **infusión** *nf, pl* **-siones** : infusion

ingeniar *vt* : invent, think up

ingeniería *nf* : engineering — **ingeniero, -ra** *n* : engineer

ingenio *nm* **1** : ingenuity **2** AGUDEZA : wit **3** MÁQUINA : device, apparatus **4 ~ azucarero** *Lat* : sugar refinery — **ingenioso, -sa** *adj* **1** : ingenious **2** AGUDO : clever, witty — **ingeniosamente** *adv* : cleverly

ingenuidad *nf* : naïveté, ingenuousness — **ingenuo, -nua** *adj* : naive

ingerir {76} *vt* : ingest, consume

ingle *nf* : groin
inglés, -glesa *adj, mpl* **-gleses** : English — **inglés** *nm* : English (language)
ingrato, -ta *adj* 1 : ungrateful 2 **un trabajo ingrato** : a thankless task — **ingratitud** *nf* : ingratitude
ingrediente *nm* : ingredient
ingresar *vt* : deposit — *vi* **~ en** : enter, be admitted into, join — **ingreso** *nm* 1 : entrance, entry 2 : admission (into a hospital, etc.) 3 **~s** *nmpl* : income, earnings
inhábil *adj* 1 : unskillful, clumsy 2 **~ para** : unsuited for — **inhabilidad** *nf* : unskillfulness
inhabitable *adj* : uninhabitable — **inhabitado, -da** *adj* : uninhabited
inhalar *vt* : inhale — **inhalación** *nf* : inhalation
inherente *adj* : inherent
inhibir *vt* : inhibit — **inhibición** *nf, pl* **-ciones** : inhibition
inhóspito, -ta *adj* : inhospitable
inhumano, -na *adj* : inhuman, inhumane — **inhumanidad** *nf* : inhumanity
iniciar *vt* : initiate, begin — **iniciación** *nf, pl* **-ciones** 1 : initiation 2 COMIENZO : beginning — **inicial** *adj & nf* : initial — **iniciativa** *nf* : initiative — **inicio** *nm* : start, beginning
inigualado, -da *adj* : unequaled
ininterrumpido, -da *adj* : uninterrupted
injerirse {76} *vr* : interfere — **injerencia** *nf* : interference
injertar *vt* : graft — **injerto** *nm* : graft
injuriar *vt* : insult — **injuria** *nf* : insult — **injurioso, -sa** *adj* : insulting, abusive
injusticia *nf* : injustice, unfairness — **injusto, -ta** *adj* : unfair, unjust
inmaculado, -da *adj* : immaculate
inmaduro, -ra *adj* 1 : immature 2 : unripe (of fruit) — **inmadurez** *nf* : immaturity
inmediaciones *nfpl* : surrounding area
inmediato, -ta *adj* 1 : immediate 2 CONTIGUO : adjoining 3 **de ~** : immediately, right away 4 **~ a** : next to, close to — **inmediatamente** *adv* : immediately
inmejorable *adj* : excellent
inmenso, -sa *adj* : immense, vast — **inmensidad** *nf* : immensity
inmerecido, -da *adj* : undeserved
inmersión *nf, pl* **-siones** : immersion
inmigrar *vi* : immigrate — **inmigración** *nf, pl* **-ciones** : immigration — **inmigrante** *adj & nmf* : immigrant
inminente *adj* : imminent, impending — **inminencia** *nf* : imminence

inmiscuirse {41} *vr* : interfere
inmobiliario, -ria *adj* : real estate, property
inmodesto, -ta *adj* : immodest
inmoral *adj* : immoral — **inmoralidad** *nf* : immorality
inmortal *adj & nmf* : immortal — **inmortalidad** *nf* : immortality
inmóvil *adj* : motionless, still — **inmovilizar** {21} *vt* : immobilize
inmueble *nm* : building, property
inmundicia *nf* : filth, trash — **inmundo, -da** *adj* : dirty, filthy
inmunizar {21} *vt* : immunize — **inmune** *adj* : immune — **inmunidad** *nf* : immunity — **inmunización** *nf, pl* **-ciones** : immunization
inmutable *adj* : unchangeable
innato, -ta *adj* : innate
innecesario, -ria *adj* : unnecessary, needless
innegable *adj* : undeniable
innoble *adj* : ignoble
innovar *vt* : introduce — *vi* : innovate — **innovación** *nf, pl* **-ciones** : innovation — **innovador, -dora** *adj* : innovative — **~** *n* : innovator
innumerable *adj* : innumerable
inocencia *nf* : innocence — **inocente** *adj & nmf* : innocent — **inocentón, -tona**, *mpl* **-tones** : naive — **~** *n* : simpleton, dupe
inocular *vt* : inoculate — **inoculación** *nf, pl* **-ciones** : inoculation
inocuo, -cua *adj* : innocuous
inodoro, -ra *adj* : odorless — **inodoro** *nm* : toilet
inofensivo, -va *adj* : inoffensive, harmless
inolvidable *adj* : unforgettable
inoperable *adj* : inoperable
inoperante *adj* : ineffective
inopinado, -da *adj* : unexpected
inoportuno, -na *adj* : untimely, inopportune
inorgánico, -ca *adj* : inorganic
inoxidable *adj* 1 : rustproof 2 **acero ~** : stainless steel
inquebrantable *adj* : unwavering
inquietar *vt* : disturb, worry — **inquietarse** *vr* : worry — **inquietante** *adj* : disturbing, worrisome — **inquieto, -ta** *adj* : anxious, worried — **inquietud** *nf* : anxiety, worry
inquilino, -na *n* : tenant
inquirir {4} *vi* : make inquiries — *vt* : investigate
insaciable *adj* : insatiable
insalubre *adj* : unhealthy

insatisfecho, -cha *adj* 1 : unsatisfied 2 DESCONTENTO : dissatisfied

inscribir {33} *vt* 1 : enroll, register 2 GRABAR : inscribe, engrave — **inscribirse** *vr* : register — **inscripción** *nf, pl* **-ciones** 1 : inscription 2 REGISTRO : registration

insecto *nm* : insect — **insecticida** *nm* : insecticide

inseguro, -ra *adj* 1 : insecure 2 PELIGROSO : unsafe 3 DUDOSO : uncertain — **inseguridad** *nf* 1 : insecurity 2 PELIGRO : lack of safety 3 DUDA : uncertainty

inseminar *vt* : inseminate — **inseminación** *nf, pl* **-ciones** : insemination

insensato, -ta *adj* : senseless, foolish — **insensatez** *nf* : foolishness, thoughtlessness

insensible *adj* 1 : insensitive, unfeeling 2 : numb (in medicine) 3 IMPERCEPTIBLE : imperceptible — **insensibilidad** *nf* : insensitivity

inseparable *adj* : inseparable

insertar *vt* : insert

insidia *nf* : snare, trap — **insidioso, -sa** *adj* : insidious

insigne *adj* : noted, famous

insignia *nf* 1 : insignia, badge 2 BANDERA : flag

insignificante *adj* : insignificant, negligible

insincero, -ra *adj* : insincere

insinuar {3} *vt* : insinuate — **insinuarse** *vr* ~ **en** : worm one's way into — **insinuación** *nf, pl* **-ciones** : insinuation — **insinuante** *adj* : insinuating, suggestive

insípido, -da *adj* : insipid

insistir *v* : insist — **insistencia** *nf* : insistence — **insistente** *adj* : insistent

insociable *adj* : unsociable

insolación *nf, pl* **-ciones** : sunstroke

insolencia *nf* : insolence — **insolente** *adj* : insolent

insólito, -ta *adj* : rare, unusual

insoluble *adj* : insoluble

insolvencia *nf* : insolvency, bankruptcy — **insolvente** *adj* : insolvent, bankrupt

insomnio *nm* : insomnia — **insomne** *nmf* : insomniac

insondable *adj* : unfathomable

insonorizado, -da *adj* : soundproof

insoportable *adj* : unbearable

insospechado, -da *adj* : unexpected

insostenible *adj* : untenable

inspeccionar *vt* : inspect — **inspección** *nf, pl* **-ciones** : inspection — **inspector, -tora** *n* : inspector

inspirar *vt* : inspire — *vi* : inhale — **inspirarse** *vr* : be inspired — **inspiración** *nf, pl* **-ciones** 1 : inspiration 2 RESPIRACIÓN : inhalation — **inspirador, -dora** *adj* : inspirational

instalar *vt* : install — **instalarse** *vr* : settle — **instalación** *nf, pl* **-ciones** : installation

instancia *nf* 1 : request 2 **en última** ~ : ultimately, as a last resort

instantáneo, -nea *adj* : instantaneous, instant — **instantánea** *nf* : snapshot — **instante** *nm* 1 : instant 2 **a cada** ~ : frequently, all the time 3 **al** ~ : immediately

instar *vt* : urge, press

instaurar *vt* : establish — **instauración** *nf, pl* **-ciones** : establishment

instigar {52} *vt* : incite, instigate — **instigador, -dora** *n* : instigator

instinto *nm* : instinct — **instintivo, -va** *adj* : instinctive

institución *nf, pl* **-ciones** : institution — **institucional** *adj* : institutional — **institucionalizar** {21} *vt* : institutionalize — **instituir** {41} *vt* : institute, establish — **instituto** *nm* : institute — **institutriz** *nf, pl* **-trices** : governess

instruir {41} *vt* : instruct — **instrucción** *nf, pl* **-ciones** 1 : instruction 2 **instrucciones** *nfpl* : instructions, directions — **instructivo, -va** *adj* : instructive — **instructor, -tora** *n* : instructor

instrumento *nm* : instrument — **instrumental** *adj* : instrumental

insubordinarse *vr* : rebel — **insubordinado, -da** *adj* : insubordinate — **insubordinación** *nf, pl* **-ciones** : insubordination

insuficiente *adj* : insufficient, inadequate — **insuficiencia** *nf* 1 : insufficiency, inadequacy 2 ~ **cardíaca** : heart failure

insufrible *adj* : insufferable

insular *adj* : insular, island

insulina *nf* : insulin

insulso, -sa *adj* 1 : insipid, bland 2 SOSO : dull

insultar *vt* : insult — **insultante** *adj* : insulting — **insulto** *nm* : insult

insuperable *adj* : insurmountable

insurgente *adj* & *nmf* : insurgent

insurrección *nf, pl* **-ciones** : insurrection, uprising

intachable *adj* : irreproachable

intacto, -ta *adj* : intact

intangible *adj* : intangible

integrar *vt* : integrate — **integrarse** *vr* : become integrated — **integración**

nf, pl **-ciones** : integration — **integral** *adj* **1** : integral **2** pan ~ : whole grain bread — **íntegro, -gra** *adj* **1** : honest, upright **2** ENTERO : whole, complete — **integridad** *nf* **1** RECTITUD : integrity **2** TOTALIDAD : wholeness

intelecto *nm* : intellect — **intelectual** *adj & nmf* : intellectual

inteligencia *nf* : intelligence — **inteligente** *adj* : intelligent — **inteligible** *adj* : intelligible

intemperie *nf* **a la** ~ : in the open air, outside

intempestivo, -va *adj* : untimely, inopportune

intención *nf, pl* **-ciones** : intention, intent — **intencionado, -da** *adj* **1** : intended **2 bien** ~ : well-meaning **3 mal** ~ : malicious — **intencional** *adj* : intentional

intensidad *nf* : intensity — **intensificar** {72} *vt* : intensify — **intensificarse** *vr* : intensify — **intensivo, -va** *adj* : intensive — **intenso, -sa** *adj* : intense

intentar *vt* : attempt, try — **intento** *nm* **1** : intention **2** TENTATIVA : attempt

interactuar {3} *vi* : interact — **interacción** *nf, pl* **-ciones** : interaction — **interactivo, -va** *adj* : interactive

intercalar *vt* : insert, intersperse

intercambio *nm* : exchange — **intercambiable** *adj* : interchangeable — **intercambiar** *vt* : exchange, trade

interceder *vi* : intercede

interceptar *vt* : intercept — **intercepción** *nf, pl* **-ciones** : interception

intercesión *nf, pl* **-siones** : intercession

interés *nm, pl* **-reses** : interest — **interesado, -da** *adj* **1** : interested **2** EGOISTA : selfish — **interesante** *adj* : interesting — **interesar** *vt* : interest — *vi* : be of interest — **interesarse** *vr* : take an interest

interfaz *nf, pl* **-faces** : interface

interferir {76} *vi* : interfere — *vt* : interfere with — **interferencia** *nf* : interference

interino, -na *adj* : temporary, interim — **interiormente** *adv* : inwardly

interior *adj* : interior, inner — ~ *nm* : interior, inside — **interiormente** *adv* : inwardly

interjección *nf, pl* **-ciones** : interjection

interlocutor, -tora *n* : speaker

intermediario, -ria *adj & n* : intermediary

intermedio, -dia *adj* : intermediate — **intermedio** *nm* : intermission

interminable *adj* : interminable, endless

intermisión *nf, pl* **-siones** : intermission, pause

intermitente *adj* : intermittent — ~ *nm* : blinker, turn signal

internacional *adj* : international

internar *vt* : commit, confine — **internarse** *vr* : penetrate — **internado** *nm* : boarding school — **interno, -na** *adj* : internal — ~ *n* **1** : boarder **2** : inmate (in a jail, etc.)

interponer {60} *vt* : interpose — **interponerse** *vr* : intervene

interpretar *vt* **1** : interpret **2** : play, perform (in theater, etc.) — **interpretación** *nf, pl* **-ciones** : interpretation — **intérprete** *nmf* TRADUCTOR : interpreter **2** : performer (of music)

interrogar {52} *vt* : interrogate, question — **interrogación** *nf, pl* **-ciones 1** : interrogation **2 signo de** ~ : question mark — **interrogativo, -va** *adj* : interrogative — **interrogatorio** *nm* : interrogation, questioning

interrumpir *v* : interrupt — **interrupción** *nf, pl* **-ciones** : interruption — **interruptor** *nm* : (electrical) switch

intersección *nf, pl* **-ciones** : intersection

intervalo *nm* : interval

intervenir {87} *vi* **1** : take part **2** MEDIAR : intervene — *vt* **1** : tap (a telephone) **2** INSPECCIONAR : audit **3** OPERAR : operate on — **intervención** *nf, pl* **-ciones 1** : intervention **2** : audit (in business) **3** *or* ~ **quirúrgica** : operation — **interventor, -tora** *n* : inspector, auditor

intestino *nm* : intestine — **intestinal** *adj* : intestinal

intimar *vi* ~ **con** : become friendly with — **intimidad** *nf* **1** : private life **2** AMISTAD : intimacy

intimidar *vt* : intimidate

íntimo, -ma *adj* **1** : intimate, close **2** PRIVADO : private

intolerable *adj* : intolerable — **intolerancia** *nf* : intolerance — **intolerante** *adj* : intolerant

intoxicar {72} *vt* : poison — **intoxicación** *nf, pl* **-ciones** : poisoning

intranquilizar {21} *vt* : make uneasy — **intranquilizarse** *vr* : be anxious — **intranquilidad** *nf* : uneasiness, anxiety — **intranquilo, -la** *adj* : uneasy, worried

intransigente *adj* : unyielding, intransigent

intransitable *adj* : impassable

intransitivo, -va *adj* : intransitive
intrascendente *adj* : unimportant, insignificant
intravenoso, -sa *adj* : intravenous
intrépido, -da *adj* : intrepid, fearless
intrigar {52} *v* : intrigue — **intriga** *nf* : intrigue — **intrigante** *adj* : intriguing
intrincado, -da *adj* : intricate, involved
intrínseco, -ca *adj* : intrinsic — **intrínsecament** *adv* : intrinsically, inherently
introducción *nf, pl* **-ciones** : introduction — **introducir** {61} *vt* 1 : introduce 2 METER : insert — **introducirse** *vr* ~ **en** : penetrate, get into — **introductorio, -ria** *adj* : introductory
intromisión *nf, pl* **-siones** : interference
introvertido, -da *adj* : introverted — ~ *n* : introvert
intrusión *nf, pl* **-siones** : intrusion — **intruso, -sa** *adj* : intrusive — ~ *n* : intruder
intuir {41} *vt* : sense — **intuición** *nf, pl* **-ciones** : intuition — **intuitivo, -va** *adj* : intuitive
inundar *vt* : flood — **inundarse** *vr* ~ **de** : be inundated with — **inundación** *nf, pl* **-ciones** : flood
inusitado, -da *adj* : unusual, uncommon
inútil *adj* 1 : useless 2 INVÁLIDO : disabled — **inutilidad** *nf* : uselessness — **inutilizar** {21} *vt* 1 : make useless 2 INCAPACITAR : disable
invadir *vt* : invade
invalidez *nf, pl* **-deces** 1 : invalidity 2 : disability (in medicine) — **inválido, -da** *adj & n* : invalid
invalorable *adj Lat* : invaluable
invariable *adj* : invariable
invasión *nf, pl* **-siones** : invasion — **invasor, -sora** *adj* : invading — ~ *n* : invader
invencible *adj* : invincible
inventar *vt* 1 : invent 2 : fabricate, make up (a word, an excuse, etc.) — **invención** *nf, pl* **-ciones** 1 : invention 2 MENTIRA : lie, fabrication
inventario *nm* : inventory
inventiva *nf* : inventiveness — **inventivo, -va** *adj* : inventive — **inventor, -tora** *n* : inventor
invernadero *nm* : greenhouse
invernal *adj* : winter
inverosímil *adj* : unlikely
inversión *nf, pl* **-siones** 1 : inversion, reversal 2 : investment (of money, time, etc.)

inverso, -sa *adj* 1 : inverse 2 CONTRARIO : opposite 3 **a la inversa** : the other way around, inversely
inversor, -sora *n* : investor
invertebrado, -da *adj* : invertebrate — **invertebrado** *nm* : invertebrate
invertir {76} *vt* 1 : invert, reverse 2 : invest (money, time, etc.) — *vi* : make an investment
investidura *nf* : investiture
investigar {52} *vt* 1 : investigate 2 ESTUDIAR : research — *vi* ~ **sobre** : do research into — **investigación** *nf, pl* **-ciones** 1 : investigation 2 ESTUDIO : research — **investigador, -dora** *n* : investigator, researcher
investir {54} *vt* : invest
inveterado, -da *adj* : deep-seated, inveterate
invicto, -ta *adj* : undefeated
invierno *nm* : winter
invisible *adj* : invisible — **invisibilidad** *nf* : invisibility
invitar *vt* : invite — **invitación** *nf, pl* **-ciones** : invitation — **invitado, -da** *n* : guest
invocar {72} *vt* : invoke — **invocación** *nf, pl* **-ciones** : invocation
involuntario, -ria *adj* : involuntary
invulnerable *adj* : invulnerable
inyectar *vt* : inject — **inyección** *nf, pl* **-ciones** : injection, shot — **inyectado, -da** *adj* **ojos inyectados** : bloodshot eyes
ion *nm* : ion — **ionizar** {21} *vt* : ionize
ir {43} *vi* 1 : go 2 FUNCIONAR : work, function 3 CONVENIR : suit 4 **¿cómo te va?** : how are you? 5 ~ **con prisa** : be in a hurry 6 ~ **por** : follow, go along 7 **vamos** : let's go — *v aux* 1 ~ **a** : be going to, be about to 2 ~ **caminando** : take a walk 3 **vamos a ver** : we shall see — **irse** *vr* : go away, be gone
ira *nf* : rage, anger — **iracundo, -da** *adj* : irate, angry
iraní *adj* : Iranian
iraquí *adj* : Iraqi
iris *nms & pl* 1 : iris (of the eye) 2 **arco** ~ : rainbow
irlandés, -desa *adj, mpl* **-deses** : Irish
ironía *nf* : irony — **irónico, -ca** *adj* : ironic, ironical
irracional *adj* : irrational
irradiar *vt* : radiate, irradiate
irrazonable *adj* : unreasonable
irreal *adj* : unreal
irreconciliable *adj* : irreconcilable
irreconocible *adj* : unrecognizable
irrecuperable *adj* : irretrievable

irreductible *adj* : unyielding
irreemplazable *adj* : irreplaceable
irreflexivo, -va *adj* : rash, unthinking
irrefutable *adj* : irrefutable
irregular *adj* : irregular — **irregulari-dad** *nf* : irregularity
irrelevante *adj* : irrelevant
irreparable *adj* : irreparable
irreprimible *adj* : irrepressible
irreprochable *adj* : irreproachable
irresistible *adj* : irresistible
irresoluto, -ta *adj* : indecisive, irresolute
irrespetuoso, -sa *adj* : disrespectful
irresponsable *adj* : irresponsible — **irresponsabilidad** *nf* : irresponsibility
irreverente *adj* : irreverent
irreversible *adj* : irreversible
irrevocable *adj* : irrevocable
irrigar {52} *vt* : irrigate — **irrigación** *nf, pl* **-ciones** : irrigation

irrisorio, -ria *adj* : laughable, ridiculous
irritar *vt* : irritate — **irritarse** *vr* : get annoyed — **irritable** *adj* : irritable — **irritación** *nf, pl* **-ciones** : irritation — **irritante** *adj* : irritating
irrompible *adj* : unbreakable
irrumpir *vi* ~ **en** : burst into
isla *nf* : island
islámico, -ca *adj* : Islamic, Muslim
islandés, -desa *adj, mpl* **-deses** : Icelandic
isleño, -ña *n* : islander
israelí *adj* : Israeli
istmo *nm* : isthmus
italiano, -na *adj* : Italian — **italiano** *nm* : Italian (language)
itinerario *nm* : itinerary
izar {21} *vt* : hoist, raise
izquierda *nf* : left — **izquierdista** *adj & nmf* : leftist — **izquierdo, -da** *adj* : left

J

j *nf* : j, tenth letter of the Spanish alphabet
jabalí *nm, pl* **-líes** : wild boar
jabalina *nf* : javelin
jabón *nm, pl* **-bones** : soap — **jabonar** *vt* : soap (up) — **jabonera** *nf* : soap dish — **jabonoso, -sa** *adj* : soapy
jaca *nf* : pony
jacinto *nm* : hyacinth
jactarse *vr* : boast, brag — **jactancia** *nf* : boastfulness, bragging — **jactancioso, -sa** *adj* : boastful
jadear *vi* : pant, gasp — **jadeante** *adj* : panting, breathless — **jadeo** *nm* : gasp, panting
jaez *nm, pl* **jaeces 1** : harness **2 jaeces** *nmpl* : trappings
jaguar *nm* : jaguar
jaiba *nf Lat* : crab
jalapeño *nm Lat* : jalapeño pepper
jalar *v Lat* : pull, tug
jalea *nf* : jelly
jaleo *nm fam* **1** : uproar, racket **2 armar un** ~ : raise a ruckus
jalón *nm, pl* **-lones** *Lat* : pull, tug
jamaicano, -na *or* **jamaiquino, -na** *adj* : Jamaican
jamás *adv* **1** : never **2 para siempre** ~ : for ever and ever
jamelgo *nm* : nag (horse)
jamón *nm, pl* **-mones 1** : ham **2** ~ **serrano** : cured ham
Januká *nmf* : Hanukkah

japonés, -nesa *adj, mpl* **-neses** : Japanese — **japonés** *nm* : Japanese (language)
jaque *nm* **1** : check (in chess) **2** ~ **mate** : checkmate
jaqueca *nf* : headache, migraine
jarabe *nm* : syrup
jardín *nm, pl* **-dines 1** : garden **2** ~ **infantil** *or* ~ **de niños** *Lat* : kindergarten — **jardinería** *nf* : gardening — **jardinero, -ra** *n* : gardener
jarra *nf* : pitcher, jug — **jarro** *nm* : pitcher — **jarrón** *nm, pl* **-rrones** : vase
jaula *nf* : cage
jauría *nf* : pack of hounds
jazmín *nm, pl* **-mines** : jasmine
jazz ['jas, 'dʒas] *nm* : jazz
jeans ['jins, 'dʒins] *nmpl* : jeans
jefe, -fa *n* **1** : chief, leader **2** PATRÓN : boss **3** ~ **de cocina** : chef — **jefatura** *nf* **1** : leadership **2** SEDE : headquarters
jengibre *nm* : ginger
jeque *nm* : sheikh, sheik
jerarquía *nf* **1** : hierarchy **2** RANGO : rank — **jerárquico, -ca** *adj* : hierarchical
jerez *nm, pl* **-reces** : sherry
jerga *nf* **1** : coarse cloth **2** ARGOT : jargon, slang
jerigonza *nf* **1** : jargon **2** GALIMATÍAS : gibberish

jeringa *or* **jeringuilla** *nf* : syringe —
  jeringar {52} *vt fam* : annoy, pester
jeroglífico *nm* : hieroglyphic
jersey *nm, pl* **-seys** : jersey
jesuita *adj & nm* : Jesuit
Jesús *nm* : Jesus
jilguero *nm* : goldfinch
jinete *nmf* : horseman, horsewoman *f*,
  rider
jirafa *nf* : giraffe
jirón *nm, pl* **-rones** : shred, tatter
jitomate *nm Lat* : tomato
jockey ['joki, 'dʒo-] *nmf, pl* **-keys** [-kis]
  : jockey
jocoso, -sa *adj* : humorous, jocular
jofaina *nf* : washbowl
jolgorio *nm* : merrymaking
jornada *nf* 1 : day's journey 2 : working
  day — **jornal** *nm* : day's pay — **jor-
  nalero, -ra** *n* : day laborer
joroba *nf* : hump — **jorobado, -da** *adj*
  : hunchbacked, humpbacked — **~** *n*
  : hunchback — **jorobar** *vt fam* : annoy
jota *nf* 1 : iota, jot 2 **no veo ni ~** : I
  can't see a thing
joven *adj, pl* **jóvenes** : young — **~**
  nmf : young man *m*, young woman *f*,
  youth
jovial *adj* : jovial, cheerful
joya *nf* : jewel — **joyería** *nf* : jewelry
  store — **joyero, -ra** *n* : jeweler —
  joyero *nm* : jewelry box
juanete *nm* : bunion
jubilación *nf, pl* **-ciones** : retirement —
  jubilado, -da *adj* : retired — **~** *nmf*
  : retiree — **jubilar** *vt* : retire, pension
  off — **jubilarse** *vr* : retire — **jubileo**
  nm : jubilee
júbilo *nm* : joy, jubilation — **jubiloso,
  -sa** *adj* : joyous, jubilant
judaísmo *nm* : Judaism
judía *nf* 1 : bean 2 *or* **~ verde** : green
  bean, string bean
judicial *adj* : judicial
judío, -día *adj* : Jewish — **~** *n* : Jew
judo ['juðo, 'dʒu-] *nm* : judo
juego *nm* 1 : game 2 : playing (of children, etc.) 3 *or* **~s de azar** : gambling 4 CONJUNTO : set 5 **estar en ~**
  : be at stake 6 **fuera de ~** : offside (in
  sports) 7 **hacer ~** : go together,
  match 8 **~ de manos** : conjuring
  trick 9 **poner en ~** : bring into play
juerga *nf fam* : spree, binge
jueves *nms & pl* : Thursday
juez *nmf, pl* **jueces** 1 : judge 2 ÁRBITRO
  : umpire, referee

jugar {44} *vi* 1 : play 2 : gamble (in a
  casino, etc.) 3 APOSTAR : bet 4 **~ (al)
  tenis** : play tennis — *vt* : play — **jugarse** *vr* : risk, gamble (away) — **ju-
  gada** *nf* 1 : play, move 2 TRETA
  : (dirty) trick — **jugador, -dora** *n*
  : player 2 : gambler
juglar *nm* : minstrel
jugo *nm* 1 : juice 2 SUSTANCIA : substance, essence — **jugoso, -sa** *adj*
  : juicy 2 SUSTANCIAL : substantial, important
juguete *nm* : toy — **juguetear** *vi* : play
  — **juguetería** *nf* : toy store — **juguetón, -tona** *adj, mpl* **-tones** : playful
juicio *nm* 1 : judgment 2 RAZÓN : reason, sense 3 **a mi ~** : in my opinion
  — **juicioso, -sa** *adj* : wise, sensible
julio *nm* : July
junco *nm* : reed, rush
jungla *nf* : jungle
junio *nm* : June
juntar *vt* 1 UNIR : join, unite 2 REUNIR
  : collect — **juntarse** *vr* 1 : join (together) 2 REUNIRSE : meet, get together — **junta** *nf* 1 : board, committee 2
  REUNIÓN : meeting 3 : (political) junta
  4 : joint, gasket — **junto, -ta** *adj* 1
  : joined 2 PRÓXIMO : close, adjacent 3
  (*used adverbially*) : together 4 **~ a**
  : next to 5 **~ con** : together with —
  juntura *nf* : joint
Júpiter *nm* : Jupiter
jurar *v* 1 : swear 2 **~ en falso** : commit
  perjury — **jurado** *nm* 1 : jury 2 : juror,
  member of a jury — **juramento** *nm*
  : oath
jurídico, -ca *adj* : legal
jurisdicción *nf, pl* **-ciones** : jurisdiction
jurisprudencia *nf* : jurisprudence
justamente *adv* 1 : fairly, justly 2 PRE-
  CISAMENTE : precisely, exactly
justicia *nf* : justice, fairness
justificar {72} *vt* 1 : justify 2 DISCULPAR
  : excuse, vindicate — **justificación** *nf,
  pl* **-ciones** : justification
justo, -ta *adj* 1 : just, fair 2 EXACTO
  : exact 3 APRETADO : tight — **justo**
  adv 1 : just, exactly 2 **~ a tiempo**
  : just in time
juvenil *adj* : youthful — **juventud** *nf* 1
  : youth 2 JÓVENES : young people
juzgar {52} *vt* 1 : try (a case in court) 2
  ESTIMAR : judge, consider 3 **a ~ por**
  : judging by — **juzgado** *nm* : court,
  tribunal

K

k *nf* : k, eleventh letter of the Spanish alphabet
kaki → **caqui**
karate *or* **kárate** *nm* : karate
kilo *nm* : kilo — **kilogramo** *nm* : kilogram

kilómetro *nm* : kilometer — **kilometraje** *nm* : distance in kilometers, mileage — **kilométrico, -ca** *adj fam* : endless
kilovatio *nm* : kilowatt
kiosco *nm* → **quiosco**

L

l *nf* : l, twelfth letter of the Spanish alphabet
la *pron* **1** : her, it **2** (*formal*) : you **3** ~ **que** : the one who — ~ *art* → **el**
laberinto *nm* : labyrinth, maze
labia *nf fam* : gift of gab
labio *nm* : lip
labor *nf* **1** : work, labor **2** TAREA : task **3** ~**es domésticas** : housework — **laborable** *adj* **día** ~ : business day — **laborar** *vi* : work — **laboratorio** *nm* : laboratory, lab — **laborioso, -sa** *adj* : laborious
labrar *vt* **1** : cultivate, till **2** : work (metals), carve (stone, wood) **3** CAUSAR : cause, bring about — **labrado, -da** *adj* **1** : cultivated, tilled **2** : carved, wrought — **labrador, -dora** *n* : farmer — **labranza** *nf* : farming
laca *nf* **1** : lacquer **2** : hair spray
lacayo *nm* : lackey
lacerar *vt* : lacerate
lacio, -cia *adj* **1** : limp **2** : straight (of hair)
lacónico, -ca *adj* : laconic
lacra *nf* : scar
lacrar *vt* : seal — **lacre** *nm* : sealing wax
lacrimógeno, -na *adj* **gas lacrimógeno** : tear gas — **lacrimoso, -sa** *adj* : tearful
lácteo, -tea *adj* **1** : dairy **2 Vía Láctea** : Milky Way
ladear *vt* : tilt — **ladearse** *vr* : lean
ladera *nf* : slope, hillside
ladino, -na *adj* : crafty
lado *nm* **1** : side **2 al** ~ : next door, nearby **3 al** ~ **de** : beside, next to **4 de** ~ : sideways **5 por otro** ~ : on the other hand **6 por todos** ~**s** : everywhere, all around
ladrar *vi* : bark — **ladrido** *nm* : bark
ladrillo *nm* : brick

ladrón, -drona *n, mpl* **-drones** : thief
lagarto *nm* : lizard — **lagartija** *nf* : (small) lizard
lago *nm* : lake
lágrima *nf* : tear
laguna *nf* **1** : lagoon **2** VACÍO : gap
laico, -ca *adj* : lay, secular — ~ *n* : layman *m*, layperson
lamentar *vt* **1** : regret, be sorry about **2 lo lamento** : I'm sorry — **lamentarse** *vr* : lament — **lamentable** *adj* **1** : deplorable **2** TRISTE : sad, pitiful — **lamento** *nm* : lament, moan
lamer *vt* **1** : lick **2** : lap (against) — **lamida** *nf* : lick
lámina *nf* **1** PLANCHA : sheet **2** DIBUJO : plate, illustration — **laminar** *vt* : laminate
lámpara *nf* : lamp
lampiño, -ña *adj* : beardless, hairless
lana *nf* **1** : wool **2 de** ~ : woolen
lance *nm* **1** : event, incident **2** : throw (of dice, etc.) **3** RIÑA : quarrel
lanceta *nf* : lancet
lancha *nf* **1** : boat, launch **2** ~ **motora** : motorboat
langosta *nf* **1** : lobster **2** : locust (insect) — **langostino** *nm* : prawn, crayfish
languidecer {53} *vi* : languish — **languidez** *nf, pl* **-deces** : languor — **lánguido, -da** *adj* : languid, listless
lanilla *nf* : nap (of fabric)
lanudo, -da *adj* : woolly
lanza *nf* : spear, lance
lanzar {21} *vt* **1** : throw **2** : shoot (a glance), give (a sigh, etc.) **3** : launch (a missile, a project) — **lanzarse** *vr* : throw oneself — **lanzamiento** *nm* : throwing, launching
lapicero *nm* : (mechanical) pencil
lápida *nf* : tombstone

lapidar *vt* : stone
lápiz *nm, pl* **-pices 1** : pencil **2** ~ **de labios** : lipstick
lapso *nm* : lapse (of time) — **lapsus** *nms & pl* : lapse, slip (of the tongue)
largar {52} *vt* **1** AFLOJAR : loosen, slacken **2** *fam* : give — **largarse** *vr fam* : go away, beat it — **largo, -ga** *adj* **1** : long **2 a la larga** : in the long run **3 a lo largo** : lengthwise **4 a lo largo de** : along — **largo** *nm* : length — **largometraje** *nm* : feature film — **largueza** *nf* : generosity
laringe *nf* : larynx — **laringitis** *nfs & pl* : laryngitis
larva *nf* : larva
las → **el**
lascivo, -va *adj* : lascivious, lewd
láser *nm* : laser
lastimar *vt* : hurt — **lastimarse** *vr* : hurt oneself — **lástima** *nf* **1** : pity **2 dar** ~ : be pitiful **3 me dan** ~ : I feel sorry for them **4 ¡qué** ~! : what a shame! — **lastimero, -ra** *adj* : pitiful, wretched — **lastimoso, -sa** *adj* : pitiful, terrible
lastre *nm* : ballast
lata *nf* **1** : tinplate **2** : (tin) can **3** *fam* : nuisance, bore **4 dar (la) lata** *a fam* : bother, annoy
latente *adj* : latent
lateral *adj* : side, lateral
latido *nm* **1** : beat, throb **2** ~ **del corazón** : heartbeat
latifundio *nm* : large estate
látigo *nm* : whip — **latigazo** *nm* : lash
latín *nm* : Latin (language)
latino, -na *adj* **1** : Latin **2** : Latin-American — ~ *n* : Latin American — **latinoamericano, -na** *adj* : Latin-American — ~ *n* : Latin American
latir *vi* : beat, throb
latitud *nf* : latitude
latón *nm, pl* **-tones** : brass
latoso, -sa *adj fam* : annoying
laúd *nm* : lute
laudable *adj* : laudable
laureado, -da *adj* : prize-winning
laurel *nm* **1** : laurel **2** : bay leaf (in cooking)
lava *nf* : lava
lavar *vt* : wash — **lavarse** *vr* **1** : wash oneself **2** ~ **las manos** : wash one's hands — **lavable** *adj* : washable — **lavabo** *nm* **1** : sink **2** RETRETE : lavatory, toilet — **lavadero** *nm* : laundry room — **lavado** *nm* : wash, washing — **lavadora** *nf* : washing machine — **lavamanos** *nms & pl* : washbowl — **lavandería** *nf* : laundry (service) — **lavaplatos** *nms & pl* **1** : dishwasher **2**

Lat : kitchen sink — **lavativa** *nf* : enema — **lavatorio** *nm* : lavatory, washroom — **lavavajillas** *nms & pl* : dishwasher
laxante *adj & nm* : laxative — **laxo, -xa** *adj* : loose
lazo *nm* **1** VÍNCULO : link, bond **2** LAZADA : bow **3** : lasso, lariat — **lazada** *nf* : bow, loop
le *pron* **1** : (to) her, (to) him, (to) it **2** (*formal*) : (to) you **3** (*as direct object*) : him, you
leal *adj* : loyal, faithful — **lealtad** *nf* : loyalty, allegiance
lebrel *nm* : hound
lección *nf, pl* **-ciones 1** : lesson **2** : lecture (in a classroom)
leche *nf* **1** : milk **2** ~ **descremada** *or* ~ **desnatada** : skim milk **3** ~ **en polvo** : powdered milk — **lechera** *nf* : milk jug — **lechería** *nf* : dairy store — **lechero, -ra** *adj* : dairy — ~ *n* : milkman *m*, milk dealer
lecho *nm* : bed
lechón, -chona *n, mpl* **-chones** : suckling pig
lechoso, -sa *adj* : milky
lechuga *nf* : lettuce
lechuza *nf* : owl
lector, -tora *n* : reader — **lectura** *nf* **1** : reading **2** ESCRITOS : reading matter
leer {20} *v* : read
legación *nf, pl* **-ciones** : legation
legado *nm* **1** : legacy **2** ENVIADO : legate, emissary
legajo *nm* : dossier, file
legal *adj* : legal — **legalidad** *nf* : legality — **legalizar** {21} *vt* : legalize — **legalización** *nf, pl* **-ciones** : legalization
legar {52} *vt* : bequeath
legendario, -ria *adj* : legendary
legible *adj* : legible
legión *nf, pl* **-giones** : legion — **legionario, -ria** *n* : legionnaire
legislar *vi* : legislate — **legislación** *nf, pl* **-ciones** : legislation — **legislador, -dora** *n* : legislator — **legislatura** *nf* : legislature
legítimo, -ma *adj* **1** : legitimate **2** GENUINO : authentic — **legitimidad** *nf* : legitimacy
lego, -ga *adj* **1** : secular, lay **2** IGNORANTE : ignorant — ~ *n* : layman *m*, layperson
legua *nf* : league
legumbre *nf* : vegetable
leído, -da *adj* : well-read
lejano, -na *adj* : distant, far away — **lejanía** *nf* : distance
lejía *nf* : bleach

lejos *adv* 1 : far (away) 2 **a lo ~** : in the distance 3 **de ~** *or* **desde ~** : from afar 4 **~ de** : far from

lelo, -la *adj* : silly, stupid

lema *nm* : motto

lencería *nf* 1 : linen 2 : (women's) lingerie

lengua *nf* 1 : tongue 2 IDIOMA : language 3 **morderse la ~** : hold one's tongue

lenguado *nm* : sole, flounder

lenguaje *nm* : language

lengüeta *nf* 1 : tongue (of a shoe) 2 : reed (of a musical instrument)

lengüetada *nf* **beber a ~s** : lap (up)

lente *nmf* 1 : lens 2 **~s** *nmpl* : eyeglasses 3 **~s de contacto** : contact lenses

lenteja *nf* : lentil — **lentejuela** *nf* : sequin

lento, -ta *adj* : slow — **lento** *adv* : slowly — **lentitud** *nf* : slowness

leña *nf* : firewood — **leñador, -dora** *n* : lumberjack, woodcutter — **leño** *nm* : log

león, -ona *n, mpl* **leones** : lion, lioness *f*

leopardo *nm* : leopard

leotardo *nm* : leotard, tights *pl*

lepra *nf* : leprosy — **leproso, -sa** *n* : leper

lerdo, -da *adj* 1 TORPE : clumsy 2 TONTO : slow-witted

les *pron* 1 : (to) them, (to) you 2 (*as direct object*) : them, you

lesbiano, -na *adj* : lesbian — **lesbiana** *nf* : lesbian — **lesbianismo** *nm* : lesbianism

lesión *nf, pl* **-siones** : lesion, wound — **lesionado, -da** *adj* : injured, wounded — **lesionar** *vt* 1 : injure, wound 2 DAÑAR : damage

letal *adj* : lethal

letanía *nf* : litany

letárgico, -ca *adj* : lethargic — **letargo** *nm* : lethargy

letra *nf* 1 : letter 2 ESCRITURA : handwriting 3 : lyrics *pl* (of a song) 4 **~ de cambio** : bill of exchange 5 **~s** *nfpl* : arts — **letrado, -da** *adj* : learned — **letrero** *nm* : sign, notice

letrina *nf* : latrine

leucemia *nf* : leukemia

levadizo, -za *adj* **puente levadizo** : drawbridge

levadura *nf* 1 : yeast 2 **~ en polvo** : baking powder

levantar *vt* 1 : lift, raise 2 RECOGER : pick up 3 CONSTRUIR : erect, put up 4 ENCENDER : rouse, stir up 5 **~ la mesa** *Lat* : clear the table — **levan-**

tarse *vr* 1 : rise, stand up 2 : get out of bed 3 SUBLEVARSE : rise up — **levantamiento** *nm* 1 : raising, lifting 2 SUBLEVACIÓN : uprising

levante *nm* 1 : east 2 : east wind

levar *vt* **~ anclas** : weigh anchor

leve *adj* 1 : light, slight 2 : minor, trivial (of wounds, sins, etc.) — **levedad** *nf* : lightness — **levemente** *adv* : lightly, slightly

léxico *nm* : vocabulary, lexicon

ley *nf* 1 : law 2 **de (buena) ~** : genuine, pure (of metals)

leyenda *nf* 1 : legend 2 : caption (of an illustration, etc.)

liar {85} *vt* 1 : bind, tie (up) 2 : roll (a cigarette) 3 CONFUNDIR : confuse, muddle — **liarse** *vr* : get mixed up

libanés, -nesa *adj, mpl* **-neses** : Lebanese

libelo *nm* 1 : libel 2 : petition (in court)

libélula *nf* : dragonfly

liberación *nf, pl* **-ciones** : liberation, deliverance

liberal *adj & nmf* : liberal — **liberalidad** *nf* : generosity, liberality

liberar *vt* : liberate, free — **libertad** *nf* 1 : freedom, liberty 2 **~ bajo fianza** : bail 3 **~ condicional** : parole 4 **en ~** : free — **libertar** *vt* : set free

libertinaje *nm* : licentiousness — **libertino, -na** *n* : libertine

libido *nf* : libido

libio, -bia *adj* : Libyan

libra *nf* 1 : pound 2 **~ esterlina** : pound sterling

librar *vt* 1 : free, save 2 : wage, fight (a battle) 3 : draw, issue (a check, etc.) — **librarse** *vr* **~ de** : free oneself from, get rid of

libre *adj* 1 : free 2 : unoccupied (of space), spare (of time) 3 **al aire ~** : in the open air 4 **~ de impuestos** : tax-free

librea *nf* : livery

libro *nm* 1 : book 2 **~ de bolsillo** : paperback — **librería** *nf* : bookstore — **librero, -ra** *n* : bookseller — **librero** *nm Lat* : bookcase — **libreta** *nf* : notebook

licencia *nf* 1 : license, permit 2 PERMISO : permission 3 : (military) leave — **licenciado, -da** *n* 1 : graduate 2 *Lat* : lawyer — **licenciar** *vt* : dismiss, discharge — **licenciarse** *vr* : graduate — **licenciatura** *nf* : degree

licencioso, -sa *adj* : licentious

liceo *nm* : high school

licitar *vt* : bid for

lícito, -ta *adj* **1** : lawful, legal **2** JUSTO : just, fair

licor *nm* **1** : liquor **2** : liqueur — **licorera** *nf* : decanter

licuadora *nf* : blender — **licuado** *nm* : milk shake — **licuar** {3} *vt* : liquefy

lid *nf* **1** : fight **2 en buena ~** : fair and square

líder *adj* : leading — **~** *nmf* : leader — **liderato** *or* **liderazgo** *nm* : leadership

lidia *nf* : bullfight — **lidiar** *v* : fight

liebre *nf* : hare

lienzo *nm* **1** : cotton or linen cloth **2** : canvas (for a painting) **3** PARED : wall

liga *nf* **1** : league **2** *Lat* : rubber band **3** : garter (for stockings) — **ligadura** *nf* **1** ATADURA : tie, bond **2** : ligature (in medicine or music) — **ligamento** *nm* : ligament — **ligar** {52} *vt* : bind, tie (up)

ligero, -ra *adj* **1** : light, lightweight **2** LEVE : slight **3** ÁGIL : agile **4** FRÍVOLO : lighthearted, superficial — **ligeramente** *adv* : lightly, slightly — **ligereza** *nf* **1** : lightness **2** : flippancy (of character), thoughtlessness (of actions) **3** AGILIDAD : agility

lija *nf* : sandpaper — **lijar** *vt* : sand

lila *nf* : lilac

lima *nf* **1** : file **2** : lime (fruit) **3 ~ para uñas** : nail file — **limar** *vt* : file

limbo *nm* : limbo

limitar *vt* : limit — *vi* **~ con** : border on — **limitación** *nf*, *pl* **-ciones** : limitation, limit — **límite** *nm* **1** : limit **2** CONFÍN : boundary, border **3 ~ de velocidad** : speed limit **4 fecha ~** : deadline — **limítrofe** *adj* : bordering

limo *nm* : slime, mud

limón *nm*, *pl* **-mones 1** : lemon **2 ~ verde** *Lat* : lime — **limonada** *nf* : lemonade

limosna *nf* **1** : alms **2 pedir ~** : beg — **limosnero, -ra** *n* : beggar

limpiabotas *nmfs & pl* : bootblack

limpiaparabrisas *nms & pl* : windshield wiper

limpiar *vt* **1** : clean, wipe (away) **2 ~ en seco** : dry-clean — **limpieza** *nf* **1** : cleanliness **2** : (act of) cleaning — **limpio** *adv* : cleanly, fairly — **limpio, -pia** *adj* **1** : clean, neat **2** HONRADO : honest **3** NETO : net, clear

limusina *nf* : limousine

linaje *nm* : lineage, ancestry

linaza *nf* : linseed

lince *nm* : lynx

linchar *vt* : lynch

lindar *vi* **~ con** : border on — **lindante** *adj* : bordering — **linde** *nmf or* **lindero** *nm* : boundary

lindo, -da *adj* **1** : pretty, lovely **2 de lo lindo** *fam* : a lot

línea *nf* **1** : line **2 ~ de conducta** : course of action **3 en ~** : on-line **4 guardar la ~** : watch one's figure — **lineal** *adj* : linear

lingote *nm* : ingot

lingüista *nmf* : linguist — **lingüística** *nf* : linguistics — **lingüístico, -ca** *adj* : linguistic

linimento *nm* : liniment

lino *nm* **1** : flax (plant) **2** : linen (fabric)

linóleo *nm* : linoleum

linterna *nf* **1** FAROL : lantern **2** : flashlight

lío *nm* **1** : bundle **2** *fam* : mess, trouble **3** *fam* : (love) affair

liofilizar {21} *vt* : freeze-dry

liquen *nm* : lichen

liquidar *vt* **1** : liquefy **2** : liquidate (merchandise, etc.) **3** : settle, pay off (a debt, etc.) — **liquidación** *nf*, *pl* **-ciones 1** : liquidation **2** REBAJA : clearance sale — **líquido, -da** *adj* **1** : liquid **2** NETO : net — **líquido** *nm* : liquid

lira *nf* : lyre

lírico, -ca *adj* : lyric, lyrical — **lírica** *nf* : lyric poetry

lirio *nm* : iris

lisiado, -da *adj* : disabled — **~** *n* : disabled person — **lisiar** *vt* : disable, cripple

liso, -sa *adj* **1** : smooth **2** PLANO : flat **3** SENCILLO : plain **4 pelo ~** : straight hair

lisonjear *vt* : flatter — **lisonja** *nf* : flattery

lista *nf* **1** : stripe **2** ENUMERACIÓN : list **3** : menu (in a restaurant) — **listado, -da** *adj* : striped

listo, -ta *adj* **1** : clever, smart **2** PREPARADO : ready

listón *nm*, *pl* **-tones 1** : ribbon **2** : strip (of wood)

lisura *nf* : smoothness

litera *nf* : bunk bed, berth

literal *adj* : literal

literatura *nf* : literature — **literario, -ria** *adj* : literary

litigar {52} *vi* : litigate — **litigio** *nm* **1** : litigation **2 en ~** : in dispute

litografía *nf* **1** : lithography **2** : lithograph (picture)

litoral *adj* : coastal — **~** *nm* : shore, seaboard

litro *nm* : liter

liturgia *nf* : liturgy — **litúrgico, -ca** *adj* : liturgical

liviano, -na *adj* **1** LIGERO : light **2** INCONSTANTE : fickle

lívido, -da *adj* : livid

llaga *nf* : sore, wound

llama *nf* **1** : flame **2** : llama (animal)

llamar *vt* **1** : call **2** : call up (on the telephone) — *vi* **1** : phone, call **2** : knock, ring (at the door) — **llamarse** *vr* **1** : be called **2 ¿cómo te llamas?** : what's your name? — **llamada** *nf* : call — **llamado, -da** *adj* : named, called — **llamamiento** *nm* : call, appeal

llamarada *nf* **1** : blaze **2** : flushing (of the face)

llamativo, -va *adj* : flashy, showy

llamear *vi* : flame, blaze

llano, -na *adj* **1** : flat **2** : straightforward (of a person, a message, etc.) **3** SENCILLO : plain, simple — **llano** *nm* : plain — **llaneza** *nf* : simplicity

llanta *nf* **1** : rim (of a wheel) **2** *Lat* : tire

llanto *nm* : crying, weeping

llanura *nf* : plain

llave *nf* **1** : key **2** *Lat* : faucet **3** INTERRUPTOR : switch **4 cerrar con ~** : lock **5 ~ inglesa** : monkey wrench — **llavero** *nm* : key chain

llegar {52} *vi* **1** : arrive, come **2** ALCANZAR : reach **3** BASTAR : be enough **4 ~ a** : manage to **5 ~ a ser** : become — **llegada** *nf* : arrival

llenar *vt* : fill (up), fill in — **lleno, -na** *adj* **1** : full **2 de lleno** : completely — **lleno** *nm* : full house

llevar *vt* **1** : take, carry **2** CONDUCIR : lead **3** : wear (clothing, etc.) **4** TENER : have **5 llevo una hora aquí** : I've been here for an hour — **llevarse** *vr* **1** : take (away) **2 ~ bien** : get along well — **llevadero, -ra** *adj* : bearable

llorar *vi* : cry, weep — **lloriquear** *vi* : whimper, whine — **lloro** *nm* : crying — **llorón, -rona** *n, mpl* **-rones** : crybaby, whiner — **lloroso, -sa** *adj* : tearful

llover {47} *v impers* : rain — **llovizna** *nf* : drizzle — **lloviznar** *v impers* : drizzle

lluvia *nf* : rain — **lluvioso, -sa** *adj* : rainy

lo *pron* **1** : him, it **2** (*formal, masculine*) : you **3 ~ que** : what, that which — **~ art 1** : the **2 ~ mejor** : the best (part) **3 sé ~ bueno que eres** : I know how good you are

loa *nf* : praise — **loable** *adj* : praiseworthy — **loar** *vt* : praise

lobo, -ba *n* : wolf

lóbrego, -ga *adj* : gloomy

lóbulo *nm* : lobe

local *adj* : local — **~** *nm* : premises *pl* — **localidad** *nf* : town, locality — **localizar** {21} *vt* **1** : localize **2** ENCONTRAR : locate — **localizarse** *vr* : be located

loción *nf, pl* **-ciones** : lotion

loco, -ca *adj* **1** : crazy, insane **2 a lo loco** : wildly, recklessly **3 volverse ~** : go mad — **~** *n* **1** : crazy person, lunatic **2 hacerse el loco** : act the fool

locomoción *nf, pl* **-ciones** : locomotion — **locomotora** *nf* : engine, locomotive

locuaz *adj, pl* **-cuaces** : talkative, loquacious

locución *nf, pl* **-ciones** : expression, phrase

locura *nf* **1** : insanity, madness **2** INSENSATEZ : crazy act, folly

locutor, -tora *n* : announcer

locutorio *nf, pl* : phone booth

lodo *nm* : mud — **lodazal** *nm* : quagmire

logaritmo *nm* : logarithm

lógica *nf* : logic — **lógico, -ca** *adj* : logical — **logística** *nf* : logistics *pl*

logotipo *nm* : logo

lograr *vt* **1** : achieve, attain **2** CONSEGUIR : get, obtain **3 ~ hacer** : manage to do — **logro** *nm* : achievement, success

loma *nf* : hill, hillock

lombriz *nf, pl* **-brices** : worm

lomo *nm* **1** : back (of an animal) **2** : spine (of a book) **3 ~ de cerdo** : pork loin

lona *nf* : canvas

loncha *nf* : slice (of bacon, etc.)

lonche *nm Lat* : lunch — **lonchería** *nf Lat* : luncheonette

longaniza *nf* : sausage

longevidad *nf* : longevity — **longevo, -va** *adj* : long-lived

longitud *nf* **1** : longitude **2** LARGO : length

lonja → loncha

loro *nm* : parrot

los, las *pron* **1** : them **2** : you **3 los que, las que** : those who, the ones who — **los** *art* → **el**

losa *nf* **1** : flagstone **2** *or* **~ sepulcral** : tombstone

lote *nm* **1** : batch, lot **2** *Lat* : plot of land

lotería *nf* : lottery

loto *nm* : lotus

loza *nf* : crockery, earthenware

lozano, -na *adj* **1** : healthy-looking, vigorous **2** : luxuriant (of plants) — **lozanía** *nf* **1** : (youthful) vigor **2** : luxuriance (of plants)

lubricar {72} *vt* : lubricate — **lubri-**

cante *adj* : lubricating — **~** *nm* : lubricant
lucero *nm* : bright star
luchar *vi* 1 : fight, struggle 2 : wrestle (in sports) — **lucha** *nf* 1 : struggle, fight 2 : wrestling (sport) — **luchador, -dora** *n* : fighter, wrestler
lucidez *nf, pl* **-deces** : lucidity — **lúcido, -da** *adj* : lucid
lucido, -da *adj* : magnificent, splendid
luciérnaga *nf* : firefly, glowworm
lucir {45} *vi* 1 : shine 2 *Lat* : appear, seem — *vt* 1 : wear, sport 2 OSTENTAR : show off — **lucirse** *vr* 1 : shine, excel 2 PRESUMIR : show off — **lucimiento** *nm* 1 : brilliance 2 ÉXITO : brilliant performance, success
lucrativo, -va *adj* : lucrative — **lucro** *nm* : profit
luego *adv* 1 : then 2 : later (on) 3 desde **~** : of course 4 ¡hasta **~**! : see you later! 5 **~** que : as soon as — **~** *conj* : therefore
lugar *nm* 1 : place 2 ESPACIO : space, room 3 dar **~** a : give rise to 4 en **~** de : instead of 5 tener **~** : take place

lugarteniente *nmf* : deputy
lúgubre *adj* : gloomy
lujo *nm* 1 : luxury 2 de **~** : deluxe — **lujoso, -sa** *adj* : luxurious
lujuria *nf* : lust
lumbre *nf* 1 : fire 2 poner en la **~** : put on the stove
luminoso, -sa *adj* : shining, luminous
luna *nf* 1 : moon 2 : (window) glass 3 ESPEJO : mirror 4 **~** de miel : honeymoon — **lunar** *adj* : lunar — **~** *nm* : mole, beauty spot
lunes *nms & pl* : Monday
lupa *nf* : magnifying glass
lúpulo *nm* : hops
lustrar *vt* : shine, polish — **lustre** *nm* 1 BRILLO : luster, shine 2 ESPLENDOR : glory — **lustroso, -sa** *adj* : lustrous, shiny
luto *nm* 1 : mourning 2 estar de **~** : be in mourning
luxación *nf, pl* **-ciones** : dislocation
luz *nf, pl* **luces** 1 : light 2 : lighting (in a room, etc.) 3 *fam* : electricity 4 a la **~** de : in light of 5 dar a **~** : give birth 6 sacar a la **~** : bring to light

M

m *nf* : m, 13th letter of the Spanish alphabet
macabro, -bra *adj* : macabre
macarrón *nm, pl* **-rrones** 1 : macaroon 2 **macarrones** *nmpl* : macaroni
maceta *nf* : flowerpot
machacar {72} *vt* : crush, grind — *vi* **~** sobre : go on about — **machacón, -cona** *adj, mpl* **-cones** : tiresome, boring
machete *nm* : machete — **machetear** *vt* : hack with a machete
macho *adj* 1 : male 2 *fam* : macho — **~** *nm* 1 : male 2 *fam* : he-man — **machista** *nm* : male chauvinist
machucar {72} *vt* 1 : beat, crush 2 : bruise (fruit)
macizo, -za *adj* : solid — **macizo** *nm* **~** de flores : flower bed
mácula *nf* : stain
madeja *nf* : skein, hank
madera *nf* 1 : wood 2 : lumber (for construction) 3 **~** dura : hardwood — **madero** *nm* : piece of lumber, plank
madre *nf* 1 : mother 2 **~** política : mother-in-law — **madrastra** *nf* : stepmother
madreselva *nf* : honeysuckle

madriguera *nf* : burrow, den
madrileño, -ña *adj* : of or from Madrid
madrina *nf* 1 : godmother 2 : bridesmaid (at a wedding)
madrugada *nf* : dawn, daybreak — **madrugador, -dora** *n* : early riser
madurar *v* 1 : mature 2 : ripen (of fruit) — **madurez** *nf, pl* **-reces** 1 : maturity 2 : ripeness (of fruit) — **maduro, -ra** *adj* 1 : mature 2 : ripe (of fruit)
maestría *nf* : mastery, skill — **maestro, -tra** *adj* : masterly, skilled — **~** *n* 1 : teacher (in grammar school) 2 EXPERTO : expert, master
Mafia *nf* : Mafia
magia *nf* : magic — **mágico, -ca** *adj* : magic, magical
magisterio *nm* : teachers *pl*, teaching profession
magistrado, -da *n* : magistrate, judge
magistral *adj* 1 : masterful 2 : magisterial (of an attitude, etc.)
magnánimo, -ma *adj* : magnanimous — **magnanimidad** *nf* : magnanimity
magnate *nmf* : magnate, tycoon
magnesia *nf* : magnesia — **magnesio** *nm* : magnesium
magnético, -ca *adj* : magnetic — **mag-**

netismo nm : magnetism — **magnetizar** {21} vt : magnetize
magnetófono nm : tape recorder
magnificencia nf : magnificence — **magnífico, -ca** adj : magnificent
magnitud nf : magnitude
magnolia nf : magnolia
mago, -ga n 1 : magician 2 **los Reyes Magos** : the Magi
magro, -gra adj 1 : lean 2 MEZQUINO : poor, meager
magullar vt : bruise — **magulladura** nf : bruise
mahometano, -na adj : Islamic, Muslim — ~ n : Muslim
maicena nf : cornstarch
maíz nm : corn
maja nf : pestle
majadero, -ra adj : foolish, silly — ~ n : fool
majar vt : crush
majestad nf 1 : majesty 2 **Su Majestad** : His/Her Majesty — **majestuoso, -sa** adj : majestic
majo, -ja adj 1 : nice 2 GUAPO : good-looking
mal adv 1 : badly, poorly 2 INCORRECTAMENTE : incorrectly 3 DIFÍCILMENTE : with difficulty, hardly 4 **de ~ en peor** : from bad to worse 5 **menos ~** : it's just as well — ~ nm 1 : evil 2 DAÑO : harm, damage 3 ENFERMEDAD : illness — ~ adj → **malo**
malabarismo nm : juggling — **malabarista** nmf : juggler
malacostumbrar vt : spoil, pamper — **malacostumbrado, -da** adj : spoiled
malaria nf : malaria
malasio, -sia adj : Malaysian
malaventura nf : misfortune — **malaventurado, -da** adj : unfortunate
malayo, -ya adj : Malay, Malayan
malcriado, -da adj : bad-mannered, spoiled
maldad nf 1 : evil 2 : evil deed
maldecir {11} vt : curse, damn — vi 1 : curse, swear 2 ~ **de** : speak ill of — **maldición** nf, pl **-ciones** : curse — **maldito, -ta** adj fam : damned
maleable adj : malleable
maleante nmf : crook
malecón nm, pl **-cones** : jetty
maleducado, -da adj : rude
maleficio nm : curse — **maléfico, -ca** adj : evil, harmful
malentendido nm : misunderstanding
malestar nm 1 : discomfort 2 INQUIETUD : uneasiness
maleta nf 1 : suitcase 2 **hacer la ~** : pack one's bags — **maletero, -ra** n

: porter — **maletero** nm : trunk (of an automobile) — **maletín** nm, pl **-tines** 1 PORTAFOLIO : briefcase 2 : overnight bag
malévolo, -la adj : malevolent — **malevolencia** nf : malevolence
maleza nf 1 : underbrush 2 MALAS HIERBAS : weeds pl
malgastar vt : waste, squander
malhablado, -da adj : foul-mouthed
malhechor, -chora n : criminal, delinquent
malhumorado, -da adj : bad-tempered, cross
malicia nf : malice — **malicioso, -sa** adj : malicious
maligno, -na adj 1 : malignant 2 PERNICIOSO : harmful, evil
malla nf 1 : mesh 2 **~s** nfpl : tights
malo, -la adj (**mal** before masculine singular nouns) 1 : bad 2 : poor (in quality) 3 ENFERMO : unwell 4 **estar de malas** : be in a bad mood — ~ n : villain, bad guy (in movies, etc.)
malograr vt : waste — **malograrse** vr 1 FRACASAR : fail 2 : die young — **malogro** nm : failure
maloliente adj : smelly
malpensado, -da adj : malicious, nasty
malsano, -na adj : unhealthy
malsonante adj : rude
malta nf : malt
maltratar vt : mistreat
maltrecho, -cha adj : battered
malvado, -da adj : evil, wicked
malvavisco nm : marshmallow
malversar vt : embezzle — **malversación** nf, pl **-ciones** : embezzlement
mama nf : teat (of an animal), breast (of a woman)
mamá nf fam : mom, mama
mamar vi 1 : suckle 2 **dar de ~ a** : breast-feed — vt 1 : suckle, nurse 2 : learn from childhood, grow up with — **mamario, -ria** adj : mammary
mamarracho nm fam : mess, sight
mambo nm : mambo
mamífero, -ra adj : mammalian — **mamífero** nm : mammal
mamografía nf : mammogram
mampara nf : screen, room divider
mampostería nf : masonry
manada nf 1 : flock, herd, pack 2 **en ~** : in droves
manar vi 1 : flow 2 ~ **en** : be rich in — **manantial** nm 1 : spring 2 ORIGEN : source
manchar vt 1 : stain, spot, mark 2 : tarnish (a reputation, etc.) — **mancharse** vr : get dirty — **mancha** nf : stain

mancillar *vt* : sully, stain

manco, -ca *adj* : one-armed, one-handed

mancomunar *vt* : combine, join — **mancomunarse** *vr* : unite — **mancomunidad** *nf* : union

mandar *vt* **1** : command, order **2** ENVIAR : send **3** *Lat* : hurl, throw — *vi* **1** : be in charge **2 ¿mande?** *Lat* : yes?, pardon? — **mandadero, -ra** *nm* : messenger — **mandado** *nm* : errand — **mandamiento** *nm* **1** : order, warrant **2** : commandment (in religion)

mandarina *nf* : mandarin orange, tangerine

mandato *nm* **1** : term of office **2** ORDEN : mandate — **mandatario, -ria** *n* **1** : leader (in politics) **2** : agent (in law)

mandíbula *nf* : jaw, jawbone

mandil *nm* : apron

mando *nm* **1** : command, leadership **2 al ～ de** : in charge of **3 ～ a distancia** : remote control

mandolina *nf* : mandolin

mandón, -dona *adj, mpl* **-dones** : bossy

manecilla *nf* : hand (of a clock), pointer

manejar *vt* **1** : handle, operate **2** : manage (a business, etc.) **3** : manipulate (a person) **4** *Lat* : drive (a car) — **manejarse** *vr* **1** : manage, get by **2** *Lat* : behave — **manejo** *nm* **1** : handling, use **2** : management (of a business, etc.)

manera *nf* **1** : way, manner **2 de ～ que** : so that **3 de ninguna ～** : by no means **4 de todas ～s** : anyway

manga *nf* **1** : sleeve **2** MANGUERA : hose

mango *nm* **1** : hilt, handle **2** : mango (fruit)

mangonear *vt fam* : boss around — *vi* **1** : be bossy **2** HOLGAZANEAR : loaf, fool around

manguera *nf* : hose

maní *nm, pl* **-níes** *Lat* : peanut

manía *nf* **1** : mania, obsession **2** MODA PASAJERA : craze, fad **3** ANTIPATÍA : dislike — **maníaco, -ca** *adj* : maniacal — **～** *n* : maniac

maniatar *vt* : tie the hands of

maniático, -ca *adj* : obsessive, fussy — **～** *n* : fussy person, fanatic

manicomio *nm* : insane asylum

manicura *nf* : manicure — **manicuro, -ra** *n* : manicurist

manido, -da *adj* : stale, hackneyed

manifestar {55} *vt* **1** : demonstrate, show **2** DECLARAR : express, declare — **manifestarse** *vr* **1** : become evident **2** : demonstrate (in politics) — **manifestación** *nf, pl* **-ciones 1** : manifestation, sign **2** : demonstration (in politics) — **manifestante** *nmf* : protester, demonstrator — **manifiesto, -ta** *adj* : manifest, evident — **manifiesto** *nm* : manifesto

manija *nf* : handle

manillar *nm* : handlebars *pl*

maniobra *nf* : maneuver — **maniobrar** *v* : maneuver

manipular *vt* **1** : manipulate **2** MANEJAR : handle — **manipulación** *nf, pl* **-ciones** : manipulation

maniquí *nmf, pl* **-quíes** : mannequin, model — **～** *nm* : mannequin, dummy

manirroto, -ta *adj* : extravagant — **～** *n* : spendthrift

manivela *nf* : crank

manjar *nm* : delicacy, special dish

mano *nf* **1** : hand **2** : coat (of paint, etc.) **3 a ～** *or* **a la ～** : at hand, nearby **4 dar la ～** : shake hands **5 de segunda ～** : secondhand **6 ～ de obra** : labor, manpower

manojo *nm* : bunch

manopla *nf* : mitten

manosear *vt* **1** : handle excessively **2** : fondle (a person)

manotazo *nm* : slap

mansalva : a ～ *adv phr* : at close range, without risk

mansarda *nf* : attic

mansedumbre *nf* **1** : gentleness **2** : tameness (of an animal)

mansión *nf, pl* **-siones** : mansion

manso, -sa *adj* **1** : gentle **2** : tame (of an animal)

manta *nf* **1** : blanket **2** *Lat* : poncho

manteca *nf* : lard, fat — **mantecoso, -sa** *adj* : greasy

mantel *nm* : tablecloth — **mantelería** *nf* : table linen

mantener {80} *vt* **1** : support **2** CONSERVAR : preserve **3** : keep up, maintain (relations, correspondence, etc.) **4** AFIRMAR : affirm — **mantenerse** *vr* **1** : support oneself **2 ～ firme** : hold one's ground — **mantenimiento** *nm* **1** : maintenance **2** SUSTENTO : sustenance

mantequilla *nf* : butter — **mantequera** *nf* : churn — **mantequería** *nf* : dairy

mantilla *nf* : mantilla

manto *nm* : cloak

mantón *nm, pl* **-tones** : shawl

manual *adj* : manual — **～** *nm* : manual, handbook

manubrio *nm* **1** : handle, crank **2** *Lat* : handlebars *pl*

manufactura *nf* **1** : manufacture **2** FÁBRICA : factory

manuscrito *nm* : manuscript— **manuscrito, -ta** *adj* : handwritten

manutención *nf, pl* **-ciones** : maintenance

manzana *nf* **1** : apple **2** : (city) block — **manzanar** *nm* : apple orchard — **manzano** *nm* : apple tree

maña *nf* **1** : skill **2** ASTUCIA : cunning, guile

mañana *adv* : tomorrow — ~ *nm* **el** ~ : the future — ~ *nf* : morning

mañoso, -sa *adj* **1** : skillful **2** *Lat* : finicky

mapa *nm* : map — **mapamundi** *nm* : map of the world

mapache *nm* : raccoon

maqueta *nf* : model, mock-up

maquillaje *nm* : makeup — **maquillarse** *vr* : put on makeup

máquina *nf* **1** : machine **2** LOCOMOTORA : locomotive **3 a toda** ~ : at full speed **4** ~ **de escribir** : typewriter — **maquinación** *nf, pl* **-ciones** : machination — **maquinal** *adj* : mechanical — **maquinaria** *nf* **1** : machinery **2** : mechanism, works *pl* (of a watch, etc.) — **maquinilla** *nf* : small machine — **maquinista** *nmf* **1** : machinist **2** : (railroad) engineer

mar *nmf* **1** : sea **2 alta** ~ : high seas *pl*

maraca *nf* : maraca

maraña *nf* **1** : thicket **2** ENREDO : tangle, mess

maratón *nm, pl* **-tones** : marathon

maravilla *nf* **1** : wonder, marvel **2** : marigold (flower) — **maravillar** *vt* : astonish — **maravillarse** *vr* : be amazed — **maravilloso, -sa** *adj* : marvelous

marca *nf* **1** : mark **2** : brand (on livestock) **3 or** ~ **de fábrica** : trademark **4** : record (in sports) — **marcado, -da** *adj* : marked — **marcador** *nm* **1** : scoreboard **2** *Lat* : marker, felt-tipped pen

marcapasos *nms & pl* : pacemaker

marcar {72} *vt* **1** : mark **2** : brand (livestock) **3** INDICAR : indicate, show **4** : dial (a telephone, etc.) **5** : score (in sports) — *vi* **1** : score **2** : dial (on the telephone, etc.)

marchar *vi* **1** : go **2** CAMINAR : walk **3** FUNCIONAR : work, run — **marcharse** *vr* : leave, go — **marcha** *nf* **1** : march **2** PASO : pace, speed **3** : gear (of an automobile) **4 poner en** ~ : put in motion

marchitarse *vr* : wither, wilt — **marchito, -ta** *adj* : withered

marcial *adj* : martial, military

marco *nm* **1** : frame **2** : goalposts *pl* (in sports) **3** ENTORNO : setting, framework

marea *nf* : tide — **marear** *vt* **1** : make nauseous or dizzy **2** CONFUNDIR : confuse — **marearse** *vr* **1** : become nauseated or dizzy **2** CONFUNDIRSE : get confused — **mareado, -da** *adj* **1** : sick, nauseous **2** ATURDIDO : dazed, dizzy

maremoto *nm* : tidal wave

mareo *nm* **1** : nausea, seasickness **2** VÉRTIGO : dizziness

marfil *nm* : ivory

margarina *nf* : margarine

margarita *nf* : daisy

margen *nm, pl* **márgenes** **1** : edge, border **2** : margin (of a page, etc.) — **marginado, -da** *adj* **1** : alienated **2** **clases marginadas** : underclass — ~ *n* : outcast — **marginal** *adj* : marginal — **marginar** *vt* : ostracize, exclude

mariachi *nm* : mariachi musician or band

maridaje *nm* : marriage, union — **marido** *nm* : husband

marihuana *or* **mariguana** *or* **marijuana** *nf* : marijuana

marimba *nf* : marimba

marina *nf* **1** : coast **2** *or* ~ **de guerra** : navy, fleet

marinada *nf* : marinade — **marinar** *vt* : marinate

marinero, -ra *adj* **1** : sea, marine **2** : seaworthy (of a ship) — **marinero** *nm* : sailor — **marino, -na** *adj* : marine — **marino** *nm* : seaman, sailor

marioneta *nf* : puppet, marionette

mariposa *nf* **1** : butterfly **2** ~ **nocturna** : moth

mariquita *nf* : ladybug

marisco *nm* **1** : shellfish **2** ~**s** *nmpl* : seafood

marisma *nf* : salt marsh

marítimo, -ma *adj* : maritime, shipping

mármol *nm* : marble

marmota *nf* ~ **de América** : groundhog

marquesina *nf* : marquee, (glass) canopy

marrano, -na *n* **1** : pig, hog **2** *fam* : slob

marrar *vt* : miss (a target) — *vi* : fail

marrón *adj & nm, pl* **-rrones** : brown

marroquí *adj* : Moroccan

marsopa *nf* : porpoise

marsupial *nm* : marsupial

Marte *nm* : Mars

martes *nms & pl* : Tuesday

martillo *nm* **1** : hammer **2** ~ **neumáti-**

co : jackhammer — **martillar** or **martillear** v : hammer

mártir nmf : martyr — **martirio** nm : martyrdom — **martirizar** {21} vt 1 : martyr 2 ATORMENTAR : torment

marxismo nm : Marxism — **marxista** adj & nmf : Marxist

marzo nm : March

mas conj : but

más adv 1 : more 2 **el/la/lo ~** : (the) most 3 (in negative constructions) : (any) longer 4 **¡qué día ~ bonito!** : what a beautiful day! — **~** adj 1 : more 2 : most 3 **¿quién ~?** : who else? — **~** prep : plus — **~** pron 1 a **lo ~** : at most 2 **de ~** : extra, spare 3 **~ o menos** : more or less 4 **¿tienes ~?** : do you have more?

masa nf 1 : mass, volume 2 : dough (in cooking) 3 **~s** nfpl : people, masses

masacre nf : massacre

masaje nm : massage — **masajear** vt : massage

mascar {72} v : chew

máscara nf : mask — **mascarada** nf : masquerade — **mascarilla** nf : mask (in medecine, etc.)

mascota nf : mascot

masculino, -na adj 1 : masculine, male 2 VARONIL : manly 3 : masculine (in grammar) — **masculinidad** nf : masculinity

mascullar v : mumble

masilla nf : putty

masivo, -va adj : mass, large-scale

masón nm, pl **-sones** : Mason, Freemason — **masónico, -ca** adj : Masonic

masoquismo nm : masochism — **masoquista** adj : masochistic — **~** nmf : masochist

masticar {72} v : chew

mástil nm 1 : mast 2 ASTA : flagpole 3 : neck (of a stringed instrument)

mastín nm, pl **-tines** : mastiff

masturbarse vr : masturbate — **masturbación** nf, pl **-ciones** : masturbation

mata nf : bush, shrub

matadero nm : slaughterhouse

matador nm : matador, bullfighter

matamoscas nms & pl : flyswatter

matar vt 1 : kill 2 : slaughter (animals) — **matarse** vr 1 : be killed 2 SUICIDARSE : commit suicide — **matanza** nf : slaughter, killing

matasanos nms & pl fam : quack

matasellos nms & pl : postmark

mate adj : matte, dull — **~** nm 1 : maté 2 **jaque ~** : checkmate

matemáticas nfpl : mathematics — **matemático, -ca** adj : mathematical — **~** n : mathematician

materia nf 1 ASUNTO : matter 2 MATERIAL : material — **material** adj 1 : material 2 **daños ~es** : property damage — **~** nm 1 : material 2 EQUIPO : equipment, gear — **materialismo** nm : materialism — **materialista** adj : materialistic — **materializar** {21} vt : bring to fruition — **materializarse** vr : materialize — **materialmente** adv : absolutely

maternal adj : maternal — **maternidad** nf 1 : motherhood 2 : maternity hospital — **materno, -na** adj 1 : maternal 2 **lengua materna** : mother tongue

matinal adj : morning

matinée or **matiné** nf : matinee

matiz nm, pl **-tices** 1 : nuance 2 : hue, shade (of colors) — **matizar** {21} vt 1 : blend (colors) 2 : qualify (a statement, etc.) 3 **~ de** : tinge with

matón nm, pl **-tones** 1 : bully 2 CRIMINAL : gangster, hoodlum

matorral nm : thicket

matraca nf 1 : rattle, noisemaker 2 **dar la ~ a** : pester

matriarcado nm : matriarchy

matrícula nf 1 : list, roll, register 2 INSCRIPCIÓN : registration 3 : license plate (of an automobile) — **matricular** vt : register — **matricularse** vr : register, matriculate

matrimonio nm 1 : marriage 2 PAREJA : (married) couple — **matrimonial** adj : marital

matriz nf, pl **-trices** 1 : matrix 2 : uterus, womb (in anatomy)

matrona nf : matron

matutino, -na adj : morning

maullar {8} vi : meow — **maullido** nm : meow

maxilar nm : jaw, jawbone

máxima nf : maxim

máxime adv : especially

máximo, -ma adj : maximum, highest — **máximo** nm 1 : maximum 2 **al ~** : to the full

maya adj : Mayan

mayo nm : May

mayonesa nf : mayonnaise

mayor adj 1 (comparative of **grande**) : bigger, larger, greater, older 2 (superlative of **grande**) : biggest, largest, greatest, oldest 3 **al por ~** : wholesale 4 **~ de edad** : of (legal) age — **~** nmf 1 : major (in the military) 2 ADULTO : adult 3 **~es** nmfpl : grown-ups — **mayoral** nm : foreman

mayordomo *nm* : butler

mayoreo *nm Lat* : wholesale

mayoría *nf* : majority

mayorista *adj* : wholesale — ~ *nmf* : wholesaler

mayormente *adv* : primarily

mayúscula *nf* : capital letter — **mayúsculo, -la** *adj* 1 : capital, uppercase 2 **un fallo mayúsculo** : a terrible mistake

maza *nf* : mace (weapon)

mazapán *nm, pl* **-panes** : marzipan

mazmorra *nf* : dungeon

mazo *nm* 1 : mallet 2 MAJA : pestle

mazorca *nf* ~ **de maíz** : corncob

me *pron* 1 (*direct object*) : me 2 (*indirect object*) : to me, for me, from me 3 (*reflexive*) : myself, to myself, for myself, from myself

mecánica *nf* : mechanics — **mecánico, -ca** *adj* : mechanical — ~ *n* : mechanic

mecanismo *nm* : mechanism — **mecanización** *nf, pl* **-ciones** : mechanization — **mecanizar** {21} *vt* : mechanize

mecanografiar {85} *vt* : type — **mecanografía** *nf* : typing — **mecanógrafo, -fa** *n* : typist

mecate *nm Lat* : rope

mecedora *nf* : rocking chair

mecenas *nmfs & pl* : patron, sponsor — **mecenazgo** *nm* : patronage, sponsorship

mecer {86} *vt* 1 : rock 2 : push (on a swing) — **mecerse** *vr* : rock, swing

mecha *nf* 1 : fuse (of a bomb, etc.) 2 : wick (of a candle)

mechero *nm* 1 : burner 2 *Spain* : cigarette lighter

mechón *nm, pl* **-chones** : lock (of hair)

medalla *nf* : medal — **medallón** *nm, pl* **-llones** 1 : medallion 2 : locket (jewelry)

media *nf* 1 : average 2 ~s *nfpl* : stockings 3 a ~s : by halves, halfway

mediación *nf, pl* **-ciones** : mediation

mediado, -da *adj* 1 : half full, half empty, half over 2 : halfway through — **mediados** *nmpl* a ~ **de** : halfway through, in the middle of

mediador, -dora *n* : mediator

medialuna *nf* 1 : crescent 2 : croissant (pastry)

medianamente *adv* : fairly

medianero, -ra *adj* **pared medianera** : dividing wall

mediano, -na *adj* 1 : medium, average 2 MEDIOCRE : mediocre

medianoche *nf* : midnight

mediante *prep* : through, by means of

mediar *vi* 1 : be in the middle 2 INTERVENIR : mediate 3 ~ **entre** : be between

medicación *nf, pl* **-ciones** : medication — **medicamento** *nm* : medicine — **medicar** {72} *vt* : medicate — **medicarse** *vr* : take medicine — **medicina** *nf* : medicine — **medicinal** *adj* : medicinal

medición *nf, pl* **-ciones** : measurement

médico, -ca *adj* : medical — ~ *n* : doctor, physician

medida *nf* 1 : measurement, measure 2 MODERACIÓN : moderation 3 GRADO : extent, degree 4 **tomar** ~s : take steps — **medidor** *nm Lat* : meter, gauge

medieval *adj* : medieval

medio, -dia *adj* 1 : half 2 MEDIANO : average 3 **una media hora** : half an hour 4 **la clase media** : the middle class — **medio** *adv* : half — ~ *nm* 1 : half 2 MANERA : means *pl*, way 3 **en** ~ **de** : in the middle of 4 ~ **ambiente** : environment 5 ~s *nmpl* : means, resources

mediocre *adj* : mediocre, average — **mediocridad** *nf* : mediocrity

mediodía *nm* : noon, midday

medioevo *nm* : Middle Ages

medir {54} *vt* 1 : measure 2 CONSIDERAR : weigh, consider — **medirse** *vr* : be moderate

meditar *vi* : meditate, contemplate — *vt* 1 : think over, consider 2 PLANEAR : plan, work out — **meditación** *nf, pl* **-ciones** : meditation

mediterráneo, -nea *adj* : Mediterranean

medrar *vt* : flourish, thrive

medroso, -sa *adj* : fearful

médula *nf* 1 : marrow 2 ~ **espinal** : spinal cord

medusa *nf* : jellyfish

megabyte *nm* : megabyte

megáfono *nm* : megaphone

mejicano → **mexicano**

mejilla *nf* : cheek

mejillón *nm, pl* **-llones** : mussel

mejor *adv* 1 (*comparative*) : better 2 (*superlative*) : best 3 a **lo** ~ : maybe, perhaps — ~ *adj* 1 (*comparative of* **bueno** *or* **bien**) : better 2 (*superlative of* **bueno** *or* **bien**) : best 3 **lo** ~ : the best thing 4 **tanto** ~ : so much the better — **mejora** *nf* : improvement

mejorana *nf* : marjoram

mejorar *vt* : improve — *vi* : improve, get better

mejunje *nm* : concoction, brew

melancolía *nf* : melancholy — **melan-cólico, -ca** *adj* : melancholic, melancholy

melaza *nf* : molasses

melena *nf* 1 : long hair 2 : mane (of a lion)

melindroso, -sa *adj* 1 : affected 2 *Lat* : finicky

mella *nf* : chip, nick — **mellado, -da** *adj* : chipped, jagged

mellizo, -za *adj & n* : twin

melocotón *nm, pl* **-tones** : peach

melodía *nf* : melody — **melódico, -ca** *adj* : melodic

melodrama *nm* : melodrama — **melo-dramático, -ca** *adj* : melodramatic

melón *nm, pl* **-lones** : melon

meloso, -sa *adj* 1 : sweet, honeyed 2 EMPALAGOSO : cloying

membrana *nf* : membrane

membrete *nm* : letterhead, heading

membrillo *nm* : quince

membrudo, -da *adj* : muscular, burly

memorable *adj* : memorable

memorándum *or* **memorando** *nm, pl* **-dums** *or* **-dos** 1 : memorandum 2 AGENDA : notebook

memoria *nf* 1 : memory 2 RECUERDO : remembrance 3 INFORME : report 4 **de ~** : by heart 5 **~s** *nfpl* : memoirs — **memorizar** {21} *vt* : memorize

mena *nf* : ore

menaje *nm* : household goods *pl*, fur-nishings *pl*

mencionar *vt* : mention, refer to — **mención** *nf, pl* **-ciones** : mention

mendaz *adj, pl* **-daces** : lying

mendigar {52} *vi* : beg — *vt* : beg for — **mendicidad** *nf* : begging — **mendigo, -ga** *n* : beggar

mendrugo *nm* : crust (of bread)

menear *vt* 1 : move, shake 2 : sway (one's hips) 3 : wag (a tail) — **men-earse** *vr* 1 : sway, shake, move 2 *fam* : hurry up

menester *nm* **ser ~** : be necessary — **menestroso, -sa** *adj* : needy

menguar *vt* : diminish, lessen — *vi* 1 : decline, decrease 2 : wane (of the moon) — **mengua** *nf* : decrease, de-cline

menopausia *nf* : menopause

menor *adj* 1 (*comparative of* **pequeño**) : smaller, lesser, younger 2 (*superla-tive of* **pequeño**) : smallest, least, youngest 3 : minor (in music) 4 **al por ~** : retail — **~** *nmf* : minor, juvenile

menos *adv* 1 (*comparative*) : less 2 (*su-perlative*) : least 3 **~ de** : fewer than — **~** *adj* 1 (*comparative*) : less, fewer 2 (*superlative*) : least, fewest — **~** *prep* 1 : minus 2 EXCEPTO : except — **~** *pron* 1 : less, fewer 2 **al ~** *or* **por lo ~** : at least 3 **a ~ que** : unless — **menoscabar** *vt* 1 : lessen 2 ESTRO-PEAR : harm, damage — **menospre-ciar** *vt* 1 DESPRECIAR : scorn 2 SUBES-TIMAR : undervalue — **menosprecio** *nm* : contempt

mensaje *nm* : message — **mensajero, -ra** *n* : messenger

menso, -sa *adj Lat fam* : foolish, stupid

menstruar {3} *vi* : menstruate — **men-struación** *nf* : menstruation

mensual *adj* : monthly — **mensuali-dad** *nf* 1 : monthly payment 2 : monthly salary

mensurable *adj* : measurable

menta *nf* 1 : mint, peppermint 2 **~ verde** : spearmint

mental *adj* : mental — **mentalidad** *nf* : mentality

mentar {55} *vt* : mention, name

mente *nf* : mind

mentir {76} *vi* : lie — **mentira** *nf* : lie — **mentirilla** *nf* : fib — **mentiroso, -sa** *adj* : lying — **~** *n* : liar

mentís *nms & pl* : denial

mentol *nm* : menthol

mentón *nm, pl* **-tones** : chin

menú *nm, pl* **-nús** : menu

menudear *vi* : occur frequently — **menudeo** *nm Lat* : retail, retailing

menudillos *nmpl* : giblets

menudo, -da *adj* 1 : small, insignificant 2 **a ~** : often

meñique *nm or* **dedo ~** : little finger, pinkie

meollo *nm* 1 : marrow 2 ESENCIA : es-sence, core

mercado *nm* 1 : market 2 **~ de va-lores** : stock market — **mercadería** *nf* : merchandise, goods *pl*

mercancía *nf* : merchandise, goods *pl* — **mercante** *nmf* : merchant, dealer — **mercantil** *adj* : commercial

mercenario, -ria *adj & n* : mercenary

mercería *nf* : notions store

mercurio *nm* : mercury

Mercurio *nm* : Mercury (planet)

merecer {53} *vt* : deserve — *vi* : be worthy — **merecedor, -dora** *adj* : de-serving, worthy — **merecido** *nm* **recibir su ~** : get one's just deserts

merendar {55} *vi* : have an afternoon snack — *vt* : have as an afternoon snack — **merendero** *nm* 1 : snack bar 2 : picnic area

merengue *nm* 1 : meringue 2 : me-rengue (dance)

meridiano, -na *adj* **1** : midday **2** CLARO : crystal-clear — **meridiano** *nm* : meridian — **meridional** *adj* : southern

merienda *nf* : afternoon snack, tea

mérito *nm* : merit, worth — **meritorio, -ria** *adj* : deserving — ~ *n* : intern, trainee

mermar *vi* : decrease — *vt* : reduce, cut down — **merma** *nf* : decrease

mermelada *nf* : marmalade, jam

mero, -ra *adj* **1** : mere, simple **2** *Lat fam* (*used as an intensifier*) : very, real — **mero** *adv Lat fam* **1** : nearly, almost **2 aquí** ~ : right here

merodear *vi* **1** : maraud **2** ~ **por** : prowl about (a place)

mes *nm* : month

mesa *nf* **1** : table **2** COMITÉ : committee, board

mesarse *vr* ~ **los cabellos** : tear one's hair

meseta *nf* : plateau

Mesías *nm* : Messiah

mesilla *nf* : small table

mesón *nm, pl* **-sones** : inn — **mesonero, -ra** *nm* : innkeeper

mestizo, -za *adj* **1** : of mixed ancestry **2** HÍBRIDO : hybrid — ~ *n* : person of mixed ancestry

mesura *nf* : moderation — **mesurado, -da** *adj* : moderate, restrained

meta *nf* : goal, objective

metabolismo *nm* : metabolism

metafísica *nf* : metaphysics — **metafísico, -ca** *adj* : metaphysical

metáfora *nf* : metaphor — **metafórico, -ca** *adj* : metaphoric, metaphorical

metal *nm* **1** : metal **2** : brass section (in an orchestra) — **metálico, -ca** *adj* : metallic, metal — **metalurgia** *nf* : metallurgy

metamorfosis *nfs & pl* : metamorphosis

metano *nm* : methane

metedura *nf* ~ **de pata** *fam* : blunder

meteoro *nm* : meteor — **meteórico, -ca** *adj* : meteoric — **meteorito** *nm* : meteorite — **meteorología** *nf* : meteorology — **meteorólogo, -ga** *adj* : meteorological, meteorologic — ~ *n* : meteorologist

meter *vt* **1** : put (in) **2** : place (in a job, etc.) **3** ENREDAR : involve **4** CAUSAR : make, cause **5** : spread (a rumor) **6** *Lat* : strike (a blow) — **meterse** *vr* **1** : get in, enter **2** ~ **en** : get involved in, meddle in **3** ~ **con** *fam* : pick a fight with

meticuloso, -sa *adj* : meticulous

método *nm* : method — **metódico, -ca**
adj : methodical — **metodología** *nf* : methodology

metomentodo *nmf fam* : busybody

metralla *nf* : shrapnel — **metralleta** *nf* : submachine gun

métrico, -ca *adj* : metric, metrical

metro *nm* **1** : meter **2** : subway (train)

metrópoli *nf or* **metrópolis** *nfs & pl* : metropolis — **metropolitano, -na** *adj* : metropolitan

mexicano, -na *adj* : Mexican — **mexicoamericano, -na** *adj* : Mexican-American

mezcla *nf* **1** : mixture **2** ARGAMASA : mortar — **mezclar** *vt* **1** : mix, blend **2** CONFUNDIR : mix up, muddle **3** INVOLUCRAR : involve — **mezclarse** *vr* **1** : get mixed up **2** : mingle (socially) — **mezcolanza** *nf* : mixture

mezclilla *nf Lat* : denim

mezquino, -na *adj* **1** : mean, petty **2** ESCASO : meager — **mezquindad** *nf* : meanness, stinginess

mezquita *nf* : mosque

mezquite *nm* : mesquite

mi *adj* : my

mí *pron* **1** : me **2** *or* ~ **mismo,** ~ **misma** : myself **3 a** ~ **no me importa** : it doesn't matter to me

miajas → **migajas**

miau *nm* : meow

mica *nf* : mica

mico *nm* : (long-tailed) monkey

microbio *nm* : microbe, germ — **microbiología** *nf* : microbiology

microbús *nm, pl* **-buses** : minibus

microcosmos *nms & pl* : microcosm

microfilm *nm, pl* **-films** : microfilm

micrófono *nm* : microphone

microondas *nms & pl* : microwave (oven)

microorganismo *nm* : microorganism

microscopio *nm* : microscope — **microscópico, -ca** *adj* : microscopic

miedo *nm* **1** : fear **2 dar** ~ : be frightening — **miedoso, -sa** *adj* : fearful

miel *nf* : honey

miembro *nm* **1** : member **2** EXTREMIDAD : limb, extremity

mientras *adv or* ~ **tanto** : meanwhile, in the meantime — ~ *conj* **1** : while, as **2** ~ **que** : while, whereas **3** ~ **viva** : as long as I live

miércoles *nms & pl* : Wednesday

mies *nf* : (ripe) corn, grain

miga *nf* : crumb — **migajas** *nfpl* **1** : breadcrumbs **2** SOBRAS : leftovers

migración *nf, pl* **-ciones** : migration

migraña *nf* : migraine

migrar *vi* : migrate

mijo *nm* : millet

mil *adj & nm* : thousand

milagro *nm* : miracle — **milagroso, -sa**
adj : miraculous

milenio *nm* : millennium

milésimo, -ma *adj* : thousandth

milicia *nf* 1 : militia 2 : military (service)

miligramo *nm* : milligram

mililitro *nm* : milliliter

milímetro *nm* : millimeter

militante *adj & nmf* : militant

militar *adj* : military — **~** *nmf* : soldier
— **militarizar** {21} *vt* : militarize

milla *nf* : mile

millar *nm* : thousand

millón *nm, pl* **-llones** 1 : million 2 **mil
millones** : billion — **millonario, -ria**
n : millionaire — **millonésimo, -ma**
adj : millionth

mimar *vt* : pamper, spoil

mimbre *nm* : wicker

mímica *nf* 1 : mime, sign language 2
IMITACIÓN : mimicry

mimo *nm* : pampering — **~** *nmf* : mime

mina *nf* 1 : mine 2 : lead (for pencils) —
minar *vt* 1 : mine 2 DEBILITAR : undermine

mineral *adj* : mineral — **~** *nm* 1 : mineral 2 : ore (of a metal)

minería *nf* : mining — **minero, -ra** *adj*
: mining — **~** *n* : miner

miniatura *nf* : miniature

minifalda *nf* : miniskirt

minifundio *nm* : small farm

minimizar {21} *vt* : minimize

mínimo, -ma *adj* 1 : minimum 2 MINÚS-
CULO : minute 3 **en lo más ~** : in the
slightest — **mínimo** *nm* : minimum

minino, -na *n fam* : pussycat

ministerio *nm* : ministry — **ministro,
-tra** *n* 1 : minister, secretary 2 **primer
ministro** : prime minister

minoría *nf* : minority

minorista *adj* : retail — **~** *nmf* : retailer

minoritario, -ria *adj* : minority

minucia *nf* : trifle, small detail — **minucioso, -sa** *adj* 1 : detailed 2 METICU-
LOSO : thorough

minué *nm* : minuet

minúsculo, -la *adj* : minuscule, tiny

minusvalía *nf* : handicap, disability —
minusválido, -da *adj* : disabled

minuta *nf* 1 : bill, fee 2 BORRADOR
: rough draft

minuto *nm* : minute — **minutero** *nm*
: minute hand

mío, mía *adj* 1 : mine 2 **una amiga mía**
: a friend of mine — **~** *pron* **el mío, la
mía** : mine, my own

miope *adj* : nearsighted

mirar *vt* 1 : look at 2 OBSERVAR : watch
3 CONSIDERAR : consider — *vi* 1 : look
2 **~ a** : face, overlook 3 **~ por** : look
after — **mirarse** *vr* 1 : look at oneself
2 : look at each other — **mira** *nf* 1
: sight (of a firearm or instrument) 2
INTENCIÓN : aim, objective — **mirada**
nf : look — **mirado, -da** *adj* 1 : careful
2 CONSIDERADO : considerate 3 **bien
~** : well thought of — **mirador** *nm* 1
BALCÓN : balcony 2 : lookout, vantage
point — **miramiento** *nm* : consideration

mirlo *nm* : blackbird

misa *nf* : Mass

miscelánea *nf* : miscellany

miserable *adj* 1 : poor 2 LASTIMOSO
: miserable, wretched — **miseria** *nf* 1
: poverty 2 DESGRACIA : misfortune,
misery

misericordia *nf* : mercy — **misericor-
dioso, -sa** *adj* : merciful

mísero, -ra *adj* : wretched, miserable

misil *nm* : missile

misión *nf, pl* **-siones** : mission — **misionero, -ra** *adj & n* : missionary

mismo *adv* (*used for emphasis*) : right,
exactly — **mismo, -ma** *adj* 1 : same 2
(*used for emphasis*) : very 3 : -self 4
por lo ~ : for that reason

misoginia *nf* : misogyny — **misógino**
nm : misogynist

misterio *nm* : mystery — **misterioso,
-sa** *adj* : mysterious

mística *nf* : mysticism — **místico, -ca**
adj : mystic, mystical — **~** *n* : mystic

mitad *nf* 1 : half 2 MEDIO : middle

mítico, -ca *adj* : mythical, mythic

mitigar {52} *vt* : mitigate

mitin *nm, pl* **mítines** : (political) meeting

mito *nm* : myth — **mitología** *nm*
: mythology — **mitológico, -ca** *adj*
: mythological

mixto, -ta *adj* 1 : mixed, joint 2 : coeducational (of a school)

mnemónico, -ca *adj* : mnemonic

mobiliario *nm* : furniture

mocasín *nm, pl* **-sines** : moccasin

mochila *nf* : backpack, knapsack

moción *nf, pl* **-ciones** : motion

moco *nm* 1 : mucus 2 **limpiarse los
~s** : wipe one's nose — **mocoso, -sa**
n fam : kid, brat

moda *nf* 1 : fashion, style 2 **a la ~ or
de ~** : in style, fashionable 3 **~
pasajera** : fad — **modal** *adj* : modal
— **modales** *nmpl* : manners —
modalidad *nf* : type, kind

modelar *vt* : model, mold — **modelo** *adj* : model — ~ *nm* : model, pattern — ~ *nmf* : model, mannequin

módem *or* **modem** ['moðem] *nm* : modem

moderar *vt* **1** : moderate **2** : reduce (speed, etc.) **3** PRESIDIR : chair (a meeting) — **moderarse** *vr* : restrain oneself — **moderación** *nf, pl* **-ciones** : moderation — **moderado, -da** *adj & n* : moderate — **moderador, -dora** *n* : moderator, chairperson

moderno, -na *adj* : modern — **modernismo** *nm* : modernism — **modernizar** {21} *vt* : modernize

modesto, -ta *adj* : modest — **modestia** *nf* : modesty

modificar {72} *vt* : modify, alter — **modificación** *nf, pl* **-ciones** : alteration

modismo *nm* : idiom

modista *nmf* **1** : dressmaker **2** : (fashion) designer

modo *nm* **1** : way, manner **2** : mood (in grammar) **3** : mode (in music) **4 a ~ de** : by way of **5 de ~ que** : so (that) **6 de todos ~s** : in any case, anyway

modorra *nf* : drowsiness

modular *vt* : modulate — **modulación** *nf, pl* **-ciones** : modulation

módulo *nm* : module, unit

mofa *nf* : ridicule, mockery — **mofarse** *vr* ~ **de** : make fun of

mofeta *nf* : skunk

moflete *nm fam* : fat cheek — **mofletudo, -da** *adj fam* : fat-cheeked, chubby

mohín *nm, pl* **-hines** : grimace — **mohíno, -na** *adj* : sulky

moho *nm* **1** : mold, mildew **2** ÓXIDO : rust — **mohoso, -sa** *adj* **1** : moldy **2** OXIDADO : rusty

moisés *nm, pl* **-seses** : bassinet, cradle

mojar *vt* **1** : wet, moisten **2** : dunk (food) — **mojarse** *vr* : get wet — **mojado, -da** *adj* : wet, damp

mojigato, -ta *adj* : prudish — ~ *n* : prude

mojón *nm, pl* **-jones** : boundary stone, marker

molar *nm* : molar

moldear *vt* : mold, shape — **molde** *nm* : mold, form — **moldura** *nf* : molding

mole[1] *nf* : mass, bulk

mole[2] *nm* **1** : Mexican chili sauce **2** : meat served with mole

molécula *nf* : molecule — **molecular** *adj* : molecular

moler {47} *vt* : grind, crush

molestar *vt* **1** : annoy, bother **2 no ~** : do not disturb — *vi* : be a nuisance — **molestarse** *vr* **1** : bother **2** OFENDERSE : take offense — **molestia** *nf* **1** : annoyance, nuisance **2** MALESTAR : discomfort — **molesto, -ta** *adj* **1** : annoyed **2** FASTIDIOSO : annoying **3** INCÓMODO : in discomfort — **molestoso, -sa** *adj* : bothersome, annoying

molido, -da *adj* **1** : ground (of meat, etc.) **2** *fam* : worn out, exhausted

molino *nm* **1** : mill **2** ~ **de viento** : windmill — **molinero, -ra** *n* : miller — **molinillo** *nm* : grinder, mill

mollera *nf* **1** : crown (of the head) **2** *fam* : brains *pl*

molusco *nm* : mollusk

momento *nm* **1** : moment, instant **2** : (period of) time **3** : momentum (in physics) **4 de ~** : for the moment **5 de un ~ a otro** : any time now — **momentáneamente** *adv* : momentarily — **momentáneo, -nea** *adj* **1** : momentary **2** PASAJERO : temporary

momia *nf* : mummy

monaguillo *nm* : altar boy

monarca *nmf* : monarch — **monarquía** *nf* : monarchy

monasterio *nm* : monastery — **monástico, -ca** *adj* : monastic

mondadientes *nms & pl* : toothpick

mondar *vt* : peel

mondongo *nm* : innards *pl*, guts *pl*

moneda *nf* **1** : coin **2** : currency (of a country) — **monedero** *nm* : change purse

monetario, -ria *adj* : monetary

monitor *nm* : monitor

monja *nf* : nun — **monje** *nm* : monk

mono, -na *n* : monkey — ~ *adj fam* : lovely, cute

monogamia *nf* : monogamy — **monógamo -ma** *adj* : monogamous

monografía *nf* : monograph

monograma *nm* : monogram

monolingüe *adj* : monolingual

monólogo *nm* : monologue

monopatín *nm, pl* **-tines** : scooter, skateboard

monopolio *nm* : monopoly — **monopolizar** {21} *vt* : monopolize

monosílabo *nm* : monosyllable — **monosilábico, -ca** *adj* : monosyllabic

monoteísmo *nm* : monotheism — **monoteísta** *adj* : monotheistic

monotonía *nf* : monotony — **monótono, -na** *adj* : monotonous

monóxido *nm* ~ **de carbono** : carbon monoxide

monstruo *nm* : monster — **monstruosidad** *nf* : monstrosity — **monstruoso, -sa** *adj* : monstrous

monta *nf* : importance, value

montaje *nm* **1** : assembly **2** : staging (in theater), editing (of films)

montaña *nf* **1** : mountain **2** ~ **rusa** : roller coaster — **montañero, -ra** *n* : mountain climber — **montañoso, -sa** *adj* : mountainous

montar *vt* **1** : mount **2** ESTABLECER : establish **3** ENSAMBLAR : assemble, put together **4** : stage (a performance) **5** : cock (a gun) — *vi* **1** ~ **a caballo** : ride horseback **2** ~ **en bicicleta** : get on a bicycle

monte *nm* **1** : mountain **2** BOSQUE : woodland **3** *or* ~ **bajo** : scrubland **4** ~ **de piedad** : pawnshop

montés *adj, pl* **-teses** : wild (of animals or plants)

montículo *nm* : mound, hillock

montón *nm, pl* **-tones 1** : heap, pile **2** **un** ~ **de** *fam* : lots of

montura *nf* **1** : mount (horse) **2** SILLA : saddle **3** : frame (of glasses)

monumento *nm* : monument — **monumental** *adj fam* : monumental, huge

monzón *nm, pl* **-zones** : monsoon

moño *nm* **1** : bun (of hair) **2** *Lat* : bow (knot)

mora *nf* **1** : mulberry **2** ZARZAMORA : blackberry

morada *nf* : residence, dwelling

morado, -da *adj* : purple — **morado** *nm* : purple

moral *adj* : moral — ~ *nf* **1** : ethics, morals *pl* **2** ÁNIMO : morale — **moraleja** *nf* : moral (of a story) — **moralidad** *nf* : morality — **moralista** *adj* : moralistic — ~ *nmf* : moralist

morar *vi* : live, reside

morboso, -sa *adj* : morbid

mordaz *adj* : caustic, scathing — **mordacidad** *nf* : bite, sharpness

mordaza *nf* : gag

morder {47} *v* : bite — **mordedura** *nf* : bite (of an animal)

mordisquear *vt* : nibble (on) — **mordisco** *nm* : nibble, bite

moreno, -na *adj* **1** : dark-haired, brunette **2** : dark-skinned — ~ *n* **1** : brunette **2** : dark-skinned person

moretón *nm, pl* **-tones** : bruise

morfina *nf* : morphine

morir {46} *vi* **1** : die **2** APAGARSE : die out, go out — **morirse** *vr* **1** ~ **de** : die of **2** ~ **por** : be dying for — **moribundo, -da** *adj* : dying

moro, -ra *adj* : Moorish — ~ *n* : Moor

moroso, -sa *adj* : delinquent, in arrears — **morosidad** *nf* : delinquency (in payment)

morral *nm* : backpack

morriña *nf* : homesickness

morro *nm* : snout

morsa *nf* : walrus

morse *nm* : Morse code

mortaja *nf* : shroud

mortal *adj* **1** : mortal **2** : deadly (of a wound, an enemy, etc.) — ~ *nmf* : mortal — **mortalidad** *nf* : mortality — **mortandad** *nf* : death toll

mortero *nm* : mortar

mortífero, -ra *adj* : deadly, lethal

mortificar {72} *vt* **1** : mortify **2** ATORMENTAR : torment — **mortificarse** *vr* : be distressed

mosaico *nm* : mosaic

mosca *nf* : fly

moscada *adj* → **nuez**

mosquearse *vr fam* **1** : become suspicious **2** ENFADARSE : get annoyed

mosquito *nm* : mosquito — **mosquitero** *nm* **1** : (window) screen **2** : mosquito net

mostachón *nm, pl* **-chones** : macaroon

mostaza *nf* : mustard

mostrador *nm* : counter (in a store)

mostrar {19} *vt* : show — **mostrarse** *vr* : show oneself, appear

mota *nf* : spot, speck — **moteado, -da** *adj* : speckled, spotted

mote *nm* : nickname

motel *nm* : motel

motín *nm, pl* **-tines 1** : riot, uprising **2** : mutiny (of troops)

motivo *nm* **1** : motive, cause **2** : motif (in art, music, etc.) — **motivación** *nf, pl* **-ciones** : motivation — **motivar** *vt* **1** : cause **2** IMPULSAR : motivate

moto *nf* : motorcycle, motorbike — **motocicleta** *nf* : motorcycle — **motociclista** *nmf* : motorcyclist

motor, -triz *or* **-tora** *adj* : motor — **motor** *nm* : motor, engine — **motorista** *nmf* **1** : motorcyclist **2** *Lat* : motorist

mover {47} *vt* **1** : move, shift **2** : shake (the head) **3** PROVOCAR : provoke — **moverse** *vr* **1** : move (over) **2** APRESURARSE : get a move on — **movedizo, -za** *adj* : movable, shifting — **movible** *adj* : movable

móvil *adj* : mobile — ~ *nm* **1** MOTIVO : motive **2** : mobile — **movilidad** *nf* : mobility — **movilizar** {21} *vt* : mobilize

movimiento *nm* **1** : movement, motion **2** ~ **sindicalista** : labor movement

mozo, -za *adj* : young — ~ *n* **1** : young man *m*, young woman *f* **2** *Lat* : waiter *m*, waitress *f*

muchacho, -cha *n* : kid, boy *m*, girl *f*
muchedumbre *nf* : crowd
mucho *adv* **1** : very much, a lot **2** : long, a long time — **mucho, -cha** *adj* **1** : a lot of, many, much **2 muchas veces** : often — **~** *pron* : a lot, many, much
mucosidad *nf* : mucus
muda *nf* **1** : molting (of animals) **2** : change (of clothing) — **mudanza** *nf* **1** : change **2** TRASLADO : move, change of residence — **mudar** *v* **1** : molt, shed **2** CAMBIAR : change — **mudarse** *vr* **1** : change (one's clothes) **2** TRASLADARSE : move (one's residence)
mudo, -da *adj* **1** : mute **2** SILENCIOSO : silent
mueble *nm* **1** : piece of furniture **2 ~s** *nmpl* : furniture, furnishings
mueca *nf* **1** : grimace, face **2 hacer ~s** : makes faces
muela *nf* **1** : tooth, molar **2 ~ de juicio** : wisdom tooth
muelle *adj* : soft — **~** *nm* **1** : wharf, jetty **2** RESORTE : spring
muérdago *nm* : mistletoe
muerte *nf* : death — **muerto, -ta** *adj* **1** : dead **2** : dull (of colors, etc.) — **~** *nm* : dead person, deceased
muesca *nf* : nick, notch
muestra *nf* **1** : sample **2** SEÑAL : sign, show
mugir {35} *vi* : moo, bellow — **mugido** *nm* : mooing, bellowing
mugre *nf* : grime, filth — **mugriento, -ta** *adj* : filthy, grimy
muguete *nm* : lily of the valley
mujer *nf* **1** : woman **2** ESPOSA : wife **3 ~ de negocios** : businesswoman
mulato, -ta *adj & n* : mulatto
muleta *nf* **1** : crutch **2** APOYO : prop, support
mullido, -da *adj* : soft, spongy
mulo, -la *n* : mule
multa *nf* : fine — **multar** *vt* : fine
multicolor *adj* : multicolored
multicultural *adj* : multicultural
multimedia *adj* : multimedia
multinacional *adj* : multinational
multiplicar {72} *v* : multiply — **multiplicarse** *vr* : multiply, reproduce — **múltiple** *adj* : multiple — **multipli-**

cación *nf, pl* **-ciones** : multiplication — **múltiplo** *nm* : multiple
multitud *nf* : crowd, multitude
mundo *nm* **1** : world **2 todo el ~** : everyone, everybody — **mundanal** *adj* : worldly — **mundano, -na** *adj* **1** : worldly, earthly **2 la vida mundana** : high society — **mundial** *adj* : world, worldwide
municiones *nfpl* : ammunition
municipal *adj* : municipal — **municipio** *nm* **1** : municipality **2** AYUNTAMIENTO : town council
muñeca *nf* **1** : doll **2** : wrist (in anatomy) — **muñeco** *nm* **1** : boy doll **2** MANIQUÍ : dummy, puppet
muñón *nm, pl* **-ñones** : stump (of an arm or leg)
mural *adj & nm* : mural — **muralla** *nf* : wall, rampart
murciélago *nm* : bat (animal)
murmullo *nm* **1** : murmur, murmuring **2** : rustling (of leaves, etc.)
murmurar *vi* **1** : murmur, whisper **2** CRITICAR : gossip
muro *nm* : wall
musa *nf* : muse
musaraña *nf* : shrew
músculo *nm* : muscle — **muscular** *adj* : muscular — **musculatura** *nf* : muscles *pl* — **musculoso, -sa** *adj* : muscular
muselina *nf* : muslin
museo *nm* : museum
musgo *nm* : moss — **musgoso, -sa** *adj* : mossy
música *nf* : music — **musical** *adj* : musical — **músico, -ca** *adj* : musical — **~** *n* : musician
musitar *vt* : mumble
muslo *nm* : thigh
musulmán, -mana *adj & n, mpl* **-manes** : Muslim
mutar *v* : mutate — **mutación** *nf, pl* **-ciones** : mutation — **mutante** *adj & nmf* : mutant
mutilar *vt* : mutilate — **mutilación** *nf, pl* **-ciones** : mutilation
mutuo, -tua *adj* : mutual
muy *adv* **1** : very, quite **2** DEMASIADO : too

N

n *nf* : n, 14th letter of the Spanish alphabet

nabo *nm* : turnip

nácar *nm* : mother-of-pearl

nacer {48} *vi* **1** : be born **2** : hatch (of an egg), sprout (of a plant) **3** SURGIR : arise, spring up — **nacido, -da** *adj & n* **recién ~** : newborn — **naciente** *adj* **1** : new, growing **2** : rising (of the sun) — **nacimiento** *nm* **1** : birth **2** : source (of a river) **3** ORIGEN : beginning **4** BELÉN : Nativity scene

nación *nf, pl* **-ciones** : nation, country — **nacional** *adj* : national — **~** *nmf* : national, citizen — **nacionalidad** *nf* : nationality — **nacionalismo** *nm* : nationalism — **nacionalista** *adj & nmf* : nationalist — **nacionalizar** {21} *vt* **1** : nationalize **2** : naturalize (as a citizen) — **nacionalizarse** *vr* : become naturalized

nada *pron* **1** : nothing **2 de ~** : you're welcome **3 ~ más** : nothing else, nothing more — **~** *adv* : not at all — **~** *nf* **la ~** : nothingness

nadar *v* : swim — **nadador, -dora** *n* : swimmer

nadería *nf* : small thing, trifle

nadie *pron* : nobody, no one

nado: a ~ *adv phr* : swimming

nafta *nf Lat* : gasoline

naipe *nm* : playing card

nalgas *nfpl* : buttocks, bottom

nana *nf* : lullaby

naranja *adj & nm* : orange (color) — **~** *nf* : orange (fruit) — **naranjal** *nm* : orange grove — **naranjo** *nm* : orange tree

narciso *nm* : narcissus, daffodil

narcótico, -ca *adj* : narcotic — **narcótico** *nm* : narcotic — **narcotizar** {21} *vt* : drug — **narcotraficante** *nmf* : drug trafficker — **narcotráfico** *nm* : drug trafficking

nariz *nf, pl* **-rices** **1** : nose **2** OLFATO : sense of smell **3 narices** *nfpl* : nostrils

narrar *vt* : narrate, tell — **narración** *nf, pl* **-ciones** : narration — **narrador, -dora** *n* : narrator — **narrativa** *nf* : narrative, storytelling

nasal *adj* : nasal

nata *nf Spain* : cream

natación *nf, pl* **-ciones** : swimming

natal *adj* : native, birth — **natalicio** *nm* : birthday — **natalidad** *nf* : birthrate

natillas *nfpl* : custard

natividad *nf* : birth, nativity

nativo, -va *adj & n* : native

natural *adj* **1** : natural **2** NORMAL : normal **3 ~ de** : native of, from — **~** *nm* **1** : temperament **2** NATIVO : native — **naturaleza** *nf* : nature — **naturalidad** *nf* : naturalness — **naturalista** *adj* : naturalistic — **naturalización** *nf, pl* **-ciones** : naturalization — **naturalizar** {21} *vt* : naturalize — **naturalizarse** *vr* : become naturalized — **naturalmente** *adv* **1** : naturally **2 POR SUPUESTO** : of course

naufragar {52} *vi* **1** : be shipwrecked **2** FRACASAR : fail — **naufragio** *nm* : shipwreck — **náufrago, -ga** *adj* : shipwrecked — **~** *n* : castaway

náusea *nf* **1** : nausea **2 dar ~s** : nauseate **3 ~s matutinas** : morning sickness — **nauseabundo, -da** *adj* : nauseating

náutico, -ca *adj* : nautical

navaja *nf* : pocketknife, penknife

naval *adj* : naval

nave *nf* **1** : ship **2** : nave (of a church) **3 ~ espacial** : spaceship

navegar {52} *v* : navigate, sail — **navegable** *adj* : navigable — **navegación** *nf, pl* **-ciones** : navigation — **navegante** *adj* : sailing, seafaring — **~** *nmf* : navigator

Navidad *nf* **1** : Christmas **2 feliz ~** : Merry Christmas — **navideño, -ña** *adj* : Christmas

naviero, -ra *adj* : shipping

nazi *adj & nmf* : Nazi — **nazismo** *nm* : Nazism

neblina *nf* : mist

nebuloso, -sa *adj* **1** : hazy, misty, foggy **2** VAGO : vague, nebulous

necedad *nf* **1** : stupidity **2 decir ~es** : talk nonsense

necesario, -ria *adj* : necessary — **necesariamente** *adv* : necessarily — **necesidad** *nf* **1** : need, necessity **2** POBREZA : poverty **3 ~es** *nfpl* : hardships — **necesitado, -da** *adj* : needy — **necesitar** *vt* : need — *vi* **~ de** : have need of

necio, -cia *adj* : silly, dumb
necrología *nf* : obituary
néctar *nm* : nectar
nectarina *nf* : nectarine
neerlandés, -desa *adj, mpl* **-deses**
: Dutch — **neerlandés** *nm* : Dutch
(language)
nefasto, -ta *adj* 1 : ill-fated 2 *fam* : terrible, awful
negar {49} *vt* 1 : deny 2 REHUSAR : refuse 3 : disown (a person) — **negarse**
vr : refuse — **negación** *nf, pl* **-ciones**
1 : denial 2 : negative (in grammar) —
negativa *nf* 1 : denial 2 RECHAZO : refusal — **negativo, -va** *adj* : negative
— **negativo** *nm* : negative (of a photograph)
negligente *adj* : negligent — **negligencia** *nf* : negligence
negociar *vt* : negotiate — *vi* : deal, do
business — **negociable** *adj* : negotiable — **negociación** *nf, pl* **-ciones**
: negotiation — **negociante** *nmf*
: businessman *m*, businesswoman *f* —
negocio *nm* 1 : business 2 TRANSAC-
CIÓN : deal 3 **~s** : business, commerce
negro, -gra *adj* : black, dark — **~** *n*
: dark-skinned person — **negro** *nm*
: black (color) — **negrura** *nf* : black-
ness — **negruzco, -ca** *adj* : blackish
nene, -na *n fam* : baby, small child
nenúfar *nm* : water lily
neón *nm* : neon
neoyorquino, -na *adj* : of or from New
York
nepotismo *nm* : nepotism
Neptuno *nm* : Neptune
nervio *nm* 1 : nerve 2 : sinew (in meat)
3 VIGOR : vigor, energy 4 **tener ~s**
: be nervous — **nerviosismo** *nf* : nervousness — **nervioso, -sa** *adj* 1
: nervous, anxious 2 **sistema nervioso** : nervous system
nervudo, -da *adj* : sinewy
neto, -ta *adj* 1 : clear, distinct 2 : net (of
weight, salaries, etc.)
neumático *nm* : tire
neumonía *nf* : pneumonia
neurología *nf* : neurology — **neu-
rológico, -ca** *adj* : neurological, neu-
rologic — **neurólogo, -ga** *n* : neurol-
ogist
neurosis *nfs & pl* : neurosis — **neurótico, -ca** *adj & n* : neurotic
neutral *adj* : neutral — **neutralidad** *nf*
: neutrality — **neutralizar** {21} *vt*
: neutralize — **neutro, -tra** *adj* 1 : neutral 2 : neuter (in biology and grammar)
neutrón *nm, pl* **-trones** : neutron
nevar {55} *v impers* : snow — **nevada**

nf : snowfall — **nevado, -da** *adj* 1
: snow-covered, snowy 2 : snow-white
— **nevasca** *nf* : snowstorm
nevera *nf* : refrigerator
nevisca *nf* : light snowfall, flurry
nexo *nm* : link, connection
ni *conj* 1 : neither, nor 2 **~ que** : as if 3
~ siquiera : not even
nicaragüense *adj* : Nicaraguan
nicho *nm* : niche
nicotina *nf* : nicotine
nidada *nf* : brood (of chicks, etc.)
nido *nm* 1 : nest 2 GUARIDA : hiding
place, den
niebla *nf* : fog, mist
nieto, -ta *n* 1 : grandson *m*, granddaughter *f* 2 **nietos** *nmpl* : grandchil-
dren
nieve *nf* : snow
nigeriano, -na *adj* : Nigerian
nilón *or* **nilon** *nm, pl* **-lones** : nylon
nimio, -mia *adj* : insignificant, trivial —
nimiedad *nf* 1 : trifle 2 INSIGNIFICAN-
CIA : triviality
ninfa *nf* : nymph
ninguno, -na (**ningún** *before masculine singular nouns*) *adj* : no, not any
— **~** *pron* 1 : neither, none 2 : no one,
nobody
niña *nf* 1 : pupil (of the eye) 2 **la ~ de
los ojos** : the apple of one's eye
niño, -ña *n* : child, boy *m*, girl *f* — **~**
adj 1 : young 2 INFANTIL : immature,
childish — **niñero, -ra** *n* : baby-sitter,
nanny — **niñez** *nf, pl* **-ñeces** : childhood
nipón, -pona *adj* : Japanese
níquel *nm* : nickel
nítido, -da *adj* : clear, sharp — **nitidez**
nf, pl **-deces** : clarity, sharpness
nitrato *nm* : nitrate
nitrógeno *nm* : nitrogen
nivel *nm* 1 : level, height 2 **~ de vida**
: standard of living — **nivelar** *vt*
: level (out)
no *adv* 1 : not 2 (*in answer to a question*) : no 3 **¡como ~!** : of course! 4
~ bien : as soon as 5 **~ fumador**
: non-smoker — **~** *nm* : no
noble *adj & nmf* : noble — **nobleza** *nf*
: nobility
noche *nf* 1 : night, evening 2 **buenas
~s** : good evening, good night 3 **de
~** *or* **por la ~** : at night 4 **hacerse de
~** : get dark — **Nochebuena** *nf*
: Christmas Eve — **nochecita** *nf* : dusk
— **Nochevieja** *nf* : New Year's Eve
noción *nf, pl* **-ciones** 1 : notion, concept 2 **nociones** *nfpl* : rudiments
nocivo, -va *adj* : harmful, noxious

nocturno, -na *adj* **1** : night **2** : nocturnal (of animals, etc.) — **nocturno** *nm* : nocturne

nogal *nm* **1** : walnut tree **2** ~ **americano** : hickory

nómada *nmf* : nomad — ~ *adj* : nomadic

nomás *adv Lat* : only, just

nombrar *vt* **1** : appoint **2** CITAR : mention — **nombrado, -da** *adj* : famous, well-known — **nombramiento** *nm* : appointment, nomination — **nombre** *nm* **1** : name **2** SUSTANTIVO : noun **3** FAMA : fame, renown **4** ~ **de pila** : first name

nómina *nf* : payroll

nominal *adj* : nominal

nominar *vt* : nominate — **nominación** *nf, pl* **-ciones** : nomination

nomo *nm* : gnome

non *adj* : odd, not even — ~ *nm* : odd number

nonagésimo, -ma *adj & n* : ninetieth

nopal *nm* : nopal, prickly pear

nordeste *or* **noreste** *adj* **1** : northeastern **2** : northeasterly (of wind, etc.) — ~ *nm* : northeast

nórdico, -ca *adj* : Scandinavian

noreste → **nordeste**

noria *nf* **1** : waterwheel **2** : Ferris wheel (at a fair, etc.)

norma *nf* : rule, norm, standard — **normal** *adj* **1** : normal **2** **escuela** ~ : teacher-training college — **normalidad** *nf* : normality — **normalizar** {21} *vt* **1** : normalize **2** ESTANDARIZAR : standardize — **normalizarse** *vr* : return to normal — **normalmente** *adv* : ordinarily, generally

noroeste *adj* **1** : northwestern **2** : northwesterly (of wind, etc.) — ~ *nm* : northwest

norte *adj* : north, northern — ~ *nm* **1** : north **2** : north wind

norteamericano, -na *adj* : North American

norteño, -ña *adj* : northern

noruego, -ga *adj* : Norwegian — **noruego** *nm* : Norwegian (language)

nos *pron* **1** (*direct object*) : us **2** (*indirect object*) : to us, for us, from us **3** (*reflexive*) : ourselves **4** : each other, one another

nosotros, -tras *pron* **1** (*subject*) : we **2** (*object*) : us **3** *or* ~ **mismos** : ourselves

nostalgia *nf* **1** : nostalgia **2** **sentir** ~ **por** : be homesick for — **nostálgico, -ca** *adj* : nostalgic

nota *nf* **1** : note **2** : grade, mark (in

school) **3** CUENTA : bill, check — **notable** *adj* : noteworthy, notable — **notar** *vt* : notice — **notarse** *vr* : be evident, seem

notario, -ria *n* : notary (public)

noticia *nf* **1** : news item, piece of news **2** ~**s** *nfpl* : news — **noticiario** *nm* : newscast — **noticiero** *nm Lat* : newscast

notificar {72} *vt* : notify — **notificación** *nf, pl* **-ciones** : notification

notorio, -ria *adj* **1** : obvious **2** CONOCIDO : well-known — **notoriedad** *nf* : fame, notoriety

novato, -ta *adj* : inexperienced — ~ *n* : beginner, novice

novecientos, -tas *adj* : nine hundred — **novecientos** *nms & pl* : nine hundred

novedad *nf* **1** : newness, innovation **2** NOTICIAS : news **3** ~**es** : novelties, latest news — **novedoso, -sa** *adj* : original, novel

novela *nf* **1** : novel **2** : soap opera (on television) — **novelesco, -ca** *adj* **1** FANTÁSTICO : fabulous — **novelista** *nmf* : novelist

noveno, -na *adj* : ninth — **noveno** *nm* : ninth

noventa *adj & nm* : ninety — **noventavo, -va** *adj* : ninetieth — **noventavo** *nm* : ninetieth

novia → **novio**

noviazgo *nm* : engagement

novicio, -cia *n* : novice

noviembre *nm* : November

novillo, -lla *n* : young bull *m*, heifer *f*

novio, -via *n* **1** : boyfriend *m*, girlfriend *f* **2** PROMETIDO : fiancé *m*, fiancée *f* **3** : bridegroom *m*, bride *f* (at a wedding)

novocaína *nf* : novocaine

nube *nf* : cloud — **nubarrón** *nm, pl* **-rrones** : storm cloud — **nublado, -da** *adj* **1** : cloudy **2** ENTURBIADO : clouded, dim — **nublado** *nm* : storm cloud — **nublar** *vt* **1** : cloud **2** OSCURECER : obscure — **nublarse** *vr* : get cloudy — **nuboso, -sa** *adj* : cloudy

nuca *nf* : nape, back of the neck

núcleo *nm* **1** : nucleus **2** CENTRO : center, core — **nuclear** *adj* : nuclear

nudillo *nm* : knuckle

nudismo *nm* : nudism — **nudista** *adj & nmf* : nudist

nudo *nm* **1** : knot **2** : crux, heart (of a problem, etc.) — **nudoso, -sa** *adj* : knotty, gnarled

nuera *nf* : daughter-in-law

nuestro, -tra *adj* : our — ~ *pron* (*with definite article*) : ours, our own

nuevamente *adv* : again, anew

nueve *adj & nm* : nine
nuevo, -va *adj* 1 : new 2 **de nuevo** : again, once more
nuez *nf, pl* **nueces** 1 : nut 2 *or* ~ **de nogal** : walnut 3 ~ **de Adán** : Adam's apple 4 ~ **moscada** : nutmeg
nulo, -la *adj* 1 *or* ~ **y sin efecto** : null and void 2 INCAPAZ : useless, inept — **nulidad** *nf* 1 : nullity 2 **es una** ~ *fam* : he's a total loss
numerar *vt* : number — **numeración** *nf, pl* **-ciones** 1 : numbering 2 NÚMEROS : numbers *pl*, numerals *pl* — **numeral** *adj* : numeral — **número** *nm* 1 : number, numeral 2 : issue (of a publication) 3 **sin** ~ : countless — **numérico, -ca** *adj* : numerical — **numeroso, -sa** *adj* : numerous
nunca *adv* 1 : never, ever 2 ~ **más** : never again 3 ~ **jamás** : never ever
nupcial *adj* : nuptial, wedding — **nupcias** *nfpl* : nuptials, wedding
nutria *nf* : otter
nutrir *vt* 1 ALIMENTAR : feed, nourish 2 FOMENTAR : fuel, foster — **nutrición** *nf, pl* **-ciones** : nutrition — **nutrido, -da** *adj* 1 : nourished 2 ABUNDANTE : considerable, abundant — **nutriente** *nm* : nutrient — **nutritivo, -va** *adj* : nourishing, nutritious

O

o¹ *nf* : o, 16th letter of the Spanish alphabet
o² *conj* (**u** *before words beginning with* o- *or* ho-) 1 : or, either 2 ~ **sea** : in other words
oasis *nms & pl* : oasis
obcecar {72} *vt* : blind (by emotions) — **obcecarse** *vr* : become stubborn
obedecer {53} *vt* : obey — *vi* 1 : obey 2 ~ **a** : respond to 3 ~ **a** : be due to — **obediencia** *nf* : obedience — **obediente** *adj* : obedient
obertura *nf* : overture
obeso, -sa *adj* : obese — **obesidad** *nf* : obesity
obispo *nm* : bishop
objetar *v* : object — **objeción** *nf, pl* **-ciones** : objection
objeto *nm* : object — **objetivo, -va** *adj* : objective — **objetivo** *nm* 1 : objective, goal 2 : lens (in photography, etc.)
objetor, -tora *n* ~ **de conciencia** : conscientious objector
oblicuo, -cua *adj* : oblique
obligar {52} *vt* : require, oblige — **obligarse** *vr* : commit oneself (to do something) — **obligación** *nf, pl* **-ciones** : obligation — **obligado, -da** *adj* 1 : obliged 2 FORZOSO : obligatory — **obligatorio, -ria** *adj* : mandatory
oblongo, -ga *adj* : oblong
oboe *nm* : oboe — *nmf* : oboist
obra *nf* 1 : work, deed 2 : work (of art, literature, etc.) 3 CONSTRUCCIÓN : construction work 4 ~ **maestra** : masterpiece 5 ~**s públicas** : public works — **obrar** *vt* : work, produce — *vi* : act, behave — **obrero, -ra** *adj* **la clase obrera** : the working class — ~ *n* : worker, laborer

obsceno, -na *adj* : obscene — **obscenidad** *nf* : obscenity
obsequiar *vt* : give, present — **obsequio** *nm* : gift, present
observar *vt* 1 : observe, watch 2 ADVERTIR : notice 3 ACATAR : observe, obey 4 COMENTAR : remark — **observación** *nf, pl* **-ciones** : observation — **observador, -dora** *adj* : observant — ~ *n* : observer — **observancia** *nf* : observance — **observatorio** *nm* : observatory
obsesionar *vt* : obsess — **obsesionarse** *vr* : be obsessed — **obsesión** *nf, pl* **-siones** : obsession — **obsesivo, -va** *adj* : obsessive — **obseso, -sa** *adj* : obsessed
obsoleto, -ta *adj* : obsolete
obstaculizar {21} *vt* : hinder — **obstáculo** *nm* : obstacle
obstante: no ~ *conj phr* : nevertheless, however — ~ *prep phr* : in spite of, despite
obstar {21} *vi* ~ **a** *or* ~ **para** : stop, prevent
obstetricia *nf* : obstetrics — **obstetra** *nmf* : obstetrician
obstinarse *vr* : be stubborn — **obstinado, -da** *adj* 1 : obstinate, stubborn 2 TENAZ : persistent
obstruir {41} *vt* : obstruct — **obstrucción** *nf, pl* **-ciones** : obstruction
obtener {80} *vt* : obtain, get
obtuso, -sa *adj* : obtuse
obviar *vt* : get around, avoid
obvio, -via *adj* : obvious — **obviamente** *adv* : obviously, clearly
oca *nf* : goose
ocasión *nf, pl* **-siones** 1 : occasion 2 OPORTUNIDAD : opportunity 3 GANGA

: bargain — **ocasional** *adj* **1** : occasional **2** ACCIDENTAL : accidental, chance — **ocasionar** *vt* : cause
ocaso *nm* **1** : sunset **2** DECADENCIA : decline
occidente *nm* **1** : west **2 el Occidente** : the West — **occidental** *adj* : western, Western
océano *nm* : ocean — **oceanografía** *nf* : oceanography
ochenta *adj & nm* : eighty
ocho *adj & nm* : eight — **ochocientos, -tas** *adj* : eight hundred — **ochocientos** *nms & pl* : eight hundred
ocio *nm* **1** : free time, leisure **2** INACTIVIDAD : idleness — **ociosidad** *nf* : idleness, inactivity — **ocioso, -sa** *adj* **1** : idle, inactive **2** INÚTIL : useless
ocre *adj & nm* : ocher
octágono *nm* : octagon — **octagonal** *adj* : octagonal
octava *nf* : octave
octavo, -va *adj & n* : eighth
octeto *nm* : byte
octogésimo, -ma *adj & n* : eightieth
octubre *nm* : October
ocular *adj* : ocular, eye — **oculista** *nmf* : ophthalmologist
ocultar *vt* : conceal, hide — **ocultarse** *vr* : hide — **oculto, -ta** *adj* : hidden, occult
ocupar *vt* **1** : occupy **2** : hold (a position, etc.) **3** : provide work for — **ocuparse** *vr* **1** ~ **de** : concern oneself with **2** ~ **de** : take care of (children, etc.) — **ocupación** *nf, pl* **-ciones** **1** : occupation **2** EMPLEO : job — **ocupado, -da** *adj* **1** : busy **2** : occupied (of a place) **3 señal de ocupado** : busy signal — **ocupante** *nmf* : occupant
ocurrir *vi* : occur, happen — **ocurrirse** *vr* ~ **a** : occur to — **ocurrencia** *nf* **1** : occurrence, event **2** SALIDA : witty remark, quip
oda *nf* : ode
odiar *vt* : hate — **odio** *nm* : hatred — **odioso, -sa** *adj* : hateful
odisea *nf* : odyssey
odontología *nf* : dentistry, dental surgery — **odontólogo, -ga** *n* : dentist, dental surgeon
oeste *adj* : west, western — ~ *nm* **1** : west **2 el Oeste** : the West
ofender *v* : offend — **ofenderse** *vr* : take offense — **ofensa** *nf* : offense, insult — **ofensiva** *nf* : offensive — **ofensivo, -va** *adj* : offensive
oferta *nf* **1** : offer **2 de** ~ : on sale **3** ~ **y demanda** : supply and demand
oficial *adj* : official — ~ *nmf* **1** : skilled worker **2** : officer (in the military)

oficina *nf* : office — **oficinista** *nmf* : office worker
oficio *nm* : trade, profession — **oficioso, -sa** *adj* : unofficial
ofrecer {53} *vt* **1** : offer **2** : provide, present (an opportunity, etc.) — **ofrecerse** *vr* : volunteer — **ofrecimiento** *nm* : offer
ofrenda *nf* : offering
oftalmología *nf* : ophthalmology — **oftalmólogo, -ga** *n* : ophthalmologist
ofuscar {72} *vt* **1** : blind, dazzle **2** CONFUNDIR : confuse — **ofuscarse** *vr* ~ **con** : be blinded by — **ofuscación** *nf, pl* **-ciones** **1** : blindness **2** CONFUSIÓN : confusion
ogro *nm* : ogre
oír {50} *vi* : hear — *vt* **1** : hear **2** ESCUCHAR : listen to **3 ¡oiga!** *or* **¡oye!** : excuse me!, listen! — **oídas: de** ~ *adv phr* : by hearsay — **oído** *nm* **1** : ear **2** : (sense of) hearing **3 duro de** ~ : hard of hearing
ojal *nm* : buttonhole
ojalá *interj* : I hope so!, if only!
ojear *vt* : eye, look at — **ojeada** *nf* : glimpse, glance
ojeriza *nf* **1** : ill will **2 tener** ~ **a** : have a grudge against
ojo *nm* **1** : eye **2** PERSPICACIA : shrewdness **3** : span (of a bridge) **4 ¡**~**!** : look out!, pay attention!
ola *nf* : wave — **oleada** *nf* : wave, surge — **oleaje** *nm* : swell (of the sea)
olé *interj* : bravo!
oleada *nf* : wave, swell — **oleaje** *nm* : waves *pl*, surf
óleo *nm* **1** : oil **2** CUADRO : oil painting — **oleoducto** *nm* : oil pipeline
oler {51} *vt* : smell — *vi* **1** : smell **2** ~ **a** : smell of — **olerse** *vr fam* : have a hunch about
olfatear *vt* **1** : sniff **2** OLER : sense, sniff out — **olfato** *nm* **1** : sense of smell **2** PERSPICACIA : nose, instinct
Olimpiada *or* **Olimpíada** *nf* : Olympics *pl*, Olympic Games *pl* — **olímpico, -ca** *adj* : Olympic
oliva *nf* : olive — **olivo** *nm* : olive tree
olla *nf* **1** : pot **2** ~ **podrida** : (Spanish) stew
olmo *nm* : elm
olor *nm* : smell — **oloroso, -sa** *adj* : fragrant
olvidar *vt* **1** : forget **2** DEJAR : leave (behind) — **olvidarse** *vr* : forget — **olvidadizo, -za** *adj* : forgetful — **olvido** *nm* **1** : forgetfulness **2** DESCUIDO : oversight
ombligo *nm* : navel
omelette *nmf Lat* : omelet

ominoso, -sa adj : ominous
omitir vt : omit — **omisión** nf, pl
-**siones** : omission
ómnibus nm, pl -**bus** or -**buses** : bus
omnipotente adj : omnipotent
omóplato or **omoplato** nm : shoulder
blade
once adj & nm : eleven — **onceavo,**
-**va** adj & n : eleventh
onda nf : wave — **ondear** vi : ripple —
ondulación nf, pl -**ciones** : undula-
tion — **ondulado, -da** adj : wavy —
ondular vt : wave (hair) — vi : undulate, ripple
ónice nmf or **ónix** nm : onyx
onza nf : ounce
opaco, -ca adj 1 : opaque 2 DESLUSTRA-
DO : dull
ópalo nm : opal
opción nf, pl -**ciones** : option — **opcional** adj : optional
ópera nf : opera
operar vt 1 : operate on 2 Lat : operate,
run (a machine) — vi 1 : operate 2 NE-
GOCIAR : deal, do business — **oper-
arse** vr 1 : have an operation 2 OCUR-
RIR : take place — **operación** nf, pl
-**ciones** 1 : operation 2 TRANSACCIÓN
: transaction, deal — **operacional** adj
: operational — **operador, -dora** n 1
: operator 2 : cameraman (for television, etc.)
opereta nf : operetta
opinar vt : think — vi : express an opinion — **opinión** nf, pl -**niones** : opinion
opio nm : opium
oponer {60} vt 1 : raise, put forward
(arguments, etc.) 2 ~ **resistencia**
: put up a fight — **oponerse** vr ~ **a**
: oppose, be against — **oponente** nmf
: opponent
oporto nm : port (wine)
oportunidad nf : opportunity — **oportunista** nmf : opportunist — **oportuno, -na** adj 1 : opportune, timely 2
APROPIADO : suitable
opositor, -tora n 1 : opponent 2 : candidate (for a position) — **oposición** nf,
pl -**ciones** : opposition
oprimir vt 1 : press, squeeze 2
TIRANIZAR : oppress — **opresión** nf, pl
-**siones** 1 : oppression 2 ~ **de pecho**
: tightness in the chest — **opresivo,
-va** adj : oppressive — **opresor, -sora**
n : oppressor
optar vi 1 ~ **a** : apply for 2 ~ **por**
: choose, opt for
óptica nf 1 : optics 2 : optician's (shop)
— **óptico, -ca** adj : optical — ~ n
: optician

optimismo nm : optimism — **optimista** adj : optimistic — ~ nmf : optimist
optometría nf : optometry — **op-
tometrista** nmf : optometrist
opuesto adj 1 : opposite 2 CONTRADIC-
TORIO : opposed, conflicting
opulencia nf : opulence — **opulento,
-ta** adj : opulent
oración nf, pl -**ciones** 1 : prayer 2
FRASE : sentence, clause
oráculo nm : oracle
orador, -dora n : speaker
oral adj : oral
orar vi : pray
órbita nf 1 : orbit (in astronomy) 2 : eye
socket — **orbitar** vi : orbit
orden nm, pl **órdenes** 1 : order 2 ~
del día : agenda (at a meeting) 3 ~
público : law and order — ~ nf, pl
órdenes 1 : order (of food) 2 ~ **religiosa** : religious order 3 ~ **de compra** : purchase order
ordenador nm Spain : computer
ordenar vt 1 : order, command 2 AR-
REGLAR : put in order 3 : ordain (a
priest) — **ordenanza** nf : orderly (in
the armed forces) — ~ nf : ordinance,
regulation
ordeñar vt : milk
ordinal adj & nm : ordinal
ordinario, -ria adj 1 : ordinary 2
GROSERO : common, vulgar
orear vt : air
orégano nm : oregano
oreja nf : ear
orfanato or **orfelinato** nm : orphanage
orfebre nmf : goldsmith, silversmith
orgánico, -ca adj : organic
organigrama nm : flowchart
organismo nm 1 : organism 2 ORGANI-
ZACIÓN : agency, organization
organista nmf : organist
organizar {21} vt : organize — **organi-
zarse** vr : get organized — **organización** nf, pl -**ciones** : organization
— **organizador, -dora** n : organizer
órgano nm : organ
orgasmo nm : orgasm
orgía nf : orgy
orgullo nm : pride — **orgulloso, -sa**
adj : proud
orientación nf, pl -**ciones** 1 : orientation 2 DIRECCIÓN : direction 3 CONSEJO
: guidance
oriental adj 1 : eastern 2 : oriental —
~ nmf : Oriental
orientar vt 1 : orient, position 2 GUIAR
: guide, direct — **orientarse** vr 1 : orient oneself 2 ~ **hacia** : turn towards

oriente *nm* **1** : east, East **2 el Oriente** : the Orient
orificio *nm* : orifice, opening
origen *nm, pl* **orígenes** : origin — **original** *adj & nm* : original — **originalidad** *nf* : originality — **originar** *vt* : give rise to — **originarse** *vr* : originate, arise — **originario, -ria** *adj* ~ **de** : native of
orilla *nf* **1** : border, edge **2** : bank (of a river), shore (of the sea)
orinar *vi* : urinate — **orina** *nf* : urine
oriol *nm* : oriole
oriundo, -da *adj* ~ **de** : native of
orla *nf* : border
ornamental *adj* : ornamental — **ornamento** *nm* : ornament
ornar *vt* : adorn
ornitología *nf* : ornithology
oro *nm* : gold
orquesta *nf* : orchestra — **orquestar** *vt* : orchestrate
orquídea *nf* : orchid
ortiga *nf* : nettle
ortodoxia *nf* : orthodoxy — **ortodoxo, -xa** *adj* : orthodox
ortografía *nf* : spelling
ortopedia *nf* : orthopedics — **ortopédico, -ca** *adj* : orthopedic
oruga *nf* : caterpillar
orzuelo *nm* : sty (in the eye)
os *pron pl Spain* **1** (*direct or indirect object*) : you, to you **2** (*reflexive*) : yourselves, to yourselves **3** : each other, to each other
osado, -da *adj* : bold, daring — **osadía** *nf* **1** : boldness, daring **2** DESCARO : audacity, nerve
osamenta *nf* : skeleton
osar *vi* : dare
oscilar *vi* **1** : swing, sway **2** FLUCTUAR : fluctuate — **oscilación** *nf, pl* **-ciones 1** : swinging **2** FLUCTUACIÓN : fluctuation
oscuro, -ra *adj* **1** : dark **2** : obscure (of ideas, persons, etc.) **3 a oscuras** : in the dark — **oscurecer** {53} *vt* **1** : darken **2** : confuse, cloud (the mind)

3 al ~ : at nightfall — *v impers* : get dark — **oscurecerse** *vr* : grow dark — **oscuridad** *nf* **1** : darkness **2** : obscurity (of ideas, persons, etc.)
óseo, ósea *adj* : skeletal, bony
oso, osa *n* **1** : bear **2** ~ **de peluche** *or* ~ **de felpa** : teddy bear
ostensible *adj* : evident, obvious
ostentar *vt* **1** : flaunt, display **2** POSEER : have, hold — **ostentación** *nf, pl* **-ciones** : ostentation — **ostentoso, -sa** *adj* : ostentatious, showy
osteopatía *n* : osteopathy — **osteópata** *nmf* : osteopath
osteoporosis *nf* : osteoporosis
ostra *nf* : oyster
ostracismo *nm* : ostracism
otear *vt* : scan, survey
otoño *nm* : autumn, fall — **otoñal** *adj* : autumn, fall
otorgar {52} *vt* **1** : grant, award **2** : draw up (a legal document)
otro, otra *adj* **1** : another, other **2 otra vez** : again — ~ *pron* **1** : another (one), other (one) **2 los otros, las otras** : the others, the rest
ovación *nf, pl* **-ciones** : ovation
óvalo *nm* : oval — **oval** *or* **ovalado, -da** *adj* : oval
ovario *nm* : ovary
oveja *nf* **1** : sheep, ewe **2** ~ **negra** : black sheep
overol *nm Lat* : overalls *pl*
ovillo *nm* **1** : ball (of yarn) **2 hacerse un** ~ : curl up (into a ball)
ovni *or* **OVNI** *nm* (*objeto volador no identificado*) : UFO
ovular *vi* : ovulate — **ovulación** *nf, pl* **-ciones** : ovulation
oxidar *vi* : rust — **oxidarse** *vr* : get rusty — **oxidación** *nf, pl* **-ciones** : rusting — **oxidado, -da** *adj* : rusty — **óxido** *nm* : rust
oxígeno *nm* : oxygen
oye → **oír**
oyente *nmf* **1** : listener **2** : auditor (student)
ozono *nm* : ozone

P

p *nf* : p, 17th letter of the Spanish alphabet
pabellón *nm, pl* **-llones 1** : pavilion **2** : block, building (in a hospital complex, etc.) **3** : summerhouse (in a garden, etc.) **4** BANDERA : flag

pabilo *nm* : wick
pacer {48} *v* : graze
paces → **paz**
paciencia *nf* : patience — **paciente** *adj & nmf* : patient
pacificar {72} *vt* : pacify, calm — **paci-**

ficarse *vr* : calm down — **pacífico, -ca** *adj* : peaceful, pacific — **pacifismo** *nm* : pacifism — **pacifista** *adj* & *nmf* : pacifist

pacotilla *nf* **de ~** : second-rate, trashy

pacto *nm* 1 : pact, agreement 2 **~** : agree on — *vi* : come to an agreement

padecer {53} *vt* : suffer, endure — *vi* **~ de** : suffer from — **padecimiento** *nm* : suffering

padre *nm* 1 : father 2 **~s** *nmpl* : parents — **~** *adj Lat fam* : great, fantastic — **padrastro** *nm* : stepfather — **padrino** *nm* 1 : godfather 2 : best man (at a wedding)

padrón *nm, pl* **-drones** : register, roll

paella *nf* : paella

paga *nf* : pay, wages *pl* — **pagadero, -ra** *adj* : payable

pagano, -na *adj* & *n* : pagan, heathen

pagar {52} *vt* : pay, pay for — *vi* : pay — **pagaré** *nm* : IOU

página *nf* : page

pago *nm* : payment

país *nm* 1 : country, nation 2 REGIÓN : region, land — **paisaje** *nm* : scenery, landscape — **paisano, -na** *n* : compatriot

paja *nf* 1 : straw 2 *fam* : nonsense

pájaro *nm* 1 : bird 2 **~ carpintero** : woodpecker — **pajarera** *nf* : aviary

pajita *nf* : (drinking) straw

pala *nf* 1 : shovel, spade 2 : blade (of an oar or a rotor) 3 : paddle, racket (in sports)

palabra *nf* 1 : word 2 HABLA : speech 3 **tener la ~** : have the floor — **palabrota** *nf* : swearword

palacio *nm* 1 : palace, mansion 2 **~ de justicia** : courthouse

paladar *nm* : palate — **paladear** *vt* : savor

palanca *nf* 1 : lever, crowbar 2 *fam* : leverage, influence 3 **~ de cambio** *or* **~ de velocidades** : gearshift

palangana *nf* : washbowl

palco *nm* : box (in a theater)

palestino, -na *adj* : Palestinian

paleta *nf* 1 : small shovel, trowel 2 : palette (in art) 3 : paddle (in sports, etc.)

paletilla *nf* : shoulder blade

paliar *vt* : alleviate, ease — **paliativo, -va** *adj* : palliative

pálido, -da *adj* : pale — **palidecer** {53} *vi* : turn pale — **palidez** *nf, pl* **-deces** : paleness, pallor

palillo *nm* 1 : small stick 2 *or* **~ de dientes** : toothpick

paliza *nf* : beating

palma *nf* 1 : palm (of the hand) 2 : palm (tree or leaf) 3 **batir ~s** : clap, applaud — **palmada** *nf* 1 : pat, slap 2 **~s** *nfpl* : clapping

palmera *nf* : palm tree

palmo *nm* 1 : span, small amount 2 **~ a ~** : bit by bit

palmotear *vi* : applaud — **palmoteo** *nm* : clapping, applause

palo *nm* 1 : stick 2 MANGO : shaft, handle 3 MÁSTIL : mast 4 POSTE : pole 5 GOLPE : blow 6 : suit (of cards)

paloma *nf* : pigeon, dove — **palomilla** *nf* : moth — **palomitas** *nfpl* : popcorn

palpar *vt* : feel, touch — **palpable** *adj* : palpable

palpitar *vi* : palpitate, throb — **palpitación** *nf, pl* **-ciones** : palpitation

palta *nf Lat* : avocado

paludismo *nm* : malaria

pampa *nf* : pampa

pan *nm* 1 : bread 2 : loaf (of bread, etc.) 3 **~ tostado** : toast

pana *nf* : corduroy

panacea *nf* : panacea

panadería *nf* : bakery, bread shop — **panadero, -ra** *n* : baker

panal *nm* : honeycomb

panameño, -ña *adj* : Panamanian

pancarta *nf* : placard, banner

pancito *nm Lat* : (bread) roll

páncreas *nms* & *pl* : pancreas

panda *nmf* : panda

pandemonio *nm* : pandemonium

pandero *nm* : tambourine — **pandereta** *nf* : (small) tambourine

pandilla *nf* : gang

panecillo *nm Spain* : (bread) roll

panel *nm* : panel

panfleto *nm* : pamphlet

pánico *nm* : panic

panorama *nm* : panorama — **panorámico, -ca** *adj* : panoramic

panqueque *nm Lat* : pancake

pantaletas *nfpl Lat* : panties

pantalla *nf* 1 : screen 2 : lampshade

pantalón *nm, pl* **-lones** 1 *or* **pantalones** *nmpl* : pants *pl*, trousers *pl* 2 **pantalones vaqueros** : jeans

pantano *nm* 1 : swamp, marsh 2 EMBALSE : reservoir — **pantanoso, -sa** *adj* : marshy, swampy

pantera *nf* : panther

pantimedias *nfpl Lat* : panty hose

pantomima *nf* : pantomime

pantorrilla *nf* : calf (of the leg)

pantufla *nf* : slipper

panza *nf* : belly, paunch — **panzón, -zona** *adj, mpl* **-zones** : potbellied

pañal *nm* : diaper
paño *nm* 1 : cloth 2 TRAPO : rag, dust cloth 3 **~ de cocina** : dishcloth 4 **~ higiénico** : sanitary napkin 5 **~s menores** : underwear
pañuelo *nm* 1 : handkerchief 2 : scarf, kerchief
papa[1] *nm* : pope
papa[2] *nf Lat* 1 : potato 2 **~s fritas** : potato chips, french fries
papá *nm fam* 1 : dad, pop 2 **~s** *nmpl* : parents, folks
papada *nf* : double chin
papagayo *nm* : parrot
papal *adj* : papal
papalote *nm Lat* : kite
papanatas *nmfs & pl fam* : simpleton
papaya *nf* : papaya
papel *nm* 1 : paper, sheet of paper 2 : role, part (in theater, etc.) 3 **~ de aluminio** : aluminum foil 4 **~ higiénico** *or* **~ de baño** : toilet paper 5 **~ de lija** : sandpaper 6 **~ pintado** : wallpaper — **papeleo** *nm* : paperwork, red tape — **papelera** *nf* : wastebasket — **papelería** *nf* : stationery store — **papeleta** *nf* 1 : ticket, slip 2 : ballot (paper)
paperas *nfpl* : mumps
papilla *nf* 1 : baby food, pap 2 **hacer ~** : smash to bits
paquete *nm* 1 : package, parcel 2 : pack (of cigarettes, etc.)
paquistaní *adj* : Pakistani
par *nm* 1 : pair, couple 2 : par (in golf) 3 NOBLE : peer 4 **abierto de ~ en ~** : wide open 5 **sin ~** : without equal — **~** *adj* : even (in number) — **~** *nf* 1 : par 2 **a la ~ que** : at the same time as
para *prep* 1 : for 2 HACIA : towards 3 : (in order) to 4 : around, by (a time) 5 **~ adelante** : forwards 6 **~ atrás** : backwards 7 **~ que** : so (that), in order that
parabienes *nmpl* : congratulations
parábola *nf* : parable
parabrisas *nms & pl* : windshield
paracaídas *nms & pl* : parachute — **paracaidista** *nmf* 1 : parachutist 2 : paratrooper (in the military)
parachoques *nms & pl* : bumper
parada *nf* 1 : stop 2 : (act of) stopping 3 DESFILE : parade — **paradero** *nm* 1 : whereabouts 2 *Lat* : bus stop — **parado, -da** *adj* 1 : idle, stopped 2 *Lat* : standing (up) 3 **bien (mal) parado** : in good (bad) shape
paradoja *nf* : paradox
parafernalia *nf* : paraphernalia

parafina *nf* : paraffin
parafrasear *vt* : paraphrase — **paráfrasis** *nfs & pl* : paraphrase
paraguas *nms & pl* : umbrella
paraguayo, -ya *adj* : Paraguayan
paraíso *nm* : paradise
paralelo, -la *adj* : parallel — **paralelo** *nm* : parallel — **paralelismo** *nm* : similarity
parálisis *nfs & pl* : paralysis — **paralítico, -ca** *adj* : paralytic — **paralizar** {21} *vt* : paralyze
parámetro *nm* : parameter
páramo *nm* : barren plateau
parangón *nm, pl* **-gones** 1 : comparison 2 **sin ~** : matchless
paraninfo *nm* : auditorium, hall
paranoia *nf* : paranoia — **paranoico, -ca** *adj & n* : paranoid
parapeto *nm* : parapet, rampart
parapléjico, -ca *adj & n* : paraplegic
parar *vt* 1 : stop 2 *Lat* : stand, prop — *vi* 1 : stop 2 **ir a ~** : end up, wind up — **pararse** *vr* 1 : stop 2 *Lat* : stand up
pararrayos *nms & pl* : lightning rod
parásito, -ta *adj* : parasitic — **parásito** *nm* : parasite
parasol *nm* : parasol
parcela *nf* : parcel, tract (of land) — **parcelar** *vt* : parcel (up)
parche *nm* : patch
parcial *adj* 1 : partial 2 **a tiempo ~** : part-time — **parcialidad** *nf* : partiality, bias
parco, -ca *adj* : sparing, frugal
pardo, -da *adj* : brownish grey
parear *vt* : pair (up)
parecer {53} *vi* 1 : seem, look 2 ASEMEJARSE A : look like, seem like 3 **me parece que** : I think that, in my opinion 4 **¿qué te parece?** : what do you think? 5 **según parece** : apparently — **parecerse** *vr* **~ a** : resemble — **~** *nm* 1 : opinion 2 ASPECTO : appearance 3 **al ~** : apparently — **parecido, -da** *adj* 1 : similar 2 **bien parecido** : good-looking — **parecido** *nm* : resemblance, similarity
pared *nf* : wall
parejo, -ja *adj* 1 : even, smooth 2 SEMEJANTE : similar — **pareja** *nf* 1 : couple, pair 2 : partner (person)
parentela *nf* : relatives *pl*, kin — **parentesco** *nm* : relationship, kinship
paréntesis *nms & pl* 1 : parenthesis 2 DIGRESIÓN : digression 3 **entre ~** : by the way
paria *nmf* : outcast
paridad *nf* : equality
pariente *nmf* : relative, relation

parir *vi* : give birth, have a baby — *vt* : give birth to

parking *nm* : parking lot

parlamentar *vi* : discuss — **parlamentario, -ria** *adj* : parliamentary — ~ *n* : member of parliament — **parlamento** *nm* : parliament

parlanchín, -china *adj, mpl* **-chines** : talkative, chatty — ~ *n* : chatterbox

parlotear *vi fam* : chatter — **parloteo** *nm fam* : chatter

paro *nm* **1** : stoppage, shutdown **2** DESEMPLEO : unemployment **3** *Lat* : strike **4** ~ **cardíaco** : cardiac arrest

parodia *nf* : parody — **parodiar** *vt* : parody

párpado *nm* : eyelid — **parpadear** *vi* **1** : blink **2** : flicker (of light), twinkle (of stars) — **parpadeo** *nm* **1** : blink **2** : flicker (of light), twinkling (of stars)

parque *nm* **1** : park **2** ~ **de atracciones** : amusement park

parqué *nm* : parquet

parquear *vt Lat* : park

parquedad *nf* : frugality, moderation

parquímetro *nm* : parking meter

parra *nf* : grapevine

párrafo *nm* : paragraph

parranda *nf fam* : party, spree

parrilla *nf* **1** : broiler, grill **2** : grate (of a chimney, etc.) — **parrillada** *nf* : barbecue

párroco *nm* : parish priest — **parroquia** *nf* **1** : parish **2** : parish church — **parroquial** *adj* : parochial — **parroquiano, -na** *nm* **1** : parishioner **2** CLIENTE : customer

parsimonia *nf* **1** : calm **2** FRUGALIDAD : thrift — **parsimonioso, -sa** *adj* **1** : calm, unhurried **2** FRUGAL : thrifty

parte *nf* **1** : part **2** PORCIÓN : share **3** LADO : side **4** : party (in negotiations, etc.) **5 de** ~ **de** : on behalf of **6 ¿de** ~ **de quién?** : who is speaking? **7 en alguna** ~ : somewhere **8 en todas** ~**s** : everywhere **9 tomar** ~ : take part — ~ *nm* **1** : report **2** ~ **meteorológico** : weather forecast

partero, -ra *n* : midwife

partición *nf, pl* **-ciones** : division, sharing

participar *vi* **1** : participate, take part **2** ~ **en** : have a share in — *vt* : notify — **participación** *nf, pl* **-ciones** **1** : participation **2** : share, interest (in a fund, etc.) **3** NOTICIA : notice — **participante** *adj* : participating — ~ *nmf* : participant — **partícipe** *nmf* : participant

participio *nm* : participle

partícula *nf* : particle

particular *adj* **1** : particular **2** PRIVADO : private — ~ *nm* **1** : matter **2** PERSONA : individual — **particularidad** *nf* : peculiarity — **particularizar** {21} *vt* : distinguish, characterize — *vi* : go into details

partir *vt* **1** : split, divide **2** ROMPER : break, crack **3** REPARTIR : share (out) — *vi* **1** : depart **2** ~ **de** : start from **3 a** ~ **de** : as of, from — **partirse** *vr* **1** : split (open) **2** RAJARSE : crack — **partida** *nf* **1** : departure **2** : entry, item (in a register, etc.) **3** JUEGO : game **4** : group (of persons) **5 mala** ~ : dirty trick **6** ~ **de nacimiento** : birth certificate — **partidario, -ria** *n* : follower, supporter — **partido** *nm* **1** : (political) party **2** : game, match (in sports) **3** PARTIDARIOS : following **4 sacar** ~ **de** : make the most of

partitura *nf* : (musical) score

parto *nm* **1** : childbirth **2 estar de** ~ : be in labor

parvulario *nm* : nursery school

pasa *nf* **1** : raisin **2** ~ **de Corinto** : currant

pasable *adj* : passable

pasada *nf* **1** : pass, wipe, coat (of paint, etc.) **2 de** ~ : in passing **3 mala** ~ : dirty trick — **pasadizo** *nm* : corridor — **pasado, -da** *adj* **1** : past **2** PODRIDO : bad, spoiled **3** ANTICUADO : out-of-date **4 el año pasado** : last year — **pasado** *nm* : past

pasador *nm* **1** CERROJO : bolt **2** : barrette (for the hair)

pasaje *nm* **1** : passage **2** BILLETE : ticket, fare **3** PASILLO : passageway **4** PASAJEROS : passengers *pl* — **pasajero, -ra** *adj* : passing — ~ *n* : passenger

pasamanos *nms & pl* : handrail, banister

pasaporte *nm* : passport

pasar *vi* **1** : pass, go (by) **2** ENTRAR : come in **3** SUCEDER : happen **4** TERMINARSE : be over, end **5** ~ **de** : exceed **6 ¿qué pasa?** : what's the matter? — *vt* **1** : pass **2** : spend (time) **3** CRUZAR : cross **4** TOLERAR : tolerate **5** SUFRIR : go through, suffer **6** : show (a movie, etc.) **7 pasarlo bien** : have a good time **8** ~ **por alto** : overlook, omit — **pasarse** *vr* **1** : pass, go away **2** ESTROPEARSE : spoil, go bad **3** OLVIDARSE : slip one's mind **4** EXCEDERSE : go too far

pasarela *nf* **1** : footbridge **2** : gangway (on a ship)

pasatiempo *nm* : pastime, hobby
Pascua *nf* 1 : Easter (Christian feast) 2 : Passover (Jewish feast) 3 NAVIDAD : Christmas
pase *nm* : pass
pasear *vi* : take a walk, go for a ride — *vt* 1 : take for a walk 2 EXHIBIR : parade, show off — **pasearse** *vr* : go for a walk, go for a ride — **paseo** *nm* 1 : walk, ride 2 *Lat* : outing
pasillo *nm* : passage, corridor
pasión *nf*, *pl* **-siones** : passion
pasivo, -va *adj* : passive — **pasivo** *nm* : liabilities *pl*
pasmar *vt* : astonish, amaze — **pasmarse** *vr* : be astonished — **pasmado, -da** *adj* : stunned, flabbergasted — **pasmo** *nm* : astonishment — **pasmoso, -sa** *adj* : astonishing
paso¹, -sa *adj* : dried (of fruit)
paso² *nm* 1 : step 2 HUELLA : footprint 3 RITMO : pace 4 CRUCE : crossing 5 PASAJE : passage, way through 6 : (mountain) pass 7 de ~ : in passing
pasta *nf* 1 : paste 2 MASA : dough 3 *or* ~s : pasta 4 ~ de dientes *or* ~ dentífrica : toothpaste
pastar *v* : graze
pastel *nm* 1 : cake 2 EMPANADA : pie 3 : pastel (crayon) — **pastelería** *nf* : pastry shop
pasteurizar {21} *vt* : pasteurize
pastilla *nf* 1 : pill, tablet 2 : bar (of chocolate, soap, etc.) 3 ~ para la tos : lozenge, cough drop
pasto *nm* 1 : pasture 2 *Lat* : grass, lawn — **pastor, -tora** *n* 1 : shepherd 2 : pastor (in religion) — **pastoral** *adj* : pastoral
pata *nf* 1 : paw, leg (of an animal) 2 : foot, leg (of furniture) 3 meter la ~ *fam* : put one's foot in it — **patada** *nf* 1 : kick 2 : stamp (of the foot) — **patalear** *vi* 1 : kick 2 : stamp (one's feet)
patata *nf Spain* : potato
patear *vt* : kick — *vi* 1 : kick 2 : stamp (one's feet)
patentar *vt* : patent — **patente** *adj* : obvious, patent — ~ *nf* : patent
paternal *adj* : fatherly, paternal — **paternidad** *nf* 1 : fatherhood 2 : paternity (in law) — **paterno, -na** *adj* : paternal
patético, -ca *adj* : pathetic, moving
patillas *nfpl* : sideburns
patinar *vi* 1 : skate 2 RESBALAR : slip, slide — **patín** *nm*, *pl* **-tines** : skate — **patinador, -dora** *n* : skater — **patinaje** *nm* : skating — **patinazo** *nm* 1 : skid 2 *fam* : blunder — **patinete** *nm* : scooter

patio *nm* 1 : courtyard, patio 2 *or* ~ de recreo : playground
pato, -ta *n* 1 : duck 2 pagar el pato *fam* : take the blame — **patito, -ta** *n* : duckling
patología *nf* : pathology — **patológico, -ca** *adj* : pathological
patraña *nf* : hoax
patria *nf* : native land
patriarca *nm* : patriarch
patrimonio *nm* 1 : inheritance 2 : (historical or cultural) heritage
patriota *adj* : patriotic — ~ *nmf* : patriot — **patriótico, -ca** *adj* : patriotic — **patriotismo** *nm* : patriotism
patrocinador, -dora *n* : sponsor — **patrocinar** *vt* : sponsor — **patrocinio** *nm* : sponsorship
patrón, -trona *n*, *mpl* **-trones** 1 : patron 2 JEFE : boss 3 : landlord, landlady *f* (of a boarding house, etc.) — **patrón** *nm*, *pl* **-trones** : pattern (in sewing) — **patronato** *nm* 1 : patronage 2 FUNDACIÓN : foundation, trust
patrulla *nf* 1 : patrol 2 : (police) cruiser — **patrullar** *v* : patrol
paulatino, -na *adj* : gradual
pausa *nf* : pause, break — **pausado, -da** *adj* : slow, deliberate
pauta *nf* : guideline
pavimento *nm* : pavement — **pavimentar** *vt* : pave
pavo, -va *n* 1 : turkey 2 pavo real : peacock
pavonearse *vr* : strut, swagger
pavor *nm* : dread, terror — **pavoroso, -sa** *adj* : terrifying
payaso, -sa *n* : clown — **payasada** *nf* : antic, buffoonery — **payasear** *vi Lat fam* : clown (around)
paz *nf*, *pl* **paces** 1 : peace 2 dejar en ~ : leave alone 3 hacer las paces : make up, reconcile
peaje *nm* : toll
peatón *nm*, *pl* **-tones** : pedestrian
peca *nf* : freckle
pecado *nm* : sin — **pecador, -dora** *adj* : sinful — ~ *n* : sinner — **pecaminoso, -sa** *adj* : sinful — **pecar** {72} *vi* : sin
pecera *nf* : fishbowl, fish tank
pecho *nm* 1 : chest 2 MAMA : breast 3 CORAZÓN : heart, courage 4 dar el ~ : breast-feed 5 tomar a ~ : take to heart — **pechuga** *nf* : breast (of fowl)
pecoso, -sa *adj* : freckled
pectoral *adj* : pectoral
peculiar *adj* 1 : particular 2 RARO : peculiar, odd — **peculiaridad** *nf* : peculiarity

pedagogía *nf* : education, pedagogy — **pedagogo, -ga** *n* : educator, teacher

pedal *nm* : pedal — **pedalear** *vi* : pedal

pedante *adj* : pedantic, pompous

pedazo *nm* **1** : piece, bit **2 hacerse ~s** : fall to pieces

pedernal *nm* : flint

pedestal *nm* : pedestal

pediatra *nmf* : pediatrician

pedigrí *nm* : pedigree

pedir {54} *vt* **1** : ask for, request **2** : order (food, merchandise, etc.) — *vi* **1** : ask **2 ~ prestado** : borrow — **pedido** *nm* **1** : order **2 hacer un ~** : place an order

pedregoso, -sa *adj* : rocky, stony

pedrería *nf* : precious stones *pl*

pegar {52} *vt* **1** : stick, glue, paste **2** : sew on (a button, etc.) **3** JUNTAR : bring together **4** GOLPEAR : hit, strike **5** PROPINAR : deal (a blow, etc.) **6** : transmit (an illness) **7 ~ un grito** : let out a scream — *vi* **1** : adhere, stick **2** GOLPEAR : hit — **pegarse** *vr* **1** : hit oneself, hit each other **2** ADHERIRSE : stick, adhere **3** CONTAGIARSE : be transmitted — **pegadizo, -za** *adj* **1** : catchy **2** CONTAGIOSO : contagious — **pegajoso, -sa** *adj* **1** : sticky **2** *Lat* : catchy — **pegamento** *nm* : glue

peinar *vt* : comb — **peinarse** *vr* : comb one's hair — **peinado** *nm* : hairstyle, hairdo — **peine** *nm* : comb — **peineta** *nf* : ornamental comb

pelado, -da *adj* **1** : shorn, hairless **2** : peeled (of fruit, etc.) **3** *fam* : bare **4** *fam* : broke, penniless

pelaje *nm* : coat (of an animal), fur

pelar *vt* **1** : cut the hair of (a person) **2** MONDAR : peel (fruit) **3** : pluck (a chicken, etc.), skin (an animal) — **pelarse** *vr* **1** : peel **2** *fam* : get a haircut

peldaño *nm* **1** : step (of stairs) **2** : rung (of a ladder)

pelear *vi* **1** : fight **2** DISCUTIR : quarrel — **pelearse** *vr* : have a fight — **pelea** *nf* **1** : fight **2** DISCUSIÓN : quarrel

peletería *nf* : fur shop

peliagudo, -da *adj* : tricky, difficult

pelícano *nm* : pelican

película *nf* : movie, film

peligro *nm* **1** : danger **2** RIESGO : risk — **peligroso, -sa** *adj* : dangerous

pelirrojo, -ja *adj* : red-haired — ~ *n* : redhead

pellejo *nm* : skin, hide

pellizcar {72} *vt* : pinch — **pellizco** *nm* : pinch

pelo *nm* **1** : hair **2** : coat, fur (of an animal) **3** : pile, nap (of fabric) **4 con ~s**

y señales : in great detail **5 no tener ~ en la lengua** *fam* : not to mince words **6 tomar el ~ a algn** *fam* : pull someone's leg — **pelón, -lona** *adj* *fam, mpl* **-lones** : bald

pelota *nf* : ball

pelotón *nm, pl* **-tones** : squad, detachment

peltre *nm* : pewter

peluca *nf* : wig

peluche *nm* **1** : plush **2 oso de ~** : teddy bear

peludo, -da *adj* : hairy, furry

peluquería *nf* : hairdresser's, barber shop — **peluquero, -ra** *n* : barber, hairdresser

pelusa *nf* : fuzz, lint

pelvis *nfs & pl* : pelvis

pena *nf* **1** : penalty **2** TRISTEZA : sorrow **3** DOLOR : suffering, pain **4** *Lat* : embarrassment **5 a duras ~s** : with great difficulty **6 ¡qué ~!** : what a shame! **7 valer la ~** : be worthwhile

penacho *nm* **1** : crest, tuft **2** : plume (ornament)

penal *adj* : penal — ~ *nm* : prison, penitentiary — **penalidad** *nf* **1** : hardship **2** : penalty (in law) — **penalizar** {21} *vt* : penalize

penalty *nm* : penalty (in sports)

penar *vt* : punish — *vi* : suffer

pendenciero, -ra *adj* : quarrelsome

pender *vi* : hang — **pendiente** *adj* **1** : pending **2 estar ~ de** : be watching out for — ~ *nf* : slope — ~ *nm Spain* : earring

pendón *nm, pl* **-dones** : banner

péndulo *nm* : pendulum

pene *nm* : penis

penetrar *vi* **1** : penetrate **2 ~ en** : go into — *vt* **1** : penetrate **2** : pierce (one's heart, etc.) **3** ENTENDER : fathom, grasp — **penetración** *nf, pl* **-ciones** : penetration **2** PERSPICACIA : insight — **penetrante** *adj* **1** : penetrating **2** : sharp (of odors, etc.), piercing (of sounds) **3** : deep (of a wound, etc.)

penicilina *nf* : penicillin

península *nf* : peninsula — **peninsular** *adj* : peninsular

penitencia *nf* **1** : penitence **2** CASTIGO : penance — **penitenciaría** *nf* : penitentiary — **penitente** *adj & nmf* : penitent

penoso, -sa *adj* **1** : painful, distressing **2** TRABAJOSO : difficult **3** *Lat* : shy

pensar {55} *vi* **1** : think **2 ~ en** : think about — *vt* **1** : think **2** CONSIDERAR : think about **3 ~ hacer algo** : intend to do sth — **pensador, -dora**

: thinker — **pensamiento** *nm* 1
: thought 2 : pansy (flower) — **pensativo, -va** *adj* : pensive, thoughtful
pensión *nf, pl* **-siones** 1 : boarding
house 2 : (retirement) pension 3 ~ **alimenticia** : alimony — **pensionista**
nmf 1 : lodger 2 JUBILADO : retiree
pentágono *nm* : pentagon
pentagrama *nm* : staff (in music)
penúltimo, -ma *adj* : next to last, penul-
timate
penumbra *nf* : half-light
penuria *nf* : dearth, shortage
peña *nf* : rock, crag — **peñasco** *nm*
: crag, large rock — **peñón** *nm, pl*
-ñones : craggy rock
peón *nm, pl* **peones** 1 : laborer, peon 2
: pawn (in chess)
peonía *nf* : peony
peor *adv* 1 (*comparative of* **mal**)
: worse 2 (*superlative of* **mal**) : worst
— ~ *adj* 1 (*comparative of* **malo**)
: worse 2 (*superlative of* **malo**) : worst
pepino *nm* : cucumber — **pepinillo** *nm*
: pickle, gherkin
pepita *nf* 1 : seed, pip 2 : nugget (of
gold, etc.)
pequeño, -ña *adj* : small, little — **pe-
queñez** *nf, pl* **-ñeces** 1 : smallness 2
NIMIEDAD : trifle
pera *nf* : pear — **peral** *nm* : pear tree
percance *nm* : mishap, setback
percatarse *vr* ~ **de** : notice
percepción *nf, pl* **-ciones** : perception
— **perceptible** *adj* : perceptible
percha *nf* 1 : perch (for birds) 2 : (coat)
hanger 3 : coatrack (on a wall)
percibir *vt* 1 : perceive 2 : receive (a
salary, etc.)
percusión *nf, pl* **-siones** : percussion
perder {56} *vt* 1 : lose 2 : miss (an opportunity, etc.) 3 DESPERDICIAR : waste
(time) — *vi* : lose — **perderse** *vr* 1
: get lost 2 DESAPARECER : disappear 3
DESPERDICIARSE : be wasted — **perdedor, -dora** *n* : loser — **pérdida** *nf* 1
: loss 2 ESCAPE : leak 3 ~ **de tiempo**
: waste of time — **perdido, -da** *adj* 1
: lost 2 **un caso perdido** *fam* : a hopeless case
perdigón *nm, pl* **-gones** : shot, pellet
perdiz *nf, pl* **-dices** : partridge
perdón *nm, pl* **-dones** : forgiveness,
pardon — **perdón** *interj* : sorry! —
perdonar *vt* 1 DISCULPAR : forgive 2
: pardon (in law)
perdurar *vi* : last, endure — **per-
durable** *adj* : lasting
perecer {53} *vi* : perish, die — **perecedero, -ra** *adj* : perishable

peregrinación *nf, pl* **-ciones** *or* **pere-
grinaje** *nm* : pilgrimage — **peregrino, -na** *adj* 1 : migratory 2 RARO : unusual, odd — ~ *n* : pilgrim
perejil *nm* : parsley
perenne *adj* & *nm* : perennial
pereza *nf* : laziness — **perezoso, -sa**
adj : lazy
perfección *nf, pl* **-ciones** : perfection
— **perfeccionar** *vt* 1 : perfect 2 MEJO-
RAR : improve — **perfeccionista** *nmf*
: perfectionist — **perfecto, -ta** *adj*
: perfect
perfidia *nf* : treachery — **pérfido, -da**
adj : treacherous
perfil *nm* 1 : profile 2 CONTORNO : outline 3 ~**es** *nmpl* RASGOS : features —
perfilar *vt* : outline — **perfilarse** *vr* 1
: be outlined 2 CONCRETARSE : take
shape
perforar *vt* 1 : perforate 2 : drill, bore (a
hole) — **perforación** *nf, pl* **-ciones**
: perforation — **perforadora** *nf*
: (paper) punch
perfume *nm* : perfume, scent — **per-
fumar** *vt* : perfume — **perfumarse** *vr*
: put perfume on
pergamino *nm* : parchment
pericia *nf* : skill
periferia *nf* : periphery, outskirts (of a
city, etc.) — **periférico, -ca** *adj* : peripheral
perilla *nf* 1 : goatee 2 *Lat* : knob 3 **venir
de** ~**s** *fam* : come in handy
perímetro *nm* : perimeter
periódico, -ca *adj* : periodic — **periódico** *nm* : newspaper — **periodismo** *nm* : journalism — **periodista** *nmf*
: journalist
período *or* **periodo** *nm* : period
periquito *nm* : parakeet
periscopio *nm* : periscope
perito, -ta *adj* & *n* : expert
perjudicar {72} *vt* : harm, damage —
perjudicial *adj* : harmful — **perjuicio**
nm 1 : harm, damage 2 **en** ~ **de** : to
the detriment of
perjurar *vi* : perjure oneself — **perjurio**
nm : perjury
perla *nf* 1 : pearl 2 **de** ~**s** *fam* : great,
just fine
permanecer {53} *vi* : remain — **permanencia** *nf* 1 : permanence 2 : stay,
staying (in a place) — **permanente**
adj : permanent — ~ *nf* : permanent
(wave)
permeable *adj* : permeable
permitir *vt* 1 : permit, allow 2 ¿**me per-
mite?** : may I? — **permitirse** *vr*
: allow oneself — **permisible** *adj*

: permissible, allowable — **permisi-vo, -va** *adj* : permissive — **permiso** *nm* **1** : permission **2** : permit, license (document) **3** : leave (in the military) **4 con ~** : excuse me

permuta *nf* : exchange

pernicioso, -sa *adj* : pernicious, destructive

pero *conj* : but — **~** *nm* **1** : fault **2** REPARO : objection

perorar *vi* : make a speech — **perorata** *nf* : (long-winded) speech

perpendicular *adj & nf* : perpendicular

perpetrar *vt* : perpetrate

perpetuar {3} *vt* : perpetuate — **perpetuo, -tua** *adj* : perpetual

perplejo, -ja *adj* : perplexed — **perplejidad** *nf* : perplexity

perro, -rra *n* **1** : dog, bitch *f* **2 perro caliente** : hot dog — **perrera** *nf* : kennel

perseguir {75} *vt* **1** : pursue, chase **2** ACOSAR : persecute — **persecución** *nf, pl* **-ciones 1** : pursuit, chase **2** ACOSO : persecution

perseverar *vi* : persevere — **perseverancia** *nf* : perseverance

persiana *nf* : (venetian) blind

persistir *vi* : persist — **persistencia** *nf* : persistence — **persistente** *adj* : persistent

persona *nf* : person — **personaje** *nm* **1** : character (in literature, etc.) **2** : important person, celebrity — **personal** *adj* : personal — **~** *nm* : personnel, staff — **personalidad** *nf* : personality — **personificar** {72} *vi* : personify

perspectiva *nf* **1** : perspective **2** VISTA : view **3** POSIBILIDAD : prospect, outlook

perspicacia *nf* : shrewdness, insight — **perspicaz** *adj, pl* **-caces** : shrewd, discerning

persuadir *vt* : persuade — **persuadirse** *vr* : become convinced — **persuasión** *nf, pl* **-siones** : persuasion — **persuasivo, -va** *adj* : persuasive

pertenecer {53} *vi* **~ a** : belong to — **perteneciente** *adj* **~ a** : belonging to — **pertenencia** *nf* **1** : ownership **2 ~s** *nfpl* : belongings

pertinaz *adj, pl* **-naces 1** OBSTINADO : obstinate **2** PERSISTENTE : persistent

pertinente *adj* : pertinent, relevant — **pertinencia** *nf* : relevance

perturbar *vt* : disturb — **perturbación** *nf, pl* **-ciones** : disturbance

peruano, -na *adj* : Peruvian

pervertir {76} *vt* : pervert — **perversión** *nf, pl* **-siones** : perversion —

perverso, -sa *adj* : perverse — **pervertido, -da** *adj* : perverted, depraved — **~** *n* : pervert

pesa *nf* **1** : weight **2 ~s** : weights (in sports) — **pesadez** *nf, pl* **-deces 1** : heaviness **2** *fam* : tediousness, drag

pesadilla *nf* : nightmare

pesado, -da *adj* **1** : heavy **2** LENTO : sluggish **3** MOLESTO : annoying **4** ABURRIDO : tedious **5** DURO : tough, difficult — **~** *n fam* : bore, pest — **pesadumbre** *nf* : grief, sorrow

pésame *nm* : condolences *pl*

pesar *vt* : weigh **2** INFLUIR : carry weight **3 pesa a** : despite — **~** *nm* **1** : sorrow, grief **2** REMORDIMIENTO : remorse **3 a ~ de** : in spite of

pescado *nm* : fish — **pesca** *nf* **1** : fishing **2** PECES : fish *pl*, catch **3 ir de ~** : go fishing — **pescadería** *nf* : fish market — **pescador, -dora** *n, mpl* **-dores** : fisherman — **pescar** {72} *vt* **1** : fish for **2** *fam* : catch (a cold, etc.) **3** *fam* : catch hold of, nab — *vi* : fish

pescuezo *nm* : neck (of an animal)

pese a → pesar

pesebre *nm* : manger

pesero *nm Lat* : minibus

peseta *nf* : peseta

pesimismo *nm* : pessimism — **pesimista** *adj* : pessimistic — **~** *nmf* : pessimist

pésimo, -ma *adj* : awful

peso *nm* **1** : weight **2** CARGA : burden **3** : peso (currency) **4 ~ pesado** : heavyweight

pesquero, -ra *adj* : fishing

pesquisa *nf* : inquiry

pestaña *nf* : eyelash — **pestañear** *vi* : blink — **pestañeo** *nm* : blink

peste *nm* **1** : plague **2** *fam* : stench, stink **3** *Lat fam* : cold, bug — **pesticida** *nm* : pesticide — **pestilencia** *nf* **1** : stench **2** PLAGA : pestilence

pestillo *nm* : bolt, latch

petaca *nf Lat* : suitcase

pétalo *nm* : petal

petardo *nm* : firecracker

petición *nf, pl* **-ciones** : petition, request

petirrojo *nm* : robin

petrificar {72} *vt* : petrify

petróleo *nm* : oil, petroleum — **petrolero, -ra** *adj* : oil — **petrolero** *nm* : oil tanker

petulante *adj* : insolent, arrogant

peyorativo, -va *adj* : pejorative

pez *nm, pl* **peces 1** : fish **2 ~ de co**

ores : goldfish 3 ~ **espada** : swordfish 4 ~ **gordo** *fam* : big shot
pezón *nm, pl* **-zones** : nipple
pezuña *nf* : hoof
piadoso, -sa *adj* 1 : compassionate 2 DEVOTO : pious, devout
piano *nm* : piano — **pianista** *nmf* : pianist, piano player
piar {85} *vi* : chirp, tweet
pibe, -ba *n Lat fam* : kid, child
pica *nf* 1 : pike, lance 2 : spade (in playing cards)
picado, -da *adj* 1 : perforated 2 : minced, chopped (of meat, etc.) 3 : decayed (of teeth) 4 : choppy (of the sea) 5 *fam* : annoyed — **picada** *nf* 1 : bite, sting 2 *Lat* : sharp descent —
picadillo *nm* : minced meat — **picadura** *nf* 1 : sting, bite 2 : (moth) hole
picante *adj* : hot, spicy
picaporte *nm* 1 : door handle 2 ALDABA : door knocker 3 PESTILLO : latch
picar {72} *vt* 1 : sting, bite 2 : peck at, nibble on (food) 3 PERFORAR : prick, puncture 4 TRITURAR : chop, mince —
vi 1 : bite, take the bait 2 ESCOCER : sting, itch 3 COMER : nibble 4 : be spicy (of food) — **picarse** *vr* 1 : get a cavity 2 ENFADARSE : take offense
picardía *nf* 1 : craftiness 2 TRAVESURA : prank — **picaresco, -ca** *adj* 1 : picaresque 2 TRAVIESO : roguish — **pícaro, -ra** *adj* 1 : mischievous 2 MALICIOSO : villainous — ~ *n* : rascal, scoundrel
picazón *nf, pl* **-zones** : itch
pichón, -chona *n, mpl* **-chones** : (young) pigeon
picnic *nm, pl* **-nics** : picnic
pico *nm* 1 : beak 2 CIMA : peak 3 PUNTA : (sharp) point 4 : pick, pickax (tool) 5 **las siete y** ~ : a little after seven —
picotazo *nm* : peck — **picotear** *vt* : peck — *vi fam* : nibble, pick — **picudo, -da** *adj* : pointy
pie *nm* 1 : foot (in anatomy) 2 : base, bottom, stem 3 **al** ~ **de la letra** : word for word 4 **dar** ~ **a** : give rise to 5 **de** ~ : standing (up) 6 **de** ~**s a cabeza** : from top to bottom
piedad *nf* 1 : pity, mercy 2 DEVOCIÓN : piety
piedra *nf* 1 : stone 2 : flint (of a lighter) 3 GRANIZO : hailstone 4 ~ **angular** : cornerstone 5 → **pómez**
piel *nf* 1 : skin 2 CUERO : leather 3 PELO : fur, pelt
pienso *nm* : feed, fodder
pierna *nf* : leg
pieza *nf* 1 : piece, part 2 *or* ~ **de teatro** : play 3 HABITACIÓN : room

pigmento *nm* : pigment — **pigmentación** *nf, pl* **-ciones** : pigmentation
pigmeo, -mea *adj* : pygmy
pijama *nm* : pajamas *pl*
pila *nf* 1 : battery 2 MONTÓN : pile 3 FREGADERO : sink 4 : basin (of a fountain, etc.)
pilar *nm* : pillar
píldora *nf* : pill
pillar *vt* 1 : catch 2 : get (a joke, etc.) — **pillaje** *nm* : pillage — **pillo, -lla** *adj* : crafty — ~ *n* : rascal, scoundrel
piloto *nmf* : pilot — **pilotar** *vt* : pilot
pimienta *nf* : pepper (condiment) — **pimiento** *nm* : pepper (fruit) — **pimentero** *nm* : pepper shaker — **pimentón** *nm, pl* **-tones** 1 : paprika 2 : cayenne pepper
pináculo *nm* : pinnacle
pincel *nm* : paintbrush
pinchar *vt* 1 : pierce, prick 2 : puncture (a tire, etc.) 3 INCITAR : goad — **pinchazo** *nm* 1 : prick 2 : puncture (of a tire, etc.)
pingüino *nm* : penguin
pino *nm* : pine (tree)
pintar *v* : paint — **pintarse** *vr* : put on makeup — **pinta** *nf* 1 : spot 2 : pint (measure) 3 *fam* : appearance — **pintada** *nf* : graffiti — **pinto, -ta** *adj* : speckled, spotted — **pintor, -tora** *n, mpl* **-tores** : painter — **pintoresco, -ca** *adj* : picturesque, quaint — **pintura** *nf* 1 : paint 2 CUADRO : painting
pinza *nf* 1 : clothespin 2 : claw, pincer (of a crab, etc.) 3 ~**s** *nfpl* : tweezers
pinzón *nm, pl* **-zones** : finch
piña *nf* 1 : pine cone 2 ANANÁS : pineapple
piñata *nf* : piñata
piñón *nm, pl* **-ñones** : pine nut
pío¹, pía *adj* 1 : pious 2 : piebald (of a horse)
pío² *nm* : peep, chirp
piojo *nm* : louse
pionero, -ra *n* : pioneer
pipa *nf* 1 : pipe (for smoking) 2 *Spain* : seed, pip
pique *nm* 1 : grudge 2 RIVALIDAD : rivalry 3 **irse a** ~ : sink, founder
piqueta *nf* : pickax
piquete *nm* : picket (line) — **piquetear** *v* : picket
piragua *nf* : canoe
pirámide *nf* : pyramid
piraña *nf* : piranha
pirata *adj* : bootleg, pirated — ~ *nmf* : pirate — **piratear** *vt* 1 : bootleg, pirate 2 : hack into (a computer)

piropo *nm* : (flirtatious) compliment

pirueta *nf* : pirouette

piruli *nm* : (cone-shaped) lollipop

pisada *nf* 1 : footstep 2 HUELLA : footprint

pisapapeles *nms & pl* : paperweight

pisar *vt* 1 : step on 2 HUMILLAR : walk all over, abuse — *vi* : step, tread

piscina *nf* 1 : swimming pool 2 : (fish) pond

piso *nm* 1 : floor, story 2 *Lat* : floor (of a room) 3 *Spain* : apartment

pisotear *vt* : trample (on)

pista *nf* 1 : trail, track 2 INDICIO : clue 3 ~ de aterrizaje : runway, airstrip 4 ~ de baile : dance floor 5 ~ de hielo : ice-skating rink

pistacho *nm* : pistachio

pistola *nf* 1 : pistol, gun 2 PULVERIZADOR : spray gun — **pistolera** *nf* : holster — **pistolero** *nm* : gunman

pistón *nm, pl* **-tones** : piston

pito *nm* 1 SILBATO : whistle 2 CLAXON : horn — **pitar** *vi* 1 : blow a whistle 2 : beep, honk (of a horn) — *vt* : whistle at — **pitido** *nm* 1 : whistle, whistling 2 : beep (of a horn) — **pitillo** *nm fam* : cigarette

pitón *nm, pl* **-tones** *nm* : python

pitorro *nm* : spout

pivote *nm* : pivot

piyama *nmf Lat* : pajamas *pl*

pizarra *nf* 1 : slate 2 ENCERADO : blackboard — **pizarrón** *nm, pl* **-rrones** *Lat* : blackboard

pizca *nf* 1 : pinch (of salt) 2 ÁPICE : speck, tiny bit 3 *Lat* : harvest

pizza ['pitsa, 'pisa] *nf* : pizza — **pizzería** *nf* : pizzeria

placa *nf* 1 : sheet, plate 2 INSCRIPCIÓN : plaque 3 : (police) badge

placenta *nf* : placenta

placer {57} *vt* : please — ~ *nm* : pleasure — **placentero, -ra** *adj* : pleasant, agreeable

plácido, -da *adj* : placid, calm

plaga *nf* 1 : plague 2 CALAMIDAD : disaster — **plagar** {52} *vt* : plague, infest

plagiar *vt* : plagiarize — **plagio** *nm* : plagiarism

plan *nm* 1 : plan 2 en ~ de : as 3 no te pongas en ese ~ *fam* : don't be that way

plana *nf* 1 : page 2 en primera ~ : on the front page

plancha *nf* 1 : iron (for ironing) 2 : grill (for cooking) 3 LÁMINA : sheet, plate — **planchar** *v* : iron — **planchado** *nm* : ironing

planear *vt* : plan — *vi* : glide — **planeador** *nm* : glider

planeta *nm* : planet

planicie *nf* : plain

planificar {72} *vt* : plan — **planificación** *nf, pl* **-ciones** : planning

planilla *nf Lat* : list, roster

plano, -na *adj* : flat — **plano** *nm* 1 : map, plan 2 : plane (surface) 3 NIVEL : level 4 de ~ : flatly, outright 5 **primer** ~ : foreground, close-up (in photography)

planta *nf* 1 : plant PISO : floor, story 3 : sole (of the foot) — **plantación** *nf, pl* **-ciones** 1 : plantation 2 : (action of) planting — **plantar** *vt* 1 : plant 2 *fam* : deal, land — **plantarse** *vr* : stand firm

plantear *vt* 1 : expound, set forth 2 : raise (a question) 3 CAUSAR : create, pose (a problem) — **plantearse** *vr* : think about, consider

plantel *nm* 1 : staff, team 2 *Lat* : educational institution

plantilla *nf* 1 : insole 2 PATRÓN : pattern, template 3 : staff (of a business, etc.)

plasma *nm* : plasma

plástico, -ca *adj* : plastic — **plástico** *nm* : plastic

plata *nf* 1 : silver 2 *Lat fam* : money 3 ~ de ley : sterling silver

plataforma *nf* 1 : platform 2 ~ petrolífera : oil rig 3 ~ de lanzamiento : launching pad

plátano *nm* 1 : banana 2 : plantain

platea *nf* : orchestra, pit (in a theater)

plateado, -da *adj* 1 : silver, silvery (color) 2 : silver-plated

platicar {72} *vi* : talk, chat — **plática** *nf* : chat, conversation

platija *nf* : flatfish, flounder

platillo *nm* 1 : saucer 2 CÍMBALO : cymbal 3 *Lat* : dish, course

platino *nm* : platinum

plato *nm* 1 : plate, dish 2 : course (of a meal) 3 ~ principal : entrée

platónico, -ca *adj* : platonic

playa *nf* 1 : beach, seashore 2 ~ de estacionamiento *Lat* : parking lot

plaza *nf* 1 : square, plaza 2 : seat (in transportation) 3 PUESTO : post, position 4 MERCADO : market, marketplace 5 ~ de toros : bullring

plazo *nm* 1 : period, term 2 PAGO : installment 3 a largo ~ : long-term

plazoleta *or* **plazuela** *nf* : small square

pleamar *nf* : high tide

plebe *nf* : common people — **plebeyo, -ya** *adj & nm* : plebeian

plegar {49} *vt* : fold, bend — **plegarse** *vr* 1 : give in, yield 2 : jackknife (of a truck) — **plegable** *or* **plegadizo, -za** *adj* : folding, collapsible

plegaria *nf* : prayer

pleito *nm* 1 : lawsuit 2 *Lat* : dispute, fight

plenilunio *nm* : full moon

pleno, -na *adj* 1 : full, complete 2 **en plena forma** : in top form 3 **en pleno día** : in broad daylight — **plenitud** *nf* : fullness, abundance

pleuresía *nf* : pleurisy

pliego *nm* : sheet (of paper) — **pliegue** *nm* 1 : crease, fold 2 : pleat (in fabric)

plisar *vt* : pleat

plomería *nf Lat* : plumbing — **plomero, -ra** *n Lat* : plumber

plomo *nm* 1 : lead 2 FUSIBLE : fuse

pluma *nf* 1 : feather 2 : (fountain) pen — **plumaje** *nm* : plumage — **plumero** *nm* : feather duster — **plumilla** *nf* : nib — **plumón** *nm, pl* **-mones** : down

plural *adj & nm* : plural — **pluralidad** *nf* : plurality

pluriempleo *nm* **hacer ~** : have more than one job

plus *nm* : bonus

plusvalía *nf* : appreciation, capital gain

plutocracia *nf* : plutocracy

Plutón *nm* : Pluto

plutonio *nm* : plutonium

pluvial *adj* : rain

poblar {19} *vt* 1 : settle, colonize 2 HABITAR : inhabit — **poblarse** *vr* : become crowded — **población** *nf, pl* **-ciones** 1 : city, town, village 2 HABITANTES : population — **poblado, -da** *adj* 1 : populated 2 : thick, bushy (of a beard, eyebrows, etc.) — **poblado** *nm* : village

pobre *adj* 1 : poor 2 **¡~ de mí!** : poor me! — **~** *nmf* 1 : poor person 2 **los ~s** : the poor 3 **¡pobre!** : poor thing! — **pobreza** *nf* : poverty

pocilga *nf* : pigsty

poción *nf, pl* **-ciones** *or* **pócima** *nf* : potion

poco, -ca *adj* 1 : little, not much, (a) few 2 **pocas veces** : rarely — **~** *pron* 1 : little, few 2 **hace poco** : not long ago 3 **poco a poco** : bit by bit, gradually 4 **por poco** : nearly, just about 5 **un poco** : a little, a bit — **poco** *adv* : little, not much

podar *vt* : prune

poder {58} *v aux* 1 : be able to, can 2 (*expressing possibility*) : might, may 3 (*expressing permission*) : can, may 4 **¿cómo puede ser?** : how can it be? 5 **¿puedo pasar?** : may I come in? — *vi* 1 : be possible 2 **~ con** : cope with, manage 3 **no puedo más** : I've

had enough — **~** *nm* 1 : power 2 POSESIÓN : possession — **poderío** *nm* : power — **poderoso, -sa** *adj* : powerful

podólogo, -ga *n* : chiropodist

podrido, -da *adj* : rotten

poema *nm* : poem — **poesía** *nf* 1 : poetry 2 POEMA : poem — **poeta** *nmf* : poet — **poético, -ca** *adj* : poetic

póker *nm* → **póquer**

polaco, -ca *adj* : Polish

polar *adj* : polar — **polarizar** {21} *vt* : polarize

polea *nf* : pulley

polémica *nf* : controversy — **polémico, -ca** *adj* : controversial — **polemizar** *vt* : argue

polen *nm, pl* **pólenes** : pollen

policía *nf* : police — **~** *nmf* : police officer, policeman *m*, policewoman *f* — **policíaco, -ca** *adj* 1 : police 2 **novela policíaca** : detective story

poliéster *nm* : polyester

poligamia *nf* : polygamy — **polígamo, -ma** *n* : polygamist

polígono *nm* : polygon

polilla *nf* : moth

polio *or* **poliomielitis** *nf* : polio, poliomyelitis

politécnico, -ca *adj* : polytechnic

política *nf* 1 : politics 2 POSTURA : policy — **político, -ca** *adj* 1 : political 2 **hermano político** : brother-in-law — **~** *n* : politician

póliza *nf or* **~ de seguros** : insurance policy

polizón *nm, pl* **-zones** : stowaway

pollo, -lla *n* 1 : chicken, chick 2 : chicken (for cooking) — **pollera** *nf Lat* : skirt — **pollería** *nf* : poultry shop — **pollito, -ta** *n* : chick

polo *nm* 1 : pole 2 : polo (sport) 3 **~ norte** : North Pole

poltrona *nf* : easy chair

polución *nf, pl* **-ciones** : pollution

polvo *nm* 1 : powder 2 SUCIEDAD : dust 3 **~s** *nmpl* : face powder 4 **hacer ~** *fam* : crush, shatter — **polvareda** *nf* : cloud of dust — **polvera** *nf* : compact (for powder) — **pólvora** *nf* : gunpowder — **polvoriento, -ta** *adj* : dusty

pomada *nf* : ointment

pomelo *nm* : grapefruit

pómez *nm or* **piedra ~** *nf* : pumice

pomo *nm* : knob, doorknob

pompa *nf* 1 : (soap) bubble 2 ESPLENDOR : pomp 3 **~s fúnebres** : funeral — **pomposo, -sa** *adj* 1 : pompous 2 ESPLÉNDIDO : splendid

pómulo *nm* : cheekbone

ponchar vt Lat : puncture — **poncha-dura** nf Lat : puncture
ponche nm : punch (drink)
poncho nm : poncho
ponderar vt 1 : consider 2 ALABAR : speak highly of
poner {60} vt 1 : put 2 AGREGAR : add 3 CONTRIBUIR : contribute 4 SUPONER : suppose 5 DISPONER : arrange, set out 6 : give (a name), call 7 ENCENDER : turn on 8 ESTABLECER : set up, establish 9 : lay (eggs) — vi : lay eggs — **ponerse** vr 1 : move (into a position) 2 : put on (clothing, etc.) 3 : set (of the sun) 4 ~ **furioso** : become angry
poniente nm 1 OCCIDENTE : west 2 : west wind
pontífice nm : pontiff
pontón nm, pl **-tones** : pontoon
ponzoña nf : poison, venom
popa nf 1 : stern 2 a ~ : astern
popelín nm, pl **-lines** : poplin
popote nm Lat : (drinking) straw
populacho nm : rabble, masses pl
popular adj 1 : popular 2 : colloquial (of language) — **popularidad** nf : popularity — **popularizar** {21} vt : popularize — **populoso, -sa** adj : populous
póquer nm : poker (card game)
por prep 1 : for 2 (indicating an approximate time) : around, during 3 (indicating an approximate place) : around, about 4 A TRAVÉS DE : through, along 5 A CAUSA DE : because of 6 (indicating rate or ratio) : per 7 or~ **medio de** : by means of 8 : times (in mathematics) 9 SEGÚN : as for, according to 10 **estar** ~ : be about to 11 ~ **ciento** : percent 12 ~ **favor** : please 13 ~ **lo tanto** : therefore 14 **¿por qué?** : why?
porcelana nf : porcelain, china
porcentaje nm : percentage
porción nf, pl **-ciones** : portion, piece
pordiosero, -ra n : beggar
porfiar {85} vi : insist — **porfiado, -da** adj : obstinate, persistent
pormenor nm : detail
pornografía nf : pornography — **pornográfico, -ca** adj : pornographic
poro nm : pore — **poroso, -sa** adj : porous
poroto nm Lat : bean
porque conj 1 : because 2 or **por que** : in order that — **porqué** nm : reason
porquería nf 1 SUCIEDAD : filth 2 : shoddy thing, junk
porra nf : nightstick, club — **porrazo** nm : blow, whack

portaaviones nms & pl : aircraft carrier
portada nf 1 : facade 2 : title page (of a book), cover (of a magazine)
portador, -dora n : bearer
portaequipajes nms & pl : luggage rack
portafolio or **portafolios** nm, pl **-lios** 1 : portfolio 2 MALETÍN : briefcase
portal nm 1 : doorway 2 VESTÍBULO : hall, vestibule
portamonedas nms & pl : purse
portar vt : carry, bear — **portarse** vr : behave
portátil adj : portable
portaviones nm → **portaaviones**
portavoz nmf, pl **-voces** : spokesperson, spokesman m, spokeswoman f
portazo nm **dar un** ~ : slam the door
porte nm 1 : transport, freight 2 ASPECTO : bearing, appearance 3 ~ **pagado** : postage paid
portento nm : marvel, wonder — **portentoso, -sa** adj : marvelous
porteño, -ña adj : of or from Buenos Aires
portería nf 1 : superintendent's office 2 : goal, goalposts pl (in sports) — **portero, -ra** n 1 : goalkeeper, goalie 2 CONSERJE : janitor, superintendent
portezuela nf : door (of an automobile)
pórtico nm : portico
portilla nf : porthole
portugués, -guesa adj, mpl **-gueses** : Portuguese — **portugués** nm : Portuguese (language)
porvenir nm : future
pos: en ~ **de** adv phr : in pursuit of
posada nf : inn
posaderas nfpl fam : backside, bottom
posar vi : pose — vt : place, lay — **posarse** vr : settle, rest
posavasos nms & pl : coaster
posdata nf : postscript
pose nf : pose
poseer {20} vt : possess, own — **poseedor, -dora** n : possessor, owner — **poseído, -da** adj : possessed — **posesión** nf, pl **-siones** : possession — **posesionarse** vr ~ **de** : take possession of, take over — **posesivo, -va** adj : possessive
posguerra nf : postwar period
posibilidad nf : possibility — **posibilitar** vt : make possible — **posible** adj 1 : possible 2 **de ser** ~ : if possible
posición nf, pl **-ciones** : position — **posicionar** vt : position — **posicionarse** vr : take a stand
positivo, -va adj : positive
poso nm : sediment, (coffee) grounds

posponer {60} vt **1** : postpone **2** RELE-GAR : put behind, subordinate

postal adj : postal — **~** nf : postcard

postdata → **posdata**

poste nm : post, pole

póster nm, pl **-ters** : poster

postergar {52} vt **1** : pass over **2** APLAZAR : postpone

posteridad nf : posterity — **posterior** adj **1** : later, subsequent **2** TRASERO : back, rear — **posteriormente** adv : subsequently, later

postigo nm **1** : small door **2** CONTRA-VENTANA : shutter

postizo, -za adj : artificial, false

postrarse vr : prostrate oneself — **postrado, -da** adj : prostrate

postre nm : dessert

postular vt **1** : advance, propose **2** Lat : nominate — **postulado** nm : postulate

póstumo, -ma adj : posthumous

postura nf : position, stance

potable adj : drinkable, potable

potaje nm : thick vegetable soup

potasio nm : potassium

pote nm : jar

potencia nf : power — **potencial** adj & nm : potential — **potente** adj : powerful

potro, -tra n : colt m, filly f — **potro** nm : horse (in gymnastics)

pozo nm **1** : well **2** : shaft (in a mine)

práctica nf **1** : practice **2 en la ~** : in practice — **practicable** adj : practicable, feasible — **practicante** adj : practicing — **~** nmf : practitioner — **practicar** {72} vt **1** : practice **2** RE-ALIZAR : perform, carry out — vi : practice — **práctico, -ca** adj : practical

pradera nf : grassland, prairie — **prado** nm : meadow

pragmático, -ca adj : pragmatic

preámbulo nm : preamble

precario, -ria adj : precarious

precaución nf, pl **-ciones 1** : precaution **2** PRUDENCIA : caution, care **3 con ~** : cautiously

precaver vt : guard against — **precavido, -da** adj : prudent, cautious

preceder v : precede — **precedencia** nf : precedence, priority — **precedente** adj : preceding, previous — **~** nm : precedent

precepto nm : precept

preciado, -da adj : prized, valuable — **preciarse** vr **~ de** : pride oneself on, boast about

precinto nm : seal

precio nm : price, cost — **preciosidad** nf **1** VALOR : value **2** : beautiful thing — **precioso, -sa** adj **1** HERMOSO : beautiful **2** VALIOSO : precious

precipicio nm : precipice

precipitar vt **1** : hasten, speed up **2** AR-ROJAR : hurl — **precipitarse** vr **1** APRESURARSE : rush **2** : act rashly **3** AR-ROJARSE : throw oneself — **precipitación** nf, pl **-ciones 1** : precipitation **2** PRISA : haste — **precipitadamente** adv : in a rush, hastily — **precipitado, -da** adj : hasty

preciso, -sa adj **1** : precise **2** NECESARIO : necessary — **precisamente** adv : precisely, exactly — **precisar** vt **1** : specify, determine **2** NECESITAR : require — **precisión** nf, pl **-siones 1** : precision **2** NECESIDAD : necessity

preconcebido adj : preconceived

precoz adj, pl **-coces 1** : early **2** : precocious (of children)

precursor, -sora n : forerunner

predecesor, -sora n : predecessor

predecir {11} vt : foretell, predict

predestinado, -da adj : predestined

predeterminar vt : predetermine

prédica nf : sermon

predicado nm : predicate

predicar {72} v : preach — **predicador, -dora** n : preacher

predicción nf, pl **-ciones 1** : prediction **2** PRONÓSTICO : forecast

predilección nf, pl **-ciones** : preference — **predilecto, -ta** adj : favorite

predisponer {60} vt : predispose — **predisposición** nf, pl **-ciones** : predisposition

predominar vi : predominate — **predominante** adj : predominant, prevailing — **predominio** nm : predominance

preeminente adj : preeminent

prefabricado, -da adj : prefabricated

prefacio nm : preface

preferir {76} vt : prefer — **preferencia** nf **1** : preference **2 de ~** : preferably — **preferente** adj : preferential — **preferible** adj : preferable — **preferido, -da** adj : favorite

prefijo nm **1** : prefix **2** Spain : area code

pregonar vt : proclaim, announce

pregunta nf **1** : question **2 hacer ~s** : ask questions — **preguntar** v : ask — **preguntarse** vr : wonder

prehistórico, -ca adj : prehistoric

prejuicio nm : prejudice

preliminar adj & nm : preliminary

preludio nm : prelude

prematrimonial adj : premarital

prematuro, -ra *adj* : premature

premeditar *vt* : premeditate — **premeditación** *nf, pl* -**ciones** : premeditation

premenstrual *adj* : premenstrual

premio *nm* 1 : prize 2 RECOMPENSA : reward 3 ~ **gordo** : jackpot — **premiado, -da** *adj* : prizewinning — **premiar** *vt* 1 : award a prize to 2 RECOMPENSAR : reward

premisa *nf* : premise

premonición *nf, pl* -**ciones** : premonition

premura *nf* : haste, urgency

prenatal *adj* : prenatal

prenda *nf* 1 : piece of clothing 2 GARANTÍA : pledge 3 : forfeit (in a game) — **prendar** *vt* : captivate — **prendarse** *vr* ~ **de** : fall in love with

prender *vt* 1 SUJETAR : pin, fasten 2 APRESAR : capture 3 : light (a match, etc.) 4 *Lat* : turn on (a light, etc.) — *vi* 1 : take root 2 ARDER : catch, burn (of fire) — **prenderse** *vr* : catch fire — **prendedor** *nm Lat* : brooch, pin

prensa *nf* : press — **prensar** *vt* : press

preñado, -da *adj* 1 : pregnant 2 ~ **de** : filled with

preocupar *vt* : worry — **preocuparse** *vr* 1 : worry 2 ~ **de** : take care of — **preocupación** *nf, pl* -**ciones** : worry

preparar *vt* : prepare — **prepararse** *vr* : get ready — **preparación** *nf, pl* -**ciones** : preparation — **preparado, -da** *adj* : prepared, ready — **preparado** *nm* : preparation — **preparativo, -va** *adj* : preparatory, preliminary — **preparativos** *nmpl* : preparations — **preparatorio, -ria** *adj* : preparatory

preposición *nf, pl* -**ciones** : preposition

prepotente *adj* : arrogant, domineering

prerrogativa *nf* : prerogative

presa *nf* 1 : catch, prey 2 DIQUE : dam 3 **hacer** ~ **en** : seize

presagiar *vt* : presage, forebode — **presagio** *nm* 1 : omen 2 PREMONICIÓN : premonition

presbítero *nm* : presbyter, priest

prescindir *vi* ~ **de** 1 : do without 2 OMITIR : dispense with

prescribir {33} *vt* : prescribe — **prescripción** *nf, pl* -**ciones** : prescription

presencia *nf* 1 : presence 2 ASPECTO : appearance — **presenciar** *vt* : be present at, witness

presentar *vt* 1 : present 2 OFRECER : offer, give 3 MOSTRAR : show 4 : introduce (persons) — **presentarse** *vr* 1 : show up 2 : arise, come up (of a

problem, etc.) 3 : introduce oneself — **presentación** *nf, pl* -**ciones** 1 : presentation 2 : introduction (of persons) 3 ASPECTO : appearance — **presentador, -dora** *n* : presenter, host of a television program, etc.)

presente *adj* 1 : present 2 **tener** ~ : keep in mind — ~ *nm* 1 : present 2 **entre los** ~**s** : among those present

presentir {76} *vt* : have a presentiment of — **presentimiento** *nm* : premonition

preservar *vt* : preserve, protect — **preservación** *nf, pl* -**ciones** : preservation — **preservativo** *nm* : condom

presidente, -ta *n* 1 : president 2 : chair, chairperson (of a meeting) — **presidencia** *nf* 1 : presidency 2 : chairmanship (of a meeting) — **presidencial** *adj* : presidential

presidio *nm* : prison — **presidiario, -ria** *n* : convict

presidir *vt* 1 : preside over, chair 2 PREDOMINAR : dominate

presión *nf, pl* -**siones** 1 : pressure 2 ~ **arterial** : blood pressure 3 **hacer** ~ : press — **presionar** *vt* 1 : press 2 COACCIONAR : put pressure on

preso, -sa *adj* : imprisoned — ~ *n* : prisoner

prestar *vt* 1 : lend, loan 2 : give (aid) 3 ~ **atención** : pay attention — **prestado, -da** *adj* 1 : borrowed, on loan 2 **pedir** ~ : borrow — **prestamista** *nmf* : moneylender — **préstamo** *nm* : loan

prestidigitación *nf, pl* -**ciones** : sleight of hand — **prestidigitador, -dora** *n* : magician

prestigio *nm* : prestige — **prestigioso, -sa** *adj* : prestigious

presto, -ta *adj* : prompt, ready — **presto** *adv* : promptly, right away

presumir *vt* : presume — *vi* : boast, show off — **presumido, -da** *adj* : conceited, vain — **presunción** *nf, pl* -**ciones** 1 : presumption 2 VANIDAD : vanity — **presunto, -ta** *adj* : presumed, alleged — **presuntuoso, -sa** *adj* : conceited

presuponer {60} *vt* : presuppose — **presupuesto** *nm* 1 : budget, estimate 2 SUPUESTO : assumption

presuroso, -sa *adj* : hasty, quick

pretender *vt* 1 : try to 2 AFIRMAR : claim 3 CORTEJAR : court, woo 4 ~ **que** : expect — **pretencioso, -sa** *adj* : pretentious — **pretendido** *adj* : supposed — **pretendiente** *nmf* 1 : candidate 2 : pretender (to a throne) — ~

nm : suitor — **pretensión** *nf, pl* **-siones** INTENCIÓN : intention, aspiration 2 : claim (to a throne, etc.) 3 **pretensiones** *nfpl* : pretensions

pretérito *nm* : past (in grammar)

pretexto *nm* : pretext, excuse

prevalecer {53} *vi* : prevail — **prevaleciente** *adj* : prevailing, prevalent

prevenir {87} *vt* 1 : prevent 2 AVISAR : warn — **prevenirse** {87} *vr* ~ **contra** *or* ~ **de** : take precautions against — **prevención** *nf, pl* **-ciones** 1 : prevention 2 PRECAUCIÓN : precaution 3 PREJUICIO : prejudice — **prevenido, -da** *adj* 1 : prepared, ready 2 PRECAVIDO : cautious — **preventivo, -va** *adj* : preventive

prever {88} *vt* 1 : foresee 2 PLANEAR : plan

previo, -via *adj* : previous, prior

previsible *adj* : foreseeable — **previsión** *nf, pl* **-siones** 1 : foresight 2 PREDICCIÓN : prediction, forecast — **previsor, -sora** *adj* : farsighted, prudent

prieto, -ta *adj* 1 CEÑIDO : tight 2 *Lat fam* : dark-skinned

prima *nf* 1 : bonus 2 : (insurance) premium 3 → **primo**

primario, -ria *adj* 1 : primary 2 **escuela primaria** : elementary school

primate *nm* : primate

primavera *nf* 1 : spring (season) 2 : primrose (flower) — **primaveral** *adj* : spring

primero, -ra *adj* (**primer** *before masculine singular nouns*) 1 : first 2 MEJOR : top, leading 3 PRINCIPAL : main, basic 4 **de primera** : first-rate — ~ *n* : first (person or thing) — **primero** *adv* 1 : first 2 MÁS BIEN : rather, sooner

primitivo, -va *adj* : primitive

primo, -ma *n* : cousin

primogénito, -ta *adj & n* : firstborn

primor *nm* : beautiful thing

primordial *adj* : basic, fundamental

primoroso, -sa *adj* 1 : exquisite, fine 2 HÁBIL : skillful

princesa *nf* : princess

principado *nm* : principality

principal *adj* : main, principal

príncipe *nm* : prince

principio *nm* 1 : principle 2 COMIENZO : beginning, start 3 ORIGEN : origin 4 **al** ~ : at first 5 **a** ~**s de** : at the beginning of — **principiante** *nmf* : beginner

pringar {52} *vt* : spatter (with grease) — **pringoso, -sa** *adj* : greasy

prioridad *nf* : priority

prisa *nf* 1 : hurry, rush 2 **a** ~ *or* **de** ~ : quickly 3 **a toda** ~ : as fast as possible 4 **darse** ~ : hurry 5 **tener** ~ : be in a hurry

prisión *nf, pl* **-siones** 1 : prison 2 ENCARCELAMIENTO : imprisonment — **prisionero, -ra** *n* : prisoner

prisma *nm* : prism — **prismáticos** *nmpl* : binoculars

privar *vt* 1 : deprive 2 PROHIBIR : forbid 3 *Lat* : knock out — **privarse** *vr* : deprive oneself — **privación** *nf, pl* **-ciones** : deprivation — **privado, -da** *adj* : private — **privativo, -va** *adj* : exclusive

privilegio *nm* : privilege — **privilegiado, -da** *adj* : privileged

pro *prep* : for, in favor of — ~ *nm* 1 : pro, advantage 2 **en** ~ **de** : for, in support of 3 **los pros y los contras** : the pros and cons

proa *nf* : bow, prow

probabilidad *nf* : probability — **probable** *adj* : probable, likely — **probablemente** *adv* : probably

probar {19} *vt* 1 : try, test 2 : try on (clothing) 3 DEMOSTRAR : prove 4 DEGUSTAR : taste — *vi* : try — **probarse** *vr* : try on (clothing) — **probeta** *nf* : test tube

problema *nm* : problem — **problemático, -ca** *adj* : problematic

proceder *vi* 1 : proceed, act 2 : be appropriate 3 ~ **de** : come from — **procedencia** *nf* : origin — **procedente** *adj* ~ **de** : coming from, originating in — **procedimiento** *nm* 1 : procedure, method 2 : proceedings *pl* (in law)

procesar *vt* 1 : prosecute 2 : process (data) — **procesador** *nm* ~ **de textos** : word processor — **procesamiento** *nm* : processing — **procesión** *nf, pl* **-siones** : procession — **proceso** *nm* 1 : process 2 : trial, proceedings *pl* (in law)

proclamar *vt* : proclaim — **proclama** *nf* : proclamation — **proclamación** *nf, pl* **-ciones** : proclamation

procrear *vi* : procreate — **procreación** *nf, pl* **-ciones** : procreation

procurar *vt* 1 : try, endeavor 2 CONSEGUIR : obtain, procure — **procurador, -dora** *n* : attorney

prodigar {52} *vt* : lavish — **prodigio** *nm* : wonder, prodigy — **prodigioso, -sa** *adj* : prodigious

pródigo, -ga *adj* : extravagant, prodigal

producir {61} *vt* 1 : produce 2 CAUSAR : cause 3 : yield, bear (interest, fruit, etc.) — **producirse** *vr* : take place —

producción *nf, pl* **-ciones** : production — **productividad** *nf* : productivity — **productivo, -va** *adj* : productive — **producto** *nm* : product — **productor, -tora** *n* : producer
proeza *nf* : exploit
profanar *vt* 1 : profane, desecrate — **profanación** *nf, pl* **-ciones** : desecration — **profano, -na** *adj* : profane
profecía *nf* : prophecy
proferir {76} *vt* 1 : utter 2 : hurl (insults)
profesar *vt* 1 : profess 2 : practice (a profession, etc.) — **profesión** *nf, pl* **-siones** : profession — **profesional** *adj & nmf* : professional — **profesor, -sora** *n* 1 : teacher 2 : professor (at a university, etc.) — **profesorado** *nm* 1 : teaching profession 2 PROFESORES : faculty
profeta *nm* : prophet — **profético, -ca** *adj* : prophetic — **profetisa** *nf* : (female) prophet — **profetizar** {21} *vt* : prophesy
prófugo, -ga *adj & n* : fugitive
profundo, -da *adj* 1 HONDO : deep 2 : profound (of thoughts, etc.) — **profundamente** *adv* : deeply, profoundly — **profundidad** *nf* : depth — **profundizar** {21} *vt* : study in depth
profuso, -sa *adj* : profuse — **profusión** *nf, pl* **-siones** : profusion
progenie *nf* : progeny, offspring
programa *nm* 1 : program 2 : curriculum (in education) — **programación** *nf, pl* **-ciones** : programming — **programador, -dora** *n* : programmer — **programar** *vt* 1 : schedule 2 : program (a computer, etc.)
progreso *nm* : progress — **progresar** *vi* : (make) progress — **progresión** *nf, pl* **-ciones** : progression — **progresista** *adj & nmf* : progressive — **progresivo, -va** *adj* : progressive, gradual
prohibir {62} *vt* : prohibit, forbid — **prohibición** *nf, pl* **-ciones** : ban, prohibition — **prohibido, -da** *adj* : forbidden — **prohibitivo, -va** *adj* : prohibitive
prójimo *nm* : neighbor, fellow man
prole *nf* : offspring
proletariado *nm* : proletariat — **proletario, -ria** *adj & n* : proletarian
proliferar *vi* : proliferate — **proliferación** *nf, pl* **-ciones** : proliferation — **prolífico, -ca** *adj* : prolific
prolijo, -ja *adj* : wordy, long-winded
prólogo *nm* : prologue, foreword
prolongar {52} *vt* 1 : prolong 2 ALARGAR : lengthen — **prolongarse** *vr* : last, continue — **prolongación** *nf, pl* **-ciones** : extension

promedio *nm* : average
promesa *nf* : promise — **prometedor, -dora** *adj* : promising, hopeful — **prometer** *vt* : promise — *vi* : show promise — **prometerse** *vr* : get engaged — **prometido, -da** *adj* : engaged — ~ *n* : fiancé *m*, fiancée *f*
prominente *adj* : prominent — **prominencia** *nf* : prominence
promiscuo, -cua *adj* : promiscuous — **promiscuidad** *nf* : promiscuity
promocionar *vt* : promote — **promoción** *nf, pl* **-ciones** : promotion
promontorio *nm* : promontory
promover {47} *vt* 1 : promote 2 CAUSAR : cause — **promotor, -tora** *n* : promoter
promulgar {52} *vt* 1 : proclaim 2 : enact (a law)
pronombre *nm* : pronoun
pronosticar {72} *vt* : predict, forecast — **pronóstico** *nm* 1 : prediction, forecast 2 : (medical) prognosis
pronto, -ta *adj* 1 : quick, prompt 2 PREPARADO : ready — **pronto** *adv* 1 : soon 2 RAPIDAMENTE : quickly, promptly 3 *de* ~ : suddenly 4 *por lo* ~ : for the time being 5 *tan* ~ *como* : as soon as
pronunciar *vt* 1 : pronounce 2 : give, deliver (a speech) — **pronunciarse** *vr* 1 : declare oneself 2 SUBLEVARSE : revolt — **pronunciación** *nf, pl* **-ciones** : pronunciation
propagación *nf, pl* **-ciones** : propagation
propaganda *nf* 1 : propaganda 2 PUBLICIDAD : advertising
propagar {52} *vt* : propagate, spread — **propagarse** *vr* : propagate
propano *nm* : propane
propasarse *vr* : go too far
propensión *nf, pl* **-siones** : inclination, propensity — **propenso, -sa** *adj* : prone, inclined
propiamente *adv* : exactly
propicio, -cia *adj* : favorable, propitious
propiedad *nf* 1 : property 2 PERTINENCIA : ownership, possession — **propietario, -ria** *n* : owner, proprietor
propina *nf* : tip
propinar *vt* : give, deal (a blow, etc.)
propio, -pia *adj* 1 : own 2 APROPIADO : proper, appropriate 3 CARACTERÍSTICO : characteristic, typical 4 MISMO : himself, herself, oneself
proponer {60} *vt* 1 : propose 2 : nominate (a person) — **proponerse** *vr* : propose, intend

proporción *nf, pl* **-ciones** : proportion — **proporcionado, -da** *adj* : proportionate — **proporcional** *adj* : proporcional — **proporcionar** *vt* **1** : provide **2** AJUSTAR : adapt, proportion

proposición *nf, pl* **-ciones** : proposal, proposition

propósito *nm* **1** : purpose, intention **2 a** ∼ : incidentally, by the way **3 a** ∼ : on purpose, intentionally

propuesta *nf* **1** : proposal **2** : offer (of employment, etc.)

propulsar *vt* **1** : propel, drive **2** PROMOVER : promote — **propulsión** *nf, pl* **-siones** : propulsion

prorrogar {52} *vt* **1** : extend **2** APLAZAR : postpone — **prórroga** *nf* **1** : extension, deferment **2** : overtime (in sports)

prorrumpir *vi* : burst forth, break out

prosa *nf* : prose

proscribir {33} *vt* **1** : prohibit, ban **2** DESTERRAR : exile — **proscripción** *nf, pl* **-ciones** **1** : ban **2** DESTIERRO : banishment — **proscrito, -ta** *adj* : banned — ∼ *n* : exile, outlaw

proseguir {75} *v* : continue — **prosecución** *nf, pl* **-ciones** : continuation

prospección *nf, pl* **-ciones** : prospecting, exploration

prospecto *nm* : prospectus

prosperar *vi* : prosper, thrive — **prosperidad** *nf* : prosperity — **próspero, -ra** *adj* : prosperous, flourishing

prostituir {41} *vt* : prostitute — **prostitución** *nf, pl* **-ciones** : prostitution — **prostituta** *nf* : prostitute

protagonista *nmf* : protagonist — **protagonizar** *vt* : star in

proteger {15} *vt* : protect — **protegerse** *vr* : protect oneself — **protección** *nf, pl* **-ciones** : protection — **protector, -tora** *adj* : protective — ∼ *n* : protector — **protegido, -da** *n* : protégé

proteína *nf* : protein

protestar *v* : protest — **protesta** *nf* : protest — **protestante** *adj & nmf* : Protestant

protocolo *nm* : protocol

prototipo *nm* : prototype

protuberancia *nf* : protuberance — **protuberante** *adj* : protuberant

provecho *nm* **1** : benefit, advantage **2** ¡buen ∼! : enjoy your meal! — **provechoso, -sa** *adj* : profitable, beneficial

proveer {63} *vt* : provide, supply — **proveedor, -dora** *n* : supplier

provenir {87} *vi* ∼ **de** : come from

proverbio *nm* : proverb — **proverbial** *adj* : proverbial

providencia *nf* **1** : providence **2** PRE-

CAUCIÓN : precaution — **providencial** *adj* : providential

provincia *nf* : province — **provincial** *adj* : provincial — **provinciano, -na** *adj* : provincial, parochial

provisión *nf, pl* **-siones** : provision — **provisional** *adj* : provisional

provocar {72} *vt* **1** : provoke, cause **2** IRRITAR : irritate — **provocación** *nf, pl* **-ciones** : provocation — **provocativo, -va** *adj* : provocative

próximo, -ma *adj* **1** CERCANO : near **2** SIGUIENTE : next — **próximamente** *adv* : shortly, soon — **proximidad** *nf* **1** : proximity **2** ∼es *nfpl* : vicinity

proyectar *vt* **1** : plan **2** LANZAR : throw, hurl **3** : cast (light) **4** : show (a film) — **proyección** *nf, pl* **-ciones** : projection — **proyectil** *nm* : missile — **proyecto** *nm* : plan, project — **proyector** *nm* : projector

prudencia *nf* : prudence, care — **prudente** *adj* : prudent, sensible

prueba *nf* **1** : proof, evidence **2** : test (in education, medicine, etc.) **3** : event (in sports) **4 a** ∼ **de agua** : waterproof

psicoanálisis *nm* : psychoanalysis — **psicoanalista** *nmf* : psychoanalyst — **psicoanalizar** {21} *vt* : psychoanalyze

psicología *nf* : psychology — **psicológico, -ca** *adj* : psychological — **psicólogo, -ga** *n* : psychologist

psicópata *nmf* : psychopath

psicosis *nfs & pl* : psychosis

psicoterapia *nf* : psychotherapy — **psicoterapeuta** *nmf* : psychotherapist

psicótico, -ca *adj & n* : psychotic

psiquiatría *nf* : psychiatry — **psiquiatra** *nmf* : psychiatrist — **psiquiátrico, -ca** *adj* : psychiatric

psíquico, -ca *adj* : psychic

púa *nf* **1** : sharp point **2** : tooth (of a comb) **3** : thorn (of a plant), quill (of a porcupine, etc.) **4** : (guitar) pick

pubertad *nf* : puberty

publicar {72} *vt* **1** : publish **2** DIVULGAR : divulge, disclose — **publicación** *nf, pl* **-ciones** : publication

publicidad *nf* **1** : publicity **2** : advertising (in marketing) — **publicista** *nmf* : publicist — **publicitar** *vt* **1** : publicize **2** : advertise (a product, etc.) — **publicitario, -ria** *adj* : advertising

público, -ca *adj* : public — **público** *nm* **1** : public **2** : audience (of theater, etc.), spectators *pl* (of sports)

puchero *nm* **1** : (cooking) pot **2** GUISADO : stew **3** hacer ∼s : pout

púdico, -ca *adj* : modest

pudiente *adj* : wealthy

pudín *nm, pl* **-dines** : pudding

pudor *nm* : modesty — **pudoroso, -sa** *adj* : modest

pudrir {59} *vt* 1 : rot 2 *fam* : annoy — **pudrirse** *vr* : rot

pueblo *nm* 1 : town, village 2 NACIÓN : people, nation

puente *nm* 1 : bridge 2 **hacer ~** : have a long weekend 3 **~ levadizo** : drawbridge

puerco, -ca *n* 1 : pig 2 **puerco espín** : porcupine — **~** *adj* : dirty, filthy

pueril *adj* : childish

puerro *nm* : leek

puerta *nf* 1 : door, gate 2 **a ~ cerrada** : behind closed doors

puerto *nm* 1 : port 2 : (mountain) pass 3 REFUGIO : haven

puertorriqueño, -ña *adj* : Puerto Rican

pues *conj* 1 : since, because 2 POR LO TANTO : so, therefore 3 (*used interjectionally*) : well, then

puesta *nf* 1 **~ a punto** : tune-up 2 **~ de sol** : sunset 3 **~ en marcha** : starting up — **puesto, -ta** *adj* 1 : put, set 2 VESTIDO : dressed — **puesto** *nm* 1 : place 2 EMPLEO : position, job 3 : stand, stall (in a market) 4 **~ avanzado** : outpost — **~ que** *conj* : since, given that

púgil *nm* : boxer

pugnar *vi* : fight — **pugna** *nf* : fight, battle

pulcro, -cra *adj* : tidy, neat

pulga *nf* 1 : flea 2 **tener malas ~s** : have a bad temper

pulgada *nf* : inch — **pulgar** *nm* 1 : thumb 2 : big toe

pulir *vt* 1 : polish 2 REFINAR : touch up, perfect

pulla *nf* : cutting remark, gibe

pulmón *nm, pl* **-mones** : lung — **pulmonar** *adj* : pulmonary — **pulmonía** *nf* : pneumonia

pulpa *nf* : pulp

pulpería *nf Lat* : grocery store

púlpito *nm* : pulpit

pulpo *nm* : octopus

pulsar *vt* 1 : press (a button), strike (a key) 2 : play (music) — **pulsación** *nf*, *pl* **-ciones** 1 : beat, throb 2 : keystroke (on a typewriter, etc.)

pulsera *nf* : bracelet

pulso *nm* 1 : pulse 2 : steadiness (of hand)

pulular *vi* : swarm

pulverizar {21} *vt* 1 : pulverize, crush 2 : spray (a liquid) — **pulverizador** *nm* : atomizer, spray

puma *nf* : puma

punitivo, -va *adj* : punitive

punta *nf* 1 : tip, end 2 : point (of a needle, etc.) 3 **~ del dedo** : fingertip 4 **sacar ~ a** : sharpen

puntada *nf* 1 : stitch 2 **~s** *nfpl* : seam

puntal *nm* : prop, support

puntapié *nm* : kick

puntear *vt* : pluck (a guitar)

puntería *nf* : aim, marksmanship

puntiagudo, -da *adj* : sharp, pointed

puntilla *nf* 1 : lace edging 2 **de ~s** : on tiptoe

punto *nm* 1 : dot, point 2 : period (in punctuation) 3 ASUNTO : item, question 4 LUGAR : spot, place 5 MOMENTO : moment 6 : point (in a score) 7 PUNTADA : stitch 8 **a las dos en ~** : at two o'clock sharp 9 **dos ~s** : colon 10 **hasta cierto ~** : up to a point 11 **~ de partida** : starting point 12 **~ muerto** : deadlock 13 **~ y coma** : semicolon

puntuación *nf, pl* **-ciones** 1 : punctuation 2 : scoring, score (in sports)

puntual *adj* 1 : prompt, punctual 2 EXACTO : accurate, detailed — **puntualidad** *nf* 1 : punctuality 2 EXACTITUD : accuracy

puntuar {3} *vt* : punctuate — *vi* : score (in sports)

punzar {21} *vt* : prick, puncture — **punzada** *nf* 1 PINCHAZO : prick 2 : sharp pain — **punzante** *adj* 1 : sharp 2 MORDAZ : biting, caustic

puñado *nm* 1 : handful 2 **a ~s** : by the handful

puñal *nm* : dagger — **puñalada** *nf* : stab

puño *nm* 1 : fist 2 : cuff (of a shirt) 3 : handle, hilt (of a sword, etc.) — **puñetazo** *nm* : punch (with the fist)

pupila *nf* : pupil (of the eye)

pupitre *nm* : desk

puré *nm* 1 : purée 2 **~ de papas** *or* **~ de patatas** *Spain* : mashed potatoes

pureza *nf* : purity

purga *nf* : purge — **purgar** {52} *vt* : purge — **purgatorio** *nm* : purgatory

purificar {72} *vt* : purify — **purificación** *nf, pl* **-ciones** : purification

puritano, -na *adj* : puritanical — **~** *n* : puritan

puro, -ra *adj* 1 : pure 2 SIMPLE : plain, simple 3 *Lat fam* : only, just — **puro** *nm* : cigar

púrpura *nf* : purple — **purpúreo, -rea** *adj* : purple

pus *nm* : pus

pusilánime *adj* : cowardly

puta *nf* : whore

putrefacción *nf, pl* **-ciones** : putrefaction, rot — **pútrido, -da** *adj* : putrid, rotten

Q

q *nf* : q, 18th letter of the Spanish alphabet

que *conj* **1** : that **2** (*in comparisons*) : than **3** (*introducing a reason or cause*) : so that, or else **4 es** ~ : the thing is that **5 yo** ~ **tú** : if I were you — ~ *pron* **1** (*referring to persons*) : who, whom **2** (*referring to things*) : that, which **3 el (la, lo, las, los)** ~ : he (she, it, they) who, whoever, the one(s) that

qué *adv* **1** : how, what **2 ¡**~ **lindo!** : how lovely! — ~ *adj* : what, which — ~ *pron* **1** : what **2 ¿**~ **crees?** : what do you think?

quebrar {55} *vt* : break — *vi* : go bankrupt — **quebrarse** *vr* : break — **quebrada** *nf* : ravine, gorge — **quebradizo, -za** *adj* : breakable, fragile — **quebrado, -da** *adj* **1** : bankrupt **2** : rough, uneven (of land, etc.) **3** ROTO : broken — **quebrado** *nm* : fraction — **quebradura** *nf* : crack, fissure — **quebrantar** *vt* **1** : break **2** DEBILITAR : weaken — **quebranto** *nm* **1** : harm, damage **2** AFLICCIÓN : grief, pain

queda *nf* → **toque**

quedar *vi* **1** PERMANECER : remain, stay **2** ESTAR : be **3** FALTAR : be left **4** : fit, look (of clothing, etc.) **5 no queda lejos** : it's not far **6** ~ **en** : agree to, agree on — **quedarse** *vr* **1** : stay **2** ~ **con** : keep

quedo, -da *adj* : quiet, still — **quedo** *adv* : softly, quietly

quehacer *nm* **1** : task **2** ~**es** *nmpl* : chores

queja *nf* : complaint — **quejarse** *vr* **1** : complain **2** GEMIR : moan, groan — **quejido** *nm* : moan, whimper — **quejoso, -sa** *adj* : complaining, whining

quemar *vt* **1** : burn **2** MALGASTAR : squander — *vi* : burn — **quemarse** *vr* **1** : burn oneself **2** : burn (up) **3** : get sunburned — **quemado, -da** *adj* **1** : burned **2** AGOTADO : burned-out **3 estar** ~ : be fed up — **quemador** *nm* : burner — **quemadura** *nf* : burn — **quemarropa: a** ~ *adj & adv phr* : point-blank

querella *nf* **1** : dispute, quarrel **2** : charge (in law)

querer {64} *vt* **1** : want **2** AMAR : love **3**

~ **decir** : mean **4 ¿quieres pasarme la leche?** : please pass the milk **5 sin** ~ : unintentionally — ~ *nm* : love — **querido, -da** *adj* : dear, beloved — ~ *n* **1** : darling **2** AMANTE : lover

queroseno *nm* : kerosene

querubín *nm, pl* **-bines** : cherub

queso *nm* : cheese — **quesadilla** *nf Lat* : quesadilla

quicio *nm* **1 estar fuera de** ~ : be beside oneself **2 sacar de** ~ : drive crazy

quiebra *nf* **1** : break **2** BANCARROTA : bankruptcy

quien *pron, pl* **quienes 1** (*subject*) : who **2** (*object*) : whom **3** (*indefinite*) : whoever, anyone, some people

quién *pron, pl* **quiénes 1** (*subject*) : who **2** (*object*) : whom **3 ¿de** ~ **es este lápiz?** : whose pencil is this?

quienquiera *pron, pl* **quienesquiera** : whoever, whomever

quieto, -ta *adj* **1** : calm, quiet **2** INMÓVIL : still — **quietud** *nf* : stillness

quijada *nf* : jaw, jawbone (of an animal)

quilate *nm* : carat, karat

quilla *nf* : keel

quimera *nf* : illusion — **quimérico, -ca** *adj* : fanciful

química *nf* : chemistry — **químico, -ca** *adj* : chemical — ~ *n* : chemist

quince *adj & nm* : fifteen — **quinceañero, -ra** *n* : fifteen-year-old, teenager — **quincena** *nf* : two-week period, fortnight — **quincenal** *adj* : semimonthly, twice a month

quincuagésimo, -ma *adj & n* : fiftieth

quinientos, -tas *adj* : five hundred — **quinientos** *nms & pl* : five hundred

quinina *nf* : quinine

quinqué *nm* : oil lamp

quinta *nf* : country house, villa

quintaesencia *nf* : quintessence

quinteto *nm* : quintet

quinto, -ta *adj & n* : fifth — **quinto** *nm* : fifth

quiosco *nm* : kiosk, newsstand

quiropráctico, -ca *n* : chiropractor

quirúrgico, -ca *adj* : surgical

quisquilloso, -sa *adj* : fastidious, fussy

quiste *nm* : cyst

quitar *vt* **1** : remove, take away **2** : take off (clothes) **3** : get rid of, relieve (pain, etc.) — **quitarse** *vr* **1** : withdraw, leave **2** : take off (one's clothes) **3** ~ **de** : give up (a habit) **4** ~ **de encima** : get rid of — **quitaesmalte** *nm* : nail-polish remover — **quita-**

manchas *nms & pl* : stain remover — **quitanieves** *nm* : snowplow — **quitasol** *nm* : parasol

quizá *or* **quizás** *adv* : maybe, perhaps

R

r *nf* : r, 19th letter of the Spanish alphabet

rábano *nm* **1** : radish **2** ~ **picante** : horseradish

rabí *nmf, pl* **-bíes** : rabbi

rabia *nf* **1** : rage, anger **2** : rabies (disease) — **rabiar** *vi* **1** : be furious **2** : be in great pain **3** ~ **por** : be dying for — **rabioso, -sa** *adj* **1** : enraged, furious **2** : rabid, having rabies

rabino, -na *n* : rabbi

rabo *nm* **1** : tail **2 el** ~ **del ojo** : the corner of one's eye

racha *nf* **1** : gust of wind **2** SERIE : series, string — **racheado, -da** *adj* : gusty

racial *adj* : racial

racimo *nm* : bunch, cluster

raciocinio *nm* : reason, reasoning

ración *nf, pl* **-ciones 1** : share, ration **2** : helping (of food)

racional *adj* : rational — **racionalizar** {21} *vt* : rationalize

racionar *vt* : ration — **racionamiento** *nm* : rationing

racismo *nm* : racism — **racista** *adj & nmf* : racist

radar *nm* : radar

radiación *nf, pl* **-ciones** : radiation

radiactivo, -va *adj* : radioactive — **radiactividad** *nf* : radioactivity

radiador *nm* : radiator

radiante *adj* : radiant

radical *adj & nmf* : radical

radicar {72} *vi* ~ **en** : lie in, be rooted in

radio *nm* **1** : radius **2** : spoke (of a wheel) **3** : radium (element) — ~ *nmf* : radio

radioactivo, -va *adj* : radioactive — **radioactividad** *nf* : radioactivity

radiodifusión *nf, pl* **-siones** : broadcasting — **radioemisora** *nf* : radio station — **radioescucha** *nmf* : listener — **radiofónico, -ca** *adj* : radio

radiografía *nf* : X ray — **radiografiar** {85} *vt* : x-ray

radiología *nf* : radiology — **radiólogo, -ga** *n* : radiologist

raer {65} *vt* : scrape off

ráfaga *nf* **1** : gust (of wind) **2** : flash (of light)

raído, -da *adj* : worn, shabby

raíz *nf, pl* **raíces 1** : root **2** ORIGEN : origin, source **3 echar raíces** : take root

raja *nf* **1** : crack, slit **2** RODAJA : slice — **rajar** *vt* : crack, split — **rajarse** *vr* **1** : crack, split open **2** *fam* : back out

rajatabla: a ~ *adv phr* : strictly, to the letter

ralea *nf* : sort, kind

ralentí *nm* : neutral (gear)

rallar *vt* : grate — **rallador** *nm* : grater

rama *nf* : branch — **ramaje** *nm* : branches *pl* — **ramal** *nm* : branch (of a railroad, etc.) — **ramificarse** {72} *vr* : branch (off) — **ramillete** *nm* **1** : bouquet **2** GRUPO : cluster, bunch — **ramo** *nm* **1** : branch **2** RAMILLETE : bouquet

rampa *nf* : ramp, incline

rana *nf* **1** : frog **2** ~ **toro** : bullfrog

rancho *nm* : ranch, farm — **ranchero, -ra** *n* : rancher, farmer

rancio, -cia *adj* **1** : rancid **2** : aged (of wine)

rango *nm* **1** : rank **2** : (social) standing

ranúnculo *nm* : buttercup

ranura *nf* : groove, slot

rapar *vt* **1** : shave **2** : crop (hair)

rapaz *adj, pl* **-paces** : rapacious, predatory

rápido, -da *adj* : rapid, quick — **rápidamente** *adv* : rapidly, fast — **rapidez** *nf* : speed — **rápido** *adv* : quickly, fast — ~ *nm* **1** : express train **2** ~**s** *nmpl* : rapids

rapiña *nf* **1** : plunder **2 ave de** ~ : bird of prey

rapsodia *nf* : rhapsody

raptar *vt* : kidnap — **rapto** *nm* : kidnapping — **raptor, -tora** *n* : kidnapper

raqueta *nf* : racket (in sports)

raro, -ra *adj* **1** : rare **2** EXTRAÑO : odd, strange — **raramente** *adv* : rarely, infrequently — **rareza** *nf* : rarity

ras *nm* **a** ~ **de** : level with

rascacielos *nms & pl* : skyscraper

rascar {72} *vt* **1** : scratch **2** RASPAR : scrape — **rascarse** *vr* : scratch oneself

rasgar {52} *vt* : rip, tear — **rasgarse** *vr* : rip

rasgo *nm* **1** : stroke (of a pen) **2** CARACTERÍSTICA : trait, characteristic **3** ~**s** *nmpl* FACCIONES : features

rasguear *vt* : strum

rasguñar *vt* : scratch — **rasguño** *nm* : scratch

raso, -sa *adj* **1** : level, flat **2** : low (of a flight) **3 soldado raso** : private (in the army) — **raso** *nm* : satin

raspar *vt* **1** : scrape **2** LIMAR : file down, smooth — *vi* : be rough — **raspadura** *nf* **1** : scratch **2** ~**s** *nfpl* : scrapings

rastra *nf* **1** : rake **2 a** ~**s** : unwillingly — **rastrear** *vt* : track, trace — **rastrero, -ra** *adj* **1** : creeping **2** DESPRECIABLE : despicable — **rastrillar** *vt* : rake — **rastrillo** *nm* : rake — **rastro** *nm* **1** : trail, track **2** SEÑAL : sign

rasurar *vt Lat* : shave — **rasurarse** *vr Lat* : shave

rata *nf* : rat

ratear *vt* : steal — **ratero, -ra** *n* : thief

ratificar {72} *vt* : ratify — **ratificación** *nf, pl* **-ciones** : ratification

rato *nm* **1** : while **2 al poco** ~ : shortly after **3 pasar el** ~ : pass the time

ratón *nm, pl* **-tones** : mouse — **ratonera** *nf* : mousetrap

raudal *nm* **1** : torrent **2 a** ~**es** : in abundance — **raudo, -da** *adj* : swift

raya *nf* **1** : line **2** LISTA : stripe **3** : part (in the hair) — **rayar** *vt* : scratch — *vi* **1 al** ~ **el día** : at daybreak **2** ~ **en** : border on — **rayarse** *vr* : get scratched

rayo *nm* **1** : ray, beam **2** : bolt of lightning **3** ~**s X** : X rays

rayón *nm* : rayon

raza *nf* **1** : (human) race **2** : breed (of animals) **3 de** ~ : thoroughbred, pedigreed

razón *nf, pl* **-zones** **1** : reason **2 dar** ~ : inform **3 en** ~ **de** : because of **4 tener** ~ : be right — **razonable** *adj* : reasonable — **razonamiento** *nm* : reasoning — **razonar** *v* : reason, think

reacción *nf, pl* **-ciones** : reaction — **reaccionar** *vi* : react — **reaccionario, -ria** *adj & n* : reactionary

reacio, -cia *adj* : resistant, stubborn

reactivar *vt* : reactivate, revive

reactor *nm* **1** : jet (airplane) **2** ~ **nuclear** : nuclear reactor

reajustar *vt* : readjust — **reajuste** *nm* : readjustment

real *adj* **1** : royal **2** VERDADERO : real, true

realce *nm* **1** : relief **2 dar** ~ : highlight

realeza *nf* : royalty

realidad *nf* **1** : reality **2 en** ~ : actually, in fact

realismo *nm* : realism — **realista** *adj* : realistic — ~ *nmf* : realist

realizar {21} *vt* **1** : carry out **2** : achieve (a goal) **3** : produce (a film or play) **4** : realize (a profit) — **realizarse** *vr* **1** : fulfill oneself **2** : come true (of a dream, etc.) — **realización** *nf, pl* **-ciones** : execution, realization

realmente *adv* : really, actually

realzar {21} *vt* : highlight, enhance

reanimar *vt* : revive

reanudar *vt* : resume, renew — **reanudarse** *vr* : resume

reaparecer {53} *vi* : reappear — **reaparición** *nf, pl* **-ciones** : reappearance

reavivar *vt* : revive

rebajar *vt* **1** : lower, reduce **2** HUMILLAR : humiliate — **rebajarse** *vr* **1** : humble oneself **2** ~ **a** : stoop to — **rebaja** *nf* **1** : reduction **2** DESCUENTO : discount **3** ~**s** *nfpl* : sales

rebanada *nf* : slice

rebaño *nm* **1** : herd **2** : flock (of sheep)

rebasar *vt* : surpass, exceed

rebatir *vt* : refute

rebelarse *vr* : rebel — **rebelde** *adj* : rebellious — ~ *nmf* : rebel — **rebeldía** *nf* : rebelliousness — **rebelión** *nf, pl* **-liones** : rebellion

reblandecer *vt* : soften

rebobinar *vt* : rewind

rebosar *vi* **1** : overflow **2** ~ **de** : be bursting with — *vt* : overflow with

rebotar *vi* : bounce, rebound — **rebote** *nm* **1** : bounce **2 de** ~ : on the rebound

rebozar {21} *vt* : coat in batter

rebuscado, -da *adj* : pretentious

rebuznar *vi* : bray

recabar *vt* **1** : obtain, collect **2** ~ **fondos** : raise money

recado *nm* **1** MENSAJE : message **2** *Spain* : errand

recaer {13} *vi* **1** : relapse **2** ~ **sobre** : fall on — **recaída** *nf* : relapse

recalcar {72} *vt* : emphasize, stress

recalcitrante *adj* : recalcitrant

recalentar {55} *vt* **1** : overheat **2** : reheat, warm up (food) — **recalentarse** *vr* : overheat

recámara *nf* **1** : chamber (of a firearm) **2** *Lat* : bedroom

recambio *nm* **1** : spare part **2** : refill (for a pen, etc.)

recapitular *vt* : recapitulate, sum up — **recapitulación** *nf, pl* **-ciones** : recapitulation

recargar {52} *vt* **1** : overload **2**

: recharge (a battery), reload (a firearm, etc.) — **recargado, -da** *adj* : overly elaborate — **recargo** *nm* : surcharge

recato *nm* : modesty — **recatado, -da** *adj* : modest, demure

recaudar *vt* : collect — **recaudación** *nf, pl* **-ciones** : collection — **recaudador, -dora** *n* ~ **de impuestos** : tax collector

recelar *vt* : distrust, fear — **recelo** *nm* : distrust, suspicion — **receloso, -sa** *adj* : distrustful, suspicious

recepción *nf, pl* **-ciones** : reception — **recepcionista** *nmf* : receptionist

receptáculo *nm* : receptacle

receptivo, -va *adj* : receptive — **receptor, -tora** *n* : recipient — **receptor** *nm* : receiver (of a radio, etc.)

recesión *nf, pl* **-siones** : recession

receso *nm Lat* : recess, adjournment

receta *nf* 1 : recipe 2 : prescription (in medicine)

rechazar {21} *vt* 1 : reject, refuse 2 REPELER : repel 3 : reflect (light) — **rechazo** *nm* 1 : rejection

rechinar *vi* 1 : squeak, creak 2 : grind, gnash (one's teeth)

rechoncho, -cha *adj fam* : chubby

recibir *vt* 1 : receive 2 ACOGER : welcome — *vi* : receive visitors — **recibidor** *nm* : vestibule, entrance hall — **recibimiento** *nm* : reception, welcome — **recibo** *nm* : receipt

reciclar *vt* 1 : recycle 2 : retrain (workers) — **reciclaje** *nm* : recycling

recién *adv* 1 : newly, recently 2 ~ **casados** : newlyweds — **reciente** *adj* : recent — **recientemente** *adv* : recently

recinto *nm* 1 : enclosure 2 ÁREA : area, site

recio, -cia *adj* : tough, strong

recipiente *nm* : container, receptacle — ~ *nmf* : recipient

recíproco, -ca *adj* : reciprocal, mutual

recitar *vt* : recite — **recital** *nm* : recital

reclamar *vt* : demand, ask for — *vi* : complain — **reclamación** *nf, pl* **-ciones** 1 : claim, demand 2 QUEJA : complaint — **reclamo** *nm* 1 : lure (in hunting) 2 *Lat* : inducement, attraction

reclinar *vt* : rest, lean — **reclinarse** *vr* : recline, lean back

recluir {41} *vt* : confine, lock up — **recluirse** *vr* : shut oneself away — **reclusión** *nf, pl* **-siones** : imprisonment — **recluso, -sa** *n* : prisoner

recluta *nmf* : recruit — **reclutamiento**

nm : recruitment — **reclutar** *vt* : recruit, enlist

recobrar *vt* : recover, regain — **recobrarse** *vr* ~ **de** : recover from

recodo *nm* : bend

recoger {15} *vt* 1 : collect, gather 2 COGER : pick up 3 LIMPIAR, ORDENAR : clean up, tidy (up) — **recogerse** *vr* : retire, withdraw — **recogedor** *nm* : dustpan — **recogido, -da** *adj* : quiet, secluded

recolección *nf, pl* **-ciones** 1 : collection 2 COSECHA : harvest

recomendar {55} *vt* : recommend — **recomendación** *nf, pl* **-ciones** : recommendation

recompensar *vt* : reward — **recompensa** *nf* : reward

reconciliar *vt* : reconcile — **reconciliarse** *vr* : be reconciled — **reconciliación** *nf, pl* **-ciones** : reconciliation

recóndito, -ta *adj* : hidden

reconfortar *vt* : comfort

reconocer {18} *vt* 1 : recognize 2 ADMITIR : admit 3 EXAMINAR : examine — **reconocible** *adj* : recognizable — **reconocido, -da** *adj* 1 : recognized, accepted 2 AGRADECIDO : grateful — **reconocimiento** *nm* 1 : recognition 2 AGRADECIMIENTO : gratitude 3 : (medical) examination

reconsiderar *vt* : reconsider

reconstruir {41} *vt* : reconstruct — **reconstrucción** *nf, pl* **-ciones** : reconstruction

recopilar *vt* 1 RECOGER : collect, gather 2 : compile — **recopilación** *nf, pl* **-ciones** : collection, compilation

récord *nm, pl* **-cords** : record

recordar {19} *vt* 1 ACORDARSE DE : remember 2 : remind — *vi* : remember — **recordatorio** *nm* : reminder

recorrer *vt* 1 : travel through 2 : cover (a distance) — **recorrido** *nm* 1 : journey, trip 2 TRAYECTO : route, course

recortar *vt* 1 : reduce 2 CORTAR : cut (out) 3 : trim (hair) — **recortarse** *vr* : stand out — **recorte** *nm* 1 : cut, cutting 2 ~**s de periódicos** : newspaper clippings

recostar {19} *vt* : lean, rest — **recostarse** *vr* : lie down

recoveco *nm* 1 : bend 2 RINCÓN : nook, corner

recrear *vt* 1 : recreate 2 ENTRETENER : entertain — **recrearse** *vr* : to enjoy oneself — **recreativo, -va** *adj* : recreational — **recreo** *nm* 1 : recreation, amusement 2 : recess, break (at school)

recriminar *vt* : reproach
recrudecer {53} *vi* : worsen — **recrudecerse** *vr* : intensify, get worse
rectángulo *nm* : rectangle — **rectangular** *adj* : rectangular
rectificar {72} *vt* **1** : rectify, correct **2** AJUSTAR : straighten (out) — **rectitud** *nf* **1** : straightness **2** : (moral) rectitude — **recto, -ta** *adj* **1** : straight **2** INTEGRO : upright, honorable — **recto** *nm* : rectum
rector, -tora *adj* : governing, managing — ~ *n* : rector — **rectoría** *nf* : rectory
recubrir {2} *vt* : cover, coat
recuento *nm* : count, recount
recuerdo *nm* **1** : memory **2** : souvenir, remembrance (of a journey, etc.) **3** ~s *nmpl* SALUDOS : regards
recuperar *vt* **1** : recover, retrieve **2** ~ el tiempo perdido : make up for lost time — **recuperarse** *vr* ~ de : recover from — **recuperación** *nf, pl* **-ciones 1** : recovery **2** ~ de datos : data retrieval
recurrir *vi* ~ a : turn to (a person), resort to (force, etc.) — **recurso** *nm* **1** : recourse, resort **2** : appeal (in law) **3** ~s *nmpl* : resources
red *nf* **1** : net **2** SISTEMA : network, system **3 la Red** : the Internet
redactar *vt* : write (up), draft — **redacción** *nf, pl* **-ciones 1** : writing, drafting **2** : editing (of a newspaper, etc.) — **redactor, -tora** *n* : editor
redada *nf* **1** : (police) raid **2** : catch (in fishing)
redescubrir {2} *vt* : rediscover
redención *nf, pl* **-ciones** : redemption — **redentor, -tora** *adj* : redeeming
redil *nm* : fold, pen
rédito *nm* : interest, yield
redoblar *vt* : redouble
redomado, -da *adj* : out-and-out
redondear *vt* **1** : make round **2** : round off (a number, etc.) — **redonda** *nf* **1** : whole note (in music) **2 a la** ~ : in the surrounding area — **redondel** *nm* **1** : ring, circle **2** : bullring — **redondo, -da** *adj* **1** : round **2** PERFECTO : excellent
reducir {61} *vt* : reduce — **reducirse** *vr* ~ a : come down to, amount to — **reducción** *nf, pl* **-ciones** : reduction — **reducido, -da** *adj* **1** : reduced, limited **2** PEQUEÑO : small
redundante *adj* : redundant — **redundancia** *nf* : redundancy
reedición *nf, pl* **-ciones** : reprint
reembolsar *vt* : refund, reimburse,

repay — **reembolso** *nm* : refund, reimbursement
reemplazar {21} *vt* : replace — **reemplazo** *nm* : replacement
reencarnación *nf, pl* **-ciones** : reincarnation
reencuentro *nm* : reunion
reestructurar *vt* : restructure
refaccionar *vt Lat* : repair, renovate — **refacciones** *nfpl Lat* : repairs, renovations
referir {76} *vt* **1** : tell **2** REMITIR : refer — **referirse** *vr* ~ a : refer to — **referencia** *nf* **1** : reference **2 hacer** ~ a : refer to — **referéndum** *nm, pl* **-dums** : referendum — **referente** *adj* ~ a : concerning
refinar *vt* : refine — **refinado, -da** *adj* : refined — **refinamiento** *nm* : refinement — **refinería** *nf* : refinery
reflector *nm* **1** : reflector **2** : spotlight, searchlight, floodlight
reflejar *vt* : reflect — **reflejarse** *vr* : be reflected — **reflejo** *nm* **1** : reflection **2** : (physical) reflex **3** ~s *nmpl* : highlights (in hair)
reflexionar *vi* : reflect, think — **reflexión** *nf, pl* **-xiones** : reflection, thought — **reflexivo, -va** *adj* **1** : reflective, thoughtful **2** : reflexive (in grammar)
reflujo *nm* : ebb (tide)
reforma *nf* **1** : reform **2** ~s *nfpl* : renovations — **reformador, -dora** *n* : reformer — **reformar** *vt* **1** : reform **2** : renovate, repair (a house, etc.) — **reformarse** *vr* : mend one's ways — **reformatorio** *nm* : reformatory
reforzar {36} *vt* : reinforce
refrán *nm, pl* **-franes** : proverb, saying
refregar {49} *vt* : scrub
refrenar *vt* **1** : rein in (a horse) **2** CONTENER : restrain — **refrenarse** *vr* : restrain oneself
refrendar *vt* : approve, endorse
refrescar {72} *vt* **1** : refresh, cool **2** : brush up on (knowledge) — *vi* : turn cooler — **refrescante** *adj* : refreshing — **refresco** *nm* : soft drink
refriega *nf* : scuffle, skirmish
refrigerar *vt* **1** : refrigerate **2** CLIMATIZAR : air-condition — **refrigeración** *nf, pl* **-ciones 1** : refrigeration **2** AIRE ACONDICIONADO : air-conditioning — **refrigerador** *nmf Lat* : refrigerator — **refrigerio** *nm* : refreshments *pl*
refrito, -ta *adj* : refried — **refrito** *nm* : rehash
refuerzo *nm* : reinforcement
refugiar *vt* : shelter — **refugiarse** *vr* : take refuge — **refugiado, -da** *n*

: refugee — **refugio** *nm* : refuge, shelter

refulgir {35} *vi* : shine brightly

refunfuñar *vi* : grumble, groan

refutar *vt* : refute

regadera *nf* 1 : watering can 2 *Lat* : shower head, shower

regalar *vt* : give (as a gift) — **regalarse** *vr* ~ : treat oneself to

regaliz *nm*, *pl* **-lices** : licorice

regalo *nm* 1 : gift, present 2 PLACER : pleasure, delight

regañadientes: a ~ *adv phr* : reluctantly, unwillingly

regañar *vt* : scold — *vi* 1 QUEJARSE : grumble 2 *Spain* : quarrel — **regañón, -ñona** *adj, mpl* **-ñones** *fam* : grumpy, irritable

regar {49} *vt* 1 : irrigate, water 2 ESPARCIR : scatter

regatear *vt* 1 : haggle over 2 ESCATIMAR : skimp on — *vi* : bargain, haggle

regazo *nm* : lap (of a person)

regenerar *vt* : regenerate

regentar *vt* : run, manage

régimen *nm*, *pl* **regímenes** 1 : regime 2 DIETA : diet 3 ~ **de vida** : lifestyle

regimiento *nm* : regiment

regio, -gia *adj* : royal, regal

región *nf*, *pl* **-giones** : region, area — **regional** *adj* : regional

regir {28} *vt* 1 : rule 2 ADMINISTRAR : manage, run 3 DETERMINAR : govern, determine — *vi* : apply, be in force — **regirse** *vr* ~ **por** : be guided by

registrar *vt* 1 : register 2 GRABAR : record, tape 3 : search (a house, etc.), frisk (a person) — **registrarse** *vr* 1 : register 2 : be recorded (of temperatures, etc.) — **registrador, -dora** *adj* : **caja registradora** : cash register — ~ *n* : registrar — **registro** *nm* 1 : registration 2 : register (book) 3 : registry (office) 4 : range (of a voice, etc.) 5 INSPECCIÓN : search

regla *nf* 1 : rule, regulation 2 : ruler (for measuring) 3 MENSTRUACIÓN : period — **reglamentación** *nf*, *pl* **-ciones** 1 : regulation 2 REGLAS : rules *pl* — **reglamentar** *vt* : regulate — **reglamentario, -ria** *adj* : regulation, official — **reglamento** *nm* : regulations *pl*, rules *pl*

regocijar *vt* : gladden, delight — **regocijarse** *vr* : rejoice — **regocijo** *nm* : delight, rejoicing

regodearse *vr* : be delighted — **regodeo** *nm* : delight

regordete *adj fam* : chubby

regresar *vi* : return, come back, go back — *vt Lat* : give back — **regresión** *nf*, *pl* **-siones** : regression — **regresivo, -va** *adj* : regressive — **regreso** *nm* 1 : return 2 **estar de** ~ : be back, be home again

reguero *nm* 1 : irrigation ditch 2 SEÑAL : trail, trace 3 **correr como un** ~ **de pólvora** : spread like wildfire

regular *adj* 1 : regular 2 MEDIANO : medium, average 3 **por lo** ~ : in general — ~ *vt* : regulate, control — **regulación** *nf*, *pl* **-ciones** : regulation, control — **regularidad** *nf* : regularity — **regularizar** {21} *vt* : normalize, make regular

rehabilitar *vt* 1 : rehabilitate 2 : reinstate (s.o. in a position) 3 : renovate (a building, etc.) — **rehabilitación** *nf* 1 : rehabilitation 2 : reinstatement (in a position) 3 : renovation (of a building, etc.)

rehacer {40} *vt* 1 : redo 2 REPARAR : repair — **rehacerse** *vr* 1 : recover 2 ~ **de** : get over

rehén *nm*, *pl* **-henes** : hostage

rehuir {41} *vt* : avoid, shun

rehusar {8} *v* : refuse

reimprimir *vt* : reprint — **reimpresión** *nf*, *pl* **-siones** : reprinting, reprint

reina *nf* : queen — **reinado** *nm* : reign — **reinante** *adj* : reigning — **reinar** *vi* 1 : reign 2 PREVALECER : prevail

reincidir *vi* : backslide, relapse

reino *nm* : kingdom, realm

reintegrar *vt* 1 : reinstate 2 : refund (money), reimburse (expenses, etc.) — **reintegrarse** *vr* ~ **a** : return to — **reintegro** *nm* : reimbursement

reír {66} *vi* : laugh — *vt* : laugh at — **reírse** *vr* : laugh

reiterar *vt* : repeat, reiterate

reivindicar {72} *vt* 1 : claim 2 RESTAURAR : restore

reja *nf* : grille, grating — **rejilla** *nf* : grille, grate, screen

rejuvenecer {53} *vt* : rejuvenate — **rejuvenecerse** *vr* : be rejuvenated

relación *nf*, *pl* **-ciones** 1 : relation, connection 2 COMUNICACIÓN : relationship, relations *pl* 3 RELATO : account 4 LISTA : list 5 **con** ~ **a** *or* **en** ~ **a** : in relation to — **relacionar** *vt* : relate, connect — **relacionarse** *vr* ~ **con** : be connected to, interact with

relajar *vt* : relax — **relajarse** *vr* : relax — **relajación** *nf*, *pl* **-ciones** : relaxation — **relajado, -da** *adj* 1 : relaxed 2 : dissolute, lax (in behavior)

relamerse *vr* : smack one's lips, lick its chops

relámpago *nm* : flash of lightning — **relampaguear** *vi* : flash

relatar *vt* : relate, tell

relativo, -va *adj* **1** : relative **2 en lo relativo a** : with regard to — **relatividad** *nf* : relativity

relato *nm* **1** : account, report **2** CUENTO : story, tale

releer {20} *vt* : reread

relegar {52} *vt* : relegate

relevante *adj* : outstanding, important

relevar *vt* **1** : relieve, take over from **2 ~ de** : exempt from — **relevo** *nm* **1** : relief, replacement **2 carrera de ~s** : relay race

relieve *nm* **1** : relief (in art, etc.) **2** IMPORTANCIA : prominence, importance **3 poner en ~** : emphasize

religión *nf, pl* **-giones** : religion — **religioso, -sa** *adj* : religious — **~** *n* : monk *m*, nun *f*

relinchar *vi* : neigh, whinny — **relincho** *nm* : neigh, whinny

reliquia *nf* **1** : relic **2 ~ de familia** : family heirloom

rellenar *vt* **1** : refill **2** : stuff, fill (in cooking) — **relleno, -na** *adj* : stuffed, filled — **relleno** *nm* : stuffing, filling

reloj *nm* **1** : clock **2** *or* **~ de pulsera** : wristwatch **3** **~ de arena** : hourglass **4 como un ~** : like clockwork

relucir {45} *vi* **1** : glitter, shine **2 sacar a ~** : bring up, mention — **reluciente** *adj* : brilliant, shining

relumbrar *vi* : shine brightly

remachar *vt* **1** : rivet **2** RECALAR : stress, drive home — **remache** *nm* : rivet

remanente *nm* : remainder, surplus

remanso *nm* : pool

remar *vi* : row

rematar *vt* **1** : conclude, finish up **2** MATAR : finish off **3** LIQUIDAR : sell off cheaply **4** *Lat* : auction — *vi* **1** : shoot (in sports) **2** TERMINAR : end — **rematado, -da** *adj* : utter, complete — **remate** *nm* **1** : shot (in sports) **2** FIN : end

remedar *vt* : imitate, mimic

remediar *vt* **1** : remedy, repair **2** : solve (a problem) **3** EVITAR : avoid — **remedio** *nm* **1** : remedy, cure **2** SOLUCIÓN : solution **3 sin ~** : hopeless

rememorar *vt* : recall

remendar {55} *vt* : mend

remesa *nf* **1** : remittance **2** : shipment (of merchandise)

remezón *nm, pl* **-zones** *Lat* : mild earthquake, tremor

remiendo *nm* : mend, patch

remilgado, -da *adj* **1** : prudish **2** AFEC-TADO : affected — **remilgo** *nm* : primness, affectation

reminiscencia *nf* : reminiscence

remisión *nf, pl* **-siones** : remission

remiso, -sa *adj* **1** : reluctant **2** NEGLIGENTE : remiss

remitir *vt* **1** : send, remit **2 ~ a** : refer to, direct to — *vi* **1** : subside, let up — **remite** *nm* : return address — **remitente** *nmf* : sender (of a letter, etc.)

remo *nm* : paddle, oar

remodelar *vt* **1** : remodel **2** : restructure (an organization)

remojar *vt* : soak, steep — **remojo** *nm* **poner en ~** : soak

remolacha *nf* : beet

remolcar {72} *vt* : tow, tug — **remolcador** *nm* : tugboat

remolino *nm* **1** : whirlwind, whirlpool **2** : crowd (of people) **3** : cowlick (of hair)

remolque *nm* **1** : towing, tow **2** : trailer (vehicle)

remontar *vt* **1** : overcome **2** SUBIR : go up — **remontarse** *vr* **1** : soar **2 ~ a** : date from, go back to

rémora *nf* : hindrance

remorder {47} *vt* : trouble, worry — **remordimiento** *nm* : remorse

remoto, -ta *adj* : remote — **remotamente** *adv* : remotely, slightly

remover {47} *vt* **1** : stir **2** : move around, turn over (earth, embers, etc.) **3** REAVIVIR : bring up again **4** DESPEDIR : fire, dismiss

remunerar *vt* : remunerate

renacer {48} *vi* : be reborn, revive — **renacimiento** *nm* **1** : rebirth, revival **2 el Renacimiento** : the Renaissance

renacuajo *nm* : tadpole, pollywog

rencilla *nf* : quarrel

renco, -ca *adj* *Lat* : lame

rencor *nm* **1** : rancor, hostility **2 guardar ~** : hold a grudge — **rencoroso, -sa** *adj* : resentful

rendición *nf, pl* **-ciones** : surrender — **rendido, -da** *adj* **1** : submissive **2** AGOTADO : exhausted

rendija *nf* : crack, split

rendir {54} *vt* **1** : render, give **2** PRODUCIR : yield, produce **3** CANSAR : exhaust — *vi* : make progress, go a long way — **rendirse** *vr* : surrender, give up — **rendimiento** *nm* **1** : performance **2** : yield, return (in finance, etc.)

renegar {49} *vt* : deny — *vi* **1** QUEJARSE : grumble **2 ~ de** ABJURAR : renounce, disown — **renegado, -da** *n* : renegade

renglón *nm, pl* **-glones 1** : line (of writing) **2** *Lat* : line (of products)
reno *nm* : reindeer
renombre *nm* : renown — **renombrado, -da** *adj* : famous, renowned
renovar {19} *vt* **1** : renew, restore **2** : renovate (a building, etc.) — **renovación** *nf, pl* **-ciones 1** : renewal **2** : renovation (of a building, etc.)
renquear *vi* : limp, hobble
rentar *vt* **1** : produce, yield **2** *Lat* : rent — **renta** *nf* **1** : income **2** ALQUILER : rent **3 impuesto sobre la ~** : income tax — **rentable** *adj* : profitable
renunciar *vi* **1** : resign **2 ~ a** : renounce, relinquish — **renuncia** *nf* **1** : renunciation **2** DIMISIÓN : resignation
reñir {67} *vi* **~ con** : argue with, fall out with — *vt* **1** : scold **2** DISPUTAR : fight — **reñido, -da** *adj* **1** : hard-fought **2 ~ con** : on bad terms with
reo, rea *n* **1** : accused, defendant **2** CULPABLE : culprit
reojo *nm* **de ~** : out of the corner of one's eye
reorganizar {21} *vt* : reorganize
repantigarse {52} *vr* : sprawl out
reparar *vt* **1** : repair, fix **2** : make amends for (an offense, etc.) — *vi* **1 ~ en** ADVERTIR : take notice of **2 ~ en** CONSIDERAR : consider — **reparación** *nf, pl* **-ciones 1** : reparation, amends **2** ARREGLO : repair — **reparo** *nm* **1** : reservation, objection **2 poner ~ a** : object to
repartir *vt* **1** : allocate **2** DISTRIBUIR : distribute **3** ESPARCIR : spread — **repartición** *nf, pl* **-ciones** : distribution — **repartidor, -dora** *n* : delivery person, distributor — **reparto** *nm* **1** : allocation **2** DISTRIBUCIÓN : delivery **3** : cast (of characters)
repasar *vt* **1** : review, go over **2** ZURCIR : mend — **repaso** *nm* **1** : review **2** : mending (of clothes)
repeler *vt* **1** : repel **2** REPUGNAR : disgust — **repelente** *adj* : repellent, repulsive
repente *nm* **1** : fit, outburst **2 de ~** : suddenly — **repentino, -na** *adj* : sudden
repercutir *vi* **1** : reverberate **2 ~ en** : have repercussions on — **repercusión** *nf, pl* **-siones** : repercussion
repertorio *nm* : repertoire
repetir {54} *vt* **1** : repeat **2** : have a second helping of (food) — **repetirse** *vr* **1** : repeat oneself **2** : recur (of an event, etc.) — **repetición** *nf, pl* **-ciones 1** : repetition **2** : rerun, repeat (of a program, etc.) — **repetido, -da**

adj **1** : repeated **2 repetidas veces** : repeatedly, time and again — **repetitivo, -va** *adj* : repetitive, repetitious
repicar {72} *vt* : ring — *vi* : ring out, peal — **repique** *nm* : ringing, pealing
repisa *nf* **1** : shelf, ledge **2 ~ de ventana** : windowsill
replegar {49} *vt* **1** : fold — **replegarse** *vr* : retreat, withdraw
repleto, -ta *adj* **1** : replete, full **2 ~ de** : packed with
replicar {72} *vt* : reply, retort — *vi* : answer back — **réplica** *nf* **1** RESPUESTA : reply **2** COPIA : replica, reproduction
repliegue *nm* **1** : fold **2** : (military) withdrawal
repollo *nm* : cabbage
reponer {60} *vt* **1** : replace **2** REPLICAR : reply — **reponerse** *vr* : recover
reportar *vt* **1** : yield, bring **2** *Lat* : report — **reportaje** *nm* : article, (news) report — **reporte** *nm* *Lat* : report — **reportero, -ra** *n* : reporter
reposar *vi* **1** DESCANSAR : rest **2** : stand, settle (of liquids, dough, etc.) — **reposado, -da** *adj* : calm, relaxed — **reposición** *nf, pl* **-ciones 1** : replacement **2** : rerun, repeat (of a program, etc.) — **reposo** *nm* : rest
repostar *vi* **1** : stock up on **2** : refuel (an airplane, etc.) — *vi* : fill up, refuel
reprender *vt* : reprimand, scold — **reprensible** *adj* : reprehensible
represalia *nf* **1** : reprisal **2 tomar ~s** : retaliate
represar *vt* : dam
representar *vt* **1** : represent **2** : perform (a play, etc.) **3** APARENTAR : look, appear as — **representación** *nf, pl* **-ciones 1** : representation **2** : performance (of a play, etc.) **3 en ~ de** : on behalf of — **representante** *nmf* **1** : representative **2** ACTOR : performer — **representativo, -va** *adj* : representative
represión *nf, pl* **-siones** : repression
reprimenda *nf* : reprimand
reprimir *vt* **1** : repress **2** : suppress (a rebellion, etc.)
reprobar {19} *vt* **1** : reprove, condemn **2** *Lat* : fail (an exam, etc.)
reprochar *vt* : reproach — **reprocharse** *vr* : reproach oneself — **reproche** *nm* : reproach
reproducir {61} *vt* : reproduce — **reproducirse** *vr* **1** : breed, reproduce **2** : recur (of an event, etc.) — **reproducción** *nf, pl* **-ciones** : reproduction — **reproductor, -tora** *adj* : reproductive
reptil *nm* : reptile

república *nf* : republic — **republicano, -na** *adj & n* : republican

repudiar *vt* : repudiate

repuesto *nm* : spare (auto) part

repugnar *vt* : disgust — **repugnancia** *nf* : disgust — **repugnante** *adj* : disgusting

repujar *vt* : emboss

repulsivo, -va *adj* : repulsive

reputar *vt* : consider, deem — **reputación** *nf, pl* **-ciones** : reputation

requerir {76} *vt* 1 : require 2 : summon, send for (a person)

requesón *nm, pl* **-sones** : cottage cheese

réquiem *nm* : requiem

requisito *nm* 1 : requirement 2 ~ **previo** : prerequisite

res *nf* 1 : beast, animal 2 *Lat or* **carne de** ~ : beef

resabio *nm* 1 VICIO : bad habit, vice 2 DEJO : aftertaste

resaca *nf* 1 : undertow 2 **tener** ~ : have a hangover

resaltar *vi* 1 : stand out 2 **hacer** ~ : bring out, highlight — *vt* : emphasize

resarcir {83} *vt* : compensate, repay — **resarcirse** *vr* ~ **de** : make up for

resbalar *vi* 1 : slip, slide 2 : skid (of an automobile) — **resbalarse** *vr* : slip, skid — **resbaladizo, -za** *adj* : slippery — **resbalón** *nm, pl* **-lones** : slip — **resbaloso, -sa** *adj Lat* : slippery

rescatar *vt* 1 : rescue, ransom 2 RECUPERAR : recover, get back — **rescate** *nm* 1 : rescue 2 : ransom (money) 3 RECUPERACIÓN : recovery

rescindir *vt* : cancel — **rescisión** *nf, pl* **-siones** : cancellation

rescoldo *nm* : embers *pl*

resecar {72} *vt* : dry (out) — **resecarse** *vr* : dry up — **reseco, -ca** *adj* : dry, dried-up

resentirse {76} *vr* 1 : suffer, be weakened 2 OFENDERSE : be offended 3 ~ **de** : feel the effects of — **resentido, -da** *adj* : resentful — **resentimiento** *nm* : resentment

reseñar *vt* 1 : review 2 DESCRIBIR : describe — **reseña** *nf* 1 : review, report 2 DESCRIPCIÓN : description

reservar *vt* 1 : reserve 2 GUARDAR : keep, save — **reservarse** *vr* 1 : save oneself 2 : keep for oneself — **reserva** *nf* 1 : reservation 2 PROVISIÓN : reserve 3 **de** ~ : spare, in reserve — **reservación** *nf, pl* **-ciones** : reservation — **reservado, -da** *adj* 1 : reserved 2 : confidential (of a document, etc.)

resfriar {85} *vt* : cool — **resfriarse** *vr* 1 : cool off 2 CONSTIPARSE : catch a cold — **resfriado** *nm* CATARRO : cold — **resfrío** *nm Lat* : cold

resguardar *vt* : protect — **resguardarse** *vr* : protect oneself — **resguardo** *nm* 1 : protection 2 RECIBO : receipt

residir *vi* 1 : reside, live 2 ~ **en** : lie in — **residencia** *nf* 1 : residence 2 *or* ~ **universitaria** : dormitory — **residencial** *adj* : residential — **residente** *adj & nmf* : resident

residuo *nm* 1 : residue 2 ~**s** *nmpl* : waste — **residual** *adj* : residual

resignar *vt* : resign — **resignarse** *vr* ~ **a** : resign oneself to — **resignación** *nf, pl* **-ciones** : resignation

resina *nf* 1 : resin 2 ~ **epoxídica** : epoxy

resistir *vt* 1 AGUANTAR : stand, bear 2 : withstand (temptation, etc.) — *vi* : resist — **resistirse** *vr* ~ **a** : be resistant to — **resistencia** *nf* 1 : resistance 2 AGUANTE : endurance, stamina — **resistente** *adj* : resistant, strong, tough

resma *nf* : ream

resollar {19} *vi* : breathe heavily, pant

resolver {89} *vt* 1 : resolve 2 DECIDIR : decide — **resolverse** *vr* : make up one's mind — **resolución** *nf, pl* **-ciones** 1 : resolution 2 DECISIÓN : decision 3 FIRMEZA : determination, resolve

resonar {19} *vi* : resound — **resonancia** *nf* 1 : resonance 2 CONSECUENCIAS : impact, repercussions *pl* — **resonante** *adj* : resonant, resounding

resoplar *vi* 1 : puff, pant 2 : snort (with annoyance)

resorte *nm* 1 MUELLE : spring 2 **tocar** ~**s** : pull strings

respaldar *vt* : back, endorse — **respaldarse** *vr* : lean back — **respaldo** *nm* 1 : back (of a chair, etc.) 2 APOYO : support, backing

respectar *vt* : concern, relate to — **respectivo, -va** *adj* : respective — **respecto** *nm* 1 **al** ~ : in this respect 2 ~ **a** : in regard to, concerning

respetar *vt* : respect — **respetable** *adj* : respectable — **respeto** *nm* 1 : respect 2 **presentar sus** ~**s** : pay one's respects — **respetuoso, -sa** *adj* : respectful

respingo *nm* : start, jump

respirar *v* : breathe — **respiración** *nf, pl* **-ciones** : respiration, breathing — **respiratorio, -ria** *adj* : respiratory — **respiro** *nm* 1 : breath 2 DESCANSO : respite, break

resplandecer {53} *vi* : shine — **resplandeciente** *adj* : shining, gleaming — **resplandor** *nm* **1** : brilliance, gleam **2** : flash (of lightning, etc.)

responder *vt* : answer, reply — *vi* **1** : answer **2** REPLICAR : answer back **3** ~ **a** : respond to **4** ~ **de** : answer for (something)

responsable *adj* : responsible — **responsabilidad** *nf* : responsibility

respuesta *nf* **1** : answer, reply **2** REACCIÓN : response

resquebrajar *vt* : split, crack — **resquebrajarse** *vr* : crack

resquicio *nm* **1** : crack, crevice **2** VESTIGIO : trace, glimmer

resta *nf* : subtraction

restablecer {53} *vt* : reestablish, restore — **restablecerse** *vr* : recover — **restablecimiento** *nm* : restoration, recovery

restallar *vi* : crack, crackle

restar *vt* **1** : deduct, subtract **2** DISMINUIR : minimize — *vi* : be left — **restante** *adj* **1** : remaining **2 lo** ~ : the rest

restauración *nf*, *pl* **-ciones** : restoration

restaurante *nm* : restaurant

restaurar *vt* : restore

restituir {41} *vt* : return, restore — **restitución** *nf*, *pl* **-ciones** : restitution

resto *nm* **1** : rest, remainder **2** ~**s** *nmpl* : leftovers **3** *or* ~**s mortales** : mortal remains

restregar {49} *vt* : rub, scrub — **restregarse** *vr* : rub

restringir {35} *vt* : restrict, limit — **restricción** *nf*, *pl* **-ciones** : restriction, limitation — **restrictivo, -va** *adj* : restrictive

resucitar *vt* : resuscitate, revive — *vi* : come back to life

resuelto, -ta *adj* : determined, resolved

resuello *nm* : heavy breathing, panting

resultar *vi* **1** : succeed, work out **2** SALIR : turn out (to be) **3** ~ **de** : be the result of **4** ~ **en** : result in — **resultado** *nm* : result, outcome

resumir *v* : summarize, sum up — **resumen** *nm*, *pl* **-súmenes 1** : summary **2 en** ~ : in short

resurgir {35} *vi* : reappear, revive — **resurgimiento** *nm* : resurgence — **resurrección** *nf*, *pl* **-ciones** : resurrection

retahíla *nf* : string, series

retal *nm* : remnant

retardar *vt* **1** RETRASAR : delay **2** POSPONER : postpone

retazo *nm* **1** : remnant, scrap **2** : fragment (of a text, etc.)

retener {80} *vt* **1** : retain, keep **2** : withhold (funds, etc.) **3** DETENER : detain — **retención** *nf*, *pl* **-ciones 1** : retention **2** : deduction, withholding (of funds)

reticente *adj* : reluctant — **reticencia** *nf* : reluctance

retina *nf* : retina

retintín *nm*, *pl* **-tines 1** : tinkling, jingle **2 con** ~ : sarcastically

retirar *vt* **1** : remove, take away **2** : withdraw (funds, statements, etc.) — **retirarse** *vr* **1** : retreat, withdraw **2** JUBILARSE : retire — **retirada** *nf* **1** : withdrawal **2 batirse en** ~ : beat a retreat — **retirado, -da** *adj* **1** : remote, secluded **2** JUBILADO : retired — **retiro** *nm* **1** : retreat **2** JUBILACIÓN : retirement **3** *Lat* : withdrawal

reto *nm* : challenge, dare

retocar {72} *vt* : touch up

retoño *nm* : sprout, shoot

retoque *nm* **1** : retouching **2 el último** ~ : the finishing touch

retorcer {14} *vt* **1** : twist, contort **2** : wring out (clothes, etc.) — **retorcerse** *vr* **1** : get twisted up **2** : squirm, writhe (in pain) — **retorcijón** *nm*, *pl* **-jones** : cramp, spasm — **retorcimiento** *nm* : twisting, wringing out

retórica *nf* : rhetoric — **retórico, -ca** *adj* : rhetorical

retornar *v* : return — **retorno** *nm* : return

retozar {21} *vi* : frolic, romp — **retozón, -zona** *adj* : playful, frisky

retractarse *vr* **1** : withdraw, back down **2** ~ **de** : take back, retract

retraer {81} *vt* : retract — **retraerse** *vr* : withdraw — **retraído, -da** *adj* : withdrawn, shy

retrasar *vt* **1** : delay, hold up **2** APLAZAR : postpone **3** : set back (a clock) — **retrasarse** *vr* **1** : be late **2** : fall behind (in work, etc.) — **retrasado, -da** *adj* **1** : retarded **2** : in arrears (of payments) **3** : backward (of a country) **4** : slow (of a clock) — **retraso** *nm* **1** : delay **2** SUBDESARROLLO : backwardness **3** ~ **mental** : mental retardation

retratar *vt* **1** : portray **2** FOTOGRAFIAR : photograph **3** DIBUJAR : paint a portrait of — **retrato** *nm* **1** : portrayal **2** DIBUJO : portrait **3** FOTOGRAFÍA : photograph

retrete *nm* : restroom, toilet

retribuir {41} *vt* **1** : pay **2** RECOMPENSAR : reward — **retribución** *nf*, *pl*

-ciones 1 : payment **2** RECOMPENSA : reward

retroactivo, -va *adj* : retroactive

retroceder *vi* **1** : go back, turn back **2** CEDER : back down — **retroceso** *nm* **1** : backward movement **2** : backing down

retrógrado, -da *adj & nmf* : reactionary

retrospectiva *nf* : hindsight — **retrospectivo, -va** *adj* : retrospective

retrovisor *nm* : rearview mirror

retumbar *vi* : resound, reverberate, rumble

reumatismo *nm* : rheumatism

reunir {68} *vt* **1** : unite, join **2** TENER : have, possess **3** RECOGER : gather, collect — **reunirse** *vr* : meet, gather — **reunión** *nf, pl* **-niones 1** : meeting **2** : (social) gathering, reunion

revalidar *vt* : confirm, ratify

revancha *nf* **1** : revenge **2** : rematch (in sports)

revelar *vt* **1** : reveal, disclose **2** : develop (film) — **revelación** *nf, pl* **-ciones** : revelation — **revelado** *nm* : developing (of film) — **revelador, -dora** *adj* : revealing

reventar {55} *v* : burst, blow up — **reventarse** *vr* : burst — **reventón** *nm, pl* **-tones** : blowout, flat tire

reverberar *vi* : reverberate — **reverberación** *nf, pl* **-ciones** : reverberation

reverenciar *vt* : revere — **reverencia** *nf* **1** : bow, curtsy **2** VENERACIÓN : reverence — **reverendo, -da** *adj & nmf* : reverend — **reverente** *adj* : reverent

reversa *nf Lat* : reverse (gear)

reverso *nm* **1** : back, reverse **2** el ∼ de la medalla : the complete opposite — **reversible** *adj* : reversible

revertir {76} *vi* **1** : revert **2** ∼ en : result in

revés *nm, pl* **-veses 1** : back, wrong side **2** CONTRATIEMPO : setback **3** BOFETADA : slap **4** : backhand (in sports) **5** al ∼ : the other way around, upside down, inside out

revestir {54} *vt* **1** : coat, cover **2** ASUMIR : take on, assume — **revestimiento** *nm* : covering, coating

revisar *vt* **1** : examine, inspect **2** : check over, overhaul (machinery, etc.) **3** MODIFICAR : revise — **revisión** *nf, pl* **-siones 1** : revision **2** INSPECCIÓN : inspection, check — **revisor, -sora** *n* : inspector

revistar *vt* : review, inspect (troops, etc.) — **revista** *nf* **1** : magazine, jour-

nal **2** : revue (in theater) **3** pasar ∼ : review, inspect

revivir *vi* : revive, come alive again — *vt* : relive

revocar {72} *vt* : revoke

revolcar {82} *vt* : knock over, knock down — **revolcarse** *vr* : roll around

revolotear *vi* : flutter, flit — **revoloteo** *nm* : fluttering, flitting

revoltijo *nm* : mess, jumble

revoltoso, -sa *adj* : rebellious

revolución *nf, pl* **-ciones** : revolution — **revolucionar** *vt* : revolutionize — **revolucionario, -ria** *adj & n* : revolutionary

revolver {89} *vt* **1** : mix, stir **2** : upset (one's stomach) **3** DESORGANIZAR : mess up — **revolverse** *vr* **1** : toss and turn **2** VOLVERSE : turn around

revólver *nm* : revolver

revuelo *nm* : commotion

revuelta *nf* : uprising, revolt — **revuelto, -ta** *adj* **1** : choppy, rough **2** DESORDENADO : messed up **3 huevos revueltos** : scrambled eggs

rey *nm* : king

reyerta *nf* : brawl, fight

rezagarse {52} *vr* : fall behind, lag

rezar {21} *vi* **1** : pray **2** DECIR : say — *vt* : say, recite — **rezo** *nm* : prayer

rezongar {52} *vi* : gripe, grumble

rezumar *v* : ooze

ría *nf* : estuary

riachuelo *nm* : brook, stream

riada *nf* : flood

ribera *nf* : bank, shore

ribetear *vt* : border, trim — **ribete** *nm* **1** : border, trim **2** : embellishment

rico, -ca *adj* **1** : rich, wealthy **2** ABUNDANTE : abundant **3** SABROSO : rich, tasty — ∼ *n* : rich person

ridiculizar {21} *vt* : ridicule — **ridículo, -la** *adj* : ridiculous — **ridículo** *nm* **1 hacer el** ∼ : make a fool of oneself **2 poner en** ∼ : ridicule

riego *nm* : irrigation

riel *nm* : rail

rienda *nf* **1** : rein **2 dar** ∼ **suelta a** : give free rein to

riesgo *nm* : risk

rifa *nf* : raffle — **rifar** *vt* : raffle (off) — **rifarse** *vr fam* : fight over

rifle *nm* : rifle

rígido, -da *adj* **1** : rigid, stiff **2** SEVERO : harsh, strict — **rigidez** *nf, pl* **-deces 1** : rigidity, stiffness **2** SEVERIDAD : harshness, strictness

rigor *nm* **1** : rigor, harshness **2** EXACTITUD : precision **3 de** ∼ : essential, obligatory — **riguroso, -sa** *adj* : rigorous

rima *nf* 1 : rhyme 2 **~s** *nfpl* : verse, poetry — **rimar** *vi* : rhyme

rimbombante *adj* : showy, pompous

rímel *nm* : mascara

rincón *nm, pl* **-cones** : corner, nook

rinoceronte *nm* : rhinoceros

riña *nf* 1 : fight, brawl 2 DISPUTA : dispute, quarrel

riñón *nm, pl* **-ñones** : kidney

río *nm* 1 : river 2 TORRENTE : torrent, stream

riqueza *nf* 1 : wealth 2 ABUNDANCIA : richness 3 **~s naturales** : natural resources

risa *nf* 1 : laughter, laugh 2 **dar ~ a algn** : make s.o. laugh 3 **morirse de la ~** *fam* : die laughing

risco *nm* : crag, cliff

risible *adj* : laughable

ristra *nf* : string, series

risueño, -ña *adj* : cheerful, smiling

ritmo *nm* 1 : rhythm 2 VELOCIDAD : pace, speed — **rítmico, -ca** *adj* : rhythmical

rito *nm* : rite, ritual — **ritual** *adj & nm* : ritual

rival *adj & nmf* : rival — **rivalidad** *nf* : rivalry, competition — **rivalizar** {21} *vi* **~ con** : rival, compete with

rizar {21} *vt* 1 : curl 2 : ripple (a surface) — **rizarse** *vr* : curl — **rizado, -da** *adj* 1 : curly 2 : choppy (of water) — **rizo** *nm* 1 : curl 2 : ripple (in water) 3 : loop (in aviation)

róbalo *nm* : bass (fish)

robar *vt* 1 : steal 2 : burglarize (a house, etc.) 3 SECUESTRAR : kidnap — **robo** *nm* : robbery, theft

roble *nm* : oak

robot *nm, pl* **-bots** : robot — **robótica** *nf* : robotics

robustecer {53} *vt* : make stronger, strengthen — **robusto, -ta** *adj* : robust, sturdy

roca *nf* : rock, boulder

roce *nm* 1 : rubbing, chafing 2 RASGUÑO : graze, scratch 3 **tener un ~ con** : have a brush with

rociar {85} *vt* : spray, sprinkle — **rocío** *nm* : dew

rocoso, -sa *adj* : rocky

rodaja *nf* : slice

rodar {19} *vi* 1 : roll, roll down, roll along 2 GIRAR : turn, go around 3 : travel (of a vehicle) 4 : film (of movies, etc.) — *vt* 1 : film, shoot 2 : break in (a vehicle) — **rodaje** *nm* 1 : filming, shooting 2 : breaking in (of a vehicle)

rodear *vt* 1 : surround, encircle 2 *Lat* : round up (cattle) — **rodearse** *vr* **~ de** : surround oneself with — **rodeo** *nm* 1 : rodeo, roundup 2 DESVÍO : detour 3 **andar con ~s** : beat around the bush

rodilla *nf* : knee

rodillo *nm* 1 : roller 2 : rolling pin (for pastry)

roer {69} *vt* 1 : gnaw 2 ATORMENTAR : eat away at, torment — **roedor** *nm* : rodent

rogar {16} *vt* : beg, request — *vi* : pray

rojo, -ja *adj* 1 : red 2 **ponerse ~** : blush — **rojo** *nm* : red — **rojez** *nf* : redness — **rojizo, -za** *adj* : reddish

rollizo, -za *adj* : plump, chubby

rollo *nm* 1 : roll, coil 2 *fam* : boring speech, lecture

romance *nm* 1 : romance 2 : Romance (language)

romano, -na *adj & n* : Roman

romántico, -ca *adj* : romantic — **romanticismo** *nm* : romanticism

romería *nf* : pilgrimage, procession

romero *nm* : rosemary

romo, -ma *adj* : blunt, dull

rompecabezas *nms & pl* : puzzle

romper {70} *vt* 1 : break 2 RASGAR : rip, tear 3 : break off (relations), break (a contract) — *vi* 1 : break (of the day, waves, etc.) 2 **~ a** : begin to, burst out with 3 **~ con** : break off with — **romperse** *vr* : break

ron *nm* : rum

roncar {72} *vi* : snore — **ronco, -ca** *adj* : hoarse

ronda *nf* 1 : rounds *pl*, patrol 2 : round (of drinks, etc.) — **rondar** *vt* 1 : patrol 2 : hang around (a place) 3 : be approximately (an age, a number, etc.) — *vi* 1 : be on patrol 2 MERODEAR : prowl about

ronquera *nf* : hoarseness

ronquido *nm* : snore

ronronear *vi* : purr — **ronroneo** *nm* : purr, purring

ronzar {21} *vt* : munch, crunch

roña *nf* 1 : mange 2 SUCIEDAD : dirt, filth — **roñoso, -sa** *adj* 1 : mangy 2 SUCIO : dirty 3 *fam* : stingy

ropa *nf* 1 : clothes *pl*, clothing 2 **~ interior** : underwear — **ropaje** *nm* : robes *pl*, regalia — **ropero** *nm* : wardrobe, closet

rosa *nf* : rose (flower) — **~** *adj* : rose-colored — **~** *nm* : rose (color) — **rosado, -da** *adj* 1 : pink 2 **vino rosado** : rosé — **rosado** *nm* : pink (color) — **rosal** *nm* : rosebush

rosario *nm* : rosary
rosbif *nm* : roast beef
rosca *nf* **1** : thread (of a screw) **2** ESPIRAL : ring, coil
roseta *nf* : rosette
rosquilla *nf* : doughnut
rostro *nm* : face
rotación *nf*, *pl* **-ciones** : rotation — **rotativo, -va** *adj* : rotary, revolving
roto, -ta *adj* : broken, torn
rotonda *nf* : traffic circle, rotary
rótula *nf* : kneecap
rótulo *nm* **1** : heading, title **2** ETIQUETA : label, sign
rotundo, -da *adj* : categorical, absolute
rotura *nf* : break, tear, fracture
rozar {21} *vt* **1** : graze, touch lightly **2** APROXIMARSE DE : touch on, border on — *vi* : scrape, rub — **rozarse** *vr* **1** : rub, chafe **2** ~ **con** *fam* : rub elbows with — **rozadura** *nf* : scratch
rubí *nm*, *pl* **rubíes** : ruby
rubicundo, -da *adj* : ruddy
rubio, -bia *adj & n* : blond
rubor *nm* : flush, blush — **ruborizarse** {21} *vr* : blush
rúbrica *nf* **1** : flourish (in writing) **2** TÍTULO : title, heading
rudeza *nf* : roughness, coarseness
rudimentos *nmpl* : rudiments, basics — **rudimentario, -ria** *adj* : rudimentary
rudo, -da *adj* **1** : rough, harsh **2** GROSERO : coarse, unpolished
rueda *nf* **1** : wheel **2** CORRO : circle, ring **3** RODAJA : (round) slice **4 ir sobre** ~**s** : go smoothly — **ruedo** *nm* : bullring

ruego *nm* : request
rugir {35} *vi* : roar — **rugido** *nm* : roar
rugoso, -sa *adj* **1** : rough **2** ARRUGADO : wrinkled
ruibarbo *nm* : rhubarb
ruido *nm* : noise — **ruidoso, -sa** *adj* : loud, noisy
ruina *nf* **1** : ruin, destruction **2** COLAPSO : collapse **3** ~**s** *nfpl* : ruins, remains — **ruinoso, -sa** *adj* : run-down, dilapidated
ruiseñor *nm* : nightingale
ruleta *nf* : roulette
rulo *nm* : curler, roller
rumano, -na *adj* : Romanian, Rumanian
rumba *nf* : rumba
rumbo *nm* **1** : direction, course **2** ESPLENDIDEZ : lavishness **3 con** ~ **a** : bound for, heading for **4 perder el** ~ : go off course
rumiar *vt* : mull over — *vi* : chew the cud — **rumiante** *adj & nm* : ruminant
rumor *nm* **1** : rumor **2** MURMULLO : murmur — **rumorearse** *or* **rumorarse** *vr* : be rumored — **rumoroso, -sa** *adj* : murmuring, babbling
ruptura *nf* **1** : break, rupture **2** : breach (of a contract) **3** : breaking off (of relations)
rural *adj* : rural
ruso, -sa *adj* : Russian — **ruso** *nm* : Russian (language)
rústico, -ca *adj* **1** : rural, rustic **2 en rústica** : in paperback
ruta *nf* : route
rutina *nf* : routine — **rutinario, -ria** *adj* : routine

S

s *nf* : s, 20th letter of the Spanish alphabet
sábado *nm* : Saturday
sábana *nf* : sheet
sabandija *nf* : bug
saber {71} *vt* **1** : know **2** SER CAPAZ DE : know how to, be able to **3** ENTERARSE : learn, find out **4 a** ~ : namely — *vi* **1** : taste **2** ~ **de** : know about — ~ *nm* : knowledge — **sabelotodo** *nmf fam* : know-it-all — **sabido, -da** *adj* : well-known — **sabiduría** *nf* **1** : wisdom **2** CONOCIMIENTO : learning, knowledge — **sabiendas: a** ~ *adv phr* : knowingly — **sabio, -bia** *adj* **1** : learned **2** PRUDENTE : wise, sensible

sabor *nm* : flavor, taste — **saborear** *vt* : savor
sabotaje *nm* : sabotage — **saboteador, -dora** *n* : saboteur — **sabotear** *vt* : sabotage
sabroso, -sa *adj* : delicious, tasty
sabueso *nm* **1** : bloodhound **2** *fam* : sleuth
sacacorchos *nms & pl* : corkscrew
sacapuntas *nms & pl* : pencil sharpener
sacar {72} *vt* **1** : take out **2** OBTENER : get, obtain **3** EXTRAER : extract, withdraw **4** : bring out (a book, a product, etc.) **5** : take (photos), make (copies) **6** QUITAR : remove **7** ~ **adelante** : bring up (children), carry out (a project,

etc.) **8 ~ la lengua** : stick out one's tongue — *vi* : serve (in sports)

sacarina *nf* : saccharin

sacerdote, -tisa *n* : priest *m*, priestess *f* — **sacerdocio** *nm* : priesthood — **sacerdotal** *adj* : priestly

saciar *vt* : satisfy

saco *nm* **1** : bag, sack **2** : sac (in anatomy) **3** *Lat* : jacket

sacramento *nm* : sacrament — **sacramental** *adj* : sacramental

sacrificar {72} *vt* : sacrifice — **sacrificarse** *vr* : sacrifice oneself — **sacrificio** *nm* : sacrifice

sacrilegio *nm* : sacrilege — **sacrílego, -ga** *adj* : sacrilegious

sacro, -cra *adj* : sacred — **sacrosanto, -ta** *adj* : sacrosanct

sacudir *vt* **1** : shake **2** GOLPEAR : beat **3** CONMOVER : shake up, shock — **sacudirse** *vr* : shake off — **sacudida** *nf* **1** : shaking **2** : jolt (of a train, etc.), tremor (of an earthquake) **3** : (emotional) shock

sádico, -ca *adj* : sadistic — **~** *n* : sadist — **sadismo** *nm* : sadism

saeta *nf* : arrow

safari *nm* : safari

sagaz *adj, pl* **-gaces** : shrewd, sagacious — **sagacidad** *nf* : shrewdness

sagrado, -da *adj* : sacred, holy

sal *nf* : salt

sala *nf* **1** : room, hall **2** : living room (of a house) **3 ~ de espera** : waiting room

salar *vt* : salt — **salado, -da** *adj* **1** : salty **2** GRACIOSO : witty **3 agua salada** : salt water

salario *nm* : salary, wage

salchicha *nf* : sausage — **salchichón** *nf, pl* **-chones** : salami-like cold cut

saldar *vt* **1** : settle, pay off **2** VENDER : sell off — **saldo** *nm* **1** : balance (of an account) **2 ~s** *nmpl* : remainders, sale items

salero *nm* : saltshaker

salir {73} *vi* **1** : go out, come out **2** PARTIR : leave **3** APARECER : appear **4** RESULTAR : turn out **5** : rise (of the sun) **6 ~ adelante** : get by **7 ~ con** : go out with, date **8 ~ de** : come from — **salirse** *vr* **1** : leave **2** ESCAPARSE : leak out, escape **3** SOLTARSE : come off **4 ~ con la suya** : get one's own way — **salida** *nf* **1** : exit **2** : (action of) leaving, departure **3** SOLUCIÓN : way out **4** : leak (of gas, liquid, etc.) **5** OCURRENCIA : witty remark **6 ~ de emergencia** : emergency exit **7 ~ del sol** : sunrise — **saliente** *adj* **1** : departing, outgoing **2** DESTACADO : outstanding

saliva *nf* : saliva

salmo *nm* : psalm

salmón *nm, pl* **-mones** : salmon

salmuera *nf* : brine

salón *nm, pl* **-lones 1** : lounge, sitting room **2 ~ de belleza** : beauty salon **3 ~ de clase** : classroom

salpicar {72} *vt* **1** : splash, spatter **2 ~ de** : pepper with — **salpicadera** *nf* *Lat* : fender — **salpicadura** *nf* : splash

salsa *nf* **1** : sauce **2** : (meat) gravy **3** : salsa (music)

saltamontes *nms & pl* : grasshopper

saltar *vi* **1** : jump, leap **2** REBOTAR : bounce **3** : come off (of a button, etc.) **4** ROMPERSE : shatter **5** ESTALLAR : explode, blow up — *vt* **1** : jump (over) **2** OMITIR : skip, miss — **saltarse** *vr* **1** : come off **2** OMITIR : skip, miss

saltear *vt* : sauté

saltimbanqui *nmf* : acrobat

salto *nm* **1** : jump, leap **2** : dive (into water) **3 ~ de agua** : waterfall — **saltón, -tona** *adj, mpl* **-tones** : bulging, protruding

salud *nf* **1** : health **2** ¡salud! : here's to your health! **3** ¡salud! *Lat* : bless you! (when someone sneezes) — **saludable** *adj* : healthy

saludar *vt* **1** : greet, say hello to **2** : salute (in the military) — **saludo** *nm* **1** : greeting **2** : (military) salute **3 ~s** : best wishes, regards

salva *nf* **~ de aplausos** : round of applause

salvación *nf, pl* **-ciones** : salvation

salvado *nm* : bran

salvador, -dora *n* : savior, rescuer

salvadoreño, -ña *adj* : (El) Salvadoran

salvaguardar *vt* : safeguard

salvaje *adj* **1** : wild **2** PRIMITIVO : savage, primitive — **~** *nmf* : savage

salvar *vt* **1** : save, rescue **2** RECORRER : cover, travel **3** SUPERAR : overcome — **salvarse** *vr* : save oneself — **salvavidas** *nms & pl* **1** : life preserver **2 bote ~** : lifeboat

salvia *nf* : sage (plant)

salvo, -va *adj* : safe — **salvo** *prep* **1** : except (for), save **2 ~ que** : unless

samba *nf* : samba

San → santo

sanar *vt* : heal, cure — *vi* : recover — **sanatorio** *nm* **1** : sanatorium **2** HOSPITAL : clinic, hospital

sanción *nf, pl* **-ciones** : sanction — **sancionar** *vt* : sanction

sandalia *nf* : sandal

sándalo *nm* : sandalwood

sandía *nf* : watermelon

sandwich ['sandwitʃ, 'saŋgwitʃ] *nm, pl* **-wiches** [-dwitʃes, -gwi-] : sandwich
saneamiento *nm* : sanitation
sangrar *vt* **1** : bleed **2** : indent (a paragraph) — *vi* : bleed — **sangrante** *adj* : bleeding — **sangre** *nf* **1** : blood **2 a ~ fría** : in cold blood — **sangriento, -ta** *adj* : bloody
sanguijuela *nf* : leech
sanguinario, -ria *adj* : bloodthirsty — **sanguíneo, -nea** *adj* : blood
sano, -na *adj* **1** : healthy **2** : (morally) wholesome **3** ENTERO : intact **4 sano y salvo** : safe and sound — **sanidad** *nf* **1** : health **2** : public health, sanitation — **sanitario, -ria** *adj* : sanitary, health — **sanitario** *nm Lat* : toilet
santiamén *nm* **en un ~** : in no time at all
santo, -ta *adj* **1** : holy **2** Santo, Santa (**San** *before masculine names except those beginning with D or T*) : Saint — **~** *n* : saint — **santo** *nm* **1** : saint's day **2** *Lat* : birthday — **santidad** *nf* : holiness, sanctity — **santiguarse** {10} *vr* : cross oneself — **santuario** *nm* : sanctuary
saña *nf* **1** : fury **2** BRUTALIDAD : viciousness
sapo *nm* : toad
saque *nm* : serve (in tennis, etc.), throw-in (in soccer)
saquear *vt* : sack, loot — **saqueador, -dora** *n* : looter — **saqueo** *nm* : sacking, looting
sarampión *nm* : measles *pl*
sarape *nm Lat* : serape
sarcasmo *nm* : sarcasm — **sarcástico, -ca** *adj* : sarcastic
sardina *nf* : sardine
sardónico, -ca *adj* : sardonic
sargento *nmf* : sergeant
sarpullido *nm* : rash
sartén *nmf, pl* **-tenes** : frying pan
sastre, -tra *n* : tailor — **sastrería** *nf* **1** : tailoring **2** : tailor's shop
Satanás *nm* : Satan — **satánico, -ca** *adj* : satanic
satélite *nm* : satellite
sátira *nf* : satire — **satírico, -ca** *adj* : satirical
satisfacer {74} *vt* **1** : satisfy **2** CUMPLIR : fulfill, meet **3** PAGAR : pay — **satisfacerse** *vr* **1** : be satisfied **2** VENGARSE : take revenge — **satisfacción** *nf, pl* **-ciones** : satisfaction — **satisfactorio, -ria** *adj* : satisfactory — **satisfecho, -cha** *adj* : satisfied
saturar *vt* : saturate — **saturación** *nf, pl* **-ciones** : saturation

Saturno *nm* : Saturn
sauce *nm* : willow
sauna *nmf* : sauna
savia *nf* : sap
saxofón *nm, pl* **-fones** : saxophone
sazón *nf, pl* **-zones** **1** : seasoning **2** MADUREZ : ripeness **3 a la ~** : at that time, then **4 en ~** : ripe, in season — **sazonar** *vt* : season
se *pron* **1** (*reflexive*) : himself, herself, itself, oneself, yourself, yourselves, themselves **2** (*indirect object*) : (to) him, (to) her, (to) you, (to) them **3** : each other, one another **4 ~ dice que** : it is said that **5 ~ habla inglés** : English spoken
sebo *nm* **1** : fat **2** : tallow (for candles, etc.) **3** : suet (for cooking)
secar {72} *v* : dry — **secarse** *vr* : dry (up) — **secador** *nm* : hair dryer — **secadora** *nf* : (clothes) dryer
sección *nf, pl* **-ciones** : section
seco, -ca *adj* **1** : dry **2** : dried (of fruits, etc.) **3** TAJANTE : sharp, brusque **4** *fam* : thin, skinny **5 a secas** : simply, just **6 en seco** : suddenly
secretar *vt* : secrete — **secreción** *nf, pl* **-ciones** : secretion
secretario, -ria *n* : secretary — **secretaría** *nf* : secretariat
secreto, -ta *adj* : secret — **secreto** *nm* **1** : secret **2 en ~** : in confidence
secta *nf* : sect
sector *nm* : sector
secuaz *nmf, pl* **-cuaces** : follower, henchman
secuela *nf* : consequence
secuencia *nf* : sequence
secuestrar *vt* **1** : kidnap **2** : hijack (an airplane, etc.) **3** EMBARGAR : confiscate, seize — **secuestrador, -dora** *n* **1** : kidnapper **2** : hijacker (of an airplane, etc.) — **secuestro** *nm* **1** : kidnapping **2** : hijacking (of an airplane, etc.) **3** : seizure (of goods)
secular *adj* : secular
secundar *vt* : support, second — **secundario, -ria** *adj* : secondary
sed *nf* **1** : thirst **2 tener ~** : be thirsty
seda *nf* : silk
sedal *nm* : fishing line
sedar *vt* : sedate — **sedante** *adj & nm* : sedative
sede *nf* **1** : seat, headquarters **2** Santa Sede : Holy See
sedentario, -ria *adj* : sedentary
sedición *nf, pl* **-ciones** : sedition — **sedicioso, -sa** *adj* : seditious
sediento, -ta *adj* : thirsty
sedimento *nm* : sediment

sedoso, -sa *adj* : silky, silken
seducir {61} *vt* 1 : seduce 2 ATRAER : captivate, charm — **seducción** *nf, pl* **-ciones** : seduction — **seductor, -tora** *adj* 1 : seductive 2 ENCANTADOR : charming — ~ *n* : seducer
segar {49} *vt* : reap — **segador, -dora** *n* : reaper, harvester
seglar *adj* : lay, secular — ~ *nm* : layperson, layman *m*, laywoman *f*
segmento *nm* : segment
segregar {52} *vt* : segregate — **segregación** *nf, pl* **-ciones** : segregation
seguir {75} *vt* : follow — *vi* : go on, continue — **seguida: en ~** *adv phr* : right away — **seguido** *adv* 1 : straight (ahead) 2 *Lat* : often — **seguido, -da** *adj* 1 : continuous 2 CONSECUTIVO : consecutive — **seguidor, -dora** *n* : follower
según *prep* : according to — ~ *adv* : it depends — ~ *conj* : as, just as
segundo, -da *adj* : second — ~ *n* : second (one) — **segundo** *nm* : second (unit of time)
seguro, -ra *adj* 1 : safe 2 FIRME : secure 3 CIERTO : sure, certain 4 FIABLE : reliable — **seguramente** *adv* : for sure, surely — **seguridad** *nf* 1 : safety 2 GARANTÍA : security 3 CERTEZA : certainty 4 CONFIANZA : confidence — **seguro** *adv* : certainly — ~ *nm* 1 : insurance 2 : safety (device)
seis *adj & nm* : six — **seiscientos, -tas** *adj* : six hundred — **seiscientos** *nms & pl* : six hundred
seísmo *nm* : earthquake
selección *nf, pl* **-ciones** : selection — **seleccionar** *vt* : select, choose — **selectivo, -va** *adj* : selective — **selecto, -ta** *adj* : choice, select
sellar *vt* 1 : seal 2 TIMBRAR : stamp — **sello** *nm* 1 : seal 2 TIMBRE : stamp 3 *or* ~ **distintivo** : hallmark
selva *nf* 1 : jungle 2 BOSQUE : forest
semáforo *nm* : traffic light
semana *nf* : week — **semanal** *adj* : weekly — **semanario** *nm* : weekly
semántica *nf* : semantics — **semántico, -ca** *adj* : semantic
semblante *nm* 1 : countenance, face 2 APARIENCIA : look
sembrar {55} *vt* 1 : sow 2 ~ **de** : strew with
semejar *vi* : resemble — **semejarse** *vr* : look alike — **semejante** *adj* 1 : similar 2 TAL : such — ~ *nm* : fellowman — **semejanza** *nf* : similarity
semen *nm* : semen — **semental** *nm* 1 : stud 2 **caballo ~** : stallion

semestre *nm* : semester
semiconductor *nm* : semiconductor
semifinal *nf* : semifinal
semilla *nf* : seed — **semillero** *nm* 1 : nursery (for plants) 2 HERVIDERO : hotbed, breeding ground
seminario *nm* 1 : seminary 2 CURSO : seminar, course
sémola *nf* : semolina
senado *nm* : senate — **senador, -dora** *n* : senator
sencillo, -lla *adj* 1 : simple 2 ÚNICO : single — **sencillez** *nf* : simplicity
senda *nf or* **sendero** *nm* : path, way
sendos, -das *adj pl* : each, both
senil *adj* : senile
seno *nm* 1 : breast, bosom 2 : sinus (in anatomy) 3 ~ **materno** : womb
sensación *nf, pl* **-ciones** : feeling, sensation — **sensacional** *adj* : sensational — **sensacionalista** *adj* : sensationalistic, lurid
sensato, -ta *adj* : sensible — **sensatez** *nf* : good sense
sensible *adj* 1 : sensitive 2 APRECIABLE : considerable, significant — **sensibilidad** *nf* : sensitivity — **sensitivo, -va** *or* **sensorial** *adj* : sense, sensory
sensual *adj* : sensual, sensuous — **sensualidad** *nf* : sensuality
sentar {55} *vt* 1 : seat, sit 2 ESTABLECER : establish, set — *vi* 1 : suit 2 ~ **bien a** : agree with (of food or drink) — **sentarse** *vr* : sit (down) — **sentado, -da** *adj* 1 : sitting, seated 2 **dar por sentado** : take for granted
sentencia *nf* 1 FALLO : sentence, judgment 2 MÁXIMA : saying — **sentenciar** *vt* : sentence
sentido, -da *adj* 1 : heartfelt, sincere 2 SENSIBLE : touchy, sensitive — **sentido** *nm* 1 : sense 2 CONOCIMIENTO : consciousness 3 DIRECCIÓN : direction 4 **doble ~** : double entendre 5 ~ **común** : common sense 6 ~ **del humor** : sense of humor 7 ~ **único** : one-way
sentimiento *nm* 1 : feeling, emotion 2 PESAR : regret — **sentimental** *adj* : sentimental — **sentimentalismo** *nm* : sentimentality
sentir {76} *vt* 1 : feel 2 OÍR : hear 3 LAMENTAR : be sorry for 4 **lo siento** : I'm sorry — *vi* : feel — **sentirse** *vr* : feel
seña *nf* 1 : sign 2 ~**s** *nfpl* DIRECCIÓN : address 3 ~**s particulares** : distinguishing marks
señal *nf* 1 : signal 2 AVISO, INDICIO : sign 3 DEPÓSITO : deposit 4 **dar ~es**

de : show signs of **5 en ~ de** : as a
token of — **señalado, -da** adj : notable — **señalar** vt **1** INDICAR : indicate, point out **2** MARCAR : mark **3**
FIJAR : fix, set — **señalarse** vr : distinguish oneself
señor, -ñora n **1** : gentleman m, man m,
lady f, woman f **2** : Sir m, Madam f **3**
: Mr. m, Mrs. f **4 señora** : wife f **5 el
Señor** : the Lord — **señorial** adj
: stately — **señorita** nf **1** : young lady,
young woman **2** : Miss
señuelo nm **1** : decoy **2** TRAMPA : bait,
lure
separar vt **1** : separate **2** QUITAR : detach, remove **3** APARTAR : move away
4 DESTITUIR : dismiss — **separarse** vr
1 APARTARSE : separate **2** : part company — **separación** nf, pl **-ciones** : separation — **separado, -da** adj **1** : separate **2** : separated (of persons) **3 por
separado** : separately
septentrional adj : northern
séptico, -ca adj : septic
septiembre nm : September
séptimo, -ma adj : seventh — ~ n
: seventh
sepulcro nm : tomb, sepulchre —
sepultar vt : bury — **sepultura** nf **1**
: burial **2** TUMBA : grave
sequedad nf : dryness — **sequía** nf
: drought
séquito nm : retinue, entourage
ser {77} vi **1** : be **2 a no ~ que** : unless **3 ¿cuánto es?** : how much is it?
4 es más : what's more **5 ~ de** : belong to **6 ~ de** : come from **7 son las
diez** : it's ten o'clock — ~ nm **1** ENTE
: being **2 ~ humano** : human being
serbio, -bia adj : Serb, Serbian
serenar vt : calm — **serenarse** vr
: calm down — **serenata** nf : serenade
— **serenidad** nf : serenity — **sereno,
-na** adj **1** : serene, calm **2** : fair, clear
(of weather) — **sereno** nm : night
watchman
serie nf **1** : series **2 fabricación en ~**
: mass production **3 fuera de ~** : extraordinary — **serial** nm : serial
serio, -ria adj **1** : serious **2** RESPONS-
ABLE : reliable **3 en serio** : seriously
— **seriedad** nf : seriousness
sermón nm, pl **-mones** : sermon —
sermonear vt : lecture, reprimand
serpentear vi : twist, wind — **serpiente** nf **1** : serpent, snake **2 ~ de cascabel** : rattlesnake
serrado, -da adj : serrated
serrano, -na adj **1** : mountain **2 jamón
serrano** : cured ham

serrar {55} vt : saw — **serrín** nm, pl
-rrines : sawdust — **serrucho** nm
: saw, handsaw
servicio nm **1** : service **2 ~s** nmpl
: restroom — **servicial** adj : obliging,
helpful — **servidor, -dora** n **1** : servant **2 su seguro servidor** : yours
truly — **servidumbre** nf **1** : servitude
2 CRIADOS : help, servants pl — **servil**
adj : servile
servilleta nf : napkin
servir {54} vt : serve — vi **1** : work,
function **2** VALER : be of use —
servirse vr **1** : help oneself **2 sírvase
sentarse** : please have a seat
sesenta adj & nm : sixty
sesgo nm : bias, slant
sesión nf, pl **-siones 1** : session **2**
: showing (of a film), performance (of
a play)
seso nm : brain — **sesudo, -da** adj **1**
: sensible **2** fam : brainy
seta nf : mushroom
setecientos, -tas adj : seven hundred
— **setecientos** nms & pl : seven hundred
setenta adj & nm : seventy
setiembre nm → **septiembre**
seto nm **1** : fence **2 ~ vivo** : hedge
seudónimo nm : pseudonym
severo, -ra adj **1** : harsh, severe **2**
: strict (of a teacher, etc.) — **severidad** nf : severity
sexagésimo, -ma adj & n : sixtieth
sexo nm : sex — **sexismo** nm : sexism
— **sexista** adj & nmf : sexist
sexteto nm : sextet
sexto, -ta adj & n : sixth
sexual adj : sexual — **sexualidad** nf
: sexuality
sexy adj, pl **sexy** or **sexys** : sexy
si conj **1** : if **2** (in indirect questions)
: whether **3 ~ bien** : although **4 ~
no** : otherwise, or else
sí¹ adv **1** : yes **2 creo que ~** : I think
so **3 porque ~** fam : (just) because —
~ nm : consent
sí² pron **1 de por ~** or **en ~** : by itself, in itself, per se **2 fuera de ~**
: beside oneself **3 para ~ (mismo)**
: to himself, to herself, for himself, for
herself **4 entre ~** : among themselves
sico- → **psico-**
SIDA or **sida** nm : AIDS
siderurgia nf : iron and steel industry
sidra nf : (hard) cider
siega nf **1** : harvesting **2** : harvest (time)
siembra nf **1** : sowing **2** : sowing season

siempre *adv* 1 : always 2 *Lat* : still 3 **para ~** : forever, for good 4 **~ que** : whenever, every time 5 **~ que** *or* **~ y cuando** : provided that
sien *nf* : temple
sierra *nf* 1 : saw 2 CORDILLERA : mountain range 3 **la ~** : the mountains *pl*
siervo, -va *n* : slave
siesta *nf* : nap, siesta
siete *adj & nm* : seven
sífilis *nf* : syphilis
sifón *nm*, *pl* **-fones** : siphon
sigilo *nm* : secrecy
sigla *nf* : acronym, abbreviation
siglo *nm* 1 : century 2 **hace ~s** : for ages
significar {72} *vt* 1 : mean, signify 2 EXPRESAR : express — **significación** *nf*, *pl* **-ciones** 1 : significance, importance 2 : meaning (of a word, etc.) — **significado, -da** *adj* : well-known — **significado** *nm* : meaning — **significativo, -va** *adj* : significant
signo *nm* 1 : sign 2 **~ de admiración** : exclamation point 3 **~ de interrogación** : question mark
siguiente *adj* : next, following
sílaba *nf* : syllable
silbar *v* 1 : whistle 2 ABUCHEAR : hiss, boo — **silbato** *nm* : whistle — **silbido** *nm* 1 : whistle, whistling 2 ABUCHEO : hiss, booing
silenciar *vt* : silence — **silenciador** *nm* : muffler — **silencio** *nm* : silence — **silencioso, -sa** *adj* : silent, quiet
silicio *nm* : silicon
silla *nf* 1 : chair 2 *or* **~ de montar** : saddle 3 **~ de ruedas** : wheelchair — **sillón** *nm*, *pl* **-llones** : armchair, easy chair
silo *nm* : silo
silueta *nf* 1 : silhouette 2 CONTORNO : outline, shape
silvestre *adj* : wild
silvicultura *nf* : forestry
símbolo *nm* : symbol — **simbólico, -ca** *adj* : symbolic — **simbolismo** *nm* : symbolism — **simbolizar** {21} *vt* : symbolize
simetría *nf* : symmetry — **simétrico, -ca** *adj* : symmetrical, symmetric
simiente *nf* : seed
símil *nm* 1 : simile 2 COMPARACIÓN : comparison — **similar** *adj* : similar, alike
simio *nm* : ape
simpatía *nf* 1 : liking, affection 2 AMABILIDAD : friendliness — **simpático, -ca** *adj* 1 : nice, likeable 2 AMABLE : pleasant, kind — **simpatizante** *nmf*

: sympathizer — **simpatizar** {21} *vi* 1 : get along, hit it off 2 **~ con** : sympathize with
simple *adj* 1 SENCILLO : simple 2 MERO : pure, sheer 3 TONTO : simpleminded — **~** *n* : fool, simpleton — **simpleza** *nf* 1 : simpleness 2 TONTERÍA : silly thing — **simplicidad** *nf* : simplicity — **simplificar** {72} *vt* : simplify
simposio *or* **simposium** *nm* : symposium
simular *vt* 1 : simulate 2 FINGIR : feign — **simulacro** *nm* : simulation, drill
simultáneo, -nea *adj* : simultaneous
sin *prep* 1 : without 2 **~ que** : without
sinagoga *nf* : synagogue
sincero, -ra *adj* : sincere — **sinceramente** *adv* : sincerely — **sinceridad** *nf* : sincerity
síncopa *nf* : syncopation
sincronizar {21} *vt* : synchronize
sindicato *nm* : (labor) union — **sindical** *adj* : union, labor
síndrome *nm* : syndrome
sinfín *nm* 1 : endless number 2 **un ~ de** : no end of
sinfonía *nf* : symphony — **sinfónico, -ca** *adj* : symphonic
singular *adj* 1 : exceptional, outstanding 2 PECULIAR : peculiar 3 : singular (in grammar) — **~** *nm* : singular — **singularizar** {21} *vt* : single out — **singularizarse** *vr* : stand out
siniestro, -tra *adj* 1 : sinister 2 IZQUIERDO : left — **siniestro** *nm* : disaster
sinnúmero *nm* → **sinfín**
sino *conj* 1 : but, rather 2 EXCEPTO : except, save
sinónimo, -ma *adj* : synonymous — **sinónimo** *nm* : synonym
sinopsis *nfs & pl* : synopsis
sinrazón *nf*, *pl* **-zones** : wrong
sintaxis *nfs & pl* : syntax
síntesis *nfs & pl* : synthesis — **sintético, -ca** *adj* : synthetic — **sintetizar** {21} *vt* 1 : synthesize 2 RESUMIR : summarize
síntoma *nm* : symptom — **sintomático, -ca** *adj* : symptomatic
sintonía *nf* 1 : tuning in (of a radio) 2 **en ~ con** : in tune with — **sintonizar** {21} *vt* : tune (in) to
sinuoso, -sa *adj* : winding
sinvergüenza *nmf* : scoundrel
sionismo *nm* : Zionism
siquiera *adv* 1 : at least 2 **ni ~** : not even — **~** *conj* : even if
sirena *nf* 1 : mermaid 2 : siren (of an ambulance, etc.)
sirio, -ria *adj* : Syrian

sirviente, -ta *n* : servant, maid *f*
sisear *vi* : hiss — **siseo** *nm* : hiss
sismo *nm* : earthquake — **sísmico, -ca** *adj* : seismic
sistema *nm* **1** : system **2 por ～** : systematically — **sistemático, -ca** *adj* : systematic
sitiar *vt* : besiege
sitio *nm* **1** : place, site **2** ESPACIO : room, space **3** CERCO : siege **4 en cualquier ～** : anywhere
situar {3} *vt* : situate, place — **situarse** *vr* **1** : be located **2** ESTABLECERSE : get oneself established — **situación** *nf, pl* **-ciones** : situation, position — **situado, -da** *adj* : situated, placed
slip *nm* : briefs *pl*, underpants *pl*
smoking *nm* : tuxedo
so *prep* : under
sobaco *nm* : armpit
sobar *vt* **1** : finger, handle **2** : knead (dough) — **sobado, -da** *adj* : worn, shabby
soberanía *nf* : sovereignty — **soberano, -na** *adj & n* : sovereign
soberbia *nf* : pride, arrogance — **soberbio, -bia** *adj* : proud, arrogant
sobornar *vt* : bribe — **soborno** *nm* **1** : bribe **2** : (action of) bribery
sobrar *vi* **1** : be more than enough **2** RESTAR : be left over — **sobra** *nf* **1** : surplus **2 de ～** : to spare **3 ～s** *nfpl* : leftovers — **sobrado, -da** *adj* : more than enough — **sobrante** *adj* : remaining
sobre[1] *nm* : envelope
sobre[2] *prep* **1** : on, on top of **2** POR ENCIMA DE : over, above **3** ACERCA DE : about **4 ～ todo** : especially, above all
sobrecama *nmf Lat* : bedspread
sobrecargar {52} *vt* : overload, overburden
sobrecoger {15} *vt* : startle — **sobrecogerse** *vr* : be startled
sobrecubierta *nf* : dust jacket
sobredosis *nfs & pl* : overdose
sobreentender {56} *vt* : infer, understand — **sobreentenderse** *vr* : be understood
sobreestimar *vt* : overestimate
sobregiro *nm* : overdraft
sobrellevar *vt* : endure, bear
sobremesa *nf* **de ～** : after-dinner
sobrenatural *adj* : supernatural
sobrenombre *nm* : nickname
sobrentender → **sobreentender**
sobrepasar *vt* : exceed
sobreponer {60} *vt* **1** : superimpose **2** ANTEPONER : put before — **sobreponerse** *vr* **～ a** : overcome

sobresalir {73} *vi* **1** : protrude **2** DESTACARSE : stand out — **sobresaliente** *adj* : outstanding
sobresaltar *vt* : startle — **sobresaltarse** *vr* : start, jump up — **sobresalto** *nm* : fright
sobrestimar → **sobreestimar**
sobretodo *nm* : overcoat
sobrevenir {87} *vi* : happen, ensue
sobrevivencia *nf* → **supervivencia**
sobreviviente *adj & nmf* → **superviviente**
sobrevivir *vi* : survive — *vt* : outlive
sobrevolar {19} *vt* : fly over
sobriedad *nf* **1** : sobriety **2** MODERACIÓN : restraint
sobrino, -na *n* : nephew *m*, niece *f*
sobrio, -bria *adj* : sober
socarrón, -rrona *adj, mpl* **-rrones** : sarcastic
socavar *vt* : undermine
sociable *adj* : sociable — **social** *adj* : social — **socialismo** *nm* : socialism — **socialista** *adj & nmf* : socialist — **sociedad** *nf* **1** : society **2** EMPRESA : company **3 ～ anónima** : incorporated company — **socio, -cia** *n* **1** : partner **2** MIEMBRO : member — **sociología** *nf* : sociology — **sociólogo, -ga** *n* : sociologist
socorrer *vt* : help — **socorrista** *nmf* : lifeguard — **socorro** *nm* : help
soda *nf* : soda (water)
sodio *nf* : sodium
sofá *nm* : couch, sofa
sofisticación *nf, pl* **-ciones** : sophistication — **sofisticado, -da** *adj* : sophisticated
sofocar {72} *vt* **1** : suffocate, smother **2** : put out (a fire), stifle (a rebellion, etc.) — **sofocarse** *vr* **1** : suffocate **2** *fam* : get upset — **sofocante** *adj* : suffocating, stifling
sofreír {66} *vt* : sauté
soga *nf* : rope
soja *nf* → **soya**
sojuzgar *vt* : subdue, subjugate
sol *nm* **1** : sun **2 hacer ～** : be sunny
solamente *adv* : only, just
solapa *nf* **1** : lapel (of a jacket) **2** : flap (of an envelope) — **solapado, -da** *adj* : secret, underhanded
solar[1] *adj* : solar, sun
solar[2] *nm* : lot, site
solariego, -ga *adj* : ancestral
solaz *nm, pl* **-laces** **1** : solace **2** DESCANSO : relaxation — **solazarse** {21} *vr* : relax
soldado *nm* **1** : soldier **2 ～ raso** : private
soldar {19} *vt* : weld, solder — **solda-**

dor *nm* : soldering iron — **soldador, -dora** *n* : welder
soleado, -da *adj* : sunny
soledad *nf* : loneliness, solitude
solemne *adj* : solemn — **solemnidad** *nf* : solemnity
soler {78} *vi* 1 : be in the habit of 2 **suele llegar tarde** : he usually arrives late
solicitar *vt* 1 : request, solicit 2 : apply for (a job, etc.) — **solicitante** *nmf* : applicant — **solícito, -ta** *adj* : solicitous, obliging — **solicitud** *nf* 1 : concern 2 PETICIÓN : request 3 : application (for a job, etc.)
solidaridad *nf* : solidarity
sólido, -da *adj* 1 : solid 2 : sound (of an argument, etc.) — **sólido** *nm* : solid — **solidez** *nf* : solidity — **solidificar** {72} *vt* : solidify — **solidificarse** *vr* : solidify, harden
soliloquio *nm* : soliloquy
solista *nmf* : soloist
sollozar {21} *vi* 1 : sob — **sollozo** *nm* : sob
solo, -la *adj* 1 : alone 2 AISLADO : lonely 3 **a solas** : alone, by oneself — **solo** *nm* : solo
sólo *adv* 1 : just, only
solomillo *nm* : sirloin
solsticio *nm* : solstice
soltar {19} *vt* 1 : release 2 DEJAR CAER : let go of, drop 3 DESATAR : unfasten, undo — **soltarse** *vr* 1 : break free 2 DESATARSE : come undone
soltero, -ra *adj* : single, unmarried — **~** *n* 1 : bachelor *m*, single woman *f* 2 **apellido de soltera** : maiden name
soltura *nf* 1 : looseness 2 : fluency (in language) 3 AGILIDAD : agility, ease
soluble *adj* : soluble
solución *nf*, *pl* -**ciones** : solution — **solucionar** *vt* : solve, resolve
solventar *vt* 1 : settle, pay 2 RESOLVER : resolve — **solvente** *adj* & *nm* : solvent
sombra *nf* 1 : shadow 2 : shade (of a tree, etc.) 3 **~s** *nfpl* : darkness, shadows — **sombreado, -da** *adj* : shady
sombrero *nm* : hat
sombrilla *nf* : parasol, umbrella
sombrío, -bría *adj* : dark, somber, gloomy
somero, -ra *adj* : superficial
someter *vt* 1 : subjugate 2 SUBORDINAR : subordinate 3 : subject (to treatment,

etc.) 4 PRESENTAR : submit, present — **someterse** *vr* 1 : submit, yield 2 **~ a** : undergo
somnífero, -ra *adj* : soporific — **somnífero** *nm* : sleeping pill — **somnoliento, -ta** *adj* : drowsy, sleepy
somos → ser
son¹ → ser
son² *nm* 1 : sound 2 **en ~ de** : as, in the manner of
sonajero *nm* : (baby's) rattle
sonámbulo, -la *n* : sleepwalker
sonar {19} *vi* 1 : sound 2 : ring (as a bell) 3 : look or sound familiar 4 **~ a** : sound like — **sonarse** *vr or* **~ las narices** : blow one's nose
sonata *nf* : sonata
sondear *vt* 1 : sound, probe 2 : survey, sound out (opinions, etc.) — **sondeo** *nm* 1 : sounding, probing 2 ENCUESTA : survey, poll
soneto *nm* : sonnet
sónico, -ca *adj* : sonic
sonido *nm* : sound
sonoro, -ra *adj* 1 : resonant, sonorous 2 RUIDOSO : loud
sonreír {66} *vi* : smile — **sonreírse** *vr* : smile — **sonriente** *adj* : smiling — **sonrisa** *nf* : smile
sonrojar *vt* : cause to blush — **sonrojarse** *vr* : blush — **sonrojo** *nm* : blush
sonrosado, -da *adj* : rosy, pink
sonsacar {72} *vt* : wheedle (out)
soñar {19} *v* 1 : dream 2 **~ con** : dream about 3 **~ despierto** : daydream — **soñador, -dora** *adj* : dreamy — **~** *n* : dreamer — **soñoliento, -ta** *adj* : sleepy, drowsy
sopa *nf* : soup
sopesar *vt* : weigh, consider
soplar *vi* : blow — *vt* : blow out, blow off, blow up — **soplete** *nm* : blowtorch — **soplo** *nm* : puff, gust
soplón, -plona *n*, *pl* -**plones** *fam* : sneak
sopor *nm* : drowsiness — **soporífero, -ra** *adj* : soporific
soportar *vt* 1 SOSTENER : support 2 AGUANTAR : bear — **soporte** *nm* : support
soprano *nmf* : soprano
sor *nf* : Sister (in religion)
sorber *vt* 1 : sip 2 ABSORBER : absorb 3 CHUPAR : suck up — **sorbete** *nm* : sherbet — **sorbo** *nm* 1 : sip, swallow 2 **beber a ~s** : sip
sordera *nf* : deafness
sórdido, -da *adj* : sordid, squalid
sordo, -da *adj* 1 : deaf 2 : muted (of a

sound) — **sordomudo, -da** *n* : deaf-mute

sorna *nf* : sarcasm

sorprender *vt* 1 : surprise — **sorprenderse** *vr* : be surprised — **sorprendente** *adj* : surprising — **sorpresa** *nf* : surprise

sortear *vt* 1 : raffle off, draw lots for 2 ESQUIVAR : dodge — **sorteo** *nm* : drawing, raffle

sortija *nf* 1 : ring 2 : ringlet (of hair)

sortilegio *nm* 1 HECHIZO : spell 2 HECHICERÍA : sorcery

sosegar {49} *vt* : calm, pacify — **sosegarse** *vr* : calm down — **sosegado, -da** *adj* : calm, tranquil — **sosiego** *nm* : calm

soslayo: **de ~** *adv phr* : obliquely, sideways

soso, -sa *adj* 1 : insipid, tasteless 2 ABURRIDO : dull

sospechar *vt* : suspect — **sospecha** *nf* : suspicion — **sospechoso, -sa** *adj* : suspicious — **~** *n* : suspect

sostener {80} *vt* 1 : support SUJETAR : hold 3 MANTENER : sustain, maintain — **sostenerse** *vr* 1 : stand (up) 2 CONTINUAR : remain 3 SUSTENTARSE : support oneself — **sostén** *nm*, *pl* **-tenes** 1 APOYO : support 2 SUSTENTO : sustenance 3 : brassiere, bra — **sostenido, -da** *adj* 1 : sustained 2 : sharp (in music) — **sostenido** *nm* : sharp

sótano *nm* : basement

soterrar {55} *vt* 1 : bury 2 ESCONDER : hide

soto *nm* : grove

soviético, -ca *adj* : Soviet

soy → ser

soya *nf* : soy

Sr. *nm* : Mr. — **Sra.** *nf* : Mrs., Ms. — **Srta.** *or* **Srita.** *nf* : Miss, Ms.

su *adj* 1 : his, her, its, their, one's 2 (*formal*) : your

suave *adj* 1 : soft 2 LISO : smooth 3 APACIBLE : gentle, mild — **suavidad** *nf* 1 : softness, smoothness 2 APACIBILIDAD : mildness, gentleness — **suavizar** {21} *vt* : soften, smooth

subalimentado, -da *adj* : undernourished, underfed

subalterno, -na *adj* 1 SUBORDINADO : subordinate 2 SECUNDARIO : secondary — **~** *n* : subordinate

subarrendar {55} *vt* : sublet

subasta *nf* : auction — **subastar** *vt* : auction (off)

subcampeón, -peona *n*, *mpl* **-peones** : runner-up

subcomité *nm* : subcommittee

subconsciente *adj* & *nm* : subconscious

subdesarrollado, -da *adj* : underdeveloped

subdirector, -tora *n* : assistant manager

súbdito, -ta *n* : subject

subdividir *vt* : subdivide — **subdivisión** *nf*, *pl* **-siones** : subdivision

subestimar *vt* : underestimate

subir *vt* 1 : climb, go up 2 LLEVAR : bring up, take up 3 AUMENTAR : raise — *vi* 1 : go up, come up 2 **~ a** : get in (a car), get on (a bus, etc.) — **subirse** *vr* 1 : climb (up) 2 **~ a** : get in (a car), get on (a bus, etc.) 3 **~ a la cabeza** : go to one's head — **subida** *nf* 1 : ascent, climb 2 AUMENTO : rise 3 PENDIENTE : slope — **subido, -da** *adj* 1 : bright, strong 2 **~ de tono** : risqué

súbito, -ta *adj* 1 : sudden 2 **de súbito** : all of a sudden, suddenly

subjetivo, -va *adj* : subjective

subjuntivo, -va *adj* : subjunctive — **subjuntivo** *nm* : subjunctive (case)

sublevar *vt* : stir up, incite to rebellion — **sublevarse** *vr* : rebel — **sublevación** *nf*, *pl* **-ciones** : uprising, rebellion

sublime *adj* : sublime

submarino, -na *adj* : underwater — **submarino** *nm* : submarine — **submarinismo** *nm* : scuba diving

subordinar *vt* : subordinate — **subordinado, -da** *adj* & *n* : subordinate

subproducto *nm* : by-product

subrayar *vt* 1 : underline 2 ENFATIZAR : emphasize, stress

subrepticio, -cia *adj* : surreptitious

subsanar *vt* 1 : rectify, correct 2 : make up for (a deficiency), overcome (an obstacle)

subscribir → suscribir

subsidio *nm* : subsidy, benefit

subsiguiente *adj* : subsequent

subsistir *vi* 1 : live, subsist 2 SOBREVIVIR : survive — **subsistencia** *nf* : subsistence

substancia *nf* → **sustancia**

subterfugio *nm* : subterfuge

subterráneo, -nea *adj* : underground, subterranean — **subterráneo** *nm* : underground passage

subtítulo *nm* : subtitle

suburbio *nm* 1 : suburb 2 : slum (outside a city) — **suburbano, -na** *adj* : suburban

subvencionar *vt* : subsidize — **sub-**

vención *nf, pl* **-ciones** : subsidy, grant

subvertir {76} *vt* : subvert — **subversión** *nf, pl* **-siones** : subversion — **subversivo, -va** *adj & n* : subversive

subyacente *adj* : underlying

subyugar {52} *vt* : subjugate, subdue

succión *nf, pl* **-ciones** : suction — **succionar** *vt* : suck up, draw in

sucedáneo *nm* : substitute

suceder *vi* **1** : happen, occur **2** ~ **a** : follow **3 suceda lo que suceda** : come what may — **sucesión** *nf, pl* **-siones** : succession — **sucesivo, -va** *adj* : successive — **suceso** *nm* **1** : event **2** INCIDENTE : incident — **sucesor, -sora** *n* : successor

suciedad *nf* **1** : dirtiness **2** MUGRE : dirt, filth

sucinto, -ta *adj* : succinct, concise

sucio, -cia *adj* : dirty, filthy

suculento, -ta *adj* : succulent

sucumbir *vi* : succumb

sucursal *nf* : branch (of a business)

sudadera *nf* : sweatshirt — **sudado, -da** *adj* : sweaty

sudafricano, -na *adj* : South African

sudamericano, -na *adj* : South American

sudar *vi* : sweat

sudeste → **sureste**

sudoeste → **suroeste**

sudor *nm* : sweat — **sudoroso, -sa** *adj* : sweaty

sueco, -ca *adj* : Swedish — **sueco** *nm* : Swedish (language)

suegro, -gra *n* **1** : father-in-law *m,* mother-in-law *f* **2 suegros** *nmpl* : in-laws

suela *nf* : sole (of a shoe)

sueldo *nm* : salary, wage

suelo *nm* **1** : ground **2** : floor (in a house) **3** TIERRA : soil, land

suelto, -ta *adj* : loose, free — **suelto** *nm* : loose change

sueño *nm* **1** : dream **2 coger el** ~ : get to sleep **3 tener** ~ : be sleepy

suero *nm* **1** : whey **2** : serum (in medicine)

suerte *nf* **1** : luck, fortune **2** AZAR : chance **3** DESTINO : fate **4** CLASE : sort, kind **5 por** ~ : luckily **6 tener** ~ : be lucky

suéter *nm* : sweater

suficiencia *nf* **1** CAPACIDAD : competence, proficiency **2** PRESUNCIÓN : smugness — **suficiente** *adj* **1** : enough, sufficient **2** PRESUNTUOSO : smug — **suficientemente** *adv* : enough

sufijo *nm* : suffix

sufragio *nm* : suffrage, vote

sufrir *vt* **1** : suffer **2** SOPORTAR : bear, stand — *vi* : suffer — **sufrido, -da** *adj* **1** : long-suffering **2** : sturdy, serviceable (of clothing) — **sufrimiento** *nm* : suffering

sugerir {76} *vt* : suggest — **sugerencia** *nf* : suggestion — **sugestión** *nf, pl* **-tiones** : suggestion — **sugestionable** *adj* : impressionable — **sugestionar** *vt* : influence — **sugestivo, -va** *adj* **1** : suggestive **2** ESTIMULANTE : interesting, stimulating

suicidio *nm* : suicide — **suicida** *adj* : suicidal — ~ *nmf* : suicide (victim) — **suicidarse** *vr* : commit suicide

suite *nf* : suite

suizo, -za *adj* : Swiss

sujetar *vt* **1** : hold (on to) **2** FIJAR : fasten **3** DOMINAR : subdue — **sujetarse** *vr* **1** ~ **a** : hold on to, cling to **2** ~ **a** : abide by — **sujeción** *nf, pl* **-ciones 1** : fastening **2** DOMINACIÓN : subjection — **sujetador** *nm Spain* : brassiere, bra — **sujetapapeles** *nms & pl* : paper clip — **sujeto, -ta** *adj* **1** : fastened **2** ~ **a** : subject to — **sujeto** *nm* **1** : individual **2** : subject (in grammar)

sulfuro *nm* : sulfur — **sulfúrico, -ca** *adj* : sulfuric

sultán *nm, pl* **-tanes** : sultan

suma *nf* **1** : sum, total **2** : addition (in mathematics) **3 en** ~ : in short — **sumamente** *adv* : extremely — **sumar** *vt* **1** : add (up) **2** TOTALIZAR : add up to, total — *vi* : add up — **sumarse** *vr* ~ **a** : join

sumario, -ria *adj* : concise — **sumario** *nm* **1** : summary **2** : indictment (in law)

sumergir {35} *vt* : submerge, plunge — **sumergirse** *vr* : be submerged — **sumergible** *adj* : waterproof (of a watch, etc.)

sumidero *nm* : drain

suministrar *vt* : supply, provide — **suministro** *nm* : supply, provision

sumir *vt* : plunge, immerse — **sumirse** *vr* ~ **en** : sink into

sumisión *nf, pl* **-siones** : submission — **sumiso, -sa** *adj* : submissive

sumo, -ma *adj* **1** : highest, supreme **2 de suma importancia** : of great importance

suntuoso, -sa *adj* : sumptuous, lavish

super *or* **súper** *nm fam* : supermarket

superabundancia *nf* : overabundance

superar *vt* **1** : surpass, outdo **2** VENCER : overcome — **superarse** *vr* : improve oneself

superávit *nm* : surplus
superestructura *nf* : superstructure
superficie *nf* 1 : surface 2 ÁREA : area — **superficial** *adj* : superficial
superfluo, -flua *adj* : superfluous
superintendente *nmf* : supervisor, superintendent
superior *adj* 1 : superior 2 : upper (of a floor, etc.) 3 ~ **a** : above, higher than — ~ *nm* : superior — **superioridad** *nf* : superiority
superlativo, -va *adj* : superlative — **superlativo** *nm* : superlative
supermercado *nm* : supermarket
superpoblado, -da *adj* : overpopulated
supersónico, -ca *adj* : supersonic
superstición *nf, pl* **-ciones** : superstition — **supersticioso, -sa** *adj* : superstitious
supervisar *vt* : supervise, oversee — **supervisión** *nf, pl* **-siones** : supervision — **supervisor, -sora** *n* : supervisor
supervivencia *nf* : survival — **superviviente** *adj* : surviving — ~ *nmf* : survivor
suplantar *vt* : supplant, replace
suplemento *nm* : supplement — **suplementario, -ria** *adj* : supplementary
suplente *adj & nmf* : substitute
suplicar {72} *vt* : beg, entreat — **súplica** *nf* : plea, entreaty
suplicio *nm* : ordeal, torture
suplir *vt* 1 : make up for 2 REEMPLAZAR : replace
supo, etc. → **saber**
suponer {60} *vt* 1 : suppose, assume 2 SIGNIFICAR : mean 3 IMPLICAR : involve, entail — **suposición** *nf, pl* **-ciones** : supposition
supositorio *nm* : suppository
supremo, -ma *adj* : supreme — **supremacía** *nf* : supremacy
suprimir *vt* 1 : suppress, eliminate 2 : delete (text) — **supresión** *nf, pl* **-siones** 1 : suppression, elimination 2 : deletion (of text)
supuesto, -ta *adj* 1 : supposed, alleged 2 **por supuesto** : of course — **supuesto** *nm* : assumption — **supuestamente** *adv* : allegedly
sur *nm* 1 : south, South 2 : south wind 3 **del ~** : south, southerly
surafricano, -na → **sudafricano**
suramericano, -na → **sudamericano**
surcar {72} *vt* 1 : plow (earth) 2 : cut through (air, water, etc.) — **surco** *nm* : groove, furrow, rut
sureño, -ña *adj* : southern, Southern — ~ *n* : Southerner

sureste *adj* 1 : southeast, southeastern 2 : southeasterly (of wind, etc.) — ~ *nm* : southeast, Southeast
surf *or* **surfing** *nm* : surfing
surgir {35} *vi* 1 : arise 2 APARECER : appear — **surgimiento** *nm* : rise, emergence
suroeste *adj* 1 : southwest, southwestern 2 : southwesterly (of wind, etc.) — ~ *nm* : southwest, Southwest
surtir *vt* 1 : supply, provide 2 ~ **efecto** : have an effect — **surtirse** *vr* ~ **de** : stock up on — **surtido, -da** *adj* 1 : assorted, varied 2 : stocked (with merchandise) — **surtido** *nm* : assortment, selection — **surtidor** *nm* : gas pump
susceptible *adj* 1 : susceptible, sensitive 2 ~ **de** : capable of — **susceptibilidad** *nf* : sensitivity
suscitar *vt* : provoke, arouse
suscribir {33} *vt* 1 : sign (a formal document) 2 RATIFICAR : endorse — **suscribirse** *vr* ~ **a** : subscribe to — **suscripción** *nf, pl* **-ciones** : subscription — **suscriptor, -tora** *n* : subscriber
susodicho, -cha *adj* : aforementioned
suspender *vt* 1 : suspend 2 COLGAR : hang 3 *Spain* : fail (an exam, etc.) — **suspensión** *nf, pl* **-siones** : suspension — **suspenso** *nm* 1 *Spain* : failure (in an exam, etc.) 2 *Lat* : suspense
suspicaz *adj, pl* **-caces** : suspicious
suspirar *vi* : sigh — **suspiro** *nm* : sigh
sustancia *nf* 1 : substance 2 **sin ~** : shallow, lacking substance — **sustancial** *adj* : substantial, significant — **sustancioso, -sa** *adj* : substantial, solid
sustantivo *nm* : noun
sustentar *vt* 1 : support 2 ALIMENTAR : sustain, nourish 3 MANTENER : maintain — **sustentarse** *vr* : support oneself — **sustentación** *nf, pl* **-ciones** : support — **sustento** *nm* 1 : means of support, livelihood 2 ALIMENTO : sustenance
sustituir {41} *vt* : replace, substitute — **sustitución** *nf, pl* **-ciones** : replacement, substitution — **sustituto, -ta** *n* : substitute
susto *nm* : fright, scare
sustraer {81} *vt* 1 : remove, take away 2 : subtract (in mathematics) — **sustraerse** *vr* ~ **a** : avoid, evade — **sustracción** *nf, pl* **-ciones** : subtraction
susurrar *vi* 1 : whisper 2 : murmur (of water) 3 : rustle (of leaves, etc.) — *vt* : whisper — **susurro** *nm* 1 : whisper 2

: murmur (of water) **3** : rustle, rustling (of leaves, etc.)
sutil *adj* **1** : delicate, fine **2** : subtle (of fragrances, differences, etc.) — **sutileza** *nf* : subtlety
sutura *nf* : suture

suyo, -ya *adj* **1** : his, her, its, one's, theirs **2** (*formal*) : yours **3 un primo suyo** : a cousin of his/hers — **~** *pron* **1** : his, hers, its (own), one's own, theirs **2** (*formal*) : yours
switch *nm Lat* : switch

T

t *nf* : t, 21st letter of the Spanish alphabet
taba *nf* : anklebone
tabaco *nm* : tobacco — **tabacalero, -ra** *adj* : tobacco
tábano *nm* : horsefly
taberna *nf* : tavern
tabicar {72} *vt* : wall up — **tabique** *nm* : thin wall, partition
tabla *nf* **1** : board, plank **2** LISTA : table, list **3 ~ de planchar** : ironing board **4 ~s** *nfpl* : stage, boards *pl* — **tablado** *nm* **1** : flooring **2** PLATAFORMA : platform **3** : (theater) stage — **tablero** *nm* **1** : bulletin board **2** : board (in games) **3** PIZARRA : blackboard **4 ~ de instrumentos** : dashboard, instrument panel
tableta *nf* **1** : tablet, pill **2** : bar (of chocolate)
tablilla *nf* : slat — **tablón** *nm, pl* **-lones** **1** : plank, beam **2 ~ de anuncios** : bulletin board
tabú *adj* : taboo — **tabú** *nm, pl* **-búes** or **-bús** : taboo
tabular *vt* : tabulate
taburete *nm* : stool
tacaño, -na *adj* : stingy, miserly
tacha *nf* **1** : flaw, defect **2 sin ~** : flawless
tachar *vt* **1** : cross out, delete **2 ~ de** : accuse of, label as
tachón *nm, pl* **-chones** : stud, hobnail — **tachuela** *nf* : tack, hobnail
tácito, -ta *adj* : tacit
taciturno, -na *adj* : taciturn
taco *nm* **1** : stopper, plug **2** *Lat* : heel (of a shoe) **3** : cue (in billiards) **4** : taco (in cooking)
tacón *nm, pl* **-cones** **1** : heel (of a shoe) **2 de ~ alto** : high-heeled
táctica *nf* : tactic, tactics *pl* — **táctico, -ca** *adj* : tactical
tacto *nm* **1** : (sense of) touch, feel **2** DELICADEZA : tact
tafetán *nm, pl* **-tanes** : taffeta
tailandés, -desa *adj* : Thai
taimado, -da *adj* : crafty, sly
tajar *vt* : cut, slice — **tajada** *nf* **1** : slice **2 sacar ~** *fam* : get one's share — **ta-**

jante *adj* : categorical — **tajo** *nm* **1** : cut, gash **2** ESCARPA : steep cliff
tal *adv* **1** : so, in such a way **2 con ~ que** : provided that, as long as **3 ¿qué ~?** : how are you?, how's it going? — **~** *adj* **1** : such, such a **2 ~ vez** : maybe, perhaps — **~** *pron* **1** : such a one, such a thing **2 ~ para cual** : two of a kind
taladrar *vt* : drill — **taladro** *nm* : drill
talante *nm* **1** HUMOR : mood **2** VOLUNTAD : willingness
talar *vt* : cut down, fell
talco *nm* : talcum powder
talego *nm* : sack
talento *nm* : talent — **talentoso, -sa** *adj* : talented
talismán *nm, pl* **-manes** : talisman, charm
talla *nf* **1** : sculpture, carving **2** ESTATURA : height **3** : size (in clothing) — **tallar** *vt* **1** : sculpt, carve **2** : measure (someone's height)
tallarín *nf, pl* **-rines** : noodle
talle *nm* **1** : waist, waistline **2** FIGURA : figure **3** : measurements *pl* (of clothing)
taller *nm* **1** : workshop **2** : studio (of an artist)
tallo *nm* : stalk, stem
talón *nm, pl* **-lones** **1** : heel (of the foot) **2** : stub (of a check) — **talonario** *nm* : checkbook
taltuza *nf* : gopher
tamal *nm* : tamale
tamaño, -ña *adj* : such a, such a big — **tamaño** *nm* **1** : size **2 de ~ natural** : life-size
tambalearse *vr* **1** : teeter, wobble **2** : stagger, totter (of persons)
también *adv* : too, as well, also
tambor *nm* : drum — **tamborilear** *vi* : drum
tamiz *nm* : sieve — **tamizar** {21} *vt* : sift
tampoco *adv* : neither, not either
tampón *nm, pl* **-pones** **1** : tampon **2** : ink pad (for stamping)
tan *adv* **1** : so, so very **2 ~ pronto como** : as soon as **3 ~ sólo** : only, merely

tanda *nf* **1** TURNO : turn, shift **2** GRUPO : batch, lot, series

tangente *nf* : tangent

tangible *adj* : tangible

tango *nm* : tango

tanque *nm* : tank

tantear *vt* **1** : feel, grope **2** SOPESAR : size up, weigh — *vi* : feel one's way — **tanteador** *nm* : scoreboard — **tanteo** *nm* **1** : weighing, sizing up **2** PUNTUACIÓN : scoring (in sports)

tanto *adv* **1** : so much **2** (*in expressions of time*) : so long — *~ nm* **1** : certain amount **2** : goal, point (in sports) **3 un ~** : somewhat, rather — **tanto, -ta** *adj* **1** : so much, so many **2** (*in comparisons*) : as much, as many **3** *fam* : however many — *~ pron* **1** : so much, so many **2 entre ~** : meanwhile **3 por lo ~** : therefore

tañer {79} *vt* **1** : ring (a bell) **2** : play (a musical instrument)

tapa *nf* **1** : cover, top, lid **2** *Spain* : snack

tapacubos *nms & pl* : hubcap

tapar *vt* **1** : cover, put a lid on **2** OCULTAR : block out **3** ENCUBRIR : cover up — **tapadera** *nf* **1** : cover, lid **2** : front (to hide a deception)

tapete *nm* **1** : small rug, mat **2** : cover (for a table)

tapia *nf* **1** : (adobe) wall, garden wall — **tapiar** *vt* **1** : wall in **2** : block off (a door, etc.)

tapicería *nf* **1** : upholstery **2** TAPIZ : tapestry — **tapicero, -ra** *n* : upholsterer

tapioca *nf* : tapioca

tapiz *nm, pl* **-pices** : tapestry — **tapizar** {21} *vt* : upholster

tapón *nm, pl* **-pones** **1** : cork **2** : cap (for a bottle, etc.) **3** : plug, stopper (for a sink)

tapujo *nm* **sin ~s** : openly, outright

taquigrafía *nf* : stenography, shorthand — **taquígrafo, -fa** *n* : stenographer

taquilla *nf* **1** : box office **2** RECAUDACIÓN : earnings *pl*, take — **taquillero, -ra** *adj* **un éxito taquillero** : a box-office hit

tarántula *nf* : tarantula

tararear *vt* : hum

tardar *vi* **1** : take a long time, be late **2 a más ~** : at the latest — *vt* : take (time) — **tardanza** *nf* : lateness, delay — **tarde** *adv* **1** : late **2 ~ o temprano** : sooner or later — *~ nf* **1** : afternoon, evening **2 ¡buenas ~s!** : good afternoon!, good evening! **3 en la ~** *or* **por la ~** : in the afternoon, in the evening — **tardío, -día** *adj* : late, tardy — **tardo, -da** *adj* : slow

tarea *nf* **1** : task, job **2** : homework (in education)

tarifa *nf* **1** : fare, rate **2** LISTA : price list **3** ARANCEL : duty, tariff

tarima *nf* : platform, stage

tarjeta *nf* **1** : card **2 ~ de crédito** : credit card **3 ~ postal** : postcard

tarro *nm* : jar, pot

tarta *nf* **1** : cake **2** TORTA : tart

tartamudear *vi* : stammer, stutter — **tartamudeo** *nm* : stutter, stammer

tartán *nm, pl* **-tanes** : tartan, plaid

tártaro *nm* : tartar

tarugo *nm* **1** : block (of wood) **2** *fam* : blockhead, dunce

tasa *nf* **1** : rate **2** IMPUESTO : tax **3** VALORACIÓN : appraisal — **tasación** *nf, pl* **-ciones** : appraisal — **tasar** *vt* **1** : set the price of **2** VALORAR : appraise, value

tasca *nf* : cheap bar, dive

tatuar {3} *vt* : tattoo — **tatuaje** *nm* : tattoo, tattooing

taurino, -na *adj* : bull, bullfighting — **tauromaquia** *nf* : (art of) bullfighting

taxi *nm, pl* **taxis** : taxi, taxicab — **taxista** *nmf* : taxi driver

taza *nf* **1** : cup **2** : (toilet) bowl — **tazón** *nm, pl* **-zones** : bowl

te *pron* **1** (*direct object*) : you **2** (*indirect object*) : for you, to you, from you **3** (*reflexive*) : yourself, for yourself, to yourself, from yourself

té *nm* : tea

teatro *nm* : theater — **teatral** *adj* : theatrical

techo *nm* **1** : roof **2** : ceiling (of a room) **3** LÍMITE : upper limit, ceiling — **techumbre** *nf* : roofing

tecla *nf* : key (of a musical instrument or a machine) — **teclado** *nm* : keyboard — **teclear** *vt* : type in, enter

técnica *nf* **1** : technique, skill **2** TECNOLOGÍA : technology — **técnico, -ca** *adj* : technical — *~ n* : technician

tecnología *nf* : technology — **tecnológico, -ca** *adj* : technological

tecolote *nm Lat* : owl

tedio *nm* : boredom — **tedioso, -sa** *adj* : tedious, boring

teja *nf* : tile — **tejado** *nm* : roof

tejer *v* **1** : knit, crochet **2** : weave (on a loom)

tejido *nm* **1** : fabric, cloth **2** : tissue (of the body)

tejón *nm, pl* **-jones** : badger

tela *nf* **1** : fabric, material **2 ~ de araña** : spiderweb — **telar** *nm* : loom — **telaraña** *nf* : spiderweb, cobweb

tele *nf fam* : TV, television

telecomunicación *nf, pl* **-ciones** : telecomunication

teledifusión *nf, pl* **-siones** : television broadcasting

teledirigido, -da *adj* : remote-controlled

telefonear *v* : telephone, call — **telefónico, -ca** *adj* : telephone — **telefonista** *nmf* : telephone operator — **teléfono** *nm* **1** : telephone **2 llamar por** **~** : make a phone call

telegrafiar {85} *v* : telegraph — **telegráfico, -ca** *adj* : telegraphic — **telégrafo** *nm* : telegraph

telegrama *nm* : telegram

telenovela *nf* : soap opera

telepatía *nf* : telepathy — **telepático, -ca** *adj* : telepathic

telescopio *nm* : telescope — **telescópico, -ca** *adj* : telescopic

telespectador, -dora *n* : (television) viewer

telesquí *nm, pl* **-squís** : ski lift

televidente *nmf* : (television) viewer

televisión *nf, pl* **-siones** : television, TV — **televisar** *vt* : televise — **televisor** *nm* : television set

telón *nm, pl* **-lones 1** : curtain (in theater) **2 ~ de fondo** : backdrop, background

tema *nm* : theme

temblar {55} *vi* **1** : tremble, shiver **2** : shake (of a building, the ground, etc.) — **temblor** *nm* **1** : shaking, trembling **2 or ~ de tierra** : tremor, earthquake — **tembloroso, -sa** *adj* : trembling, shaky

temer *vt* : fear, dread — *vi* : be afraid — **temerario, -ria** *adj* : reckless — **temeridad** *nf* **1** : recklessness **2** : rash act — **temeroso, -sa** *adj* : fearful — **temor** *nm* : fear, dread

temperamento *nm* : temperament — **temperamental** *adj* : temperamental

temperatura *nf* : temperature

tempestad *nf* : storm — **tempestuoso, -sa** *adj* : stormy

templar *vt* **1** : temper (steel) **2** : moderate (temperature) **3** : tune (a musical instrument) — **templarse** *vr* : warm up, cool down — **templado, -da** *adj* **1** : temperate, mild **2 TIBIO** : lukewarm **3 VALIENTE** : courageous — **templanza** *nf* **1** : moderation **2** : mildness (of weather)

templo *nm* : temple, synagogue

tempo *nm* : tempo

temporada *nf* **1** : season, time **2 PERÍODO** : period, spell — **temporal** *adj* **1** : temporal **2 PROVISIONAL** : temporary — **~** *nm* : storm — **temporero, -ra** *n* : temporary or seasonal worker

temporizador *nm* : timer

temprano, -na *adj* : early — **temprano** *adv* : early

tenaz *adj, pl* **-naces** : tenacious — **tenaza** *nf or* **tenazas** *nfpl* **1** : pliers **2** : tongs (for the fireplace, etc.) **3** : claw (of a crustacean)

tendedero *nm* : clothesline

tendencia *nf* : tendency, trend

tender {56} *vt* **1** : spread out, stretch out **2** : hang out (clothes) **3** : lay (cables, etc.) **4** : set (a trap) — *vi* **~ a** : have a tendency towards — **tenderse** *vr* : stretch out, lie down

tendero, -ra *n* : shopkeeper

tendido *nm* **1** : laying (of cables, etc.) **2** : seats *pl*, stand (at a bullfight)

tendón *nm, pl* **-dones** : tendon

tenebroso, -sa *adj* **1** : gloomy, dark **2 SINIESTRO** : sinister

tenedor, -dora *n* **1** : holder **2 ~ de libros** : bookkeeper — **tenedor** *nm* : table fork — **teneduría** *nf* **~ de libros** : bookkeeping

tener {80} *vt* **1** : have, possess **2 SUJETAR** : hold **3 TOMAR** : take **4 ~ frío** **(hambre,** *etc.***)** : be cold (hungry, etc.) **5 ... años** : be ... years old **6 ~** **por** : think, consider — *v aux* **1 ~** **que** : have to, ought to **2 tenía pensado escribirte** : I've been thinking of writing to you — **tenerse** *vr* **1** : stand up **2 ~ por** : consider oneself

tenería *nf* : tannery

tengo → **tener**

tenia *nf* : tapeworm

teniente *nmf* : lieutenant

tenis *nms & pl* **1** : tennis **2 ~** *nmpl* : sneakers — **tenista** *nmf* : tennis player

tenor *nm* **1** : tenor **2** : tone, sense (in style)

tensar *vt* **1** : tense, make taut **2** : draw (a bow) — **tensarse** *vr* : become tense — **tensión** *nf, pl* **-siones 1** : tension **2 ~ arterial** : blood pressure — **tenso, -sa** *adj* : tense

tentación *nf, pl* **-ciones** : temptation

tentáculo *nm* : tentacle

tentar {55} *vt* **1** : feel, touch **2 ATRAER** : tempt — **tentador, -dora** *adj* : tempting

tentativa *nf* : attempt

tentempié *nm fam* : snack

tenue *adj* **1** : tenuous **2** : faint, weak (of sounds) **3** : light, fine (of thread, rain, etc.)

teñir {67} *vt* **1** : dye **2 ~ de** : tinge with

teología *nf* : theology — **teólogo, -ga** *n* : theologian

teorema nm : theorem
teoría nf : theory — **teórico, -ca** adj : theoretical
tequila nm : tequila
terapia nf 1 : therapy 2 ~ **ocupacional** : occupational therapy — **terapeuta** nmf : therapist — **terapéutico, -ca** adj : therapeutic
tercermundista adj : third-world
tercero, -ra adj (tercer before masculine singular nouns) 1 : third 2 **el Tercer Mundo** : the Third World — ~ n : third (in a series)
terciar vt : sling (sth over one's shoulders), tilt (a hat) — vi 1 : intervene 2 ~ **en** : take part in
tercio nm : third
terciopelo nm : velvet
terco, -ca adj : obstinate, stubborn
tergiversar vt : distort, twist
termal adj : thermal, hot — **termas** nfpl : hot springs
terminar vt : conclude, finish — vi 1 : finish 2 ACABARSE : come to an end — **terminarse** vr 1 : run out 2 ACABARSE : come to an end — **terminación** nf, pl **-ciones** : termination, conclusion — **terminal** adj : terminal, final — ~ nm (in some regions f) : (electric or electronic) terminal — ~ nf (in some regions m) : terminal, station — **término** nm 1 : end 2 PLAZO : period, term 3 ~ **medio** : happy medium 4 ~**s** nmpl : terms — **terminología** nf : terminology
termita nf : termite
termo nm : thermos
termómetro nm : thermometer
termóstato nm : thermostat
ternero, -ra n : calf — **ternera** nf : veal
ternura nf : tenderness
terquedad nf : obstinacy, stubbornness
terracota nf : terra-cotta
terraplén nm, pl **-plenes** : embankment
terráqueo, -quea adj : earth, terrestrial
terrateniente nmf : landowner
terraza nf 1 : terrace 2 BALCÓN : balcony
terremoto nm : earthquake
terreno nm 1 : terrain 2 SUELO : earth, ground 3 SOLAR : plot, tract of land — **terreno, -na** adj : earthly — **terrestre** adj : terrestrial
terrible adj : terrible
terrier nmf : terrier
territorio nm : territory — **territorial** adj : territorial
terrón nm, pl **-rones** 1 : clod (of earth) 2 ~ **de azúcar** : lump of sugar
terror nm : terror — **terrorífico, -ca** adj

: terrifying — **terrorismo** nm : terrorism — **terrorista** adj & nmf : terrorist
terroso, -sa adj : earthy
terso, -sa adj 1 : smooth 2 : polished, flowing (of a style) — **tersura** nf : smoothness
tertulia nf : gathering, group
tesis nfs & pl : thesis
tesón nm : persistence, tenacity
tesoro nm 1 : treasure 2 : thesaurus (book) 3 **el Tesoro** : the Treasury — **tesorero, -ra** n : treasurer
testaferro nm : figurehead
testamento nm : testament, will — **testamentario, -ria** n : executor, executrix f — **testar** vi : draw up a will
testarudo, -da adj : stubborn
testículo nm : testicle
testificar {72} v : testify — **testigo** nmf 1 : witness 2 ~ **ocular** : eyewitness — **testimoniar** vi : testify — **testimonio** nm : testimony
tétano or **tétanos** nm : tetanus
tetera nf : teapot
tetilla nf 1 : teat, nipple (of a man) 2 : nipple (of a baby bottle) — **tetina** nf : nipple (of a baby bottle)
tétrico, -ca adj : somber, gloomy
textil adj & nm : textile
texto nm : text — **textual** adj 1 : textual 2 EXACTO : literal, exact
textura nf : texture
tez nf, pl **teces** : complexion
ti pron 1 : you 2 ~ **mismo,** ~ **misma** : yourself
tía → **tío**
tianguis nms & pl Lat : open-air market
tibio, -bia adj : lukewarm
tiburón nm, pl **-rones** : shark
tic nm : tic
tiempo nm 1 : time 2 ÉPOCA : age, period 3 : weather (in meteorology) 4 : halftime (in sports) 5 : tempo (in music) 6 : tense (in grammar)
tienda nf 1 : store, shop 2 or ~ **de campaña** : tent
tiene → **tener**
tienta nf **andar a** ~**s** : feel one's way, grope around
tierno, -na adj 1 : tender, fresh, young 2 CARIÑOSO : affectionate
tierra nf 1 : land 2 SUELO : ground, earth 3 or ~ **natal** : native land 4 **la Tierra** : the Earth 5 **por** ~ : overland 6 ~ **adentro** : inland
tieso, -sa adj 1 : stiff, rigid 2 ERGUIDO : erect 3 ENGREÍDO : haughty
tiesto nm : flowerpot
tifoideo, -dea adj **fiebre tifoidea** : typhoid fever

tifón *nm, pl* **-fones** : typhoon

tifus *nm* : typhus

tigre, -gresa *n* 1 : tiger, tigress *f* 2 *Lat* : jaguar

tijera *nf or* **tijeras** *nfpl* : scissors — **tijeretada** *nf* : cut, snip

tildar *vt* ~ **de** : brand as, call

tilde *nf* 1 : tilde 2 ACENTO : accent mark

tilo *nm* : linden (tree)

timar *vt* : swindle, cheat

timbre *nm* 1 : bell 2 : tone, timbre (of a voice, etc.) 3 SELLO : seal, stamp 4 *Lat* : postage stamp — **timbrar** *vt* : stamp

tímido, -da *adj* : timid, shy — **timidez** *nf* : timidity, shyness

timo *nm fam* : swindle, hoax

timón *nm, pl* **-mones** 1 : rudder 2 **coger el** ~ : take the helm, take charge

tímpano *nm* 1 : eardrum 2 ~**s** *nmpl* : timpani, kettledrums

tina *nf* 1 : vat 2 BAÑERA : bathtub

tinieblas *nfpl* 1 : darkness 2 **estar en** ~ **sobre** : be in the dark about

tino *nm* 1 : good judgment, sense 2 TACTO : tact

tinta *nf* 1 : ink 2 **saberlo de buena** ~ : have it on good authority — **tinte** *nm* 1 : dye, coloring 2 MATIZ : overtone — **tintero** *nm* : inkwell

tintinear *vi* : jingle, tinkle, clink — **tintineo** *nm* : jingle, tinkle, clink

tinto, -ta *adj* 1 : dyed, stained 2 : red (of wine)

tintorería *nf* : dry cleaner (service)

tintura *nf* 1 : dye, tint 2 ~ **de yodo** : tincture of iodine

tiña *nf* : ringworm

tío, tía *n* : uncle *m*, aunt *f*

tiovivo *nm* : merry-go-round

típico, -ca *adj* : typical

tiple *nm* : soprano

tipo *nm* 1 : type, kind 2 FIGURA : figure (of a woman), build (of a man) 3 : rate (of interest, etc.) 4 : (printing) type, typeface — **tipo, -pa** *n fam* : guy *m*, gal *f*

tipografía *nf* : typography, printing — **tipográfico, -ca** *adj* : typographical — **tipógrafo, -fa** *n* : printer

tique *or* **tíquet** *nm* : ticket — **tiquete** *nm Lat* : ticket

tira *nf* 1 : strip, strap 2 ~ **cómica** : comic strip

tirabuzón *nf, pl* **-zones** 1 : corkscrew 2 RIZO : curl, coil

tirada *nf* 1 : throw 2 DISTANCIA : distance 3 IMPRESIÓN : printing, issue — **tirador** *nm* : handle, knob — **tirador, -dora** *n* : marksman *m*, markswoman *f*

tiranía *nf* : tyranny — **tiránico, -ca** *adj* : tyrannical — **tiranizar** {21} *vt* : tyrannize — **tirano, -na** *adj* : tyrannical — ~ *n* : tyrant

tirante *adj* 1 : taut, tight 2 : tense (of a situation, etc.) — ~ *nm* 1 : (shoulder) strap 2 ~**s** *nmpl* : suspenders

tirar *vt* 1 : throw 2 DESECHAR : throw away 3 DERRIBAR : knock down 4 DISPARAR : shoot, fire 5 IMPRIMIR : print — *vi* 1 : pull 2 DISPARAR : shoot 3 ATRAER : attract 4 *fam* : get by, manage 5 ~ **a** : tend towards — **tirarse** *vr* 1 : throw oneself 2 *fam* : spend (time)

tiritar *vi* : shiver

tiro *nm* 1 : shot, gunshot 2 : shot, kick (in sports) 3 : team (of horses, etc.) 4 **a** ~ : within range

tiroides *nmf* : thyroid (gland)

tirón *nm, pl* **-rones** 1 : pull, yank 2 **de un** ~ : in one go

tirotear *vt* : shoot at — **tiroteo** *nm* : shooting

tisis *nfs & pl* : tuberculosis

títere *nm* : puppet

titilar *vi* : flicker

titiritero, -ra *n* 1 : puppeteer 2 ACRÓBATA : acrobat

titubear *vi* 1 : hesitate 2 BALBUCEAR : stutter, stammer — **titubeante** *adj* : hesitant, faltering — **titubeo** *nm* : hesitation

titular *vt* : title, call — **titularse** *vr* 1 : be called, be titled 2 LICENCIARSE : receive a degree — ~ *adj* : titular, official — ~ *nm* : headline — ~ *nmf* : holder, incumbent — **título** *nm* 1 : title 2 : degree, qualification (in education)

tiza *nf* : chalk

tiznar *vt* : blacken (with soot, etc.) — **tizne** *nm* : soot

toalla *nf* : towel — **toallero** *nm* : towel rack

tobillo *nm* : ankle

tobogán *nm, pl* **-ganes** 1 : toboggan, sled 2 : slide (in a playground, etc.)

tocadiscos *nms & pl* : record player

tocado, -da *adj fam* : touched, not all there — **tocado** *nm* : headgear, headdress

tocador *nm* : dressing table

tocar {72} *vt* 1 : touch, feel 2 MENCIONAR : touch on, refer to 3 : play (a musical instrument) — *vi* 1 : knock, ring 2 ~ **en** : touch on, border on

tocayo, -ya *n* : namesake

tocino *nm* 1 : bacon 2 : salt pork (for cooking) — **tocineta** *nf Lat* : bacon

tocólogo, -ga *n* : obstetrician

tocón *nm, pl* **-cones** : stump (of a tree)

todavía *adv* **1** AÚN : still **2** (*in comparisons*) : even **3** ~ **no** : not yet

todo, -da *adj* **1** : all **2** CADA, CUALQUIER : every, each **3 a toda velocidad** : at top speed **4 todo el mundo** : everyone, everybody — ~ *pron* **1** : everything, all **2 todos, -das** *pl* : everybody, everyone, all — **todo** *nm* : whole — **todopoderoso, -sa** *adj* : almighty, all-powerful

toga *nf* **1** : toga **2** : gown, robe (of a judge, etc.)

toldo *nm* : awning, canopy

tolerar *vt* : tolerate — **tolerancia** *nf* : tolerance — **tolerante** *adj* : tolerant

toma *nf* **1** : capture **2** DOSIS : dose **3** : take (in film) **4** ~ **de corriente** : wall socket, outlet **5** ~ **y daca** : give-and-take — **tomar** *vt* **1** : take **2** : have (food or drink) **3** CAPTURAR : capture, seize **4** ~ **el sol** : sunbathe **5** ~ **tierra** : land — *vi* : drink (alcohol) — **tomarse** *vr* **1** : take (time, etc.) **2** : drink, eat, have (food, drink)

tomate *nm* : tomato

tomillo *nm* : thyme

tomo *nm* : volume

ton *nm* **sin** ~ **ni son** : without rhyme or reason

tonada *nf* : tune

tonel *nm* : barrel, cask

tonelada *nf* : ton — **tonelaje** *nm* : tonnage

tónica *nf* **1** : tonic (water) **2** TENDENCIA : trend, tone — **tónico, -ca** *adj* : tonic — **tónico** *nm* : tonic (in medicine)

tono *nm* **1** : tone **2** : shade (of colors) **3** : key (in music)

tontería *nf* **1** : silly thing or remark **2** ESTUPIDEZ : foolishness **3 decir** ~**s** : talk nonsense — **tonto, -ta** *adj* **1** : stupid, silly **2 a tontas y a locas** : haphazardly — ~ *n* : fool, idiot

topacio *nm* : topaz

toparse *vr* ~ **con** : run into, come across

tope *nm* **1** : limit, end **2** *or* ~ **de puerta** : doorstop **3** *Lat* : bump — ~ *adj* : maximum

tópico, -ca *adj* **1** : topical, external **2** MANIDO : trite — **tópico** *nm* : cliché

topo *nm* : mole (animal)

toque *nm* **1** : (light) touch **2** : ringing, peal (of a bell) **3** ~ **de queda** : curfew **4** ~ **de diana** : reveille — **toquetear** *vt* : finger, handle

tórax *nms & pl* : thorax

torbellino *nm* : whirlwind

torcer {14} *vt* **1** : twist, bend **2** : turn (a corner) **3** : wring (out) — *vi* : turn —

torcerse *vr* **1** : twist, sprain **2** FRUSTRARSE : go wrong **3** DESVIARSE : go astray — **torcedura** *nf* **1** : twisting **2** ESGUINCE : sprain — **torcido, -da** *adj* : twisted, crooked

tordo, -da *adj* : dappled — **tordo** *nm* : thrush (bird)

torear *vt* **1** : fight (bulls) **2** ELUDIR : dodge, sidestep — *vi* : fight bulls — **toreo** *nm* : bullfighting — **torero, -ra** *n* : bullfighter

tormenta *nf* : storm — **tormento** *nm* **1** : torture **2** ANGUSTIA : torment, anguish — **tormentoso, -sa** *adj* : stormy

tornado *nm* : tornado

tornar *vt* CONVERTIR : render, turn — *vi* : go back, return — **tornarse** *vr* : become, turn into

torneo *nm* : tournament

tornillo *nm* : screw

torniquete *nm* **1** : turnstile **2** : tourniquet (in medicine)

torno *nm* **1** : winch **2** : (carpenter's) lathe **3** ~ **de alfarero** : (potter's) wheel **4** ~ **de banco** : vise **5 en** ~ **a** : around, about

toro *nm* **1** : bull **2** ~**s** *nmpl* : bullfight

toronja *nf* : grapefruit

torpe *adj* **1** : clumsy, awkward **2** ESTÚPIDO : stupid, dull

torpedear *vt* : torpedo — **torpedo** *nm* : torpedo

torpeza *nf* **1** : clumsiness, awkwardness **2** ESTUPIDEZ : slowness, stupidity

torre *nf* **1** : tower **2** : turret (on a ship, etc.) **3** : rook, castle (in chess)

torrente *nm* **1** : torrent **2** ~ **sanguíneo** : bloodstream — **torrencial** *adj* : torrential

tórrido, -da *adj* : torrid

torsión *nf, pl* **-siones** : twisting

torta *nf* **1** : torte, cake **2** *Lat* : sandwich

tortazo *nm fam* : blow, wallop

tortícolis *nfs & pl* : stiff neck

tortilla *nf* **1** : tortilla **2** *or* ~ **de huevo** : omelet

tórtola *nf* : turtledove

tortuga *nf* **1** : turtle, tortoise **2** ~ **de agua dulce** : terrapin

tortuoso, -sa *adj* : tortuous, winding

tortura *nf* : torture — **torturar** *vt* : torture

tos *nf* **1** : cough **2** ~ **ferina** : whooping cough

tosco, -ca *adj* : rough, coarse

toser *vi* : cough

tosquedad *nf* : coarseness

tostar {19} *vt* **1** : toast **2** BRONCEAR : tan — **tostarse** *vr* : get a tan — **tostada**

nf **1** : piece of toast **2** *Lat* : tostada — **tostador** *nm* : toaster

tostón *nm, pl* **-tones** *Lat* : fried plantain chip

total *adj & nm* : total — ~ *adv* : so, after all — **totalidad** *nf* : whole — **totalitario, -ria** *adj & n* : totalitarian — **totalitarismo** *nm* : totalitarianism — **totalizar** {21} *vt* : total, add up to

tóxico, -ca *adj* : toxic, poisonous — **tóxico** *nm* : poison — **toxicomanía** *nf* : drug addiction — **toxicómano, -na** *n* : drug addict — **toxina** *nf* : toxin

tozudo, -da *adj* : stubborn

traba *nf* : obstacle, hindrance

trabajar *vi* **1** : work **2** : act, perform (in theater, etc.) — *vt* **1** : work (metal) **2** : knead (dough) **3** MEJORAR : work on, work at — **trabajador, -dora** *adj* : hard-working — ~ *n* : worker — **trabajo** *nm* **1** : work **2** EMPLEO : job **3** TAREA : task **4** ESFUERZO : effort **5** costar ~ : be difficult **6** ~ en equipo : teamwork **7** ~s *nmpl* : hardships, difficulties — **trabajoso, -sa** *adj* : hard, laborious

trabalenguas *nms & pl* : tongue twister

trabar *vt* **1** : join, connect **2** OBSTACULIZAR : impede **3** : strike up (a conversation, etc.) **4** : thicken (sauces) — **trabarse** *vr* **1** : jam **2** ENREDARSE : become entangled **3** se le traba la lengua : he gets tongue-tied

trabucar {72} *vt* : mix up

tracción *nf* : traction

tractor *nm* : tractor

tradición *nf, pl* **-ciones** : tradition — **tradicional** *adj* : traditional

traducir {61} *vt* : translate — **traducción** *nf, pl* **-ciones** : translation — **traductor, -tora** *n* : translator

traer {81} *vt* **1** : bring **2** CAUSAR : cause, bring about **3** CONTENER : carry, have **4** LLEVAR : wear — **traerse** *vr* **1** : bring along **2** traérselas : be difficult

traficar {72} *vi* ~ en : traffic in — **traficante** *nmf* : dealer, trafficker — **tráfico** *nm* **1** : trade (of merchandise) **2** : traffic (of vehicles)

tragaluz *nf, pl* **-luces** : skylight

tragar {52} *vt* **1** : swallow **2** *fam* : put up with — *vi* : swallow — **tragarse** *vr* **1** : swallow **2** ABSORBER : absorb, swallow up

tragedia *nf* : tragedy — **trágico, -ca** *adj* : tragic

trago *nm* **1** : swallow, swig **2** *fam* : drink, liquor — **tragón, -gona** *adj fam* : greedy — ~ *nmf fam* : glutton

traicionar *vt* : betray — **traición** *nf, pl*

-ciones 1 : betrayal **2** : treason (in law) — **traidor, -dora** *adj* : traitorous, treacherous — ~ *n* : traitor

trailer *nm* : trailer

traje *nm* **1** : dress, costume **2** : (man's) suit **3** ~ de baño : bathing suit

trajinar *vi fam* : rush around — **trajín** *nm, pl* **-jines** *fam* : hustle and bustle

trama *nf* **1** : plot **2** : weave, weft (of fabric) — **tramar** *vt* **1** : plot, plan **2** : weave (fabric)

tramitar *vt* : negotiate — **trámite** *nm* : procedure, step

tramo *nm* **1** : stretch, section **2** : flight (of stairs)

trampa *nf* **1** : trap **2** hacer ~s : cheat — **trampear** *vt* : cheat

trampilla *nf* : trapdoor

trampolín *nm, pl* **-lines 1** : diving board **2** : trampoline (in a gymnasium, etc.)

tramposo, -sa *adj* : crooked, cheating — ~ *n* : cheat, swindler

tranca *nf* **1** : cudgel, club **2** : bar (for a door or window)

trance *nm* **1** : critical juncture **2** : (hypnotic) trance **3** en ~ de : in the process of

tranquilo, -la *adj* : calm, tranquil — **tranquilidad** *nf* : tranquility, peace — **tranquilizante** *nm* : tranquilizer — **tranquilizar** {21} *vt* : calm, soothe — **tranquilizarse** *vr* : calm down

trans- *see also* **tras-**

transacción *nf, pl* **-ciones** : transaction

transatlántico, -ca *adj* : transatlantic — **transatlántico** *nm* : ocean liner

transbordador *nm* **1** : ferry **2** ~ espacial : space shuttle — **transbordar** *vt* : transfer — *vi* : change (of trains, etc.) — **transbordo** *nm* hacer ~ : change (trains, etc.)

transcribir {33} *vt* : transcribe — **transcripción** *nf, pl* **-ciones** : transcription

transcurrir *vi* : elapse, pass — **transcurso** *nm* : course, progression

transeúnte *nmf* : passerby

transferir {76} *vt* : transfer — **transferencia** *nf* : transfer, transference

transformar *vt* **1** : transform, change **2** CONVERTIR : convert — **transformarse** *vr* : be transformed — **transformación** *nf, pl* **-ciones** : transformation — **transformador** *nm* : transformer

transfusión *nf, pl* **-siones** : transfusion

transgredir {1} *vt* : transgress — **transgresión** *nf* : transgression

transición *nf, pl* **-ciones** : transition

transido, -da *adj* : overcome, stricken

transigir {35} *vi* : give in, compromise
transistor *nm* : transistor
transitar *vi* : go, travel — **transitable**
adj : passable
transitivo, -va *adj* : transitive
tránsito *nm* **1** : transit **2** TRÁFICO : traffic **3 hora de máximo ~** : rush hour
— **transitorio, -ria** *adj* : transitory
transmitir *vt* **1** : transmit **2** : broadcast
(radio, TV, etc.) **3** CEDER : pass on —
transmisión *nf, pl* **-siones 1** : broadcast **2** TRANSFERENCIA : transfer **3**
: transmission (of an automobile) —
transmisor *nm* : transmitter
transparentarse *vr* : be transparent —
transparente *adj* : transparent
transpirar *vi* : perspire, sweat — **transpiración** *nf, pl* **-ciones** : perspiration,
sweat
transponer {60} *vt* : transpose, move
— **transponerse** *vr* **1** : set (of the sun,
etc.) **2** DORMITAR : doze off
transportar *vt* : transport, carry —
transportarse *vr* : get carried away
— **transporte** *nm* : transport, transportation
transversal *adj* **corte ~** : cross section
tranvía *nm* : streetcar, trolley
trapear *vt Lat* : mop
trapecio *nm* : trapeze
trapisonda *nf* : scheme, plot
trapo *nm* **1** : cloth, rag **2 ~s** *nmpl fam*
: clothes
tráquea *nf* : trachea, windpipe
traquetear *vi* : rattle around, shake —
traqueteo *nm* : rattling
tras *prep* **1** DESPUÉS DE : after **2** DETRÁS
DE : behind
tras- *see also* **trans-**
trascender {56} *vi* **1** : leak out, become
known **2** EXTENDERSE : spread **3 ~ de**
: transcend — **trascendencia** *nf* : importance — **trascendental** *adj* **1**
: transcendental **2** IMPORTANTE : important
trasegar *vt* : move around
trasero, -ra *adj* : rear, back — **trasero**
nm : buttocks *pl*
trasfondo *nm* **1** : background **2** : undercurrent (of suspicion, etc.)
trasladar *vt* **1** : transfer, move **2**
POSPONER : postpone — **trasladarse**
vr : move, relocate — **traslado** *nm* **1**
: transfer, move **2** COPIA : copy
traslapar *vt* : overlap — **traslaparse** *vr*
: overlap
traslucirse {45} *vr* **1** : be translucent **2**
REVELARSE : be revealed — **traslúcido, -da** : translucent

trasnochar *vi* : stay up all night
traspasar *vt* **1** : pierce, go through **2**
EXCEDER : go beyond **3** ATRAVESAR
: cross, go across **4** : transfer (a business, etc.) — **traspaso** *nm* : transfer,
sale
traspié *nm* **1** : stumble, trip **2** ERROR
: blunder
trasplantar *vt* : transplant — **trasplante** *nm* : transplant
trasquilar *vt* : shear
traste *nm* **1** : fret (on a guitar, etc.) **2** *Lat*
: (kitchen) utensil **3 dar al ~ con**
: ruin **4 irse al ~** : fall through
trastos *nmpl fam* : pieces of junk, stuff
trastornar *vt* **1** : disturb, disrupt **2**
VOLVER LOCO : drive crazy — **trastornarse** *vr* : go crazy — **trastornado,
-da** *adj* : disturbed, deranged — **trastorno** *nm* **1** : disturbance, disruption **2**
: (medical or psychological) disorder
trastrocar *vt* : change, switch around
tratable *adj* : friendly, sociable
tratar *vi* **1 ~ con** : deal with **2 ~ de**
: try to **3 ~ de** *or* **~ sobre** : be
about, concern **4 ~ en** : deal in — *vt*
1 : treat **2** MANEJAR : deal with, handle
— **tratarse** *vr* **~ de** : be about, concern — **tratado** *nm* **1** : treatise **2** CONVENIO : treaty — **tratamiento** *nm*
: treatment — **trato** *nm* **1** : treatment **2**
ACUERDO : deal, agreement **3 ~s**
nmpl : dealings
trauma *nm* : trauma — **traumático, -ca**
adj : traumatic
través *nm* **1 a ~ de** : across, through **2**
de ~ : sideways
travesaño *nm* : crosspiece
travesía *nf* : voyage, crossing (of the
sea)
travesura *nf* **1** : prank **2 ~s** *nfpl* : mischief — **travieso, -sa** *adj* : mischievous, naughty
trayecto *nm* **1** : trajectory, path **2** VIAJE
: journey **3** RUTA : route — **trayectoria**
nf : path, trajectory
traza *nf* **1** : design, plan **2** ASPECTO : appearance — **trazado** *nm* **1** : outline,
sketch **2** DISEÑO : plan, layout —
trazar {21} *vt* **1** : trace, outline **2**
: draw up (a plan, etc.) — **trazo** *nm* **1**
: stroke, line
trébol *nm* **1** : clover, shamrock **2 ~es**
nmpl : clubs (in playing cards)
trece *adj & nm* : thirteen — **treceavo,
-va** *adj* : thirteenth — **treceavo** *nm*
: thirteenth (fraction)
trecho *nm* **1** : stretch, period **2** DISTANCIA : distance **3 de ~ a ~** : at intervals

tregua *nf* **1** : truce **2 sin ~** : without respite

treinta *adj & nm* : thirty — **treintavo, -va** *adj* : thirtieth — **treintavo** *nm* : thirtieth (fraction)

tremendo, -da *adj* : tremendous, enormous

trementina *nf* : turpentine

trémulo, -la *adj* : trembling, flickering

tren *nm* **1** : train **2 ~ de aterrizaje** : landing gear

trenza *nf* : braid, pigtail — **trenzar** {21} *vt* : braid — **trenzarse** *vr Lat* : get involved

trepar *vi* **1** : climb **2** : creep, spread (of a plant) — **treparse** *vr* : climb (up) — **trepador, -dora** *adj* : climbing — **trepadora** *nf* **1** : climbing plant **2** *fam* : social climber

trepidar *vi* : shake, vibrate

tres *adj & nm* : three — **trescientos, -tas** *adj* : three hundred — **trescientos** *nms & pl* : three hundred

treta *nf* : trick

triángulo *nm* : triangle — **triangular** *adj* : triangular

tribu *nf* : tribe — **tribal** *adj* : tribal

tribulación *nf, pl* **-ciones** : tribulation

tribuna *nf* **1** : dais, platform **2** : grandstand, bleachers *pl* (in a stadium)

tribunal *nm* : court, tribunal

tributar *vt* : pay, render — *vi* : pay taxes — **tributo** *nm* **1** : tribute **2** IMPUESTO : tax

triciclo *nm* : tricycle

tricolor *adj* : tricolored

tridimensional *adj* : three-dimensional

trigésimo, -ma *adj & n* : thirtieth

trigo *nm* : wheat

trigonometría *nf* : trigonometry

trillado, -da *adj* : trite

trillar *vt* : thresh — **trilladora** *nf* : threshing machine

trillizo, -za *n* : triplet

trilogía *nf* : trilogy

trimestral *adj* : quarterly

trinar *vi* : warble

trinchar *vt* : carve

trinchera *nf* **1** : trench, ditch **2** IMPERMEABLE : trench coat

trineo *nm* : sled, sleigh

trinidad *nf* : trinity

trino *nm* : trill, warble

trío *nm* : trio

tripa *nf* **1** : gut, intestine **2 ~s** *nfpl fam* : belly, tummy

triple *adj & nm* : triple — **triplicar** {72} *vt* : triple

trípode *nm* : tripod

tripular *vt* : man — **tripulación** *nf, pl*

-ciones : crew — **tripulante** *nmf* : crew member

tris *nm* **estar en un ~ de** : be within an inch of

triste *adj* **1** : sad **2** SOMBRÍO : dismal, gloomy **3** MISERABLE : sorry, miserable — **tristeza** *nf* : sadness, grief

tritón *nm, pl* **-tones** : newt

triturar *vt* : crush, grind

triunfar *vi* : triumph, win — **triunfal** *adj* : triumphal — **triunfante** *adj* : triumphant — **triunfo** *nm* : triumph, victory

trivial *adj* : trivial

triza *nf* **1** : shred, bit **2 hacer ~s** : smash to pieces

trocar {82} *vt* **1** CONVERTIR : change **2** INTERCAMBIAR : exchange

trocha *nf* : path, trail

trofeo *nm* : trophy

trombón *nm, pl* **-bones 1** : trombone **2** : trombonist (musician)

trombosis *nf* : thrombosis

trompa *nf* **1** : trunk (of an elephant), snout **2** : horn (musical instrument) **3** : tube (in anatomy)

trompeta *nf* : trumpet — **trompetista** *nmf* : trumpet player

trompo *nm* : top (toy)

tronada *nf* : thunderstorm — **tronar** {19} *vi* : thunder, rage — *vt Lat fam* : shoot — *v impers* : thunder

tronchar *vt* **1** : snap **2** TRUNCAR : cut short

tronco *nm* **1** : trunk (of a tree) **2** : torso (of a person) **3 dormir como un ~** : sleep like a log

trono *nm* : throne

tropa *nf* : troops *pl*, soldiers *pl*

tropel *nm* : mob

tropezar {29} *vi* **1** : trip, stumble **2 ~ con** : come up against, run into — **tropezón** *nm, pl* **-zones 1** : stumble **2** EQUIVOCACIÓN : mistake, slip

trópico *nm* : tropic — **tropical** *adj* : tropical

tropiezo *nm* **1** CONTRATIEMPO : snag, setback **2** EQUIVOCACIÓN : mistake, slip

trotar *vi* **1** : trot **2** *fam* : rush about — **trote** *nm* **1** : trot **2** *fam* : rush, bustle **3 al ~** : at a trot, quickly

trozo *nm* : piece, bit, chunk

trucha *nf* : trout

truco *nm* **1** : knack **2** ARDID : trick

trueno *nm* : thunder

trueque *nm* : barter, exchange

trufa *nf* : truffle

truncar {72} *vt* **1** : cut short **2** : thwart, spoil (plans, etc.)

tu *adj* : your
tú *pron* : you
tuba *nf* : tuba
tuberculosis *nf* : tuberculosis
tubo *nm* **1** : tube, pipe **2** ~ **de escape** : exhaust pipe (of a vehicle) **3** ~ **de desagüe** : drainpipe — **tubería** *nf* : pipes *pl*, tubing
tuerca *nf* : nut (for a screw)
tuerto, -ta *adj* : one-eyed, blind in one eye
tuétano *nm* : marrow
tufo *nm* **1** : vapor **2** *fam* : stench, stink
tugurio *nm* : hovel
tulipán *nm, pl* **-panes** : tulip
tullido, -da *adj* : crippled, paralyzed
tumba *nf* : tomb, grave
tumbar *vt* : knock down, knock over — **tumbarse** *vr* : lie down — **tumbo** *nm* **dar** ~**s** : jolt, bump around
tumor *nm* : tumor
tumulto *nm* **1** : commotion, tumult **2** MOTÍN : riot — **tumultuoso, -sa** *adj* : tumultuous
tuna *nf* : prickly pear
túnel *nm* : tunnel
túnica *nf* : tunic
tupé *nm* : toupee
tupido, -da *adj* : dense, thick
turba *nf* **1** : peat **2** MUCHEDUMBRE : mob, throng

turbación *nf, pl* **-ciones 1** : disturbance **2** CONFUSIÓN : confusion
turbante *nm* : turban
turbar *vt* **1** : disturb, upset **2** CONFUNDIR : confuse, bewilder
turbina *nf* : turbine
turbio, -bia *adj* **1** : cloudy, murky **2** : blurred (of vision, etc.) — **turbión** *nm, pl* **-biones** : squall
turbulencia *nf* : turbulence — **turbulento, -ta** *adj* : turbulent
turco, -ca *adj* : Turkish — **turco** *nm* : Turkish (language)
turista *nmf* : tourist — **turismo** *nm* : tourism, tourist industry — **turístico, -ca** *adj* : tourist, travel
turnarse *vr* : take turns, alternate — **turno** *nm* **1** : turn **2** ~ **de noche** : night shift
turquesa *nf* : turquoise
turrón *nm, pl* **-rrones** : nougat
tutear *vt* : address as *tú*
tutela *nf* **1** : guardianship (in law) **2** **bajo la** ~ **de** : under the protection of
tuteo *nm* : addressing as *tú*
tutor, -tora *n* **1** : guardian **2** : tutor (in education)
tuyo, -ya *adj* : yours, of yours — ~ *pron* **1** **el tuyo, la tuya, lo tuyo, los tuyos, las tuyas** : yours **2** **los tuyos** : your family, your friends

U

u¹ *nf* : u, 22d letter of the Spanish alphabet
u² *conj* (*used before words beginning with o- or ho-*) : or
uapití *nm* : American elk, wapiti
ubicar {72} *vt Lat* **1** COLOCAR : place, position **2** LOCALIZAR : find — **ubicarse** *vr* : be located
ubre *nf* : udder
Ud., Uds. → **usted**
ufanarse *vr* ~ **de** : boast about — **ufano, -na** *adj* **1** : proud **2** ENGREÍDO : self-satisfied
ujier *nm* : usher
úlcera *nf* : ulcer
ulterior *adj* : later, subsequent — **ulteriormente** *adv* : subsequently
últimamente *adv* : lately, recently
ultimar *vt* **1** : complete, finish **2** *Lat* : kill — **ultimátum** *nm, pl* **-tums** : ultimatum
último, -ma *adj* **1** : last **2** : latest, most

recent (in time) **3** : farthest (in space) **4 por último** : finally
ultrajar *vt* : outrage, insult — **ultraje** *nm* : outrage, insult
ultramar *nm* **de** ~ **or en** ~ : overseas — **ultramarino, -na** *adj* : overseas — **ultramarinos** *nmpl* **tienda de** ~ : grocery store
ultranza: a ~ *adv phr* : to the extreme — **a** ~ *adj phr* : out-and-out, complete
ultrasonido *nm* : ultrasound
ultravioleta *adj* : ultraviolet
ulular *vi* **1** : hoot (of an owl) **2** : howl (of a wolf, the wind, etc.) — **ululato** *nm* : hoot (of an owl)
umbilical *adj* : umbilical
umbral *nm* : threshold
un, una *art, mpl* **unos 1** : a, an **2 unos** *or* **unas** *pl* : some, a few **3 unos** *or* **unas** *pl* : about, approximately — **un** *adj* → **uno**

unánime *adj* : unanimous — **unanimidad** *nf* : unanimity
uncir {83} *vt* : yoke
undécimo, -ma *adj & n* : eleventh
ungir {35} *vt* : anoint — **ungüento** *nm* : ointment
único, -ca *adj* **1** : only, sole **2** EXCEPCIONAL : unique — **~** *n* : only one — **únicamente** *adv* : only
unicornio *nm* : unicorn
unidad *nf* **1** : unit **2** ARMONÍA : unity — **unido, -da** *adj* **1** : united **2** : close (of friends, etc.)
unificar {72} *vt* : unify — **unificación** *nf, pl* **-ciones** : unification
uniformar *vt* **1** : standardize **2** : put into uniform — **uniformado, -da** *adj* : uniformed — **uniforme** *adj & nm* : uniform — **uniformidad** *nf* : uniformity
unilateral *adj* : unilateral
unir *vt* **1** : unite, join **2** COMBINAR : combine, mix together — **unirse** *vr* **1** : join together **2 ~ a** : join — **unión** *nf, pl* **uniones 1** : union **2** JUNTURA : joint, coupling
unísono *nm* **al ~** : in unison
unitario, -ria *adj* : unitary
universal *adj* : universal
universidad *nf* : university, college — **universitario, -ria** *adj* : university, college
universo *nm* : universe
uno, una (**un** *before masculine singular nouns*) *adj* : one — **~** *pron* **1** : one **2 unos, unas** *pl* : some **3 uno(s) a otro(s)** : one another, each other **4 uno y otro** : both — **uno** *nm* : one (number)
untar *vt* **1** : smear, grease **2** *fam* : bribe — **untuoso, -sa** *adj* : greasy, sticky
uña *nf* **1** : nail, fingernail **2** : claw (of a cat, etc.), hoof (of a horse, etc.)
uranio *nm* : uranium

Urano *nm* : Uranus
urbano, -na *adj* : urban, city — **urbanidad** *nf* : politeness, courtesy — **urbanización** *nf, pl* **-ciones** : housing development — **urbanizar** *vt* : develop, urbanize — **urbe** *nf* : large city
urdir *vt* **1** : warp **2** PLANEAR : plot — **urdimbre** *nf* : warp (of a fabric)
urgir {35} *v impers* : be urgent, be pressing — **urgencia** *nf* **1** : urgency **2** EMERGENCIA : emergency — **urgente** *adj* : urgent
urinario, -ria *adj* : urinary — **urinario** *nm* : urinal (place)
urna *nf* **1** : urn **2** : ballot box (for voting)
urraca *nf* : magpie
uruguayo, -ya *adj* : Uruguayan
usar *vt* **1** : use **2** LLEVAR : wear — **usarse** *vr* **1** EMPLEARSE : be used **2** : be worn, be in fashion — **usado, -da** *adj* **1** : used **2** GASTADO : worn, worn-out — **usanza** *nf* : custom, usage — **uso** *nm* **1** : use **2** DESGASTE : wear and tear **3** USANZA : custom, usage
usted *pron* **1** (*used in formal address; often written as* **Ud.** *or* **Vd.**) : you **2 ~es** *pl* (*often written as* **Uds.** *or* **Vds.**) : you (all)
usual *adj* : usual
usuario, -ria *n* : user
usura *nf* : usury — **usurero, -ra** *n* : usurer
usurpar *vt* : usurp
utensilio *nm* : utensil, tool
útero *nm* : uterus, womb
utilizar {21} *vt* : use, utilize — **útil** *adj* : useful — **útiles** *nmpl* : implements, tools — **utilidad** *nf* : utility, usefulness — **utilitario, -ria** *adj* : utilitarian — **utilización** *nf, pl* **-ciones** : utilization, use
uva *nf* : grape

V

v *nf* : v, 23d letter of the Spanish alphabet
va → ir
vaca *nf* : cow
vacaciones *nfpl* **1** : vacation **2 estar de ~** : be on vacation **3 irse de ~** : go on vacation
vacante *adj* : vacant — **~** *nf* : vacancy
vaciar {85} *vt* **1** : empty (out) **2** AHUECAR : hollow out **3** : cast, mold (a statue, etc.)

vacilar *vi* **1** : hesitate, waver **2** : flicker (of light) **3** TAMBALEARSE : be unsteady, wobble **4** *fam* : joke, fool around — **vacilación** *nf, pl* **-ciones** : hesitation — **vacilante** *adj* **1** : hesitant **2** OSCILANTE : unsteady
vacío, -cía *adj* : empty — **vacío** *nm* **1** : void **2** : vacuum (in physics) **3** HUECO : space, gap
vacuna *nf* : vaccine — **vacunación** *nf,*

pl **-ciones** : vaccination — **vacunar** *vt*
: vaccinate
vacuno, -na *adj* : bovine
vadear *vt* : ford — **vado** *nm* : ford
vagabundear *vi* : wander — **vagabun-**
do, -da *adj* **1** : vagrant **2** : stray (of a
dog, etc.) — **~** *n* : hobo, bum — **va-**
gancia *nf* **1** : vagrancy **2** PEREZA : laziness, idleness — **vagar** {52} *vi*
: roam, wander
vagina *nf* : vagina
vago, -ga *adj* **1** : vague **2** PEREZOSO
: lazy, idle — **~** *n* : idler, loafer
vagón *nm, pl* **-gones** : car (of a train)
vahído *nm* : dizzy spell
vaho *nm* **1** : breath **2** VAPOR : vapor,
steam
vaina *nf* **1** : sheath, scabbard **2** : pod (in
botany) **3** *Lat fam* : bother, pain
vainilla *nf* : vanilla
vaivén *nm, pl* **-venes** **1** : swinging,
swaying **2** : coming and going (of
people, etc.) **3** **vaivenes** *nmpl* : ups
and downs
vajilla *nf* : dishes *pl*
vale *nm* **1** : voucher **2** PAGARÉ : IOU —
valedero, -ra *adj* : valid
valentía *nf* : courage, bravery
valer {84} *vt* **1** : be worth **2** COSTAR
: cost **3** GANAR : gain, earn **4** EQUI-
VALER A : be equal to — *vi* **1** : have
value, cost **2** SER VÁLIDO : be valid,
count **3** SERVIR : be of use **4** **hacerse**
~ : assert oneself **5** **más vale** : it's
better — **valerse** *vr* **1** **~ de** : take advantage of **2** **~ solo** *or* **~ por sí**
mismo : look after oneself
valeroso, -sa *adj* : courageous
valga, etc. → **valer**
valía *nf* : worth
validar *vt* : validate — **validez** *nf* : validity — **válido, -da** *adj* : valid
valiente *adj* **1** : brave **2** (*used ironical-*
ly) : fine, great
valija *nf* : case, valise
valioso, -sa *adj* : valuable
valla *nf* **1** : fence **2** : hurdle (in sports)
— **vallar** *vt* : put a fence around
valle *nm* : valley
valor *nm* **1** : value, worth **2** VALENTÍA
: courage, valor **3** **objetos de ~**
: valuables **4** **sin ~** : worthless **5**
~es *nmpl* : values, principles **6** **~es**
nmpl : securities, bonds — **valoración**
nf, pl **-ciones** : valuation — **valorar** *vt*
: evaluate, assess
vais *etc.* → **ir**
válvula *nf* : valve
vamos → **ir**
vampiro *nm* : vampire

van → **ir**
vanagloriarse *vr* : boast, brag
vándalo *nm* : vandal — **vandalismo**
: vandalism
vanguardia *nf* **1** : vanguard **2** : avant-
garde (in art, music, etc.) **3** **a la ~**
: at/in the forefront
vanidad *nf* : vanity — **vanidoso, -sa**
adj : vain, conceited
vano, -na *adj* **1** INÚTIL : vain, useless **2**
SUPERFICIAL : empty, hollow **3** **en**
vano : in vain
vapor *nm* **1** : steam, vapor **2** **al ~**
: steamed — **vaporizador** *nm* : vapor-
izer — **vaporizar** {21} *vt* : vaporize
vaquero, -ra *n* : cowboy *m*, cowgirl *f* —
vaqueros *nmpl* : jeans
vara *nf* **1** : stick, rod **2** : staff (of office)
varado, -da *adj* : stranded
variar {85} *vt* **1** : vary **2** CAMBIAR
: change, alter — *vi* : vary, change —
variable *adj & nf* : variable — **vari-**
ación *nf, pl* **-ciones** : variation —
variado, -da *adj* : varied — **variante**
nf : variant
varicela *nf* : chicken pox
varicoso, -sa *adj* : varicose
variedad *nf* : variety
varilla *nf* : rod, stick
vario, -ria *adj* **1** : varied **2** **~s** *pl* : several
varita *nf* : wand
variz *nf, pl* **-rices** *or* **várices** : varicose
vein
varón *nm, pl* **-rones** **1** : man, male **2**
NIÑO : boy — **varonil** *adj* : manly
vas → **ir**
vasco, -ca *adj* : Basque — **vasco** *nm*
: Basque (language)
vasija *nf* : container, vessel
vaso *nm* **1** : glass **2** : vessel (in anatomy)
vástago *nm* **1** : offspring, descendent **2**
BROTE : shoot **3** VARILLA : rod
vasto, -ta *adj* : vast
vaticinar *vt* : prophesy, predict —
vaticinio *nm* : prophecy
vatio *nm* : watt
vaya, etc. → **ir**
Vd., Vds. → **usted**
ve, etc. → **ir, ver**
vecinal *adj* : local
vecino, -na *n* **1** : neighbor **2** HABITANTE
: resident, inhabitant — **~** *adj*
: neighboring — **vecindad** *nf* : neighborhood, vicinity — **vecindario** *nm* **1**
: neighborhood **2** VECINOS : community, residents *pl*
vedar *vt* : prohibit — **veda** *nf* **1** : prohibition, ban **2** : closed season (for hunt-

ing and fishing) — **vedado** *nm* : preserve (for game, etc.)

vega *nf* : fertile lowland

vegetal *nm* : vegetable, plant — ~ *adj*
: vegetable — **vegetación** *nf, pl*
-ciones : vegetation — **vegetar** *vi*
: vegetate — **vegetariano, -na** *adj & n*
: vegetarian

vehemente *adj* : vehement

vehículo *nm* : vehicle

veinte *adj & nm* : twenty — **veinteavo,**
-va *adj* : twentieth — **veinteavo** *nm*
: twentieth — **veintena** *nf* : group of
twenty, score

vejar *vt* : mistreat, humiliate — **ve-**
jación *nf, pl* **-ciones** : humiliation

vejez *nf* : old age

vejiga *nf* 1 : bladder 2 AMPOLLA : blister

vela *nf* 1 : candle 2 : sail (of a ship) 3
VIGILIA : vigil 4 **pasar la noche en ~**
: have a sleepless night

velada *nf* : evening (party)

velar *vt* 1 : hold a wake over 2 CUIDAR
: watch over 3 : blur (a photograph) 4
OCULTAR : veil, mask — *vi* 1 : stay
awake 2 **~ por** : watch over — **vela-**
do, -da *adj* 1 : veiled, hidden 2
: blurred (of a photograph)

velero *nm* : sailing ship

veleta *nf* : weather vane

vello *nm* 1 : body hair 2 PELUSA : down,
fuzz — **vellón** *nm, pl* **-llones** : fleece
— **velloso, -sa** *adj* : downy, fluffy —
velludo, -da *adj* : hairy

velo *nm* : veil

veloz *adj, pl* **-loces** : fast, quick — **ve-**
locidad *nf* 1 : speed, velocity 2 MAR-
CHA : gear (of an automobile) — **ve-**
locímetro *nm* : speedometer

vena *nf* 1 : vein 2 : grain (of wood) 3
DISPOSICIÓN : mood 4 **tener ~ de**
: have a talent for

venado *nm* 1 : deer 2 : venison (in
cooking)

vencer {86} *vt* 1 : beat, defeat 2 SUPER-
AR : overcome — *vi* 1 : win 2 CADUCAR
: expire — **vencerse** *vr* : collapse,
give way — **vencedor, -dora** *adj*
: winning — ~ *n* : winner — **venci-**
do, -da *adj* 1 : beaten, defeated 2 CAD-
UCADO : expired 3 : due, payable (in
finance) 4 **darse por ~** : give up —
vencimiento *nm* 1 : expiration 2 : maturity (of a loan)

venda *nf* : bandage — **vendaje** *nm*
: bandage, dressing — **vendar** *vt* 1
: bandage 2 **~ los ojos** : blindfold

vendaval *nm* : gale

vender *vt* : sell — **venderse** *vr* 1 : be
sold 2 **se vende** : for sale — **vende-**

dor, -dora *n* 1 : seller 2 : salesman *m,*
saleswoman *f* (in a store)

vendimia *nf* : grape harvest

vendrá, etc. → **venir**

veneno *nm* 1 : poison 2 : venom (of a
snake, etc.) — **venenoso, -sa** *adj*
: poisonous

venerar *vt* : venerate, revere — **venera-**
ble *adj* : venerable — **veneración** *nf,*
pl **-ciones** : veneration, reverence

venéreo, -rea *adj* : venereal

venezolano, -na *adj* : Venezuelan

venga → **venir**

vengar {52} *vt* : avenge — **vengarse**
vr : get even, take revenge — **vengan-**
za *nf* : vengeance, revenge — **venga-**
tivo, -va *adj* : vindictive, vengeful

venia *nf* 1 : permission 2 : pardon (in
law)

venial *adj* : venial, petty

venir {87} *vi* 1 : come 2 LLEGAR : arrive
3 HALLARSE : be, appear 4 QUEDAR : fi
5 **que viene** : coming, next 6 **~ a se**
: turn out to be 7 **~ bien** : be suitable
— **venirse** *vr* 1 : come 2 **~ abaje**
: fall apart, collapse — **venida** *nf* 1
: arrival, coming 2 REGRESO : return —
venidero, -ra *adj* : coming

venta *nf* 1 : sale, selling 2 **en ~** : fo
sale

ventaja *nf* : advantage — **ventajoso**
-sa *adj* : advantageous

ventana *nf* 1 : window 2 **~ de la nari.**
: nostril — **ventanilla** *nf* 1 : window
(of a vehicle or airplane) 2 : ticke
window, box office (of a theater, etc.)

ventilar *vt* : ventilate, air (out) — **venti**
lación *nf, pl* **-ciones** : ventilation —
ventilador *nm* : fan, ventilator

ventisca *nf* : blizzard — **ventisquer**
nm : snowdrift

ventoso, -sa *adj* : windy — **ventos**
dad *nf* : wind, flatulence

ventrílocuo, -cua *n* : ventriloquist

ventura *nf* 1 : fortune, luck 2 SATISFAC
CIÓN : happiness 3 **a la ~** : at randon
— **venturoso, -sa** *adj* : fortunate
happy

ver {88} *vt* 1 : see 2 : watch (television
etc.) — *vi* 1 : see 2 **a ~** *or* **vamos**
~ : let's see 3 **no tener nada que ~**
con : have nothing to do with 4 **y**
veremos : we'll see — **verse** *vr*
: see oneself 2 HALLARSE : find onese
3 ENCONTRARSE : see each other, me

vera *nf* 1 : side, edge 2 : bank (of
river)

veracidad *nf* : truthfulness

verano *nm* : summer — **veranean**
nmf : summer vacationer — **verane**

vi : spend the summer — **veraniego, -ga** *adj* : summer

veras *nfpl* **de ~** : really

veraz *adj, pl* **-races** : truthful

verbal *adj* : verbal

verbena *nf* : festival, fair

verbo *nm* : verb — **verboso, -sa** *adj* : verbose

verdad *nf* **1** : truth **2 de ~** : really, truly **3 ¿verdad?** : right?, isn't that so? — **verdaderamente** *adv* : really, truly — **verdadero, -dera** *adj* : true, real

verde *adj* **1** : green **2** : dirty, risqué (of a joke, etc.) — **~** *nm* : green — **verdor** *nm* : greenness

verdugo *nm* **1** : executioner, hangman **2** : cruel person, tyrant

verdura *nf* : vegetable(s), green(s)

vereda *nf* **1** : path, trail **2** *Lat* : sidewalk

veredicto *nm* : verdict

vergüenza *nf* **1** : shame **2** TIMIDEZ : bashfulness, shyness — **vergonzoso, -sa** *adj* **1** : shameful **2** TÍMIDO : bashful, shy

verídico, -ca *adj* : true, truthful

verificar {72} *vt* **1** : verify, confirm **2** EXAMINAR : test, check out — **verificarse** *vr* **1** : take place **2** : come true (of a prophecy, etc.) — **verificación** *nf, pl* **-ciones** : verification

verja *nf* **1** : (iron) gate **2** : rails *pl* (of a fence) **3** ENREJADO : grating, grille

vermut *nm, pl* **-muts** : vermouth

vernáculo, -la *adj* : vernacular

verosímil *adj* **1** : probable, likely **2** CREÍBLE : credible

verraco *nm* : boar

verruga *nf* : wart

versar *vi* **~ sobre** : deal with, be about — **versado, -da** *adj* **~ en** : versed in

versátil *adj* **1** : versatile **2** VOLUBLE : fickle

versión *nf, pl* **-siones** **1** : version **2** TRADUCCIÓN : translation

verso *nm* **1** : poem, verse **2** : line (of poetry)

vértebra *nf* : vertebra

verter {56} *vt* **1** : pour (out) **2** DERRAMAR : spill **3** TIRAR : dump — *vi* : flow — **vertedero** *nm* **1** : dump, landfill **2** DESAGÜE : drain, outlet

vertical *adj & nf* : vertical

vértice *nm* : vertex, apex

vertiente *nf* : slope

vértigo *nm* : vertigo, dizziness — **vertiginoso, -sa** *adj* : dizzy

vesícula *nf* **1** : blister **2 ~ biliar** : gallbladder

vestíbulo *nm* : vestibule, hall, foyer

vestido *nm* **1** : dress **2** ROPA : clothing, clothes *pl*

vestigio *nm* : vestige, trace

vestir {54} *vt* **1** : dress, clothe **2** LLEVAR : wear — *vi* : dress — **vestirse** *vr* : get dressed — **vestimenta** *nf* : clothing — **vestuario** *nm* **1** : wardrobe, clothes *pl* **2** : dressing room (in a theater), locker room (in sports)

veta *nf* **1** : vein, seam **2** : grain (of wood)

vetar *vt* : veto

veteado, -da *adj* : streaked, veined

veterano, -na *adj & n* : veteran

veterinaria *nf* : veterinary medicine — **veterinario, -ria** *adj* : veterinary — *n* : veterinarian

veto *nm* : veto

vetusto, -ta *adj* : ancient

vez *nf, pl* **veces** **1** : time **2** TURNO : turn **3 a la ~** : at the same time **4 a veces** : sometimes **5 de una ~** : all at once **6 de una ~ para siempre** : once and for all **7 de ~ en cuando** : from time to time **8 dos veces** : twice **9 en ~ de** : instead of **10 una ~** : once

vía *nf* **1** : way, road, route **2** MEDIO : means **3** : track, line (of a railroad) **4** : (anatomical) tract **5 en ~ de** : in the process of — **~** *prep* : via

viable *adj* : viable, feasible — **viabilidad** *nf* : viability

viaducto *nm* : viaduct

viajar *vi* : travel — **viajante** *nmf* : traveling salesperson — **viaje** *nm* : trip, journey — **viajero, -ra** *adj* : traveling — *n* **1** : traveler **2** PASAJERO : passenger

vial *adj* : road, traffic

víbora *nf* : viper

vibrar *vi* : vibrate — **vibración** *nf, pl* **-ciones** : vibration — **vibrante** *adj* : vibrant

vicario, -ria *n* : vicar

vicepresidente, -ta *n* : vice president

viceversa *adv* : vice versa

vicio *nm* **1** : vice **2** MALA COSTUMBRE : bad habit **3** DEFECTO : defect — **viciado, -da** *adj* **1** : corrupt **2** : stuffy, stale (of air, etc.) — **viciar** *vt* **1** : corrupt **2** ESTROPEAR : spoil, pollute — **vicioso, -sa** *adj* : depraved, corrupt

vicisitud *nf* : vicissitude

víctima *nf* : victim

victoria *nf* : victory — **victorioso, -sa** *adj* : victorious

vid *nf* : vine, grapevine

vida *nf* **1** : life **2** DURACIÓN : lifetime **3 de por ~** : for life **4 estar con ~** : be alive

video *or* **vídeo** *nm* 1 : video 2 : VCR, videocassette recorder

vidrio *nm* : glass — **vidriado** *nm* : glaze — **vidriar** *vt* : glaze — **vidriera** *nf* 1 : stained-glass window 2 : glass door 3 *Lat* : shopwindow — **vidrioso, -sa** *adj* 1 : delicate (of a subject, etc.) 2 **ojos vidriosos** : glassy eyes

vieira *nf* : scallop

viejo, -ja *adj* : old — ~ *n* 1 : old man *m*, old woman *f* 2 **hacerse** ~ : get old

viene, etc. → **venir**

viento *nm* : wind

vientre *nm* 1 : abdomen, belly 2 MATRIZ : womb 3 INTESTINO : bowels *pl*

viernes *nms & pl* 1 : Friday 2 **Viernes Santo** : Good Friday

vietnamita *adj & nm* : Vietnamese

viga *nf* : beam, girder

vigencia *nf* 1 : validity 2 **entrar en** ~ : go into effect — **vigente** *adj* : valid, in force

vigésimo, -ma *adj & n* : twentieth

vigía *nmf* : lookout

vigilar *vt* : look after, watch over — *vi* : keep watch — **vigilancia** *nf* 1 : vigilance 2 **bajo** ~ : under surveillance — **vigilante** *adj* : vigilant — ~ *nmf* : watchman, guard — **vigilia** *nf* 1 : wakefulness 2 : vigil (in religion)

vigor *nm* 1 : vigor 2 **entrar en** ~ : go into effect — **vigorizante** *adj* : invigorating — **vigoroso, -sa** *adj* : vigorous

VIH *nm* : HIV

vil *adj* : vile, despicable — **vileza** *nf* 1 : vileness 2 : despicable act — **vilipendiar** *vt* : revile

villa *nf* 1 : town, village 2 : villa (house)

villancico *nm* : (Christmas) carol

villano, -na *n* : villain

vilo *en* ~ : suspended, in the air

vinagre *nm* : vinegar — **vinagrera** *nf* : cruet — **vinagreta** *nf* : vinaigrette

vincular *vt* : tie, link — **vínculo** *nm* : link, tie, bond

vindicar *vt* 1 : vindicate 2 VENGAR : avenge

vino¹, etc. → **venir**

vino² *nm* : wine

viña *nf or* **viñedo** *nm* : vineyard

vio, etc. → **ver**

viola *nf* : viola

violar *vt* 1 : violate (a law, etc.) 2 : rape (a person) — **violación** *nf, pl* **-ciones** 1 : violation, offense 2 : rape (of a person)

violencia *nf* : violence, force — **violentar** *vt* 1 : force 2 : break into (a house, etc.) — **violentarse** *vr* 1 : force one-

self 2 AVERGONZARSE : be embarrassed — **violento, -ta** *adj* 1 : violent 2 INCÓMODO : awkward, embarrassing

violeta *adj & nm* : violet (color) — ~ *nf* : violet (flower)

violín *nm, pl* **-lines** : violin — **violinista** *nmf* : violinist — **violoncelista** *or* **violonchelista** *nmf* : cellist — **violoncelo** *or* **violonchelo** *nm* : cello, violoncello

virar *vi* : turn, change direction — **viraje** *nm* 1 : turn, swerve 2 CAMBIO : change

virgen *adj & nmf, pl* **vírgenes** : virgin — **virginal** *adj* : virginal — **virginidad** *nf* : virginity

viril *adj* : virile — **virilidad** *nf* : virility

virtual *adj* : virtual

virtud *nf* 1 : virtue 2 **en** ~ **de** : by virtue of — **virtuoso, -sa** *adj* : virtuous — ~ *n* : virtuoso

viruela *nf* 1 : smallpox 2 **picado de** ~**s** : pockmarked

virulento, -ta *adj* : virulent

virus *nms & pl* : virus

visa *nf Lat* : visa — **visado** *nm Spain* : visa

vísceras *nfpl* : entrails — **visceral** *adj* : visceral

viscoso, -sa *adj* : viscous — **viscosidad** *nf* : viscosity

visera *nf* : visor

visible *adj* : visible — **visibilidad** *nf* : visibility

visión *nf, pl* **-siones** 1 : eyesight 2 APARICIÓN : vision, illusion 3 PUNTO DE VISTA : view, perspective — **visionario, -ria** *adj & n* : visionary

visitar *vt* : visit — **visita** *nf* 1 : visit 2 **tener** ~ : have company — **visitante** *adj* : visiting — ~ *nmf* : visitor

vislumbrar *vt* : make out, discern — **vislumbre** *nf* 1 : glimpse, sign 2 RESPLANDOR : glimmer, gleam

viso *nm* 1 : sheen 2 **tener** ~**s de** : seem, show signs of

visón *nm, pl* **-sones** : mink

víspera *nf* : eve, day before

vista *nf* 1 : vision, eyesight 2 MIRADA : look, gaze 3 PANORAMA : view, vista 4 : hearing (in court) 5 **a primera** ~ *or* **a simple** ~ : at first sight 6 **hacer la** ~ **gorda** : turn a blind eye — **vistazo** *nm* 1 : glance 2 **echar un** ~ : have a look

visto, -ta *adj* 1 : clear, obvious 2 COMÚN : commonly seen 3 **estar bien** ~ : be approved of 4 **estar mal** ~ : be frowned upon 5 **nunca** ~ : unheard of **6 por lo visto** : apparently **7 visto que** : since, given that — **visto** nm — **bueno** : approval — ~ pp → **ver**

vistoso, -sa adj : colorful, bright

visual adj : visual — **visualizar** {21} vt : visualize

vital adj : vital — **vitalicio, -cia** adj : life, for life — **vitalidad** nf : vitality

vitamina nf : vitamin

viticultor, -tora n : winegrower — **viticultura** nf : wine growing

vitorear vt : cheer, acclaim

vítreo, -trea adj : glassy

vitrina nf **1** : showcase, display case **2** Lat : shopwindow

vituperar vt : censure — **vituperio** nm : censure

viudo, -da n : widower m, widow f — ~ adj : widowed — **viudez** nf : widowerhood, widowhood

viva nm **dar** ~**s** : cheer

vivacidad nf : vivacity, liveliness

vivamente adv **1** : vividly **2** PROFUNDAMENTE : deeply, acutely

vivaz adj, pl **-vaces 1** : lively, vivacious **2** AGUDO : vivid, sharp

víveres nmpl : provisions, supplies

vivero nm **1** : nursery (for plants) **2** : (fish) hatchery, (oyster) bed

viveza nf **1** : liveliness **2** : vividness (of colors, descriptions, etc.) **3** ASTUCIA : sharpness (of mind) — **vívido, -da** adj : vivid

vividor, -dora n : freeloader

vivienda nf **1** : housing **2** MORADA : dwelling

viviente adj : living

vivificar {72} vt : enliven

vivir vi **1** : live, be alive **2** ~ **de** : live on — vt : experience, live (through) — ~ nm **1** : life, lifestyle **2 de mal** ~ : disreputable — **vivo, -va** adj **1** : alive **2** INTENSO : intense, bright **3** ANIMADO : lively **4** ASTUTO : sharp, quick **5 en vivo** : live

vocablo nm : word — **vocabulario** nm : vocabulary

vocación nf, pl **-ciones** : vocation — **vocacional** adj : vocational

vocal adj : vocal — ~ nmf : member (of a committee, etc.) — ~ nf : vowel — **vocalista** nmf : singer, vocalist

vocear v : shout — **vocerío** nm : shouting

vociferar vi : shout

vodka nmf : vodka

volar {19} vi **1** : fly **2** : blow away (of papers, etc.) **3** fam : disappear **4 irse volando** : rush off — vt : blow up — **volador, -dora** adj : flying — **volan-**

das: **en** ~ adv phr : in the air — **volante** adj : flying — ~ nm **1** : steering wheel **2** : shuttlecock (in badminton) **3** : flounce (of fabric) **4** Lat : flier, circular

volátil adj : volatile

volcán nm, pl **-canes** : volcano — **volcánico, -ca** adj : volcanic

volcar {82} vt **1** : upset, knock over **2** VACIAR : empty out — vi : overturn — **volcarse** vr **1** : overturn, tip over **2** ~ **en** : throw oneself into

voleibol nm : volleyball

voltaje nm : voltage

voltear vt : turn over, turn upside down — **voltearse** vr Lat : turn (around) — **voltereta** nf : somersault

voltio nm : volt

voluble adj : fickle

volumen nm, pl **-lúmenes** : volume — **voluminoso, -sa** adj : voluminous

voluntad nf **1** : will **2** DESEO : wish **3** INTENCIÓN : intention **4 a** ~ : at will **5 buena** ~ : goodwill **6 mala** ~ : ill will **7 fuerza de** ~ : willpower — **voluntario, -ria** adj : voluntary — ~ n : volunteer — **voluntarioso, -sa** adj **1** : willing **2** TERCO : stubborn, willful

voluptuoso, -sa adj : voluptuous

volver {89} vi **1** : return, come or go back **2** ~ **a** : return to, do again **3** ~ **en sí** : come to — vt **1** : turn, turn over, turn inside out **2** CONVERTIR EN : turn (into) **3** ~ **loco** : drive crazy — **volverse** vr **1** : turn (around) **2** HACERSE : become

vomitar vi : vomit — vt **1** : vomit **2** : spew (out) — **vómito** nm **1** : (action of) vomiting **2** : vomit

voraz adj, pl **-races** : voracious

vos pron Lat : you

vosotros, -tras pron Spain : you, yourselves

votar vi : vote — vt : vote for — **votación** nf, pl **-ciones** : vote, voting — **votante** nmf : voter — **voto** nm **1** : vote **2** : vow (in religion)

voy → **ir**

voz nf, pl **voces 1** : voice **2** GRITO : shout, yell **3** VOCABLO : word **4** RUMOR : rumor **5 dar voces** : shout **6 en** ~ **alta** : loudly **7 en** ~ **baja** : softly

vuelco nm : upset, overturning

vuelo nm **1** : flight **2** : (action of) flying **3** : flare (of clothing) **4 al** ~ : on the wing

vuelta nf **1** : turn **2** REVOLUCIÓN : circle, revolution **3** CURVA : bend, curve **4** REGRESO : return **5** : round, lap (in sports)

6 PASEO : walk, drive, ride **7** REVÉS : back, other side **8** *Spain* : change **9** **dar —s** : spin **10 estar de ~** : be back — **vuelto** *nm Lat* : change

vuestro, -tra *adj Spain* : your, of yours — **~** *pron Spain* (*with definite article*) : yours

vulgar *adj* **1** : vulgar **2** CORRIENTE : common — **vulgaridad** *nf* **1** : vulgarity **2** BANALIDAD : banality — **vulgo** *nm* **el ~** : the masses, common people

vulnerable *adj* : vulnerable — **vulnerabilidad** *nf* : vulnerability

WXYZ

w *nf* : w, 24th letter of the Spanish alphabet

wáter *nm Spain* : toilet

whisky *nm, pl* **-skys** *or* **-skies** : whiskey

x *nf* : x, 25th letter of the Spanish alphabet

xenofobia *nf* : xenophobia

xilófono *nm* : xylophone

y[1] *nf* : y, 26th letter of the Spanish alphabet

y[2] *conj* : and

ya *adv* **1** : already **2** AHORA : (right) now **3** MÁS TARDE : later, soon **4 — no** : no longer **5 ~ que** : now that, since, inasmuch as

yacer {90} *vi* : lie (on or in the ground) — **yacimiento** *nm* : bed, deposit

yanqui *adj & nmf* : Yankee

yate *nm* : yacht

yegua *nf* : mare

yelmo *nm* : helmet

yema *nf* **1** : bud, shoot **2** : yolk (of an egg) **3** *or* **~ del dedo** : fingertip

yerba *nf* **1** *or* **~ mate** : maté **2** → **hierba**

yermo, -ma *adj* : barren, deserted — **yermo** *nm* : wasteland

yerno *nm* : son-in-law

yerro *nm* : blunder, mistake

yerto, -ta *adj* : stiff

yesca *nf* : tinder

yeso *nm* **1** : gypsum **2** : plaster (for art, construction)

yo *pron* **1** (*subject*) : I **2** (*object*) : me **3 soy ~** : it is I, it's me — **~** *nm* : ego, self

yodo *nm* : iodine

yoga *nm* : yoga

yogurt *or* **yogur** *nm* : yogurt

yuca *nf* : yucca

yugo *nm* : yoke (of oxen)

yugoslavo, -va *adj* : Yugoslavian

yugular *adj* : jugular

yunque *nm* : anvil

yunta *nf* : yoke

yuxtaponer {60} *vt* : juxtapose — **yuxtaposición** *nf, pl* **-ciones** : juxtaposition

z *nf* : z, 27th letter of the Spanish alphabet

zacate *nm Lat* : grass

zafar *vt Lat* : loosen, untie — **zafarse** *vr* **1** : come undone **2** : get free of (an obligation, etc.)

zafio, -fia *adj* : coarse

zafiro *nm* : sapphire

zaga *nf* **a la ~** *or* **en ~** : behind, in the rear

zaguán *nm, pl* **-guanes** : (entrance) hall

zaherir {76} *vt* : hurt (s.o.'s feelings)

zaino, -na *adj* : chestnut (color)

zalamería *nf* : flattery — **zalamero, -ra** *adj* : flattering — **~** *n* : flatterer

zambullirse {38} *vr* : dive, plunge — **zambullida** *nf* : dive, plunge

zanahoria *nf* : carrot

zancada *nf* : stride, step — **zancadilla** *nf* **1** : trip, stumble **2 hacer una ~ a algn** : trip s.o. up

zancos *nmpl* : stilts

zancudo *nm Lat* : mosquito

zángano, -na *n fam* : lazy person, slacker — **zángano** *nm* : drone (bee)

zanja *nf* : ditch, trench — **zanjar** *vt* : settle, resolve

zapallo *nm Lat* : pumpkin — **zapallito** *nm Lat* : zucchini

zapapico *nm* : pickax

zapato *nm* : shoe — **zapatería** *nf* : shoe store — **zapatero, -ra** *n* : shoemaker, cobbler — **zapatilla** *nf* **1** : slipper **2** : sneaker (for sports, etc.)

zar *nm* : czar

zarandear *vt* **1** : sift **2** SACUDIR : shake

zarcillo *nm* : earring

zarpa *nf* : paw

zarpar *vi* : set sail, raise anchor

zarza *nf* : bramble — **zarzamora** *n,* : blackberry

zigzag *nm, pl* **-zags** *or* **-zagues** : zigzag — **zigzaguear** *vi* : zigzag

zinc *nm* : zinc
zíper *nm Lat* : zipper
zircón *nm, pl* **-cones** : zircon
zócalo *nm* **1** : base (of a column, etc.) **2** : baseboard (of a wall) **3** *Lat* : main square, plaza
zodíaco *nm* : zodiac
zona *nf* : zone, area
zoo *nm* : zoo — **zoología** *nf* : zoology — **zoológico, -ca** *adj* : zoological — **zoológico** *nm* : zoo — **zoólogo, -ga** *n* : zoologist
zopilote *nm Lat* : buzzard
zoquete *nmf fam* : oaf, blockhead

zorrillo *nm Lat* : skunk
zorro, -rra *n* : fox, vixen *f* — ~ *adj* : foxy, sly
zozobra *nf* : anxiety, worry — **zozobrar** *vi* : capsize
zueco *nm* : clog (shoe)
zumbar *vi* : buzz — *vt fam* : hit, beat — **zumbido** *nm* : buzzing
zumo *nf* : juice
zurcir {83} *vt* : darn, mend
zurdo, -da *adj* : left-handed — ~ *n* : left-handed person — **zurda** *nf* : left hand
zutano, -na → fulano

English-Spanish
Dictionary

A

a¹ ['eɪ] *n*, *pl* **a's** *or* **as** ['eɪz] : a *f*, primera letra del alfabeto inglés

a² [ə, 'eɪ] *art* (**an** [ən, æn] *before vowel or silent h*) **1** : un *m*, una *f* **2** PER : por, a la, al

aback [ə'bæk] *adv* **be taken ~** : quedarse desconcertado

abacus ['æbəkəs] *n*, *pl* **abaci** ['æbə,saɪ, -,kiː] *or* **abacuses** : ábaco *m*

abandon [ə'bændən] *vt* **1** DESERT : abandonar **2** GIVE UP : renunciar a — **~** *n* : desenfreno *m* — **abandonment** [ə'bændənmənt] *n* : abandono *m*

abashed [ə'bæʃt] *adj* : avergonzado

abate [ə'beɪt] *vi* **abated; abating** : amainar, disminuir

abattoir ['æbə,twɑr] *n* : matadero *m*

abbey ['æbi] *n*, *pl* **-beys** : abadía *f* — **abbot** ['æbət] *n* : abad *m*

abbreviate [ə'briːvi,eɪt] *vt* **-ated; -ating** : abreviar — **abbreviation** [ə,briːvi-'eɪʃən] *n* : abreviatura *f*, abreviación *f*

abdicate ['æbdɪ,keɪt] *v* **-cated; -cating** : abdicar — **abdication** [,æbdɪ'keɪəən] *n* : abdicación *f*

abdomen ['æbdəmən, æb'do:mən] *n* : abdomen *m*, vientre *m* — **abdominal** [æb'dɑmənəl] *adj* : abdominal

abduct [æb'dʌkt] *vt* : secuestrar — **abduction** [æb'dʌkʃən] *n* : secuestro *m*

aberration [,æbə'reɪʃən] *n* : aberración *f*

abet [ə'bɛt] *vt* **abetted; abetting** *or* **aid and ~** : ser cómplice de

abeyance [ə'beɪəns] *n* : desuso *m*

abhor [əb'hɔr, æb-] *vt* **-horred; -horring** : aborrecer

abide [ə'baɪd] *v* **abode** [ə'boːd] *or* **abided; abiding** *vt* : soportar, tolerar — *vi* **1** DWELL : morar **2 ~ by** : atenerse a

ability [ə'bɪləti] *n*, *pl* **-ties 1** CAPABILITY : aptitud *f*, capacidad *f* **2** SKILL : habilidad *f*

abject ['æb,dʒɛkt, æb'-] *adj* : miserable, desdichado

ablaze [ə'bleɪz] *adj* : en llamas

able ['eɪbəl] *adj* **abler; ablest 1** CAPABLE : capaz, hábil **2** COMPETENT : competente

abnormal [æb'nɔrməl] *adj* : anormal — **abnormality** [,æbnɔr'mæləti, -nɔr-] *n*, *pl* **-ties** : anormalidad *f*

aboard [ə'bord] *adv* : a bordo — **~** *prep* : a bordo de

abode *n* : morada *f*, domicilio *m*

abolish [ə'bɑlɪʃ] *vt* : abolir, suprimir — **abolition** [,æbə'lɪʃən] *n* : abolición *f*

abominable [ə'bɑmənəbəl] *adj* : abominable, aborrecible — **abomination** [ə,bɑmə'neɪʃən] *n* : abominación *f*

aborigine [,æbə'rɪdʒəni] *n* : aborigen *mf*

abort [ə'bɔrt] *vt* : abortar — **abortion** [ə'bɔrʃən] *n* : aborto *m* — **abortive** [ə'bɔrtɪv] *adj* UNSUCCESSFUL : malogrado

abound [ə'baʊnd] *vi* **~ in** : abundar en

about [ə'baʊt] *adv* **1** APPROXIMATELY : aproximadamente, más o menos **2** AROUND : alrededor **3 be ~ to** : estar a punto de **4 be up and ~** : estar levantado — **~** *prep* **1** AROUND : alrededor de **2** CONCERNING : acerca de, sobre

above [ə'bʌv] *adv* : arriba — **~** *prep* **1** : encima de **2 ~ all** : sobre todo — **aboveboard** *adj* : honrado

abrasive [ə'breɪsɪv] *adj* **1** : abrasivo **2** BRUSQUE : brusco, mordaz

abreast [ə'brɛst] *adv* **1** : al lado **2 keep ~ of** : mantenerse al corriente de

abridge [ə'brɪdʒ] *vt* **abridged; abridging** : abreviar

abroad [ə'brɔd] *adv* **1** : en el extranjero **2** WIDELY : por todas partes **3 go ~** : ir al extranjero

abrupt [ə'brʌpt] *adj* **1** SUDDEN : repentino **2** BRUSQUE : brusco

abscess ['æb,sɛs] *n* : absceso *m*

absence ['æbsəns] *n* **1** : ausencia *f* **2** LACK : falta *f*, carencia *f* — **absent** ['æbsənt] *adj* : ausente — **absentee** [,æbsən'tiː] *n* : ausente *mf* — **absentminded** [,æbsənt'maɪndəd] *adj* : distraído, despistado

absolute ['æbsə,luːt, ,æbsə'luːt] *adj* : absoluto — **absolutely** [,æbsə'luːtli] *adv* : absolutamente

absolve [əb'zɑlv, æb-, -'sɑlv] *vt* **-solved; -solving** : absolver

absorb [əb'zɔrb, æb-, -'sɔrb] *vt* : absorber — **absorbent** [əb'zɔrbənt, æb-, -'sɔr-] *adj* : absorbente — **absorption** [əb'zɔrpʃən, æb-, -'sɔrp-] *n* : absorción *f*

abstain [əb'steɪn, æb-] *vi* **~ from** : abstenerse de — **abstinence** ['æbstə-nənts] *n* : abstinencia *f*

abstract [æb'strækt, 'æb,-] *adj* : abstracto — ~ *vt* : extraer — ~ ['æb,strækt] *n* : resumen *m* — **abstraction** [æb-'stræk∫ən] *n* : abstracción *f*

absurd [əb'sərd, -'zərd] *adj* : absurdo — **absurdity** [əb'sərdəṭi, -'zərdəṭi] *n, pl* **-ties** : absurdo *m*

abundant [ə'bʌndənt] *adj* : abundante — **abundance** [ə'bʌndəns] *n* : abundancia *f*

abuse [ə'bju:z] *vt* **abused; abusing 1** MISUSE : abusar de **2** MISTREAT : maltratar **3** REVILE : insultar — ~ [ə'bju:s] *n* **1** : abuso *m* **2** INSULTS : insultos *mpl* — **abusive** [ə'bju:sɪv] *adj* : injurioso

abut [ə'bʌt] *vi* **abutted; abutting** ~ **on** : colindar con

abyss [ə'bɪs, 'æbɪs] *n* : abismo *m* — **abysmal** [ə'bɪzməl] *adj* : atroz, pésimo

academy [ə'kædəmi] *n, pl* **-mies** : academia *f* — **academic** [ˌækə'demɪk] *adj* **1** : académico **2** THEORETICAL : teórico

accelerate [ɪk'seləˌreɪt, æk-] *v* **-ated; -ating** : acelerar — **acceleration** [ɪk-ˌseləˈreɪʃən, æk-] *n* : aceleración *f*

accent ['æk,sent, æk'sent] *vt* : acentuar — ~ ['æk,sent, sənt] *n* : acento *m* — **accentuate** [ɪk'sentæʊˌeɪt, æk-] *vt* **-ated; -ating** : acentuar, subrayar

accept [ɪk'sept, æk-] *vt* : aceptar — **acceptable** [ɪk'septəbəl, æk-] *adj* : aceptable — **acceptance** [ɪk'septəns, æk-] *n* **1** : aceptación *f* **2** APPROVAL : aprobación *f*

access ['æk,ses] *n* : acceso *m* — **accessible** [ɪk'sesəbəl, æk-] *adj* : accesible, asequible

accessory *n, pl* **-ries 1** : accesorio *m* **2** ACCOMPLICE : cómplice *mf*

accident ['æksədənt] *n* **1** MISHAP : accidente *m* **2** CHANCE : casualidad *f* — **accidental** [ˌæksə'dentəl] *adj* : accidental — **accidentally** [ˌæksə'dentəli, -'dentli] *adv* **1** BY CHANCE : por casualidad **2** UNINTENTIONALLY : sin querer

acclaim [ə'kleɪm] *vt* : aclamar — ~ *n* : aclamación *f*

acclimatize [ə'klaɪməˌtaɪz] *vt* **-tized; -tizing** : aclimatar

accommodate [ə'kaməˌdeɪt] *vt* **-dated; -dating 1** ADAPT : acomodar, adaptar **2** SATISFY : complacer, satisfacer **3** HOLD : tener cabida para — **accomodation** [əˌkaməˈdeɪʃən] *n* **1** : adaptación *f* **2** ~**s** *npl* LODGING : alojamiento *m*

accompany [ə'kʌmpəni, -kəm-] *vt* **-nied; -nying** : acompañar

accomplice [ə'kampləs, -'kʌm-] *n* : cómplice *mf*

accomplish [ə'kamplɪʃ, -'kʌm-] *vt* : re-alizar, llevar a cabo — **accomplishment** [ə'kamplɪʃmənt, -kʌm-] *n* **1** COMPLETION : realización *f* **2** ACHIEVEMENT : logro *m*, éxito *m*

accord *n* **1** AGREEMENT : acuerdo *m* **2** of one's own ~ : voluntariamente — **accordance** [ə'kordəns] *n* in ~ with : conforme a, de acuerdo con — **accordingly** [ə'kordɪŋli] *adv* : en consecuencia — **according to** [ə'kordɪŋ] *prep* : según

accordion [ə'kordiən] *n* : acordeón *m*

accost [ə'kost] *vt* : abordar

account [ə'kaunt] *n* **1** : cuenta *f* **2** REPORT : relato *m*, informe *m* **3** WORTH : importancia *f* **4** on ~ of : a causa de, debido a **5** on no ~ : de ninguna manera — ~ *vi* — **for** : dar cuenta de, explicar — **accountable** [ə'kauntəbəl] *adj* : responsable — **accountant** [ə'kauntənt] *n* : contador *m*, -dora *f Lat*; contable *mf Spain* — **accounting** [ə'kauntɪŋ] *n* : contabilidad *f*

accrue [ə'kru:] *vi* **-crued; -cruing** : acumularse

accumulate [ə'kju:mjəˌleɪt] *v* **-lated; -lating** *vt* : acumular — *vi* : acumularse — **accumulation** [əˌkju:mjə-'leɪʃən] *n* : acumulación *f*

accurate ['ækjərət] *adj* : exacto, preciso — **accuracy** ['ækjərəsi] *n* : exactitud *f*, precisión *f*

accuse [ə'kju:z] *vt* **-cused; -cusing** : acusar — **accusation** [ˌækjəˈzeɪʃən] *n* : acusación *f*

accustomed [ə'kʌstəmd] *adj* **1** : acostumbrado **2** become ~ to : acostumbrarse a

ace ['eɪs] *n* : as *m*

ache ['eɪk] *vi* **ached; aching** : doler — ~ *n* : dolor *m*

achieve [ə'tʃi:v] *vt* **achieved; achieving** : lograr, realizar — **achievement** [ə'tʃi:vmənt] *n* : logro *m*, éxito *m*

acid ['æsəd] *adj* : ácido — ~ *n* : ácido *m*

acknowledge [ɪk'nɑlɪdʒ, æk-] *vt* **-edged; -edging 1** ADMIT : admitir **2** RECOGNIZE : reconocer **3** ~ **receipt of** : acusar recibo de — **acknowledgment** [ɪk'nɑlɪdʒmənt, æk-] *n* **1** : reconocimiento *m* **2** THANKS : agradecimiento *m* **3** ~ **of receipt** : acuse *m* de recibo

acne ['ækni] *n* : acné *m*

acorn ['eɪˌkɔrn, -kərn] *n* : bellota *f*

acoustic [ə'ku:stɪk] *or* **acoustical** [-stɪkəl] *adj* : acústico — **acoustics** [ə'ku:stɪks] *ns & pl* : acústica *f*

acquaint [ə'kweɪnt] *vt* **1** ~ **s.o. with**

: poner a algn al corriente de **2 be ~ed with** : conocer a (una persona), saber (un hecho) — **acquaintance** [ə'kweɪntʃ] n **1** : conocimiento m **2** : conocido m, -da f (persona)

acquire [ə'kwaɪr] vt **-quired; -quiring** : adquirir — **acquisition** [ækwə'zɪʃən] n : adquisición f

acquit [ə'kwɪt] vt **-quitted; -quitting** : absolver

acre ['eɪkər] n : acre m — **acreage** ['eɪkərɪdʒ] n : superficie f en acres

acrid ['ækrəd] adj : acre

acrobat ['ækrəbæt] n : acróbata mf — **acrobatic** [ækrə'bætɪk] adj : acrobático

acronym ['ækrənɪm] n : siglas fpl

across [ə'krɔs] adv **1** : de un lado a otro **2** CROSSWISE : a través **3 go ~ the street** : al otro lado de la calle — ~ prep **1** : a través de **2**

acrylic [ə'krɪlɪk] n : acrílico m

act ['ækt] vi **1** : actuar **2** PRETEND : fingir **3** FUNCTION : funcionar **4 ~ as** : servir de — vt : interpretar (un papel) — ~ n **1** ACTION : acto m, acción f **2** DECREE : ley f **3** : acto m (en una obra de teatro), número m (en un espectáculo) — **acting** adj : interino

action ['ækʃən] n **1** : acción f **2** LAWSUIT : demanda f **3 take ~** : tomar medidas

activate ['æktəveɪt] vt **-vated; -vating** : activar

active ['æktɪv] adj **1** : activo **2** LIVELY : enérgico **3 ~ volcano** : volcán m en actividad — **activity** [æk'tɪvəti] n, pl **-ties** : actividad f

actor ['æktər] n : actor m — **actress** ['æktrəs] n : actriz f

actual ['æktʃuəl] adj : real, verdadero — **actually** [æktʃuəli, -æʃli] adv : realmente, en realidad

acupuncture ['ækjupʌŋktʃər] n : acupuntura f

acute [ə'kjut] adj **acuter; acutest 1** : agudo **2** PERCEPTIVE : perspicaz

ad ['æd] → **advertisement**

adamant ['ædəmənt, -mænt] adj : inflexible

adapt [ə'dæpt] vt : adaptar — vi : adaptarse — **adaptable** [ə'dæptəbəl] adj : adaptable — **adaptation** [ædæp'teɪʃən, -dəp-] n : adaptación f — **adapter** [ə'dæptər] n : adaptador m

add ['æd] vt **1** : añadir **2 or ~ up** : sumar — vi : sumar

addict ['ædɪkt] n **1** : adicto m, -ta f **2 or drug ~** : drogadicto m, -ta f; toxicómano m, -na f — **addiction** [ə'dɪkʃən] n : dependencia f

addition [ə'dɪʃən] n **1** : suma f (en matemáticas) **2** ADDING : adición f **3 in ~** : además — **additional** [ə'dɪʃənəl] adj : adicional — **additive** ['ædəṭɪv] n : aditivo m

address [ə'dres] vt **1** : dirigirse a (una persona) **2** : ponerle la dirección a (una carta) **3** : tratar (un asunto) — ~ [ə'dres, 'ædres] n **1** : dirección f, domicilio m **2** SPEECH : discurso m

adept [ə'dept] adj : experto, hábil

adequate ['ædɪkwət] adj : adecuado, suficiente

adhere [æd'hɪr, əd-] vi **-hered; -hering 1** STICK : adherirse **2 ~ to** : observar — **adherence** [æd'hɪrənts, əd-] n **1** : adhesión f **2** : observancia f (de una ley, etc.) — **adhesive** [æd'hiːsɪv, əd-, -zɪv] adj : adhesivo — ~ n : adhesivo m

adjacent [ə'dʒeɪsənt] adj : adyacente, contiguo

adjective ['ædʒɪktɪv] n : adjetivo m

adjoining [ə'dʒɔɪnɪŋ] adj : contiguo, vecino

adjourn [ə'dʒərn] vt : aplazar, suspender — vi : suspenderse

adjust [ə'dʒʌst] vt : ajustar, arreglar — vi : adaptarse — **adjustable** [ə'dʒʌstəbəl] adj : ajustable — **adjustment** [ə'dʒʌstmənt] n : ajuste m (a una máquina, etc.), adaptación f (de una persona)

ad–lib [æd'lɪb] v **-libbed; -libbing** : improvisar

administer [æd'mɪnəstər, əd-] vt : administrar — **administration** [ædmɪnə'streɪʃən, əd-] n : administración f — **administrative** [æd'mɪnəstreɪṭɪv, əd-] adj : administrativo — **administrator** [æd'mɪnəstreɪṭər, əd-] n : administrador m, -dora f

admirable ['ædmərəbəl] adj : admirable

admiral ['ædmərəl] n : almirante m

admire [æd'maɪr] vt **-mired; -miring** : admirar — **admiration** [ædmə'reɪʃən] n : admiración f — **admirer** [æd'maɪrər] n : admirador m, -dora f

admit [æd'mɪt, əd-] vt **-mitted; -mitting 1** : admitir, dejar entrar **2** ACKNOWLEDGE : reconocer — **admission** [æd'mɪʃən] n **1** ADMITTANCE : entrada f, admisión f **2** ACKNOWLEDGMENT : reconocimiento m — **admittance** [æd'mɪtənts, əd-] n : admisión f, entrada f

admonish [æd'mɑnɪʃ, əd-] vt : amonestar, reprender

ado [ə'du] n **1** : alboroto m, bulla f **2 without further ~** : sin más (preámbulos)

adolescent [ˌædəl'ɛsənt] *n* : adolescente *mf* — **adolescence** [ˌædəl'ɛsənts] *n* : adolescencia *f*

adopt [ə'dɑpt] *vt* : adoptar — **adoption** [ə'dɑpʃən] *n* : adopción *f*

adore [ə'dor] *vt* **adored; adoring** 1 : adorar 2 LIKE, LOVE : encantarle (algo a uno) — **adorable** [ə'dorəbəl] *adj* : adorable — **adoration** [ˌædə'reɪæən] *n* : adoración *f*

adorn [ə'dorn] *vt* : adornar — **adornment** [ə'dornmənt] *n* : adorno *m*

adrift [ə'drɪft] *adj & adv* : a la deriva

adroit [ə'drɔɪt] *adj* : diestro, hábil

adult [ə'dʌlt, 'æˌdʌlt] *adj* : adulto — ~ *n* : adulto *m*, -ta *f*

adultery [ə'dʌltəri] *n*, *pl* -**teries** : adulterio *m*

advance [əd'vænts, əd-] *v* -**vanced; -vancing** *vt* : adelantar — *vi* : avanzar, adelantarse — ~ *n* 1 : avance *m* 2 PROGRESS : adelanto *m* 3 **in** ~ : por adelantado — **advancement** [əd'væntsmənt, əd-] *n* : adelanto *m*, progreso *m*

advantage [əd'væntɪdʒ, æd-] *n* 1 : ventaja *f* 2 **take** ~ **of** : aprovecharse de — **advantageous** [ˌæd,væn'teɪdʒəs, -vən-] *adj* : ventajoso

advent [æd,vent] *n* 1 ARRIVAL : llegada *f* 2 **Advent** : Adviento *m*

adventure [əd'ventʃər, əd-] *n* : aventura *f* — **adventurous** [æd'ventʃərəs, əd-] *adj* 1 : intrépido 2 RISKY : arriesgado

adverb [æd,vərb] *n* : adverbio *m*

adversary ['ædvərˌseri] *n*, *pl* -**saries** : adversario *m*, -ria *f*

adverse [æd'vərs, 'æd-] *adj* : adverso, desfavorable — **adversity** [æd'vərsəti, əd-] *n*, *pl* -**ties** : adversidad *f*

advertise ['ædvərˌtaɪz] *v* -**tised; -tising** *vt* : anunciar — *vi* : hacer publicidad — **advertisement** ['ædvər,taɪzmənt] *n* : anuncio *m* — **advertiser** ['ædvər,taɪzər] *n* : anunciante *mf* — **advertising** ['ædvər,taɪzɪŋ] *n* : publicidad *f*

advice [æd'vaɪs] *n* : consejo *m*

advise [æd'vaɪz, əd-] *vt* -**vised; -vising** 1 COUNSEL : aconsejar, asesorar 2 RECOMMEND : recomendar 3 INFORM : informar — **advisable** [æd'vaɪzəbəl, əd-] *adj* : aconsejable — **adviser** [æd'vaɪzər, əd-] *n* : consejero *m*, -ra *f*; asesor *m*, -sora *f* — **advisory** [æd'vaɪzəri, əd-] *adj* : consultivo

advocate ['ædvəˌkeɪt] *vt* -**cated; -cating** : recomendar — ~ ['ædvəkət] *n* : defensor *m*, -sora *f*

aerial ['æriəl] *adj* : aéreo — ~ *n* : antena *f*

aerobics [ˌær'o:bɪks] *ns & pl* : aeróbic *m*

aerodynamic [ˌæro:daɪ'næmɪk] *adj* : aerodinámico

aerosol ['ærəˌsɔl] *n* : aerosol *m*

aesthetic [ɛs'θɛtɪk] *adj* : estético

afar [ə'fɑr] *adv* : lejos

affable ['æfəbəl] *adj* : afable

affair [ə'fær] *n* 1 : asunto *m*, cuestión *f* 2 **or love** ~ : amorío *m*, aventura *f*

affect [ə'fɛkt, æ-] *vt* 1 : afectar 2 FEIGN : fingir — **affection** [ə'fɛkʃən] *n* : afecto *m*, cariño *m* — **affectionate** [ə'fɛkʃənət] *adj* : afectuoso, cariñoso

affinity [ə'fɪnəti] *n*, *pl* -**ties** : afinidad *f*

affirm [ə'fərm] *vt* : afirmar — **affirmative** [ə'fərmətɪv] *adj* : afirmativo

affix [ə'fɪks] *vt* : fijar, pegar

afflict [ə'flɪkt] *vt* : afligir — **affliction** [ə'flɪkʃən] *n* : aflicción *f*

affluent ['æˌfluːənt; æ'fluː-, ə-] *adj* : próspero, adinerado

afford [ə'ford] *vt* 1 : tener los recursos para, permitirse (el lujo de) 2 PROVIDE : brindar

affront [ə'frʌnt] *n* : afrenta *f*

afloat [ə'flot] *adv & adv* : a flote

afoot [ə'fut] *adj* : en marcha

afraid [ə'freɪd] *adj* 1 **be** ~ : tener miedo 2 **I'm** ~ **not** : me temo que no

African ['æfrɪkən] *adj* : africano

after ['æftər] *adv* 1 AFTERWARD : después 2 BEHIND : detrás, atrás — ~ *conj* : después de (que) — ~ *prep* 1 : después de 2 ~ **all** : después de todo 3 **it's ten** ~ **five** : son las cinco y diez

aftereffect ['æftərə,fɛkt] *n* : efecto *m* secundario

aftermath ['æftər,mæθ] *n* : consecuencias *fpl*

afternoon [ˌæftər'nuːn] *n* : tarde *f*

afterward ['æftərwərd] *or* **afterwards** [-wərdz] *adv* : después, más tarde

again [ə'gɛn, -'gɪn] *adv* 1 : otra vez, de nuevo 2 ~ **and** ~ : una y otra vez 3 **then** ~ : por otra parte

against [ə'gɛntst, -'gɪntst] *prep* : contra, en contra de

age ['eɪdʒ] *n* 1 : edad *f* 2 ERA : era *f*, época *f* 3 **be of** ~ : ser mayor de edad 4 **for** ~**s** : hace siglos 5 **old** ~ : vejez *f* — ~ *vi* **aged; aging** : envejecer — **aged** *adj* 1 ['eɪdʒəd, 'eɪdʒd] OLD : anciano, viejo 2 ['eɪdʒd] **children** ~ **10 to 17** : niños de 10 a 17 años

agency ['eɪdʒəntsi] *n*, *pl* -**cies** : agencia *f*

agenda [ə'dʒɛndə] *n* : orden *m* del día

agent ['eɪdʒənt] *n* : agente *mf*, representante *mf*

aggravate ['ægrəˌveɪt] *vt* -**vated; -vating**

1 WORSEN : agravar, empeorar **2** ANNOY : irritar

aggregate ['ægrɪgət] *adj* : total, global — ~ *n* : total *m*

aggression [ə'grɛʃən] *n* : agresión *f* — **aggressive** [ə'grɛsɪv] *adj* : agresivo — **aggressor** [ə'grɛsər] *n* : agresor *m*, -sora *f*

aghast [ə'gæst] *adj* : horrorizado

agile ['ædʒəl] *adj* : ágil — **agility** [ə'dʒɪləti] *n, pl* **-ties** : agilidad *f*

agitate ['ædʒə,teɪt] *v* **-tated; -tating** *vt* **1** SHAKE : agitar **2** TROUBLE : inquietar — **agitation** [,ædʒə'teɪʃən] *n* : agitación *f*, inquietud *f*

agnostic [æg'nɑstɪk] *n* : agnóstico *m*, -ca *f*

ago [ə'goː] *adv* **1** : hace **2** long ~ : hace mucho tiempo

agony ['ægəni] *n, pl* **-nies 1** PAIN : dolor *m* **2** ANGUISH : angustia *f* — **agonize** ['ægə,naɪz] *vi* **-nized; -nizing** : atormentarse — **agonizing** ['ægə,naɪzɪŋ] *adj* : angustioso

agree [ə'griː] *v* **agreed; agreeing** *vt* **1** : acordar *m* — *vi* **1** : estar de acuerdo de que — *vi* **1** : estar de acuerdo **2** CORRESPOND : concordar **3** ~ to : acceder a **4** this climate ~s with me : este clima me sienta bien — **agreeable** [ə'griːəbəl] *adj* **1** PLEASING : agradable **2** WILLING : dispuesto — **agreement** [ə'griːmənt] *n* : acuerdo *m*

agriculture ['ægrɪ,kʌltʃər] *n* : agricultura *f* — **agricultural** [,ægrɪ'kʌltʃərəl] *adj* : agrícola

aground [ə'graʊnd] *adv* run ~ : encallar

ahead [ə'hɛd] *adv* **1** IN FRONT : delante, adelante **2** BEFOREHAND : por adelantado **3** LEADING : a la delantera **4** get ~ : adelantar — **ahead of** *prep* **1** : delante de, antes de **2** get ~ of : adelantarse a

aid [eɪd] *vt* : ayudar — ~ *n* : ayuda *f*, asistencia *f*

AIDS ['eɪdz] *n* : SIDA *m*, sida *m*

ail ['eɪl] *vi* : estar enfermo — **ailment** ['eɪlmənt] *n* : enfermedad *f*

aim ['eɪm] *vt* : apuntar (un arma), dirigir (una observación) — *vi* **1** : apuntar **2** ASPIRE : aspirar — ~ *n* **1** : puntería *f* **2** GOAL : propósito *m*, objetivo *m* — **aimless** ['eɪmləs] *adj* : sin objetivo

air ['ær] *vt or* ~ out : airear **2** EXPRESS : expresar **3** BROADCAST : emitir — ~ *n* **1** : aire *m* **2** be on the ~ : estar en el aire — **air-conditioning** [,ærkən'dɪʃənɪŋ] *n* : aire *m* acondicionado — **air conditioned** ['ærkən,dɪʃənd] *n*

: climatizado — **aircraft** ['ær,kræft] *ns & pl* **1** : avión *m*, aeronave *f* **2** ~ **carrier** : portaaviones *m* — **air force** *n* : fuerza *f* aérea — **airline** ['ær,laɪn] *n* : aerolínea *f*, línea *f* aérea — **airliner** ['ær,laɪnər] *n* : avión *m* de pasajeros — **airmail** *n* : correo *m* aéreo — **airplane** ['ær,pleɪn] *n* : avión *m* — **airport** ['ær,port] *n* : aeropuerto *m* — **airstrip** ['ær,strɪp] *n* : pista *f* de aterrizaje — **airtight** ['ær,taɪt] *adj* : hermético — **airy** ['æri] *adj* **airier** [-iər]; **-est** : aireado, bien ventilado

aisle ['aɪl] *n* **1** : pasillo *m* **2** : nave *f* lateral (de una iglesia)

ajar [ə'dʒɑr] *adj* : entreabierto

akin [ə'kɪn] *adj* ~ to : semejante a

alarm [ə'lɑrm] *n* **1** : alarma *f* **2** ANXIETY : inquietud *f* — *vt* : alarmar, asustar — **alarm clock** : despertador *m*

alas [ə'læs] *interj* : ¡ay!

album ['ælbəm] *n* : álbum *m*

alcohol ['ælkə,hɔl] *n* : alcohol *m* — **alcoholic** [,ælkə'hɔlɪk] *adj* : alcohólico — ~ *n* : alcohólico *m*, -ca *f* — **alcoholism** ['ælkəhə,lɪzəm] *n* : alcoholismo *m*

alcove ['æl,koːv] *n* : nicho *m*, hueco *m*

ale ['eɪl] *n* : cerveza *f*

alert [ə'lərt] *adj* **1** WATCHFUL : alerta, atento **2** LIVELY : vivo — ~ *n* : alerta *f* — *vt* : alertar, poner sobre aviso

alfalfa [æl'fælfə] *n* : alfalfa *f*

alga ['ælgə] *n, pl* **-gae** [-dʒiː] : alga *f*

algebra ['ældʒəbrə] *n* : álgebra *f*

alias ['eɪliəs] *adv* : alias — ~ *n* : alias *m*

alibi ['ælə,baɪ] *n* : coartada *f*

alien ['eɪliən] *adj* : extranjero — ~ *n* **1** FOREIGNER : extranjero *m*, -ra *f* **2** EXTRATERRESTRIAL : extraterrestre *mf*

alienate ['eɪliə,neɪt] *vt* **-ated; -ating** : enajenar — **alienation** [,eɪliə'neɪæn] *n* : enajenación *f*

alight [ə'laɪt] *vi* **1** LAND : posarse **2** ~ **from** : apearse de

align [ə'laɪn] *vt* : alinear — **alignment** [ə'laɪnmənt] *n* : alineación *f*

alike [ə'laɪk] *adv* : igual, del mismo modo — ~ *adj* : parecido

alimony ['ælə,moʊni] *n, pl* **-nies** : pensión *f* alimenticia

alive [ə'laɪv] *adj* **1** LIVING : vivo, viviente **2** LIVELY : animado, activo

all ['ɔl] *adv* **1** COMPLETELY : todo, completamente **2** ~ **the better** : tanto mejor **3** ~ **the more** : aún más, todavía más — ~ *adj* : todo — ~ *pron* **1** : todo, -da **2** **in** ~ : en general **3** **not at** ~ : de ninguna manera —

all–around [,ɔlə'raʊnd] *adj* VERSATILE : completo

allay [ə'leɪ] *vt* 1 ALLEVIATE : aliviar 2 CALM : aquietar

allege [ə'ledʒ] *vt* -leged; -leging : alegar — allegation [,ælɪ'geɪʃən] *n* : alegato *m*, acusación *f* — alleged [ə'ledʒd, ə'ledʒəd] *adj* : presunto — allegedly [ə'ledʒədli] *adv* : supuestamente

allegiance [ə'liːdʒənts] *n* : lealtad *f*

allegory ['æləgori] *n*, *pl* -ries : alegoría *f* — allegorical [,ælə'gɔrɪkəl] *adj* : alegórico

allergy ['ælərdʒi] *n*, *pl* -gies : alergia *f* — allergic [ə'lərdʒɪk] *adj* : alérgico

alleviate [ə'liːviˌeɪt] *vt* -ated; -ating : aliviar

alley ['æli] *n*, *pl* -leys : callejón *m*

alliance [ə'laɪənts] *n* : alianza *f*

alligator ['æləˌgeɪtər] *n* : caimán *m*

allocate ['æləˌkeɪt] *vt* -cated; -cating : asignar — allocation [,ælə'keɪʃən] *n* : asignación *f*, reparto *m*

allot [ə'lɑt] *vt* -lotted; -lotting : asignar — allotment [ə'lɑtmənt] *n* : reparto *m*, asignación *f*

allow [ə'laʊ] *vt* 1 PERMIT : permitir 2 GRANT : dar, conceder 3 ADMIT : admitir 4 CONCEDE : reconocer — *vi* ~ for : tener en cuenta — allowance [ə'laʊənts] *n* 1 : pensión *f*, subsidio *m* 2 make ~s for : tener en cuenta, disculpar

alloy ['æˌlɔɪ, ə'lɔɪ] *n* : aleación *f*

all right *adv* 1 YES : sí, de acuerdo 2 WELL : bien 3 DEFINITELY : bien, sin duda — ~ *adj* : bien, bueno

allude [ə'luːd] *vi* -luded; -luding : aludir

allure [ə'lʊr] *vt* -lured; -luring : atraer — alluring [ə'lʊrɪŋ] *adj* : atrayente, seductor

allusion [ə'luːʒən] *n* : alusión *f*

ally [ə'laɪ, 'æˌlaɪ] *vi* -lied; -lying ~ oneself with : aliarse con — ~ ['æˌlaɪ, ə'laɪ] *n* : aliado *m*, -da *f*

almanac ['ɔlməˌnæk, 'æl-] *n* : almanaque *m*

almighty [ɔl'maɪti] *adj* : omnipotente, todopoderoso

almond ['ɑmənd, 'ɑl-, 'æ-, 'æl-] *n* : almendra *f*

almost ['ɔlˌmoːst, ɔl'moːst] *adv* : casi

alms ['ɑmz, 'ɑlmz, 'ælmz] *ns* & *pl* : limosna *f*

alone [ə'loːn] *adv* : sólo, solamente, únicamente — ~ *adj* : solo

along [ə'lɔŋ] *adv* 1 FORWARD : adelante 2 ~ with : con, junto con 3 all ~ : desde el principio — ~ *prep* : por, a lo largo de — alongside [ə,lɔŋ'saɪd]

adv : al costado — ~ or ~ of *prep* : al lado de

aloof [ə'luːf] *adj* : distante, reservado

aloud [ə'laʊd] *adv* : en voz alta

alphabet ['ælfəˌbɛt] *n* : alfabeto *m* — alphabetical [,ælfə'bɛtɪkəl] *or* alphabetic [-'bɛtɪk] *adj* : alfabético

already [ɔl'rɛdi] *adv* : ya

also ['ɔlˌsoː] *adv* : también, además

altar ['ɔltər] *n* : altar *m*

alter ['ɔltər] *vt* : alterar, modificar — alteration [,ɔltə'reɪʃən] *n* : alteración *f*, modificación *f*

alternate ['ɔltərnət] *adj* : alterno — ~ ['ɔltərˌneɪt] *v* -nated; -nating : alternar — alternating current *n* : corriente *f* alterna — alternative [ɔl'tərnəˌtɪv] *adj* : alternativo — ~ *n* : alternativa *f*

although [ɔl'ðoː] *conj* : aunque

altitude ['æltəˌtuːd, -ˌtjuːd] *n* : altitud *f*

altogether [,ɔltə'gɛðər] *adv* 1 COMPLETELY : completamente, del todo 2 ON THE WHOLE : en suma, en general

aluminum [ə'luːmənəm] *n* : aluminio *m*

always ['ɔlwiz, -ˌweɪz] *adv* 1 : siempre 2 FOREVER : para siempre

am → be

amass [ə'mæs] *vt* : amasar, acumular

amateur ['æmətˌʃər, -tər, -ˌtʊr, -ˌtjʊr] *adj* : amateur — ~ *n* : amateur *mf*; aficionado *m*, -da *f*

amaze [ə'meɪz] *vt* amazed; amazing : asombrar — amazement [ə'meɪzmənt] *n* : asombro *m* — amazing [ə'meɪzɪŋ] *adj* : asombroso

ambassador [æm'bæsədər] *n* : embajador *m*, -dora *f*

amber ['æmbər] *n* : ámbar *m*

ambiguous [æm'bɪgjuəs] *adj* : ambiguo — ambiguity [,æmbə'gjuːəˌti] *n*, *pl* -ties : ambigüedad *f*

ambition [æm'bɪʃən] *n* : ambición *f* — ambitious [æm'bɪʃəs] *adj* : ambicioso

ambivalence [æm'bɪvələnts] *n* : ambivalencia *f* — ambivalent [æm'bɪvələnt] *adj* : ambivalente

amble ['æmbəl] *vi* *or* ~ along : andar sin prisa

ambulance ['æmbjələnts] *n* : ambulancia *f*

ambush ['æmˌbʊʃ] *vt* : emboscar — ~ *n* : emboscada *f*

amen ['eɪˌmɛn, 'ɑ-] *interj* : amén

amenable [ə'miːnəbəl, -'mɛ-] *adj* ~ to : receptivo a

amend [ə'mɛnd] *vt* : enmendar — amendment [ə'mɛndmənt] *n* : enmienda *f* — amends [ə'mɛndz] *ns* & *p* make ~ for : reparar

amenities [ə'menəţiz, -'mi:-] *npl* : servicios *mpl*, comodidades *fpl*
American [ə'merɪkən] *adj* : americano
amethyst ['æməθəst] *n* : amatista *f*
amiable ['eɪmiəbəl] *adj* : amable, agradable
amicable ['æmɪkəbəl] *adj* : amigable, amistoso
amid [ə'mɪd] *or* **amidst** [ə'mɪdst] *prep* : en medio de, entre
amiss [ə'mɪs] *adv* **1** : mal **2 take sth ~** : tomar algo a mal — **~** *adj* **1** WRONG : malo **2 something is ~** : algo anda mal
ammonia [ə'mo:njə] *n* : amoníaco *m*
ammunition [ˌæmjə'nɪʃən] *n* : municiones *fpl*
amnesia [æm'ni:ʒə] *n* : amnesia *f*
amnesty ['æmnəsti] *n*, *pl* **-ties** : amnistía *f*
among [ə'mʌŋ] *prep* : entre
amorous ['æmərəs] *adj* : amoroso
amount [ə'maʊnt] *vi* **1 ~ to** : equivaler a **2 ~ to** TOTAL : sumar, ascender a — **~** *n* : cantidad *f*
amphibian [æm'fɪbiən] *n* : anfibio *m* — **amphibious** [æm'fɪbiəs] *adj* : anfibio
amphitheater ['æmfəˌθi:əţər] *n* : anfiteatro *m*
ample ['æmpəl] *adj* **-pler; -plest 1** SPACIOUS : amplio, extenso **2** ABUNDANT : abundante
amplify ['æmpləˌfaɪ] *vt* **-fied; -fying** : amplificar — **amplifier** ['æmpləˌfaɪər] *n* : amplificador *m*
amputate ['æmpjəˌteɪt] *vt* **-tated; -tating** : amputar — **amputation** [ˌæmpjə'teɪʃən] *n* : amputación *f*
amuse [ə'mju:z] *vt* **amused; amusing** : hacer reír, divertir **2** ENTERTAIN : entretener — **amusement** [ə'mju:zmənt] *n* : diversión *f* — **amusing** *adj* : divertido
an → a²
analogy [ə'nælədʒi] *n*, *pl* **-gies** : analogía *f* — **analogous** [ə'næləgəs] *adj* : análogo
analysis [ə'næləsəs] *n*, *pl* **-yses** [-ˌsi:z] : análisis *m* — **analytic** [ˌænə'lɪţɪk] *or* **analytical** [-ţɪkəl] *adj* : analítico — **analyze** ['ænəˌlaɪz] *vt* **-lyzed; -lyzing** : analizar
anarchy ['ænərki, -nɑr-] *n* : anarquía *f*
anatomy [ə'næţəmi] *n*, *pl* **-mies** : anatomía *f* — **anatomic** [ˌænə'tɑmɪk] *or* **anatomical** [-mɪkəl] *adj* : anatómico
ancestor ['ænˌsestər] *n* : antepasado *m*, -da *f* — **ancestral** [æn'sestrəl] *adj* : ancestral — **ancestry** ['ænˌsestri] *n* **1** DE-

SCENT : linaje *m*, abolengo *m* **2** ANCESTORS : antepasados *mpl*, -das *fpl*
anchor ['æŋkər] *n* **1** : ancla *f* **2** : presentador *m*, -dora *f* (en televisión) — **~** *vt* **1** : anclar **2** FASTEN : sujetar — *vi* : anclar
anchovy ['ænˌtʃo:vi, æn'tʃo:-] *n*, *pl* **-vies** *or* **-vy** : anchoa *f*
ancient ['eɪntʃənt] *adj* : antiguo, viejo
and ['ænd] *conj* **1** : y (e *before words beginning with i-* or *hi-*) **2 come ~ see** : ven a ver **3 more ~ more** : cada vez más **4 try ~ finish it soon** : trata de terminarlo pronto
anecdote ['ænɪkˌdoːt] *n* : anécdota *f*
anemia [ə'ni:miə] *n* : anemia *f* — **anemic** [ə'ni:mɪk] *adj* : anémico
anesthesia [ˌænəs'θi:ʒə] *n* : anestesia *f* — **anesthetic** [ˌænəs'θeţɪk] *adj* : anestésico — **~** *n* : anestésico *m*
anew [ə'nu:, -'nju:] *adv* : de nuevo, nuevamente
angel ['eɪndʒəl] *n* : ángel *m* — **angelic** [æn'dʒelɪk] *or* **angelical** [-lɪkəl] *adj* : angélico
anger ['æŋɡər] *vt* : enojar, enfadar — **~** *n* : ira *f*, enojo *m*, enfado *m*
angle *n* **1** : ángulo *m* **2** POINT OF VIEW : perspectiva *f*, punto de vista — **angler** ['æŋɡlər] *n* : pescador *m*, -dora *f*
Anglo–Saxon [ˌæŋɡlo'sæksən] *adj* : anglosajón
angry ['æŋɡri] *adj* **-grier; -est** : enojado, enfadado
anguish ['æŋɡwɪʃ] *n* : angustia *f*
angular ['æŋɡjələr] *adj* **1** : angular **2 ~ features** : rasgos *mpl* angulosos
animal ['ænəməl] *n* : animal *m*
animate ['ænəmət] *adj* : animado — **~** ['ænəˌmeɪt] *vt* **-mated; -mating** : animar — **animated** *adj* **1** : animado **2 ~ cartoon** : dibujos *mpl* animados — **animation** [ˌænə'meɪʃən] *n* : animación *f*
animosity [ˌænə'mɑsəţi] *n*, *pl* **-ties** : animosidad *f*
anise ['ænəs] *n* : anís *m*
ankle ['æŋkəl] *n* : tobillo *m*
annals ['ænəlz] *npl* : anales *mpl*
annex [ə'neks, 'æˌneks] *vt* : anexar — **~** ['æˌneks, -nɪks] *n* : anexo *m*
annihilate [ə'naɪəˌleɪt] *vt* **-lated; -lating** : aniquilar — **annihilation** [əˌnaɪə'leɪʃən] *n* : aniquilación *f*
anniversary [ˌænə'vərsəri] *n*, *pl* **-ries** : aniversario *m*
annotate ['ænəˌteɪt] *vt* **-tated; -tating** : anotar — **annotation** [ˌænə'teɪʃən] *n* : anotación *f*
announce [ə'naʊns] *vt* **-nounced;**

-nouncing : anunciar — **announce-ment** [ə'naʊntsmənt] n : anuncio m — **announcer** [ə'naʊntsər] n : locutor m, -tora f

annoy [ə'nɔɪ] vt : fastidiar, molestar — **annoyance** [ə'nɔɪənts] n : fastidio m, molestia f — **annoying** [ə'nɔɪɪŋ] adj : molesto, fastidioso

annual ['ænjuəl] adj : anual — ~ n : anuario m

annuity [ə'nuːəti] n, pl **-ties** : anualidad f

annul [ə'nʌl] vt **annulled; annulling** : anular — **annulment** [ə'nʌlmənt] n : anulación f

anoint [ə'nɔɪnt] vt : ungir

anomaly [ə'nɑməli] n, pl **-lies** : anomalía f

anonymous [ə'nɑnəməs] adj : anónimo — **anonymity** [ˌænə'nɪməti] n : anonimato m

another [ə'nʌðər] adj 1 : otro 2 **in** ~ **minute** : en un minuto más — ~ pron : otro, otra

answer ['æntsər] n 1 REPLY : respuesta f, contestación f 2 SOLUTION : solución f — ~ vt 1 : contestar a, responder a 2 ~ **the door** : abrir la puerta — vi : contestar, responder

ant ['ænt] n : hormiga f

antagonize [æn'tægə,naɪz] vt **-nized; -nizing** : provocar la enemistad de — **antagonism** [æn'tægə,nɪzəm] n : antagonismo m

antarctic [æn'tɑrktɪk, -'ɑrt̬ɪk] adj : antártico

antelope ['æntəl,oːp] n, pl **-lope** or **-lopes** : antílope m

antenna [æn'tenə] n, pl **-nae** [-ˌniː, -ˌnaɪ] or **-nas** : antena f

anthem ['ænθəm] n : himno m

anthology [æn'θɑlədʒi] n, pl **-gies** : antología f

anthropology [ˌænθrə'pɑlədʒi] n : antropología f

antibiotic [ˌæntibai'ɑtɪk, ˌæntaɪ-, -bi-] adj : antibiótico — ~ n : antibiótico m

antibody ['ænti,bɑdi] n, pl **-bodies** : anticuerpo m

anticipate [æn'tɪsə,peɪt] vt **-pated; -pating** 1 FORESEE : anticipar, prever 2 EXPECT : esperar — **anticipation** [æn,tɪsə'peɪʃən] n : anticipación f, expectación f

antics ['ænt̬ɪks] npl : payasadas fpl

antidote ['ænti,doːt] n : antídoto m

antifreeze ['ænti,friːz] n : anticongelante m

antipathy [æn'tɪpəθi] n, pl **-thies** : antipatía f

antiquated ['æntə,kweɪt̬əd] adj : anticuado

antique [æn'tiːk] adj : antiguo — ~ n : antigüedad f — **antiquity** [æn'tɪkwə-ti] n, pl **-ties** : antigüedad f

anti–Semitic [ˌæntisə'mɪt̬ɪk, ˌæntaɪ-] adj : antisemita

antiseptic [ˌæntə'septɪk] adj : antiséptico — ~ n : antiséptico m

antisocial [ˌænti'soː'ʃəl, ˌæntaɪ-] adj 1 : antisocial 2 UNSOCIABLE : poco sociable

antithesis [æn'tɪθəsɪs] n, pl **-eses** [-ˌsiːz] : antítesis f

antlers ['æntlərz] npl : cornamenta f

antonym ['æntə,nɪm] n : antónimo m

anus ['eɪnəs] n : ano m

anvil ['ænvəl, -vɪl] n : yunque m

anxiety [æŋk'zaɪəti] n, pl **-eties** 1 APPREHENSION : inquietud f, ansiedad f 2 EAGERNESS : anhelo m — **anxious** ['æŋkʃəs] adj 1 WORRIED : inquieto, preocupado 2 EAGER : ansioso — **anxiously** ['æŋkʃəsli] adv : con ansiedad

any ['eni] adv 1 SOMEWHAT : algo, un poco 2 **it's not** ~ **good** : no sirve para nada 3 **we can't wait** ~ **longer** : no podemos esperar más — ~ adj 1 : alguno 2 (in negative constructions) : ningún 3 WHATEVER : cualquier 4 **in** ~ **case** : en todo caso — ~ pron 1 : alguno, -na 2 : ninguno, -na 3 **do you want** ~ **more rice?** : ¿quieres más arroz?

anybody ['eni,bʌdi, -,bɑ-] → **anyone**

anyhow ['eni,haʊ] adv 1 : de todas formas 2 HAPHAZARDLY : de cualquier modo

anymore [ˌeni'mor] adv **not** ~ : ya no

anyone ['eni,wʌn] pron 1 SOMEONE : alguien 2 WHOEVER : quienquiera 3 **I don't see** ~ : no veo a nadie

anyplace ['eni,pleɪs] → **anywhere**

anything ['eni,θɪŋ] pron 1 SOMETHING : algo, alguna cosa 2 (in negative constructions) : nada 3 WHATEVER : cualquier cosa, lo que sea

anytime ['eni,taɪm] adv : en cualquier momento

anyway ['eni,weɪ] → **anyhow**

anywhere ['eni,ʰwer] adv 1 : en cualquier parte, dondequiera 2 (used in questions) : en algún sitio 3 **I can't find it** ~ : no lo encuentro por ningun na parte

apart [ə'pɑrt] adv 1 : aparte 2 ~ **fron** : excepto, aparte de 3 **fall** ~ : deshac erse, hacerse pedazos 4 **live** ~ : vivi separados 5 **take** ~ : desmontar, des mantelar

apartment [ə'partmənt] n : apartamento m

apathy ['æpəθi] n : apatía f — **apathetic** [,æpə'θεtɪk] adj : apático, indiferente

ape n : simio m

aperture ['æpərtʃər, -,tʃʊr] n : abertura f

apex ['eɪ,pεks] n, pl **apexes** or **apices** ['eɪpə,siːz, 'æ-] : ápice m, cumbre f

apiece [ə'piːs] adv : cada uno

aplomb [ə'plam, -'plʌm] n : aplomo m

apology [ə'palədʒi] n, pl **-gies** : disculpa f — **apologetic** [ə,palə'dʒεtɪk] adj : lleno de disculpas — **apologize** [ə'palə,dʒaɪz] vi **-gized; -gizing** : disculparse, pedir perdón

apostle [ə'pasəl] n : apóstol m

apostrophe [ə'pastrə,fiː] n : apóstrofo m

appall [ə'pɔl] vt : horrorizar — **appalling** [ə'pɔlɪŋ] adj : horroroso

apparatus [,æpə'rætəs, -'reɪ-] n, pl **-tuses** or **-tus** : aparato m

apparel [ə'pærəl] n : ropa f

apparent [ə'pærənt] adj 1 OBVIOUS : claro, evidente 2 SEEMING : aparente — **apparently** [ə'pærəntli] adv : al parecer, por lo visto

apparition [,æpə'rɪʃən] n : aparición f

appeal [ə'piːl] vi 1 ~ **for** : solicitar 2 ~ **to** : apelar a (la bondad de algn, etc.) 3 ~ **to** ATTRACT : atraer a — ~ n 1 : apelación f (en derecho) 2 REQUEST : llamamiento m 3 ATTRACTION : atractivo m — **appealing** [ə'piːlɪŋ] adj : atractivo

appear [ə'pɪr] vi 1 : aparecer 2 : comparecer (ante un tribunal), actuar (en el teatro) 3 SEEM : parecer — **appearance** [ə'pɪrəns] n 1 : aparición f 2 LOOK : apariencia f, aspecto m

appease [ə'piːz] vt **-peased; -peasing** : apaciguar, aplacar

appendix [ə'pεndɪks] n, pl **-dixes** or **-dices** [-də,siːz] : apéndice m — **appendicitis** [ə,pεndə'saɪtəs] n : apendicitis f

appetite ['æpə,taɪt] n : apetito m — **appetizer** ['æpə,taɪzər] n : aperitivo m — **appetizing** ['æpə,taɪzɪŋ] adj : apetitoso

applaud [ə'plɔd] v : aplaudir — **applause** [ə'plɔz] n : aplauso m

apple ['æpəl] n : manzana f

appliance [ə'plaɪəns] n : aparato m

apply [ə'plaɪ] v **-plied; -plying** vt 1 : aplicar 2 ~ **oneself** : aplicarse — vi 1 : aplicarse 2 ~ **for** : solicitar, pedir — **applicable** ['æplɪkəbəl, ə'plɪkə-] adj : aplicable — **applicant** ['æplɪkənt] n : solicitante mf, candidato m, -ta f — **application** [,æplə'keɪʃən] n 1 : apli-

cación f 2 : solicitud f (para un empleo, etc.)

appoint [ə'pɔɪnt] vt 1 NAME : nombrar 2 FIX, SET : fijar, señalar — **appointment** [ə'pɔɪntmənt] n 1 APPOINTING : nombramiento m 2 ENGAGEMENT : cita f

apportion [ə'porʃən] vt : distribuir, repartir

appraise [ə'preɪz] vt **-praised; -praising** : evaluar, valorar — **appraisal** [ə-'preɪzəl] n : evaluación f

appreciate [ə'priːʃi,eɪt, -'prɪ-] v **-ated; -ating** vt 1 VALUE : apreciar 2 UNDERSTAND : darse cuenta de 3 I ~ **your help** : te agradezco tu ayuda — vi : aumentar en valor — **appreciation** [ə,priːʃi'eɪʃən, -,prɪ-] n 1 GRATITUDE : agradecimiento m 2 VALUING : apreciación f, valoración f — **appreciative** [ə'priːʃəṭɪv, -'prɪ-; ə'priːʃi,eɪ-] adj 1 : apreciativo 2 GRATEFUL : agradecido

apprehend [,æprɪ'hεnd] vt 1 ARREST : aprehender, detener 2 DREAD : temer 3 COMPREHEND : comprender — **apprehension** [,æprɪ'hεntʃən] n 1 ARREST : detención f, aprehensión f 2 ANXIETY : aprensión f, temor m — **apprehensive** [,æprɪ'hεntsɪv] adj : aprensivo, inquieto

apprentice [ə'prεntɪs] n : aprendiz m, -diza f

approach [ə'proːtʃ] vt 1 NEAR : acercarse a 2 : dirigirse a (algn), abordar (un problema, etc.) — vi : acercarse — ~ n 1 NEARING : acercamiento m 2 POSITION : enfoque m 3 ACCESS : acceso m — **approachable** [ə'proːtʃəbəl] adj : accesible, asequible

appropriate [ə'proːpri,eɪt] vt **-ated; -ating** : apropiarse de — ~ [ə'proːpriət] adj : apropiado

approve [ə'pruːv] vt **-proved; -proving** : aprobar — **approval** [ə'pruːvəl] n : aprobación f

approximate [ə'praksəmət] adj : aproximado — ~ [ə'praksə,meɪt] vt **-mated; -mating** : aproximarse a — **approximately** [ə'praksəmətli] adv : aproximadamente

apricot ['æprə,kat, 'eɪ-] n : albaricoque m, chabacano m Lat

April ['eɪprəl] n : abril m

apron ['eɪprən] n : delantal m

apropos [,æprə'poː, 'æprə,poː] adv : a propósito

apt ['æpt] adj 1 FITTING : apto, apropiado 2 LIABLE : propenso — **aptitude** ['æptə,tuːd, -,tjuːd] n : aptitud f

aquarium [ə'kwæriəm] n, pl **-iums** or **-ia** [-iə] : acuario m

aquatic [ə'kwɑtɪk, -'kwæ-] adj : acuático

aqueduct ['ækwə,dʌkt] n : acueducto m

Arab ['ærəb] adj : árabe — **Arabic** ['ærəbɪk] adj : árabe — ~ n : árabe m (idioma)

arbitrary ['ɑrbə,treri] adj : arbitrario

arbitrate ['ɑrbə,treɪt] v -**trated**; -**trating** : arbitrar — **arbitration** [,ɑrbə'treɪʃən] n : arbitraje m

arc ['ɑrk] n : arco m

arcade [ɑr'keɪd] n 1 : arcada f 2 **shopping** ~ : galería f comercial

arch ['ɑrtʃ] n : arco m — ~ vt : arquear — vi : arquearse

archaeology or **archeology** [,ɑrki'ɑlədʒi] n : arqueología f — **archaeological** [,ɑrkiə'lɑdʒɪkəl] adj : arqueológico — **archaeologist** [,ɑrki'ɑlədʒɪst] n : arqueólogo m, -ga f

archaic [ɑr'keɪɪk] adj : arcaico

archbishop [ɑrtʃ'bɪʃəp] n : arzobispo m

archery ['ɑrtʃəri] n : tiro m al arco

archipelago [,ɑrkə'pelə,goː, ,ɑrtʃə-] n, pl -**goes** or -**gos** [-goːz] : archipiélago m

architecture ['ɑrkə,tektʃər] n : arquitectura f — **architect** ['ɑrkə,tekt] n : arquitecto m, -ta f — **architectural** [,ɑrkə'tektʃərəl] adj : arquitectónico

archives ['ɑr,kaɪvz] npl : archivo m

archway ['ɑrtʃ,weɪ] n : arco m (de entrada)

arctic ['ɑrktɪk, 'ɑrt-] adj : ártico

ardent ['ɑrdənt] adj : ardiente, fervoroso — **ardor** ['ɑrdər] n : ardor m, fervor m

arduous ['ɑrdʒuəs] adj : arduo

are → **be**

area ['æriə] n 1 REGION : área f, zona f 2 FIELD : campo m 3 ~ **code** : código m de la zona Lat, prefijo m Spain

arena [ə'riːnə] n : arena f, ruedo m

aren't ['ɑrnt, 'ɑrənt] (contraction of **are not**) → **be**

Argentine ['ɑrdʒən,taɪn, -,tiːn] or **Argentinean** or **Argentinian** [,ɑrdʒən'tɪniən] adj : argentino

argue ['ɑr,gjuː] v -**gued**; -**guing** vi 1 QUARREL : discutir 2 ~ **against** : argumentar contra — vt : argumentar, sostener — **argument** ['ɑrgjəmənt] n 1 QUARREL : disputa f, discusión f 2 REASONING : argumentos mpl

arid ['ærəd] adj : árido — **aridity** [ə'rɪdəti, æ-] n : aridez f

arise [ə'raɪz] vi **arose** [ə'roːz]; **arisen** [ə'rɪzən]; **arising** 1 : levantarse 2 ~ **from** : surgir de

aristocracy [,ærə'stɑkrəsi] n, pl -**cies** : aristocracia f — **aristocrat** [ə'rɪstə-

,kræt] n : aristócrata mf — **aristocratic** [ə,rɪstə'krætɪk] adj : aristocrático

arithmetic [ə'rɪθmə,tɪk] n : aritmética f

ark ['ɑrk] n : arca f

arm ['ɑrm] n 1 : brazo m 2 WEAPON : arma f — ~ vt : armar — **armament** ['ɑrməmənt] n : armamento m — **armchair** ['ɑrm,tʃer] n : sillón m — **armed** ['ɑrmd] adj 1 ~ **forces** : fuerzas fpl armadas 2 ~ **robbery** : robo m a mano armada

armistice ['ɑrməstɪs] n : armisticio m

armor or Brit **armour** ['ɑrmər] n : armadura f — **armored** or Brit **armoured** ['ɑrmərd] adj : blindado, acorazado — **armory** or Brit **armoury** ['ɑrmri, 'ɑrməri] : arsenal m

armpit ['ɑrm,pɪt] n : axila f, sobaco m

army ['ɑrmi] n, pl -**mies** : ejército m

aroma [ə'roːmə] n : aroma m — **aromatic** [,ærə'mætɪk] adj : aromático

around [ə'raʊnd] adv 1 : de circunferencia 2 NEARBY : por ahí 3 APPROXIMATELY : más o menos, aproximadamente 4 **all** ~ : por todos lados, todo alrededor 5 **turn** ~ : voltearse — ~ prep 1 SURROUNDING : alrededor de 2 THROUGHOUT : por 3 NEAR : cerca de 4 ~ **the corner** : a la vuelta de la esquina

arouse [ə'raʊz] vt **aroused**; **arousing** 1 AWAKE : despertar 2 EXCITE : excitar

arrange [ə'reɪndʒ] vt -**ranged**; -**ranging** : arreglar, poner en orden — **arrangement** [ə'reɪndʒmənt] n 1 ORDER : arreglo m 2 ~**s** npl : preparativos mpl

array [ə'reɪ] n : selección f, surtido m

arrears [ə'rɪrz] npl 1 : atrasos mpl 2 **be in** ~ : estar atrasado en pagos

arrest [ə'rest] vt : detener — ~ n 1 : arresto m, detención f 2 **under** ~ : detenido

arrive [ə'raɪv] vi -**rived**; -**riving** : llegar — **arrival** [ə'raɪvəl] n : llegada f

arrogance ['ærəgənts] n : arrogancia f — **arrogant** ['ærəgənt] adj : arrogante

arrow ['æroː] n : flecha f

arsenal ['ɑrsənəl] n : arsenal m

arsenic ['ɑrsənɪk] n : arsénico m

arson ['ɑrsən] n : incendio m premeditado

art ['ɑrt] n 1 : arte m 2 ~**s** npl : letras fpl (en educación) 3 **fine** ~**s** : bellas artes fpl

artefact Brit → **artifact**

artery ['ɑrtəri] n, pl -**teries** : arteria f

artful ['ɑrtfəl] adj : astuto, taimado

arthritis [ɑr'θraɪtəs] n, pl -**tides** [ɑr'θrɪtə,diːz] : artritis f — **arthritic** [ɑr'θrɪtɪk] adj : artrítico

artichoke [ˈɑrtəˌtʃoːk] n : alcachofa f
article [ˈɑrtɪkəl] n : artículo m
articulate [ɑrˈtɪkjəˌleɪt] vt **-lated; -lating** : articular — ~ [ɑrˈtɪkjələt] adj be ~ : expresarse bien
artifact or Brit **artefact** [ˈɑrtəˌfækt] n : artefacto m
artificial [ˌɑrtəˈfɪʃəl] adj : artificial
artillery [ɑrˈtɪləri] n, pl **-leries** : artillería f
artisan [ˈɑrtəzən, -sən] n : artesano m, -na f
artist [ˈɑrtɪst] n : artista mf — **artistic** [ɑrˈtɪstɪk] adj : artístico
as [ˈæz] adv 1 : tan, tanto 2 ~ **much** : tanto como 3 ~ **tall** : tan alto como 4 ~ **well** : también — ~ conj 1 WHILE : mientras 2 (referring to manner) : como 3 SINCE : ya que 4 THOUGH : por más que — ~ prep 1 : de 2 LIKE : como — ~ pron : que
asbestos [æzˈbɛstəs, æs-] n : asbesto m, amianto m
ascend [əˈsɛnd] vi : ascender, subir — vt : subir (a) — **ascent** [əˈsɛnt] n : ascensión f, subida f
ascertain [ˌæsərˈteɪn] vt : averiguar, determinar
ascribe [əˈskraɪb] vt **-cribed; -cribing** : atribuir
as for prep : en cuanto a
ash¹ [ˈæʃ] n : ceniza f
ash² n : fresno m (árbol)
ashamed [əˈʃeɪmd] adj : avergonzado, apenado Lat
ashore [əˈʃor] adv 1 : en tierra 2 go ~ : desembarcar
ashtray [ˈæʃˌtreɪ] n : cenicero m
Asian [ˈeɪʒən, -ʃən] adj : asiático
aside [əˈsaɪd] adv 1 : a un lado 2 APART : aparte 3 set ~ : guardar — **aside from** prep 1 BESIDES : además de 2 EXCEPT : aparte de, menos
as if conj : como si
ask [ˈæsk] vt 1 : preguntar 2 REQUEST : pedir 3 INVITE : invitar — vi : preguntar
askance [əˈskænts] adv look ~ : mirar de soslayo
askew [əˈskju:] adj : torcido, ladeado
asleep [əˈsliːp] adj 1 : dormido 2 fall ~ : dormirse, quedarse dormido
as of prep : desde, a partir de
asparagus [əˈspærəgəs] n : espárrago m
aspect [ˈæˌspɛkt] n : aspecto m
asphalt [ˈæsˌfɔlt] n : asfalto m
asphyxiate [æsˈfɪksiˌeɪt] v **-ated; -ating** vt : asfixiar — **asphyxiation** [æsˌfɪksiˈeɪʃən] n : asfixia f
aspire [əˈspaɪr] vi **-pired; -piring** : aspirar — **aspiration** [ˌæspəˈreɪʃən] n : aspiración f
aspirin [ˈæsprən, ˈæspə-] n, pl **aspirin** or **aspirins** : aspirina f
ass [ˈæs] n 1 : asno m 2 IDIOT : imbécil mf, idiota mf
assail [əˈseɪl] vt : atacar, asaltar — **assailant** [əˈseɪlənt] n : asaltante mf, atacante mf
assassin [əˈsæsən] n : asesino m, -na f — **assassinate** [əˈsæsənˌeɪt] vt **-nated; -nating** : asesinar — **assassination** [əˌsæsənˈeɪʃən] n : asesinato m
assault [əˈsɔlt] n 1 : ataque m, asalto m 2 : agresión f (contra algn) — ~ vt : atacar, asaltar
assemble [əˈsɛmbəl] v **-bled; -bling** vt 1 GATHER : reunir, juntar 2 CONSTRUCT : montar — vi : reunirse — **assembly** [əˈsɛmbli] n, pl **-blies** 1 MEETING : reunión f, asamblea f 2 CONSTRUCTING : montaje m
assent [əˈsɛnt] vi : asentir, consentir — ~ n : asentimiento m
assert [əˈsərt] vt 1 : afirmar 2 ~ oneself : hacerse valer — **assertion** [əˈsərʃən] n : afirmación f — **assertive** [əˈsərtɪv] adj : firme, enérgico
assess [əˈsɛs] vt : evaluar, valorar — **assessment** [əˈsɛsmənt] n : evaluación f, valoración f
asset [ˈæˌsɛt] n 1 : ventaja f, recurso m 2 ~s npl : bienes mpl, activo m
assiduous [əˈsɪdʒuəs] adj : asiduo
assign [əˈsaɪn] vt 1 APPOINT : designar, nombrar 2 ALLOT : asignar — **assignment** [əˈsaɪnmənt] n 1 TASK : misión f 2 HOMEWORK : tarea f 3 ASSIGNING : asignación f
assimilate [əˈsɪməˌleɪt] vt **-lated; -lating** : asimilar
assist [əˈsɪst] vt : ayudar — **assistance** [əˈsɪstənts] n : ayuda f — **assistant** [əˈsɪstənt] n : ayudante mf
associate [əˈsoːʃiˌeɪt, -si-] v **-ated; -ating** vt : asociar — vi : asociarse — ~ [əˈsoːʃiət, -siət] n : asociado m, -da f; socio m, -cia f — **association** [əˌsoːʃiˈeɪʃən, -si-] n : asociación f
as soon as conj : tan pronto como
assorted [əˈsɔrtəd] adj : surtido — **assortment** [əˈsɔrtmənt] n : surtido m, variedad f
assume [əˈsuːm] vt **-sumed; -suming** 1 SUPPOSE : suponer 2 UNDERTAKE : asumir 3 TAKE ON : adquirir, tomar — **assumption** [əˈsʌmpʃən] n : suposición f
assure [əˈʃur] vt **-sured; -suring** : asegurar — **assurance** [əˈʃurənts] n 1

CERTAINTY : certeza *f*, garantía *f* 2 CON-
FIDENCE : confianza *f*, seguridad *f* (de
sí mismo)

asterisk ['æstərˌrɪsk] *n* : asterisco *m*

asthma ['æzmə] *n* : asma *m*

as though → as if

as to *prep* : sobre, acerca de

astonish [ə'stɑnɪʃ] *vt* : asombrar — **as-tonishing** [ə'stɑnɪʃɪŋ] *adj* : asombroso
— **astonishment** [ə'stɑnɪʃmənt] *n*
: asombro *m*

astound [ə'staʊnd] *vt* : asombrar, pas-mar — **astounding** [ə'staʊndɪŋ] *adj*
: asombroso, pasmoso

astray [ə'streɪ] *adv* 1 go ~ : extraviarse
2 lead ~ : llevar por mal camino

astrology [ə'strɑlədʒi] *n* : astrología *f*

astronaut ['æstrəˌnɔt] *n* : astronauta *mf*

astronomy [ə'strɑnəmi] *n, pl* **-mies**
: astronomía *f* — **astronomer** [ə-
'strɑnəmər] *n* : astrónomo *m*, -ma *f* —
astronomical [ˌæstrə'nɑmɪkəl] *adj* : astronómico

astute [ə'stuːt, -'stjuːt] *adj* : astuto, sagaz
— **astuteness** [ə'stuːtnəs, -'stjuːt-] *n*
: astucia *f*

as well as *conj* : tanto como — ~ *prep*
: además de, aparte de

asylum [ə'saɪləm] *n* 1 : asilo *m* 2 **insane**
~ : manicomio *m*

at ['æt] *prep* 1 : a 2 ~ **home** : en casa 3
~ **night** : en la noche, por la noche 4
~ **two o'clock** : a las dos 5 **be angry**
~ : estar enojado con 6 **laugh**
~ : reírse de — **at all** *adv* **not** ~ : en absoluto, nada

ate → eat

atheist ['eɪθiːɪst] *n* : ateo *m*, atea *f* —
atheism *n* ['eɪθiˌɪzəm] : ateísmo *m*

athlete ['æθˌliːt] *n* : atleta *mf* — **athletic**
[æθ'lɛtɪk] *adj* : atlético — **athletics**
[æθ'lɛtɪks] *ns & pl* : atletismo *m*

atlas ['ætləs] *n* : atlas *m*

atmosphere ['ætməˌsfɪr] *n* 1 : atmósfera
f 2 AMBIENCE : ambiente *m* — **atmospheric** [ˌætmə'sfɪrɪk, -'sfɛr-] *adj* : atmosférico

atom ['ætəm] *n* : átomo *m* — **atomic** [ə-
'tɑmɪk] *adj* : atómico

atomizer ['ætəˌmaɪzər] *n* : atomizador *m*

atone [ə'toːn] *vt* **atoned; atoning** ~ **for**
: expiar

atrocity [ə'trɑsəti] *n, pl* **-ties** : atrocidad
f — **atrocious** [ə'troːʃəs] *adj* : atroz

atrophy ['ætrəfi] *vi* **-phied; -phying**
: atrofiarse

attach [ə'tætʃ] *vt* 1 : sujetar, atar 2 : adjuntar (un documento, etc.) 3 ~ **importance to** : atribuir importancia a 4
become ~**ed to s.o.** : encariñarse

con algn — **attachment** [ə'tætʃmənt] *n*
1 ACCESSORY : accesorio *m* 2 FOND-
NESS : cariño *m*

attack [ə'tæk] *v* : atacar — ~ *n* : ataque
m — **attacker** [ə'tækər] *n* : agresor *m*,
-sora *f*

attain [ə'teɪn] *vt* : lograr, alcanzar — **attainment** [ə'teɪnmənt] *n* : logro *m*

attempt [ə'tɛmpt] *vt* : intentar — ~ *n*
: intento *m*

attend [ə'tɛnd] *vt* : asistir a — *vi* 1 : asistir 2 ~ **to** : ocuparse de — **attendance** [ə'tɛndənts] *n* 1 : asistencia *f* 2
TURNOUT : concurrencia *f* — **attendant** *n* : encargado *m*, -da *f*; asistente
mf

attention [ə'tɛntʃən] *n* 1 : atención *f* 2
pay ~ : prestar atención, hacer caso
— **attentive** [ə'tɛntɪv] *adj* : atento

attest [ə'tɛst] *vt* : atestiguar

attic ['ætɪk] *n* : desván *m*

attire [ə'taɪr] *n* : atavío *m*

attitude ['ætəˌtuːd, -ˌtjuːd] *n* 1 : actitud *f* 2
POSTURE : postura *f*

attorney [ə'tərni] *n, pl* **-neys** : abogado
m, -da *f*

attract [ə'trækt] *vt* : atraer — **attraction**
[ə'trækʃən] *n* 1 : atracción *f* 2 APPEAL
: atractivo *m* — **attractive** [ə'træktɪv]
adj : atractivo, atrayente

attribute ['ætrəˌbjuːt] *n* : atributo *m* — ~
[ə'trɪˌbjuːt] *vt* **-tributed; -tributing**
: atribuir, imputar

auburn ['ɔbərn] *adj* : castaño rojizo

auction ['ɔkʃən] *n* : subasta *f* — ~ *vt or*
~ **off** : subastar

audacious [ɔ'deɪʃəs] *adj* : audaz — **audacity** [ɔ'dæsəti] *n, pl* **-ties** : audacia *f*,
atrevimiento *m*

audible ['ɔdəbəl] *adj* : audible

audience ['ɔdiənts] *n* 1 INTERVIEW : audiencia *f* 2 PUBLIC : público *m*

audiovisual [ˌɔdio'vɪʒʊəl] *adj* : audiovisual

audition [ɔ'dɪʃən] *n* : audición *f*

auditor ['ɔdətər] *n* 1 : auditor *m*, -tora *f*
(de finanzas) 2 STUDENT : oyente *mf*

auditorium [ˌɔdə'toriəm] *n, pl* **-riums** *or*
-ria [-riæ] : auditorio *m*

augment [ɔg'mɛnt] *vt* : aumentar

augur ['ɔgər] *vi* ~ **well** : ser de buen
agüero

August ['ɔgəst] *n* : agosto *m*

aunt ['ænt, 'ɑnt] *n* : tía *f*

aura ['ɔrə] *n* : aura *f*

auspices ['ɔspəsəz, -ˌsiːz] *npl* : auspicios
mpl

auspicious [ɔ'spɪʃəs] *adj* : propicio,
prometedor

austere [ɔ'stɪr] *adj* : austero — **austerity** [ɔ'sterəṭi] *n, pl* **-ties** : austeridad *f*

Australian [ɔ'streɪljən] *adj* : australiano

authentic [ə'θentɪk, ɔ-] *adj* : auténtico

author ['ɔθər] *n* : autor *m*, -tora *f*

authority [ə'θɔrəṭi, ɔ-] *n, pl* **-ties** : autoridad *f* — **authoritarian** [ə,θɔrə'terjən, ə-] *adj* : autoritario — **authoritative** [əθɔrəˌteɪṭIV, ɔ-] *adj* **1** RELIABLE : autorizado **2** DICTATORIAL : autoritario — **authorization** [,ɔθərə'zeɪʃən] *n* : autorización *f* — **authorize** ['ɔθə,raɪz] *vt* **-rized; -rizing** : autorizar

autobiography [,ɔṭobaɪ'ɑgrəfi] *n, pl* **-phies** : autobiografía *f* — **autobiographical** [,ɔṭo,baɪə'græfɪkəl] *adj* : autobiográfico

autograph ['ɔṭə,græf] *n* : autógrafo *m* — ~ *vt* : autografiar

automatic [,ɔṭə'mæṭɪk] *adj* : automático — **automate** ['ɔṭə,meɪt] *vt* **-mated; -mating** : automatizar — **automation** [,ɔṭə'meɪʃən] *n* : automatización *f*

automobile [,ɔṭəmo'biːl, -'moːbiːl] *n* : automóvil *m*

autonomy [ɔ'tɑnəmi] *n, pl* **-mies** : autonomía *f* — **autonomous** [ɔ'tɑnəməs] *adj* : autónomo

autopsy ['ɔ,tɑpsi, -təp-] *n, pl* **-sies** : autopsia *f*

autumn ['ɔṭəm] *n* : otoño *m*

auxiliary [ɔg'zɪljəri, -'zɪləri] *adj* : auxiliar — ~ *n, pl* **-ries** : auxiliar *mf*

avail [ə'veɪl] *vt* ~ **oneself of** : aprovecharse de — ~ *n* **to no** ~ : en vano — **available** [ə'veɪləbəl] *adj* : disponible — **availability** [ə,veɪlə'bɪləṭi] *n, pl* **-ties** : disponibilidad *f*

avalanche ['ævə,læntʃ] *n* : avalancha *f*

avarice ['ævərəs] *n* : avaricia *f*

avenge [ə'vendʒ] *vt* **avenged; avenging** : vengar

avenue ['ævə,nuː, -,njuː] *n* **1** : avenida *f* **2** MEANS : vía *f*

average ['ævrɪdʒ, 'ævə-] *n* : promedio *m* — ~ *adj* **1** MEAN : medio **2** ORDINARY : regular, ordinario — ~ *vt* **-aged; -aging 1** : hacer un promedio de **2** *or* ~ **out** : calcular el promedio de

averse [ə'vərs] *adj* **be** ~ **to** : sentir aversión por — **aversion** [ə'vərʒən] *n* : aversión *f*

avert [ə'vərt] *vt* **1** AVOID : evitar, prevenir **2** ~ **one's eyes** : apartar los ojos

aviation [,eɪvi'eɪʃən] *n* : aviación *f* — **aviator** ['eɪvi,eɪṭər] *n* : aviador *m*, -dora *f*

avid ['ævɪd] *adj* : ávido — **avidly** *adv* : con avidez

avocado [,ævə'kɑdo, ,ɑvə-] *n, pl* **-dos** : aguacate *m*

avoid [ə'vɔɪd] *vt* : evitar — **avoidable** [ə'vɔɪdəbəl] *adj* : evitable

await [ə'weɪt] *vt* : esperar

awake [ə'weɪk] *v* **awoke** [ə'woːk]; **awoken** [ə'woːkən] *or* **awaked; awaking** : despertar — ~ *adj* : despierto — **awaken** [ə'weɪkən] *v* → **awake**

award [ə'wɔrd] *vt* **1** : otorgar, conceder (un premio, etc.) **2** : adjudicar (daños y perjuicios) — ~ *n* **1** PRIZE : premio *m* **2** : adjudicación *f*

aware [ə'wær] *adj* **be** ~ **of** : estar consciente de — **awareness** [ə'wærnəs] *n* : conciencia *f*

away [ə'weɪ] *adv* (*referring to distance*) : de aquí, de distancia **2 far** ~ : lejos **3 give** ~ : regalar **4 go** ~ : irse **5 right** ~ : en seguida **6 take** ~ : quitar — ~ *adj* **1** ABSENT : ausente **2** ~ **game** : partido *m* fuera de casa

awe [ɔ] *n* : temor *m* reverencial — **awesome** ['ɔsəm] *adj* : imponente, formidable

awful ['ɔfəl] *adj* **1** : terrible, espantoso **2 an** ~ **lot** : muchísimo — **awfully** ['ɔfəli] *adv* : terriblemente

awhile [ə'hwaɪl] *adv* : un rato

awkward ['ɔkwərd] *adj* **1** CLUMSY : torpe **2** EMBARRASSING : embarazoso, delicado **3** DIFFICULT : difícil — **awkwardly** *adv* **1** : con dificultad **2** CLUMSILY : de manera torpe

awning ['ɔnɪŋ] *n* : toldo *m*

awry [ə'raɪ] *adj* **1** ASKEW : torcido **2 go** ~ : salir mal

ax *or* **axe** ['æks] *n* : hacha *f*

axiom ['æksiəm] *n* : axioma *m*

axis ['æksɪs] *n, pl* **axes** [-,siːz] : eje *m*

axle ['æksəl] *n* : eje *m*

B

b ['biː] *n*, *pl* **b's** *or* **bs** ['biːz] : b, segunda letra del alfabeto inglés

babble ['bæbəl] *vi* **-bled; -bling 1** : balbucear **2** MURMUR : murmurar — **~** *n* : balbuceo *m* (de bebé), murmullo *m* (de voces, de un arroyo)

baboon [bæˈbuːn] *n* : babuino *m*

baby ['beɪbi] *n*, *pl* **-bies** : bebé *m*; niño *m*, -ña *f* — baby *vt* **-bied; -bying** : mimar, consentir — **babyish** ['beɪbiɪʃ] *adj* : infantil — baby–sit ['beɪbi-ˌsɪt] *vi* **-sat** [-ˌsæt]; **-sitting** : cuidar a los niños

bachelor ['bætʃ[ə]lər] *n* **1** : soltero *m* **2** GRADUATE : licenciado *m*, -da *f*

back ['bæk] *n* **1** : espalda *f* **2** : reverso *m*, dorso *m*, revés *m* **3** REAR : fondo *m*, parte *f* trasera **4** : defensa *mf* (en deportes) — **~** *adv* **1** : atrás **2 be ~** : estar de vuelta **3 go ~** : volver **4 two years ~** : hace dos años — **~** *adj* **1** REAR : de atrás, trasero **2** OVERDUE : atrasado — *vt* **1** SUPPORT : apoyar **2** *or* **~ up** : dar marcha atrás a (un vehículo) — *vi* **1 ~ down** : volverse atrás **2 ~ up** : retroceder — **backache** ['bæk,eɪk] *n* : dolor *m* de espalda — **backbone** ['bæk,boːn] *n* : columna *f* vertebral — **backfire** ['bæk,faɪr] *vi* **-fired; -firing** : petardear — **background** ['bæk,graʊnd] *n* **1** : fondo *m* (de un cuadro, etc.), antecedentes *mpl* (de una situación) **2** EXPERIENCE : formación *f* — **backhand** ['bæk,hænd] *adv* : de revés, con el revés — **backhanded** ['bæk,hændəd] *adj* : indirecto — **backing** ['bækɪŋ] *n* : apoyo *m*, respaldo *m* — **backlash** ['bæk,læʃ] *n* : reacción *f* violenta — **backlog** ['bæk,lɔg] *n* : atrasos *mpl* — **backpack** ['bæk,pæk] *n* : mochila *f* — **backstage** [,bæk'steɪdʒ, 'bæk,-] *adv* & *adj* : entre bastidores — **backtrack** ['bæk,træk] *vi* : dar marcha atrás — **backup** ['bæk,ʌp] *n* **1** SUPPORT : respaldo *m*, apoyo *m* **2** : copia *f* de seguridad (para computadoras) — **backward** ['bækwərd] *or* **backwards** [-wərdz] *adv* **1** : hacia atrás **2 do it ~** : hacerlo al revés **3 fall ~** : caer de espaldas **4 bend over ~** : hacer todo lo posible — **backward** *adj* **1** : hacia atrás **2** RETARDED : retrasado

3 SHY : tímido **4** UNDERDEVELOPED : atrasado

bacon ['beɪkən] *n* : tocino *m*, tocineta *f* *Lat*, bacon *m* *Spain*

bacteria [bæk'tɪriə] : bacterias *fpl*

bad ['bæd] *adj* **worse** ['wərs]; **worst** ['wərst] **1** : malo **2** ROTTEN : podrido **3** SEVERE : grave **4 from ~ to worse** : de mal en peor **5 too ~!** : ¡qué lástima! — **~** *adv* → **badly**

badge ['bædʒ] *n* : insignia *f*, chapa *f*

badger ['bædʒər] *n* : tejón *m* — **~** *vt* : acosar

badly ['bædli] *adv* **1** : mal **2** SEVERELY : gravemente **3 want ~** : desear mucho

baffle ['bæfəl] *vi* **-fled; -fling** : desconcertar

bag ['bæg] *n* **1** : bolsa *f*, saco *m* **2** HANDBAG : bolso *m*, cartera *f* *Lat* **3** SUITCASE : maleta *f* — *vt* **bagged; bagging** : ensacar, poner en una bolsa

baggage ['bægɪdʒ] *n* : equipaje *m*

baggy ['bægi] *adj* **-gier; -est** : holgado

bail ['beɪl] *n* : fianza *f* — **~** *vt* **1** : achicar (agua de un bote) **2 ~ out** RELEASE : poner en libertad bajo fianza **3 ~ out** EXTRICATE : sacar de apuros

bailiff ['beɪlɪf] *n* : alguacil *mf*

bait ['beɪt] *vt* **1** : cebar **2** HARASS : acosar — **~** *n* : cebo *m*, carnada *f*

bake ['beɪk] *v* **baked; baking** *vt* : cocer al horno — *vi* : cocerse (al horno) — **baker** ['beɪkər] *n* : panadero *m*, -ra *f* — **bakery** ['beɪkəri] *n*, *pl* **-ries** : panadería *f*

balance ['bælənts] *n* **1** SCALES : balanza *f* **2** COUNTERBALANCE : contrapeso *m* **3** EQUILIBRIUM : equilibrio *m* **4** REMAINDER : resto *m* **5** *or* **bank ~** : saldo *m* — **~** *v* **-anced; -ancing** *vt* **1** : hacer el balance de (una cuenta) **2** EQUALIZE : equilibrar **3** WEIGH : sopesar — *vi* **1** : sostenerse en equilibrio **2** : cuadrar (dícese de una cuenta)

balcony ['bælkəni] *n*, *pl* **-nies 1** : balcón *m* **2** : galería *f* (de un teatro)

bald ['bɔld] *adj* **1** : calvo **2** WORN : pelado **3 the ~ truth** : la pura verdad

bale *n* : bala *f*, fardo *m*

baleful ['beɪlfəl] *adj* : siniestro

balk ['bɔk] *vi* **~ at** : resistirse a

ball ['bɔl] n 1 : pelota f, bola f, balón m 2 DANCE : baile m 3 ~ **of string** : ovillo m de cuerda

ballad ['bæləd] n : balada f

ballast n : lastre m

ball bearing n : cojinete m de bola

ballerina [ˌbælə'riːnə] n : bailarina f

ballet ['bæˌleɪ, bæ'leɪ] n : ballet m

ballistic [bə'lɪstɪk] adj : balístico

balloon n : globo m

ballot ['bælət] n 1 : papeleta f (de voto) 2 VOTING : votación f

ballpoint pen ['bɔlˌpɔɪnt] n : bolígrafo m

ballroom ['bɔlˌruːm, -ˌrʊm] n : sala f de baile

balm ['bam, 'balm] n : bálsamo m — **balmy** ['bami, 'bal-] adj **balmier; -est** : templado, agradable

baloney [bə'loːni] n NONSENSE : tonterías fpl

bamboo [bæm'buː] n : bambú m

bamboozle [bæm'buːzəl] vt **-zled; -zling** : engañar, embaucar

ban ['bæn] vt **banned; banning** : prohibir — ~ n : prohibición f

banal [bə'nal, bə'næl, 'beɪnəl] adj : banal

banana [bə'nænə] n : plátano m, banana f Lat, banano m Lat

band ['bænd] n 1 STRIP : banda f 2 GROUP : banda f, grupo m, conjunto m — ~ vi ~ **together** : unirse, juntarse

bandage ['bændɪdʒ] n : vendaje m, venda f — ~ vt **-daged; -daging** : vendar

bandit ['bændət] n : bandido m, -da f

bandy ['bændi] vt **-died; -dying** ~ **about** : circular, repetir

bang ['bæŋ] vt 1 STRIKE : golpear 2 SLAM : cerrar de un golpe — vi 1 SLAM : cerrarse de un golpe 2 ~ **on** : golpear — ~ n 1 BLOW : golpe m 2 NOISE : estrépito m 3 SLAM : portazo m

bangle ['bæŋgəl] n : brazalete m, pulsera f

bangs ['bæŋz] npl : flequillo m

banish ['bænɪʃ] vt : desterrar

banister ['bænəstər] n : pasamanos m, barandal m

bank ['bæŋk] n 1 : banco m 2 : orilla f, ribera f (de un río) 3 EMBANKMENT : terraplén m — ~ vt : depositar — vi 1 : ladearse (dícese de un avión) 2 : tener una cuenta (en un banco) 3 ~ **on** : contar con — **banker** ['bæŋkər] n : banquero m, -ra f — **banking** ['bæŋkɪŋ] n : banca f

bankrupt ['bæŋˌkrʌpt] adj : en bancarrota, en quiebra — **bankruptcy** ['bæŋˌkrʌptsi] n, pl **-cies** : quiebra f, bancarrota f

banner ['bænər] n : bandera f, pancarta f

banquet ['bæŋkwət] n : banquete m

banter ['bæntər] n : bromas fpl — ~ vi : hacer bromas

baptize [bæp'taɪz, 'bæpˌtaɪz] vt **-tized; -tizing** : bautizar — **baptism** ['bæpˌtɪzəm] n : bautismo m

bar ['bar] n 1 : barra f 2 BARRIER : barrera f, obstáculo m 3 COUNTER : mostrador m, barra f 4 TAVERN : bar m 5 **behind ~s** : entre rejas 6 ~ **of soap** : pastilla f de jabón — ~ vt **barred; barring** 1 OBSTRUCT : obstruir, bloquear 2 EXCLUDE : excluir 3 PROHIBIT : prohibir — ~ prep 1 : excepto 2 ~ **none** : sin excepción

barbarian [bar'bæriən] n : bárbaro m, -ra f

barbecue ['barbɪˌkjuː] vt **-cued; -cuing** : asar a la parrilla — ~ n : barbacoa f

barbed wire ['barbd'waɪr] n : alambre m de púas

barber ['barbər] n : barbero m, -ra f

bare ['bær] adj 1 : desnudo 2 EMPTY : vacío 3 MINIMUM : mero, esencial — **barefaced** ['bærˌfeɪst] adj : descarado — **barefoot** ['bærˌfʊt] or **barefooted** [-ˌfʊtəd] adv & adj : descalzo — **barely** ['bærli] adv : apenas, por poco

bargain ['bargən] n 1 AGREEMENT : acuerdo m 2 BUY : ganga f — ~ vi 1 : regatear, negociar 2 ~ **for** : contar con

barge ['bardʒ] n : barcaza f — ~ vi **barged; barging** ~ **in** : entrometerse, interrumpir

baritone ['bærəˌtoːn] n : barítono m

bark¹ ['bark] vi : ladrar — ~ n : ladrido m (de un perro)

bark² ['bark] n : corteza f (de un árbol)

barley ['barli] n : cebada f

barn ['barn] n : granero m — **barnyard** ['barnˌjard] n : corral m

barometer [bə'ramətər] n : barómetro m

baron ['bærən] n : barón m — **baroness** ['bærənɪs, -nəs, -ˌnɛs] n : baronesa f

barracks ['bærəks] ns & pl : cuartel m

barrage [bə'raʒ, -'radʒ] n 1 : descarga f (de artillería) 2 : aluvión m (de preguntas, etc.)

barrel ['bærəl] n 1 : barril m, tonel m 2 : cañón m (de un arma de fuego)

barren ['bærən] adj : estéril

barricade ['bærəˌkeɪd, ˌbærə'-] vt **-caded; -cading** : cerrar con barricadas — ~ n : barricada f

barrier ['bæriər] n : barrera f

barring ['barɪŋ] prep : salvo

barrio ['bario, 'bær-] n : barrio m

bartender ['bɑr,tendər] n : camarero m, -ra f

barter ['bɑrtər] vt : cambiar, trocar — ~ n : trueque m

base ['beɪs] n, pl **bases** : base f — ~ vt **based; basing** : basar, fundamentar — ~ adj **baser; basest** : vil

baseball ['beɪs,bɔl] n : beisbol m, béisbol m

basement ['beɪsmənt] n : sótano m

bash ['bæʃ] vt : golpear violentamente — ~ n 1 BLOW : golpe m 2 PARTY: fiesta f

bashful ['bæʃfəl] adj : tímido, vergonzoso

basic ['beɪsɪk] adj : básico, fundamental — **basically** ['beɪsɪkli] adv : fundamentalmente

basil ['beɪzəl, 'bæzəl] n : albahaca f

basin ['beɪsən] n 1 WASHBOWL : palangana f, lavabo m 2 : cuenca f (de un río)

basis ['beɪsəs] n, pl **bases** [-,siːz] : base f

bask ['bæsk] vi ~ **in the sun** : tostarse al sol

basket ['bæskət] n : cesta f, cesto m — **basketball** ['bæskət,bɔl] n : baloncesto m, basquetbol m Lat

bass¹ ['bæs] n, pl **bass** or **basses** : róbalo m (pesca)

bass² ['beɪs] n : bajo m (tono, voz, instrumento)

bassoon [bə'suːn, bæ-] n : fagot m

bastard ['bæstərd] n : bastardo m, -da f

baste ['beɪst] vt **basted; basting** 1 STITCH : hilvanar 2 : bañar (carne)

bat¹ ['bæt] n : murciélago m (animal)

bat² n : bate m — ~ vt **batted; batting** : batear

batch ['bætʃ] n : hornada f (de pasteles, etc.), lote m (de mercancías), montón m (de trabajo), grupo m (de personas)

bath ['bæθ, 'bɑθ] n, pl **baths** ['bæðz, 'bæθs, 'bɑðz, 'bɑθs] 1 : baño m 2 BATHROOM : baño m, cuarto m de baño 3 **take a ~** : bañarse — **bathe** ['beɪð] v **bathed; bathing** vt : bañar, lavar — vi : bañarse — **bathrobe** ['bæθ,roːb] n : bata f (de baño) — **bathroom** ['bæθ,ruːm, -,rʊm] n : baño m, cuarto m de baño — **bathtub** ['bæθ,tʌb] n : bañera f, tina f (de baño)

baton [bə'tɑn] n : batuta f

battalion [bə'tæljən] n : batallón m

batter ['bætər] vt 1 BEAT : golpear 2 MISTREAT : maltratar — ~ n 1 : masa f para rebozar 2 HITTER : bateador m, -dora f

battery ['bætəri] n, pl **-teries** : batería f, pila f (de electricidad)

battle ['bætəl] n 1 : batalla f 2 STRUGGLE : lucha f — ~ vi **-tled; -tling** : luchar — **battlefield** ['bætəl,fiːld] n : campo m de batalla — **battleship** ['bætəl,ʃɪp] n : acorazado m

bawl ['bɔl] vi : llorar a gritos

bay¹ ['beɪ] n INLET : bahía f

bay² n or ~ **leaf** : laurel m

bay³ vi : aullar — ~ n : aullido m

bayonet [,beɪə'nɛt, 'beɪə,nɛt] n : bayoneta f

bay window n : ventana f en saliente

bazaar [bə'zɑr] n 1 : bazar m 2 SALE : venta f benéfica

be ['biː] v **was** ['wʌz, 'wɑz], **were** ['wər]; **been** ['bɪn]; **being; am** ['æm], **is** ['ɪz], **are** ['ɑr] vi 1 : ser 2 (expressing location) : estar 3 (expressing existence) : ser, existir 4 (expressing a state of being) : estar, tener — v impers 1 (indicating time) : hacer, estar — v aux 1 (expressing occurrence) : ser 2 (expressing possibility) : poderse 3 (expressing obligation) : deber 4 (expressing progression) : estar

beach ['biːtʃ] n : playa f

beacon ['biːkən] n : faro m

bead ['biːd] n 1 : cuenta f 2 DROP : gota f 3 —s npl NECKLACE : collar m

beak ['biːk] n : pico m

beam ['biːm] n 1 : viga f (de madera, etc.) 2 RAY : rayo m — ~ vi SHINE : brillar — vt BROADCAST : transmitir, emitir

bean ['biːn] n 1 : habichuela f, frijol m 2 **coffee ~** : grano m 3 **string ~** : judía f

bear¹ ['bær] n, pl **bears** or **bear** : oso m, osa f

bear² v **bore** ['bor]; **borne** ['bɔrn]; **bearing** vt 1 CARRY : portar 2 ENDURE : soportar — vi ~ **right/left** : doble a la derecha/a la izquierda — **bearable** ['bærəbəl] adj : soportable

beard ['bɪrd] n : barba f

bearer ['bærər] n : portador m, -dora f

bearing ['bærɪŋ] n 1 MANNER : comportamiento m 2 SIGNIFICANCE : relación f, importancia f 3 **get one's ~s** : orientarse

beast ['biːst] n : bestia f

beat ['biːt] v **beat; beaten** ['biːtən] or **beat; beating** vt 1 HIT : golpear 2 : batir (huevos, etc.) 3 DEFEAT : derrotar — vi : latir (dícese del corazón) — ~ n 1 : golpe m, latido m (del corazón) 3 RHYTHM : ritmo m, tiempo m — **beating** ['biːtɪŋ] n 1 : paliza f 2 DEFEAT : derrota f

beauty ['bjuːṭi] *n, pl* **-ties** : belleza *f* — **beautiful** ['bjuːṭifəl] *adj* : hermoso, lindo — **beautifully** ['bjuːṭifəli] *adv* WONDERFULLY : maravillosamente — **beautify** ['bjuːṭifaɪ] *vt* **-fied; -fying** : embellecer

beaver ['biːvər] *n* : castor *m*

because [bɪˈkʌz, -ˈkɔz] *conj* : porque — **because of** *prep* : por, a causa de, debido a

beckon ['bɛkən] *vt* : llamar, hacer señas a — *vi* : hacer una seña

become [bɪˈkʌm] *v* **-came** [-ˈkeɪm], **-come, -coming** *vi* : hacerse, ponerse — *vt* SUIT : favorecer — **becoming** [bɪˈkʌmɪŋ] *adj* 1 SUITABLE : apropiado 2 FLATTERING : favorecedor

bed ['bɛd] *n* 1 : cama *f* 2 : cauce *m* (de un río), fondo *m* (del mar) 3 : macizo *m* (de flores) 4 **go to ~** : irse a la cama — **bedclothes** ['bɛdˌkloːz, -ˌkloːðz] *npl* : ropa *f* de cama

bedlam ['bɛdləm] *n* : confusión *f*, caos *m*

bedraggled [bɪˈdrægəld] *adj* : desaliñado, sucio

bedridden ['bɛdˌrɪdən] *adj* : postrado en cama

bedroom ['bɛdˌruːm, -ˌrʊm] *n* : dormitorio *m*, recámara *f Lat*

bedspread ['bɛdˌsprɛd] *n* : colcha *f*

bedtime ['bɛdˌtaɪm] *n* : hora *f* de acostarse

bee ['biː] *n* : abeja *f*

beech ['biːtʃ] *n, pl* **beeches** *or* **beech** : haya *f*

beef ['biːf] *n* : carne *f* de vaca, carne *f* de res *Lat* — **beefsteak** ['biːfˌsteɪk] *n* : bistec *m*

beehive ['biːˌhaɪv] *n* : colmena *f*

beeline ['biːˌlaɪn] *n* **make a ~ for** : irse derecho a

beep ['biːp] *n* : pitido *m* — **~** *v* : pitar

beer ['bɪr] *n* : cerveza *f*

beet ['biːt] *n* : remolacha *f*

beetle ['biːṭəl] *n* : escarabajo *m*

before [bɪˈfor] *adv* 1 : antes 2 **the month ~** : el mes anterior — **~** *prep* 1 (*in space*) : delante de, ante 2 (*in time*) : antes de — **~** *conj* : antes de que — **beforehand** [bɪˈforˌhænd] *adv* : antes

befriend [bɪˈfrɛnd] *vt* : hacerse amigo de

beg ['bɛg] *v* **begged; begging** *vt* 1 : pedir, mendigar 2 ENTREAT : suplicar — *vi* : mendigar, pedir limosna — **beggar** ['bɛgər] *n* : mendigo *m*, -ga *f*

begin [bɪˈgɪn] *v* **-gan** [-ˈgæn]; **-gun** [-ˈgʌn]; **-ginning** : empezar, comenzar — **beginner** [bɪˈgɪnər] *n* : principiante

mf — **beginning** [bɪˈgɪnɪŋ] *n* : principio *m*, comienzo *m*

begrudge [bɪˈgrʌdʒ] *vt* **-grudged; -grudging** 1 : dar de mala gana 2 ENVY : envidiar

behalf [bɪˈhæf, -ˈhaf] *n* **on ~ of** : de parte de, en nombre de

behave [bɪˈheɪv] *vi* **-haved; -having** : comportarse, portarse — **behavior** [bɪˈheɪvjər] *n* : comportamiento *m*, conducta *f*

behind [bɪˈhaɪnd] *adv* 1 : detrás 2 **fall ~** : atrasarse — **~** *prep* 1 : atrás de, detrás de 2 **be ~ schedule** : ir retrasado 3 **her friends are ~ her** : tiene el apoyo de sus amigos

behold [bɪˈhoːld] *vt* **-held; -holding** : contemplar

beige ['beɪʒ] *adj & nm* : beige

being ['biːɪŋ] *n* 1 : ser *m* 2 **come into ~** : nacer

belated [bɪˈleɪṭəd] *adj* : tardío

belch ['bɛltʃ] *vi* : eructar — **~** *n* : eructo *m*

Belgian ['bɛldʒən] *adj* : belga

belie [bɪˈlaɪ] *vt* **-lied; -lying** : contradecir, desmentir

belief [bɪˈliːf] *n* 1 TRUST : confianza *f* 2 CONVICTION : creencia *f*, convicción *f* 3 FAITH : fe *f* — **believable** [bəˈliːvəbəl] *adj* : creíble — **believe** [bəˈliːv] *v* **-lieved; -lieving** : creer — **believer** [bəˈliːvər] *n* : creyente *mf*

belittle [bɪˈlɪṭəl] *vt* **-littled; -littling** : menospreciar

Belizean [bəˈliːziən] *adj* : beliceño *m*, -ña *f*

bell ['bɛl] *n* 1 : campana *f* 2 : timbre *m* (de teléfono, de la puerta, etc.)

belligerent [bəˈlɪdʒərənt] *adj* : beligerante

bellow ['bɛˌloː] *vi* : bramar, mugir — *vt or* **~ out** : gritar

bellows ['bɛˌloːz] *ns & pl* : fuelle *m*

belly ['bɛli] *n, pl* **-lies** : vientre *m*

belong [bɪˈlɔŋ] *vi* 1 **~ to** : pertenecer a, ser propiedad de 2 **~ to** : ser miembro de (un club, etc.) 3 **where does it ~** : ¿dónde va? — **belongings** [bɪˈlɔŋɪŋz] *npl* : pertenencias *fpl*, efectos *mpl* personales

beloved [bɪˈlʌvəd, -ˈlʌvd] *adj* : querido, amado — **~** *n* : querido *m*, -da *f*

below [bɪˈloː] *adv* : abajo — **~** *prep* 1 : abajo de, debajo de 2 **~ average** : por debajo del promedio 3 **~ zero** : bajo cero

belt ['bɛlt] *n* 1 : cinturón *m* 2 BAND, STRAP : cinta *f*, correa *f* 3 AREA : frente

m, zona f — ~ vt 1 : ceñir con un cinturón 2 THRASH : darle una paliza a
bench ['bent∫] n 1 : banco m 2 WORKBENCH : mesa f de trabajo 3 COURT : tribunal m
bend ['bend] v bent ['bent]; bending vt : doblar, torcer — vi 1 : torcerse 2 ~ over : inclinarse — ~ n : curva f, ángulo m
beneath [bi'ni:θ] adv : abajo, debajo — ~ prep : bajo, debajo de
benediction [,benə'dik∫ən] n : bendición f
benefactor ['benə,fæktər] n : benefactor m, -tora f
benefit ['benəfit] n 1 ADVANTAGE : ventaja f, provecho m 2 AID : asistencia f, beneficio m — ~ vt : beneficiar — vi : beneficiarse — **beneficial** [,benə'fi∫əl] adj : beneficioso — **beneficiary** [,benə'fi∫i,eri, -'fi∫əri] n, pl -ries : beneficiario m, -ria f
benevolent [bə'nevələnt] adj : benévolo
benign [bi'nain] adj 1 KIND : benévolo, amable 2 : benigno (en medicina)
bent ['bent] adj 1 : encorvado 2 be ~ on : estar empeñado en — ~ n : aptitud f, inclinación f
bequeath [bi'kwi:θ, -'kwi:ð] vt : legar — **bequest** [bi'kwest] n : legado m
berate [bi'reit] vt -rated; -rating : reprender, regañar
bereaved [bi'ri:vd] adj : desconsolado, a luto
beret [bə'rei] n : boina f
berry ['beri] n, pl -ries : baya f
berserk [bər'sərk, -'zərk] adj 1 : enloquecido 2 go ~ : volverse loco
berth ['bərθ] n 1 MOORING : atracadero m 2 BUNK : litera f
beseech [bi'si:t∫] vt -sought [-'sɔt] or -seeched; -seeching : suplicar, implorar
beset [bi'set] vt -set; -setting 1 HARASS : acosar 2 SURROUND : rodear
beside [bi'said] prep 1 : al lado de, junto a 2 be ~ oneself : estar fuera de sí — **besides** [bi'saidz] adv : además — ~ prep 1 : además de 2 EXCEPT : excepto
besiege [bi'si:dʒ] vt -sieged; -sieging : asediar
best ['best] adj (superlative of **good**) : mejor — ~ adv (superlative of **well**) : mejor — ~ n 1 at ~ : a lo más 2 do one's ~ : hacer todo lo posible 3 the ~ : lo mejor — **best man** n : padrino m (de boda)
bestow [bi'sto:] vt : otorgar, conceder
bet ['bet] n : apuesta f — ~ v bet; bet-

ting vt : apostar — vi ~ on sth : apostarle a algo
betray [bi'trei] vt : traicionar — **betrayal** [bi'treiəl] n : traición f
better ['betər] adj (comparative of **good**) 1 : mejor 2 get ~ : mejorar — ~ adv (comparative of **well**) 1 : mejor 2 all the ~ : tanto mejor — ~ n 1 the ~ : el mejor, la mejor 2 get the ~ of : vencer a — ~ vt 1 IMPROVE : mejorar 2 SURPASS : superar
between [bi'twi:n] prep : entre — ~ adv or in ~ : en medio
beverage ['bevridʒ, 'bevə-] n : bebida f
beware [bi'wær] vi ~ of : tener cuidado con
bewilder [bi'wildər] vt : desconcertar — **bewilderment** [bi'wildərmənt] n : desconcierto m
bewitch [bi'wit∫] vt : hechizar, encantar
beyond [bi'jand] adv : más allá, más lejos (en el espacio), más adelante (en el tiempo) — ~ prep : más allá de
bias ['baiəs] n 1 PREJUDICE : prejuicio m 2 TENDENCY : inclinación f, tendencia f — **biased** ['baiəst] adj : parcial
bib ['bib] n : babero m (para niños)
Bible ['baibəl] n : Biblia f — **biblical** ['biblikəl] adj : bíblico
bibliography [,bibli'agrəfi] n, pl -phies : bibliografía f
bicarbonate of soda [bai'karbənət, ,neit] n : bicarbonato m de soda
biceps ['bai,seps] ns & pl : bíceps m
bicker ['bikər] vi : reñir
bicycle ['baisikəl, -,si-] n : bicicleta f — ~ vi -cled; -cling : ir en bicicleta
bid ['bid] vt **bade** ['bæd, 'beid] or **bid**; **bidden** ['bidən] or **bid**; **bidding** 1 OFFER : ofrecer 2 ~ **farewell** : decir adios — ~ n 1 OFFER : oferta f 2 ATTEMPT : intento m, tentativa f
bide ['baid] vt **bode** ['bo:d] or **bided**; **bided**; **biding** ~ **one's time** : esperar el momento oportuno
bifocals ['bai,fo:kəlz] npl : anteojos mpl bifocales
big ['big] adj **bigger; biggest** : grande
bigamy ['bigəmi] n : bigamía f
bigot ['bigət] n : intolerante mf — **bigotry** ['bigətri] n, pl -tries : intolerancia f, fanatismo m
bike ['baik] n 1 BICYCLE : bici f fam 2 MOTORCYCLE : moto f
bikini [bə'ki:ni] n : bikini m
bile ['bail] n : bilis f
bilingual [bai'liŋgwəl] adj : bilingüe
bill ['bil] n 1 BEAK : pico m 2 INVOICE : cuenta f, factura f 3 BANKNOTE : billete m 4 LAW : proyecto m de ley, ley f

— ~ *vt* : pasarle la cuenta a — **bill-board** ['bɪl‚bord] *n* : cartelera *f* — **bill-fold** ['bɪl‚fold] *n* : billetera *f*, cartera *f*

billiards ['bɪljərdz] *n* : billar *m*

billion ['bɪljən] *n, pl* **billions** *or* **billion** : mil millones *mpl*

billow ['bɪlo] *vi* : ondular, hincharse

billy goat ['bɪli‚got] *n* : macho *m* cabrío

bin ['bɪn] *n* : cubo *m*, cajón *m*

binary ['baɪnəri, -‚neri] *adj* : binario *m*

bind ['baɪnd] *vt* **bound** ['baʊnd]; **binding 1** TIE : atar **2** OBLIGATE : obligar **3** UNITE : unir **4** BANDAGE : vendar **5** : encuadernar (un libro) — **binder** ['baɪndər] *n* FOLDER : carpeta *f* — **binding** ['baɪndɪŋ] *n* : encuadernación *f* (de libros)

binge ['bɪndʒ] *n* : juerga *f fam*

bingo ['bɪŋgo] *n, pl* **-gos** : bingo *m*

binoculars [bə‚nɑkjələrz, baɪ-] *npl* : binoculares *mpl*, gemelos *mpl*

biochemistry [‚baɪo'kemɪstri] *n* : bioquímica *f*

biography [baɪ'ɑgrəfi, bi:-] *n, pl* **-phies** : biografía *f* — **biographer** [baɪ'ɑgrəfər] *n* : biógrafo *m*, -fa *f* — **biographical** [‚baɪə'græfɪkəl] *adj* : biográfico

biology [baɪ'ɑlədʒi] *n* : biología *f* — **biological** [-dʒɪkəl] *adj* : biológico — **biologist** [baɪ'ɑlədʒɪst] *n* : biólogo *m*, -ga *f*

birch ['bərtʃ] *n* : abedul *m*

bird ['bərd] *n* : pájaro *m* (pequeño), ave *f* (grande)

birth ['bərθ] *n* **1** : nacimiento *m*, parto *m* **2 give ~ to** : dar a luz a — **birthday** ['bərθ‚deɪ] *n* : cumpleaños *m* — **birthmark** ['bərθ‚mɑrk] *n* : mancha *f* de nacimiento — **birthplace** ['bərθ‚pleɪs] *n* : lugar *m* de nacimiento — **birthrate** ['bərθ‚reɪt] *n* : índice *m* de natalidad

biscuit ['bɪskət] *n* : bizcocho *m*

bisect [baɪ‚sekt, -'-] *vt* : bisecar

bisexual [‚baɪ'sekʃəwəl, -'sekʃəl] *adj* : bisexual

bishop ['bɪʃəp] *n* : obispo *m*

bison ['baɪzən, -sən] *ns & pl* : bisonte *m*

bit[1] ['bɪt] *n* : bocado *m* (de una brida)

bit[2] ['bɪt] *n* **1** : trozo *m*, pedazo *m* **2** : bit *m* (de información) **3 a ~** : un poco

bitch ['bɪtʃ] *n* : perra *f* — ~ *vi* COMPLAIN : quejarse, reclamar

bite ['baɪt] *v* **bit** ['bɪt]; **bitten** ['bɪtən]; **biting** *vt* **1** : morder **2** STING : picar — *vi* : morder — *n* **1** : picadura *f* (de un insecto), mordedura *f* (de un animal) **2** SNACK : bocado *m* — **biting** *adj* **1** PENETRATING : cortante, penetrante **2** CAUSTIC : mordaz

bitter ['bɪtər] *adj* **1** : amargo **2 it's ~ cold** : hace un frío glacial **3 to the ~ end** : hasta el final — **bitterness** ['bɪtərnəs] *n* : amargura *f*

bizarre [bə'zɑr] *adj* : extraño

black ['blæk] *adj* : negro — ~ *n* **1** : negro *m* (color) **2** : negro *m*, -gra *f* (persona) — **black–and–blue** [‚blækən'blu:] *adj* : amoratado — **blackberry** ['blæk‚beri] *n, pl* **-ries** : mora *f* — **blackbird** ['blæk‚bərd] *n* : mirlo *m* — **blackboard** ['blæk‚bord] *n* : pizarra *f*, pizarrón *m Lat* — **blacken** ['blækən] *vt* : ennegrecer — **blackmail** ['blæk‚meɪl] *n* : chantaje *m* — ~ *vt* : chantajear — **black market** *n* : mercado *m* negro — **blackout** ['blæk‚aʊt] *n* **1** : apagón *m* (de poder eléctrico) **2** FAINT : desmayo *m* — **blacksmith** ['blæk‚smɪθ] *n* : herrero *m* — **blacktop** ['blæk‚tɑp] *n* : asfalto *m*

bladder ['blædər] *n* : vejiga *f*

blade ['bleɪd] *n* **1** : hoja *f* (de un cuchillo), cuchilla *f* (de un patín) **2** : pala *f* (de un remo, una hélice, etc.) **3 ~ of grass** : brizna *f* (de hierba)

blame ['bleɪm] *vt* **blamed; blaming** : culpar, echar la culpa a — ~ *n* : culpa *f* — **blameless** ['bleɪmləs] *adj* : inocente

bland ['blænd] *adj* : soso, insulso

blank ['blæŋk] *adj* **1** : en blanco (dícese de un papel), liso (dícese de una pared) **2** EMPTY : vacío — ~ *n* : espacio *m* en blanco

blanket ['blæŋkət] *n* **1** : manta *f*, cobija *f Lat* **2 ~ of snow** : manto *m* de nieve — ~ *vt* : cubrir

blare ['blær] *vi* **blared; blaring** : resonar

blasphemy ['blæsfəmi] *n, pl* **-mies** : blasfemia *f*

blast ['blæst] *n* **1** GUST : ráfaga *f* **2** EXPLOSION : explosión *f* **3** : toque *m* (de trompeta, etc.) — ~ *vt* BLOW UP : volar — **blast-off** ['blæst‚ɔf] *n* : despegue *m*

blatant ['bleɪtənt] *adj* : descarado

blaze ['bleɪz] *n* **1** FIRE : fuego *m* **2** BRIGHTNESS : resplandor *m*, brillantez *f* **3 ~ of anger** : arranque *m* de cólera — ~ *v* **blazed; blazing** *vi* : arder, brillar — *vt* **~ a trail** : abrir un camino

blazer ['bleɪzər] *n* : chaqueta *f* deportiva

bleach ['bli:tʃ] *vt* : blanquear, decolorar — ~ *n* : lejía *f*, blanqueador *m Lat* — **bleachers** ['bli:tʃərz] *ns & pl* : gradas *fpl*

bleak ['bli:k] *adj* **1** DESOLATE : desolado **2** GLOOMY : triste, sombrío

bleary–eyed ['blɪri‚aɪd] *adj* : con los ojos nublados

bleat ['bli:t] *vi* : balar — ~ *n* : balido *m*

bleed ['bli:d] v **bled** ['bled]; **bleeding** : sangrar

blemish ['blemɪʃ] vt : manchar, marcar — ~ n : mancha f, marca f

blend ['blend] vt : mezclar, combinar — ~ n : mezcla f, combinación f — **blender** ['blendər] n : licuadora f

bless ['bles] vt **blessed** ['blest]; **blessing** : bendecir — **blessed** ['blesəd] or **blest** ['blest] adj : bendito — **blessing** ['blesɪŋ] n : bendición f

blew → **blow**

blind ['blaɪnd] adj : ciego — ~ vt 1 : cegar, dejar ciego 2 DAZZLE : deslumbrar — ~ n 1 : persiana f (para una ventana) 2 **the** ~ : los ciegos — **blindfold** ['blaɪndˌfoːld] vt : vendar los ojos — ~ n : venda f (para los ojos) — **blindly** ['blaɪndli] adv : ciegamente — **blindness** ['blaɪndnəs] n : ceguera f

blink ['blɪŋk] vi 1 : parpadear 2 FLICKER : brillar intermitentemente — ~ n : parpadeo m — **blinker** ['blɪŋkər] n : intermitente m, direccional f Lat

bliss ['blɪs] n : dicha f, felicidad f (absoluta) — **blissful** ['blɪsfəl] adj : feliz

blister ['blɪstər] n : ampolla f — ~ vi : ampollarse

blitz ['blɪts] n : bombardeo m aéreo

blizzard ['blɪzərd] n : ventisca f (de nieve)

bloated ['bloːtəd] adj : hinchado

blob ['blab] n 1 DROP : gota f 2 SPOT : mancha f

block ['blak] n 1 : bloque m 2 OBSTRUCTION : obstrucción f 3 : manzana f, cuadra f Lat (de edificios) 4 or **building** ~ : cubo m de construcción — ~ vt : obstruir, bloquear — **blockade** [bla'keɪd] n : bloqueo m — **blockage** ['blakɪdʒ] n : obstrucción f

blond or **blonde** ['bland] adj : rubio — ~ n : rubio m, -bia f

blood ['blʌd] n : sangre f — **bloodhound** ['blʌdˌhaʊnd] n : sabueso m — **blood pressure** n : tensión f (arterial) — **bloodshed** ['blʌdˌʃed] n : derramamiento m de sangre — **bloodshot** ['blʌdˌʃat] adj : inyectado de sangre — **bloodstained** ['blʌdˌsteɪnd] adj : manchado de sangre — **bloodstream** ['blʌdˌstriːm] n : sangre f, torrente m sanguíneo — **bloody** ['blʌdi] adj **bloodier; -est** : ensangrentado, sangriento

bloom ['bluːm] n 1 : flor f 2 **in full** ~ : en plena floración — ~ vi : florecer

blossom ['blasəm] n : flor f — ~ vi : florecer

blot ['blat] n 1 : borrón m (de tinta, etc.)

2 BLEMISH : mancha f — ~ vt **blotted**; **blotting** 1 : emborronar 2 DRY : secar

blotch ['blatʃ] n : mancha f, borrón m — **blotchy** ['blatʃi] adj **blotchier; -est** : lleno de manchas

blouse ['blaʊs, 'blaʊz] n : blusa f

blow ['bloː] v **blew** ['bluː]; **blown** ['bloːn]; **blowing** vi 1 : soplar 2 SOUND : sonar 3 or ~ **out** : fundirse (dícese de un fusible eléctrico), reventarse (dícese de una llanta) — vt 1 : soplar 2 SOUND : tocar, sonar 3 BUNGLE : echar a perder — ~ n : golpe m — **blowout** ['bloːˌaʊt] n : reventón m — **blow up** vi : estallar, hacer explosión — vt 1 EXPLODE : volar 2 INFLATE : inflar

blubber ['blʌbər] n : esperma f de ballena

bludgeon ['blʌdʒən] vt : aporrear

blue ['bluː] adj **bluer; bluest** 1 : azul 2 MELANCHOLY : triste — ~ n : azul m — **blueberry** ['bluːˌberi] n, pl **-ries** : arándano f — **bluebird** ['bluːˌbərd] n : azulejo m — **blue cheese** n : queso m azul — **blueprint** ['bluːˌprɪnt] n PLAN : proyecto m — **blues** ['bluːz] npl 1 SADNESS : tristeza f 2 : blues m (en música)

bluff ['blʌf] vi : hacer un farol — ~ n : farol m

blunder ['blʌndər] vi : meter la pata fam — ~ n : metedura f de pata fam

blunt ['blʌnt] adj 1 DULL : desafilado 2 DIRECT : directo, franco

blur ['blər] n : imágen f borrosa — ~ vt **blurred; blurring** : hacer borroso

blurb ['blərb] n : nota f publicitaria

blurt ['blərt] vt or ~ **out** : espetar

blush ['blʌʃ] n : rubor m — ~ vi : ruborizarse

blustery ['blʌstəri] adj : borrascoso, tempestuoso

boar ['bor] n : cerdo m macho

board ['bord] n 1 PLANK : tabla f, tablón m 2 COMMITTEE : junta f, consejo m 3 : tablero m (de juegos) 4 **room and** ~ : comida f y alojamiento — ~ vt 1 : subir a bordo de (una nave, un avión, etc.), subir a (un tren) 2 LODGE : hospedar 3 ~ **up** : cerrar con tablas — **boarder** ['bordər] n : huésped mf

boast ['boːst] vi : jactancia f — ~ vi : alardear, jactarse — **boastful** ['boːstfəl] adj : jactancioso

boat ['boːt] n : barco m (grande), barca f (pequeña)

bob ['bab] vi **bobbed; bobbing** or ~ **up and down** : subir y bajar

bobbin ['babən] n : bobina f, carrete m

bobby pin ['babiˌpɪn] n : horquilla f

body ['bɑdi] *n, pl* **bodies 1** : cuerpo *m* **2** CORPSE : cadáver *m* **3** : carrocería (de un automóvil, etc.) **4** COLLECTION : conjunto *m* **5** ~ **of water** : masa *f* de agua — **bodily** *adj* : corporal — **bodyguard** ['bɑdi,gɑrd] *n* : guardaespaldas *mf*

bog ['bɑg, 'bɔg] *n* : ciénaga *f* — ~ *vt* **bogged; bogging** *or* ~ **down** : empantanarse

bogus ['bo:gəs] *adj* : falso

boil ['bɔil] *v* : hervir — **boiler** ['bɔilər] *n* : caldera *f*

bold ['bo:ld] *adj* **1** DARING : audaz **2** IMPUDENT : descarado — **boldness** ['bo:ldnəs] *n* : audacia *f*

Bolivian [bə'liviən] *adj* : boliviano *m*, -na *f*

bologna [bə'lo:ni] *n* : salchicha *f* ahumada

bolster ['bo:lstər] *vt* **-stered; -stering** *or* ~ **up** : reforzar

bolt ['bo:lt] *n* **1** LOCK : cerrojo *m* **2** SCREW : tornillo *m* **3** ~ **of lightning** : relámpago *m*, rayo *m* — ~ *vt* **1** FASTEN : atornillar **2** LOCK : echar el cerrojo a — *vi* FLEE : salir corriendo

bomb ['bɑm] *n* : bomba *f* — ~ *vt* : bombardear — **bombard** [bɑm'bɑrd, bəm-] *vt* : bombardear — **bombardment** [bɑm'bɑrdmənt] *n* : bombardeo *m* — **bomber** ['bɑmər] *n* : bombardero *m*

bond ['bɑnd] *n* **1** TIE : vínculo *m*, lazo *m* **2** SURETY : fianza *f* **3** : bono *m* (en finanzas) — ~ *vi* STICK : adherirse

bondage ['bɑndidʒ] *n* : esclavitud *f*

bone ['bo:n] *n* : hueso *m* — ~ *vt* **boned; boning** : deshuesar

bonfire ['bɑn,fair] *n* : hoguera *f*

bonus ['bo:nəs] *n* **1** PAY : prima *f* **2** BENEFIT : beneficio *m* adicional

bony ['bo:ni] *adj* **bonier; -est 1** : huesudo *m* **2** : lleno de espinas (dícese de pescados)

boo ['bu:] *n, pl* **boos** : abucheo *m* — ~ *vt* : abuchear

book ['buk] *n* **1** : libro *m* **2** NOTEBOOK : libreta *f*, cuaderno *m* — ~ *vt* : reservar — **bookcase** ['buk,keis] *n* : estantería *f* — **bookkeeping** ['buk,ki:piŋ] *n* : teneduría *f* de libros, contabilidad *f* — **booklet** ['buklət] *n* : folleto *m* — **bookmark** ['buk,mɑrk] *n* : marcador *m* de libros — **bookseller** ['buk,selər] *n* : librero *m*, -ra *f* — **bookshelf** ['buk,ʃelf] *n, pl* **-shelves** : estante *m* — **bookstore** ['buk,stor] *n* : librería *f*

boom ['bu:m] *vi* **1** : tronar, resonar — PROSPER : estar en auge, prosperar —

~ *n* **1** : bramido *m*, estruendo *m* **2** : auge *m* (económico)

boon ['bu:n] *n* : ayuda *f*, beneficio *m*

boost ['bu:st] *vt* **1** LIFT : levantar **2** INCREASE : aumentar — ~ *n* **1** INCREASE : aumento *m* **2** ENCOURAGEMENT : estímulo *m*

boot ['bu:t] *n* : bota *f*, botín *m* — ~ *vt* **1** : dar una patada a **2** *or* ~ **up** : cargar (un ordenador)

booth ['bu:θ] *n, pl* **booths** ['bu:ðz, 'bu:θs] : cabina *f* (de teléfono, de votar), caseta *f* (de información)

booty ['bu:ti] *n, pl* **-ties** : botín *m*

booze ['bu:z] *n* : trago *m*, bebida *f* (alcohólica)

border ['bordər] *n* **1** EDGE : borde *m*, orilla *f* **2** TRIM : ribete *m* **3** FRONTIER : frontera *f*

bore[1] ['bor] *vt* **bored; boring** DRILL : taladrar

bore[2] *vt* TIRE : aburrir — ~ *n* : pesado *m*, -da *fam f* (persona), lata *f fam* (cosa, situación) — **boredom** ['bordəm] *n* : aburrimiento *m* — **boring** ['boriŋ] *adj* : aburrido, pesado

born ['born] *adj* **1** : nacido **2 be** ~ : nacer

borough ['bəro] *n* : distrito *m* municipal

borrow ['bɑro] *vt* : pedir prestado, tomar prestado

Bosnian ['bɑzniən, 'boz-] *adj* : bosnio *m*, -nia *f*

bosom ['buzəm, 'bu:-] *n* BREAST : pecho *m*, seno *m* — ~ *adj* ~ **friend** : amigo *m* íntimo

boss ['bɔs] *n* : jefe *m*, -fa *f*; patrón *m*, -trona *f* — ~ *vt* SUPERVISE : dirigir — **bossy** ['bɔsi] *adj* **bossier; -est** : autoritario

botany ['bɑtəni] *n* : botánica *f* — **botanical** [bə'tænikəl] *adj* : botánico

botch ['bɑtʃ] *vt* : hacer una chapuza de, estropear

both ['bo:θ] *adj* : ambos, los dos, las dos — ~ *pron* : ambos *m*, -bas *f*; los dos, las dos

bother ['bɑðər] *vt* TROUBLE : preocupar **2** PESTER : molestar, fastidiar — *vi* ~ **to** : molestarse en — ~ *n* : molestia *f*

bottle ['bɑtəl] *n* **1** : botella *f*, frasco *m* **2** *or* **baby** ~ : biberón *m* — ~ *vt* **bottled; bottling** : embotellar — **bottleneck** ['bɑtəl,nek] *n* : embotellamiento *m*

bottom ['bɑtəm] *n* **1** : fondo *m* (de una caja, del mar, etc.), pie *m* (de una escalera, una montaña, etc.), final *m* (de una lista) **2** BUTTOCKS : nalgas *fpl*, trasero *m* — ~ *adj* : más bajo, inferior, de abajo — **bottomless** ['bɑṭəmləs] *adj* : sin fondo

bough ['baʊ] *n* : rama *f*

bought → buy

bouillon ['bu:jɑn; 'bʊljɑn, -jən] *n* : caldo *m*

boulder ['boːldər] *n* : canto *m* rodado

boulevard ['bʊlə,vɑrd, 'buː-] *n* : bulevar *m*

bounce ['baʊnts] *v* **bounced; bouncing** *vt* : hacer rebotar — *vi* : rebotar — **~** *n* : rebote *m*

bound[1] ['baʊnd] *adj* be **~** for : ir rumbo a

bound[2] *adj* 1 OBLIGED : obligado 2 DETERMINED : decidido 3 be **~** to : tener que

bound[3] *n* out of **~s** : (en) zona prohibida — **boundary** ['baʊndri, -dəri] *n, pl* **-aries** : límite *m* — **boundless** ['baʊndləs] *adj* : sin límites

bouquet [boːˈkeɪ, buː-] *n* : ramo *m*

bourgeois ['bʊrʒ,wɑ, bʊrʒ'wɑ] *adj* : burgués

bout ['baʊt] *n* 1 : combate *m* (en deportes) 2 : ataque *m* (de una enfermedad) 3 : período *m* (de actividad)

bow[1] ['baʊ] *vi* : inclinarse — *vt* **~** one's head : inclinar la cabeza — **~** ['baʊ] *n* : reverencia *f*, inclinación *f*

bow[2] ['boː] *n* 1 : arco *m* 2 **tie a ~** : hacer un lazo

bow[3] ['baʊ] *n* : proa *f* (de un barco)

bowels ['baʊəls] *npl* 1 : intestinos *mpl* 2 DEPTHS : entrañas *fpl*

bowl[1] ['boːl] *n* : tazón *m*, cuenco *m*

bowl[2] *vi* : jugar a los bolos — **bowling** ['boːlɪŋ] *n* : bolos *mpl*

box[1] ['bɑks] *vi* FIGHT : boxear — **boxer** ['bɑksər] *n* : boxeador *m*, -dora *f* — **boxing** ['bɑksɪŋ] *n* : boxeo *m*

box[2] *n* 1 : caja *f*, cajón *m* : palco *m* (en el teatro) — **~** *vt* : empaquetar — **box office** *n* : taquilla *f*, boletería *f Lat*

boy ['bɔɪ] *n* : niño *m*, chico *m*

boycott ['bɔɪ,kɑt] *vt* : boicotear — **~** *n* : boicot *m*

boyfriend ['bɔɪ,frɛnd] *n* : novio *m*

bra ['brɑ] → **brassiere**

brace ['breɪs] *n* 1 SUPPORT : abrazadera *f* 2 **~s** *npl* : aparatos *mpl* (para dientes) — **~** *vi* **~ oneself for** : prepararse para

bracelet ['breɪslət] *n* : brazalete *m*

bracket ['brækət] *n* 1 SUPPORT : soporte *m* 2 : corchete *m* (marca de puntuación) 3 CATEGORY : categoría *f* — **~** *vt* 1 : poner entre corchetes 2 CATEGORIZE : catalogar

brag ['bræg] *vi* **bragged; bragging** : jactarse

braid ['breɪd] *vt* : trenzar — **~** *n* : trenza *f*

braille ['breɪl] *n* : braille *m*

brain ['breɪn] *n* 1 : cerebro *m* 2 **~s** *npl* : inteligencia *f* — **brainstorm** ['breɪn,stɔrm] *n* : idea *f* genial — **brainwash** ['breɪn,wɔʃ, -,wɑʃ] *vt* : lavar el cerebro — **brainy** ['breɪni] *adj* **brainier; -est** : inteligente, listo

brake ['breɪk] *n* : freno *m* — **~** *v* **braked; braking** : frenar

bramble ['bræmbəl] *n* : zarza *f*

bran ['bræn] *n* : salvado *m*

branch ['bræntʃ] *n* 1 : rama *f* (de una planta) 2 DIVISION : ramal *m* (de un camino, etc.), sucursal *f* (de una empresa), agencia *f* (del gobierno) — *vi or* **~ off** : ramificarse, bifurcarse

brand ['brænd] *n* 1 : marca *f* (de ganado) 2 *or* **~ name** : marca *f* de fábrica — **~** *vt* 1 : marcar (ganado) 2 LABEL : tachar, tildar

brandish ['brændɪʃ] *vt* : blandir

brand-new ['brænd'nuː, -'njuː] *adj* : flamante

brandy ['brændi] *n, pl* **-dies** : brandy *m*, coñac *m*

brass ['bræs] *n* 1 : latón *m* 2 : metales *mpl* (de una orquesta)

brassiere [brəˈzɪr, brɑ-] *n* : sostén *m*, brasier *m Lat*

brat ['bræt] *n* : mocoso *m*, -sa *f fam*

bravado [brəˈvɑdo] *n, pl* **-does** *or* **-dos** : bravuconadas *fpl*

brave ['breɪv] *adj* **braver; bravest** : valiente, valeroso — **~** *vt* **braved; braving** : afrontar, hacer frente a — **~** *n* : guerrero *m* indio — **bravery** ['breɪvəri] *n* : valor *m*, valentía *f*

brawl ['brɔl] *n* : pelea *f*, reyerta *f*

brawn ['brɔn] *n* : músculos *mpl* — **brawny** ['brɔni] *adj* **brawnier; -est** : musculoso

bray ['breɪ] *vi* : rebuznar

brazen ['breɪzən] *adj* : descarado

Brazilian [brəˈzɪljən] *adj* : brasileño *m*, -ña *f*

breach ['briːtʃ] *n* 1 VIOLATION : infracción *f*, violación *f* 2 GAP : brecha *f*

bread ['brɛd] *n* 1 : pan *m* 2 **~ crumbs** : migajas *fpl*

breadth ['brɛtθ] *n* : anchura *f*

break ['breɪk] *v* **broke** ['broːk]; **broken** ['broːkən]; **breaking** *vt* 1 : romper, quebrar 2 VIOLATE : infringir, violar 3 INTERRUPT : interrumpir 4 : batir (un récord, etc.) 5 **~ a habit** : quitarse una costumbre 6 **~ the news** : dar la noticia — *vi* 1 : romperse, quebrarse 2 **~ away** : escapar **3 ~ down** : estropearse (dícese de una máquina), fallar (dícese de un sistema, etc.) **4 ~ into** : entrar en **5 ~ off** : interrumpirse **6 ~ out of** : escaparse de **7 ~ up** SEPARATE : separarse — **~** n **1** : ruptura f, fractura f **2** GAP : interrupción f, claro m (entre las nubes) **3 lucky ~** : golpe m de suerte **4 take a ~** : tomar(se) un descanso — **breakable** ['breɪkəbəl] adj : quebradizo, frágil — **breakdown** ['breɪk,daʊn] n **1** : avería f (de máquinas), interrupción f (de comunicaciones), fracaso m (de negociaciones) **2** or **nervous ~** : crisis f nerviosa

breakfast ['brɛkfəst] n : desayuno m

breast ['brɛst] n **1** : seno m (de una mujer) **2** CHEST : pecho m — **breast–feed** ['brɛst,fiːd] vt **-fed** [-,fɛd]; **-feeding** : amamantar

breath ['brɛθ] n : aliento m, respiración f — **breathe** ['briːð] v **breathed**; **breathing** : respirar — **breathless** ['brɛθləs] adj : sin aliento, jadeante — **breathtaking** ['brɛθ,teɪkɪŋ] adj : impresionante

breed ['briːd] v **bred** ['brɛd]; **breeding** vt **1** : criar (animales) **2** ENGENDER : engendrar, producir — vi **1** : reproducirse — **~** n **1** : raza f **2** CLASS : clase f, tipo m

breeze ['briːz] n : brisa f — **breezy** ['briːzi] adj **breezier; -est 1** WINDY : ventoso **2** NONCHALANT : despreocupado

brevity ['brɛvəṭi] n, pl **-ties** : brevedad f

brew ['bruː] vt : hacer (cerveza, etc.), preparar (té) — vi **1** : fabricar cerveza **2** : amenazar (dícese de una tormenta) — **brewery** ['bruːəri, 'brʊri] n, pl **-eries** : cervecería f

bribe ['braɪb] n : soborno m — **~** vt **bribed; bribing** : sobornar — **bribery** ['braɪbəri] n, pl **-eries** : soborno m

brick ['brɪk] n : ladrillo m — **bricklayer** ['brɪk,leɪər] n : albañil mf

bride ['braɪd] n : novia f — **bridal** ['braɪdəl] adj : nupcial, de novia — **bridegroom** ['braɪd,gruːm] n : novio m — **bridesmaid** ['braɪdz,meɪd] n : dama f de honor

bridge ['brɪdʒ] n **1** : puente m **2** : caballete m (de la nariz) **3** : bridge m (juego de naipes) — **~** vt **bridged; bridging 1** : tender un puente sobre **2 ~ the gap** : salvar las diferencias

bridle ['braɪdəl] n : brida f — **~** vt **-dled; -dling** : embridar

brief ['briːf] adj : breve — **~** n **1** : resumen m, sumario m **2 ~s** npl UN-

DERPANTS : calzoncillos mpl — **~** vt ['briːf,keɪs] n : portafolio m, maletín m — **briefly** ['briːfli] adv : brevemente

bright ['braɪt] adj **1** : brillante, claro **2** CHEERFUL : alegre, animado **3** INTELLIGENT : listo, inteligente — **brighten** ['braɪtən] vi **1** : hacerse más brillante **2** or **~ up** : animarse, alegrarse — vt **1** ILLUMINATE : iluminar **2** ENLIVEN : alegrar, animar

brilliant ['brɪljənt] adj : brillante — **brilliance** ['brɪljənts] n **1** BRIGHTNESS : resplandor m, brillantez f **2** INTELLIGENCE : inteligencia f

brim ['brɪm] n **1** : borde m (de una taza, etc.) **2** : ala f (de un sombrero) — **~** vi **brimmed; brimming** or **~ over** : desbordarse, rebosar

brine ['braɪn] n : salmuera f

bring ['brɪŋ] vt **brought** ['brɔt]; **bringing 1** : traer **2 ~ about** : ocasionar **3 ~ around** PERSUADE : convencer **4 ~ back** : devolver **5 ~ down** : derribar **6 ~ on** CAUSE : provocar **7 ~ out** : sacar **8 ~ to an end** : terminar (con) **9 ~ up** REAR : criar **10 ~ up** MENTION : sacar

brink ['brɪŋk] n : borde m

brisk ['brɪsk] adj **1** FAST : rápido **2** LIVELY : enérgico

bristle ['brɪsəl] n : cerda f (de un animal), pelo m (de una planta) — **~** vi **-tled; -tling** : erizarse

British ['brɪtɪʃ] adj : británico

brittle ['brɪtəl] adj **-tler; -tlest** : frágil, quebradizo

broach ['broːtʃ] vt : abordar

broad ['brɔd] adj **1** WIDE : ancho **2** GENERAL : general **3 in ~ daylight** : en pleno día

broadcast ['brɔd,kæst] vt **-cast; -casting** : emitir — **~** n : emisión f

broaden ['brɔdən] vt : ampliar, ensanchar — vi : ensancharse — **broadly** ['brɔdli] adv : en general — **broad–minded** ['brɔd'maɪndəd] adj : de miras amplias, tolerante

broccoli ['brɑkəli] n : brócoli m, brécol m

brochure [broˈʃʊr] n : folleto m

broil ['brɔɪl] vt : asar a la parrilla

broke ['broːk] → **break** — **~** adj : pelado fam — **broken** ['broːkən] adj : roto, quebrado — **brokenhearted** [,broːkən'hɑrtəd] adj : desconsolado, con el corazón destrozado

broker ['broːkər] n : corredor m, -dora f

bronchitis [brɑnˈkaɪtəs, brɑŋ-] n : bronquitis f

bronze ['branz] n : bronce m

brooch ['broːtʃ, 'bruːtʃ] n : broche m

brood ['bruːd] n : nidada f (de pájaros), camada f (de mamíferos) — ~ vi IN-CUBATE : empollar 2 ~ **about** : dar vueltas a, pensar demasiado en

brook ['brʊk] n : arroyo m

broom ['bruːm, 'brʊm] n : escoba f — **broomstick** ['bruːm,stɪk, 'brʊm-] n : palo m de escoba

broth ['brɔθ] n, pl **broths** ['brɔθs, 'brɔðz] : caldo m

brothel ['braθəl, 'brɔ-] n : burdel m

brother ['brʌðər] n : hermano m — **brotherhood** ['brʌðər,hʊd] n : fraternidad f — **brother–in–law** ['brʌðərin-,lɔ] n, pl **brothers–in–law:** cuñado m — **brotherly** ['brʌðərli] adj : fraternal

brought → **bring**

brow ['braʊ] n 1 EYEBROW : ceja f 2 FOREHEAD : frente f 3 : cima f (de una colina)

brown ['braʊn] adj : marrón, castaño (dícese del pelo), moreno (dícese de la piel) — ~ n : marrón m — ~ vt : dorar (en cocinar)

browse ['braʊz] vi **browsed; browsing** : mirar, echar un vistazo

bruise ['bruːz] vt **bruised; bruising 1** : contusionar, magullar (a una persona) **2** : machucar (frutas) — ~ n : cardenal m, magulladura f

brunch ['brʌntʃ] n : brunch m

brunet or **brunette** [bruːˈnɛt] adj : moreno — ~ n : moreno m, -na f

brunt ['brʌnt] n **bear the ~ of** : aguantar el mayor impacto de

brush ['brʌʃ] n 1 : cepillo m, pincel m (de artista), brocha f (de pintor) 2 UN-DERBRUSH : maleza f — ~ vt 1 : cepillar 2 GRAZE : rozar 3 ~ **aside** : rechazar 4 ~ **off** DISREGARD : hacer caso omiso de — vi ~ **up on** : repasar — **brush–off** ['brʌʃ,ɔf] n **give the ~ to** : dar calabazas a

brusque ['brʌsk] adj : brusco

brutal ['bruːtəl] adj : brutal — **brutality** [bruːˈtæləti] n, pl **-ties** : brutalidad f

brute ['bruːt] adj : bruto — ~ n : bestia f; bruto m, -ta f

bubble ['bʌbəl] n : burbuja f — ~ vi **-bled; -bling** : burbujear

buck ['bʌk] n, pl **buck** or **bucks 1** : animal m macho, ciervo m (macho) **2** DOLLAR : dólar m — ~ vi **1** : corcovear (dícese de un caballo) **2** ~ **up** : animarse, levantar el ánimo — vt OP-POSE : oponerse a, ir en contra de

bucket ['bʌkət] n : cubo m

buckle ['bʌkəl] n : hebilla f — ~ v **-led;** **-ling** vt **1** FASTEN : abrochar **2** BEND : combar, torcer — vi **1** : combarse, torcerse **2** : doblarse (dícese de las rodillas)

bud ['bʌd] n 1 : brote m **2** or **flower ~** : capullo m — ~ vi **budded; budding** : brotar, hacer brotes

Buddhism ['buː,dɪzəm, 'bʊ-] n : budismo m — **Buddhist** ['buːdɪst, 'bʊ-] adj : budista — ~ n : budista mf

buddy ['bʌdi] n, pl **-dies** : compañero m, -ra f

budge ['bʌdʒ] vi **budged; budging 1** MOVE : moverse **2** YIELD : ceder

budget ['bʌdʒət] n : presupuesto m — ~ vi : presupuestar — **budgetary** ['bʌdʒə,tɛri] adj : presupuestario

buff ['bʌf] n 1 : beige m, color m de ante **2** ENTHUSIAST : aficionado m, -da f — ~ adj : beige — ~ vt POLISH : pulir

buffalo ['bʌfə,loː] n, pl **-lo** or **-loes** : búfalo m

buffet [,bʌˈfeɪ, ,buː-] n 1 : bufé m (comida) **2** SIDEBOARD : aparador m

bug ['bʌg] n 1 INSECT : bicho m, insecto m **2** FLAW : defecto m **3** GERM : microbio m **4** MICROPHONE : micrófono m (oculto) — ~ vt **bugged; bugging 1** PESTER : fastidiar, molestar **2** : ocultar micrófonos en (una habitación, etc.)

buggy ['bʌgi] n, pl **-gies 1** CARRIAGE : calesa f **2** or **baby ~** : cochecito m (para niños)

bugle ['bjuːgəl] n : clarín m, corneta f

build ['bɪld] v **built** ['bɪlt]; **building** vt **1** : construir **2** DEVELOP : desarrollar — vi **1** or ~ **up** INTENSIFY : aumentar, intensificar **2** or ~ **up** ACCUMULATE : acumularse — ~ n PHYSIQUE : físico m, complexión f — **builder** ['bɪldər] n : constructor m, -tora f — **building** ['bɪldɪŋ] n 1 STRUCTURE : edificio m **2** CONSTRUCTION : construcción f — **built–in** ['bɪlt'ɪn] adj : empotrado

bulb ['bʌlb] n 1 : bulbo m (de una planta) **2** LIGHTBULB : bombilla f

bulge ['bʌldʒ] vi **bulged; bulging** : sobresalir — ~ n : bulto m, protuberancia f

bulk ['bʌlk] n 1 VOLUME : volumen m, bulto m **2 in ~** : en grandes cantidades — **bulky** ['bʌlki] adj **bulkier; -est** : voluminoso

bull ['bʊl] n 1 : toro m **2** MALE : macho m

bulldog ['bʊl,dɔg] n : buldog m

bulldozer ['bʊl,doːzər] n : bulldozer m

bullet ['bʊlət] n : bala f

bulletin ['bʊlətən, -ləʒən] n : boletín m — **bulletin board** n : tablón m de anuncios

bulletproof [ˈbʊlətˌpruːf] *adj* : a prueba de balas

bullfight [ˈbʊlˌfaɪt] *n* : corrida *f* (de toros) — **bullfighter** [ˈbʊlˌfaɪtər] *n* : torero *m*, -ra *f*; matador *m*

bullion [ˈbʊljən] *n* : oro *m* en lingotes, plata *f* en lingotes

bull's-eye [ˈbʊlzˌaɪ] *n, pl* **bull's-eyes** : diana *f*

bully [ˈbʊli] *n, pl* **-lies** : matón *m* — *vt* **-lied; -lying** : intimidar

bum [ˈbʌm] *n* : vagabundo *m*, -da *f*

bumblebee [ˈbʌmbəlˌbiː] *n* : abejorro *m*

bump [ˈbʌmp] *n* **1** BULGE : bulto *m*, protuberancia *f* **2** IMPACT : golpe *m* **3** JOLT : sacudida *f* — ~ *vt* : chocar contra — *vi* ~ **into** MEET : encontrarse con — **bumper** [ˈbʌmpər] *n* : parachoques *mpl* — ~ *adj* : extraordinario, récord — **bumpy** [ˈbʌmpi] *adj* **bumpier; -est** **1** : desigual, lleno de baches (dícese de un camino) **2 a** ~ **flight** : un vuelo agitado

bun [ˈbʌn] *n* : bollo *m*

bunch [ˈbʌntʃ] *n* : grupo *m* (de personas), racimo *m* (de frutas, etc.), ramo *m* (de flores), manojo *m* (de llaves) — ~ *vi or* ~ **up** : amontonar, agruparse

bundle [ˈbʌndəl] *n* **1** : lío *m*, bulto *m*, atado *m*, haz *m* (de palos) **2** PARCEL : paquete *m* **3** ~ **of nerves** : manojo *m* de nervios — ~ *vt* **-dled; -dling** *or* ~ **up** : liar, atar

bungalow [ˈbʌŋgəˌloː] *n* : casa *f* de un solo piso

bungle [ˈbʌŋgəl] *vt* **-gled; -gling** : echar a perder

bunion [ˈbʌnjən] *n* : juanete *m*

bunk [ˈbʌŋk] *n or* **bunk bed** : litera *f*

bunny [ˈbʌni] *n, pl* **-nies** : conejo *m*, -ja *f*

buoy [ˈbuːi, ˈbɔɪ] *n* : boya *f* — ~ *vt or* ~ **up** HEARTEN : animar, levantar el ánimo a — **buoyant** [ˈbɔɪənt, ˈbuːjənt] *adj* **1** : boyante, flotante **2** LIGHTHEARTED : alegre, optimista

burden [ˈbərdən] *n* : carga *f* — ~ *vt* ~ **s.o. with** : cargar a algn con — **burdensome** [ˈbərdənsəm] *adj* : oneroso

bureau [ˈbjʊro] *n* **1** : cómoda *f* (mueble) **2** : departamento *m* (del gobierno) AGENCY : agencia *f* — **bureaucracy** [bjʊˈrɑkrəsi] *n, pl* **-cies** : burocracia *f* — **bureaucrat** [ˈbjʊrəˌkræt] *n* : burócrata *mf* — **bureaucratic** [ˌbjʊrəˈkrætɪk] *adj* : burocrático

burglar [ˈbərglər] *n* : ladrón *m*, -drona *f* — **burglarize** [ˈbərgləˌraɪz] *vt* **-ized; -izing** : robar — **burglary** [ˈbərgləri] *n, pl* **-glaries** : robo *m*

burgundy [ˈbərgəndi] *n, pl* **-dies** : borgoña *m*, vino *m* de Borgoña

burial [ˈbɛriəl] *n* : entierro *m*

burly [ˈbərli] *adj* **-lier; -liest** : fornido

burn [ˈbərn] *v* **burned** [ˈbərnd, ˈbərnt] *or* **burnt** [ˈbərnt]; **burning** *vt* **1** : quemar **2** *or* ~ **down** : incendiar **3** ~ **up** : consumir — *vi* **1** : arder (dícese de un fuego), quemarse (dícese de la comida, etc.) **2** : estar encendido (dícese de una luz) **3** ~ **out** : apagarse — ~ *n* : quemadura *f* — **burner** [ˈbərnər] *n* : quemador *m*

burnish [ˈbərnɪʃ] *vt* : pulir

burp [ˈbərp] *vi* : eructar — ~ *n* : eructo *m*

burro [ˈbɛro, ˈbʊr-] *n, pl* **-os** : burro *m*

burrow [ˈbɛro] *n* : madriguera *f* — ~ *vi* **1** : cavar **2** ~ **into** : hurgar en

bursar [ˈbərsər] *n* : tesorero *m*, -ra *f*

burst [ˈbərst] *v* **burst** *or* **bursted; bursting** *vi* : reventarse — *vt* : reventar — ~ *n* **1** EXPLOSION : estallido *m*, explosión *f* **2** OUTBURST : arranque *m*, arrebato *m* **3** ~ **of laughter** : carcajada *f*

bury [ˈbɛri] *vt* **buried; burying** **1** INTER : enterrar **2** HIDE : esconder

bus [ˈbʌs] *n, pl* **buses** *or* **busses** : autobús *m*, bus *m* — ~ *v* **bused** *or* **bussed** [ˈbʌst]; **busing** *or* **bussing** [ˈbʌsɪŋ] *vt* : transportar en autobús — *vi* : viajar en autobús

bush [ˈbʊʃ] *n* SHRUB : arbusto *m*; mata *f*

bushel [ˈbʊʃəl] *n* : medida *f* de áridos igual a 35.24 litros

bushy [ˈbʊʃi] *adj* **bushier; -est** : poblado, espeso

busily [ˈbɪzəli] *adv* : afanosamente

business [ˈbɪznəs, -nəz] *n* **1** COMMERCE : negocios *mpl*, comercio *m* **2** COMPANY : empresa *f*, negocio *m* **3 it's none of your** ~ : no es asunto tuyo — **businessman** [ˈbɪznəsˌmæn, -nəz-] *n, pl* **-men** [-mən, -ˌmɛn] : empresario *m*, hombre *m* de negocios — **businesswoman** [ˈbɪznəsˌwʊmən, -nəz-] *n, pl* **-women** [-ˌwɪmən] : empresaria *f*, mujer *f* de negocios

bust[1] [ˈbʌst] *vt* BREAK : romper

bust[2] *n* **1** : busto *m* (en la escultura) **2** BREASTS : pecho *m*, senos *mpl*

bustle [ˈbʌsəl] *vi* **-tled; -tling** *or* ~ **about** : ir y venir, ajetrearse — ~ *n or* **hustle and** ~ : bullicio *m*, ajetreo *m*

busy [ˈbɪzi] *adj* **busier; -est 1** : ocupado **2** BUSTLING : concurrido

but [ˈbʌt] *conj* **1** : pero **2 not one** ~ **two** : no uno sino dos — ~ *prep* : excepto, menos

butcher ['butʃər] n : carnicero m, -ra f — ~ vt 1 : matar 2 BOTCH : hacer una carnicería de

butler ['bʌtlər] n : mayordomo m

butt ['bʌt] vt : embestir (con los cuernos), darle un cabezazo a — vi ~ **in** : interrumpir — ~ n 1 BUTTING : embestida f (de cuernos) 2 TARGET : blanco m 3 : extremo m, culata f (de un rifle), colilla f (de un cigarillo)

butter ['bʌtər] n : mantequilla f — ~ vt : untar con mantequilla

buttercup ['bʌtər,kʌp] n : ranúnculo m

butterfly ['bʌtər,flaɪ] n, pl **-flies** : mariposa f

buttocks ['bʌtəks, -,taks] npl : nalgas fpl

button ['bʌtən] n : botón m — ~ vt : abotonar — vi or ~ **up** : abotonarse — **buttonhole** ['bʌtən,hoːl] n : ojal m — ~ vt **-holed; -holing** : acorralar

buy ['baɪ] vt **bought** ['bɔt], **buying** : comprar — ~ n : compra f — **buyer** ['baɪər] n : comprador m, -dora f

buzz ['bʌz] vi : zumbar — ~ n : zumbido m

buzzard ['bʌzərd] n : buitre m

buzzer ['bʌzər] n : timbre m

by ['baɪ] prep 1 NEAR : cerca de 2 VIA : por 3 PAST : por, por delante de 4 DURING : de, durante 5 (in expressions of time) : para 6 (indicating cause or agent) : por, de, a — ~ adv 1 ~ **and** ~ : poco después 2 ~ **and large** : en general 3 go ~ : pasar 4 stop ~ : pasar por casa

bygone ['baɪ,gɔn] adj : pasado — ~ n let ~s be ~s : lo pasado, pasado está

bypass ['baɪ,pæs] n : carretera f de circunvalación — ~ vt : evitar

by-product ['baɪ,prɑdəkt] n : subproducto m

bystander ['baɪ,stændər] n : espectador m, -dora f

byte ['baɪt] n : byte m, octeto m

byword ['baɪ,wərd] n be a ~ for : estar sinónimo de

C

c ['siː] n, pl **c's** or **cs** : c, tercera letra del alfabeto inglés

cab ['kæb] n 1 : taxi m 2 : cabina f (de un camión, etc.)

cabbage ['kæbɪdʒ] n : col f, repollo m

cabin ['kæbən] n 1 : cabaña f 2 : cabina f (de un avión, etc.), camarote m (de un barco)

cabinet ['kæbnət] n 1 CUPBOARD : armario m 2 : gabinete m (del gobierno) 3 or medicine ~ : botiquín m

cable ['keɪbəl] n : cable m — **cable television** n : televisión f por cable

cackle ['kækəl] vi **-led; -ling 1** CLUCK : cacarear 2 LAUGH : reírse a carcajadas

cactus ['kæktəs] n, pl **cacti** [-,taɪ] or **-tuses** : cactus m

cadence ['keɪdənts] n : cadencia f, ritmo m

cadet [kə'dɛt] n : cadete mf

café [kæ'feɪ, kə-] n : café m, cafetería f — **cafeteria** [,kæfə'tɪriə] n : restaurante m autoservicio, cantina f

caffeine [kæ'fiːn] n : cafeína f

cage ['keɪdʒ] n : jaula f — ~ vt **caged; caging** : enjaular

cajole [kə'dʒoːl] vt **-joled; -joling** : engatusar

cake ['keɪk] n 1 : pastel m, torta f 2 : pastilla f (de jabón) 3 take the ~ : ser el colmo — **caked** ['keɪkt] adj ~ **with** : cubierto de

calamity [kə'læməti] n, pl **-ties** : calamidad f

calcium ['kælsiəm] n : calcio m

calculate ['kælkjə,leɪt] v **-lated; -lating** : calcular — **calculating** ['kælkjə,leɪtɪŋ] adj : calculador — **calculation** [,kælkjə'leɪʃən] n : cálculo m — **calculator** ['kælkjə,leɪtər] n : calculadora f

calendar ['kæləndər] n : calendario m

calf¹ ['kæf, 'kaf] n, pl **calves** ['kævz, 'kavz] 1 : becerro m, -rra f; ternero m, -ra f (de vacunos) 2 : cría f (de otros mamíferos)

calf² n, pl **calves** : pantorrilla f (de la pierna)

caliber or **calibre** ['kæləbər] n : calibre m

call ['kɔl] vi 1 : llamar 2 VISIT : pasar, hacer (una) visita 3 ~ **for** : requerir — vt 1 : llamar 2 ~ **off** : cancelar — ~ n 1 : llamada f 2 SHOUT : grito m 3 VISIT : visita f 4 DEMAND : petición f — **calling** ['kɔlɪŋ] n : vocación f

callous ['kæləs] adj : insensible, cruel

calm ['kɑm, 'kɑlm] n : calma f, tranquilidad f — ~ vt : calmar — vi or ~ **down** : calmarse — ~ adj : tranquilo, en calma — **calmly** ['kɑmli, 'kɑlm-] adv : con calma

calorie ['kæləri] n : caloría f

came → **come**

camel ['kæməl] n : camello m

camera ['kæmrə, 'kæmərə] n : cámara f

camouflage ['kæmə,flɑʒ, -,flɑdʒ] n : camuflaje m — ~ vt **-flaged; -flaging** : camuflar

camp ['kæmp] n **1** : campamento m **2** FACTION : bando m — ~ vi : acampar, ir de camping

campaign [kæm'peɪn] n : campaña f — ~ vi : hacer (una) campaña

camping ['kæmpɪŋ] n : camping m

campus ['kæmpəs] n : ciudad f universitaria

can¹ ['kæn] v aux, past could ['kʊd]; present s & pl **can 1** (expressing possibility or permission) : poder **2** (expressing knowledge or ability) : saber **3** that cannot be! : ¡no puede ser!

can² ['kæn] n : lata f — ~ vt **canned; canning** : enlatar

Canadian [kə'neɪdiən] adj : canadiense

canal [kə'næl] n : canal m

canary [kə'neri] n, pl **-naries** : canario m

cancel ['kæntsəl] vt **-celed** or **-celled; -celing** or **-celling** : cancelar — **cancellation** [,kæntsə'leɪʃən] n : cancelación f

cancer ['kæntsər] n : cáncer m — **cancerous** ['kæntsərəs] adj : canceroso

candelabra [,kændə'lɑbrə, -'læ-] n, pl **-bra** or **-bras** : candelabro m

candid ['kændɪd] adj : franco

candidate ['kændə,deɪt, -dət] n : candidato m, -ta f — **candidacy** ['kændədəsi] n, pl **-cies** : candidatura f

candle ['kændəl] n : vela f — **candlestick** ['kændəl,stɪk] n : candelero m

candor or Brit **candour** ['kændər] n : franqueza f

candy ['kændi] n, pl **-dies** : dulce m, caramelo m

cane ['keɪn] n **1** : bastón m (para andar), vara f (para castigar) **2** REED : caña f, mimbre m — ~ vt **caned; caning 1** : tapizar con mimbre **2** FLOG : azotar

canine ['keɪ,naɪn] n or ~ **tooth** : colmillo m, diente m canino — ~ adj : canino

canister ['kænəstər] n : lata f, bote m Spain

cannibal ['kænəbəl] n : caníbal mf

cannon ['kænən] n, pl **-nons** or **-non** : cañón m

cannot (can not) ['kæn,ɑt, kə'nɑt] → **can¹**

canny ['kæni] adj **cannier; -est** : astuto

canoe [kə'nuː] n : canoa f, piragua f — ~ vt **-noed; -noeing** : ir en canoa

canon ['kænən] n : canon m — **canonize** ['kænə,naɪz] vt **-ized; -izing** : canonizar

can opener n : abrelatas m

canopy ['kænəpi] n, pl **-pies** : dosel m

can't ['kænt, 'kɑnt] (contraction of **can not**) → **can¹**

cantaloupe ['kæntəl,oːp] n : melón m, cantalupo m

cantankerous [kæn'tæŋkərəs] adj : irritable, irascible

canteen [kæn'tiːn] n **1** FLASK : cantimplora f **2** CAFETERIA : cantina f

canter ['kæntər] vi : ir a medio galope — ~ n : medio galope m

canvas ['kænvəs] n **1** : lona f (tela) **2** : lienzo m (de pintar)

canvass ['kænvəs] vt **1** : solicitar votos de, hacer campaña entre **2** POLL : sondear — ~ n **1** : solicitación f (de votos) **2** POLL : sondeo m

canyon ['kænjən] n : cañón m

cap n **1** : gorra f, gorro m **2** TOP : tapa f, tapón m (de botellas) **3** LIMIT : tope m — ~ ['kæp] vt **capped; capping 1** COVER : tapar, cubrir **2** OUTDO : superar

capable ['keɪpəbəl] adj : capaz, competente — **capability** [,keɪpə'bɪləti] n, pl **-ties** : capacidad f

capacity [kə'pæsəti] n, pl **-ties 1** : capacidad f **2** ROLE : calidad f

cape¹ ['keɪp] n : cabo m (en geografía)

cape² n CLOAK : capa f

caper¹ ['keɪpər] n : alcaparra f

caper² n PRANK : broma f, travesura f

capital ['kæpəṭəl] adj **1** : capital **2** : mayúsculo (dícese de las letras) — ~ n **1** or ~ **city** : capital f **2** WEALTH : capital m **3** or ~ **letter** : mayúscula f — **capitalism** ['kæpəṭəl,ɪzəm] n : capitalismo m — **capitalist** ['kæpəṭəlɪst] or **capitalistic** [,kæpəṭəl'ɪstɪk] adj : capitalista — **capitalize** ['kæpəṭəl,aɪz] vt **-ized; -izing 1** FINANCE : capitalizar **2** : escribir con mayúscula — vi ~ **on** : sacar partido de

capitol ['kæpəṭəl] n : capitolio m

capitulate [kə'pɪtʃəleɪt] vi **-lated; -lating** : capitular

capsize ['kæp,saɪz, kæp'saɪz] v **-sized; -sizing** vt : hacer volcar — vi : zozobrar, volcar(se)

capsule ['kæpsəl, -,suːl] n : cápsula f

captain ['kæptən] n : capitán m, -tana f

caption ['kæpʃən] n **1** : leyenda f (al pie de una ilustración) **2** SUBTITLE : subtítulo m

captivate ['kæptə,veɪt] vt **-vated; -vating** : cautivar, encantar

captive ['kæptɪv] adj : cautivo — ~ n
: cautivo m, -va f — **captivity** [kæp-
'tɪvət̬i] n : cautiverio m

capture ['kæptʃər] n : captura f, apresamiento m — ~ vt **-tured; -turing 1**
SEIZE : capturar, apresar 2 ~ **one's interest** : captar el interés de uno

car ['kɑr] n 1 : automóvil m, coche m,
carro m Lat 2 or **railroad** ~ : vagón m

carafe [kə'ræf, -'rɑf] n : garrafa f

caramel ['kærməl; 'kærəməl, -,mɛl] n
: caramelo m, azúcar f quemada

carat ['kærət] n : quilate m

caravan ['kærə,væn] n : caravana f

carbohydrate [,kɑrbo'haɪ,dreɪt, -drət] n
: carbohidrato m, hidrato m de carbono

carbon ['kɑrbən] n : carbono m — **carbon copy** n : copia f, duplicado m

carburetor ['kɑrbə,reɪt̬ər, -bjə-] n : carburador m

carcass ['kɑrkəs] n : cuerpo m (de un
animal muerto)

card ['kɑrd] n 1 : tarjeta f 2 or **playing
~** : carta f, naipe m — **cardboard**
['kɑrd,bord] n : cartón m

cardiac ['kɑrdi,æk] adj : cardíaco

cardigan ['kɑrdɪgən] n : cárdigan m

cardinal ['kɑrdənəl] n : cardenal m — ~
adj : cardinal, fundamental

care ['kær] n 1 : cuidado m 2 WORRY
: preocupación 3 **take** ~ **of** : cuidar
(de) — ~ vi **cared; caring 1** : preocuparse, inquietarse 2 ~ **for** TEND
: cuidar (de), atender 3 ~ **for** LIKE
: querer 4 **I don't** ~ : no me importa

career [kə'rɪr] n : carrera f — ~ vi : ir a
toda velocidad

carefree ['kær,fri:, ,kær'-] adj : despreocupado

careful ['kærfəl] adj : cuidadoso —
carefully ['kærfəli] adv : con cuidado,
cuidadosamente — **careless** ['kærləs]
adj : descuidado — **carelessness**
['kærləsnəs] n : descuido m

caress [kə'res] n : caricia f — ~ vt
: acariciar

cargo ['kɑr,goː] n, pl **-goes** or **-gos**
: cargamento m, carga f

caricature ['kærɪkə,tʃʊr] n : caricatura f
— ~ vt **-tured; -turing** : caricaturizar

caring ['kærɪŋ] adj : solícito, afectuoso

carnage ['kɑrnɪdʒ] n : matanza f, carnicería f

carnal ['kɑrnəl] adj : carnal

carnation [kɑr'neɪʃən] n : clavel m

carnival ['kɑrnəvəl] n : carnaval m

carol ['kærəl] n : villancico m

carp ['kɑrp] vi ~ **at** : quejarse de

carpenter ['kɑrpəntər] n : carpintero m,

-ra f — **carpentry** ['kɑrpəntri] n : carpintería f

carpet ['kɑrpət] n : alfombra f

carriage ['kærɪdʒ] n 1 : transporte m (de
mercancías) 2 BEARING : porte m 3 or
baby ~ : cochecito m 4 or **horse-
drawn** ~ : carruaje m, coche m

carrier ['kæriər] n 1 : transportista mf,
empresa f de transportes 2 : portador
m, -dora f (de una enfermedad)

carrot ['kærət] n : zanahoria f

carry ['kæri] v **-ried; -rying** vt 1 : llevar
2 TRANSPORT : transportar 3 STOCK
: vender 4 ENTAIL : acarrear, implicar 5
~ **oneself** : portarse — vi : oírse
(dícese de sonidos) — **carry away** vt
get carried away : exaltarse, entusiasmarse — **carry on** vt CONDUCT : realizar — vi 1 : portarse inapropiada-
mente 2 CONTINUE : seguir, continuar
— **carry out** vt 1 PERFORM : llevar a
cabo, realizar 2 FULFILL : cumplir

cart ['kɑrt] n : carreta f, carro m — ~ vt
or ~ **around** : acarrear

cartilage ['kɑrt̬əlɪdʒ] n : cartílago m

carton ['kɑrtən] n : caja f (de cartón)

cartoon [kɑr'tuːn] n 1 : caricatura f 2
COMIC STRIP : historieta f 3 or **animated** ~ : dibujos mpl animados

cartridge ['kɑrtrɪdʒ] n : cartucho m

carve ['kɑrv] vt **carved; carving 1** : tallar, esculpir 2 : trinchar (carne)

case n 1 : caso m 2 BOX : caja f 3 **in any**
~ : en todo caso 4 **in** ~ **of** : en caso
de 5 **just in** ~ : por si acaso

cash ['kæʃ] n : efectivo m, dinero m en
efectivo — ~ vt : convertir en efectivo, cobrar

cashew ['kæ,ʃuː, kə'ʃuː] n : anacardo m

cashier [kæ'ʃɪr] n : cajero m, -ra f

cashmere ['kæʒ,mɪr, 'kæʃ-] n : cachemira f

cash register n : caja f registradora

casino [kə'siː,noː] n, pl **-nos** : casino m

cask ['kæsk] n : barril m

casket ['kæskət] n : ataúd m

casserole ['kæsə,roːl] n 1 or ~ **dish**
: cazuela f 2 : guiso m (comida)

cassette [kə'set, kæ-] n : cassette mf

cast ['kæst] vt **cast; casting 1** THROW
: arrojar, lanzar 2 : depositar (un voto)
3 : repartir (papeles dramáticos) 4
MOLD : fundir — ~ n 1 : elenco m,
reparto m (de actores) 2 or **plaster** ~
: molde m de yeso, escayola f

castanets [,kæstə'nets] npl : castañuelas
fpl

castaway ['kæstə,weɪ] n : náufrago m,
-ga f

cast iron n : hierro m fundido

castle ['kæsəl] *n* 1 : castillo *m* 2 : torre *f* (en ajedrez)
castrate ['kæs̩treɪt] *vt* **-trated; -trating** : castrar
casual ['kæʒuəl] *adj* 1 CHANCE : casual, fortuito 2 INDIFFERENT : despreocupado 3 INFORMAL : informal — **casually** ['kæʒuəli, 'kæʒəli] *adv* 1 : de manera despreocupada 2 INFORMALLY : informalmente
casualty ['kæʒuəlti, 'kæʒəl-] *n, pl* **-ties** 1 : accidente *m* 2 VICTIM : víctima *f*; herido *m*, -da *f* 3 **casualties** *npl* : bajas *fpl* (militares)
cat ['kæt] *n* : gato *m*, -ta *f*
catalog *or* **catalogue** ['kætə̩lɔg] *n* : catálogo *m* — *vt* **-loged** *or* **-logued; -loging** *or* **-loguing** : catalogar
catapult ['kætə̩pʌlt, -pʊlt] *n* : catapulta *f*
cataract ['kætə̩rækt] *n* : catarata *f*
catastrophe [kə'tæstrə̩fiː] *n* : catástrofe *f* — **catastrophic** [,kætə'strɑfɪk] *adj* : catastrófico
catch ['kætʃ, 'ketʃ] *v* **caught** ['kɔt]; **catching** *vt* 1 CAPTURE, TRAP : capturar, atrapar 2 SURPRISE : sorprender 3 GRASP : agarrar, captar 4 SNAG : enganchar 5 : tomar (un tren, etc.) 6 **~ a cold** : resfriarse — *vi* 1 SNAG : engancharse 2 **~ fire** : prender fuego — **catching** ['kætʃɪŋ, 'ke-] *adj* : contagioso — **catchy** ['kætʃi, 'ke-] *adj* **catchier; -est** : pegadizo, pegajoso *Lat*
category ['kætə̩gɔri] *n, pl* **-ries** : categoría *f* — **categorical** [,kætə'gɔrɪkəl] *adj* : categórico
cater ['keɪtər] *vi* 1 : proveer comida 2 **~ to** : atender a — **caterer** ['keɪtərər] *n* : proveedor *m*, -dora *f* de comida
caterpillar ['kætər̩pɪlər] *n* : oruga *f*
catfish ['kæt̩fɪʃ] *n* : bagre *m*
cathedral [kə'θiːdrəl] *n* : catedral *f*
catholic ['kæθəlɪk] *adj* 1 : universal 2 **Catholic** : católico — **catholicism** [kə'θɑlə̩sɪzəm] *n* : catolicismo *m*
cattle ['kæt̩əl] *npl* : ganado *m* (vacuno)
caught → **catch**
cauldron ['kɔldrən] *n* : caldera *f*
cauliflower ['kɑlɪ̩flaʊər, 'kɔ-] *n* : coliflor *f*
cause ['kɔz] *n* 1 : causa *f* 2 REASON : motivo *m* — *vt* **caused; causing** : causar
caustic ['kɔstɪk] *adj* : cáustico
caution ['kɔʃən] *n* 1 WARNING : advertencia *f* 2 CARE : precaución *f*, cautela *f* — *vt* : advertir — **cautious** ['kɔʃəs] *adj* : cauteloso, precavido —

cautiously ['kɔʃəsli] *adv* : con precaución
cavalier [,kævə'lɪr] *adj* : arrogante, desdeñoso
cavalry ['kævəlri] *n, pl* **-ries** : caballería *f*
cave ['keɪv] *n* : cueva *f* — **~** *vi* **caved; caving** *or* **~ in** : hundirse
cavern ['kævərn] *n* : caverna *f*
cavity ['kævəti] *n, pl* **-ties** 1 : cavidad *f* 2 : caries *f* (dental)
cavort [kə'vɔrt] *vi* : brincar
CD [,siːˈdiː] *n* : CD *m*, disco *m* compacto
cease ['siːs] *v* **ceased; ceasing** *vt* : dejar de — *vi* : cesar — **cease-fire** ['siːs̩faɪr] *n* : alto *m* el fuego — **ceaseless** ['siːsləs] *adj* : incesante
cedar ['siːdər] *n* : cedro *m*
ceiling ['siːlɪŋ] *n* : techo *m*
celebrate ['selə̩breɪt] *v* **-brated; -brating** *vt* : celebrar — *vi* : divertirse — **celebrated** ['selə̩breɪtəd] *adj* : célebre — **celebration** [,selə'breɪʃən] *n* 1 : celebración *f* 2 FESTIVITY : fiesta *f* — **celebrity** [sə'lebrəti] *n, pl* **-ties** : celebridad *f*
celery ['seləri] *n, pl* **-eries** : apio *m*
cell ['sel] *n* 1 : célula *f* 2 : celda *f* (en una cárcel, etc.)
cellar ['selər] *n* 1 BASEMENT : sótano *m* 2 : bodega *f* (de vinos)
cello ['tʃe̩loː] *n, pl* **-los** : violoncelo *m*
cellular ['seljələr] *adj* : celular
cement [sɪˈment] *n* : cemento *m* — *vt* : cementar
cemetery ['semə̩teri] *n, pl* **-teries** : cementerio *m*
censor ['sensər] *vt* : censurar — **censorship** ['sensər̩ʃɪp] *n* : censura *f* — **censure** ['sensər] *n* : censura *f* — *vt* **-sured; -suring** : censurar, criticar
census ['sensəs] *n* : censo *m*
cent ['sent] *n* : centavo *m*
centennial [sen'teniəl] *n* : centenario *m*
center *or Brit* **centre** ['sentər] *n* : centro *m* — *v* **centered** *or Brit* **centred; centering** *or Brit* **centring** *vt* : centrar — *vi* **~ on** : centrarse en
centigrade ['sentə̩greɪd, 'sɑn-] *adj* : centígrado
centimeter ['sentə̩miːtər, 'sɑn-] *n* : centímetro *m*
centipede ['sentə̩piːd] *n* : ciempiés *m*
central ['sentrəl] *adj* 1 : central 2 **a ~ location** : un lugar céntrico — **centralize** ['sentrə̩laɪz] *vt* **-ized; -izing** : centralizar
centre ['sentər] → **center**
century ['sentʃəri] *n, pl* **-ries** : siglo *m*
ceramics [sə'ræmɪks] *npl* : cerámica *f*

cereal ['sıriəl] *n* : cereal *m*

ceremony ['serə,mo:ni] *n, pl* **-nies** : ceremonia *f* — **ceremonial** [,serə'mo:niəl] *adj* : ceremonial

certain ['sərtən] *adj* **1** : cierto **2 be ~ of** : estar seguro de **3 for ~** : seguro, con toda seguridad **4 make ~ of** : asegurarse de — **certainly** ['sərtənli] *adv* : desde luego, por supuesto — **certainty** ['sərtənti] *n, pl* **-ties** : certeza *f*, seguridad *f*

certify ['sərtə,faı] *vt* **-fied; -fying** : certificar — **certificate** [sər'tıfıkət] *n* : certificado *m*, partida *f*, acta *f*

chafe ['tʃeɪf] *v* **chafed; chafing** *vi* : rozarse — *vt* : rozar

chain ['tʃeɪn] *n* **1** : cadena *f* **2 ~ of events** : serie *f* de acontecimientos — **~** *vt* : encadenar

chair ['tʃer] *n* **1** : silla *f* **2** : cátedra *f* (en una universidad) — **~** *vt* : presidir — **chairman** ['tʃermən] *n, pl* **-men** [-mən, -,men] : presidente *m* — **chairperson** ['tʃer,pərsən] *n* : presidente *m*, -ta *f*

chalk ['tʃɔk] *n* : tiza *f*, gis *m Lat*

challenge ['tʃælɪndʒ] *vt* **-lenged; -lenging 1** DISPUTE : disputar, poner en duda **2** DARE : desafiar — **~** *n* : reto *m*, desafío *m* — **challenging** ['tʃælɪndʒɪŋ] *adj* : estimulante

chamber ['tʃeɪmbər] *n* : cámara *f* — **chambermaid** ['tʃeɪmbər,meɪd] *n* : camarera *f*

champagne [ʃæm'peɪn] *n* : champaña *m*, champán *m*

champion ['tʃæmpiən] *n* : campeón *m*, -peona *f* — **~** *vt* : defender — **championship** ['tʃæmpiən,ʃɪp] *n* : campeonato *m*

chance ['tʃænts] *n* **1** LUCK : azar *m*, suerte *f* **2** OPPORTUNITY : oportunidad *f* **3** LIKELIHOOD : probabilidad *f* **4 by ~** : por casualidad **5 take a ~** : arriesgarse — **~** *vt* **chanced; chancing** RISK : arriesgar — **~** *adj* : fortuito

chandelier [,ʃændə'lır] *n* : araña *f* (de luces)

change ['tʃeɪndʒ] *v* **changed; changing** *vt* **1** : cambiar **2** SWITCH : cambiar de — *vi* **1** : cambiar **2** *or* **clothes** : cambiarse (de ropa) — **~** *n* : cambio *m* — **changeable** ['tʃeɪndʒəbəl] *adj* : cambiable

channel ['tʃænəl] *n* **1** : canal *m* **2** : cauce *m* (de un río) **3** MEANS : vía *f*, medio *m*

chant ['tʃænt] *v* : cantar — **~** *n* : canto *m*

chaos ['keɪ,ɑs] *n* : caos *m* — **chaotic** [keɪ'ɑtɪk] *adj* : caótico

chap[1] ['tʃæp] *vi* **chapped; chapping** : agrietarse

chap[2] *n* : tipo *m fam*

chapel ['tʃæpəl] *n* : capilla *f*

chaperon *or* **chaperone** ['ʃæpə,ro:n] *n* : acompañante *mf*

chaplain ['tʃæplɪn] *n* : capellán *m*

chapter ['tʃæptər] *n* : capítulo *m*

char ['tʃɑr] *vt* **charred; charring** : carbonizar

character ['kærɪktər] *n* **1** : carácter *m* **2** : personaje *m* (en una novela, etc.) — **characteristic** [,kærɪktə'rɪstɪk] *adj* : característico — **~** *n* : característica *f* — **characterize** ['kærɪktə,raɪz] *vt* **-ized; -izing** : caracterizar

charcoal ['tʃɑr,ko:l] *n* : carbón *m*

charge ['tʃɑrdʒ] *n* **1** : carga *f* (eléctrica) **2** COST : precio *m* **3** BURDEN : carga *f*, peso *m* **4** ACCUSATION : cargo *m*, acusación *f* **5 in ~ of** : encargado de **6 take ~ of** : hacerse cargo de — **~** *v* **charged; charging** *vt* **1** : cargar **2** ENTRUST : encargar **3** COMMAND : ordenar, mandar **4** ACCUSE : acusar — *vi* **1** : cargar **2 ~ too much** : cobrar demasiado

charisma [kə'rɪzmə] *n* : carisma *m* — **charismatic** [,kærəz'mætɪk] *adj* : carismático

charity ['tʃærəti] *n, pl* **-ties 1** : organización *f* benéfica **2** GOODWILL : caridad *f*

charlatan ['ʃɑrlətən] *n* : charlatán *m*, -tana *f*

charm ['tʃɑrm] *n* **1** : encanto *m* **2** SPELL : hechizo *m* — **~** *vt* : encantar, cautivar — **charming** ['tʃɑrmɪŋ] *adj* : encantador

chart ['tʃɑrt] *n* **1** MAP : carta *f* **2** DIAGRAM : gráfico *m*, tabla *f* — **~** *vt* : trazar un mapa de

charter ['tʃɑrtər] *n* : carta *f* — **~** *vt* : alquilar, fletar

chase ['tʃeɪs] *n* : persecución *f* — **~** *vt* **chased; chasing 1** PURSUE : perseguir **2** *or* **away** : ahuyentar

chasm ['kæzəm] *n* : abismo *m*

chaste ['tʃeɪst] *adj* **chaster; -est** : casto — **chastity** ['tʃæstəti] *n* : castidad *f*

chat ['tʃæt] *vi* **chatted; chatting** : charlar — **~** *n* : charla *f* — **chatter** ['tʃætər] *vi* **1** : parlotear *fam* **2** : castañetear (dícese de los dientes) — **~** *n* **1** : parloteo *m*, cháchara *f* — **chatterbox** ['tʃætər,bɑks] *n* : parlanchín *m*, -china *f* — **chatty** ['tʃæti] *adj* **chattier; chattiest 1** : parlanchín **2** INFORMAL : familiar

chauffeur ['ʃo:fər, ʃo'fər] *n* : chofer *mf*

chauvinist ['ʃo:vənɪst] *or* **chauvinistic**

[ˌʃoːvəˈnɪstɪk] *adj* : chauvinista, patriotero

cheap [ˈtʃiːp] *adj* **1** INEXPENSIVE : barato **2** SHODDY : de baja calidad — ~ *adv* : barato — **cheapen** [ˈtʃiːpən] *vt* : rebajar — **cheaply** [ˈtʃiːpli] *adv* : barato, a precio bajo

cheat [ˈtʃiːt] *vt* : defraudar, estafar — *vi* **1** : hacer trampa(s) **2** ~ **on s.o.** : engañar a algn — ~ *or* **cheater** [ˈtʃiːtər] *n* : tramposo *m*, -sa *f*

check [ˈtʃek] *n* **1** RESTRAINT : freno *m* **2** INSPECTION : inspección *f*, comprobación *f* **3** DRAFT : cheque *m* **4** BILL : cuenta *f* **5** : jaque *m* (en ajedrez) **6** : tela *f* a cuadros — ~ *vt* **1** RESTRAIN : frenar, contener **2** INSPECT : revisar **3** VERIFY : comprobar **4** : dar jaque (en ajedrez) **5** ~ **in** : enregistrarse (en un hotel) **6** ~ **out** : irse (de un hotel) **7** ~ **out** VERIFY : verificar, comprobar

checkers [ˈtʃekərz] *n* : damas *fpl*

checkmate [ˈtʃekˌmeɪt] *n* : jaque *m* mate

checkpoint [ˈtʃekˌpɔɪnt] *n* : puesto *m* de control

checkup [ˈtʃekˌʌp] *n* : chequeo *m*, examen *m* médico

cheek [ˈtʃiːk] *n* : mejilla *f*

cheer [ˈtʃɪr] *n* **1** CHEERFULNESS : alegría *f* **2** APPLAUSE : aclamación *f* **3** ~ **s!** : ¡salud! — ~ *vt* **1** GLADDEN : alegrar **2** APPLAUD, SHOUT : aclamar, aplaudir — **cheerful** [ˈtʃɪrfəl] *adj* : alegre

cheese [ˈtʃiːz] *n* : queso *m*

cheetah [ˈtʃiːtə] *n* : guepardo *m*

chef [ˈʃef] *n* : chef *m*

chemical [ˈkemɪkəl] *adj* : químico — ~ *n* : sustancia *f* química — **chemist** [ˈkemɪst] *n* : químico *m*, -ca *f* — **chemistry** [ˈkemɪstri] *n*, *pl* **-tries** : química *f*

cheque [ˈtʃek] *Brit* → **check**

cherish [ˈtʃerɪʃ] *vt* **1** : querer, apreciar **2** HARBOR : abrigar (un recuerdo, una esperanza, etc.)

cherry [ˈtʃeri] *n*, *pl* **-ries** : cereza *f*

chess [ˈtʃes] *n* : ajedrez *m*

chest [ˈtʃest] *n* **1** BOX : cofre *m* **2** : pecho *m* (del cuerpo) **3** *or* ~ **of drawers** : cómoda *f*

chestnut [ˈtʃesˌnʌt] *n* : castaña *f*

chew [ˈtʃuː] *vt* : masticar, mascar — **chewing gum** *n* : chicle *m*

chic [ˈʃiːk] *adj* : elegante

chick [ˈtʃɪk] *n* : polluelo *m* — **chicken** [ˈtʃɪkən] *n* : pollo *m* — **chicken pox** *n* : varicela *f*

chicory [ˈtʃɪkəri] *n*, *pl* **-ries 1** : endivia *f* (para ensaladas) **2** : achicoria *f* (aditivo de café)

m, -fa *f* — **chiefly** [ˈtʃiːfli] *adv* : principalmente

child [ˈtʃaɪld] *n*, *pl* **children** [ˈtʃɪldrən] **1** : niño *m*, -ña *f* **2** OFFSPRING : hijo *m*, -ja *f* — **childbirth** [ˈtʃaɪldˌbərθ] *n* : parto *m* — **childhood** [ˈtʃaɪldˌhʊd] *n* : infancia *f*, niñez *f* — **childish** [ˈtʃaɪldɪʃ] *adj* : infantil — **childlike** [ˈtʃaɪldˌlaɪk] *adj* : infantil, inocente — **childproof** [ˈtʃaɪldˌpruːf] *adj* : a prueba de niños

Chilean [ˈtʃɪliən, tʃɪˈleɪən] *adj* : chileno

chili *or* **chile** *or* **chilli** [ˈtʃɪli] *n*, *pl* **chilies** *or* **chiles** *or* **chillies 1** *or* ~ **pepper** : chile *m* **2** : chile *m* con carne

chill [ˈtʃɪl] *n* **1** CHILLINESS : frío *m* **2 catch a** ~ : resfriarse **3 there's a** ~ **in the air** : hace fresco — ~ *adj* : frío — ~ *v* : enfriar — **chilly** [ˈtʃɪli] *adj* **chillier; -est** : fresco, frío

chime [ˈtʃaɪm] *vi* **chimed; chiming** : repicar, sonar — ~ *n* : carillón *m*

chimney [ˈtʃɪmni] *n*, *pl* **-neys** : chimenea *f*

chimpanzee [ˌtʃɪmpænˈziː, ʃɪmˈ; tʃɪmˈpænzi, ʃɪmˈ] *n* : chimpancé *m*

chin [ˈtʃɪn] *n* : barbilla *f*

china [ˈtʃaɪnə] *n* : porcelana *f*, loza *f*

Chinese [tʃaɪˈniːz, -ˈniːs] *adj* : chino — ~ *n* : chino *m* (idioma)

chink [ˈtʃɪŋk] *n* : grieta *f*

chip [ˈtʃɪp] *n* **1** : astilla *f* (de madera o vidrio), lasca *f* (de piedra) **2** : ficha *f* (de póker, etc.) **3** NICK : desportilladura *f* **4** *or* **computer** ~ : chip *m* **5** ~ **potato chips** — ~ *v* **chipped; chipping** *vt* : desportillar — *vi* **1** : desportillarse **2** ~ **in** : contribuir

chipmunk [ˈtʃɪpˌmʌŋk] *n* : ardilla *f* listada

chiropodist [kəˈrɑpədɪst, ʃə-] *n* : podólogo *m*, -ga *f*

chiropractor [ˈkaɪrəˌpræktər] *n* : quiropráctico *m*, -ca *f*

chirp [ˈtʃərp] *vi* : piar, gorjear

chisel [ˈtʃɪzəl] *n* : cincel *m* (para piedras, etc.), formón *m*, escoplo *m* (para madera) — ~ *vt* **-eled** *or* **-elled; -eling** *or* **-elling** : cincelar, tallar

chit [ˈtʃɪt] *n* : nota *f*

chitchat [ˈtʃɪtˌtʃæt] *n* : cháchara *f* *fam*

chivalrous [ˈʃɪvəlrəs] *adj* : caballeroso — **chivalry** [ˈʃɪvəlri] *n*, *pl* **-ries** : caballerosidad *f*

chive [ˈtʃaɪv] *n* : cebollino *m*

chlorine [ˈklorˌiːn] *n* : cloro *m*

chock-full [ˈtʃɑkˌfʊl, ˈtʃʌk-] *adj* : repleto, atestado

chocolate [ˈtʃɑkələt, ˈtʃɔk-] *n* : chocolate *m*

choice [ˈtʃɔɪs] *n* **1** : elección *f*, selección

f **2** PREFERENCE : preferencia *f* — ~
adj **choicer; -est** : selecto

choir ['kwaɪr] *n* : coro *m*

choke ['tʃoːk] *v* **choked; choking** *vt*
1 : asfixiar, estrangular **2** BLOCK : atascar — *vi* : asfixiarse, atragantarse (con comida) — ~ *n* : estárter *m* (de un motor)

choose ['tʃuːz] *v* **chose** ['tʃoːz]; **chosen**
['tʃoːzən]; **choosing** *vt* **1** SELECT : escoger, elegir **2** DECIDE : decidir — *vi*
: escoger *or* **choosy** *or* **choosey**
['tʃuːzi] *adj* **choosier; -est** : exigente

chop ['tʃɑp] *vt* **chopped; chopping 1**
: cortar, picar (carne, etc.) **2** ~ **down**
: talar — ~ *n* : chuleta *f* (de cerdo,
etc.) — **choppy** ['tʃɑpi] *adj* **-pier; -est**
: picado, agitado

chopsticks ['tʃɑpˌstɪks] *npl* : palillos
mpl

chord ['kɔrd] *n* : acorde *m* (en música)

chore ['tʃor] *n* **1** : tarea *f* **2 household**
~**s** : faenas *fpl* domésticas

choreography [ˌkori'ɑɡrəfi] *n, pl* **-phies**
: coreografía *f*

chortle ['tʃɔrtəl] *vi* **-tled; -tling** : reírse
(con satisfacción o júbilo)

chorus ['korəs] *n* **1** : coro *m* (grupo de
personas) **2** REFRAIN : estribillo *m*

chose, chosen → **choose**

christen ['krɪsən] *vt* : bautizar — **christening** ['krɪsənɪŋ] *n* : bautizo *m*

Christian ['krɪstʃən] *n* : cristiano *m*, -na *f*
— ~ *adj* : cristiano — **Christianity**
[ˌkrɪstʃi'ænəti, ˌkrɪs'tʃæ-] *n* : cristianismo *m*

Christmas ['krɪsməs] *n* : Navidad *f*

chrome ['kroːm] *n* : cromo *m*

chronic ['krɑnɪk] *adj* : crónico

chronicle ['krɑnɪkəl] *n* : crónica *f*

chronology [krə'nɑlədʒi] *n, pl* **-gies**
: cronología *f* — **chronological**
[ˌkrɑnə'ɑdʒɪkəl] *adj* : cronológico

chrysanthemum [krɪ'sænθəməm] *n*
: crisantemo *m*

chubby ['tʃʌbi] *adj* **-bier; -est** : regordete *fam*, rechoncho *fam*

chuck ['tʃʌk] *vt* : tirar, arrojar

chuckle ['tʃʌkəl] *vi* **-led; -ling** : reírse
(entre dientes) — ~ *n* : risa *f* ahogada

chum ['tʃʌm] *n* : amigo *m*, -ga *f*; compinche *mf fam* — **chummy** ['tʃʌmi] *adj*
-mier; -est : muy amigable

chunk ['tʃʌŋk] *n* : trozo *m*, pedazo *m*

church ['tʃərtʃ] *n* : iglesia *f*

churn ['tʃərn] *n* : mantequera *f* — ~ *vt*
1 : agitar **2** ~ **out** : producir en
grandes cantidades

chute ['ʃuːt] *n* **1** : vertedor *m* **2** SLIDE : tobogán *m*

cider ['saɪdər] *n* : sidra *f*

cigar [sɪ'ɡɑr] *n* : puro *m* — **cigarette**
[ˌsɪɡə'ret, 'sɪɡəˌret] *n* : cigarrillo *m*, cigarro *m*

cinch ['sɪntʃ] *n* **it's a** ~ : es pan comido

cinema ['sɪnəmə] *n* : cine *m*

cinnamon ['sɪnəmən] *n* : canela *f*

cipher ['saɪfər] *n* **1** ZERO : cero *m* **2** CODE
: cifra *f*

circa ['sərkə] *prep* : hacia

circle ['sərkəl] *n* : círculo *m* — ~ *v*
-cled; -cling *vt* **1** : dar vueltas alrededor de **2** : trazar un círculo alrededor
de (un número, etc.) — *vi* : dar vueltas

circuit ['sərkət] *n* : circuito *m* — **circuitous** [ˌsər'kjuːətəs] *adj* : tortuoso

circular ['sərkjələr] *adj* : circular — ~ *n*
LEAFLET : circular *f*

circulate ['sərkjəˌleɪt] *v* **-lated; -lating** *vi*
: hacer circular — *vi* : circular — **circulation** [ˌsərkjə'leɪʃən] *n* **1** : circulación *f* **2** : tirada *f* (de una publicación)

circumcise ['sərkəmˌsaɪz] *vt* **-cised;
-cising** : circuncidar — **circumcision**
[ˌsərkəm'sɪʒən, 'sərkəm,-] *n* : circuncisión *f*

circumference [sər'kʌmfrənts] *n* : circunferencia *f*

circumspect ['sərkəmˌspekt] *adj* : circunspecto, prudente

circumstance ['sərkəmˌstænts] *n* **1** : circunstancia *f* **2 under no** ~**s** : bajo
ningún concepto

circus ['sərkəs] *n* : circo *m*

cistern ['sɪstərn] *n* : cisterna *f*

cite ['saɪt] *vt* **cited; citing** : citar — **citation** [saɪ'teɪʃən] *n* : citación *f*

citizen ['sɪtəzən] *n* : ciudadano *m*, -na *f*
— **citizenship** ['sɪtəzənˌʃɪp] *n* : ciudadanía *f*

citrus ['sɪtrəs] *n, pl* **-rus** *or* **-ruses** *or* ~
fruit : cítrico *m*

city ['sɪti] *n, pl* **cities** : ciudad *f*

civic ['sɪvɪk] *adj* : cívico — **civics**
['sɪvɪks] *ns & pl* : civismo *m*

civil ['sɪvəl] *adj* : civil — **civilian** [sə'vɪljən] *n* : civil *mf* — **civility** [sə'vɪləti]
n, pl **-ties** : cortesía *f* — **civilization**
[ˌsɪvələ'zeɪʃən] *n* : civilización *f* — **civilize** ['sɪvəˌlaɪz] *vt* **-lized; -lizing** : civilizar

clad ['klæd] *adj* ~ **in** : vestido de

claim ['kleɪm] *vt* **1** DEMAND : reclamar **2**
MAINTAIN : afirmar, sostener **3** ~ **responsibility** : atribuirse la responsabilidad — ~ *n* **1** DEMAND : demanda
f, reclamación *f* **2** ASSERTION : afirmación *f*

clam ['klæm] *n* : almeja *f*

clamber ['klæmbər] *vi* : trepar (con torpeza)

clammy ['klæmi] *adj* **-mier; -est** : húmedo y algo frío

clamor ['klæmər] *n* : clamor *m* — ~ *vi* : clamar

clamp ['klæmp] *n* : abrazadera *f* — ~ *vt* : sujetar con abrazaderas — *vi* ~ **down on** : reprimir

clan ['klæn] *n* : clan *m*

clandestine [klæn'destɪn] *adj* : clandestino

clang ['klæŋ] *n* : ruido *m* metálico

clap ['klæp] *v* **clapped; clapping** *vt* **1** : aplaudir **2** ~ **one's hands** : dar palmadas — *vi* : aplaudir — ~ *n* : palmada *f*

clarify ['klærə,faɪ] *vt* **-fied; -fying** : aclarar — **clarification** [,klærəfə-'keɪʃən] *n* : clarificación *f*

clarinet [,klærə'nɛt] *n* : clarinete *m*

clarity ['klærəti] *n* : claridad *f*

clash ['klæʃ] *vi* **1** : chocar, enfrentarse **2** CONFLICT : estar en conflicto — ~ *n* **1** CRASH : choque *m* **2** CONFLICT : conflicto *m*

clasp ['klæsp] *n* : broche *m*, cierre *m* — ~ *vt* **1** : abrazar (a una persona), agarrar (una cosa) **2** FASTEN : abrochar

class ['klæs] *n* : clase *f*

classic ['klæsɪk] *or* **classical** ['klæsɪkəl] *adj* : clásico — **classic** *n* : clásico *m*

classify ['klæsə,faɪ] *vt* **-fied; -fying** : clasificar — **classification** [,klæsəfə-'keɪʃən] *n* : clasificación *f* — **classified** ['klæsə,faɪd] *adj* RESTRICTED : secreto

classmate ['klæs,meɪt] *n* : compañero *m*, -ra *f* de clase

classroom ['klæs,ru:m] *n* : aula *f*, salón *m* de clase

clatter ['klætər] *vi* : hacer ruido — ~ *n* : estrépito *m*

clause ['klɔz] *n* : cláusula *f*

claustrophobia [,klɔstrə'fo:biə] *n* : claustrofobia *f*

claw ['klɔ] *n* : garra *f*, uña *f* (de un gato), pinza *f* (de un crustáceo) — ~ *v* : arañar

clay ['kleɪ] *n* : arcilla *f*

clean ['kli:n] *adj* **1** : limpio **2** UNADULTERATED : puro **3** SPOTLESS : impecable — ~ *adv* : limpio — **cleaner** ['kli:nər] *n* **1** : limpiador *m*, -dora *f* **2** DRY CLEANER : tintorería *f* — **cleanliness** ['klɛnlinəs] *n* : limpieza *f* — **cleanse** ['klɛnz] *vt* **cleansed; cleansing** : limpiar, purificar

clear ['klɪr] *adj* **1** : claro **2** TRANSPARENT : transparente **3** UNOBSTRUCTED : despejado, libre — ~ *vt* **1** : despejar (una superficie), desatascar (un tubo, etc.) **2** EXONERATE : absolver **3** : saltar por encima de (un obstáculo) **4** ~ **the table** : levantar la mesa **5** ~ **up** RESOLVE : aclarar, resolver — *vi* **1** ~ **up** BRIGHTEN : despejarse (dícese del tiempo, etc.) **2** ~ **up** VANISH : desaparecer (dícese de una infección, etc.) — ~ *adv* **1 make oneself** ~ : explicarse **2 stand** ~ ! : ¡aléjate! — **clearance** ['klɪrənts] *n* **1** SPACE : espacio *m* (libre) **2** AUTHORIZATION : autorización *f* **3** ~ **sale** : liquidación *f* — **clearing** ['klɪrɪŋ] *n* : claro *m* — **clearly** ['klɪrli] *adv* **1** DISTINCTLY : claramente **2** OBVIOUSLY : obviamente

cleaver ['kli:vər] *n* : cuchillo *m* de carnicero

clef ['klɛf] *n* : clave *f*

cleft ['klɛft] *n* : hendidura *f*, grieta *f*

clement ['klɛmənt] *adj* : clemente — **clemency** ['klɛməntsi] *n* : clemencia *f*

clench ['klɛntʃ] *vt* : apretar

clergy ['klərdʒi] *n, pl* **-gies** : clero *m* — **clergyman** ['klərdʒimən] *n, pl* **-men** [-mən, -mɛn] : clérigo *m* — **clerical** ['klɛrɪkəl] *adj* **1** : clerical **2** ~ **work** : trabajo *m* de oficina

clerk ['klərk, *Brit* 'klɑrk] *n* **1** : oficinista *mf*; empleado *m*, -da *f* de oficina **2** SALESPERSON : dependiente *m*, -ta *f*

clever ['klɛvər] *adj* **1** SKILLFUL : ingenioso, hábil **2** SMART : listo, inteligente — **cleverly** ['klɛvərli] *adv* : ingeniosamente — **cleverness** ['klɛvərnəs] *n* **1** SKILL : ingenio *m* **2** INTELLIGENCE : inteligencia *f*

cliché [kli'ʃeɪ] *n* : cliché *m*

click ['klɪk] *vt* : chasquear — *vi* **1** : chasquear **2** GET ALONG : llevarse bien — ~ *n* : chasquido *m*

client ['klaɪənt] *n* : cliente *m*, -ta *f* — **clientele** [,klaɪən'tɛl, ,kli:-] *n* : clientela *f*

cliff ['klɪf] *n* : acantilado *m*

climate ['klaɪmət] *n* : clima *m*

climax ['klaɪ,mæks] *n* : clímax *m*, punto *m* culminante

climb ['klaɪm] *vt* : escalar, subir a, trepar a — *vi* **1** RISE : subir **2** *or* ~ **up** : subirse, treparse — ~ *n* : subida *f*

clinch ['klɪntʃ] *vt* : cerrar (un acuerdo, etc.)

cling ['klɪŋ] *vi* **clung** ['klʌŋ]; **clinging** : adherirse, pegarse

clinic ['klɪnɪk] *n* : clínica *f* — **clinical** ['klɪnɪkəl] *adj* : clínico

clink ['klɪŋk] *vi* : tintinear

clip ['klɪp] *vt* **clipped; clipping 1** CUT

: cortar, recortar **2** FASTEN : sujetar (con un clip) — **~** *n* **1** FASTENER : clip *m* **2 at a good ~** : a buen trote **3 → paper clip** — **clippers** ['klɪpərz] *npl* **1** : maquinilla *f* para cortar el pelo **2** *or* **nail ~** : cortauñas *m*

cloak ['kloːk] *n* : capa *f*

clock ['klɑk] **1** : reloj *m* (de pared) **2 around the ~** : las veinticuatro horas — **clockwise** ['klɑk,waɪz] *adv* & *adj* : en el sentido de las agujas del reloj — **clockwork** ['klɑk,wərk] *n* **1** : mecanismo *m* de relojería **2 like ~** : con precisión

clog ['klɑg] *n* : zueco *m* — **~** *v* **clogged; clogging 1** : atascar, obstruir — *vi or* **~ up** : atascarse

cloister ['klɔɪstər] *n* : claustro *m*

close¹ ['kloːz] *v* **closed; closing** *vt* : cerrar — *vi* **1** : cerrarse **2** TERMINATE : terminar **3 ~ in** : acercarse — **~** *n* : final *m*

close² ['kloːs] *adj* **closer; closest 1** NEAR : cercano, próximo **2** INTIMATE : íntimo **3** STRICT : estricto **4** STUFFY : sofocante **5 a ~ game** : un juego reñido — **~** *adv* : cerca, de cerca — **closely** ['kloːsli] *adv* : cerca, de cerca — **closeness** ['kloːsnəs] *n* **1** NEARNESS : cercanía *f* **2** INTIMACY : intimidad *f*

closet ['klɑzət] *n* : armario *m*, clóset *m* *Lat*

closure ['kloːʒər] *n* : cierre *m*

clot ['klɑt] *n* : coágulo *m* — **~** *v* **clotted; clotting** *vt* : coagular, cuajar — *vi* : coagularse

cloth ['klɔθ] *n*, *pl* **cloths** ['klɔðz, 'klɔθs] **1** FABRIC : tela *f* **2** RAG : trapo *m*

clothe ['kloːð] *vt* **clothed** *or* **clad** ['klæd]; **clothing** : vestir — **clothes** ['kloːz, 'kloːðz] *npl* **1** : ropa *f* **2 put on one's ~** : vestirse — **clothespin** ['kloːz,pɪn] *n* : pinza *f* (para la ropa) — **clothing** ['kloːðɪŋ] *n* : ropa *f*

cloud ['klaʊd] *n* : nube *f* — **~** *vt* : nublar — *vi or* **~ over** : nublarse — **cloudy** ['klaʊdi] *adj* **cloudier; -est** : nublado

clout ['klaʊt] *n* **1** BLOW : golpe *m*, tortazo *m fam* **2** INFLUENCE : influencia *f*

clove ['kloːv] *n* **1** : clavo *m* **2** : diente *m* (de ajo)

clover ['kloːvər] *n* : trébol *m*

clown ['klaʊn] *n* : payaso *m*, -sa *f* — **~** *or* **~ around** *vi* : payasear

cloying ['klɔɪŋ] *adj* : empalagoso

club ['klʌb] *n* **1** : garrote *m*, porra *f* **2** ASSOCIATION : club *m* **3 ~s** *mpl* : tréboles *mpl* (en los naipes) — **~** *vt* **clubbed; clubbing** : aporrear

cluck ['klʌk] *vi* : cloquear

clue ['kluː] *n* **1** : pista *f*, indicio *m* **2 I haven't got a ~** : no tengo la menor idea

clump ['klʌmp] *n* : grupo *m* (de arbustos)

clumsy ['klʌmzi] *adj* **-sier; -est** : torpe — **clumsiness** ['klʌmzinəs] *n* : torpeza *f*

cluster ['klʌstər] *n* : grupo *m*, racimo *m* (de uvas, etc.) — **~** *vi* : agruparse

clutch ['klʌtʃ] *vt* : agarrar, asir — *vi* **~ at** : tratar de agarrarse de — **~** *n* : embrague *m*, clutch *m Lat* (de un automóvil)

clutter ['klʌtər] *vt* : llenar desordenadamente — **~** *n* : desorden *m*, revoltijo *m*

coach ['koːtʃ] *n* **1** CARRIAGE : carruaje *m*, carroza *f* **2** : vagón *m* de pasajeros (de un tren) **3** BUS : autobús *m* **4** : pasaje *m* aéreo de segunda clase **5** TRAINER : entrenador *m*, -dora *f* — *vt* : entrenar (un atleta), dar clases particulares a (un alumno)

coagulate [koˈæɡjə,leɪt] *v* **-lated; -lating** *vt* : coagular — *vi* : coagularse

coal ['koːl] *n* : carbón *m*

coalition [,koːəˈlɪʃən] *n* : coalición *f*

coarse ['koːrs] *adj* **coarser; -est 1** : tosco, basto **2** CRUDE, VULGAR : grosero, ordinario — **coarseness** ['koːrsnəs] *n* : aspereza *f*, tosquedad *f*

coast ['koːst] *n* : costa *f* — **~** *vi* : ir en punto muerto (dícese de un automóvil), deslizarse (dícese de una bicicleta) — **coastal** ['koːstəl] *adj* : costero

coaster ['koːstər] *n* : posavasos *m*

coast guard *n* : guardacostas *mpl*

coastline ['koːst,laɪn] *n* : litoral *m*

coat ['koːt] *n* **1** : abrigo *m* **2** : pelaje *m* (de un animal) **3** : mano *f* (de pintura) — **~** *vt* : cubrir, revestir — **coating** ['koːtɪŋ] *n* : capa *f* — **coat of arms** *n* : escudo *m* de armas

coax ['koːks] *vt* : engatusar

cob ['kɑb] **→ corncob**

cobblestone ['kɑbəl,stoːn] *n* : adoquín *m*

cobweb ['kɑb,wɛb] *n* : telaraña *f*

cocaine [koˈkeɪn, 'koː,keɪn] *n* : cocaína *f*

cock ['kɑk] *n* **1** ROOSTER : gallo *m* **2** FAUCET : grifo *m* **3** : martillo *m* (de un arma de fuego) — **~** *vt* **1** : amartillar (un arma de fuego) **2 ~ one's head** : ladear la cabeza — **cockeyed** ['kɑk,aɪd] *adj* **1** ASKEW : ladeado **2** ABSURD : absurdo

cockpit ['kɑk,pɪt] *n* : cabina *f*

cockroach ['kɑk,roːtʃ] *n* : cucaracha *f*

cocktail ['kɑk,teɪl] *n* : coctel *m*, cóctel *m*

cocky ['kɑki] *adj* **cockier; -est** : engreído, arrogante

cocoa ['ko:,ko:] *n* **1** : cacao *m* **2** : chocolate *m* (bebida)

coconut ['ko:kə,nʌt] *n* : coco *m*

cocoon [kə'ku:n] *n* : capullo *m*

cod ['kɑd] *ns & pl* : bacalao *m*

coddle ['kɑdəl] *vt* **-dled; -dling** : mimar

code ['ko:d] *n* : código *m*

coeducational [,ko:,edʒə'keɪʃənəl] *adj* : mixto

coerce [ko'ərs] *vt* **-erced; -ercing** : coaccionar, forzar — **coercion** [ko-'ərʒən, -ʃən] *n* : coacción *f*

coffee ['kɔfi] *n* : café *m* — **coffeepot** ['kɔfi,pɑt] *n* : cafetera *f*

coffer ['kɔfər] *n* : cofre *m*

coffin ['kɔfən] *n* : ataúd *m*, féretro *m*

cog ['kɑg] *n* : diente *m* (de una rueda)

cogent ['ko:dʒənt] *adj* : convincente, persuasivo

cognac ['ko:n,jæk] *n* : coñac *m*

cogwheel ['kɑg,hwi:l] *n* : rueda *f* dentada

coherent [ko'hirənt] *adj* : coherente

coil ['kɔɪl] *vt* : enrollar — *vi* : enrollarse — **~** *n* **1** ROLL : rollo *m* **2** : tirabuzón *m* (de pelo), espiral *f* (de humo)

coin ['kɔɪn] *n* : moneda *f* — **~** *vt* : acuñar

coincide [,ko:ɪn'saɪd, 'ko:ɪn,saɪd] *vi* **-cided; -ciding** : coincidir — **coincidence** [ko'ɪntsədənts] *n* : coincidencia *f*, casualidad *f* — **coincidental** [ko-,ɪntsə'dentəl] *adj* : casual, fortuito

coke ['ko:k] *n* : coque *m* (combustible)

colander ['kɑləndər, 'kʌ-] *n* : colador *m*

cold ['ko:ld] *adj* **1** : frío **2 be ~** : tener frío **3 it's ~ today** : hace frío hoy — **~** *n* **1** : frío *m* **2** : resfriado *m* (en medicina) **3 catch a ~** : resfriarse

coleslaw ['ko:l,slɔ] *n* : ensalada *f* de col

colic ['kɑlɪk] *n* : cólico *m*

collaborate [kə'læbə,reɪt] *vi* **-rated; -rating** : colaborar — **collaboration** [kə,læbə'reɪʃən] *n* : colaboración *f* — **collaborator** [kə'læbə,reɪtər] *n* : colaborador *m*, -dora *f*

collapse [kə'læps] *vi* **-lapsed; -lapsing** **1** : derrumbarse, hundirse **2** : sufrir un colapso (físico o mental) — **~** *n* **1** FALL : derrumbamiento *m* **2** BREAKDOWN : colapso *m* — **collapsible** [kə'læpsəbəl] *adj* : plegable

collar ['kɑlər] *n* : cuello *m* (de camisa, etc.), collar *m* (para animales) — **collarbone** ['kɑlər,bo:n] *n* : clavícula *f*

colleague ['kɑ,li:g] *n* : colega *mf*

collect [kə'lekt] *vt* **1** GATHER : reunir **2** : coleccionar, juntar (timbres, etc.) **3** : recaudar (fondos, etc.) — *vi* **1** ACCUMULATE : acumularse, juntarse **2** CONGREGATE : congregarse, reunirse — **~** *adv* **call ~** : llamar a cobro revertido, llamar por cobrar *Lat* — **collection** [kə'lekʃən] *n* **1** : colección *f* **2** : colecta *f* (de contribuciones) — **collective** [kə'lektɪv] *adj* : colectivo — **collector** [kə'lektər] *n* **1** : coleccionista *mf* **2** : cobrador *m*, -dora *f* (de deudas)

college ['kɑlɪdʒ] *n* **1** : instituto *m* (a nivel universitario) **2** : colegio *m* (electoral, etc.)

collide [kə'laɪd] *vi* **-lided; -liding** : chocar, colisionar — **collision** [kə-'lɪʒən] *n* : choque *m*, colisión *f*

colloquial [kə'lo:kwiəl] *adj* : coloquial, familiar

cologne [kə'lo:n] *n* : colonia *f*

Colombian [kə'lʌmbiən] *adj* : colombiano

colon[1] ['ko:lən] *n, pl* **colons** *or* **cola** [-lə] : colon *m* (en anatomía)

colon[2] *n, pl* **colons** : dos puntos *mpl* (signo de puntuación)

colonel ['kərnəl] *n* : coronel *m*

colony ['kɑləni] *n, pl* **-nies** : colonia *f* — **colonial** [kə'lo:niəl] *adj* : colonial — **colonize** ['kɑlə,naɪz] *vt* **-nized; -nizing** : colonizar

color *or Brit* **colour** ['kʌlər] *n* : color *m* — **~** *vi* : colorear, pintar — *vi* BLUSH : sonrojarse — **color-blind** *or Brit* **colour-blind** ['kʌlər,blaɪnd] *adj* : daltónico — **colored** *or Brit* **coloured** ['kʌlərd] *adj* : de color — **colorful** *or Brit* **colourful** ['kʌlərfəl] *adj* **1** : de vivos colores **2** PICTURESQUE : pintoresco — **colorless** *or Brit* **colourless** ['kʌlərləs] *adj* : incoloro

colossal [kə'lɑsəl] *adj* : colosal

colt ['ko:lt] *n* : potro *m*

column ['kɑləm] *n* : columna *f* — **columnist** ['kɑləmnɪst, -ləmɪst] *n* : columnista *mf*

coma ['ko:mə] *n* : coma *m*

comb ['ko:m] *n* **1** : peine *m* **2** : cresta *f* (de un gallo) — **~** *vt* : peinar

combat ['kɑm,bæt] *n* : combate *m* — **~** [kəm'bæt, 'kɑm,bæt] *vt* **-bated** *or* **-batted; -bating** *or* **-batting** : combatir — **combatant** [kəm'bætənt] *n* : combatiente *mf*

combine [kəm'baɪn] *v* **-bined; -bining** *vt* : combinar — *vi* : combinarse — **~** ['kɑm,baɪn] *n* HARVESTER : cosechadora *f* — **combination** [,kɑmbə'neɪʃən] *n* : combinación *f*

combustion [kəm'bʌstʃən] *n* : combustión *f*

come ['kʌm] *vi* **came** ['keɪm]; **come**; **coming 1** : venir **2** ARRIVE : llegar **3** ~ **about** : suceder **4** ~ **back** : regresar, volver **5** ~ **from** : venir de, provenir de **6** ~ **in** : entrar **7** ~ **out** : salir **8** ~ **to** REVIVE : volver en sí **9** ~ **on!** : ¡ándale! **10** ~ **up** OCCUR : surgir **11 how** ~? : ¿por qué? — **comeback** ['kʌm,bæk] *n* **1** RETURN : retorno *m* **2** RETORT : réplica *f*

comedy ['kɑmədi] *n*, *pl* **-dies** : comedia *f* — **comedian** [kə'miːdiən] *n* : cómico *m*, -ca *f*

comet ['kɑmət] *n* : cometa *m*

comfort ['kʌmpfərt] *vt* : consolar — ~ *n* **1** : comodidad *f* **2** SOLACE : consuelo *m* — **comfortable** ['kʌmpfərtəbəl, 'kʌmpftə-] *adj* : cómodo

comic ['kɑmɪk] *or* **comical** ['kɑmɪkəl] *adj* : cómico — ~ *n* **1** COMEDIAN : cómico *m*, -ca *f* **2** *or* ~ **book** : revista *f* de historietas, cómic *m* — **comic strip** *n* : tira *f* cómica, historieta *f*

coming ['kʌmɪŋ] *adj* : próximo, que viene

comma ['kɑmə] *n* : coma *f*

command [kə'mænd] *vt* **1** ORDER : ordenar, mandar **2** : estar al mando de (un barco, etc.) **3** ~ **respect** : inspirar (el) respeto — *vi* : dar órdenes — ~ *n* **1** ORDER : orden *f* **2** LEADERSHIP : mando *m* **3** MASTERY : maestría *f*, dominio *m* — **commander** [kə'mændər] *n* : comandante *mf* — **commandment** [kə'mændmənt] *n* : mandamiento *m*

commemorate [kə'memə,reɪt] *vt* **-rated; -rating** : conmemorar — **commemoration** [kə,memə'reɪʃən] *n* : conmemoración *f*

commence [kə'mɛns] *v* **-menced; -mencing** : comenzar, empezar — **commencement** [kə'mɛnsmənt] *n* **1** BEGINNING : comienzo *m* **2** GRADUATION : ceremonia *f* de graduación

commend [kə'mend] *vt* **1** ENTRUST : encomendar **2** PRAISE : alabar — **commendable** [kə'mendəbəl] *adj* : loable

comment ['kɑment] *n* : comentario *m*, observación *f* — ~ *vi* : hacer comentarios — **commentary** ['kɑmən,teri] *n*, *pl* **-taries** : comentario *m* — **commentator** ['kɑmən,teɪtər] *n* : comentarista *mf*

commerce ['kɑmərs] *n* : comercio *m* — **commercial** [kə'mərʃəl] *adj* : comercial — ~ *n* : anuncio *m*, aviso *m* *Lat* — **commercialize** [kə'mərʃə,laɪz] *vt* **-ized; -izing** : comercializar

commiserate [kə'mɪzə,reɪt] *vi* **-ated; -ating** : compadecerse

commission [kə'mɪʃən] *n* : comisión *f* — ~ *vt* : encargar (una obra de arte) — **commissioner** [kə'mɪʃənər] *n* : comisario *m*, -ria *f*

commit [kə'mɪt] *vt* **-mitted; -mitting 1** ENTRUST : confiar **2** : cometer (un crimen) **3** : internar (a algn en un hospital) **4** ~ **oneself** : comprometerse **5** ~ **to memory** : aprender de memoria — **commitment** [kə'mɪtmənt] *n* : compromiso *m*

committee [kə'mɪt̬i] *n* : comité *m*, comisión *f*

commodity [kə'mɑdət̬i] *n*, *pl* **-ties** : artículo *m* de comercio, producto *m*

common ['kɑmən] *adj* **1** : común **2** ORDINARY : ordinario, común y corriente — ~ **in** ~ : en común — **commonly** ['kɑmənli] *adv* : comúnmente — **commonplace** ['kɑmən,pleɪs] *adj* : común, banal — **common sense** *n* : sentido *m* común

commotion [kə'moːʃən] *n* : alboroto *m*, jaleo *m*

commune[1] ['kɑmjuːn, kə'mjuːn] *n* : comuna *f* — **communal** [kə'mjuːnəl] *adj* : comunal

commune[2] [kə'mjuːn] *vi* **-muned; -muning** ~ **with** : comunicarse con

communicate [kə'mjuːnə,keɪt] *v* **-cated; -cating** *vt* : comunicar — *vi* : comunicarse — **communicable** [kə'mjuːnɪkəbəl] *adj* : transmisible — **communication** [kə,mjuːnə'keɪʃən] *n* : comunicación *f* — **communicative** [kə'mjuːnɪ,keɪt̬ɪv, -kət̬ɪv] *adj* : comunicativo

communion [kə'mjuːnjən] *n* : comunión *f*

Communism ['kɑmjə,nɪzəm] *n* : comunismo *m* — **Communist** ['kɑmjə,nɪst] *adj* : comunista — ~ *n* : comunista *mf*

community [kə'mjuːnət̬i] *n*, *pl* **-ties** : comunidad *f*

commute [kə'mjuːt] *v* **-muted; -muting** *vt* : conmutar, reducir (una sentencia) — *vi* : viajar de la residencia al trabajo

compact [kəm'pækt, 'kɑm,pækt] *adj* : compacto — ~ ['kɑm,pækt] *n* **1** *or* ~ **car** : auto *m* compacto **2** *or* **powder** ~ : polvera *f* — **compact disc** ['kɑm,pækt'dɪsk] *n* : disco *m* compacto

companion [kəm'pænjən] *n* : compañero *m*, -ra *f* — **companionship** [kəm'pænjən,ʃɪp] *n* : compañerismo *m*

company ['kʌmpəni] *n*, *pl* **-nies 1** : compañía *f* **2** GUESTS : visita *f*

compare [kəm'pær] *v* **-pared; -paring**

vt : comparar — *vi* ~ **with** : poderse
comparar con — **comparable**
['kɑmpərəbəl] *adj* : comparable —
comparative [kəm'pærəṭiv] *adj* : comparativo, relativo — **comparison**
[kəm'pærəsən] *n* : comparación *f*

compartment [kəm'pɑrtmənt] *n* : compartimento *m*

compass ['kʌmpəs, 'kɑm-] *n* **1** : compás
m **2 points of the** ~ : puntos *mpl*
cardinales

compassion [kəm'pæʃən] *n* : compasión *f* — **compassionate** [kəm'pæ-
ʃənət] *adj* : compasivo

compatible [kəm'pæṭəbəl] *adj* : compatible, afín — **compatibility** [kəm,pæṭə-
'bɪləṭi] *n* : compatibilidad *f*

compel [kəm'pɛl] *vt* **-pelled; -pelling**
: obligar — **compelling** [kəm'pɛlɪŋ]
adj : convincente

compensate ['kɑmpən,seɪt] *v* **-sated;
-sating** *vi* ~ **for** : compensar — *vt*
: indemnizar, compensar — **compensation** [,kɑmpən'seɪʃən] *n* : compensación *f*, indemnización *f*

compete [kəm'piːt] *vi* **-peted; -peting**
: competir — **competent** ['kɑmpəṭənt]
adj : competente — **competition**
[,kɑmpə'tɪʃən] *n* **1** : competencia *f* **2**
CONTEST : concurso *m* — **competitor**
[kəm'pɛṭəṭər] *n* : competidor *m*, -dora *f*

compile [kəm'paɪl] *vt* **-piled; -piling**
: compilar, recopilar

complacency [kəm'pleɪsəntsi] *n* : satisfacción *f* consigo mismo — **compla-
cent** [kəm'pleɪsənt] *adj* : satisfecho de
sí mismo

complain [kəm'pleɪn] *vi* : quejarse —
complaint [kəm'pleɪnt] *n* **1** : queja *f* **2**
AILMENT : enfermedad *f*

complement ['kɑmpləmənt] *n* : complemento *m* — ~ ['kɑmplə,mɛnt] *vt* : complementar — **complementary** [,kɑm-
plə'mɛntəri] *adj* : complementario

complete [kəm'pliːt] *adj* **-pleter; -est 1**
WHOLE : completo, entero **2** FINISHED
: terminado **3** TOTAL : total — ~ *vt*
-pleted; -pleting : completar — **completion** [kəm'pliːʃən] *n* : conclusión *f*

complex [kɑm'plɛks, kəm-; 'kɑm,plɛks]
adj : complejo — ~ ['kɑm,plɛks] *n*
: complejo *m*

complexion [kəm'plɛkʃən] *n* : cutis *m*,
tez *f*

complexity [kəm'plɛksəṭi, kɑm-] *n*, *pl*
-ties : complejidad *f*

compliance [kəm'plaɪənts] *n* **1** : acatamiento *m* **2 in** ~ **with** : conforme a —
compliant [kəm'plaɪənt] *adj* : sumiso

complicate ['kɑmplə,keɪt] *vt* **-cated;**

-cating : complicar — **complicated**
['kɑmplə,keɪṭəd] *adj* : complicado —
complication [,kɑmplə'keɪʃən] *n* : complicación *f*

compliment ['kɑmpləmənt] *n* **1** : cumplido *m* **2** ~**s** *npl* : saludos *mpl* — ~
['kɑmplə,mɛnt] *vt* : felicitar — **compli-
mentary** [,kɑmplə'mɛntəri] *adj* **1** FLAT-
TERING : halagador, halagüeño **2** FREE
: de cortesía, gratis

comply [kəm'plaɪ] *vi* **-plied; -plying** ~
with : cumplir, obedecer

component [kəm'poːnənt, 'kɑm,poː-] *n*
: componente *m*

compose [kəm'poːz] *vt* **-posed;
-posing 1** : componer **2** ~ **oneself**
: serenarse — **composer** [kəm'poːzər]
n : compositor *m*, -tora *f* — **composition** [,kɑmpə'zɪʃən] *n* **1** : composición *f*
2 ESSAY : ensayo *m* — **composure**
[kəm'poːʒər] *n* : calma *f*

compound[1] [kɑm'paʊnd, kəm-; 'kɑm-
,paʊnd] *vt* **1** COMPOSE : componer **2**
: agravar (un problema, etc.) — ~
['kɑm,paʊnd; kɑm'paʊnd, kəm-] *adj*
: compuesto — ~ ['kɑm,paʊnd] *n*
: compuesto *m*

compound[2] ['kɑm,paʊnd] *n* ENCLOSURE
: recinto *m*

comprehend [,kɑmprɪ'hɛnd] *vt* : comprender — **comprehension** [,kɑmprɪ-
'hɛnʃən] *n* : comprensión *f* — **compre-
hensive** [,kɑmprɪ'hɛnsɪv] *adj* **1**
INCLUSIVE : inclusivo **2** BROAD : amplio

compress [kəm'prɛs] *vt* : comprimir —
compression [kəm'prɛʃən] *n* : compresión *f*

comprise [kəm'praɪz] *vt* **-prised;
-prising** : comprender

compromise ['kɑmprə,maɪz] *n* : acuerdo
m, arreglo *m* — ~ *v* **-mised; -mising**
vi : llegar a un acuerdo — *vt* : comprometer

compulsion [kəm'pʌlʃən] *n* **1** COERCION
: coacción *f* **2** URGE : impulso *m* —
compulsive [kəm'pʌlsɪv] *adj* : compulsivo — **compulsory** [kəm'pʌlsəri]
adj : obligatorio

compute [kəm'pjuːt] *vt* **-puted; -puting**
: computar — **computer** [kəm'pjuːṭər]
n : computadora *f*, computador *m*, ordenador *m* *Spain* — **computerize**
[kəm'pjuːṭə,raɪz] *vt* **-ized; -izing** : informatizar

comrade ['kɑm,ræd] *n* : camarada *mf*

con ['kɑn] *vt* **conned; conning** : estafar
— ~ *n* **1** SWINDLE : estafa *f* **2 the pros
and** ~**s** : los pros y los contras

concave [kɑn'keɪv, 'kɑn,keɪv] *adj* : cóncavo

conceal [kən'siːl] *vt* : ocultar
concede [kən'siːd] *vt* **-ceded; -ceding** : conceder, admitir
conceit [kən'siːt] *n* : vanidad *f* — **conceited** [kən'siːtəd] *adj* : engreído
conceive [kən'siːv] *v* **-ceived; -ceiving** *vt* : concebir — *vi* **of** : concebir — **conceivable** [kən'siːvəbəl] *adj* : concebible
concentrate ['kɑntsən,treɪt] *v* **-trated; -trating** *vt* : concentrar — *vi* : concentrarse — **concentration** [kɑntsən'treɪʃən] *n* : concentración *f*
concept ['kɑn,sɛpt] *n* : concepto *m* — **conception** [kən'sɛpʃən] *n* : concepción *f*
concern [kən'sərn] *vt* **1** : concernir **2 oneself about** : preocuparse por — **n 1** AFFAIR : asunto *m* **2** WORRY : preocupación *f* **3** BUSINESS : negocio *m* — **concerned** [kən'sərnd] *adj* **1** ANXIOUS : ansioso **2 as far as I'm** : en cuanto a mí — **concerning** [kən'sərnɪŋ] *prep* : con respecto a
concert ['kɑn,sərt] *n* : concierto *m* — **concerted** [kən'sərtəd] *adj* : concertado
concession [kən'sɛʃən] *n* : concesión *f*
concise [kən'saɪs] *adj* : conciso
conclude [kən'kluːd] *v* **-cluded; -cluding** : concluir — **conclusion** [kən'kluːʒən] *n* : conclusión *f* — **conclusive** [kən'kluːsɪv] *adj* : concluyente
concoct [kən'kɑkt, kɑn-] *vt* **1** PREPARE : confeccionar **2** DEVISE : inventarse, tramar — **concoction** [kən'kɑkʃən] *n* : mezcla *f*, brebaje *m*
concourse ['kɑn,kors] *n* : vestíbulo *m*, salón *m*
concrete [kɑn'kriːt, 'kɑn,kriːt] *adj* : concreto — **~** ['kɑn,kriːt, kɑn'kriːt] *n* : hormigón *m*, concreto *m Lat*
concur [kən'kər] *vi* **concurred; concurring** AGREE : estar de acuerdo
concussion [kən'kʌʃən] *n* : conmoción *f* cerebral
condemn [kən'dɛm] *vt* : condenar — **condemnation** [kɑn,dɛm'neɪʃən] *n* : condenación *f*
condense [kən'dɛnts] *v* **-densed; -densing** *vt* : condensar — *vi* : condensarse — **condensation** [kɑn,dɛn'seɪʃən, -dən-] *n* : condensación *f*
condescending [kɑndɪ'sɛndɪŋ] *adj* : condescendiente
condiment ['kɑndəmənt] *n* : condimento *m*
condition [kən'dɪʃən] *n* **1** : condición *f* **2 in good ~** : en buen estado — **conditional** [kən'dɪʃənəl] *adj* : condicional

condolences [kən'doːləntsəz] *npl* : pésame *m*
condom ['kɑndəm] *n* : condón *m*
condominium [,kɑndə'mɪniəm] *n*, *pl* **-ums** : condominio *m Lat*
condone [kən'doːn] *vt* **-doned; -doning** : aprobar
conducive [kən'duːsɪv, -'djuː-] *adj* : propicio, favorable
conduct ['kɑn,dʌkt] *n* : conducta *f* — **~** [kən'dʌkt] *vt* **1** DIRECT, GUIDE : conducir, dirigir **2** CARRY OUT : llevar a cabo **3 ~ oneself** : conducirse, comportarse — **conductor** [kən'dʌktər] *n* : revisor *m*, -sora *f* (en un tren); cobrador *m*, -dora *f* (en un autobús); director *m*, -tora *f* (de una orquesta)
cone ['koːn] *n* **1** : cono *m* **2 or ice-cream ~** : cucurucho *m*, barquillo *m Lat*
confection [kən'fɛkʃən] *n* : dulce *m*
confederation [kən,fɛdə'reɪʃən] *n* : confederación *f*
confer [kən'fər] *v* **-ferred; -ferring** *vt* : conferir, otorgar — *vi* **~ with** : consultar — **conference** ['kɑnfrənts, -fərənts] *n* : conferencia *f*
confess [kən'fɛs] *vt* : confesar — *vi* **1** : confesarse **2 ~ to** : confesar, admitir — **confession** [kən'fɛʃən] *n* : confesión *f*
confetti [kən'fɛti] *n* : confeti *m*
confide [kən'faɪd] *v* **-fided; -fiding** : confiar — **confidence** ['kɑnfədənts] *n* **1** TRUST : confianza *f* **2** SELF-ASSURANCE : confianza *f* en sí mismo **3** SECRET : confidencia *f* — **confident** ['kɑnfədənt] *adj* **1** SURE : seguro **2** SELF-ASSURED : confiado, seguro de sí mismo — **confidential** [,kɑnfə'dɛntʃəl] *adj* : confidencial
confine [kən'faɪn] *vt* **-fined; -fining 1** LIMIT : confinar, limitar **2** IMPRISON : encerrar — **confines** ['kɑn,faɪnz] *npl* : confines *mpl*
confirm [kən'fərm] *vt* : confirmar — **confirmation** [,kɑnfər'meɪʃən] *n* : confirmación *f* — **confirmed** *adj* : inveterado
confiscate ['kɑnfə,skeɪt] *vt* **-cated; -cating** : confiscar
conflict ['kɑn,flɪkt] *n* : conflicto *m* — **~** [kən'flɪkt] *vi* : estar en conflicto, oponerse
conform [kən'form] *vi* **1** COMPLY : ajustarse **2 ~ with** : corresponder a — **conformity** [kən'forməti] *n*, *pl* **-ties** : conformidad *f*
confound [kən'faʊnd, kɑn-] *vt* : confundir, desconcertar

confront [kən'frʌnt] *vt* : afrontar, encarar — **confrontation** [ˌkɑnfrən'teɪʃən] *n* : confrontación *f*

confuse [kən'fjuːz] *vt* **-fused; -fusing** : confundir — **confusing** [kən'fjuːzɪŋ] *adj* : confuso, desconcertante — **confusion** [kən'fjuːʒən] *n* : confusión *f*, desconcierto *m*

congeal [kən'dʒiːl] *vi* : coagularse

congenial [kən'dʒiːniəl] *adj* : agradable

congested [kən'dʒestəd] *adj* : congestionado — **congestion** [kən'dʒestʃən] *n* : congestión *f*

congratulate [kən'grædʒəˌleɪt, -'grætʃə-] *vt* **-lated; -lating** : felicitar — **congratulations** [kənˌgrædʒə'leɪʃən, -'grætʃə-] *npl* : felicitaciones *fpl*

congregate ['kɑŋgrɪˌgeɪt] *vi* **-gated; -gating** : congregarse — **congregation** [ˌkɑŋgrɪ'geɪʃən] *n* : feligreses *mpl* (en religión)

congress ['kɑŋgrəs] *n* : congreso *m* — **congressional** [kən'greʃənəl, kɑŋ-] *adj* : del congreso — **congressman** ['kɑŋgrəsmən] *n, pl* **-men** [-mən, -ˌmen] : congresista *mf*

conjecture [kən'dʒektʃər] *n* : conjetura *f*, presunción *f* — ~ *v* **-tured; -turing** *vt* : conjeturar — *vi* : hacer conjeturas

conjugal ['kɑndʒɪgəl, kən'dʒuː-] *adj* : conyugal

conjugate ['kɑndʒəˌgeɪt] *vt* **-gated; -gating** : conjugar — **conjugation** [ˌkɑndʒə'geɪʃən] *n* : conjugación *f*

conjunction [kən'dʒʌŋkʃən] *n* **1** : conjunción *f* **2 in ~ with** : en combinación con

conjure ['kɑndʒər, 'kʌn-] *v* **-jured; -juring** *vi* : hacer juegos de manos — ~ *vt or* ~ **up** : evocar

connect [kə'nekt] *vi* : conectarse — *vt* **1** JOIN : conectar, juntar **2** ASSOCIATE : asociar — **connection** [kə'nekʃən] *n* **1** : conexión *f* **2** : enlace *m* (con un tren, etc.) **3** ~**s** *npl* : relaciones *fpl* (personas)

connoisseur [ˌkɑnə'sər, -'sʊr] *n* : conocedor *m*, -dora *f*

connote [kə'noːt] *vt* **-noted; -noting** : connotar, implicar

conquer ['kɑŋkər] *vt* : conquistar — **conqueror** ['kɑŋkərər] *n* : conquistador *m*, -dora *f* — **conquest** ['kɑnˌkwest, 'kɑŋ-] *n* : conquista *f*

conscience ['kɑntʃənts] *n* : conciencia *f* — **conscientious** [ˌkɑntʃi'entʃəs] *adj* : concienzudo

conscious ['kɑntʃəs] *adj* **1** AWARE : consciente **2** INTENTIONAL : intencional — **consciously** *adv* : deliberadamente

— **consciousness** ['kɑntʃəsnəs] *n* **1** AWARENESS : conciencia *f* **2 lose ~** : perder el conocimiento

consecrate ['kɑntsəˌkreɪt] *vt* **-crated; -crating** : consagrar — **consecration** [ˌkɑntsə'kreɪʃən] *n* : consagración *f*

consecutive [kən'sekjətɪv] *adj* : consecutivo, sucesivo

consensus [kən'sentsəs] *n* : consenso *m*

consent [kən'sent] *vi* : consentir — ~ *n* : consentimiento *m*

consequence ['kɑntsəˌkwents, -kwənts] *n* **1** : consecuencia *f* **2 of no ~** : sin importancia — **consequent** ['kɑntsəkwənt, -ˌkwent] *adj* : consiguiente — **consequently** ['kɑntsəkwəntli, -ˌkwent-] *adv* : por consiguiente

conserve [kən'sərv] *vt* **-served; -serving** : conservar, preservar — **conservation** [ˌkɑntsər'veɪʃən] *n* : conservación *f* — **conservative** [kən'sərvətɪv] *adj* **1** : conservador **2** CAUTIOUS : moderado, prudente — ~ *n* : conservador *m*, -dora *f* — **conservatory** [kən'sərvəˌtori] *n, pl* **-ries** : conservatorio *m*

consider [kən'sɪdər] *vt* **1** : considerar **2 all things considered** : teniéndolo todo en cuenta — **considerable** [kən'sɪdərəbəl] *adj* : considerable — **considerate** [kən'sɪdərət] *adj* : considerado — **consideration** [kənˌsɪdə'reɪʃən] *n* **1** : consideración *f* **2 take into ~** : tener en cuenta — **considering** [kən'sɪdərɪŋ] *prep* : teniendo en cuenta

consign [kən'saɪn] *vt* **1** : relegar **2** SEND : enviar — **consignment** [kən'saɪnmənt] *n* : envío *m*

consist [kən'sɪst] *vi* **1** ~ **in** : consistir en **2** ~ **of** : constar de, componerse de — **consistency** [kən'sɪstəntsi] *n, pl* **-cies 1** TEXTURE : consistencia *f* **2** COHERENCE : coherencia *f* **3** UNIFORMITY : regularidad *f* — **consistent** [kən'sɪstənt] *adj* **1** UNCHANGING : constante, regular **2** ~ **with** : consecuente con

console [kən'soːl] *vt* **-soled; -soling** : consolar — **consolation** [ˌkɑntsə'leɪʃən] *n* **1** : consuelo *m* **2** ~ **prize** : premio *m* de consolación

consolidate [kən'sɑləˌdeɪt] *vt* **-dated; -dating** : consolidar — **consolidation** [kənˌsɑlə'deɪʃən] *n* : consolidación *f*

consonant ['kɑntsənənt] *n* : consonante *f*

conspicuous [kən'spɪkjuəs] *adj* **1** OBVIOUS : visible, evidente **2** STRIKING : llamativo — **conspicuously** [kən'spɪkjuəsli] *adv* : de manera llamativa

conspire [kən'spaɪr] *vi* **-spired;**
-spiring : conspirar — **conspiracy**
[kən'spɪrəsi] *n, pl* **-cies** : conspiración *f*
constant ['kɑntstənt] *adj* : constante —
constantly ['kɑntstəntli] *adv* : constantemente
constellation [ˌkɑntstə'leɪʃən] *n* : constelación *f*
constipated ['kɑntstə.peɪtəd] *adj* : estre-
ñido — **constipation** [ˌkɑntstə'peɪʃən]
n : estreñimiento *m*
constituent [kən'stɪtʃuənt] *n* 1 COMPO-
NENT : componente *m* 2 VOTER : elector *m*, -tora *f*
constitute ['kɑntstə.tuːt, -'tjuːt] *vt* **-tuted;**
-tuting : constituir — **constitution**
[ˌkɑntstə'tuːʃən, -'tjuː-] *n* : constitución
f — **constitutional** [ˌkɑntstə'tuːʃənəl,
-'tjuː-] *adj* : constitucional
constraint [kən'streɪnt] *n* : restricción *f*,
limitación *f*
construct [kən'strʌkt] *vt* : construir —
construction [kən'strʌkʃən] *n* : construcción *f* — **constructive** [kən-
'strʌktɪv] *adj* : constructivo
construe [kən'struː] *vt* **-strued; -struing**
: interpretar
consul ['kɑntsəl] *n* : cónsul *mf* — **con-**
sulate ['kɑntsələt] *n* : consulado *m*
consult [kən'sʌlt] *v* : consultar — **con-**
sultant [kən'sʌltənt] *n* : asesor *m*, -sora
f; consultor *m*, -tora *f* — **consultation**
[ˌkɑntsəl'teɪʃən] *n* : consulta *f*
consume [kən'suːm] *vt* **-sumed;**
-suming : consumir — **consumer**
[kən'suːmər] *n* : consumidor *m*, -dora *f*
— **consumption** [kən'sʌmpʃən] *n*
: consumo *m*
contact ['kɑn.tækt] *n* : contacto *m* — **~**
['kɑn.tækt, kən'-] *vt* : ponerse en contacto con — **contact lens** ['kɑn.tækt'lenz]
n : lente *mf* (de contacto)
contagious [kən'teɪdʒəs] *adj* : contagioso
contain [kən'teɪn] *vt* 1 : contener 2 **~**
oneself : contenerse — **container**
[kən'teɪnər] *n* : recipiente *m*, envase *m*
contaminate [kən'tæmə.neɪt] *vt* **-nated;**
-nating : contaminar — **contamina-**
tion [kən.tæmə'neɪʃən] *n* : contaminación *f*
contemplate ['kɑntəm.pleɪt] *v* **-plated;**
-plating *vt* 1 : contemplar 2 CONSIDER
: considerar, pensar en — *vi* : reflexionar — **contemplation** [ˌkɑntəm-
'pleɪʃən] *n* : contemplación *f*
contemporary [kən'tempə.reri] *adj*
: contemporáneo — **~** *n, pl* **-raries**
: contemporáneo *m*, -nea *f*
contempt [kən'tempt] *n* : desprecio *m* —

contemptible [kən'temptəbəl] *adj*
: despreciable — **contemptuous** [kən-
'temptʃuəs] *adj* : desdeñoso
contend [kən'tend] *vi* 1 COMPETE : contender, competir 2 **~** **with** : enfrentarse a — *vt* : sostener, afirmar —
contender [kən'tendər] *n* : contendiente *mf*
content[1] ['kɑn.tent] *n* 1 : contenido *m* 2
table of ~s : índice *m* de materias
content[2] [kən'tent] *adj* : contento — *vt*
~ **oneself with** : contentarse con
— **contented** [kən'tentəd] *adj* : satisfecho, contento
contention [kən'tentʃən] *n* 1 DISPUTE
: disputa *f* 2 OPINION : argumento *m*,
opinión *f*
contentment [kən'tentmənt] *n* : satisfacción *f*
contest [kən'test] *vt* : disputar — **~**
['kɑn.test] *n* 1 STRUGGLE : contienda *f* 2
COMPETITION : concurso *m*, competencia *f* — **contestant** [kən'testənt] *n*
: concursante *mf*, contendiente *mf*
context ['kɑn.tekst] *n* : contexto *m*
continent ['kɑntənənt] *n* : continente *m*
— **continental** [ˌkɑntən'entəl] *adj*
: continental
contingency [kən'tɪndʒəntsi] *n, pl* **-cies**
: contingencia *f*
continue [kən'tɪnjuː] *v* **-tinued; -tinuing**
: continuar — **continual** [kən'tɪnjuəl]
adj : continuo, constante — **continua-**
tion [kən.tɪnju'eɪʃən] *n* : continuación *f*
— **continuity** [ˌkɑntən'uːəti, -'juː-] *n, pl*
-ties : continuidad *f* — **continuous**
[kən'tɪnjuəs] *adj* : continuo
contort [kən'tɔrt] *vt* : retorcer — **con-**
tortion [kən'tɔrʃən] *n* : contorsión *f*
contour ['kɑn.tur] *n* 1 : contorno *m* 2 *or*
~ line : curva *f* de nivel
contraband ['kɑntrə.bænd] *n* : contrabando *m*
contraception [ˌkɑntrə'sepʃən] *n* : anticoncepción *f* — **contraceptive** [ˌkɑn-
trə'septɪv] *adj* : anticonceptivo — **~** *n*
: anticonceptivo *m*
contract ['kɑn.trækt] *n* : contrato *m* —
~ [kən'trækt] *vt* : contraer — *vi* : contraerse — **contraction** [kən'trækʃən] *n*
: contracción *f* — **contractor** ['kɑn-
.træktər, kən'træk-] *n* : contratista *mf*
contradiction [ˌkɑntrə'dɪkʃən] *n* : contradicción *f* — **contradict** [ˌkɑntrə'dɪkt]
vt : contradecir — **contradictory**
[ˌkɑntrə'dɪktəri] *adj* : contradictorio
contraption [kən'træpʃən] *n* : artilugio
m, artefacto *m*
contrary ['kɑn.treri] *n, pl* **-traries** 1
: contrario 2 **on the ~** : al contrario

— ~ ['kɑn₁treri] *adj* **1** : contrario, opuesto **2** ~ **to** : en contra de
contrast [kən'træst] *v* : contrastar — ~ ['kɑn₁træst] *n* : contraste *m*
contribute [kən'trɪbjət] *v* **-uted; -uting** : contribuir — **contribution** [₁kɑntrə'bjuːʃən] *n* : contribución *f* — **contributor** [kən'trɪbjətər] *n* **1** : contribuyente *mf* **2** : colaborador *m*, -dora *f* (en periodismo)
contrite ['kɑn₁traɪt, kən'traɪt] *adj* : arrepentido
contrive [kən'traɪv] *vt* **-trived; -triving 1** DEVISE : idear **2** ~ **to do sth** : lograr hacer algo
control [kən'troːl] *vt* **-trolled; -trolling** : controlar — ~ *n* **1** : control *m* **2** ~**s** *npl* : mandos *mpl*
controversy ['kɑntrə₁vərsi] *n, pl* **-sies** : controversia *f* — **controversial** [₁kɑntrə'vərʃəl, -siəl] *adj* : polémico
convalescence [₁kɑnvə'lesənts] *n* : convalecencia *f* — **convalescent** [₁kɑnvə'lesənt] *adj* : convaleciente — ~ *n* : convaleciente *mf*
convene [kən'viːn] *v* **-vened; -vening** *vt* : convocar — *vi* : reunirse
convenience [kən'viːnjənts] *n* : conveniencia *f*, comodidad *f* — **convenient** [kən'viːnjənt] *adj* : conveniente
convent ['kɑnvənt, -₁vent] *n* : convento *m*
convention [kən'ventʃən] *n* : convención *f* — **conventional** [kən'ventʃənəl] *adj* : convencional
converge [kən'vərdʒ] *vi* **-verged; -verging** : converger, convergir
converse[1] [kən'vərs] *vi* **-versed; -versing** : conversar — **conversation** [₁kɑnvər'seɪʃən] *n* : conversación *f* — **conversational** [₁kɑnvər'seɪʃənəl] *adj* : familiar
converse[2] [kən'vərs, 'kɑn₁vərs] *adj* : contrario, opuesto — **conversely** [kən'vərsli, 'kɑn₁vərs-] *adv* : a la inversa
conversion [kən'vərʒən] *n* : conversión *f* — **convert** [kən'vərt] *vt* : convertir — *vi* : convertirse — **convertible** [kən'vərtəbəl] *adj* : convertible — ~ *n* : descapotable *m*, convertible *m Lat*
convex [kɑn'veks, 'kɑn-, kən'-] *adj* : convexo
convey [kən'veɪ] *vt* **1** TRANSPORT : llevar, transportar **2** TRANSMIT : comunicar
convict [kən'vɪkt] *vt* : declarar culpable a — ~ ['kɑn₁vɪkt] *n* : presidiario *m*, -ria *f* — **conviction** [kən'vɪkʃən] *n* **1** : condena *f* (de un acusado) **2** BELIEF : convicción *f*

convince [kən'vɪnts] *vt* **-vinced; -vincing** : convencer — **convincing** [kən'vɪntsɪŋ] *adj* : convincente
convoke [kən'voːk] *vt* **-voked; -voking** : convocar
convoluted ['kɑnvə₁luːtəd] *adj* : complicado
convulsion [kən'vʌlʃən] *n* : convulsión *f* — **convulsive** [kən'vʌlsɪv] *adj* : convulsivo
cook ['kʊk] *n* : cocinero *m*, -ra *f* — *vi* : cocinar, guisar — *vt* : preparar (comida) — **cookbook** ['kʊk₁bʊk] *n* : libro *m* de cocina
cookie *or* **cooky** ['kʊki] *n, pl* **-ies** : galleta *f* (dulce)
cooking *n* : cocina *f*
cool ['kuːl] *adj* **1** : fresco **2** CALM : tranquilo **3** UNFRIENDLY : frío — ~ *vt* : enfriar — *vi* : enfriarse — ~ *n* **1** : fresco *m* **2** COMPOSURE : calma *f* — **cooler** ['kuːlər] *n* : nevera *f* portátil — **coolness** ['kuːlnəs] *n* : frescura *f*
coop ['kuːp, 'kʊp] *n* : gallinero *m* — ~ *vt or* ~ **up** : encerrar
cooperate [ko'ɑpə₁reɪt] *vi* **-ated; -ating** : cooperar — **cooperation** [ko₁ɑpə'reɪʃən] *n* : cooperación *f* — **cooperative** [ko'ɑpərət̬ɪv, -₁ɑpə₁reɪt̬ɪv] *adj* : cooperativo
coordinate [ko'ɔrdən₁eɪt] *v* **-nated; -nating** *vt* : coordinar — **coordination** [ko₁ɔrdən'eɪʃən] *n* : coordinación *f*
cop ['kɑp] *n* **1** : poli *mf fam* **2 the** ~**s** : la poli
cope ['koːp] *vi* **coped; coping 1** : arreglárselas **2** ~ **with** : hacer frente a, poder con
copier ['kɑpiər] *n* : fotocopiadora *f*
copious ['koːpiəs] *adj* : copioso
copper ['kɑpər] *n* : cobre *m*
copy ['kɑpi] *n, pl* **copies 1** : copia *f* **2** : ejemplar *m* (de un libro), número *m* (de una revista) — ~ *vt* **copied; copying 1** DUPLICATE : hacer una copia de **2** IMITATE : copiar — **copyright** ['kɑpi₁raɪt] *n* : derechos *mpl* de autor
coral ['kɔrəl] *n* : coral *m*
cord ['kɔrd] *n* **1** : cuerda *f* **2** *or* **electric** ~ : cable *m* (eléctrico)
cordial ['kɔrdʒəl] *adj* : cordial
corduroy ['kɔrdə₁rɔɪ] *n* : pana *f*
core ['kor] *n* **1** : corazón *m* (de una fruta) **2** CENTER : núcleo *m*, centro *m*
cork ['kɔrk] *n* : corcho *m* — **corkscrew** ['kɔrk₁skruː] *n* : sacacorchos *m*
corn ['kɔrn] *n* **1** : grano *m* **2** *or* **Indian** ~ : maíz *m* **3** : callo *m* (del pie) — **corncob** ['kɔrn₁kɑb] *n* : mazorca *f*

corner ['kɔrnər] *n* : ángulo *m*, rincón *m* (en una habitación), esquina *f* (de una intersección) — ~ *vt* **1** TRAP : acorralar **2** MONOPOLIZE : acaparar (un mercado) — **cornerstone** ['kɔrnər,sto:n] *n* : piedra *f* angular

cornmeal ['kɔrn,mi:l] *n* : harina *f* de maíz — **cornstarch** ['kɔrn,stɑrtʃ] *n* : maicena *f*

corny ['kɔrni] *adj* : cursi, sentimental

coronary ['kɔrə,neri] *n, pl* **-naries** : trombosis *f* coronaria

coronation [,kɔrə'neɪʃən] *n* : coronación *f*

corporal ['kɔrpərəl] *n* : cabo *m*

corporation [,kɔrpə'reɪʃən] *n* : sociedad *f* anónima, compañía *f* — **corporate** ['kɔrpərət] *adj* : corporativo

corps ['kor] *n, pl* **corps** ['korz] : cuerpo *m*

corpse ['kɔrps] *n* : cadáver *m*

corpulent ['kɔrpjələnt] *adj* : obeso, gordo

corpuscle ['kɔr,pʌsəl] *n* : glóbulo *m*

corral [kə'ræl] *n* : corral *m* — ~ *vt* **-ralled; -ralling** : acorralar

correct [kə'rekt] *vt* : corregir — ~ *adj* : correcto — **correction** [kə'rekʃən] *n* : corrección *f*

correlation [,kɔrə'leɪʃən] *n* : correlación *f*

correspond [,kɔrə'spɑnd] *vi* **1** WRITE : corresponderse **2** ~ **to** : corresponder a — **correspondence** [,kɔrə-'spɑndənts] *n* : correspondencia *f*

corridor ['kɔrədər, -,dɔr] *n* : pasillo *m*

corroborate [kə'rɑbə,reɪt] *vt* **-rated; -rating** : corroborar

corrode [kə'ro:d] *v* **-roded; -roding** *vt* : corroer — *vi* : corroerse — **corrosion** [kə'ro:ʒən] *n* : corrosión *f* — **corrosive** [kə'ro:sɪv] *adj* : corrosivo

corrugated ['kɔrə,geɪtəd] *adj* : ondulado

corrupt [kə'rʌpt] *vt* : corromper — ~ *adj* : corrupto, corrompido — **corruption** [kə'rʌpʃən] *n* : corrupción *f*

corset ['kɔrsət] *n* : corsé *m*

cosmetic [kɑz'metɪk] *n* : cosmético *m* — ~ *adj* : cosmético

cosmic ['kɑzmɪk] *adj* : cósmico

cosmopolitan [,kɑzmə'pɑlətən] *adj* : cosmopolita

cosmos ['kɑzməs, -,mo:s, -,mɑs] *n* : cosmos *m*

cost ['kɔst] *n* : costo *m*, coste *m* — ~ *vi* **cost; costing 1** : costar **2 how much does it ~?** : ¿cuánto cuesta?, ¿cuánto vale?

Costa Rican [,kɑstə'ri:kən] *adj* : costarricense

costly ['kɔstli] *adj* : costoso

costume ['kɑs,tu:m, -,tju:m] *n* **1** OUTFIT : traje *m* **2** DISGUISE : disfraz *m*

cot ['kɑt] *n* : catre *m*

cottage ['kɑtɪdʒ] *n* : casita *f* (de campo) — **cottage cheese** *n* : requesón *m*

cotton ['kɑtən] *n* : algodón *m*

couch ['kaʊtʃ] *n* : sofá *m*

cough ['kɔf] *vi* : toser — ~ *n* : tos *f*

could ['kʊd] → **can¹**

council ['kaʊntsəl] *n* **1** : concejo *m* **2 or city ~** : ayuntamiento *m* — **councillor** *or* **councilor** ['kaʊntsələr] *n* : concejal *m*, -jala *f*

counsel *n* **1** ADVICE : consejo *m* **2** LAWYER : abogado *m*, -da *f* — ~ ['kaʊntsəl] *vt* **-seled** *or* **-selled; -seling** *or* **-selling** : aconsejar — **counselor** *or* **counsellor** ['kaʊntsələr] *n* : consejero *m*, -ra *f*

count¹ ['kaʊnt] *vt* : contar — *vi* **1** : contar **2** ~ **on** : contar con **3 that doesn't ~** : eso no vale — ~ *n* **1** : recuento *m* **2 keep ~ of** : llevar la cuenta de

count² *n* : conde *m* (noble)

counter¹ ['kaʊntər] *n* **1** : mostrador *m* (de un negocio) **2** TOKEN : ficha *f* (de un juego)

counter² *vt* : oponerse a — *vi* : contraatacar — *adv* ~ **to** : contrario a — **counteract** [,kaʊntər'ækt] *vt* : contrarrestar — **counterattack** ['kaʊntərə-,tæk] *n* : contraataque *m* — **counterbalance** [,kaʊntər'bæləns] *n* : contrapeso *m* — **counterclockwise** [,kaʊntər'klɑk,waɪz] *adv* & *adj* : en sentido opuesto a las agujas del reloj — **counterfeit** ['kaʊntər,fɪt] *vt* : falsificar — ~ *adj* : falsificado — ~ *n* : falsificación *f* — **counterpart** ['kaʊntər,pɑrt] *n* : homólogo *m* (de una persona), equivalente *m* (de una cosa) — **counterproductive** [,kaʊntərprə'dʌktɪv] *adj* : contraproducente

countess ['kaʊntɪs] *n* : condesa *f*

countless ['kaʊntləs] *adj* : incontable, innumerable

country ['kʌntri] *n, pl* **-tries 1** NATION : país *m* **2** COUNTRYSIDE : campo *m* — ~ *adj* : campestre, rural — **countryman** ['kʌntrimən] *n, pl* **-men** [-mən, -,men] *or* **fellow ~** : compatriota *mf* — **countryside** ['kʌntri,saɪd] *n* : campo *m*, campiña *f*

county ['kaʊnti] *n, pl* **-ties** : condado *m*

coup ['ku:] *n, pl* **coups** ['ku:z] *or* ~ **d'etat** : golpe *m* (de estado)

couple ['kʌpəl] *n* **1** : pareja *f* (de per-

sonas) **2 a ~ of** : un par de — **~** vt
-pled; -pling : acoplar, unir
coupon ['ku:pɑn, 'kju:-] n : cupón m
courage ['kɘrɪdʒ] n : valor m — **coura-**
geous [kɘ'reɪdʒɘs] adj : valiente
courier ['kʊriɘr, 'kɔriɘr] n : mensajero m,
-ra f
course ['kors] n **1** : curso m **2** : plato m
(de una cena) **3 or golf ~** : campo m
de golf **4 in the ~ of** : en el transcurso de **5 of ~** : desde luego, por
supuesto
court ['kort] n **1** : corte f (de un rey, etc.)
2 : cancha f, pista f (en deportes) **3** TRI-
BUNAL : corte f, tribunal m — **~** vt
: cortejar
courteous ['kɘrtiɘs] adj : cortés —
courtesy ['kɘrtɘsi] n, pl **-sies** : cortesía f
courthouse ['kort,haʊs] n : palacio m de
justicia, juzgado m — **courtroom**
['kort,ru:m] n : sala f (de un tribunal)
courtship ['kort,ʃɪp] n : cortejo m, noviazgo m
courtyard ['kort,jɑrd] n : patio m
cousin ['kʌzən] n : primo m, -ma f
cove ['ko:v] n : ensenada f, cala f
covenant ['kʌvɘnɘnt] n : pacto m, convenio m
cover ['kʌvɘr] vt **1** : cubrir **2 or ~ up**
: encubrir, ocultar **3** TREAT : tratar —
~ n **1** : cubierta f **2** SHELTER : abrigo
m, refugio m **3** LID : tapa f **4** : cubierta
f (de un libro), portada f (de una revista) **5 ~s** npl BEDCLOTHES : mantas
fpl, cobijas fpl Lat **6 take ~** : ponerse
a cubierto **7 under ~ of** : al amparo
de — **coverage** ['kʌvɘrɪdʒ] n : cobertura f — **covert** ['ko:,vɘrt, 'kʌvɘrt] adj
: encubierto — **cover-up** ['kʌvɘr,ʌp] n
: encubrimiento m
covet ['kʌvɘt] vt : codiciar — **covetous**
['kʌvɘtɘs] adj : codicioso
cow ['kaʊ] n : vaca f — **~** vt : intimidar,
acobardar
coward ['kaʊɘrd] n : cobarde mf —
cowardice ['kaʊɘrdɪs] n : cobardía f —
cowardly ['kaʊɘrdli] adj : cobarde
cowboy ['kaʊ,bɔɪ] n : vaquero m
cower ['kaʊɘr] vi : encogerse (de miedo)
coy ['kɔɪ] adj : tímido y coqueto
coyote [kaɪ'o:ti, 'kaɪ,o:t] n, pl **coyotes**
or coyote : coyote m
cozy ['ko:zi] adj **-zier; -est** : acogedor
crab ['kræb] n : cangrejo m, jaiba f Lat
crack ['kræk] vt **1** SPLIT : rajar, partir
2 : cascar (nueces, huevos) **3** : chasquear (un látigo, etc.) **4 ~ down on**
: tomar medidas enérgicas contra —
vi **1** SPLIT : rajarse, agrietarse **2**

: chasquear (dícese de un látigo) **3 ~**
up : sufrir una crisis nerviosa — **~** n
1 CRACKING : chasquido m, crujido m **2**
CREVICE : raja f, grieta f **3 have a ~ at**
: intentar
cracker ['krækɘr] n : galleta f (de soda,
etc.)
crackle ['krækəl] vi **-led; -ling** : crepitar,
chisporrotear — **~** n : crujido m,
chisporroteo m
cradle ['kreɪdəl] n : cuna f — **~** vt
-dled; -dling : acunar
craft ['kræft] n **1** TRADE : oficio m **2** CUN-
NING : astucia f **3 → craftsmanship 4**
pl usually **craft** BOAT : embarcación f
— **craftsman** ['kræftsmɘn] n, pl **-men**
[-mɘn, -,mɛn] : artesano m, -na f —
craftsmanship ['kræftsmɘn,ʃɪp] n
: artesanía f, destreza f — **crafty**
['kræfti] adj **craftier; -est** : astuto,
taimado
crag ['kræg] n : peñasco m
cram ['kræm] v **crammed; cramming**
vt **1** STUFF : embutir **2 ~ with** : atiborrar de — vi : estudiar a última hora
cramp ['kræmp] n **1** : calambre m, espasmo m (de los músculos) **2 ~s** npl
: retorcijones mpl
cranberry ['kræn,beri] n, pl **-berries**
: arándano m (rojo y agrio)
crane ['kreɪn] n **1** : grulla f (ave) **2** : grúa
f (máquina) — **~** vt **craned; craning**
: estirar (el cuello)
crank ['kræŋk] n **1** : manivela f **2** ECCEN-
TRIC : excéntrico m, -ca f — **cranky**
['kræŋki] adj **crankier; -est** : malhumorado
crash ['kræʃ] vi **1** : caerse con estrépito
2 COLLIDE : estrellarse, chocar — vt
: estrellar — **~** n **1** DIN : estrépito m **2**
COLLISION : choque m
crass ['kræs] adj : burdo, grosero
crate ['kreɪt] n : cajón m (de madera)
crater ['kreɪtɘr] n : cráter m
crave ['kreɪv] vt **craved; craving** : ansiar — **craving** ['kreɪvɪŋ] n : ansia f
crawl ['krɔl] vi : arrastrarse, gatear
(dícese de un bebé) — **~** n **at a ~** : a
paso lento
crayon ['kreɪ,ɑn, -ən] n : lápiz m de cera
craze ['kreɪz] n : moda f pasajera, manía
f
crazy ['kreɪzi] adj **-zier; -est 1** : loco **2**
go ~ : volverse loco — **craziness**
['kreɪzɪnɘs] : locura f
creak ['kri:k] vi : chirriar, crujir — **~** n
: chirrido m, crujido m
cream ['kri:m] n : crema f, nata f Spain
— **cream cheese** n : queso m crema

— creamy ['kri:mi] *adj* **creamier; -est** : cremoso

crease ['kri:s] *n* : pliegue *m*, raya *f* (del pantalón) **— ~** *vt* **creased; creasing** : plegar, poner una raya en (el pantalón)

create [kri'eɪt] *vt* **-ated; -ating** : crear **— creation** [kri'eɪʃən] *n* : creación *f* **— creative** [kri'eɪtɪv] *adj* : creativo **— creator** [kri'eɪtər] *n* : creador *m*, -dora *f*

creature ['kri:tʃər] *n* : criatura *f*, animal *m*

credence ['kri:dənts] **n lend ~ to** : dar crédito a

credentials [krɪ'dentʃəlz] *npl* : credenciales *fpl*

credible ['kredəbəl] *adj* : creíble **— credibility** [ˌkredə'bɪləṭi] *n* : credibilidad *f*

credit ['kredɪt] *n* **1** : crédito *m* **2** RECOGNITION : reconocimiento *m* **3 be a ~ to** : ser el orgullo de **— ~** *vt* **1** BELIEVE : creer **2** : abonar (en una cuenta) **3 ~ s.o. with sth** : atribuir algo a algn **— credit card** *n* : tarjeta *f* de crédito

credulous ['kredʒələs] *adj* : crédulo

creed ['kri:d] *n* : credo *m*

creek ['kri:k, 'krɪk] *n* : arroyo *m*, riachuelo *m*

creep ['kri:p] *vi* **crept** ['krept]; **creeping 1** CRAWL : arrastrarse **2** SLINK : ir a hurtadillas **— ~** *n* **1** CRAWL : paso *m* lento **2 the ~s** : escalofríos *mpl* **— creeping** *adj* **~ plant** : planta *f* trepadora

cremate ['kri:meɪt] *vt* **-mated; -mating** : incinerar

crescent ['kresənt] *n* : media luna *f*

cress ['kres] *n* : berro *m*

crest ['krest] *n* : cresta *f* **— crestfallen** ['krest,fɔlən] *adj* : alicaído

crevice ['krevɪs] *n* : grieta *f*

crew ['kru:] *n* **1** : tripulación *f* (de una nave) **2** TEAM : equipo *m*

crib ['krɪb] *n* : cuna *f* (de un bebé)

cricket ['krɪkət] *n* **1** : grillo *m* (insecto) **2** : críquet *m* (juego)

crime ['kraɪm] *n* : crimen *m* **— criminal** ['krɪmənəl] *adj* : criminal **— ~** *n* : criminal *mf*

crimp ['krɪmp] *vt* : rizar

crimson ['krɪmzən] *n* : carmesí *m*

cringe ['krɪndʒ] *vi* **cringed; cringing** : encogerse

crinkle ['krɪŋkəl] *vt* **-kled; -kling** : arrugar

cripple ['krɪpəl] *vt* **-pled; -pling 1** DISABLE : lisiar, dejar inválido **2** INCAPACITATE : inutilizar, paralizar

crisis ['kraɪsɪs] *n*, *pl* **crises** [-ˌsi:z] : crisis *f*

crisp ['krɪsp] *adj* **1** CRUNCHY : crujiente **2** : frío y vigorizante (dícese del aire) **— crispy** ['krɪspi] *adj* **crispier; -est** : crujiente

crisscross ['krɪsˌkrɔs] *vt* : entrecruzar

criterion [kraɪ'tɪriən] *n*, *pl* **-ria** [-ɪə] : criterio *m*

critic ['krɪtɪk] *n* : crítico *m*, -ca *f* **— critical** ['krɪtɪkəl] *adj* : crítico **— criticism** ['krɪtəˌsɪzəm] *n* : crítica *f* **— criticize** ['krɪtəˌsaɪz] *vt* **-cized; -cizing** : criticar

croak ['kro:k] *vi* : croar

crock ['krak] *n* : vasija *f* de barro **— crockery** ['krakəri] *n* : vajilla *f*, loza *f*

crocodile ['krakəˌdaɪl] *n* : cocodrilo *m*

crony ['kro:ni] *n*, *pl* **-nies** : amigote *m fam*

crook ['krʊk] *n* **1** STAFF : cayado *m* **2** THIEF : ratero *m*, -ra *f*; ladrón *m*, -drona *f* **3** BEND : pliegue *m* **— crooked** ['krʊkəd] *adj* **1** BENT : torcido, chueco *Lat* **2** DISHONEST : deshonesto

crop ['krap] *n* **1** WHIP : fusta *f* **2** HARVEST : cosecha *f* **3** : cultivo *m* (de maíz, tabaco, etc.) **— ~** *v* **cropped; cropping** *vt* TRIM : recortar, cortar **— vi ~ up** : surgir

cross ['krɔs] *n* **1** : cruz *f* **2** HYBRID : cruce *m* **— ~** *vt* **1** : cruzar, atravesar **2** CROSSBREED : cruzar **3** *or* **~ out** : tachar **— ~** *adj* **1** : que atraviesa **2** ANGRY : enojado **— crossbreed** ['krɔsˌbri:d] *vt* **-bred** [-bred]; **-breeding** : cruzar **— cross–examine** *vt* : interrogar **— cross–eyed** ['krɔsˌaɪd] *adj* : bizco **— cross fire** *n* : fuego *m* cruzado **— crossing** ['krɔsɪŋ] *n* **1** INTERSECTION : cruce *m*, paso *m* **2** VOYAGE : travesía *f* (del mar) **— cross–reference** [ˌkrɔs'refrənts, -'refərənts] *n* : referencia *f* **— crossroads** ['krɔsˌro:dz] *n* : cruce *m* **— cross section** *n* **1** : corte *m* transversal **2** SAMPLE : muestra *f* representativa **— crosswalk** ['krɔsˌwɔk] *n* : cruce *m* peatonal, paso *m* de peatones **— crossword puzzle** ['krɔsˌwərd] *n* : crucigrama *m*

crotch ['krɑtʃ] *n* : entrepierna *f*

crouch ['kraʊtʃ] *vi* : agacharse

crouton ['kru:ˌtɑn] *n* : crutón *m*

crow ['kro:] *n* : cuervo *m* **— ~** *vi* **crowed** *or Brit* **crew; crowing** : cacarear

crowbar ['kro:ˌbɑr] *n* : palanca *f*

crowd ['kraʊd] *vi* : amontonarse **— vt** : atestar, llenar **— ~** *n* : multitud *f*, muchedumbre *f*

crown ['kraʊn] *n* **1** : corona *f* **2** : cima *f* (de una colina) — ~ *vt* : coronar

crucial ['kruːʃəl] *adj* : crucial

crucify ['kruːsəˌfaɪ] *vt* **-fied; -fying** : crucificar — **crucifix** ['kruːsəˌfɪks] *n* : crucifijo *m* — **crucifixion** [ˌkruːsəˈfɪkʃən] *n* : crucifixión *f*

crude ['kruːd] *adj* **cruder; -est 1** RAW : crudo **2** VULGAR : grosero **3** ROUGH : tosco, rudo

cruel ['kruːəl] *adj* **-eler** *or* **-eller; -elest** *or* **-ellest** : cruel — **cruelty** ['kruːəlti] *n, pl* **-ties** : crueldad *f*

cruet ['kruːɪt] *n* : vinagrera *f*

cruise ['kruːz] *vi* **cruised; cruising 1** : hacer un crucero **2** : ir a velocidad de crucero — ~ *n* : crucero *m* — **cruiser** ['kruːzər] *n* **1** WARSHIP : crucero *m* **2** : patrulla *f* (de policía)

crumb ['krʌm] *n* : miga *f*, migaja *f*

crumble ['krʌmbəl] *v* **-bled; -bling** : desmenuzar — *vi* : desmenuzarse, desmoronarse

crumple ['krʌmpəl] *vt* **-pled; -pling** : arrugar

crunch ['krʌntʃ] *vt* : ronzar (con los dientes), hacer crujir (con los pies, etc.) — **crunchy** ['krʌntʃi] *adj* **crunchier; -est** : crujiente

crusade [kruːˈseɪd] *n* : cruzada *f*

crush ['krʌʃ] *vt* : aplastar, apachurrar *Lat* — ~ *n* **have a** ~ **on** : estar chiflado por

crust ['krʌst] *n* : corteza *f*

crutch ['krʌtʃ] *n* : muleta *f*

crux ['krʌks, 'krʊks] *n* : quid *m*

cry ['kraɪ] *v* **cried; crying 1** SHOUT : gritar **2** WEEP : llorar — ~ *n, pl* **cries** : grito *m*

crypt ['krɪpt] *n* : cripta *f*

crystal ['krɪstəl] *n* : cristal *m*

cub ['kʌb] *n* : cachorro *m*, -rra *f*

Cuban ['kjuːbən] *adj* : cubano

cube ['kjuːb] *n* : cubo *m* — **cubic** ['kjuːbɪk] *adj* : cúbico

cubicle ['kjuːbɪkəl] *n* : cubículo *m*

cuckoo ['kuːˌkuː, 'kʊ-] *n* : cuco *m*, cuclillo *m*

cucumber ['kjuːˌkʌmbər] *n* : pepino *m*

cuddle ['kʌdəl] *v* **-dled; -dling** *vi* : acurrucarse, abrazarse — *vt* : abrazar

cudgel ['kʌdʒəl] *n* : porra *f* — ~ *vt* **-geled** *or* **-gelled; -geling** *or* **-gelling** : aporrear

cue[1] ['kjuː] *n* SIGNAL : señal *f*

cue[2] *n* : taco *m* (de billar)

cuff[1] ['kʌf] **1** : puño *m* (de una camisa) **2** ~**s** *npl* → **handcuffs**

cuff[2] *vt* : bofetear — ~ *n* SLAP : bofetada *f*

cuisine [kwɪˈziːn] *n* : cocina *f*

culinary ['kʌləˌneri, 'kjuːlə-] *adj* : culinario

cull ['kʌl] *vt* : seleccionar, entresacar

culminate ['kʌlməˌneɪt] *vi* **-nated; -nating** : culminar — **culmination** [ˌkʌlməˈneɪʃən] *n* : culminación *f*

culprit ['kʌlprɪt] *n* : culpable *mf*

cult ['kʌlt] *n* : culto *m*

cultivate ['kʌltəˌveɪt] *vt* **-vated; -vating** : cultivar — **cultivation** [ˌkʌltəˈveɪʃən] *n* : cultivo *m*

culture ['kʌltʃər] *n* **1** : cultura *f* **2** : cultivo *m* (en biología) — **cultural** ['kʌltʃərəl] *adj* : cultural — **cultured** ['kʌltʃərd] *adj* : culto

cumbersome ['kʌmbərsəm] *adj* : torpe (y pesado), difícil de manejar

cumulative ['kjuːmjələˌtɪv, -ˌleɪtɪv] *adj* : acumulativo

cunning ['kʌnɪŋ] *adj* : astuto, taimado — ~ *n* : astucia *f*

cup ['kʌp] *n* **1** : taza *f* **2** TROPHY : copa *f*

cupboard ['kʌbərd] *n* : alacena *f*, armario *m*

curator ['kjʊrˌeɪtər, kjʊˈreɪtər] *n* : conservador *m*, -dora *f*; director *m*, -tora *f*

curb ['kərb] *n* **1** RESTRAINT : freno *m* **2** : borde *m* de la acera — ~ *vt* : refrenar

curdle ['kərdəl] *v* **-dled; -dling** *vi* : cuajarse — *vt* : cuajar

cure ['kjʊr] *n* : cura *f*, remedio *m* — ~ *vt* **cured; curing** : curar

curfew ['kərˌfjuː] *n* : toque *m* de queda

curious ['kjʊriəs] *adj* : curioso — **curio** ['kjʊriˌoː] *n, pl* **-rios** : curiosidad *f* — **curiosity** [ˌkjʊriˈɑsəṭi] *n, pl* **-ties** : curiosidad *f*

curl ['kərl] *vt* **1** : rizar **2** COIL : enrollar, enroscar — *vi* **1** : rizarse **2** ~ **up** : acurrucarse — ~ *n* : rizo *m* — **curler** ['kərlər] *n* : rulo *m* — **curly** ['kərli] *adj* **curlier; -est** : rizado

currant ['kərənt] *n* **1** : grosella *f* (fruta) **2** RAISIN : pasa *f* de Corinto

currency ['kərəntsi] *n, pl* **-cies 1** MONEY : moneda *f* **2 gain** ~ : ganar aceptación

current ['kərənt] *adj* **1** PRESENT : actual **2** PREVALENT : corriente — ~ *n* : corriente *f*

curriculum [kəˈrɪkjələm] *n, pl* **-la** [-lə] : plan *m* de estudios

curry ['kəri] *n, pl* **-ries** : curry *m*

curse ['kərs] *n* : maldición *f* — ~ *v* **cursed; cursing** : maldecir

cursor ['kərsər] *n* : cursor *m*

cursory ['kərsəri] *adj* : superficial

curt ['kərt] *adj* : corto, seco

curtail [kər'teɪl] *vt* : acortar

curtain ['kərtən] *n* : cortina *f* (de una ventana), telón *m* (en un teatro)

curtsy ['kərtsi] *vi* **-sied** *or* **-seyed; -sying** *or* **-seying** : hacer una reverencia — ~ *n* : reverencia *f*

curve ['kərv] *v* **curved; curving** *vi* : hacer una curva — *vt* : encorvar — ~ *n* : curva *f*

cushion ['kʊʃən] *n* : cojín *m* — ~ *vt* : amortiguar

custard ['kʌstərd] *n* : natillas *fpl*

custody ['kʌstədi] *n, pl* **-dies 1** : custodia *f* **2 be in** ~ : estar detenido — **custodian** [kʌ'stoʊdiən] *n* : custodio *m*, -dia *f*; guardián, -diana *f*

custom ['kʌstəm] *n* : costumbre *f* — **customary** ['kʌstə,meri] *adj* : habitual, acostumbrado — **customer** ['kʌstəmər] *n* : cliente *m*, -ta *f* — **customs** ['kʌstəmz] *npl* : aduana *f*

cut ['kʌt] *v* **cut; cutting** *vt* **1** : cortar **2** REDUCE : reducir, rebajar **3** ~ **oneself** : cortarse **4** ~ **up** : cortar en pedazos — *vi* **1** : cortar **2** ~ **in** : interrumpir —

~ *n* **1** : corte *m* **2** REDUCTION : rebaja *f*, reducción *f*

cute ['kjuːt] *adj* **cuter; -est** : mono *fam*, lindo

cutlery ['kʌtləri] *n* : cubiertos *mpl*

cutlet ['kʌtlət] *n* : chuleta *f*

cutting ['kʌtɪŋ] *adj* : cortante, mordaz

cyanide ['saɪə,naɪd, -nɪd] *n* : cianuro *m*

cycle ['saɪkəl] *n* **1** : ciclo *m* **2** BICYCLE : bicicleta *f* — ~ *vi* **-cled; -cling** : ir en bicicleta — **cyclic** ['saɪklɪk, 'sɪ-] *or* **cyclical** [-klɪkəl] *adj* : cíclico — **cyclist** ['saɪklɪst] *n* : ciclista *mf*

cyclone ['saɪ,kloʊn] *n* : ciclón *m*

cylinder ['sɪləndər] *n* : cilindro *m* — **cylindrical** [sə'lɪndrɪkəl] *adj* : cilíndrico

cymbal ['sɪmbəl] *n* : platillo *m*, címbalo *m*

cynic ['sɪnɪk] *n* : cínico *m*, -ca *f* — **cynical** ['sɪnɪkəl] *adj* : cínico — **cynicism** ['sɪnə,sɪzəm] *n* : cinismo *m*

cypress ['saɪprəs] *n* : ciprés *m*

cyst ['sɪst] *n* : quiste *m*

czar ['zɑr, 'sɑr] *n* : zar *m*

Czech ['tʃɛk] *adj* : checo — ~ *n* : checo *m* (idioma)

D

d ['diː] *n, pl* **d's** *or* **ds** ['diːz] : d *f*, cuarta letra del alfabeto inglés

dab ['dæb] *n* : toque *m* — ~ *vt* **dabbed; dabbing** : dar toques ligeros a, aplicar suavemente

dabble ['dæbəl] *vi* **-bled; -bling** ~ **in** : interesarse superficialmente en — **dabbler** *n* : aficionado *m*, -da *f*

dad ['dæd] *n* : papá *m fam* — **daddy** ['dædi] *n, pl* **-dies** : papá *m fam*

daffodil ['dæfə,dɪl] *n* : narciso *m*

dagger ['dægər] *n* : daga *f*, puñal *m*

daily ['deɪli] *adj* : diario — ~ *adv* : diariamente

dainty ['deɪnti] *adj* **-tier; -est** : delicado

dairy ['dæri] *n, pl* **-ies 1** : lechería *f* (tienda) **2** *or* ~ **farm** : granja *f* lechera

daisy ['deɪzi] *n, pl* **-sies** : margarita *f*

dam ['dæm] *n* : presa *f* — ~ *vt* **dammed; damming** : represar

damage ['dæmɪdʒ] *n* **1** : daño *m*, perjuicio *m* **2** ~**s** *npl* : daños y perjuicios *mpl* — ~ *vt* **-aged; -aging** : dañar

damn ['dæm] *vt* **1** CONDEMN : condenar **2** CURSE : maldecir — ~ **not give a** ~ : no importarse un comino *fam* — ~ *or* **damned** ['dæmd] *adj* : maldito *fam*

damp ['dæmp] *adj* : húmedo — **dampen** ['dæmpən] *vt* **1** MOISTEN : humede-

cer **2** DISCOURAGE : desalentar, desanimar — **dampness** ['dæmpnəs] *n* : humedad *f*

dance ['dænts] *v* **danced; dancing** : bailar — ~ *n* : baile *m* — **dancer** ['dæntsər] *n* : bailarín *m*, -rina *f*

dandelion ['dændəl,aɪən] *n* : diente *m* de león

dandruff ['dændrəf] *n* : caspa *f*

dandy ['dændi] *adj* **-dier; -est** : de primera, excelente

danger ['deɪndʒər] *n* : peligro *m* — **dangerous** ['deɪndʒərəs] *adj* : peligroso

dangle ['dæŋgəl] *v* **-gled; -gling** *vi* HANG : colgar, pender — *vt* : hacer oscilar

Danish ['deɪnɪʃ] *adj* : danés — ~ *n* : danés *m* (idioma)

dank ['dæŋk] *adj* : frío y húmedo

dare ['dær] *v* **dared; daring** *vt* : desafiar — *vi* : osar — ~ *n* : desafío *m* — **daredevil** ['dær,dɛvəl] *n* : persona *f* temeraria — **daring** ['dærɪŋ] *adj* : atrevido, audaz — ~ *n* : audacia *f*

dark ['dɑrk] *adj* **1** : oscuro **2** : moreno (dícese del pelo o de la piel) **3** GLOOMY : sombrío **4 get** ~ : hacerse de noche — **darken** ['dɑrkən] *vt* : oscurecer — *vi* : oscurecerse — **darkness** ['dɑrknəs] *n* : oscuridad *f*

darling ['dɑrlɪŋ] n BELOVED : querido m, -da f — ~ adj : querido
darn ['dɑrn] vt : zurcir — ~ adj : maldito fam
dart ['dɑrt] n 1 : dardo m 2 ~s npl : juego m de dardos — ~ vi : precipitarse
dash ['dæʃ] vt 1 SMASH : romper 2 HURL : lanzar 3 ~ off : hacer (algo) rápidamente — vi : lanzarse, irse corriendo — ~ n 1 : guión m largo (signo de puntuación) 2 PINCH : poquito m, pizca f 3 RACE : carrera f — **dashboard** ['dæʃˌbord] n : tablero m de instrumentos — **dashing** ['dæʃɪŋ] adj : gallardo, apuesto
data ['deɪtə, 'dæ-, 'dɑ-] ns & pl : datos mpl — **database** ['deɪtəˌbeɪs, 'dæ-, 'dɑ-] n : base f de datos
date[1] ['deɪt] n : dátil m (fruta)
date[2] n 1 : fecha f 2 APPOINTMENT : cita f — ~ v dated; dating vt 1 : fechar (una carta, etc.) 2 : salir con (algn) — vi ~ from : datar de — **dated** ['deɪtəd] adj : pasado de moda
daub ['dɔb] vt : embadurnar
daughter ['dɔtər] n : hija f — **daughter-in-law** ['dɔtərɪnˌlɔ] n, pl **daughters-in-law** : nuera f
daunt ['dɔnt] vt : intimidar
dawdle ['dɔdəl] vi -dled; -dling : entretenerse, perder tiempo
dawn ['dɔn] vi 1 : amanecer 2 it ~ed on him that : cayó en la cuenta de que — ~ n : amanecer m
day ['deɪ] n 1 : día m 2 or working ~ : jornada f 3 the ~ before : el día anterior 4 the ~ before yesterday : anteayer 5 the ~ after : el día siguiente 6 the ~ after tomorrow : pasada mañana — **daybreak** ['deɪˌbreɪk] n : amanecer m — **daydream** ['deɪˌdriːm] n : ensueño m — ~ vi : soñar despierto — **daylight** ['deɪˌlaɪt] n : luz f del día — **daytime** ['deɪˌtaɪm] n : día m
daze ['deɪz] vt dazed; dazing : aturdir — ~ n in a ~ : aturdido
dazzle ['dæzəl] vt -zled; -zling : deslumbrar
dead ['dɛd] adj 1 LIFELESS : muerto 2 NUMB : entumecido — ~ n 1 in the ~ of night : en plena noche 2 the ~ : los muertos — ~ adv ABSOLUTELY : absolutamente — **deaden** ['dɛdən] vt 1 : atenuar (dolores) 2 MUFFLE : amortiguar — **dead end** ['dɛdˌɛnd] n : callejón m sin salida — **deadline** ['dɛdˌlaɪn] n : fecha f límite — **deadlock** ['dɛdˌlɑk] n : punto m muerto — **deadly**

['dɛdli] adj -lier; -est 1 : mortal, letal 2 ACCURATE : certero, preciso
deaf ['dɛf] adj : sordo — **deafen** ['dɛfən] vt : ensordecer — **deafness** ['dɛfnəs] n : sordera f
deal ['diːl] n 1 TRANSACTION : trato m, transacción f 2 : reparto m (de naipes) 3 a good ~ : mucho — ~ v dealt; dealing vt 1 : dar 2 : repartir, dar (naipes) 3 ~ a blow : asestar un golpe — vi 1 ~ : dar, repartir (en juegos de naipes) 2 ~ in : comerciar en 3 ~ with CONCERN : tratar de 4 ~ with s.o. : tratar con algn — **dealer** ['diːlər] n : comerciante mf — **dealings** npl : trato m, relaciones fpl
dean ['diːn] n : decano m, -na f
dear ['dɪr] adj : querido — ~ n : querido m, -da f — **dearly** ['dɪrli] adv 1 : mucho 2 pay ~ : pagar caro
death ['dɛθ] n : muerte f
debar [dɪ'bɑr] vt : excluir
debate [dɪ'beɪt] n : debate m, discusión f — ~ vt -bated; -bating : debatir, discutir
debit ['dɛbɪt] vt : adeudar, cargar — ~ n : débito m, debe m
debris [də'briː, deɪ-; 'deɪˌbriː] n, pl -bris [-'briːz, -'briːz] : escombros mpl
debt ['dɛt] n : deuda f — **debtor** ['dɛtər] n : deudor m, -dora f
debunk [dɪ'bʌŋk] vt : desmentir
debut ['deɪˌbjuː, deɪ'bjuː] n : debut m — ~ vi : debutar
decade ['dɛˌkeɪd, dɛ'keɪd] n : década f
decadence ['dɛkədənts] n : decadencia f — **decadent** ['dɛkədənt] adj : decadente
decal ['diːˌkæl, dɪ'kæl] n : calcomanía f
decanter [dɪ'kæntər] n : licorera f
decapitate [dɪ'kæpəˌteɪt] vt -tated; -tating : decapitar
decay [dɪ'keɪ] vi 1 DECOMPOSE : descomponerse 2 DETERIORATE : deteriorarse 3 : cariarse (dícese de los dientes) — ~ n 1 : descomposición f 2 : deterioro m (de un edificio, etc.) 3 : caries f (de los dientes)
deceased [dɪ'siːst] adj : difunto — ~ n the ~ : el difunto, la difunta
deceive [dɪ'siːv] vt -ceived; -ceiving : engañar — **deceit** [dɪ'siːt] n : engaño m — **deceitful** [dɪ'siːtfəl] adj : engañoso
December [dɪ'sɛmbər] n : diciembre m
decent ['diːsənt] adj 1 : decente 2 KIND : bueno, amable — **decency** ['diːsəntsi] n, pl -cies : decencia f
deception [dɪ'sɛpʃən] n : engaño m — **deceptive** [dɪ'sɛptɪv] adj : engañoso

decide [dɪ'saɪd] *v* **-cided; -ciding** *vt*
: decidir — *vi* : decidirse — **decided**
[dɪ'saɪdəd] *adj* **1** UNQUESTIONABLE : indudable **2** RESOLUTE : decidido — **de-**
cidedly [dɪ'saɪdədli] *adv* **1** DEFINITELY
: decididamente **2** RESOLUTELY : con
decisión

decimal ['dɛsəməl] *adj* : decimal — ~
n : número *m* decimal — **decimal**
point *n* : coma *f* decimal

decipher [dɪ'saɪfər] *vt* : descifrar

decision [dɪ'sɪʒən] *n* : decisión *f* — **de-**
cisive [dɪ'saɪsɪv] *adj* **1** RESOLUTE : decidido **2** CONCLUSIVE : decisivo

deck ['dɛk] *n* **1** : cubierta *f* (de un barco)
2 *or* ~ **of cards** : baraja *f* (de naipes)
3 TERRACE : entarimado *m*

declare [dɪ'klær] *vt* **-clared; -claring**
: declarar — **declaration** [ˌdɛklə-
'reɪʃən] *n* : declaración *f*

decline [dɪ'klaɪn] *v* **-clined; -clining** *vt*
REFUSE : declinar, rehusar — *vi* DE-
CREASE : disminuir — ~ *n* **1** DETERIO-
RATION : decadencia *f*, deterioro *m* **2**
DECREASE : disminución *f*

decode [di'ko:d] *vt* **-coded; -coding**
: descodificar

decompose [ˌdi:kəm'po:z] *vt* **-posed;**
-posing : descomponer — *vi* : descomponerse

decongestant [ˌdi:kən'dʒestənt] *n* : descongestionante *m*

decorate ['dɛkəˌreɪt] *vt* **-rated; -rating**
: decorar — **decor** *or* **décor** [deɪˈkɔr,
'deɪˌkɔr] *n* : decoración *f* — **decora-**
tion [ˌdɛkə'reɪʃən] *n* : decoración *f* —
decorator ['dɛkəˌreɪtər] *n* : decorador
m, -dora *f*

decoy ['di:ˌkɔɪ, di'-] *n* : señuelo *m*

decrease [dɪ'kri:s] *v* **-creased; -creas-**
ing : disminuir — ~ ['di:ˌkri:s] *n* : disminución *f*

decree [dɪ'kri:] *n* : decreto *m* — ~ *vt*
-creed; -creeing : decretar

decrepit [dɪ'krɛpɪt] *adj* **1** FEEBLE : decrépito **2** DILAPIDATED : ruinoso

dedicate ['dɛdɪˌkeɪt] *vt* **-cated; -cating 1**
: dedicar **2** ~ **oneself to** : consa-
grarse a — **dedication** [ˌdɛdɪ'keɪʃən] *n*
1 DEVOTION : dedicación *f* **2** INSCRIP-
TION : dedicatoria *f*

deduce [dɪ'du:s, -'dju:s] *vt* **-duced;**
-ducing : deducir — **deduct** [dɪ'dʌkt]
vt : deducir — **deduction** [dɪ'dʌkʃən] *n*
: deducción *f*

deed ['di:d] *n* **1** : acción *f*, hecho *m*

deem ['di:m] *vt* : considerar, juzgar

deep ['di:p] *adj* **1** : hondo, profundo — ~
adv **1** DEEPLY : profundamente **2** ~
down : en el fondo **3 dig** ~ : cavar

hondo — **deepen** ['di:pən] *vt* : ahondar
— *vi* : hacerse más profundo —
deeply ['di:pli] *adv* : hondo, profundamente

deer ['dɪr] *ns & pl* : ciervo *m*

deface [dɪ'feɪs] *vt* **-faced; -facing** : desfigurar

default [dɪ'fɔlt, 'di:ˌfɔlt] *n* **by** ~ : en rebeldía — *vi* **1** ~ **on** : no pagar (una
deuda) **2** : no presentarse (en deportes)

defeat [dɪ'fi:t] *vt* **1** BEAT : vencer, derrotar **2** FRUSTRATE : frustrar — ~ *n*
: derrota *f*

defect ['di:ˌfɛkt, dɪ'fɛkt] *n* : defecto *m* —
~ [dɪ'fɛkt] *vi* : desertar — **defective**
[dɪ'fɛktɪv] *adj* : defectuoso

defend [dɪ'fɛnd] *vt* : defender — **defen-**
dant [dɪ'fɛndənt] *n* : acusado *m*, -da *f*
— **defense** *or Brit* **defence** [dɪ'fɛnts,
'di:ˌfɛnts] *n* : defensa *f* — **defenseless**
or Brit **defenceless** *adj* : indefenso
— **defensive** [dɪ'fɛntsɪv] *adj* : defensivo — ~ *n* **on the** ~ : a la defensiva

defer [dɪ'fər] *v* **-ferred; -ferring** *vt*
: diferir, aplazar — *vi* ~ **to** : deferir a
— **deference** ['dɛfərənts] *n* : deferencia *f* — **deferential** [ˌdɛfə'rɛntʃəl] *adj*
: deferente

defiance [dɪ'faɪənts] *n* **1** : desafío *m* **2 in**
~ **of** : a despecho de — **defiant** [dɪ-
'faɪənt] *adj* : desafiante

deficiency [dɪ'fɪʃəntsi] *n, pl* **-cies** : deficiencia *f* — **deficient** [dɪ'fɪʃənt] *adj*
: deficiente

deficit ['dɛfəsɪt] *n* : déficit *m*

defile [dɪ'faɪl] *vt* **-filed; -filing 1** DIRTY
: ensuciar **2** DESECRATE : profanar

define [dɪ'faɪn] *v* **-fined; -fining**
: definir — **definite** ['dɛfənɪt] *adj* **1**
: definido **2** CERTAIN : seguro, incuestionable — **definition** [ˌdɛfə'nɪʃən] *n*
: definición *f* — **definitive** [dɪ'fɪnətɪv]
adj : definitivo

deflate [dɪ'fleɪt] *v* **-flated; -flating** *vt*
: desinflar (una llanta, etc.) — *vi*
: desinflarse

deflect [dɪ'flɛkt] *vt* : desviar — *vi* : desviarse

deform [dɪ'fɔrm] *vt* : deformar — **defor-**
mity [dɪ'fɔrməti] *n, pl* **-ties** : deformidad *f*

defraud [dɪ'frɔd] *vt* : defraudar

defrost [dɪ'frɔst] *vt* : descongelar — *vi*
: descongelarse

deft ['dɛft] *adj* : hábil, diestro

defy [dɪ'faɪ] *vt* **-fied; -fying 1** CHAL-
LENGE : desafiar **2** RESIST : resistir

degenerate [dɪ'dʒɛnəˌreɪt] *vi* : degenerar
— ~ [dɪ'dʒɛnərət] *adj* : degenerado

degrade [dɪ'greɪd] *vt* **-graded; -grading** : degradar — **degrading** *adj* : degradante

degree [dɪ'griː] *n* **1** : grado *m* **2** *or* **academic ~** : título *m*

dehydrate [diˈhaɪˌdreɪt] *vt* **-drated; -drating** : deshidratar

deign ['deɪn] *vi* **~ to** : dignarse (a)

deity ['diːəti, 'deɪ-] *n, pl* **-ties** : deidad *f*

dejected [dɪˈdʒektəd] *adj* : abatido — **dejection** [dɪˈdʒekʃən] *n* : abatimiento *m*

delay [dɪˈleɪ] *n* : retraso *m* — **~** *vt* **1** POSTPONE : aplazar **2** HOLD UP : retrasar — *vi* : demorar

delectable [dɪˈlektəbəl] *adj* : delicioso

delegate ['delɪgət, -ˌgeɪt] *n* : delegado *m*, -da *f* — **~** ['delɪˌgeɪt] *v* **-gated; -gating** : delegar — **delegation** [ˌdelɪˈgeɪʃən] *n* : delegación *f*

delete [dɪˈliːt] *vt* **-leted; -leting** : borrar

deliberate [dɪˈlɪbəˌreɪt] *v* **-ated; -ating** *vt* : deliberar sobre — *vi* : deliberar — **~** [dɪˈlɪbərət] *adj* : deliberado — **deliberately** [dɪˈlɪbərətli] *adv* INTENTIONALLY : a propósito — **deliberation** [dɪˌlɪbəˈreɪʃən] *n* : deliberación *f*

delicacy ['delɪkəsi] *n, pl* **-cies 1** : delicadeza *f* **2** FOOD : manjar *m*, exquisitez *f* — **delicate** ['delɪkət] *adj* : delicado

delicatessen [ˌdelɪkəˈtesən] *n* : charcutería *f*

delicious [dɪˈlɪʃəs] *adj* : delicioso

delight [dɪˈlaɪt] *n* : placer *m*, deleite *m* — **~** *vt* : deleitar, encantar — *vi* **~ in** : deleitarse con — **delightful** [dɪˈlaɪtfəl] *adj* : delicioso, encantador

delinquent [dɪˈlɪŋkwənt] *adj* : delincuente — **~** *n* : delincuente *mf*

delirious [dɪˈlɪriəs] *adj* : delirante — **delirium** [dɪˈlɪriəm] *n* : delirio *m*

deliver [dɪˈlɪvər] *vt* **1** DISTRIBUTE : entregar, repartir **2** FREE : liberar **3** : asistir en el parto de (un niño) **4** : pronunciar (un discurso, etc.) **5** DEAL : asestar (un golpe, etc.) — **delivery** [dɪˈlɪvəri] *n, pl* **-eries 1** DISTRIBUTION : entrega *f*, reparto *m* **2** LIBERATION : liberación *f* **3** CHILDBIRTH : parto *m*, alumbramiento *m*

delude [dɪˈluːd] *vt* **-luded; -luding 1** : engañar **2 ~ oneself** : engañarse

deluge ['delˌjuːdʒ, -ˌjuːʒ] *n* : diluvio *m*

delusion [dɪˈluːʒən] *n* : ilusión *f*

deluxe [dɪˈlʌks, -ˈlʊks] *adj* : de lujo

delve ['delv] *vi* **delved; delving 1** : escarbar **2 ~ into** PROBE : investigar

demand [dɪˈmænd] *n* **1** REQUEST : petición *f* **2** CLAIM : reclamación *f*, exigencia *f* **3 → supply** — **~** *vt* : exigir — **demanding** *adj* : exigente

demean [dɪˈmiːn] *vt* **~ oneself** : rebajarse

demeanor [dɪˈmiːnər] *n* : comportamiento *m*

demented [dɪˈmentəd] *adj* : demente, loco

demise [dɪˈmaɪz] *n* : fallecimiento *m*

democracy [dɪˈmɑkrəsi] *n, pl* **-cies** : democracia *f* — **democrat** ['deməˌkræt] *n* : demócrata *mf* — **democratic** [ˌdeməˈkrætɪk] *adj* : democrático

demolish [dɪˈmɑlɪʃ] *vt* : demoler — **demolition** [ˌdeməˈlɪʃən, ˌdiː-] *n* : demolición *f*

demon ['diːmən] *n* : demonio *m*

demonstrate ['demənˌstreɪt] *v* **-strated; -strating** *vt* : demostrar — *vi* RALLY : manifestarse — **demonstration** [ˌdemənˈstreɪʃən] *n* **1** : demostración *f* **2** RALLY : manifestación *f*

demoralize [dɪˈmɔrəˌlaɪz] *vt* **-ized; -izing** : desmoralizar

demote [dɪˈmoːt] *vt* **-moted; -moting** : bajar de categoría

demure [dɪˈmjʊr] *adj* : recatado

den ['den] *n* LAIR : guarida *f*

denial [dɪˈnaɪəl] *n* **1** : negación *f*, rechazo *m* **2** REFUSAL : denegación *f*

denim ['denəm] *n* : tela *f* vaquera, mezclilla *f* Lat

denomination [dɪˌnɑməˈneɪʃən] *n* **1** : confesión *f* (religiosa) **2** : valor *m* (de una moneda)

denounce [dɪˈnaʊnts] *vt* **-nounced; -nouncing** : denunciar

dense ['dents] *adj* **denser; -est 1** THICK : denso **2** STUPID : estúpido — **density** ['dentsəti] *n, pl* **-ties** : densidad *f*

dent ['dent] *vt* : abollar — **~** *n* : abolladura *f*

dental ['dentəl] *adj* : dental — **dental floss** *n* : hilo *m* dental — **dentist** ['dentɪst] *n* : dentista *mf* — **dentures** ['dentʃərz] *npl* : dentadura *f* postiza

deny [dɪˈnaɪ] *vt* **-nied; -nying 1** : negar **2** REFUSE : denegar

deodorant [diˈoːdərənt] *n* : desodorante *m*

depart [dɪˈpɑrt] *vi* **1** : salir **2 ~ from** : apartarse de (la verdad, etc.)

department [dɪˈpɑrtmənt] *n* : sección *f* (de una tienda, etc.), departamento *m* (de una empresa, etc.), ministerio *m* (del gobierno) — **department store** *n* : grandes almacenes *mpl*

departure [dɪˈpɑrtʃər] *n* **1** : salida *f* **2** DEVIATION : desviación *f*

depend [dɪˈpend] *vi* **1 ~ on** : depender

de 2 ~ **on s.o.** : contar con algn **3 that ~s** : eso depende — **dependable** [di'pendəbəl] *adj* : digno de confianza — **dependence** [di'pendənts] *n* : dependencia *f* — **dependent** [di'pendənt] *adj* : dependiente

depict [di'pikt] *vt* 1 PORTRAY : representar 2 DESCRIBE : describir

deplete [di'pli:t] *vt* **-pleted; -pleting** : agotar, reducir

deplore [di'plor] *vt* **-plored; -ploring** : deplorar, lamentar — **deplorable** [di'plorəbəl] *adj* : lamentable

deploy [di'plɔɪ] *vt* : desplegar

deport [di'port] *vt* : deportar, expulsar (de un país) — **deportation** [ˌdiˌpor'teɪʃən] *n* : deportación *f*

depose [di'po:z] *vt* **-posed; -posing** : deponer

deposit [di'pazət] *vt* **-ited; -iting** : depositar — ~ *n* 1 : depósito *m* 2 DOWN PAYMENT : entrega *f* inicial

depot [*in sense 1 usu* 'de.po:, 2 *usu* 'di:-] *n* 1 WAREHOUSE : almacén *m*, depósito *m* 2 STATION : terminal *mf*

depreciate [di'pri:ʃiˌeɪt] *vi* **-ated; -ating** : depreciarse — **depreciation** [diˌpri:ʃi'eɪʃən] *n* : depreciación *f*

depress [di'pres] *vt* 1 : deprimir 2 PRESS : apretar — **depressed** [di'prest] *adj* : abatido, deprimido — **depressing** [di'presɪŋ] *adj* : deprimente — **depression** [di'preʃən] *n* : depresión *f*

deprive [di'praɪv] *vt* **-prived; -priving** : privar

depth [depθ] *n, pl* **depths** ['depθs, 'deps] 1 : profundidad *f* 2 **in the ~s of night** : en lo más profundo de la noche

deputy ['depjuˌti] *n, pl* **-ties** : suplente *mf*; sustituto *m*, -ta *f*

derail [di'reɪl] *vt* : hacer descarrilar

deranged [di'reɪndʒd] *adj* : trastornado

derelict ['derəˌlɪkt] *adj* : abandonado

deride [di'raɪd] *vt* **-rided; -riding** : burlarse de — **derision** [di'rɪʒən] *n* : mofa *f*

derive [di'raɪv] *vi* **-rived; -riving** : derivar — **derivation** [ˌderə'veɪʃən] *n* : derivación *f*

derogatory [di'ragəˌtori] *adj* : despectivo

descend [di'send] *v* : descender, bajar — **descendant** [di'sendənt] *n* : descendiente *mf* — **descent** [di'sent] *n* 1 : descenso *m* 2 LINEAGE : descendencia *f*

describe [di'skraɪb] *vt* **-scribed; -scribing** : describir — **description** [di'skrɪpʃən] *n* : descripción *f* — **descriptive** [di'skrɪptɪv] *adj* : descriptivo

desecrate ['desɪˌkreɪt] *vt* **-crated; -crating** : profanar

desert ['dezərt] *n* : desierto *m* — ~ *adj* ~ **island** : isla *f* desierta — ~ [di'zərt] *vt* : abandonar — *vi* : desertar — **deserter** [di'zərtər] *n* : desertor *m*, -tora *f*

deserve [di'zərv] *vt* **-served; -serving** : merecer

design [di'zaɪn] *vt* 1 DEVISE : diseñar 2 PLAN : proyectar — ~ *n* 1 : diseño *m* 2 PLAN : plan *m*, proyecto *m*

designate ['dezɪgˌneɪt] *vt* **-nated; -nating** : nombrar, designar

designer [di'zaɪnər] *n* : diseñador *m*, -dora *f*

desire [di'zaɪr] *vt* **-sired; -siring** : desear — ~ *n* : deseo *m* — **desirable** [di'zaɪrəbəl] *adj* : deseable

desk ['desk] *n* : escritorio *m*, pupitre *m* (en la escuela)

desolate ['desələt, -zə-] *adj* : desolado

despair [di'spær] *vi* : desesperar — ~ *n* : desesperación *f*

desperate ['despərət] *adj* : desesperado — **desperation** [ˌdespə'reɪʃən] *n* : desesperación *f*

despise [di'spaɪz] *vt* **-spised; -spising** : despreciar — **despicable** [di'spɪkəbəl, 'despɪ-] *adj* : despreciable

despite [də'spaɪt] *prep* : a pesar de

despondent [di'spandənt] *adj* : desanimado

dessert [di'zərt] *n* : postre *m*

destination [ˌdestə'neɪʃən] *n* : destino *m* — **destined** [di'destənd] *adj* 1 : destinado 2 **for** : con destino a — **destiny** ['destəni] *n, pl* **-nies** : destino *m*

destitute ['destəˌtu:t, -ˌtju:t] *adj* : indigente

destroy [di'strɔɪ] *vt* : destruir — **destruction** [di'strʌkʃən] *n* : destrucción *f* — **destructive** [di'strʌktɪv] *adj* : destructivo

detach [di'tætʃ] *vt* : separar — **detached** [di'tætʃt] *adj* 1 : separado 2 IMPARTIAL : objetivo

detail [di'teɪl, 'di:ˌteɪl] *n* 1 : detalle *m* 2 **go into ~** : entrar en detalles — ~ *vt* : detallar — **detailed** *adj* : detallado

detain [di'teɪn] *vt* 1 : detener (un prisionero) 2 DELAY : entretener

detect [di'tekt] *vt* : detectar — **detection** [di'tekʃən] *n* : detección *f*, descubrimiento *m* — **detective** [di'tektɪv] *n* : detective *mf*

detention [di'tentʃən] *n* : detención *m*

deter [di'tər] *vt* **-terred; -terring** : disuadir

detergent [di'tərdʒənt] *n* : detergente *m*

deteriorate [dɪ'tɪriəˌreɪt] *vi* **-rated; -rating** : deteriorarse — **deterioration** [dɪˌtɪriə'reɪʃən] *n* : deterioro *m*

determine [dɪ'tərmən] *vt* **-mined; -mining** : determinar — **determined** [dɪ'tərmənd] *adj* RESOLUTE : decidido — **determination** [dɪˌtərmə'neɪʃən] *n* : determinación *f*

deterrent [dɪ'tərənt] *n* : medida *f* disuasiva

detest [dɪ'tɛst] *vt* : detestar — **detestable** [dɪ'tɛstəbəl] *adj* : odioso

detonate ['dɛtənˌeɪt] *v* **-nated; -nating** *vt* : hacer detonar — *vi* EXPLODE : detonar, estallar — **detonation** [ˌdɛtə'neɪʃən, ˌdɛtə-] *n* : detonación *f*

detour ['diːˌtʊr, dɪ'tʊr] *n* **1** : desviación *f* **2 make a ~** : dar un rodeo — **~** *vi* : desviarse

detract [dɪ'trækt] *vi* **~ from** : aminorar, restar importancia a

detrimental [ˌdɛtrə'mɛntəl] *adj* : perjudicial

devalue [diː'væljuː] *vt* **-ued; -uing** : devaluar

devastate ['dɛvəˌsteɪt] *vt* **-tated; -tating** : devastar — **devastating** *adj* : devastador — **devastation** [ˌdɛvə'steɪʃən] *n* : devastación *f*

develop [dɪ'vɛləp] *vt* **1** : desarrollar **2 ~ an illness** : contraer una enfermedad — *vi* **1** GROW : desarrollarse **2** HAPPEN : aparecer — **development** [dɪ'vɛləpmənt] *n* : desarrollo *m*

deviate ['diːviˌeɪt] *v* **-ated; -ating** *vi* : desviarse — **deviation** [ˌdiːvi'eɪʃən] *n* : desviación *f*

device [dɪ'vaɪs] *n* : dispositivo *m*, mecanismo *m*

devil ['dɛvəl] *n* : diablo *m*, demonio *m* — **devilish** ['dɛvəlɪʃ] *adj* : diabólico

devious ['diːviəs] *adj* **1** CRAFTY : taimado **2** WINDING : tortuoso

devise [dɪ'vaɪz] *vt* **-vised; -vising** : idear, concebir

devoid [dɪ'vɔɪd] *adj* **~ of** : desprovisto de

devote [dɪ'voːt] *vt* **-voted; -voting** : consagrar, dedicar — **devoted** [dɪ'voːtəd] *adj* : leal — **devotee** [ˌdɛvə'tiː, -'teɪ] *n* : devoto *m*, -ta *f* — **devotion** [dɪ'voːʃən] *n* **1** : devoción *f*, dedicación *f* **2** : oración *f* (en religión)

devour [dɪ'vaʊər] *vt* : devorar

devout [dɪ'vaʊt] *adj* : devoto

dew ['duː, 'djuː] *n* : rocío *m*

dexterity [dɛk'stɛrəti] *n, pl* **-ties** : destreza *f*

diabetes [ˌdaɪə'biːtiz] *n* : diabetes *f* —

diabetic [ˌdaɪə'bɛtɪk] *adj* : diabético — **~** *n* : diabético *m*, -ca *f*

diabolic [ˌdaɪə'bɑlɪk] *or* **diabolical** [-lɪkəl] *adj* : diabólico

diagnosis [ˌdaɪɪg'noːsɪs] *n, pl* **-noses** [-'noːˌsiːz] : diagnóstico *m* — **diagnose** ['daɪɪgˌnoːs, ˌdaɪɪg'noːs] *vt* **-nosed; -nosing** : diagnosticar — **diagnostic** [ˌdaɪɪg'nɑstɪk] *adj* : diagnóstico

diagonal [daɪ'ægənəl] *adj* : diagonal, en diagonal — **~** *n* : diagonal *f*

diagram ['daɪəˌgræm] *n* : diagrama *m*

dial ['daɪl] *n* : esfera *f* (de un reloj), dial *m* (de un radio, etc.) — **~** *v* **dialed** *or* **dialled; dialing** *or* **dialling** : marcar

dialect ['daɪəˌlɛkt] *n* : dialecto *m*

dialogue ['daɪəˌlɔg] *n* : diálogo *m*

diameter [daɪ'æmətər] *n* : diámetro *m*

diamond ['daɪmənd, 'daɪə-] *n* **1** : diamante *m* **2** : rombo *m* (forma) **3** *or* **baseball ~** : cuadro *m*, diamante *m*

diaper ['daɪpər, 'daɪə-] *n* : pañal *m*

diaphragm ['daɪəˌfræm] *n* : diafragma *m*

diarrhea [ˌdaɪə'riːə] *n* : diarrea *f*

diary ['daɪəri] *n, pl* **-ries** : diario *m*

dice ['daɪs] *ns & pl* : dados *mpl* (juego)

dictate ['dɪkˌteɪt, dɪk'teɪt] *vt* **-tated; -tating** : dictar — **dictation** [dɪk'teɪʃən] *n* : dictado *m* — **dictator** [dɪk'teɪtər] *n* : dictador *m*, -dora *f* — **dictatorship** [dɪk'teɪtərˌʃɪp, 'dɪk-] *n* : dictadura *f*

dictionary ['dɪkʃəˌnɛri] *n, pl* **-naries** : diccionario *m*

did → do

die[1] ['daɪ] *vi* **died** ['daɪd]; **dying** ['daɪɪŋ] **1** : morir **2 ~ down** : amainar, disminuir **3 ~ out** : extinguirse **4 be dying for** : morirse por

die[2] ['daɪ] *n* **1** *pl* **dice** ['daɪs] : dado *m* (para jugar) **2** *pl* **dies** ['daɪz] MOLD : molde *m*

diesel ['diːzəl, -səl] *n* : diesel *m*

diet ['daɪət] *n* **1** FOOD : alimentación *f* **2 go on a ~** : ponerse a régimen — **~** *vi* : estar a régimen

differ ['dɪfər] *vi* **-ferred; -ferring 1** : diferir, ser distinto **2** DISAGREE : no estar de acuerdo — **difference** ['dɪfrəns, 'dɪfərənts] *n* : diferencia *f* — **different** ['dɪfrənt, 'dɪfərənt] *adj* : distinto, diferente — **differentiate** [ˌdɪfə'rɛntʃiˌeɪt] *v* **-ated; -ating** *vt* : diferenciar — *vi* : distinguir — **differently** ['dɪfrəntli, 'dɪfərənt-] *adv* : de otra manera

difficult ['dɪfɪˌkʌlt] *adj* : difícil — **difficulty** ['dɪfɪˌkʌlti] *n, pl* **-ties** : dificultad *f*

diffident ['dɪfədənt] *adj* : tímido, que falta confianza

dig ['dɪg] *v* **dug** ['dʌg]; **digging** *vt* **1** : cavar **2** ~ **up** : desenterrar — *vi* : cavar — ~ *n* **1** GIBE : pulla *f* **2** EXCAVATION : excavación *f*

digest ['daɪ,dʒest] *n* : resumen *m* — ~ [daɪ'dʒest] *vt* **1** SUMMARIZE : resumir — **digestible** [daɪ'dʒestəbəl, dɪ-] *adj* : digerible — **digestion** [daɪ'dʒestʃən, dɪ-] *n* : digestión *f* — **digestive** [daɪ'dʒestɪv, dɪ-] *adj* : digestivo

digit ['dɪdʒət] *n* **1** NUMERAL : dígito *m*, número *m* **2** FINGER, TOE : dedo *m* — **digital** ['dɪdʒətəl] *adj* : digital

dignity ['dɪgnəti] *n*, *pl* **-ties** : dignidad *f* — **dignified** ['dɪgnə,faɪd] *adj* : digno, decoroso

digress [daɪ'gres, də-] *vi* : desviarse del tema, divagar — **digression** [daɪ'greʃən, də-] *n* : digresión *f*

dike ['daɪk] *n* : dique *m*

dilapidated [də'læpə,deɪtəd] *adj* : ruinoso

dilate [daɪ'leɪt, 'daɪ,leɪt] *v* **-lated; -lating** *vt* : dilatar — *vi* : dilatarse

dilemma [dɪ'lemə] *n* : dilema *m*

diligence ['dɪlədʒənts] *n* : diligencia *f* — **diligent** ['dɪlədʒənt] *adj* : diligente

dilute [daɪ'luːt, də-] *vt* **-luted; -luting** : diluir

dim ['dɪm] *v* **dimmed; dimming** *vt* : atenuar — *vi* : irse atenuando — ~ *adj* **dimmer; dimmest 1** DARK : oscuro **2** FAINT : débil, tenue

dime ['daɪm] *n* : moneda *f* de diez centavos

dimension [də'mentʃən, daɪ-] *n* : dimensión *f*

diminish [də'mɪnɪʃ] *v* : disminuir

diminutive [də'mɪnjʊtɪv] *adj* : diminuto

dimple ['dɪmpəl] *n* : hoyuelo *m*

din ['dɪn] *n* : estrépito *m*

dine ['daɪn] *vi* **dined; dining** : cenar — **diner** ['daɪnər] *n* **1** : comensal *mf* (persona) **2** : cafetería *f* (restaurante)

dingy ['dɪndʒi] *adj* **-gier; -est** : sucio, deslucido

dinner ['dɪnər] *n* : cena *f*, comida *f*

dinosaur ['daɪnə,sɔr] *n* : dinosaurio *m*

dint ['dɪnt] *n* **by** ~ **of** : a fuerza de

dip ['dɪp] *v* **dipped; dipping** *vt* : mojar — *vi* : bajar, descender — ~ *n* **1** DROP : descenso *m*, caída *f* **2** SWIM : chapuzón *m* **3** SAUCE : salsa *f*

diploma [də'ploːmə] *n*, *pl* **-mas** : diploma *m*

diplomacy [də'ploːməsi] *n* : diplomacia *f* — **diplomat** ['dɪplə,mæt] *n* : diplomático *m*, **-ca** *f* — **diplomatic** [,dɪplə-'mætɪk] *adj* : diplomático

dire ['daɪr] *adj* **direr; direst 1** : grave, terrible **2** EXTREME : extremo

direct [də'rekt, daɪ-] *vt* **1** : dirigir **2** ORDER : mandar — ~ *adj* **1** STRAIGHT : directo **2** FRANK : franco — ~ *adv* **1** : directamente — **direct current** *n* : corriente *f* continua — **direction** [də-'rekʃən, daɪ-] *n* **1** : dirección *f* **2** ask ~**s** : pedir indicaciones — **directly** [də'rektli, daɪ-] *adv* **1** STRAIGHT : directamente **2** IMMEDIATELY : en seguida — **director** [də'rektər, daɪ-] *n* **1** : director *m*, **-tora** *f* **2 board of** ~**s** : directorio *m* — **directory** [də'rektəri, daɪ-] *n*, *pl* **-ries** : guía *f* (telefónica)

dirt ['dərt] *n* **1** : suciedad *f* **2** SOIL : tierra *f* — **dirty** ['dərti] *adj* **dirtier; -est 1** : sucio **2** INDECENT : obsceno, cochino *fam*

disability [,dɪsə'bɪləti] *n*, *pl* **-ties** : minusvalía *f*, invalidez *f* — **disable** [dɪs-'eɪbəl] *vt* **-abled; -abling** : incapacitar — **disabled** [dɪs'eɪbəld] *adj* : minusválido

disadvantage [,dɪsəd'væntɪdʒ] *n* : desventaja *f*

disagree [,dɪsə'griː] *vi* **1** : no estar de acuerdo (con algn) **2** CONFLICT : no coincidir — **disagreeable** [,dɪsə'griːəbəl] *adj* : desagradable — **disagreement** [,dɪsə'griːmənt] *n* **1** : desacuerdo *m* **2** ARGUMENT : discusión *f*

disappear [,dɪsə'pɪr] *vi* : desaparecer — **disappearance** [,dɪsə'pɪrənts] *n* : desaparición *f*

disappoint [,dɪsə'pɔɪnt] *vt* : decepcionar, desilusionar — **disappointment** [,dɪsə'pɔɪntmənt] *n* : decepción *f*, desilusión *f*

disapprove [,dɪsə'pruːv] *vi* **-proved; -proving** ~ **of** : desaprobar — **disapproval** [,dɪsə'pruːvəl] *n* : desaprobación *f*

disarm [dɪs'ɑrm] *vt* : desarmar — **disarmament** [dɪs'ɑrməmənt] *n* : desarme *m*

disarray [,dɪsə'reɪ] *n* : desorden *m*

disaster [dɪ'zæstər] *n* : desastre *m* — **disastrous** [dɪ'zæstrəs] *adj* : desastroso

disbelief [,dɪsbɪ'liːf] *n* : incredulidad *f*

disc → **disk**

discard [dɪs'kɑrd, 'dɪs,kɑrd] *vt* : desechar, deshacerse de

discern [dɪ'sərn, -'zərn] *vt* : percibir, discernir — **discernible** [dɪ'sərnəbəl, -'zər-] *adj* : perceptible

discharge [dɪs'tʃɑrdʒ, 'dɪs,-] *vt* **-charged; -charging 1** UNLOAD : descargar **2** RELEASE : liberar, poner en libertad **3** DISMISS : despedir **4**

CARRY OUT : cumplir con (una obligación) — **~** ['dɪstʃɑrdʒ, dɪs-'] *n* **1** : descarga *f* (de electricidad), emisión *f* (de humo, etc.) **2** DISMISSAL : despido *m* **3** RELEASE : alta *f* (de un paciente), puesta *f* en libertad (de un preso) **4** : supuración *f* (en medicina)

disciple [dɪ'saɪpəl] *n* : discípulo *m*, -la *f*

discipline ['dɪsəplən] *n* **1** : disciplina *f* **2** PUNISHMENT : castigo *m* — **~** *vt* **-plined; -plining 1** CONTROL : disciplinar **2** PUNISH : castigar

disclaim [dɪs'kleɪm] *vt* : negar

disclose [dɪs'kloːz] *vt* **-closed; -closing** : revelar — **disclosure** [dɪs'kloʒər] *n* : revelación *f*

discomfort [dɪs'kʌmfərt] *n* **1** : incomodidad *f* **2** PAIN : malestar *m* **3** UNEASINESS : inquietud *f*

disconcert [,dɪskən'sərt] *vt* : desconcertar

disconnect [,dɪskə'nekt] *vt* : desconectar

disconsolate [dɪs'kɑntsələt] *adj* : desconsolado

discontented [,dɪskən'tentəd] *adj* : descontento

discontinue [,dɪskən'tɪnjuː] *vt* **-ued; -uing** : suspender, descontinuar

discount ['dɪs,kaʊnt, dɪs-'] *n* : descuento *m*, rebaja *f* — **~** *vt* **1** : descontar (precios) **2** DISREGARD : descartar

discourage [dɪs'kɔrɪdʒ] *vt* **-aged; -aging** : desalentar, desanimar — **discouragement** [dɪs'kɔrɪdʒmənt] *n* : desánimo *m*, desaliento *m*

discover [dɪs'kʌvər] *vt* : descubrir — **discovery** [dɪs'kʌvəri] *n*, *pl* **-ries** : descubrimiento *m*

discredit [dɪs'kredət] *vt* : desacreditar — **~** *n* : descrédito *m*

discreet [dɪs'kriːt] *adj* : discreto

discrepancy [dɪs'krepəntsi] *n*, *pl* **-cies** : discrepancia *f*

discretion [dɪs'kreʃən] *n* : discreción *f*

discriminate [dɪs'krɪmə,neɪt] *vi* **-nated; -nating 1 ~ against** : discriminar **2 ~ between** : distinguir entre — **discrimination** [dɪsˌkrɪmə'neɪʃən] *n* **1** PREJUDICE : discriminación *f* **2** DISCERNMENT : discernimiento *m*

discuss [dɪs'kʌs] *vt* : hablar de, discutir — **discussion** [dɪs'kʌʃən] *n* : discusión *f*

disdain [dɪs'deɪn] *n* : desdén *m* — **~** *vt* : desdeñar

disease [dɪ'ziːz] *n* : enfermedad *f* — **diseased** [dɪ'ziːzd] *adj* : enfermo

disembark [,dɪsɪm'bɑrk] *vi* : desembarcar

disengage [,dɪsɪn'geɪdʒ] *vt* **-gaged;**

-gaging 1 RELEASE : soltar **2 ~ the clutch** : desembragar

disentangle [,dɪsɪn'tæŋɡəl] *vt* **-gled; -gling** : desenredar

disfavor [dɪs'feɪvər] *n* : desaprobación *f*

disfigure [dɪs'fɪɡjər] *vt* **-ured; -uring** : desfigurar

disgrace [dɪs'kreɪs] *vt* **-graced; -gracing** : deshonrar — **~** *n* **1** DISHONOR : deshonra *f* **2** SHAME : vergüenza *f* — **disgraceful** [dɪs'kreɪsfəl] *adj* : vergonzoso, deshonroso

disgruntled [dɪs'ɡrʌntəld] *adj* : descontento

disguise [dɪs'kaɪz] *vt* **-guised; -guising** : disfrazar — **~** *n* : disfraz *m*

disgust [dɪs'kʌst] *n* : asco *m*, repugnancia *f* — **~** *vt* : asquear — **disgusting** [dɪs'kʌstɪŋ] *adj* : asqueroso

dish ['dɪʃ] *n* **1** : plato *m* **2** *or* **serving ~** : fuente *f* **3 wash the ~es** : lavar los platos — **~** *vt or* **~ up** : servir — **dishcloth** ['dɪʃ,klɔθ] *n* : paño *m* de cocina (para secar), trapo *m* de fregar (para lavar)

dishearten [dɪs'hɑrtən] *vt* : desanimar

disheveled *or* **dishevelled** [dɪ'ʃevəld] *adj* : desaliñado, despeinado (dícese del pelo)

dishonest [dɪ'sɑnəst] *adj* : deshonesto — **dishonesty** [dɪ'sɑnəsti] *n*, *pl* **-ties** : falta *f* de honradez

dishonor [dɪ'sɑnər] *n* : deshonra *f* — **~** *vt* : deshonrar — **dishonorable** [dɪ'sɑnərəbəl] *adj* : deshonroso

dishwasher ['dɪʃ,wɔʃər] *n* : lavaplatos *m*, lavavajillas *m*

disillusion [,dɪsə'luːʒən] *vt* : desilusionar — **disillusionment** [,dɪsə'luːʒənmənt] *n* : desilusión *f*

disinfect [,dɪsɪn'fekt] *vt* : desinfectar — **disinfectant** [,dɪsɪn'fektənt] *n* : desinfectante *m*

disintegrate [dɪs'ɪntə,greɪt] *vi* **-grated; -grating** : desintegrarse

disinterested [dɪs'ɪntərəstəd, -,res-] *adj* : desinteresado

disk *or* **disc** ['dɪsk] *n* : disco *m*

dislike [dɪs'laɪk] *n* : aversión *f*, antipatía *f* — **~** *vt* **-liked; -liking 1** : tener aversión a **2 I ~ dancing** : no me gusta bailar

dislocate ['dɪslo,keɪt, dɪs'lo:-] *vt* **-cated; -cating** : dislocar

dislodge [dɪs'lɑdʒ] *vt* **-lodged; -lodging** : sacar, desalojar

disloyal [dɪs'lɔɪəl] *adj* : desleal — **disloyalty** [dɪs'lɔɪəlti] *n*, *pl* **-ties** : deslealtad *f*

dismal ['dɪzməl] *adj* : sombrío, deprimente

dismantle [dɪs'mæntəl] *vt* **-tled; -tling** : desmontar, desarmar

dismay [dɪs'meɪ] *vt* : consternar — **~** *n* : consternación *f*

dismiss [dɪs'mɪs] *vt* **1** DISCHARGE : despedir, destituir **2** REJECT : descartar, rechazar — **dismissal** [dɪs'mɪsəl] *n* **1** : despido *m* (de un empleado), destitución *f* (de un funcionario) **2** REJECTION : rechazo *m*

dismount [dɪs'maʊnt] *vi* : desmontar

disobey [ˌdɪsə'beɪ] *v* : desobedecer — **disobedience** [ˌdɪsə'biːdiənts] *n* : desobediencia *f* — **disobedient** [-ənt] *adj* : desobediente

disorder [dɪs'ɔrdər] *n* **1** : desorden *m* **2** AILMENT : afección *f*, problema *m* — **disorderly** [dɪs'ɔrdərli] *adj* : desordenado

disorganize [dɪs'ɔrgənaɪz] *vt* **-nized; -nizing** : desorganizar

disown [dɪs'on] *vt* : renegar de

dispassionate [dɪs'pæʃənət] *adj* : desapasionado

dispatch [dɪs'pætʃ] *vt* : despachar, enviar

dispel [dɪs'pel] *vt* **-pelled; -pelling** : disipar

dispensation [ˌdɪspen'seɪʃən] *n* EXEMPTION : exención *m*, dispensa *f*

dispense [dɪs'pents] *v* **-pensed; -pensing** *vt* : repartir, distribuir — *vi* **~ with** : prescindir de

disperse [dɪs'pərs] *v* **-persed; -persing** *vt* : dispersar — *vi* : dispersarse

displace [dɪs'pleɪs] *vt* **-placed; -placing 1** : desplazar **2** REPLACE : reemplazar

display [dɪs'pleɪ] *vt* **1** EXHIBIT : exponer, exhibir **2 ~ anger** : manifestar la ira — **~** *n* : muestra *f*, exposición *f*

displease [dɪs'pliːz] *vt* **-pleased; -pleasing** : desagradar — **displeasure** [dɪs'plɛʒər] *n* : desagrado *m*

dispose [dɪs'poːz] *vt* **-posed; -posing** *vt* : disponer — *vi* **~ of** : deshacerse de — **disposable** [dɪs'poːzəbəl] *adj* : desechable — **disposal** [dɪs'poːzəl] *n* **1** REMOVAL : eliminación *f* **2 have at one's ~** : tener a su disposición — **disposition** [ˌdɪspə'zɪʃən] *n* **1** ARRANGEMENT : disposición *f* **2** TEMPERAMENT : temperamento *m*, carácter *m*

disprove [dɪs'pruːv] *vt* **-proved; -proving** : refutar

dispute [dɪs'pjuːt] *v* **-puted; -puting** *vt* QUESTION : cuestionar — *vi* ARGUE : discutir — **~** *n* : disputa *f*, conflicto *m*

disqualification [ˌdɪsˌkwɑləfə'keɪʃən] *n* : descalificación *f* — **disqualify** [dɪs'kwɑləfaɪ] *vt* **-fied; -fying** : descalificar

disregard [ˌdɪsri'gard] *vt* : ignorar, hacer caso omiso de — **~** *n* : indiferencia *f*

disrepair [ˌdɪsri'pær] *n* : mal estado *m*

disreputable [dɪs'rɛpjʊtəbəl] *adj* : de mala fama

disrespect [ˌdɪsri'spɛkt] *n* : falta *f* de respeto — **disrespectful** [ˌdɪsri'spɛktfəl] *adj* : irrespetuoso

disrupt [dɪs'rʌpt] *vt* : trastornar, perturbar — **disruption** [dɪs'rʌpʃən] *n* : trastorno *m*

dissatisfaction [dɪsˌsætəs'fækʃən] *n* : descontento *m* — **dissatisfied** [dɪs'sætəsˌfaɪd] *adj* : descontento

dissect [dɪ'sɛkt] *vt* : disecar

disseminate [dɪ'sɛməneɪt] *vt* **-nated; -nating** : diseminar, difundir

dissent [dɪ'sɛnt] *vi* : disentir — **~** *n* : disentimiento *m*

dissertation [ˌdɪsər'teɪʃən] THESIS : tesis *f*

disservice [dɪs'sərvɪs] *n* **do a ~ to** : no hacer justicia a

dissident ['dɪsədənt] *n* : disidente *mf*

dissimilar [dɪ'sɪmələr] *adj* : distinto

dissipate ['dɪsəpeɪt] *vt* **-pated; -pating 1** DISPEL : disipar **2** SQUANDER : desperdiciar

dissolve [dɪ'zɑlv] *v* **-solved; -solving** *vt* : disolver — *vi* : disolverse

dissuade [dɪ'sweɪd] *vt* **-suaded; -suading** : disuadir

distance ['dɪstənts] *n* **1** : distancia *f* **2 in the ~** : a lo lejos — **distant** ['dɪstənt] *adj* : distante

distaste [dɪs'teɪst] *n* : desagrado *m* — **distasteful** [dɪs'teɪstfəl] *adj* : desagradable

distend [dɪs'tɛnd] *vt* : dilatar — *vi* : dilatarse

distill [dɪ'stɪl] *or Brit* **distil** *vt* **-tilled; -tilling** : destilar

distinct [dɪ'stɪŋkt] *adj* **1** DIFFERENT : distinto **2** CLEAR : claro — **distinction** [dɪ'stɪŋkʃən] *n* : distinción *f* — **distinctive** [dɪ'stɪŋktɪv] *adj* : distintivo

distinguish [dɪs'tɪŋgwɪʃ] *vt* : distinguir — **distinguished** [dɪs'tɪŋgwɪʃt] *adj* : distinguido

distort [dɪ'stɔrt] *vt* : deformar, distorsionar — **distortion** [dɪ'stɔrʃən] *n* : deformación *f*

distract [dɪ'strækt] *vt* : distraer — **distraction** [dɪ'strækʃən] *n* : distracción *f*

distraught [dɪ'strɔt] *adj* : muy afligido

distress [dɪ'strɛs] *n* **1** : angustia *f*, aflicción *f* **2 in ~** : en peligro — **~** *vt*

: afligir — **distressing** [dɪ'stresɪŋ] *adj*
: penoso
distribute [dɪ'strɪ,bjuːt, -bjʊt] *vt* **-uted;**
-uting : distribuir, repartir — **distribu-**
tion [,dɪstrə'bjuːʃən] *n* : distribución *f* —
distributor [dɪ'strɪbjʊtər] *n* : distribuidor *m*, -dora *f*
district ['dɪs,trɪkt] *n* **1** REGION : región *f*,
zona *f*, barrio *m* (de una ciudad) **2**
: distrito *m* (zona política)
distrust [dɪs'trʌst] *n* : desconfianza *f* —
~ *vt* : desconfiar de
disturb [dɪ'stərb] *vt* **1** BOTHER : molestar,
perturbar **2** WORRY : inquietar — **dis-**
turbance [dɪ'stərbənts] *n* **1** COMMOTION
: alboroto *m*, disturbio *m* **2** INTERRUP-
TION : interrupción *f*
disuse [dɪs'juːs] *n* **fall into** ~ : caer en
desuso
ditch [dɪtʃ] *n* : zanja *f*, cuneta *f* — ~ *vt*
DISCARD : deshacerse de, botar
ditto ['dɪtoː] *n, pl* **-tos 1** : ídem *m* **2** ~
marks : comillas *fpl*
dive ['daɪv] *vi* **dived** *or* **dove** ['doːv];
dived; diving 1 : zambullirse, tirarse
al agua **2** DESCEND : bajar en picada
(dícese de un avión, etc.) — ~ *n* **1**
: zambullida *f*, clavado *m* Lat **2** DE-
SCENT : descenso *m* en picada — **diver**
['daɪvər] *n* : saltador *m*, -dora *f*
diverge [də'vərdʒ, daɪ-] *vi* **-verged;**
-verging : divergir
diverse [daɪ'vərs, də-, 'daɪ,vərs] *adj* : diverso — **diversify** [daɪ'vərsə,faɪ, də-] *v*
-fied; -fying *vt* : diversificar — *vi* : di-
versificarse
diversion [daɪ'vərʒən, də-] *n* **1**
: desviación *f* **2** AMUSEMENT : diversión *f*, distracción *f*
diversity [daɪ'vərsəti, də-] *n, pl* **-ties**
: diversidad *f*
divert [də'vərt, daɪ-] *vt* **1** : desviar **2** DIS-
TRACT : distraer **3** AMUSE : divertir
divide [də'vaɪd] *v* **-vided; -viding** *vt* : dividir — *vi* : dividirse
dividend ['dɪvə,dend, -dənd] *n* : dividendo *m*
divine [də'vaɪn] *adj* **-viner; -est** : divino
— **divinity** [də'vɪnəti] *n, pl* **-ties** : divinidad *f*
division [dɪ'vɪʒən] *n* : división *f*
divorce [də'vors] *n* : divorcio *m* — ~ *v*
-vorced; -vorcing *vt* : divorciar — *vi*
: divorciarse — **divorcée** [dɪ,vor'seɪ,
-'siː; -'vor,-] *n* : divorciada *f*
divulge [də'vʌldʒ, daɪ-] *vt* **-vulged;**
-vulging : revelar, divulgar
dizzy ['dɪzi] *adj* **dizzier; -est 1** : mareado **2 a ~ speed** : una velocidad ver-

tiginosa — **dizziness** ['dɪzinəs] *n*
: mareo *m*, vértigo *m*
DNA [,diː,en'eɪ] *n* : AND *m*
do ['duː] *v* **did** ['dɪd]; **done** ['dʌn]; **doing;**
does ['dʌz] *vt* **1** : hacer **2** PREPARE
: preparar — *vi* **1** BEHAVE : hacer **2**
FARE : estar, ir, andar **3** SUFFICE : ser
suficiente **4** ~ **away with** : abolir,
eliminar **5 how are you doing?**
: ¿cómo estás? — *v aux* **1** (*used in in-*
terrogative sentences) **do you know**
her? : ¿la conoces? **2** (*used in nega-*
tive statements) **I don't know** : yo no
se **3** (*used as a substitute verb to*
avoid repetition) **do you speak Eng-**
lish? yes, I do : ¿habla inglés? sí
dock ['dɑk] *n* : muelle *m* — ~ *vt* : descontar dinero de (un sueldo) — *vi*
ANCHOR : fondear, atracar
doctor ['dɑktər] *n* **1** : doctor *m*, -tora *f*
(en derecho, etc.) **2** PHYSICIAN : médi-
co *m*, -ca *f*; doctor *m*, -tora *f* — ~ *vt*
ALTER : alterar, falsificar
doctrine ['dɑktrɪn] *n* : doctrina *f*
document ['dɑkjəmənt] *n* : documento
m — ~ ['dɑkjʊ,ment] *vt* : documentar
— **documentary** [,dɑkjʊ'mentəri] *n, pl*
-ries : documental *m*
dodge ['dɑdʒ] *n* : artimaña *f*, truco *m* —
~ *v* **dodged; dodging** *vt* : esquivar,
eludir — *vi* : echarse a un lado
doe ['doː] *n, pl* **does** *or* **doe** : gama *f*,
cierva *f*
does → **do**
dog ['dɔg, 'dag] *n* : perro *m*, -rra *f* — ~
vt **dogged; dogging** : perseguir —
dogged ['dɔgəd] *adj* : tenaz
dogma ['dɔgmə] *n* : dogma *m* — **dog-**
matic [dɔg'mætɪk] *adj* : dogmático
doily ['dɔɪli] *n, pl* **-lies** : tapete *m*
doings ['duːɪŋz] *npl* : actividades *fpl*
doldrums ['doːldrəmz, 'dɑl-] *npl* **be in**
the ~ : estar abatido
dole ['doːl] *n* : subsidio *m* de desempleo
— ~ *vt* **doled; doling** *or* ~ **out**
: repartir
doleful ['doːlfəl] *adj* : triste, lúgubre
doll ['dɑl, 'dɔl] *n* : muñeco *m*, -ca *f*
dollar ['dɑlər] *n* : dólar *m*
dolphin ['dɑlfən, 'dɔl-] *n* : delfín *m*
domain [doː'meɪn, də-] *n* **1** TERRITORY
: dominio *m* **2** FIELD : campo *m*, esfera
f
dome ['doːm] *n* : cúpula *f*
domestic [də'mestɪk] *adj* **1** : doméstico
2 INTERNAL : nacional — ~ *n* SERVANT
: empleado *m* doméstico, empleada *f*
doméstica — **domesticate** [də'mesti-
,keɪt] *vt* **-cated; -cating** : domesticar
domination [,dɑmə'neɪʃən] *n* : domi-

nación f — **dominant** ['dɑmənənt] adj : dominante — **dominate** ['dɑmə,neɪt] v **-nated; -nating** : dominar — **domineer** [,dɑmə'nɪr] vi : dominar, tiranizar

dominos ['dɑmə,noːz] n : dominó m (juego)

donate ['doː,neɪt, doː'-] vt **-nated; -nating** : donar, hacer un donativo de — **donation** [doː'neɪʃən] n : donativo m

done ['dʌn] → **do** — ~ adj 1 FINISHED : terminado, hecho 2 COOKED : cocido

donkey ['dɑŋki, 'dʌŋ-] n, pl **-keys** : burro m

donor ['doːnər] n : donante mf

don't ['doːnt] (contraction of **do not**) → **do**

doodle ['duːdəl] v **-dled; -dling** : garabatear — ~ n : garabato m

doom ['duːm] n : perdición f, fatalidad f — ~ vt : condenar

door ['dor] n 1 : puerta f 2 ENTRANCE : entrada f — **doorbell** ['dor,bɛl] n : timbre m — **doorknob** ['dor,nɑb] n : pomo m — **doorman** ['dormən] n, pl **-men** [-mən, -,mɛn] : portero m — **doormat** ['dor,mæt] n : felpudo m — **doorstep** ['dor,stɛp] n : umbral m — **doorway** ['dor,weɪ] n : entrada f, portal m

dope ['doːp] n 1 DRUG : droga f 2 IDIOT : idiota mf — ~ vt **doped; doping** : drogar

dormant ['dɔrmənt] adj : inactivo, latente

dormitory ['dɔrmə,tori] n, pl **-ries** : dormitorio m

dose ['doːs] n : dosis f — **dosage** ['doːsɪdʒ] n : dosis f

dot ['dɑt] n 1 : punto m 2 **on the** ~ : en punto

dote ['doːt] vi **doted; doting** ~ **on** : adorar

double ['dʌbəl] adj : doble — ~ v **-bled; -bling** vt : doblar — vi : doblarse — ~ adv : (el) doble — ~ n : doble mf — **double bass** n : contrabajo m — **double-cross** [,dʌbəl-'krɔs] vt : traicionar — **doubly** ['dʌbli] adv : doblemente

doubt ['daʊt] vt 1 : dudar 2 DISTRUST : desconfiar de, dudar de — ~ n : duda f — **doubtful** ['daʊtfəl] adj : dudoso — **doubtless** ['daʊtləs] adv : sin duda

dough ['doː] n : masa f — **doughnut** ['doː,nʌt] n : rosquilla f, dona f Lat

douse ['daʊs, 'daʊz] vt **doused; dousing** 1 DRENCH : empapar, mojar 2 EXTINGUISH : apagar

dove[1] ['dəv] → **dive**

dove[2] ['dʌv] n : paloma f

dowdy ['daʊdi] adj **dowdier; -est** : poco elegante

down ['daʊn] adv 1 DOWNWARD : hacia abajo 2 **come/go** ~ : bajar 3 ~ **here** : aquí abajo 4 **fall** ~ : caer 5 **lie** ~ : acostarse 6 **sit** ~ : sentarse — ~ prep 1 ALONG : a lo largo de 2 THROUGH : a través de 3 ~ **the hill** : cuesta abajo — ~ adj 1 DESCENDING : de bajada 2 DOWNCAST : abatido — ~ n : plumón m — **downcast** ['daʊn,kæst] adj : triste, abatido — **downfall** ['daʊn,fɔl] n : ruina f — **downhearted** ['daʊn,hɑrtəd] adj : desanimado — **downhill** ['daʊn,hɪl] adv & adj : cuesta abajo — **down payment** n : entrega f inicial — **downpour** ['daʊn,por] n : chaparrón m — **downright** ['daʊn,raɪt] adv : absolutamente — ~ adj : absoluto, categórico — **downstairs** ['daʊn'stærz] adv : abajo — ~ ['daʊn,stærz] adj : de abajo — **downstream** ['daʊn'striːm] adv : río abajo — **down–to–earth** [,daʊntu'ərθ] adj : realista — **downtown** [,daʊn'taʊn, 'daʊn,taʊn] n : centro m (de la ciudad) — ~ [,daʊn'taʊn] adv : al centro, en el centro — ~ adj : del centro — **downward** ['daʊnwərd] or **downwards** [-wərdz] adv & adj : hacia abajo

dowry ['daʊri] n, pl **-ries** : dote f

doze ['doːz] vi **dozed; dozing** : dormitar

dozen ['dʌzən] n, pl **dozens** or **dozen** : docena f

drab ['dræb] adj **drabber; drabbest** : monótono, apagado

draft ['dræft, 'draft] n 1 : corriente f de aire 2 or **rough** ~ : borrador m 3 : conscripción f (militar) 4 or ~ **beer** : cerveza f de barril — ~ vt 1 SKETCH : hacer el borrador de 2 CONSCRIPT : reclutar — **drafty** ['dræfti] adj **draftier; -est** : con corrientes de aire

drag ['dræg] v **dragged; dragging** vt 1 : arrastrar 2 DREDGE : dragar — vi : arrastrar(se) — ~ n 1 RESISTANCE : resistencia f (aerodinámica) 2 BORE : pesadez f, plomo m fam

dragon ['drægən] n : dragón m — **dragonfly** ['drægən,flaɪ] n, pl **-flies** : libélula f

drain ['dreɪn] vt 1 EMPTY : vaciar, drenar 2 EXHAUST : agotar — vi 1 : escurrir(se) (se dice de los platos) 2 or ~ **away** : desaparecer poco a poco — ~ n 1 : desagüe m 2 SEWER : alcantarilla f 3 DEPLETION : agotamiento m — **drainage** ['dreɪnɪdʒ] n : drenaje m — **drainpipe** ['dreɪn,paɪp] n : tubo m de desagüe

drama ['drɑmə, 'dræ-] n : drama m —

dramatic [drə'mæṭɪk] *adj* : dramático
— **dramatist** ['dræməṭɪst, 'drɑ-] *n* : dramaturgo *m*, -ga *f* — **dramatize** ['dræmə,taɪz, 'drɑ-] *vt* **-tized; -tizing** : dramatizar

drank → drink

drape ['dreɪp] *vt* **draped; draping** 1 COVER : cubrir (con tela) 2 HANG : drapear — **drapes** *npl* CURTAINS : cortinas *fpl*

drastic ['dræstɪk] *adj* : drástico

draught ['dræft, 'draft] → **draft**

draw ['drɔ] *v* **drew** ['dru:]; **drawn** ['drɔn]; **drawing** *vt* 1 PULL : tirar de 2 ATTRACT : atraer 3 SKETCH : dibujar, trazar 4 : sacar (una espada, etc.) 5 ~ **a conclusion** : llegar a una conclusión 6 ~ **up** DRAFT : redactar — *vi* 1 SKETCH : dibujar 2 ~ **near** : acercarse — ~ *n* 1 DRAWING : sorteo *m* 2 TIE : empate *m* 3 ATTRACTION : atracción *f* — **drawback** ['drɔ,bæk] *n* : desventaja *f* — **drawer** ['drɔr, 'drɔər] *n* : gaveta *f*, cajón *m* (en un mueble) — **drawing** ['drɔɪŋ] *n* 1 LOTTERY : sorteo *m* 2 SKETCH : dibujo *m*

drawl ['drɔl] *n* : habla *f* lenta y con vocales prolongadas

dread ['drɛd] *vt* : temer — ~ *n* : pavor *m*, temor *m* — **dreadful** ['drɛdfəl] *adj* : espantoso, terrible

dream ['dri:m] *n* : sueño *m* — ~ *v* **dreamed** ['drɛmpt, 'dri:md] *or* **dreamt** ['drɛmpt]; **dreaming** *vi* : soñar — *vt* 1 : soñar 2 ~ **up** : idear — **dreamer** ['dri:mər] *n* : soñador *m*, -dora *f* — **dreamy** ['dri:mi] *adj* **dreamier; -est** : soñador

dreary ['drɪri] *adj* **-rier; -est** : sombrío, deprimente

dredge ['drɛdʒ] *vt* **dredged; dredging** : dragar — ~ *n* : draga *f*

dregs ['drɛgz] *npl* : heces *fpl*

drench ['drɛntʃ] *vt* : empapar

dress ['drɛs] *vt* 1 : vestir 2 : preparar (pollo o pescado), aliñar (ensalada) — *vi* 1 : vestirse 2 ~ **up** : ponerse elegante — ~ *n* 1 CLOTHING : ropa *f* 2 : vestido *m* (de mujer) — **dresser** ['drɛsər] *n* : cómoda *f* con espejo — **dressing** ['drɛsɪŋ] *n* 1 : aliño *m* (de ensalada), relleno *m* (de pollo) 2 BANDAGE : vendaje *m* — **dressmaker** ['drɛs,meɪkər] *n* : modista *mf* — **dressy** ['drɛsi] *adj* **dressier; -est** : elegante

drew → draw

dribble ['drɪbəl] *vi* **-bled; -bling** 1 DRIP : gotear 2 DROOL : babear 3 : driblar (en basquetbol) — ~ *n* 1 TRICKLE : goteo *m*, hilo *m* 2 DROOL : baba *f*

drier, driest → dry

drift ['drɪft] *n* 1 MOVEMENT : movimiento *m* 2 HEAP : montón *m* (de arena, etc.), ventisquero *m* (de nieve) 3 MEANING : sentido *m* — ~ *vi* 1 : ir a la deriva 2 ACCUMULATE : amontonarse

drill ['drɪl] *n* 1 : taladro *m* 2 : ejercicio *m* (en educación), simulacro *m* (de incendio, etc.) — ~ *vt* 1 : perforar, taladrar 2 TRAIN : instruir por repetición — *vi* ~ **for** : perforar en busca de

drink ['drɪŋk] *v* **drank** ['dræŋk]; **drunk** ['drʌŋk] *or* **drank; drinking** : beber — ~ *n* : bebida *f*

drip ['drɪp] *vi* **dripped; dripping** : gotear — ~ *n* 1 DROP : gota *f* 2 DRIPPING : goteo *m*

drive ['draɪv] *v* **drove** ['dro:v]; **driven** ['drɪvən]; **driving** *vt* 1 : manejar 2 IMPEL : impulsar 3 ~ **crazy** : volver loco 4 ~ **s.o. to (do sth)** : llevar a algn a (hacer algo) — *vi* : manejar, conducir — ~ *n* 1 : paseo *m* (en coche) 2 CAMPAIGN : campaña *f* 3 VIGOR : energía *f* 4 NEED : instinto *m*

drivel ['drɪvəl] *n* : tonterías *fpl*

driver ['draɪvər] *n* : conductor *m*, -tora *f*; chofer *m*

driveway ['draɪv,weɪ] *n* : camino *m* de entrada

drizzle ['drɪzəl] *n* : llovizna *f* — ~ *vi* **-zled; -zling** : lloviznar

drone ['dro:n] *n* 1 BEE : zángano *m* 2 HUM : zumbido *m* — ~ *vi* **droned; droning** 1 BUZZ : zumbar 2 *or* ~ **on** : hablar con monotonía

drool ['dru:l] *vi* : babear — ~ *n* : baba *f*

droop ['dru:p] *vi* : inclinarse (dícese de la cabeza), encorvarse (dícese de los escombros), marchitarse (dícese de las flores)

drop ['drɑp] *n* 1 : gota *f* (de líquido) 2 DECLINE, FALL : caída *f* — ~ *v* **dropped; dropping** *vt* 1 : dejar caer 2 LOWER : bajar 3 ABANDON : abandonar, dejar 4 ~ **off** LEAVE : dejar — *vi* 1 FALL : caer(se) 2 DECREASE : bajar, descender 3 ~ **by** *or* ~ **in** : pasar

drought ['draut] *n* : sequía *f*

drove → drive

droves ['dro:vz] *in* ~ : en manada

drown ['draun] *vt* : ahogar — *vi* : ahogarse

drowsy ['drauzi] *adj* **drowsier; -est** : somnoliento

drudgery ['drʌdʒəri] *n*, *pl* **-eries** : trabajo *m* pesado

drug ['drʌg] *n* 1 MEDICATION : medicamento *m* 2 NARCOTIC : droga *f*, estupefaciente *m* — ~ *vt* **drugged; drugging** : drogar — **drugstore** ['drʌg,stɔr] *n* : farmacia *f*

drum ['drʌm] n 1 : tambor m 2 or oil ~ : bidón m (de petróleo) — ~ v **drummed; drumming** vi : tocar el tambor — vt : tamborilear con (los dedos, etc.) — **drumstick** ['drʌm,stɪk] n 1 : palillo m (de tambor) 2 : muslo m (de pollo)

drunk ['drʌŋk] → **drink** — ~ adj : borracho — ~ or **drunkard** ['drʌŋkərd] n : borracho m, -cha f — **drunken** ['drʌŋkən] adj : borracho, ebrio

dry ['draɪ] adj **drier; driest** : seco — ~ v **dried; drying** vt : secar — vi : secarse — **dry-clean** ['draɪ,kli:n] vt : limpiar en seco — **dry cleaner** n : tintorería f (servicio) — **dry cleaning** n : limpieza f en seco — **dryer** ['draɪər] n : secadora f — **dryness** ['draɪnəs] n : sequedad f, aridez f

dual ['du:əl, 'dju:-] adj : doble

dub ['dʌb] vt **dubbed; dubbing** 1 CALL : apodar 2 : doblar (una película)

dubious ['du:biəs, 'dju:-] adj 1 UNCERTAIN : dudoso 2 QUESTIONABLE : sospechoso

duchess ['dʌtʃəs] n : duquesa f

duck ['dʌk] n, pl **duck** or **ducks** : pato m, -ta f — ~ vt 1 LOWER : agachar, bajar 2 EVADE : eludir, esquivar — vi : agacharse — **duckling** ['dʌklɪŋ] n : patito m, -ta f

duct ['dʌkt] n : conducto m

due ['du:, 'dju:] adj 1 PAYABLE : pagadero 2 APPROPRIATE : debido, apropiado 3 EXPECTED : esperado 4 ~ **to** : debido a — ~ n 1 **give s.o. their** ~ : hacer justicia a algn 2 ~**s** npl : cuota f — ~ adv ~ **east** : justo al este

duel ['du:əl, 'dju:-] n : duelo m

duet ['du:,et, 'dju:-] n : dúo m

dug → **dig**

duke ['du:k, 'dju:k] n : duque m

dull ['dʌl] adj 1 STUPID : torpe 2 BLUNT : desafilado 3 BORING : aburrido 4 LACKLUSTER : apagado — ~ vt : entorpecer (los sentidos), aliviar (el dolor)

dumb ['dʌm] adj 1 MUTE : mudo 2 STUPID : estúpido

dumbfound or **dumfound** [,dʌm'faʊnd] vt : dejar sin habla

dummy ['dʌmi] n, pl **-mies** 1 SHAM : imitación f 2 MANNEQUIN : maniquí m 3 IDIOT : tonto m, -ta f

dump ['dʌmp] vt : descargar, verter — ~ n 1 : vertedero m, tiradero m Lat 2 **down in the** ~**s** : triste, deprimido

dumpling ['dʌmplɪŋ] n : bola f de masa hervida

dumpy ['dʌmpi] adj **dumpier; -est** : regordete

dunce ['dʌnts] n : burro m, -rra f fam

dune ['du:n, 'dju:n] n : duna f

dung ['dʌŋ] n 1 : excrementos mpl 2 MANURE : estiércol m

dungarees [,dʌŋgə'ri:z] npl JEANS : vaqueros mpl, jeans mpl

dungeon ['dʌndʒən] n : calabozo m

dunk ['dʌŋk] vt : mojar

duo ['du:o:, 'dju:-] n, pl **duos** : dúo m

dupe ['du:p, dju:p] vt **duped; duping** : engañar — ~ n : inocentón m, -tona f

duplex ['du:,pleks, 'dju:-] n : casa f de dos viviendas, dúplex m

duplicate ['du:plɪkət, 'dju:-] adj : duplicado — ~ ['du:plɪ,keɪt, 'dju:-] vt **-cated; -cating** : duplicar, hacer copias de — ~ ['du:plɪkət, 'dju:-] n : duplicado m, copia f

durable ['durəbəl, 'djur-] adj : duradero

duration [du'reɪ ʃən, dju-] n : duración f

duress [du'res, dju-] n : coacción f

during ['durɪŋ, 'djur-] prep : durante

dusk ['dʌsk] n : anochecer m, crepúsculo m

dust ['dʌst] n : polvo m — ~ vt 1 : quitar el polvo a 2 SPRINKLE : espolvorear — **dustpan** ['dʌst,pæn] n : recogedor m — **dusty** ['dʌsti] adj **dustier; -est** : polvoriento

Dutch ['dʌtʃ] adj : holandés — ~ n 1 : holandés m (idioma) 2 **the** ~ : los holandeses

duty ['du:ti, 'dju:-] n, pl **-ties** 1 OBLIGATION : deber m 2 TAX : impuesto m 3 **on** ~ : de servicio — **dutiful** ['du:tɪfəl, 'dju:-] adj : obediente

dwarf ['dwɔrf] n, pl **dwarfs** ['dwɔrfs] or **dwarves** ['dwɔrvz] : enano m, -na f — ~ vt : hacer parecer pequeño

dwell ['dwɛl] vi **dwelled** or **dwelt** ['dwɛlt]; **dwelling** 1 RESIDE : morar, vivir 2 ~ **on** : pensar demasiado en — **dweller** ['dwɛlər] n : habitante mf — **dwelling** ['dwɛlɪŋ] n : morada f, vivienda f

dwindle ['dwɪndəl] vi **-dled; -dling** : disminuir

dye ['daɪ] n : tinte m — ~ vt **dyed; dyeing** : teñir

dying → **die**[1]

dynamic [daɪ'næmɪk] adj : dinámico

dynamite ['daɪnə,maɪt] n : dinamita f

dynamo ['daɪnə,mo:] n, pl **-mos** : dínamo m

dynasty ['daɪnəsti, -,næs-] n, pl **-ties** : dinastía f

dysentery ['dɪsən,teri] n, pl **-teries** : disentería f

E

e ['iː] *n, pl* **e's** *or* **es** ['iːz] : e *f*, quinta letra del alfabeto inglés

each ['iːtʃ] *adj* : cada — ~ *pron* **1** : cada uno *m*, cada una *f* **2** ~ **other** : el uno al otro **3 they hate** ~ **other** : se odian — ~ *adv* : cada uno, por persona

eager ['iːɡər] *adj* **1** ENTHUSIASTIC : entusiasta **2** IMPATIENT : impaciente — **eagerness** ['iːɡərnəs] *n* : entusiasmo *m*, impaciencia *f*

eagle ['iːɡəl] *n* : águila *f*

ear ['ɪr] *n* **1** : oreja *f* **2** ~ **of corn** : mazorca *f*, choclo *m* *Lat* — **eardrum** ['ɪr,drʌm] *n* : tímpano *m*

earl ['ərl] *n* : conde *m*

earlobe ['ɪr,loːb] *n* : lóbulo *m* de la oreja

early ['ərli] *adv* **earlier; -est 1** : temprano **2 as** ~ **as possible** : lo más pronto posible **3 ten minutes** ~ : diez minutos de adelanto — ~ *adj* **earlier; -est 1** FIRST : primero **2** ANCIENT : primitivo, antiguo **3 an** ~ **death** : una muerte prematura **4 be** ~ : llegar temprano **5 in the** ~ **spring** : a principios de la primavera

earmark ['ɪr,mɑrk] *vt* : destinar

earn ['ərn] *vt* **1** : ganar **2** DESERVE : merecer

earnest ['ərnəst] *adj* : serio — ~ *n* **in** ~ : en serio

earnings ['ərnɪŋz] *npl* **1** WAGES : ingresos *mpl* **2** PROFITS : ganancias *fpl*

earphone ['ɪr,foːn] *n* : audífono *m*

earring ['ɪr,rɪŋ] *n* : pendiente *m*, arete *m* *Lat*

earshot ['ɪr,ʃɑt] *n* **within** ~ : al alcance del oído

earth ['ərθ] *n* : tierra *f* — **earthenware** ['ərθən,wær, -ðən-] *n* : loza *f* — **earthly** ['ərθli] *adj* : terrenal — **earthquake** ['ərθ,kweɪk] *n* : terremoto *m* — **earthworm** ['ərθ,wərm] *n* : lombriz *f* (de tierra) — **earthy** ['ərθi] *adj* **earthier; -est 1** : terroso **2** COARSE, CRUDE : grosero

ease ['iːz] *n* **1** FACILITY : facilidad *f* **2** COMFORT : comodidad *f* **3 feel at** ~ : sentir cómodo — ~ *v* **eased; easing** *vt* **1** ALLEVIATE : aliviar, calmar **2** FACILITATE : facilitar — *vi* **1** : calmarse **2** ~ **up** : disminuir

easel ['iːzəl] *n* : caballete *m*

easily ['iːzəli] *adv* **1** : fácilmente, con facilidad **2** UNQUESTIONABLY : con mucho, de lejos *Lat*

east ['iːst] *adv* : al este — ~ *adj* : este, del este — ~ *n* **1** : este *m* **2 the East** : el Oriente

Easter ['iːstər] *n* : Pascua *f*

easterly ['iːstərli] *adv & adj* : del este

eastern ['iːstərn] *adj* **1** : del este **2 Eastern** : oriental, del este

easy ['iːzi] *adj* **easier; -est 1** : fácil **2** RELAXED : relajado — **easygoing** [ˌiːzi'ɡoːɪŋ] *adj* : tolerante, relajado

eat ['iːt] *v* **ate** ['eɪt]; **eaten** ['iːtən]; **eating** *vt* : comer — *vi* **1** : comer **2** ~ **into** CORRODE : corroer **3** ~ **into** DEPLETE : comerse — **eatable** ['iːtəbəl] *adj* : comestible

eaves ['iːvz] *npl* : alero *m* — **eavesdrop** ['iːvz,drɑp] *vi* **-dropped; -dropping** : escuchar a escondidas

ebb ['ɛb] *n* : reflujo *m* — ~ *vi* **1** : bajar (dícese de la marea) **2** DECLINE : decaer

ebony ['ɛbəni] *n, pl* **-nies** : ébano *m*

eccentric [ɪk'sɛntrɪk] *adj* : excéntrico — ~ *n* : excéntrico *m*, -ca *f* — **eccentricity** [ˌɛksen'trɪsəti] *n, pl* **-ties** : excentricidad *f*

echo ['ɛ,koː] *n, pl* **echoes** : eco *m* — ~ *v* **echoed; echoing** *vt* : repetir — *vi* : hacer eco, resonar

eclipse [ɪ'klɪps] *n* : eclipse *m* — ~ *vt* **eclipsed; eclipsing** : eclipsar

ecology [ɪ'kɑlədʒi, ɛ-]. *n, pl* **-gies** : ecología *f* — **ecological** [ˌiːkə'lɑdʒɪkəl, ˌɛkə-] *adj* : ecológico

economy [ɪ'kɑnəmi] *n, pl* **-mies** : economía *f* — **economic** [ˌiːkə'nɑmɪk, ˌɛkə-] *or* **economical** [ˌiːkə'nɑmɪkəl, ˌɛkə-] *adj* : económico — **economics** [ˌiːkə'nɑmɪks, ˌɛkə-] *n* : economía *f* — **economist** [ɪ'kɑnəmɪst] *n* : economista *mf* — **economize** [ɪ'kɑnə,maɪz] *v* **-mized; -mizing** : economizar

ecstasy ['ɛkstəsi] *n, pl* **-sies** : éxtasis *m* — **ecstatic** [ɛk'stætɪk, ɪk-] *adj* : extático

Ecuadoran [ˌɛkwə'dorən] *or* **Ecuadorean** *or* **Ecuadorian** [ˌɛkwə'doriən] *adj* : ecuatoriano

edge ['ɛdʒ] *n* **1** BORDER : borde *m* **2** : filo *m* (de un cuchillo) **3** ADVANTAGE : ventaja *f* — ~ *v* **edged; edging** *vt* : bordear, ribetear — *vi* : avanzar poco a poco — **edgewise** ['ɛdʒ₁waɪz] *adv* : de lado — **edgy** ['ɛdʒi] *adj* **edgier; -est** : nervioso

edible ['ɛdəbəl] *adj* : comestible

edit ['ɛdɪt] *vt* **1** : editar, redactar, corregir **2** ~ **out** : suprimir, cortar — **edition** [ɪ'dɪʃən] *n* : edición *f* — **editor** ['ɛdɪt̬ər] *n* : director *m*, -tora *f* (de un periódico); redactor *m*, -tora *f* (de un libro) — **editorial** [ˌɛdɪ'toriəl] *n* : editorial *m*

educate ['ɛdʒə₁keɪt] *vt* **-cated; -cating 1** TEACH : educar, instruir **2** INFORM : informar — **education** [ˌɛdʒə'keɪʃən] *n* : educación *f* — **educational** [ˌɛdʒə-'keɪʃənəl] *adj* **1** : educativo, instructivo **2** TEACHING : docente — **educator** ['ɛdʒə₁keɪt̬ər] *n* : educador *m*, -dora *f*

eel ['iːl] *n* : anguila *f*

eerie ['ɪri] *adj* **-rier; -est** : extraño e inquietante, misterioso

effect [ɪ'fɛkt] *n* **1** : efecto *m* **2 go into ~** : entrar en vigor — ~ *vt* : efectuar, llevar a cabo — **effective** [ɪ'fɛktɪv] *adj* **1** : eficaz **2** ACTUAL : efectivo, vigente — **effectiveness** [ɪ'fɛktɪvnəs] *n* : eficacia *f*

effeminate [ə'fɛmənət] *adj* : afeminado

effervescent [ˌɛfər'vɛsənt] *adj* : efervescente

efficient [ɪ'fɪʃənt] *adj* : eficiente — **efficiency** [ɪ'fɪʃəntsi] *n, pl* **-cies** : eficiencia *f*

effort ['ɛfərt] *n* **1** : esfuerzo *m* **2 it's not worth the ~** : no vale la pena — **effortless** ['ɛfərtləs] *adj* : fácil, sin esfuerzo

egg ['ɛg] *n* : huevo *m* — ~ *vt* ~ **on** : incitar — **eggplant** ['ɛg₁plænt] *n* : berenjena *f* — **eggshell** ['ɛg₁ʃɛl] *n* : cascarón *m*

ego ['iː₁goː] *n, pl* **egos 1** SELF : ego *m*, yo *m* **2** SELF-ESTEEM : amor *m* propio — **egotism** ['iːgə₁tɪzəm] *n* : egotismo *m* — **egotist** ['iːgət̬ɪst] *n* : egotista *mf* — **egotistic** [ˌiːgə'tɪstɪk] *or* **egotistical** [-'tɪstɪkəl] *adj* : egotista

eiderdown ['aɪdər₁daʊn] *n* **1** DOWN : plumón *m* **2** COMFORTER : edredón *m*

eight ['eɪt] *n* : ocho *m* — ~ *adj* : ocho — **eight hundred** *n* : ochocientos *m*

eighteen [eɪt'tiːn] *n* : dieciocho *m* — ~ *adj* : dieciocho — **eighteenth** [eɪt-'tiːnθ] *adj* : decimoctavo — ~ *n* **1** : decimoctavo *m*, -va *f* (en una serie) **2** : dieciochoavo *m*, dieciochoava parte *f*

eighth ['eɪtθ] *n* **1** : octavo *m*, -va *f* (en una serie) **2** : octavo *m*, octava parte *f* — ~ *adj* : octavo

eighty ['eɪt̬i] *n, pl* **eighties** : ochenta *m* — ~ *adj* : ochenta

either ['iːðər, 'aɪ-] *adj* **1** : cualquiera (de los dos) **2** (*in negative constructions*) : ninguno (de los dos) **3** EACH : cada — ~ *pron* **1** : cualquiera *mf* (de los dos) **2** (*in negative constructions*) : ninguno *m*, -na *f* (de los dos) **3** *or* ~ **one** : algún *m*, alguna *f* — ~ *conj* **1** : o **2** (*in negative constructions*) : ni

eject [ɪ'dʒɛkt] *vt* : expulsar, expeler

eke ['iːk] *vt* **eked; eking** *or* ~ **out** : ganar a duras penas

elaborate [ɪ'læbərət] *adj* **1** DETAILED : detallado **2** COMPLEX : complicado — ~ [ɪ'læbə₁reɪt] *v* **-rated; -rating** *vt* : elaborar — *vi* : entrar en detalles

elapse [ɪ'læps] *vi* **elapsed; elapsing** : transcurrir

elastic [ɪ'læstɪk] *adj* : elástico — ~ *n* **1** : elástico *m* **2** RUBBER BAND : goma *f* (elástica) — **elasticity** [ɪˌlæs'tɪsət̬i, ˌiːˌlæs-] *n, pl* **-ties** : elasticidad *f*

elated [ɪ'leɪt̬əd] *adj* : regocijado

elbow ['ɛl₁boː] *n* : codo *m*

elder ['ɛldər] *adj* : mayor — ~ *n* **1** : mayor *mf* **2** : anciano *m*, -na *f* (de una tribu, etc.) — **elderly** ['ɛldərli] *adj* : mayor, anciano

elect [ɪ'lɛkt] *vt* : elegir — ~ *adj* : electo — **election** [ɪ'lɛkʃən] *n* : elección *f* — **electoral** [ɪ'lɛktərəl] *adj* : electoral — **electorate** [ɪ'lɛktərət] *n* : electorado *m*

electricity [ɪˌlɛk'trɪsət̬i] *n, pl* **-ties** : electricidad *f* — **electric** [ɪ'lɛktrɪk] *or* **electrical** [-trɪkəl] *adj* : eléctrico — **electrician** [ɪˌlɛk'trɪʃən] *n* : electricista *mf* — **electrify** [ɪ'lɛktrə₁faɪ] *vt* **-fied; -fying** : electrificar — **electrocute** [ɪ'lɛktrə₁kjuːt] *vt* **-cuted; -cuting** : electrocutar

electron [ɪ'lɛk₁tran] *n* : electrón *m* — **electronic** [ɪˌlɛk'tranɪk] *adj* : electrónico — **electronic mail** *n* : correo *m* electrónico — **electronics** [ɪˌlɛk-'tranɪks] *n* : electrónica *f*

elegant ['ɛlɪgənt] *adj* : elegante — **elegance** ['ɛlɪgənts] *n* : elegancia *f*

element ['ɛləmənt] *n* **1** : elemento *m* **2** ~**s** *npl* BASICS : elementos *mpl*, rudimentos *mpl* — **elementary** [ˌɛlə-'mɛntri] *adj* : elemental — **elementary school** *n* : escuela *f* primaria

elephant ['ɛləfənt] *n* : elefante *m*, -ta *f*

elevate ['ɛlə₁veɪt] *vt* **-vated; -vating** : elevar — **elevator** ['ɛlə₁veɪt̬ər] *n* : ascensor *m*

eleven [ɪ'lɛvən] *n* : once *m* — ~ *adj* : once — **eleventh** [ɪ'lɛvənθ] *adj* : undécimo — ~ *n* **1** : undécimo *m*, -ma *f* (en una serie) **2** : onceavo *m*, onceava parte *f*

elf ['elf] *n*, *pl* **elves** ['elvz] : duende *m*

elicit [ɪ'lɪsət] *vt* : provocar

eligible ['elədʒəbəl] *adj* : elegible

eliminate [ɪ'lɪmə,neɪt] *vt* **-nated; -nating** : eliminar — **elimination** [ɪ,lɪmə'neɪ-ʃən] *n* : eliminación *f*

elite [eɪ'liːt, i-] *n* : elite *f*

elk ['elk] *n* : alce *m* (de Europa), uapití *m* (de América)

elliptical [ɪ'lɪptɪkəl, ɛ-] *or* **elliptic** [-tɪk] *adj* : elíptico

elm ['elm] *n* : olmo *m*

elongate [i'lɔŋgeɪt] *vt* **-gated; -gating** : alargar

elope [i'loːp] *vi* **eloped; eloping** : fugarse — **elopement** [i'loːpmənt] *n* : fuga *f*

eloquence ['eləkwənts] *n* : elocuencia *f* — **eloquent** ['eləkwənt] *adj* : elocuente

else ['els] *adv* **1** how ~ ? : ¿de qué otro modo? **2** where ~ ? : ¿en qué otro sitio? **3 or** ~ : si no, de lo contrario — ~ *adj* **1** everyone ~ : todos los demás **2** nobody ~ : ningún otro, nadie más **3** nothing ~ : nada más **4** what ~ ? : ¿qué más? — **elsewhere** ['els,hwer] *adv* : en otra parte

elude [i'luːd] *vt* **eluded; eluding** : eludir, esquivar — **elusive** [i'luːsɪv] *adj* : esquivo

elves → **elf**

emaciated [i'meɪʃi,eɪtəd] *adj* : escuálido, demacrado

E-mail ['iː,meɪl] → **electronic mail**

emanate ['emə,neɪt] *vi* **-nated; -nating** : emanar

emancipate [i'mæntsə,peɪt] *vt* **-pated; -pating** : emancipar — **emancipation** [i,mæntsə'peɪʃən] *n* : emancipación *f*

embalm [ɪm'bam, ɛm-, -'balm] *vt* : embalsamar

embankment [ɪm'bæŋkmənt, ɛm-] *n* : terraplén *m*, dique *m* (de un río)

embargo [ɪm'bargo, ɛm-] *n*, *pl* **-goes** : embargo *m*

embark [ɪm'bark, ɛm-] *vt* : embarcar — *vi* **1** : embarcarse **2** ~ upon : emprender — **embarkation** [,ɛm,bar-'keɪʃən] *n* : embarque *m*, embarco *m*

embarrass [ɪm'bærəs, ɛm-] *vt* : avergonzar — **embarrassing** [ɪm'bærəsɪŋ, ɛm-] *adj* : embarazoso — **embarrassment** [ɪm'bærəsmənt, ɛm-] *n* : vergüenza *f*

embassy ['embəsi] *n*, *pl* **-sies** : embajada *f*

embed [ɪm'bed, ɛm-] *vt* **-bedded; -bedding** : incrustar, enterrar

embellish [ɪm'belɪʃ, ɛm-] *vt* : adornar, embellecer — **embellishment** [ɪm-'belɪʃmənt, ɛm-] *n* : adorno *m*

embers ['embəz] *npl* : ascuas *fpl*

embezzle [ɪm'bezəl, ɛm-] *vt* **-zled; -zling** : desfalcar, malversar — **embezzlement** [ɪm'bezəlmənt, ɛm-] *n* : desfalco *m*, malversación *f*

emblem ['embləm] *n* : emblema *m*

embody [ɪm'badi, ɛm-] *vt* **-bodied; -bodying** : encarnar, personificar

emboss [ɪm'bas, ɛm-, -'bɔs] *vt* : repujar, grabar en relieve

embrace [ɪm'breɪs, ɛm-] *v* **-braced; -bracing** *vt* : abrazar — *vi* : abrazarse — ~ *n* : abrazo *m*

embroider [ɪm'brɔɪdər, ɛm-] *vt* : bordar — **embroidery** [ɪm'brɔɪdəri, ɛm-] *n*, *pl* **-deries** : bordado *m*

embryo ['embri,o] *n*, *pl* **embryos** : embrión *m*

emerald ['emrəld, 'emə-] *n* : esmeralda *f*

emerge [i'mərdʒ] *vi* **emerged; emerging** : salir, aparecer — **emergence** [i'mərdʒənts] *n* : aparición *f*

emergency [i'mərdʒəntsi] *n*, *pl* **-cies** **1** : emergencia *f* **2** ~ exit : salida *f* de emergencia **3** ~ room : sala *f* de urgencias, sala *f* de guardia

emery ['eməri] *n*, *pl* **-eries** **1** : esmeril *m* **2** ~ board : lima *f* de uñas

emigrant ['emɪgrənt] *n* : emigrante *mf* — **emigrate** ['emə,greɪt] *vi* **-grated; -grating** : emigrar — **emigration** [,emə'greɪʃən] *n* : emigración *f*

eminence ['emənənts] *n* : eminencia *f* — **eminent** ['emənənt] *adj* : eminente

emission [i'mɪʃən] *n* : emisión *f* — **emit** [i'mɪt] *vt* **emitted; emitting** : emitir

emotion [i'moːʃən] *n* : emoción *f* — **emotional** [i'moːʃənəl] *adj* **1** : emocional **2** MOVING : emotivo

emperor ['empərər] *n* : emperador *m*

emphasis ['emfəsɪs] *n*, *pl* **-phases** [-,siːz] : énfasis *m* — **emphasize** ['emfə,saɪz] *vt* **-sized; -sizing** : subrayar, hacer hincapié en — **emphatic** [ɪm-'fætɪk, ɛm-] *adj* : enérgico, categórico

empire ['em,paɪr] *n* : imperio *m*

employ [ɪm'plɔɪ, ɛm-] *vt* : emplear — **employee** [ɪm,plɔri:, ɛm-, -'plɔɪ,i:] *n* : empleado *m*, -da *f* — **employer** [ɪm-'plɔɪər, ɛm-] *n* : patrón *m*, -trona *f*; empleador *m*, -dora *f* — **employment** [ɪm'plɔɪmənt, ɛm-] *n* : trabajo *m*, empleo *m*

empower [ɪm'paʊər, ɛm-] *vt* : autorizar

empress ['emprəs] *n* : emperatriz *f*

empty ['empti] *adj* **emptier; -est 1** : vacío **2** MEANINGLESS : vano — ~ *v*

-tied; -tying *vt* : vaciar — *vi* : vaciarse — **emptiness** ['emptinəs] *n* : vacío *m*

emulate ['emjə,leɪt] *vt* **-lated; -lating** : emular

enable [r'neɪbəl, ɛ-] *vt* **-abled; -abling** : hacer posible, permitir

enact [r'nækt, ɛ-] *vt* **1** : promulgar (un ley o un decreto) **2** PERFORM : representar

enamel [r'næməl] *n* : esmalte *m*

encampment [ɪn'kæmpmənt, ɛn-] *n* : campamento *m*

encase [ɪn'keɪs, ɛn-] *vt* **-cased; -casing** : encerrar, revestir

enchant [ɪn'tʃænt, ɛn-] *vt* : encantar — **enchanting** [ɪn'tʃæntɪŋ, ɛn-] *adj* : encantador — **enchantment** [ɪn'tʃæntmənt, ɛn-] *n* : encanto *m*

encircle [ɪn'sərkəl, ɛn-] *vt* **-cled; -cling** : rodear

enclose [ɪn'kloːz, ɛn-] *vt* **-closed; -closing 1** SURROUND : encerrar, cercar **2** INCLUDE : adjuntar (a una carta) — **enclosure** [ɪn'kloːʒər, ɛn-] *n* **1** AREA : recinto *m* **2** : anexo *m* (con una carta)

encompass [ɪn'kʌmpəs, ɛn-, -'kɑm-] *vt* **1** ENCIRCLE : cercar **2** INCLUDE : abarcar

encore ['ɑn,kor] *n* : bis *m*

encounter [ɪn'kaʊntər, ɛn-] *vt* : encontrar — ~ *n* : encuentro *m*

encourage [ɪn'kərɪdʒ, ɛn-] *vt* **-aged; -aging 1** : animar, alentar **2** FOSTER : promover, fomentar — **encouragement** [ɪn'kərɪdʒmənt, ɛn-] *n* **1** : aliento *m* **2** PROMOTION : fomento *m*

encroach [ɪn'kroːtʃ, ɛn-] *vi* ~ on : invadir, usurpar, quitar (el tiempo)

encyclopedia [ɪn,saɪklə'piːdiə, ɛn-] *n* : enciclopedia *f*

end ['ɛnd] *n* **1** : fin *m* **2** EXTREMITY : extremo *m*, punta *f* **3** come to an ~ : llegar a su fin **4** in the ~ : por fin — ~ *vt* : terminar, poner fin a — *vi* : terminar(se)

endanger [ɪn'deɪndʒər, ɛn-] *vt* : poner en peligro

endearing [ɪn'dɪrɪŋ, ɛn-] *adj* : simpático

endeavor *or Brit* **endeavour** [ɪn'dɛvər, ɛn-] *vi* ~ **to** : esforzarse por — ~ *n* : esfuerzo *m*

ending ['ɛndɪŋ] *n* : final *m*, desenlace *m*

endive ['ɛn,daɪv, 'ɑn'diːv] *n* : endibia *f*, endivia *f*

endless ['ɛndləs] *adj* **1** INTERMINABLE : interminable **2** INNUMERABLE : innumerable **3** ~ **possibilities** : posibilidades *fpl* infinitas

endorse [ɪn'dors, ɛn-] *vt* **-dorsed; -dorsing 1** SIGN : endosar **2** APPROVE : aprobar — **endorsement** [ɪn'dorsmənt, ɛn-] *n* APPROVAL : aprobación *f*

endow [ɪn'daʊ, ɛn-] *vt* : dotar

endure [ɪn'dʊr, ɛn-, -'dʒʊr] *v* **-dured; -during 1** *vt* : soportar, aguantar — *vi* LAST : durar — **endurance** [ɪn'dʊrənts, ɛn-, -'dʒʊr-] *n* : resistencia *f*

enemy ['ɛnəmi] *n, pl* **-mies** : enemigo *m*, -ga *f*

energy ['ɛnərdʒi] *n, pl* **-gies** : energía *f* — **energetic** [,ɛnər'dʒɛtɪk] *adj* : enérgico

enforce [ɪn'fors, ɛn-] *vt* **-forced; -forcing 1** : hacer cumplir (un ley, etc.) **2** IMPOSE : imponer — **enforced** *adj* : forzoso — **enforcement** [ɪn'forsmənt, ɛn-] *n* : imposición *f* del cumplimiento

engage [ɪn'geɪdʒ, ɛn-] *v* **-gaged; -gaging 1** *vt* : captar, atraer (la atención, etc.) **2** ~ **the clutch** : embragar — *vi* ~ **in** : dedicarse a, entrar en — **engagement** [ɪn'geɪdʒmənt, ɛn-] *n* **1** APPOINTMENT : cita *f*, hora *f* **2** BETROTHAL : compromiso *m* — **engaging** [ɪn'geɪdʒɪŋ, ɛn-] *adj* : atractivo

engine ['ɛndʒən] *n* **1** : motor *m* **2** LOCOMOTIVE : locomotora *f* — **engineer** [,ɛndʒə'nɪr] *n* **1** : ingeniero *m*, -ra *f* **2** : maquinista *mf* (de locomotoras) — ~ *vt* **1** CONSTRUCT : construir **2** CONTRIVE : tramar — **engineering** [,ɛndʒə'nɪrɪŋ] *n* : ingeniería *f*

English ['ɪŋglɪʃ, 'ɪŋlɪʃ] *adj* : inglés — ~ *n* : inglés *m* (idioma) — **Englishman** ['ɪŋglɪʃmən, 'ɪŋlɪʃ-] *n* : inglés *m* — **Englishwoman** ['ɪŋglɪʃ,wʊmən, 'ɪŋlɪʃ-] *n* : inglesa *f*

engrave [ɪn'greɪv, ɛn-] *vt* **-graved; -graving** : grabar — **engraving** [ɪn'greɪvɪŋ, ɛn-] *n* : grabado *m*

engross [ɪn'groːs, ɛn-] *vt* : absorber

engulf [ɪn'gʌlf, ɛn-] *vt* : envolver

enhance [ɪn'hænts, ɛn-] *vt* **-hanced; -hancing** : aumentar, mejorar

enjoy [ɪn'dʒɔɪ, ɛn-] *vt* **1** : disfrutar, gozar de **2** ~ **oneself** : divertirse — **enjoyable** [ɪn'dʒɔɪəbəl, ɛn-] *adj* : agradable — **enjoyment** [ɪn'dʒɔɪmənt, ɛn-] *n* : placer *m*

enlarge [ɪn'lardʒ, ɛn-] *v* **-larged; -larging 1** *vt* : agrandar, ampliar — *vi* **1** : agrandarse **2** ~ **upon** : extenderse sobre — **enlargement** [ɪn'lardʒmənt, ɛn-] *n* : ampliación *f*

enlighten [ɪn'laɪtən, ɛn-] *vt* : aclarar, iluminar

enlist [ɪn'lɪst, ɛn-] *vt* **1** ENROLL : alistar **2** OBTAIN : conseguir — *vi* : alistarse

enliven [ɪn'laɪvən, ɛn-] *vt* : animar

enmity ['ɛnməti] *n, pl* **-ties** : enemistad *f*
enormous [ɪ'nɔrməs] *adj* : enorme
enough [ɪ'nʌf] *adj* : bastante, suficiente — ~ *adv* : bastante — ~ *pron* **1** : (lo) suficiente, (lo) bastante **2 it's not** ~ : no basta **3 I've had** ~ **!** : ¡estoy harto!
enquire [ɪn'kwaɪr, ɛn-], **enquiry** ['ɪn,kwaɪri, 'ɛn-, 'ɛn-kwəri; ɪn'kwaɪri, ɛn'-] → **inquire, inquiry**
enrage [ɪn'reɪdʒ, ɛn-] *vt* **-raged; -raging** : enfurecer
enrich [ɪn'rɪtʃ, ɛn-] *vt* : enriquecer
enroll *or* **enrol** [ɪn'roːl, ɛn-] *v* **-rolled; -rolling** *vt* : matricular, inscribir — *vi* : matricularse, inscribirse
ensemble [ɑn'sɑmbəl] *n* : conjunto *m*
ensign ['ɛnsən, 'ɛn,saɪn] *n* **1** FLAG : enseña *f* **2** : alférez *mf* (de fragata)
enslave [ɪn'sleɪv, ɛn-] *vt* **-slaved; -slaving** : esclavizar
ensue [ɪn'suː, ɛn-] *vi* **-sued; -suing** : seguir, resultar
ensure [ɪn'ʃʊr, ɛn-] *vt* **-sured; -suring** : asegurar
entail [ɪn'teɪl, ɛn-] *vt* : suponer, conllevar
entangle [ɪn'tæŋgəl, ɛn-] *vt* **-gled; -gling** : enredar — **entanglement** [ɪn'tæŋgəlmənt, ɛn-] *n* : enredo *m*
enter ['ɛntər] *vt* **1** : entrar en **2** RECORD : inscribir — *vi* **1** : entrar **2** ~ **into** : firmar (un acuerdo), entablar (negociaciones, etc.)
enterprise ['ɛntər,praɪz] *n* **1** : empresa *f* **2** INITIATIVE : iniciativa *f* — **enterprising** ['ɛntər,praɪzɪŋ] *adj* : emprendedor
entertain [,ɛntər'teɪn] *vt* **1** AMUSE : entretener, divertir **2** CONSIDER : considerar **3** ~ **guests** : recibir invitados — **entertainment** [,ɛntər'teɪnmənt] *n* : entretenimiento *m*, diversión *f*
enthrall *or* **enthral** [ɪn'θrɔl, ɛn-] *vt* **-thralled; -thralling** : cautivar, embelesar
enthusiasm [ɪn'θuːzi,æzəm, ɛn-, -'θjuː-] *n* : entusiasmo *m* — **enthusiast** [ɪn'θuːzi,æst, ɛn-, -'θjuː-, -əst] *n* : entusiasta *mf* — **enthusiastic** [ɪn,θuːzi'æstɪk, ɛn-, -,θjuː-] *adj* : entusiasta
entice [ɪn'taɪs, ɛn-] *vt* **-ticed; -ticing** : atraer, tentar
entire [ɪn'taɪr, ɛn-] *adj* : entero, completo — **entirely** [ɪn'taɪrli, ɛn-] *adv* : completamente — **entirety** [ɪn'taɪrti, ɛn-, -'taɪrəti] *n, pl* **-ties** : totalidad *f*
entitle [ɪn'taɪtəl, ɛn-] *vt* **-tled; -tling 1** NAME : titular **2** AUTHORIZE : dar derecho a — **entitlement** [ɪn'taɪtəlmənt, ɛn-] *n* : derecho *m*
entity ['ɛntəti] *n, pl* **-ties** : entidad *f*

entrails ['ɛn,treɪlz, -trəlz] *npl* : entrañas *fpl*, vísceras *fpl*
entrance¹ [ɪn'træns, ɛn-] *vt* **-tranced; -trancing** : encantar, fascinar
entrance² ['ɛntrənts] *n* : entrada *f* — **entrant** ['ɛntrənt] *n* : participante *mf*
entreat [ɪn'triːt, ɛn-] *vt* : suplicar
entrée *or* **entree** ['ɑn,treɪ, 'ɑn'-] *n* : plato *m* principal
entrepreneur [,ɑntrəprə'nər, -'njʊr] *n* : empresario *m*, -ria *f*
entrust [ɪn'trʌst, ɛn-] *vt* : confiar
entry ['ɛntri] *n, pl* **-tries 1** ENTRANCE : entrada *f* **2** NOTATION : entrada *f*, anotación *f*
enumerate [ɪ'nuːmə,reɪt, ɛ-, -'njuː-] *vt* **-ated; -ating** : enumerar
enunciate [ɪ'nʌntsi,eɪt, ɛ-] *vt* **-ated; -ating 1** STATE : enunciar **2** PRONOUNCE : articular
envelop [ɪn'vɛləp, ɛn-] *vt* : envolver — **envelope** ['ɛnvə,loːp, 'ɑn-] *n* : sobre *m*
envious ['ɛnviəs] *adj* : envidioso — **enviously** *adv* : con envidia
environment [ɪn'vaɪrənmənt, ɛn-, -'vaɪ-ərn-] *n* : medio *m* ambiente — **environmental** [ɪn,vaɪrən'mɛntəl, ɛn-, -,vaɪ-ərn-] *adj* : ambiental — **environmentalist** [ɪn,vaɪrən'mɛntəlɪst, ɛn-, -,vaɪərn-] *n* : ecologista *mf*
envision [ɪn'vɪʒən, ɛn-] *vt* : prever, imaginar
envoy ['ɛn,vɔɪ, 'ɑn-] *n* : enviado *m*, -da *f*
envy ['ɛnvi] *n, pl* **envies** : envidia *f* — ~ *vt* **-vied; -vying** : envidiar
enzyme ['ɛn,zaɪm] *n* : enzima *f*
epic ['ɛpɪk] *adj* : épico — ~ *n* : epopeya *f*
epidemic [,ɛpə'dɛmɪk] *n* : epidemia *f* — ~ *adj* : epidémico
epilepsy ['ɛpə,lɛpsi] *n, pl* **-sies** : epilepsia *f* — **epileptic** [,ɛpə'lɛptɪk] *adj* : epiléptico — ~ *n* : epiléptico *m*, -ca *f*
episode ['ɛpə,soːd] *n* : episodio *m*
epitaph ['ɛpə,tæf] *n* : epitafio *m*
epitome [ɪ'pɪtəmi] *n* : personificación *f* — **epitomize** [ɪ'pɪtə,maɪz] *vt* **-mized; -mizing** : ser la personificación de, personificar
epoch ['ɛpək, 'ɛ,pɑk, 'iː,pɑk] *n* : época *f*
equal ['iːkwəl] *adj* **1** SAME : igual **2 be** ~ **to** : estar a la altura de (una tarea, etc.) — ~ *n* : igual *mf* — ~ *vt* **equaled** *or* **equalled; equaling** *or* **equalling 1** : igualar **2** : ser igual a (en matemáticas) — **equality** [ɪ'kwɑləti] *n, pl* **-ties** : igualdad *f* — **equalize** ['iːkwə,laɪz] *vt* **-ized; -izing** : igualar — **equally** ['iːkwəli] *adv* **1** : igual-

mente 2 ~ important : igual de importante

equate [r'kweɪt] *vt* **equated; equating** ~ **with** : equiparar con — **equation** [r'kweɪʒən] *n* : ecuación *f*

equator [r'kweɪt̬ər] *n* : ecuador *m*

equilibrium [ˌiːkwə'lɪbriəm, ˌɛ-] *n, pl* **-riums** *or* **-ria** [-briə] : equilibrio *m*

equinox [ˈiːkwəˌnɑks, 'ɛ-] *n* : equinoccio *m*

equip [r'kwɪp] *vt* **equipped; equipping** : equipar — **equipment** [r'kwɪpmənt] *n* : equipo *m*

equity ['ɛkwət̬i] *n, pl* **-ties 1** FAIRNESS : equidad *f* **2 equities** *npl* STOCKS : acciones *fpl* ordinarias

equivalent [r'kwɪvələnt] *adj* : equivalente — ~ *n* : equivalente *m*

era ['ɪrə, 'ɛrə, 'iːrə] *n* : era *f*, época *f*

eradicate [r'rædə,keɪt] *vt* **-cated; -cating** : erradicar

erase [r'reɪs] *vt* **erased; erasing** : borrar — **eraser** [r'reɪsər] *n* : goma *f* de borrar, borrador *m*

erect [r'rɛkt] *adj* : erguido — ~ *vt* : erigir, levantar — **erection** [r'rɛkʃən] *n* **1** BUILDING : construcción *f* **2** : erección *f* (en fisiología)

erode [r'roːd] *vt* **eroded; eroding** : erosionar (el suelo), corroer (metales) — **erosion** [r'roːʒən] *n* : erosión *f*, corrosión *f*

erotic [r'rɑt̬ɪk] *adj* : erótico

err ['ɛr, 'ər] *vi* : equivocarse, errar

errand ['ɛrənd] *n* : mandado *m*, recado *m* Spain

erratic [r'ræt̬ɪk] *adj* : errático, irregular

error ['ɛrər] *n* : error *m* — **erroneous** [r'roːniəs, ɛ-] *adj* : erróneo

erupt [r'rʌpt] *vi* **1** : hacer erupción (dícese de un volcán) **2** : estallar (dícese de la cólera, la violencia, etc.) — **eruption** [r'rʌpʃən] *n* : erupción *f*

escalate ['ɛskəˌleɪt] *vi* **-lated; -lating** : intensificarse

escalator ['ɛskəˌleɪt̬ər] *n* : escalera *f* mecánica

escapade ['ɛskəˌpeɪd] *n* : aventura *f*

escape [r'skeɪp, ɛ-] *v* **-caped; -caping** *vt* : escapar a, evitar — *vi* : escaparse, fugarse — ~ *n* **1** : fuga *f* **2** ~ **from reality** : evasión *f* de la realidad — **escapee** [ˌɪskeɪ'piː, ˌɛ-] *n* : fugitivo *m*, -va *f*

escort ['ɛsˌkɔrt] *n* **1** GUARD : escolta *f* COMPANION : acompañante *mf* — ~ [r'skɔrt, ɛ-] *vt* **1** : escoltar **2** ACCOMPANY : acompañar

Eskimo ['ɛskəˌmoː] *adj* : esquimal

especially [r'spɛʃəli] *adv* : especialmente

espionage ['ɛspiəˌnɑʒ, -ˌnɑdʒ] *n* : espionaje *m*

espresso [ɛ'sprɛˌsoː] *n, pl* **-sos** : café *m* exprés

essay ['ɛˌseɪ] *n* : ensayo *m* (literario), composición *f* (académica)

essence ['ɛsənts] *n* : esencia *f* — **essential** [r'sɛntʃəl] *adj* : esencial — ~ *n* **1** : elemento *m* esencial **2 the** ~**s** : lo indispensable

establish [r'stæblɪʃ, ɛ-] *vt* : establecer — **establishment** [r'stæblɪʃmənt, ɛ-] *n* : establecimiento *m*

estate [r'steɪt, ɛ-] *n* **1** POSSESSIONS : bienes *mpl* **2** LAND, PROPERTY : finca *f*

esteem [r'stiːm, ɛ-] *n* : estima *f* — ~ *vt* : estimar

esthetic [ɛs'θɛt̬ɪk] → **aesthetic**

estimate ['ɛstəˌmeɪt] *vt* **-mated; -mating** : calcular, estimar — ~ ['ɛstəmət] *n* **1** : cálculo *m* (aproximado) **2** *or* ~ **of costs** : presupuesto *m* — **estimation** [ˌɛstə'meɪʃən] *n* **1** JUDGMENT : juicio *m* **2** ESTEEM : estima *f*

estuary ['ɛstʃuˌweri] *n, pl* **-aries** : estuario *m*, ría *f*

eternal [r'tərnəl, iː-] *adj* : eterno — **eternity** [r'tərnət̬i, iː-] *n, pl* **-ties** : eternidad *f*

ether ['iːθər] *n* : éter *m*

ethical ['ɛθɪkəl] *adj* : ético — **ethics** ['ɛθɪks] *ns & pl* : ética *f*, moralidad *f*

ethnic ['ɛθnɪk] *adj* : étnico

etiquette ['ɛt̬ɪkət, -ˌkɛt] *n* : etiqueta *f*

Eucharist ['juːkərɪst] *n* : Eucaristía *f*

eulogy ['juːlədʒi] *n, pl* **-gies** : elogio *m*, panegírico *m*

euphemism ['juːfəˌmɪzəm] *n* : eufemismo *m*

euphoria [juˈforiə] *n* : euforia *f*

European [ˌjurəˈpiːən, -ˌpiːn] *adj* : europeo

evacuate [r'vækjuˌeɪt] *vt* **-ated; -ating** : evacuar — **evacuation** [ˌvækjuˈeɪʃən] *n* : evacuación *f*

evade [r'veɪd] *vt* **evaded; evading** : evadir, eludir

evaluate [r'væljuˌeɪt] *vt* **-ated; -ating** : evaluar

evaporate [r'væpəˌreɪt] *vi* **-rated; -rating** : evaporarse

evasion [r'veɪʒən] *n* : evasión *f* — **evasive** [r'veɪsɪv] *adj* : evasivo

eve ['iːv] *n* : víspera *f*

even ['iːvən] *adj* **1** REGULAR, STEADY : regular, constante **2** LEVEL : plano, llano **3** SMOOTH : liso **4** EQUAL : igual **5** ~ **number** : número *m* par **6 get** ~ **with** : desquitarse con — ~ *adv* **1** : hasta, incluso **2** ~ **better** : aún

mejor, todavía mejor **3 ~ if** : aunque
4 ~ so : aun así — **~** *vt* : igualar —
vi or **~ out** : nivelarse
evening ['i:vnɪŋ] *n* : tarde *f*, noche *f*
event [ɪ'vɛnt] *n* **1** : acontecimiento *m*,
suceso *m* **2** : prueba *f* (en deportes) **3**
in the ~ of : en caso de — **eventful**
[ɪ'vɛntfəl] *adj* : lleno de incidentes
eventual [ɪ'vɛntʃuəl] *adj* : final — **even-**
tuality [ɪ,vɛntʃu'æləti] *n, pl* **-ties**
: eventualidad *f* — **eventually** [ɪ-
'vɛntʃuəli] *adv* : al fin, finalmente
ever ['ɛvər] *adv* **1** ALWAYS : siempre **2 ~**
since : desde entonces **3 hardly ~**
: casi nunca **4 have you ~** done it?
: ¿lo has hecho alguna vez?
evergreen ['ɛvər,gri:n] *n* : planta *f* de
hoja perenne
everlasting [,ɛvər'læstɪŋ] *adj* : eterno
every ['ɛvri] *adj* **1** EACH : cada **2 ~**
month : todos los meses **3 ~ other**
day : cada dos días — **everybody**
['ɛvri,bɑdi, -ba-] *pron* : todos *mpl*, -das
fpl; todo el mundo — **everyday** [,ɛvri-
'deɪ, 'ɛvri,-] *adj* : cotidiano, de todos los
días — **everyone** ['ɛvri,wʌn] → **every-**
body — **everything** ['ɛvri ,θɪŋ] *pron*
: todo — **everywhere** ['ɛvri ,hwɛr] *adv*
: en todas partes, por todas partes
evict [ɪ'vɪkt] *vt* : desahuciar, desalojar —
eviction [ɪ'vɪkʃən] *n* : desahucio *m*
evidence ['ɛvədənts] *n* **1** PROOF : prue-
bas *fpl* **2** TESTIMONY : testimonio *m*,
declaración *f* — **evident** ['ɛvidənt] *adj*
: evidente — **evidently** ['ɛvidəntli, ,ɛvi-
'dɛntli] *adv* **1** OBVIOUSLY : obviamente
2 APPARENTLY : evidentemente, al
parecer
evil ['i:vəl, -vɪl] *adj* **eviler** *or* **eviller**;
evilest *or* **evillest** : malvado, malo —
~ *n* : mal *m*, maldad *f*
evoke [i'vo:k] *vt* **evoked; evoking**
: evocar
evolution [,ɛvə'lu:ʃən, ,i:-] *n* : evolución
f, desarrollo *m* — **evolve** [i'vɑlv] *vi*
evolved; evolving : evolucionar, desarrollarse
exact [ɪg'zækt, ɛg-] *adj* : exacto, preciso
— **~** *vt* : exigir — **exacting** [ɪg-
'zæktɪŋ, ɛg-] *adj* : exigente — **exactly**
[ɪg'zæktli, ɛg-] *adv* : exactamente
exaggerate [ɪg'zædʒə,reɪt, ɛg-] *v* **-ated;**
-ating : exagerar — **exaggeration** [ɪg-
,zædʒə'reɪʃən, ɛg-] *n* : exageración *f*
examine [ɪg'zæmən, ɛg-] *vt* **-ined;**
-ining 1 : examinar **2** INSPECT : revisar
3 QUESTION : interrogar — **exam** [ɪg-
'zæm, ɛg-] *n* : examen *m* — **examina-**
tion [ɪg,zæmə'neɪʃən, ɛg-] *n* : examen
m

example [ɪg'zæmpəl, ɛg-] *n* : ejemplo *m*
exasperate [ɪg'zæspə,reɪt, ɛg-] *vt* **-ated;**
-ating : exasperar — **exasperation**
[ɪg,zæspə'reɪʃən, ɛg-] *n* : exasperación *f*
excavate ['ɛkskə,veɪt] *vt* **-vated; -vating**
: excavar — **excavation** [,ɛkskə'veɪʃən]
n : excavación *f*
exceed [ɪk'si:d, ɛk-] *vt* : exceder, sobrepasar — **exceedingly** [ɪk'si:dɪŋli,
ɛk-] *adv* : extremadamente
excel [ɪk'sɛl, ɛk-] *v* **-celled; -celling** *vi*
: sobresalir — *vt* SURPASS : superar —
excellence ['ɛksələnts] *n* : excelencia *f*
— **excellent** ['ɛksələnt] *adj* : excelente
except [ɪk'sɛpt] *prep or* **~ for** : excepto, menos, salvo — **~** *vt* : exceptuar
— **exception** [ɪk'sɛpʃən] *n* : excepción
f — **exceptional** [ɪk'sɛpʃənəl] *adj* : excepcional
excerpt ['ɛk,sərpt, 'ɛg,zərpt] *n* : extracto
m
excess [ɪk'sɛs, 'ɛk,sɛs] *n* : exceso *m* —
~ ['ɛk,sɛs, ɪk'sɛs] *adj* : excesivo, de
sobra — **excessive** [ɪk'sɛsɪv, ɛk-] *adj*
: excesivo
exchange [ɪks'tʃeɪndʒ, ɛks-; 'ɛks,tʃeɪndʒ]
n **1** : intercambio *m* **2** : cambio *m* (en
finanzas) — *vt* **-changed; -chang-**
ing : cambiar, intercambiar
excise [ɪk'saɪz, ɛk-] *n* **~ tax** : impuesto
m interno, impuesto *m* sobre el consumo
excite [ɪk'saɪt, ɛk-] *vt* **-cited; -citing**
: excitar, emocionar — **excited** [ɪk-
'saɪtəd, ɛk-] *adj* : excitado, entusias-
mado — **excitement** [ɪk'saɪtmənt, ɛk-]
n : entusiasmo *m*, emoción *f*
exclaim [ɪks'kleɪm, ɛk-] *v* : exclamar —
exclamation [,ɛksklə'meɪʃən] *n* : exclamación *f* — **exclamation point** *n*
: signo *m* de admiración
exclude [ɪks'klu:d, ɛks-] *vt* **-cluded;**
-cluding : excluir — **excluding** [ɪks-
'klu:dɪŋ, ɛks-] *prep* : excepto, con excepción de — **exclusion** [ɪks'klu:ʒən,
ɛks-] *n* : exclusión *f* — **exclusive** [ɪks-
'klu:sɪv, ɛks-] *adj* : exclusivo
excrement ['ɛkskrəmənt] *n* : excremento *m*
excruciating [ɪk'skru:ʃi,eɪtɪŋ, ɛk-] *adj*
: insoportable, atroz
excursion [ɪk'skərʒən, ɛk-] *n* : excursión *f*
excuse [ɪk'skju:z, ɛk-] *vt* **-cused;**
-cusing 1 : perdonar **2 ~ me**
: perdóne, perdón — **~** [ɪk'skju:s, ɛk-]
n : excusa *f*
execute ['ɛksɪ,kjut] *vt* **-cuted; -cuting**
: ejecutar — **execution** [,ɛksɪ'kju:ʃən] *n*
: ejecución *f* — **executioner** [,ɛksɪ-
'kju:ʃənər] *n* : verdugo *m*

executive [ɪg'zɛkjəˌtɪv, ɛg-] *adj* : ejecutivo — **~** *n* **1** MANAGER : ejecutivo *m*, -va *f* **2** *or* **~ branch** : poder *m* ejecutivo

exemplify [ɪg'zɛmpləˌfaɪ, ɛg-] *vt* **-fied; -fying** : ejemplificar — **exemplary** [ɪg'zɛmpləri, ɛg-] *adj* : ejemplar

exempt [ɪg'zɛmpt, ɛg-] *adj* : exento — **~** *vt* : dispensar — **exemption** [ɪg'zɛmpʃən, ɛg-] *n* : exención *f*

exercise ['ɛksərˌsaɪz] *n* : ejercicio *m* — **~** *v* **-cised; -cising** *vt* USE : ejercer, hacer uso de — *vi* : hacer ejercicio

exert [ɪg'zərt, ɛg-] *vt* **1** : ejercer **2 ~ oneself** : esforzarse — **exertion** [ɪg'zərʃən, ɛg-] *n* : esfuerzo *m*

exhale [ɛks'heɪl] *v* **-haled; -haling** : exhalar

exhaust [ɪg'zɔst, ɛg-] *vt* : agotar — **~** *n* **1** *or* **~ fumes** : gases *mpl* de escape *m or* **~ pipe** : tubo *m* de escape — **exhaustion** [ɪg'zɔstʃən, ɛg-] *n* : agotamiento *m* — **exhaustive** [ɪg'zɔstɪv, ɛg-] *adj* : exhaustivo

exhibit [ɪg'zɪbət, ɛg-] *vt* **1** DISPLAY : exponer **2** SHOW : mostrar — **~** *n* **1** : objeto *m* expuesto **2** EXHIBITION : exposición *f* — **exhibition** [ˌɛksə'bɪʃən] *n* : exposición *f*

exhilarate [ɪg'zɪləˌreɪt, ɛg-] *vt* **-rated; -rating** : alegrar — **exhilaration** [ɪgˌzɪlə'reɪʃən, ɛg-] *n* : regocijo *m*

exile ['ɛgˌzaɪl, 'ɛkˌsaɪl] *n* **1** : exilio *m* **2** OUTCAST : exiliado *m*, -da *f* — **~** *vt* **exiled; exiling** : exiliar

exist [ɪg'zɪst, ɛg-] *vi* : existir — **existence** [ɪg'zɪstənts, ɛg-] *n* : existencia *f* — **existing** *adj* : existente

exit ['ɛgzət, 'ɛksət] *n* : salida *f* — **~** *vi* : salir

exodus ['ɛksədəs] *n* : éxodo *m*

exonerate [ɪg'zɑnəˌreɪt, ɛg-] *vt* **-ated; -ating** : exonerar, disculpar

exorbitant [ɪg'zɔrbətənt, ɛg-] *adj* : exorbitante, excesivo

exotic [ɪg'zɑtɪk, ɛg-] *adj* : exótico

expand [ɪk'spænd, ɛk-] *vt* **1** : ampliar, extender **2** : dilatar (metales, etc.) — *vi* **1** : ampliarse, extenderse **2** : dilatarse (dícese de metales, etc.) — **expanse** [ɪk'spænts, ɛk-] *n* : extensión *f* — **expansion** [ɪk'spænʃən, ɛk-] *n* : expansión *f*

expatriate [ɛks'peɪtriət, -ˌeɪt] *n* : expatriado *m*, -da *f* — **~** *vt* : expatriado

expect [ɪk'spɛkt, ɛk-] *vt* **1** : esperar **2** REQUIRE : contar con — *vi* **be expecting** : estar embarazada — **expectancy** [ɪk'spɛktəntsi, ɛk-] *n, pl* **-cies** : esperanza *f* — **expectant** [ɪk'spɛktənt, ɛk-] *adj* **1**

: expectante **2 ~ mother** : futura madre *f* — **expectation** [ˌɛkˌspɛk'teɪʃən] *n* : esperanza *f*

expedient [ɪk'spidiənt, ɛk-] *adj* : conveniente — **~** *n* : expediente *m*, recurso *m*

expedition [ˌɛkspə'dɪʃən] *n* : expedición *f*

expel [ɪk'spɛl, ɛk-] *vt* **-pelled; -pelling** : expulsar (a una persona), expeler (humo, etc.)

expend [ɪk'spɛnd, ɛk-] *vt* : gastar — **expendable** [ɪk'spɛndəbəl, ɛk-] *adj* : prescindible — **expenditure** [ɪk'spɛndɪtʃər, ɛk-, -ˌtʃur] *n* : gasto *m* — **expense** [ɪk'spɛnts, ɛk-] *n* **1** : gasto *m* **2 ~s** *npl* : gastos *mpl*, expensas *fpl* **3 at the ~ of** : a expensas de — **expensive** [ɪk'spɛntsɪv, ɛk-] *adj* : caro

experience [ɪk'spɪriənts, ɛk-] *n* : experiencia *f* — **~** *vt* **-enced; -encing** : experimentar — **experienced** [ɪk'spɪriəntst, ɛk-] *adj* : experimentado — **experiment** [ɪk'spɛrəmənt, ɛk-, -ˌspɪr-] *n* : experimento *m* — **~** *vi* : experimentar — **experimental** [ɪkˌspɛrə'mɛntəl, ɛk-, -ˌspɪr-] *adj* : experimental

expert ['ɛkˌspərt, ɪk'spərt] *adj* : experto — **~** ['ɛkˌspərt] *n* : experto *m*, -ta *f* — **expertise** [ˌɛkspər'tiːz] *n* : pericia *f*, competencia *f*

expire [ɪk'spaɪr, ɛk-] *vi* **-pired; -piring 1** : caducar, vencer **2** DIE : expirar, morir — **expiration** [ˌɛkspə'reɪʃən] *n* : vencimiento *m*, caducidad *f*

explain [ɪk'spleɪn, ɛk-] *vt* : explicar — **explanation** [ˌɛksplə'neɪʃən] *n* : explicación *f* — **explanatory** [ɪk'splænəˌtori, ɛk-] *adj* : explicativo

explicit [ɪk'splɪsət, ɛk-] *adj* : explícito

explode [ɪk'sploːd, ɛk-] *v* **-ploded; -ploding** *vt* : hacer explotar — *vi* : explotar, estallar

exploit ['ɛkˌsploɪt] *n* : hazaña *f*, proeza *f* — **~** [ɪk'sploɪt, ɛk-] *vt* : explotar — **exploitation** [ˌɛksploɪ'teɪʃən] *n* : explotación *f*

exploration [ˌɛksplə'reɪʃən] *n* : exploración *f* — **explore** [ɪk'splor, ɛk-] *vt* **-plored; -ploring** : explorar — **explorer** [ɪk'splorər, ɛk-] *n* : explorador *m*, -dora *f*

explosion [ɪk'sploːʒən, ɛk-] *n* : explosión *f* — **explosive** [ɪk'sploːsɪv, ɛk-] *adj* : explosivo — **~** *n* : explosivo *m*

export ['ɛkˌsport, 'ɛkˌsport] *vt* : exportar — **~** ['ɛkˌsport] *n* : exportación *f*

expose [ɪk'spoːz, ɛk-] *vt* **-posed; -posing 1** : exponer **2** REVEAL : descubrir, revelar — **exposed** [ɪk'spoːzd, ɛk-]

: expuesto, al descubierto — **exposure** [ɪk'spoːʒər, ɛk-] n : exposición f

express [ɪk'spres, ɛk-] adj **1** SPECIFIC : expreso, específico **2** FAST : expreso, rápido — ~ adv : por correo urgente — ~ n or ~ **train** : expreso m — ~ vt : expresar — **expression** [ɪk'spreʃən, ɛk-] n : expresión f — **expressive** [ɪk'spresɪv, ɛk-] adj : expresivo — **expressly** [ɪk'spresli, ɛk-] adv : expresamente — **expressway** [ɪk'spres₁weɪ, ɛk-] n : autopista f

expulsion [ɪk'spʌlʃən, ɛk-] n : expulsión f

exquisite [ɛk'skwɪzət, 'ɛk₁skwɪ-] adj : exquisito

extend [ɪk'stend, ɛk-] vt **1** STRETCH : extender **2** LENGTHEN : prolongar **3** ENLARGE : ampliar **4** ~ **one's hand** : tender la mano — vi : extenderse — **extension** [ɪk'stentʃən, ɛk-] n **1** : extensión f **2** LENGTHENING : prolongación f **3** ANNEX : ampliación f, anexo m **4** ~ **cord** : alargador m — **extensive** [ɪk'stenɪsɪv, ɛk-] adj : extenso — **extent** [ɪk'stent, ɛk-] n **1** SIZE : extensión f **2** DEGREE : alcance m, grado m **3** **to a certain** ~ : hasta cierto punto

extenuating [ɪk'stenjə₁weɪtɪŋ, ɛk-] adj ~ **circumstances** : circunstancias fpl atenuantes

exterior [ɛk'stɪriər] adj : exterior — ~ n : exterior m

exterminate [ɪk'stərmə₁neɪt, ɛk-] vt **-nated; -nating** : exterminar — **extermination** [ɪk₁stərmə'neɪʃən, ɛk-] n : exterminación f

external [ɪk'stərnəl, ɛk-] adj : externo — **externally** [ɪk'stərnəli, ɛk-] adv : exteriormente

extinct [ɪk'stɪŋkt, ɛk-] adj : extinto — **extinction** [ɪk'stɪŋkʃən, ɛk-] n : extinción f

extinguish [ɪk'stɪŋgwɪʃ, ɛk-] vt : extinguir, apagar — **extinguisher** [ɪk'stɪŋgwɪʃər, ɛk-] n : extintor m

extol [ɪk'stoːl, ɛk-] vt **-tolled; -tolling** : ensalzar, alabar

extort [ɪk'stɔrt, ɛk-] vt : arrancar (algo a algn) por la fuerza — **extortion** [ɪk'stɔrʃən, ɛk-] n : extorsión f

extra ['ɛkstrə] adj : suplementario, de

más — ~ n : extra m — ~ adv **1** : extra, más **2** ~ **special** : super especial

extract [ɪk'strækt, ɛk-] vt : extraer, sacar — ~ ['ɛk₁strækt] n : extracto m — **extraction** [ɪk'strækʃən, ɛk-] n : extracción f

extracurricular [₁ɛkstrəkə'rɪkjələr] adj : extracurricular

extradite ['ɛkstrə₁daɪt] vt **-dited; -diting** : extraditar

extraordinary [ɪk'strɔrdən₁eri, ₁ɛkstrə'ɔrd-] adj : extraordinario

extraterrestrial [₁ɛkstrətə'restriəl] adj : extraterrestre — ~ n : extraterrestre mf

extravagant [ɪk'strævəgənt, ɛk-] adj **1** WASTEFUL : despilfarrador, derrochador **2** EXAGGERATED : extravagante, exagerado — **extravagance** [ɪk'strævəgənts, ɛk-] n **1** WASTEFULNESS : derroche m, despilfarro m **2** LUXURY : lujo m **3** EXAGGERATION : extravagancia f

extreme [ɪk'striːm, ɛk-] adj : extremo — ~ n : extremo m — **extremely** [ɪk'striːmli, ɛk-] adv : extremadamente — **extremity** [ɪk'streməʧi, ɛk-] n, pl **-ties** : extremidad f

extricate ['ɛkstrə₁keɪt] vt **-cated; -cating** : librar, (lograr) sacar

extrovert ['ɛkstrə₁vərt] n : extrovertido m, -da f — **extroverted** ['ɛkstrə₁vərtəd] adj : extrovertido

exuberant [ɪg'zuːbərənt, ɛg-] adj **1** JOYOUS : eufórico **2** LUSH : exuberante — **exuberance** [ɪg'zuːbərənts, ɛg-] n **1** JOYOUSNESS : euforia f **2** VIGOR : exuberancia f

exult [ɪg'zʌlt, ɛg-] vi : exultar

eye ['aɪ] n **1** : ojo m **2** VISION : visión f, vista f **3** GLANCE : mirada f — ~ vt **eyed; eyeing** or **eying** : mirar — **eyeball** ['aɪ₁bɔl] n : globo m ocular — **eyebrow** ['aɪ₁braʊ] n : ceja f — **eyeglasses** ['aɪ₁glæsəz] npl : anteojos mpl, lentes mpl — **eyelash** ['aɪ₁læʃ] n : pestaña f — **eyelid** ['aɪ₁lɪd] n : párpado m — **eyesight** ['aɪ₁saɪt] n : vista f, visión f — **eyesore** ['aɪ₁sor] n : monstruosidad f — **eyewitness** ['aɪ₁wɪtnəs] n : testigo mf ocular

F

f ['ef] *n, pl* **f's** *or* **fs** ['efs] : f, sexta letra del alfabeto inglés
fable ['feɪbəl] *n* : fábula *f*
fabric ['fæbrɪk] *n* : tela *f*, tejido *m*
fabulous ['fæbjələs] *adj* : fabuloso
facade [fə'sɑd] *n* : fachada *f*
face ['feɪs] *n* **1** : cara *f*, rostro *m* (de una persona) **2** APPEARANCE : fisonomía *f*, aspecto *m* **3** : cara *f* (de una moneda), fachada *f* (de un edificio) **4** ~ **value** : valor *m* nominal **5** **in the** ~ **of** : en medio de, ante **6** **lose** ~ : desprestigiarse **7** **make** ~**s** : hacer muecas — ~ **faced; facing** *vt* **1** : estar frente a **2** CONFRONT : enfrentarse a **3** OVERLOOK : dar a — *vi* ~ **to the north** : mirar hacia el norte — **facedown** ['feɪs,daʊn] *adv* : boca abajo — **faceless** ['feɪsləs] *adj* : anónimo — **face–lift** ['feɪs,lɪft] *n* : estiramiento *m* facial
facet ['fæsət] *n* : faceta *f*
face–to–face *adv & adj* : cara a cara
facial ['feɪʃəl] *adj* : de la cara, facial — ~ *n* : limpieza *f* de cutis
facetious [fə'si:ʃəs] *adj* : gracioso, burlón
facility [fə'sɪləti] *n, pl* **-ties 1** EASE : facilidad *f* **2** CENTER : centro *m* **3** **facilities** *npl* : comodidades *fpl*, servicios *mpl*
facsimile [fæk'sɪməli] *n* : facsímile *m*, facsímil *m*
fact ['fækt] *n* **1** : hecho *m* **2** **in** ~ : en realidad, de hecho
faction ['fækʃən] *n* : facción *m*, bando *m*
factor ['fæktər] *n* : factor *m*
factory ['fæktəri] *n, pl* **-ries** : fábrica *f*
factual ['fæktʃʊəl] *adj* : basado en hechos
faculty ['fækəlti] *n, pl* **-ties** : facultad *f*
fad ['fæd] *n* : moda *f* pasajera, manía *f*
fade ['feɪd] *v* **faded; fading** *vi* **1** WITHER : marchitarse **2** DISCOLOR : desteñirse, decolorarse **3** DIM : apagarse **4** VANISH : desvanecerse — *vt* : desteñir
fail ['feɪl] *vi* **1** : fracasar (dícese de una empresa, un matrimonio, etc.) **2** BREAK DOWN : fallar **3** ~ **in** : faltar a, no cumplir con **4** FLUNK : suspender *Spain*, ser reprobado *Lat* **5** ~ **to do sth** : no hacer algo — *vt* **1** DISAPPOINT : fallar **2** FLUNK : suspender *Spain*, reprobar *Lat* — ~ *n* **without** ~ : sin

falta — **failing** ['feɪlɪŋ] *n* : defecto *m* —
failure ['feɪljər] *n* **1** : fracaso *m* **2** BREAKDOWN : falla *f*
faint ['feɪnt] *adj* **1** WEAK : débil **2** INDISTINCT : tenue, indistinto **3** **feel** ~ : estar mareado — ~ *vi* : desmayarse — ~ *n* : desmayo *m* — **fainthearted** ['feɪnt'hɑrtəd] *adj* : cobarde, pusilánime — **faintly** ['feɪntli] *adv* **1** WEAKLY : débilmente **2** SLIGHTLY : ligeramente, levemente
fair[1] ['fær] *n* : feria *f*
fair[2] *adj* **1** BEAUTIFUL : bello, hermoso **2** : bueno (dícese del tiempo) **3** JUST : justo **4** : rubio (dícese del pelo), blanco (dícese de la tez) **5** ADEQUATE : adecuado — ~ *adv* **play** ~ : jugar limpio — **fairly** ['færli] *adv* **1** JUSTLY : justamente **2** QUITE : bastante — **fairness** ['færnəs] *n* : justicia *f*
fairy ['færi] *n, pl* **fairies 1** : hada *f* **2** ~ **tale** : cuento *m* de hadas
faith ['feɪθ] *n, pl* **faiths** ['feɪθs, 'feɪðz] : fe *f* — **faithful** ['feɪθfəl] *adj* : fiel — **faithfully** *adv* : fielmente — **faithfulness** ['feɪθfəlnəs] *n* : fidelidad *f*
fake ['feɪk] *v* **faked; faking** *vt* **1** FALSIFY : falsificar, falsear **2** FEIGN : fingir — *vi* PRETEND : fingir — ~ *adj* : falso — ~ *n* **1** IMITATION : falsificación *f* **2** IMPOSTOR : impostor *m*, -tora *f*
falcon ['fælkən, 'fɔl-] *n* : halcón *m*
fall ['fɔl] *vi* **fell** ['fɛl]; **fallen** ['fɔlən]; **falling 1** : caer, bajar (dícese de los precios), descender (dícese de la temperatura) **2** ~ **asleep** : dormirse **3** ~ **back** : retirarse **4** ~ **back on** : recurrir a **5** ~ **down** : caerse **6** ~ **in love** : enamorarse **7** ~ **out** QUARREL : pelearse **8** ~ **through** : fracasar — ~ *n* **1** : caída *f*, bajada *f* (de precios), descenso *m* (de temperatura) **2** AUTUMN : otoño *m* **3** ~**s** *npl* WATERFALL : cascada *f*, catarata *f*
fallacy ['fæləsi] *n, pl* **-cies** : concepto *m* erróneo
fallible ['fæləbəl] *adj* : falible
fallow ['fælo] *adj* **lie** ~ : estar en barbecho
false ['fɔls] *adj* **falser; falsest 1** : falso **2** ~ **alarm** : falsa alarma *f* **3** ~ **teeth** : dentadura *f* postiza — **falsehood** ['fɔls,hʊd] *n* : mentira — **falseness**

['fɔlsnəs] n : falsedad f — **falsify** ['fɔlsə,faɪ] vt **-fied; -fying** : falsificar, falsear

falter ['fɔltər] vi **-tered; -tering 1** STUMBLE : tambalearse **2** WAVER : vacilar

fame ['feɪm] n : fama f

familiar [fə'mɪljər] adj **1** : familiar **2 be ~ with** : estar familiarizado con — **familiarity** [fə,mɪli'ærəti, -,mɪl'jær-], pl **-ties** : familiaridad f — **familiarize** [fə'mɪljə,raɪz] vt **-ized; -izing ~ oneself** : familiarizarse

family ['fæmli, 'fæmə-] n, pl **-lies** : familia f

famine ['fæmən] n : hambre f, hambruna f

famished ['fæmɪʃt] adj : famélico

famous ['feɪməs] adj : famoso

fan ['fæn] n **1** : ventilador m, abanico m **2** : aficionado m, -da f (a un pasatiempo); admirador m, -dora f (de una persona) — ~ vt **fanned; fanning** : abanicar (a una persona), avivar (un fuego)

fanatic [fə'næt̬ɪk] or **fanatical** [-t̬ɪkəl] adj : fanático — ~ n : fanático m, -ca f — **fanaticism** [fə'næt̬ə,sɪzəm] n : fanatismo m

fancy ['fænsi] vt **-cied; -cying 1** IMAGINE : imaginarse **2** DESIRE : apetecerle (algo a uno) — ~ adj **-cier; -est 1** ELABORATE : elaborado **2** LUXURIOUS : lujoso, elegante — ~ n, pl **-cies 1** WHIM : capricho m **2** IMAGINATION : imaginación f **3 take a ~ to** : aficionarse a (una cosa), tomar cariño a (una persona) — **fanciful** ['fænt̬sɪfəl] adj **1** CAPRICIOUS : caprichoso **2** IMAGINATIVE : imaginativo

fanfare ['fæn,fær] n : fanfarria f

fang ['fæŋ] n : colmillo m (de un animal), diente m (de una serpiente)

fantasy ['fænt̬əsi] n, pl **-sies** : fantasía f — **fantasize** ['fænt̬ə,saɪz] vi **-sized; -sizing** : fantasear — **fantastic** [fæn'tæstɪk] adj : fantástico

far ['fɑr] adv **farther** ['fɑrðər] or **further** ['fər-]; **farthest** or **furthest** [-ðəst] **1** : lejos **2** MUCH : muy, mucho **3 as ~ as** : hasta (un lugar), con respecto a (un tema) **4 by ~** : con mucho **5 ~ and wide** : por todas partes **6 ~ away** : a lo lejos **7 ~ from it!** : ¡todo lo contrario! **8 so ~** : hasta ahora, todavía — ~ adj **farther** or **further; farthest** or **furthest 1** REMOTE : lejano **2** EXTREME : extremo — **faraway** ['fɑrə,weɪ] adj : remoto, lejano

farce ['fɑrs] n : farsa f

fare ['fær] vi **fared; faring** : irle a uno —

~ n **1** : precio m del pasaje **2** FOOD : comida f

farewell [fær'wel] n : despedida f — ~ adj : de despedida

far-fetched ['fɑr'fetʃt] adj : improbable, exagerado

farm ['fɑrm] n : granja f, hacienda f — ~ vt : cultivar (la tierra), criar (animales) — vi : ser agricultor — **farmer** ['fɑrmər] n : agricultor m, -tora f; granjero m, -jera f — **farmhand** ['fɑrm,hænd] n : peón m — **farmhouse** ['fɑrm,haʊs] n : granja f, casa f de hacienda — **farming** ['fɑrmɪŋ] n : agricultura f, cultivo m (de plantas), crianza f (de animales) — **farmyard** ['fɑrm,jɑrd] n : corral m

far-off ['fɑr,ɔf, -'ɔf] adj : lejano

far-reaching ['fɑr'riːtʃɪŋ] adj : de gran alcance

farsighted ['fɑr,saɪt̬əd] adj **1** : hipermétrope **2** PRUDENT : previsor

farther ['fɑrðər] adv **1** : más lejos **2** MORE : más — adj : más lejano — **farthest** adv **1** : lo más lejos **2** MOST : más — adj : más lejano

fascinate ['fæsən,eɪt] vt **-nated; -nating** : fascinar — **fascination** [,fæsən'eɪʃən] n : fascinación f

fascism ['fæ∫,ɪzəm] n : fascismo m — **fascist** ['fæ∫ɪst] adj : fascista — ~ n : fascista mf

fashion ['fæ∫ən] n **1** MANNER : manera f **2** STYLE : moda f **3 out of ~** : pasada de moda — **fashionable** ['fæ∫ənəbəl] adj : de moda

fast[1] ['fæst] vi : ayunar — ~ n : ayuno m

fast[2] adj **1** SWIFT : rápido **2** SECURE : firme, seguro **3** : adelantado (dícese de un reloj) **4 ~ friends** : amigos mpl leales — ~ adv **1** SECURELY : firmemente **2** SWIFTLY : rápidamente **3 ~ asleep** : profundamente dormido

fasten ['fæsən] vt : sujetar (papeles, etc.), abrochar (una blusa, etc.), cerrar (una maleta, etc.) — vi : abrocharse, cerrar — **fastener** ['fæsənər] n : cierre m

fat ['fæt] adj **fatter; fattest 1** : gordo **2** THICK : grueso — ~ n : grasa f

fatal ['feɪt̬əl] adj **1** : mortal **2** FATEFUL : fatal, fatídico — **fatality** [feɪ'tælət̬i, fə-] n, pl **-ties** : víctima f mortal

fate ['feɪt] n **1** : destino m **2** LOT : suerte f — **fateful** ['feɪtfəl] adj : fatídico

father ['fɑðər] n : padre m — ~ vt : engendrar — **fatherhood** ['fɑðər,hʊd] n : paternidad f — **father-in-law** ['fɑðərn,lɔ] n, pl **fathers-in-law** : suegro *m* — **fatherly** ['fɑðərli] *adj* : paternal

fathom ['fæðəm] *vt* : comprender

fatigue [fə'tiːg] *n* : fatiga *f* — ~ *vt* -tigued; -tiguing : fatigar

fatten ['fætən] *vt* : engordar — **fattening** *adj* : que engorda

fatty ['fæti] *adj* **fattier; -est** : graso

faucet ['fɔsət] *n* : llave *f Lat*, grifo *m Spain*

fault ['fɔlt] *n* 1 FLAW : defecto *m* 2 RESPONSIBILITY : culpa *f* 3 : falla *f* (geológica) — *vt* : encontrar defectos a — **faultless** ['fɔltləs] *adj* : impecable — **faulty** ['fɔlti] *adj* **faultier; -est** : defectuoso

fauna ['fɔnə] *n* : fauna *f*

favor *or Brit* **favour** ['feɪvər] *n* 1 : favor *m* 2 **in** ~ **of** : a favor de — ~ *vt* 1 : favorecer 2 SUPPORT : estar a favor de 3 PREFER : preferir — **favorable** *or Brit* **favourable** ['feɪvərəbəl] *adj* : favorable — **favorite** *or Brit* **favourite** ['feɪvərət] *n* : favorito *m*, -ta *f* — ~ *adj* : favorito — **favoritism** *or Brit* **favouritism** ['feɪvərə,tɪzəm] *n* : favoritismo *m*

fawn[1] ['fɔn] *vi* ~ **over** : adular

fawn[2] *n* : cervato *m*

fax ['fæks] *n* : fax *m* — ~ *vt* : faxear, enviar por fax

fear ['fɪr] *v* : temer — ~ *n* 1 : miedo *m*, temor *m* 2 **for** ~ **of** : por temor a — **fearful** ['fɪrfəl] *adj* 1 FRIGHTENING : espantoso 2 AFRAID : temeroso

feasible ['fiːzəbəl] *adj* : viable, factible

feast ['fiːst] *n* 1 BANQUET : banquete *m*, festín *m* 2 FESTIVAL : fiesta *f* — ~ *vi* 1 : banquetear 2 ~ **upon** : darse un festín de

feat ['fiːt] *n* : hazaña *f*

feather ['feðər] *n* : pluma *f*

feature ['fiːtʃər] *n* 1 : rasgo *m* (de la cara) 2 CHARACTERISTIC : característica *f* 3 : artículo *m* (en un periódico) 4 ~ **film** : largometraje *m* — ~ *v* -**tured; -turing** *vt* 1 PRESENT : presentar 2 EMPHASIZE : destacar — *vi* : figurar

February ['febju̇ˌeri, 'febu̇-, 'febru̇-] *n* : febrero *m*

feces ['fiːˌsiːz] *npl* : excremento *mpl*

federal ['fedrəl, -dərəl] *adj* : federal — **federation** [fedə'reɪʃən] *n* : federación *f*

fed up *adj* : harto

fee ['fiː] *n* 1 : honorarios *mpl* 2 **entrance** ~ : entrada *f*

feeble ['fiːbəl] *adj* -**bler; -blest** 1 : débil 2 **a ~ excuse** : una pobre excusa

feed ['fiːd] *v* **fed** ['fed]; **feeding** *vt* 1 : dar de comer a, alimentar 2 SUPPLY : alimentar — *vi* : comer, alimentarse — ~ *n* : pienso *m*

feel ['fiːl] *v* **felt** ['felt]; **feeling** *vt* 1 : sentir (una sensación, etc.) 2 TOUCH : tocar, palpar 3 BELIEVE : creer — *vi* 1 : sentirse (bien, cansado, etc.) 2 SEEM : parecer 3 ~ **hot/thirsty** : tener calor/sed 4 ~ **like doing** : tener ganas de hacer — ~ *n* : tacto *m*, sensación *f* — **feeling** ['fiːlɪŋ] *n* 1 SENSATION : sensación *f* 2 EMOTION : sentimiento *m* 3 OPINION : opinión *f* 4 **hurt s.o.'s ~s** : herir los sentimientos de algn

feet → **foot**

feign ['feɪn] *vt* : fingir

feline ['fiːˌlaɪn] *adj* : felino — ~ *n* : felino *m*, -na *f*

fell[1] → **fall**

fell[2] ['fel] *vt* : talar (un árbol)

fellow ['feˌloː] *n* 1 COMPANION : compañero *m*, -ra *f* 2 MEMBER : socio *m*, -cia *f* 3 MAN : tipo *m* — **fellowship** ['feloˌʃɪp] *n* 1 : compañerismo *m* 2 ASSOCIATION : fraternidad *f* 3 GRANT : beca *f*

felon ['felən] *n* : criminal *mf* — **felony** ['feləni] *n*, *pl* -**nies** : delito *m* grave

felt[1] → **feel**

felt[2] ['felt] *n* : fieltro *m*

female ['fiːˌmeɪl] *adj* : femenino — ~ *n* 1 : hembra *f* (animal) 2 WOMAN : mujer *f*

feminine ['femənən] *adj* : femenino — **femininity** [femə'nɪnəṭi] *n* : femineidad *f* — **feminism** ['feməˌnɪzəm] *n* : feminismo *m* — **feminist** ['femənɪst] *adj* : feminista — ~ *n* : feminista *mf*

fence ['fens] *n* : cerca *f*, valla *f*, cerco *m Lat* — ~ *v* **fenced; fencing** *vt* or ~ **in** : vallar, cercar — *vi* : hacer esgrima — **fencing** ['fensɪŋ] *n* : esgrima *m* (deporte)

fend ['fend] *vt* ~ **off** : rechazar (un enemigo), eludir (una pregunta) — *vi* ~ **for oneself** : valerse por sí mismo — **fender** ['fendər] *n* : guardabarros *mpl*

fennel ['fenəl] *n* : hinojo *m*

ferment [fər'ment] *v* : fermentar — **fermentation** [ˌfərmən'teɪʃən, -ˌmen-] *n* : fermentación *f*

fern ['fərn] *n* : helecho *m*

ferocious [fə'roːʃəs] *adj* : feroz — **ferocity** [fə'rɑsəṭi] *n* : ferocidad *f*

ferret ['ferət] *n* : hurón *m* — ~ *vt* ~ **out** : descubrir

Ferris wheel ['ferɪs] *n* : noria *f*

ferry ['feri] *vt* -**ried; -rying** : transportar — ~ *n*, *pl* -**ries** : ferry *m*

fertile ['fərt̬əl] *adj* : fértil — **fertility** [fər-'tɪlət̬i] *n* : fertilidad *f* — **fertilize** ['fərt̬əlˌaɪz] *vt* **-ized; -izing** : fecundar (un huevo), abonar (el suelo) — **fertilizer** ['fərt̬əlˌaɪzər] *n* : fertilizante *m*, abono *m*

fervent ['fərvənt] *adj* : ferviente — **fervor** *or Brit* **fervour** ['fərvər] *n* : fervor *m*

fester ['fɛstər] *vi* : enconarse

festival ['fɛstəvəl] *n* **1** : fiesta *f* **2** film ~ : festival *m* de cine — **festive** ['fɛstɪv] *adj* : festivo — **festivity** [fɛs'tɪvət̬i] *n*, *pl* **-ties** : festividad *f*

fetch ['fɛtʃ] *vt* **1** : ir a buscar **2** : venderse por (un precio)

fête ['feɪt, 'fɛt] *n* : fiesta *f*

fetid ['fɛt̬əd] *adj* : fétido

fetish ['fɛt̬ɪʃ] *n* : fetiche *m*

fetters ['fɛt̬ərz] *npl* : grillos *mpl* — **fetter** ['fɛt̬ər] *vt* : encadenar

fetus ['fit̬əs] *n* : feto *m*

feud ['fjuːd] *n* : enemistad *f* (entre familiares) — *vi* : pelear

feudal ['fjuːdəl] *adj* : feudal — **feudalism** ['fjuːdəlˌɪzəm] *n* : feudalismo *m*

fever ['fivər] *n* : fiebre *f* — **feverish** ['fivərɪʃ] *adj* : febril

few ['fjuː] *adj* **1** : pocos **2 a ~ times** : varias veces — *pron* **1** : pocos **2 a ~** : algunos, unos cuantos **3 quite a ~** : muchos — **fewer** ['fjuːər] *adj & pron* : menos

fiancé, fiancée [ˌfiːɑnˈseɪ, ˌfiːˈɑnˌseɪ] *n* : prometido *m*, -da *f*; novio *m*, -via *f*

fiasco [fiˈæsˌkoː] *n*, *pl* **-coes** : fiasco *m*

fib ['fɪb] *n* : mentirilla *f* — *vi* **fibbed; fibbing** : decir mentirillas

fiber *or* **fibre** ['faɪbər] *n* : fibra *f* — **fiberglass** ['faɪbərˌglæs] *n* : fibra *f* de vidrio — **fibrous** ['faɪbrəs] *adj* : fibroso

fickle ['fɪkəl] *adj* : inconstante

fiction ['fɪkʃən] *n* : ficción *f* — **fictional** ['fɪkʃənəl] *or* **fictitious** [fɪkˈtɪʃəs] *adj* : ficticio

fiddle ['fɪdəl] *n* : violín *m* — *vi* **-dled; -dling 1** : tocar el violín **2 ~ with** : juguetear con

fidelity [fəˈdɛlət̬i, faɪ-] *n*, *pl* **-ties** : fidelidad *f*

fidget ['fɪdʒət] *vi* **1** : estarse inquieto, moverse **2 ~ with** : juguetear con — **fidgety** ['fɪdʒət̬i] *adj* : inquieto, nervioso

field ['fild] *n* : campo *m* — *vt* : interceptar (una pelota), sortear (una pregunta) — **field glasses** : binoculares *mpl*, gemelos *mpl* — **field trip** *n* : viaje *m* de estudio

fiend ['find] *n* **1** : demonio *m* **2** FANATIC : fanático *m*, -ca *f* — **fiendish** ['findɪʃ] *adj* : diabólico

fierce ['fɪrs] *adj* **fiercer; -est 1** : feroz **2** INTENSE : fuerte (dícese del viento), acalorado (dícese de un debate) — **fierceness** ['fɪrsnəs] *n* : ferocidad *f*

fiery ['faɪəri] *adj* **fierier; -est 1** BURNING : llameante **2** SPIRITED : ardiente, fogoso — **fieriness** ['faɪərinəs] *n* : pasión *f*, ardor *m*

fifteen [fɪfˈtin] *n* : quince *m* — ~ *adj* : quince — **fifteenth** [fɪfˈtinθ] *adj* : decimoquinto — ~ *n* **1** : decimoquinto *m*, -ta *f* (en una serie) **2** : quinceavo *m* (en matemáticas)

fifth ['fɪfθ] *n* **1** : quinto *m*, -ta *f* (en una serie) **2** : quinto *m* (en matemáticas) — ~ *adj* : quinto

fiftieth ['fɪftiəθ] *adj* : quincuagésimo — ~ *n* **1** : quincuagésimo *m*, -ma *f* (en una serie) **2** : cincuentavo *m* (en matemáticas)

fifty ['fɪfti] *n*, *pl* **-ties** : cincuenta *m* — ~ *adj* : cincuenta — **fifty-fifty** [ˌfɪfti-ˈfɪfti] *adv* : a medias, mitad y mitad — ~ *adj* **a ~ chance** : un cincuenta por ciento de posibilidades

fig ['fɪg] *n* : higo *m*

fight ['faɪt] *v* **fought** ['fɔt]; **fighting** *vi* **1** BATTLE : luchar **2** QUARREL : pelear **3 ~ back** : defenderse — *vt* : luchar contra — ~ *n* **1** STRUGGLE : lucha *f* **2** QUARREL : pelea *f* — **fighter** ['faɪt̬ər] *n* **1** : luchador *m*, -dora *f* **2** *or* **~ plane** : avión *m* de caza

figment ['fɪgmənt] *n* **~ of the imagination** : producto *m* de la imaginación

figurative ['fɪgjərət̬ɪv, -gə-] *adj* : figurado

figure ['fɪgjər, -gər] *n* **1** NUMBER : número *m*, cifra *f* **2** PERSON, SHAPE : figura *f* **3 ~ of speech** : figura *f* retórica **4 watch one's ~** : cuidar la línea — ~ *v* **-ured; -uring** *vt* : calcular — *vi* **1** : figurar **2 that ~s!** : ¡no me extraña! — **figurehead** ['fɪgjərˌhɛd, -gər-] *n* : testaferro *m* — **figure out** *vt* **1** UNDERSTAND : entender **2** RESOLVE : resolver

file¹ ['faɪl] *n* : lima *f* (instrumento) — ~ *vt* **filed; filing** : limar

file² *vt* **filed; filing 1** : archivar (documentos) **2 ~ charges** : presentar cargos — ~ *n* : archivo *m*

file³ *n* LINE : fila *f* — *vi* **~ in/out** : entrar/salir en fila

fill ['fɪl] *vt* **1** : llenar, rellenar **2** : cumplir con (un requisito) **3** : tapar (un agujero), empastar (un diente) — *vi* **1 ~ in for** : reemplazar **2** *or* **~ up**

: llenarse — ~ n 1 **eat one's ~** : comer lo suficiente 2 **have one's ~ of** : estar harto de

fillet ['fɪlət, fɪ'leɪ, 'fɪˌleɪ] n : filete m

filling ['fɪlɪŋ] n 1 : relleno m 2 : empaste m (de dientes) 3 **~ station** → **service station**

filly ['fɪli] n, pl **-lies** : potra f

film ['fɪlm] n : película f — ~ vt : filmar

filter ['fɪltər] n : filtro m — ~ vt : filtrar

filth ['fɪlθ] n : mugre f — **filthy** ['fɪlθi] adj **filthier; -est** 1 : mugriento 2 OBSCENE : obsceno

fin ['fɪn] n : aleta f

final ['faɪnəl] adj 1 LAST : último 2 DEFINITIVE : definitivo 3 ULTIMATE : final — ~ n 1 : final f (en deportes) 2 **~s** npl : exámenes mpl finales — **finalist** ['faɪnəlɪst] n : finalista mf — **finalize** ['faɪnəlˌaɪz] vt **-ized; -izing** : finalizar — **finally** ['faɪnəli] adv : finalmente

finance [fə'næns, 'faɪˌnæns] n 1 : finanzas fpl 2 **~s** npl : recursos mpl financieros — ~ vt **-nanced; -nancing** : financiar — **financial** [fə'næntʃəl, faɪ-] adj : financiero — **financially** [fə'næntʃəli, faɪ-] adv : económicamente

find ['faɪnd] vt **found** ['faʊnd]; **finding** 1 LOCATE : encontrar 2 REALIZE : darse cuenta de 3 **~ guilty** : declarar culpable 4 or **~ out** : descubrir — vi **~ out** : enterarse — ~ n : hallazgo m — **finding** ['faɪndɪŋ] n 1 FIND : hallazgo m 2 **~s** npl : conclusiones fpl

fine¹ ['faɪn] n : multa f — ~ vt **fined; fining** : multar

fine² adj **finer; -est** 1 DELICATE : fino 2 EXCELLENT : excelente 3 SUBTLE : sutil 4 : bueno (dícese del tiempo) 5 **~ print** : letra f menuda 6 **it's ~ with me** : me parece bien — ~ adv OK : bien — **fine arts** npl : bellas artes fpl — **finely** ['faɪnli] adv 1 EXCELLENTLY : excelentemente 2 PRECISELY : con precisión 3 MINUTELY : fino, menudo

finger ['fɪŋgər] n : dedo m — ~ vt : tocar, toquetear — **fingernail** ['fɪŋgərˌneɪl] n : uña f — **fingerprint** ['fɪŋgərˌprɪnt] n : huella f digital — **fingertip** ['fɪŋgərˌtɪp] n : punta f del dedo

finicky ['fɪnɪki] adj : maniático, mañoso Lat

finish ['fɪnɪʃ] v : acabar, terminar — ~ n 1 END : fin m, final m 2 or **~ line** : meta f 3 SURFACE : acabado m

finite ['faɪˌnaɪt] adj : finito

fir ['fər] n : abeto m

fire ['faɪr] n 1 : fuego m 2 CONFLAGRATION : incendio m 3 **catch ~** : incendiarse (dícese de bosques, etc.), prenderse (dícese de fósforos, etc.) 4 **on ~** : en llamas 5 **open ~ on** : abrir fuego sobre — ~ vt **fired; firing** 1 DISMISS : despedir 2 SHOOT : disparar — vi : disparar — **fire alarm** n : alarma f contra incendios — **firearm** ['faɪrˌarm] n : arma f de fuego — **firecracker** ['faɪrˌkrækər] n : petardo m — **fire engine** n : carro m de bomberos Lat, coche m de bomberos Spain — **fire escape** n : escalera f de incendios — **fire extinguisher** n : extintor m (de incendios) — **firefighter** ['faɪrˌfaɪtər] n : bombero m, -ra f — **firefly** ['faɪrˌflaɪ] n, pl **-flies** : luciérnaga f — **firehouse** → **fire station** — **fireman** ['faɪrmən] n, pl **-men** [-mən, -ˌmen] → **firefighter** — **fireplace** ['faɪrˌpleɪs] n : hogar m, chimenea f — **fireproof** ['faɪrˌpruːf] adj : ignífugo — **fireside** ['faɪrˌsaɪd] n : hogar m — **fire station** n : estación f de bomberos Lat, parque m de bomberos Spain — **firewood** ['faɪrˌwʊd] n : leña f — **fireworks** ['faɪrˌwərk] npl : fuegos mpl artificiales

firm¹ ['fərm] n : empresa f

firm² adj : firme — **firmly** ['fərmli] adv : firmemente — **firmness** ['fərmnəs] n : firmeza f

first ['fərst] adj 1 : primero 2 **at ~ sight** : a primera vista 3 **for the ~ time** : por primera vez — ~ adv 1 : primero 2 **~ and foremost** : ante todo 3 **~ of all** : en primer lugar — ~ n 1 : primero m, -ra f 2 **at ~** : al principio — **first aid** n : primeros auxilios mpl — **first-class** ['fərst'klæs] adv : en primera — ~ adj : de primera f — **firsthand** ['fərst'hænd] adv : directamente — ~ adj : de primera mano — **firstly** ['fərstli] adv : en primer lugar — **first name** n : nombre m de pila — **first-rate** ['fərst'reɪt] adj → **first-class**

fiscal ['fɪskəl] adj : fiscal

fish ['fɪʃ] n, pl **fish** or **fishes** : pez m (vivo), pescado m (para comer) — ~ vi 1 : pescar 2 **~ for** SEEK : buscar 3 **go ~ing** : ir de pesca — **fisherman** ['fɪʃərmən] n, pl **-men** [-mən, -ˌmen] : pescador m, -dora f — **fishhook** ['fɪʃˌhʊk] n : anzuelo m — **fishing** ['fɪʃɪŋ] n : pesca f — **fishing pole** n : caña f de pescar — **fish market** n : pescadería f — **fishy** ['fɪʃi] adj **fishier; -est** 1 : a pescado (dícese de sabores, etc.) 2 SUSPICIOUS : sospechoso

fist ['fɪst] n : puño m

fit¹ ['fɪt] n 1 : ataque m 2 **he had a ~** : le dio un ataque

fit² *adj* **fitter; fittest 1** SUITABLE : apropiado **2** HEALTHY : en forma **3 be ~ for** : ser apto para — *~ v* **fitted; fitting** *vt* **1** : encajar en (un hueco, etc.) **2** *(relating to clothing)* : quedar bien a **3** SUIT : ser apropiado para **4** MATCH : coincidir con **5** *or* **~ out** : equipar — *vi* **1** : caber (en una caja, etc.), encajar (en un hueco, etc.) **2** *or* **~ in** BELONG : encajar **3 this dress doesn't ~** : este vestido no me queda bien — *~ n* **it's a good fit** : me queda bien — **fitful** ['fɪtfəl] *adj* : irregular — **fitness** ['fɪtnəs] *n* **1** HEALTH : salud *f* **2** SUITABILITY : idoneidad *f* — **fitting** ['fɪt ɪŋ] *adj* : apropiado

five ['faɪv] *n* : cinco *m* — *~ adj* : cinco — **five hundred** *n* : quinientos *m* — *~ adj* : quinientos

fix ['fɪks] *vt* **1** ATTACH : fijar, sujetar **2** REPAIR : arreglar **3** PREPARE : preparar — *~ n* PREDICAMENT : aprieto *m*, apuro *m* — **fixed** ['fɪkst] *adj* : fijo — **fixture** ['fɪkstʃər] *n* : instalación *f*

fizz ['fɪz] *vi* : burbujear — *~ n* : efervescencia *f*

fizzle ['fɪzəl] *vi* **-zled; -zling** *or* **~ out** : quedar en nada

flabbergasted ['flæbərˌgæstəd] *adj* : estupefacto, pasmado

flabby ['flæbi] *adj* **-bier; -est** : fofo

flaccid ['flæksəd, 'flæsəd] *adj* : fláccido

flag¹ ['flæg] *vi* WEAKEN : flaquear

flag² *n* : bandera *f* — *~ vt* **flagged; flagging** *or* **~ down** : hacer señales de parada a — **flagpole** ['flæg.poːl] *n* : asta *f*

flagrant ['fleɪɡrənt] *adj* : flagrante

flair ['flær] *n* : don *m*, facilidad *f*

flake ['fleɪk] *n* : copo *m* (de nieve), escama *f* (de pintura, de la piel) — *~ vi* **flaked; flaking** : pelarse

flamboyant [flæm'bɔɪənt] *adj* : extravagante

flame ['fleɪm] *n* **1** : llama *f* **2 burst into ~s** : estallar en llamas **3 go up in ~s** : incendiarse

flamingo [flə'mɪŋɡo] *n*, *pl* **-gos** : flamenco *m*

flammable ['flæməbəl] *adj* : inflamable

flank ['flæŋk] *n* : ijado *m* (de un animal), flanco *m* (militar) — *~ vt* : flanquear

flannel ['flænəl] *n* : franela *f*

flap ['flæp] *n* : solapa *f* (de un sobre, un libro, etc.), tapa *f* (de un recipiente) — *~ v* **flapped; flapping** *vi* : agitarse — *vt* : batir, agitar

flapjack ['flæp.dʒæk] → **pancake**

flare ['flær] *vi* **flared; flaring 1 ~ up** BLAZE : llamear **2 ~ up** EXPLODE,

ERUPT : estallar, explotar — *~ n* **1** BLAZE : llamarada *f* **2** SIGNAL : (luz *f* de) bengala *f*

flash ['flæʃ] *vi* **1** : brillar, destellar **2 ~ past** : pasar como un rayo — *vt* **1** : dirigir (una luz) **2** SHOW : mostrar **3 ~ a smile** : sonreír — *~ n* **1** : destello *m* **2 ~ of lightning** : relámpago *m* **3 in a ~** : de repente — **flashlight** ['flæʃ.laɪt] *n* : linterna *f* — **flashy** ['flæʃi] *adj* **flashier; -est** : ostentoso

flask ['flæsk] *n* : frasco *m*

flat ['flæt] *adj* **flatter; flattest 1** LEVEL : plano, llano **2** DOWNRIGHT : categórico **3** FIXED : fijo **4** MONOTONOUS : monótono **5** : bemol (en la música) **6 ~ tire** : neumático *m* desinflado — *~ n* **1** : bemol *m* (en la música) **2** *Brit* APARTMENT : apartamento *m*, departamento *m* *Lat* **3** PUNCTURE : pinchazo *m* — *~ adv* **1 ~ broke** : pelado *m* **2 in one hour ~** : en una hora justa — **flatly** ['flætli] *adv* : categóricamente — **flat-out** ['flæt.aʊt] *adj* **1** : frenético **2** DOWNRIGHT : categórico — **flatten** ['flætən] *vt* **1** LEVEL : aplanar, allanar **2** KNOCK DOWN : arrasar

flatter ['flætər] *vt* **1** : halagar **2** BECOME : favorecer — **flatterer** ['flætərər] *n* : adulador *m*, -dora *f* — **flattering** ['flætərɪŋ] *adj* **1** : halagador **2** BECOMING : favorecedor — **flattery** ['flætəri] *n*, *pl* **-ries** : halagos *mpl*

flaunt ['flɔnt] *vt* : hacer alarde de

flavor *or Brit* **flavour** ['fleɪvər] *n* : gusto *m*, sabor *m* — *~ vt* : sazonar — **flavorful** *or Brit* **flavourful** ['fleɪvərfəl] *adj* : sabroso — **flavoring** *or Brit* **flavouring** ['fleɪvərɪŋ] *n* : condimento *m*, sazón *f*

flaw ['flɔ] *n* : defecto *m* — **flawless** ['flɔləs] *adj* : perfecto

flax ['flæks] *n* : lino *m*

flea ['fliː] *n* : pulga *f*

fleck ['flek] *n* **1** PARTICLE : mota *f* **2** SPOT : pinta *f*

flee ['fliː] *v* **fled** ['fled]; **fleeing** *vi* : huir — *vt* : huir de

fleece ['fliːs] *n* : vellón *m* — *~ vt* **fleeced; fleecing 1** SHEAR : esquilar **2** DEFRAUD : desplumar

fleet ['fliːt] *n* : flota *f*

fleeting ['fliːtɪŋ] *adj* : fugaz

Flemish ['flemɪʃ] *adj* : flamenco

flesh ['fleʃ] *n* **1** : carne *f* **2** PULP : pulpa *f* **3 in the ~** : en persona — **fleshy** ['fleʃi] *adj* **fleshier; -est 1** : gordo **2** PULPY : carnoso

flew → **fly**

flex ['fleks] *vt* : flexionar — **flexibility**

[ˌfleksəˈbiləʧi] n, pl -ties : flexibilidad f — **flexible** [ˈfleksəbəl] adj : flexible

flick [ˈflɪk] n : golpecito m — ~ vt : dar un golpecito a — vi ~ **through** : hojear

flicker [ˈflɪkər] vi : parpadear — ~ n 1 : parpadeo m 2 a ~ **of hope** : un rayo de esperanza

flier [ˈflaɪər] n 1 AVIATOR : aviador m, -dora f 2 or **flyer** LEAFLET : folleto m, volante m Lat

flight¹ [ˈflaɪt] n 1 : vuelo m 2 TRAJECTORY : trayectoria f 3 ~ **of stairs** : tramo m

flight² n ESCAPE : huida f

flimsy [ˈflɪmzi] adj flimsier; -est 1 LIGHT : ligero 2 SHAKY : poco sólido 3 a ~ **excuse** : una excusa floja

flinch [ˈflɪntʃ] vi ~ **from** : encogerse ante

fling [ˈflɪŋ] vt flung [ˈflʌŋ]; flinging 1 : arrojar 2 ~ **open** : abrir de un golpe — ~ n 1 AFFAIR : aventura f 2 **have a** ~ **at** : intentar

flint [ˈflɪnt] n : pedernal m

flip [ˈflɪp] v flipped; flipping vt 1 or ~ **over** : dar la vuelta a 2 ~ **a coin** : echarlo a cara o cruz — vi 1 or ~ **over** : volcarse 2 ~ **through** : hojear — ~ n SOMERSAULT : voltereta f

flippant [ˈflɪpənt] adj : ligero, frívolo

flipper [ˈflɪpər] n : aleta f

flirt [ˈflərt] vi : coquetear — ~ n : coqueto m, -ta f — **flirtatious** [flərˈteɪʃəs] adj : coqueto

flit [ˈflɪt] vi flitted; flitting : revolotear

float [ˈfloːt] n 1 : flotador m 2 : carroza f (en un desfile) — ~ vi : flotar — vt : hacer flotar

flock [ˈflɑk] n : rebaño m (de ovejas), bandada f (de pájaros) — ~ vi : congregarse

flog [ˈflɑg] vt flogged; flogging : azotar

flood [ˈflʌd] n 1 : inundación f 2 : torrente m (de palabras, de lágrimas, etc.) — ~ vt : inundar — **floodlight** [ˈflʌdˌlaɪt] n : foco m

floor [ˈflor] n 1 : suelo m, piso m Lat 2 STORY : piso m 3 **dance** ~ : pista f de baile 4 **ground** ~ : planta f baja — ~ vt 1 KNOCK DOWN : derribar 2 NONPLUS : desconcertar — **floorboard** [ˈflorˌbord] n : tabla f del suelo

flop [ˈflɑp] vi flopped; flopping 1 FLAP : agitarse 2 COLLAPSE : dejarse caer 3 FAIL : fracasar — ~ n FAILURE : fracaso m — **floppy** [ˈflɑpi] adj -pier; -est : flojo, flexible — **floppy disk** n : diskette m, disquete m

flora [ˈflorə] n : flora f — **floral** [ˈflorəl]

adj : floral — **florid** [ˈflorɪd] adj 1 FLOWERY : florido 2 RUDDY : rojizo —

florist [ˈflorɪst] n : florista mf

floss [ˈflɔs] n → **dental floss**

flounder¹ [ˈflaʊndər] n, pl **flounder** or **flounders** : platija f

flounder² vi 1 or ~ **about** : resbalarse, revolcarse 2 : titubear (en un discurso)

flour [ˈflaʊər] n : harina f

flourish [ˈflərɪʃ] vi : florecer — vt BRANDISH : blandir — ~ n : floritura f — **flourishing** [ˈflərɪʃɪŋ] adj : floreciente

flout [ˈflaʊt] vt : desacatar, burlarse de

flow [ˈfloː] vi : fluir, correr — ~ n 1 : flujo m, circulación f 2 : corriente f (de información, etc.)

flower [ˈflaʊər] n : flor f — ~ vi : florecer — **flowered** [ˈflaʊərd] adj : floreado — **flowerpot** [ˈflaʊərˌpɑt] n : maceta f — **flowery** [ˈflaʊəri] adj : florido

flown → **fly**

flu [ˈfluː] n : gripe f

fluctuate [ˈflʌktʃuˌeɪt] vi -ated; -ating : fluctuar — **fluctuation** [ˌflʌktʃuˈeɪʃən] n : fluctuación f

fluency [ˈfluːənsi] n : fluidez f — **fluent** [ˈfluːənt] adj 1 : fluido 2 **be** ~ **in** : hablar con fluidez — **fluently** [ˈfluːəntli] adv : con fluidez

fluff [ˈflʌf] n : pelusa f — **fluffy** [ˈflʌfi] adj fluffier; -est : de pelusa, velloso

fluid [ˈfluːɪd] adj : fluido — ~ n : fluido m

flung → **fling**

flunk [ˈflʌŋk] vt : reprobar Lat, suspender Spain — vi : ser reprobado Lat, suspender Spain

fluorescence [ˌflʊrˈɛsəns, ˌflɔr-] n : fluorescencia f — **fluorescent** [ˌflʊrˈɛsənt, ˌflɔr-] adj : fluorescente

flurry [ˈfləri] n, pl -ries 1 GUST : ráfaga f 2 or **snow** ~ : nevisca f 3 ~ **of questions** : aluvión m de preguntas

flush [ˈflʌʃ] vi BLUSH : ruborizarse, sonrojarse — vt ~ **the toilet** : tirar de la cadena, jalarle a la cadena Lat — ~ n BLUSH : rubor m, sonrojo m — ~ adj ~ **with** : a nivel con, a ras de — ~ adv : al mismo nivel, a ras

fluster [ˈflʌstər] vt : poner nervioso

flute [ˈfluːt] n : flauta f

flutter [ˈflʌtər] vi 1 FLIT : revolotear 2 WAVE : ondear 3 or ~ **about** : ir y venir — ~ n 1 : revoloteo m (de alas) 2 STIR : revuelo m

flux [ˈflʌks] n **be in a state of** ~ : cambiar continuamente

fly¹ [ˈflaɪ] v flew [ˈfluː]; flown [ˈfloːn]; flying vi 1 : volar 2 TRAVEL : ir en avión 3 WAVE : ondear 4 RUSH : correr 5 ~

by : pasar volando — *vt* 1 PILOT : pilotar 2 : hacer volar (una cometa), enarbolar (una bandera) — ~ *n, pl* **flies** : bragueta *f* (de un pantalón)

fly² *n, pl* **flies** : mosca *f* (insecto)

flyer → **flier**

flying saucer *n* : platillo *m* volador *Lat*, platillo *m* volante *Spain*

flyswatter ['flaɪ,swɑt̬ər] *n* : matamoscas *m*

foal ['foːl] *n* : potro *m*, -tra *f*

foam ['foːm] *n* : espuma *f* — ~ *vi* : hacer espuma — **foamy** ['foːmi] *adj* **foamier; -est** : espumoso

focus ['foːkəs] *n, pl* **-ci** ['foː,saɪ, -,kaɪ] 1 : foco *m* 2 **be in** ~ : estar enfocado 3 ~ **of attention** : centro *m* de atención — ~ *v* **-cused** *or* **-cussed; -cusing** *or* **-cussing** *vt* 1 : enfocar 2 : centrar (la atención, etc.) — *vi* ~ **on** : enfocar (con los ojos), concentrarse en (con la mente)

fodder ['fɑdər] *n* : forraje *m*

foe ['foː] *n* : enemigo *m*, -ga *f*

fog ['fɔg, 'fag] *n* : niebla *f* — ~ *v* **fogged; fogging** *vt* : empañar — *vi* *or* ~ **up** : empañarse — **foggy** ['fɔgi, 'fa-] *adj* **foggier; -est** : nebuloso — **foghorn** ['fɔg,hɔrn, 'fag-] *n* : sirena *f* de niebla

foil¹ ['fɔɪl] *vt* : frustrar

foil² *n or* **aluminum** ~ : papel *m* de aluminio

fold¹ ['foːld] *n* 1 : redil *m* (para ovejas) 2 **return to the** ~ : volver al redil

fold² *vt* 1 : doblar, plegar 2 ~ **one's arms** : cruzar los brazos — *vi* 1 *or* ~ **up** : doblarse, plegarse 2 FAIL : fracasar — ~ *n* : pliegue *m* — **folder** ['foːldər] *n* : carpeta *f*

foliage ['foːliɪdʒ, -lɪdʒ] *n* : follaje *m*

folk ['foːk] *n, pl* **folk** *or* **folks** 1 : gente *f* 2 ~**s** *npl* PARENTS : padres *mpl* — ~ *adj* : popular 2 ~ **dance** : danza *f* folklórica — **folklore** ['foːk,lor] *n* : folklore *m*

follow ['falo] *vt* 1 : seguir 2 UNDERSTAND : entender 3 ~ **up** : seguir — *vi* 1 : seguir 2 UNDERSTAND : entender 3 ~ **up on** : seguir con — **follower** ['faloər] *n* : seguidor *m*, -dora *f* — **following** ['faloɪŋ] *adj* : siguiente — ~ *n* : seguidores *mpl* — ~ *prep* : después de

folly ['fali] *n, pl* **-lies** : locura *f*

fond ['fand] *adj* 1 : cariñoso 2 **be** ~ **of sth** : ser aficionado a algo 3 **be** ~ **of s.o.** : tener cariño a algn

fondle ['fandəl] *vt* **-dled; -dling** : acariciar

fondness ['fandnəs] *n* 1 LOVE : cariño *m* 2 LIKING : afición *f*

food ['fuːd] *n* : comida *f*, alimento *m* — **foodstuffs** ['fuːd,stʌfs] *npl* : comestibles *mpl*

fool ['fuːl] *n* 1 : idiota *mf* 2 JESTER : bufón *m*, -fona *f* — ~ *vi* 1 JOKE : bromear 2 ~ **around** : perder el tiempo — *vt* TRICK : engañar — **foolhardy** ['fuːl,hardi] *adj* : temerario — **foolish** ['fuːlɪʃ] *adj* : tonto — **foolishness** ['fuːlɪʃnəs] *n* : tontería *f* — **foolproof** ['fuːl,pruːf] *adj* : infalible

foot ['fut] *n, pl* **feet** ['fiːt] : pie *m* — **footage** ['fut̬ɪdʒ] *n* : secuencias *fpl* (cinemáticas) — **football** ['fut,bɔl] *n* : fútbol *m* americano — **footbridge** ['fut,brɪdʒ] *n* : pasarela *f*, puente *m* peatonal — **foothills** ['fut,hɪlz] *npl* : estribaciones *fpl* — **foothold** ['fut,hoːld] *n* : punto *m* de apoyo — **footing** ['fut̬ɪŋ] *n* 1 BALANCE : equilibrio *m* 2 **on equal** ~ : en igualdad — **footlights** ['fut,laɪts] *npl* : candilejas *fpl* — **footnote** ['fut,noːt] *n* : nota *f* al pie de la página — **footpath** ['fut,pæθ] *n* : sendero *m* — **footprint** ['fut,prɪnt] *n* : huella *f* — **footstep** ['fut,step] *n* : paso *m* — **footstool** ['fut,stuːl] *n* : escabel *m* — **footwear** ['fut,wær] *n* : calzado *m*

for ['fɔr] *prep* 1 (*indicating purpose, etc.*) : para 2 (*indicating motivation, etc.*) : por 3 (*indicating duration*) : durante 4 **we walked** ~ **3 miles** : andamos 3 millas 5 AS FOR : con respecto a — ~ *conj* : puesto que, porque

forage ['fɔrɪdʒ] *n* : forraje *m* — ~ *vi* **-aged; -aging** 1 : forrajear 2 ~ **for** : buscar

foray ['fɔr,eɪ] *n* : incursión *f*

forbid [fərbɪd] *vt* **-bade** [-'bæd, -'beɪd] *or* **-bad** [-'bæd]; **-bidden** [-'bɪdən]; **-bidding** : prohibir — **forbidding** [fər'bɪdɪŋ] *adj* : intimidante, severo

force ['fɔrs] *n* 1 : fuerza *f* 2 **by** ~ : por la fuerza 3 **in** ~ : en vigor, en vigencia 4 **armed** ~**s** : fuerzas *fpl* armadas — ~ *vt* **forced; forcing** 1 : forzar 2 OBLIGATE : obligar — **forced** ['fɔrst] *adj* : forzado, forzoso — **forceful** ['fɔrsfəl] *adj* : fuerte, energético

forceps ['fɔrsəps, -,seps] *ns & pl* : fórceps *m*

forcibly [-bli] *adv* : por la fuerza

ford ['fɔrd] *n* : vado *m* — ~ *vt* : vadear

fore ['fɔr] *n* **come to the** ~ : empezar a destacarse

forearm ['fɔr,arm] *n* : antebrazo *m*

foreboding [fɔr'boːdɪŋ] *n* : premonición *f*, presentimiento *m*

forecast ['for,kæst] vt -cast; -casting : predecir, pronosticar — ~ n : predicción f, pronóstico m

forefathers ['for,fɑðərz] n : antepasados mpl

forefinger ['for,fiŋgər] n : índice m, dedo m índice

forefront ['for,frʌnt] n at/in the ~ : a la vanguardia

forego [for'go:] → forgo

foregone [for'gɔn] adj ~ conclusion : resultado m inevitable

foreground ['for,graund] n : primer plano m

forehead ['forəd, 'for,hed] n : frente f

foreign ['forən] adj 1 : extranjero 2 ~ trade : comercio m exterior — foreigner ['forənər] n : extranjero m, -ra f

foreman ['formən] n, pl -men [-mən, -,men] : capataz mf

foremost ['for,mo:st] adj : principal — ~ adv first and ~ : ante todo

forensic [fə'rensik] adj : forense

forerunner ['for,rʌnər] n : precursor m, -sora f

foresee [for'si:] vt -saw; -seen; -seeing : prever — foreseeable [for'si:əbəl] adj : previsible

foreshadow [for'ʃædo:] vt : presagiar

foresight ['for,sait] n : previsión f

forest ['forəst] n : bosque m — forestry ['forəstri] n : silvicultura f

foretaste ['for,teist] n : anticipo m

foretell [for'tel] vt -told; -telling : predecir

forethought ['for,θɔt] n : reflexión f previa

forever [fər'evər] adv 1 ETERNALLY : para siempre 2 CONTINUALLY : siempre, constantemente

forewarn [for'worn] vt : advertir, prevenir

foreword ['forword] n : prólogo m

forfeit ['forfət] n 1 PENALTY : pena f 2 : prenda f (en un juego) — ~ vt : perder

forge ['fordʒ] n : forja f — ~ v forged; forging vt 1 : forjar (metal, etc.) 2 COUNTERFEIT : falsificar — vi ~ ahead : avanzar, seguir adelante — forger ['fordʒər] n : falsificador m, -dora f — forgery ['fordʒəri] n, pl -eries : falsificación f

forget [fər'get] v -got [-'gɑt]; -gotten [-'gɑtən] or -got; -getting vt : olvidar, olvidarse de — vi ~ : olvidarse 2 I forgot : se me olvidó — forgetful [fər'getfəl] adj : olvidadizo

forgive [fər'giv] vt -gave [-'geiv]; -given

[-'givən]; -giving : perdonar — forgiveness [fər'givnəs] n : perdón m

forgo or forego [for'go:] vt -went; -gone; -going : privarse de, renunciar a

fork ['fork] n 1 : tenedor m 2 PITCHFORK : horca f 3 : bifurcación f (de un camino, etc.) — vi : ramificarse, bifurcarse — vt ~ over : desembolsar

forlorn [fər'lorn] adj : triste

form ['form] n 1 : forma f 2 DOCUMENT : formulario m 3 KIND : tipo m — ~ vt 1 : formar 2 ~ a habit : adquirir un hábito — vi : formarse

formal ['forməl] adj : formal — ~ n 1 BALL : baile m (formal) 2 or ~ dress : traje m de etiqueta — formality [for'mæləṭi] n, pl -ties : formalidad f

format ['for,mæt] n : formato m — ~ vt -matted; -matting : formatear

formation [for'meiʃən] n 1 : formación f 2 SHAPE : forma f

former ['formər] adj 1 PREVIOUS : antiguo, anterior 2 : primero (de dos) — formerly ['formərli] adv : anteriormente, antes

formidable ['formədəbəl, for'midə-] adj : formidable

formula ['formjələ] n, pl -las or -lae [-,li:, -,lai] 1 : fórmula f 2 or baby ~ : preparado m para biberón

forsake [fər'seik] vt -sook [-'suk]; -saken [-'seikən]; -saking : abandonar

fort ['fort] n : fuerte m

forth ['forθ] adv 1 and so ~ : etcétera 2 back and ~ → back 3 from this day ~ : de hoy en adelante — forthcoming [forθ'kʌmiŋ, 'forθ,-] adj 1 COMING : próximo 2 OPEN : comunicativo — forthright ['forθ,rait] adj : directo, franco

fortieth ['forṭiəθ] adj : cuadragésimo — ~ n 1 : cuadragésimo m, -ma f (en una serie) 2 : cuarentavo m, cuarentava parte f

fortify ['forṭə,fai] vt -fied; -fying : fortificar — fortification [,forṭəfə'keiʃən] n : fortificación f

fortitude ['forṭə,tu:d, -,tju:d] n : fortaleza f

fortnight ['fort,nait] n : quince días mpl, quincena f

fortress ['fortrəs] n : fortaleza f

fortunate ['fortʃənət] adj : afortunado — fortunately ['fortʃənətli] adv : afortunadamente — fortune ['fortʃən] n : fortuna f — fortune–teller ['fortʃən,telər] n : adivino m, -na f

forty ['forṭi] n, pl forties : cuarenta m — ~ adj : cuarenta

forum ['fɔrəm] *n, pl* **-rums** : foro *m*
forward ['fɔrwərd] *adj* **1** : hacia adelante (en dirección), delantero (en posición) **2** BRASH : descarado — ～ *adv* **1** : (hacia) adelante **2 from this day** ～ : de aquí en adelante — ～ *vt* : remitir, enviar — ～ *n* : delantero *m*, -ra *f* (en deportes) — **forwards** ['fɔrwərdz] *adv* → **forward**
fossil ['fɑsəl] *n* : fósil *m*
foster ['fɔstər] *adj* : adoptivo — ～ *vt* : promover, fomentar
fought → **fight**
foul ['faul] *adj* **1** REPULSIVE : asqueroso **2** ～ **language** : palabrotas *fpl* **3** ～ **play** : actos *mpl* criminales **4** ～ **weather** : mal tiempo *m* — ～ *n* : falta *f* (en deportes) — ～ *vi* : cometer faltas (en deportes) — *vt* : ensuciar
found¹ ['faund] → **find**
found² *vt* : fundar, establecer — **foundation** [faun'deɪʃən] *n* **1** : fundación *f* **2** BASIS : fundamento *m* **3** : cimientos *mpl* (de un edificio)
founder¹ ['faundər] *n* : fundador *m*, -dora *f*
founder² *vi* SINK : hundirse
fountain ['fauntən] *n* : fuente *f*
four ['fɔr] *n* : cuatro *m* — ～ *adj* : cuatro — **fourfold** ['fɔr,fo:ld, -'fo:ld] *adj* : cuadruple — **four hundred** *adj* : cuatrocientos — ～ *n* : cuatrocientos *m*
fourteen [fɔr'ti:n] *n* : catorce *m* — ～ *adj* : catorce — **fourteenth** [fɔr'ti:nθ] *adj* : decimocuarto — ～ *n* **1** : decimocuarto *m*, -ta *f* (en una serie) **2** : catorceavo *m*, catorceava parte *f*
fourth ['fɔrθ] *n* **1** : cuarto *m*, -ta *f* (en una serie) **2** : cuarto *m*, cuarta parte *f* — ～ *adj* : cuarto
owl ['faul] *n, pl* **fowl** *or* **fowls** : ave *f*
ox ['fɑks] *n, pl* **foxes** : zorro *m*, -ra *f* — ～ *vt* TRICK : engañar — **foxy** ['fɑksi] *adj* **foxier; -est** SHREWD : astuto
oyer ['fɔɪər, 'fɔɪˌjeɪ] *n* : vestíbulo *m*
raction ['frækʃən] *n* : fracción *f*
racture ['fræktʃər] *n* : fractura *f* — ～ *vt* **-tured; -turing** : fracturar
ragile ['frædʒəl, -dʒaɪl] *adj* : frágil
ragment ['frægmənt] *n* : fragmento *m*
ragrant ['freɪɡrənt] *adj* : fragante — **fragrance** ['freɪɡrənts] *n* : fragancia *f*, aroma *m*
rail ['freɪl] *adj* : débil, delicado
rame ['freɪm] *vt* **framed; framing 1** ENCLOSE : enmarcar **2** COMPOSE, DRAFT : formular **3** INCRIMINATE : incriminar — ～ *n* **1** : armazón *mf* (de un edificio, etc.) **2** : marco *m* (de un cuadro, una puerta, etc.) **3** *or* ～**s** *npl* : montura *f*

(para anteojos) **4** ～ **of mind** : estado *m* de ánimo — **framework** ['freɪm,wərk] *n* : armazón *f*
franc ['fræŋk] *n* : franco *m*
frank ['fræŋk] *adj* : franco — **frankly** *adv* : francamente — **frankness** ['fræŋknəs] *n* : franqueza *f*
frantic ['fræntɪk] *adj* : frenético
fraternal [frə'tərnəl] *adj* : fraterno, fraternal — **fraternity** [frə'tərnəti] *n, pl* **-ties** : fraternidad *f* — **fraternize** ['frætər,naɪz] *vi* **-nized; -nizing** : confraternizar
fraud ['frɔd] *n* **1** DECEIT : fraude *m* **2** IMPOSTOR : impostor *m*, -tora *f* — **fraudulent** ['frɔdʒələnt] *adj* : fraudulento
fraught ['frɔt] *adj* ～ **with** : lleno de, cargado de
fray¹ ['freɪ] *n* **1 join the** ～ : salir a la palestra **2 return to the** ～ : volver a la carga
fray² *vt* : crispar (los nervios) — *vi* : deshilacharse
freak ['fri:k] *n* **1** ODDITY : fenómeno *m* **2** ENTHUSIAST : entusiasta *mf* — **freakish** ['fri:kɪʃ] *adj* : anormal
freckle ['frekəl] *n* : peca *f*
free ['fri:] *adj* **freer; freest 1** : libre **2** *or* ～ **of charge** : gratuito, gratis **3** LOOSE : suelto — ～ *vt* **freed; freeing 1** : liberar, poner en libertad **2** RELEASE, UNFASTEN : soltar, desatar — ～ *adv or* **for** ～ : gratis — **freedom** ['fri:dəm] *n* : libertad *f* — **freelance** ['fri:,lænts] *adj* : por cuenta propia — **freely** ['fri:li] *adv* **1** : libremente **2** LAVISHLY : con generosidad — **freeway** ['fri:,weɪ] *n* : autopista *f* — **free will** *n* **1** : libre albedrío *m* **2 of one's own** ～ : por su propia voluntad
freeze ['fri:z] *v* **froze** ['fro:z]; **frozen** ['fro:zən]; **freezing** *vi* **1** : congelarse, helarse **2** STOP : quedarse inmóvil — *vt* : helar (agua, etc.), congelar (alimentos, precios, etc.) — **freeze-dry** ['fri:z-'draɪ] *vt* **-dried; -drying** : liofilizar — **freezer** ['fri:zər] *n* : congelador *m* — **freezing** ['fri:zɪŋ] *adj* **1** CHILLY : helado **2 it's freezing!** : ¡hace un frío espantoso!
freight ['freɪt] *n* **1** SHIPPING : porte *m*, flete *m Lat* **2** CARGO : carga *f*
French ['frentʃ] *adj* : francés — ～ *n* **1** : francés *m* (idioma) **2 the** ～ *npl* : los franceses — **Frenchman** ['frentʃmən] *n* : francés *m* — **Frenchwoman** ['frentʃ,wumən] *n* : francesa *f* — **french fries** ['frentʃ,fraɪz] *npl* : papas *fpl* fritas
frenetic [frɪ'netɪk] *adj* : frenético

frenzy ['frenzi] *n, pl* **-zies** : frenesí *m* —
frenzied ['frenzid] *adj* : frenético
frequent — ~ ['fri:kwənt, fri:'kwənt] *vt* : frecuentar — ~ ['fri:kwənt] *adj* : frecuen-
te — **frequency** ['fri:kwəntsi] *n, pl*
-cies : frecuencia *f* — **frequently** *adv*
: a menudo, frecuentemente
fresco ['freskoː] *n, pl* **-coes** : fresco *m*
fresh ['freʃ] *adj* **1** : fresco **2** IMPUDENT
: descarado **3** CLEAN : limpio **4** NEW
: nuevo **5** ~ **water** : agua *m* dulce —
freshen ['freʃən] *vt* : refrescar — *vi* ~
up : arreglarse — **freshly** ['freʃli] *adv*
: recién — **freshman** ['freʃmən] *n, pl*
-men [-mən, -men] : estudiante *mf* de
primer año — **freshness** ['freʃnəs] *n*
: frescura *f*
fret ['fret] *vi* **fretted; fretting** : preocuparse — **fretful** ['fretfəl] *adj* : nervioso,
irritable
friar ['fraɪər] *n* : fraile *m*
friction ['frɪkʃən] *n* : fricción *f*
Friday ['fraɪdeɪ, -di] *n* : viernes *m*
friend ['frend] *n* : amigo *m*, -ga *f* —
friendliness ['frendlinəs] *n* : simpatía *f*
— **friendly** ['frendli] *adj* **-lier; -est**
: simpático, amable — **friendship**
['frendʃɪp] *n* : amistad *f*
frigate ['frɪgət] *n* : fragata *f*
fright ['fraɪt] *n* : miedo *m*, susto *m* —
frighten ['fraɪtən] *vt* : asustar, espantar
— **frightened** ['fraɪtənd] *adj* **1** : asustado, temeroso **2 be** ~ **of** : tener miedo
de — **frightening** ['fraɪtənɪŋ] *adj* : espantoso — **frightful** ['fraɪtfəl] *adj* : espantoso, terrible
frigid ['frɪdʒɪd] *adj* : frío, glacial
frill ['frɪl] *n* **1** RUFFLE : volante *m* **2** LUX-
URY : lujo *m*
fringe ['frɪndʒ] *n* **1** : fleco *m* **2** EDGE
: periferia *f*, margen *m* **3** ~ **benefits**
: incentivos *mpl*, extras *mpl*
frisk ['frɪsk] *vt* SEARCH : cachear, registrar — **frisky** ['frɪski] *adj* **friskier; -est**
: retozón, juguetón
fritter ['frɪtər] *n* : buñuelo *m* — ~ *vt or*
~ **away** : malgastar (dinero), desperdiciar (tiempo)
frivolous ['frɪvələs] *adj* : frívolo — **frivolity** [frɪ'valəti] *n, pl* **-ties** : frivolidad
f
frizzy ['frɪzi] *adj* **frizzier; -est** : rizado,
crespo
fro ['froː] *adv* **to and** ~ → **to**
frock ['frak] *n* : vestido *m*
frog ['frɔg, 'frag] *n* **1** : rana *f* **2 have a** ~
in one's throat : tener carraspera
frolic ['fralɪk] *vi* **-icked; -icking** : retozar
from ['frʌm, 'fram] *prep* **1** : de **2** (*indicating a starting point*) : desde **3** (*in-

dicating a cause*) : de, por **4** ~ **now
on** : a partir de ahora
front ['frʌnt] *n* **1** : parte *f* delantera **2**
: delantera *f* (de un vestido, etc.),
fachada *f* (de un edificio), frente *m*
(militar) **3 cold** ~ : frente *m* frío **4 in
~ of** : delante de, adelante de *Lat* —
~ *vi or* ~ **on** : dar a, estar orientado
a — ~ *adj* **1** : delantero, de adelante **2**
the ~ **row** : la primera fila
frontier [frʌn'tɪr] *n* : frontera *f*
frost ['frɔst] *n* **1** : helada *f* **2** : escarcha *f*
(en una superficie) — ~ *vt* ICE : bañar
(pasteles) — **frostbite** ['frɔst,baɪt] *n*
: congelación *f* — **frosting** ['frɔstɪŋ] *n*
ICING : baño *m* — **frosty** ['frɔsti] *adj*
frostier; -est 1 : cubierto de escarcha
2 CHILLY : helado, frío
froth ['frɔθ] *n, pl* **froths** ['frɔθs, 'frɔðz]
: espuma *f* — **frothy** ['frɔθi] *adj* **froth-
ier; -est** : espumoso
frown ['fraun] *vi* **1** : fruncir el ceño,
fruncir el entrecejo **2** ~ **at** : mirar con
ceño **3** ~ **upon** : desaprobar — ~ *n*
: ceño *m* (fruncido)
froze, frozen → **freeze**
frugal ['fru:gəl] *adj* : frugal
fruit ['fru:t] *n* **1** : fruta *f* **2** PRODUCT, RE-
SULT : fruto *m* — **fruitcake** ['fru:t,keɪk]
n : pastel *m* de frutas — **fruitful**
['fru:tfəl] *adj* : fructífero — **fruition**
[fru'ɪʃən] *n* **come to** ~ : realizarse —
fruitless ['fru:tləs] *adj* : infructuoso —
fruity ['fru:ti] *adj* **fruitier; -est** : (con
sabor) a fruta
frustrate ['frʌs,treɪt] *vt* **-trated; -trating**
: frustrar — **frustrating** ['frʌs,treɪtɪŋ]
adj : frustrante — **frustration** [frʌs-
'treɪʃən] *n* : frustración *f*
fry ['fraɪ] *vt* **fried; frying** : freír — ~ *n,
pl* **fries 1 small** ~ : gente *f* de poca
monta **2 fries** *npl* → **french fries** —
frying pan *n* : sartén *mf*
fudge ['fʌdʒ] *n* : dulce *m* blando de
chocolate y leche
fuel ['fju:əl] *n* : combustible *m* — ~ *v*
-eled *or* **-elled; -eling** *or* **-elling**
: alimentar (un horno), abastecer de
combustible (un avión) **2** STIMULATE
: estimular
fugitive ['fju:dʒətɪv] *n* : fugitivo *m*, -va
fulfill *or* **fulfil** [fʊl'fɪl] *vt* **-filled; -filling**
: cumplir con (una obligación), desa-
rrollar (potencial) **2** FILL, MEET
: cumplir — **fulfillment** [fʊl'fɪlmənt] *n*
1 ACCOMPLISHMENT : cumplimiento *m*
2 SATISFACTION : satisfacción *f*
full ['fʊl, 'fal] *adj* **1** FILLED : lleno **2** COM-
PLETE : complete, detallado **3** : redon-
do (dícese de la cara), amplio (dícese

de ropa) **4 at ~ speed** : a toda velocidad **5 in ~ bloom** : en plena flor — *adv* **1** DIRECTLY : de lleno **2 know ~ well** : saber muy bien — ~ *n* **1 pay in ~** : pagar en su totalidad **2 to the ~** : al máximo — **full-fledged** ['ful'fledʒd] *adj* : hecho y derecho — **fully** ['fuli] *adv* **1** COMPLETELY : completamente **2** AT LEAST : al menos, por lo menos

fumble ['fʌmbəl] *vi* **-bled; -bling 1** RUMMAGE : hurgar **2 ~ with** : manejar con torpeza

fume ['fju:m] *vi* **fumed; fuming 1** SMOKE : echar humo, humear **2** RAGE : estar furioso — **fumes** *npl* : gases *mpl*

fumigate ['fju:məgeɪt] *vt* **-gated; -gating** : fumigar

fun ['fʌn] *n* **1** AMUSEMENT : diversión *f* **2 have ~** : divertirse **3 make ~ of** : reírse de, burlarse de — ~ *adj* : divertido

function ['fʌŋkʃən] *n* **1** : función *f* **2** GATHERING : recepción *f*, reunión *f* social — ~ *vi* : funcionar — **functional** ['fʌŋkʃənəl] *adj* : funcional

fund ['fʌnd] *n* **1** : fondo *m* **2 ~s** *npl* RESOURCES : fondos *mpl* — ~ *vt* : financiar

fundamental [,fʌndə'mentəl] *adj* : fundamental — **fundamentals** *npl* : fundamentos *mpl*

funeral ['fju:nərəl] *adj* : funeral, fúnebre — ~ *n* : funeral *m*, funerales *mpl* — **funeral home** or **funeral parlor** *n* : funeraria *f*

fungus ['fʌŋgəs] *n, pl* **fungi** ['fʌn,dʒaɪ, 'fʌŋ,gaɪ] : hongo *m*

funnel ['fʌnəl] *n* **1** : embudo *m* **2** SMOKESTACK : chimenea *f*

funny ['fʌni] *adj* **funnier; -est 1** : divertido, gracioso **2** STRANGE : extraño, raro — **funnies** ['fʌniz] *npl* : tiras *fpl* cómicas

fur ['fər] *n* **1** : pelaje *m*, pelo *m* (de un animal) **2** or **~ coat** : (prenda *f* de) piel *f* — ~ *adj* : de piel

furious ['fjʊriəs] *adj* : furioso

furnace ['fərnəs] *n* : horno *m*

furnish ['fərnɪʃ] *vt* **1** SUPPLY : proveer **2** : amueblar (una casa, etc.) — **furnishings** ['fərnɪʃɪŋz] *npl* : muebles *mpl*, mobiliario *m* — **furniture** ['fərnɪtʃər] *n* : muebles *mpl*, mobiliario *m*

furrow ['fəro:] *n* : surco *m*

furry ['fəri] *adj* **furrier; -est** : peludo (dícese de un animal), de peluche (dícese de un juguete, etc.)

further ['fərðər] *adv* **1** FARTHER : más lejos **2** MOREOVER : además **3** MORE : más — ~ *vt* : promover, fomentar — ~ *adj* **1** FARTHER : más lejano **2** ADDITIONAL : adicional, más **3 until ~ notice** : hasta nuevo aviso — **furthermore** ['fərðər,mor] *adv* : además — **furthest** ['fərðəst] → **farthest**

furtive ['fərtɪv] *adj* : furtivo

fury ['fjʊri] *n, pl* **-ries** : furia *f*

fuse[1] or **fuze** ['fju:z] *n* : mecha *f* (de una bomba, etc.)

fuse[2] *v* **fused; fusing** *vt* **1** MELT : fundir **2** UNITE : fusionar — *vi* : fundirse, fusionarse — ~ *n* **1** : fusible *m* **2 blow a ~** : fundir un fusible — **fusion** ['fju:ʒən] *n* : fusión *f*

fuss ['fʌs] *n* **1** : jaleo *m*, alboroto *m* **2 make a ~** : armar un escándalo — ~ *vi* **1** WORRY : preocuparse **2** COMPLAIN : quejarse — **fussy** ['fʌsi] *adj* **fussier; -est 1** IRRITABLE : irritable **2** ELABORATE : recargado **3** FINICKY : quisquilloso

futile ['fju:təl, 'fju:taɪl] *adj* : inútil, vano — **futility** [fju:'tɪləti] *n, pl* **-ties** : inutilidad *f*

future ['fju:tʃər] *adj* : futuro — ~ *n* : futuro *m*

fuze → **fuse**[1]

fuzz ['fʌz] *n* : pelusa *f* — **fuzzy** ['fʌzi] *adj* **fuzzier; -est 1** FURRY : con pelusa, peludo **2** BLURRY : borroso **3** VAGUE : confuso

G

['dʒi:] *n, pl* **g's** or **gs** ['dʒi:z] : g *f*, séptima letra del alfabeto inglés

gab ['gæb] *vi* **gabbed; gabbing** : charlar, cotorrear *fam* — ~ *n* CHATTER : charla *f*

gable ['geɪbəl] *n* : aguilón *m*

gadget ['gædʒət] *n* : artilugio *m*

gag ['gæg] *v* **gagged; gagging** *vt*

: amordazar — *vi* CHOKE : atragantarse — ~ *n* **1** : mordaza *f* **2** JOKE : chiste *m*

gage → **gauge**

gaiety ['geɪəti] *n, pl* **-eties** : alegría *f* — **gaily** ['geɪli] *adv* : alegremente

gain ['geɪn] *n* **1** PROFIT : ganancia *f* **2** INCREASE : aumento *m* — ~ *vt* **1** OBTAIN : ganar, adquirir **2 ~ weight** : aumen-

tar de peso — *vi* **1** PROFIT : beneficiarse **2** : adelantar(se) (dícese de un reloj) —
gainful ['geɪnfəl] *adj* : lucrativo
gait ['geɪt] *n* : modo *m* de andar
gala ['geɪlə, 'gæ-, 'gɑ-] *n* : fiesta *f*
galaxy ['gæləksi] *n, pl* **-axies** : galaxia *f*
gale ['geɪl] *n* **1** : vendaval *f* **2** **~s of laughter** : carcajadas *fpl*
gall ['gɔl] *n* **have the ~ to** : tener el descaro de
gallant ['gælənt] *adj* **1** BRAVE : valiente **2** CHIVALROUS : galante
gallbladder ['gɔl,blædər] *n* : vesícula *f* biliar
gallery ['gæləri] *n, pl* **-leries** : galería *f*
gallon ['gælən] *n* : galón *m*
gallop ['gæləp] *vi* : galopar — **~** *n* : galope *m*
gallows ['gæ,loːz] *n, pl* **-lows** *or* **-lowses** [-,loːzəz] : horca *f*
gallstone ['gɔl,stoːn] *n* : cálculo *m* biliar
galore [gə'lor] *adj* : en abundancia
galoshes [gə'lɑʃ] *n* : galochas *fpl*, chanclos *mpl*
galvanize ['gælvən,aɪz] *vt* **-nized; -nizing** : galvanizar
gamble ['gæmbəl] *v* **-bled; -bling** *vi* : jugar — *vt* : jugarse — **~** *n* **1** BET : apuesta *f* **2** RISK : riesga *f* — **gambler** ['gæmbələr] *n* : jugador *m*, -dora *f*
game ['geɪm] *n* **1** : juego *m* **2** MATCH : partido *m* **3** *or* **~ animals** : caza *f* — **~** *adj* READY : listo, dispuesto
gamut ['gæmət] *n* : gama *f*
gang ['gæŋ] *n* : banda *f*, pandilla *f* — **~** *vi* **~ up on** : unirse contra
gangplank ['gæŋ,plæŋk] *n* : pasarela *f*
gangrene ['gæŋ,griːn, 'gæn-; gæŋ'-, gæn-'-] *n* : gangrena *f*
gangster ['gæŋstər] *n* : gángster *mf*
gangway ['gæŋ,weɪ] *n* → **gangplank**
gap ['gæp] *n* **1** OPENING : espacio *m* **2** INTERVAL : intervalo *m* **3** DISPARITY : brecha *f*, distancia *f* **4** DEFICIENCY : laguna *f*
gape ['geɪp] *vi* **gaped; gaping 1** OPEN : estar abierto **2** STARE : mirar boquiabierto
garage [gə'rɑʒ, -'rɑdʒ] *n* : garaje *m* — **~** *vt* **-raged; -raging** : dejar en un garaje
garb ['gɑrb] *n* : vestido *m*
garbage ['gɑrbɪdʒ] *n* : basura *f* — **garbage can** *n* : cubo *m* de la basura
garble ['gɑrbəl] *vt* **-bled; -bling** : tergiversar — **garbled** ['gɑrbəld] *adj* : confuso, incomprensible
garden [gə'rɑʒ] *n* : jardín *m* — *vi* : trabajar en el jardín — **gardener** ['gɑrdənər] *n* : jardinero *m*, -ra *f* — **gardening** ['gɑrdənɪŋ] *n* : jardinería *f*

gargle ['gɑrgəl] *vi* **-gled; -gling** : hacer gárgaras
garish ['gærɪʃ] *adj* : chillón
garland ['gɑrlənd] *n* : guirnalda *f*
garlic ['gɑrlɪk] *n* : ajo *m*
garment ['gɑrmənt] *n* : prenda *f*
garnish ['gɑrnɪʃ] *vt* : guarnecer — **~** *n* : adorno *m*, guarnición *f*
garret ['gærət] *n* : buhardilla *f*
garrison ['gærəsən] *n* : guarnición *f*
garrulous ['gærələs] *adj* : charlatán, parlanchín
garter ['gɑrtər] *n* : liga *f*
gas ['gæs] *n, pl* **gases** ['gæsəz] **1** : gas *m* **2** GASOLINE : gasolina *f* — **~** *v* **gassed; gassing** *vt* : asfixiar con gas — *vi* **~ up** : llenar el tanque con gasolina
gash ['gæʃ] *n* : tajo *m* — **~** *vt* : hacer un tajo en, cortar
gasket ['gæskət] *n* : junta *f*
gasoline ['gæsə,liːn, ,gæsə'-] *n* : gasolina *f*
gasp ['gæsp] *vi* **1** : dar un grito ahogado **2** PANT : jadear — **~** *n* : grito *m* ahogado
gas station *n* : gasolinera *f*
gastric ['gæstrɪk] *adj* : gástrico
gastronomy [gæs'trɑnəmi] *n* : gastronomía *f*
gate ['geɪt] *n* **1** DOOR : puerta *f* **2** BARRIER : barrera *f* — **gateway** ['geɪt,weɪ] *n* : puerta *f*
gather ['gæðər] *vt* **1** ASSEMBLE : reunir **2** COLLECT : recoger **3** CONCLUDE : deducir **4** : fruncir (una tela) **5** **~ speed** : acelerar — *vi* : reunirse (dícese de personas), acumularse (dícese de cosas) — **gathering** ['gæðərɪŋ] *n* : reunión *f*
gaudy ['gɔdi] *adj* **gaudier; -est** : chillón, llamativo
gauge ['geɪdʒ] *n* **1** INDICATOR : indicador *m* **2** CALIBER : calibre *m* — **~** *vt* **gauged; gauging 1** MEASURE : medir **2** ESTIMATE : calcular, evaluar
gaunt ['gɔnt] *adj* : demacrado, descarnado
gauze ['gɔz] *n* : gasa *f*
gave → **give**
gawky ['gɔki] *adj* **gawkier; -est** : desgarbado
gay ['geɪ] *adj* **1** : alegre **2** HOMOSEXUAL : gay, homosexual
gaze ['geɪz] *vi* **gazed; gazing** : mirar (fijamente) — **~** *n* : mirada *f*
gazelle [gə'zel] *n* : gacela *f*
gazette [gə'zet] *n* : gaceta *f*
gear ['gɪr] *n* **1** EQUIPMENT : equipo *m* **2** POSSESSIONS : efectos *mpl* personales

3 : marcha *f* (de un vehículo) **4** *or* ~ **wheel** : rueda *f* dentada — ~ *vt* : orientar, adaptar — *vi* ~ **up** : prepararse — **gearshift** ['gɪr,ʃɪft] *n* : palanca *f* de cambio, palanca *f* de velocidades *Lat*

geese → **goose**

gelatin ['dʒelətən] *n* : gelatina *f*

gem ['dʒɛm] *n* : gema *f*, piedra *f* preciosa — **gemstone** ['dʒɛm,sto:n] *n* : piedra *f* preciosa

gender ['dʒɛndər] *n* **1** SEX : sexo *m* **2** : género *m* (en la gramática)

gene ['dʒi:n] *n* : gen *m*, gene *m*

genealogy [,dʒi:ni'alədʒi, ,dʒe-, -'æ-] *n*, *pl* **-gies** : genealogía *f*

general ['dʒɛnrəl, 'dʒɛnə-] *adj* : general — ~ *n* **1** : general *mf* (militar) **2 in** ~ : en general, por lo general — **generalize** ['dʒɛnrə,laɪz, 'dʒɛnərə-] *v* **-ized; -izing** : generalizar — **generally** ['dʒɛnrəli, 'dʒɛnərə-] *adv* : generalmente, en general — **general practitioner** *n* : médico *m*, -ca *f* de cabecera

generate ['dʒɛnə,reɪt] *vt* **-ated; -ating** : generar — **generation** [,dʒɛnə'reɪʃən] *n* : generación *f* — **generator** ['dʒɛnə,reɪtər] *n* : generador *m*

generous ['dʒɛnərəs] *adj* **1** : generoso **2** AMPLE : abundante — **generosity** [,dʒɛnə'rasəti] *n*, *pl* **-ties** : generosidad *f*

genetic [dʒə'nɛtɪk] *adj* : genético — **genetics** [dʒə'nɛtɪks] *n* : genética *f*

genial ['dʒi:niəl] *adj* : afable, simpático

genital ['dʒɛnət̬əl] *adj* : genital — **genitals** ['dʒɛnət̬əlz] *npl* : genitales *mpl*

genius ['dʒi:njəs] *n* : genio *m*

genocide ['dʒɛnə,saɪd] *n* : genocidio *m*

genteel [dʒɛn'ti:l] *adj* : refinado

gentle ['dʒɛnt̬əl] *adj* **-tler; -tlest 1** MILD : suave, dulce **2** LIGHT : ligero **3 a** ~ **hint** : una indirecta discreta — **gentleman** ['dʒɛnt̬əlmən] *n*, *pl* **-men** [-mən, -,mɛn] **1** MAN : caballero *m*, señor *m* **2 a perfect** ~ : un perfecto caballero — **gentleness** ['dʒɛnt̬əlnəs] *n* : delicadeza *f*, ternura *f*

genuine ['dʒɛnjuwən] *adj* **1** AUTHENTIC : verdadero, auténtico **2** SINCERE : sincero

geography [dʒi'agrəfi] *n*, *pl* **-phies** : geografía *f* — **geographic** [,dʒi:ə'græfɪk] *or* **geographical** [-fɪkəl] *adj* : geográfico

geology [dʒi'alədʒi] *n* : geología *f* — **geologic** [,dʒi:ə'ladʒɪk] *or* **geological** [-dʒɪkəl] *adj* : geológico

geometry [dʒi'amətri] *n*, *pl* **-tries** : geometría *f* — **geometric** [,dʒi:ə'mɛtrɪk] *or* **geometrical** [-trɪkəl] *adj* : geométrico

geranium [dʒə'reɪniəm] *n* : geranio *m*

geriatric [,dʒɛri'ætrɪk] *adj* : geriátrico — **geriatrics** [,dʒɛri'ætrɪks] *n* : geriatría *f*

germ ['dʒərm] *n* **1** : germen *m* **2** MICROBE : microbio *m*

German ['dʒərmən] *adj* : alemán — ~ *n* : alemán *m* (idioma)

germinate ['dʒərmə,neɪt] *v* **-nated; -nating** *vi* : germinar — *vt* : hacer germinar

gestation [dʒɛ'steɪʃən] *n* : gestación *f*

gesture ['dʒɛstʃər] *n* : gesto *m* — ~ *vi* **-tured; -turing 1** : hacer gestos **2** ~ **to** : hacer señas a

get ['gɛt] *v* **got** ['gɑt]; **got** *or* **gotten** ['gɑtən]; **getting** *vt* **1** OBTAIN : conseguir, obtener **2** RECEIVE : recibir **3** EARN : ganar **4** FETCH : traer **5** CATCH : coger, agarrar *Lat* **6** UNDERSTAND : entender **7** PREPARE : preparar **8** ~ **one's hair cut** : cortarse el pelo **9** ~ **s.o. to do sth** : lograr que uno haga algo **10 have got** : tener **11 have got to** : tener que — *vi* **1** BECOME : ponerse, hacerse **2** GO, MOVE : ir **3** PROGRESS : avanzar **4** ~ **ahead** : progresar **5** ~ **at** MEAN : querer decir **6** ~ **away** : escaparse **7** ~ **away with** : salir impune de **8** ~ **back at** : desquitarse con **9** ~ **by** : arreglárselas **10** ~ **home** : llegar a casa **11** ~ **out** : salir **12** ~ **over** : reponerse de, consolarse de **13** ~ **together** : reunirse **14** ~ **up** : levantarse — **getaway** ['gɛt̬ə,weɪ] *n* : fuga *f*, huida *f* — **get-together** *n* : reunión *f*

geyser ['gaɪzər] *n* : géiser *m*

ghastly ['gæstli] *adj* **-lier; -est** : horrible, espantoso

ghetto ['gɛt̬o] *n*, *pl* **-tos** *or* **-toes** : gueto *m*

ghost ['go:st] *n* : fantasma *f*, espectro *m* — **ghostly** ['go:stli] *adv* : fantasmal

giant ['dʒaɪənt] *n* : gigante *m*, -ta *f* — ~ *adj* : gigantesco

gibberish ['dʒɪbərɪʃ] *n* : galimatías *m*, jerigonza *f*

gibe ['dʒaɪb] *vi* **gibed; gibing** ~ **at** : mofarse de — ~ *n* : pulla *f*, mofa *f*

giblets ['dʒɪbləts] *npl* : menudillos *mpl*

giddy ['gɪdi] *adj* **-dier; -est** : mareado, vertiginoso — **giddiness** ['gɪdinəs] *n* : vértigo *m*

gift ['gɪft] *n* **1** PRESENT : regalo *m* **2** TALENT : don *m* — **gifted** ['gɪftəd] *adj* : talentoso, de talento

gigantic [dʒaɪ'gæntɪk] *adj* : gigantesco

giggle ['gɪgəl] *vi* **-gled; -gling** : reírse tontamente — ~ *n* : risa *f* tonta

gild ['gɪld] *vt* **gilded** ['gɪldəd] *or* **gilt** ['gɪlt]; **gilding** : dorar

gill ['gɪl] *n* : agalla *f*, branquia *f*

gilt ['gɪlt] *adj* : dorado

gimmick ['gɪmɪk] *n* : truco *m*, ardid *m*

gin ['dʒɪn] *n* : ginebra *f*

ginger ['dʒɪndʒər] *n* : jengibre *m* — **ginger ale** *n* : refresco *m* de jengibre — **gingerbread** ['dʒɪndʒər,brɛd] *n* : pan *m* de jengibre — **gingerly** ['dʒɪndʒərli] *adv* : con cuidado, cautelosamente

giraffe [dʒəˈræf] *n* : jirafa *f*

girder ['gərdər] *n* : viga *f*

girdle ['gərdəl] *n* CORSET : faja *f*

girl ['gərl] *n* 1 : niña *f*, muchacha *f*, chica *f* — **girlfriend** ['gərl,frɛnd] *n* : novia *f*, amiga *f*

girth ['gərθ] *n* : circunferencia *f*

gist ['dʒɪst] *n* **get the ~ of** : comprender lo esencial de

give ['gɪv] *v* **gave** ['geɪv]; **given** ['gɪvən]; **giving** *vt* 1 : dar 2 INDICATE : señalar 3 PRESENT : presentar 4 **~ away** : regalar 5 **~ back** : devolver 6 **~ out** : repartir 7 **~ up smoking** : dejar de fumar — *vi* 1 YIELD : ceder 2 COLLAPSE : romperse 3 **~ out** : agotarse 4 **~ up** : rendirse — **~** *n* : elasticidad *f* — **given** ['gɪvən] *adj* 1 SPECIFIED : determinado 2 INCLINED : dado, inclinado — **given name** *n* : nombre *m* de pila

glacier ['gleɪʃər] *n* : glaciar *m*

glad ['glæd] *adj* **gladder; gladdest** 1 : alegre, contento 2 **be ~** : alegrarse 3 **~ to meet you!** : ¡mucho gusto! — **gladden** ['glædən] *vt* : alegrar — **gladly** ['glædli] *adv* : con mucho gusto — **gladness** ['glædnəs] *n* : alegría *f*, gozo *m*

glade ['gleɪd] *n* : claro *m*

glamor *or* **glamour** ['glæmər] *n* : atractivo *m*, encanto *m* — **glamorous** ['glæmərəs] *adj* : atractivo

glance ['glænts] *v* **glanced; glancing** 1 **~ at** : mirar, dar un vistazo a 2 **~ off** : rebotar en — **~** *n* : mirada *f*, vistazo *m*

gland ['glænd] *n* : glándula *f*

glare ['glær] *vi* **glared; glaring** 1 : brillar, relumbrar 2 **~ at** : lanzar una mirada feroz a — **~** *n* 1 : luz *f* deslumbrante 2 STARE : mirada *f* feroz — **glaring** ['glærɪŋ] *adj* 1 BRIGHT : deslumbrante 2 FLAGRANT : flagrante

glass ['glæs] *n* 1 : vidrio *m*, cristal *m* 2 **a ~ of milk** : un vaso de leche 3 **~es** *npl* SPECTACLES : anteojos *mpl*, lentes *fpl* — **~** *adj* : de vidrio — **glassware** ['glæs,wær] *n* : cristalería *f* — **glassy** ['glæsi] *adj* **glassier; -est** 1 : vítreo 2 **~ eyes** : ojos *mpl* vidriosos

glaze ['gleɪz] *vt* **glazed; glazing** 1 : poner vidrios a (una ventana, etc.) 2 : vidriar (cerámica) 3 ICE : glasear — **~** *n* 1 : vidriado *m*, barniz *m* (de cerámica) 2 ICING : glaseado *m*

gleam ['gliːm] *n* 1 : destello *m* 2 **a ~ of hope** : un rayo de esperanza — **~** *vi* : destellar, relucir

glee ['gliː] *n* : alegría *f* — **gleeful** ['gliːfəl] *adj* : lleno de alegría

glib ['glɪb] *adj* **glibber; glibbest** 1 : de mucha labia 2 **a ~ reply** : una respuesta simplista — **glibly** ['glɪbli] *adv* : con mucha labia

glide ['glaɪd] *vi* **glided; gliding** : deslizarse (en una superficie), planear (en el aire) — **glider** ['glaɪdər] *n* : planeador *m*

glimmer ['glɪmər] *vi* : brillar con luz trémula — **~** *n* : luz *f* trémula, luz *f* tenue

glimpse ['glɪmps] *vt* **glimpsed; glimpsing** : vislumbrar — **~** *n* : vislumbre *f*

glint ['glɪnt] *vi* : destellar — **~** *n* : destello *m*

glisten ['glɪsən] *vi* : brillar

glitter ['glɪtər] *vi* : relucir, brillar

gloat ['gloɪt] *vi* **~ over** : regodearse con

globe ['gloːb] *n* : globo *m* — **global** ['gloːbəl] *adj* : global, mundial

gloom ['gluːm] *n* 1 DARKNESS : oscuridad *f* 2 SADNESS : tristeza *f* — **gloomy** ['gluːmi] *adj* **gloomier; -est** 1 DARK : sombrío, tenebroso 2 DISMAL : deprimente, lúgubre 3 PESSIMISTIC : pesimista

glory ['glori] *n*, *pl* **-ries** : gloria *f* — **glorify** ['glorə,faɪ] *vt* **-fied; -fying** : glorificar — **glorious** ['gloriəs] *adj* : glorioso, espléndido

gloss ['glɔs, 'glɑs] *n* : lustre *m*, brillo *m* — **~** *vt* **~ over** : minimizar (la importancia de algo)

glossary ['glɔsəri, 'glɑ-] *n*, *pl* **-ries** : glosario *m*

glossy ['glɔsi, 'glɑ-] *adj* **glossier; -est** : lustroso, brillante

glove ['glʌv] *n* : guante *m*

glow ['gloː] *vi* 1 : brillar, resplandecer 2 **~ with health** : rebosar de salud — **~** *n* : resplandor *m*, brillo *m*

glue ['gluː] *n* : pegamento *m*, cola *f* — **~** *vt* **glued; gluing** *or* **glueing** : pegar

glum ['glʌm] *adj* **glummer; glummest** : sombrío, triste

glut ['glʌt] *n* : superabundancia *f*, exceso *m*

glutton ['glʌtən] *n* : glotón *m*, -tona *f* — **gluttonous** ['glʌtənəs] *adj* : glotón — **gluttony** ['glʌtəni] *n, pl* **-tonies** : glotonería *f*

gnarled ['nɑrld] *adj* : nudoso

gnash ['næʃ] *vt* ~ **one's teeth** : hacer rechinar los dientes

gnat ['næt] *n* : jején *m*

gnaw ['nɔ] *vt* : roer

go ['goː] *v* **went** ['wɛnt]; **gone** ['gɔn, 'gɑn]; **going**; **goes** ['goːz] *vi* 1 : ir 2 LEAVE : irse, salir 3 EXTEND : ir, extenderse 4 SELL : venderse 5 FUNCTION : funcionar, marchar 6 DISAPPEAR : desaparecer 7 ~ **back on one's word** : faltar a su palabra 8 ~ **crazy** : volverse loco 9 ~ **for** LIKE : gustar 10 ~ **off** EXPLODE : estallar 11 ~ **with** MATCH : armonizar con 12 ~ **without** : pasar sin — *v aux* **be going to** : ir a — ~ *n, pl* **goes** 1 **be on the** ~ : no parar 2 **have a** ~ **at** : intentar

goad ['goːd] *vt* : aguijonear (un animal), incitar (a una persona)

goal ['goːl] *n* 1 AIM : meta *m*, objetivo *m* 2 : gol *m* (en deportes) — **goalkeeper** ['goːlˌkiːpər] *or* **goalie** ['goːli] *n* : portero *m*, -ra *f*; arquero *m*, -ra *f*

goat ['goːt] *n* : cabra *f*

goatee [goːtiː] *n* : barba *f* de chivo

gobble ['gɑbəl] *vt* **-bled; -bling** *or* ~ **up** : engullir

goblet ['gɑblət] *n* : copa *f*

goblin ['gɑblən] *n* : duende *m*

god ['gɑd, 'gɔd] *n* 1 : dios *m* 2 **God** : Dios *m* — **goddess** ['gɑdəs, 'gɔ-] *n* : diosa *f* — **godchild** ['gɑdˌtʃaɪld, 'gɔd-] *n, pl* **-children** : ahijado *m*, -da *f* — **godfather** ['gɑdˌfɑðər, 'gɔd-] *n* : padrino *m* — **godmother** ['gɑdˌmʌðər, 'gɔd-] *n* : madrina *f* — **godparents** ['gɑdˌpærənt, 'gɔd-] *npl* : padrinos *mpl* — **godsend** ['gɑdˌsɛnd, 'gɔd-] *n* : bendición *f* (del cielo)

goes → **go**

goggles ['gɑgəlz] *npl* : gafas *fpl* (protectoras), anteojos *mpl*

goings-on [ˌgoːɪŋzˈɑn, -ˈɔn] *npl* : sucesos *mpl*

gold ['goːld] *n* : oro *m* — **golden** ['goːldən] *adj* 1 : (hecho) de oro 2 : dorado, de color oro — **goldfish** ['goːldˌfɪʃ] *n* : pez *m* de colores — **goldsmith** ['goːldˌsmɪθ] *n* : orfebre *mf*

golf ['gɑlf, 'gɔlf] *n* : golf *m* — ~ *vi* : jugar (al) golf — **golf ball** *n* : pelota *f* de golf — **golf course** *n* : campo *m* de golf — **golfer** ['gɑlfər, 'gɔl-] *n* : golfista *mf*

gone ['gɔn] *adj* 1 : ido, pasado 2 DEAD : muerto 3 LOST : desaparecido

good ['gʊd] *adj* **better** ['bɛt̬ər]; **best** ['bɛst] 1 : bueno 2 KIND : amable 3 ~ **afternoon (evening)** : buenas tardes 4 **be** ~ **at** : tener facilidad para 5 **feel** ~ : sentirse bien 6 ~ **for a cold** : beneficioso para los resfriados 7 **have a** ~ **time** : divertirse 8 ~ **morning** : buenos días 9 ~ **night** : buenas noches — ~ *n* 1 : bien *m* 2 GOODNESS : bondad *f* 3 ~ **s** *npl* PROPERTY : bienes *mpl* 4 ~ **s** *npl* WARES : mercancías *fpl*, mercaderías *fpl* 5 **for** ~ : para siempre — ~ *adv* : bien — **good-bye** *or* **good-by** ['gʊdˈbaɪ] *n* : adiós *m* — **Good Friday** *n* : Viernes *m* Santo — **good-looking** ['gʊdˈlʊkɪŋ] *adj* : bello, guapo — **goodness** ['gʊdnəs] *n* 1 : bondad *f* 2 **thank** ~ ! : ¡gracias a Dios!, ¡menos mal! — **goodwill** [ˌgʊdˈwɪl] *n* : buena voluntad *f* — **goody** ['gʊdi] *n, pl* **goodies** : golosina *f*

gooey ['guːi] *adj* **gooier; gooiest** : pegajoso

goof *n* ['guːf] : pifia *f fam* — ~ *vi* 1 *or* ~ **up** : cometer un error 2 ~ **around** : hacer tonterías

goose ['guːs] *n, pl* **geese** ['giːs] : ganso *m*, -sa *f*; oca *f* — **goose bumps** *or* **goose pimples** *npl* : carne *f* de gallina

gopher ['goːfər] *n* : taltuza *f*

gore[1] ['gor] *n* BLOOD : sangre *f*

gore[2] *vt* **gored; goring** : cornear

gorge ['gɔrdʒ] *n* RAVINE : cañón *m* — *vt* **gorged; gorging** ~ **oneself** : hartarse

gorgeous ['gɔrdʒəs] *adj* : magnífico, espléndido

gorilla [gəˈrɪlə] *n* : gorila *m*

gory ['gori] *adj* **gorier; -est** : sangriento

gospel ['gɑspəl] *n* 1 : evangelio *m* 2 **the Gospel** : el Evangelio

gossip ['gɑsɪp] *n* 1 : chismoso *m*, -sa *f* (persona) 2 RUMOR : chisme *m* — ~ *vi* : chismear, contar chismes — **gossipy** ['gɑsɪpi] *adj* : chismoso

got → **get**

Gothic ['gɑθɪk] *adj* : gótico

gotten → **get**

gourmet ['gʊrˌmeɪ, gʊrˈmeɪ] *n* : gastrónomo *m*, -ma *f*

gout ['gaʊt] *n* : gota *f*

govern ['gʌvərn] *v* : gobernar — **governess** ['gʌvərnəs] *n* : institutriz *f* — **government** ['gʌvərmənt] *n* : gobierno *m* — **governor** ['gʌvənər, 'gʌvərnər] *n* : gobernador *m*, -dora *f*

gown ['gaʊn] *n* **1** : vestido *m* **2** : toga *f* (de magistrados, etc.)

grab ['græb] *v* **grabbed; grabbing** *vt* : agarrar, arrebatar

grace ['greɪs] *n* **1** : gracia *f* **2 say ~** : bendecir la mesa — **~** *vt* **graced; gracing 1** HONOR : honrar **2** ADORN : adornar — **graceful** ['greɪsfəl] *adj* : lleno de gracia, grácil — **gracious** ['greɪʃəs] *adj* : cortés, gentil

grade ['greɪd] *n* **1** QUALITY : calidad *f* **2** RANK : grado *m*, rango *m* (militar) **3** YEAR : grado *m*, año *m* (a la escuela) **4** MARK : nota *f* **5** SLOPE : cuesta *f* — **~** *vt* **graded; grading 1** CLASSIFY : clasificar **2** MARK : calificar (exámenes, etc.) — **grade school → elementary school**

gradual ['grædʒʊəl] *adj* : gradual — **gradually** ['grædʒʊəli, 'grædʒəli] *adv* : gradualmente, poco a poco

graduate ['grædʒʊət] *n* : licenciado *m*, -da *f* (de la universidad), bachiller *mf* (de la escuela secundaria) — **~** ['grædʒʊˌeɪt] *v* **-ated; -ating** *vi* : graduarse, licenciarse — *vt* CALIBRATE : graduar — **graduation** [ˌgrædʒʊˈeɪʃən] *n* : graduación *f*

graffiti [grəˈfiːti, græ-] *npl* : graffiti *mpl*

graft ['græft] *n* : injerto *m* — **~** *vt* : injertar

grain ['greɪn] *n* **1** : grano *m* **2** CEREALS : cereales *mpl* **3** : veta *f*, vena *f* (de madera)

gram ['græm] *n* : gramo *m*

grammar ['græmər] *n* : gramática *f* — **grammar school → elementary school**

grand ['grænd] *adj* **1** : magnífico, espléndido **2** FABULOUS, GREAT : fabuloso, estupendo — **grandchild** ['grændˌtʃaɪld] *n, pl* **-children** : nieto *m*, -ta *f* — **granddaughter** ['grændˌdɔtər] *n* : nieta *f* — **grandeur** ['grændʒər] *n* : grandiosidad *f* — **grandfather** ['grændˌfɑðər] *n* : abuelo *m* — **grandiose** ['grændiˌoːs, ˌgrændiˈ-] *adj* : grandioso — **grandmother** ['grændˌmʌðər] *n* : abuela *f* — **grandparents** ['grændˌpærənt] *npl* : abuelos *mpl* — **grandson** ['grændˌsʌn] *n* : nieto *m* — **grandstand** ['grændˌstænd] *n* : tribuna *f*

granite ['grænɪt] *n* : granito *m*

grant ['grænt] *vt* **1** : conceder **2** ADMIT : reconocer, admitir **3 take for granted** : dar (algo) por sentado — **~** *n* **1** SUBSIDY : subvención *f* **2** SCHOLARSHIP : beca *f*

grape ['greɪp] *n* : uva *f*

grapefruit ['greɪpˌfruːt] *n* : toronja *f*, pomelo *m*

grapevine ['greɪpˌvaɪn] *n* **1** : vid *f*, parra *f* **2 I heard it through the ~** : me lo dijo un pajarito *fam*

graph ['græf] *n* : gráfica *f*, gráfico *m* — **graphic** ['græfɪk] *adj* : gráfico

grapple ['græpəl] *vi* **-pled; -pling ~ with** : forcejear con (una persona), luchar con (un problema)

grasp ['græsp] *vt* **1** : agarrar **2** UNDERSTAND : comprender, captar — **~** *n* **1** : agarre *m* **2** UNDERSTANDING : comprensión *f* **3** REACH : alcance *m*

grass ['græs] *n* **1** : hierba *f* (planta) **2** LAWN : césped *m*, pasto *m* *Lat* — **grasshopper** ['græsˌhɑpər] *n* : saltamontes *m* — **grassy; -est** : cubierto de hierba

grate¹ ['greɪt] *v* **grated; -ing** *vt* **1** : rallar (en cocina) **2 ~ one's teeth** : hacer rechinar los dientes — *vi* RASP : chirriar

grate² *n* GRATING : reja *f*, rejilla *f*

grateful ['greɪtfəl] *adj* : agradecido — **gratefully** ['greɪtfəli] *adv* : con agradecimiento — **gratefulness** ['greɪtfəlnəs] *n* : gratitud *f*, agradecimiento *m*

grater ['greɪtər] *n* : rallador *m*

gratify ['grætəˌfaɪ] *vt* **-fied; -fying 1** PLEASE : complacer **2** SATISFY : satisfacer

grating ['greɪtɪŋ] *n* : reja *f*, rejilla *f*

gratitude ['grætəˌtuːd, -ˌtjuːd] *n* : gratitud *f*

gratuitous [grəˈtuːətəs] *adj* : gratuito

grave¹ ['greɪv] *n* : tumba *f*, sepultura *f*

grave² *adj* **graver; -est** : grave

gravel ['grævəl] *n* : grava *f*, gravilla *f*

gravestone ['greɪvˌstoːn] *n* : lápida *f* — **graveyard** ['greɪvˌjɑrd] *n* : cementerio *m*

gravity ['grævəti] *n, pl* **-ties** : gravedad *f*

gravy ['greɪvi] *n, pl* **-vies** : salsa *f* (preparada con jugo de carne)

gray ['greɪ] *adj* **1** : gris **2 ~ hair** : pelo *m* canoso — **~** *n* : gris *m* — **~** *vi* **turn ~** : encanecer, ponerse gris

graze¹ ['greɪz] *vi* **grazed; grazing** : pastar, pacer

graze² *vt* **1** TOUCH : rozar **2** SCRATCH : rasguñarse

grease ['griːs] *n* : grasa *f* — **~** ['griːs, 'griːz] *vt* **greased; greasing** : engrasar — **greasy** ['griːsi, -zi] *adj* **greasier; -est 1** : grasiento **2** OILY : graso, grasoso

great ['greɪt] *adj* **1** : grande **2** FANTASTIC : estupendo, fabuloso — **great-grandchild** [ˌgreɪtˈgrændˌtʃaɪld] *n, pl*

-children [-ˌtʃɪldrən] : bisnieto *m*, **-ta** *f* — **great-grandfather** [ˌɡreɪtˈɡrænd-ˌfɑðər] *n* : bisabuelo *m* — **great-grandmother** [ˌɡreɪtˈɡrændˌmʌðər] *n* : bisabuela *f* — **greatly** [ˈɡreɪtli] *adv* 1 MUCH : mucho 2 VERY : muy — **greatness** [ˈɡreɪtnəs] *n* : grandeza *f*

greed [ˈɡriːd] *n* 1 : codicia *f*, avaricia *f* 2 GLUTTONY : glotonería *f* — **greedily** [ˈɡriːdəli] *adv* : con avaricia — **greedy** [ˈɡriːdi] *adj* **greedier; -est** 1 : codicioso, avaro 2 GLUTTONOUS : glotón

Greek [ˈɡriːk] *adj* : griego — ~ *n* : griego *m* (idioma)

green [ˈɡriːn] *adj* 1 : verde 2 INEXPERIENCED : novato — ~ *n* 1 : verde *m* (color) 2 ~**s** *npl* : verduras *fpl* — **greenery** [ˈɡriːnəri] *n, pl* **-eries** : vegetación *f* — **greenhouse** [ˈɡriːnˌhaus] *n* : invernadero *m*

greet [ˈɡriːt] *vt* 1 : saludar 2 WELCOME : recibir — **greeting** [ˈɡriːtɪŋ] *n* 1 : saludo *m* 2 ~ *npl* REGARDS : saludos *mpl*, recuerdos *mpl*

gregarious [ɡrɪˈɡæriəs] *adj* : sociable

grenade [ɡrəˈneɪd] *n* : granada *f*

grew → **grow**

grey → **gray**

greyhound [ˈɡreɪˌhaund] *n* : galgo *m*

grid [ˈɡrɪd] *n* 1 GRATING : rejilla *f* 2 NETWORK : red *f* 3 : cuadriculado *m* (de un mapa)

griddle [ˈɡrɪdəl] *n* : plancha *f*

grief [ˈɡriːf] *n* : pena *f*, pesar *m* — **grievance** [ˈɡriːvəns] *n* : queja *f* — **grieve** [ˈɡriːv] *v* **grieved; grieving** *vt* : entristecer — *vi* ~ **for** : llorar (a), lamentar — **grievous** [ˈɡriːvəs] *adj* : grave, doloroso

grill [ˈɡrɪl] *vt* 1 : asar a la parrilla 2 INTERROGATE : interrogar — ~ *n* : parrilla *f* (para cocinar) — **grille** *or* **grill** [ˈɡrɪl] GRATING *n* : reja *f*, rejilla *f*

grim [ˈɡrɪm] *adj* **grimmer; grimmest** 1 STERN : severo 2 GLOOMY : sombrío

grimace [ˈɡrɪməs, ɡrɪˈmeɪs] *n* : mueca *f* — ~ *vi* **-maced; -macing** : hacer muecas

grime [ˈɡraɪm] *n* : mugre *f*, suciedad *f* — **grimy** [ˈɡraɪmi] *adj* **grimier; -est** : mugriento, sucio

grin [ˈɡrɪn] *vi* **grinned; grinning** : sonreír (abiertamente) — ~ *n* : sonrisa *f* (abierta)

grind [ˈɡraɪnd] *v* **ground** [ˈɡraund]; **grinding** *vt* 1 : moler (el café, etc.) 2 SHARPEN : afilar 3 ~ **one's teeth** : rechinar los dientes — *vi* : rechinar — ~ *n* **the daily** ~ : la rutina diaria — **grinder** [ˈɡraɪndər] *n* : molinillo *m*

grip [ˈɡrɪp] *vt* **gripped; gripping** 1 : agarrar, asir 2 INTEREST : captar el interés de — ~ *n* 1 GRASP : agarre *m* 2 CONTROL : control *m*, dominio *m* 3 HANDLE : empuñadura *f* 4 **come to** ~**s with** : llegar a entender de

gripe [ˈɡraɪp] *vi* **griped; griping** : quejarse — ~ *n* : queja *f*

grisly [ˈɡrɪzli] *adj* **-lier; -est** : espeluznante, horrible

gristle [ˈɡrɪsəl] *n* : cartílago *m*

grit [ˈɡrɪt] *n* 1 : arena *f*, grava *f* 2 GUTS : agallas *fpl fam* 3 ~**s** *npl* : sémola *f* de maíz — ~ *vt* **gritted; gritting** ~ **one's teeth** : acorazarse

groan [ˈɡroːn] *vi* : gemir — ~ *n* : gemido *m*

grocery [ˈɡroːsəri, -ʃəri] *n, pl* **-ceries** 1 *or* ~ **store** : tienda *f* de comestibles, tienda *f* de abarrotes *Lat* 2 **groceries** *npl* : comestibles *mpl*, abarrotes *mpl* *Lat* — **grocer** [ˈɡroːsər] *n* : tendero *m*, -ra *f*

groggy [ˈɡrɑɡi] *adj* **-gier; -est** : atontado, grogui *fam*

groin [ˈɡrɔɪn] *n* : ingle *f*

groom [ˈɡruːm, ˈɡrʊm] *n* BRIDEGROOM : novio *m* — ~ *vt* 1 : almohazar (un animal) 2 PREPARE : preparar

groove [ˈɡruːv] *n* : ranura *f*, surco *m*

grope [ˈɡroːp] *vi* **groped; groping** 1 : andar a tientas 2 ~ **for:** buscar a tientas

gross [ˈɡroːs] *adj* 1 SERIOUS : grave 2 OBESE : obeso 3 TOTAL : bruto 4 VULGAR : grosero, basto — ~ **income** : ingresos *mpl* brutos 2 *pl* ~ : gruesa *f* (12 docenas) — **grossly** [ˈɡroːsli] *adv* 1 EXTREMELY : enormemente 2 CRUDELY : groseramente

grotesque [ɡroːˈtɛsk] *adj* : grotesco

grouch [ˈɡraʊtʃ] *n* : gruñón *m*, -ñona *f fam* — **grouchy** [ˈɡraʊtʃi] *adj* **grouchier; -est** : gruñón *fam*

ground[1] [ˈɡraund] → **grind**

ground[2] *n* 1 : suelo *m*, tierra *f* 2 *or* ~**s** LAND : terreno *m* 3 ~**s** REASON : razón *f*, motivos *mpl* 4 ~**s** DREGS : pozo *m* (de café) — ~ *vt* 1 BASE : fundar, basar 2 : conectar a tierra (un aparato eléctrico) 3 : restringir (un avión o un piloto) a la tierra — **groundhog** [ˈɡraundˌhɑɡ] *n* : marmota *f* (de América) — **groundless** [ˈɡraundləs] *adj* : infundado — **groundwork** [ˈɡraundˌwərk] *n* : trabajo *m* preparatorio

group [ˈɡruːp] *n* : grupo *m* — ~ *vt* : agrupar — *vi or* ~ **together** : agruparse

grove [ˈɡroːv] *n* : arboleda *f*

grovel ['grɑvəl, 'grʌ-] *vi* **-eled** *or* **-elled;** **-eling** *or* **-elling** : arrastrarse, humillarse

grow ['groː] *v* **grew** ['gruː]; **grown** ['groːn]; **growing** *vi* **1** : crecer **2** INCREASE : aumentar **3** BECOME : volverse, ponerse **4** ~ **dark** : oscurecerse **5** ~ **up** : hacerse mayor — *vt* **1** CULTIVATE : cultivar **2** : dejarse crecer (el pelo, etc.) — **grower** ['groːər] *n* : cultivador *m*, -dora *f*

growl ['grɑʊl] *vi* : gruñir — ~ *n* : gruñido *m*

grown-up ['groːnˌəp] *adj* : mayor — ~ *n* : persona *f* mayor

growth ['groːθ] *n* **1** : crecimiento *m* **2** INCREASE : aumento *m* **3** DEVELOPMENT : desarrollo *m* **4** TUMOR : tumor *m*

grub ['grʌb] *n* **1** LARVA : larva *f* **2** FOOD : comida *f*

grubby ['grʌbi] *adj* **grubbier; -est** : mugriento, sucio

grudge ['grʌdʒ] *vt* **grudged; grudging** : dar de mala gana — ~ *n* **hold a** ~ : guardar rencor

grueling *or* **gruelling** ['gruːlɪŋ, 'gruːə-] *adj* : extenuante, agotador

gruesome ['gruːsəm] *adj* : horripilante

gruff ['grʌf] *adj* **1** BRUSQUE : brusco **2** HOARSE : bronco

grumble ['grʌmbəl] *vi* **-bled; -bling** : refunfuñar, rezongar

grumpy ['grʌmpi] *adj* **grumpier; -est** : malhumorado, gruñón *fam*

grunt ['grʌnt] *vi* : gruñir — ~ *n* : gruñido *m*

guarantee [ˌgærən'tiː] *n* : garantía *f* — ~ *vt* **-teed; -teeing** : garantizar

guard ['gɑrd] *n* **1** : guardia *f* **2** PRECAUTION : protección *f* — ~ *vt* : proteger, vigilar — *vi* ~ **against** : protegerse contra — **guardian** ['gɑrdiən] *n* **1** : tutor *m*, -tora *f* (de niños) **2** PROTECTOR : guardián *m*, -diana *f*

guava ['gwɑvə] *n* : guayaba *f*

guerrilla *or* **guerilla** [gə'rɪlə] *n* **1** : guerrillero *m*, -ra *f* **2** ~ **warfare** : guerra *f* de guerrillas

guess ['gɛs] *vt* **1** : adivinar **2** SUPPOSE : suponer, creer — *vi* ~ **at** : adivinar — ~ *n* : conjetura *f*, suposición *f*

guest ['gɛst] *n* **1** : invitado *m*, -da *f* **2** : huésped *mf* (a un hotel)

guide ['gaɪd] *n* : guía *mf* (persona), guía *f* (libro, etc.) — ~ *vt* **guided; guiding** : guiar — **guidance** ['gaɪdənts] *n* : orientación *f* — **guidebook** ['gaɪdˌbʊk] *n* : guía *f* — **guideline** ['gaɪdˌlaɪn] *n* : pauta *f*, directriz *f*

guild ['gɪld] *n* : gremio *m*

guile ['gaɪl] *n* : astucia *f*

guilt ['gɪlt] *n* : culpa *f*, culpabilidad *f* — **guilty** ['gɪlti] *adj* **guiltier; -est** : culpable

guinea pig ['gɪni-] *n* : conejillo *m* de Indias, cobaya *f*

guise ['gaɪz] *n* : apariencia *f*

guitar [gə'tɑr, gɪ-] *n* : guitarra *f*

gulf ['gʌlf] *n* **1** : golfo *m* **2** ABYSS : abismo *m*

gull ['gʌl] *n* : gaviota *f*

gullet ['gʌlət] *n* **1** THROAT : garganta *f* **2** ESOPHAGUS : esófago *m*

gullible ['gʌləbəl] *adj* : crédulo

gully ['gʌli] *n, pl* **-lies** : barranco *m*

gulp ['gʌlp] *vt or* ~ **down** : tragarse, engullir — *vi* : tragar saliva — ~ *n* : trago *m*

gum¹ ['gʌm] *n* : encía *f* (de la boca)

gum² *n* **1** : resina *f* (de plantas) **2** CHEWING GUM : goma *f* de mascar, chicle *m*

gumption ['gʌmpʃən] *n* : iniciativa *f*, agallas *fpl fam*

gun ['gʌn] *n* **1** FIREARM : arma *f* de fuego **2** *or* **spray** ~ : pistola *f* **3** → **cannon, pistol, revolver, rifle** — ~ *vt* **gunned; gunning 1** *or* ~ **down** : matar a tiros, asesinar **2** ~ **the engine** : acelerar (el motor) — **gunboat** ['gʌnˌboːt] *n* : cañonero *m* — **gunfire** ['gʌnˌfaɪr] *n* : disparos *mpl* — **gunman** ['gʌnmən] *n, pl* **-men** [-mən, -ˌmɛn] : pistolero *m*, gatillero *m Lat* — **gunpowder** ['gʌnˌpaʊdər] *n* : pólvora *f* — **gunshot** ['gʌnˌʃɑt] *n* : disparo *m*, tiro *m*

gurgle ['gərgəl] *vi* **-gled; -gling 1** : borbotar, gorgotear **2** : gorjear (dícese de un niño)

gush ['gʌʃ] *vi* **1** SPOUT : salir a chorros **2** ~ **with praise** : deshacerse en elogios

gust ['gʌst] *n* : ráfaga *f*

gusto ['gʌsˌtoː] *n, pl* **gustoes** : entusiasmo *m*

gusty ['gʌsti] *adj* **gustier; -est** : racheado, ventoso

gut ['gʌt] *n* **1** : intestino *m* **2** ~**s** *npl* INNARDS : tripas *fpl* **3** ~**s** *npl* COURAGE : agallas *fpl fam* — ~ *vt* **gutted; gutting 1** EVISCERATE : destripar (un pollo, etc.), limpiar (un pescado) **2** : destruir el interior de (un edificio)

gutter ['gʌtər] *n* : canaleta *f* (de un techo), cuneta *f* (de una calle)

guy ['gaɪ] *n* : tipo *m fam*

guzzle ['gʌzəl] *vt* **-zled; -zling** : chupar *fam*, tragar

gym ['dʒɪm] *or* **gymnasium** [dʒɪm-'neɪziəm, -ʒəm] *n, pl* **-siums** *or* **-sia** [-ziːə, -ʒə] : gimnasio *m* — **gymnast**

H

h ['eɪtʃ] *n, pl* **h's** *or* **hs** ['eɪtʃəz] : h *f*, octava letra del alfabeto inglés

habit ['hæbɪt] *n* **1** CUSTOM : hábito *m*, costumbre *f* **2** : hábito *m* (religioso)

habitat ['hæbɪ,tæt] *n* : hábitat *m*

habitual [hə'bɪtʃʊəl] *adj* **1** CUSTOMARY : habitual **2** INVETERATE : empedernido → **have**

hack¹ ['hæk] *n* **1** : caballo *m* de alquiler **2** *or* ~ **writer** : escritorzuelo *m*, -la *f*

hack² *vt* : cortar — *vi or* ~ **into** : piratear (un sistema informático)

hackneyed ['hæknid] *adj* : manido, trillado

hacksaw ['hæk,sɔ] *n* : sierra *f* para metales

had → **have**

haddock ['hædək] *ns & pl* : eglefino *m*

hadn't ['hædənt] (*contraction of* **had not**) → **have**

hag ['hæg] *n* : bruja *f*

haggard ['hægərd] *adj* : demacrado

haggle ['hægəl] *vi* -**gled**; -**gling** : regatear

hail¹ ['heɪl] *vt* **1** GREET : saludar **2** : llamar (un taxi)

hail² *n* : granizo *m* (en meteorología) — ~ *vi* : granizar — **hailstone** ['heɪl,stoʊn] *n* : piedra *f* de granizo

hair ['hær] *n* **1** : pelo *m*, cabello *m* **2** : vello *m* (en las piernas, etc.) — **hairbrush** ['hær,brʌʃ] *n* : cepillo *m* (para el pelo) — **haircut** ['hær,kʌt] *n* **1** : corte *m* de pelo **2 get a** ~ : cortarse el pelo — **hairdo** ['hær,du:] *n, pl* -**dos** : peinado *m* — **hairdresser** ['hær,drɛsər] *n* : peluquero *m*, -ra *f* — **hairless** ['hærləs] *adj* : sin pelo, calvo — **hairpin** ['hær,pɪn] *n* : horquilla *f* — **hair-raising** ['hær,reɪzɪŋ] *adj* : espeluznante — **hairstyle** ['hær,staɪl] → **hairdo** — **hair spray** *n* : laca *f* (para el pelo) — **hairy** ['hæri] *adj* **hairier**; -**est** : peludo, velludo

hale ['heɪl] *adj* : saludable, robusto

half ['hæf, 'haf] *n, pl* **halves** ['hævz, 'havz] **1** : mitad *f* **2** *or* **halftime** : tiempo *m* (en deportes) **3 in** ~ : por la mitad — ~ *adj* **1** : medio **2** ~ **an hour** : una media hora — ~ *adv* : medio — **half brother** *n* : medio hermano *m*, hermanastro *m* — **halfhearted** ['hæf'hɑrtəd] *adj* : sin ánimo, poco entusiasta — **half sister** *n* : media hermana *f*, hermanastra *f* — **halfway** ['hæf'weɪ] *adv* : a medio camino — ~ *adj* : medio

halibut ['hælɪbət] *ns & pl* : halibut *m*

hall ['hɔl] *n* **1** HALLWAY : corredor *m*, pasillo *m* **2** AUDITORIUM : sala *f* **3** LOBBY : vestíbulo *m* **4** DORMITORY : residencia *f* universitaria

hallmark ['hɔl,mɑrk] *n* : sello *m* (distintivo)

Halloween [,hælə'wi:n, ,hɑ-] *n* : víspera *f* de Todos los Santos

hallucination [hə,lu:sən'eɪʃən] *n* : alucinación *f*

hallway ['hɔl,weɪ] *n* **1** ENTRANCE : entrada *f* **2** CORRIDOR : corredor *m*, pasillo *m*

halo ['heɪ,loʊ] *n, pl* -**los** *or* -**loes** : aureola *f*, halo *m*

halt ['hɔlt] *n* **1 call a** ~ **to** : poner fin a **2 come to a** ~ : pararse — ~ *vi* : pararse — *vt* : parar

halve ['hæv, 'hav] *vt* **halved**; **halving 1** DIVIDE : partir por la mitad **2** REDUCE : reducir a la mitad — **halves** → **half**

ham ['hæm] *n* : jamón *m*

hamburger ['hæm,bərgər] *or* **hamburg** [-,bərg] *n* **1** : carne *f* molida **2** *or* ~ **patty** : hamburguesa *f*

hammer ['hæmər] *n* : martillo *m* — ~ *v* : martillar, martillear

hammock ['hæmək] *n* : hamaca *f*

hamper¹ ['hæmpər] *vt* : obstaculizar, dificultar

hamper² *n* : cesto *m*, canasta *f* (para ropa sucia)

hamster ['hæmpstər] *n* : hámster *m*

hand ['hænd] *n* **1** : mano *f* **2** : manecilla *f*, aguja *f* (de un reloj, etc.) **3** HANDWRITING : letra *f*, escritura *f* **4** WORKER : obrero *m*, -ra *f* **5 by** ~ : a mano **6 lend a** ~ : echar una mano **7 on** ~ : a mano, disponible **8 on the other** ~ : por otro lado — *vt* **1** : pasar, dar **2** ~ **out** : distribuir **3** ~ **over** : entregar — **handbag** ['hænd,bæg] *n* : cartera *f Lat*, bolso *m Spain* — **handbook** ['hænd,bʊk] *n* : manual *m* — **handcuffs** ['hænd,kʌfs] *npl* : esposas *fpl* — **handful** ['hænd,fʊl] *n* : puñado *m* — **handgun** ['hænd,gʌn] *n* : pistola *f*, revólver *m*

handicap ['hændi,kæp] *n* **1** : minusvalía *f*

(física) **2** : hándicap *m* (en deportes) — ~ *vt* **-capped; -capping 1** : asignar un handicap a (en deportes) **2** HAMPER : obstaculizar — **handicapped** ['hændi,kæpt] *adj* : minusválido

handicrafts ['hændi,kræfts] *npl* : artesanía(s) *f(pl)*

handiwork ['hændi,wərk] *n* : trabajo *m* (manual)

handkerchief ['hæŋkərtʃəf, -,tʃiːf] *n, pl* **-chiefs** : pañuelo *m*

handle ['hændəl] *n* : asa *m* (de una taza, etc.), mango *m* (de un utensilio), pomo *m* (de una puerta), tirador *m* (de un cajón) — ~ *vt* **-dled; -dling 1** TOUCH : tocar **2** MANAGE : tratar, manejar — **handlebars** ['hændəl,bɑrz] *npl* : manillar *m*, manubrio *m* Lat

handmade ['hænd,meɪd] *adj* : hecho a mano

handout ['hænd,aʊt] *n* **1** ALMS : dádiva *f*, limosna *f* **2** LEAFLET : folleto *m*

handrail ['hænd,reɪl] *n* : pasamanos *m*

handshake ['hænd,ʃeɪk] *n* : apretón *m* de manos

handsome ['hæntsəm] *adj* **-somer; -est 1** ATTRACTIVE : apuesto, guapo **2** GENEROUS : generoso **3** SIZABLE : considerable

handwriting ['hænd,raɪtɪŋ] *n* : letra *f*, escritura *f* — **handwritten** ['hænd,rɪtən] *adj* : escrito a mano

handy ['hændi] *adj* **handier; -est 1** NEARBY : a mano **2** USEFUL : práctico, útil **3** DEFT : habilidoso — **handyman** ['hændi,mən] *n, pl* **-men** [-mən, -,mɛn] : hombre *m* habilidoso

hang ['hæŋ] *v* **hung** ['hʌŋ]; **hanging** *vt* **1** : colgar **2** (*past tense often* **hanged**) EXECUTE : ahorcar **3** ~ **one's head** : bajar la cabeza — *vi* **1** : colgar, pender **2** : caer (dícese de la ropa, etc.) **3** ~ **up on s.o.** : colgar a algn — ~ *n* **1** DRAPE : caída *f* **2** **get the** ~ **of** : agarrar la onda de

hangar ['hæŋər, 'hæŋgər] *n* : hangar *m*

hanger ['hæŋər] *n* : percha *f*, gancho *m* (para ropa) Lat

hangover ['hæŋ,oːvər] *n* : resaca *f*

hanker ['hæŋkər] *vi* ~ **for** : tener ansias de — **hankering** ['hæŋkərɪŋ] *n* : ansia *f*, anhelo *m*

haphazard [hæp'hæzərd] *adj* : casual, fortuito

happen ['hæpən] *vi* **1** : pasar, suceder, ocurrir **2** ~ **to do sth** : hacer algo por casualidad **3 it so happens that...** : da la casualidad de que... — **happening** ['hæpənɪŋ] *n* : suceso *m*, acontecimiento *m*

happy ['hæpi] *adj* **-pier; -est 1** : feliz **2 be** ~ : alegrarse **3 be** ~ **with** : estar contento con **4 be** ~ **to do sth** : hacer algo con mucho gusto — **happily** ['hæpəli] *adv* : alegremente — **happiness** ['hæpinəs] *n* : felicidad *f* — **happy—go—lucky** ['hæpigo'lʌki] *adj* : despreocupado

harass [hə'ræs, 'hærəs] *vt* : acosar — **harassment** [hə'ræsmənt, 'hærəsmənt] *n* : acoso *m*

harbor *or Brit* **harbour** ['hɑrbər] *n* : puerto *m* — ~ *vt* **1** SHELTER : albergar **2** ~ **a grudge against** : guardar rencor a

hard ['hɑrd] *adj* **1** : duro **2** DIFFICULT : difícil **3 be a** ~ **worker** : ser muy trabajador **4** ~ **liquor** : bebidas *fpl* fuertes **5** ~ **water** : agua *f* dura — ~ *adv* **1** FORCEFULLY : fuerte **2 work** ~ : trabajar duro **3 take sth** ~ : tomarse algo muy mal — **harden** ['hɑrdən] *vt* : endurecer — **hardheaded** [,hɑrd'hɛdəd] *adj* : testarudo, terco — **hard—hearted** [,hɑrd'hɑrtəd] *adj* : duro de corazón — **hardly** ['hɑrdli] *adv* **1** : apenas **2** ~ **ever** : casi nunca — **hardness** ['hɑrdnəs] *n* **1** : dureza *f* **2** DIFFICULTY : dificultad *f* — **hardship** ['hɑrd,ʃɪp] *n* : dificultad *f* — **hardware** ['hɑrd,wær] *n* **1** : ferretería *f* **2** : hardware *m* (en informática) — **hardworking** ['hɑrd'wərkɪŋ] *adj* : trabajador

hardy ['hɑrdi] *adj* **-dier; -est** : fuerte (dícese de personas), resistente (dícese de las plantas)

hare ['hær] *n, pl* **hare** *or* **hares** : liebre *f*

harm ['hɑrm] *n* : daño *m* — ~ *vt* : hacer daño a (una persona), dañar (una cosa), perjudicar (la reputación de algn, etc.) — **harmful** ['hɑrmfəl] *adj* : perjudicial — **harmless** ['hɑrmləs] *adj* : inofensivo

harmonica [hɑr'mɑnɪkə] *n* : armónica *f*

harmony ['hɑrməni] *n, pl* **-nies** : armonía *f* — **harmonious** [hɑr'moːniəs] *adj* : armonioso — **harmonize** ['hɑrmə,naɪz] *v* **-nized; -nizing** : armonizar

harness ['hɑrnəs] *n* : arnés *m* — ~ *vt* **1** : enjaezar **2** UTILIZE : utilizar

harp ['hɑrp] *n* : arpa *m* — ~ *vi* ~ **on** : insistir sobre

harpoon [hɑr'puːn] *n* : arpón *m*

harpsichord ['hɑrpsɪ,kɔrd] *n* : clavicémbalo *m*

harsh ['hɑrʃ] *adj* **1** ROUGH : áspero **2** SEVERE : duro, severo **3** : fuerte (dícese de una luz), discordante (dícese de sonidos) — **harshness** ['hɑrʃnəs] *n* : severidad *f*

harvest ['hɑrvəst] *n* : cosecha *f* — ∼ *v* : cosechar

has → **have**

hash ['hæʃ] *vt* **1** CHOP : picar **2** ∼ **over** DISCUSS : discutir — ∼ *n* : picadillo *m* (comida)

hasn't ['hæzənt] (*contraction of* **has not**) → **has**

hassle ['hæsəl] *n* : problemas *mpl*, lío *m* — ∼ *vt* **-sled; -sling** : fastidiar

haste ['heɪst] *n* **1** : prisa *f*, apuro *m Lat* **2 make** ∼ : darse prisa, apurarse *Lat* — **hasten** ['heɪsən] *vt* : acelerar — *vi* : apresurarse, apurarse *Lat* — **hasty** ['heɪsti] *adj* **hastier; -est** : precipitado

hat ['hæt] *n* : sombrero *m*

hatch ['hætʃ] *n* : escotilla *f* — ∼ *vt* **1** : empollar (huevos) **2** CONCOCT : tramar — *vi* : salir del cascarón

hatchet ['hætʃət] *n* : hacha *f*

hate ['heɪt] *n* : odio *m* — ∼ *vt* **hated; hating** : odiar, aborrecer — **hateful** ['heɪtfəl] *adj* : odioso, aborrecible — **hatred** ['heɪtrəd] *n* : odio *m*

haughty ['hɔti] *adj* **-tier; -est** : altanero, altivo

haul ['hɔl] *vt* : arrastrar, jalar *Lat* — ∼ *n* **1** CATCH : redada *f* (de peces) **2** LOOT : botín *m* **3 a long** ∼ : un trayecto largo

haunch ['hɔntʃ] *n* : cadera *f* (de una persona), anca *f* (de un animal)

haunt ['hɔnt] *vt* **1** : frecuentar, rondar **2** TROUBLE : inquietar — ∼ *n* : sitio *m* predilecto — **haunted** ['hɔntəd] *adj* : embrujado

have ['hæv, *in sense 3 as an auxiliary verb usu* 'hæf] *v* **had** ['hæd]; **having; has** ['hæz, *in sense 3 as an auxiliary verb usu* 'hæs] *vt* **1** : tener **2** CONSUME : comer, tomar **3** ALLOW : permitir **4** : dar (una fiesta, etc.), convocar (una reunión) **5** ∼ **one's hair cut** : cortarse el pelo **6** ∼ **sth done** : mandar hacer algo — *v aux* **1** : haber **2** ∼ **just done sth** : acabar de hacer algo **4 you've finished, haven't you?** : has terminado, ¿no?

haven ['heɪvən] *n* : refugio *m*

havoc ['hævək] *n* : estragos *mpl*

hawk¹ ['hɔk] *n* : halcón *m*

hawk² *vt* : pregonar (mercancías)

hay ['heɪ] *n* : heno *m* — **hay fever** *n* : fiebre *f* del heno — **haystack** ['heɪ,stæk] *n* : almiar *m* — **haywire** ['heɪ,waɪr] *adj* **go** ∼ : estropearse

hazard ['hæzərd] *n* : peligro *m*, riesgo *m* — ∼ *vt* : arriesgar, aventurar — **hazardous** ['hæzərdəs] *adj* : arriesgado, peligroso

haze ['heɪz] *n* : bruma *f*, neblina *f*

hazel ['heɪzəl] *n* : color *m* avellana — **hazelnut** ['heɪzəl,nʌt] *n* : avellana *f*

hazy ['heɪzi] *adj* **hazier; -est** : nebuloso

he ['hi] *pron* : él

head ['hɛd] *n* **1** : cabeza *f* **2** END, TOP : cabeza *f* (de un clavo, etc.), cabecera *f* (de una mesa) **3** LEADER : jefe *m*, -fa *f* **4 be out of one's** ∼ : estar loco **5 come to a** ∼ : llegar a un punto crítico **6** ∼**s or tails** : cara o cruz **7 per** ∼ : por cabeza — ∼ *adj* MAIN : principal — ∼ *vt* : encabezar — *vi* : dirigirse — **headache** ['hɛd,eɪk] *n* : dolor *m* de cabeza — **headband** ['hɛd,bænd] *n* : cinta *f* del pelo — **headdress** ['hɛd,drɛs] *n* : tocado *m* — **headfirst** ['hɛd'fərst] *adv* : de cabeza — **heading** ['hɛdɪŋ] *n* : encabezamiento *m*, título *m* — **headland** ['hɛdlənd, -,lænd] *n* : cabo *m* — **headlight** ['hɛd,laɪt] *n* : faro *m* — **headline** ['hɛd,laɪn] *n* : titular *m* — **headlong** ['hɛd,lɔŋ] *adv* **1** HEADFIRST : de cabeza **2** HASTILY : precipitadamente — **headmaster** ['hɛd,mæstər] *n* : director *m* — **headmistress** ['hɛd,mɪstrəs, -'mɪs-] *n* : directora *f* — **head-on** ['hɛd'ɑn, -'ɔn] *adv & adj* : de frente — **headphones** ['hɛd,foʊnz] *npl* : auriculares *mpl*, audífonos *mpl Lat* — **headquarters** ['hɛd,kwɔrtərz] *ns & pl* : oficina *f* central (de una compañía), cuartel *m* general (de los militares) — **head start** *n* : ventaja *f* — **headstrong** ['hɛd'strɔŋ] *adj* : testarudo, obstinado — **headwaiter** ['hɛd'weɪtər] *n* : jefe *m*, -fa *f* de comedor — **headway** ['hɛd,weɪ] *n* **1** : progreso *m* **2 make** ∼ : avanzar — **heady** ['hɛdi] *adj* **headier; -est** : embriagador

heal ['hil] *vt* : curar — *vi* : cicatrizar

health ['hɛlθ] *n* : salud *f* — **healthy** ['hɛlθi] *adj* **healthier; -est** : sano, saludable

heap ['hip] *n* : montón *m* — ∼ *vt* : amontonar

hear ['hɪr] *v* **heard** ['hərd]; **hearing** *vt* : oír — *vi* **1** : oír **2** ∼ **about** : enterarse de **3** ∼ **from** : tener noticias de — **hearing** ['hɪrɪŋ] *n* **1** : oído *m* **2** : vista *f* (en un tribunal) — **hearing aid** *n* : audífono *m* — **hearsay** ['hɪr,seɪ] *n* : rumores *mpl*

hearse ['hərs] *n* : coche *m* fúnebre

heart ['hɑrt] *n* **1** : corazón *m* **2 at** ∼ : en el fondo **3 by** ∼ : de memoria **4 lose** ∼ : descorazonarse **5 take** ∼ : animarse — **heartache** ['hɑrt,eɪk] *n* : pena *f*, dolor *m* — **heart attack** *n* : infarto *m*, ataque *m* al corazón — **heartbeat**

['hɑrt.biːt] n : latido m (del corazón) —
heartbreak ['hɑrt.breɪk] n : congoja f,
angustia f — **heartbroken** ['hɑrt-
,broːkən] adj : desconsolado — **heart-
burn** ['hɑrt.bərn] n : acidez f estomacal
hearth ['hɑrθ] n : hogar m
heartily ['hɑrtəli] adv : de buena gana
heartless ['hɑrtləs] adj : de mal corazón, cruel
hearty ['hɑrti] adj **heartier; -est 1** : cordial, caluroso **2** : abundante (dícese de
una comida)
heat ['hiːt] vt : calentar — vi or ~ **up**
: calentarse — ~ n **1** : calor m **2** HEAT-
ING : calefacción f — **heated** ['hiːtəd]
adj : acalorado — **heater** ['hiːtər] n
: calentador m
heath ['hiːθ] n : brezal m
heathen ['hiːðən] adj : pagano — ~ n,
pl **-thens** or **-then** : pagano m, -na f
heather ['hɛðər] n : brezo m
heave ['hiːv] v **heaved** or **hove** ['hoːv];
heaving 1 LIFT : levantar (con esfuerzo) **2** HURL : lanzar, tirar **3** ~ **a
sigh** : suspirar — ~ vi or ~ **up** : levantarse
heaven ['hɛvən] n : cielo m — **heavenly** ['hɛvənli] adj **1** : celestial **2** ~ **body**
: cuerpo m celeste
heavy ['hɛvi] adj **heavier; -est 1** : pesado **2** INTENSE : fuerte **3** ~ **sigh** : suspiro m profundo **4** ~ **traffic** : tráfico
m denso — **heavily** ['hɛvəli] adv **1**
: pesadamente **2** EXCESSIVELY : mucho
— **heaviness** ['hɛvinəs] n : peso m,
pesadez f — **heavyweight** ['hɛvi.weɪt]
n : peso m pesado
Hebrew ['hiː.bruː] adj : hebreo — ~ n
: hebreo m (idioma)
heckle ['hɛkəl] vt **-led; -ling** : interrumpir (a un orador) con preguntas mo-
lestas
hectic ['hɛktɪk] adj : agitado, ajetreado
he'd ['hiːd] (contraction of **he had** or **he
would**) → **have, would**
hedge ['hɛdʒ] n : seto m vivo — ~ v
hedged; hedging vt ~ **one's bets**
: cubrirse — vi : contestar con evasi-
vas — **hedgehog** ['hɛdʒ.hɔɡ, -.hɑɡ] n
: erizo m
heed ['hiːd] vt : prestar atención a, hacer
caso de — ~ n **take** ~ : tener cuidado — **heedless** ['hiːdləs] adj **be** ~ **of**
: hacer caso omiso de
heel ['hiːl] n : talón m (del pie), tacón m
(de un zapato)
hefty ['hɛfti] adj **heftier; -est** : robusto y
pesado
heifer ['hɛfər] n : novilla f
height ['haɪt] n **1** : estatura f (de una per-

sona), altura f (de un objeto) **2** PEAK
: cumbre f **3** the ~ **of folly** : el colmo
de la locura **4 what is your** ~ **?**
: ¿cuánto mides? — **heighten** ['haɪtən]
vt : aumentar, intensificar
heir ['ær] n : heredero m, -ra f —
heiress ['æras] n : heredera f — **heirloom** ['ær.luːm] n : reliquia f de familia
held → **hold**
helicopter ['hɛlə.kɑptər] n : helicóptero
m
hell ['hɛl] n : infierno m — **hellish**
['hɛlɪʃ] adj : infernal
he'll ['hiːl, 'hɪl] (contraction of **he shall**
or **he will**) → **shall, will**
hello [hə'loː, hɛ-] interj : ¡hola!
helm ['hɛlm] n : timón m
helmet ['hɛlmət] n : casco m
help ['hɛlp] vt **1** : ayudar **2** ~ **oneself**
: servirse **3 I can't** ~ **it** : no lo puedo
remediar — ~ n **1** : ayuda f **2** STAFF
: personal m **3 help!** : ¡socorro!, ¡auxilio! — **helper** ['hɛlpər] n : ayudante
mf — **helpful** ['hɛlpfəl] adj **1** OBLIGING
: servicial, amable **2** USEFUL : útil —
helping ['hɛlpɪŋ] n : porción f — **helpless** ['hɛlpləs] adj **1** POWERLESS : incapaz **2** DEFENSELESS : indefenso
hem ['hɛm] n : dobladillo m — ~ vt
hemmed; hemming ~ **in** : encerrar
hemisphere ['hɛmə.sfɪr] n : hemisferio
m
hemorrhage ['hɛmərɪdʒ] n : hemorragia
f
hemorrhoids ['hɛmə.rɔɪdz, 'hɛm.rɔɪdz]
npl : hemorroides fpl, almorranas fpl
hemp ['hɛmp] n : cáñamo m
hen ['hɛn] n : gallina f
hence ['hɛns] adv **1** : de aquí, de ahí **2**
THEREFORE : por lo tanto **3 ten years**
~ : de aquí a 10 años — **henceforth**
['hɛns.forθ, 'hɛns'-] adv : de ahora en
adelante
henpeck ['hɛn.pɛk] vt : dominar (al
marido)
hepatitis [.hɛpə'taɪtəs] n, pl **-titides**
[-'tɪtə.diːz] : hepatitis f
her ['hər] adj : su, sus — ~ ['hər, ər]
pron **1** (used as direct object) : la **2**
(used as indirect object) : le, se **3**
(used as object of a preposition) : ella
herald ['hɛrəld] vt : anunciar
herb ['ərb, 'hərb] n : hierba f
herd ['hərd] n : manada f — ~ vt : conducir (en manada) — vi or ~ **together** : reunir
here ['hɪr] adv **1** : aquí, acá **2** ~ **you
are!** : ¡toma! — **hereabouts** ['hɪrə-
,baʊts] or **hereabout** [-.baʊt] adv : por
aquí (cerca) — **hereafter** [hɪr'æftər]

adv : en el futuro — **hereby** [hɪr'baɪ]
adv : por este medio
hereditary [hə'redə,teri] *adj* : hereditario
— **heredity** [hə'redəṭi] *n* : herencia *f*
heresy ['herəsi] *n, pl* **-sies** : herejía *f*
herewith [hɪr'wɪθ] *adv* : adjunto
heritage ['herəṭɪdʒ] *n* **1** : herencia *f* **2**
: patrimonio *m* (nacional)
hermit ['hərmət] *n* : ermitaño *m*, -ña *f*
hernia ['hərniə] *n, pl* **-nias** *or* **-niae**
[-niˌiː, -niˌaɪ] : hernia *f*
hero ['hiːroː, 'hɪroː] *n, pl* **-roes** : héroe *m*
— **heroic** [hɪ'roːɪk] *adj* : heroico —
heroine ['heroən] *n* : heroína *f* —
heroism ['heroˌɪzəm] *n* : heroísmo *m*
heron ['herən] *n* : garza *f*
herring ['herɪŋ] *n, pl* **-ring** *or* **-rings**
: arenque *m*
hers ['hərz] *pron* **1** : (el) suyo, (la) suya,
(los) suyos, (las) suyas **2 some
friends of ~** : unos amigos suyos,
unos amigos de ella — **herself** [hər-
'self] *pron* **1** (*used reflexively*) : se **2**
(*used emphatically*) : ella misma
he's ['hiːz] (*contraction of* **he is** *or* **he
has**) → **be, have**
hesitant ['hezətənt] *adj* : titubeante,
vacilante — **hesitate** ['hezəˌteɪt] *vi*
-tated; -tating : vacilar, titubear —
hesitation [ˌhezə'teɪʃən] *n* : vacilación
f, titubeo *m*
heterosexual [ˌheṭəroˈsekʃʊəl] *adj* : heterosexual — ~ *n* : heterosexual *mf*
hexagon ['heksəˌɡɑn] *n* : hexágono *m*
hey ['heɪ] *interj* : ¡eh!, ¡oye!
heyday ['heɪˌdeɪ] *n* : auge *m*, apogeo *m*
hi ['haɪ] *interj* : ¡hola!
hibernate ['haɪbərˌneɪt] *vi* **-nated; -nat-
ing** : hibernar
hiccup ['hɪkəp] *n* **have the ~s** : tener
hipo — ~ *vi* **-cuped; -cuping** : tener
hipo
hide[1] ['haɪd] *n* : piel *f*, cuero *m*
hide[2] *v* **hid** ['hɪd]; **hidden** ['hɪdən] *or*
hid; hiding *vt* **1** : esconder **2** : ocultar
(motivos, etc.) — *vi* : esconderse —
hide-and-seek ['haɪdəndˌsiːk] *n* : escondite *m*, escondidas *fpl Lat*
hideous ['hɪdiəs] *adj* : horrible, espantoso
hideout ['haɪdˌaʊt] *n* : escondite *m*, guarida *f*
hierarchy ['haɪəˌrɑrki] *n, pl* **-chies** : jerarquía *f* — **hierarchical** [ˌhaɪəˈrɑrkɪkəl]
adj : jerárquico
high ['haɪ] *adj* **1** : alto **2** INTOXICATED
: borracho, drogado **3 a ~ voice** : una
voz aguda **4 it's two feet ~** : tiene
dos pies de alto **5 ~ winds** : fuertes
vientos *mpl* — ~ *adv* : alto — ~ *n*

: récord *m*, máximo *m* — **higher**
['haɪər] *adj* **1** : superior **2 ~ education** : enseñanza *f* superior — **highlight** ['haɪˌlaɪt] *n* : punto *m* culminante
— **highly** ['haɪli] *adv* **1** VERY : muy,
sumamente **2 think ~ of** : tener en
mucho a — **Highness** ['haɪnəs] *n*
His/Her ~ : Su Alteza *f* — **high
school** *n* : escuela *f* secundaria — **high**
secundaria — **high-strung** ['haɪ'strʌŋ]
adj : nervioso, excitable — **highway**
['haɪˌweɪ] *n* : carretera *f*
hijack ['haɪˌdʒæk] *vt* : secuestrar — **hijacker** ['haɪˌdʒækər] *n* : secuestrador
m, -dora *f* — **hijacking** *n* : secuestro
m
hike ['haɪk] *v* **hiked; hiking** *vi* : ir de
caminata — *vt or* **~ up** RAISE : subir
— ~ *n* : caminata *f*, excursión *f* —
hiker ['haɪkər] *n* : excursionista *mf*
hilarious [hɪ'læriəs, haɪ-] *adj* : muy divertido — **hilarity** [hɪ'læreṭi, haɪ-] *n*
: hilaridad *f*
hill ['hɪl] *n* **1** : colina *f*, cerro *m* **2** SLOPE
: cuesta *f* — **hillside** ['hɪl,saɪd] *n*
: ladera *f*, cuesta *f* — **hilly** ['hɪli] *adj*
hillier; -est : accidentado
hilt ['hɪlt] *n* : puño *m*
him ['hɪm, əm] *pron* **1** (*used as direct object*) : lo **2** (*used as indirect object*)
: le, se **3** (*used as object of a preposition*) : él — **himself** [hɪm'self] *pron* **1**
(*used reflexively*) : se **2** (*used emphatically*) : él mismo
hind ['haɪnd] *adj* : trasero, posterior
hinder ['hɪndər] *vt* : dificultar, estorbar
— **hindrance** ['hɪndrəns] *n* : obstáculo
m
hindsight ['haɪnd,saɪt] *n* **in ~** : en retrospectiva
Hindu ['hɪnˌduː] *adj* : hindú
hinge ['hɪndʒ] *n* : bisagra *f*, gozne *m* —
~ *vi* **hinged; hinging ~ on** : depender de
hint ['hɪnt] *n* **1** : indirecta *f* **2** TIP : consejo *m* **3** TRACE : asomo *m*, toque *m* —
~ *vt* : dar a entender — *vi* **~ at** : insinuar
hip ['hɪp] *n* : cadera *f*
hippopotamus [ˌhɪpə'pɑṭəməs] *n, pl*
-muses *or* **-mi** [-ˌmaɪ] : hipopótamo *m*
hire ['haɪr] *n* **1** : alquiler *m* **2 for ~** : se
alquila — ~ *vt* **hired; hiring 1** EM-
PLOY : contratar, emplear **2** RENT
: alquilar
his ['hɪz, ɪz] *adj* : su, sus, de él — ~
pron **1** : (el) suyo, (la) suya, (los)
suyos, (las) suyas **2 some friends of
~** : unos amigos suyos, unos amigos
de él

Hispanic [hɪ'spænɪk] *adj* : hispano, hispánico

hiss ['hɪs] *vi* : silbar — *n* : silbido *m*

history ['hɪstəri] *n, pl* **-ries 1** : historia *f* **2** BACKGROUND : historial *m* — **historian** [hɪ'stɔriən] *n* : historiador *m*, -dora *f* — **historic** [hɪ'stɔrɪk] *or* **historical** [-ɪkəl] *adj* : histórico

hit ['hɪt] *v* **hit; hitting** *vt* **1** : golpear, pegar **2** : dar (con un proyectil) **3** AFFECT : afectar **4** REACH : alcanzar **5 the car ~ a tree** : el coche chocó contra un árbol — *vi* : pegar — *n* **1** : golpe *m* **2** SUCCESS : éxito *m*

hitch ['hɪtʃ] *vt* **1** ATTACH : enganchar **2** *or* **~ up** RAISE : subirse **3 ~ a ride** : hacer autostop — *~ n* PROBLEM : problema *m* — **hitchhike** ['hɪtʃ,haɪk] *vi* **-hiked; -hiking** : hacer autostop — **hitchhiker** ['hɪtʃ,haɪkər] *n* : autostopista *mf*

hitherto ['hɪðər,tu:, ,hɪðər'-] *adv* : hasta ahora

HIV [,eɪtʃ,aɪ'vi:] *n* : VIH *m*, virus *m* del sida

hive ['haɪv] *n* : colmena *f*

hives ['haɪvz] *ns & pl* : urticaria *f*

hoard ['hɔrd] *n* : tesoro *m* (de dinero), reserva *f* (de provisiones) — *~ vt* : acumular

hoarse ['hɔrs] *adj* **hoarser; -est** : ronco

hoax ['ho:ks] *n* : engaño *m*

hobble ['hɑbəl] *vi* **-bled; -bling** : cojear

hobby ['hɑbi] *n, pl* **-bies** : pasatiempo *m*

hobo ['ho:bo:] *n, pl* **-boes** : vagabundo *m*, -da *f*

hockey ['hɑki] *n* : hockey *m*

hoe ['ho:] *n* : azada *f* — *~ vt* **hoed; hoeing** : azadonar

hog ['hɔg, 'hɑg] *n* : cerdo *m* — *~ vt* **hogged; hogging** MONOPOLIZE : acaparar

hoist ['hɔɪst] *vt* **1** : izar (una vela, etc.) **2** LIFT : levantar — *~ n* : grúa *f*

hold[1] ['ho:ld] *n* : bodega *f* (en un barco o un avión)

hold[2] *v* **held** ['hɛld]; **holding** *vt* **1** GRIP : agarrar **2** POSSESS : tener **3** SUPPORT : sostener **4** : celebrar (una reunión, etc.), mantener (una conversación) **5** CONTAIN : contener **6** CONSIDER : considerar **7** *or* **~ back** : detener **8 ~ hands** : agarrarse de la mano **9 ~ up** ROB : atracar **10 ~ up** DELAY : retrasar — *vi* **1** LAST : durar, continuar **2** APPLY : ser válido — *n* **1** GRIP : agarre *m* **2 get ~ of** : conseguir **3 get ~ of oneself** : controlarse — **holder** ['ho:ldər] *n* : tenedor *m*, -dora *f* — **holdup** ['ho:ld-

hole ['ho:l] *n* : agujero *m*, hoyo *m*

holiday ['hɑlə,deɪ] *n* **1** : día *m* feriado, fiesta *f* **2** *Brit* VACATION : vacaciones *fpl*

holiness ['ho:linəs] *n* : santidad *f*

holler ['hɑlər] *vi* : gritar — *~ n* : grito *m*

hollow ['hɑlo:] *n* **1** : hueco *m* **2** VALLEY : hondonada *f* — *~ adj* **-lower; -est 1** : hueco **2** FALSE : vacío, falso — *~ vt or* **~ out** : ahuecar

holly ['hɑli] *n, pl* **-lies** : acebo *m*

holocaust ['hɑlə,kɔst, 'ho:-, 'hɔ-] *n* : holocausto *m*

holster ['ho:lstər] *n* : pistolera *f*

holy ['ho:li] *adj* **-lier; -est** : santo, sagrado

homage ['ɑmɪdʒ, 'hɑ-] *n* : homenaje *m*

home ['ho:m] *n* **1** : casa *f* **2** FAMILY : hogar *m* **3** INSTITUTION : residencia *f*, asilo *m* **4 at ~ and abroad** : dentro y fuera del país — *~ adv* **go ~** : ir a casa — **homeland** ['ho:m,lænd] *n* : patria *f* — **homeless** ['ho:mləs] *adj* : sin hogar — **homely** ['ho:mli] *adj* **-lier; -est 1** DOMESTIC : casero **2** UGLY : feo — **homemade** ['ho:m'meɪd] *adj* : casero, hecho en casa — **homemaker** ['ho:m,meɪkər] *n* : ama *f* de casa — **home run** *n* : jonrón *m* — **homesick** ['ho:m,sɪk] *adj* **be ~** : echar de menos a la familia — **homeward** ['ho:mwərd] *adj* : de vuelta, de regreso — **homework** ['ho:m,wərk] *n* : tarea *f*, deberes *mpl* — **homey** ['ho:mi] *adj* **homier; -est** : hogareño, acogedor

homicide ['hɑmə,saɪd, 'ho:-] *n* : homicidio *m*

homogeneous [,ho:mə'dʒi:niəs, -njəs] *adj* : homogéneo

homosexual [,ho:mə'sɛkʃʊəl] *adj* : homosexual — *~ n* : homosexual *mf* — **homosexuality** [,ho:mə,sɛkʃʊ'æləti] *n* : homosexualidad *f*

honest ['ɑnəst] *adj* **1** : honrado **2** FRANK : sincero — **honestly** *adv* : sinceramente — **honesty** ['ɑnəsti] *n, pl* **-ties** : honradez *f*

honey ['hʌni] *n, pl* **-eys** : miel *f* — **honeycomb** ['hʌni,ko:m] *n* : panal *m* — **honeymoon** ['hʌni,mu:n] *n* : luna *f* de miel

honk ['hɑŋk, 'hɔŋk] *vi* : tocar la bocina — *~ n* : bocinazo *m*

honor *or Brit* **honour** ['ɑnər] *n* : honor *m* — *~ vt* **1** : honrar **2** : aceptar (un cheque, etc.), cumplir con (una promesa) — **honorable** *or Brit* **honourable** ['ɑnərəbəl] *adj* : honorable, honroso — **honorary** ['ɑnə,reri] *adj* : honorario

hood ['hʊd] n 1 : capucha f (de un abrigo, etc.) 2 : capó m (de un automóvil)
hoodlum ['hʊdləm, 'huːd-] n : matón m
hoodwink ['hʊd,wɪŋk] vt : engañar
hoof ['hʊf, 'huːf] n, pl **hooves** ['hʊvz, 'huːvz] or **hoofs** : pezuña f (de una vaca, etc.), casco m (de un caballo)
hook ['hʊk] n 1 : gancho m 2 or ~ **and eye** : corchete m 3 → **fishhook 4 off the** ~ : descolgado — ~ vt : enganchar — vi : engancharse
hoop ['huːp] n : aro m
hooray [hʊ'reɪ] → **hurrah**
hoot ['huːt] vi 1 : ulular (dícese de un búho) 2 ~ **with laughter** : reírse a carcajadas — ~ n 1 : ululato m (de un búho) 2 **I don't give a** ~ : me importa un comino
hop[1] ['hɑp] vi **hopped; hopping** : saltar a la pata coja — ~ n : salto m a la pata coja
hop[2] n ~**s** : lúpulo m (planta)
hope ['hoːp] v **hoped; hoping** vi : esperar — vt : esperar que — ~ n : esperanza f — **hopeful** ['hoːpfəl] adj : esperanzado — **hopefully** adv 1 : con esperanza 2 ~ **it will help** : se espera que ayude — **hopeless** ['hoːpləs] adj : desesperado — **hopelessly** ['hoːpləsli] adv : desesperadamente
horde ['hɔrd] n : horda f
horizon [hə'raɪzən] n : horizonte m — **horizontal** [,hɔrə'zɑntəl] adj : horizontal
hormone ['hɔr,moːn] n : hormona f
horn ['hɔrn] n 1 : cuerno m (de un animal) 2 : trompa f (instrumento musical) 3 : bocina f, claxon m (de un vehículo)
hornet ['hɔrnət] n : avispón m
horoscope ['hɔrə,skoːp] n : horóscopo m
horror ['hɔrər] n : horror m — **horrendous** [hɔ'rendəs] adj : horrendo — **horrible** ['hɔrəbəl] adj : horrible — **horrid** ['hɔrɪd] adj : horroroso, horrible — **horrify** ['hɔrə,faɪ] vt **-fied; -fying** : horrorizar
hors d'oeuvre [ɔr'dərv] n, pl **hors d'oeuvres** [-'dərvz] : entremés m
horse ['hɔrs] n : caballo m — **horseback** ['hɔrs,bæk] n **on** ~ : a caballo — **horsefly** ['hɔrs,flaɪ] n, pl **-flies** : tábano m — **horseman** ['hɔrsmən] n, pl **-men** [-mən, -,men] : jinete m — **horseplay** ['hɔrs,pleɪ] n : payasadas fpl — **horsepower** ['hɔrs,paʊər] n : caballo m de fuerza — **horseradish** ['hɔrs,rædɪʃ] n : rábano m picante — **horseshoe** ['hɔrs,ʃuː] n : herradura f — **horse-**

woman ['hɔrs,wʊmən] n, pl **-women** [-,wɪmən] : jinete f
horticulture ['hɔrtə,kʌltʃər] n : horticultura f
hose ['hoːz] n 1 pl **hoses** : manguera f, manga f 2 **hose** pl STOCKINGS : medias fpl — ~ vt **hosed; hosing** : regar (con manguera) — **hosiery** ['hoːʒəri, 'hoːʒə-] n : calcetería f
hospice ['hɑspəs] n : hospicio m
hospital ['hɑs,pɪtəl] n : hospital m — **hospitable** [hɑ'spɪtəbəl, 'hɑs,pɪ-] adj : hospitalario — **hospitality** [,hɑspə'tæləti] n, pl **-ties** : hospitalidad f — **hospitalize** ['hɑs,pɪtəl,aɪz] vt **-ized; -izing** : hospitalizar
host[1] ['hoːst] n **a** ~ **of** : toda una serie de
host[2] n 1 : anfitrión m, -triona f 2 : presentador m, -dora f (de televisión, etc.) — ~ vt : presentar (un programa de televisión, etc.)
host[3] n EUCHARIST : hostia f, Eucaristía f
hostage ['hɑstɪdʒ] n : rehén m
hostel ['hɑstəl] n or **youth** ~ : albergue m juvenil
hostess ['hoːstɪs] n : anfitriona f
hostile ['hɑstəl, -,taɪl] adj : hostil — **hostility** [hɑs'tɪləti] n, pl **-ties** : hostilidad f
hot ['hɑt] adj **hotter; hottest 1** : caliente, caluroso (dícese del tiempo), cálido (dícese del clima) **2** SPICY : picante **3 feel** ~ : tener calor **4 have a** ~ **temper** : tener mal genio **5** ~ **news** : noticias fpl de última hora **6 it's** ~ **today** : hace calor
hot dog n : perro m caliente
hotel [hoː'tel] n : hotel m
hotheaded ['hɑt'hedəd] adj : exaltado
hound ['haʊnd] n : perro m (de caza) — ~ vt : acosar, perseguir
hour ['aʊər] n : hora f — **hourglass** ['aʊər,glæs] n : reloj m de arena — **hourly** ['aʊərli] adv & adj : cada hora, por hora
house ['haʊs] n, pl **houses** ['haʊzəz, -səz] **1** : casa f **2** : cámara f (del gobierno) **3 publishing** ~ : editorial f — ~ ['haʊz] vt **housed; housing** : albergar — **houseboat** ['haʊs,boːt] n : casa f flotante — **housefly** ['haʊs,flaɪ] n, pl **-flies** : mosca f común — **household** ['haʊs,hoːld] adj **1** : doméstico **2** ~ **name** : nombre m muy conocido — ~ n : casa f — **housekeeper** ['haʊs,kiːpər] n : ama f de llaves — **housekeeping** ['haʊs,kiːpɪŋ] n : gobierno m de la casa — **housewarming** ['haʊs,wɔrmɪŋ] n : fiesta f de estreno de

una casa — **housewife** ['haʊs,waɪf] *n*, *pl* **-wives** : ama *f* de casa — **housework** ['haʊs,wərk] *n* : faenas *fpl* domésticas — **housing** ['haʊzɪŋ] *n* 1 : viviendas *fpl* 2 CASE : caja *f* protectora

hove → **heave**

hovel ['hʌvəl, 'hɑ-] *n* : casucha *f*, tugurio *m*

hover ['hʌvər, 'hɑ-] *vi* 1 : cernerse 2 ~ **about** : rondar

how ['haʊ] *adv* 1 : cómo 2 (*used in exclamations*) : qué 3 ~ **are you?** : ¿cómo está Ud.? 4 ~ **come** : por qué 5 ~ **much** : cuánto 6 ~ **do you do?** : mucho gusto 7 ~ **old are you?** : ¿cuántos años tienes? — ~ *conj* : como

however [haʊˈɛvər] *conj* 1 : de cualquier manera que 2 ~ **you like** : como quieras — ~ *adv* 1 NEVERTHELESS : sin embargo, no obstante 2 ~ **difficult it is** : por difícil que sea 3 ~ **hard I try** : por más que me esfuerce

howl ['haʊl] *vi* : aullar — ~ *n* : aullido *m*

hub ['hʌb] *n* 1 CENTER : centro *m* 2 : cubo *m* (de una rueda)

hubbub ['hʌ,bʌb] *n* : alboroto *m*, jaleo *m*

hubcap ['hʌb,kæp] *n* : tapacubos *m*

huddle ['hʌdəl] *vi* **-dled; -dling** *or* ~ **together** : apiñarse

hue ['hju:] *n* : color *m*, tono *m*

huff ['hʌf] *n* **be in a** ~ : estar enojado

hug ['hʌg] *vt* **hugged; hugging** : abrazar — ~ *n* : abrazo *m*

huge ['hju:dʒ] *adj* **huger; hugest** : inmenso, enorme

hull ['hʌl] *n* : casco *m* (de un barco, etc.)

hum ['hʌm] *v* **hummed; humming** *vi* 1 : tararear 2 BUZZ : zumbar — *vt* : tararear (una melodía) — ~ *n* : zumbido *m*

human ['hju:mən, 'ju:-] *adj* : humano — ~ *n* : (ser *m*) humano *m* — **humane** [hju:ˈmeɪn, ju:-] *adj* : humano, humanitario — **humanitarian** [hju:,mænəˈteriən, ju:-] *adj* : humanitario — **humanity** [hju:ˈmænəti, ju:-] *n*, *pl* **-ties** : humanidad *f*

humble ['hʌmbəl] *vt* **-bled; -bling** 1 : humillar 2 ~ **oneself** : humillarse — ~ *adj* **-bler; -blest** : humilde

humdrum ['hʌm,drʌm] *adj* : monótono, rutinario

humid ['hju:məd, 'ju:-] *adj* : húmedo — **humidity** [hju:ˈmɪdəti, ju:-] *n*, *pl* **-ties** : humedad *f*

humiliate [hju:ˈmɪli,eɪt, ju:-] *vt* **-ated; -ating** : humillar — **humiliating** [hju:ˈmɪli,eɪtɪŋ, ju:-] *adj* : humillante — **humiliation** [hju:,mɪliˈeɪʃən, ju:-] *n* : humillación *f* — **humility** [hju:ˈmɪləti, ju:-] *n* : humildad *f*

humor *or Brit* **humour** ['hju:mər, 'ju:-] *n* : humor *m* — ~ *vt* : seguir la corriente a, complacer — **humorous** ['hju:mərəs, 'ju:-] *adj* : humorístico, cómico

hump ['hʌmp] *n* : joroba *f*

hunch ['hʌntʃ] *vi or* ~ **over** : encorvarse — ~ *n* : presentimiento *m*

hundred ['hʌndrəd] *adj* : cien, ciento — ~ *n*, *pl* **-dreds** *or* **-dred** : ciento *m* — **hundredth** ['hʌndrədθ] *adj* : centésimo — ~ *n* 1 : centésimo *m*, -ma *f* (en una serie) 2 : centésimo *m* (en matemáticas)

hung → **hang**

Hungarian [hʌŋˈgæriən] *adj* : húngaro — ~ *n* : húngaro *m* (idioma)

hunger ['hʌŋgər] *n* : hambre *m* — ~ *vi* 1 : tener hambre 2 ~ **for** : ansiar, anhelar — **hungry** ['hʌŋgri] *adj* **-grier; -est** 1 : hambriento 2 **be** ~ : tener hambre

hunk ['hʌŋk] *n* : pedazo *m* (grande)

hunt ['hʌnt] *vt* 1 : cazar 2 ~ **for** : buscar — ~ *n* 1 : caza *f*, cacería *f* 2 SEARCH : búsqueda *f*, busca *f* — **hunter** ['hʌntər] *n* : cazador *m*, -dora *f* — **hunting** ['hʌntɪŋ] *n* 1 : caza *f* 2 **go** ~ : ir de caza

hurdle ['hərdəl] *n* 1 : valla *f* (en deportes) 2 OBSTACLE : obstáculo *m*

hurl ['hərl] *vt* : lanzar, arrojar

hurrah [hʊˈrɑ, -ˈrɔ] *interj* : ¡hurra!

hurricane ['hərə,keɪn] *n* : huracán *m*

hurry ['həri] *n* : prisa *f*, apuro *f Lat* — ~ *vb* **-ried; -rying** *vi* : darse prisa, apurarse *Lat* — *vt* : apurar, dar prisa a — **hurried** ['hərid] *adj* : apresurado — **hurriedly** ['hərədli] *adv* : apresuradamente, de prisa

hurt ['hərt] *v* **hurt; hurting** *vt* 1 INJURE : hacer daño a, lastimar 2 OFFEND : ofender, herir — *vi* 1 : doler 2 **my foot** ~**s** : me duele el pie — ~ *n* 1 INJURY : herida *f* 2 DISTRESS : dolor *m*, pena *f* — **hurtful** ['hərtfəl] *adj* : hiriente, doloroso

hurtle ['hərtəl] *vi* **-tled; -tling** : lanzarse, precipitarse

husband ['hʌzbənd] *n* : esposo *m*, marido *m*

hush ['hʌʃ] *vt* : hacer callar, acallar — ~ *n* : silencio *m*

husk ['hʌsk] *n* : cáscara *f*

husky[1] ['hʌski] *adj* **-kier; -est** HOARSE : ronco

husky[2] *n*, *pl* **-kies** : perro *m*, -rra *f* esquimal

husky³ adj BURLY : fornido
hustle ['həsəl] v **-tled; -tling** vt : dar prisa a, apurar *Lat* — vi : darse prisa, apurarse *Lat* — ～ n ～ **and bustle** : ajetreo m, bullicio m
hut ['hʌt] n : cabaña f
hutch ['hʌtʃ] n or **rabbit** ～ : conejera f
hyacinth ['haɪəsɪnθ] n : jacinto m
hybrid ['haɪbrɪd] n : híbrido m — ～ adj : híbrido
hydrant ['haɪdrənt] n or **fire** ～ : boca f de incendios
hydraulic [haɪˈdrɔlɪk] adj : hidráulico
hydroelectric [ˌhaɪdroɪˈlɛktrɪk] adj : hidroeléctrico
hydrogen ['haɪdrədʒən] n : hidrógeno m
hyena [haɪˈiːnə] n : hiena f
hygiene ['haɪdʒiːn] n : higiene f — **hygienic** [haɪˈdʒɛnɪk, -'dʒiː-; ˌhaɪdʒiˈɛnɪk] adj : higiénico
hymn ['hɪm] n : himno m

hyperactive [ˌhaɪpərˈæktɪv] adj : hiperactivo
hyphen ['haɪfən] n : guión m
hypnosis [hɪpˈnoːsɪs] n, pl **-noses** [-ˌsiːz] : hipnosis f — **hypnotic** [hɪpˈnɑtɪk] adj : hipnótico — **hypnotism** ['hɪpnəˌtɪzəm] n : hipnotismo m — **hypnotize** ['hɪpnəˌtaɪz] vt **-tized; -tizing** : hipnotizar
hypochondriac [ˌhaɪpəˈkɑndriˌæk] n : hipocondríaco m, -ca f
hypocrisy [hɪpˈɑkrəsi] n, pl **-sies** : hipocresía f — **hypocrite** ['hɪpəˌkrɪt] n : hipócrita mf — **hypocritical** [ˌhɪpəˈkrɪtɪkəl] adj : hipócrita
hypothesis [haɪˈpɑθəsɪs] n, pl **-eses** [-ˌsiːz] : hipótesis f — **hypothetical** [ˌhaɪpəˈθɛtɪkəl] adj : hipotético
hysteria [hɪsˈtɛriə, -ˈtɪr-] n : histeria f, histerismo m — **hysterical** [hɪsˈtɛrɪkəl] adj : histérico

I

i ['aɪ] n, pl **i's** or **is** ['aɪz] : i f, novena letra del alfabeto inglés
I ['aɪ] pron : yo
ice ['aɪs] n : hielo m — ～ v **iced; icing** vt **1** FREEZE : congelar **2** CHILL : enfriar **3** : bañar (pasteles, etc.) — ～ vi or ～ **up** : helarse, congelarse — **iceberg** ['aɪsˌbərg] n : iceberg m — **icebox** ['aɪs-ˌbɑks] → **refrigerator** — **ice-cold** ['aɪsˈkoːld] adj : helado — **ice cream** n : helado m — **ice cube** n : cubito m de hielo — **ice-skate** ['aɪsˌskeɪt] vi **-skated; -skating** : patinar — **ice skate** n : patín m de cuchilla — **icicle** ['aɪˌsɪkəl] n : carámbano m — **icing** ['aɪsɪŋ] n : baño m
icon ['aɪˌkɑn, -kən] n : icono m
icy ['aɪsi] adj **icier; -est 1** : cubierto de hielo (dícese de pavimento, etc.) **2** FREEZING : helado
I'd ['aɪd] (contraction of **I should** or **I would**) → **should, would**
idea [aɪˈdiːə] n : idea f
ideal [aɪˈdiːəl] adj : ideal — ～ n : ideal m — **idealist** [aɪˈdiːəlɪst] n : idealista mf — **idealistic** [aɪˌdiːəˈlɪstɪk] adj : idealista — **idealize** [aɪˈdiːəˌlaɪz] vt **-ized; -izing** : idealizar
identity [aɪˈdɛntəti] n, pl **-ties** : identidad f — **identical** [aɪˈdɛntɪkəl] adj : idéntico — **identify** [aɪˈdɛntəˌfaɪ] v **-fied; -fying** vt : identificar — vi ～ **with** : identificarse con — **identifica-**

tion [aɪˌdɛntəfəˈkeɪʃən] n **1** : identificación f **2** ～ **card** : carnet m, carné m
ideology [ˌaɪdiˈɑlədʒi, ˌɪ-] n, pl **-gies** : ideología f — **ideological** [ˌaɪdiə-ˈlɑdʒɪkəl, ˌɪ-] adj : ideológico
idiocy ['ɪdiəsi] n, pl **-cies** : idiotez f
idiom ['ɪdiəm] n EXPRESSION : modismo m — **idiomatic** [ˌɪdiəˈmætɪk] adj : idiomático
idiosyncrasy [ˌɪdioˈsɪŋkrəsi] n, pl **-sies** : idiosincrasia f
idiot ['ɪdiət] n : idiota mf — **idiotic** [ˌɪdiˈɑtɪk] adj : idiota
idle ['aɪdəl] adj **idler; idlest 1** LAZY : haragán, holgazán **2** INACTIVE : parado (dícese de una máquina) **3** UNEMPLOYED : desocupado **4** VAIN : frívolo, vano **5 out of** ～ **curiosity** : por pura curiosidad — ～ v **idled; idling** vi : andar al ralentí (dícese de un motor) — vt ～ **away the hours** : pasar el rato — **idleness** ['aɪdəlnəs] n : ociosidad f
idol ['aɪdəl] n : ídolo m — **idolize** ['aɪdəˌlaɪz] vt **-ized; -izing** : idolatrar
idyllic [aɪˈdɪlɪk] adj : idílico
if ['ɪf] conj **1** : si **2** THOUGH : aunque, si bien **3** ～ **so** : si es así
igloo ['ɪˌgluː] n, pl **-loos** : iglú m
ignite [ɪgˈnaɪt] v **-nited; -niting** vt : encender — vi : encenderse — **ignition** [ɪgˈnɪʃən] n **1** : ignición f **2** or ～ **switch** : encendido m

ignore [ɪg'nor] vt **-nored; -noring** : ignorar, no hacer caso de — **ignorance** [ˈɪgnərənts] n : ignorancia f — **ignorant** [ˈɪgnərənt] adj 1 : ignorante 2 be ~ of : desconocer, ignorar

ilk ['ɪlk] n : tipo m, clase f

ill ['ɪl] adj worse ['wərs]; worst ['wərst] 1 SICK : enfermo 2 BAD : malo — adv worse; worst : mal — **ill-advised** [ˌɪlædˈvaɪzd, -əd-] : imprudente — **ill at ease** adj : incómodo

I'll ['aɪl] (contraction of **I shall** or **I will**) → **shall, will**

illegal [ɪˈliːgəl] adj : ilegal

illegible [ɪˈledʒəbəl] adj : ilegible

illegitimate [ˌɪlɪˈdʒɪtəmət] adj : ilegítimo — **illegitimacy** [ˌɪlɪˈdʒɪtəməsi] n : ilegitimidad f

illicit [ɪˈlɪsət] adj : ilícito

illiterate [ɪˈlɪtərət] adj : analfabeto — **illiteracy** [ɪˈlɪtərəsi] n, pl **-cies** : analfabetismo m

ill-mannered [ˌɪlˈmænərd] adj : descortés, maleducado

ill-natured [ˌɪlˈneɪtʃərd] adj : de mal genio

illness ['ɪlnəs] n : enfermedad f

illogical [ɪˈlɑdʒɪkəl] adj : ilógico

ill-treat [ˌɪlˈtriːt] vt : maltratar

illuminate [ɪˈluːməˌneɪt] vt **-nated; -nating** : iluminar — **illumination** [ɪˌluːməˈneɪʃən] n : iluminación f

illusion [ɪˈluːʒən] n : ilusión f — **illusory** [ɪˈluːsəri, -zəri] adj : ilusorio

illustrate ['ɪləsˌtreɪt] v **-trated; -trating** : ilustrar — **illustration** [ˌɪləˈstreɪʃən] n 1 : ilustración f 2 EXAMPLE : ejemplo m — **illustrative** [ɪˈlʌstrətɪv, ˈɪləˌstreɪtɪv] adj : ilustrativo

illustrious [ɪˈlʌstriəs] adj : ilustre, glorioso

ill will n : animadversión f, mala voluntad f

I'm ['aɪm] (contraction of **I am**) → **be**

image ['ɪmɪdʒ] n : imagen f — **imaginary** [ɪˈmædʒəˌneri] adj : imaginario — **imagination** [ɪˌmædʒəˈneɪʃən] n : imaginación f — **imaginative** [ɪˈmædʒənətɪv, -əˌneɪtɪv] adj : imaginativo — **imagine** [ɪˈmædʒən] vt **-ined; -ining** : imaginar(se)

imbalance [ɪmˈbælənts] n : desequilibrio m

imbecile ['ɪmbəsəl, -ˌsɪl] n : imbécil mf

imbue [ɪmˈbjuː] vt **-bued; -buing** : imbuir

imitation [ˌɪməˈteɪʃən] n : imitación f — ~ adj : de imitación, artificial — **imitate** ['ɪməˌteɪt] vt **-tated; -tating** : imitar, remedar — **imitator** ['ɪməˌteɪtər] n : imitador m, -dora f

immaculate [ɪˈmækjələt] adj : inmaculado

immaterial [ˌɪməˈtɪriəl] adj : irrelevante, sin importancia

immature [ˌɪməˈtʃʊr, -ˈtjʊr, -ˈtʊr] adj : inmaduro — **immaturity** [ˌɪməˈtʃʊrəti, -ˈtjʊr-, -ˈtʊr-] n, pl **-ties** : inmadurez f

immediate [ɪˈmiːdiət] adj : inmediato — **immediately** [ɪˈmiːdiətli] adv : inmediatamente

immense [ɪˈments] adj : inmenso — **immensity** [ɪˈmentsəti] n, pl **-ties** : inmensidad f

immerse [ɪˈmərs] vt **-mersed; -mersing** : sumergir — **immersion** [ɪˈmərʒən] n : inmersión f

immigrate ['ɪməˌgreɪt] vi **-grated; -grating** : inmigrar — **immigrant** ['ɪmɪgrənt] n : inmigrante mf — **immigration** [ˌɪməˈgreɪʃən] n : inmigración f

imminent ['ɪmənənt] adj : inminente — **imminence** ['ɪmənənts] n : inminencia f

immobile [ɪmˈoːbəl] adj : inmóvil — **immobilize** [ɪˈmoːbəˌlaɪz] vt **-lized; -lizing** : inmovilizar

immoral [ɪˈmɔrəl] adj : inmoral — **immorality** [ˌɪmɔˈræləti, ˌɪmə-] n, pl **-ties** : inmoralidad f

immortal [ɪˈmɔrtəl] adj : inmortal — ~ n : inmortal mf — **immortality** [ˌɪmɔrˈtæləti] n : inmortalidad f

immune [ɪˈmjuːn] adj : inmune — **immunity** [ɪˈmjuːnəti] n, pl **-ties** : inmunidad f — **immunization** [ˌɪmjənəˈzeɪʃən] n : inmunización f — **immunize** ['ɪmjʊˌnaɪz] vt **-nized; -nizing** : inmunizar

imp ['ɪmp] n RASCAL : diablillo m

impact ['ɪmˌpækt] n : impacto m

impair [ɪmˈpær] vt : dañar, perjudicar

impart [ɪmˈpɑrt] vt : impartir (información), conferir (una calidad, etc.)

impartial [ɪmˈpɑrʃəl] adj : imparcial — **impartiality** [ɪmˌpɑrʃiˈæləti] n, pl **-ties** : imparcialidad f

impassable [ɪmˈpæsəbəl] adj : intransitable

impasse ['ɪmˌpæs] n : impasse m

impassioned [ɪmˈpæʃənd] adj : apasionado

impassive [ɪmˈpæsɪv] adj : impasible

impatience [ɪmˈpeɪʃənts] n : impaciencia f — **impatient** [ɪmˈpeɪʃənt] adj : impaciente — **impatiently** [ɪmˈpeɪʃəntli] adv : con impaciencia

impeccable [ɪmˈpekəbəl] adj : impecable

impede [ɪm'piːd] vt **-peded; -peding** : dificultar — **impediment** [ɪm'pedəmənt] n : impedimento m, obstáculo m

impel [ɪm'pel] vt **-pelled; -pelling** : impeler

impending [ɪm'pendɪŋ] adj : inminente

impenetrable [ɪm'penətrəbəl] adj : impenetrable

imperative [ɪm'perətɪv] adj **1** COMMANDING : imperativo **2** NECESSARY : imprescindible — ~ n : imperativo m

imperceptible [ˌɪmpər'septəbəl] adj : imperceptible

imperfection [ˌɪmpər'fekʃən] n : imperfección f — **imperfect** [ɪm'pərfɪkt] adj : imperfecto — ~ n or ~ **tense** : imperfecto m

imperial [ɪm'pɪriəl] adj : imperial — **imperialism** [ɪm'pɪriəˌlɪzəm] n : imperialismo m — **imperious** [ɪm'pɪriəs] adj : imperioso

impersonal [ɪm'pərsənəl] adj : impersonal

impersonate [ɪm'pərsənˌeɪt] vt **-ated; -ating** : hacerse pasar por, imitar — **impersonation** [ɪmˌpərsən'eɪʃən] n : imitación f — **impersonator** [ɪm'pərsənˌeɪtər] n : imitador m, -dora f

impertinent [ɪm'pərtənənt] adj : impertinente — **impertinence** [ɪm'pərtənənts] n : impertinencia f

impervious [ɪm'pərviəs] adj ~ **to** : impermeable a

impetuous [ɪm'petʃuəs] adj : impetuoso, impulsivo

impetus ['ɪmpətəs] n : ímpetu m, impulso m

impinge [ɪm'pɪndʒ] vi **-pinged; -pinging** ~ **on** : afectara, incidir en

impish ['ɪmpɪʃ] adj : pícaro, travieso

implant [ɪm'plænt] vt : implantar

implausible [ɪm'plɔːzəbəl] adj : inverosímil

implement ['ɪmpləmənt] n : instrumento m, implemento m Lat — ~ ['ɪmpləˌment] vt : poner en práctica

implicate ['ɪmpləˌkeɪt] vt **-cated; -cating** : implicar — **implication** [ˌɪmplə'keɪʃən] n **1** INVOLVEMENT : implicación f **2** CONSEQUENCE : consecuencia f **3 by** ~ : de forma indirecta

implicit [ɪm'plɪsət] adj **1** : implícito **2** UNQUESTIONING : absoluto, incondicional

implore [ɪm'plɔr] vt **-plored; -ploring** : implorar, suplicar

imply [ɪm'plaɪ] vt **-plied; -plying 1** HINT : insinuar **2** ENTAIL : implicar

impolite [ˌɪmpə'laɪt] adj : descortés, maleducado

import [ɪm'pɔrt] vt : importar (mercancías) — **important** [ɪm'pɔrtənt] adj : importante — **importance** [ɪm'pɔrtənts] n : importancia f — **importation** [ˌɪmpɔr'teɪʃən] n : importación f — **importer** [ɪm'pɔrtər] n : importador m, -dora f

impose [ɪm'pɔːz] v **-posed; -posing** vt : imponer — vi ~ **on** : importunar, molestar — **imposing** [ɪm'pɔːzɪŋ] adj : imponente — **imposition** [ˌɪmpə'zɪʃən] n **1** ENFORCEMENT : imposición f **2 be an** ~ **on** : molestar

impossible [ɪm'pɑsəbəl] adj : imposible — **impossibility** [ɪmˌpɑsə'bɪlətʃi] n, pl **-ties** : imposibilidad f

impostor or **imposter** [ɪm'pɑstər] n : impostor m, -tora f

impotent ['ɪmpətənt] adj : impotente — **impotence** ['ɪmpətənts] n : impotencia f

impound [ɪm'paʊnd] vt : incautar, embargar

impoverished [ɪm'pɑvərɪʃt] adj : empobrecido

impracticable [ɪm'præktɪkəbəl] adj : impracticable

impractical [ɪm'præktɪkəl] adj : poco práctico

imprecise [ˌɪmprɪ'saɪs] adj : impreciso — **imprecision** [ˌɪmprɪ'sɪʒən] n : imprecisión f

impregnable [ɪm'pregnəbəl] adj : impenetrable

impregnate [ɪm'pregˌneɪt] vt **-nated; -nating 1** : impregnar **2** FERTILIZE : fecundar

impress [ɪm'pres] vt **1** : causar una buena impresión a **2** AFFECT : impresionar **3** ~ **sth on s.o.** : recalcar algo a algn — vi : impresionar — **impression** [ɪm'preʃən] n : impresión f — **impressionable** [ɪm'preʃənəbəl] adj : impresionable — **impressive** [ɪm'presɪv] adj : impresionante

imprint [ɪm'prɪnt, 'ɪm,-] vt : imprimir — ~ ['ɪm,prɪnt] n MARK : impresión f, huella f

imprison [ɪm'prɪzən] vt : encarcelar — **imprisonment** [ɪm'prɪzənmənt] n : encarcelamiento m

improbable [ɪm'prɑbəbəl] adj : improbable — **improbability** [ɪmˌprɑbə'bɪlətʃi] n, pl **-ties** : improbabilidad f

impromptu [ɪm'prɑmpˌtuː, -ˌtjuː] adj : improvisado

improper [ɪm'prɑpər] adj **1** UNSEEMLY : indecoroso **2** INCORRECT : impropio

— **impropriety** [ˌɪmprə'praɪəti] *n*, *pl* **-eties** : inconveniencia *f*

improve [ɪm'pruːv] *v* **-proved; -proving** : mejorar — **improvement** [ɪm'pruːvmənt] *n* : mejora *f*

improvise ['ɪmprə,vaɪz] *v* **-vised; -vising** : improvisar — **improvisation** [ˌɪmprəvə'zeɪʃən, ˌɪmprəvə-] *n* : improvisación *f*

impudent ['ɪmpjədənt] *adj* : insolente — **impudence** ['ɪmpjədənts] *n* : insolencia *f*

impulse ['ɪmpʌls] *n* **1** : impulso *m* **2 on ~** : sin reflexionar — **impulsive** [ɪm'pʌlsɪv] *adj* : impulsivo — **impulsiveness** [ɪm'pʌlsɪvnəs] *n* : impulsividad *f*

impunity [ɪm'pjuːnəti] *n* **1** : impunidad *f* **2 with ~** : impunemente

impure [ɪm'pjʊr] *adj* : impuro — **impurity** [ɪm'pjʊrəti] *n*, *pl* **-ties** : impureza *f*

in ['ɪn] *prep* **1** : en **2** DURING : por, en *Lat* **3** WITHIN : dentro de **4 dressed ~ red** : vestido de rojo **5 ~ the rain** : bajo la lluvia **6 ~ the sun** : al sol **7 ~ this way** : de esta manera **8 the best ~ the world** : el mejor del mundo **9 written ~ ink/French** : escrito con tinta/en francés — *adv* **1** INSIDE : dentro, adentro **2 be ~** : estar (en casa) **3 be ~ on** : participar en **4 come in!** : ¡entre!, ¡pase! **5 he's ~ for a shock** : se va a llevar un shock — *~ adj* : de moda

inability [ˌɪnə'bɪləti] *n*, *pl* **-ties** : incapacidad *f*

inaccessible [ˌɪnɪk'sɛsəbəl] *adj* : inaccesible

inaccurate [ɪn'ækjərət] *n* : inexacto

inactive [ɪn'æktɪv] *n* : inactivo — **inactivity** [ˌɪn,æk'tɪvəti] *n*, *pl* **-ties** : inactividad *f*

inadequate [ɪn'ædɪkwət] *adj* : insuficiente

inadvertently [ˌɪnəd'vərtəntli] *adv* : sin querer

inadvisable [ˌɪnæd'vaɪzəbəl] *adj* : desaconsejable

inane [ɪ'neɪn] *adj* **inaner; -est** : estúpido, tonto

inanimate [ɪn'ænəmət] *adj* : inanimado

inapplicable [ɪn'æplɪkəbəl, ˌɪnə'plɪkəbəl] *adj* : inaplicable

inappropriate [ˌɪnə'proːpriət] *adj* : impropio, inoportuno

inarticulate [ˌɪnɑr'tɪkjələt] *adj* : incapaz de expresarse

inasmuch as [ˌɪnəz'mʌtʃæz] *conj* : ya que, puesto que

inattentive [ˌɪnə'tɛntɪv] *adj* : poco atento

inaudible [ɪn'ɒdəbəl] *adj* : inaudible

inaugural [ɪ'nɒgjərəl, -gərəl] *adj* **1** : inaugural **2 ~ address** : discurso *m* de investidura — **inaugurate** [ɪ'nɒgjə,reɪt, -gə-] *vt* **-rated; -rating 1** : investir (a un presidente, etc.) **2** BEGIN : inaugurar — **inauguration** [ɪ,nɒgjə'reɪʃən, -gə-] *n* : investidura *f* (de una persona), inauguración *f* (de un edificio, etc.)

inborn ['ɪn,bɒrn] *adj* : innato

inbred ['ɪn,brɛd] *adj* INNATE : innato

incalculable [ɪn'kælkjələbəl] *adj* : incalculable

incapable [ɪn'keɪpəbəl] *adj* : incapaz — **incapacitate** [ˌɪnkə'pæsə,teɪt] *vt* **-tated; -tating** : incapacitar — **incapacity** [ˌɪnkə'pæsəti] *n*, *pl* **-ties** : incapacidad *f*

incarcerate [ɪn'kɑrsə,reɪt] *vt* **-ated; -ating** : encarcelar

incarnate [ɪn'kɑrnət, -,neɪt] *adj* : encarnado — **incarnation** [ˌɪn,kɑr'neɪʃən] *n* : encarnación *f*

incendiary [ɪn'sɛndi,ɛri] *adj* : incendiario

incense[1] ['ɪn,sɛnts] *n* : incienso *m*

incense[2] [ɪn'sɛnts] *vt* **-censed; -censing** : indignar, enfurecer

incentive [ɪn'sɛntɪv] *n* : incentivo *m*

inception [ɪn'sɛpʃən] *n* : comienzo *m*, principio *m*

incessant [ɪn'sɛsənt] *adj* : incesante

incest ['ɪn,sɛst] *n* : incesto *m* — **incestuous** [ɪn'sɛstʃʊəs] *adj* : incestuoso

inch ['ɪntʃ] *n* : pulgada *f* — *~ v* : avanzar poco a poco

incident ['ɪnsədənt] *n* : incidente *m* — **incidence** ['ɪnsədənts] *n* : índice *m* (de crímenes, etc.) — **incidental** [ˌɪnsə'dɛntəl] *adj* **1** MINOR : incidental **2** CHANCE : casual — **incidentally** [ˌɪnsə'dɛntəli, -'dɛntli] *adv* : a propósito

incinerate [ɪn'sɪnə,reɪt] *vt* **-ated; -ating** : incinerar — **incinerator** [ɪn'sɪnə,reɪtər] *n* : incinerador *m*

incision [ɪn'sɪʒən] *n* : incisión *f*

incite [ɪn'saɪt] *vt* **-cited; -citing** : incitar, instigar

incline [ɪn'klaɪn] *v* **-clined; -clining** *vt* **1** BEND : inclinar **2 be ~ed to** : inclinarse a, tender a — *~ vi* : inclinarse — *~* ['ɪn,klaɪn] *n* : pendiente *f* — **inclination** [ˌɪnklə'neɪʃən] *n* **1** : inclinación *f* **2** DESIRE : deseo *m*, ganas *fpl*

include [ɪn'kluːd] *vt* **-cluded; -cluding** : incluir — **inclusion** [ɪn'kluːʒən] *n* : inclusión *f* — **inclusive** [ɪn'kluːsɪv] *adj* : inclusivo

incognito [ˌɪn,kɑg'niːto, ɪn'kɑgnə,to:] *adv & adj* : de incógnito

incoherent [ˌɪnko'hɪrənt, -'hɛr-] *adj* : incoherente — **incoherence** [ˌɪnko-ˈhɪrənts, -her-] n : incoherencia f

income [ˈɪnˌkʌm] n : ingresos mpl — **income tax** n : impuesto m sobre la renta

incomparable [ɪnˈkɑmpərəbəl] adj : incomparable

incompatible [ˌɪnkəmˈpæt̬əbəl] adj : incompatible

incompetent [ɪnˈkɑmpət̬ənt] adj : incompetente — **incompetence** [ɪnˈkɑmpət̬ənts] n : incompetencia f

incomplete [ˌɪnkəmˈpliːt] adj : incompleto

incomprehensible [ˌɪnˌkɑmprɪˈhentsə-bəl] adj : incomprensible

inconceivable [ˌɪnkənˈsiːvəbəl] adj : inconcebible

inconclusive [ˌɪnkənˈkluːsɪv] adj : no concluyente

incongruous [ɪnˈkɑŋgruəs] adj : incongruente

inconsiderate [ˌɪnkənˈsɪdərət] adj : desconsiderado

inconsistent [ˌɪnkənˈsɪstənt] adj 1 : inconsecuente 2 be ~ with : no concordar con — **inconsistency** [ˌɪnkən-ˈsɪstəntsi] n, pl -cies : inconsecuencia f

inconspicuous [ˌɪnkənˈspɪkjuəs] adj : que no llama la atención

inconvenient [ˌɪnkənˈviːnjənt] adj : incómodo, inconveniente — **inconvenience** [ˌɪnkənˈviːnjənts] n 1 BOTHER : incomodidad f, molestia f 2 DRAWBACK : inconveniente m — ~ vt -nienced; -niencing vt : importunar, molestar

incorporate [ɪnˈkɔrpəˌreɪt] vt -rated; -rating : incorporar

incorrect [ˌɪnkəˈrekt] adj : incorrecto

increase [ˈɪnˌkriːs, ɪnˈkriːs] n : aumento m — ~ [ɪnˈkriːs, ˈɪnˌkriːs] v -creased; -creasing : aumentar — **increasingly** [ɪnˈkriːsɪŋli] adv : cada vez más

incredible [ɪnˈkredəbəl] adj : increíble

incredulous [ɪnˈkredʒələs] adj : incrédulo

incriminate [ɪnˈkrɪməˌneɪt] vt -nated; -nating : incriminar

incubator [ˈɪŋkjuˌbeɪt̬ər, ˈɪn-] n : incubadora f

incumbent [ɪnˈkʌmbənt] n : titular mf

incur [ɪnˈkər] vt incurred; incurring : provocar (al enojo, etc.), incurrir en (gastos)

incurable [ɪnˈkjurəbəl] adj : incurable

indebted [ɪnˈdet̬əd] adj 1 : endeudado 2 be ~ to s.o. : estar en deuda con algn

indecent [ɪnˈdiːsənt] adj : indecente — **indecency** [ɪnˈdiːsəntsi] n, pl -cies : indecencia f

indecisive [ˌɪndɪˈsaɪsɪv] adj : indeciso

indeed [ɪnˈdiːd] adv 1 TRULY : verdaderamente, sin duda 2 IN FACT : en efecto 3 ~? : ¿de veras?

indefinite [ɪnˈdefənət] adj 1 : indefinido 2 VAGUE : impreciso — **indefinitely** [ɪnˈdefənət̬li] adv : indefinidamente

indelible [ɪnˈdeləbəl] adj : indeleble

indent [ɪnˈdent] vt : sangrar (un párrafo) — **indentation** [ˌɪnˌdenˈteɪʃən] n DENT, NOTCH : mella f

independent [ˌɪndəˈpendənt] adj : independiente — **independence** [ˌɪndə-ˈpendənts] n : independencia f

indescribable [ˌɪndɪˈskraɪbəbəl] adj : indescriptible

indestructible [ˌɪndɪˈstrʌktəbəl] adj : indestructible

index [ˈɪnˌdeks] n, pl **-dexes** or **-dices** [ˈɪndəˌsiːz] : índice m — ~ vt : incluir en un índice — **index finger** n : dedo m índice

Indian [ˈɪndiən] adj : indio m, -dia f

indication [ˌɪndəˈkeɪʃən] n : indicio m, señal f — **indicate** [ˈɪndəˌkeɪt] vt -cated; -cating : indicar — **indicative** [ɪnˈdɪkət̬ɪv] adj : indicativo — **indicator** [ˈɪndəˌkeɪt̬ər] n : indicador m

indict [ɪnˈdaɪt] vt : acusar (de un crimen) — **indictment** [ɪnˈdaɪtmənt] n : acusación f

indifferent [ɪnˈdɪfrənt, -dɪfə-] adj 1 : indiferente 2 MEDIOCRE : mediocre — **indifference** [ɪnˈdɪfrənts, -dɪfə-] n : indiferencia f

indigenous [ɪnˈdɪdʒənəs] adj : indígena

indigestion [ˌɪndaɪˈdʒestʃən, -dɪ-] n : indigestión f — **indigestible** [ˌɪndaɪ-ˈdʒestəbəl, -dɪ-] adj : indigesto

indignation [ˌɪndɪgˈneɪʃən] n : indignación f — **indignant** [ɪnˈdɪgnənt] adj : indignado — **indignity** [ɪnˈdɪgnət̬i] n, pl **-ties** : indignidad f

indigo [ˈɪndɪˌgoː] n, pl **-gos** or **-goes** : añil m

indirect [ˌɪndəˈrekt, -daɪ-] adj : indirecto

indiscreet [ˌɪndɪˈskriːt] adj : indiscreto — **indiscretion** [ˌɪndɪˈskreʃən] n : indiscreción f

indiscriminate [ˌɪndɪˈskrɪmənət] adj : indiscriminado

indispensable [ˌɪndɪˈspentsəbəl] adj : indispensable, imprescindible

indisputable [ˌɪndɪˈspjuːt̬əbəl, ɪnˈdɪspjuːt̬ə-] adj : indiscutible

indistinct [ˌɪndɪˈstɪŋkt] adj : indistinto

individual [ˌɪndəˈvɪdʒuəl] adj 1 : individual 2 PARTICULAR : particular — ~ n : individuo m — **individuality** [ˌɪndə-ˌvɪdʒuˈælət̬i] n, pl **-ties** : individualidad *f* — **individually** [ˌɪndə'vɪdʒʊəli, -dʒəli] *adv* : individualmente

indoctrinate [ɪn'dɑktrəˌneɪt] *vt* **-nated; -nating** : adoctrinar — **indoctrination** [ɪnˌdɑktrə'neɪʃən] *n* : adoctrinamiento *m*

indoor ['ɪn'dor] *adj* **1** : (de) interior **2** ~ **plant** : planta *f* de interior **3** ~ **pool** : piscina *f* cubierta **4** ~ **sports** : deportes *mpl* bajo techo — **indoors** ['ɪn'dorz] *adv* : adentro, dentro

induce [ɪn'dus, -'djus] *vt* **-duced; -ducing 1** : inducir **2** CAUSE : provocar — **inducement** [ɪn'dusmənt, -'djus-] *n* : incentivo *m*

indulge [ɪn'dʌldʒ] *v* **-dulged; -dulging** *vt* **1** GRATIFY : satisfacer **2** PAMPER : consentir — *vi* ~ **in** : permitirse — **indulgence** [ɪn'dʌldʒənts] *n* **1** : indulgencia *f* **2** SATISFYING : satisfacción *f* — **indulgent** [ɪn'dʌldʒənt] *adj* : indulgente

industry ['ɪndəstri] *n, pl* **-tries 1** : industria *f* **2** DILIGENCE : diligencia *f* — **industrial** [ɪn'dʌstriəl] *adj* : industrial — **industrialize** [ɪn'dʌstriəˌlaɪz] *vt* **-ized; -izing** : industrializar — **industrious** [ɪn'dʌstriəs] *adj* : diligente, trabajador

inebriated [ɪ'niːbriˌeɪtəd] *adj* : ebrio, embriagado

inedible [ɪn'ɛdəbəl] *adj* : no comestible

ineffective [ˌɪnɪ'fɛktɪv] *adj* **1** : ineficaz **2** INCOMPETENT : incompetente — **ineffectual** [ˌɪnɪ'fɛktʃʊəl] *adj* : inútil, ineficaz

inefficient [ˌɪnɪ'fɪʃənt] *adj* **1** : ineficiente **2** INCOMPETENT : incompetente — **inefficiency** [ˌɪnɪ'fɪʃəntsi] *n, pl* **-cies** : ineficiencia *f*

ineligible [ɪn'ɛlədʒəbəl] *adj* : ineligible

inept [ɪ'nɛpt] *adj* **1** : inepto **2** ~ **at** : incapaz para

inequality [ˌɪnɪ'kwɑləti] *n, pl* **-ties** : desigualdad *f*

inert [ɪ'nərt] *adj* : inerte — **inertia** [ɪ'nərʃə] *n* : inercia *f*

inescapable [ˌɪnɪ'skeɪpəbəl] *adj* : ineludible

inevitable [ɪ'nɛvət̬əbəl] *adj* : inevitable — **inevitably** [-bli] *adv* : inevitablemente

inexcusable [ˌɪnɪk'skjuːzəbəl] *adj* : inexcusable

inexpensive [ˌɪnɪk'spɛntsɪv] *adj* : barato, económico

inexperienced [ˌɪnɪk'spɪriəntst] *adj* : inexperto

inexplicable [ˌɪnɪk'splɪkəbəl] *adj* : inexplicable

infallible [ɪn'fæləbəl] *adj* : infalible

infamous ['ɪnfəməs] *adj* : infame

infancy ['ɪnfəntsi] *n, pl* **-cies** : infancia *f* — **infant** ['ɪnfənt] *n* : bebé *m;* niño *m,* -ña *f* — **infantile** ['ɪnfənˌtaɪl, -təl, -ˌtiːl] *adj* : infantil

infantry ['ɪnfəntri] *n, pl* **-tries** : infantería *f*

infatuated [ɪn'fætʃʊˌeɪt̬əd] *adj* be ~ **with** : estar encaprichado con — **infatuation** [ɪnˌfætʃʊ'eɪʃən] *n* : encaprichamiento *m*

infect [ɪn'fɛkt] *vt* : infectar — **infection** [ɪn'fɛkʃən] *n* : infección *f* — **infectious** [ɪn'fɛkʃəs] *adj* : contagioso

infer [ɪn'fər] *vt* **inferred; inferring** : deducir, inferir — **inference** ['ɪnfərənts] *n* : deducción *f*

inferior [ɪn'firiər] *adj* : inferior — ~ *n* : inferior *mf* — **inferiority** [ɪnˌfiri'ɔrəti] *n, pl* **-ties** : inferioridad *f*

infernal [ɪn'fərnəl] *adj* : infernal — **inferno** [ɪn'fərˌnoː] *n, pl* **-nos** : infierno *m*

infertile [ɪn'fərt̬əl, -ˌtaɪl] *adj* : estéril — **infertility** [ˌɪnfər'tɪləti] *n* : esterilidad *f*

infest [ɪn'fɛst] *vt* : infestar

infidelity [ˌɪnfə'dɛlət̬i, -faɪ-] *n, pl* **-ties** : infidelidad *f*

infiltrate [ɪn'fɪlˌtreɪt, 'ɪnfɪl-] *v* **-trated; -trating** *vt* : infiltrar — *vi* : infiltrarse

infinite ['ɪnfənət] *adj* : infinito

infinitive [ɪn'fɪnət̬ɪv] *n* : infinitivo *m*

infinity [ɪn'fɪnət̬i] *n, pl* **-ties 1** : infinito *m* **2 an** ~ **of** : una infinidad de

infirm [ɪn'fərm] *adj* : enfermizo, endeble — **infirmary** [ɪn'fərməri] *n, pl* **-ries** : enfermería *f* — **infirmity** [ɪn'fərmət̬i] *n, pl* **-ties 1** FRAILTY : endeblez *f* **2** AILMENT : enfermedad *f*

inflame [ɪn'fleɪm] *vt* **-flamed; -flaming** : inflamar — **inflammable** [ɪn'flæməbəl] *adj* : inflamable — **inflammation** [ˌɪnflə'meɪʃən] *n* : inflamación *f* — **inflammatory** [ɪn'flæməˌtori] *adj* : inflamatorio

inflate [ɪn'fleɪt] *vt* **-flated; -flating** : inflar — **inflation** [ɪn'fleɪʃən] *n* : inflación *f* — **inflationary** [ɪn'fleɪʃəˌneri] *adj* : inflacionario, inflacionista

inflexible [ɪn'flɛksɪbəl] *adj* : inflexible

inflict [ɪn'flɪkt] *vt* : infligir

influence ['ɪnˌfluːənts, ɪn'fluːənts] *n* **1** : influencia *f* **2 under the** ~ : embriagado — ~ *vt* **-enced; -encing** : influir en, influenciar — **influential** [ˌɪnflu'entʃəl] *adj* : influyente

influenza [ˌɪnflu'enzə] *n* : gripe *f,* influenza *f*

influx ['ɪnˌflʌks] *n* : afluencia *f*

inform [ɪn'form] *vt* **1** : informar **2 keep me** ~**ed** : manténme al corriente — *vi* ~ **on** : delatar, denunciar

informal [ɪnˈfɔrməl] *adj* **1** : informal **2**
: familiar (dícese del lenguaje) — **in-
formality** [ˌɪnfɔrˈmæləṭi, -fər-] *n, pl*
-ties : falta *f* de ceremonia — **informally** [ɪnˈfɔrməli] *adv* : de manera informal

information [ˌɪnfərˈmeɪʃən] *n* : información *f* — **informative** [ɪnˈfɔrməṭɪv] *adj*
: informativo — **informer** [ɪnˈfɔrmər] *n*
: informante *mf*

infrared [ˌɪnfrəˈrɛd] *adj* : infrarrojo

infrastructure [ˈɪnfrəˌstrʌktʃər] *n* : infraestructura *f*

infrequent [ɪnˈfriːkwənt] *adj* : infrecuente — **infrequently** [ɪnˈfriːkwəntli]
adv : raramente

infringe [ɪnˈfrɪndʒ] *v* **-fringed; -fringing**
vt : infringir — *vi* ~ **on** : violar — **in-
fringement** [ɪnˈfrɪndʒmənt] *n* : violación *f*

infuriate [ɪnˈfjʊriˌeɪt] *vt* **-ated; -ating**
: enfurecer, poner furioso — **infuriat-
ing** [ɪnˈfjʊriˌeɪtɪŋ] *adj* : exasperante

infuse [ɪnˈfjuːz] *vt* **-fused; -fusing** : infundir — **infusion** [ɪnˈfjuːʒən] *n* : infusión *f*

ingenious [ɪnˈdʒiːnjəs] *adj* : ingenioso
— **ingenuity** [ˌɪndʒəˈnuːəṭi, -ˈnjuː-] *n, pl*
-ities : ingenio

ingenuous [ɪnˈdʒɛnjʊəs] *adj* : ingenuo

ingest [ɪnˈdʒɛst] *vt* : ingerir

ingot [ˈɪŋɡət] *n* : lingote *m*

ingrained [ɪnˈɡreɪnd] *adj* : arraigado

ingratiate [ɪnˈɡreɪʃiˌeɪt] *vt* **-ated; -ating**
~ **oneself with** : congraciarse con

ingratitude [ɪnˈɡræṭəˌtuːd, -ˌtjuːd] *n* : ingratitud *f*

ingredient [ɪnˈɡriːdiənt] *n* : ingrediente *m*

ingrown [ˈɪnˌɡroːn] *adj* ~ **nail** : uña *f* en-
carnada

inhabit [ɪnˈhæbət] *vt* : habitar — **inhabitant** [ɪnˈhæbətənt] *n* : habitante *mf*

inhale [ɪnˈheɪl] *v* **-haled; -haling** *vt* : inhalar, aspirar — *vi* : inspirar

inherent [ɪnˈhɪrənt, -ˈher-] *adj* : inherente
— **inherently** [ɪnˈhɪrəntli, -ˈher-] *adv*
: intrínsecamente

inherit [ɪnˈherət] *vt* : heredar — **inheritance** [ɪnˈherətənts] *n* : herencia *f*

inhibit [ɪnˈhɪbət] *vt* IMPEDE : inhibir —
inhibition [ˌɪnhəˈbɪʃən, ˌɪnə-] *n* : inhibición *f*

inhuman [ɪnˈhjuːmən, -ˈjuː-] *adj* : inhumano — **inhumane** [ˌɪnhjuˈmeɪn, -ju-]
adj : inhumano — **inhumanity** [ˌɪnhju-
ˈmænəṭi, -ju-] *n, pl* **-ties** : inhumanidad
f

initial [ɪˈnɪʃəl] *adj* : inicial — *n* : inicial *f*
— *vt* **-tialed** *or* **-tialled; -tialing** *or*
-tialling : poner las iniciales a

initiate [ɪˈnɪʃiˌeɪt] *vt* **-ated; -ating 1**
BEGIN : iniciar **2** ~ **s.o. into sth** : iniciar a algn en algo — **initiation** [ɪˌnɪʃi-
ˈeɪʃən] *n* : iniciación *f* — **initiative** [ɪˈnɪ-
ʃəṭɪv] *n* : iniciativa *f*

inject [ɪnˈdʒɛkt] *vt* : inyectar — **injection** [ɪnˈdʒɛkʃən] *n* : inyección *f*

injure [ˈɪndʒər] *vt* **-jured; -juring 1**
: herir **2** ~ **oneself** : hacerse daño —
injurious [ɪnˈdʒʊriəs] *adj* : perjudicial
— **injury** [ˈɪndʒəri] *n, pl* **-ries 1** : herida
f **2** HARM : perjuicio *m*

injustice [ɪnˈdʒʌstəs] *n* : injusticia *f*

ink [ˈɪŋk] *n* : tinta *f* — **inkwell** [ˈɪŋkˌwɛl] *n*
: tintero *m*

inland [ˈɪnˌlænd, -lənd] *adj* : interior —
~ *adv* : hacia el interior, tierra adentro

in-laws [ˈɪnˌlɔz] *npl* : suegros *mpl*

inlet [ˈɪnˌlɛt, -lət] *n* : ensenada *f*, cala *f*

inmate [ˈɪnˌmeɪt] *n* **1** PATIENT : paciente
mf **2** PRISONER : preso *m*, -sa *f*

inn [ˈɪn] *n* : posada *f*, hostería *f*

innards [ˈɪnərdz] *npl* : entrañas *fpl*, tripas *fpl fam*

innate [ɪˈneɪt] *adj* : innato

inner [ˈɪnər] *adj* : interior, interno — **in-
nermost** [ˈɪnərˌmoːst] *adj* : más íntimo,
más profundo

inning [ˈɪnɪŋ] *n* : entrada *f*

innocent [ˈɪnəsənt] *adj* : inocente — ~
n : inocente *mf* — **innocence** [ˈɪnə-
sənts] *n* : inocencia *f*

innocuous [ɪˈnɑkjəwəs] *adj* : inocuo

innovate [ˈɪnəˌveɪt] *vi* **-vated; -vating**
: innovar — **innovation** [ˌɪnəˈveɪʃən] *n*
: innovación *f* — **innovative** [ˈɪnə-
ˌveɪṭɪv] *adj* : innovador — **innovator**
[ˈɪnəˌveɪtər] *n* : innovador *m*, -dora *f*

innuendo [ˌɪnjʊˈɛndo] *n, pl* **-dos** *or*
-does : insinuación *f*, indirecta *f*

innumerable [ɪˈnuːmərəbəl, -ˈnjuː-] *adj*
: innumerable

inoculate [ɪˈnɑkjəˌleɪt] *vt* **-lated; -lating**
: inocular — **inoculation** [ɪˌnɑkjə-
ˈleɪʃən] *n* : inoculación *f*

inoffensive [ˌɪnəˈfɛntsɪv] *adj* : inofensivo

inpatient [ˈɪnˌpeɪʃənt] *n* : paciente *mf*
hospitalizado

input [ˈɪnˌpʊt] *n* **1** : contribución *f* **2** : entrada *f* (de datos) — ~ *vt* **-putted** *or*
-put; -putting : entrar (datos, etc.)

inquire [ɪnˈkwaɪr] *v* **-quired; -quiring** *vt*
: preguntar — *vi* **1** ~ **about** : informarse sobre **2** ~ **into** : investigar —
inquiry [ˈɪnkwaɪri, ɪnˈkwaɪri; ˈɪnkwəri,
ˈɪŋ-] *n, pl* **-ries 1** QUESTION : pregunta *f*
2 INVESTIGATION : investigación *f* —
inquisition [ˌɪnkwəˈzɪʃən, ˌɪŋ-] *n* : in-

quisición *f* — **inquisitive** [ɪnˈkwɪzət̬ɪv] *adj* : curioso
insane [ɪnˈseɪn] *adj* : loco — **insanity** [ɪnˈsænət̬i] *n, pl* **-ties** : locura *f*
insatiable [ɪnˈseɪʃəbəl] *adj* : insaciable
inscribe [ɪnˈskraɪb] *vt* **-scribed; -scribing** : inscribir — **inscription** [ɪnˈskrɪpʃən] *n* : inscripción *f*
inscrutable [ɪnˈskruːt̬əbəl] *adj* : inescrutable
insect [ˈɪnˌsɛkt] *n* : insecto *m* — **insecticide** [ɪnˈsɛktəˌsaɪd] *n* : insecticida *m*
insecure [ˌɪnsɪˈkjʊr] *adj* : inseguro, poco seguro — **insecurity** [ˌɪnsɪˈkjʊrət̬i] *n, pl* **-ties** : inseguridad *f*
insensitive [ɪnˈsɛnsət̬ɪv] *adj* : insensible — **insensitivity** [ɪnˌsɛnsəˈtɪvət̬i] *n, pl* **-ties** : insensibilidad *f*
inseparable [ɪnˈsɛpərəbəl] *adj* : inseparable
insert [ɪnˈsərt] *vt* : insertar (texto), introducir (una moneda, etc.)
inside [ɪnˈsaɪd, ˈɪnˌsaɪd] *n* **1** : interior *m* **2** ~ **out** : al revés — *adv* : dentro, adentro — ~ *adj* : interior — ~ *prep* **1** or ~ **of** : dentro de **2** ~ **an hour** : en menos de una hora
insidious [ɪnˈsɪdiəs] *adj* : insidioso
insight [ˈɪnˌsaɪt] *n* : perspicacia *f*
insignia [ɪnˈsɪgniə] or **insigne** [-niː] *n, pl* **-nia** or **-nias** : insignia *f*, enseña *f*
insignificant [ˌɪnsɪgˈnɪfɪkənt] *adj* : insignificante
insincere [ˌɪnsɪnˈsɪr] *adj* : insincero
insinuate [ɪnˈsɪnjuˌeɪt] *vt* **-ated; -ating** : insinuar — **insinuation** [ɪnˌsɪnjuˈeɪʃən] *n* : insinuación *f*
insipid [ɪnˈsɪpəd] *adj* : insípido
insist [ɪnˈsɪst] *v* : insistir — **insistent** [ɪnˈsɪstənt] *adj* : insistente
insofar as [ˌɪnsoˈfɑrˌæz] *conj* : en la medida en que
insole [ˈɪnˌsoːl] *n* : plantilla *f*
insolent [ˈɪnsələnt] *adj* : insolente — **insolence** [ˈɪnsələnts] *n* : insolencia *f*
insolvent [ɪnˈsɑlvənt] *adj* : insolvente
insomnia [ɪnˈsɑmniə] *n* : insomnio *m*
inspect [ɪnˈspɛkt] *vt* : inspeccionar, revisar — **inspection** [ɪnˈspɛkʃən] *n* : inspección *f* — **inspector** [ɪnˈspɛktər] *n* : inspector *m*, -tora *f*
inspire [ɪnˈspaɪr] *vt* **-spired; -spiring** : inspirar — **inspiration** [ˌɪnspəˈreɪʃən] *n* : inspiración *f* — **inspirational** [ˌɪnspəˈreɪʃənəl] *adj* : inspirador
instability [ˌɪnstəˈbɪlət̬i] *n, pl* **-ties** : inestabilidad *f*
install [ɪnˈstɔl] *vt* **-stalled; -stalling** : instalar — **installation** [ˌɪnstəˈleɪʃən] *n* : instalación *f* — **installment** [ɪnˈstɔlmənt] *n* **1** PAYMENT : plazo *m*, cuota *f* **2** : entrega *f* (de una publicación o telenovela)
instance [ˈɪnstənts] *n* **1** : ejemplo *m* **2** **for** ~ : por ejemplo **3** **in this** ~ : en este caso
instant [ˈɪnstənt] *n* : instante *m* — ~ *adj* **1** IMMEDIATE : inmediato **2** ~ **coffee** : café *m* instantáneo — **instantaneous** [ˌɪnstənˈteɪniəs] *adj* : instantáneo — **instantly** [ˈɪnstəntli] *adv* : al instante, instantáneamente
instead [ɪnˈstɛd] *adv* **1** : en cambio **2** **I went** ~ : fui en su lugar — **instead of** *prep* : en vez de, en lugar de
instep [ˈɪnˌstɛp] *n* : empeine *m*
instigate [ˈɪnstəˌgeɪt] *vt* **-gated; -gating** : instigar a — **instigation** [ˌɪnstəˈgeɪʃən] *n* : instigación *f* — **instigator** [ˈɪnstəˌgeɪt̬ər] *n* : instigador *m*, -dora *f*
instill [ɪnˈstɪl] or *Brit* **instil** *vt* **-stilled; -stilling** : inculcar, infundir
instinct [ˈɪnstɪŋkt] *n* : instinto *m* — **instinctive** [ɪnˈstɪŋktɪv] or **instinctual** [ɪnˈstɪŋktʃuəl] *adj* : instintivo
institute [ˈɪnstəˌtuːt, -ˌtjuːt] *vt* **-tuted; -tuting** **1** : instituir **2** INITIATE : iniciar — ~ *n* : instituto *m* — **institution** [ˌɪnstəˈtuːʃən, -ˈtjuː-] *n* : institución *f*
instruct [ɪnˈstrʌkt] *vt* **1** : instruir **2** COMMAND : mandar — **instruction** [ɪnˈstrʌkʃən] *n* : instrucción *f* — **instructor** [ɪnˈstrʌktər] *n* : instructor *m*, -tora *f*
instrument [ˈɪnstrəmənt] *n* : instrumento *m* — **instrumental** [ˌɪnstrəˈmɛntəl] *adj* **1** : instrumental **2** **be** ~ **in** : jugar un papel fundamental en
insubordinate [ˌɪnsəˈbɔrdənət] *adj* : insubordinado — **insubordination** [ˌɪnsəˌbɔrdənˈeɪʃən] *n* : insubordinación *f*
insufferable [ɪnˈsʌfərəbəl] *adj* : insoportable
insufficient [ˌɪnsəˈfɪʃənt] *adj* : insuficiente
insular [ˈɪnt̬sələr, -ˌsjʊ-] *adj* **1** : insular **2** NARROW-MINDED : estrecho de miras
insulate [ˈɪntsəˌleɪt] *vt* **-lated; -lating** : aislar — **insulation** [ˌɪntsəˈleɪʃən] *n* : aislamiento *m*
insulin [ˈɪntsələn] *n* : insulina *f*
insult [ɪnˈsʌlt] *vt* : insultar — ~ [ˈɪnˌsʌlt] *n* : insulto *m* — **insulting** [ɪnˈsʌltɪŋ] *adj* : insultante, ofensivo
insure [ɪnˈʃʊr] *vt* **-sured; -suring** : asegurar — **insurance** [ɪnˈʃʊrənts, ˈɪnˌʃʊr-] *n* : seguro *m*
insurmountable [ˌɪnsərˈmaʊntəbəl] *adj* : insuperable
intact [ɪnˈtækt] *adj* : intacto

intake ['ɪn,teɪk] *n* : consumo *m* (de alimentos), entrada *f* (de aire, etc.)
intangible [ɪn'tændʒəbəl] *adj* : intangible
integral ['ɪntɪgrəl] *adj* : integral
integrate ['ɪntəgreɪt] *v* **-grated; -grating** *vt* : integrar — *vi* : integrarse
integrity [ɪn'tegrəti] *n* : integridad *f*
intellect ['ɪntə,lekt] *n* : intelecto *m* — **intellectual** [,ɪntə'lektʃuəl] *adj* : intelectual — ~ *n* : intelectual *mf* — **intelligence** [ɪn'telədʒənts] *n* : inteligencia *f* — **intelligent** [ɪn'telədʒənt] *adj* : inteligente — **intelligible** [ɪn'telədʒəbəl] *adj* : inteligible
intend [ɪn'tend] *vt* **1 be ~ed for** : ser para **2 ~ to do** : pensar hacer, tener la intención de hacer — **intended** [ɪn'tendəd] *adj* : intencionado, deliberado
intense [ɪn'tents] *adj* : intenso — **intensely** [ɪn'tentsli] *adv* : sumamente, profundamente — **intensify** [ɪn'tentsə,faɪ] *v* **-fied; -fying** *vt* : intensificar — *vi* : intensificarse — **intensity** [ɪn'tentsəti] *n*, *pl* **-ties** : intensidad *f* — **intensive** [ɪn'tentsɪv] *adj* : intensivo
intent [ɪn'tent] *n* : intención *f* — ~ *adj* **1** : atento, concentrado **2 ~ on doing** : resuelto a hacer — **intention** [ɪn'tentʃən] *n* : intención *f* — **intentional** [ɪn'tentʃənəl] *adj* : intencional, deliberado — **intently** [ɪn'tentli] *adv* : atentamente, fijamente
interact [,ɪntər'ækt] *vi* **1** : interactuar **2 ~ with** : relacionarse con — **interaction** [,ɪntər'ækʃən] *n* : interacción *f* — **interactive** [,ɪntər'æktɪv] *adj* : interactivo
intercede [,ɪntər'siːd] *vi* **-ceded; -ceding** : interceder
intercept [,ɪntər'sept] *vt* : interceptar
interchange [,ɪntər'tʃeɪndʒ] *vt* **-changed; -changing** : intercambiar — ~ ['ɪntər,tʃeɪndʒ] *n* **1** : intercambio *m* **2** JUNCTION : enlace *m* — **interchangeable** [,ɪntər'tʃeɪndʒəbəl] *adj* : intercambiable
intercourse ['ɪntər,kɔrs] *n* : relaciones *fpl* (sexuales)
interest ['ɪntrəst, -tə,rest] *n* : interés *m* — ~ *vt* : interesar — **interested** [-əd] *adj* : interesado — **interesting** ['ɪntrəstɪŋ, -tə,restɪŋ] *adj* : interesante
interface ['ɪntər,feɪs] *n* : interfaz *mf* (de una computadora)
interfere [,ɪntər'fɪr] *vi* **-fered; -fering 1 ~ in** : entrometerse en, interferir en **2 ~ with** DISRUPT : afectar (una actividad, etc.) — **interference** [,ɪntər-'fɪrənts] *n* **1** : interferencia *f* **2** : intromisión *f* (en el radio, etc.)
interim ['ɪntərəm] *n* **1** : interín *m* **2 in the ~** : mientras tanto — ~ *adj* : interino, provisional
interior [ɪn'tɪriər] *adj* : interior — ~ *n* : interior *m*
interjection [,ɪntər'dʒekʃən] *n* : interjección *f*
interlock [,ɪntər'lɑk] *vt* : engranar
interloper [,ɪntər'loːpər] *n* : intruso *m*, -sa *f*
interlude ['ɪntər,luːd] *n* **1** : intervalo *m* **2** : interludio *m* (en música, etc.)
intermediate [,ɪntər'miːdiət] *adj* : intermedio — **intermediary** [,ɪntər'miːdi,eri] *n*, *pl* **-aries** : intermediario *m*, -ria *f*
interminable [ɪn'tərmənəbəl] *adj* : interminable
intermission [,ɪntər'mɪʃən] *n* : intervalo *m*, intermedio *m*
intermittent [,ɪntər'mɪtənt] *adj* : intermitente
intern[1] ['ɪn,tərn, ɪn'tərn] *vt* : confinar
intern[2] ['ɪn,tərn] *vi* : hacer las prácticas — ~ *n* : interno *m*, -na *f*
internal [ɪn'tərnəl] *adj* : interno
international [,ɪntər'næʃənəl] *adj* : internacional
interpret [ɪn'tərprət] *vt* : interpretar — **interpretation** [ɪn,tərprə'teɪʃən] *n* : interpretación *f* — **interpreter** [ɪn'tərprə-tər] *n* : intérprete *mf*
interrogate [ɪn'terəgeɪt] *vt* **-gated; -gating** : interrogar — **interrogation** [ɪn,terə'geɪʃən] *n* QUESTIONING : interrogatorio *m* — **interrogative** [,ɪntə-'rɑgətɪv] *adj* : interrogativo
interrupt [,ɪntər'ʌpt] *v* : interrumpir — **interruption** [,ɪntər'ʌpʃən] *n* : interrupción *f*
intersect [,ɪntər'sekt] *vt* : cruzar (dícese de calles), cortar (dícese de líneas) — *vi* : cruzarse, cortarse — **intersection** [,ɪntər'sekʃən] *n* : cruce *m*, intersección *f*
intersperse [,ɪntər'spərs] *vt* **-spersed; -spersing** : intercalar
interstate [,ɪntər'steɪt] *n* or ~ **highway** : carretera *f* interestatal
intertwine [,ɪntər'twaɪn] *vi* **-twined; -twining** : entrelazarse
interval ['ɪntərvəl] *n* : intervalo *m*
intervene [,ɪntər'viːn] *vi* **-vened; -vening 1** : intervenir **2** ELAPSE : transcurrir, pasar — **intervention** [,ɪntər'ven-tʃən] *n* : intervención *f*
interview ['ɪntər,vjuː] *n* : entrevista *f* — ~ *vt* : entrevistar — **interviewer** ['ɪntər,vjuːər] *n* : entrevistador *m*, -dora *f*

intestine ['ɪn'tɛstən] n : intestino m — **intestinal** ['ɪn'tɛstənəl] adj : intestinal

intimate[1] ['ɪntəˌmeɪt] vt **-mated; -mating** : insinuar, dar a entender

intimate[2] ['ɪntəmət] adj : íntimo — **intimacy** ['ɪntəməsi] n, pl **-cies** : intimidad f

intimidate [ɪn'tɪməˌdeɪt] vt **-dated; -dating** : intimidar — **intimidation** [ɪnˌtɪmə'deɪʃəd] n : intimidación f

into ['ɪnˌtuː] prep **1** : en, a **2** bump ∼ : darse contra **3** (used in mathematics) **3** ∼ **12** : 12 dividido por 3

intolerable [ɪn'tɑlərəbəl] adj : intolerable — **intolerance** [ɪn'tɑlərənts] n : intolerancia f — **intolerant** [ɪn'tɑlərənt] adj : intolerante

intoxicate [ɪn'tɑksəˌkeɪt] vt **-cated; -cating** : embriagar — **intoxicated** [ɪn'tɑksəˌkeɪtəd] adj **1** : embriagado **2** ∼ **with** : ebrio de

intransitive [ɪn'træntsətɪv, -'trænzə-] adj : intransitivo

intravenous [ˌɪntrə'viːnəs] adj : intravenoso

intrepid [ɪn'trɛpəd] adj : intrépido

intricate ['ɪntrɪkət] adj : complicado, intrincado — **intricacy** ['ɪntrɪkəsi] n, pl **-cies** : complejidad f

intrigue ['ɪnˌtriːg, ɪn'triːg] n : intriga f — ∼ [ɪn'triːg] v **-trigued; -triguing** : intrigar — **intriguing** [ɪn'triːgɪŋli] adj : intrigante

intrinsic [ɪn'trɪnzɪk, -'trɪntsɪk] adj : intrínseco

introduce [ˌɪntrə'duːs, -'djuːs] vt **-duced; -ducing** **1** : introducir **2** : presentar (a una persona) — **introduction** [ˌɪntrə'dʌkʃən] n **1** : introducción f **2** : presentación f (de una persona) — **introductory** [ˌɪntrə'dʌktəri] adj : introductorio

introvert ['ɪntrəˌvərt] n : introvertido m, -da f — **introverted** ['ɪntrəˌvərtəd] adj : introvertido

intrude [ɪn'truːd] vi **-truded; -truding 1** : entrometerse **2** ∼ **on s.o.** : molestar a algn — **intruder** [ɪn'truːdər] n : intruso m, -sa f — **intrusion** [ɪn'truːʒən] n : intrusión f — **intrusive** [ɪn'truːsɪv] adj : intruso

intuition [ˌɪntu'ɪʃən, -tju-] n : intuición f — **intuitive** [ɪn'tuːətɪv, -tju-] adj : intuitivo

inundate ['ɪnənˌdeɪt] vt **-dated; -dating** : inundar

invade [ɪn'veɪd] vt **-vaded; -vading** : invadir

invalid[1] [ɪn'væləd] adj : inválido

invalid[2] ['ɪnvələd] n : inválido m, -da f

invaluable [ɪn'væljəbəl, -'væljuə-] adj : inestimable, invalorable Lat

invariable [ɪn'væriəbəl] adj : invariable

invasion [ɪn'veɪʒən] n : invasión f

invent [ɪn'vɛnt] vt : inventar — **invention** [ɪn'vɛntʃən] n : invención f — **inventive** [ɪn'vɛntɪv] adj : inventivo — **inventor** [ɪn'vɛntər] n : inventor m, -tora f

inventory ['ɪnvənˌtɔri] n, pl **-ries** : inventario m

invert [ɪn'vərt] vt : invertir

invertebrate [ɪn'vərtəˌbreɪt, -ˌbreɪt] adj : invertebrado — ∼ n : invertebrado m

invest [ɪn'vɛst] vt : invertir

investigate [ɪn'vɛstəˌgeɪt] v **-gated; -gating** : investigar — **investigation** [ɪnˌvɛstə'geɪʃən] n : investigación f — **investigator** [ɪn'vɛstəˌgeɪtər] n : investigador m, -dora f

investment [ɪn'vɛstmənt] n : inversión f — **investor** [ɪn'vɛstər] n : inversor m, -sora f

inveterate [ɪn'vɛtərət] adj : inveterado

invigorating [ɪn'vɪgəˌreɪtɪŋ] adj : vigorizante

invincible [ɪn'vɪntsəbəl] adj : invencible

invisible [ɪn'vɪzəbəl] adj : invisible

invitation [ˌɪnvə'teɪʃən] n : invitación f — **invite** [ɪn'vaɪt] vt **-vited; -viting 1** : invitar **2** SEEK : buscar (problemas, etc.) — **inviting** [ɪn'vaɪtɪŋ] adj : atrayente

invoice ['ɪnˌvɔɪs] n : factura f

invoke [ɪn'voːk] vt **-voked; -voking** : invocar

involuntary [ɪn'vɑlənˌtɛri] adj : involuntario

involve [ɪn'vɑlv] vt **-volved; -volving 1** CONCERN : concernir, afectar **2** ENTAIL : suponer — **involved** [ɪn'vɑlvd] adj **1** COMPLEX : complicado **2** CONCERNED : afectado — **involvement** [ɪn'vɑlvmənt] n : participación f

invulnerable [ɪn'vʌlnərəbəl] adj : invulnerable

inward ['ɪnwərd] adj INNER : interior, interno — ∼ or **inwards** [-wərdz] adv : hacia adentro, hacia el interior

iodine ['aɪəˌdaɪn, -dən] n : yodo m, tintura f de yodo

ion ['aɪən, 'aɪˌɑn] n : ion m

iota [aɪ'oːtə] n : pizca f, ápice m

IOU [ˌaɪˌoː'juː] n : pagaré m, vale m

Iranian [ɪ'reɪniən, -'ræ-, -'rɑ-; aɪ'-] adj : iraní

Iraqi [ɪ'rɑki, -'ræk-] adj : iraquí

ire ['aɪr] n : ira f — **irate** [aɪ'reɪt] adj : furioso

iris ['aɪrəs] n, pl **irises** or **irides** ['aɪrə-

,di:z, 'ır-] **1** : iris *m* (del ojo) **2** : lirio *m* (planta)

Irish ['aırıʃ] *adj* : irlandés

irksome ['ərksəm] *adj* : irritante, fastidioso

iron ['aıərn] *n* **1** : hierro *m*, fierro *m Lat* (metal) **2** : plancha *f* (para la ropa) — **~** *v* : planchar

ironic [aı'ranık] *or* **ironical** [-nıkəl] *adj* : irónico

ironing board *n* : tabla *f* (de planchar)

irony ['aırəni] *n, pl* **-nies** : ironía *f*

irrational [ı'ræʃənəl] *adj* : irracional

irreconcilable [ı,rekən'saıləbəl] *adj* : irreconciliable

irrefutable [ı,rı'fju:təbəl, ı'refjə-] *adj* : irrefutable

irregular [ı'regjələr] *adj* : irregular — **irregularity** [ı,regjə'lærəṭi] *n, pl* **-ties** : irregularidad *f*

irrelevant [ı'reləvənt] *adj* : irrelevante

irreparable [ı'repərəbəl] *adj* : irreparable

irreplaceable [ı,rı'pleısəbəl] *adj* : irreemplazable

irresistible [ı,rı'zıstəbəl] *adj* : irresistible

irresolute [ı'rezə,lu:t] *adj* : irresoluto

irrespective of [ı,rı'spektıvəv] *prep* : sin tener en cuenta

irresponsible [ı,rı'spansəbəl] *adj* : irresponsable — **irresponsibility** [ı,rı,spansə'bıləṭi] *n, pl* **-ties** : irresponsabilidad *f*

irreverent [ı'revərənt] *adj* : irreverente

irreversible [ı,rı'vərsəbəl] *adj* : irreversible, irrevocable

irrigate ['ırə,geıt] *vt* **-gated; -gating** : irrigar, regar — **irrigation** [ı,rə'geıʃən] *n* : irrigación *f*, riego *m*

irritate ['ırə,teıt] *vt* **-tated; -tating** : irritar — **irritable** ['ırəṭəbəl] *adj* : irritable — **irritably** ['ırəṭəbli] *adv* : con irritación — **irritating** ['ırə,teıṭıŋ] *adj* : irritante — **irritation** [,ırə'teıʃən] *n* : irritación *f*

is → **be**

Islam [ıs'lam, ız-, -'læm; 'ıs,lam, 'ız-, -,læm] *n* : el Islam — **Islamic** [ıs'lamık, ız-, -'læ-] *adj* : islámico

island ['aılənd] *n* : isla *f* — **isle** ['aıl] *n* : isla *f*

isolate ['aısə,leıt] *vt* **-lated; -lating** : aislar — **isolation** [,aısə'leıʃən] *n* : aislamiento *m*

Israeli [ız'reıli] *adj* : israelí

issue ['ı,ʃu:] *n* **1** MATTER : asunto *m*, cuestión *f* **2** : número *m* (de una revista, etc.) **3 make an ~ of** : insistir demasiado sobre **4 take ~ with** : disentir de — **~** *v* **-sued; -suing** *vi* **from** : surgir de — *vt* **1** : emitir (sellos, etc.), distribuir (provisiones, etc.) **2** PUBLISH : publicar

isthmus ['ısməs] *n* : istmo *m*

it ['ıt] *pron* **1** (*as subject*) : él, ella **2** (*as indirect object*) : le, se **3** (*as direct object*) : lo, la **4** (*as object of a preposition*) : él, ella **5 it's raining** : está lloviendo **6 it's 8 o'clock** : son las ocho **7 it's hot out** : hace calor **8 ~ is necessary** : es necesario **9 who is ~?** : ¿quién es? **10 it's me** : soy yo

Italian [ı'tæljən, aı-] *adj* : italiano — **~** *n* : italiano *m* (idioma)

italics [ı'tælıks, aı-] *n* : cursiva *f*

itch ['ıtʃ] *vi* **1** : picar **2 be ~ing to** : morirse por — **~** *n* : picazón *f* — **itchy** ['ıtʃi] *adj* **itchier; -est** : que pica

it'd ['ıṭəd] (*contraction of* **it had** *or* **it would**) → **have, would**

item ['aıṭəm] *n* **1** : artículo *m* **2** : punto *m* (en una agenda) **3 ~ of clothing** : prenda *f* de vestir **4 news ~** : noticia *f* — **itemize** ['aıṭə,maız] *vt* **-ized; -izing** : detallar, enumerar

itinerant [aı'tınərənt] *adj* : ambulante

itinerary [aı'tınə,reri] *n, pl* **-aries** : itinerario *m*

it'll ['ıṭəl] (*contraction of* **it shall** *or* **it will**) → **shall, will**

its ['ıts] *adj* : su, sus

it's ['ıts] (*contraction of* **it is** *or* **it has**) → **be, have**

itself [ıt'self] *pron* **1** (*used reflexively*) : se **2** (*used for emphasis*) : (él) mismo, (ella) misma, sí (mismo) **3 by ~** : solo

I've ['aıv] (*contraction of* **I have**) → **have**

ivory ['aıvəri] *n, pl* **-ries** : marfil *m*

ivy ['aıvi] *n, pl* **ivies** : hiedra *f*

J

j ['dʒeɪ] *n, pl* **j's** *or* **js** ['dʒeɪz] : j *f*, décima
letra del alfabeto inglés

jab ['dʒæb] *vt* **jabbed; jabbing 1** PIERCE
: pinchar **2** POKE : golpear (con la
punta de algo) — ~ *n* **1** PRICK : pinchazo *m* **2** POKE : golpe *m* abrupto

jabber ['dʒæbər] *vi* : farfullar

jack ['dʒæk] *n* **1** : gato *m* (mecanismo)
: sota *f* (de naipes) — ~ *vt or* ~ **up 1**
: levantar (con un gato) **2** INCREASE
: subir

jackal ['dʒækəl] *n* : chacal *m*

jackass ['dʒækæs] *n* : asno *m*, burro *m*

jacket ['dʒækət] *n* **1** : chaqueta *f* **2** : sobrecubierta *f* (de un libro), carátula *f*
(de un disco)

jackhammer ['dʒæk,hæmər] *n* : martillo
m neumático

jackknife ['dʒæk,naɪf] *n* : navaja *f* — ~
vi **-knifed; -knifing** : plegarse (dícese
de un camión)

jack-o'-lantern ['dʒækə,læntərn] *n* : linterna *f* hecha de una calabaza

jackpot ['dʒæk,pɑt] *n* : premio *m* gordo

jaded ['dʒeɪdəd] *adj* **1** TIRED : agotado **2**
BORED : hastiado

jagged ['dʒægəd] *adj* : dentado

jail ['dʒeɪl] *n* : cárcel *f* — ~ *vt* : encarcelar — **jailer** *or* **jailor** ['dʒeɪlər] *n*
: carcelero *m*, -ra *f*

jalapeño [,hɑlə'peɪnjo, ,hæ-, -'piːno] *n*
: jalapeño *m Lat*

jam¹ ['dʒæm] *v* **jammed; jamming** *vt* **1**
CRAM : apiñar, embutir **2** BLOCK : atascar, atorar — *vi* : atascarse, atrancarse
— ~ *n* **1** *or* **traffic** ~ : embotellamiento *m* (de tráfico) **2** FIX : lío *m*,
aprieto *m*

jam² *n* PRESERVES : mermelada *f*

jangle ['dʒæŋgəl] *v* **-gled; -gling** *vi*
: hacer un ruido metálico — *vt* : hacer
sonar — ~ *n* : ruido *m* metálico

janitor ['dʒænətər] *n* : portero *m*, -ra *f*;
conserje *mf*

January ['dʒænju,ɛri] *n* : enero *m*

Japanese [,dʒæpə'niːz, -'niːs] *adj*
: japonés — *n* : japonés *m* (idioma)

jar¹ ['dʒɑr] *v* **jarred; jarring** *vi* **1** GRATE
: chirriar **2** CLASH : desentonar **3** ~ **on**
IRRITATE : crispar, enervar (a algn) —
vt JOLT : sacudir — ~ *n* : sacudida *f*

jar² *n* : tarro *m*

jargon ['dʒɑrgən] *n* : jerga *f*

jaundice ['dʒɔndɪs] *n* : ictericia *f*

jaunt ['dʒɔnt] *n* : excursión *f*

jaunty ['dʒɔnti] *adj* **-tier; -est** : garboso,
desenvuelto

jaw ['dʒɔ] *n* : mandíbula *f* (de una persona), quijada *f* (de un animal) — **jawbone** ['dʒɔ,boʊn] *n* : mandíbula *f*, quijada *f*

jay ['dʒeɪ] *n* : arrendajo *m*

jazz ['dʒæz] *n* : jazz *m* — ~ *vt or* ~ **up**
: animar, alegrar — **jazzy** ['dʒæzi] *adj*
jazzier; -est FLASHY : llamativo

jealous ['dʒɛləs] *adj* : celoso — **jealousy** ['dʒɛləsi] *n* : celos *mpl*, envidia *f*

jeans ['dʒiːnz] *npl* : jeans *mpl*, vaqueros
mpl

jeer ['dʒɪr] *vt* **1** BOO : abuchear **2** MOCK
: mofarse de — *vi* ~ **at** : mofarse de
— ~ *n* : mofa *f*

jell ['dʒɛl] *vi* : cuajar

jelly ['dʒɛli] *n, pl* **-lies** : jalea *f* — **jellyfish** ['dʒɛli,fɪʃ] *n* : medusa *f*

jeopardy ['dʒɛpərdi] *n* : peligro *m*, riesgo *m* — **jeopardize** ['dʒɛpər,daɪz] *vt*
-dized; -dizing : arriesgar, poner en
peligro

jerk ['dʒərk] *n* **1** JOLT : sacudida *f* brusca
2 FOOL : idiota *mf* — ~ *vt* : sacudir —
vi JOLT : dar sacudidas

jersey ['dʒərzi] *n, pl* **-seys** : jersey *m*

jest ['dʒɛst] *n* : broma *f* — ~ *vi*
: bromear — **jester** ['dʒɛstər] *n* : bufón
m

Jesus ['dʒiːzəs, -zəz] *n* : Jesús *m*

jet ['dʒɛt] *n* **1** STREAM : chorro *m* **2** *or* ~
airplane : avión *m* a reacción, reactor
m — **jet-propelled** *adj* : a reacción

jettison ['dʒɛtəsən] *vt* **1** : echar al mar **2**
DISCARD : deshacerse de

jetty ['dʒɛti] *n, pl* **-ties** : desembarcadero *m*, muelle *m*

jewel ['dʒuːəl] *n* **1** : joya *f* **2** GEM : piedra
f preciosa — **jeweler** *or* **jeweller**
['dʒuːələr] *n* : joyero *m*, -ra *f* — **jewelry**
['dʒuːəlri] *n* : joyas *fpl*, alhajas *fpl*

Jewish ['dʒuːɪʃ] *adj* : judío

jibe ['dʒaɪb] *vi* **jibed; jibing** AGREE
: concordar

jiffy ['dʒɪfi] *n, pl* **-fies** : santiamén *m*, segundo *m*

jig ['dʒɪg] *n* : giga *f*

jiggle ['dʒɪgəl] *vt* **-gled; -gling** : sacudir,
zarandear — ~ *n* : sacudida *f*

jigsaw ['dʒɪɡ,sɔ] n **1** : sierra f de vaivén **2** or ~ **puzzle** : rompecabezas m

jilt ['dʒɪlt] vt : dejar plantado

jingle ['dʒɪŋɡəl] v **-gled; -gling** vi : tintinear — vt : hacer sonar — ~ n TINKLE : tintineo m

jinx ['dʒɪŋks] n CURSE : maldición f

jitters ['dʒɪt̬ərz] npl **have the** ~ : estar nervioso — **jittery** ['dʒɪt̬əri] adj : nervioso

job ['dʒɑb] n **1** EMPLOYMENT : empleo m, trabajo m **2** TASK : trabajo m

jockey ['dʒɑki] n, pl **-eys** : jockey mf

jog ['dʒɑɡ] v **jogged; jogging** vt ~ **s.o.'s memory** : refrescar la memoria a algn — vi : hacer footing — **jogging** n : footing m

join ['dʒɔɪn] vt **1** UNITE : unir, juntar **2** MEET : reunirse con **3** : hacerse socio de (una organización, etc.) — vi **1** or ~ **together** : unirse **2** : hacerse socio (de una organización, etc.)

joint ['dʒɔɪnt] n **1** : articulación f (en anatomía) **2** JUNCTURE : juntura f, unión f — ~ adj : conjunto — **jointly** ['dʒɔɪntli] adv : conjuntamente

joke ['dʒoːk] n : chiste m, broma f — vi **joked; joking** : bromear — **joker** ['dʒoːkər] n **1** : bromista mf **2** : comodín m (en los naipes)

jolly ['dʒɑli] adj **-lier; -est** : alegre, jovial

jolt ['dʒoːlt] vt : sacudir — ~ n **1** : sacudida f brusca **2** SHOCK : golpe m (emocional)

jostle ['dʒɑsəl] v **-tled; -tling** vt : empujar, dar empujones — vi : empujarse

jot ['dʒɑt] vt **jotted; jotting** or ~ **down** : anotar, apuntar

journal ['dʒərnəl] n **1** DIARY : diario m **2** PERIODICAL : revista f — **journalism** ['dʒərnəl,ɪzəm] n : periodismo m — **journalist** ['dʒərnəlɪst] n : periodista mf

journey ['dʒərni] n, pl **-neys** : viaje m — ~ vi **-neyed; -neying** : viajar

jovial ['dʒoːviəl] adj : jovial

joy ['dʒɔɪ] n : alegría f — **joyful** ['dʒɔɪfəl] adj : alegre, feliz — **joyous** ['dʒɔɪəs] adj : jubiloso, alegre

jubilant ['dʒuːbələnt] adj : jubiloso — **jubilee** ['dʒuːbə,liː] n : aniversario m especial

Judaism ['dʒuːdə,ɪzəm, 'dʒuːdi-, 'dʒuːdeɪ-] n : judaísmo m

judge ['dʒʌdʒ] vt **judged; judging** : juzgar — ~ n : juez mf — **judgment** or **judgement** ['dʒʌdʒmənt] n **1** RULING : fallo m, sentencia f **2** VIEW : juicio m

judicial [dʒuˈdɪʃəl] adj : judicial — **judicious** [dʒuˈdɪʃəs] adj : juicioso

jug ['dʒʌɡ] n : jarra f

juggle ['dʒʌɡəl] vi **-gled; -gling** : hacer juegos malabares — **juggler** ['dʒʌɡələr] n : malabarista mf

jugular vein ['dʒʌɡjʊlər-] n : vena f yugular

juice ['dʒuːs] n : jugo m — **juicy** ['dʒuːsi] adj **juicier; -est** : jugoso

jukebox ['dʒuːk,bɑks] n : máquina f de discos

July [dʒʊˈlaɪ] n : julio m

jumble ['dʒʌmbəl] vt **-bled; -bling** : mezclar — ~ n : revoltijo m

jumbo ['dʒʌm,boː] adj : gigante

jump ['dʒʌmp] vi **1** LEAP : saltar **2** START : sobresaltarse **3** RISE : subir de un golpe **4** ~ **at** : no dejar escapar (una oportunidad, etc.) — vt : saltar — ~ n **1** LEAP : salto m **2** INCREASE : aumento m — **jumper** ['dʒʌmpər] n **1** : saltador m, -dora f (en deportes) **2** : jumper m (vestido) — **jumpy** ['dʒʌmpi] adj **jumpier; -est** : nervioso

junction ['dʒʌŋkʃən] n **1** JOINING : unión f **2** : cruce m (de calles), empalme m (de un ferrocarril) — **juncture** ['dʒʌŋktʃər] n : coyuntura f

June ['dʒuːn] n : junio m

jungle ['dʒʌŋɡəl] n : selva f

junior ['dʒuːnjər] adj **1** YOUNGER : más joven **2** SUBORDINATE : subalterno — ~ n **1** : persona f de menor edad **2** SUBORDINATE : subalterno m, -na f **3** : estudiante mf de penúltimo año

junk ['dʒʌŋk] n **1** : trastos mpl (viejos) — ~ vt : echar a la basura

junta ['hʊntə, 'dʒʌn-, 'hʌn-] n : junta f (militar)

jurisdiction [,dʒʊrəsˈdɪkʃən] n : jurisdicción f

jury ['dʒʊri] n, pl **-ries** : jurado m — **juror** ['dʒʊrər] n : jurado mf

just ['dʒʌst] adj : justo — ~ adv **1** BARELY : apenas **2** EXACTLY : exactamente **3** ONLY : sólo, solamente **4** ~ **now** : ahora mismo **5** she has ~ **left** : acaba de salir **6** we were ~ **leaving** : justo íbamos a salir

justice ['dʒʌstɪs] n **1** : justicia f **2** JUDGE : juez mf

justify ['dʒʌstə,faɪ] vt **-fied; -fying** : justificar — **justification** [,dʒʌstəfəˈkeɪʃən] n : justificación f

jut ['dʒʌt] vi **jutted; jutting** or ~ **out** : sobresalir

juvenile ['dʒuːvə,naɪl, -vənəl] adj **1** YOUNG : juvenil **2** CHILDISH : infantil — ~ n : menor mf

juxtapose ['dʒʌkstə,poːz] vt **-posed; -posing** : yuxtaponer

K

k ['keɪ] *n, pl* **k's** *or* **ks** ['keɪz] : k *f*, undécima letra del alfabeto inglés

kaleidoscope [kə'laɪdə,skoːp] *n* : calidoscopio *m*

kangaroo [,kæŋgə'ruː] *n, pl* **-roos** : canguro *m*

karat ['kærət] *n* : quilate *m*

karate [kə'rɑti] *n* : karate *m*

keel ['kiːl] *n* : quilla *f* — *vi or* ~ **over** : volcarse (dícese de un barco), desplomarse (dícese de una persona)

keen ['kiːn] *adj* **1** SHARP : afilado **2** PENETRATING : cortante, penetrante **3** ENTHUSIASTIC : entusiasta **4** ~ **eyesight** : visión *f* aguda

keep ['kiːp] *v* **kept** ['kept]; **keeping** *vt* **1** : guardar **2** : cumplir (una promesa), acudir a (una cita) **3** DETAIN : hacer quedar, detener **4** PREVENT : impedir **5** ~ **up** : mantener — *vi* **1** REMAIN : mantenerse **2** LAST : conservarse **3** *or* ~ **on** CONTINUE : no dejar — ~ **1** CARE : cuidado *m* **2** **in** ~ **with** : de acuerdo con — **keepsake** ['kiːp,seɪk] *n* : recuerdo *m*

keg ['keg] *n* : barril *m*

kennel ['kenəl] *n* : caseta *f* para perros, perrera *f*

kept → **keep**

kerchief ['kərtʃəf, -,tʃiːf] *n* : pañuelo *m*

kernel ['kərnəl] *n* **1** : almendra *f* **2** CORE : meollo *m*

kerosene *or* **kerosine** ['kerə,siːn, ,kerə'-] *n* : queroseno *m*

ketchup ['ketʃəp, 'kæ-] *n* : salsa *f* de tomate

kettle ['ketəl] *n* : hervidor *m*, tetera *f* (para hervir)

key ['kiː] *n* **1** : llave *f* **2** : tecla *f* (de un piano o una máquina) — ~ *vt* **be keyed up** : estar nervioso — ~ *adj* : clave — **keyboard** ['kiː,bord] *n* : teclado *m* — **keyhole** ['kiː,hoːl] *n* : ojo *m* (de la cerradura) — **keynote** ['kiː,noːt] *n* : tónica *f* — **key ring** *n* : llavero *m*

khaki ['kæki, 'kɑ-] *adj* : caqui

kick ['kɪk] *vt* **1** : dar una patada a **2** ~ **out** : echar a patadas — *vi* **1** : dar patadas (dícese de una persona), cocear (dícese de un animal) **2** RECOIL : dar un culatazo — ~ *n* **1** : patada *f*, coz *f* (de un animal) **2** RECOIL : culatazo *m* **3** PLEASURE, THRILL : placer *m*

kid ['kɪd] *n* **1** GOAT : chivo *m*, -va *f*; cabrito *m* **2** CHILD : niño *m*, -ña *f* — ~ *v* **kidded; kidding** *vi or* ~ **around** : bromear — *vt* TEASE : tomar el pelo a — **kidnap** ['kɪd,næp] *vt* **-napped** *or* **-naped** [-,næpt]; **-napping** *or* **-naping** [-,næpɪŋ] : secuestrar, raptar

kidney ['kɪdni] *n, pl* **-neys** : riñón *m*

kidney bean *n* : frijol *m*

kill ['kɪl] *vt* **1** : matar **2** DESTROY : acabar con **3** ~ **time** : matar el tiempo — ~ *n* **1** KILLING : matanza *f* **2** PREY : presa *f* — **killer** ['kɪlər] *n* : asesino *m*, -na *f* — **killing** ['kɪlɪŋ] *n* **1** : matanza *f* **2** MURDER : asesinato *m*

kiln ['kɪl, 'kɪln] *n* : horno *m*

kilo ['kiː,loː] *n, pl* **-los** : kilo *m* — **kilogram** ['kɪlə,græm, 'kiː-] *n* : kilogramo *m* — **kilometer** [kɪ'lɑmətər, 'kɪlə,miː-] *n* : kilómetro *m* — **kilowatt** ['kɪlə,wɑt] *n* : kilovatio *m*

kin ['kɪn] *n* : parientes *mpl*

kind ['kaɪnd] *n* : tipo *m*, clase *f* — ~ *adj* : amable

kindergarten ['kɪndər,gɑrtən, -dən] *n* : jardín *m* infantil, jardín *m* de niños *Lat*

kindhearted [,kaɪnd'hɑrtəd] *adj* : de buen corazón

kindle ['kɪndəl] *vt* **-dled; -dling 1** : encender (un fuego) **2** AROUSE : despertar

kindly ['kaɪndli] *adj* **-lier; -est** : bondadoso, amable — ~ *adv* **1** : amablemente **2 take** ~ **to** : aceptar de buena gana **3 we** ~ **ask you not smoke** : les rogamos que no fumen — **kindness** ['kaɪndnəs] *n* : bondad *f* — **kind of** *adv* SOMEWHAT : un tanto, algo

kindred ['kɪndrəd] *adj* **1** : emparentado **2** ~ **spirit** : alma *f* gemela

king ['kɪŋ] *n* : rey *m* — **kingdom** ['kɪŋdəm] *n* : reino *m*

kink ['kɪŋk] *n* **1** TWIST : vuelta *f*, curva *f* **2** FLAW : problema *m*

kinship ['kɪn,ʃɪp] *n* : parentesco *m*

kiss ['kɪs] *vt* : besar — *vi* : besarse — ~ *n* : beso *m*

kit ['kɪt] *n* **1** : juego *m*, kit *m* **2 first–aid**

~ : botiquín *m* **3 tool** ~ : caja *f* de herramientas

kitchen ['kɪtʃən] *n* : cocina *f*

kite ['kaɪt] *n* : cometa *f*, papalote *m Lat*

kitten ['kɪtən] *n* : gatito *m*, -ta *f* — **kitty** ['kɪti] *n, pl* **-ties** FUND : fondo *m* común

knack ['næk] *n* : maña *f*, facilidad *f*

knapsack ['næp,sæk] *n* : mochila *f*

knead ['niːd] *vt* **1** : amasar, sobar **2** MASSAGE : masajear

knee ['niː] *n* : rodilla *f* — **kneecap** ['niː,kæp] *n* : rótula *f*

kneel ['niːl] *vi* **knelt** ['nɛlt] *or* **kneeled** ['niːld]; **kneeling** : arrodillarse

knew → **know**

knickknack ['nɪk,næk] *n* : chuchería *f*

knife ['naɪf] *n, pl* **knives** ['naɪvz] : cuchillo *m* — ~ *vt* **knifed** ['naɪft]; **knifing** : acuchillar

knight ['naɪt] *n* **1** : caballero *m* **2** : caballo *m* (en ajedrez) — **knighthood** ['naɪt,hʊd] *n* : título *m* de Sir

knit ['nɪt] *v* **knit** *or* **knitted** ['nɪtəd]; **knitting** *v* : tejer — ~ *n* : prenda *f* tejida

knob ['nɑb] *n* : tirador *m*, botón *m*, perilla *f Lat*

knock ['nɑk] *vt* **1** : golpear **2** CRITICIZE : criticar **3** ~ **down** : derribar, echar al suelo — *vi* **1** : dar un golpe, llamar (a la puerta) **2** COLLIDE : darse, chocar — ~ *n* : golpe *m*, llamada *f* (a la puerta)

knot ['nɑt] *n* : nudo *m* — ~ *vt* **knotted**; **knotting** : anudar — **knotty** ['nɑti] *adj* **-tier; -est 1** : nudoso **2** : enredado (dícese de un problema)

know ['noː] *v* **knew** ['nuː, 'njuː]; **known** ['noːn]; **knowing** *vt* **1** : saber **2** : conocer (a una persona, un lugar) **3** ~ **how to** : saber — *vi* : saber — **knowing** ['noːɪŋ] *adj* : cómplice — **knowingly** ['noːɪŋli] *adv* **1** : de manera cómplice **2** DELIBERATELY : a sabiendas — **know—it—all** ['noːɪt,ɔl] *n* : sabelotodo *mf fam* — **knowledge** ['nɑlɪdʒ] *n* **1** : conocimiento *m* **2** LEARNING : conocimientos *mpl*, saber *m* — **knowledgeable** ['nɑlɪdʒəbəl] *adj* : informado, entendido

knuckle ['nʌkəl] *n* : nudillo *m*

Koran [kə'ran, -'ræn] *n* **the Koran** : el Corán *m*

Korean [kə'riːən] *adj* : coreano *m*, -na *f* — ~ *n* : coreano *m* (idioma)

kosher ['koːʃər] *adj* : aprobado por la ley judía

L

l ['ɛl] *n, pl* **l's** *or* **ls** ['ɛlz] : l *f*, duodécima letra del alfabeto inglés

lab ['læb] → **laboratory**

label ['leɪbəl] *n* **1** TAG : etiqueta *f* **2** BRAND : marca *f* — ~ *vt* **-beled** *or* **-belled; -beling** *or* **-belling** : etiquetar

labor ['leɪbər] *n* **1** : trabajo *m* **2** WORKERS : mano *f* de obra **3** **in** ~ : de parto — ~ *vi* **1** : trabajar **2** STRUGGLE : avanzar penosamente — *vt* BELABOR : insistir en (un punto)

laboratory ['læbrə,tori, lə'borə-] *n, pl* **-ries** : laboratorio *m*

laborer ['leɪbərər] *n* : trabajador *m*, -dora *f*

laborious [lə'boriəs] *adj* : laborioso

lace ['leɪs] *n* **1** : encaje *m* **2** SHOELACE : cordón *m* (de zapatos), agujeta *f Lat* — ~ *vt* **laced; lacing 1** TIE : atar **2 be laced with** : echar licor a (una bebida, etc.)

lacerate ['læsə,reɪt] *vt* **-ated; -ating** : lacerar

lack ['læk] *vt* : carecer de, no tener — *vi* **be lacking** : faltar — ~ *n* : falta *f*, carencia *f*

lackadaisical [,lækə'deɪzɪkəl] *adj* : apático, indolente

lackluster ['læk,lʌstər] *adj* : sin brillo, apagado

laconic [lə'kɑnɪk] *adj* : lacónico

lacquer ['lækər] *n* : laca *f*

lacrosse [lə'krɔs] *n* : lacrosse *f*

lacy ['leɪsi] *adj* **lacier; -est** : como de encaje

lad ['læd] *n* : muchacho *m*, niño *m*

ladder ['lædər] *n* : escalera *f*

laden ['leɪdən] *adj* : cargado

ladle ['leɪdəl] *n* : cucharón *m* — ~ *vt* **-dled; -dling** : servir con cucharón

lady ['leɪdi] *n, pl* **-dies** : señora *f*, dama *f* — **ladybug** ['leɪdi,bʌg] *n* : mariquita *f* — **ladylike** ['leɪdi,laɪk] *adj* : elegante, como señora

lag ['læg] *n* **1** DELAY : retraso *m* **2** INTERVAL : intervalo *m* — ~ *vi* **lagged; lagging** : quedarse atrás, rezagarse

lager ['lɑgər] *n* : cerveza *f* rubia

lagoon [lə'guːn] *n* : laguna *f*

laid *pp* → **lay**[1]

lain *pp* → **lie**[1]

lair ['lær] *n* : guarida *f*

lake ['leɪk] *n* : lago *m*

lamb ['læm] *n* : cordero *m*

lame ['leɪm] *adj* **lamer; lamest 1** : cojo, renco **2 a ~ excuse** : una excusa poco convincente

lament [lə'mɛnt] *vt* **1** MOURN : llorar **2** DEPLORE : lamentar — **~** *n* : lamento *m* — **lamentable** ['læməntəbəl, lə-'mɛntə-] *adj* : lamentable

laminate ['læmə,neɪt] *vt* **-nated; -nating** : laminar

lamp ['læmp] *n* : lámpara *f* — **lamppost** ['læmp,poːst] *n* : farol *m* — **lampshade** ['læmp,ʃeɪd] *n* : pantalla *f*

lance ['læns] *n* : lanza *f* — **~** *vt* **lanced; lancing** : abrir con lanceta (en medecina)

land ['lænd] *n* **1** : tierra *f* **2** COUNTRY : país *m* **3** *or* **plot of ~** : terreno *m* — **~** *vt* **1** : desembarcar (pasajeros de un barco), hacer aterrizar (un avión) **2** CATCH : sacar (un pez) del agua **3** SE-CURE : conseguir (empleo, etc.) — *vi* **1** : aterrizar (dícese de un avión) **2** FALL : caer — **landing** ['lændɪŋ] *n* **1** : aterrizaje *m* (de aviones) **2** : desembarco *m* (de barcos) **3** : descanso *m* (de una escalera) — **landlady** ['lænd,leɪdi] *n*, *pl* **-dies** : casera *f* — **landlord** ['lænd,lord] *n* : casero *m* — **landmark** ['lænd,mɑrk] *n* **1** : punto de referencia **2** MONU-MENT : monumento *m* histórico — **landowner** ['lænd,oːnər] *n* : hacendado *m*, **-da** *f*; terrateniente *mf* — **land-scape** ['lænd,skeɪp] *n* : paisaje *m* — **~** *vt* **-scaped; -scaping** : ajardinar — **landslide** ['lænd,slaɪd] *n* **1** : desprendimiento *m* de tierras **2** *or* **~ victory** : victoria *f* arrolladora

lane ['leɪn] *n* **1** : carril *m* (de una carretera) **2** PATH, ROAD : camino *m*

language ['læŋgwɪdʒ] *n* **1** : idioma *m*, lengua *f* **2** SPEECH : lenguaje *m*

languid ['læŋgwɪd] *adj* : lánguido — **languish** ['læŋgwɪʃ] *vi* : languidecer

lanky ['læŋki] *adj* **lankier; -est** : delgado, larguirucho *fam*

lantern ['læntərn] *n* : linterna *f*

lap ['læp] *n* **1** : regazo *m* (de una persona) **2** : vuelta *f* (en deportes) — **~** *v* **lapped; lapping** *vt or* **~ up** : beber a lengüetadas — *vi* **~ against** : lamer

lapel [lə'pɛl] *n* : solapa *f*

lapse ['læps] *n* **1** : lapsus *m*, falla *f* (de memoria, etc.) **2** INTERVAL : lapso *m*, intervalo *m* — **~** *vi* **lapsed; lapsing 1** EXPIRE : caducar **2** ELAPSE : transcurrir, pasar **3 ~ into** : caer en

laptop ['læp,tɑp] *adj* : portátil

larceny ['lɑrsəni] *n*, *pl* **-nies** : robo *m*

lard ['lɑrd] *n* : manteca *f* de cerdo

large ['lɑrdʒ] *adj* **larger; largest 1** : grande **2 at ~** : en libertad **3 by and ~** : por lo general — **largely** ['lɑrdʒli] *adv* : en gran parte

lark ['lɑrk] *n* **1** : alondra *f* (pájaro) **2 for a ~** : por divertirse

larva ['lɑrvə] *n*, *pl* **-vae** [-,viː, -,vaɪ] : larva *f*

larynx ['lærɪŋks] *n*, *pl* **-rynges** [lə'rɪn-,dʒiːz] *or* **-ynxes** ['lærɪŋksəz] : laringe *f* — **laryngitis** [,lærən'dʒaɪtəs] *n* : laringitis *f*

lasagna [lə'zɑnjə] *n* : lasaña *f*

laser ['leɪzər] *n* : láser *m*

lash ['læʃ] *vt* **1** WHIP : azotar **2** BIND : amarrar — *vi* **~ out at** : arremeter contra — **~** *n* **1** BLOW : latigazo *m* (con un látigo) **2** EYELASH : pestaña *f*

lass ['læs] *or* **lassie** ['læsi] *n* : muchacha *f*, chica *f*

lasso ['læsoː, læ'suː] *n*, *pl* **-sos** *or* **-soes** : lazo *m*

last ['læst] *vi* : durar — **~** *n* **1** : último *m*, **-ma** *f* **2 at ~** : por fin, finalmente — **~** *adv* **1** : por última vez, en último lugar **2 arrive ~** : llegar el último — **~** *adj* **1** : último **2 ~ year** : el año pasado — **lastly** ['læstli] *adv* : por último, finalmente

latch ['lætʃ] *n* : picaporte *m*, pestillo *m*

late ['leɪt] *adj* **later; latest 1** : tarde **2** : avanzado (dícese de la hora) **3** DE-CEASED : difunto **4** RECENT : reciente — **~** *adv* **later; latest** : tarde — **late-ly** ['leɪtli] *adv* : recientemente, última-mente — **lateness** ['leɪtnəs] *n* **1** : retraso *m* **2** : lo avanzado (de la hora)

latent ['leɪtənt] *adj* : latente

lateral ['lætərəl] *adj* : lateral

latest ['leɪtəst] *n* **at the ~** : a más tardar

lathe ['leɪð] *n* : torno *m*

lather ['læðər] *n* : espuma *f* — **~** *vt* : enjabonar — *vi* : hacer espuma

Latin–American [,lætənə'merɪkən] *adj* : latinoamericano

latitude ['lætə,tuːd, -,tjuːd] *n* : latitud *f*

latter ['lætər] *adj* **1** : último **2** SECOND : segundo — **~** *pron* **the ~** : éste, ésta, éstos *pl*, éstas *pl*

lattice ['lætəs] *n* : enrejado *m*

laugh ['læf] *vi* : reír(se) — **~** *n* : risa *f* — **laughable** ['læfəbəl] *adj* : risible, ridículo — **laughter** ['læftər] *n* : risa *f*, risas *fpl*

launch ['lɔntʃ] *vt* : lanzar — **~** *n* : lanzamiento *m*

launder ['lɔndər] *vt* **1** : lavar y planchar (ropa) **2** : blanquear, lavar (dinero) — **laundry** ['lɔndri] *n*, *pl* **-dries 1** : ropa *f* sucia **2** : lavandería *f* (servicio) **3 do the ~** : lavar la ropa

lava ['lɑvə, 'læ-] *n* : lava *f*

lavatory ['lævə,tori] *n, pl* **-ries** BATH-ROOM : baño *m*, cuarto *m* de baño

lavender ['lævəndər] *n* : lavanda *f*

lavish ['lævɪʃ] *adj* **1** EXTRAVAGANT : pródigo **2** ABUNDANT : abundante **3** LUXURIOUS : lujoso — ~ *vt* : prodigar

law ['lɔ] *n* **1** : ley *f* **2** : derecho *m* (profesión, etc.) **3 practice ~** : ejercer la abogacía — **lawful** ['lɔfəl] *adj* : legal, legítimo

lawn ['lɔn] *n* : césped *m* — **lawn mower** *n* : cortadora *f* de césped

lawsuit ['lɔˌsuːt] *n* : pleito *m*

lawyer ['lɔɪər, 'lɔjər] *n* : abogado *m*, -da *f*

lax ['læks] *adj* : poco estricto, relajado

laxative ['læksətɪv] *n* : laxante *m*

lay¹ ['leɪ] *vt* **laid** ['leɪd]; **laying 1** PLACE, PUT : poner, colocar **2 ~ eggs** : poner huevos **3 ~ off** : despedir (un empleado) **4 ~ out** PRESENT : presentar, exponer **5 ~ out** DESIGN : diseñar (el trazado de)

lay² *pp* → **lie¹**

lay³ *adj* **1** SECULAR : laico **2** NONPROFESSIONAL : lego, profano

layer ['leɪər] *n* : capa *f*

layman ['leɪmən] *n, pl* **-men** : lego *m*, laico *m* (en religión)

layout ['leɪˌaʊt] *n* ARRANGEMENT : disposición *f*

lazy ['leɪzi] *adj* **-zier; -est** : perezoso — **laziness** ['leɪzinəs] *n* : pereza *f*

lead¹ ['liːd] *vt* **led** ['lɛd]; **leading 1** GUIDE : conducir **2** DIRECT : dirigir **3** HEAD : encabezar, ir al frente de — *vi* : llevar, conducir (a algo) — ~ *n* **1** : delantera *f* **2 follow s.o.'s ~** : seguir el ejemplo de algn

lead² ['lɛd] *n* **1** : plomo *m* (metal) **2** GRAPHITE : mina *f* — **leaden** ['lɛdən] *adj* **1** : de plomo **2** HEAVY : pesado

leader ['liːdər] *n* : jefe *m*, -fa *f* — **leadership** ['liːdərˌʃɪp] *n* : mando *m*, dirección *f*

leaf ['liːf] *n, pl* **leaves** ['liːvz] **1** : hoja *f* **2 turn over a new ~** : hacer borrón y cuenta nueva — *vi* **~ through** : hojear (un libro, etc.) — **leaflet** ['liːflət] *n* : folleto *m*

league ['liːg] *n* **1** : liga *f* **2 be in ~ with** : estar confabulado con

leak ['liːk] *vi* **1** : dejar escapar (un líquido o un gas) **2** : filtrar (información) — *vi* **1** : gotear, escaparse (dícese de un líquido o un gas) **2** : filtrarse (dícese de información) — ~ *n* **1** : agujero *m* (de un cubo, etc.), gotera *f*

(de un techo) **2** : fuga *f*, escape *m* (de un líquido o un gas) **3** : filtración *f* (de información) — **leaky** ['liːki] *adj* **leakier; -est** : que hace agua

lean¹ ['liːn] *v* **leaned** *or Brit* **leant** ['lɛnt]; **leaning** *vi* **1** BEND : inclinarse **2 ~ against** : apoyarse contra — *vt* : apoyar

lean² *adj* **1** THIN : delgado **2** : sin grasa (dícese de la carne)

leaning ['liːnɪŋ] *n* : inclinación *f*

leanness ['liːnnəs] *n* : delgadez *f* (de una persona), lo magro (de la carne)

leap ['liːp] *vi* **leapt** *or* **leaped** ['liːpt, 'lɛpt]; **leaping** : saltar, brincar — ~ *n* : salto *m*, brinco *m* — **leap year** *n* : año *m* bisiesto

learn ['lərn] *v* **learned** ['lərnd, 'lərnt]; **learning** : aprender — **learned** ['lərnəd] *adj* : sabio, erudito — **learner** ['lərnər] *n* : principiante *mf*, estudiante *mf* — **learning** ['lərnɪŋ] *n* : erudición *f*, saber *m*

lease ['liːs] *n* : contrato *m* de arrendamiento — ~ *vt* **leased; leasing** : arrendar

leash ['liːʃ] *n* : correa *f*

least ['liːst] *adj* **1** : menor **2** SLIGHTEST : más mínimo — ~ *n* **1 at ~** : por lo menos **2 the ~** : lo menos **3 to say the ~** : por no decir más — ~ *adv* : menos

leather ['lɛðər] *n* : cuero *m*

leave ['liːv] *v* **left** ['lɛft]; **leaving** *vt* **1** : dejar **2** : salir(se) de (un lugar) **3 ~ out** : omitir — *vi* DEPART : irse — ~ *n* **1** *or* **~ of absence** : permiso *m*, licencia *f* **2 take one's ~** : despedirse

leaves → **leaf**

lecture ['lɛktʃər] *n* **1** TALK : conferencia *f* **2** REPRIMAND : sermón *m*, reprimenda *f* — ~ *v* **-tured; -turing** *vt* : sermonear — *vi* : dar clase, dar una conferencia

led *pp* → **lead¹**

ledge ['lɛdʒ] *n* : antepecho *m* (de una ventana), saliente *m* (de una montaña)

leech ['liːtʃ] *n* : sanguijuela *f*

leek ['liːk] *n* : puerro *m*

leer ['lɪr] *vi* : lanzar una mirada lasciva — ~ *n* : mirada *f* lasciva

leery ['lɪri] *adj* : receloso

leeway ['liːˌweɪ] *n* : libertad *f* de acción, margen *m*

left¹ → **leave**

left² ['lɛft] *adj* : izquierdo — ~ *adv* : a la izquierda — ~ *n* : izquierda *f* — **left–handed** ['lɛftˈhændəd] *adj* : zurdo

leftovers ['lɛftˌoːvərz] *npl* : restos *mpl*, sobras *fpl*

leg ['leg] n 1 : pierna f (de una persona, de ropa), pata f (de un animal, de muebles) 2 : etapa f (de un viaje)
legacy ['legəsi] n, pl **-cies** : legado m
legal ['li:gəl] adj 1 LAWFUL : legítimo, legal 2 JUDICIAL : legal, jurídico — **legality** [li'gæləti] n, pl **-ties** : legalidad f — **legalize** ['li:gə,laɪz] vt **-ized; -izing** : legalizar
legend ['ledʒənd] n : leyenda f — **legendary** ['ledʒən,deri] adj : legendario
legible ['ledʒəbəl] adj : legible
legion ['li:dʒən] n : legión f
legislate ['ledʒəs,leɪt] vi **-lated; -lating** : legislar — **legislation** [,ledʒəs'leɪʃən] n : legislación f — **legislative** ['ledʒəs,leɪtɪv] adj : legislativo, legislador — **legislature** ['ledʒəs,leɪtʃər] n : asamblea f legislativa
legitimate [lɪ'dʒɪtəmət] adj : legítimo — **legitimacy** [lɪ'dʒɪtəməsi] n : legitimidad f
leisure ['li:ʒər, 'le-] n 1 : ocio m, tiempo m libre 2 **at your ~** : cuando te venga bien — **leisurely** ['li:ʒərli, 'le-] adj & adv : lento, sin prisas
lemon ['lemən] n : limón m — **lemonade** [,lemə'neɪd] n : limonada f
lend ['lend] vt **lent** ['lent]; **lending** : prestar
length ['leŋkθ] n 1 : largo m 2 DURATION : duración f 3 **at ~** FINALLY : por fin 4 **at ~** : EXTENSIVELY : extensamente 5 **go to any ~s** : hacer todo lo posible — **lengthen** ['leŋkθən] vt 1 : alargar 2 PROLONG : prolongar — vi : alargarse — **lengthways** ['leŋkθ,weɪz] or **lengthwise** ['leŋkθ,waɪz] adv : a lo largo — **lengthy** ['leŋkθi] adj **lengthier; -est** : largo
lenient ['li:niənt] adj : indulgente — **leniency** ['li:niəntsi] n, pl **-cies** : indulgencia f
lens ['lenz] n 1 : cristalino m (del ojo) 2 : lente mf (de un instrumento) 3 → **contact lens**
Lent ['lent] n : Cuaresma f
lentil ['lentəl] n : lenteja f
leopard ['lepərd] n : leopardo m
leotard ['li:ə,tard] n : leotardo m, malla f
lesbian ['lezbiən] n : lesbiana f
less ['les] adv (comparative of **little**) : menos — **~** adj (comparative of **little**) : menos — **~** pron : menos — **~** prep MINUS : menos — **lessen** ['lesən] v : disminuir — **lesser** ['lesər] adj : menor
lesson ['lesən] n 1 CLASS : clase f, curso m 2 **learn one's ~** : aprender la lección

lest ['lest] conj **~ we forget** : para que no olvidemos
let ['let] vt **let; letting** 1 ALLOW : dejar, permitir 2 RENT : alquilar 3 **~'s go!** : ¡vamos!, ¡vámonos! 4 **~ down** DISAPPOINT : fallar 5 **~ in** : dejar entrar 6 **~ off** FORGIVE : perdonar 7 **~ up** ABATE : amainar, disminuir
letdown ['let,daʊn] n : chasco m, decepción f
lethal ['li:θəl] adj : letal
lethargic [lɪ'θardʒɪk] adj : letárgico
let's ['lets] (contraction of **let us**) → **let**
letter ['letər] n 1 : carta f 2 : letra f (del alfabeto)
lettuce ['letəs] n : lechuga f
letup ['let,əp] n : pausa f, descanso m
leukemia [lu:'ki:miə] n : leucemia f
level ['levəl] n 1 : nivel m 2 **be on the ~** : ser honrado — **~** vt **-eled** or **-elled; -eling** or **-elling** 1 : nivelar 2 AIM : apuntar 3 RAZE : arrasar — **~** adj 1 FLAT : llano, plano 2 : nivel (de altura) — **levelheaded** ['levəl'hedəd] adj : sensato, equilibrado
lever ['levər, 'li:-] n : palanca f — **leverage** ['levərɪdʒ, 'li:-] n 1 : apalancamiento m (en física) 2 INFLUENCE : influencia f
levity ['levəti] n : ligereza f
levy ['levi] n, pl **levies** : impuesto m — **~** vt **levied; levying** : imponer, exigir (un impuesto)
lewd ['lu:d] adj : lascivo
lexicon ['leksi,kɑn] n, pl **-ica** [-kə] or **-icons** : léxico m, lexicón m
liable ['laɪəbəl] adj 1 : responsable 2 LIKELY : probable 3 SUSCEPTIBLE : propenso — **liability** [,laɪə'biləti] n, pl **-ties** 1 RESPONSIBILITY : responsabilidad f 2 DRAWBACK : desventaja f 3 **liabilities** npl DEBTS : deudas fpl, pasivo m
liaison ['li:ə,zan, li'eɪ-] n 1 : enlace m 2 AFFAIR : amorío m
liar ['laɪər] n : mentiroso m, -sa f
libel ['laɪbəl] n : libelo m, difamación f — **~** vt **-beled** or **-belled; -beling** or **-belling** : difamar
liberal ['lɪbrəl, 'lɪbərəl] adj : liberal — **~** n : liberal mf
liberate ['lɪbə,reɪt] vt **-ated; -ating** : liberar — **liberation** [,lɪbə'reɪʃən] n : liberación f
liberty ['lɪbərti] n, pl **-ties** : libertad f
library ['laɪ,breri] n, pl **-braries** : biblioteca f — **librarian** [laɪ'breriən] n : bibliotecario m, -ria f
lice → **louse**
license or **licence** ['laɪsənts] n 1 PERMIT

: licencia *f* **2** FREEDOM : libertad *f* **3** AUTHORIZATION : permiso *m* — ~ *vt* **licensed; licensing** : autorizar

licorice [ˈlɪkərɪʃ, -rəs] *n* : regaliz *m*

lick [ˈlɪk] *vt* **1** : lamer **2** DEFEAT : dar una paliza a *fam* — ~ *n* : lamida *f*

lid [ˈlɪd] *n* **1** : tapa *f* **2** EYELID : párpado *m*

lie¹ [ˈlaɪ] *vi* **lay** [ˈleɪ]; **lain** [ˈleɪn]; **lying** [ˈlaɪɪŋ] **1** *or* ~ **down** : acostarse, echarse **2** BE : estar, encontrarse

lie² *vi* **lied; lying** [ˈlaɪɪŋ] : mentir — ~ *n* : mentira *f*

lieutenant [luːˈtɛnənt] *n* : teniente *mf*

life [ˈlaɪf] *n, pl* **lives** [ˈlaɪvz] : vida *f* — **lifeboat** [ˈlaɪf.boːt] *n* : bote *m* salvavidas — **lifeguard** [ˈlaɪf.gɑrd] *n* : socorrista *mf* — **lifeless** [ˈlaɪfləs] *adj* : sin vida — **lifelike** [ˈlaɪf.laɪk] *adj* : natural, realista — **lifelong** [ˈlaɪf.lɔŋ] *adj* : de toda la vida — **life preserver** *n* : salvavidas *m* — **lifestyle** [ˈlaɪf.staɪl] *n* : estilo *m* de vida — **lifetime** [ˈlaɪf.taɪm] *n* : vida *f*

lift [ˈlɪft] *vt* **1** RAISE : levantar **2** STEAL : robar — *vi* **1** CLEAR UP : despejarse *or* ~ **off** : despegar (dícese de un avión, etc.) — ~ *n* **1** LIFTING : levantamiento *m* **2** give s.o. a ~ : llevar en coche a algn — **liftoff** [ˈlɪft.ɔf] *n* : despegue *m*

light¹ [ˈlaɪt] *n* **1** : luz *f* **2** LAMP : lámpara *f* **3** HEADLIGHT : faro *m* **4 do you have a ~?** : ¿tienes fuego? — ~ *adj* **1** BRIGHT : bien iluminado **2** : claro (dícese de los colores), rubio (dícese del pelo) — ~ *v* **lit** [ˈlɪt] *or* **lighted; lighting** *vt* **1** : encender (un fuego) **2** ILLUMINATE : iluminar — *vi or* ~ **up** : iluminarse — **lightbulb** [ˈlaɪt.bʌlb] *n* : bombilla *f*, bombillo *m* Lat — **lighten** [ˈlaɪtən] *vt* BRIGHTEN : iluminar — **lighter** [ˈlaɪtər] *n* : encendedor *m* — **lighthouse** [ˈlaɪt.haʊs] *n* : faro *m* — **lighting** [ˈlaɪtɪŋ] *n* : alumbrado *m* — **lightning** [ˈlaɪtnɪŋ] *n* : relámpago *m*, rayo *m* — **light-year** [ˈlaɪt.jɪr] *n* : año *m* luz

light² *adj* : ligero — **lighten** [ˈlaɪtən] *vt* : aligerar — **lightly** [ˈlaɪtli] *adv* **1** : suavemente **2 let off ~** : tratar con indulgencia — **lightness** [ˈlaɪtnəs] *n* : ligereza *f* — **lightweight** [ˈlaɪt.weɪt] *adj* : ligero

like¹ [ˈlaɪk] *v* **liked; liking** *vt* **1** : gustarle (a uno) **2** WANT : querer — *vi* **if you ~** : si quieres — **likes** *npl* : preferencias *fpl*, gustos *mpl* — **likable** *or* **likeable** [ˈlaɪkəbəl] *adj* : simpático

like² *adj* SIMILAR : parecido — ~ *prep* : como — ~ *conj* **1** AS : como **2** AS IF

: como si — **likelihood** [ˈlaɪkliˌhʊd] *n* : probabilidad *f* — **likely** [ˈlaɪkli] *adj* **-lier; -est** : probable — **liken** [ˈlaɪkən] *vt* : comparar — **likeness** [ˈlaɪknəs] *n* : semejanza *f*, parecido *m* — **likewise** [ˈlaɪk.waɪz] *adv* **1** : lo mismo **2** ALSO : también

liking [ˈlaɪkɪŋ] *n* : afición *f* (por una cosa), simpatía *f* (por una persona)

lilac [ˈlaɪlək, -læk, -lɑk] *n* : lila *f*

lily [ˈlɪli] *n, pl* **lilies** : lirio *m*, azucena *f* — **lily of the valley** *n* : lirio *m* de los valles

lima bean [ˈlaɪmə] *n* : frijol *m* de media luna

limb [ˈlɪm] *n* **1** : miembro *m* (en anatomía) **2** : rama *f* (de un árbol)

limber [ˈlɪmbər] *vi or* ~ **up** : calentarse, hacer ejercicios preliminares — ~ *adj* : ágil

limbo [ˈlɪm.boː] *n, pl* **-bos** : limbo *m*

lime [ˈlaɪm] *n* : lima *f*, limón *m* verde Lat — **limelight** [ˈlaɪm.laɪt] *n* **be in the ~** : estar en el candelero

limerick [ˈlɪmərɪk] *n* : poema *m* jocoso de cinco versos

limestone [ˈlaɪm.stoːn] *n* : (piedra *f*) caliza *f*

limit [ˈlɪmət] *n* : límite *m* — ~ *vt* : limitar, restringir — **limitation** [ˌlɪmə-ˈteɪʃən] *n* : limitación *f*, restricción *f* — **limited** [ˈlɪmətəd] *adj* : limitado

limousine [ˈlɪməˌziːn, ˌlɪmə'-] *n* : limusina *f*

limp¹ [ˈlɪmp] *vi* : cojear — ~ *n* : cojera *f*

limp² *adj* : flojo, fláccido

line [ˈlaɪn] *n* **1** : línea *f* **2** ROPE : cuerda *f* **3** ROW : fila *f* **4** QUEUE : cola *f* **5** WRINKLE : arruga *f* **6 drop a ~** : mándar unas líneas — ~ *v* **lined; lining** *vt* **1** : forrar (un vestido, etc.), cubrir (las paredes, etc.) **2** MARK : rayar, trazar líneas en **3** BORDER : bordear — *vi* ~ **up** : ponerse en fila, hacer cola

lineage [ˈlɪniːɪdʒ] *n* : linaje *m*

linear [ˈlɪniːər] *adj* : lineal

linen [ˈlɪnən] *n* : lino *m*

liner [ˈlaɪnər] *n* **1** LINING : forro *m* **2** SHIP : buque *m*, transatlántico *m*

lineup [ˈlaɪn.əp] *n* **1** *or* **police ~** : fila *f* de sospechosos **2** : alineación *f* (en deportes)

linger [ˈlɪŋgər] *vi* **1** : quedarse, entretenerse **2** PERSIST : persistir

lingerie [ˌlɑːndʒəˈreɪ, ˌlænʒˈriː] *n* : ropa *f* íntima femenina, lencería *f*

lingo [ˈlɪŋgoː] *n, pl* **-goes** JARGON : jerga *f*

linguistics [lɪŋˈgwɪstɪks] *n* : lingüística *f* — **linguist** [ˈlɪŋgwɪst] *n* : lingüista *mf*

— **linguistic** [lɪŋ'gwɪstɪk] *adj* : lingüís-tico

lining ['laɪnɪŋ] *n* : forro *m*

link ['lɪŋk] *n* **1** : eslabón *m* (de una cade-na) **2** BOND : lazo *m* **3** CONNECTION : conexión *f* — *vt* : enlazar, conec-tar — *vi* ~ **up** : unirse, conectar

linoleum [lə'noːliəm] *n* : linóleo *m*

lint ['lɪnt] *n* : pelusa *f*

lion ['laɪən] *n* : león *m* — **lioness** ['laɪə-nɪs] *n* : leona *f*

lip ['lɪp] *n* **1** : labio *m* **2** EDGE : borde *m* — **lipstick** ['lɪp,stɪk] *n* : lápiz *m* de labios

liqueur [lɪ'kʊr, -'kər, -'kjʊr] *n* : licor *m*

liquid ['lɪkwəd] *adj* : líquido — *n* : líquido *m* — **liquidate** ['lɪkwə,deɪt] *vt* **-dated; -dating** : liquidar — **liquida-tion** [,lɪkwə'deɪʃən] *n* : liquidación *f*

liquor ['lɪkər] *n* : bebidas *fpl* alcohólicas

lisp ['lɪsp] *vi* : cecear — *n* : ceceo *m*

list¹ ['lɪst] *n* : lista *f* — *vt* **1** ENUMER-ATE : hacer una lista de, enumerar **2** IN-CLUDE : incluir (en una lista)

list² *vi* : escorar (dícese de un barco)

listen ['lɪsən] *vi* **1** : escuchar **2** ~ **to** HEED : hacer caso de **3** ~ **to reason** : atender a razones — **listener** ['lɪsənər] *n* : oyente *mf*

listless ['lɪstləs] *adj* : apático

lit ['lɪt] *pp* → **light**

litany ['lɪtəni] *n, pl* **-nies** : letanía *f*

liter ['liːtər] *n* : litro *m*

literacy ['lɪtərəsi] *n* : alfabetismo *m*

literal ['lɪtərəl] *adj* : literal — **literally** *adv* : literalmente, al pie de la letra

literate ['lɪtərət] *adj* : alfabetizado

literature ['lɪtərə,tʃʊr, -tʃər] *n* : literatura *f* — **literary** ['lɪtə,reri] *adj* : literario

lithe ['laɪð, 'laɪθ] *adj* : ágil y grácil

litigation [,lɪtə'geɪʃən] *n* : litigio *m*

litre → **liter**

litter ['lɪtər] *n* **1** RUBBISH : basura *f* **2** : ca-mada *f* (de animales) **3** *or* **kitty** ~ : arena *f* higiénica — *vt* : tirar ba-sura en, ensuciar — *vi* : tirar basura

little ['lɪtəl] *adj* **littler** *or* **less** ['lɛs] *or* **lesser** ['lɛsər]; **littlest** *or* **least** ['liːst] **1** SMALL : pequeño **2 a** ~ SOME : un poco de **3 he speaks** ~ **English** : habla poco inglés — ~ *adv* **less** ['lɛs]; **least** ['liːst] : poco — ~ *pron* **1** : poco *m*, -ca *f* **2** **a** ~ **by** ~ : poco a poco

liturgy ['lɪtərdʒi] *n, pl* **-gies** : liturgia *f* — **liturgical** [lə'tərdʒɪkəl] *adj* : litúrgico

live ['lɪv] *vi* **lived; living 1** : vivir **2** RE-SIDE : residir **3** ~ **on** : vivir de — *vt* : vivir, llevar (una vida) — ~ ['laɪv] *adj* **1** : vivo **2** : con corriente (dícese de cables eléctricos) **3** : en vivo, en di-

recto (dícese de programas de tele-visión, etc.) — **livelihood** ['laɪvli,hʊd] *n* : sustento *m*, medio *m* de vida —

lively ['laɪvli] *adj* **-lier; -est** : animado, alegre — **liven** ['laɪvən] *vt or* ~ **up** : animar — *vi* : animarse

liver ['lɪvər] *n* : hígado *m*

livestock ['laɪv,stak] *n* : ganado *m*

livid ['lɪvəd] *adj* **1** : lívido **2** ENRAGED : furioso

living ['lɪvɪŋ] *adj* : vivo — ~ *n* **make a** ~ : ganarse la vida — **living room** *n* : living *m*, sala *f* (de estar)

lizard ['lɪzərd] *n* : lagarto *m*

llama ['lɑmə, 'jɑ-] *n* : llama *f*

load ['loːd] *n* **1** CARGO : carga *f* **2** BURDEN : carga *f*, peso *m* **3** ~**s of** : un montón de — *vt* : cargar

loaf¹ ['loːf] *n, pl* **loaves** ['loːvz] : pan *m*, barra *f* (de pan)

loaf² *vi* : holgazanear — **loafer** ['loːfər] *n* **1** : holgazán *m*, -zana *f* **2** : mocasín *m* (zapato)

loan ['loːn] *n* : préstamo *m* — ~ *vt* : prestar

loathe ['loːð] *vt* **loathed; loathing** : odiar — **loathsome** ['loːθsəm, 'loːð-] *adj* : odioso

lobby ['labi] *n, pl* **-bies 1** : vestíbulo *m* **2** *or* **political** ~ : grupo *m* de presión, lobby *m* — ~ *v* **-bied; -bying** *vt* : ejercer presión sobre

lobe ['loːb] *n* : lóbulo *m*

lobster ['labstər] *n* : langosta *f*

local ['loːkəl] *adj* : local — ~ *n* **the** ~**s** : los vecinos del lugar — **locale** [lo-'kæl] *n* : escenario *m* — **locality** [lo-'kæləti] *n, pl* **-ties** : localidad *f*

locate ['loːkeɪt, loː'keɪt] *vt* **-cated; -cating 1** SITUATE : situar, ubicar **2** FIND : localizar — **location** [loː'keɪʃən] *n* : situación *f*, lugar *m*

lock¹ ['lak] *n* : mechón *m* (de pelo)

lock² *n* **1** : cerradura *f* (de una puerta, etc.) **2** : esclusa *f* (de un canal) — ~ *vt* **1** : cerrar (con llave) **2** *or* ~ **up** CON-FINE : encerrar — *vi* **1** : cerrarse con llave **2** : bloquearse (dícese de una rueda, etc.) — **locker** ['lakər] *n* : ar-mario *m* — **locket** ['lakət] *n* : medallón *m* — **locksmith** ['lak,smɪθ] *n* : cerra-jero *m*, -ra *f*

locomotive [,loːkə'moːtɪv] *n* : locomoto-ra *f*

locust ['loːkəst] *n* : langosta *f*, chapulí *m Lat*

lodge ['ladʒ] *v* **lodged; lodging** *vt* HOUSE : hospedar, alojar **2** FILE : pre-sentar — *vi* : hospedarse, alojarse — ~ *n* : pabellón *m* — **lodger** ['ladʒər]

: huésped *m*; -peda *f* — **lodging** [ˈlɑdʒɪŋ] *n* 1 : alojamiento *m* 2 **~s** *npl* : habitaciones *fpl*

loft [ˈlɒft] *n* 1 : desván *m* (en una casa) 2 HAYLOFT : pajar *m* — **lofty** [ˈlɔfti] *adj* **loftier; -est** 1 : noble, elevado 2 HAUGHTY : altanero

log [ˈlɔg, ˈlɑg] *n* 1 : tronco *m*, leño *m* 2 RECORD : diario *m* — **~** *vi* **logged; logging** 1 : talar (árboles) 2 RECORD : registrar, anotar 3 **~ on** : entrar (en el sistema) 4 **~ off** : salir (del sistema) — **logger** [ˈlɔgər, ˈlɑ-] *n* : leñador *m*, -dora *f*

logic [ˈlɑdʒɪk] *n* : lógica *f* — **logical** [ˈlɑdʒɪkəl] *adj* : lógico — **logistics** [ləˈdʒɪstɪks, lo-] *ns & pl* : logística *f*

logo [ˈloːgoː] *n*, *pl* **logos** [-ˌgoːz] : logotipo *m*

loin [ˈlɔɪn] *n* : lomo *m*

loiter [ˈlɔɪtər] *vi* : vagar, holgazanear

lollipop *or* **lollypop** [ˈlɑliˌpɑp] *n* : pirulí *m*, chupete *m* *Lat*

lone [ˈloːn] *adj* : solitario — **loneliness** [ˈloːnlinəs] *n* : soledad *f* — **lonely** [ˈloːnli] *adj* **-lier; -est** : solitario, solo — **loner** [ˈloːnər] *n* : solitario *m*, -ria *f* — **lonesome** [ˈloːnsəm] *adj* : solo, solitario

long[1] [ˈlɔŋ] *adj* **longer** [ˈlɔŋgər]; **longest** [ˈlɔŋgəst] : largo — **~** *adv* 1 : mucho tiempo 2 **all day ~** : todo el día 3 **as ~ as** : mientras 4 **no ~er** : ya no 5 **so ~!** : ¡hasta luego!, ¡adiós! — **~** *n* 1 **before ~** : dentro de poco 2 **the ~ and the short** : lo esencial

long[2] *vi* **~ for** : anhelar, desear

longevity [lɑnˈdʒevəʈi] *n* : longevidad *f*

longing [ˈlɔŋɪŋ] *n* : ansia *f*, anhelo *m*

longitude [ˈlɑndʒəˌtuːd, -ˌtjuːd] *n* : longitud *f*

look [ˈlʊk] *vi* 1 : mirar 2 SEEM : parecer 3 **~ after** : cuidar (de) 4 **~ for** EXPECT : esperar 5 **~ for** SEEK : buscar 6 **~ into** : investigar 7 **~ out** : tener cuidado 8 **~ over** EXAMINE : revisar 9 **~ up to** : respetar — *vt* : mirar — **~** *n* 1 : mirada *f* 2 APPEARANCE : aspecto *m*, aire *m* — **lookout** [ˈlʊkˌaʊt] *n* 1 : puesto *m* de observación 2 WATCHMAN : vigía *mf* 3 **be on the ~ for** : estar al acecho de

loom[1] [ˈluːm] *n* : telar *m*

loom[2] *vi* 1 APPEAR : aparecer, surgir 2 APPROACH : ser inminente

loop [ˈluːp] *n* : lazada *f*, lazo *m* — **~** *vt* : hacer lazadas con — **loophole** [ˈluːpˌhoːl] *n* : escapatoria *f*

loose [ˈluːs] *adj* **looser; -est** 1 MOVABLE : flojo, suelto 2 SLACK : flojo 3 ROOMY : holgado 4 APPROXIMATE : libre, aproximado 5 FREE : suelto 6 IMMORAL : relajado — **loosely** [ˈluːsli] *adv* 1 : sin apretar 2 ROUGHLY : aproximadamente — **loosen** [ˈluːsən] *vt* : aflojar

loot [ˈluːt] *n* : botín *m* — **~** *vt* : saquear, robar — **looter** [ˈluːtər] *n* : saqueador *m*, -dora *f* — **looting** [ˈluːtɪŋ] *n* : saqueo *m*

lop [ˈlɑp] *vt* **lopped; lopping** : cortar, podar

lopsided [ˈlɑpˌsaɪdəd] *adj* : torcido, chueco *Lat*

lord [ˈlɔrd] *n* 1 : señor *m*, noble *m* 2 **the Lord** : el Señor

lore [ˈlor] *n* : saber *m* popular, tradición *f*

lose [ˈluːz] *v* **lost** [ˈlɔst]; **losing** [ˈluːzɪŋ] *vt* 1 : perder 2 **~ one's way** : perderse 3 **~ time** : atrasarse (dícese de un reloj) — *vi* : perder — **loser** [ˈluːzər] *n* : perdedor *m*, -dora *f* — **loss** [ˈlɔs] *n* 1 : pérdida *f* 2 DEFEAT : derrota *f* 3 **be at a ~ for words** : no encontrar palabras — **lost** [ˈlɔst] *adj* 1 : perdido 2 **get ~** : perderse

lot [ˈlɑt] *n* 1 FATE : suerte *f* 2 PLOT : solar *m* 3 **a ~ of** *or* **~s of** : mucho, un montón de

lotion [ˈloːʃən] *n* : loción *f*

lottery [ˈlɑtəri] *n*, *pl* **-teries** : lotería *f*

loud [ˈlaʊd] *adj* 1 : alto, fuerte 2 NOISY : ruidoso 3 FLASHY : llamativo — **~** *adv* 1 : fuerte 2 **out ~** : en voz alta — **loudly** [ˈlaʊdli] *adv* : en voz alta — **loudspeaker** [ˈlaʊdˌspiːkər] *n* : altavoz *m*

lounge [ˈlaʊndʒ] *vi* **lounged; lounging** 1 : repantigarse 2 *or* **~ about** : holgazanear — **~** *n* : salón *m*

louse [ˈlaʊs] *n*, *pl* **lice** [ˈlaɪs] : piojo *m* — **lousy** [ˈlaʊzi] *adj* **lousier; -est** 1 : piojoso 2 BAD : pésimo, muy malo

love [ˈlʌv] *n* 1 : amor *m* 2 **fall in ~** : enamorarse — **~** *v* **loved; loving** : querer, amar — **lovable** [ˈlʌvəbəl] *adj* : adorable, amoroso *Lat* — **lovely** [ˈlʌvli] *adj* **-lier; -est** : lindo, precioso — **lover** [ˈlʌvər] *n* : amante *mf* — **loving** [ˈlʌvɪŋ] *adj* : cariñoso

low [ˈloː] *adj* **lower** [ˈloːər]; **-est** 1 : bajo 2 SCARCE : escaso 3 DEPRESSED : deprimido — **~** *adv* 1 : bajo 2 **turn the lights down ~** : bajar las luces — **~** *n* 1 : punto *m* bajo 2 *or* **~ gear** : primera velocidad *f* — **lower** [ˈloːər] *adj* : inferior, más bajo — **~** *vt* : bajar — **lowly** [ˈloːli] *adj* **-lier; -est** : humilde

loyal [ˈlɔɪəl] *adj* : leal, fiel — **loyalty** [ˈlɔɪəlti] *n*, *pl* **-ties** : lealtad *f*

lozenge ['lɑzəndʒ] *n* : pastilla *f*
lubricate ['lu:brɪˌkeɪt] *vt* **-cated; -cating**
: lubricar — **lubricant** ['lu:brɪkənt] *n*
: lubricante *m* — **lubrication** [ˌlu:brɪ-
'keɪʃən] *n* : lubricación *f*
lucid ['lu:səd] *adj* : lúcido — **lucidity**
[lu:'sɪdət̬i] *n* : lucidez *f*
luck ['lʌk] *n* **1** : suerte *f* **2** **good**
~!: ¡buena suerte! — **luckily** ['lʌkəli]
adv : afortunadamente — **lucky** ['lʌki]
adj **luckier; -est 1** : afortunado **2 ~**
charm : amuleto *m* (de la suerte)
lucrative ['lu:krət̬ɪv] *adj* : lucrativo
ludicrous ['lu:dəkrəs] *adj* : ridículo, absurdo
lug ['lʌg] *vt* **lugged; lugging** : arrastrar
luggage ['lʌgɪdʒ] *n* : equipaje *m*
lukewarm ['lu:k'wɔrm] *adj* : tibio
lull ['lʌl] *vt* **1** CALM : calmar **2 ~ to**
sleep : adormecer — **~** *n* : período *m*
de calma, pausa *f*
lullaby ['lʌlə̩baɪ] *n, pl* **-bies** : canción *f*
de cuna, nana *f*
lumber ['lʌmbər] *n* : madera *f* — **lum-**
berjack ['lʌmbərˌdʒæk] *n* : leñador *m*,
-dora *f*
luminous ['lu:mənəs] *adj* : luminoso
lump ['lʌmp] *n* **1** CHUNK, PIECE : pedazo
m, trozo *m* **2** SWELLING : bulto *m* **3**
: grumo *m* (en un líquido) — **~** *vt or*
~ together : juntar, agrupar —
lumpy ['lʌmpi] *adj* **lumpier; -est**
: grumoso (dícese de una salsa), lleno
de bultos (dícese de un colchón)
lunacy ['lu:nəsi] *n, pl* **-cies** : locura *f*
lunar ['lu:nər] *adj* : lunar
lunatic ['lu:nəˌtɪk] *n* : loco *m*, -ca *f*

lunch ['lʌntʃ] *n* : almuerzo *m*, comida *f*
— **~** *vi* : almorzar, comer — **lunch-**
eon ['lʌntʃən] *n* : comida *f*, almuerzo *m*
lung ['lʌŋ] *n* : pulmón *m*
lunge ['lʌndʒ] *vi* **lunged; lunging 1**
: lanzarse **2 ~ at** : arremeter contre
lurch[1] ['lərtʃ] *vi* **1** STAGGER : tambalearse
2 : dar bandazos (dícese de un vehícu-
lo)
lurch[2] *n* **leave in a ~** : dejar en la estacada
lure ['lʊr] *n* **1** BAIT : señuelo *m* **2** AT-
TRACTION : atractivo *m* — **~** *vt* **lured;**
luring : atraer
lurid ['lʊrəd] *adj* **1** GRUESOME : espeluznante **2** SENSATIONAL : sensacionalista
3 GAUDY : chillón
lurk ['lərk] *vi* : estar al acecho
luscious ['lʌʃəs] *adj* : delicioso, exquisito
lush ['lʌʃ] *adj* : exuberante, suntuoso
lust ['lʌst] *n* **1** : lujuria *f* **2** CRAVING
: ansia *f*, anhelo *m* — **~** *vi* **~ after**
: desear (a una persona), codiciar
(riquezas, etc.)
luster *or* **lustre** ['lʌstər] *n* : lustre *m*
lusty ['lʌsti] *adj* **lustier; -est** : fuerte
vigoroso
luxurious [ˌlʌg'ʒʊriəs, ˌlʌk'ʃʊr-] *adj* : lujoso — **luxury** ['lʌkʃəri, 'lʌgʒə-] *n, p*
-ries : lujo *m*
lye ['laɪ] *n* : lejía *f*
lying → lie
lynch ['lɪntʃ] *vt* : linchar
lynx ['lɪŋks] *n* : lince *m*
lyric ['lɪrɪk] *or* **lyrical** ['lɪrɪkəl] *adj* : líric
— **lyrics** *npl* : letra *f* (de una canción

M

m ['ɛm] *n, pl* **m's** *or* **ms** ['ɛmz] : m *f*, de-
cimotercera letra del alfabeto inglés
ma'am ['mæm] → **madam**
macabre [mə'kɑb, -'kɑbər, -'kɑbrə] *adj*
: macabro
macaroni [ˌmækə'ro:ni] *n* : macarrones
mpl
mace ['meɪs] *n* **1** : maza *f* (arma o símbolo) **2** : macis *f* (especia)
machete [mə'ʃɛt̬i] *n* : machete *m*
machine [mə'ʃi:n] *n* : máquina *f* — **ma-**
chinery [mə'ʃi:nəri] *n, pl* **-eries 1**
: maquinaria *f* **2** WORKS : mecanismo
m — **machine gun** *n* : ametralladora *f*
mad ['mæd] *adj* **madder; maddest 1**
INSANE : loco **2** FOOLISH : insensato **3**
ANGRY : furioso

madam ['mædəm] *n, pl* **mesdame**
[meɪ'dɑm] : señora *f*
madden ['mædən] *vt* : enfurecer
made → make
madly ['mædli] *adv* : como un loco, lo
camente — **madman** ['mædˌmæ
-mən] *n, pl* **-men** [-mən, -ˌmen] : loc
m — **madness** ['mædnəs] *n* : locur
f
Mafia ['mɑfiə] *n* : Mafia *f*
magazine ['mægəˌzi:n] *n* **1** PERIODICA
: revista *f* **2** : recámara *f* (de un arm
de fuego)
maggot ['mægət] *n* : gusano *m*
magic ['mædʒɪk] *n* : magia *f* — **~** *n*
magical ['mædʒɪkəl] *adj* : mágico -
magician [mə'dʒɪʃən] *n* : mago *m*, -ga

magistrate ['mædʒə,streıt] n : magistra-do m, -da f

magnanimous [mæg'nænəməs] adj : magnánimo

magnate ['mæg,neıt, -nət] n : magnate mf

magnet ['mægnət] n : imán m — **magnetic** [mæg'netɪk] adj : magnético — **magnetism** ['mægnə,tızəm] n : magnetismo m — **magnetize** ['mægnə,taız] vt **-tized; -tizing** : magnetizar

magnificent [mæg'nıfəsənt] adj : magnífico — **magnificence** [mæg'nıfəsənts] n : magnificencia f

magnify ['mægnə,faı] vt **-fied; -fying** 1 ENLARGE : ampliar 2 EXAGGERATE : exagerar — **magnifying glass** n : lupa f

magnitude ['mægnə,tu:d, -,tju:d] n : magnitud f

magnolia [mæg'no:ljə] n : magnolia f

mahogany [mə'hɑgəni] n, pl **-nies** : caoba f

maid ['meıd] n : sirvienta f, criada f, muchacha f — **maiden** ['meıdən] adj FIRST : inaugural — **maiden name** n : nombre m de soltera

mail ['meıl] n 1 : correo m 2 LETTERS : correspondencia f — ~ vt : enviar por correo — **mailbox** ['meıl,bɑks] n : buzón m — **mailman** ['meıl,mæn, -mən] n, pl **-men** [-mən, -,men] : cartero m

maim ['meım] vt : mutilar

main ['meın] n : tubería f principal (de agua o gas), cable m principal (de un circuito) — ~ adj : principal — **mainframe** ['meın,freım] n : computadora f central — **mainland** ['meın,lænd, -lənd] n : continente m — **mainly** ['meınli] adv : principalmente — **mainstay** ['meın,steı] n : sostén m (principal) — **mainstream** ['meın,stri:m] n : corriente f principal — ~ adj : dominante, convencional

maintain [meın'teın] vt : mantener — **maintenance** ['meıntənənts] n : mantenimiento m

maize ['meız] n : maíz m

majestic [mə'dʒestɪk] adj : majestuoso — **majesty** ['mædʒəsti] n, pl **-ties** : majestad f

major ['meıdʒər] adj 1 : muy importante, principal 2 : mayor (en música) — ~ n 1 : mayor mf, comandante mf (en las fuerzas armadas) 2 : especialidad f (universitaria) — ~ vi **-jored; -joring** : especializarse — **majority** [mə'dʒɔrəti] n, pl **-ties** : mayoría f

make ['meık] v **made** ['meıd]; **making** vt 1 : hacer 2 MANUFACTURE : fabricar 3 CONSTITUTE : constituir 4 PREPARE : preparar 5 RENDER : poner 6 COMPEL : obligar 7 ~ **a decision** : tomar una decisión 8 ~ **a living** : ganar la vida — vi 1 ~ **do** : arreglárselas 2 ~ **for** : dirigirse a 3 ~ **good** SUCCEED : tener éxito — ~ n BRAND : marca f — **make-believe** [,meıkbə'li:v] n : fantasía f — ~ adj : imaginario — **make out** vt 1 : hacer (un cheque, etc.) 2 DISCERN : distinguir 3 UNDERSTAND : comprender — vi **how did you** ~? : ¿qué tal te fue? — **maker** ['meıkər] n MANUFACTURER : fabricante mf — **makeshift** ['meık,ʃıft] adj : improvisado — **makeup** ['meık,ʌp] n 1 COMPOSITION : composición f 2 COSMETICS : maquillaje m — **make up** vt 1 PREPARE : preparar 2 INVENT : inventar 3 CONSTITUTE : formar — vi RECONCILE : hacer las paces

maladjusted [,mælə'dʒʌstəd] adj : inadaptado

malaria [mə'leriə] n : malaria f, paludismo m

male ['meıl] n : macho m (de animales o plantas), varón m (de personas) — ~ adj 1 : macho 2 MASCULINE : masculino

malevolent [mə'levələnt] adj : malévolo

malfunction [mæl'fʌŋkʃən] vi : funcionar mal — ~ n : mal funcionamiento m

malice ['mælıs] n : mala intención f, rencor m — **malicious** [mə'lıʃəs] adj : malicioso

malign [mə'laın] adj : maligno — ~ vt : calumniar

malignant [mə'lıgnənt] adj : maligno

mall ['mɔl] n or **shopping** ~ : centro m comercial

malleable ['mæliəbəl] adj : maleable

mallet ['mælət] n : mazo m

malnutrition [,mælnu'trıʃən, -nju-] n : desnutrición f

malpractice [,mæl'præktəs] n : mala práctica f, negligencia f

malt ['mɔlt] n : malta f

mama or **mamma** ['mɑmə] n : mamá f

mammal ['mæməl] n : mamífero m

mammogram ['mæmə,græm] n : mamografía f

mammoth ['mæməθ] adj : gigantesco

man ['mæn] n, pl **men** ['men] : hombre m — ~ vt **manned; manning** : tripular (un barco o avión), encargarse de (un servicio)

manage ['mænıdʒ] v **-aged; -aging** vt 1 HANDLE : manejar 2 DIRECT : administrar, dirigir — vi COPE : arreglárselas

— **manageable** ['mænɪdʒəbəl] *adj* : manejable — **management** ['mænɪdʒmənt] *n* : dirección *f* — **manager** ['mænɪdʒər] *n* : director *m*, -tora *f*; gerente *mf* — **managerial** [,mænə'dʒɪriəl] *adj* : directivo

mandarin ['mændərən] *n or* ～ **orange** : mandarina *f*

mandate ['mæn,deɪt] *n* : mandato *m* — **mandatory** ['mændə,tori] *adj* : obligatorio

mane ['meɪn] *n* : crin *f* (de un caballo), melena *f* (de un león)

maneuver [mə'nu:vər, -'nju:-] *n* : maniobra *f* — ～ *v* -**vered; -vering** : maniobrar

mangle ['mæŋgəl] *vt* -**gled; -gling** : destrozar

mango ['mæŋgo:] *n, pl* -**goes** : mango *m*

mangy ['meɪndʒi] *adj* **mangier; -est** : sarnoso

manhandle ['mæn,hændəl] *vi* -**dled; -dling** : maltratar

manhole ['mæn,ho:l] *n* : boca *f* de alcantarilla

manhood ['mæn,hʊd] *n* **1** : madurez *f* (de un hombre) **2** VIRILITY : virilidad *f*

mania ['meɪniə, -njə] *n* : manía *f* — **maniac** ['meɪni,æk] *n* : maníaco *m*, -ca *f*

manicure ['mænə,kjʊr] *n* : manicura *f* — ～ *vt* -**cured; -curing** : hacer la manicura a

manifest ['mænə,fest] *adj* : manifiesto, patente — ～ *vt* : manifestar — **manifesto** [,mænə'fes,to:] *n, pl* -**tos** *or* -**toes** : manifiesto *m*

manipulate [mə'nɪpjə,leɪt] *vt* -**lated; -lating** : manipular — **manipulation** [mə,nɪpjə'leɪʃən] *n* : manipulación *f*

mankind ['mæn'kaɪnd, ,kaɪnd] *n* : género *m* humano, humanidad *f*

manly ['mænli] *adj* -**lier; -est** : viril — **manliness** ['mænlinəs] *n* : virilidad *f*

man-made ['mæn'meɪd] *adj* : artificial

mannequin ['mænɪkən] *n* : maniquí *m*

manner ['mænər] *n* **1** : manera *f* **2** KIND : clase *f* **3** ～**s** *npl* ETIQUETTE : modales *mpl*, educación *f* — **mannerism** ['mænə,rɪzəm] *n* : peculiaridad *f* (de una persona)

manoeuvre *Brit* → **maneuver**

manor ['mænər] *n* : casa *f* solariega

manpower ['mæn,paʊər] *n* : mano *f* de obra

mansion ['mæntʃən] *n* : mansión *f*

manslaughter ['mæn,slɔtər] *n* : homicidio *m* sin premeditación

mantel ['mæntəl] *or* **mantelpiece** ['mæntəl,pi:s] *n* : repisa *f* de la chimenea

manual ['mænjʊəl] *adj* : manual — ～ *n* : manual *m*

manufacture [,mænjə'fæktʃər] *n* : fabricación *f* — ～ *vt* -**tured; -turing** : fabricar — **manufacturer** [,mænjə'fæktʃərər] *n* : fabricante *mf*

manure [mə'nʊr, -'njʊr] *n* : estiércol *m*

manuscript ['mænjə,skrɪpt] *n* : manuscrito *m*

many ['meni] *adj* **more** ['mor]; **most** ['mo:st] **1** : muchos **2 as** ～ : tantos **3 how** ～ : cuántos **4 too** ～ : demasiados — ～ *pron* : muchos *pl*, -chas *pl*

map ['mæp] *n* : mapa *m* — ～ *vt* **mapped; mapping 1** : trazar el mapa de **2** *or* ～ **out** : planear, proyectar

maple ['meɪpəl] *n* : arce *m*

mar ['mar] *vt* **marred; marring** : estropear

marathon ['mærə,θɑn] *n* : maratón *m*

marble ['marbəl] *n* **1** : mármol *m* **2** ～**s** *npl* : canicas *fpl* (para jugar)

march ['martʃ] *n* : marcha *f* — ～ *vi* : marchar, desfilar

March ['martʃ] *n* : marzo *m*

mare ['mær] *n* : yegua *f*

margarine ['mardʒərən] *n* : margarina *f*

margin ['mardʒən] *n* : margen *m* — **marginal** ['mardʒənəl] *adj* : marginal

marigold ['mærə,go:ld] *n* : caléndula *f*

marijuana [,mærə'hwanə] *n* : marihuana *f*

marinate ['mærə,neɪt] *vt* -**nated; -nating** : marinar

marine [mə'ri:n] *adj* : marino — ～ *n* : soldado *m* de marina

marionette [,mæriə'net] *n* : marioneta *f*

marital ['mærətəl] *adj* **1** : matrimonial **2** ～ **status** : estado *m* civil

maritime ['mærə,taɪm] *adj* : marítimo

mark ['mark] *n* **1** : marca *f* **2** STAIN : mancha *f* **3** IMPRINT : huella *f* **4** TARGET : blanco *m* **5** GRADE : nota *f* — ～ *vt* **1** : marcar **2** STAIN : manchar **3** POINT OUT : señalar **4** : calificar (un examen, etc.) **5** COMMEMORATE : conmemorar **6** CARACTERIZE : caracterizar **7** ～ **off** : delimitar — **marked** ['markt] *adj* : marcado, notable — **markedly** ['markədli] *adv* : notablemente — **marker** ['markər] *n* : marcador *m*

market ['markət] *n* : mercado *m* — ～ *vt* : vender, comercializar — **marketable** ['markətəbəl] *adj* : vendible — **marketplace** ['markət,pleɪs] *n* : mercado *m*

marksman ['marksmən] *n, pl* -**men** [-mən, -,men] : tirador *m* — **marksmanship** ['marksmən,ʃɪp] *n* : puntería *f*

marmalade ['marmə,leɪd] *n* : mermelada *f*

maroon[1] [məˈruːn] vt : abandonar, aislar
maroon[2] n : rojo m oscuro
marquee [mɑrˈkiː] n CANOPY : marquesina f
marriage [ˈmærɪdʒ] n 1 : matrimonio m 2 WEDDING : casamiento m, boda f — **married** [ˈmærid] adj 1 : casado 2 get ~ : casarse
marrow [ˈmæroː] n : médula f, tuétano m
marry [ˈmæri] v -ried; -rying vt 1 : casar 2 WED : casarse con — vi : casarse
Mars [ˈmɑrz] n : Marte m
marsh [ˈmɑrʃ] n 1 : pantano m 2 or salt ~ : marisma f
marshal [ˈmɑrʃəl] n : mariscal m (en el ejército); jefe m, -fa f (de policía, de bomberos, etc.) — ~ vt -shaled or -shalled; -shaling or -shalling : poner en orden (los pensamientos, etc.), reunir (las tropas)
marshmallow [ˈmɑrʃˌmɛloː, -ˌmæloː] n : malvavisco m
marshy [ˈmɑrʃi] adj marshier; -est : pantanoso
mart [ˈmɑrt] n : mercado m
martial [ˈmɑrʃəl] adj : marcial
martyr [ˈmɑrtər] n : mártir mf — ~ vt : martirizar
marvel [ˈmɑrvəl] n : maravilla f — ~ vi -veled or -velled; -veling or -velling : maravillarse — **marvelous** [ˈmɑrvələs] or **marvellous** adj : maravilloso
mascara [mæsˈkærə] n : rímel m
mascot [ˈmæsˌkɑt, -kət] n : mascota f
masculine [ˈmæskjələn] adj : masculino — **masculinity** [ˌmæskjəˈlinəţi] n : masculinidad f
mash [ˈmæʃ] vt 1 CRUSH : aplastar, majar 2 PUREE : hacer puré de — **mashed potatoes** npl : puré m de patatas, puré m de papas Lat
mask [ˈmæsk] n : máscara f — ~ vt : enmascarar
masochism [ˈmæsəˌkizəm, ˈmæzə-] n : masoquismo m — **masochist** [ˈmæsəkɪst, ˈmæzə-] n : masoquista mf — **masochistic** [ˌmæsəˈkɪstɪk, ˌmæzə-] adj : masoquista
mason [ˈmeɪsən] n : albañil mf — **masonry** [ˈmeɪsənri] n, pl -ries : albañilería f
masquerade [ˌmæskəˈreɪd] n : mascarada f — ~ vi -aded; -ading ~ as : disfrazarse de, hacerse pasar por
mass [ˈmæs] n 1 : masa f 2 MULTITUDE : cantidad f 3 the ~es : las masas
Mass [ˈmæs] n : misa f
massacre [ˈmæsɪkər] n : masacre f — ~ vt -cred; -cring : masacrar

massage [məˈsɑʒ, -ˈsɑdʒ] n : masaje m — ~ vt -saged; -saging : dar masaje a, masajear — **masseur** [mæˈsər] n : masajista m — **masseuse** [mæˈsəz, -ˈsərz, -ˈsuːz] n : masajista f
massive [ˈmæsɪv] adj 1 BULKY, SOLID : macizo 2 HUGE : enorme, masivo
mast [ˈmæst] n : mástil m
master [ˈmæstər] n 1 : amo m, señor m (de la casa) 2 EXPERT : maestro m, -tra f 3 ~'s degree : maestría f — ~ vt : dominar — **masterful** [ˈmæstərfəl] adj : magistral — **masterpiece** [ˈmæstərˌpiːs] n : obra f maestra — **mastery** [ˈmæstəri] n : maestría f
masturbate [ˈmæstərˌbeɪt] v -bated; -bating vi : masturbarse — **masturbation** [ˌmæstərˈbeɪʃən] n : masturbación f
mat [ˈmæt] n 1 DOORMAT : felpudo m 2 RUG : estera f
matador [ˈmætəˌdɔr] n : matador m
match [ˈmætʃ] n 1 EQUAL : igual mf 2 : fósforo m, cerilla f (para encender) 3 GAME : partido m, combate m (en boxeo) 4 be a good ~ : hacer buena pareja — ~ vt 1 or ~ up : emparejar 2 EQUAL : igualar 3 : combinar con, hacer juego con (ropa, colores, etc.) — vi : concordar, coincidir
mate [ˈmeɪt] n 1 COMPANION : compañero m, -ra f; amigo m, -ga f 2 : macho m, hembra f (de animales) — ~ vi mated; mating : aparearse
material [məˈtiriəl] adj 1 : material 2 IMPORTANT : importante — ~ n 1 : material m 2 CLOTH : tela f, tejido m — **materialistic** [məˌtiriəˈlɪstɪk] adj : materialista — **materialize** [məˈtiriəˌlaɪz] vi -ized; -izing : aparecer
maternal [məˈtərnəl] adj : maternal — **maternity** [məˈtərnəţi] n, pl -ties : maternidad f — ~ adj 1 : de maternidad 2 ~ clothes : ropa f de futura mamá
math [ˈmæθ] → **mathematics**
mathematics [ˌmæθəˈmætɪks] ns & pl : matemáticas fpl — **mathematical** [ˌmæθəˈmætɪkəl] adj : matemático — **mathematician** [ˌmæθəməˈtɪʃən] n : matemático m, -ca f
matinee or **matinée** [ˌmætənˈeɪ] n : matiné(e) f, función f de tarde
matrimony [ˈmætrəˌmoːni] n : matrimonio m — **matrimonial** [ˌmætrəˈmoːniəl] adj : matrimonial
matrix [ˈmeɪtrɪks] n, pl -trices [ˈmeɪtrəˌsiːz, ˈmæ-] or -trixes [ˈmeɪtrɪksəz] : matriz f
matte [ˈmæt] adj : mate
matter [ˈmætər] n 1 SUBSTANCE : materia

f **2** QUESTION : asunto *m*, cuestión *f* **3**
as a ~ of fact : en efecto, en realidad
4 for that : de hecho **5 to make
~s worse** : para colmo de males **6
what's the ~?** : ¿qué pasa? — *vi*
: importar

mattress ['mætrəs] *n* : colchón *m*

mature [mə'tʊr, -'tjʊr, -'tʃʊr] *adj* **-turer;
-est** : maduro — **~** *vi* **-tured; -turing**
: madurar — **maturity** [mə'tʊrəṭi, -'tjʊr-,
-'tʃʊr-] *n* : madurez *f*

maul ['mɔl] *vt* : maltratar, aporrear

mauve ['moːv, 'mɔv] *n* : malva *m*

maxim ['mæksəm] *n* : máxima *f*

maximum ['mæksəməm] *n, pl* **-ma**
['mæksəmə] *or* **-mums** : máximo *m*
— **~** *adj* : máximo — **maximize**
['mæksəˌmaɪz] *vt* **-mized; -mizing** : llevar al máximo

may ['meɪ] *v aux, past* **might** ['maɪt];
present s & pl **may 1** : poder **2 come
what ~** : pase lo que pase **3 it ~
happen** : puede pasar **4 ~ the best
man win** : que gane el mejor

May ['meɪ] *n* : mayo *m*

maybe ['meɪbi] *adv* : quizás, tal vez

mayhem ['meɪˌhem, 'meɪəm] *n* : alboroto
m

mayonnaise ['meɪəˌneɪz] *n* : mayonesa *f*

mayor ['meɪər, 'mer] *n* : alcalde *m*, -desa
f

maze ['meɪz] *n* : laberinto *m*

me ['miː] *pron* **1** : me **2 for ~** : para mí
3 give it to ~! : ¡dámelo! **4 it's ~**
: soy yo **5 with ~** : conmigo

meadow ['medoː] *n* : prado *m*, pradera *f*

meager ['miːɡər] *or* **meagre** *adj* : escaso

meal ['miːl] *n* **1** : comida *f* **2** : harina *f* (de
maíz, etc.) — **mealtime** ['miːlˌtaɪm] *n*
: hora *f* de comer

mean¹ ['miːn] *vt* **meant** ['ment]; **meaning 1** SIGNIFY : querer decir **2** INTEND
: querer, tener la intención de **3 be
meant for** : estar destinado a **4 he
didn't ~ it** : no lo dijo en serio

mean² *adj* **1** UNKIND : malo **2** STINGY
: mezquino, tacaño **3** HUMBLE : humilde

mean³ *adj* AVERAGE : medio — **~** *n*
: promedio *m*

meander [mi'ændər] *vi* **-dered; -dering
1** WIND : serpentear **2** WANDER : vagar

meaning ['miːnɪŋ] *n* : significado *m*,
sentido *m* — **meaningful** ['miːnɪŋfəl]
adj : significativo — **meaningless**
['miːnɪŋləs] *adj* : sin sentido

meanness ['miːnnəs] *n* **1** UNKINDNESS
: maldad *f* **2** STINGINESS : mezquindad
f

means ['miːnz] *n* **1** : medio *m* **2 by all
~** : por supuesto **3 by ~ of** : por
medio de **4 by no ~** : de ninguna
manera

meantime ['miːnˌtaɪm] *n* **1** : interín *m* **2
in the ~** : mientras tanto — **~** *adv* →
meanwhile

meanwhile ['miːnˌhwaɪl] *adv* : mientras
tanto — **~** *n* → **meantime**

measles ['miːzəlz] *npl* : sarampión *m*

measly ['miːzli] *adj* **-slier; -est** : miserable, misero

measure ['meʒər, 'meɪ-] *n* : medida *f* —
~ *v* **-sured; -suring** : medir — **measurable** ['meʒərəbəl, 'meɪ-] *adj* : mensurable — **measurement** ['meʒərmənt,
'meɪ-] *n* : medida *f* — **measure up** *vi*
~ to : estar a la altura de

meat ['miːt] *n* : carne *f* — **meatball**
['miːtˌbɔl] *n* : albóndiga *f* — **meaty**
['miːti] *adj* **meatier; -est 1** : carnoso **2**
SUBSTANTIAL : sustancioso

mechanic [mɪ'kænɪk] *n* : mecánico *m*,
-ca *f* — **mechanical** [mɪ'kænɪkəl] *adj*
: mecánico — **mechanics** [mɪ'kænɪks]
ns & pl **1** : mecánica *f* **2** WORKINGS
: mecanismo *m* — **mechanism**
['mekəˌnɪzəm] *n* : mecanismo *m* —
mechanize ['mekəˌnaɪz] *vt* **-nized;
-nizing** : mecanizar

medal ['medəl] *n* : medalla *f* — **medallion** [mə'dæljən] *n* : medallón *m*

meddle ['medəl] *vi* **-dled; -dling** : entrometerse

media ['miːdiə] *or* **mass ~** *npl* : me-
dios *mpl* de comunicación

median ['miːdiən] *adj* : medio

mediate ['miːdiˌeɪt] *vi* **-ated; -ating**
: mediar — **mediation** [ˌmiːdi'eɪʃən] *n*
: mediación *f* — **mediator** ['miːdiˌeɪtər]
n : mediador *m*, -dora *f*

medical ['medɪkəl] *adj* : médico —
medicated ['medəˌkeɪtəd] *adj* : medicinal — **medication** [ˌmedə'keɪʃən] *n*
: medicamento *m* — **medicinal** [mə-
'dɪsənəl] *adj* : medicinal — **medicine**
['medəsən] *n* **1** : medicina *f* **2** MEDICA-
TION : medicina *f*, medicamento *m*

medieval *or* **mediaeval** [mɪ'diːvəl, ˌmiː-,
ˌme-, -di'iːvəl] *adj* : medieval

mediocre [ˌmiːdi'oːkər] *adj* : mediocre —
mediocrity [ˌmiːdi'ɑkrəṭi] *n, pl* **-ties**
: mediocridad *f*

meditate ['medəˌteɪt] *vi* **-tated; -tating**
: meditar — **meditation** [ˌmedə'teɪʃən]
n : meditación *f*

medium ['miːdiəm] *n, pl* **-diums** *or* **-dia**
['miːdiə] *n* **1** MEANS : medio *m* **2** MEAN
: punto *m* medio, término *m* medio **3**
→ **media** — **~** *adj* : mediano

medley ['medli] *n, pl* **-leys 1** : mezcla *f*
2 : popurrí *m* (de canciones)

meek ['miːk] *adj* : dócil

meet ['miːt] *v* **met** ['met]; **meeting** *vt* **1**
ENCOUNTER : encontrarse con **2** SATIS-
FY : satisfacer **3 pleased to ~ you**
: encantado de conocerlo — *vi* **1** : encontrarse **2** ASSEMBLE : reunirse **3** BE
INTRODUCED : conocerse — **~** *n* : encuentro *m* — **meeting** ['miːtɪŋ] *n* : reunión *f*

megabyte ['megəˌbaɪt] *n* : megabyte *m*

megaphone ['megəˌfoːn] *n* : megáfono
m

melancholy ['melənˌkɑli] *n, pl* **-cholies**
: melancolía *f* — **~** *adj* : melancólico,
triste

mellow ['meloː] *adj* **1** : suave, dulce **2**
CALM : apacible **3** : maduro (dícese de
frutas), añejo (dícese de vinos) — **~**
vt : suavizar, endulzar — *vi* : suavizarse

melody ['melədi] *n, pl* **-dies** : melodía *f*

melon ['melən] *n* : melón *m*

melt ['melt] *vi* : derretirse, fundirse — *vt*
: derretir

member ['membər] *n* : miembro *m* —
membership ['membərˌʃɪp] *n* **1** : calidad *f* de miembro **2** MEMBERS : miem-
bros *mpl*

membrane ['memˌbreɪn] *n* : membrana *f*

memory ['memri, 'memə-] *n, pl* **-ries 1**
: memoria *f* **2** RECOLLECTION : recuerdo *m* — **memento** [mɪ'menˌtoː] *n, pl*
-tos *or* **-toes** : recuerdo *m* — **memo**
['memoː] *n, pl* **memos** *or* **memorandum** [ˌmemə'rændəm] *n, pl* **-dums** *or*
-da [-də] : memorándum *m* — **memoirs** ['memˌwɑrz] *npl* : memorias *fpl* —
memorable ['memərəbəl] *adj* : memorable — **memorial** [mə'moːriəl] *adj*
: conmemorativo — **~** *n* : monumento *m* (conmemorativo) — **memorize**
['meməˌraɪz] *vt* **-rized; -rizing** : aprender de memoria

men → **man**

menace ['menəs] *n* : amenaza *f* — **~** *vt*
-aced; -acing : amenazar — **menac-
ing** ['menəsɪŋ] *adj* : amenazador

mend ['mend] *vt* **1** : reparar, arreglar **2**
DARN : zurcir — *vi* HEAL : curarse

menial ['miːniəl] *adj* : servil, bajo

meningitis [ˌmenən'dʒaɪtəs] *n, pl*
-gitides [-'dʒɪtəˌdiːz] : meningitis *f*

menopause ['menəˌpɔz] *n* : menopausia
f

menstruate ['menstruˌeɪt] *vi* **-ated;
-ating** : menstruar — **menstruation**
[ˌmenstru'eɪʃən] *n* : menstruación *f*

mental ['mentəl] *adj* : mental — **men-**

tality [men'tæləti] *n, pl* **-ties** : mentalidad *f*

mention ['mentʃən] *n* : mención *f* —
mention *vt* **1** : mencionar **2 don't ~
it!** : ¡de nada!, ¡no hay de qué!

menu ['menjuː] *n* : menú *m*

meow [miˈaʊ] *n* : maullido *m*, miau *m*
— **~** *vi* : maullar

mercenary ['mərsənˌeri] *n, pl* **-naries**
: mercenario *m*, -ria *f* — **~** *adj* : mercenario

merchant ['mərtʃənt] *n* : comerciante *mf*
— **merchandise** ['mərtʃənˌdaɪs, -ˌdaɪs]
n : mercancía *f*, mercadería *f*

merciful ['mərsɪfəl] *adj* : misericor-
dioso, compasivo — **merciless** ['mər-
sɪləs] *adj* : despiadado

mercury ['mərkjəri] *n, pl* **-ries** : mercurio *m*

Mercury *n* : Mercurio *m*

mercy ['mərsi] *n, pl* **-cies 1** : misericordia *f*, compasión *f* **2 at the ~ of** : a la
merced de

mere ['mɪr] *adj, superlative* **merest**
: mero, simple — **merely** ['mɪrli] *adv*
: simplemente

merge ['mərdʒ] *v* **merged; merging** *vi*
: unirse, fusionarse (dícese de las
compañías), confluir (dícese de los
ríos, las calles, etc.) — *vt* : unir, fusionar, combinar — **merger** ['mərdʒər]
n : unión *f*, fusión *f*

merit ['merət] *n* : mérito *m* — **~** *vt*
: merecer

mermaid ['mərˌmeɪd] *n* : sirena *f*

merry ['meri] *adj* **-rier; -est** : alegre —
merry–go–round ['merigoˌraʊnd] *n*
: tiovivo *m*

mesa ['meɪsə] *n* : mesa *f*

mesh ['meʃ] *n* : malla *f*

mesmerize ['mezməˌraɪz] *vt* **-ized;
-izing** : hipnotizar

mess ['mes] *n* **1** : desorden *m* **2** MUDDLE
: lío *m* **3** : rancho *m* (militar) — **~** *vt*
1 *or* **~ up** SOIL : ensuciar **2 ~ up** DIS-
ARRANGE : desordenar **3 ~ up** BUN-
GLE : echar a perder — *vi* **1 ~ around**
PUTTER : entretenerse **2 ~ with** PRO-
VOKE : meterse con

message ['mesɪdʒ] *n* : mensaje *m* —
messenger ['mesəndʒər] *n* : mensajero
m, -ra *f*

messy ['mesi] *adj* **messier; -est** : desordenado, sucio

met → **meet**

metabolism [mə'tæbəˌlɪzəm] *n* : metabolismo *m*

metal ['metəl] *n* : metal *m* — **metallic**
[mə'tælɪk] *adj* : metálico

metamorphosis [ˌmɛtəˈmɔrfəsɪs] n, pl **-phoses** [-ˌsiːz] : metamorfosis f

metaphor [ˈmɛtəˌfɔr, -fər] n : metáfora f

meteor [ˈmiːtiər, -tiˌɔr] n : meteoro m — **meteorological** [ˌmiːtiˌɔrəˈlɑdʒɪkəl] adj : meteorológico — **meteorologist** [ˌmiːtiəˈrɑlədʒɪst] n : meteorólogo m, -ga f — **meteorology** [ˌmiːtiəˈrɑlədʒi] n : meteorología f

meter or Brit **metre** [ˈmiːtər] n 1 : metro m 2 : contador m (de electricidad, etc.)

method [ˈmɛθəd] n : método m — **methodical** [məˈθɑdɪkəl] adj : metódico

meticulous [məˈtɪkjələs] adj : meticuloso

metric [ˈmɛtrɪk] or **metrical** [-trɪkəl] adj : métrico

metropolis [məˈtrɑpələs] n : metrópoli f — **metropolitan** [ˌmɛtrəˈpɑlətən] adj : metropolitano

Mexican [ˈmɛksɪkən] adj : mexicano

mice → **mouse**

microbe [ˈmaɪˌkroːb] n : microbio m

microfilm [ˈmaɪkroˌfɪlm] n : microfilm m

microphone [ˈmaɪkrəˌfoːn] n : micrófono m

microscope [ˈmaɪkrəˌskoːp] n : microscopio m — **microscopic** [ˌmaɪkrəˈskɑpɪk] adj : microscópico

microwave [ˈmaɪkrəˌweɪv] n or **~ oven** : microondas m

mid [ˈmɪd] adj 1 **~ morning** : a media mañana 2 **in ~-August** : a mediados de agosto 3 **she is in her mid thirties** : tiene alrededor de 35 años — **midair** [ˈmɪdˈær] n **in ~** : en el aire — **midday** [ˈmɪdˌdeɪ] n : mediodía m

middle [ˈmɪdəl] adj : de en medio, del medio — ~ n 1 : medio m, centro m 2 **in the ~ of** : en medio de (un espacio), a mitad de (una actividad) 3 **in the ~ of the month** : a mediados del mes — **middle–aged** [ˌmɪdəlˈeɪdʒd] adj : de mediana edad — **Middle Ages** npl : Edad f Media — **middle class** n : clase f media — **middleman** [ˈmɪdəlˌmæn] n, pl **-men** [-mən, -ˌmɛn] : intermediario m, -ria f

midget [ˈmɪdʒət] n : enano m, -na f

midnight [ˈmɪdˌnaɪt] n : medianoche f

midriff [ˈmɪdˌrɪf] n : diafragma m

midst [ˈmɪdst] n 1 **in the ~ of** : en medio de 2 **in our ~** : entre nosotros

midsummer [ˈmɪdˈsʌmər, -ˌsʌ-] n : pleno verano m

midway [ˈmɪdˌweɪ] adv : a mitad de camino, a medio camino

midwife [ˈmɪdˌwaɪf] n, pl **-wives** [-ˌwaɪvz] : comadrona f

midwinter [ˈmɪdˈwɪntər, -ˌwɪn-] n : pleno invierno m

miff [ˈmɪf] vt : ofender

might[1] n [ˈmaɪt] (used to express permission or possibility or as a polite alternative to **may**) → **may**

might[2] n : fuerza f, poder m — **mighty** [ˈmaɪti] adj **mightier; -est** 1 : fuerte, poderoso 2 GREAT : enorme — ~ adv : muy

migraine [ˈmaɪˌgreɪn] n : jaqueca f, migraña f

migrate [ˈmaɪˌgreɪt] vi **-grated; -grating** : emigrar — **migrant** [ˈmaɪgrənt] n : trabajador m, -dora f ambulante

mild [ˈmaɪld] adj 1 GENTLE : suave 2 LIGHT : leve 3 **a ~ climate** : una clima templada

mildew [ˈmɪlˌduː, -ˌdjuː] n : moho m

mildly [ˈmaɪldli] adv : ligeramente, suavemente — **mildness** [ˈmaɪldnəs] n : apacibilidad f (de personas), suavedad f (de sabores, etc.)

mile [ˈmaɪl] n : milla f — **mileage** [ˈmaɪlɪdʒ] n : distancia f recorrida (en millas), kilometraje m — **milestone** [ˈmaɪlˌstoːn] n : hito m

military [ˈmɪləˌteri] adj : militar — ~ n **the ~** : las fuerzas armadas — **militant** [ˈmɪlətənt] adj : militante — ~ n : militante mf — **militia** [məˈlɪʃə] n : milicia f

milk [ˈmɪlk] n : leche f — ~ vt 1 : ordeñar (una vaca, etc.) 2 EXPLOIT : explotar — **milky** [ˈmɪlki] adj **milkier; -est** : lechoso — **Milky Way** n **the ~** : la Vía Láctea

mill [ˈmɪl] n 1 : molino m 2 FACTORY : fábrica f 3 GRINDER : molinillo m — ~ vt : moler — vi or **~ about** : arremolinarse

millennium [məˈlɛniəm] n, pl **-nia** [-niə] or **-niums** : milenio m

miller [ˈmɪlər] n : molinero m, -ra f

milligram [ˈmɪləˌgræm] n : miligramo m — **millimeter** or Brit **millimetre** [ˈmɪləˌmiːtər] n : milímetro m

million [ˈmɪljən] n, pl **millions** or **million** 1 : millón m 2 **a ~ people** : un millón de personas — ~ adj **a ~** : un millón de — **millionaire** [ˌmɪljəˈnær, ˈmɪljəˌnær] n : millonario m, -ria f — **millionth** [ˈmɪljənθ] adj : millonésimo

mime [ˈmaɪm] n 1 : mimo mf 2 PANTOMIME : pantomima f — ~ v **mimed; miming** vt : imitar — vi : hacer la mímica — **mimic** [ˈmɪmɪk] vt **-icked; -icking** : imitar, remedar — ~ n : imitador m, -dora f — **mimicry** [ˈmɪmɪkri] n, pl **-ries** : imitación f

mince ['mɪnts] v **minced; mincing** vt **1** : picar, moler **2 not to ~ one's words** : no tener pelos en la lengua

mind ['maɪnd] n **1** : mente f **2** INTELLECT : capacidad f intelectual **3** OPINION : opinión f **4** REASON : razón f **5 have a ~ to** : tener intención de — ~ vt **1** TEND : cuidar **2** OBEY : obedecer **3** WATCH : tener cuidado con **4 I don't ~ the heat** : no me molesta el calor — vi **1** OBEY : obedecer **2 I don't ~** : no me importa, me es igual — **mindful** ['maɪndfəl] adj : atento — **mindless** ['maɪndləs] adj **1** SENSELESS : estúpido, sin sentido **2** DULL : aburrido

mine¹ ['maɪn] pron **1** : (el) mío, (la) mía, (los) míos, (las) mías **2 a friend of ~** : un amigo mío

mine² n : mina f — ~ vt **mined; mining 1** : extraer (oro, etc.) **2** : minar (con artefactos explosivos) — **minefield** ['maɪn,fiːld] n : campo m de minas — **miner** ['maɪnər] n : minero m, -ra f

mineral ['mɪnərəl] n : mineral m

mingle ['mɪŋɡəl] v **-gled; -gling** vt : mezclar — vi **1** : mezclarse **2** : circular (a una fiesta, etc.)

miniature ['mɪniətʃur, 'mɪni,tʃur, -tʃər] n : miniatura f — ~ adj : en miniatura

minimal ['mɪnəməl] adj : mínimo — **minimize** ['mɪnə,maɪz] vt **-mized; -mizing** : minimizar — **minimum** ['mɪnəməm] adj : mínimo — ~ n, pl **-ma** ['mɪnəmə] or **-mums** : mínimo m

mining ['maɪnɪŋ] n : minería f

minister ['mɪnəstər] n **1** : pastor m, -tora f (de una iglesia) **2** : ministro m, -tra f (en política) — ~ vi **to ~ to** : cuidar (de), atender a — **ministerial** [,mɪnə'stɪriəl] adj : ministerial — **ministry** ['mɪnəstri] n, pl **-tries** : ministerio m

mink ['mɪŋk] n, pl **mink** or **minks** : visón m

minnow ['mɪnoː] n, pl **-nows** : pececillo m de agua dulce

minor ['maɪnər] adj **1** : menor **2** INSIGNIFICANT : sin importancia — ~ n **1** : menor mf (de edad) **2** : asignatura f secundaria (de estudios) — **minority** [mə'nɔrəti, maɪ-] n, pl **-ties** : minoría f

mint¹ ['mɪnt] n **1** : menta f (planta) **2** : pastilla f de menta (dulce)

mint² n **1 the U.S. Mint** : la casa de la moneda de los EE.UU. **2 be worth a ~** : valer un dineral — ~ vt : acuñar — ~ adj **in ~ condition** : como nuevo

minus ['maɪnəs] prep **1** : menos **2** WITHOUT : sin — ~ n or **~ sign** : signo m de menos

minuscule ['mɪnəs,kjuːl, mɪ'nʌs-] adj : minúsculo

minute¹ [maɪ'nuːt, mɪ-, -'njuːt] n **1** : minuto m **2** MOMENT : momento m **3 ~s** npl : actas fpl (de una reunión)

minute² ['mɪnət] adj **-nuter; -est 1** TINY : diminuto, minúsculo **2** DETAILED : minucioso

miracle ['mɪrɪkəl] n : milagro m — **miraculous** [mə'rækjələs] adj : milagroso

mirage [mɪ'rɑʒ, 'mɪr,ɑʒ] n : espejismo m

mire ['maɪr] n : lodo m, fango m

mirror ['mɪrər] n : espejo m — ~ vt : reflejar

mirth ['mərθ] n : alegría f, risas fpl

misapprehension [,mɪs,æprə'hentʃən] n : malentendido m

misbehave [,mɪsbɪ'heɪv] vi **-haved; -having** : portarse mal — **misbehavior** [,mɪsbɪ'heɪvjər] n : mala conducta f

miscalculate [mɪs'kælkjə,leɪt] v **-lated; -lating** : calcular mal

miscarriage [mɪs'kærɪdʒ, 'mɪs,kærɪdʒ] n **1** : aborto m **2 ~ of justice** : error m judicial

miscellaneous [,mɪsə'leɪniəs] adj : diverso, vario

mischief ['mɪstʃəf] n : travesuras fpl — **mischievous** ['mɪstʃəvəs] adj : travieso

misconception [,mɪskən'sepʃən] n : concepto m erróneo

misconduct [mɪs'kandəkt] n : mala conducta f

misdeed [mɪs'diːd] n : fechoría f

misdemeanor [,mɪsdɪ'miːnər] n : delito m menor

miser ['maɪzər] n : avaro m, -ra f; tacaño m, -ña f

miserable ['mɪzərəbəl] adj **1** UNHAPPY : triste **2** WRETCHED : miserable **3 ~ weather** : tiempo m malo — **miserly** ['maɪzərli] adj : mezquino

misery ['mɪzəri] n, pl **-eries 1** : sufrimiento m **2** WRETCHEDNESS : miseria f

misfire [mɪs'faɪr] vi **-fired; -firing** : fallar

misfit ['mɪs,fɪt, mɪs'fɪt] n : inadaptado m, -da f

misfortune [mɪs'fɔrtʃən] n : desgracia f

misgiving [mɪs'ɡɪvɪŋ] n : duda f

misguided [mɪs'ɡaɪdəd] adj : descaminado, equivocado

mishap ['mɪs,hæp] n : contratiempo m

misinform [,mɪsɪn'fɔrm] vt : informar mal

misinterpret [,mɪsɪn'tərprət] vt : interpretar mal

misjudge [mɪs'dʒʌdʒ] vt **-judged; -judging** : juzgar mal

mislay ['mɪsˌleɪ] *vt* **-laid** [-leɪd]; **-laying** : extraviar, perder

mislead [mɪs'liːd] *vt* **-led** [-'led]; **-leading** : engañar — **misleading** [mɪs'liːdɪŋ] *adj* : engañoso

misnomer [mɪs'noːmər] *n* : nombre *m* inapropiado

misplace [mɪs'pleɪs] *vt* **-placed**; **-placing** : extraviar, perder

misprint ['mɪsˌprɪnt, mɪs'-] *n* : errata *f*, error *m* de imprenta

miss ['mɪs] *vt* **1** : errar, faltar **2** OVERLOOK : pasar por alto **3** : perder (una oportunidad, un vuelo, etc.) **4** AVOID : evitar **5** OMIT : saltarse **6 I** ~ **you** : te echo de menos — ~ *n* **1** : fallo *m* (de un tiro, etc.) **2** FAILURE : fracaso *m*

Miss ['mɪs] *n* : señorita *f*

missile ['mɪsəl] *n* **1** : misil *m* **2** PROJECTILE : proyectil *m*

missing ['mɪsɪŋ] *adj* : perdido, desaparecido

mission ['mɪʃən] *n* : misión *f* — **missionary** ['mɪʃəˌneri] *n, pl* **-aries** : misionero *m*, -ra *f*

misspell [mɪs'spel] *vt* : escribir mal

mist ['mɪst] *n* : neblina *f*, bruma *f*

mistake [mɪ'steɪk] *vt* **mistook** [-'stʊk]; **mistaken** [-'steɪkən]; **-taking 1** MISINTERPRET : entender mal **2** CONFUSE : confundir — ~ *n* **1** : error *m* **2 make a** ~ : equivocarse — **mistaken** [mɪ'steɪkən] *adj* : equivocado

mister ['mɪstər] *n* : señor *m*

mistletoe ['mɪsəlˌtoː] *n* : muérdago *m*

mistreat [mɪs'triːt] *vt* : maltratar

mistress ['mɪstrəs] *n* **1** : dueña *f*, señora *f* (de una casa) **2** LOVER : amante *f*

mistrust [mɪs'trʌst] *n* : desconfianza *f* — ~ *vt* : desconfiar de

misty ['mɪsti] *adj* **mistier; -est** : neblinoso, nebuloso

misunderstand [ˌmɪsˌʌndər'stænd] *vt* **-stood; -standing** : entender mal — **misunderstanding** [ˌmɪsˌʌndər'stændɪŋ] *n* : malentendido *m*

misuse [mɪs'juːz] *vt* **-used; -using 1** : emplear mal **2** MISTREAT : maltratar — ~ [mɪs'juːs] *n* : mal empleo *m*, abuso *m*

mitigate ['mɪtəˌgeɪt] *vt* **-gated; -gating** : mitigar

mitt ['mɪt] *n* : manopla *f*, guante *m* (de béisbol) — **mitten** ['mɪtən] *n* : manopla *f*, mitón *m*

mix ['mɪks] *vt* **1** : mezclar **2** ~ **up** : confundir — *vi* : mezclarse — ~ *n* : mezcla *f* — **mixture** ['mɪkstʃər] *n* : mezcla *f* — **mix-up** ['mɪksˌʌp] *n* : confusión *f*, lío *m fam*

moan ['moːn] *n* : gemido *m* — ~ *vi* : gemir

mob ['mab] *n* : muchedumbre *f* — ~ *vt* **mobbed; mobbing** : acosar

mobile ['moːbəl, -ˌbiːl, -ˌbaɪl] *adj* : móvil — ~ ['moːˌbiːl] *n* : móvil *m* — **mobile home** *n* : caravana *f* — **mobility** [moː'bɪləti] *n* : movilidad *f* — **mobilize** ['moːbəˌlaɪz] *vt* **-lized; -lizing** : movilizar

moccasin ['makəsən] *n* : mocasín *m*

mock ['mak, 'mɔk] *vt* : burlarse de, mofarse de — ~ *adj* : falso — **mockery** ['makəri, 'mɔ-] *n, pl* **-eries** : burla *f* — **mock-up** ['makˌʌp] *n* : maqueta *f*

mode ['moːd] *n* **1** : modo *m* **2** FASHION : moda *f*

model ['madəl] *n* **1** : modelo *m* **2** MOCK-UP : maqueta *f* **3** : modelo *mf* (persona) — ~ *v* **-eled** *or* **-elled; -eling** *or* **-elling** *vt* **1** SHAPE : modelar **2** WEAR : lucir — *vi* : trabajar de modelo — ~ *adj* : modelo

modem ['moːdəm, -ˌdem] *n* : módem *m*

moderate ['madərət] *adj* : moderado — ~ *n* : moderado *m*, -da *f* — ~ ['madəˌreɪt] *v* **-ated; -ating** *vt* : moderar — *vi* : moderarse — **moderation** [ˌmadə'reɪʃən] *n* : moderación *f* — **moderator** ['madəˌreɪtər] *n* : moderador *m*, -dora *f*

modern ['madərn] *adj* : moderno — **modernize** ['madərˌnaɪz] *vt* **-ized; -izing** : modernizar

modest ['madəst] *adj* : modesto — **modesty** ['madəsti] *n* : modestia *f*

modify ['madəˌfaɪ] *vt* **-fied; -fying** : modificar

moist ['mɔɪst] *adj* : húmedo — **moisten** ['mɔɪsən] *vt* : humedecer — **moisture** ['mɔɪstʃər] *n* : humedad *f* — **moisturizer** ['mɔɪstʃəˌraɪzər] *n* : crema *f* hidratante

molar ['moːlər] *n* : muela *f*

molasses [mə'læsəz] *n* : melaza *f*

mold¹ ['moːld] *n* FORM : molde *m* — ~ *vt* : moldear, formar

mold² *n* FUNGUS : moho *m* — **moldy** ['moːldi] *adj* **moldier; -est** : mohoso

mole¹ ['moːl] *n* : lunar *m* (en la piel)

mole² *n* : topo *m* (animal)

molecule ['malɪˌkjuːl] *n* : molécula *f*

molest [mə'lest] *vt* **1** HARASS : importunar **2** : abusar (sexualmente)

molten ['moːltən] *adj* : fundido

mom ['mam, 'mʌm] *n* : mamá *f*

moment ['moːmənt] *n* : momento *m* — **momentarily** [ˌmoːmən'terəli] *adv* **1** : momentáneamente **2** SOON : dentro de poco, pronto — **momentary** ['moːmənˌteri] *adj* : momentáneo

momentous [mo'mɛntəs] *adj* : muy importante

momentum [mo'mɛntəm] *n, pl* **-ta** [-tə] *or* **-tums 1** : momento *m* (en física) **2** IMPETUS : ímpetu *m*

monarch ['mɑ,nɑrk, -nərk] *n* : monarca *mf* — **monarchy** ['mɑ,nɑrki, -nər-] *n, pl* **-chies** : monarquía *f*

monastery ['mɑnə,stɛri] *n, pl* **-teries** : monasterio *m*

Monday ['mʌn,deɪ, -di] *n* : lunes *m*

money ['mʌni] *n, pl* **-eys** *or* **-ies** : dinero *m* — **monetary** ['mɑnə,tɛri, 'mʌnə-] *adj* : monetario — **money order** *n* : giro *m* postal

mongrel ['mɑŋgrəl, 'mʌŋ-] *n* : perro *m* mestizo

monitor ['mɑnətər] *n* : monitor *m* (de una computadora, etc.) — ~ *vt* : controlar

monk ['mʌŋk] *n* : monje *m*

monkey ['mʌŋki] *n, pl* **-keys** : mono *m*, -na *f* — **monkey wrench** *n* : llave *f* inglesa

monogram ['mɑnə,græm] *n* : monograma *m*

monologue ['mɑnə,lɔg] *n* : monólogo *m*

monopoly [mə'nɑpəli] *n, pl* **-lies** : monopolio *m* — **monopolize** [mə'nɑpə,laɪz] *vt* **-lized; -lizing** : monopolizar

monotonous [mə'nɑtənəs] *adj* : monótono — **monotony** [mə'nɑtəni] *n* : monotonía *f*

monster ['mɑntstər] *n* : monstruo *m* — **monstrosity** [mɑn'strɑsəti] *n, pl* **-ties** : monstruosidad *f* — **monstrous** ['mɑntstrəs] *adj* **1** : monstruoso **2** HUGE : gigantesco

month ['mʌnθ] *n* : mes *m* — **monthly** ['mʌnθli] *adv* : mensualmente — ~ *adj* : mensual

monument ['mɑnjəmənt] *n* : monumento *m* — **monumental** [,mɑnjə'mɛntəl] *adj* : monumental

moo ['mu:] *vi* : mugir — ~ *n* : mugido *m*

mood ['mu:d] *n* : humor *m* — **moody** ['mu:di] *adj* **moodier; -est 1** GLOOMY : melancólico, deprimido **2** IRRITABLE : malhumorado **3** TEMPERAMENTAL : de humor variable

moon ['mu:n] *n* : luna *f* — **moonlight** ['mu:n,laɪt] *n* : luz *f* de la luna

moor[1] ['mʊr, 'mɔr] *n* : brezal *m*, páramo *m*

moor[2] *vt* : amarrar — **mooring** ['mʊrɪŋ, 'mɔr-] *n* : atracadero *m*

moose ['mu:s] *ns & pl* : alce *m*

moot ['mu:t] *adj* : discutible

mop ['mɑp] *n* **1** : trapeador *m* Lat, fregona *f* Spain **2** *or* ~ **of hair** : pelambrera *f* — ~ *vt* **mopped; mopping** : trapear Lat, pasar la fregona a Spain

mope ['mo:p] *vi* **moped; moping** : andar deprimido

moped ['mo:,pɛd] *n* : ciclomotor *m*

moral ['mɔrəl] *adj* : moral — ~ *n* **1** : moraleja *f* (de un cuento, etc.) **2** ~**s** *npl* : moral *f*, moralidad *f* — **morale** [mə'ræl] *n* : moral *f* — **morality** [mə'rælətɪ] *n, pl* **-ties** : moralidad *f*

morbid ['mɔrbɪd] *adj* : morboso

more ['mɔr] *adj* : más — ~ *adv* **1** : más **2** ~ **and** ~ : cada vez más **3** ~ **or less** : más o menos **4 once** ~ : una vez más — ~ *n* : más *m* — ~ *pron* : más — **moreover** [mɔr'o:vər] *adv* : además

morgue ['mɔrg] *n* : depósito *m* de cadáveres

morning ['mɔrnɪŋ] *n* **1** : mañana *f* **2 good** ~! : ¡buenos días! **3 in the** ~ : por la mañana

moron ['mɔr,ɑn] *n* : estúpido *m*, -da *f*; imbécil *mf*

morose [mə'ro:s] *adj* : malhumorado

morphine ['mɔr,fi:n] *n* : morfina *f*

morsel ['mɔrsəl] *n* **1** BITE : bocado *m* **2** FRAGMENT : pedazo *m*

mortal ['mɔrtəl] *adj* : mortal — ~ *n* : mortal *mf* — **mortality** [mɔr'tælətɪ] : mortalidad *f*

mortar ['mɔrtər] *n* : mortero *m*

mortgage ['mɔrgɪdʒ] *n* : hipoteca *f* — ~ *vt* **-gaged; -gaging** : hipotecar

mortify ['mɔrtə,faɪ] *vt* **-fied; -fying 1** : mortificar **2** HUMILIATE : avergonzar

mosaic [mo'zeɪk] *n* : mosaico *m*

Moslem ['mɑzləm] → **Muslim**

mosque ['mɑsk] *n* : mezquita *f*

mosquito [mə'ski:to] *n, pl* **-toes** : mosquito *m*, zancudo *m* Lat

moss ['mɔs] *n* : musgo *m*

most ['mo:st] *adj* **1** : la mayoría de, la mayor parte de **2 (the)** ~ : más — ~ *adv* : más — ~ *n* : más *m*, máximo *m* — ~ *pron* : la mayoría, la mayor parte — **mostly** ['mo:stli] *adv* **1** MAINLY : en su mayor parte, principalmente **2** USUALLY : normalmente

motel [mo'tɛl] *n* : motel *m*

moth ['mɔθ] *n* : palomilla *f*, polilla *f*

mother ['mʌðər] *n* : madre *f* — ~ *vt* **1** : cuidar de **2** SPOIL : mimar — **motherhood** ['mʌðər,hʊd] *n* : maternidad *f* — **mother–in–law** ['mʌðərɪn,lɔ] *n, pl* **mothers–in–law** : suegra *f* — **motherly** ['mʌðərli] *adj* : maternal — **mother–of–pearl** [,mʌðərəv'pərl] *n* : nácar *m*

motif [mo'ti:f] *n* : motivo *m*

motion ['moːʃən] *n* **1** : movimiento *m* **2** PROPOSAL : moción *f* **3 set in ~** : poner en marcha — **~** *vi* **~ to s.o.** : hacer una señal a algn — **motionless** ['moːʃənləs] *adj* : inmóvil — **motion picture** *n* : película *f*

motive ['moːṭɪv] *n* : motivo *m* — **motivate** ['moːṭəˌveɪt] *vt* -**vated**; -**vating** : motivar — **motivation** [ˌmoːṭəˈveɪʃən] *n* : motivación *f*

motor ['moːṭər] *n* : motor *m* — **motorbike** ['moːṭərˌbaɪk] *n* : motocicleta *f* (pequeña), moto *f* — **motorboat** ['moːṭərˌboːt] *n* : lancha *f* motora — **motorcycle** ['moːṭərˌsaɪkəl] *n* : motocicleta *f* — **motorcyclist** ['moːṭərˌsaɪkəlɪst] *n* : motociclista *mf* — **motorist** ['moːṭərɪst] *n* : automovilista *mf*, motorista *mf Lat*

motto ['moːṭoː] *n, pl* -**toes** : lema *m*

mould ['moːld] → **mold**

mound ['maʊnd] *n* **1** PILE : montón *m* **2** HILL : montículo *m*

mount¹ ['maʊnt] *n* **1** HORSE : montura *f* **2** SUPPORT : soporte *m* — **~** *vt* : montar (un caballo, etc.), subir (una escalera) — *vi* INCREASE : aumentar

mount² *n* HILL : monte *m* — **mountain** ['maʊntən] *n* : montaña *f* — **mountainous** ['maʊntənəs] *adj* : montañoso

mourn ['moːrn] *vt* : llorar (por) — *vi* : lamentarse — **mourner** ['moːrnər] *n* : doliente *mf* — **mournful** ['moːrnfəl] *adj* : triste — **mourning** ['moːrnɪŋ] *n* : luto *m*

mouse ['maʊs] *n, pl* **mice** ['maɪs] : ratón *m* — **mousetrap** ['maʊsˌtræp] *n* : ratonera *f*

moustache ['mʌˌstæʃ, məˈstæʃ] → **mustache**

mouth ['maʊθ] *n* : boca *f* (de una persona o un animal), desembocadura *f* (de un río) — **mouthful** ['maʊθˌfʊl] *n* : bocado *m* — **mouthpiece** ['maʊθˌpiːs] *n* : boquilla *f* (de un instrumento musical)

move ['muːv] *v* **moved**; **moving** *vi* **1** GO : ir **2** RELOCATE : mudarse **3** STIR : moverse **4** ACT : tomar medidas — *vt* **1** : mover **2** AFFECT : conmover **3** TRANSPORT : transportar, trasladar **4** PROPOSE : proponer — **~** *n* **1** MOVEMENT : movimiento *m* **2** RELOCATION : mudanza *f* **3** STEP : medida *f* — **movable** ['muːvəbəl] *or* **moveable** *adj* : movible, móvil — **movement** ['muːvmənt] *n* : movimiento *m*

movie ['muːvi] *n* **1** : película *f* **2 ~s** *npl* : cine *m*

mow ['moː] *vt* **mowed**; **mowed** *or* **mown** ['moːn]; **mowing** : cortar (la hierba) — **mower** ['moːər] → **lawn mower**

Mr. ['mɪstər] *n, pl* **Messrs.** ['mɛsərz] : señor *m*

Mrs. ['mɪsəz, -səs, *esp South* 'mɪzəz, -zəs] *n, pl* **Mesdames** [meɪˈdeɪm, -ˈdæm] : señora *f*

Ms. ['mɪz] *n* : señora *f*, señorita *f*

much ['mʌtʃ] *adj* **more**; **most** : mucho — **~** *adv* **more** ['mor]; **most** ['moːst] **1** : mucho **2 as ~ as** : tanto como **3 how ~?** : ¿cuánto? **4 too ~** : demasiado — **~** *pron* : mucho, -cha

muck ['mʌk] *n* **1** DIRT : mugre *f*, suciedad *f* **2** MANURE : estiércol *m*

mucus ['mjuːkəs] *n* : mucosidad *f*

mud ['mʌd] *n* : barro *m*, lodo *m*

muddle ['mʌdəl] *v* -**dled**; -**dling** *vt* **1** CONFUSE : confundir **2** JUMBLE : desordenar — *vi* **~ through** : arreglárselas — **~** *n* : confusión *f*, lío *m fam*

muddy ['mʌdi] *adj* -**dier**; -**est** : fangoso, lleno de barro

muffin ['mʌfən] *n* : mollete *m*

muffle ['mʌfəl] *vt* -**fled**; -**fling** : amortiguar (un sonido) — **muffler** ['mʌflər] *n* **1** SCARF : bufanda *f* **2** : silenciador *m*, mofle *m Lat* (de un automóvil)

mug ['mʌg] *n* CUP : tazón *m* — **~** *vt* : asaltar, atracar — **mugger** ['mʌgər] *n* : atracador *m*, -dora *f*

muggy ['mʌgi] *adj* -**gier**; -**est** : bochornoso

mule ['mjuːl] *n* : mula *f*

mull ['mʌl] *vt or* **~ over** : reflexionar sobre

multicolored [ˌmʌltiˈkʌlərd, ˌmʌltaɪ-] *adj* : multicolor

multimedia [ˌmʌltiˈmiːdiə, ˌmʌltaɪ-] *adj* : multimedia

multinational [ˌmʌltiˈnæʃənəl, ˌmʌltaɪ-] *adj* : multinacional

multiple ['mʌltəpəl] *adj* : múltiple — **~** *n* : múltiplo *m* — **multiplication** [ˌmʌltəpləˈkeɪʃən] *n* : multiplicación *f* — **multiply** ['mʌltəˌplaɪ] *v* -**plied**; -**plying** *vt* : multiplicar — *vi* : multiplicarse

multitude ['mʌltəˌtuːd, -ˌtjuːd] *n* : multitud *f*

mum ['mʌm] *adj* **keep ~** : guardar silencio

mumble ['mʌmbəl] *v* -**bled**; -**bling** *vt* : mascullar — *vi* : hablar entre dientes

mummy ['mʌmi] *n, pl* -**mies** : momia *f*

mumps ['mʌmps] *ns & pl* : paperas *fpl*

munch ['mʌntʃ] *v* : mascar, masticar

mundane [ˌmʌnˈdeɪn, 'mʌn-] *adj* : rutinario, ordinario

municipal [mjʊ'nɪsəpəl] *adj* : municipal — **municipality** [mjʊ,nɪsə'pælət̬i] *n, pl* **-ties** : municipio *m*

munitions [mjʊ'nɪʃənz] *npl* : municiónes *fpl*

mural ['mjʊrəl] *n* : mural *m*

murder ['mərdər] *n* : asesinato *m*, homicidio *m* — ~ *vt* : asesinar, matar — *vi* : matar — **murderer** ['mərdərər] *n* : asesino *m*, -na *f*; homicida *mf* — **murderous** ['mərdərəs] *adj* : asesino, homicida

murky ['mərki] *adj* **-kier; -est** : turbio, oscuro

murmur ['mərmər] *n* : murmullo *m* — **murmur** *v* : murmurar

muscle ['mʌsəl] *n* : músculo *m* — ~ *vi* **-cled; -cling** *or* ~ **in** : meterse por la fuerza en — **muscular** ['mʌskjələr] *adj* **1** : muscular **2** STRONG : musculoso

muse[1] ['mjuːz] *n* : musa *f*

muse[2] *vi* **mused; musing** : meditar

museum [mjʊ'ziːəm] *n* : museo *m*

mushroom ['mʌʃ,ruːm, -,rʊm] *n* **1** : hongo *m*, seta *f* **2** : champiñón *m* (en la cocina) — ~ *vi* GROW : crecer rápidamente, multiplicarse

mushy ['mʌʃi] *adj* **mushier; -est 1** SOFT : blando **2** MAWKISH : sensiblero

music ['mjuːzɪk] *n* : música *f* — **musical** ['mjuːzɪkəl] *adj* : musical — ~ *n* : comedia *f* musical — **musician** [mjʊ'zɪʃən] *n* : músico *m*, -ca *f*

Muslim ['mʌzləm, 'mʊs-, 'mʊz-] *adj* : musulmán — ~ *n* : musulmán *m*, -mana *f*

muslin ['mʌzlən] *n* : muselina *f*

mussel ['mʌsəl] *n* : mejillón *m*

must ['mʌst] *v aux* **1** : deber, tener que **2** you ~ **come** : tienes que venir **3** you

~ **be tired** : debes (de) estar cansado — ~ *n* : necesidad *f*

mustache ['mʌ,stæʃ, mʌ'stæʃ] *n* : bigote *m*, bigotes *mpl*

mustang ['mʌ,stæŋ] *n* : mustang *m*

mustard ['mʌstərd] *n* : mostaza *f*

muster ['mʌstər] *vt* **1** : reunir **2** *or* ~ **up** : armarse de, cobrar (valor, fuerzas, etc.)

musty ['mʌsti] *adj* **mustier; -est** : que huele a cerrado

mute ['mjuːt] *adj* **muter; mutest** : mudo — ~ *n* : mudo *m*, -da *f*

mutilate ['mjuːtə,leɪt] *vt* **-lated; -lating** : mutilar

mutiny ['mjuːtəni] *n, pl* **-nies** : motín *m* — ~ *vi* **-nied; -nying** : amotinarse

mutter ['mʌtər] *vi* : murmurar

mutton ['mʌtən] *n* : carne *f* de carnero

mutual ['mjuːtʃʊəl] *adj* **1** : mutuo **2** COMMON : común — **mutually** ['mjuːtʃʊəli, -tʃəli] *adv* : mutuamente

muzzle ['mʌzəl] *n* **1** SNOUT : hocico *m* **2** : bozal *m* (para un perro, etc.) **3** : boca *f* (de un arma de fuego) — ~ *vt* **-zled; -zling** : poner un bozal a (un animal)

my ['maɪ] *adj* : mi

myopia [maɪ'oːpiə] *n* : miopía *f* — **myopic** [maɪ'oːpɪk, -'ɑ-] *adj* : miope

myself [maɪ'sɛlf] *pron* **1** (*reflexive*) : me **2** (*emphatic*) : yo mismo **3** by ~ : solo

mystery ['mɪstəri] *n, pl* **-teries** : misterio *m* — **mysterious** [mɪ'stɪriəs] *adj* : misterioso

mystic ['mɪstɪk] *adj or* **mystical** ['mɪstɪkəl] : místico

mystify ['mɪstə,faɪ] *vt* **-fied; -fying** : dejar perplejo, confundir

mystique [mɪ'stiːk] *n* : aura *f* de misterio

myth ['mɪθ] *n* : mito *m* — **mythical** ['mɪθɪkəl] *adj* : mítico

N

n ['ɛn] *n, pl* **n's** *or* **ns** ['ɛnz] : n *f*, decimocuarta letra del alfabeto inglés

nab ['næb] *vt* **nabbed; nabbing 1** ARREST : pescar *fam* **2** GRAB : agarrar

nag ['næg] *v* **nagged; nagging** *vi* COMPLAIN : quejarse — *vt* **1** ANNOY : fastidiar, dar la lata a **2** SCOLD : regañar — **nagging** *adj* : persistente

nail ['neɪl] *n* **1** : clavo *m* **2** : uña *f* (de un dedo) — ~ *vt or* ~ **down** : clavar — **nail file** *n* : lima *f* de uñas

naive *or* **naïve** [nɑ'iːv] *adj* **-iver; -est** : ingenuo — **naïveté** [nɑ,iːvə'teɪ, nɑ-'iːvə,-] *n* : ingenuidad *f*

naked ['neɪkəd] *adj* **1** : desnudo **2** the ~ **truth** : la pura verdad **3** to the ~ **eye** : a simple vista

name ['neɪm] *n* **1** : nombre *m* **2** REPUTATION : fama *f* **3** what is your ~? : ¿cómo se llama? **4** → **first name, surname** — ~ *vt* **named; naming 1** : poner nombre a **2** APPOINT : nombrar **3** ~ **a price** : fijar un precio — **nameless** ['neɪmləs] *adj* : anónimo — **namely** ['neɪmli] *adv* : a saber — **namesake** ['neɪm,seɪk] *n* : tocayo *m*, -ya *f*

nap[1] ['næp] *vi* **napped; napping** : echarse una siesta — ~ *n* : siesta *f*

nap² n : pelo m (de una tela)
nape ['neɪp, 'næp] n or **~ of the neck** : nuca f
napkin ['næpkən] n 1 : servilleta f 2 → **sanitary napkin**
narcotic [nɑr'kɑtɪk] n : narcótico m, estupefaciente m
narrate ['nær,eɪt] vt **-rated; -rating** : narrar — **narration** [næ'reɪʃən] n : narración f — **narrative** ['nærətɪv] n : narración f — **narrator** ['nær,eɪtər] n : narrador m, -dora f
narrow ['nær,o:] adj 1 : estrecho, angosto 2 RESTRICTED : limitado — vi : estrecharse — vt 1 : estrechar 2 or **~ down** : limitar — **narrowly** ['næroli] adv : por poco — **narrow—minded** [,næro'maɪndəd] adj : de miras estrechas
nasal ['neɪzəl] adj : nasal
nasty ['næsti] adj **-tier; -est 1** MEAN : malo, cruel 2 UNPLEASANT : desagradable 3 REPUGNANT : asqueroso — **nastiness** ['næstinəs] n : maldad f
nation ['neɪʃən] n : nación f — **national** ['næʃənəl] adj : nacional — **nationalism** ['næʃənə,lɪzəm] n : nacionalismo m — **nationality** [,næʃə'nælət̬i] n, pl **-ties** : nacionalidad f — **nationalize** ['næʃənə,laɪz] vt **-ized; -izing** : nacionalizar — **nationwide** ['neɪʃən'waɪd] adj : por todo el país
native ['neɪt̬ɪv] adj 1 : natal (dícese de un país, etc.) 2 INNATE : innato 3 **~ language** : lengua f materna — n 1 : nativo m, -va f 2 **be a ~ of** : ser natural de — **Native American** : indio m americano, india f americana — **nativity** [nə'tɪvət̬i, neɪ-] n, pl **-ties the Nativity** : la Navidad
nature ['neɪt̬ʃər] n 1 : naturaleza f 2 KIND : índole f, clase f 3 DISPOSITION : carácter m, natural m — **natural** ['næt̬ʃərəl] adj : natural — **naturalize** ['næt̬ʃərə,laɪz] vt **-ized; -izing** : naturalizar — **naturally** ['næt̬ʃərəli] adv : naturalmente
naught ['nɔt] n 1 NOTHING : nada f 2 ZERO : cero m
naughty ['nɔt̬i] adj **-tier; -est 1** : travieso, pícaro 2 RISQUÉ : picante
nausea ['nɔziə, 'nɔʃə] n : náuseas fpl — **nauseating** adj : nauseabundo — **nauseous** ['nɔʃəs, -ziəs] adj 1 **feel ~** : sentir náuseas 2 SICKENING : nauseabundo
nautical ['nɔt̬ɪkəl] adj : náutico
naval ['neɪvəl] adj : naval
nave ['neɪv] n : nave f (de una iglesia)
navel ['neɪvəl] n : ombligo m

navigate ['nævə,geɪt] v **-gated; -gating** vi : navegar — vt 1 : gobernar (un barco), pilotar (un avión) 2 : navegar por (un río, etc.) — **navigable** ['nævɪgəbəl] adj : navegable — **navigation** [,nævə'geɪʃən] n : navegación f — **navigator** ['nævə,geɪt̬ər] n : navegante mf
navy ['neɪvi] n, pl **-vies 1** : marina f de guerra 2 or **~ blue** : azul m marino
near ['nɪr] adv : cerca — **~ prep** : cerca de — **~ adj** : cercano, próximo — vt : acercarse a — **nearby** [nɪr'baɪ, 'nɪr,baɪ] adv : cerca — **~ adj** : cercano — **nearly** ['nɪrli] adv : casi — **nearsighted** ['nɪr,saɪt̬əd] adj : miope, corto de vista
neat ['ni:t] adj 1 TIDY : muy arreglado 2 CLEVER : hábil, ingenioso — **neatly** ['ni:tli] adv 1 : ordenadamente 2 CLEVERLY : hábilmente — **neatness** ['ni:tnəs] n : pulcritud f, orden m
nebulous ['nebjʊləs] adj : nebuloso
necessary ['nesə,seri] adj : necesario — **necessarily** [,nesə'serəli] adv : necesariamente — **necessitate** [nɪ'sesə,teɪt] vt **-tated; -tating** : exigir, requerir — **necessity** [nɪ'sesət̬i] n, pl **-ties 1** : necesidad f 2 **necessities** npl : cosas fpl indispensables
neck ['nek] n 1 : cuello m (de una persona o una botella), pescuezo m (de un animal) 2 COLLAR : cuello m — **necklace** ['nekləs] n : collar m — **necktie** ['nek,taɪ] n : corbata f
nectar ['nektər] n : néctar m
nectarine [,nektə'ri:n] n : nectarina f
need ['ni:d] n 1 : necesidad f 2 **if ~ be** : si hace falta — **~ vt 1** : necesitar, exigir 2 **~ to** : tener que — v aux : tener que
needle ['ni:dəl] n : aguja f — **~ vt -dled; -dling** : pinchar
needless ['ni:dləs] adj 1 : innecesario 2 **~ to say** : de más está decir
needlework ['ni:dəl,wərk] n : bordado m
needn't ['ni:dənt] (contraction of need not) → **need**
needy ['ni:di] adj **needier; -est** adj : necesitado
negative ['negət̬ɪv] adj : negativo — n 1 : negación f (en gramática) 2 : negativo m (en fotografía)
neglect [nɪ'glekt] vt : descuidar — n : descuido m, abandono m
negligee [,neglə'ʒeɪ] n : negligé m
negligence ['neglɪdʒənts] n : negligencia f, descuido m — **negligent** ['neglɪdʒənt] adj : negligente, descuidado
negligible ['neglɪdʒəbəl] adj : insignificante

negotiate [nɪˈgoːʃiˌeɪt] *v* **-ated; -ating** : negociar — **negotiable** [nɪˈgoːʃəbəl, -ʃiə-] *adj* : negociable — **negotiation** [nɪˌgoːʃiˈeɪʃən, -siˈeɪ-] *n* : negociación *f* — **negotiator** [nɪˈgoːʃiˌeɪtər, -siˌeɪ-] *n* : negociador *m*, -dora *f*

Negro [ˈniːˌgroː] *n, pl* **-groes** *sometimes considered offensive* : negro *m*, -gra *f*

neigh [ˈneɪ] *vi* : relinchar — ~ *n* : relincho *m*

neighbor *or Brit* **neighbour** [ˈneɪbər] *n* : vecino *m*, -na *f* — **neighborhood** *or Brit* **neighbourhood** [ˈneɪbərˌhʊd] *n* **1** : barrio *m*, vecindario *m* **2 in the ~ of** : alrededor de — **neighborly** *or Brit* **neighbourly** [ˈneɪbərli] *adv* : amable

neither [ˈniːðər, ˈnaɪ-] *conj* **1** ...**nor** : ni...ni **2 ~ am/do I** : yo tampoco — ~ *pron* : ninguno, -na — ~ *adj* : ninguno (de los dos)

neon [ˈniːˌɑn] *n* : neón *m*

nephew [ˈneˌfjuː, *chiefly British* ˈneˌvjuː] *n* : sobrino *m*

Neptune [ˈneptuːn, -ˌtjuːn] *n* : Neptuno *m*

nerve [ˈnərv] *n* **1** : nervio *m* **2** COURAGE : coraje *m* **3** GALL : descaro *m* **4 ~s** *npl* JITTERS : nervios *mpl* — **nervous** [ˈnərvəs] *adj* : nervioso — **nervousness** [ˈnərvəsnəs] *n* : nerviosismo *m* — **nervy** [ˈnərvi] *adj* **nervier; -est** : descarado

nest [ˈnest] *n* : nido *m* — ~ *vi* : anidar

nestle [ˈnesəl] *vi* **-tled; -tling** : acurrucarse

net¹ [ˈnet] *n* : red *f* — ~ *vt* **netted; netting** : pescar, atrapar (con una red)

net² *adj* : neto — ~ *vt* **netted; netting** YIELD : producir neto

nettle [ˈnetəl] *n* : ortiga *f*

network [ˈnetˌwərk] *n* : red *f*

neurology [nʊˈrɑlədʒi, njʊ-] *n* : neurología *f*

neurosis [nʊˈroːsɪs, njʊ-] *n, pl* **-roses** [-ˌsiːz] : neurosis *f* — **neurotic** [nʊˈrɑtɪk, njʊ-] *adj* : neurótico

neuter [ˈnuːtər, ˈnjuː-] *adj* : neutro — ~ *vt* : castrar

neutral [ˈnuːtrəl, ˈnjuː-] *n* : punto *m* muerto (de un automóvil) — ~ *adj* **1** : neutral **2** : neutro (en electrotecnia o química) — **neutrality** [nuːˈtrælətiː, njuː-] *n* : neutralidad *f* — **neutralize** [ˈnuːtrəˌlaɪz, ˈnjuː-] *vt* **-ized; -izing** : neutralizar

neutron [ˈnuːtrɑn, ˈnjuː-] *n* : neutrón *m*

never [ˈnevər] *adv* **1** : nunca, jamás **2** NOT : no **3** ~ **again** : nunca más **4** ~ **mind** : no importa — **nevermore** [ˌnevərˈmor] *adv* : nunca jamás — **nev-**

ertheless [ˌnevərðəˈles] *adv* : sin embargo, no obstante

new [ˈnuː, ˈnjuː] *adj* : nuevo — **newborn** [ˈnuːˌbɔrn, ˈnjuː-] *adj* : recién nacido — **newcomer** [ˈnuːˌkʌmər, ˈnjuː-] *n* : recién llegado *m*, -da *f* — **newly** [ˈnuːli, ˈnjuː-] *adv* : recién, recientemente — **newlywed** [ˈnuːliˌwed, ˈnjuː-] *n* : recién casado *m*, -da *f* — **news** [ˈnuːz, ˈnjuːz] *n* : noticias *fpl* — **newscast** [ˈnuːzˌkæst, ˈnjuːz-] *n* : noticiario *m*, noticiero *m Lat* — **newscaster** [ˈnuːzˌkæstər, ˈnjuːz-] *n* : presentador *m*, -dora *f* (de un noticiario) — **newsletter** [ˈnuːzˌletər, ˈnjuːz-] *n* : boletín *m* informativo — **newspaper** [ˈnuːzˌpeɪpər, ˈnjuːz-] *n* : periódico *m*, diario *m* — **newsstand** [ˈnuːzˌstænd, ˈnjuːz-] *n* : puesto *m* de periódicos

newt [ˈnuːt, ˈnjuːt] *n* : tritón *m*

New Year's Day *n* : día *m* del Año Nuevo

next [ˈnekst] *adj* **1** : próximo **2** FOLLOWING : siguiente — ~ *adv* **1** : la próxima vez **2** AFTERWARD : después, luego **3** NOW : ahora — **next-door** [ˈnekstˈdor] *adj* : de al lado — **next to** *adv* ALMOST : casi — ~ *prep* BESIDE : al lado de

nib [ˈnɪb] *n* : plumilla *f*

nibble [ˈnɪbəl] *vt* **-bled; -bling** : mordisquear

Nicaraguan [ˌnɪkəˈrɑgwən] *adj* : nicaragüense

nice [ˈnaɪs] *adj* **nicer; nicest 1** PLEASANT : agradable, bueno **2** KIND : amable — **nicely** [ˈnaɪsli] *adv* **1** WELL : bien **2** KINDLY : amablemente — **niceness** [ˈnaɪsnəs] *n* : amabilidad *f* — **niceties** [ˈnaɪsətiz] *npl* : detalles *mpl*, sutilezas *fpl*

niche [ˈnɪtʃ] *n* **1** : nicho *m* **2 find one's ~** : hacerse su hueco

nick [ˈnɪk] *n* **1** : corte *m* pequeño, muesca *f* **2 in the ~ of time** : justo a tiempo — ~ *vt* : hacer una muesca en

nickel [ˈnɪkəl] *n* **1** : níquel *m* (metal) **2** : moneda *f* de cinco centavos

nickname [ˈnɪkˌneɪm] *n* : apodo *m*, sobrenombre *m* — ~ *vt* **-named; -naming** : apodar

nicotine [ˈnɪkəˌtiːn] *n* : nicotina *f*

niece [ˈniːs] *n* : sobrina *f*

niggling [ˈnɪgəlɪŋ] *adj* **1** PETTY : insignificante **2** PERSISTENT : constante

night [ˈnaɪt] *n* **1** : noche *f* **2 at ~** : de noche **3 last ~** : anoche **4 tomorrow ~** : mañana por la noche — **nightclub** [ˈnaɪtˌklʌb] *n* : club *m* nocturno — **nightfall** [ˈnaɪtˌfɔl] *n* : anochecer *m* — **nightgown** [ˈnaɪtˌgaʊn] *n* : camisón *m* (de noche) — **nightly** ['naɪt] *adj* : de todas las noches — **~** *adv* : cada noche — **nightmare** ['naɪt,mær] *n* : pesadilla *f* — **nighttime** ['naɪt,taɪm] *n* : noche *f*

nil ['nɪl] *n* NOTHING : nada *f*

nimble ['nɪmbəl] *adj* **-bler; -blest** : ágil

nine ['naɪn] *adj* : nueve — **~** *n* : nueve *m* — **nine hundred** *adj* : novecientos — **~** *n* : novecientos *m* — **nineteen** [naɪn'tiːn] *adj* : diecinueve — **~** *n* : diecinueve *m* — **nineteenth** [naɪn'tiːnθ] *adj* : decimonoveno, decimonono — **~** *n* **1** : decimonoveno *m*, -na *f*; decimonono *m*, -na *f* (en una serie) **2** : diecinueveavo *m* (en matemáticas) — **ninetieth** ['naɪntiəθ] *adj* : nonagésimo — **~** *n* **1** : nonagésimo *m*, -ma *f* (en una serie) **2** : noventavo *m* (en matemáticas) — **ninety** ['naɪnti] *adj* : noventa — **~** *n* : noventa *m* — **ninth** ['naɪnθ] *adj* : noveno — **~** *n* **1** : noveno *m*, -na *f* (en una serie) **2** : noveno *m* (en matemáticas)

nip ['nɪp] *vt* **nipped; nipping 1** PINCH : pellizcar **2** BITE : mordisquear **3** — **in the bud** : cortar de raíz — **~** *n* **1** PINCH : pellizco *m* **2** NIBBLE : mordisco *m*

nipple ['nɪpəl] *n* **1** : pezón *m* (de una mujer) **2** : tetilla *f* (de un hombre o un biberón)

nitrogen ['naɪtrədʒən] *n* : nitrógeno *m*

nitwit ['nɪt,wɪt] *n* : idiota *mf*

no ['noː] *adv* : no — **~** *adj* **1** : ninguno **2 I have ~ money** : no tengo dinero **3 it's ~ trouble** : no es ningún problema **4 ~ smoking** : prohibido fumar — **~** *n, pl* **noes** *or* **nos** ['noːz] : no *m*

noble ['noːbəl] *adj* **-bler; -blest** : noble — **~** *n* : noble *mf* — **nobility** [noʊ'bɪləṭi] *n* : nobleza *f*

nobody ['noːbɑdi, -,bɑdi] *pron* : nadie

nocturnal [nɑk'tərnəl] *adj* : nocturno

nod ['nɑd] *v* **nodded; nodding** *vi* **1** *or* **~ yes** : asentir con la cabeza **2 ~ off** : dormirse — *vt* **~ one's head** : asentir con la cabeza — **~** *n* : señal *m* con la cabeza

noes → **no**

noise ['nɔɪz] *n* : ruido *m* — **noisily** ['nɔɪzəli] *adv* : ruidosamente — **noisy** ['nɔɪzi] *adj* **noisier; -est** : ruidoso

nomad ['noːmæd] *n* : nómada *mf* — **nomadic** [noʊ'mædɪk] *adj* : nómada

nominal ['nɑmənəl] *adj* : nominal

nominate ['nɑmə,neɪt] *vt* **-nated; -nating 1** : proponer, postular *Lat* **2** APPOINT : nombrar — **nomination**

[nɑmə'neɪʃən] *n* **1** : propuesta *f*, postulación *f Lat* **2** APPOINTMENT : nombramiento *m*

nonalcoholic [,nɑnælkə'hɔlɪk] *adj* : no alcohólico

nonchalant [,nɑnʃə'lɑnt] *adj* : despreocupado

noncommissioned officer [,nɑnkə'mɪʃənd] *n* : suboficial *mf*

noncommittal [,nɑnkə'mɪṭəl] *adj* : evasivo

nondescript [,nɑndɪ'skrɪpt] *adj* : anodino, soso

none ['nʌn] *pron* **1** : ninguno, ninguna **2 there are ~ left** : no hay más — **~** *adv* **1 be ~ the worse** : no sufrir daño alguno **2 ~ too happy** : nada contento **3 ~ too soon** : a buena hora

nonentity [,nɑn'entəṭi] *n, pl* **-ties** : persona *f* insignificante

nonetheless [,nʌnðə'les] *adv* : sin embargo, no obstante

nonexistent [,nɑnɪg'zɪstənt] *adj* : inexistente

nonfat [,nɑn'fæt] *adj* : sin grasa

nonfiction [,nɑn'fɪkʃən] *n* : no ficción *f*

nonprofit [,nɑn'prɑfət] *adj* : sin fines lucrativos

nonsense ['nɑn,sents, 'nɑntsənts] *n* : tonterías *fpl*, disparates *mpl* — **nonsensical** [nɑn'sentsɪkəl] *adj* : absurdo

nonsmoker [,nɑn'smoːkər] *n* : no fumador *m*, -dora *f*

nonstop [,nɑn'stɑp] *adj* : directo — **~** *adv* : sin parar

noodle ['nuːdəl] *n* : fideo *m*

nook ['nʊk] *n* : rincón *m*

noon ['nuːn] *n* : mediodía *m*

no one *pron* : nadie

noose ['nuːs] *n* **1** : dogal *m*, soga *f* **2** LASSO : lazo *m*

nor ['nɔr] *conj* **1 neither...~** : ni...ni **2 ~ I** : yo tampoco

norm ['nɔrm] *n* **1** : norma *f* **2 the ~** : lo normal — **normal** ['nɔrməl] *adj* : normal — **normality** [nɔr'mæləṭi] *n* : normalidad *f* — **normally** *adv* : normalmente

north ['nɔrθ] *adv* : al norte — **~** *adj* : norte, del norte — **~** *n* : norte *m* **2 the North** : el Norte — **North American** *adj* : norteamericano — **northeast** [nɔrθ'iːst] *adv* : hacia el nordeste — **~** *adj* : nordeste, del nordeste — **~** *n* : nordeste *m*, noreste *m* — **northeastern** [nɔrθ'iːstərn] *adj* : nordeste, del nordeste — **northerly** ['nɔrðərli] *adj* : del norte — **northern** ['nɔrðərn] *adj* : del norte, norteño — **northwest** [nɔrθ'west] *adv* : hacia el noroeste —

~ *adj* : noroeste, del noroeste — **~** *n* : noroeste *m* — **northwestern** [,nɔrθ-'wɛstərn] *adj* : noroeste, del noroeste
Norwegian [nɔr'wiːdʒən] *adj* : noruego
nose ['noːz] *n* **1** : nariz *f* (de una persona), hocico *m* (de un animal) **2 blow one's ~** : sonarse las narices — **~** *vi* **nosed; nosing** *or* **~ around** : meter las narices — **nosebleed** ['noːz,bliːd] *n* : hemorragia *f* nasal — **nosedive** ['noːz,daɪv] *n* : descenso *m* en picada
nostalgia [nɑ'stældʒə, nə-] *n* : nostalgia *f* — **nostalgic** [nɑ'stældʒɪk, nə-] *adj* : nostálgico
nostril ['nɑstrəl] *n* : ventana *f* de la nariz
nosy *or* **nosey** ['noːzi] *adj* **nosier; -est** : entrometido
not ['nɑt] *adv* **1** : no **2 he's ~ tired** : no esta cansado **3 I hope ~** : espero que no **4 ~ ... anything** : no...nada
notable ['noːţəbəl] *adj* : notable — **~** *n* : personaje *m* — **notably** ['noːţəbli] *adv* : notablemente
notary public ['noːţəri-] *n, pl* **notaries public** *or* **notary publics** : notario *m*, -ria *f*
notation [noːteɪʃən] *n* : anotación *f*
notch ['nɑtʃ] *n* : muesca *f*, corte *m* — **~** *vt* : hacer un corte en
note ['noːt] *vt* **noted; noting 1** NOTICE : observar, notar **2** RECORD : anotar — **~** *n* **1** : nota *f* **2 of ~** : destacado **3 take ~ of** : prestar atención a **4 take ~s** : apuntar — **notebook** ['noːt,bʊk] *n* : libreta *f*, cuaderno *m* — **noted** ['noːţəd] *adj* : renombrado, célebre — **noteworthy** ['noːt,wərði] *adj* : notable
nothing ['nʌθɪŋ] *pron* **1** : nada **2 be ~ but** : no ser más que **3 for ~ FREE** : gratis — **~** *n* **1** ZERO : zero *m* **2** TRIFLE : nimiedad *f*
notice ['noːţɪs] *n* **1** SIGN : letrero *m*, aviso *m* **2 at a moment's ~** : sin previo aviso **3 be given one's ~** : ser despedido **4 take ~ of** : prestar atención a — **~** *vt* **-ticed; -ticing** : notar — **noticeable** ['noːţɪsəbəl] *adj* : perceptible, evidente
notify ['noːţə,faɪ] *vt* **-fied; -fying** : notificar, avisar — **notification** [,noːţəfə-'keɪʃən] *n* : notificación *f*, aviso *m*
notion ['noːʃən] *n* **1** : noción *f*, idea *f* **2 ~s** *npl* : artículos *mpl* de mercería
notorious [noːto:riəs] *adj* : de mala fama — **notoriety** [,noːţə'raɪəţi] *n* : mala fama *f*, notoriedad *f*
notwithstanding [,nɑtwɪθ'stændɪŋ, -wɪð-] *prep* : a pesar de, no obstante — **~** *adv* : sin embargo — **~** *conj* : a pesar de que

nougat ['nuːgət] *n* : turrón *m*
nought ['nɔt, 'nɑt] → **naught**
noun ['naʊn] *n* : nombre *m*, sustantivo *m*
nourish ['nərɪʃ] *vt* : nutrir — **nourishing** ['nərɪʃɪŋ] *adj* : nutritivo — **nourishment** ['nərɪʃmənt] *n* : alimento *m*
novel ['nɑvəl] *adj* : original, novedoso — **~** *n* : novela *f* — **novelist** ['nɑvəlɪst] *n* : novelista *mf* — **novelty** ['nɑvəlţi] *n, pl* **-ties** : novedad *f*
November [no'vembər] *n* : noviembre *m*
novice ['nɑvɪs] *n* : novato *m*, -ta *f*; principiante *mf*
now ['naʊ] *adv* **1** : ahora **2** THEN : entonces **3 from ~ on** : de ahora en adelante **4 ~ and then** : de vez en cuando **5 right ~** : ahora mismo — **~** *conj or* **~ that** : ahora que, ya que — **~** *n* **1 a year from ~** : dentro de un año **2 by ~** : ya **3 until ~** : hasta ahora — **nowadays** ['naʊə,deɪz] *adv* : hoy en día
nowhere ['noː,hwɛr] *adv* **1** (*indicating location*) : por ninguna parte, por ningún lado **2** (*indicating motion*) : a ninguna parte, a ningún lado **3 I'm ~ near finished** : aún me falta mucho para terminar **4 it's ~ near here** : queda bastante lejos de aquí — **~** *n* : ninguna parte *f*
nozzle ['nɑzəl] *n* : boca *f* (de una manguera, etc.)
nuance ['nuː,ɑns, 'nju-] *n* : matiz *m*
nucleus ['nuːkliəs, 'nju-] *n, pl* **-clei** [-kli,aɪ] : núcleo *m* — **nuclear** ['nuːkliər, 'nju-] *adj* : nuclear
nude ['nuːd, 'njuːd] *adj* **nuder; nudest** : desnudo — **~** *n* : desnudo *m*
nudge ['nʌdʒ] *vt* **nudged; nudging** : dar un codazo a — **~** *n* : toque *m* (con el codo)
nudity ['nuːdəţi, 'nju-] *n* : desnudez *f*
nugget ['nʌgət] *n* : pepita *f* (de oro, etc.)
nuisance ['nuːsənts, 'nju-] *n* **1** ANNOYANCE : fastidio *m*, molestia *f* **2** PEST : pesado *m*, -da *f fam*
null ['nʌl] *adj* **~ and void** : nulo y sin efecto
numb ['nʌm] *adj* **1** : entumecido, dormido **2 ~ with fear** : paralizado de miedo — **~** *vt* : entumecer, adormecer
number ['nʌmbər] *n* **1** : número *m* **2 a ~ of** : varios — **~** *vt* **1** : numerar **2** INCLUDE : contar, incluir **3** TOTAL : ascender a
numeral ['nuːmərəl, 'nju-] *n* : número *m* — **numeric** [nu'mɛrɪk, nju-] *or* **numerical** [nu'mɛrɪkəl, nju-] *adj* : numérico — **numerous** ['nuːmərəs, 'nju-] *adj* : numeroso

nun ['nʌn] *n* : monja *f*
nuptial ['nʌpʃəl] *adj* : nupcial
nurse ['nərs] *n* **1** : enfermero *m*, -ra *f* **2** — **nursemaid** — **~** *vt* **nursed; nursing 1** : cuidar (de), atender **2** SUCKLE : amamantar — **nursemaid** ['nərs‚meɪd] *n* : niñera *f* — **nursery** ['nərsəri] *n*, *pl* **-eries 1** : cuarto *m* de los niños **2** *or* **day ~** : guardería *f* **3** : vivero *m* (de plantas) — **nursing home** *n* : asilo *m* de ancianos
nurture ['nərtʃər] *vt* **-tured; -turing 1** NOURISH : nutrir **2** EDUCATE : criar, educar **3** FOSTER : alimentar
nut ['nʌt] *n* **1** : nuez *f* **2** LUNATIC : loco *m*, -ca *f* **3** ENTHUSIAST : fanático *m*, -ca *f* **4** **~s and bolts** : tuercas y tornillos

nutcracker ['nʌt‚krækər] *n* : cascanueces *m*
nutmeg ['nʌt‚meg] *n* : nuez *f* moscada
nutrient ['nu:triənt, 'nju:-] *n* : nutriente *m*
nutrition [nu'trɪʃən, nju-] *n* : nutrición *f* — **nutritional** [nu'trɪʃənəl, nju-] *adj* : nutritivo — **nutritious** [nu'trɪʃəs, nju-] *adj* : nutritivo
nuts ['nʌts] *adj* : loco
nutshell ['nʌt‚ʃel] *n* **1** : cáscara *f* de nuez **2 in a ~** : en pocas palabras
nutty ['nʌti] *adj* **-tier; -tiest** : loco
nuzzle ['nʌzəl] *v* **-zled; -zling** *vi* : acurrucarse — *vt* : acariciar con el hocico
nylon ['naɪ‚lɑn] *n* **1** : nilón *m* **2 ~s** *npl* : medias *fpl* de nilón
nymph ['nɪmpf] *n* : ninfa *f*

O

o ['oː] *n*, *pl* **o's** *or* **os** ['oːz] **1** : o *f*, decimoquinta letra del alfabeto inglés **2** ZERO : cero *m*
O ['oː] → **oh**
oaf ['oːf] *n* : zoquete *m*
oak ['oːk] *n*, *pl* **oaks** *or* **oak** : roble *m*
oar ['or] *n* : remo *m*
oasis [o'eɪsɪs] *n*, *pl* **oases** [-‚siːz] : oasis *m*
oath ['oːθ] *n*, *pl* **oaths** ['oːðz, 'oːθs] **1** : juramento *m* **2** SWEARWORD : palabrota *f*
oats ['oːts] *npl* : avena *f* — **oatmeal** ['oːt‚miːl] *n* : harina *f* de avena
obedient [o'biːdiənt] *adj* : obediente — **obedience** [o'biːdiəns] *n* : obediencia *f*
obese [o'biːs] *adj* : obeso — **obesity** [o'biːsəti] *n* : obesidad *f*
obey [o'beɪ] *v* **obeyed; obeying** : obedecer
obituary [ə'bɪtʃu‚eri] *n*, *pl* **-aries** : obituario *m*
object ['ɑbdʒɪkt] *n* **1** : objeto *m* **2** AIM : objetivo *m* **3** : complemento *m* (en gramática) — **~** [əb'dʒekt] *vt* : objetar — *vi* **~ to** : oponerse a — **objection** [əb'dʒekʃən] *n* : objeción *f* — **objectionable** [əb'dʒekʃənəbəl] *adj* : desagradable — **objective** [əb'dʒektɪv] *adj* : objetivo — **~** *n* : objetivo *m*
oblige [ə'blaɪdʒ] *vt* **obliged; obliging 1** : obligar **2 be much ~d** : estar muy agradecido **3 ~ s.o.** : hacer un favor a algn — **obligation** [‚ɑblə'geɪʃən] *n* : obligación *f* — **obligatory** [ə'blɪgə‚tori] *adj* : obligatorio — **obliging** [ə'blaɪdʒɪŋ] *adj* : atento, servicial

oblique [o'bliːk] *adj* **1** SLANTING : oblicuo **2** INDIRECT : indirecto
obliterate [ə'blɪtə‚reɪt] *vt* **-ated; -ating 1** ERASE : borrar **2** DESTROY : arrasar
oblivion [ə'blɪviən] *n* : olvido *m* — **oblivious** [ə'blɪviəs] *adj* : inconsciente
oblong ['ɑ‚blɔŋ] *adj* : oblongo — **~** *n* : rectángulo *m*
obnoxious [ɑb'nɑkʃəs, əb-] *adj* : odioso
oboe ['oː‚boː] *n* : oboe *m*
obscene [ɑb'siːn, əb-] *adj* : obsceno — **obscenity** [ɑb'senəti, əb-] *n*, *pl* **-ties** : obscenidad *f*
obscurity [ɑb'skjurəti, əb-] *n*, *pl* **-ties** : oscuridad *f* — **obscure** [ɑb'skjur, əb-] *adj* : oscuro — **~** *vt* **-scured; -scuring 1** DARKEN : oscurecer **2** HIDE : ocultar
observe [əb'zərv] *v* **-served; -serving** *vt* : observar — *vi* WATCH : mirar — **observance** [əb'zərvəns] *n* **1** : observancia *f* **2 religious ~s** : prácticas *fpl* religiosas — **observant** [əb'zərvənt] *adj* : observador — **observation** [‚ɑbsər'veɪʃən, -zər-] *n* : observación *f* — **observatory** [əb'zərvə‚tori] *n*, *pl* **-ries** : observatorio *m*
obsess [əb'ses] *vt* : obsesionar — **obsession** [əb'seʃən, ɑb-] *n* : obsesión *f* — **obsessive** [ɑb'sesɪv, əb-] *adj* : obsesivo
obsolete [‚ɑbsə'liːt, 'ɑbsə‚-] *adj* : obsoleto, desusado
obstacle ['ɑbstɪkəl] *n* : obstáculo *m*
obstetrics [əb'stetrɪks] *n* : obstetricia *f*
obstinate ['ɑbstənət] *adj* : obstinado
obstruct [əb'strʌkt] *vt* **1** BLOCK : obstru-

ir 2 HINDER : obstaculizar — **obstruction** [əb'strʌkʃən] n : obstrucción f

obtain [əb'teɪn] vt : obtener, conseguir — **obtainable** [əb'teɪnəbəl] adj : asequible

obtrusive [əb'tru:sɪv] adj : entrometido (dícese de las personas), demasiado prominente (dícese de las cosas)

obtuse [ɑb'tu:s, əb-, -'tju:s] adj : obtuso

obvious ['ɑbviəs] adj : obvio, evidente — **obviously** ['ɑbviəsli] adv 1 CLEARLY : obviamente 2 OF COURSE : claro, por supuesto

occasion [ə'keɪʒən] n 1 : ocasión f 2 on ~ : de vez en cuando — ~ vt : ocasionar — **occasional** [ə'keɪʒənəl] adj : poco frecuente, ocasional — **occasionally** [ə'keɪʒənəli] adv : de vez en cuando

occult [ə'kʌlt, 'ɑ,kʌlt] adj : oculto

occupy ['ɑkjə,paɪ] vt **-pied; -pying** 1 : ocupar 2 ~ **oneself** : entretenerse — **occupancy** ['ɑkjəpəntsi] n, pl **-cies** : ocupación f — **occupant** ['ɑkjəpənt] n : ocupante mf — **occupation** [,ɑkjə'peɪʃən] n : ocupación f — **occupational** [,ɑkjə'peɪʃənəl] adj : profesional

occur [ə'kər] vi **occurred; occurring** 1 : ocurrir 2 APPEAR : encontrarse 3 ~ **to s.o.** : ocurrirse a algn — **occurrence** [ə'kərənts] n 1 EVENT : acontecimiento m, suceso m 2 INCIDENCE : incidencia f

ocean ['oʃən] n : océano m

ocher or **ochre** ['oʃkər] n : ocre m

o'clock [ə'klɑk] adv 1 **at 6** ~ : a las seis 2 **it's one** ~ : es la una 3 **it's ten** ~ : son las diez

octagon ['ɑktə,gɑn] n : octágono m — **octagonal** [ɑk'tægənəl] adj : octagonal

octave ['ɑktɪv] n : octava f

October [ɑk'to:bər] n : octubre m

octopus ['ɑktəpus, -pəs] n, pl **-puses** or **-pi** [-,paɪ] : pulpo m

oculist ['ɑkjəlɪst] n : oculista mf

odd ['ɑd] adj 1 STRANGE : extraño, raro 2 : sin pareja (dícese de un calcetín, etc.) 3 **forty** ~ **years** : cuarenta y tantos años 4 ~ **jobs** : algunos trabajos mpl 5 ~ **number** : número m impar — **oddity** ['ɑdəţi] n, pl **-ties** : rareza f — **oddly** ['ɑdli] adv : de manera extraña — **odds** ['ɑdz] npl 1 CHANCES : probabilidades fpl 2 **at** ~ : en desacuerdo 3 **five to one** ~ : cinco contra uno (en apuestas) — **odds and ends** npl : cosas fpl sueltas

ode ['o:d] n : oda f

odious ['o:diəs] adj : odioso

odor or Brit **odour** ['o:dər] n : olor m —

odorless or Brit **odourless** ['o:dərləs] adj : inodoro

of ['ʌv, 'ɑv] prep 1 : de 2 **five minutes** ~ **ten** : las diez menos cinco 3 **the eighth** ~ **April** : el ocho de abril

off ['ɔf] adv 1 **be** ~ LEAVE : irse 2 **cut** ~ : cortar 3 **day** ~ : día m de descanso 4 **fall** ~ : caerse 5 **doze** ~ : dormirse 6 **far** ~ : lejos 7 ~ **and on** : de vez en cuando 8 **shut** ~ : apagar 9 **ten miles** ~ : a diez millas de aquí — ~ prep 1 : de 2 **be** ~ **duty** : estar libre 3 ~ **center** : descentrado — ~ adj 1 CANCELED : cancelado 2 OUT : apagado 3 **an** ~ **chance** : una posibilidad remota

offend [ə'fend] vt : ofender — **offender** [ə'fendər] n : delincuente mf — **offense** or **offence** [ə'fents, 'ɔ,fents] n 1 AFFRONT : afrenta f 2 ASSAULT : ataque m 3 : ofensiva f (en deportes) 4 CRIME : delito m 5 **take** ~ : ofenderse — **offensive** [ə'fentsɪv,'ɔ,fent-] adj : ofensivo — ~ n : ofensiva f

offer ['ɔfər] vt : ofrecer — ~ n : oferta f — **offering** ['ɔfərɪŋ] n : ofrenda f

offhand ['ɔf,hænd] adv : de improviso, en este momento — ~ adj : improvisado

office ['ɔfəs] n 1 : oficina f 2 POSITION : cargo m 3 **run for** ~ : presentarse como candidato — **officer** ['ɔfəsər] n 1 : oficial mf 2 or **police** ~ : agente mf (de policía) — **official** [ə'fɪʃəl] n 1 : funcionario m, -ria f — ~ adj : oficial

offing ['ɔfɪŋ] n **in the** ~ : en perspectiva

offset ['ɔf,set] vt **-set; -setting** : compensar

offshore ['ɔf,ʃor] adv : a una distancia de la costa

offspring ['ɔf,sprɪŋ] ns & pl : prole f, progenie f

often ['ɔfən, 'ɔftən] adv 1 : muchas veces, a menudo, con frecuencia 2 **every so** ~ : de vez en cuando

ogle ['o:gəl] vt **ogled; ogling** : comerse con los ojos

ogre ['o:gər] n : ogro m

oh ['o:] interj 1 : ¡oh!, ¡ah! 2 ~ **no!** : ¡ay no! 3 ~ **really?** : ¿de veras?

oil ['ɔɪl] n 1 : aceite m 2 PETROLEUM : petróleo m 3 or ~ **painting** : óleo m — ~ vt : lubricar — **oilskin** ['ɔɪl,skɪn] n : hule m — **oily** ['ɔɪli] adj **oilier; -est** : aceitoso, grasiento

ointment ['ɔɪntmənt] n : ungüento m, pomada f

OK or **okay** [o:'keɪ] adv 1 : muy bien 2 ~ **!** : ¡de acuerdo!, ¡bueno! — ~ adj 1

ALL RIGHT : bien 2 it's ~ with me
: por mí no hay problema — ~ n
: visto m bueno — ~ [ˌoːˈkeɪ] vt OK'd
or okayed [ˌoːˈkeɪd]; OK'ing or okay-
ing : dar el visto bueno a

okra ['oːkrə, *South also* -krɪ] n : quin-
gombó m

old ['oːld] adj 1 : viejo 2 FORMER : antiguo 3 any ~ : cualquier 4 be ten
years ~ : tener diez años (de edad) 5
~ age : vejez f 6 ~ man : anciano m
7 ~ woman : anciana f — ~ n the
~ : los viejos, los ancianos —
old–fashioned ['oːldˈfæʃənd] adj : anticuado

olive ['ɑlɪv, -ləv] n 1 : aceituna f (fruta) 2
or ~ green : verde m oliva

Olympic [oˈlɪmpɪk] adj : olímpico —
Olympics [oˈlɪmpɪks] npl the ~ : las
Olimpiadas, las Olimpíadas

omelet or omelette ['ɑmlət, 'ɑmə-] n
: omelette mf Lat, tortilla f francesa
Spain

omen ['oːmən] n : agüero m — ominous
['ɑmənəs] adj : ominoso, de mal
agüero

omit [oˈmɪt] vt omitted; omitting : omitir — omission [oˈmɪʃən] n : omisión f

omnipotent [ɑmˈnɪpətənt] adj : omnipotente

on ['ɑn, 'ɔn] prep 1 : en 2 ABOUT :
sobre 3 ~ foot : a pie 4 ~ Monday : el
lunes 5 ~ the right : a la derecha 6
~ vacation : de vacaciones 7 talk ~
the phone : hablar por teléfono — ~
adv 1 and so ~ : etcétera 2 from that
moment ~ : a partir de ese momento
3 keep ~ : seguir 4 later ~ : más
tarde 5 ~ and ~ : sin parar 6 put ~
: ponerse (ropa), poner (música, etc.)
7 turn ~ : encender (una luz, etc.),
abrir (una llave) — ~ adj 1 : encendido (dícese de luces, etc.), abierto
(dícese de llaves) 2 be ~ to : estar
enterado de

once ['wʌnts] adv 1 : una vez 2 FORMER-
LY : antes — ~ n 1 at ~ TOGETHER
: al mismo tiempo 2 at ~ IMMEDIATE-
LY : inmediatamente — ~ conj : una
vez que

oncoming ['ɑnˌkʌmɪŋ, 'ɔn-] adj : que
viene

one ['wʌn] adj 1 : un, uno 2 ONLY : único
3 or ~ and the same : el mismo —
~ n 1 : uno m (número) 2 ~ by ~
: uno a uno — ~ pron 1 : uno, una 2
~ another : el uno al otro 3 ~ never
knows : nunca se sabe 4 that ~
: aquél, aquella 5 which ~? : ¿cuál?
— oneself [ˌwʌnˈself] pron 1 (*used re-*

flexively*) : se 2 (*used after prepositions*) : sí mismo, sí misma 3 (*used emphatically*) : uno mismo, una misma 4
by ~ : solo — one–sided ['wʌn-
ˈsaɪdəd] adj 1 UNEQUAL : desigual 2 BI-
ASED : parcial — one–way ['wʌnˈweɪ]
adj 1 : de sentido único (dícese de una
calle) 2 ~ ticket : boleto m de ida

ongoing ['ɑnˌgoɪŋ] adj : en curso, corriente

onion ['ʌnjən] n : cebolla f

only ['oːnli] adj : único — ~ adv 1
: sólo, solamente 2 if ~ : ojalá, por lo
menos — ~ conj BUT : pero

onset ['ɑnˌsɛt] n : comienzo m, llegada f

onslaught ['ɑnˌslɔt, 'ɔn-] n : ataque m,
arremetida f

onto ['ɑnˌtuː, 'ɔn-] prep : sobre

onus ['oːnəs] n : responsabilidad f

onward ['ɑnwərd, 'ɔn-] adv & adj : hacia
adelante

onyx ['ɑnɪks] n : ónix m

ooze ['uːz] v oozed; oozing : rezumar

opal ['oːpəl] n : ópalo m

opaque [oˈpeɪk] adj : opaco

open ['oːpən] adj 1 : abierto 2 AVAILABLE
: vacante, libre 3 an ~ question
: una cuestión pendiente — ~ vt
: abrir — vi 1 : abrirse 2 BEGIN : comenzar — ~ n in the ~ 1 OUTDOORS
: al aire libre 2 KNOWN : sacado a la luz
— open–air ['oːpənˈær] adj : al aire
libre — opener ['oːpənər] n 1 : abridor
m 2 or bottle ~ : abrebotellas m 3 or
can ~ : abrelatas m — opening
['oːpənɪŋ] n 1 : abertura f 2 BEGINNING
: comienzo m, apertura f 3 OPPORTUNI-
TY : opportunidad f — openly ['oːpən-
li] adv : abiertamente

opera ['ɑprə, 'ɑpərə] n : ópera f

operate ['ɑpəˌreɪt] v -ated; -ating vi 1
FUNCTION : funcionar 2 ~ on s.o.
: operar a algn — vt 1 : hacer funcionar (una máquina) 2 MANAGE : dirigir, manejar — operation [ˌɑpəˈreɪʃən]
n 1 : operación f 2 FUNCTIONING : funcionamiento m — operational [ˌɑpə-
ˈreɪʃənəl] adj : operacional — opera-
tive ['ɑpərəˌtɪv, -rət-] adj : en vigor —
operator ['ɑpəˌreɪtər] n 1 : operador m,
-dora f 2 or machine ~ : operario m,
-ria f

opinion [əˈpɪnjən] n : opinión f — opin-
ionated [əˈpɪnjəˌneɪtəd] adj : dogmático

opium ['oːpiəm] n : opio m

opossum [əˈpɑsəm] n : zarigüeya f, opo-
sum m

opponent [əˈpoːnənt] n : adversario m,
-ria f; contrincante mf (en deportes)

opportunity [,apǝr'tu:nǝti, -'tju:-] *n, pl* **-ties** : oportunidad *f* — **opportune** [,apǝr'tu:n, -'tju:n] *adj* : oportuno — **opportunist** [,apǝr'tu:nɪst, -'tju:-] *n* : oportunista *mf*

oppose [ǝ'po:z] *vt* **-posed; -posing** : oponerse a — **opposed** *adj* ~ **to** : en contra de

opposite ['apǝzǝt] *adj* **1** FACING : de enfrente **2** CONTRARY : opuesto — ~ *n* **the** ~ : lo contrario, lo opuesto — ~ *adv* : enfrente — ~ *prep* : enfrente de, frente a — **opposition** [,apǝ'zɪʃǝn] *n* **1** : oposición *f* **2** **in** ~ **to** : en contra de

oppress [ǝ'prɛs] *vt* : oprimir — **oppression** [ǝ'prɛʃǝn] *n* : opresión *f* — **oppressive** [ǝ'prɛsɪv] *adj* **1** STIFLING : agobiante — **oppressor** [ǝ'prɛsǝr] *n* : opresor *m*, -sora *f*

opt ['apt] *vi* ~ **for** : optar por

optic ['aptɪk] *or* **optical** [-tɪkǝl] *adj* : óptico — **optician** [ap'tɪʃǝn] *n* : óptico *m*, -ca *f*

optimism ['aptǝ,mɪzǝm] *n* : optimismo *f* — **optimist** ['aptǝmɪst] *n* : optimista *mf* — **optimistic** [,aptǝ'mɪstɪk] *adj* : optimista

optimum ['aptǝmǝm] *n, pl* **-ma** [-'mǝ] : lo óptimo, lo ideal

option ['apʃǝn] *n* **1** : opción *f* **2** **have no** ~ : no tener más remedio — **optional** ['apʃǝnǝl] *adj* : facultativo, opcional

opulence ['apjǝlǝnts] *n* : opulencia *f* — **opulent** ['apjǝlǝnt] *adj* : opulento

or ['ɔr] *conj* **1** (*indicating an alternative*) : o (u *before o- or ho-*) **2** (*following a negative*) : ni **3** ~ **else** : si no

oracle ['ɔrǝkǝl] *n* : oráculo *m*

oral ['ɔrǝl] *adj* : oral

orange ['ɔrɪndʒ] *n* **1** : naranja *f* (fruta) **2** : naranja *m* (color)

orator ['ɔrǝtǝr] *n* : orador *m*, -dora *f*

orbit ['ɔrbǝt] *n* : órbita *f* — ~ *vt* : girar alrededor de — *vi* : orbitar

orchard ['ɔrtʃǝrd] *n* : huerto *m*

orchestra ['ɔrkǝstrǝ] *n* : orquesta *f*

orchid ['ɔrkɪd] *n* : orquídea *f*

ordain [ɔr'deɪn] *vt* **1** : ordenar (un sacerdote, etc.) **2** DECREE : decretar

ordeal [ɔr'di:l, 'ɔr,di:l] *n* : prueba *f* dura

order ['ɔrdǝr] *vt* **1** : ordenar **2** : pedir (mercancías, etc.) — *vi* : hacer un pedido — ~ *n* **1** ARRANGEMENT : orden *m* **2** COMMAND : orden *f* **3** REQUEST : pedido *m* **4** : orden *f* (religiosa) **5** **in** ~ **that** : para que **6** **in** ~ **to** : para **7** **out of** ~ : averiado, descompuesto *Lat* — **orderly** ['ɔrdǝrli] *adj* : ordenado — ~ *n, pl* **-lies 1** : ordenanza *m* (en el ejército) **2** : camillero *m* (en un hospital)

ordinary ['ɔrdǝn,ɛri] *adj* **1** : normal, corriente **2** MEDIOCRE : ordinario — **ordinarily** [,ɔrdǝn'ɛrǝli] *adv* : generalmente

ore ['ɔr] *n* : mena *f*

oregano [ǝ'rɛgǝ,no:] *n* : orégano *m*

organ ['ɔrgǝn] *n* : órgano *m* — **organic** [ɔr'gænɪk] *adj* : orgánico — **organism** ['ɔrgǝ,nɪzǝm] *n* : organismo *m* — **organist** ['ɔrgǝnɪst] *n* : organista *mf* — **organize** ['ɔrgǝ,naɪz] *vt* **-nized; -nizing** : organizar — **organization** [,ɔrgǝnǝ'zeɪʃǝn] *n* : organización *f* — **organizer** ['ɔrgǝ,naɪzǝr] *n* : organizador *m*, -dora *f*

orgasm ['ɔr,gæzǝm] *n* : orgasmo *m*

orgy ['ɔrdʒi] *n, pl* **-gies** : orgía *f*

Orient ['ɔri,ɛnt] *n* **the** ~ : el Oriente — **orient** *vt* : orientar — **oriental** [,ɔri'ɛntǝl] *adj* : del Oriente, oriental — **orientation** [,ɔriǝn'teɪʃǝn] *n* : orientación *f*

orifice ['ɔrǝfǝs] *n* : orificio *m*

origin ['ɔrǝdʒǝn] *n* : origen *m* — **original** [ǝ'rɪdʒǝnǝl] *n* : original *m* — ~ *adj* : original — **originality** [ǝ,rɪdʒǝ'nælǝti] *n* : originalidad *f* — **originally** [ǝ'rɪdʒǝnǝli] *adv* : originariamente — **originate** [ǝ'rɪdʒǝ,neɪt] *v* **-nated; -nating** *vt* : originar — *vi* **1** : originarse **2** ~ **from** : provenir de — **originator** [ǝ'rɪdʒǝ,neɪtǝr] *n* : creador *m*, -dora *f*

ornament ['ɔrnǝmǝnt] *n* : adorno *m* — ~ *vt* : adornar — **ornamental** [,ɔrnǝ'mɛntǝl] *adj* : ornamental, de adorno — **ornate** [ɔr'neɪt] *adj* : elaborado, adornado

ornithology [,ɔrnǝ'θalǝdʒi] *n, pl* **-gies** : ornitología *f*

orphan ['ɔrfǝn] *n* : huérfano *m*, -na *f* — ~ *vt* : dejar huérfano — **orphanage** ['ɔrfǝnɪdʒ] *n* : orfelinato *m*, orfanato *m*

orthodox ['ɔrθǝ,daks] *adj* : ortodoxo — **orthodoxy** ['ɔrθǝ,daksi] *n, pl* **-doxies** : ortodoxia *f*

orthopedic [,ɔrθǝ'pi:dɪk] *adj* : ortopédico

oscillation [,asǝ'leɪʃǝn] *n* : oscilación *f* — **oscillate** ['asǝ,leɪt] *vi* **-lated; -lating** : oscilar

ostensible [a'stɛntsǝbǝl] *adj* : aparente, ostensible

ostentation [,astǝn'teɪʃǝn] *n* : ostentación *f* — **ostentatious** [,astǝn'teɪʃǝs] *adj* : ostentoso

osteopath ['astiǝ,pæθ] *n* : osteópata *f*

ostracism ['astrǝ,sɪzǝm] *n* : ostracismo *m* — **ostracize** ['astrǝ,saɪz] *vt* **-cized; -cizing** : aislar

ostrich ['astrɪtʃ, 'ɔs-] *n* : avestruz *m*

other ['ʌðər] *adj* 1 : otro 2 **every ~ day** : cada dos días 3 **on the ~ hand** : por otra parte, por otro lado — ~ *pron* 1 : otro, otra 2 **the ~s** : los otros, las otras, los demás, las demás — **other than** *prep* : aparte de, fuera de — **otherwise** ['ʌðər,waɪz] *adv* 1 : eso aparte, por lo demás 2 DIFFERENTLY : de otro modo 3 OR ELSE : si no

otter ['ɑtər] *n* : nutria *f*

ought ['ɔt] *v aux* 1 : deber 2 **you ~ to have done it** : deberías haberlo hecho

ounce ['aʊnts] *n* : onza *f*

our ['ɑr, 'aʊr] *adj* : nuestro — **ours** ['aʊrz, 'ɑrz] *pron* 1 : (el) nuestro, (la) nuestra, (los) nuestros, (las) nuestras 2 **a friend of ~** : un amigo nuestro — **ourselves** [ɑr'sɛlvz, aʊr-] *pron* 1 (*used reflexively*) : nos 2 (*used after prepositions*) : nosotros, nosotras 3 (*used for emphasis*) : nosotros mismos, nosotras mismas

oust ['aʊst] *vt* : desbancar

out ['aʊt] *adv* 1 OUTSIDE : fuera, afuera 2 **cry ~** : gritar 3 **eat ~** : comer afuera 4 **go ~** : salir 5 **look ~** : mirar para afuera 6 **run ~ of** : agotar 7 **turn ~** : apagar (una luz) 8 **take ~** REMOVE : sacar — ~ *prep* → **out of** — ~ *adj* 1 ABSENT : ausente 2 UNFASHIONABLE : fuera de moda 3 EXTINGUISHED : apagado 4 **the sun is ~** : hace sol

outboard motor ['aʊt,bord] *n* : motor *m* fuera de borde

outbreak ['aʊt,breɪk] *n* : brote *m* (de una enfermedad), comienzo *m* (de guerra)

outburst ['aʊt,bərst] *n* : arranque *m*, arrebato *m*

outcast ['aʊt,kæst] *n* : paria *mf*

outcome ['aʊt,kʌm] *n* : resultado *m*

outcry ['aʊt,kraɪ] *n*, *pl* **-cries** : protesta *f*

outdated [,aʊt'deɪtəd] *adj* : anticuado

outdo [aʊt'du:] *vt* **-did** [-'dɪd]; **-done** [-'dʌn]; **-doing**; **-does** [-'dʌz] : superar

outdoor [aʊt'dor] *adj* : al aire libre — **outdoors** ['aʊt'dorz] *adv* : al aire libre

outer ['aʊtər] *adj* : exterior — **outer space** *n* : espacio *m* exterior

outfit ['aʊt,fɪt] *n* 1 EQUIPMENT : equipo *m* 2 CLOTHES : conjunto *m* — ~ *vt* **-fitted; -fitting** EQUIP : equipar

outgoing ['aʊt,go:ɪŋ] *adj* 1 SOCIABLE : extrovertido 2 ~ **mail** : correo *m* (para enviar) 3 ~ **president** : presidente *m*, -ta *f* saliente

outgrow [aʊt'gro:] *vt* **-grew** [-'gru:]; **-grown** [-'gro:n]; **-growing** : crecer más que

outing ['aʊtɪŋ] *n* : excursión *f*

outlandish [aʊt'lændɪʃ] *adj* : estrafalario

outlast [aʊt'læst] *vt* : durar más que

outlaw ['aʊt,lɔ] *n* : forajido *m*, -da *f* — ~ *vt* : declarar ilegal

outlay ['aʊt,leɪ] *n* : desembolso *m*

outlet ['aʊt,lɛt, -lət] *n* 1 EXIT : salida *f* 2 RELEASE : desahogo *m* 3 *or* **electrical ~** : toma *f* de corriente 4 *or* **retail ~** : tienda *f* al por menor

outline ['aʊt,laɪn] *n* 1 CONTOUR : contorno *m* 2 SKETCH : bosquejo *m*, boceto *m* 3 SUMMARY : esquema *m* — ~ *vt* **-lined; -lining** 1 SKETCH : bosquejar 2 EXPLAIN : delinear, esbozar

outlive [aʊt'lɪv] *vt* **-lived; -living** : sobrevivir a

outlook ['aʊt,lʊk] *n* 1 PROSPECTS : perspectivas *fpl* 2 VIEWPOINT : punto *m* de vista

outlying ['aʊt,laɪɪŋ] *adj* : alejado, distante

outmoded [,aʊt'mo:dəd] *adj* : pasado de moda, anticuado

outnumber [,aʊt'nʌmbər] *vt* : superar en número a

outpatient ['aʊt,peɪʃənt] *n* : paciente *m* externo

outpost ['aʊt,po:st] *n* : puesto *m* avanzado

output ['aʊt,pʊt] *n* 1 : producción *f*, rendimiento *m* 2 : salida *f* (informática) — ~ *vt* **-putted** *or* **-put; -putting** : producir

outrage ['aʊt,reɪdʒ] *n* 1 : atrocidad *f*, escándalo *m* 2 ANGER : ira *f*, indignación *f* — ~ *vt* **-raged; -raging** : ultrajar — **outrageous** [,aʊt'reɪdʒəs] *adj* : escandaloso

outright [aʊt'raɪt] *adv* 1 COMPLETELY : por completo 2 INSTANTLY : en el acto — ~ ['aʊt,raɪt] *adj* : completo, absoluto

outset ['aʊt,sɛt] *n* : comienzo *m*, principio *m*

outside [aʊt'saɪd, 'aʊt-] *n* 1 : exterior *m* 2 **from the ~** : desde fuera, desde afuera — ~ *adj* 1 : exterior, externo 2 **an ~ chance** : una posibilidad remota — ~ *adv* : fuera, afuera — ~ *prep* *or* ~ **of** : fuera de — **outsider** [aʊt'saɪdər] *n* : forastero *m*, -ra *f*

outskirts ['aʊt,skərts] *npl* : afueras *fpl*, alrededores *mpl*

outspoken [,aʊt'spo:kən] *adj* : franco, directo

outstanding [,aʊt'stændɪŋ] *adj* 1 UNPAID : pendiente 2 EXCELLENT : excepcional

outstretched [,aʊt'stretʃt] *adj* : extendido

outstrip [aʊt'strɪp] *vt* **-stripped** *or* **-stript** [-'strɪpt]; **-stripping** : aventajar

outward ['aʊtwərd] *adj* 1 : hacia afuera 2 EXTERNAL : externo, external — ~ *or* **outwards** [-wərdz] *adv* : hacia afuera — **outwardly** ['aʊtwərdli] *adv* APPARENTLY : aparentemente

outweigh [aʊt'weɪ] *vt* : pesar más que

outwit [,aʊt'wɪt] *vt* **-witted; -witting** : ser más listo que

oval ['o:vəl] *n* : óvalo *m* — ~ *adj* : ovalado

ovary ['o:vəri] *n*, *pl* **-ries** : ovario *m*

ovation [o'veɪʃən] *n* : ovación *f*

oven ['ʌvən] *n* : horno *m*

over ['o:vər] *adv* 1 ABOVE : por encima 2 AGAIN : otra vez, de nuevo 3 MORE : más 4 all ~ : por todas partes 5 ask ~ : invitar 6 cross ~ : cruzar 7 fall ~ : caerse 8 ~ and ~ : una y otra vez 9 ~ here : aquí 10 ~ there : allí — ~ *prep* 1 ABOVE, UPON : encima de, sobre 2 ACROSS : por encima de, sobre 3 DURING : en, durante 4 fight ~ : pelearse por 5 ~ $5 : más de $5 6 ~ the phone : por teléfono — ~ *adj* : terminado, acabado

overall [,o:vər'ɔl] *adv* GENERALLY : en general — *adj* : total, en conjunto — **overalls** ['o:vər,ɔlz] *npl* : overol *m Lat*

overbearing [,o:vər'bærɪŋ] *adj* : dominante, imperioso

overboard ['o:vər,bord] *adv* fall ~ : caer al agua

overburden [,o:vər'bərdən] *vt* : sobrecargar

overcast [,o:vər,kæst] *adj* : nublado

overcharge [,o:vər'tʃardʒ] *vt* **-charged; -charging** : cobrar demasiado

overcoat ['o:vər,ko:t] *n* : abrigo *m*

overcome [,o:vər'kʌm] *v* **-came** [-'keɪm]; **-come; -coming** *vt* 1 CONQUER : vencer 2 OVERWHELM : agobiar — *vi* : vencer

overcook [,o:vər'kʊk] *vt* : cocer demasiado

overcrowded [,o:vər'kraʊdəd] *adj* : abarrotado de gente

overdo [,o:vər'du:] *vt* **-did** [-'dɪd]; **-done** [-'dʌn]; **-doing; -does** [-'dʌz] 1 : hacer demasiado 2 EXAGGERATE : exagerar 3 → overcook

overdose ['o:vər,do:s] *n* : sobredosis *f*

overdraw [,o:vər'drɔ] *vt* **-drew** [-'dru:]; **-drawn** [-'drɔn]; **-drawing** : girar en descubierto — **overdraft** ['o:vər,dræft] *n* : sobregiro *m*, descubierto *m*

overdue [,o:vər'du:] *adj* : fuera de plazo (dícese de pagos, libros, etc.)

overeat [,o:vər'i:t] *vi* **-ate** [-'eɪt]; **-eaten** [-'eɪtən]; **-eating** : comer demasiado

overestimate [,o:vər'estə,meɪt] *vt* **-mated; -mating** : sobreestimar

overflow [,o:vər'flo:] *vt* : desbordar — *vi* : desbordarse — ~ ['o:vər,flo:] *n* : desbordamiento *m* (de un río)

overgrown [,o:vər'gro:n] *adj* : cubierto (de malas hierbas, etc.)

overhand ['o:vər,hænd] *adv* : por encima de la cabeza

overhang [,o:vər'hæŋ] *v* **-hung** [-'hʌŋ]; **-hanging** : sobresalir

overhaul [,o:vər'hɔl] *vt* : revisar (un motor, etc.)

overhead [,o:vər'hed] *adv* : por encima — ~ [-vər,hed] *adj* : de arriba — ~ ['o:vər,hed] *n* : gastos *mpl* generales

overhear [,o:vər'hɪr] *vt* **-heard; -hearing** : oír por casualidad

overheat [,o:vər'hi:t] *vt* : calentar demasiado — *vi* : recalentarse

overjoyed [,o:vər'dʒɔɪd] *adj* : encantado

overland ['o:vər,lænd, -lənd] *adv & adj* : por tierra

overlap [,o:vər'læp] *v* **-lapped; -lapping** *vt* : traslapar — *vi* : traslaparse

overload [,o:vər'lo:d] *vt* : sobrecargar

overlook [,o:vər'lʊk] *vt* 1 : dar a (un jardín, el mar, etc.) 2 MISS : pasar por alto

overly ['o:vərli] *adv* : demasiado

overnight [,o:vər'naɪt] *adv* 1 : por la noche 2 SUDDENLY : de la noche a la mañana — ~ ['o:vər,naɪt] *adj* 1 : de noche 2 SUDDEN : repentino

overpass ['o:vər,pæs] *n* : paso *m* elevado

overpopulated [,o:vər'papjə,leɪtəd] *adj* : superpoblado

overpower [,o:vər'paʊər] *vt* 1 SUBDUE : dominar 2 OVERWHELM : agobiar, abrumar

overrated [,o:vər'reɪtəd] *adj* : sobreestimado

override [,o:vər'raɪd] *vt* **-rode** [-'ro:d]; **-ridden** [-'rɪdən]; **-riding** 1 : predominar sobre 2 : anular (una decisión, etc.)

overrule [,o:vər'ru:l] *vt* **-ruled; -ruling** : anular (una decisión), rechazar (una protesta)

overrun [,o:vər'rʌn] *vt* **-ran** [-'ræn]; **-running** 1 INVADE : invadir 2 EXCEED : exceder

overseas [,o:vər'si:z] *adv* : en el extranjero — **∼** ['o:vər,si:z] *adj* : extranjero, exterior
oversee [,o:vər'si:] *vt* **-saw** [-'sɔ]; **-seen** [-'si:n]; **-seeing** : supervisar
overshadow [,o:vər'ʃædo:] *vt* : eclipsar
oversight ['o:vər,saɪt] *n* : descuido *m*
oversleep [,o:vər'sli:p] *vi* **-slept** [-'slɛpt]; **-sleeping** : quedarse dormido
overstep [,o:vər'stɛp] *vt* **-stepped**; **-stepping** : sobrepasar
overt [o'vərt, 'o:,vərt] *adj* : manifiesto
overtake [,o:vər'teɪk] *vt* **-took** [-'tʊk]; **-taken** [-'teɪkən]; **-taking 1** PASS : adelantar **2** SURPASS : superar
overthrow [,o:vər'θro:] *vt* **-threw** [-'θru:]; **-thrown** [-'θro:n]; **-throwing** : derrocar
overtime ['o:vər,taɪm] *n* **1** : horas *fpl* extras (de trabajo) **2** : prórroga *f* (en deportes)
overtone ['o:vər,to:n] *n* SUGGESTION : tinte *m*, insinuación *f*
overture ['o:vər,tʃʊr, -,tʃər] *n* : obertura *f* (en música)
overturn [,o:vər'tərn] *vt* **1** : dar la vuelta a **2** NULLIFY : anular — *vi* : volcar

overweight [,o:vər'weɪt] *adj* : demasiado gordo
overwhelm [,o:vər'hwɛlm] *vt* **1** : abrumar, agobiar **2** : aplastar (a un enemigo) — **overwhelming** [,o:vər'hwɛlmɪŋ] *adj* : abrumador, apabullante
overwork [,o:vər'wərk] *vt* : hacer trabajar demasiado — *vi* : trabajar demasiado
overwrought [,o:vər'rɔt] *adj* : alterado, sobreexitado
owe ['o:] *vt* **owed; owing** : deber — **owing to** *prep* : debido a
owl ['aʊl] *n* : búho *m*
own ['o:n] *adj* : propio — **∼** *vt* : poseer, tener — *vi* **∼ up** : confesar — **∼** *pron* **1 my (your, his/her/their, our) ∼** : el mío, la mía; el tuyo, la tuya; el suyo, la suya; el nuestro, la nuestra **2 be on one's ∼** : estar solo **3 to each his ∼** : cada uno a lo suyo — **owner** ['o:nər] *n* : propietario *m*, -ria *f* — **ownership** ['o:nər,ʃɪp] *n* : propiedad *f*
ox ['ɑks] *n*, *pl* **oxen** ['ɑksən] : buey *m*
oxygen ['ɑksɪdʒən] *n* : oxígeno *m*
oyster ['ɔɪstər] *n* : ostra *f*
ozone ['o:,zo:n] *n* : ozono *m*

P

p ['pi:] *n*, *pl* **p's** *or* **ps** ['pi:z] : p *f*, decimosexta letra del alfabeto inglés
pace ['peɪs] *n* **1** STEP : paso *m* **2** RATE : ritmo *m* **3 keep ∼ with** : andar al mismo paso que — **∼** *vi* **paced; pacing** *or* **∼ up and down** : caminar de arriba para abajo
pacify ['pæsə,faɪ] *vt* **-fied; -fying** : apaciguar — **pacifier** ['pæsə,faɪər] *n* : chupete *m* — **pacifist** ['pæsəfɪst] *n* : pacifista *mf*
pack ['pæk] *n* **1** BUNDLE : fardo *m* **2** BACKPACK : mochila *f* **3** PACKAGE : paquete *m* **4** : baraja *f* (de naipes) **5** : manada *f* (de lobos, etc.), jauría *f* (de perros) — **∼** *vt* **1** PACKAGE : empaquetar **2** FILL : llenar **3** : hacer (una maleta) — *vi* : hacer las maletas — **package** ['pækɪdʒ] *vt* **-aged; -aging** : empaquetar — **∼** *n* : paquete *m* — **packet** ['pækət] *n* : paquete *m*
pact ['pækt] *n* : pacto *m*, acuerdo *m*
pad ['pæd] *n* **1** CUSHION : almohadilla *f* **2** TABLET : bloc *m* (de papel) **3** *or* **ink ∼** ~~tampón~~ *m* **4 launching ∼** : plataforma ~~(de lanzamiento)~~ — **∼** *vt* ~~padding~~ : rellenar — **pad-**

ding ['pædɪŋ] *n* **1** : relleno *m* **2** : paja *f* (en un discurso, etc.)
paddle ['pædəl] *n* **1** : canalete *m* (de una canoa) **2** : pala *f*, paleta *f* (en deportes) — **∼** *vt* **-dled; -dling** : hacer avanzar (una canoa) con canalete
padlock ['pæd,lɑk] *n* : candado *m* — **∼** *vt* : cerrar con candado
pagan ['peɪgən] *n* : pagano *m*, -na *f* — **∼** *adj* : pagano
page¹ ['peɪdʒ] *vt* **paged; paging** : llamar por altavoz
page² *n* : página *f* (de un libro, etc.)
pageant ['pædʒənt] *n* : espectáculo *m* — **pageantry** ['pædʒəntri] *n* : pompa *f*, boato *m*
paid → **pay**
pail ['peɪl] *n* : cubo *m* Spain, cubeta *f* Lat
pain ['peɪn] *n* **1** : dolor *m* **2** : pena *f* (mental) **3** **∼s** *npl* EFFORT : esfuerzos *mpl* — **∼** *vt* : doler — **painful** ['peɪnfəl] *adj* : doloroso — **painkiller** ['peɪn,kɪlər] *n* : analgésico *m* — **painless** ['peɪnləs] *adj* : indoloro, sin dolor — **painstaking** ['peɪn,steɪkɪŋ] *adj* : meticuloso, esmerado
paint ['peɪnt] *v* : pintar — **∼** *n* : pintura

f — **paintbrush** ['peɪnt̬brʌʃ] *n* : pincel *m* (de un artista), brocha *f* (para pintar casas, etc.) — **painter** ['peɪntər] *n* : pintor *m*, -tora *f* — **painting** ['peɪntɪŋ] *n* : pintura *f*

pair ['pær] *n* **1** : par *m* **2** COUPLE : pareja *f* — *vt* : emparejar

pajamas [pəˈdʒɑməz, -ˈdʒæ-] *npl* : pijama *m*, piyama *mf Lat*

Pakistani [ˌpækɪˈstæni, ˌpɑkɪˈstɑni] *adj* : paquistaní

pal ['pæl] *n* : amigo *m*, -ga *f*

palace ['pæləs] *n* : palacio *m*

palate ['pælət] *n* : paladar *m* — **palatable** ['pælət̬əbəl] *adj* : sabroso

pale ['peɪl] *adj* **paler; palest 1** PALLID : pálido **2** : claro (dícese de los colores, etc.) — *~ vi* **paled; paling** : palidecer — **paleness** ['peɪlnəs] *n* : palidez *f*

Palestinian [ˌpæləˈstɪniən] *adj* : palestino

palette ['pælət] *n* : paleta *f*

pallbearer ['pɔlˌberər] *n* : portador *m*, -dora *f* del féretro

pallid ['pæləd] *adj* : pálido — **pallor** ['pælər] *n* : palidez *f*

palm[1] ['pɑm, 'pɑlm] *n* : palma *f* (de la mano)

palm[2] *or ~* **tree** : palmera *f* — **Palm Sunday** *n* : Domingo *m* de Ramos

palpitate ['pælpəˌteɪt] *vi* **-tated; -tating** : palpitar — **palpitation** [ˌpælpəˈteɪʃən] *n* : palpitación *f*

paltry ['pɔltri] *adj* **-trier; -est** : mísero, mezquino

pamper ['pæmpər] *vt* : mimar

pamphlet ['pæmflət] *n* : panfleto *m*, folleto *m*

pan ['pæn] *n* **1** SAUCEPAN : cacerola *f* **2** FRYING PAN : sartén *mf* — *~ vt* **panned; panning** CRITICIZE : poner por los suelos

pancake ['pænˌkeɪk] *n* : crepe *mf*, panqueque *m Lat*

panda ['pændə] *n* : panda *mf*

pandemonium [ˌpændəˈmoːniəm] *n* : pandemonio *m*

pander ['pændər] *vi ~* **to** : complacer a

pane ['peɪn] *n* : cristal *m*, vidrio *m*

panel ['pænəl] *n* **1** : panel *m* **2** GROUP : jurado *m* **3** *or* **instrument ~** : tablero *m* (de instrumentos) — *~ vt* **-eled** *or* **-elled; -eling** *or* **-elling** : adornar con paneles — **paneling** ['pænəlɪŋ] *n* : paneles *mpl*

pang ['pæŋ] *n* : punzada *f*

panic ['pænɪk] *n* : pánico *m* — *~ v* **-icked; -icking** *vt* : llenar del pánico — *vi* : ser presa del pánico — **panicky** ['pæniki] *adj* : presa de pánico

panorama [ˌpænəˈræmə, -ˈrɑ-] *n* : panorama *m* — **panoramic** [ˌpænəˈræmɪk, -ˈrɑ-] *adj* : panorámico

pansy ['pænzi] *n*, *pl* **-sies** : pensamiento *m*

pant ['pænt] *vi* : jadear, resoplar

panther ['pænθər] *n* : pantera *f*

panties ['pæntiz] *npl* : bragas *fpl Spain*, calzones *mpl Lat*

pantomime ['pæntəˌmaɪm] *n* : pantomima *f*

pantry ['pæntri] *n*, *pl* **-tries** : despensa *f*

pants ['pænts] *npl* TROUSERS : pantalón *m*, pantalones *mpl*

papa ['pɑpə] *n* : papá *m fam*

papal ['peɪpəl] *adj* : papal

papaya [pəˈpaɪə] *n* : papaya *f*

paper ['peɪpər] *n* **1** : papel *m* **2** DOCUMENT : documento *m* **3** NEWSPAPER : periódico *m* — *~ vt* WALLPAPER : empapelar — *~ adj* : de papel — **paperback** ['peɪpərˌbæk] *n* : libro *m* en rústica — **paper clip** *n* : clip *m*, sujetapapeles *m* — **paperweight** ['peɪpərˌweɪt] *n* : pisapapeles *m* — **paperwork** ['peɪpərˌwɔrk] *n* : papeleo *m*

paprika [pəˈpriːkə, pæ-] *n* : pimentón *m*

par ['pɑr] *n* **1** : par *m* (en golf) **2 below ~** : debajo de la par **3 on a ~ with** : al nivel de

parable ['pærəbəl] *n* : parábola *f*

parachute ['pærəˌʃuːt] *n* : paracaídas *m* — *~ vi* **-chuted; -chuting** : lanzarse en paracaídas

parade [pəˈreɪd] *n* **1** : desfile *m* **2** DISPLAY : alarde *m* — *~ v* **-raded; -rading** *vi* MARCH : desfilar — *vt* DISPLAY : hacer alarde de

paradise ['pærəˌdaɪs, -ˌdaɪz] *n* : paraíso *m*

paradox ['pærəˌdɑks] *n* : paradoja *f* — **paradoxical** [ˌpærəˈdɑksɪkəl] *adj* : paradójico

paraffin ['pærəfən] *n* : parafina *f*

paragraph ['pærəˌgræf] *n* : párrafo *m*

Paraguayan [ˌpærəˈgwaɪən, -ˈgweɪ-] *adj* : paraguayo

parakeet ['pærəˌkiːt] *n* : periquito *m*

parallel ['pærəˌlel, -ləl] *adj* : paralelo — *~ n* **1** : paralelo *m* (en geografía) **2** SIMILARITY : paralelismo *m*, semejanza *f* — *~ vt* : ser paralelo a

paralysis [pəˈræləsɪs] *n*, *pl* **-yses** [-ˌsiːz] : parálisis *f* — **paralyze** *or Brit* **paralise** ['pærəˌlaɪz] *vt* **-lyzed** *or Brit* **-lised; -lyzing** *or Brit* **-lising** : paralizar

parameter [pəˈræmət̬ər] *n* : parámetro *m*

paramount ['pærəˌmaunt] *adj* **of ~ importance** : de suma importancia

paranoia [ˌpærəˈnɔɪə] *n* : paranoia *f* —
paranoid [ˈpærəˌnɔɪd] *adj* : paranoico
paraphernalia [ˌpærəfəˈneɪljə, -fər-] *ns*
& *pl* : parafernalia *f*
paraphrase [ˈpærəˌfreɪz] *n* : paráfrasis *f*
— ~ *vt* **-phrased; -phrasing** : parafrasear
paraplegic [ˌpærəˈpliːdʒɪk] *n* : parapléjico *m*, -ca *f*
parasite [ˈpærəˌsaɪt] *n* : parásito *m*
paratrooper [ˈpærəˌtruːpər] *n* : paracaidista *mf* (militar)
parcel [ˈpɑrsəl] *n* : paquete *m*
parch [ˈpɑrtʃ] *vt* : resecar
parchment [ˈpɑrtʃmənt] *n* : pergamino
m
pardon [ˈpɑrdən] *n* **1** : perdón *m* **2** RE-
PRIEVE : indulto *m* **3 I beg your** ~
: perdone Ud., disculpe Ud. *Lat* — ~
vt **1** : perdonar **2** REPRIEVE : indultar (a
un delincuente)
parent [ˈpærənt] *n* **1** : madre *f*, padre *m* **2**
~**s** *npl* : padres *mpl* — **parental** [pə-
ˈrentəl] *adj* : de los padres
parenthesis [pəˈrenθəsɪs] *n*, *pl* **-theses**
[-ˌsiːz] : paréntesis *m*
parish [ˈpærɪʃ] *n* : parroquia *f* — **parishioner** [pəˈrɪʃənər] *n* : feligrés *m*, -gresa
f
parity [ˈpærəti] *n*, *pl* **-ties** : igualdad *f*
park [ˈpɑrk] *n* : parque *m* — ~ *v* : estacionar, parquear *Lat*
parka [ˈpɑrkə] *n* : parka *f*
parking [ˈpɑrkɪŋ] *n* : estacionamiento *m*
parliament [ˈpɑrləmənt, ˈpɑrljə-] *n* : parlamento *m* — **parliamentary** [ˌpɑrlə-
ˈmentəri, ˌpɑrljə-] *adj* : parlamentario
parlor *or Brit* **parlour** [ˈpɑrlər] *n* : salón
m
parochial [pəˈroːkiəl] *adj* **1** : parroquial
2 PROVINCIAL : de miras estrechas
parody [ˈpærədi] *n*, *pl* **-dies** : parodia *f*
— ~ *vt* **-died; -dying** : parodiar
parole [pəˈroːl] *n* : libertad *f* condicional
parrot [ˈpærət] *n* : loro *m*, papagayo *m*
parry [ˈpæri] *vt* **-ried; -rying 1** : parar
(un golpe) **2** EVADE : eludir (una pregunta, etc.)
parsley [ˈpɑrsli] *n* : perejil *m*
parsnip [ˈpɑrsnɪp] *n* : chirivía *f*
parson [ˈpɑrsən] *n* : clérigo *m*
part [ˈpɑrt] *n* **1** : parte *f* **2** PIECE : pieza *f*
3 ROLE : papel *m* **4** : raya *f* (del pelo) —
~ *vi* **1** *or* ~ **company** : separarse **2**
~ **with** : dehacerse de — *vt* SEPARATE
: separar
partake [pɑrˈteɪk, pər-] *vi* **-took; -taken;
-taking** ~ **in** : participar en
partial [ˈpɑrʃəl] *adj* **1** : parcial **2 be** ~
to : ser aficionado a

participate [pərˈtɪsəˌpeɪt, pɑr-] *vi* **-pated;
-pating** : participar — **participant**
[pərˈtɪsəpənt, pɑr-] *n* : participante *mf*
participle [ˈpɑrtəˌsɪpəl] *n* : participio *m*
particle [ˈpɑrtɪkəl] *n* : partícula *f*
particular [pərˈtɪkjələr] *adj* **1** : particular
2 FUSSY : exigente — ~ *n* **1 in** ~ : en
particular, en especial **2** ~**s** *npl* DE-
TAILS : detalles *mpl* — **particularly**
[pərˈtɪkjələrli] *adv* : especialmente
partisan [ˈpɑrtəzən, -sən] *n* : partidario
m, -ria *f*
partition [pərˈtɪʃən, pɑr-] *n* **1** DISTRIBU-
TION : partición *f* **2** DIVIDER : tabique *m*
— ~ *vt* : dividir
partly [ˈpɑrtli] *adv* : en parte
partner [ˈpɑrtnər] *n* **1** : pareja *f* (en un
juego, etc.) **2** *or* **business** ~ : socio
m, -cia *f* — **partnership** [ˈpɑrtnərˌʃɪp] *n*
: asociación *f*
party [ˈpɑrti] *n*, *pl* **-ties 1** : partido *m*
(político) **2** GATHERING : fiesta *f* **3**
GROUP : grupo *m*
pass [ˈpæs] *vi* **1** : pasar **2** CEASE
: pasarse **3** : aprobar (en un examen) **4**
or ~ **away** DIE : morir **5** ~ **for** : pasar
por **6** ~ **out** FAINT : desmayarse — *vt*
1 : pasar **2** *or* ~ **in front of** : pasar
por **3** OVERTAKE : adelantar **4** : aprobar (un
examen, una ley, etc.) **5** ~ **down**
: transmitir — ~ *n* **1** PERMIT : pase *m*,
permiso *m* **2** : pase *m* (en deportes) **3**
or **mountain** ~ : paso *m* de montaña
— **passable** [ˈpæsəbəl] *adj* **1** ADE-
QUATE : adecuado **2** : transitable
(dícese de un camino, etc.) — **pas-
sage** [ˈpæsɪdʒ] *n* **1** : paso *m* **2** CORRI-
DOR : pasillo *m* (dentro de un edificio),
pasaje *m* (entre edificios) **3** VOYAGE
: travesía *f* (por el mar) — **passageway** [ˈpæsɪdʒˌweɪ] *n* : pasillo *m*, corredor *m*
passenger [ˈpæsəndʒər] *n* : pasajero *m*,
-ra *f*
passerby [ˌpæsərˈbaɪ, ˈpæsər-] *n*, *pl*
passersby : transeúnte *mf*
passion [ˈpæʃən] *n* : pasión *f* — **passionate** [ˈpæʃənət] *adj* : apasionado
passive [ˈpæsɪv] *adj* : pasivo
Passover [ˈpæsˌoːvər] *n* : Pascua *f* (en el
judaísmo)
passport [ˈpæsˌport] *n* : pasaporte *m*
password [ˈpæsˌwərd] *n* : contraseña *f*
past [ˈpæst] *adj* **1** : pasado **2** FORMER
: anterior **3 the** ~ **few months** : los
últimos meses — ~ *prep* **1** IN FRONT
OF : por delante de **2** BEYOND : más
allá de **3 half** ~ **two** : las dos y media
— ~ *n* : pasado *m* — ~ *adv* : por delante

pasta ['pɑstə, 'pæs-] n : pasta f
paste ['peɪst] n 1 : pasta f 2 GLUE : engrudo m — ~ vt **pasted; pasting** : pegar
pastel [pæ'stɛl] n : pastel m — ~ adj : pastel
pasteurize ['pæstʃəˌraɪz, 'pæstjə-] vt **-ized; -izing** : pasteurizar
pastime ['pæsˌtaɪm] n : pasatiempo m
pastor ['pæstər] n : pastor m, -tora f
pastry ['peɪstri] n, pl **-ries** : pasteles mpl
pasture ['pæstʃər] n : pasto m
pasty ['peɪsti] adj **pastier; -est 1** DOUGHY : pastoso 2 PALLID : pálido
pat ['pæt] n 1 : palmadita f 2 **a ~ of** butter : una porción de mantequilla — ~ vt **patted; patting** : dar palmaditas a — ~ adv **have down** ~ : saberse de memoria — ~ adj GLIB : fácil
patch ['pætʃ] n 1 : parche m, remiendo m (para la ropa) 2 SPOT : mancha f, trozo m 3 PLOT : parcela f (de tierra) — ~ vt 1 MEND : remendar 2 ~ **up** : arreglar — **patchy** ['pætʃi] adj **patchier; -est 1** : desigual 2 INCOMPLETE : parcial, incompleto
patent adj ['pætənt] **1** or **patented** ['pætəntəd] : patentado 2 ['pætənt, 'peɪt-] OBVIOUS : patente, evidente — ~ ['pætənt] n : patente f — ~ ['pætənt] vt : patentar
paternal [pə'tərnəl] adj **1** FATHERLY : paternal 2 ~ **grandmother** : abuela f paterna — **paternity** [pə'tərnəṭi] n : paternidad f
path ['pæθ, 'paθ] n **1** TRACK, TRAIL : camino m, sendero m 2 COURSE : trayectoria f
pathetic [pə'θɛṭɪk] adj : patético
pathology [pə'θɑlədʒi] n, pl **-gies** : patología f
pathway ['pæθˌweɪ] n : camino m, sendero m
patience ['peɪʃənts] n : paciencia f — **patient** ['peɪʃənt] adj : paciente — ~ n : paciente mf — **patiently** adv : con paciencia
patio ['pæṭiˌoː] n, pl **-tios** : patio m
patriot ['peɪtriət] n : patriota mf — **patriotic** [ˌpeɪtri'ɑṭɪk] adj : patriótico
patrol [pə'troːl] n : patrulla f — ~ v **-trolled; -trolling** : patrullar
patron ['peɪtrən] n **1** SPONSOR : patrocinador m, -dora f 2 CUSTOMER : cliente m, -ta f — **patronage** ['peɪtrənɪdʒ, 'pæ-] n 1 SPONSORSHIP : patrocinio m 2 CLIENTELE : clientela f — **patronize** ['peɪtrəˌnaɪz, 'pæ-] vt **-ized; -izing 1** : ser cliente de (una tienda, etc.) 2 : tratar (a algn) con condescencia

patter ['pæṭər] n : tamborileo m (de la lluvia), correteo m (de los pies)
pattern ['pæṭərn] n **1** MODEL : modelo m 2 DESIGN : diseño m 3 STANDARD : pauta f, modo m 4 : patrón m (en costura) — ~ vt : basar (en un modelo)
paunch ['pɔntʃ] n : panza f
pause ['pɔz] n : pausa f — ~ vi **paused; pausing** : hacer una pausa
pave ['peɪv] vt **paved; paving** : pavimentar — **pavement** ['peɪvmənt] n : pavimento m
pavilion [pə'vɪljən] n : pabellón m
paw ['pɔ] n **1** : pata f 2 : garra f (de un gato) — ~ vt : tocar con la pata
pawn[1] ['pɔn] n : peón m (en ajedrez)
pawn[2] vt : empeñar — **pawnbroker** ['pɔnˌbroːkər] n : prestamista mf — **pawnshop** ['pɔnˌʃɑp] n : casa f de empeños
pay ['peɪ] v **paid** ['peɪd]; **paying** vt **1** : pagar 2 ~ **attention** : prestar atención 3 ~ **back** : devolver 4 ~ **one's respects** : presentar uno sus respetos 5 ~ **a visit** : hacer una visita — vi **1** : pagar 2 **crime doesn't** ~ : no hay crimen sin castigo — ~ n : paga f — **payable** ['peɪəbəl] adj : pagadero — **paycheck** ['peɪˌtʃɛk] n : cheque m del sueldo — **payment** ['peɪmənt] n **1** : pago m 2 INSTALLMENT : plazo m, cuota f Lat — **payroll** n : nómina f
PC [ˌpiːˈsiː] n, pl **PCs** or **PC's** : PC mf, computadora f personal
pea ['piː] n : guisante m, arveja f Lat
peace ['piːs] n : paz f — **peaceful** ['piːsfəl] adj **1** : pacífico 2 CALM : tranquilo
peach ['piːtʃ] n : melocotón m, durazno m Lat
peacock ['piːˌkɑk] n : pavo m real
peak ['piːk] n **1** SUMMIT : cumbre f, cima f, pico m (de una montaña) 2 APEX : nivel m máximo — ~ adj : máximo — ~ vi : alcanzar su nivel máximo
peal ['piːl] n **1** : repique m 2 ~**s of laughter** : carcajadas fpl
peanut ['piːˌnʌt] n : cacahuete m, maní m Lat
pear ['pær] n : pera f
pearl ['pərl] n : perla f
peasant ['pɛzənt] n : campesino m, -na f
peat ['piːt] n : turba f
pebble ['pɛbəl] n : guijarro m
pecan [pɪ'kɑn, -'kæn, 'piːˌkæn] n : pacana f, nuez f Lat
peck ['pɛk] vt : picar, picotear — ~ n **1** : picotazo m (de un pájaro) 2 KISS : besito
peculiar [pɪ'kjuːljər] adj **1** DISTINCTIVE

: peculiar, característico **2** STRANGE
: extraño, raro — **peculiarity** [pɪˌkjuːl-
ˈjærət̬i, -kjuːliʹær-] n, pl **-ties 1** : peculiaridad f **2** ODDITY : rareza f

pedal [ˈpɛdəl] n : pedal m — ~ vi **-aled**
or **-alled; -aling** or **-alling** : pedalear

pedantic [prˈdæntɪk] adj : pedante

peddle [ˈpɛdəl] vt **-dled; -dling** : vender
en las calles — **peddler** [ˈpɛdlər] n
: vendedor m, **-dora** f ambulante

pedestal [ˈpɛdəstəl] n : pedestal m

pedestrian [pəˈdɛstriən] n : peatón m,
-tona f — ~ adj ~ **crossing** : paso m
de peatones

pediatrics [ˌpiːdiˈætrɪks] ns & pl : pedi-
atría f — **pediatrician** [ˌpiːdiəˈtrɪʃən] n
: pediatra mf

pedigree [ˈpɛdəˌgriː] n : pedigrí m (de un
animal), linaje m (de una persona)

peek [ˈpiːk] vi : mirar a hurtadillas — ~
n : miradita f (furtiva)

peel [ˈpiːl] vt : pelar (fruta, etc.) — vi
: pelarse (dícese de la piel), descon-
charse (dícese de la pintura) — ~ n
: piel f, cáscara f

peep[1] [ˈpiːp] vi CHEEP : piar — ~ n : pío
m (de un pajarito)

peep[2] vi **1** PEEK : mirar a hurtadillas **2**
or ~ **out** : asomar — ~ n GLANCE
: mirada f (furtiva)

peer[1] [ˈpɪr] n : par mf

peer[2] vi : mirar (con atención)

peeve [ˈpiːv] vt : irritar — **peevish**
[ˈpiːvɪʃ] adj : malhumorado

peg [ˈpɛg] n **1** : clavija f **2** HOOK : gancho
m

pelican [ˈpɛlɪkən] n : pelícano m

pellet [ˈpɛlət] n **1** : bolita f **2** SHOT
: perdigón m

pelt[1] [ˈpɛlt] n : piel f (de un animal)

pelt[2] vt : lanzar (algo a algn)

pelvis [ˈpɛlvɪs] n, pl **-vises** or **-ves** [ˈpɛl-
ˌviːz] : pelvis f — **pelvic** [ˈpɛlvɪk] adj
: pélvico

pen[1] [ˈpɛn] vt **penned; penning** EN-
CLOSE : encerrar — ~ n : corral m,
redil m

pen[2] n **1** or **ballpoint** ~ : bolígrafo m **2**
or **fountain** ~ : pluma f

penal [ˈpiːnəl] adj : penal — **penalize**
[ˈpiːnəˌlaɪz, ˈpɛn-] vt **-ized; -izing** : penalizar — **penalty** [ˈpɛnəlti] n, pl **-ties**
1 : pena f, castigo m **2** : penalty m (en
deportes)

penance [ˈpɛnənts] n : penitencia f

pencil [ˈpɛntsəl] n : lápiz m — **pencil
sharpener** n : sacapuntas m

pendant [ˈpɛndənt] n : colgante m

pending [ˈpɛndɪŋ] adj : pendiente — ~
prep : en espera de

penetrate [ˈpɛnəˌtreɪt] v **-trated; -trating**
: penetrar — **penetrating** [ˈpɛnəˌtreɪ-
tɪŋ] adj : penetrante — **penetration**
[ˌpɛnəˈtreɪʃən] n : penetración f

penguin [ˈpɛŋgwɪn, ˈpɛn-] n : pingüino
m

penicillin [ˌpɛnəˈsɪlən] n : penicilina f

peninsula [pəˈnɪntsələ, -ˈnɪntʃʊlə] n : península f

penis [ˈpiːnəs] n, pl **-nes** [-ˌniːz] or
-nises : pene m

penitentiary [ˌpɛnəˈtɛntʃəri] n, pl **-ries**
: penitenciaría f

pen name n : seudónimo m

pennant [ˈpɛnənt] n : banderín m

penny [ˈpɛni] n, pl **-nies** or **pence**
[ˈpɛnts] : centavo m (de los Estados
Unidos), penique m (del Reino Unido)
— **penniless** [ˈpɛniləs] adj : sin un
centavo

pension [ˈpɛntʃən] n : pensión m, jubilación f

pensive [ˈpɛntsɪv] adj : pensativo

pentagon [ˈpɛntəˌgɑn] n : pentágono m

penthouse [ˈpɛntˌhaʊs] n : ático m

pent–up [ˈpɛntˌʌp] adj : reprimido

people [ˈpiːpəl] ns & pl **1** people npl
: gente f, personas fpl **2** pl ~**s**
: pueblo m

pep [ˈpɛp] n : energía f, vigor m — ~ vt
or ~ **up** : animar

pepper [ˈpɛpər] n **1** : pimienta f (condimento) **2** : pimiento m (fruta) — **peppermint** [ˈpɛpərˌmɪnt] n : menta f

per [ˈpər] prep **1** : por **2** ACCORDING TO
: según **3** ~ **day** : al día **4 miles** ~
hour : millas fpl por hora

perceive [pərˈsiːv] vt **-ceived; -ceiving**
: percibir

percent [pərˈsɛnt] adv : por ciento —
percentage [pərˈsɛntɪdʒ] n : porcentaje m

perception [pərˈsɛpʃən] n : percepción f
— **perceptive** [pərˈsɛptɪv] adj : perspicaz

perch[1] [ˈpərtʃ] n : percha f (para los pájaros) — ~ vi : posarse

perch[2] n : perca f (pez)

percolate [ˈpərkəˌleɪt] vi **-lated; -lating**
: filtrarse — **percolator** [ˈpərkəˌleɪt̬ər]
n : cafetera f de filtro

percussion [pərˈkʌʃən] n : percusión f

perennial [pəˈrɛniəl] adj : perenne — ~
n : planta f perenne

perfect [ˈpərfɪkt] adj : perfecto — ~
[pərˈfɛkt] vt : perfeccionar — **perfection** [pərˈfɛkʃən] n : perfección f —
perfectionist [pərˈfɛkʃənɪst] n : perfeccionista mf

perforate ['pərfə‚reɪt] *vt* **-rated; -rating** : perforar

perform [pər'fɔrm] *vt* **1** CARRY OUT : realizar, hacer **2** : representar (una obra teatral), interpretar (una obra musical) — *vi* **1** FUNCTION : funcionar **2** ACT : actuar — **performance** [pər'fɔrmənt̬s] *n* **1** : realización *f* **2** INTERPRETATION : interpretación *f* **3** PRESENTATION : representación *f* — **performer** [pər'fɔrmər] *n* : actor *m*, -triz *f*; intérprete *mf* (de música)

perfume ['pər‚fjuːm, pər-] *n* : perfume *m*

perhaps [pər'hæps] *adv* : tal vez, quizá, quizás

peril ['perəl] *n* : peligro *m* — **perilous** ['perələs] *adj* : peligroso

perimeter [pə'rɪmət̬ər] *n* : perímetro *m*

period ['pɪriəd] *n* **1** : período *m* (de tiempo) **2** : punto *m* (en puntuación) **3** ERA : época *f* — **periodic** [‚pɪri'ɑdɪk] *adj* : periódico — **periodical** [‚pɪri'ɑdɪkəl] *n* : revista *f*

peripheral [pə'rɪfərəl] *adj* : periférico

perish ['perɪʃ] *vi* : perecer — **perishable** ['perɪʃəbəl] *adj* : perecedero — **perishables** ['perɪʃəbəlz] *npl* : productos *mpl* perecederos

perjury ['pərdʒəri] *n* : perjurio *m*

perk ['pərk] *vi* ~ **up** : animarse, reanimarse — ~ *n* : extra *m* — **perky** ['pərki] *adj* **perkier; -est** : alegre

permanence ['pərmənənt̬s] *n* : permanencia *f* — **permanent** ['pərmənənt] *adj* : permanente — ~ *n* : permanente *f*

permeate ['pərmi‚eɪt] *v* **-ated; -ating** : penetrar

permission [pər'mɪʃən] *n* : permiso *m* — **permissible** [pər'mɪsəbəl] *adj* : permisible — **permissive** [pər'mɪsɪv] *adj* : permisivo — **permit** [pər'mɪt] *vt* **-mitted; -mitting** : permitir — ~ ['pər‚mɪt, pər-] *n* : permiso *m*

peroxide [pə'rɑk‚saɪd] *n* : peróxido *m*

perpendicular [‚pərpən'dɪkjələr] *adj* : perpendicular

perpetrate ['pərpə‚treɪt] *vt* **-trated; -trating** : cometer — **perpetrator** ['pərpə‚treɪt̬ər] *n* : autor *m*, -tora *f* (de un delito)

perpetual [pər'pet̬ʃuəl] *adj* : perpetuo

perplex [pər'pleks] *vt* : dejar perplejo — **perplexing** [pər'pleksɪŋ] *adj* : desconcertante — **perplexity** [pər'pleksət̬i] *n*, *pl* **-ties** : perplejidad *f*

persecute ['pərsɪ‚kjuːt] *vt* **-cuted; -cuting** : perseguir — **persecution** [‚pərsɪ'kjuːʃən] *n* : persecución *f*

persevere [‚pərsə'vɪr] *vi* **-vered; -vering**

: perseverar — **perseverance** [‚pərsə'vɪrənt̬s] *n* : perseverancia *f*

persist [pər'sɪst] *vi* : persistir — **persistence** [pər'sɪstənt̬s] *n* : persistencia *f* — **persistent** [pər'sɪstənt] *adj* : persistente

person ['pərsən] *n* : persona *f* — **personal** ['pərsənəl] *adj* : personal — **personality** [‚pərsən'ælət̬i] *n*, *pl* **-ties** : personalidad *f* — **personally** ['pərsənəli] *adv* : personalmente, en persona — **personnel** [‚pərsən'el] *n* : personal *m*

perspective [pər'spektɪv] *n* : perspectiva *f*

perspiration [‚pərspə'reɪʃən] *n* : transpiración *f* — **perspire** [pər'spaɪr] *vi* **-spired; -spiring** : transpirar

persuade [pər'sweɪd] *vt* **-suaded; -suading** : persuadir — **persuasion** [pər'sweɪʒən] *n* : persuasión *f*

pertain [pər'teɪn] *vi* ~ **to** : estar relacionado con — **pertinent** ['pərtənənt] *adj* : pertinente

perturb [pər'tərb] *vt* : perturbar

Peruvian [pə'ruːviən] *adj* : peruano

pervade [pər'veɪd] *vt* **-vaded; -vading** : penetrar — **pervasive** [pər'veɪsɪv, -zɪv] *adj* : penetrante

perverse [pər'vərs] *adj* **1** CORRUPT : perverso **2** STUBBORN : obstinado — **pervert** ['pər‚vərt] *n* : pervertido *m*, -da *f*

peso ['peɪ‚soː] *n*, *pl* **-sos** : peso *m*

pessimism ['pesə‚mɪzəm] *n* : pesimismo *m* — **pessimist** ['pesəmɪst] *n* : pesimista *mf* — **pessimistic** [‚pesə'mɪstɪk] *adj* : pesimista

pest ['pest] *n* **1** : insecto *m* nocivo, animal *m* nocivo **2** : peste *f fam* (persona)

pester ['pestər] *vt* **-tered; -tering** : molestar

pesticide ['pestə‚saɪd] *n* : pesticida *m*

pet ['pet] *n* **1** : animal *m* doméstico **2** FAVORITE : favorito *m*, -ta *f* — ~ *vt* **petted; petting** : acariciar

petal ['pet̬əl] *n* : pétalo *m*

petite [pə'tiːt] *adj* : chiquita

petition [pə'tɪʃən] *n* : petición *f* — ~ *vt* : dirigir una petición a

petrify ['petrə‚faɪ] *vt* **-fied; -fying** : petrificar

petroleum [pə'troːliəm] *n* : petróleo *m*

petticoat ['pet̬i‚koːt] *n* : enagua *f*, fondo *m Lat*

petty ['pet̬i] *adj* **-tier; -est 1** UNIMPORTANT : insignificante, nimio **2** MEAN : mezquino — **pettiness** ['pet̬inəs] *n* : mezquindad *f*

petulant ['petʃələnt] *adj* : irritable, de mal genio

pew ['pjuː] *n* : banco *m* (de iglesia)

pewter ['pju:t̬ər] *n* : peltre *m*

phallic ['fælɪk] *adj* : fálico

phantom ['fæntəm] *n* : fantasma *m*

pharmacy ['fɑrməsi] *n, pl* **-cies** : farmacia *f* — **pharmacist** ['fɑrməsɪst] *n* : farmacéutico *m*, -ca *f*

phase ['feɪz] *n* : fase *f* — ~ *vt* **phased; phasing 1** ~ **in** : introducir progresivamente **2** ~ **out** : retirar progresivamente

phenomenon [fɪ'nɑmənɑn, -nən] *n, pl* **-na** [-nə] *or* **-nons** : fenómeno *m* — **phenomenal** [fɪ'nɑmənəl] *adj* : fenomenal

philanthropy [fə'lænθrəpi] *n, pl* **-pies** : filantropía *f* — **philanthropist** [fə'lænθrəpɪst] *n* : filántropo *m*, -pa *f*

philosophy [fə'lɑsəfi] *n, pl* **-phies** : filosofía *f* — **philosopher** [fə'lɑsəfər] *n* : filósofo *m*, -fa *f*

phlegm ['flɛm] *n* : flema *f*

phobia ['fo:biə] *n* : fobia *f*

phone ['fo:n] → **telephone**

phonetic [fə'nɛt̬ɪk] *adj* : fonético

phony *or* **phoney** ['fo:ni] *adj* **-nier; -est** : falso — ~ *n, pl* **-nies** : farsante *mf*

phosphorus ['fɑsfərəs] *n* : fósforo *m*

photo ['fo:t̬o:] *n, pl* **-tos** : foto *f* — **photocopier** ['fo:t̬o,kɑpiər] *n* : fotocopiadora *f* — **photocopy** ['fo:t̬o,kɑpi] *n, pl* **-copies** : fotocopia *f* — ~ *vt* **-copied; -copying** : fotocopiar — **photograph** ['fo:t̬ə,græf] *n* : fotografía *f*, foto *f* — ~ *vt* : fotografiar — **photographer** [fə'tɑgrəfər] *n* : fotógrafo *m*, -fa *f* — **photographic** [,fo:t̬ə'græfɪk] *adj* : fotográfico — **photography** [fə'tɑgrəfi] *n* : fotografía *f*

phrase ['freɪz] *n* : frase *f* — ~ *vt* **phrased; phrasing** : expresar

physical ['fɪzɪkəl] *adj* : físico — ~ *n* : reconocimiento *m* médico

physician [fə'zɪʃən] *n* : médico *m*, -ca *f*

physics ['fɪzɪks] *ns & pl* : física *f* — **physicist** ['fɪzəsɪst] *n* : físico *m*, -ca *f*

physiology [,fɪzi'ɑlədʒi] *n* : fisiología *f*

physique [fə'zi:k] *n* : físico *m*

piano [pi'æno:] *n, pl* **-anos** : piano *m* — **pianist** [pi'ænɪst, 'pi:ənɪst] *n* : pianista *mf*

pick ['pɪk] *vt* **1** CHOOSE : escoger **2** GATHER : recoger **3** REMOVE : quitar (poco a poco) **4** ~ **a fight** : buscar camorra — *vi* **1** ~ **and choose** : ser exigente **2** ~ **on** : meterse con — ~ *n* **1** CHOICE : selección *f* **2** *or* **pickax** ['pɪk,æks] : pico *m* **3 the** ~ **of** : lo mejor de

picket ['pɪkət] *n* **1** STAKE : estaca *f* **2** ~ **line** : piquete *m* — ~ *v* : piquetear

pickle ['pɪkəl] *n* **1** : pepinillo *m* (encurtido) **2** JAM : lío *m fam*, apuro *m* — ~ *vt* **-led; -ling** : encurtir

pickpocket ['pɪk,pɑkət] *n* : carterista *mf*

pickup ['pɪk,əp] *n* **1** IMPROVEMENT : mejora *f* **2** *or* ~ **truck** : camioneta *f* — **pick up** *vt* **1** LIFT : levantar **2** TIDY : arreglar, ordenar — *vi* IMPROVE : mejorar

picnic ['pɪk,nɪk] *n* : picnic *m* — ~ *vi* **-nicked; -nicking** : ir de picnic

picture ['pɪkt̬ʃər] *n* **1** PAINTING : cuadro *m* **2** DRAWING : dibujo *m* **3** PHOTO : fotografía *f* **4** IMAGE : imagen *f* **5** MOVIE : película *f* — ~ *vt* **-tured; -turing 1** DEPICT : representar **2** IMAGINE : imaginarse — **picturesque** [,pɪkt̬ʃə'rɛsk] *adj* : pintoresco

pie ['paɪ] *n* : pastel *m* (con fruta o carne), empanada *f* (con carne)

piece ['pi:s] *n* **1** : pieza *f* **2** FRAGMENT : trozo *m*, pedazo *m* **3 a** ~ **of advice** : un consejo — ~ *vt* **pieced; piecing** *or* ~ **together** : juntar, componer — **piecemeal** ['pi:s,mi:l] *adv* : poco a poco — ~ *adj* : poco sistemático

pier ['pɪr] *n* : muelle *m*

pierce ['pɪrs] *vt* **pierced; piercing** : perforar — **piercing** *adj* : penetrante

piety ['paɪət̬i] *n, pl* **-eties** : piedad *f*

pig ['pɪg] *n* : cerdo *m*, -da *f*; puerco *m*, -ca *f*

pigeon ['pɪdʒən] *n* : paloma *f* — **pigeonhole** ['pɪdʒən,ho:l] *n* : casilla *f*

piggyback ['pɪgi,bæk] *adv & adj* : a cuestas

pigment ['pɪgmənt] *n* : pigmento *m*

pigpen ['pɪg,pɛn] *n* : pocilga *f*

pigtail ['pɪg,teɪl] *n* : coleta *f*, trenza *f*

pile¹ ['paɪl] *n* HEAP : montón *m*, pila *f* — ~ *v* **piled; piling** *vt* : amontonar, apilar — *vi* ~ **up** : amontonarse, acumularse

pile² *n* NAP : pelo *m* (de telas)

pilfer ['pɪlfər] *vt* : robar, hurtar

pilgrim ['pɪlgrəm] *n* : peregrino *m*, -na *f* — **pilgrimage** ['pɪlgrəmɪdʒ] *n* : peregrinación *f*

pill ['pɪl] *n* : pastilla *f*, píldora *f*

pillage ['pɪlɪdʒ] *n* : saqueo *m* — ~ *vt* **-laged; -laging** : saquear

pillar ['pɪlər] *n* : pilar *m*, columna *f*

pillow ['pɪ,lo:] *n* : almohada *f* — **pillowcase** ['pɪ,lo:,keɪs] *n* : funda *f* (de almohada)

pilot ['paɪlət] *n* : piloto *mf* — ~ *vt* : pilotar, pilotear — **pilot light** *n* : piloto *m*

pimp ['pɪmp] *n* : proxeneta *m*

pimple ['pɪmpəl] *n* : grano *m*

pin ['pɪn] *n* **1** : alfiler *m* **2** BROOCH

: broche *m* **3** *or* **bowling** ~ : bolo *m*
— ~ *vt* **pinned; pinning 1** FASTEN
: prender, sujetar (con alfileres) **2** *or*
~ **down** : inmovilizar

pincers ['pɪntsərz] *npl* : tenazas *fpl*

pinch ['pɪntʃ] *vt* **1** : pellizcar **2** STEAL
: robar — *vi* : apretar — ~ *n* **1** : pellizco *m* **2** BIT : pizca *f* **3 in a** ~ : en
caso necesario

pine¹ ['paɪn] *n* : pino *m* (árbol)

pine² *vi* **pined; pining 1** LANGUISH
: languidecer **2** ~ **for** : suspirar por

pineapple ['paɪnˌæpəl] *n* : piña *f*, ananás
m

pink ['pɪŋk] *n* : rosa *m*, rosado *m* — ~
adj : rosa, rosado

pinnacle ['pɪnɪkəl] *n* : pináculo *m*

pinpoint ['pɪnˌpɔɪnt] *vt* : localizar, precisar

pint ['paɪnt] *n* : pinta *f*

pioneer [ˌpaɪəˈnɪr] *n* : pionero *m*, -ra *f*

pious ['paɪəs] *adj* : piadoso

pipe ['paɪp] *n* **1** : tubo *m*, caño *m* **2** : pipa
f (para fumar) — **pipeline** ['paɪpˌlaɪn] *n*
1 : conducto *m*, oleoducto *m* (para
petróleo)

piquant ['piːkənt, 'pɪkwənt] *adj* : picante

pique ['piːk] *n* : resentimiento *m*

pirate ['paɪrət] *n* : pirata *mf*

pistachio [pəˈstæʃiˌoː, -ˈstɑ-] *n, pl* **-chios**
: pistacho *m*

pistol ['pɪstəl] *n* : pistola *f*

piston ['pɪstən] *n* : pistón *m*

pit ['pɪt] *n* **1** HOLE : hoyo *m*, fosa *f* **2** MINE
: mina *f* **3** : hueso *m* (de una fruta) **4** ~
of the stomach : boca *f* del estómago
— ~ *vt* **pitted; pitting 1** : marcar de
hoyos **2** : deshuesar (una fruta) **3** ~
against : enfrentar a

pitch ['pɪtʃ] *vt* **1** : armar (una tienda) **2**
THROW : lanzar — *vi* **1** *or* ~ **forward**
: caerse **2** LURCH : cabecear (dícese de
un barco o un avión) — ~ *n* **1** DE-
GREE, LEVEL : grado *m*, punto *m* **2**
TONE : tono *m* **3** THROW : lanzamiento
m **4** *or* **sales** ~ : presentación *f* (de
un vendedor)

pitcher ['pɪtʃər] *n* **1** JUG : jarro *m* **2** : lan-
zador *m*, -dora *f* (en béisbol, etc.)

pitchfork ['pɪtʃˌfɔrk] *n* : horquilla *f*,
horca *f*

pitfall ['pɪtˌfɔl] *n* : riesgo *m*, dificultad *f*

pith ['pɪθ] *n* **1** : médula *f* (de un hueso,
etc.) **2** CORE : meollo *m* — **pithy** ['pɪθi]
adj **pithier; -est** : conciso y sustancioso

pity ['pɪti] *n, pl* **pities 1** COMPASSION
: compasión *f* **2 what a** ~! : ¡qué lástima! — ~ *vt* **pitied; pitying** : compadecerse de — **pitiful** ['pɪtɪfəl] *adj*

: lastimoso — **pitiless** ['pɪtɪləs] *adj*
: despiadado

pivot ['pɪvət] *n* : pivote *m* — ~ *vi* **1**
: girar sobre un eje **2** ~ **on** : depender
de

pizza ['piːtsə] *n* : pizza *f*

placard ['plækərd, -ˌkɑrd] *n* POSTER : cartel *m*, póster *m*

placate ['pleɪˌkeɪt, 'plæ-] *vt* **-cated;**
-cating : apaciguar

place ['pleɪs] *n* **1** : sitio *m*, lugar *m* **2**
SEAT : asiento *m* **3** POSITION : puesto *m*
4 ROLE : papel *m* **5 take** ~ : tener
lugar **6 take the** ~ **of** : sustituir a —
~ *vt* **placed; placing 1** PUT, SET
: poner, colocar **2** IDENTIFY : identificar, recordar **3** ~ **an order** : hacer
un pedido — **placement** ['pleɪsmənt] *n*
: colocación *f*

placid ['plæsəd] *adj* : plácido, tranquilo

plagiarism ['pleɪdʒəˌrɪzəm] *n* : plagio *m*
— **plagiarize** ['pleɪdʒəˌraɪz] *vt* **-rized;**
-rizing : plagiar

plague ['pleɪg] *n* **1** : plaga *f* (de insectos,
etc.) **2** : peste *f* (en medicina)

plaid ['plæd] *n* : tela *f* escocesa — ~ *adj*
: escocés

plain ['pleɪn] *adj* **1** SIMPLE : sencillo **2**
CLEAR : claro, evidente **3** CANDID
: franco **4** HOMELY : poco atractivo **5 in**
~ **sight** : a la vista (de todos) — ~ *n*
: llanura *f*, planicie *f* — **plainly** ['pleɪn-
li] *adv* **1** CLEARLY : claramente **2**
FRANKLY : francamente **3** SIMPLY : sencillamente

plaintiff ['pleɪntɪf] *n* : demandante *mf*

plan ['plæn] *n* **1** : plan *m*, proyecto *m* **2**
DIAGRAM : plano *m* — ~ *v* **planned;**
planning 1 : planear, proyectar **2**
INTEND : tener planeado — *vi* : hacer
planes

plane¹ ['pleɪn] *n* **1** LEVEL : plano *m*,
nivel *m* **2** AIRPLANE : avión *m*

plane² *n or* **carpenter's** ~ : cepillo *m*

planet ['plænət] *n* : planeta *m*

plank ['plæŋk] *n* : tabla *f*

planning ['plænɪŋ] *n* : planificación *f*

plant ['plænt] *vt* : plantar (flores, árboles), sembrar (semillas) — ~ *n* **1**
: planta *f* **2** FACTORY : fábrica *f*

plantain ['plæntən] *n* : plátano *m* (grande)

plantation [plænˈteɪʃən] *n* : plantación *f*

plaque ['plæk] *n* : placa *f*

plaster ['plæstər] *n* : yeso *m* — ~ *vt* **1**
: enyesar **2** COVER : cubrir — **plaster**
cast *n* : escayola *f*

plastic ['plæstɪk] *adj* **1** : de plástico **2**
FLEXIBLE : plástico, flexible **3** ~ **sur-**
gery : cirugía *f* plástica — ~ *n* : plástico *m*

plate 334 **pneumatic**

plate ['pleɪt] n 1 SHEET : placa f 2 DISH
: plato m 3 ILLUSTRATION : lámina f —
~ vt **plated; plating** : chapar (en
metal)

plateau [plæ'to:] n, pl **-teaus** or **-teaux**
[-'to:z] : meseta f

platform ['plæt,fɔrm] n 1 : plataforma f 2
: andén m (de una estación de ferrocarril) 3 or **political** ~ : programa m
electoral

platinum ['plæt̬ənəm] n : platino m

platitude ['plæt̬ə,tu:d, -,tju:d] n : lugar m
común

platoon [plə'tu:n] n : sección f (en el
ejército)

platter ['plæt̬ər] n : fuente f

plausible ['plɔzəbəl] adj : creíble, verosímil

play ['pleɪ] n 1 : juego m 2 DRAMA : obra
f de teatro — ~ vi 1 : jugar 2 ~ **in a
band** : tocar en un grupo — vt 1
: jugar (deportes, etc.), jugar a (juegos) 2 : tocar (música o un instrumento) 3 ~ **the role of** : representar el
papel de — **player** ['pleɪər] n 1 : jugador m, -dora f 2 ACTOR : actor m, actriz f 3 MUSICIAN : músico m, -ca f —
playful ['pleɪfəl] adj : juguetón —
playground ['pleɪ,graʊnd] n : patio m
de recreo — **playing card** : naipe m,
carta f 2 — **playmate** ['pleɪ,meɪt] n
: compañero m, -ra f de juego —
play-off ['pleɪ,ɔf] n : desempate m —
playpen ['pleɪ,pɛn] n : corral m (para
niños) — **plaything** ['pleɪ,θɪŋ] n
: juguete m — **playwright** ['pleɪ,raɪt] n
: dramaturgo m, -ga f

plea ['pli:] n 1 : acto m de declararse (en
derecho) 2 APPEAL : ruego m, súplica f
— **plead** ['pli:d] v **pleaded** or **pled**
['plɛd]; **pleading** vi 1 ~ **for** : suplicar
2 ~ **guilty** : declararse culpable 3 ~
not guilty : negar la acusación — vt 1
: alegar, pretextar 2 ~ **a case** : defender un caso

pleasant ['plɛzənt] adj : agradable,
grato — **please** ['pli:z] v **pleased;
pleasing** vt 1 GRATIFY : complacer 2
SATISFY : satisfacer — vi 1 : agradar 2
do as you ~ : haz lo que quieras —
~ adv : por favor — **pleased** ['pli:zd]
adj : contento — **pleasing** ['pli:zɪŋ]
adj : agradable — **pleasure** ['plɛʒər] n
: placer m, gusto m

pleat ['pli:t] vt : plisar — ~ n : pliegue
m

pledge ['plɛdʒ] n 1 SECURITY : prenda f 2
PROMISE : promesa f — ~ vt **pledged;
pledging** 1 PAWN : empeñar 2 PROMISE
: prometer

plenty ['plɛnt̬i] n 1 : abundancia f 2 ~
of time : tiempo m de sobra — **plentiful** ['plɛnt̬ɪfəl] adj : abundante

pliable ['plaɪəbəl] adj : flexible

pliers ['plaɪərz] npl : alicates mpl

plight ['plaɪt] n : situación f difícil

plod ['plɑd] vi **plodded; plodding** 1
: caminar con paso pesado 2 DRUDGE
: trabajar laboriosamente

plot ['plɑt] n 1 LOT : parcela f 2 : argumento m (de una novela, etc.) 3 CON-
SPIRACY : complot m, intriga f — ~ v
plotted; plotting vt : tramar (un plan),
trazar (una gráfica, etc.) — vi CON-
SPIRE : conspirar

plow or **plough** ['plaʊ] n 1 : arado m 2
→ **snowplow** — ~ v : arar

ploy ['plɔɪ] n : estratagema f

pluck ['plʌk] vt 1 : arrancar 2 : desplumar (un pollo, etc.) 3 : recoger
(flores) 4 ~ **one's eyebrows** : de-
pilarse las cejas

plug ['plʌg] n 1 STOPPER : tapón m 2
: enchufe m (eléctrico) — ~ vt
plugged; plugging 1 BLOCK : tapar 2
ADVERTISE : dar publicidad a 3 ~ **in**
: enchufar

plum ['plʌm] n : ciruela f

plumb ['plʌm] adj : a plomo, vertical —
plumber ['plʌmər] n : fontanero m, -ra
f; plomero m, -ra f Lat — **plumbing**
['plʌmɪŋ] n 1 : fontanería f, plomería f
Lat 2 PIPES : cañerías fpl

plume ['plu:m] n : pluma f

plummet ['plʌmət] vi : caer en picado

plump ['plʌmp] adj : rechoncho fam

plunder ['plʌndər] vi : saquear, robar —
~ n : botín m

plunge ['plʌndʒ] v **plunged; plunging**
vt 1 IMMERSE : sumergir 2 THRUST
: hundir — vi 1 : zambullirse (en el
agua) 2 DESCEND : descender en picada — ~ n 1 DIVE : zambullida f 2
DROP : descenso m abrupto

plural ['plʊrəl] adj : plural — ~ n : plural m

plus ['plʌs] adj : positivo — ~ n 1 or
~ **sign** : signo m (de) más 2 ADVAN-
TAGE : ventaja f — ~ prep : más — ~
conj : y, además

plush ['plʌʃ] n : felpa f — ~ adj 1 : de
felpa 2 LUXURIOUS : lujoso

plutonium [plu'to:niəm] n : plutonio
m

ply ['plaɪ] vt **plied; plying** 1 : ejercer (un
oficio) 2 ~ **with questions** : acosar
con preguntas

plywood ['plaɪ,wʊd] n : contrachapado m

pneumatic [nʊ'mæt̬ɪk, njʊ-] adj : neumático

pneumonia [nʊ'moːnjə, njʊ-] n : pulmonía f

poach[1] ['poːtʃ] vt : cocer a fuego lento

poach[2] vt or ~ **game** : cazar ilegalmente — **poacher** ['poːtʃər] n : cazador m furtivo, cazadora f furtiva

pocket ['pɑkət] n : bolsillo m — ~ vt : meterse en el bolsillo — **pocketbook** ['pɑkət,bʊk] n : cartera f, bolsa f Lat — **pocketknife** ['pɑkət,naɪf] n, pl **-knives** : navaja f

pod ['pɑd] n : vaina f

poem ['poːəm] n : poema m — **poet** ['poːət] n : poeta mf — **poetic** [po'ɛtɪk] or **poetical** [-tɪkəl] adj : poético — **poetry** ['poːətri] n : poesía f

poignant ['pɔɪnjənt] adj : conmovedor

point ['pɔɪnt] n 1 : punto m 2 PURPOSE : sentido m 3 TIP : punta f 4 FEATURE : cualidad f 5 be beside the ~ : no venir al caso 6 there's no ~ ... : no sirve de nada... — ~ vt 1 AIM : apuntar 2 or ~ **out** : señalar, indicar — vi ~ **at** : señalar (con el dedo) — **point–blank** ['pɔɪnt'blæŋk] adv : a quemarropa — **pointer** ['pɔɪntər] n 1 NEEDLE : aguja f 2 : perro m de muestra 3 TIP : consejo m — **pointless** ['pɔɪntləs] adj : inútil — **point of view** n : perspectiva f, punto m de vista

poise ['pɔɪz] n 1 : elegancia f 2 COMPOSURE : aplomo m

poison ['pɔɪzən] n : veneno m — ~ vt : envenenar — **poisonous** ['pɔɪzənəs] adj : venenoso (dícese de una culebra, etc.), tóxico (dícese de una sustancia)

poke ['poːk] vt **poked; poking** 1 JAB : golpear (con la punta de algo), dar 2 THRUST : introducir, asomar — ~ n : golpe m abrupto (con la punta de algo)

poker[1] ['poːkər] n : atizador m (para el fuego)

poker[2] n : póquer m (juego de naipes)

polar ['poːlər] adj : polar — **polar bear** n : oso m blanco — **polarize** ['poːlə,raɪz] or **-ised; -ising** : polarizar

pole[1] ['poːl] n : palo m, poste m

pole[2] n : polo m (en geografía)

police [pə'liːs] vt **-liced; -licing** : mantener el orden en — ~ ns & pl **the ~** : la policía — **policeman** [pə'liːsmən] n, pl **-men** [-mən, -ˌmɛn] : policía m — **police officer** n : policía mf, agente mf de policía — **policewoman** [pə'liːsˌwʊmən] n, pl **-women** [-ˌwɪmən] : (mujer f) policía f

policy ['pɑləsi] n, pl **-cies** 1 : política f 2 or **insurance ~** : póliza f de seguros

polio ['poːliˌoː] or **poliomyelitis** [ˌpoːliˌoːˌmaɪə'laɪtəs] n : polio f, poliomielitis f

polish ['pɑlɪʃ] vt 1 : pulir 2 : limpiar (zapatos), encerar (un suelo) — ~ n 1 LUSTER : brillo m, lustre m 2 : betún m (para zapatos), cera f (para suelos y muebles), esmalte m (para las uñas)

Polish ['poːlɪʃ] adj : polaco — ~ n : polaco m (idioma)

polite [pə'laɪt] adj **-liter; -est** : cortés — **politeness** [pə'laɪtnəs] n : cortesía f

political [pə'lɪtɪkəl] adj : político — **politician** [ˌpɑlə'tɪʃən] n : político m, -ca f — **politics** ['pɑlə,tɪks] ns & pl : política f

polka ['poːlkə, 'poːkə] n : polka f — **polka dot** ['poːkə,dɑt] n : lunar m

poll ['poːl] n 1 : encuesta f, sondeo m 2 **the ~s** : las urnas — ~ vt 1 : obtener (votos) 2 CANVASS : encuestar, sondear

pollen ['pɑlən] n : polen m

pollute [pə'luːt] vt **-luted; -luting** : contaminar — **pollution** [pə'luːʃən] n : contaminación f

polyester ['pɑliˌɛstər, ˌpɑli'-] n : poliéster m

polygon ['pɑliˌɡɑn] n : polígono m

pomegranate ['pɑməˌɡrænət, 'pɑmˌɡrænət] n : granada f

pomp ['pɑmp] n : pompa f — **pompous** ['pɑmpəs] adj : pomposo

pond ['pɑnd] n : charca f (natural), estanque m (artificial)

ponder ['pɑndər] vt : considerar — vi ~ **over** : reflexionar sobre

pony ['poːni] n, pl **-nies** : poni m — **ponytail** ['poːniˌteɪl] n : cola f de caballo

poodle ['puːdəl] n : caniche m

pool ['puːl] n 1 PUDDLE : charco m 2 : fondo m común (de recursos) 3 BILLIARDS : billar m 4 or **swimming** ~ : piscina f — ~ vt : hacer un fondo común de

poor ['pʊr, 'por] adj 1 : pobre 2 INFERIOR : malo 3 **the ~** : los pobres — **poorly** ['pʊrli, 'por-] adv : mal

pop[1] ['pɑp] v **popped; popping** vt 1 : hacer reventar 2 ~ **sth into** : meter algo en — vi 1 BURST : reventarse, estallar 2 ~ **in** : entrar (un momento) 3 ~ **out** : saltar (dícese de los ojos) 4 ~ **up** APPEAR : aparecer — ~ n 1 : ruido m seco 2 or **soda pop**

pop[2] n or ~ **music** : música f popular

popcorn ['pɑp,kɔrn] n : palomitas fpl

pope ['poːp] n : papa m

poplar ['pɑplər] n : álamo m

poppy ['pɑpi] n, pl **-pies** : amapola f

popular ['pɑpjələr] adj : popular — **pop-**

ularity [ˌpɑpjə'lærəti] *n* : popularidad *f* — **popularize** ['pɑpjələˌraɪz] *vt* -**ized**; -**izing** : popularizar

populate ['pɑpjəˌleɪt] *vt* -**lated**; -**lating** : poblar — **population** [ˌpɑpjə'leɪʃən] *n* : población *f*

porcelain ['pɔrsələn] *n* : porcelana *f*

porch ['pɔrtʃ] *n* : porche *m*

porcupine ['pɔrkjəˌpaɪn] *n* : puerco *m* espín

pore¹ ['pɔr] *vi* **pored**; **poring** ~ **over** : estudiar esmeradamente

pore² *n* : poro *m*

pork ['pɔrk] *n* : carne *f* de cerdo

pornography [pɔr'nɑgrəfi] *n* : pornografía *f* — **pornographic** [ˌpɔrnə'græfɪk] *adj* : pornográfico

porous ['pɔrəs] *adj* : poroso

porpoise ['pɔrpəs] *n* : marsopa *f*

porridge ['pɔrɪdʒ] *n* : avena *f* (cocida), gachas *fpl* (de avena)

port¹ ['pɔrt] *n* HARBOR : puerto *m*

port² *n or* ~ **side** : babor *m*

port³ *n* : oporto *m* (vino)

portable ['pɔrtəbəl] *adj* : portátil

portent ['pɔrˌtent] *n* : presagio *m*

porter ['pɔrtər] *n* : maletero *m*, mozo *m* (de estación)

portfolio [pɔrt'foˌlioˌ] *n*, *pl* -**lios** : cartera *f*

porthole ['pɔrtˌhoːl] *n* : portilla *f*

portion ['pɔrʃən] *n* : porción *f*

portrait ['pɔrtrət, -ˌtreɪt] *n* : retrato *m*

portray [pɔr'treɪ] *vt* **1** : representar, retratar **2** : interpretar (un personaje)

Portuguese [ˌpɔrtʃə'giːz, -'giːs] *adj* : portugués — ~ *n* : portugués *m* (idioma)

pose ['poːz] *v* **posed**; **posing** *vt* : plantear (una pregunta, etc.), representar (una amenaza) — *vi* **1** : posar *f* **2** ~ **as** : hacerse pasar por — ~ *n* : pose *f*

posh ['pɑʃ] *adj* : elegante, de lujo

position [pə'zɪʃən] *n* **1** : posición *f* **2** JOB : puesto *m* — ~ *vt* : colocar, situar

positive ['pɑzətɪv] *adj* **1** : positivo **2** CERTAIN : seguro

possess [pə'zes] *vt* : poseer — **possession** [pə'zeʃən] *n* **1** : posesión *f* **2** ~**s** *npl* BELONGINGS : bienes *mpl* — **possessive** [pə'zesɪv] *adj* : posesivo

possible ['pɑsəbəl] *adj* : posible — **possibility** [ˌpɑsə'bɪləti] *n*, *pl* -**ties** : posibilidad *f* — **possibly** ['pɑsəbli] *adv* : posiblemente

post¹ ['poːst] *n* POLE : poste *m*, palo *m*

post² *n* POSITION : puesto *m*

post³ *n* MAIL : cartas *fpl* — ~ *vt* **1** : echar al correo **2 keep** ~**ed** : tener al corriente — **postage** ['poːstɪdʒ] *n*

: franqueo *m* — **postal** ['poːstəl] *adj* : postal — **postcard** ['poːstˌkɑrd] *n* : tarjeta *f* postal

poster ['poːstər] *n* : cartel *m*

posterity [pɑ'sterəti] *n* : posteridad *f*

posthumous ['pɑstʃəməs] *adj* : póstumo

postman ['poːstmən, -ˌmæn] → **mailman** — **post office** *n* : oficina *f* de correos

postpone [ˌpoːst'poːn] *vt* -**poned**; -**poning** : aplazar — **postponement** [ˌpoːst'poːnmənt] *n* : aplazamiento *m*

postscript ['poːstˌskrɪpt] *n* : posdata *f*

posture ['pɑstʃər] *n* : postura *f*

postwar [poːst'wɔr] *adj* : de (la) posguerra

pot ['pɑt] *n* **1** : olla *f* (de cocina) **2** FLOWERPOT : maceta *f* **3** ~**s and pans** : cacharros *mpl*

potassium [pə'tæsiəm] *n* : potasio *m*

potato [pə'teɪtoˌ] *n*, *pl* -**toes** : patata *f*, papa *f Lat*

potent ['poːtənt] *adj* **1** POWERFUL : poderoso **2** EFFECTIVE : eficaz

potential [pə'tentʃəl] *adj* : potencial — ~ *n* : potencial *m*

pothole ['pɑtˌhoːl] *n* : bache *m*

potion ['poːʃən] *n* : poción *f*

pottery ['pɑtəri] *n*, *pl* -**teries** : cerámica *f*

pouch ['paʊtʃ] *n* **1** BAG : bolsa *f* pequeña **2** : bolsa *f* (de un animal)

poultry ['poːltri] *n* : aves *fpl* de corral

pounce ['paʊns] *vi* **pounced**; **pouncing** : abalanzarse

pound¹ ['paʊnd] *n* : libra *f* (unidad de dinero o de peso)

pound² *n or* **dog** ~ : perrera *f*

pound³ *vt* **1** CRUSH : machacar **2** HIT : golpear — *vi* : palpitar (dícese del corazón)

pour ['pɔr] *vt* : verter — *vi* **1** FLOW : fluir, salir **2 it's** ~**ing** : está lloviendo a cántaros

pout ['paʊt] *vi* : hacer pucheros — ~ *n* : puchero *m*

poverty ['pɑvərti] *n* : pobreza *f*

powder ['paʊdər] *vt* **1** : empolvar **2** CRUSH : pulverizar — ~ *n* **1** : polvo *m* **2 or face** ~ : polvos *mpl* — **powdery** ['paʊdəri] *adj* : polvoriento

power ['paʊər] *n* **1** CONTROL : poder *m* **2** ABILITY : capacidad *f* **3** STRENGTH : fuerza *f* **4** : potencia *f* (política) **5** ENERGY : energía *f* **6** ELECTRICITY : electricidad *f* — ~ *vt* : impulsar — **powerful** ['paʊərfəl] *adj* : poderoso — **powerless** ['paʊərləs] *adj* : impotente

practical ['præktɪkəl] *adj* : práctico — **practically** ['præktɪkli] *adv* : casi, prácticamente

practice *or* **practise** ['præktəs] *v* -**ticed**

or **-tised; -ticing** *or* **-tising** *vt* **1** : practicar **2** : ejercer (una profesión) — *vi* : practicar — **practice** *n* **1** : práctica *f* **2** CUSTOM : costumbre *f* **3** : ejercicio *m* (de una profesión) **4 be out of ~** : no estar en forma — **practitioner** [præk-'tɪʃənər] *n* **1** : profesional *mf* **2 general ~** : médico *m*, -ca *f* de medicina general

pragmatic [præg'mætɪk] *adj* : pragmático

prairie ['preri] *n* : pradera *f*

praise ['preɪz] *vt* **praised; praising** : elogiar, alabar — **~** *n* : elogio *m*, alabanza *f* — **praiseworthy** ['preɪz,wərði] *adj* : loable

prance ['præns] *vi* **pranced; prancing** : hacer cabriolas

prank ['præŋk] *n* : travesura *f*

prawn ['prɔn] *n* : gamba *f*

pray ['preɪ] *vi* **1** : rezar **2 ~ for** : rogar — **prayer** ['prɛr] *n* : oración *f*

preach ['priːtʃ] *v* : predicar — **preacher** ['priːtʃər] *n* MINISTER : pastor *m*, -tora *f*

precarious [prɪ'kæriəs] *adj* : precario

precaution [prɪ'kɔʃən] *n* : precaución *f*

precede [prɪ'siːd] *vt* **-ceded; -ceding** : preceder a — **precedence** ['presədənts, prɪ'siːdənts] *n* : precedencia *f* — **precedent** ['presədənt] *n* : precedente *m*

precinct ['priː,sɪŋkt] *n* **1** DISTRICT : distrito *m* **2 ~s** *npl* : recinto *m*

precious ['preʃəs] *adj* : precioso

precipice ['presəpəs] *n* : precipicio *m*

precipitate [prɪ'sɪpə,teɪt] *vt* **-tated; -tating** : precipitar — **precipitation** [prɪ,sɪpə'teɪʃən] *n* **1** HASTE : precipitación *f* **2** : precipitaciones *fpl* (en meteorología)

precise [prɪ'saɪs] *adj* : preciso — **precisely** *adv* : precisamente — **precision** [prɪ'sɪʒən] *n* : precisión *f*

preclude [prɪ'kluːd] *vt* **-cluded; -cluding 1** PREVENT : impedir **2** EXCLUDE : excluir

precocious [prɪ'koːʃəs] *adj* : precoz

preconceived [,priːkən'siːv] *adj* : preconcebido

predator ['predətər] *n* : depredador *m*

predecessor ['predə,sesər, 'priː-] *n* : antecesor *m*, -sora *f*; predecesor *m*, -sora *f*

predicament [prɪ'dɪkəmənt] *n* : apuro *m*

predict [prɪ'dɪkt] *vt* : pronosticar, predecir — **predictable** [prɪ'dɪktəbəl] *adj* : previsible — **prediction** [prɪ'dɪkʃən] *n* : pronóstico *m*, predicción *f*

predispose [,priːdɪ'spoːz] *vt* **-posed; -posing** : predisponer

predominant [prɪ'dɑmənənt] *adj* : predominante

preeminent [prɪ'emənənt] *adj* : preeminente

preempt [prɪ'empt] *vt* : adelantarse a (un ataque, etc.)

preen ['priːn] *v* **1** : arreglarse (las plumas) **2 ~ oneself** : acicalarse

prefabricated [,priː'fæbrə,keɪtəd] *adj* : prefabricado

preface ['prefəs] *n* : prefacio *m*, prólogo *m*

prefer [prɪ'fər] *vt* **-ferred; -ferring** : preferir — **preferable** ['prefərəbəl] *adj* : preferible — **preference** ['prefrənts, 'prefər-] *n* : preferencia *f* — **preferential** [,prefə'rentʃəl] *adj* : preferente

prefix ['priː,fɪks] *n* : prefijo *m*

pregnancy ['pregnəntsi] *n*, *pl* **-cies** : embarazo *m* — **pregnant** ['pregnənt] *adj* : embarazada

prehistoric [,priːhɪs'tɔrɪk] *or* **prehistorical** [-ɪkəl] *adj* : prehistórico

prejudice ['predʒədəs] *n* **1** BIAS : prejuicio *m* **2** HARM : perjuicio *m* — **~** *vt* **-diced; -dicing 1** BIAS : predisponer **2** HARM : perjudicar — **prejudiced** ['predʒədəst] *adj* : parcial

preliminary [prɪ'lɪmə,neri] *adj* : preliminar

prelude ['prel,uːd, 'prel,juːd; 'preɪ,luːd, 'priː-] *n* : preludio *m*

premarital [,priː'mærətəl] *adj* : prematrimonial

premature [,priːmə'tur, -'tjur, -'tʃur] *adj* : prematuro

premeditated [priː'medə,teɪtəd] *adj* : premeditado

premier [prɪ'mɪr, -'mjɪr; 'priː,mɪər] *adj* : principal — **~** *n* PRIME MINISTER : primer ministro *m*, primera ministra *f*

premiere [prɪ'mjer, -'mɪr] *n* : estreno *m*

premise ['premɪs] *n* **1** : premisa *f* (de un argumento) **2 ~s** *npl* : recinto *m*, local *m*

premium ['priːmiəm] *n* **1** : premio *m* **2** *or* **insurance ~** : prima *f* (de seguro)

preoccupied [pri'ɑkjə,paɪd] *adj* : preocupado

prepare [prɪ'pær] *v* **-pared; -paring** *vt* : preparar — *vi* : prepararse — **preparation** [prepə'reɪʃən] *n* **1** : preparación *f* **2 ~s** *npl* ARRANGEMENTS : preparativos *mpl* — **preparatory** [prɪ'pærə,tori] *adj* : preparatorio

prepay [prɪ'peɪ] *vt* **-paid; -paying** : pagar por adelantado

preposition [,prepə'zɪʃən] *n* : preposición *f*

preposterous [prɪ'pɑstərəs] *adj* : absurdo, ridículo

prerequisite [pri'rɛkwəzət] *n* : requisito *m* previo

prerogative [prɪ'rɑgəṭɪv] *n* : prerrogativa *f*

prescribe [prɪ'skraɪb] *vt* **-scribed; -scribing 1** : prescribir **2** : recetar (en medicina) — **prescription** [prɪ'skrɪpʃən] *n* : receta *f*

presence ['prɛzənts] *n* : presencia *f*

present[1] ['prɛzənt] *adj* **1** CURRENT : actual **2 be ~ at** : estar presente en — **~** *n* **1** : presente *m* **2 at ~** : actualmente

present[2] ['prɛzənt] *n* GIFT : regalo *m* — **~** [prɪ'zɛnt] *vt* **1** INTRODUCE : presentar **2** GIVE : entregar — **presentation** [ˌpriːzən'teɪʃən, ˌprɛzən-] *n* **1** : presentación *f* **2 or ~ ceremony** : ceremonia *f* de entrega

presently ['prɛzəntli] *adv* **1** SOON : dentro de poco **2** NOW : actualmente

preserve [prɪ'zərv] *vt* **-served; -serving 1** : conservar **2** MAINTAIN : mantener — **~** *n* **1** JAM : confitura *f* **2** *or* **game ~** : coto *m* de caza — **preservation** [ˌprɛzər'veɪʃən] *n* : preservación *f*, conservación *f* — **preservative** [prɪ'zərvəṭɪv] *n* : conservante *m*

president ['prɛzədənt] *n* : presidente *m*, -ta *f* — **presidency** ['prɛzədəntsi] *n*, *pl* **-cies** : presidencia *f* — **presidential** [ˌprɛzə'dɛntʃəl] *adj* : presidencial

press ['prɛs] *n* : prensa *f* — **~** *vt* **1** : apretar **2** IRON : planchar — *vi* **1** : apretar **2** URGE : presionar — **pressing** ['prɛsɪŋ] *adj* : urgente — **pressure** ['prɛʃər] *n* : presión *f* — **~** *vt* **-sured; -suring** : presionar, apremiar

prestige [prɛ'stiːʒ, -'stiːdʒ] *n* : prestigio *m* — **prestigious** [prɛ'stɪdʒəs] *adj* : prestigioso

presume [prɪ'zuːm] *vt* **-sumed; -suming** : presumir — **presumably** [prɪ'zuːməbli] *adv* : es de suponer, supuestamente — **presumption** [prɪ'zʌmpʃən] *n* : presunción *f* — **presumptuous** [prɪ'zʌmptʃuəs] *adj* : presuntuoso

pretend [prɪ'tɛnd] *vt* **1** CLAIM : pretender **2** FEIGN : fingir — *vi* : fingir — **pretense** *or* **pretence** ['priːˌtɛns, prɪ'tɛns] *n* **1** CLAIM : pretensión *f* **2 under false ~s** : con pretextos falsos — **pretentious** [prɪ'tɛntʃəs] *adj* : pretencioso

pretext ['priːˌtɛkst] *n* : pretexto *m*

pretty ['prɪṭi] *adj* **-tier; -est** : lindo, bonito — **~** *adv* FAIRLY : bastante

pretzel ['prɛtsəl] *n* : galleta *f* salada

prevail [prɪ'veɪl] *vi* **1** TRIUMPH : prevalecer **2** PREDOMINATE : predominar **3 ~ upon** : persuadir — **prevalent** ['prɛvələnt] *adj* : extendido

prevent [prɪ'vɛnt] *vt* : impedir — **prevention** [prɪ'vɛntʃən] *n* : prevención *f* — **preventive** [prɪ'vɛntɪv] *adj* : preventivo

preview ['priːˌvjuː] *n* : preestreno *m*

previous ['priːviəs] *adj* : previo, anterior — **previously** ['priːviəsli] *adv* : anteriormente

prey ['preɪ] *n*, *pl* **preys** : presa *f* — **prey on** *vt* **1** : alimentarse de **2 ~ on one's mind** : atormentar a algn

price ['praɪs] *n* : precio *m* — **~** *vt* **priced; pricing** : poner un precio a — **priceless** ['praɪsləs] *adj* : inestimable

prick ['prɪk] *n* : pinchazo *m* — **~** *vt* **1** : pinchar **2 ~ up one's ears** : levantar las orejas — **prickly** ['prɪkəli] *adj* : espinoso

pride ['praɪd] *n* : orgullo *m* — **~** *vt* **prided; priding ~ oneself on** : enorgullecerse de

priest ['priːst] *n* : sacerdote *m* — **priesthood** ['priːstˌhʊd] *n* : sacerdocio *m*

prim ['prɪm] *adj* **primmer; primmest** : remilgado

primary ['praɪˌmɛri, 'praɪməri] *adj* **1** FIRST : primario **2** PRINCIPAL : principal — **primarily** [praɪ'mɛrəli] *adv* : principalmente

prime[1] ['praɪm] *vt* **primed; priming 1** : cebar (un arma de fuego, etc.) **2** PREPARE : preparar

prime[2] *n* **the ~ of one's life** : la flor de la vida — **~** *adj* **1** MAIN : principal, primero **2** EXCELLENT : excelente — **prime minister** *n* : primero ministro *m*, primera ministra *f*

primer[1] ['praɪmər] *n* : base *f* (de pintura)

primer[2] ['prɪmər] *n* READER : cartilla *f*

primitive ['prɪmɪṭɪv] *adj* : primitivo

primrose ['prɪmˌroːz] *n* : primavera *f*

prince ['prɪnts] *n* : príncipe *m* — **princess** ['prɪntsəs, 'prɪnˌsɛs] *n* : princesa *f*

principal ['prɪntsəpəl] *adj* : principal — **~** *n* : director *m*, -tora *f* (de un colegio)

principle ['prɪntsəpəl] *n* : principio *m*

print ['prɪnt] *n* **1** MARK : huella *f* **2** LETTERING : letra *f* **3** ENGRAVING : grabado *m* **4** : estampado *m* (de tela) **5** : copia *f* (en fotografía) **6 out of ~** : agotado — **~** *vt* : imprimir (libros, etc.) — *vi* : escribir con letra de molde — **printer** ['prɪntər] *n* **1** : impresor *m*, -sora *f* (persona) **2** : impresora *f* (máquina) — **printing** ['prɪntɪŋ] *n* **1** : impresión *f* **2**

: imprenta *f* (profesión) **3** LETTERING
: letras *fpl* de molde
prior ['praɪər] *adj* **1** : previo **2** ~ **to**
: antes de — **priority** [praɪ'ɔrət̬i] *n, pl*
-ties : prioridad *f*
prison ['prɪzən] *n* : prisión *f*, cárcel *f* —
prisoner ['prɪzənər] *n* **1** : preso *m*, -sa *f*
2 ~ **of war** : prisionero *m*, -ra *f* de
guerra
privacy ['praɪvəsi] *n, pl* **-cies** : intimidad
f — **private** ['praɪvət] *adj* **1** : privado *f*
SECRET : secreto — ~ *n* : soldado *m*
raso — **privately** ['praɪvətli] *adv* : en
privado
privilege ['prɪvlɪdʒ, 'prɪvə-] *n* : privilegio
m — **privileged** ['prɪvlɪdʒd, 'prɪvə-] *adj*
: privilegiado
prize ['praɪz] *n* : premio *m* — ~ *vt* **prized;**
prizing — **prizefighter**
['praɪz,faɪt̬ər] *n* : boxeador *m*, -dora *f*
profesional — **prizewinning** ['praɪz-
ˌwɪnɪŋ] *adj* : premiado
pro ['proː] *n* **1** → **professional 2** the ~s
and cons : los pros y los contras
probability [ˌprɑbə'bɪlət̬i] *n, pl* **-ties**
: probabilidad *f* — **probable** ['prɑbə-
bəl] *adj* : probable — **probably** [-bli]
adv : probablemente
probation [proˈbeɪʃən] *n* **1** : período *m*
de prueba (de un empleado, etc.) **2**
: libertad *f* condicional (de un preso)
probe ['proːb] *n* **1** : sonda *f* (en medicina, etc.) **2** INVESTIGATION : investigación *f* — ~ *vt* **probed; probing 1**
: sondar **2** INVESTIGATE : investigar
problem ['prɑbləm] *n* : problema *m*
procedure [prəˈsiːdʒər] *n* : procedimiento *m*
proceed [proˈsiːd] *vi* **1** ACT : proceder **2**
CONTINUE : continuar **3** ADVANCE
: avanzar — **proceedings** [proˈsiːdɪŋz]
npl **1** EVENTS : actos *mpl* **2** : proceso *m*
(en derecho) — **proceeds** ['proːˌsiːdz]
npl : ganancias *fpl*
process ['prɑˌsɛs, 'proː-] *n, pl* **-cesses**
['prɑˌsɛsəz, 'proː-, -səsəz, -sə̩siːz] **1** : proceso *m* **2 in the** ~ **of** : en vías de —
~ *vt* : procesar — **procession** [prə-
'sɛʃən] *n* : desfile *m*
proclaim [proˈkleɪm] *vt* : proclamar —
proclamation [ˌprɑklə'meɪʃən] *n* : proclamación *f*
procrastinate [prəˈkræstə̩neɪt] *vi* **-nated;**
-nating : demorar, aplazar
procure [prəˈkjʊr] *vt* **-cured; -curing**
: obtener
prod ['prɑd] *vt* **prodded; prodding**
: pinchar, aguijonear
prodigal ['prɑdɪgəl] *adj* : pródigo

prodigy ['prɑdədʒi] *n, pl* **-gies** : prodigio
m
produce [prəˈduːs, -ˈdjuːs] *vt* **-duced;**
-ducing 1 : producir **2** CAUSE : causar
3 SHOW : presentar, mostrar **4** : poner
en escena (una obra de teatro) — ~
['prɑˌduːs, 'proː-, -ˌdjuːs] *n* : productos
mpl agrícolas — **producer** [prəˈduːsər,
-ˈdjuː-] *n* : productor *m*, -tora *f* — **prod-**
uct ['prɑˌdʌkt] *n* : producto *m* — **pro-**
ductive [prəˈdʌktɪv] *adj* : productivo
profane [proˈfeɪn] *adj* **1** : profano **2** IR-
REVERENT : blasfemo — **profanity**
[proˈfænət̬i] *n, pl* **-ties** : blasfemia *f*
profess [prəˈfɛs] *vt* : profesar — **profes-**
sion [prəˈfɛʃən] *n* : profesión *f* —
professional [prəˈfɛʃənəl] *adj* : profesional — ~ *n* : profesional *mf* —
professor [prəˈfɛsər] *n* : profesor *m*,
-sora *f*
proficiency [prəˈfɪʃənsi] *n* : competencia *f* — **proficient** [prəˈfɪʃənt] *adj*
: competente
profile ['proːˌfaɪl] *n* **1** : perfil *m* **2 keep a**
low ~ : no llamar la atención
profit ['prɑfət] *n* : beneficio *m*, ganancia
f — ~ *vi* : sacar provecho (de), beneficiarse (de) — **profitable** ['prɑfət̬əbəl]
adj : provechoso
profound [prəˈfaʊnd] *adj* : profundo
profuse [prəˈfjuːs] *adj* : profuso — **pro-**
fusion [prəˈfjuːʒən] *n* : profusión *f*
prognosis [prɑgˈnoːsɪs] *n, pl* **-noses**
[-ˌsiːz] : pronóstico *m*
program ['proːˌgræm, -grəm] *n* : programa *m* — ~ *vt* **-grammed** *or*
-gramed; -gramming *or* **-graming**
: programar
progress ['prɑgrəs, -grɛs] *n* **1** : progreso
m **2** ADVANCE : avance *m* — ~ [prə-
'grɛs] *vi* : progresar, avanzar — **pro-**
gressive [prəˈgrɛsɪv] *adj* **1** : progresista (dícese de la política, etc.) **2**
INCREASING : progresiva
prohibit [proˈhɪbət] *vt* : prohibir — **pro-**
hibition [ˌproːəˈbɪʃən, ˌproːhə-] *n* : prohibición *f*
project ['prɑdʒɛkt, -dʒɪkt] *n* : proyecto *m*
— ~ [prəˈdʒɛkt] *vt* : proyectar — *vi*
PROTRUDE : sobresalir — **projectile**
[prəˈdʒɛktəl, -ˌtaɪl] *n* : proyectil *m* —
projection [prəˈdʒɛkʃən] *n* **1** : proyección *f* **2** PROTRUSION : saliente *m* —
projector [prəˈdʒɛktər] *n* : proyector *m*
proliferate [prəˈlɪfə̩reɪt] *vi* **-ated; -ating**
: proliferar — **proliferation** [prəˌlɪfə-
'reɪʃən] *n* : proliferación *f* — **prolific**
[prəˈlɪfɪk] *adj* : prolífico
prologue ['proːˌlɔg] *n* : prólogo *m*
prolong [prəˈlɔŋ] *vt* : prolongar

prom ['pram] *n* : baile *m* formal (en un colegio)
prominent ['prɑmənənt] *adj* : prominente — **prominence** ['prɑmənənts] *n* **1** : prominencia *f* **2** IMPORTANCE : eminencia *f*
promiscuous [prə'mɪskjʊəs] *adj* : promiscuo
promise ['prɑməs] *n* : promesa *f* — ～ *v* **-ised; -ising** : prometer — **promising** ['prɑməsɪŋ] *adj* : prometedor
promote [prə'moːt] *vt* **-moted; -moting** **1** : ascender (a un alumno o un empleado) **2** FURTHER : promover, fomentar **3** ADVERTISE : promocionar — **promoter** [prə'moːtər] *n* : promotor *m*, -tora *f*; empresario *m*, -ria *f* (en deportes) — **promotion** [prə'moːʃən] *n* **1** : ascenso *m* (de un alumno o un empleado) **2** ADVERTISING : publicidad *f*, propaganda *f*
prompt ['prɑmpt] *vt* **1** INCITE : provocar (una cosa), inducir (a una persona) **2** : apuntar (a un actor, etc.) — ～ *adj* **1** : rápido **2** PUNCTUAL : puntual
prone ['proːn] *adj* **1** : boca abajo, decúbito prono **2 be ～ to** : ser propenso a
prong ['prɔŋ] *n* : punta *f*, diente *m*
pronoun ['proː,naʊn] *n* : pronombre *m*
pronounce [prə'naʊnts] *vt* **-nounced; -nouncing** : pronunciar — **pronouncement** [prə'naʊntsmənt] *n* : declaración *f* — **pronunciation** [prə,nʌntsi'eɪʃən] *n* : pronunciación *f*
proof ['pruːf] *n* : prueba *f* — ～ *adj* **~ against** : a prueba de — **proofread** ['pruːf,riːd] *vt* **-read; -reading** : corregir
prop ['prɑp] *n* **1** SUPPORT : puntal *m*, apoyo *m* **2** : accesorio *m* (en teatro) — ～ *vt* **propped; propping 1 ～ against** : apoyar contra **2 ～ up** SUPPORT : apoyar
propaganda [,prɑpə'gændə, ,proː-] *n* : propaganda *f*
propagate ['prɑpə,geɪt] *v* **-gated; -gating** *vt* : propagar — *vi* : propagarse
propel [prə'pɛl] *vt* **-pelled; -pelling** : propulsar — **propeller** [prə'pɛlər] *n* : hélice *f*
propensity [prə'pɛntsəti] *n, pl* **-ties** : propensión *f*
proper ['prɑpər] *adj* **1** SUITABLE : apropiado **2** REAL : verdadero **3** CORRECT : correcto **4** GENTEEL : cortés **5 ～ name** : nombre *m* propio — **properly** ['prɑpərli] *adv* : correctamente
property ['prɑpərti] *n, pl* **-ties 1** : propiedad *f* **2** BUILDING : inmueble *m* **3** LAND, LOT : parcela *f*

prophet ['prɑfət] *n* : profeta *m*, profetisa *f* — **prophecy** ['prɑfəsi] *n, pl* **-cies** : profecía *f* — **prophesy** ['prɑfə,saɪ] *v* **-sied; -sying** *vt* : profetizar — *vi* : hacer profecías — **prophetic** [prə'fɛtɪk] *adj* : profético
proportion [prə'porʃən] *n* **1** : proporción *f* **2** SHARE : parte *f* — **proportional** [prə'porʃənəl] *adj* : proporcional — **proportionate** [prə'porʃənət] *adj* : proporcional
proposal [prə'poːzəl] *n* : propuesta *f*
propose [prə'poːz] *v* **-posed; -posing** *vt* **1** SUGGEST : proponer **2 ～ to do sth** : pensar hacer algo — *vi* : proponer matrimonio — **proposition** [,prɑpə'zɪʃən] *n* : proposición *f*
proprietor [prə'praɪətər] *n* : propietario *m*, -ria *f*
propriety [prə'praɪəti] *n, pl* **-eties** : decencia *f*, decoro *m*
propulsion [prə'pʌlʃən] *n* : propulsión *f*
prose ['proːz] *n* : prosa *f*
prosecute ['prɑsɪ,kjuːt] *vt* **-cuted; -cuting** : procesar — **prosecution** [,prɑsɪ'kjuːʃən] *n* **1** : procesamiento *m* **2 the ～** : la acusación — **prosecutor** ['prɑsɪ,kjuːtər] *n* : acusador *m*, -dora *f*
prospect ['prɑ,spɛkt] *n* **1** : perspectiva *f* **2** POSSIBILITY : posibilidad *f* — **prospective** [prə'spɛktɪv, 'prɑ,spɛk-] *adj* : futuro, posible
prosper ['prɑspər] *vi* : prosperar — **prosperity** [prɑ'spɛrəti] *n* : prosperidad *f* — **prosperous** ['prɑspərəs] *adj* : próspero
prostitute ['prɑstə,tuːt, -,tjuːt] *n* : prostituta *f* — **prostitution** [,prɑstə'tuːʃən, -'tjuː-] *n* : prostitución *f*
prostrate ['prɑ,streɪt] *adj* : postrado
protagonist [proː'tægənɪst] *n* : protagonista *mf*
protect [prə'tɛkt] *vt* : proteger — **protection** [prə'tɛkʃən] *n* : protección *f* — **protective** [prə'tɛktɪv] *adj* : protector — **protector** [prə'tɛktər] *n* : protector *m*, -tora *f*
protégé ['proːtə,ʒeɪ] *n* : protegido *m*, -da *f*
protein ['proː,tiːn] *n* : proteína *f*
protest ['proː,tɛst] *n* : protesta *f* — ～ [proː'tɛst] *vi* : protestar — *vi* **～ against** : protestar contra — **Protestant** ['prɑtəstənt] *n* : protestante *mf* — **protester** *or* **protestor** ['proː,tɛstər, proː'-] *n* : manifestante *mf*
protocol ['proːtə,kɔl] *n* : protocolo *m*
prototype ['proːtə,taɪp] *n* : prototipo *m*
protract [proː'trækt] *vt* : prolongar
protrude [proː'truːd] *vi* **-truded; -truding** : sobresalir

proud ['praud] *adj* : orgulloso
prove ['pru:v] *v* **proved; proved** *or*
  proven ['pru:vən]; **proving** *vt* : probar
  — *vi* : resultar
proverb ['prɑ,vərb] *n* : proverbio *m*, refrán *m* — **proverbial** [prə'vərbiəl] *adj*
  : proverbial
provide [prə'vaɪd] *v* **-vided; -viding** *vt*
  : proveer — *vi* ~ **for** SUPPORT : mantener — **provided** [prə'vaɪdəd] *or* ~
  that *conj* : con tal (de) que, siempre
  que — **providence** ['prɑvədəns] *n*
  : providencia *f*
province ['prɑvɪnts] *n* **1** : provincia *f* **2**
  SPHERE : campo *m*, competencia *f* —
  provincial [prə'vɪntʃəl] *adj* : provinciano
provision [prə'vɪʒən] *n* **1** : provisión *f*,
  suministro *m* **2** STIPULATION : condición *f* **3** ~ **s** *npl* : víveres *mpl* — **provisional** [prə'vɪʒənəl] *adj* : provisional
  — **proviso** [prə'vaɪ,zo:] *n, pl* **-sos** *or*
  -soes : condición *f*
provoke [prə'vo:k] *vt* **-voked; -voking**
  : provocar — **provocation** [,prɑvə-
  'keɪʃən] *n* : provocación *f* — **provocative** [prə'vɑkətɪv] *adj* : provocador,
  provocativo
prow ['prau] *n* : proa *f*
prowess ['prauəs] *n* **1** BRAVERY : valor *m*
  2 SKILL : habilidad *f*
prowl ['praul] *vi* : merodear, rondar — *vt*
  : merodear por — **prowler** ['praulər] *n*
  : merodeador *m*, -dora *f*
proximity [prɑk'sɪmət̮i] *n* : proximidad *f*
  — **proxy** ['prɑksi] *n, pl* **proxies by** ~
  : por poder
prude ['pru:d] *n* : mojigato *m*, -ta *f*
prudence ['pru:dənts] *n* : prudencia *f* —
  prudent ['pru:dənt] *adj* : prudente
prune[1] ['pru:n] *n* : ciruela *f* pasa
prune[2] *vt* **pruned; pruning** : podar (arbustos, etc.)
pry ['praɪ] *v* **pried; prying** *vi* ~ **into**
  : entrometerse en — *vt* ~ **or** ~ **open**
  : abrir (a la fuerza)
psalm ['sɑm, 'sɑlm] *n* : salmo *m*
pseudonym ['su:də,nɪm] *n* : seudónimo
  m
psychiatry [sə'kaɪətri, saɪ-] *n* : psiquiatría *f* — **psychiatric** [,saɪki'ætrɪk] *adj*
  : psiquiátrico — **psychiatrist** [sə-
  'kaɪətrɪst, saɪ-] *n* : psiquiatra *mf*
psychic ['saɪkɪk] *adj* : psíquico
psychoanalysis [,saɪko:ə'næləsɪs] *n, pl*
  -yses : psicoanálisis *m* — **psychoanalyst** [saɪko:'ænəlɪst] *n* : psicoanalista
  mf — **psychoanalyze** [,saɪko:'ænəl,aɪz]
  vt **-lyzed; -lyzing** : psicoanalizar
psychology [saɪ'kɑlədʒi] *n, pl* **-gies**

  : psicología *f* — **psychological**
  [,saɪkə'lɑdʒɪkəl] *adj* : psicológico —
  psychologist [saɪ'kɑlədʒɪst] *n* : psicólogo *m*, -ga *f*
psychopath ['saɪkə,pæθ] *n* : psicópata *mf*
psychotherapy [,saɪko'θerəpi] *n, pl*
  -pies : psicoterapia *f*
psychotic [saɪ'kɑtɪk] *adj* : psicótico
puberty ['pju:bərt̮i] *n* : pubertad *f*
pubic ['pju:bɪk] *adj* : púbico
public ['pʌblɪk] *adj* : público — ~ *n*
  : público *m* — **publication** [,pʌblə-
  'keɪʃən] *n* : publicación *f* — **publicity**
  [pə'blɪsət̮i] *n* : publicidad *f* — **publicize** ['pʌblə,saɪz] *vt* **-cized; -cizing**
  : publicitar, divulgar
publish ['pʌblɪʃ] *vt* : publicar — **publisher** ['pʌblɪʃər] *n* **1** : editor *m*, -tora *f*
  (persona) **2** : casa *f* editorial (negocio)
pucker ['pʌkər] *vt* : fruncir, arrugar — *vi*
  : arrugarse
pudding ['pudɪŋ] *n* : budín *m*, pudín *m*
puddle ['pʌdəl] *n* : charco *m*
pudgy ['pʌdʒi] *adj* **pudgier; -est** : rechoncho *fam*
Puerto Rican [,pwertə'ri:kən, ,pɔrt̮ə-] *adj*
  : puertorriqueño
puff ['pʌf] *vi* **1** BLOW : soplar **2** PANT : resoplar **3** ~ **up** SWELL : hincharse — *vt*
  ~ **out** : hinchar — ~ *n* **1** : bocanada
  f (de humo) **2** : chupada *f* (a un cigarrillo) **3** *or* **cream** ~ : pastelito *m* de
  crema **4** *or* **powder** ~ : borla *f* —
  puffy ['pʌfi] *adj* **puffier; -est** : hinchado
pull ['pul, 'pʌl] *vt* **1** : tirar de **2** EXTRACT
  : sacar **3** TEAR : desgarrarse (un músculo, etc.) **4** ~ **off** REMOVE : quitar **5**
  ~ **oneself together** : calmarse **6** ~
  up : levantar, subir — *vi* **1** : tirar **2** ~
  through RECOVER : reponerse **3** ~ **together** COOPERATE : reunir **4** ~ **up**
  STOP : parar — ~ *n* **1** : tirón *m* **2** INFLUENCE : influencia *f* — **pulley** ['puli]
  n, pl **-leys** : polea *f* — **pullover** ['pul-
  ,o:vər] *n* : suéter *m*
pulp ['pʌlp] *n* **1** : pulpa *f* (de frutas, etc.)
  2 *or* **wood** ~ : pasta *f* de papel
pulpit ['pul,pɪt] *n* : púlpito *m*
pulsate ['pʌl,seɪt] *vi* **-sated; -sating**
  : palpitar — **pulse** ['pʌls] *n* : pulso *m*
pulverize ['pʌlvə,raɪz] *vt* **-ized; -izing**
  : pulverizar
pummel ['pʌməl] *vt* **-meled; -meling**
  : aporrear
pump[1] ['pʌmp] *n* : bomba *f* — ~ *vt* **1**
  : bombear **2** ~ **up** : inflar
pump[2] *n* SHOE : zapato *m* de tacón
pumpernickel ['pʌmpər,nɪkəl] *n* : pan *m*
  negro de centeno

pumpkin ['pʌmpkɪn, 'pʌŋkən] n : calabaza f, zapallo m Lat

pun ['pʌn] n : juego m de palabras — vi **punned; punning** : hacer juegos de palabras

punch[1] ['pʌntʃ] vt 1 : dar un puñetazo a 2 PERFORATE : perforar (papeles, etc.), picar (un boleto) — ~ n 1 : golpe m, puñetazo m 2 or **paper** ~ : perforadora f

punch[2] n : ponche m (bebida)

punctual ['pʌŋktʃuəl] adj : puntual — **punctuality** [,pʌŋktʃu'ælət̬i] n : puntualidad f

punctuate ['pʌŋktʃu,eɪt] vt **-ated; -ating** : puntuar — **punctuation** [,pʌŋktʃu-'eɪʃən] n : puntuación f

puncture ['pʌŋktʃər] n : pinchazo m, ponchadura f Lat — ~ vt **-tured; -turing** : pinchar, ponchar Lat

pungent ['pʌndʒənt] adj : acre

punish ['pʌnɪʃ] vt : castigar — **punishment** ['pʌnɪʃmənt] n : castigo m — **punitive** ['pju:nət̬ɪv] adj : punitivo

puny ['pju:ni] adj **-nier; -est** : enclenque

pup ['pʌp] n : cachorro m, -rra f (de un perro); cría f (de otros animales)

pupil[1] ['pju:pəl] n : alumno m, -na f (de colegio)

pupil[2] n : pupila f (del ojo)

puppet ['pʌpət] n : títere m

puppy ['pʌpi] n, pl **-pies** : cachorro m, -rra f

purchase ['pərtʃəs] vt **-chased; -chasing** : comprar — ~ n : compra f

pure ['pjʊr] adj **purer; purest** : puro

puree [pjʊ'reɪ, -'ri:] n : puré m

purely ['pjʊrli] adv : puramente

purgatory ['pərgə,tori] n, pl **-ries** : purgatorio m — **purge** ['pərdʒ] vt **purged; purging** : purgar — ~ n : purga f

purify ['pjʊrə,faɪ] vt **-fied; -fying** : purificar — **purification** [,pjʊrəfə'keɪʃən] n : purificación f

puritanical [,pjʊrə'tænɪkəl] adj : puritano

purity ['pjʊrət̬i] n : pureza f

purple ['pərpəl] n : morado m

purport [pər'port] vt ~ **to be** : pretender ser

purpose ['pərpəs] n 1 : propósito m 2 RESOLUTION : determinación f 3 **on** ~ : a propósito — **purposeful** ['pərpəs-fəl] adj : resuelto — **purposely** ['pər-pəsli] adv : a propósito

purr ['pər] n : ronroneo m — ~ vi : ronronear

purse ['pərs] n 1 or **change** ~ : monedero m 2 HANDBAG : cartera f, bolso m Spain, bolsa f Lat — ~ vt **pursed; pursing** : fruncir

pursue [pər'su:] vt **-sued; -suing** 1 CHASE : perseguir 2 SEEK : buscar — **pursuer** [pər'su:ər] n : perseguidor m, -dora f — **pursuit** [pər'su:t] n 1 CHASE : persecución f 2 SEARCH : búsqueda f 3 OCCUPATION : actividad f

pus ['pʌs] n : pus m

push ['pʊʃ] vt 1 SHOVE : empujar 2 PRESS : apretar 3 URGE : presionar 4 ~ **around** BULLY : mangonear — vi 1 : empujar 2 ~ **for** : presionar para — ~ n 1 SHOVE : empujón m 2 DRIVE : dinamismo m 3 EFFORT : esfuerzo m — **pushy** ['pʊʃi] adj **pushier; -est** : mandón, prepotente

pussy ['pʊsi] n, pl **pussies** : gatito m, -ta f; minino m, -na f

put ['pʊt] v **put; putting** vt 1 : poner 2 INSERT : meter 3 EXPRESS : decir 4 ~ **one's mind to sth** : proponerse hacer algo — vi ~ **up with** : aguantar — **put away** vt 1 STORE : guardar 2 or ~ **aside** : dejar a un lado — **put down** vt 1 SUPPRESS : aplastar, sofocar 2 ATTRIBUTE : atribuir — **put off** vt DEFER : aplazar, posponer — **put on** vt 1 ASSUME : adoptar 2 PRESENT : presentar (una obra de teatro, etc.) 3 WEAR : ponerse — **put out** vt INCONVENIENCE : incomodar — **put up** vt 1 BUILD : construir 2 LODGE : alojar 3 PROVIDE : poner (dinero)

putrefy ['pju:trə,faɪ] vi **-fied; -fying** : pudrirse

putty ['pʌt̬i] n, pl **-ties** : masilla f

puzzle ['pʌzəl] v **-zled; -zling** vt : confundir, dejar perplejo — vi ~ **over** : tratar de descifrar — ~ n 1 : rompecabezas m 2 MYSTERY : enigma m

pylon ['paɪ,lɑn, -lən] n : pilón m

pyramid ['pɪrə,mɪd] n : pirámide f

python ['paɪ,θɑn, -θən] n : pitón f

Q

q ['kju:] *n*, *pl* **q's** *or* **qs** ['kju:z] : q *f*, decimoséptima letra del alfabeto inglés

quack¹ ['kwæk] *vi* : graznar (dícese del pato) — ~ *n* : graznido *m*

quack² *n* CHARLATAN : charlatán *m*, -tana *f*

quadruple [kwɑ'dru:pəl, -'drʌ-; 'kwɑdrə-] *v* **-pled; -pling** *vt* : cuadruplicar — *vi* : cuadruplicarse

quagmire ['kwæg,maɪr, 'kwɑg-] *n* : atolladero *m*

quail ['kweɪl] *n*, *pl* **quail** *or* **quails** : codorniz *f*

quaint ['kweɪnt] *adj* 1 ODD : curioso 2 PICTURESQUE : pintoresco

quake ['kweɪk] *vi* **quaked; quaking** : temblar — ~ *n* → **earthquake**

qualify ['kwɑlə,faɪ] *v* **-fied; -fying** *vt* 1 LIMIT : matizar 2 : calificar (en gramática) 3 EQUIP : habilitar — *vi* 1 : titularse (de abogado, etc.) 2 : clasificarse (en deportes) — **qualification** [,kwɑləfə'keɪʃən] *n* 1 REQUIREMENT : requisito *m* 2 ~s *npl* ABILITY : capacidad *f* 3 without ~ : sin reservas — **qualified** ['kwɑlə,faɪd] *adj* : capacitado

quality ['kwɑləti] *n*, *pl* **-ties** 1 : calidad *f* 2 PROPERTY : cualidad *f*

qualm ['kwɑm, 'kwɑlm, 'kwɔm] *n* 1 DOUBT : duda *f* 2 have no ~s about : no tener ningún escrúpulo en

quandary ['kwɑndri] *n*, *pl* **-ries** : dilema *m*

quantity ['kwɑntəti] *n*, *pl* **-ties** : cantidad *f*

quarantine ['kwɔrən,ti:n] *n* : cuarentena *f* — ~ *vt* **-tined; -tining** : poner en cuarentena

quarrel ['kwɔrəl] *n* : pelea *f*, riña *f* — ~ *vi* **-reled** *or* **-relled; -reling** *or* **-relling** : pelearse, reñir — **quarrelsome** ['kwɔrəlsəm] *adj* : pendenciero

quarry¹ ['kwɔri] *n*, *pl* **quarries** PREY : presa *f*

quarry² *n*, *pl* **quarries** EXCAVATION : cantera *f*

quart ['kwɔrt] *n* : cuarto *m* de galón

quarter ['kwɔrtər] *n* 1 : cuarto *m* (en matemáticas) 2 : moneda *f* de 25 centavos 3 DISTRICT : barrio *m* 4 ~ after three : las tres y cuarto 5 ~s *npl* LODGING : alojamiento *m* — ~ *vt* 1

: dividir en cuatro partes 2 : acuartelar (tropas) — **quarterly** ['kwɔrtərli] *adv* : cada tres meses — ~ *adj* : trimestral — ~ *n*, *pl* **-lies** : publicación *f* trimestral

quartet [kwɔr'tet] *n* : cuarteto *m*

quartz ['kwɔrts] *n* : cuarzo *m*

quash ['kwɑʃ, 'kwɔʃ] *vt* 1 ANNUL : anular 2 SUPPRESS : aplastar, sofocar

quaver ['kweɪvər] *vi* : temblar

quay ['ki:, 'keɪ, 'kweɪ] *n* : muelle *m*

queasy ['kwi:zi] *adj* **-sier; -est** : mareado

queen ['kwi:n] *n* : reina *f*

queer ['kwɪr] *adj* ODD : extraño

quell ['kwel] *vt* SUPPRESS : sofocar, aplastar

quench ['kwentʃ] *vt* 1 EXTINGUISH : apagar 2 ~ one's thirst : quitar la sed

query ['kwɪri, 'kwɛr-] *n*, *pl* **-ries** : pregunta *f* — ~ *vt* **-ried; -rying** 1 ASK : preguntar 2 QUESTION : cuestionar

quest ['kwest] *n* : búsqueda *f*

question ['kwestʃən] *n* 1 QUERY : pregunta *f* 2 ISSUE : cuestión *f* 3 be out of the ~ : ser indiscutible 4 call into ~ : poner en duda 5 without ~ : sin duda — ~ *vt* 1 ASK : preguntar 2 DOUBT : cuestionar 3 INTERROGATE : interrogar — *vi* : preguntar — **questionable** ['kwestʃənəbəl] *adj* : discutible — **question mark** *n* : signo *m* de interrogación — **questionnaire** [,kwestʃə'nær] *n* : cuestionario *m*

queue ['kju:] *n* : cola *f* — ~ *vi* **queued; queuing** *or* **queueing** : hacer cola

quibble ['kwɪbəl] *vi* **-bled; -bling** : discutir, quejarse por nimiedades

quick ['kwɪk] *adj* 1 : rápido 2 CLEVER : agudo — ~ *n* to the ~ : en lo vivo — ~ *adv* : rápidamente — **quicken** ['kwɪkən] *vt* : acelerar — **quickly** ['kwɪkli] *adv* : rápidamente — **quicksand** ['kwɪk,sænd] *n* : arena *f* movediza — **quick-tempered** ['kwɪk'tempərd] *adj* : irascible — **quick-witted** ['kwɪk'wɪtəd] *adj* : agudo

quiet ['kwaɪət] *n* 1 : silencio *m* 2 CALM : tranquilidad *f* — ~ *adj* 1 : silencioso 2 CALM : tranquilo 3 RESERVED : callado 4 : discreto (dícese de colores, etc.) — ~ *vt* 1 SILENCE : hacer callar 2 CALM : calmar — *vi or* ~ **down** : cal-

marse — **quietly** *adv* **1** : silenciosa-
mente **2** CALMLY : tranquilamente
quilt ['kwɪlt] *n* : edredón *m*
quintet [kwɪn'tɛt] *n* : quinteto *m*
quip ['kwɪp] *n* : ocurrencia *f*, salida *f* —
~ *vt* **quipped; quipping** : decir bro-
meando
quirk ['kwərk] *n* : peculiaridad *f*
quit ['kwɪt] *v* **quit; quitting** *vt* **1** LEAVE
: dejar, abandonar **2** ~ **doing** : dejar
de hacer — *vi* **1** STOP : parar **2** RESIGN
: dimitir, renunciar
quite ['kwaɪt] *adv* **1** COMPLETELY : completamente **2** RATHER : bastante

quits ['kwɪts] *adj* **call it** ~ : quedar en
paz
quiver ['kwɪvər] *vi* : temblar
quiz ['kwɪz] *n, pl* **quizzes** TEST : prueba
f — ~ *vt* **quizzed; quizzing** : interrogar
quota ['kwoːtə] *n* : cuota *f*, cupo *m*
quotation [kwo'teɪʃən] *n* **1** : cita *f* **2** ESTI-
MATE : presupuesto *m* — **quotation
marks** *npl* : comillas *fpl* — **quote**
['kwoːt] *vt* **quoted; quoting 1** CITE
: citar **2** : cotizar (en finanzas) — ~ *n*
1 → **quotation 2** ~**s** *npl* → **quotation
marks**
quotient ['kwoːʃənt] *n* : cociente *m*

R

r ['ɑr] *n, pl* **r's** *or* **rs** ['ɑrz] : r *f*, decimoc-
tava letra del alfabeto inglés
rabbi ['ræˌbaɪ] *n* : rabino *m*, -na *f*
rabbit ['ræbət] *n, pl* **-bit** *or* **-bits** : conejo *m*, -ja *f*
rabble ['ræbəl] *n* : chusma *f*, populacho
m
rabies ['reɪbiːz] *ns* & *pl* : rabia *f* — **rabid**
['ræbɪd] *adj* **1** : rabioso **2** FANATIC
: fanático
raccoon [ræ'kuːn] *n, pl* **-coon** *or*
-coons : mapache *m*
race¹ ['reɪs] *n* **1** : raza *f* **2 human** ~
: género *m* humano
race² *n* : carrera *f* (competitiva) — ~ *vi*
raced; racing 1 : correr (en una carrera) **2** RUSH : ir corriendo — **race-
horse** ['reɪs,hors] *n* : caballo *m* de carreras — **racetrack** ['reɪs,træk] *n* : pista
f (de carreras)
racial ['reɪʃəl] *adj* : racial — **racism**
['reɪ,sɪzəm] *n* : racismo *m* — **racist**
['reɪsɪst] *n* : racista *mf*
rack ['ræk] *n* **1** SHELF : estante *m* **2** lug-
gage ~ : portaequipajes *m* — ~ *vt* **1**
~**ed with** : atormentado por **2** ~
one's brains : devanarse los sesos
racket¹ ['rækət] *n* : raqueta *f* (en deportes)
racket² *n* **1** DIN : alboroto *m*, bulla *f* **2**
SWINDLE : estafa *f*
racy ['reɪsi] *adj* **racier; -est** : subido de
tono, picante
radar ['reɪ,dɑr] *n* : radar *m*
radiant ['reɪdiənt] *adj* : radiante — **radi-
ance** ['reɪdiənts] *n* : resplandor *m* —
radiate ['reɪdi,eɪt] *v* **-ated; -ating** *vt*
: irradiar — *vi* **1** : irradiar **2** *or* ~ **out**
: extenderse (desde un centro) — **radi-**

ation [ˌreɪdi'eɪʃən] *n* : radiación *f* —
radiator ['reɪdi,eɪtər] *n* : radiador *m*
radical ['rædɪkəl] *adj* : radical — ~ *n*
: radical *mf*
radii → **radius**
radio ['reɪdi,oː] *n, pl* **-dios** : radio *mf*
(aparato), radio *f* (medio) — ~ *vt*
: transmitir por radio — **radioactive**
['reɪdioˈæktɪv] *adj* : radioactivo, radiactivo
radish ['rædɪʃ] *n* : rábano *m*
radius ['reɪdiəs] *n, pl* **radii** [-di,aɪ] : radio
m
raffle ['ræfəl] *vt* **-fled; -fling** : rifar — ~
n : rifa *f*
raft ['ræft] *n* : balsa *f*
rafter ['ræftər] *n* : cabrio *m*
rag ['ræg] *n* **1** : trapo *m* **2** ~**s** *npl* TAT-
TERS : harapos *mpl*, andrajos *mpl*
rage ['reɪdʒ] *n* **1** : cólera *f*, rabia *f* **2 be
all the** ~ : hacer furor — ~ *vi*
raged; raging 1 : estar furioso **2** : bramar (dícese del viento, etc.)
ragged ['rægəd] *adj* **1** UNEVEN : irregular **2** TATTERED : andrajoso, harapiento
raid ['reɪd] *n* **1** : invasión *f* (militar) **2**
: asalto *m* (por delincuentes), redada *f*
(por la policía) — ~ *vt* **1** INVADE : invadir **2** ROB : asaltar **3** : hacer una
redada en (dícese de la policía) —
raider ['reɪdər] *n* ATTACKER : asaltante
mf
rail¹ ['reɪl] *vi* ~ **at s.o.** : recriminar a
algn
rail² *n* **1** BAR : barra *f* **2** HANDRAIL
: pasamanos *m* **3** TRACK : riel *m* **4 by**
~ : por ferrocarril — **railing** ['reɪlɪŋ] *n*
1 : baranda *f* (de un balcón),
pasamanos *m* (de una escalera) **2**

RAILS : reja *f* — **railroad** ['reɪl,roːd] *n* : ferrocarril *m* — **railway** ['reɪl,weɪ] → **railroad**

rain ['reɪn] *n* : lluvia *f* — *vi* : llover — **rainbow** ['reɪn,boː] *n* : arco *m* iris — **raincoat** ['reɪn,koːt] *n* : impermeable *m* — **rainfall** ['reɪn,fɔl] *n* : precipitación *f* — **rainy** ['reɪni] *adj* **rainier; -est** : lluvioso

raise ['reɪz] *vt* **raised; raising 1** : levantar **2** COLLECT : recaudar **3** REAR : criar **4** GROW : cultivar **5** INCREASE : aumentar **6** : sacar (objeciones, etc.) — *n* : aumento *m*

raisin ['reɪzən] *n* : pasa *f*

rake ['reɪk] *n* : rastrillo *m* — *vt* **raked; raking** : rastrillar

rally ['ræli] *v* **-lied; -lying** *vi* **1** : unirse, reunirse **2** RECOVER : recuperarse — *vt* : conseguir (apoyo), unir a (la gente) — *n*, *pl* **-lies** : reunión *f*, mitin *m*

ram *n* ['ræm] : carnero *m* (animal) — *vt* **rammed; ramming 1** CRAM : meter con fuerza **2** *or* **~ into** : chocar contra

RAM ['ræm] *n* : RAM *f*

ramble ['ræmbəl] *vi* **-bled; -bling 1** WANDER : pasear **2** *or* **~ on** : divagar — *n* : paseo *m*, excursión *f*

ramp ['ræmp] *n* : rampa *f*

rampage ['ræm,peɪdʒ, ,ræm'peɪdʒ] *vi* **-paged; -paging** : andar arrasando todo — *n* ['ræm,peɪdʒ] : frenesí *m* (de violencia)

rampant ['ræmpənt] *adj* : desenfrenado

rampart ['ræm,pɑrt] *n* : muralla *f*

ramshackle ['ræm,ʃækəl] *adj* : destartalado

ran → **run**

ranch ['ræntʃ] *n* : hacienda *f* — **rancher** ['ræntʃər] *n* : hacendado *m*, -da *f*

rancid ['ræntsɪd] *adj* : rancio

rancor ['ræŋkər] *n* : rencor *m*

random ['rændəm] *adj* **1** : aleatorio **2 at ~** : al azar

rang → **ring**

range ['reɪndʒ] *n* **1** GRASSLAND : pradera *f* **2** STOVE : cocina *f* **3** VARIETY : gama *f* **4** SCOPE : amplitud *f* **5** *or* **mountain ~** : cordillera *f* — *v* **~ed; ranging 1** EXTEND : extenderse **2** **~ from...to...** : variar entre...y... — **ranger** ['reɪndʒər] *n* *or* **forest ~** : guardabosque *mf*

rank¹ ['ræŋk] *adj* **1** SMELLY : fétido **2** OUTRIGHT : completo

rank² *n* **1** ROW : fila *f* **2** : rango *m* (militar) **3** **~s** *npl* : soldados *mpl* rasos **4 the ~ and file** : las bases — *vt* RATE : clasificar — *vi* : clasificarse

rankle ['ræŋkəl] *vi* **-kled; -kling** : causar rencor, doler

ransack ['ræn,sæk] *vt* **1** SEARCH : registrar **2** LOOT : saquear

ransom ['ræntsəm] *n* : rescate *m* — *vt* : rescatar

rant ['rænt] *vi* *or* **~ and rave** : despotricar

rap¹ ['ræp] *n* KNOCK : golpecito *m* — *v* **rapped; rapping** : golpear

rap² *n* *or* **~ music** : rap *m*

rapacious [rə'peɪʃəs] *adj* : rapaz

rape ['reɪp] *vt* **raped; raping** : violar — *n* : violación *f*

rapid ['ræpɪd] *adj* : rápido — **rapids** ['ræpɪdz] *npl* : rápidos *mpl*

rapist ['reɪpɪst] *n* : violador *m*, -dora *f*

rapport [ræ'por] *n* **have a good ~** : entenderse bien

rapt ['ræpt] *adj* : absorto, embelesado

rapture ['ræptʃər] *n* : éxtasis *m*

rare ['rær] *adj* **rarer; rarest 1** FINE : excepcional **2** UNCOMMON : raro **3** : poco cocido (dícese de la carne) — **rarely** ['rærli] *adv* : raramente — **rarity** ['rærə,ti] *n*, *pl* **-ties** : rareza *f*

rascal ['ræskəl] *n* : pillo *m*, -lla *f*; pícaro *m*, -ra *f*

rash¹ ['ræʃ] *adj* : imprudente, precipitado

rash² *n* : sarpullido *m*, erupción *f*

rasp ['ræsp] *vt* SCRAPE : raspar — *n* : escofina *f*

raspberry ['ræz,bɛri] *n*, *pl* **-ries** : frambuesa *f*

rat ['ræt] *n* : rata *f*

rate ['reɪt] *n* **1** PACE : velocidad *f*, ritmo *m* **2** : tipo *m*, tasa *m* (de interés, etc.) **3** PRICE : tarifa *f* **4 at any ~** : de todos modos **5 birth ~** : índice *m* de natalidad — *vt* **rated; rating 1** REGARD : considerar **2** DESERVE : merecer

rather ['ræðər, 'rʌ-, 'rɑ-] *adv* **1** FAIRLY : bastante **2 I'd ~...** : prefiero... **3** *or* **~** : o mejor dicho

ratify ['rætə,faɪ] *vt* **-fied; -fying** : ratificar — **ratification** [,rætəfə'keɪʃən] *n* : ratificación *f*

rating ['reɪtɪŋ] *n* **1** : clasificación *f* **2** **~s** *npl* : índice *m* de audiencia

ratio ['reɪʃio] *n*, *pl* **-tios** : proporción *f*

ration ['ræʃən, 'reɪʃən] *n* **1** : ración *f* **2** **~s** *npl* PROVISIONS : víveres *mpl* — *vt* **rationed; rationing** : racionar

rational ['ræʃənəl] *adj* : racional — **rationale** [,ræʃə'næl] *n* : lógica *f*, razones *fpl* — **rationalize** ['ræʃənə,laɪz] *vt* **-ized; -izing** : racionalizar

rattle ['rætəl] *v* **-tled; -tling** *vi* : traquetear — *vt* **1** SHAKE : agitar **2** UPSET : desconcertar 3 ~ off : decir de corrido — ~ n 1 : traqueteo m 2 or baby's ~ : sonajero m — rattlesnake ['ræt̬əl,sneɪk] n : serpiente f de cascabel

raucous ['rɔkəs] adj 1 HOARSE : ronco 2 BOISTEROUS : bullicioso

ravage ['rævɪdʒ] vt -aged; -aging : estragar, asolar — ravages ['rævɪdʒəz] npl : estragos mpl

rave ['reɪv] vi raved; raving 1 : delirar 2 ~ about : hablar con entusiasmo sobre

raven ['reɪvən] n : cuervo m

ravenous ['rævənəs] adj 1 HUNGRY : hambriento 2 VORACIOUS : voraz

ravine [rə'viːn] n : barranco m

ravishing ['rævɪʃɪŋ] adj : encantador

raw ['rɔ] adj rawer; rawest 1 UNCOOKED : crudo 2 INEXPERIENCED : inexperto 3 CHAFED : en carne viva 4 : frío y húmedo (dícese del tiempo) 5 ~ deal : trato m injusto 6 ~ materials : materias fpl primas

ray ['reɪ] n : rayo m

rayon ['reɪɑn] n : rayón m

raze ['reɪz] vt razed; razing : arrasar

razor ['reɪzər] n : maquinilla f de afeitar — razor blade n : hoja f de afeitar

reach ['riːtʃ] vt 1 : alcanzar 2 or ~ out : extender 3 : llegar a (un acuerdo, un límite, etc.) 4 CONTACT : contactar — vi : extenderse 2 ~ for : tratar de agarrar — ~ n 1 : alcance m 2 within ~ : al alcance

react [ri'ækt] vi : reaccionar — reaction [ri'ækʃən] n : reacción f — reactionary [ri'ækʃə,neri] adj : reaccionario m, -ria f — reactor [ri'æktər] n : reactor m

read ['riːd] v read ['red]; reading vt 1 : leer 2 INTERPRET : interpretar 3 SAY : decir 4 INDICATE : marcar — vi 1 : leer 2 it ~s as follows : dice lo siguiente — readable ['riːdəbəl] adj : legible — reader ['riːdər] n : lector m, -tora f

readily ['redəli] adv 1 WILLINGLY : de buena gana 2 EASILY : fácilmente

reading ['riːdɪŋ] n : lectura f

readjust [,riːə'dʒʌst] vt : reajustar — vi : volverse a adaptar

ready ['redi] adj readier; -est 1 : listo, preparado 2 WILLING : dispuesto 3 AVAILABLE : disponible 4 get ~ : prepararse — ~ vt readied; readying : preparar

real ['riːl] adj 1 : verdadero, real 2 GENUINE : auténtico — ~ adv VERY : muy — real estate n : propiedad f inmobiliaria, bienes mpl raices — realism

['riːə,lɪzəm] n : realismo m — realist ['riːəlɪst] n : realista mf — realistic [,riːə'lɪstɪk] adj : realista — reality [ri'ælət̬i] n, pl -ties : realidad f

realize ['riːə,laɪz] vt -ized; -izing 1 : darse cuenta de 2 ACHIEVE : realizar — realization [,riːələ'zeɪʃən] n 1 : comprensión f 2 FULFILLMENT : realización f

really ['riːli, 'rɪ-] adv : verdaderamente

realm ['relm] n 1 KINGDOM : reino m 2 SPHERE : esfera f

ream ['riːm] n : resma f (de papel)

reap ['riːp] v : cosechar

reappear [,riːə'pɪr] vi : reaparecer

rear1 ['rɪr] vt 1 RAISE : levantar 2 : criar (niños, etc.) — vi or ~ up : encabritarse

rear2 n 1 BACK : parte f de atrás 2 BUTTOCKS : trasero m fam — ~ adj : trasero, posterior

rearrange [,riːə'reɪndʒ] vt -ranged; -ranging : reorganizar, cambiar

reason ['riːzən] n : razón f — ~ vt THINK : pensar — vi : razonar — reasonable ['riːzənəbəl] adj : razonable — reasoning ['riːzənɪŋ] n : razonamiento m

reassure [,riːə'ʃʊr] vt -sured; -suring : tranquilizar — reassurance [,riːə'ʃʊrəns] n : (palabras fpl de) consuelo m

rebate ['riː,beɪt] n : reembolso m

rebel ['rebəl] n : rebelde mf — ~ [rɪ'bel] vi -belled; -belling : rebelarse — rebellion [rɪ'beljən] n : rebelión f — rebellious [rɪ'beljəs] adj : rebelde

rebirth [,riː'bərθ] n : renacimiento m

rebound ['riː,baʊnd, ,riː'baʊnd] vi : rebotar — ~ ['riː,baʊnd] n : rebote m

rebuff [rɪ'bʌf] vt : rechazar — ~ n : desaire m

rebuild [,riː'bɪld] vt -built; -building : reconstruir

rebuke [rɪ'bjuːk] vt -buked; -buking : reprender — ~ n : reprimenda f

rebut [rɪ'bʌt] vt -butted; -butting : rebatir — rebuttal [rɪ'bʌt̬əl] n : refutación f

recall [rɪ'kɔl] vt 1 : llamar (al servicio, etc.) 2 REMEMBER : recordar 3 REVOKE : revocar — ~ [rɪ'kɔl, 'riː,kɔl] n 1 : retirada f 2 MEMORY : memoria f

recant [rɪ'kænt] vi : retractarse

recapitulate [,riːkə'pɪtʃə,leɪt] v -lated; -lating : recapitular

recapture [,riː'kæptʃər] vt -tured; -turing 1 : recobrar 2 RELIVE : revivir

recede [ri'siːd] vi -ceded; -ceding : retirarse

receipt [rɪ'siːt] *n* **1** : recibo *m* **2** ∼s *npl* : ingresos *mpl*
receive [rɪ'siːv] *vt* -ceived; -ceiving : recibir — **receiver** [rɪ'siːvər] *n* **1** : receptor *m* (de radio, etc.) **2** *or* tele-phone ∼ : auricular *m*
recent ['riːsənt] *adj* : reciente — **recently** [-li] *adv* : recientemente
receptacle [rɪ'sɛptɪkəl] *n* : receptáculo *m*, recipiente *m*
reception [rɪ'sɛpʃən] *n* : recepción *f* — **receptionist** [rɪ'sɛpʃənɪst] *n* : recepcionista *mf* — **receptive** [rɪ'sɛptɪv] *adj* : receptivo
recess ['riːˌsɛs, rɪ'sɛs] *n* **1** ALCOVE : hueco *m* **2** : recreo *m* (escolar) **3** ADJOURNMENT : suspensión *f* de actividades *Spain*, receso *m* *Lat* — **recession** [rɪ'sɛʃən] *n* : recesión *f*
recharge [ˌriː'tʃɑrdʒ] *vt* -charged; -charging : recargar — **rechargeable** [ˌriː'tʃɑrdʒəbəl] *adj* : recargable
recipe ['rɛsəˌpi] *n* : receta *f*
recipient [rɪ'sɪpiənt] *n* : recipiente *mf*
reciprocal [rɪ'sɪprəkəl] *adj* : recíproco
recite [rɪ'saɪt] *vt* -cited; -citing **1** : recitar (un poema, etc.) **2** LIST : enumerar — **recital** [rɪ'saɪtəl] *n* : recital *m*
reckless ['rɛkləs] *adj* : imprudente — **recklessness** ['rɛkləsnəs] *n* : imprudencia *f*
reckon ['rɛkən] *vt* **1** COMPUTE : calcular **2** CONSIDER : considerar — **reckoning** ['rɛkənɪŋ] *n* : cálculos *mpl*
reclaim [rɪ'kleɪm] *vt* **1** : reclamar **2** RECOVER : recuperar
recline [rɪ'klaɪn] *vi* -clined; -clining : reclinarse — **reclining** *adj* : reclinable (dícese de un asiento, etc.)
recluse ['rɛˌkluːs, rɪ'kluːs] *n* : solitario *m*, -ria *f*
recognition [ˌrɛkɪg'nɪʃən] *n* : reconocimiento *m* — **recognizable** ['rɛkɪgˌnaɪzəbəl] *adj* : reconocible — **recognize** ['rɛkɪgˌnaɪz] *vt* -nized; -nizing : reconocer
recoil [rɪ'kɔɪl] *vi* : retroceder — ∼ ['riːˌkɔɪl, rɪ'-] *n* : culatazo *m* (de un arma de fuego)
recollect [ˌrɛkə'lɛkt] *v* : recordar — **recollection** [ˌrɛkə'lɛkʃən] *n* : recuerdo *m*
recommend [ˌrɛkə'mɛnd] *vt* : recomendar — **recommendation** [ˌrɛkəmən'deɪʃən] *n* : recomendación *f*
reconcile ['rɛkənˌsaɪl] *v* -ciled; -ciling *vt* **1** : reconciliar (personas), conciliar (datos, etc.) **2** ∼ **oneself to** : resignarse a — *vi* MAKE UP : reconciliarse — **reconciliation** [ˌrɛkənˌsɪli'eɪʃən] *n* : reconciliación *f*

reconnaissance [rɪ'kɑnəzənts, -sənts] *n* : reconocimiento *m* (militar)
reconsider [ˌriːkən'sɪdər] *vt* : reconsiderar
reconstruct [ˌriːkən'strʌkt] *vt* : reconstruir
record [rɪ'kɔrd] *vt* **1** WRITE DOWN : anotar, apuntar **2** REGISTER : registrar **3** : grabar (música, etc.) — ∼ ['rɛkərd] *n* **1** DOCUMENT : documento *m* **2** REGISTER : registro *m* **3** HISTORY : historial *m* **4** : disco *m* (de música, etc.) **5** criminal ∼ : antecedentes *mpl* penales **6** world ∼ : récord *m* mundial — **recorder** [rɪ'kɔrdər] *n* **1** : flauta *f* dulce **2** *or* tape ∼ : grabadora *f* — **recording** [-ɪŋ] *n* : disco *m* — **record player** *n* : tocadiscos *m*
recount[1] [rɪ'kaʊnt] *vt* NARRATE : narrar, relatar
recount[2] ['riːˌkaʊnt, ˌriː'-] *vt* : volver a contar (votos, etc.) — ∼ *n* : recuento *m*
recourse ['riːˌkɔrs, rɪ'-] *n* **1** : recurso *m* **2** have ∼ to : recurrir a
recover [rɪ'kʌvər] *vt* : recobrar — *vi* RECUPERATE : recuperarse — **recovery** [rɪ'kʌvəri] *n*, *pl* -eries : recuperación *f*
recreation [ˌrɛkri'eɪʃən] *n* : recreo *m* — **recreational** [ˌrɛkri'eɪʃənəl] *adj* : de recreo
recruit [rɪ'kruːt] *vt* : reclutar — ∼ *n* : recluta *mf* — **recruitment** [rɪ'kruːtmənt] *n* : reclutamiento *m*
rectangle ['rɛkˌtæŋgəl] *n* : rectángulo *m* — **rectangular** [rɛk'tæŋgjələr] *adj* : rectangular
rectify ['rɛktəˌfaɪ] *vt* -fied; -fying : rectificar
rector ['rɛktər] *n* **1** : párroco *m* (clérigo) **2** : rector *m*, -tora *f* (de una universidad) — **rectory** ['rɛktəri] *n*, *pl* -ries : rectoría *f*
rectum ['rɛktəm] *n*, *pl* -tums *or* -ta [-tə] : recto *m*
recuperate [rɪ'kuːpəˌreɪt, -'kjuː-] *v* -ated; -ating *vt* : recuperar — *vi* : recuperarse — **recuperation** [rɪˌkuːpə'reɪʃən, -ˌkjuː-] *n* : recuperación *f*
recur [rɪ'kər] *vi* -curred; -curring : repetirse — **recurrence** [rɪ'kərənts] *n* : repetición *f* — **recurrent** [rɪ'kərənt] *adj* : que se repite
recycle [rɪ'saɪkəl] *vt* -cled; -cling : reciclar
red ['rɛd] *adj* : rojo — ∼ *n* : rojo *m* — **redden** ['rɛdən] *vt* : enrojecer — *vi* : enrojecerse — **reddish** ['rɛdɪʃ] *adj* : rojizo
redecorate [ˌriː'dɛkəˌreɪt] *vt* -rated; -rating : pintar de nuevo
redeem [rɪ'diːm] *vt* **1** SAVE : salvar,

rescatar **2** : desempeñar (de un monte de piedad) **3** : canjear (cupones, etc.) — **redemption** [ri'dempʃən] n : redención f

red–handed ['red'hændəd] adv or adj : con las manos en la masa

redhead ['red,hed] n : pelirrojo m, -ja f

red–hot ['red'hɑt] adj : al rojo vivo

redness ['rednəs] n : rojez f

redo [,ri:'du:] vt **-did** [-dɪd]; **-done** [-'dʌn]; **-doing** : hacer de nuevo

redouble [ri'dʌbəl] vt **-bled**; **-bling** : redoblar

red tape n : papeleo m

reduce [ri'du:s, -'dju:s] v **-duced**; **-ducing** vt : reducir — vi SLIM : adelgazar — **reduction** [ri'dʌkʃən] n : reducción f

redundant [ri'dʌndənt] adj : redundante

reed ['ri:d] n **1** : caña f **2** : lengüeta f (de un instrumento)

reef ['ri:f] n : arrecife m

reek ['ri:k] vi : apestar

reel ['ri:l] n **1** : carrete m (de hilo, etc.) — ~ vt **1** ~ **in** : enrollar (un sedal), sacar (un pez) del agua **2** ~ **off** : enumerar — vi **1** SPIN : dar vueltas **2** STAGGER : tambalearse

reestablish [,ri:ɪ'stæblɪʃ] vt : restablecer

refer [ri'fər] v **-ferred**; **-ferring** vt DIRECT : enviar, mandar **2** SUBMIT : remitir — vi ~ **to 1** MENTION : referirse a **2** CONSULT : consultar

referee [,refə'ri:] n : árbitro m, -tra f — ~ **-eed**; **-eeing** : arbitrar

reference ['refrəns, 'refə-] n **1** : referencia f **2** CONSULTATION : consulta f **3** or ~ **book** : libro m de consulta **4 in** ~ **to** : con referencia a

refill [ri'fɪl] vt : rellenar — ~ ['ri;fɪl] n : recambio m

refine [ri'faɪn] vt **-fined**; **-fining** : refinar — **refined** [ri'faɪnd] adj : refinado — **refinement** [ri'faɪnmənt] n : refinamiento m — **refinery** [ri'faɪnəri] n, pl **-eries** : refinería f

reflect [ri'flekt] vt : reflejar — vi **1** : reflejarse **2** ~ **upon** : reflexionar sobre — **reflection** [ri'flekʃən] n **1** : reflexión f **2** IMAGE : reflejo m — **reflector** [ri'flektər] n : reflector m

reflex ['ri:,fleks] n : reflejo m

reflexive [ri'fleksɪv] adj : reflexivo

reform [ri'form] vt : reformar — vi : reformarse — ~ n : reforma f — **reformer** [ri'formər] n : reformador m, -dora f

refrain[1] [ri'freɪn] vi ~ **from** : abstenerse de

refrain[2] n : estribillo m (en música)

refresh [ri'freʃ] vt : refrescar — **refreshments** [ri'freʃmənts] npl : refrigerio m

refrigerate [ri'frɪdʒə,reɪt] vt **-ated**; **-ating** : refrigerar — **refrigeration** [ri,frɪdʒə'reɪʃən] n : refrigeración f — **refrigerator** [ri'frɪdʒə,reɪtər] n : nevera f, refrigerador m Lat, frigorífico m Spain

refuel [ri:'fju:əl] v **-eled** or **-elled**; **-eling** or **-elling** vt : llenar de carburante — vi : repostar

refuge ['re,fju:dʒ] n : refugio m — **refugee** [,refju'dʒi:] n : refugiado m, -da f

refund [ri'fʌnd, 'ri:,fʌnd] vt : reembolsar — ~ ['ri:,fʌnd] n : reembolso m

refurbish [ri'fərbɪʃ] vt : renovar, restaurar

refuse[1] [ri'fju:z] v **-fused**; **-fusing** vt **1** : rehusar, rechazar **2** ~ **to do sth** : negarse a hacer algo — vi : negarse — **refusal** [ri'fju:zəl] n : negativa f

refuse[2] ['re,fju:s, -,fju:z] n : residuos mpl, desperdicios mpl

refute [ri'fju:t] vt **-futed**; **-futing** : refutar

regain [ri'geɪn] vt : recuperar, recobrar

regal ['ri:gəl] adj : regio, majestuoso — **regalia** [ri'geɪljə] n : ropaje m, insignias fpl

regard [ri'gard] n **1** : consideración f **2** ESTEEM : estima f **3 in this** ~ : en este sentido **4** ~**s** npl : saludos mpl **5 with** ~ **to** : respecto a — ~ vt **1** : mirar (con recelo, etc.) **2** HEED : tener en cuenta **3** ESTEEM : estimar **4 as** ~**s** : en lo que se refiere a **5** ~ **as** : considerar — **regarding** [ri'gardɪŋ] prep : respecto a — **regardless** [ri'gardləs] adv : a pesar de todo — **regardless of** prep **1** : sin tener en cuenta **2** IN SPITE OF : a pesar de

regent ['ri:dʒənt] n : regente mf

regime [reɪ'ʒi:m, rɪ-] n : régimen m — **regimen** ['redʒəmən] n : régimen m

regiment ['redʒəmənt] n : regimiento m

region ['ri:dʒən] n : región f — **regional** ['ri:dʒənəl] adj : regional

register ['redʒəstər] n : registro m — ~ vt **1** : registrar (a personas), matricular (vehículos) **2** SHOW : marcar, manifestar **3** : certificar (correo) — vi ENROLL : inscribirse, matricularse — **registrar** ['redʒə,strar] n : registrador m, -dora f oficial — **registration** [,redʒə'streɪʃən] n **1** : inscripción f, matriculación f **2** or ~ **number** : número m de matrícula — **registry** ['redʒəstri] n, pl **-tries** : registro m

regret [ri'gret] vt **-gretted**; **-gretting** : lamentar — ~ n **1** REMORSE : arrepentimiento m **2** SORROW : pesar m

— **regrettable** [ri'grɛṭəbəl] *adj* : lamentable

regular ['rɛgjələr] *adj* **1** : regular **2** CUSTOMARY : habitual — ~ *n* : cliente *mf* habitual — **regularity** [,rɛgjə'læræṭi] *n*, *pl* **-ties** : regularidad *f* — **regularly** ['rɛgjələrli] *adv* : regularmente — **regulate** ['rɛgjə,leɪt] *vt* **-lated; -lating** : regular — **regulation** [,rɛgjə'leɪʃən] *n* **1** CONTROL : regulación *f* **2** RULE : regla *f*

rehabilitate [,riːhə'bɪlə,teɪt, ,riːə-] *vt* **-tated; -tating** : rehabilitar — **rehabilitation** [,riːhə,bɪlə'teɪʃən, ,riːə-] *n* : rehabilitación *f*

rehearse [ri'hərs] *v* **-hearsed; -hearsing** : ensayar — **rehearsal** [ri'hərsəl] *n* : ensayo *m*

reign ['reɪn] *n* : reinado *m* — ~ *vi* : reinar

reimburse [,riːəm'bərs] *vt* **-bursed; -bursing** : reembolsar — **reimbursement** [,riːəm'bərsmənt] *n* : reembolso *m*

rein ['reɪn] *n* : rienda *f*

reincarnation [,riːɪn,kɑr'neɪʃən] *n* : reencarnación *f*

reindeer ['reɪn,dɪr] *n* : reno *m*

reinforce [,riːən'fors] *vt* **-forced; -forcing** : reforzar — **reinforcement** [,riːən'forsmənt] *n* : refuerzo *m*

reinstate [,riːən'steɪt] *vt* **-stated; -stating** **1** : restablecer **2** : restituir (a algn en su cargo)

reiterate [ri'ɪṭə,reɪt] *vt* **-ated; -ating** : reiterar

reject [ri'dʒɛkt] *vt* : rechazar — **rejection** [ri'dʒɛkʃən] *n* : rechazo *m*

rejoice [ri'dʒɔɪs] *vi* **-joiced; -joicing** : regocijarse

rejuvenate [ri'dʒuːvə,neɪt] *vt* **-nated; -nating** : rejuvenecer

rekindle [,riː'kɪndəl] *vt* **-dled; -dling** : reavivar

relapse ['riːˌlæps, ri'læps] *n* : recaída *f* — ~ [ri'læps] *vi* **-lapsed; -lapsing** : recaer

relate [ri'leɪt] *v* **-lated; -lating** *vt* **1** TELL : relatar **2** ASSOCIATE : relacionar — *vi* ~ **to 1** CONCERN : estar relacionado con **2** UNDERSTAND : identificarse con **3** : relacionarse con (socialmente) — **related** [ri'leɪṭəd] *adj* ~ **to** : emparentado con — **relation** [ri'leɪʃən] *n* **1** CONNECTION : relación *f* **2** RELATIVE : pariente *mf* **3 in** ~ **to** : en relación con **4** ~**s** *npl* : relaciones *fpl* — **relationship** [ri'leɪʃən,ʃɪp] *n* **1** : relación *f* **2** KINSHIP : parentesco *m* — **relative** ['rɛləṭɪv] *n* : pariente *mf* — ~ *adj* : relativo — **relatively** *adv* : relativamente

relax [ri'læks] *vt* : relajar — *vi* : relajarse — **relaxation** [,riː,læk'seɪʃən] *n* **1** : relajación *f* **2** RECREATION : esparcimiento *m*

relay ['riːˌleɪ] *n* **1** : relevo *m* **2 or** ~ **race** : carrera *f* de relevos — ~ ['riːˌleɪ, ri'leɪ] *vt* **-layed; -laying** : transmitir

release [ri'liːs] *vt* **-leased; -leasing 1** FREE : liberar, poner en libertad **2** : soltar (un freno, etc.) **3** EMIT : despedir **4** : sacar (un libro, etc.), estrenar (una película) — ~ *n* **1** : liberación *f* **2** : estreno *m* (de una película), publicación *f* (de un libro) **3** : fuga *f* (de gases)

relegate ['rɛləˌgeɪt] *vt* **-gated; -gating** : relegar

relent [ri'lɛnt] *vi* : ceder — **relentless** [ri'lɛntləs] *adj* : implacable

relevant ['rɛləvənt] *adj* : pertinente — **relevance** ['rɛləvənts] *n* : pertinencia *f*

reliable [ri'laɪəbəl] *adj* : fiable (dícese de personas), fidedigno (dícese de información, etc.) — **reliability** [ri,laɪə'bɪlə,ṭi] *n*, *pl* **-ties** : fiabilidad *f* (de una cosa), responsabilidad *f* (de una persona) — **reliance** [ri'laɪənts] *n* **1** : dependencia *f* **2** TRUST : confianza *f* — **reliant** [ri'laɪənt] *adj* : dependiente

relic ['rɛlɪk] *n* : reliquia *f*

relief [ri'liːf] *n* **1** : alivio *m* **2** AID : ayuda *f* **3** : relieve *m* (en la escultura) **4** REPLACEMENT : relevo *m* — **relieve** [ri'liːv] *vt* **-lieved; -lieving 1** : aliviar **2** REPLACE : relevar (a algn) **3** ~ **s.o. of** : liberar a algn de

religion [ri'lɪdʒən] *n* : religión *f* — **religious** [ri'lɪdʒəs] *adj* : religioso

relinquish [ri'lɪŋkwɪʃ, -'lɪn-] *vt* : renunciar a, abandonar

relish ['rɛlɪʃ] *n* **1** : salsa *f* (condimento) **2 with** ~ : con gusto — ~ *vt* : saborear

relocate [,riːˈloˌkeɪt, ,riːlo'keɪt] *vt* **-cated; -cating** : trasladar — *vi* : trasladarse — **relocation** [,riːloˈkeɪʃən] *n* : traslado *m*

reluctance [ri'lʌktənts] *n* : reticencia *f*, desgana *f* — **reluctant** [ri'lʌktənt] *adj* : reacio, reticente — **reluctantly** [ri'lʌktəntli] *adv* : a regañadientes

rely [ri'laɪ] *vi* **-lied; -lying** ~ **on 1** DEPEND ON : depender de **2** TRUST : confiar (en)

remain [ri'meɪn] *vi* **1** : quedar **2** STAY : quedarse **3** CONTINUE : seguir, continuar — **remainder** [ri'meɪndər] *n* : resto *m* — **remains** [ri'meɪnz] *npl* : restos *mpl*

remark [ri'mɑrk] *n* : comentario *m*, observación *f* — ~ *vt* : observar — *vi* ~

on : observar — **remarkable** [ri-'mɑrkəbəl] *adj* : extraordinario, notable

remedy ['remədi] *n, pl* **-dies** : remedio *m* — **~** *vt* **-died; -dying** : remediar — **remedial** [ri'miːdiəl] *adj* : correctivo

remember [ri'membər] *vt* **1** : acordarse de, recordar **2 ~ to** : acordarse de — *vi* : acordarse, recordar — **remembrance** [ri'membrəns] *n* : recuerdo *m*

remind [ri'maɪnd] *vt* : recordar — **reminder** [ri'maɪndər] *n* : recordatorio *m*

reminiscence [remə'nɪsənts] *n* : recuerdo *m*, reminiscencia *f* — **reminisce** [remə'nɪs] *vi* **-nisced; -niscing** : rememorar los viejos tiempos — **reminiscent** [remə'nɪsənt] *adj* **be ~ of** : recordar

remiss [ri'mɪs] *adj* : negligente, remiso

remit [ri'mɪt] *vt* **-mitted; -mitting 1** PARDON : perdonar **2** : enviar (dinero) — **remission** [ri'mɪʃən] *n* : remisión *f*

remnant ['remnənt] *n* **1** : resto *m* **2** TRACE : vestigio *m*

remorse [ri'mɔrs] *n* : remordimiento *m* — **remorseful** [ri'mɔrsfəl] *adj* : arrepentido

remote [ri'moːt] *adj* **-moter; -est 1** : remoto *m* **2** ALOOF : distante **3 ~ from** : apartado de, alejado de — **remote control** *n* : control *m* remoto — **remotely** [ri'moːtli] *adv* SLIGHTLY : remotamente

remove [ri'muːv] *vt* **-moved; -moving 1** : quitar (una tapa, etc.), quitarse (ropa) **2** EXTRACT : sacar **3** DISMISS : destituir **4** ELIMINATE : eliminar — **removable** [ri'muːvəbəl] *adj* : separable, de quita y pon — **removal** [ri'muːvəl] *n* **1** : eliminación *f* **2** EXTRACTION : extracción *f*

remunerate [ri'mjuːnəˌreɪt] *vt* **-ated; -ating** : remunerar

render ['rendər] *vt* **1** : rendir (homenaje), prestar (ayuda) **2** MAKE : hacer **3** TRANSLATE : traducir

rendezvous ['rɑndiˌvuː, -deɪ-] *ns & pl* : cita *f*

rendition [ren'dɪʃən] *n* : interpretación *f*

renegade ['renɪˌgeɪd] *n* : renegado *m*, -da *f*

renew [ri'nuː, -'njuː] *vt* **1** : renovar **2** RESUME : reanudar — **renewal** [ri'nuːəl, -'njuː-] *n* : renovación *f*

renounce [ri'naʊnts] *vt* **-nounced; -nouncing** : renunciar a

renovate ['renəˌveɪt] *vt* **-vated; -vating** : renovar — **renovation** [renə'veɪʃən] *n* : renovación *f*

renown [ri'naʊn] *n* : renombre *m* — **renowned** [ri'naʊnd] *adj* : célebre, renombrado

rent ['rent] *n* **1** : alquiler *m*, arrendamiento *m*, renta *f* **2 for ~** : se alquila — **~** *vt* : alquilar — **rental** ['rentəl] *n* : alquiler *m* — **~** *adj* : de alquiler — **renter** ['rentər] *n* : arrendatario *m*, -ria *f*

renunciation [riˌnʌntsi'eɪʃən] *n* : renuncia *f*

reopen [riː'oːpən] *vt* : volver a abrir

reorganize [riːˈɔrgəˌnaɪz] *vt* **-nized; -nizing** : reorganizar — **reorganization** [riːˌɔrgənə'zeɪʃən] *n* : reorganización *f*

repair [ri'pær] *vt* : reparar, arreglar — **~** *n* **1** : reparación *f*, arreglo *m* **2 in bad ~** : en mal estado

repay [ri'peɪ] *vt* **-paid; -paying 1** : devolver (dinero), pagar (una deuda) **2** : corresponder a (un favor, etc.)

repeal [ri'piːl] *vt* : abrogar, revocar — **~** *n* : abrogación *f*, revocación *f*

repeat [ri'piːt] *vt* : repetir — **~** *n* : repetición *f* — **repeatedly** [ri'piːtədli] *adv* : repetidas veces

repel [ri'pel] *vt* **-pelled; -pelling** : repeler — **repellent** [ri'pelənt] *n* : repelente *m*

repent [ri'pent] *vi* : arrepentirse — **repentance** [ri'pentənts] *n* : arrepentimiento *m*

repercussion [ˌriːpər'kʌʃən, ˌrepər-] *n* : repercusión *f*

repertoire ['repərˌtwɑr] *n* : repertorio *m*

repetition [ˌrepə'tɪʃən] *n* : repetición *f* — **repetitious** [ˌrepə'tɪʃəs] *adj* : repetitivo — **repetitive** [ri'petətɪv] *adj* : repetitivo

replace [ri'pleɪs] *vt* **-placed; -placing 1** : reponer **2** SUBSTITUTE : reemplazar, sustituir **3** EXCHANGE : cambiar — **replacement** [ri'pleɪsmənt] *n* **1** : sustitución *f* **2** : sustituto *m*, -ta *f* (persona) **3** *or* **~ part** : repuesto *m*

replenish [ri'plenɪʃ] *vt* **1** : reponer **2** REFILL : rellenar

replete [ri'pliːt] *adj* **~ with** : repleto de

replica ['replɪkə] *n* : réplica *f*

reply [ri'plaɪ] *vi* **-plied; -plying** : contestar, responder — **~** *n, pl* **-plies** : respuesta *f*

report [ri'pɔrt] *n* **1** : informe *m* **2** RUMOR : rumor *m* **3** *or* **news ~** : reportaje *m* **4 weather ~** : boletín *m* meteorológico — **~** *vt* **1** RELATE : anunciar **2 ~ a crime** : denunciar un delito **3** *or* **~ on** : informar sobre — *vi* **1** : informar **2 ~ for duty** : presentarse — **report card** *n* : boletín *m* de calificaciones — **reportedly** [ri'pɔrtədli] *adv*

: según se dice — **reporter** [ri'pɔrtər]
n : periodista *mf*; reportero *m*, -ra *f*
repose [ri'po:z] *vi* -**posed; -posing** : reposar — ~ *n* : reposo *m*
reprehensible [ˌrepri'hentsəbəl] *adj*
: reprensible
represent [ˌrepri'zent] *vt* 1 : representar
2 PORTRAY : presentar — **representation** [ˌrepriˌzen'teiʃən, -zən-] *n* : representación *f* — **representative** [ˌrepri-
'zentətɪv] *adj* : representativo — ~ *n*
: representante *mf*
repress [ri'pres] *vt* : reprimir — **repression** [ri'preʃən] *n* : represión *f*
reprieve [ri'pri:v] *n* : indulto *m*
reprimand ['reprəˌmænd] *n* : reprimenda
f — ~ *vt* : reprender
reprint [ri'print] *vt* : reimprimir — ~
['ri:ˌprint, ri'print] *n* : reedición *f*
reprisal [ri'praizəl] *n* : represalia *f*
reproach [ri'pro:tʃ] *n* 1 : reproche *m* 2
beyond ~ : irreprochable — ~ *vt*
: reprochar — **reproachful** [ri'pro:tʃfəl]
adj : de reproche
reproduce [ˌri:prə'du:s, -'dju:s] *v* -**duced;
-ducing** *vt* : reproducir — *vi* : reproducirse — **reproduction** [ˌri:prə'dʌk-
ʃən] *n* : reproducción *f* — **reproductive** [ˌri:prə'dʌktɪv] *adj* : reproductor
reproof [ri'pru:f] *n* : reprobación *f*
reptile ['reptail] *n* : reptil *m*
republic [ri'pʌblik] *n* : república *f* — **republican** [ri'pʌblikən] *n* : republicano
m, -na *f* — ~ *adj* : republicano
repudiate [ri'pju:diˌeit] *vt* -**ated; -ating**
: repudiar
repugnant [ri'pʌgnənt] *adj* : repugnante,
asqueroso — **repugnance** [ri-
'pʌgnənts] *n* : repugnancia *f*
repulse [ri'pʌls] *vt* -**pulsed; -pulsing**
: repeler, rechazar — **repulsive** [ri-
'pʌlsɪv] *adj* : repulsivo
reputation [ˌrepjə'teiʃən] *n* : reputación *f*
— **reputable** ['repjətəbəl] *adj* : de confianza, acreditado — **reputed** [ri'pju:-
təd] *adj* : supuesto
request [ri'kwest] *n* : petición *f* — ~ *vt*
: pedir
requiem ['rekwiəm, 'rei-] *n* : réquiem *m*
require [ri'kwair] *vt* -**quired; -quiring**
CALL FOR : requerir 2 NEED : necesitar
— **requirement** [ri'kwairmənt] *n* 1
NEED : necesidad *f* 2 DEMAND : requisito *m* — **requisite** ['rekwəzit] *adj*
: necesario
resale ['ri:ˌseil, ˌri:'seil] *n* : reventa *f*
rescind [ri'sind] *vt* : rescindir (un contrato), revocar (una ley), etc.)
rescue ['reskju:] *vt* -**cued; -cuing**
: rescatar, salvar — ~ *n* : rescate *m* —

rescuer ['reskjuər] *n* : salvador *m*,
-dora *f*
research [ri'sərtʃ, 'ri:ˌsərtʃ] *n* : investigación *f* — ~ *vt* : investigar — **researcher** [ri'sərtʃər, 'ri:-] *n* : investigador *m*, -dora *f*
resemble [ri'zembəl] *vt* -**sembled;
-sembling** : parecerse a — **resemblance** [ri'zemblənts] *n* : parecido *m*
resent [ri'zent] *vt* : resentirse de, ofenderse por — **resentful** [ri'zentfəl] *adj*
: resentido — **resentment** [ri-
'zentmənt] *n* : resentimiento *m*
reserve [ri'zərv] *vt* -**served; -serving**
: reservar — ~ *n* 1 : reserva *f* 2 ~**s**
npl : reservas *fpl* (militares) — **reservation** [ˌrezər'veiʃən] *n* : reserva *f* —
reserved [ri'zərvd] *adj* : reservado —
reservoir ['rezərˌvwar, -ˌvwɔr, -ˌvɔr] *n*
: embalse *m*
reset [ˌri:'set] *vt* -**set; -setting** : volver a
poner (un reloj, etc.)
residence ['rezədənts] *n* : residencia *f* —
reside [ri'zaid] *vi* -**sided; -siding** : residir — **resident** ['rezədənt] *adj* : residente — ~ *n* : residente *mf* — **residential** [ˌrezə'dentʃəl] *adj* : residencial
residue ['rezəˌdu:, -ˌdju:] *n* : residuo *m*
resign [ri'zain] *vt* 1 QUIT : dimitir 2 ~
oneself to : resignarse a — **resignation** [ˌrezig'neiʃən] *n* 1 : dimisión *f* 2
ACCEPTANCE : resignación *f*
resilient [ri'ziljənt] *adj* 1 : resistente
(dícese de personas) 2 ELASTIC : elástico — **resilience** [ri'ziljənts] *n* 1 : resistencia *f* 2 ELASTICITY : elasticidad *f*
resin ['rezən] *n* : resina *f*
resist [ri'zist] *vt* : resistir — *vi* : resistirse — **resistance** [ri'zistənts] *n* : resistencia *f* — **resistant** [ri'zistənt] *adj*
: resistente
resolve [ri'zalv] *vt* -**solved; -solving**
: resolver — ~ *n* : resolución *f* —
resolution [ˌrezə'lu:ʃən] *n* 1 : resolución *f* 2 DECISION, INTENTION : propósito *m* — **resolute** ['rezəˌlu:t] *adj* : resuelto
resonance ['rezənənts] *n* : resonancia *f*
— **resonant** ['rezənənt] *adj* : resonante
resort [ri'zɔrt] *n* 1 RECOURSE : recurso *m*
2 *or* **tourist** ~ : centro *m* turístico —
~ *vi* ~ **to** : recurrir a
resounding [ri'zaundiŋ] *adj* 1 RESONANT
: resonante 2 ABSOLUTE : rotundo
resource ['ri:ˌsɔrs, ri'sɔrs] *n* : recurso *m*
— **resourceful** [ri'sɔrsfəl, -ˌzɔrs-] *adj*
: ingenioso
respect [ri'spekt] *n* 1 ESTEEM : respeto *m*
2 **in some** ~**s** : en algún sentido 3
pay one's ~**s** : presentar uno sus re-

spetos 4 with ~ to : (con) respecto a — ~ *vt* : respetar — **respectable** [ri'spektəbəl] *adj* : respetable — **respectful** [ri'spektfəl] *adj* : respetuoso — **respective** [ri'spektɪv] *adj* : respectivo — **respectively** *adv* : respectivamente

respiration [,respə'reɪʃən] *n* : respiración *f* — **respiratory** ['respərə,tori, rɪ'spaɪrə-] *adj* : respiratorio

respite ['respɪt, rɪ'spaɪt] *n* : respiro *m*

response [rɪ'spɑns] *n* : respuesta *f* — **respond** [rɪ'spɑnd] *vi* : responder — **responsibility** [rɪ,spɑntsə'biləʈi] *n*, *pl* **-ties** : responsabilidad *f* — **responsible** [rɪ'spɑntsəbəl] *adj* : responsable — **responsive** [rɪ'spɑntsɪv] *adj* : sensible, receptivo

rest[1] ['rest] *n* **1** : descanso *m* **2** SUPPORT : apoyo *m* **3** : silencio *m* (en música) — ~ *vi* **1** : descansar **2** LEAN : apoyarse **3** ~ **on** DEPEND ON : depender de — ~ *vt* **1** RELAX : descansar **2** LEAN : apoyar

rest[2] *n* REMAINDER : resto *m*

restaurant ['restə,rɑnt, -rənt] *n* : restaurante *m*

restful ['restfəl] *adj* : tranquilo, apacible

restitution [,restə'tu:ʃən, -'tju:-] *n* : restitución *f*

restless ['restləs] *adj* : inquieto, agitado

restore [rɪ'stor] *vt* **-stored; -storing 1** RETURN : devolver **2** REESTABLISH : restablecer **3** REPAIR : restaurar — **restoration** [,restə'reɪʃən] *n* **1** : restablecimiento *m* **2** REPAIR : restauración *f*

restrain [rɪ'streɪn] *vt* **1** : contener **2** ~ **oneself** : contenerse — **restrained** [rɪ'streɪnd] *adj* : comedido, moderado — **restraint** [rɪ'streɪnt] *n* **1** : restricción *f* **2** SELF-CONTROL : moderación *f*, control *m* de sí mismo

restriction [rɪ'strɪkʃən] *n* : restricción *f* — **restrict** [rɪ'strɪkt] *vt* : restringir — **restricted** [rɪ'strɪktəd] *adj* : restringido — **restrictive** [rɪ'strɪktɪv] *adj* : restrictivo

result [rɪ'zʌlt] *vi* : resultar — ~ *n* **1** : resultado *m* **2 as a ~ of** : como consecuencia de

resume [rɪ'zu:m] *v* **-sumed; -suming** *vt* : reanudar — *vi* : reanudarse

résumé *or* **resume** *or* **resumé** [ˈrezə,meɪ, ,rezə'-] *n* : currículum *m* (vitae)

resumption [rɪ'zʌmpʃən] *n* : reanudación *f*

resurgence [rɪ'sərdʒənts] *n* : resurgimiento *m*

resurrection [,rezə'rekʃən] *n* : resurrección *f* — **resurrect** [,rezə'rekt] *vt* : resucitar

resuscitate [rɪ'sʌsə,teɪt] *vt* **-tated; -tating** : resucitar

retail ['ri:,teɪl] *vt* : vender al por menor — ~ *n* : venta *f* al por menor — ~ *adj* : detallista, minorista — ~ *adv* : al detalle, al por menor — **retailer** ['ri:,teɪlər] *n* : detallista *mf*, minorista *mf*

retain [rɪ'teɪn] *vt* : retener

retaliate [rɪ'tæli,eɪt] *vi* **-ated; -ating** : tomar represalias — **retaliation** [rɪ,tæli'eɪʃən] *n* : represalias *fpl*

retard [rɪ'tɑrd] *vt* : retardar, retrasar — **retarded** [rɪ'tɑrdəd] *adj* : retrasado

retention [rɪ'tentʃən] *n* : retención *f*

reticence ['retəsənts] *n* : reticencia *f* — **reticent** ['retəsənt] *adj* : reticente

retina ['retənə] *n*, *pl* **-nas** *or* **-nae** [-əni, -ən,aɪ] : retina *f*

retinue ['retən,u:, -,ju:] *n* : séquito *m*

retire [rɪ'taɪr] *vi* **-tired; -tiring 1** WITHDRAW : retirarse **2** : jubilarse, retirarse (de un trabajo) **3** : acostarse (en la cama) — **retirement** [rɪ'taɪrmənt] *n* : jubilación *f* — **retiring** [rɪ'taɪrɪŋ] *adj* SHY : retraído

retort [rɪ'tort] *vt* : replicar — ~ *n* : réplica *f*

retrace [,ri:'treɪs] *vt* **-traced; -tracing ~ one's steps** : volver sobre sus pasos

retract [rɪ'trækt] *vt* **1** WITHDRAW : retirar **2** : retraer (garras, etc.) — *vi* : retractarse

retrain [,ri:'treɪn] *vt* : reciclar

retreat [rɪ'tri:t] *n* **1** : retirada *f* **2** REFUGE : refugio *m* — ~ *vi* : retirarse

retribution [,retrə'bju:ʃən] *n* : castigo *m*

retrieve [rɪ'tri:v] *vt* **-trieved; -trieving 1** : cobrar, recuperar **2** RESCUE : salvar — **retrieval** [rɪ'tri:vəl] *n* : recuperación *f* — **retriever** [rɪ'tri:vər] *n* : perro *m* cobrador

retroactive [,retro'æktɪv] *adj* : retroactivo

retrospect ['retrə,spekt] *n* **in ~** : mirando hacia atrás — **retrospective** [,retro'spektɪv] *adj* : retrospectivo

return [rɪ'tərn] *vi* **1** : volver, regresar **2** REAPPEAR : reaparecer — *vt* **1** : devolver **2** YIELD : producir — ~ *n* **1** : regreso *m*, vuelta *f* **2** : devolución *f* (de algo prestado) **3** YIELD : rendimiento *m* **4 in ~ for** : a cambio de **5** *or* **tax ~** : declaración *f* de impuestos — ~ *adj* : de vuelta

reunite [,ri:ju'naɪt] *vt* **-nited; -niting** : reunir — **reunion** [ri'ju:njən] *n* : reunión *f*

revamp [,ri'væmp] *vt* : renovar

reveal [rɪ'vi:l] *vt* **1** : revelar **2** SHOW : dejar ver

revel ['rɛvəl] *vi* **-eled** *or* **-elled; -eling** *or* **-elling** ~ **in** : deleitarse en

revelation [,rɛvəˈleɪʃən] *n* : revelación *f*

revelry ['rɛvəlri] *n, pl* **-ries** : jolgorio *m*, regocijos *mpl*

revenge [riˈvɛndʒ] *vt* **-venged; -venging** : vengar — ~ *n* **1** : venganza *f* **2 take** ~ **on** : vengarse de

revenue ['rɛvəˌnuː, -ˌnjuː] *n* : ingresos *mpl*

reverberate [riˈvərbəˌreɪt] *vi* **-ated; -ating** : retumbar, resonar

reverence ['rɛvərənts] *n* : reverencia *f*, veneración *f* — **revere** [riˈvɪr] *vt* **-vered; -vering** : venerar — **reverend** ['rɛvərənd] *adj* : reverendo — **reverent** ['rɛvərənt] *adj* : reverente

reverie ['rɛvəri] *n, pl* **-eries** : ensueño *m*

reverse [riˈvərs] *adj* : inverso, contrario — ~ *v* **-versed; -versing** *vt* **1** : invertir **2** : cambiar (una política), revocar (una decisión) **3** : dar marcha atrás a (un automóvil) — *vi* : invertirse — ~ *n* **1** BACK : dorso *m*, revés *m* **2** *or* ~ **gear** : marcha *f* atrás **3 the** ~ : lo contrario — **reversible** [riˈvərsəbəl] *adj* : reversible — **reversal** [riˈvərsəl] *n* **1** : inversión *f* **2** CHANGE : cambio *m* total **3** SETBACK : revés *m* — **revert** [riˈvərt] *vi* : revertir

review [riˈvjuː] *n* **1** : revisión *f* **2** OVERVIEW : resumen *m* **3** CRITIQUE : reseña *f*, crítica *f* **4** : repaso *m* (para un examen) — ~ *vt* **1** EXAMINE : examinar **2** : repasar (una lección) **3** CRITIQUE : reseñar — **reviewer** [riˈvjuːər] *n* : crítico *m*, -ca *f*

revile [riˈvaɪl] *vt* **-viled; -viling** : injuriar

revise [riˈvaɪz] *vt* **-vised; -vising 1** : modificar (una política, etc.) **2** : revisar, corregir (una publicación) — **revision** [riˈvɪʒən] *n* : corrección *f*, modificación *f*

revive [riˈvaɪv] *v* **-vived; -viving** *vt* **1** : reanimar, reactivar **2** : resucitar (a una persona) **3** RESTORE : restablecer — *vi* **1** : reanimarse, reactivarse **2** COME TO : volver en sí — **revival** [riˈvaɪvəl] *n* : reanimación *f*, reactivación *f*

revoke [riˈvoːk] *vt* **-voked; -voking** : revocar

revolt [riˈvoːlt] *vi* : rebelarse, sublevarse — *vt* : dar asco a — ~ *n* : revuelta *f*, sublevación *f* — **revolting** [riˈvoːltɪŋ] *adj* : asqueroso

revolution [,rɛvəˈluːʃən] *n* : revolución *f* — **revolutionary** [,rɛvəˈluːʃənˌɛri] *adj* : revolucionario — ~ *n, pl* **-aries** : revolucionario *m*, -ria *f* — **revolutionize** [,rɛvəˈluːʃənˌaɪz] *vt* **-ized; -izing** : revolucionar

revolve [riˈvalv] *v* **-volved; -volving** *vt* : hacer girar — *vi* : girar

revolver [riˈvalvər] *n* : revólver *m*

revue [riˈvjuː] *n* : revista *f* (teatral)

revulsion [riˈvʌlʃən] *n* : repugnancia *f*

reward [riˈwɔrd] *vt* : recompensar — ~ *n* : recompensa *f*

rewrite [,riːˈraɪt] *vt* **-wrote; -written; -writing** : volver a escribir

rhetoric ['rɛtərɪk] *n* : retórica *f* — **rhetorical** [riˈtɔrɪkəl] *adj* : retórico

rheumatism ['ruːməˌtɪzəm, 'ru-] *n* : reumatismo *m* — **rheumatic** [ruˈmæʈɪk] *adj* : reumático

rhino ['raɪˌnoː] *n, pl* **-no** *or* **-nos** → **rhinoceros** — **rhinoceros** [raɪˈnɑsərəs] *n, pl* **-noceroses** *or* **-noceros** *or* **-noceri** [-ˌraɪ] : rinoceronte *m*

rhubarb ['ruːˌbɑrb] *n* : ruibarbo *m*

rhyme ['raɪm] *n* **1** : rima *f* **2** VERSE : verso *m* (en rima) — ~ *vi* **rhymed; rhyming** : rimar

rhythm ['rɪðəm] *n* : ritmo *m* — **rhythmic** ['rɪðmɪk] *or* **rhythmical** [-mɪkəl] *adj* : rítmico

rib ['rɪb] *n* : costilla *f* — ~ *vt* TEASE : tomar el pelo a

ribbon ['rɪbən] *n* : cinta *f*

rice ['raɪs] *n* : arroz *m*

rich ['rɪtʃ] *adj* **1** : rico **2** ~ **foods** : comidas *fpl* pesadas — **riches** ['rɪtʃəz] *npl* : riquezas *fpl* — **richness** ['rɪtʃnəs] *n* : riqueza *f*

rickety ['rɪkəti] *adj* : desvencijado, destartalado

ricochet ['rɪkəˌʃeɪ, -ˌʃɛt] *n* : rebote *m* — ~ *vi* **-cheted** [-ˌʃeɪd] *or* **-chetted** [-ˌʃɛtəd]; **-cheting** [-ˌʃeɪŋ] *or* **-chetting** [-ˌʃɛtɪŋ] : rebotar

rid ['rɪd] *vt* **rid; ridding 1** : librar **2 get** ~ **of** : deshacerse de — **riddance** ['rɪdənts] *n* **good** ~**!** : ¡adiós y buen viaje!

riddle¹ ['rɪdəl] *n* : acertijo *m*, adivinanza *f*

riddle² *vt* **-dled; -dling 1** : acribillar **2 riddled with** : lleno de

ride ['raɪd] *v* **rode** ['roːd]; **ridden** ['rɪdən]; **riding** *vt* **1** : montar (a caballo, en bicicleta), ir (en autobús, etc.) **2** TRAVERSE : recorrer — *vi* **1** *or* ~ **horseback** : montar a caballo **2** : ir (en auto, etc.) — ~ *n* **1** : paseo *m*, vuelta *f* **2** : aparato *m* (en un parque de diversiones) — **rider** ['raɪdər] *n* **1** : jinete *mf* (a caballo) **2** CYCLIST : ciclista *mf*, motociclista *mf*

ridge ['rɪdʒ] *n* : cadena *f* (de montañas)

ridiculous [rəˈdɪkjələs] *adj* : ridículo — **ridicule** ['rɪdəˌkjuːl] *n* : burlas *fpl* — ~ *vt* **-culed; -culing** : ridiculizar

rife ['raɪf] *adj* **1** : extendido **2 be ~ with** : estar plagado de

rifle¹ ['raɪfəl] *vi* **-fled; -fling ~ through** : revolver

rifle² *n* : rifle *m*, fusil *m*

rift ['rɪft] *n* **1** : grieta *f* **2** : ruptura *f* (entre personas)

rig¹ ['rɪg] *vt* : amañar (una elección)

rig² *vt* **rigged; rigging 1** : aparejar (un barco) **2** EQUIP : equipar **3** *or* **~ out** DRESS : vestir **4** *or* **~ up** CONSTRUCT : construir — **~** *n* **1** : aparejo *m* (de un barco) **2** *or* **oil ~** : plataforma *f* petrolífera — **rigging** ['rɪgɪŋ, -gən] *n* : aparejo *m*

right ['raɪt] *adj* **1** JUST : bueno, justo **2** CORRECT : correcto **3** APPROPRIATE : apropiado, adecuado **4** STRAIGHT : recto **5 be ~** : tener razón **6 ~** ENTITLEMENT : derecho **~** *n* **1** GOOD : bien *m* **2** *or* **~ side** : derecha *f* — **~** *adv* **1** WELL : bien **2** PRECISELY : justo **3** DIRECTLY : derecho **4** IMMEDIATELY : inmediatamente **5** COMPLETELY : completamente **6** *or* **to the ~** : a la derecha — **~** *vt* **1** STRAIGHTEN : enderezar **2 ~ a wrong** : reparar un daño — **right angle** *n* : ángulo *m* recto — **righteous** ['raɪtʃəs] *adj* : recto, honrado — **rightful** ['raɪtfəl] *adj* : legítimo — **right-hand** ['raɪtˈhænd] *adj* : derecho — **right-handed** ['raɪtˈhændəd] *adj* : diestro — **rightly** ['raɪtli] *adv* **1** : justamente **2** CORRECTLY : correctamente — **right-wing** ['raɪtˈwɪŋ] *adj* : derechista

rigid ['rɪdʒɪd] *adj* : rígido

rigor *or Brit* **rigour** ['rɪgər] *n* : rigor *m* — **rigorous** ['rɪgərəs] *adj* : riguroso

rim ['rɪm] *n* **1** EDGE : borde *m* **2** : llanta *f* (de una rueda) **3** : montura *f* (de anteojos)

rind ['raɪnd] *n* : corteza *f*

ring¹ ['rɪŋ] *v* **rang** ['ræŋ]; **rung** ['rʌŋ]; **ringing** *vi* **1** : sonar (dícese de un timbre, etc.) **2** RESOUND : resonar — *vt* **1** : tocar (un timbre, etc.) — **~** *n* **1** : toque *m* (de un timbre, etc.) **2** CALL : llamada *f* (por teléfono)

ring² *n* **1** : anillo *m*, sortija *f* **2** BAND, HOOP : aro *m* **3** CIRCLE : círculo *m* **4** *or* **boxing ~** : cuadrilátero *m* **5** NETWORK : red *f* — **~** *vt* : cercar, rodear — **ringleader** ['rɪŋˌliːdər] *n* : cabecilla *mf*

ringlet ['rɪŋlət] *n* : rizo *m*, bucle *m*

rink ['rɪŋk] *n* : pista *f* (de patinaje)

rinse ['rɪnts] *vt* **rinsed; rinsing** : enjuagar — **~** *n* : enjuague *m*

riot ['raɪət] *n* : disturbio *m* — **~** *vi* : causar disturbios — **rioter** ['raɪətər] *n* : alborotador *m*, -dora *f*

rip ['rɪp] *v* **ripped; ripping** *vt* **1** : rasgar, desgarrar **2 ~ off** : arrancar — *vi* : rasgarse — **~** *n* : rasgón *m*, desgarrón *m*

ripe ['raɪp] *adj* **riper; ripest 1** : maduro **2 ~ for** : listo por — **ripen** ['raɪpən] *v* : madurar — **ripeness** ['raɪpnəs] *n* : madurez *f*

rip-off ['rɪpˌɔf] *n* : timo *m fam*

ripple ['rɪpəl] *v* **-pled; -pling** *vi* : rizarse (dícese de agua) — *vt* : rizar — **~** *n* : onda *f*, rizo *m*

rise ['raɪz] *vi* **rose** ['roːz]; **risen** ['rɪzən]; **rising 1** GET UP : levantarse **2** : salir (dícese del sol, etc.) **3** ASCEND : subir **4** INCREASE : aumentar **5 ~ up** REBEL : sublevarse — **~** *n* **1** ASCENT : subida *f* **2** INCREASE : aumento *m* **3** SLOPE : cuesta *f* — **riser** ['raɪzər] *n* **1 early ~** : madrugador *m*, -dora *f* **2 late ~** : dormilón *m*, -lona *f*

risk ['rɪsk] *n* : riesgo *m* — **~** *vt* : arriesgar — **risky** ['rɪski] *adj* **riskier; -est** : arriesgado, riesgoso *Lat*

rite ['raɪt] *n* : rito *m* — **ritual** ['rɪtʃʊəl] *adj* : ritual — **~** *n* : ritual *m*

rival ['raɪvəl] *n* : rival *mf* — **~** *adj* : rival — **~** *vt* **-valed** *or* **-valled; -valing** *or* **-valling** : rivalizar con — **rivalry** ['raɪvəlri] *n, pl* **-ries** : rivalidad *f*

river ['rɪvər] *n* : río *m*

rivet ['rɪvət] *n* : remache *m* — **~** *vt* **1** : remachar **2** FIX : fijar (los ojos, etc.) **3 be ~ed by** : estar fascinado con

roach ['roːtʃ] → **cockroach**

road ['roːd] *n* **1** : carretera *f* **2** STREET : calle *f* **3** PATH : camino *m* — **roadblock** ['roːdˌblɑk] *n* : control *m* — **roadside** ['roːdˌsaɪd] *n* : borde *m* de la carretera — **roadway** ['roːdˌweɪ] *n* : carretera *f*

roam ['roːm] *vi* : vagar — *vt* : vagar por

roar ['ror] *vi* **1** : rugir **2 ~ with laughter** : reírse a carcajadas — *vt* : decir a gritos — **~** *n* **1** : rugido *m* (de un animal), estruendo *m* (de un avión, etc.)

roast ['roːst] *vt* : asar (carne, etc.), tosta (café, etc.) — *vi* : asarse — **~** *n* : asado *m* — **~** *adj* : asado — **roas beef** *n* : rosbif *m*

rob ['rɑb] *v* **robbed; robbing** *vt* **1** : roba **2 ~ of** : privar de — *vi* : robar — **robber** ['rɑbər] *n* : ladrón *m*, -drona *f* — **robbery** ['rɑbəri] *n, pl* **-beries** : robo *n*

robe ['roːb] *n* **1** : toga *f* (de un magistra do, etc.) **2** → **bathrobe**

robin ['rɑbən] *n* : petirrojo *m*

robot ['roːbʌt, -bət] *n* : robot *m*

robust [roˈbʌst, ˈroːbʌst] *adj* : robusto

rock[1] ['rɑk] *vt* **1** : acunar (a un niño), mecer (una cuna) **2** SHAKE : sacudir — *vi* : mecerse — **~** *n or* **~ music** : música *f* rock

rock[2] *n* **1** : roca *f* (sustancia) **2** BOULDER : peña *f*, peñasco *m* **3** STONE : piedra *f*

rocket ['rɑkət] *n* : cohete *m*

rocking chair *n* : mecedora *f*

rocky ['rɑki] *adj* **rockier; -est 1** : rocoso **2** SHAKY : tambaleante

rod ['rɑd] *n* **1** : varilla *f* **2** *or* **fishing ~** : caña *f* de pescar

rode → ride

rodent ['roːdənt] *n* : roedor *m*

rodeo ['roːdiˌoː, roˈdeɪˌoː] *n, pl* **-deos** : rodeo *m*

roe ['roː] *n* : hueva *f*

rogue ['roːg] *n* : pícaro *m*, -ra *f*

role ['roːl] *n* : papel *m*

roll ['roːl] *n* **1** : rollo *m* (de película, etc.) **2** LIST : lista *f* **3** : redoble *m* (de un tambor) **4** SWAYING : balanceo *m* **5** BUN : pancito *m* *Lat*, panecillo *m* *Spain* — **~** *vt* **1** : hacer rodar **2** *or* **~ out** : estirar (masa) **3 ~ up** : enrollar (papel, etc.), arremangar (una manga) — *vi* **1** : rodar **2** SWAY : balancearse **3 ~ around** : revolcarse **4 ~ over** : darse la vuelta — **roller** ['roːlər] *n* **1** : rodillo *m* **2** CURLER : rulo *m* — **roller coaster** ['roːlərˌkoːstər] *n* : montaña *f* rusa — **roller-skate** ['roːlərˌskeɪt] *vi* **-skated; -skating** : patinar (sobre ruedas) — **roller skate** *n* : patín *m* (de ruedas)

Roman ['roːmən] *adj* : romano — **Roman Catholic** *adj* : católico

romance [roˈmænts, ˈroːˌmænts] *n* **1** : novela *f* romántica **2** AFFAIR : romance *m*

Romanian [ruˈmeɪniən, roː-] *adj* : rumano — **~** *n* : rumano *m* (idioma)

romantic [roˈmæntɪk] *adj* : romántico

romp ['rɑmp] *n* : retozo *m* — **~** *vi* : retozar

roof ['ruːf, 'rʊf] *n, pl* **roofs** ['ruːfs, 'rʊfs; 'ruːvz, 'rʊvz] **1** : tejado *m*, techo *m* **2 ~ of the mouth** : paladar *m* — **roofing** ['ruːfɪŋ, 'rʊfɪŋ] *n* : techumbre *f* — **rooftop** ['ruːfˌtɑp, 'rʊf-] *n* : tejado *m*, techo *m*

rook[1] ['rʊk] *n* : grajo *m* (ave)

rook[2] *n* : torre *f* (en ajedrez)

rookie ['rʊki] *n* : novato *m*, -ta *f*

room ['ruːm, 'rʊm] *n* **1** : cuarto *m*, habitación *f* **2** BEDROOM : dormitorio *m* **3** SPACE : espacio *m* **4** OPPORTUNITY : posibilidad *f* — **roommate** ['ruːmˌmeɪt, 'rʊm-] *n* : compañero *m*, -ra *f* de

cuarto — **roomy** ['ruːmi, 'rʊmi] *adj* **roomier; -est** : espacioso

roost ['ruːst] *n* : percha *f* — **~** *vi* : posarse — **rooster** ['ruːstər, 'rʊs-] *n* : gallo *m*

root[1] ['ruːt, 'rʊt] *n* : raíz *f* — **~** *vt* **~ out** : extirpar

root[2] *vi* **~ around in** : hurgar en

root[3] *vi* **~ for** SUPPORT : alentar

rope ['roːp] *n* : cuerda *f* — **~** *vt* **roped; roping 1** : atar (con cuerda) **2 ~ off** : acordonar

rosary ['roːzəri] *n, pl* **-ries** : rosario *m*

rose[1] **→ rise**

rose[2] ['roːz] *n* **1** : rosa *f* (flor), rosa *m* (color) — **~** *adj* : rosa — **rosebush** ['roːzˌbʊʃ] *n* : rosal *m*

rosemary ['roːzˌmeri] *n, pl* **-maries** : romero *m*

Rosh Hashanah [ˌrɑʃhɑˈʃɑnə, ˌroːʃ-] *n* : el Año Nuevo judío

roster ['rɑstər] *n* : lista *f*

rostrum ['rɑstrəm] *n, pl* **-tra** *or* **-trums** [-trə] : tribuna *f*

rosy ['roːzi] *adj* **rosier; -est 1** : sonrosado **2** PROMISING : halagüeno

rot ['rɑt] *v* **rotted; rotting** *vi* : pudrirse — *vt* : pudrir — **~** *n* : putrefacción *f*

rotary ['roːtəri] *adj* : rotativo — **~** *n* : rotonda *f*, glorieta *f* *Spain*

rotate ['roːteɪt] *v* **-tated; -tating** *vi* : girar — *vt* **1** : girar **2** ALTERNATE : alternar — **rotation** [roˈteɪʃən] *n* : rotación *f*

rote ['roːt] *n* **by ~** : de memoria

rotor ['roːtər] *n* : rotor *m*

rotten ['rɑtən] *adj* **1** : podrido **2** BAD : malo

rouge ['ruːʒ, 'ruːdʒ] *n* : colorete *m*

rough ['rʌf] *adj* **1** COARSE : áspero **2** RUGGED : accidentado **3** CHOPPY : agitado **4** DIFFICULT : duro **5** FORCEFUL : brusco **6** APPROXIMATE : aproximado **7** UNREFINED : tosco **8 ~ draft** : borrador *m* — **~** *vt* **1 → roughen 2 ~ up** BEAT : dar una paliza a — **roughage** ['rʌfɪdʒ] *n* : fibra *f* — **roughen** ['rʌfən] *vt* : poner áspero — *vi* : ponerse áspero — **roughly** ['rʌfli] *adv* **1** : bruscamente **2** ABOUT : aproximadamente — **roughness** ['rʌfnəs] *n* : COARSENESS : aspereza *f*

roulette [ruˈlet] *n* : ruleta *f*

round ['raʊnd] *adj* : redondo — **~** *adv* **→ around** — **~** *n* **1** : círculo *m* **2** : ronda *f* (de bebidas, negociaciones, etc.) **3** : asalto *m* (en boxeo), vuelta *f* (en juegos) **4 ~ of applause** : aplauso *m* **5 ~s** *npl* : visitas *fpl* (de un médico), rondas *fpl* (de un policía, etc.) — **~** *vt* **1** TURN : doblar **2 ~ off**

: redondear **3 ~ off** or **~ out** COMPLETE : rematar **4 ~ up** GATHER : reunir (personas), rodear (ganado) — **~** *prep* → **around** — **roundabout** ['raʊndə,baʊt] *adj* : indirecto — **round-trip** ['raʊnd,trɪp] *n* : viaje *m* de ida y vuelta — **roundup** ['raʊnd,ʌp] *n* : rodeo *m* (de animales), redada *f* (de delincuentes, etc.)

rouse ['raʊz] *vt* **roused; rousing 1** AWAKEN : despertar **2** EXCITE : excitar

rout ['raʊt] *n* : derrota *f* aplastante — **~** *vt* : derrotar

route ['ruːt, 'raʊt] *n* **1** : ruta *f* or **delivery ~** : recorrido *m*

routine [ruː'tiːn] *n* : rutina *f* — **~** *adj* : rutinario

rove ['roːv] *v* **roved; roving** *vi* : errar, vagar — *vt* : errar por

row¹ ['roː] *vt* **1** : llevar a remo **2 ~ a boat** : remar — *vi* : remar

row² *n* **1** : fila *f* (de gente o asientos), hilera *f* (de casas, etc.) **2 in a ~** SUCCESSIVELY : seguido

row³ ['raʊ] *n* **1** RACKET : bulla *f* **2** QUARREL : pelea *f*

rowboat ['roː,boːt] *n* : bote *m* de remos

rowdy ['raʊdi] *adj* **-dier; -est** : escandaloso, alborotador — **~** *n, pl* **-dies** : alborotador *m*, -dora *f*

royal ['rɔɪəl] *adj* : real — **royalty** ['rɔɪəlti] *n, pl* **-ties 1** : realeza *f* **2 royalties** *npl* : derechos *mpl* de autor

rub ['rʌb] *v* **rubbed; rubbing** *vt* **1** : frotar **2** CHAFE : rozar **3 ~ in** : aplicar frotando — *vi* **1 ~ against** : rozar **2 ~ off** : salir (al frotar) — **~** *n* : frotamiento *m*

rubber ['rʌbər] *n* **1** : goma *f*, caucho *m* **2 ~s** *npl* : chanclos *mpl* — **rubber band** *n* : goma *f* (elástica) — **rubber stamp** *n* : sello *m* (de goma) — **rubbery** ['rʌbəri] *adj* : gomoso

rubbish ['rʌbɪʃ] *n* **1** : basura *f* **2** NONSENSE : tonterías *fpl*

rubble ['rʌbəl] *n* : escombros *mpl*

ruby ['ruːbi] *n, pl* **-bies** : rubí *m*

rudder ['rʌdər] *n* : timón *m*

ruddy ['rʌdi] *adj* **-dier; -est** : rubicundo

rude ['ruːd] *adj* **ruder; rudest 1** IMPOLITE : grosero, mal educado **2** ABRUPT : brusco — **rudely** ['ruːdli] *adv* : groseramente — **rudeness** ['ruːdnəs] *n* : mala educación *f*

rudiment ['ruːdəmənt] *n* : rudimento *m* — **rudimentary** [,ruːdə'mentəri] *adj* : rudimentario

rue ['ruː] *vt* **rued; ruing** : lamentar — **rueful** ['ruːfəl] *adj* : triste, arrepentido

ruffle ['rʌfəl] *vt* **-fled; -fling 1** : des-

peinar (pelo), erizar (plumas) **2** VEX : alterar, contrariar — **~** *n* : volante *m* (de un vestido, etc.)

rug ['rʌg] *n* : alfombra *f*, tapete *m*

rugged ['rʌgəd] *adj* **1** : escabroso (dícese del terreno), escarpado (dícese de montañas) **2** HARSH : duro **3** STURDY : fuerte

ruin ['ruːən] *n* : ruina *f* — **~** *vt* : arruinar

rule ['ruːl] *n* **1** : regla *f* **2** CONTROL : dominio *m* **3 as a ~** : por lo general — **~** *v* **ruled; ruling** *vt* **1** GOVERN : gobernar **2** : fallar (dícese de un juez) **3 ~ out** : descartar — *vi* : gobernar, reinar — **ruler** ['ruːlər] *n* **1** : gobernante *mf*; soberano *m*, -na *f* **2** : regla *f* (para medir) — **ruling** ['ruːlɪŋ] *n* VERDICT : fallo *m*

rum ['rʌm] *n* : ron *m*

Rumanian [ruˈmeɪniən] → **Romanian**

rumble ['rʌmbəl] *vi* **-bled; -bling 1** : retumbar **2** : hacer ruidos (dícese del estómago) — **~** *n* : retumbo *m*, estruendo *m*

rummage ['rʌmɪdʒ] *vi* **-maged; -maging** : hurgar

rumor ['ruːmər] *n* : rumor *m* — **~** *vt* **be ~ed** : rumorearse

rump ['rʌmp] *n* **1** : grupa *f* (de un animal) **2 ~ steak** : filete *m* de cadera

rumpus ['rʌmpəs] *n* **1** : lío *m*, jaleo *m* *fam*

run ['rʌn] *v* **ran** ['ræn]; **run; running** *vi* **1** : correr **2** FUNCTION : funcionar **3** LAST : durar **4** : desteñir (dícese de colores) **5** EXTEND : correr, extenderse **6** : presentarse (como candidato) **7 ~ away** : huir **8 ~ into** ENCOUNTER : tropezar con **9 ~ into** HIT : chocar contra **10 ~ late** : ir retrasado **11 ~ out of** : quedarse sin **12 ~ over** : atropellar — *vt* **1** : correr **2** OPERATE : hacer funcionar **3** : hacer correr (agua) **4** MANAGE : dirigir **5 ~ a fever** : tener fiebre — **~** *n* **1** : carrera *f* **2** TRIP : viaje *m*, paseo *m* (en coche) **3** SERIES : serie *f* **4 in the long ~** : a la larga **5 in the short ~** : a corto plazo — **runaway** ['rʌnə,weɪ] *n* : fugitivo *m*, -va *f* — **~** *adj* : fugitivo — **rundown** ['rʌn,daʊn] *n* : resumen *m* — **run-down** ['rʌn'daʊn] *adj* **1** : destartalado **2** EXHAUSTED : agotado

rung¹ → **ring¹**

rung² ['rʌŋ] *n* : peldaño *m* (de una escalera, etc.)

runner ['rʌnər] *n* **1** : corredor *m*, -dora *f* **2** : patín *m* (de un trineo), riel *m* (de un cajón, etc.) — **runner-up** [,rʌnər'ʌp] *n, pl* **runners-up** : subcampeón *m*, -peona *f* — **running** ['rʌnɪŋ] *adj* **1**

FLOWING : corriente **2** CONTINUOUS : continuo **3** CONSECUTIVE : seguido
runt ['rʌnt] *n* : animal *m* más pequeño (de una camada)
runway ['rʌn,weɪ] *n* : pista *f* de aterrizaje
rupture ['rʌptʃər] *n* : ruptura *f* — ~ *v* **-tured; -turing** *vt* : romper — *vi* : reventar
rural ['rʊrəl] *adj* : rural
ruse ['ruːs, 'ruːz] *n* : ardid *m*
rush¹ ['rʌʃ] *n* : junco *m* (planta)
rush² *vi* : ir de prisa — *vt* **1** : apresurar, apurar **2** ATTACK : asaltar **3** : llevar rápidamente (al hospital, etc.) — ~ *n* **1** : prisa *f*, apuro *m* **2** : ráfaga *f* (de aire), torrente *m* (de agua) — ~ *adj* : urgente — **rush hour** *n* : hora *f* punta
russet ['rʌsət] *n* : color *m* rojizo
Russian ['rʌʃən] *adj* : ruso — ~ *n* : ruso *m* (idioma)
rust ['rʌst] *n* : herrumbre *f*, óxido *m* — ~ *vi* : oxidarse — *vt* : oxidar
rustic ['rʌstɪk] *adj* : rústico
rustle ['rʌsəl] *v* **-tled; -tling** *vt* **1** : hacer susurrar **2** : robar (ganado) — *vi* : susurrar — ~ *n* : susurro *m*
rusty ['rʌsti] *adj* **rustier; -est** : oxidado
rut ['rʌt] *n* **1** : surco *m* **2 be in a** ~ : ser esclavo de la rutina
ruthless ['ruːθləs] *adj* : despiadado, cruel
rye ['raɪ] *n* : centeno *m*

S

s ['ɛs] *n, pl* **s's** *or* **ss** ['ɛsəz] : s *f*, decimonovena letra del alfabeto inglés
Sabbath ['sæbəθ] *n* **1** : sábado *m* (día santo judío) **2** : domingo *m* (día santo cristiano)
sabotage ['sæbə,tɑʒ] *n* : sabotaje *m* — *vt* **-taged; -taging** : sabotear
saccharin ['sækərən] *n* : sacarina *f*
sack ['sæk] *n* : saco *m* — ~ *vt* **1** FIRE : despedir **2** PLUNDER : saquear
sacrament ['sækrəmənt] *n* : sacramento *m*
sacred ['seɪkrəd] *adj* : sagrado
sacrifice ['sækrə,faɪs] *n* : sacrificio *m* — *vt* **-ficed; -ficing** : sacrificar
sacrilege ['sækrəlɪdʒ] *n* : sacrilegio *m* — **sacrilegious** [,sækrə'lɪdʒəs, -'liː-] *adj* : sacrílego
sad ['sæd] *adj* **sadder; saddest** : triste — **sadden** ['sædən] *vt* : entristecer
saddle ['sædəl] *n* : silla *f* (de montar) — ~ *vt* **-dled; -dling 1** : ensillar (un caballo, etc.) **2** ~ **s.o. with sth** : cargar a algn con algo
sadistic [sə'dɪstɪk] *adj* : sádico
sadness ['sædnəs] *n* : tristeza *f*
safari [sə'fɑri, -'fær-] *n* : safari *m*
safe ['seɪf] *adj* **safer; safest 1** : seguro **2** UNHARMED : ileso **3** CAREFUL : prudente **4** ~ **and sound** : sano y salvo — ~ *n* : caja *f* fuerte — **safeguard** ['seɪf,gɑrd] *n* : salvaguarda *f* — ~ *vt* : salvaguardar — **safely** ['seɪfli] *adv* **1** : sin peligro **2** arrive ~ : llegar sin novedad — **safety** ['seɪfti] *n, pl* **-ties** : seguridad *f* — **safety belt** *n* : cinturón *m* de seguridad — **safety pin** *n* : imperdible *m*
saffron ['sæfrən] *n* : azafrán *m*
sag ['sæg] *vi* **sagged; sagging 1** : combarse **2** GIVE : aflojarse **3** FLAG : flaquear
saga ['sɑgə, 'sæ-] *n* : saga *f*
sage¹ ['seɪdʒ] *n* : salvia *f* (planta)
sage² *adj* **sager; -est** : sabio — ~ *n* : sabio *m*, **-bia** *f*
said → **say**
sail ['seɪl] *n* **1** : vela *f* (de un barco) **2 go for a** ~ : salir a navegar **3 set** ~ : zarpar — ~ *vi* : navegar — *vt* : gobernar (un barco), navegar (el mar) — **sailboat** ['seɪl,boːt] *n* : velero *m* — **sailor** ['seɪlər] *n* : marinero *m*
saint ['seɪnt, *before a name* ,seɪnt *or* sənt] *n* : santo *m*, **-ta** *f* — **saintly** ['seɪntli] *adj* **saintlier; -est** : santo
sake ['seɪk] *n* **1 for goodness'** ~**!** : ¡por Dios! **2 for the** ~ **of** : por (el bien de)
salad ['sæləd] *n* : ensalada *f*
salamander ['sælə,mændər] *n* : salamandra *f*
salami [sə'lɑmi] *n* : salami *m*
salary ['sæləri] *n, pl* **-ries** : sueldo *m*
sale ['seɪl] *n* **1** : venta *f* **2 for** ~ : se vende **3 on** ~ : de rebaja — **salesman** ['seɪlzmən] *n, pl* **-men** [-mən, -,men] : vendedor *m*, dependiente *m* — **saleswoman** ['seɪlz,wʊmən] *n, pl* **-women** [-,wɪmən] : vendedora *f*, dependienta *f*
salient ['seɪljənt] *adj* : saliente
saliva [sə'laɪvə] *n* : saliva *f*
sallow ['sælo:] *adj* : amarillento, cetrino
salmon ['sæmən] *ns & pl* : salmón *m*
salon [sə'lɑn, 'sæ,lɑn] *n* → **beauty salon**

saloon [sə'luːn] n : bar m

salsa ['sɔlsə, 'sɑl-] n : salsa f mexicana, salsa f picante

salt ['sɔlt] n : sal f — ~ vt : salar — **saltwater** ['sɔlt,wɔt̬ər, -,wɑ-] adj : de agua salada — **salty** ['sɔlti] adj **saltier; -est** : salado

salute [sə'luːt] v **-luted; -luting** vt : saludar — vi : hacer un saludo — ~ n : saludo m

salvage ['sælvɪdʒ] n : salvamento m — ~ vt **-vaged; -vaging** : salvar

salvation [sæl'veɪʃən] n : salvación f

salve ['sæv, 'sav] n : ungüento m

same ['seɪm] adj 1 : mismo 2 be the ~ (as) : ser igual (que) 3 the ~ thing (as) : la misma cosa (que) — ~ pron 1 all the ~ : igual 2 the ~ : lo mismo — ~ adv the ~ : igual

sample ['sæmpəl] n : muestra f — ~ vt **-pled; -pling** : probar

sanatorium [,sænə'tɔriəm] n, pl **-riums** or **-ria** [-iə] : sanatorio m

sanctify ['sæŋktə,faɪ] vt **-fied; -fying** : santificar

sanction n ['sæŋkʃən] : sanción f — ~ vt : sancionar

sanctity ['sæŋktət̬i] n, pl **-ties** : santidad f

sanctuary ['sæŋkt̬ʃuˌeri] n, pl **-aries** : santuario m

sand ['sænd] n : arena f — ~ vt : lijar (madera)

sandal ['sændəl] n : sandalia f

sandpaper ['sænd,peɪpər] n : papel m de lija — ~ vt : lijar

sandwich ['sænd,wɪtʃ] n : sandwich m, bocadillo m Spain — ~ vt ~ between : meter entre

sandy ['sændi] adj **sandier; -est** : arenoso

sane ['seɪn] adj **saner; sanest** 1 : cuerdo 2 SENSIBLE : sensato

sang → sing

sanitarium [,sænə'teriəm] n, pl **-iums** or **-ia** [-iə] → **sanatorium**

sanitary ['sænəˌteri] adj 1 : sanitario 2 HYGIENIC : higiénico — **sanitary napkin** n : compresa f (higiénica) — **sanitation** [,sænə'teɪʃən] n : sanidad f

sanity ['sænət̬i] n : cordura f

sank → sink

Santa Claus ['sæntəˌklɔz] n : Papá m Noel

sap¹ ['sæp] n 1 : savia f (de una planta) 2 SUCKER : inocentón m, -tona f

sap² vt **sapped; sapping** : minar (la fuerza, etc.)

sapphire ['sæˌfaɪr] n : zafiro m

sarcasm ['sɑrˌkæzəm] n : sarcasmo m — **sarcastic** [sɑr'kæstɪk] adj : sarcástico

sardine [sɑr'diːn] n : sardina f

sash ['sæʃ] n : faja f (de un vestido), fajín m (de un uniforme)

sat → sit

satanic [sə'tænɪk, seɪ-] adj : satánico

satchel ['sætʃəl] n : cartera f

satellite ['sæt̬əˌlaɪt] n : satélite m

satin ['sætən] n : raso m

satire ['sæˌtaɪr] n : sátira f — **satiric** [sə'tɪrɪk] or **satirical** [-ɪkəl] adj : satírico

satisfaction [,sæt̬əs'fækʃən] n : satisfacción f — **satisfactory** [,sæt̬əs'fæktəri] adj : satisfactorio — **satisfy** ['sæt̬əsˌfaɪ] v **-fied; -fying** vt 1 : satisfacer 2 CONVINCE : convencer — **satisfying** adj : satisfactorio

saturate ['sætʃəˌreɪt] vt **-rated; -rating** 1 : saturar 2 DRENCH : empapar — **saturation** [,sætʃə'reɪʃən] n : saturación f

Saturday ['sæt̬ərˌdeɪ, -di] n : sábado m

Saturn ['sæt̬ərn] n : Saturno m

sauce ['sɔs] n : salsa f — **saucepan** ['sɔsˌpæn] n : cacerola f — **saucer** ['sɔsər] n : platillo m — **saucy** ['sɔsi] adj **saucier; -est** IMPUDENT : descarado

sauna ['sɔnə, 'saunə] n : sauna mf

saunter ['sɔntər, 'san-] vi : pasear

sausage ['sɔsɪdʒ] n : salchicha f

sauté [sɔˈteɪ, soː-] vt **-téed** or **-téd; -téing** : saltear, sofreír

savage ['sævɪdʒ] adj : salvaje, feroz — ~ n : salvaje mf — **savagery** ['sævɪdʒri, -dʒəri] n, pl **-ries** : ferocidad f

save ['seɪv] v **saved; saving 1** RESCUE : salvar 2 RESERVE : guardar 3 : ahorrar (dinero, tiempo, etc.) — ~ prep EXCEPT : salvo

savior ['seɪvjər] n : salvador m, -dora f

savor ['seɪvər] vt : saborear — **savory** ['seɪvəri] adj : sabroso

saw¹ → see

saw² ['sɔ] n : sierra f — ~ vt **sawed; sawed** or **sawn; sawing** : serrar — **sawdust** ['sɔˌdʌst] n : serrín m, aserrín m

saxophone ['sæksəˌfoːn] n : saxofón m

say ['seɪ] v **said** ['sed]; **saying; says** ['sez] vt 1 : decir 2 INDICATE : marcar (dícese de relojes, etc.) — vi 1 : decir 2 that is to ~ : es decir — ~ n, pl **says** ['seɪz] 1 have no ~ : no tener ni voz ni voto 2 have one's ~ : dar su opinión — **saying** ['seɪŋ] n : refrán m

scab ['skæb] n 1 : costra f (en una herida) 2 STRIKEBREAKER : esquirol mf

scaffold ['skæfəld, -ˌfoːld] n : andamio m (en construcción)

scald ['skɔld] vt : escaldar

scale¹ ['skeɪl] *n* : balanza *f* (para pesar)
scale² *n* : escama *f* (de un pez, etc.) —
~ *vt* **scaled; scaling** : escamar
scale³ *vt* **scaled; scaling 1** CLIMB : escalar **2** ~ **down** : reducir — ~ *n* : escala *f* (musical, salarial, etc.)
scallion ['skæljən] *n* : cebolleta *f*
scallop ['skɑləp, 'skæ-] *n* : vieira *f*
scalp ['skælp] *n* : cuero *m* cabelludo
scam ['skæm] *n* : estafa *f*, timo *m fam*
scamper ['skæmpər] *vi* ~ **away** : irse
corriendo
scan ['skæn] *vt* **scanned; scanning 1**
: escandir **2** EXAMINE : escudriñar **3** SKIM : echar un vistazo a **4** : escanear (en informática)
scandal ['skændəl] *n* **1** : escándalo *m* **2**
GOSSIP : habladurías *fpl* — **scandalous** ['skændələs] *adj* : escandaloso
Scandinavian [,skændə'neɪviən] *adj*
: escandinavo
scant ['skænt] *adj* : escaso
scapegoat ['skeɪp,goːt] *n* : chivo *m* expiatorio
scar ['skɑr] *n* : cicatriz *f* — ~ *v*
scarred; scarring *vt* : dejar una cicatriz en — *vi* : cicatrizar
scarce ['skɛrs] *adj* **scarcer; -est** : escaso — **scarcely** ['skɛrsli] *adv* : apenas
— **scarcity** ['skɛrsəti] *n, pl* **-ties** : escasez *f*
scare ['skɛr] *vt* **scared; scaring 1**
: asustar **2 be** ~**d of** : tener miedo a
— ~ *n* **1** FRIGHT : susto *m* **2** ALARM
: pánico *m* — **scarecrow** ['skɛr,kroː] *n*
: espantapájaros *m*, espantajo *m*
scarf ['skɑrf] *n, pl* **scarves** ['skɑrvz] *or*
scarfs **1** : bufanda *f* **2** KERCHIEF
: pañuelo *m*
scarlet ['skɑrlət] *adj* : escarlata — **scarlet fever** *n* : escarlatina *f*
scary ['skɛri] *adj* **scarier; -est** : que da
miedo
scathing ['skeɪðɪŋ] *adj* : mordaz
scatter ['skætər] *vt* **1** STREW : esparcir **2**
DISPERSE : dispersar — *vi* : dispersarse
scavenger ['skævəndʒər] *n* : carroñero
m, -ra *f* (animal)
scenario [sə'næriːoː, -'nɑr-] *n, pl* **-ios 1**
: guión *m* (cinemático) **2 the worst-case** ~ : el peor de los casos
scene ['sim] *n* **1** : escena *f* **2 behind the**
~**s** : entre bastidores **3 make a** ~
: armar un escándalo — **scenery** ['siːnəri] *n, pl* **-eries 1** : decorado *m* **2**
LANDSCAPE : paisaje *m* — **scenic** ['siːnɪk] *adj* : pintoresco
scent ['sɛnt] *n* **1** : aroma *m* **2** PERFUME
: perfume *m* **3** TRAIL : rastro *m* —
scented ['sɛntəd] *adj* : perfumado

sceptic ['skɛptɪk] → **skeptic**
schedule ['skɛdʒuːl, -dʒəl, *esp Brit* 'ʃɛdjuːl] *n* **1** : programa *m* **2** TIMETABLE
: horario *m* **3 behind** ~ : atrasado,
con retraso **4 on** ~ : según lo previsto — ~ *vt* **-uled; -uling** : planear,
programar
scheme ['skiːm] *n* **1** PLAN : plan *m* **2**
PLOT : intriga *f* **3** DESIGN : esquema *f* —
~ *vi* **schemed; scheming** : intrigar
schism ['sɪzəm, 'skɪ-] *n* : cisma *m*
schizophrenia [,skɪtsə'friniːə, ,skɪzə-,
-'frɛ-] *n* : esquizofrenia *f* — **schizophrenic** [,skɪtsə'frɛnɪk, ,skɪzə-] *adj* : esquizofrénico
scholar ['skɑlər] *n* : erudito *m*, -ta *f* —
scholarly ['skɑlərli] *adj* : erudito —
scholarship ['skɑlər,ʃɪp] *n* **1** : erudición *f* **2** GRANT : beca *f*
school¹ ['skuːl] *n* : banco *m* (de peces)
school² *n* **1** : escuela *f* **2** COLLEGE : universidad *f* **3** DEPARTMENT : facultad *f* —
~ *vt* : instruir — **schoolboy** ['skuːl,bɔɪ] *n* : colegial *m* — **schoolgirl** ['skuːl,gərl] *n* : colegiala *f* — **schoolteacher** ['skuːl,tiːtʃər] *n* → **teacher**
science ['saɪəns] *n* : ciencia *f* — **scientific** [,saɪən'tɪfɪk] *adj* : científico — **scientist** ['saɪəntɪst] *n* : científico *m*, -ca *f*
scissors ['sɪzərz] *npl* : tijeras *fpl*
scoff ['skɑf] *vi* ~ **at** : burlarse de, mofarse de
scold ['skoːld] *vt* : regañar
scoop ['skuːp] *n* **1** : pala *f* **2** : noticia *f*
exclusiva (en periodismo) — ~ *vt* **1**
: sacar (con pala) **2** ~ **out** : ahuecar **3**
~ **up** : recoger
scoot ['skuːt] *vi* : ir rápidamente —
scooter ['skuːtər] *n* **1** : patinete *m* **2** *or*
motor ~ : escúter *m*
scope ['skoːp] *n* **1** RANGE : alcance *m* **2**
OPPORTUNITY : posibilidades *fpl*
scorch ['skɔrtʃ] *vt* : chamuscar
score ['skor] *n, pl* **scores 1** : tanteo *m*
(en deportes) **2** RATING : puntuación *f* **3**
: partitura *f* (musical) **4** *or* ~ *pl* **score**
TWENTY : veintena *f* **5 keep** ~ : llevar
la cuenta **6 on that** ~ : en ese sentido
— ~ *v* **scored; scoring** *vt* **1** : marcar,
anotarse *Lat* (un tanto) **2** : sacar (una
nota) — *vi* : marcar (en deportes)
scorn ['skɔrn] *n* : desdén *m* — ~ *vt*
: desdeñar — **scornful** ['skɔrnfəl] *adj*
: desdeñoso
scorpion ['skɔrpiən] *n* : alacrán *m*, escorpión *m*
Scot ['skɑt] *n* : escocés *m*, -cesa *f* —
Scotch ['skɑtʃ] *adj* → **Scottish** — ~
n or ~ **whiskey** : whisky *m* escocés
— **Scottish** ['skɑtɪʃ] *adj* : escocés

scoundrel ['skaʊndrəl] *n* : sinvergüenza *mf*

scour ['skaʊər] *vt* 1 SCRUB : fregar 2 SEARCH : registrar

scourge ['skərdʒ] *n* : azote *m*

scout ['skaʊt] *n* : explorador *m*, -dora *f*

scowl ['skaʊl] *vi* : fruncir el ceño — ~ *n* : ceño *m* fruncido

scram ['skræm] *vi* **scrammed; scramming** : largarse

scramble ['skræmbəl] *v* **-bled; -bling** *vi* 1 CLAMBER : trepar 2 ~ **for** : pelearse por — *vt* : mezclar — ~ *n* : rebatiña *f*, pelea *f* — **scrambled eggs** *npl* : huevos *mpl* revueltos

scrap¹ ['skræp] *n* 1 PIECE : pedazo *m* 2 *or* ~ **metal** : chatarra *f* 3 ~**s** *npl* : sobras — ~ *vt* **scrapped; scrapping** : desechar

scrap² *n* FIGHT : pelea *f*

scrapbook ['skræp,bʊk] *n* : álbum *m* de recortes

scrape ['skreɪp] *v* **scraped; scraping** *vt* 1 : rascar 2 : rasparse (la rodilla, etc.) 3 ~ **off** : raspar 4 ~ **together** : reunir — *vi* 1 RUB : rozar 2 ~ **by** : arreglárselas — ~ *n* 1 : rasguño *m* 2 PREDICAMENT : apuro *m*

scratch ['skrætʃ] *vt* 1 CLAW : arañar 2 MARK : rayar 3 : rascarse (la cabeza, etc.) 4 ~ **out** : tachar — ~ *n* 1 : arañazo *m* 2 MARK : rayón *m* 3 **start from** ~ : empezar desde cero

scrawl ['skrɔl] *v* : garabatear — ~ *n* : garabato *m*

scrawny ['skrɔni] *adj* **scrawnier; -est** : escuálido

scream ['skri:m] *vi* : gritar, chillar — ~ *n* : grito *m*, chillido *m*

screech ['skri:tʃ] *n* 1 : chillido *m* (de personas) 2 : chirrido *m* (de frenos, etc.) — ~ *vi* 1 : chillar 2 : chirriar (dícese de los frenos, etc.)

screen ['skri:n] *n* 1 : pantalla *f* 2 PARTITION : mampara *f* 3 *or* **window** ~ : mosquitero *m* — ~ *vt* 1 SHIELD : proteger 2 HIDE : ocultar 3 : seleccionar (candidatos, etc.)

screw ['skru:] *n* : tornillo *m* — ~ *vt* 1 : atornillar 2 ~ **up** RUIN : fastidiar — **screwdriver** ['skru:,draɪvər] *n* : destornillador *m*

scribble ['skrɪbəl] *v* **-bled; -bling** : garabatear — ~ *n* : garabato *m*

script ['skrɪpt] *n* 1 HANDWRITING : escritura *f* 2 : guión *m* (de cine, etc.) — **scripture** ['skrɪptʃər] *n* 1 : escritos *mpl* sagrados 2 **the Scriptures** *npl* : las Escrituras *fpl*

scroll ['skro:l] *n* : rollo *m* (de pergamino, etc.)

scrounge ['skraʊndʒ] *v* **scrounged; scrounging** *vt* : gorrear *fam* — *vi* ~ **around for sth** : andar buscando algo

scrub¹ ['skrʌb] *n* UNDERBRUSH : maleza *f*

scrub² *vt* **scrubbed; scrubbing** SCOUR : fregar — ~ *n* : fregado *m*

scruff ['skrʌf] *n* **by the** ~ **of the neck** : por el pescuezo

scruple ['skru:pəl] *n* : escrúpulo *m* — **scrupulous** ['skru:pjələs] *adj* : escrupuloso

scrutiny ['skru:təni] *n, pl* **-nies** : análisis *m* cuidadoso — **scrutinize** ['skru:tən,aɪz] *vt* **-nized; -nizing** : escudriñar

scuff ['skʌf] *vt* : raspar, rayar

scuffle ['skʌfəl] *n* : refriega *f*

sculpture ['skʌlptʃər] *n* : escultura *f* — **sculpt** ['skʌlpt] *v* : esculpir — **sculptor** ['skʌlptər] *n* : escultor *m*, -tora *f*

scum ['skʌm] *n* 1 FROTH : espuma *f* 2 : escoria *f* (dícese de personas)

scurry ['skəri] *vi* **-ried; -rying** : corretear

scuttle¹ ['skʌtəl] *n* : cubo *m* (para carbón)

scuttle² *vt* **-tled; -tling** : hundir (un barco)

scuttle³ *vi* SCAMPER : corretear

sea ['si:] *n* 1 : mar *mf* 2 **at** ~ : en el mar — ~ *adj* : del mar — **seafarer** ['si:,færər] *n* : marinero *m* — **seafood** ['si:,fu:d] *n* : mariscos *mpl* — **seagull** ['si:,gʌl] *n* : gaviota *f*

seal¹ ['si:l] *n* : foca *f* (animal)

seal² *n* 1 STAMP : sello *m* 2 CLOSURE : cierre *m* (hermético) — ~ *vt* : sellar

seam ['si:m] *n* 1 : costura *f* 2 VEIN : veta *f*

seaman ['si:mən] *n, pl* **-men** [-mən, -,men] : marinero *m*

seamy ['si:mi] *adj* **seamier; -est** : sórdido

seaplane ['si:,pleɪn] *n* : hidroavión *m*

seaport ['si:,port] *n* : puerto *m* marítimo

search ['sərtʃ] *vt* : registrar — *vi* ~ **for** : buscar — ~ *n* 1 : registro *m* 2 HUNT : búsqueda *f* — **searchlight** ['sərtʃ,laɪt] *n* : reflector *m*

seashell ['si:,ʃel] *n* : concha *f* (marina) — **seashore** ['si:,ʃor] *n* : orilla *f* del mar — **seasick** ['si:,sɪk] *adj* 1 : mareado 2 **be** ~ : marearse — **seasickness** ['si:,sɪknəs] *n* : mareo *m*

season ['si:zən] *n* 1 : estación *f* (del año) 2 : temporada *f* (en deportes, etc.) — ~ *vt* 1 FLAVOR : sazonar 2 : secar (madera) — **seasonal** ['si:zənəl] *adj*

: estacional — **seasoned** *adj* EXPERI-
ENCED : veterano — **seasoning**
['si:zənɪŋ] *n* : condimento *m*

seat ['si:t] *n* **1** : asiento *m* **2** : fondillos
mpl (de un pantalón) **3** BUTTOCKS
: trasero *m* **4** CENTER : sede *f* — *vt* **1**
be ~ed : sentarse **2** the bus ~s 30
: el autobús tiene cabida para 30 —
seat belt *n* : cinturón *m* de seguridad

seaweed ['si:,wi:d] *n* : alga *f* marina

secede [sɪ'si:d] *vi* **-ceded; -ceding**
: separarse (de una nación, etc.)

secluded [sɪ'klu:dəd] *adj* : aislado —
seclusion [sɪ'klu:ʒən] *n* : aislamiento
m

second ['sekənd] *adj* : segundo — *or*
secondly ['sekəndli] *adv* : en segundo
lugar — ~ *n* **1** : segundo *m*, -da *f* **2**
MOMENT : segundo *m* **3** have ~s
: repetir (en una comida) — ~ *vt* : secundar — **secondary** ['sekən,deri] *adj*
: secundario — **secondhand** ['sekənd-
'hænd] *adj* : de segunda mano — **second–rate** ['sekənd'reɪt] *adj* : mediocre

secret ['si:krət] *adj* : secreto — ~ *n*
: secreto *m* — **secrecy** ['si:krəsi] *n*, *pl*
-cies : secreto *m*

secretary ['sekrə,teri] *n*, *pl* **-taries 1**
: secretario *m*, -ria *f* **2** : ministro *m*, -tra
f (del gobierno)

secretion [sɪ'kri:ʃən] *n* : secreción *f* —
secrete [sɪ'kri:t] *vt* **-creted; -creting**
: secretar

secretive ['si:krətɪv, sɪ'kri:tɪv] *adj*
: reservado — **secretly** ['si:krətli] *adv*
: en secreto

sect ['sekt] *n* : secta *f*

section ['sekʃən] *n* : sección *f*, parte *f*

sector ['sektər] *n* : sector *m*

secular ['sekjələr] *adj* : secular

security [sɪ'kjorəti] *n*, *pl* **-ties 1** : seguridad *f* **2** GUARANTEE : garantía *f* **3** securities *npl* : valores *mpl* — **secure** [sɪ-
'kjor] *adj* **-curer; -est** : seguro — ~ *vt*
-cured; -curing 1 FASTEN : asegurar **2**
GET : conseguir

sedan [sɪ'dæn] *n* : sedán *m*

sedate [sɪ'deɪt] *adj* : sosegado

sedative ['sedətɪv] *adj* : sedante — ~ *n*
: sedante *m*

sedentary ['sedən,teri] *adj* : sedentario

sediment ['sedəmənt] *n* : sedimento *m*

seduce [sɪ'du:s, -'dju:s] *vt* **-duced; -duc-
ing** : seducir — **seduction** [sɪ'dʌkʃən]
n : seducción *f* — **seductive** [sɪ'dʌktɪv]
adj : seductor

see ['si:] *v* **saw** ['sɔ]; **seen** ['si:n]; **seeing**
vt **1** : ver **2** UNDERSTAND : entender **3**
ESCORT : acompañar **4** ~ s.o. off : despedirse de algn **5** ~ sth through : ll-

evar algo a cabo **6** ~ you later!
: ¡hasta luego! — *vi* **1** : ver **2** UNDER-
STAND : entender **3** let's ~ : vamos a
ver **4** ~ to : ocuparse de

seed ['si:d] *n*, *pl* **seed** *or* **seeds 1**
: semilla *f* **2** SOURCE : germen *m* —
seedy ['si:di] *adj* **seedier; -est**
SQUALID : sórdido

seek ['si:k] *v* **sought** ['sɔt]; **seeking** *vt* **1**
or ~ **out** : buscar **2** REQUEST : pedir **3**
~ **to** : tratar de — *vi* SEARCH : buscar

seem ['si:m] *vi* : parecer

seep ['si:p] *vi* : filtrarse

seesaw ['si:,sɔ] *n* : balancín *m*

seethe ['si:ð] *vi* **seethed; seething** : rabiar, estar furioso

segment ['segmənt] *n* : segmento *m*

segregate ['segrɪ,geɪt] *vt* **-gated;
-gating** : segregar — **segregation**
[,segrɪ'geɪʃən] *n* : segregación *f*

seize ['si:z] *v* **seized; seizing** *vt* **1**
GRASP : agarrar **2** CAPTURE : tomar **3**
: aprovechar (una oportunidad) — *vi*
or ~ **up** : agarrotarse — **seizure**
['si:ʒər] *n* **1** CAPTURE : toma *f* **2** : ataque
m (en medicina)

seldom ['seldəm] *adv* : pocas veces,
raramente

select [sə'lekt] *adj* : selecto — ~ *vt*
: seleccionar — **selection** [sə'lekʃən] *n*
: selección *f* — **selective** [sə'lektɪv]
adj : selectivo

self ['self] *n*, *pl* **selves** ['selvz] **1** : ser *m*
2 her better ~ : su lado bueno —
self–addressed [,selfə'drest] *adj* : con
la dirección del remitente — **self–as-
sured** [,selfə'ʃord] *adj* : seguro de sí
mismo — **self–centered** [,self'sentərd]
adj : egocéntrico — **self–confidence**
[,self'kɑnfədənts] *n* : confianza *f* en sí
mismo — **self–confident** [,self'kɑn-
fədənt] *adj* : seguro de sí mismo —
self–conscious [,self'kɑntʃəs] *adj*
: cohibido — **self–control** [,selfkən-
'tro:l] *n* : dominio *m* de sí mismo —
self–defense [,selfdɪ'fents] *n* : defensa
f propia — **self–employed** [,selfɪm-
'plɔɪd] *adj* : que trabaja por cuenta
propia — **self–esteem** [,selfɪ'sti:m] *n*
: amor *m* propio — **self–evident** [,self-
'evədənt] *adj* : evidente — **self–help**
[,self'help] *n* : autoayuda *f* — **self–
important** [,selfɪm'pɔrtənt] *adj* : presumido — **self–interest** [,self'ɪntrəst,
-tərest] *n* : interés *m* personal — **selfish** ['selfɪʃ] *adj* : egoísta — **selfish-
ness** ['selfɪʃnəs] *n* : egoísmo *m* — **self-
less** ['selfləs] *adj* : desinteresado —
self–pity [,self'pɪti] *n*, *pl* **-ties** : autocompasión *f* — **self–portrait** [,self-

'pɔrtrət] n : autorretrato m — **self-respect** [ˌselfri'spekt] n : amor m propio — **self-righteous** [ˌself'raitʃəs] adj : santurrón — **self-service** [ˌself-'sərvis] adj : de autoservicio — **self-sufficient** [ˌselfsə'fiʃənt] adj : autosuficiente — **self-taught** [ˌself'tɔt] adj : autodidacta

sell ['sel] v **sold** ['sold]; **selling** vt : vender — vi : venderse — **seller** ['selər] n : vendedor m, -dora f

selves → **self**

semantics [si'mæntiks] ns & pl : semántica f

semblance ['semblənts] n : apariencia f

semester [sə'mestər] n : semestre m

semicolon ['semiˌko:lən, ˌse.mai-] n : punto y coma m

semifinal ['semiˌfainəl, ˌse.mai-] n : semifinal f

seminary ['seməˌneri] n, pl **-naries** : seminario m — **seminar** ['seməˌnɑr] n : seminario m

senate ['senət] n : senado m — **senator** ['senətər] n : senador m, -dora f

send ['send] vt **sent** ['sent]; **sending 1** : mandar, enviar **2 ~ away for** : pedir **3 ~ back** : devolver (mercancías, etc.) **4 ~ for** : mandar a buscar — **sender** ['sendər] n : remitente mf

senile ['si:ˌnail] adj : senil — **senility** [si'nilət̬i] n : senilidad f

senior ['si:njər] n **1** SUPERIOR : superior m **2** : estudiante mf de último año (en educación) **3** or **~ citizen** : persona f mayor **4 be s.o.'s ~** : ser mayor que algn — **~** adj **1** : superior (en rango) **2** ELDER : mayor — **seniority** [ˌsi:-'njɔrət̬i] n : antigüedad f

sensation [sen'seiʃən] n : sensación f — **sensational** [sen'seiʃənəl] adj : sensacional

sense ['sents] n **1** : sentido m **2** FEELING : sensación f **3** COMMON SENSE : sentido m común **4 make ~** : tener sentido — **~** vt **sensed**; **sensing** : sentir — **senseless** ['sentsləs] adj **1** : sin sentido **2** UNCONSCIOUS : inconsciente — **sensible** ['sentsəbəl] adj : sensato, práctico — **sensibility** [ˌsentsə'bilət̬i] n, pl **-ties** : sensibilidad f — **sensitive** ['sentsət̬iv] adj **1** : sensible **2** TOUCHY : susceptible — **sensitivity** [ˌsentsə-'tivət̬i] n, pl **-ties** : sensibilidad f — **sensual** ['sentʃʊəl] adj : sensual — **sensuous** ['sentʃʊəs] adj : sensual

sent → **send**

sentence ['sentənts, -ənz] n **1** : frase f **2** JUDGMENT : sentencia f — **~** vt **-tenced**; **-tencing** : sentenciar

sentiment ['sentəmənt] n **1** : sentimiento m **2** BELIEF : opinión f — **sentimental** [ˌsentə'mentəl] adj : sentimental — **sentimentality** [ˌsentəmen'tælət̬i] n, pl **-ties** : sentimentalismo m

sentry ['sentri] n, pl **-tries** : centinela m

separation [ˌsepə'reiʃən] n : separación f — **separate** ['sepəˌreit] v **-rated**; **-rating** vt **1** DISTINGUISH : distinguir — vi : separarse — **~** ['seprət, 'sepə-] adj **1** : separado **2** DETACHED : aparte **3** DISTINCT : distinto — **separately** ['seprət̬li, 'sepə-] adv : por separado

September [sep'tembər] n : septiembre m, setiembre m

sequel ['si:kwəl] n **1** : continuación f **2** CONSEQUENCE : secuela f

sequence ['si:kwənts] n **1** ORDER : orden m **2** : secuencia f (de números o escenas)

Serb ['sərb] or **Serbian** ['sərbiən] adj : serbio

serene [sə'ri:n] adj : sereno — **serenity** [sə'renət̬i] n : serenidad f

sergeant ['sɑrdʒənt] n : sargento mf

serial ['siriəl] adj : seriado — **~** n : serial m — **series** ['sir.i:z] n, pl **series** : serie f

serious ['siriəs] adj : serio — **seriously** ['siriəsli] adv **1** : seriamente **2** GRAVELY : gravemente **3 take ~** : tomar en serio

sermon ['sərmən] n : sermón m

serpent ['sərpənt] n : serpiente f

servant ['sərvənt] n : criado m, -da f

serve ['sərv] v **served**; **serving** vi **1** : servir **2** : sacar (en deportes) **3 ~ as** : servir de — vt **1** : servir **2 ~ time** : cumplir una condena — **server** ['sərvər] n **1** WAITER : camarero m, -ra f **2** : servidor m (en informática)

service ['sərvəs] n **1** : servicio m **2** CEREMONY : oficio m **3** MAINTENANCE : revisión f **4 armed ~s** : fuerzas fpl armadas — **~** vt **-viced**; **-vicing** : revisar (un vehículo, etc.) — **serviceman** ['sərvəsˌmæn, -mən] n, pl **-men** [-mən, -ˌmen] : militar m — **service station** n : estación f de servicio — **serving** ['sərvɪŋ] n : porción f, ración f

session ['seʃən] n : sesión f

set ['set] n **1** : juego m (de platos, etc.) **2** : set m (en tenis, etc.) **3** or **stage ~** : decorado m **4 television ~** : aparato m de televisión — **~** v **set**; **setting** vt **1** or **~ down** : poner **2** : poner en hora (un reloj) **3** FIX : fijar (una fecha, etc.) **4 ~ fire to** : prender fuego a **5 ~ free** : poner en libertad **6 ~ off**

: hacer sonar (una alarma), hacer estallar (una bomba) **7 ~ out to (do sth)** : proponerse (hacer algo) **8 ~ up** ASSEMBLE : montar, armar **9 ~ up** ESTABLISH : establecer — *vi* **1** : cuajarse (dícese de la gelatina, etc.), fraguar (dícese del cemento) **2** : ponerse (dícese del sol, etc.) **3 ~ in** BEGIN : empezar **4 ~ off** *or* **~ out** : salir (de viaje) — *~ adj* **1** FIXED : fijo **2** READY : listo, preparado — **setback** ['sɛt,bæk] *n* : revés *m* — **setting** ['sɛtɪŋ] *n* **1** : posición *f* (de un control) **2** MOUNTING : engaste *m* (de joyas) **3** SCENE : escenario *m*

settle ['sɛtəl] *v* **settled; settling** *vi* **1** : asentarse (dícese de polvo, colonos, etc.) **2 ~ down** RELAX : calmarse **3 ~ for** : conformarse con **4 ~ in** : instalarse — *vt* **1** DECIDE : fijar, decidir **2** RESOLVE : resolver **3** PAY : pagar **4** CALM : calmar **5** COLONIZE : colonizar — **settlement** ['sɛtəlmənt] *n* **1** PAYMENT : pago *m* **2** COLONY : colonia *f*, poblado *m* **3** AGREEMENT : acuerdo *m* — **settler** ['sɛtələr] *n* : colono *m*, -na *f*

seven ['sɛvən] *adj* : siete — *~ n* : siete *m* — **seven hundred** *adj* : setecientos — *~ n* : setecientos *m* — **seventeen** [,sɛvən'tiːn] *adj* : diecisiete — *~ n* **1** : diecisiete *m* — **seventeenth** [,sɛvən'tiːnθ] *adj* : decimoséptimo — *~ n* **1** : decimoséptimo *m*, -ma *f* (en una serie) **2** : diecisieteavo *m* (en matemáticas) — **seventh** ['sɛvənθ] *adj* : séptimo — *~ n* **1** : séptimo *m*, -ma *f* (en una serie) **2** : séptimo *m* (en matemáticas) — **seventieth** ['sɛvəntiəθ] *adj* : septuagésimo — *~ n* **1** : septuagésimo *m*, -ma *f* (en una serie) **2** : setentavo *m* (en matemáticas) — **seventy** ['sɛvənti] *adj* : setenta — *~ n, pl* **-ties** : setenta *m*

sever ['sɛvər] *vt* **-ered; -ering** : cortar, romper

several ['sɛvrəl, 'sɛvə-] *adj* : varios — *~ pron* : varios, varias

severance ['sɛvrənts, sɛvə-] *n* : ruptura *f*

severe [sə'vɪr] *adj* **severer; -est 1** : severo **2** SERIOUS : grave — **severely** *adv* **1** : severamente **2** SERIOUSLY : gravemente — **severity** [sə'vɛrəti] *n* **1** : severidad *f* **2** SERIOUSNESS : gravedad *f*

sew ['soː] *v* **sewed; sewn** ['soːn] *or* **sewed; sewing** : coser

sewer ['suːər] *n* : cloaca *f* — **sewage** ['suːɪdʒ] *n* : aguas *fpl* negras

sewing ['soːɪŋ] *n* : costura *f*

sex ['sɛks] *n* **1** : sexo *m* **2** INTERCOURSE

: relaciones *fpl* sexuales — **sexism** ['sɛk,sɪzəm] *n* : sexismo *m* — **sexist** ['sɛksɪst] *adj* : sexista — **sexual** ['sɛkʃʊəl] *adj* : sexual — **sexuality** [,sɛkʃʊ'ælət̬i] *n* : sexualidad *f* — **sexy** ['sɛksi] *adj* **sexier; -est** : sexy

shabby ['ʃæbi] *adj* **shabbier; -est 1** WORN : gastado **2** UNFAIR : malo, injusto

shack ['ʃæk] *n* : choza *f*

shackle ['ʃækəl] *n* : grillete *m*

shade ['ʃeɪd] *n* **1** : sombra *f* **2** : tono *m* (de un color) **3** NUANCE : matiz *m* **4** *or* **lampshade** : pantalla *f* **5** *or* **window ~** : persiana *f* — *vt* **shaded; shading** : proteger de la luz — **shadow** ['ʃædoː] *n* : sombra *f* — **shadowy** ['ʃædowi] *adj* INDISTINCT : vago — **shady** ['ʃeɪdi] *adj* **shadier; -est 1** : sombreado **2** DISREPUTABLE : sospechoso

shaft ['ʃæft] *n* **1** : asta *f* (de una flecha, etc.) **2** HANDLE : mango *m* **3** AXLE : eje *m* **4** : rayo *m* (de luz) **5** *or* **mine ~** : pozo *m*

shaggy ['ʃægi] *adj* **shaggier; -est** : peludo

shake ['ʃeɪk] *v* **shook** ['ʃʊk]; **shaken** ['ʃeɪkən]; **shaking** *vt* **1** : sacudir **2** MIX : agitar **3 ~ hands with s.o.** : dar la mano a algn **4 ~ one's head** : negar con la cabeza **5 ~ up** UPSET : afectar — *vi* : temblar — *~ n* **1** : sacudida *f* **2 ~ handshake** — **shaker** ['ʃeɪkər] *n* **1 salt ~** : salero *m* **2 pepper ~** : pimentero *m* — **shaky** ['ʃeɪki] *adj* **shakier; -est 1** : tembloroso **2** UNSTABLE : poco firme

shall ['ʃæl] *v aux, past* **should** ['ʃʊd]; *pres sing & pl* **shall 1** (*expressing volition or futurity*) → **will 2** (*expressing possibility or obligation*) → **should 3 ~ we go?** : ¿nos vamos?

shallow ['ʃæloː] *adj* **1** : poco profundo **2** SUPERFICIAL : superficial

sham ['ʃæm] *n* : farsa *f* — *~ v* **shammed; shamming** : fingir

shambles ['ʃæmbəlz] *ns & pl* : caos *m*, desorden *m*

shame ['ʃeɪm] *n* **1** : vergüenza *f* **2 what a ~!** : ¡qué lástima! — *~ vt* **shamed; shaming** : avergonzar — **shameful** ['ʃeɪmfəl] *adj* : vergonzoso — **shameless** ['ʃeɪmləs] *adj* : desvergonzado

shampoo [ʃæm'puː] *vt* : lavar (el pelo) — *~ n, pl* **-poos** : champú *m*

shamrock ['ʃæm,rɑk] *n* : trébol *m*

shan't ['ʃænt] (*contraction of* **shall not**) → **shall**

shape ['ʃeɪp] v shaped; shaping vt 1
: formar 2 DETERMINE : determinar 3
be ~d like : tener forma de — vi or
~ up : tomar forma — ~ n 1 : forma
f 2 get in ~ : ponerse en forma —
shapeless ['ʃeɪpləs] adj : informe

share ['ʃer] n 1 : porción f 2 : acción f
(en una compañía) — ~ v shared;
sharing vt 1 : compartir 2 DIVIDE : dividir — vi : compartir — shareholder
['ʃer,hoʊldər] n : accionista mf

shark ['ʃɑrk] n : tiburón m

sharp ['ʃɑrp] adj 1 : afilado 2 POINTY
: puntiagudo 3 ACUTE : agudo 4 HARSH
: duro, severo 5 CLEAR : nítido 6
: sostenido (en música) 7 a ~ curve
: una curva cerrada — ~ adv at two
o'clock ~ : a las dos en punto — ~
n : sostenido (en música) — sharpen
['ʃɑrpən] vt : afilar (un cuchillo, etc.),
sacar punta a (un lápiz) — sharpener
['ʃɑrpənər] n 1 or knife ~ : afilador m
2 or pencil ~ : sacapuntas m —
sharply ['ʃɑrpli] adv : bruscamente

shatter ['ʃætər] vt 1 : hacer añicos 2
DEVASTATE : destrozar — vi : hacerse
añicos

shave ['ʃeɪv] v shaved; shaved or
shaven ['ʃeɪvən]; shaving vt 1 : afeitar 2 SLICE : cortar — vi : afeitarse
— ~ n : afeitada f — shaver ['ʃeɪvər] n
: máquina f de afeitar

shawl ['ʃɔl] n : chal m

she ['ʃiː] pron : ella

sheaf ['ʃiːf] n, pl sheaves ['ʃiːvz] 1
: gavilla f 2 : fajo m (de papeles)

shear ['ʃɪr] vt sheared; sheared or
shorn ['ʃorn]; shearing : esquilar —
shears ['ʃɪrz] npl : tijeras fpl (grandes)

sheath ['ʃiːθ] n, pl sheaths ['ʃiːðz, 'ʃiːθs]
: funda f, vaina f

shed¹ ['ʃed] v shed; shedding vt 1
: derramar (lágrimas, etc.) 2 : mudar
(de piel, etc.), quitarse (ropa) 3 ~
light on : aclarar

shed² n : cobertizo m

she'd ['ʃiːd] (contraction of she had or
she would) → have, would

sheen ['ʃiːn] n : brillo m, lustre m

sheep ['ʃiːp] n, pl sheep : oveja f —
sheepish ['ʃiːpɪʃ] adj : avergonzado

sheer ['ʃɪr] adj 1 THIN : transparente 2
PURE : puro 3 STEEP : escarpado

sheet ['ʃiːt] n 1 : sábana f (de la cama) 2
: hoja f (de papel) 3 : capa f (de hielo,
etc.) 4 PLATE : placa f, lámina f

shelf ['ʃelf] n, pl shelves ['ʃelvz] : estante m

shell ['ʃel] n 1 : concha f 2 : caparazón
m (de un crustáceo, etc.) 3 : cáscara f

(de un huevo, etc.) 4 : armazón mf (de
un edificio, etc.) 5 POD : vaina f 6 MIS-
SILE : proyectil m — ~ vt 1 : pelar
(nueces, etc.) 2 BOMBARD : bombardear

she'll ['ʃiːl, 'ʃɪl] (contraction of she
shall or she will) → shall, will

shellfish ['ʃel,fɪʃ] n : marisco m

shelter ['ʃeltər] n 1 : refugio m 2 take
~ : refugiarse — ~ vt 1 PROTECT
: proteger 2 HARBOR : albergar

shelve ['ʃelv] vt shelved; shelving
DEFER : dar carpetazo a

shepherd ['ʃepərd] n : pastor m — ~ vt
GUIDE : conducir, guiar

sherbet ['ʃɑrbət] n : sorbete m

sheriff ['ʃerɪf] n : sheriff m

sherry ['ʃeri] n, pl -ries : jerez m

she's ['ʃiːz] (contraction of she is or
she has) → be, have

shield ['ʃiːld] n : escudo m — ~ vt
: proteger

shier, shiest → shy

shift ['ʃɪft] vt 1 MOVE : mover 2 SWITCH
: transferir — vi CHANGE : cambiar 2
MOVE : moverse 3 or ~ gears : cambiar de velocidad — ~ n 1 CHANGE
: cambio m 2 : turno m (de trabajo) —
shiftless ['ʃɪftləs] adj : holgazán —
shifty ['ʃɪfti] adj shiftier; -est : sospechoso

shimmer ['ʃɪmər] vi : brillar, relucir

shin ['ʃɪn] n : espinilla f

shine ['ʃaɪn] v shone ['ʃoʊn] or shined;
shining : brillar — vt 1 : alumbrar
(una luz) 2 POLISH : sacar brillo a —
~ n : brillo m

shingle ['ʃɪŋgəl] n : teja f plana y delga-
da (en construcción) — ~ vt -gled;
-gling : techar — shingles ['ʃɪŋgəlz]
npl : herpes m

shiny ['ʃaɪni] adj shinier; -est : brillante

ship ['ʃɪp] n 1 : barco m, buque m 2 →
spaceship — ~ vt shipped; shipping : transportar, enviar (por barco)
— shipbuilding ['ʃɪp,bɪldɪŋ] n : construcción f naval — shipment
['ʃɪpmənt] n : envío m — shipping
['ʃɪpɪŋ] n 1 : transporte m 2 SHIPS : barcos mpl — shipshape ['ʃɪp,ʃeɪp] adj
: ordenado — shipwreck ['ʃɪp,rek] n
: naufragio m — ~ vt be ~ed
: naufragar — shipyard ['ʃɪp,jɑrd] n
: astillero m

shirk ['ʃɑrk] vt : esquivar

shirt ['ʃɑrt] n : camisa f

shiver ['ʃɪvər] vi : temblar (del frío, etc.)
— ~ n : escalofrío m

shoal ['ʃoʊl] n : banco m

shock [ˈʃɑk] *n* **1** IMPACT : choque *m* **2** SURPRISE, UPSET : golpe *m* emocional **3** : shock *m* (en medicina) **4** *or* **electric ~** : descarga *f* (eléctrica) — **~** *vt* : escandalizar — **shock absorber** *n* : amortiguador *m* — **shocking** [ˈʃɑkɪŋ] *adj* : escandaloso

shoddy [ˈʃɑdi] *adj* **shoddier; -est** : de mala calidad

shoe [ˈʃuː] *n* : zapato *m* — **~** *vt* **shod** [ˈʃɑd]; **shoeing** : herrar (un caballo) — **shoelace** [ˈʃuːˌleɪs] *n* : cordón *m* (de zapato) — **shoemaker** [ˈʃuːˌmeɪkər] *n* : zapatero *m*, -ra *f*

shone → **shine**

shook → **shake**

shoot [ˈʃuːt] *v* **shot** [ˈʃɑt]; **shooting** *vt* **1** : disparar **2** : echar (una mirada) **3** PHOTOGRAPH : fotografiar **4** FILM : rodar — *vi* **1** : disparar **2 ~ by** : pasar como una bala — **~** *n* : brote *m*, retoño *m* (de una planta) — **shooting star** *n* : estrella *f* fugaz

shop [ˈʃɑp] *n* **1** : tienda *f* **2** WORKSHOP : taller *m* — **~** *vi* **shopped; shopping 1** : hacer compras **2 go shopping** : ir de compras — **shopkeeper** [ˈʃɑpˌkiːpər] *n* : tendero *m*, -ra *f* — **shoplift** [ˈʃɑpˌlɪft] *vi* : hurtar mercancía (en tiendas) — **shoplifter** [ˈʃɑpˌlɪftər] *n* : ladrón *m*, -drona *f* (que roba en tiendas) — **shopper** [ˈʃɑpər] *n* : comprador *m*, -dora *f*

shore [ˈʃor] *n* : orilla *f*

shorn → **shear**

short [ˈʃort] *adj* **1** : corto **2** : bajo (de estatura) **3** CURT : brusco **4 a ~ time ago** : hace poco **5 be ~ of** : estar corto de — **~** *adv* **1 stop ~** : parar en seco **2 fall ~** : quedarse corto — **shortage** [ˈʃortɪdʒ] *n* : escasez *f*, carencia *f* — **shortcake** [ˈʃortˌkeɪk] *n* : tarta *f* de fruta — **shortcoming** [ˈʃortˌkʌmɪŋ] *n* : defecto *m* — **shortcut** [ˈʃortˌkʌt] *n* : atajo *m* — **shorten** [ˈʃortən] *vt* : acortar — **shorthand** [ˈʃortˌhænd] *n* : taquigrafía *f* — **short-lived** [ˈʃortˈlɪvd, -ˈlaɪvd] *adj* : efímero — **shortly** [ˈʃortli] *adv* : dentro de poco — **shortness** [ˈʃortnəs] *n* **1** : lo corto (de una cosa), baja estatura *f* (de una persona) **2 ~ of breath** : falta *f* de aliento — **shorts** *npl* : shorts *mpl*, pantalones *mpl* cortos — **shortsighted** [ˈʃortˌsaɪtəd] → **nearsighted**

shot [ˈʃɑt] *n* **1** : disparo *m*, tiro *m* **2** : tiro *m* (en deportes) **3** ATTEMPT : intento *m* **4** PHOTOGRAPH : foto *f* **5** INJECTION : inyección *f* **6** : trago *m* (de licor) — **shotgun** [ˈʃɑtˌgʌn] *n* : escopeta *f*

should [ˈʃʊd] *past of* **shall 1** if she **~** call : si llama **2 I ~ have gone** : debería haber ido **3 they ~ arrive soon** : deben llegar pronto **4 what ~ we do?** : ¿qué hacemos?

shoulder [ˈʃoːldər] *n* **1** : hombro *m* **2** : arcén *m* (de una carretera) — **~** *vt* : cargar con (la responsabilidad, etc.) — **shoulder blade** *n* : omóplato *m*

shouldn't [ˈʃʊdənt] *(contraction of should not)* → **should**

shout [ˈʃaʊt] *v* : gritar — **~** *n* : grito *m*

shove [ˈʃʌv] *v* **shoved; shoving** : empujar — **~** *n* : empujón *m*

shovel [ˈʃʌvəl] *n* : pala *f* — **~** *vt* **-veled** *or* **-velled; -veling** *or* **-velling 1** : mover (tierra, etc.) con una pala **2** DIG : cavar (con una pala)

show [ˈʃoː] *v* **showed; shown** [ˈʃoːn] *or* **showed; showing** *vt* **1** : mostrar **2** TEACH : enseñar **3** PROVE : demostrar **4** ESCORT : acompañar **5** : proyectar (una película), dar (un programa de televisión) **6 ~ off** : hacer alarde de — *vi* **1** : notarse, verse **2 ~ off** : lucirse **3 ~ up** ARRIVE : aparecer — **~** *n* **1** : demostración *f* **2** EXHIBITION : exposición *f* **3** : espectáculo *m* (teatral), programa *m* (de televisión, etc.) — **showdown** [ˈʃoːˌdaʊn] *n* : confrontación *f*

shower [ˈʃaʊər] *n* **1** : ducha *f* **2** : chaparrón *m* (en meteorología) **3** PARTY : fiesta *f* — **~** *vt* **1** SPRAY : regar **2 ~ s.o. with** : colmar a algn de — *vi* **1** : ducharse **2** RAIN : llover

showy [ˈʃoːi] *adj* **showier; -est** : llamativo, ostentoso

shrank → **shrink**

shrapnel [ˈʃræpnəl] *ns & pl* : metralla *f*

shred [ˈʃred] *n* **1** : tira *f* (de tela, etc.) **2** IOTA : pizca *f* — **~** *vt* **shredded; shredding 1** : hacer tiras **2** GRATE : rallar

shrewd [ˈʃruːd] *adj* : astuto

shriek [ˈʃriːk] *vi* : chillar — **~** *n* : chillido *m*, alarido *m*

shrill [ˈʃrɪl] *adj* : agudo, estridente

shrimp [ˈʃrɪmp] *n* : camarón *m*

shrine [ˈʃraɪn] *n* **1** TOMB : sepulcro *m* **2** SANCTUARY : santuario *m*

shrink [ˈʃrɪŋk] *v* **shrank** [ˈʃræŋk]; **shrunk** [ˈʃrʌŋk] *or* **shrunken** [ˈʃrʌŋkən]; **shrinking** *vt* : encoger — *vi* **1** : encogerse (dícese de ropa), reducirse (dícese de números, etc.) **2 ~ back** : retroceder

shrivel [ˈʃrɪvəl] *vi* **-veled** *or* **-velled; -veling** *or* **-velling** *or* **~ up** : arrugarse, marchitarse

shroud ['ʃraʊd] *n* **1** : sudario *m*, mortaja *f* **2** VEIL : velo *m* — ~ *vt* : envolver
shrub ['ʃrʌb] *n* : arbusto *m*, mata *f*
shrug ['ʃrʌg] *vi* **shrugged; shrugging** : encogerse de hombros
shrunk → **shrink**
shudder ['ʃʌdər] *vi* : estremecerse — ~ *n* : estremecimiento *m*
shuffle ['ʃʌfəl] *v* **-fled; -fling** *vt* : barajar (naipes), revolver (papeles, etc.) — *vi* : caminar arrastrando los pies
shun ['ʃʌn] *vi* **shunned; shunning** : evitar, esquivar
shut ['ʃʌt] *v* **shut; shutting** *vt* **1** CLOSE : cerrar **2** ~ **off** → **turn off 3** ~ **up** CONFINE : encerrar — *vi* **1** *or* ~ **down** : cerrarse **2** ~ **up!** : ¡cállate! — **shutter** ['ʃʌtər] *n* **1** *or* **window** ~ : contraventana *f* **2** : obturador *m* (de una cámara)
shuttle ['ʃʌtəl] *n* **1** : lanzadera *f* (para tejer) **2** *or* ~ **bus** : autobús *m* (de corto recorrido) **3** → **space shuttle** — ~ *v* **-tled; -tling** *vt* : transportar — *vi* : ir y venir
shy ['ʃaɪ] *adj* **shier** *or* **shyer** ['ʃaɪər]; **shiest** *or* **shyest** ['ʃaɪəst] : tímido — ~ *vi* **shied; shying** *or* ~ **away** : retroceder — **shyness** ['ʃaɪnəs] *n* : timidez *f*
sibling ['sɪblɪŋ] *n* : hermano *m*, hermana *f*
sick ['sɪk] *adj* **1** : enfermo **2 be** ~ VOMIT : vomitar **3 be** ~ **of** : estar harto de **4 feel** ~ : tener náuseas — **sicken** ['sɪkən] *vt* DISGUST : dar asco a — **sickening** ['sɪkənɪŋ] *adj* : nauseabundo
sickle ['sɪkəl] *n* : hoz *f*
sickly ['sɪkli] *adj* **sicklier; -est 1** UNHEALTHY : enfermizo **2** → **sickening** — **sickness** ['sɪknəs] *n* : enfermedad *f*
side ['saɪd] *n* **1** : lado *m* **2** : costado *m* (de una persona), ijada *f* (de un animal) **3** : parte *f* (en una disputa, etc.) **4** ~ **by** ~ : uno al lado de otro **5 take** ~**s** : tomar partido — ~ *vi* ~ **with** : ponerse de parte de — **sideboard** ['saɪdbord] *n* : aparador *m* — **sideburns** ['saɪdbərnz] *npl* : patillas *fpl* — **side effect** *n* : efecto *m* secundario — **sideline** ['saɪdlaɪn] *n* : línea *f* de banda (en deportes) — **sidestep** ['saɪdstɛp] *vt* **-stepped; -stepping** : eludir, esquivar — **sidetrack** ['saɪdtræk] *vt* **get** ~**ed** : distraerse — **sidewalk** ['saɪdwɔk] *n* : acera *f* — **sideways** ['saɪdweɪz] *adj & adv* : de lado — **siding** ['saɪdɪŋ] *n* : revestimiento *m* exterior
siege ['siːdʒ, 'siːʒ] *n* : sitio *m*

sieve ['sɪv] *n* : tamiz *m*, cedazo *m*
sift ['sɪft] *vt* **1** : cerner, tamizar **2** *or* ~ **through** : pasar por el tamiz
sigh ['saɪ] *vi* : suspirar — ~ *n* : suspiro *m*
sight ['saɪt] *n* **1** : vista *f* **2** SPECTACLE : espectáculo *m* **3** : lugar *m* de interés (turístico) **4 catch** ~ **of** : avistar — ~ *vt* : avistar — **sightseer** ['saɪtsiːər] *n* : turista *mf*
sign ['saɪn] *n* **1** : signo *m* **2** NOTICE : letrero *m* **3** GESTURE : seña *f*, señal *f* — ~ *vt* : firmar (un cheque, etc.) — *vi* **1** : firmar **2** ~ **up** ENROLL : inscribirse
signal ['sɪgnəl] *n* : señal *f* — ~ *v* **-naled** *or* **-nalled; -naling** *or* **-nalling** *vt* **1** : hacer señas a **2** INDICATE : señalar — *vi* **1** : hacer señas **2** : señalizar (en un vehículo)
signature ['sɪgnətʃʊr] *n* : firma *f*
significance [sɪg'nɪfɪkənts] *n* **1** : significado *m* **2** IMPORTANCE : importancia *f* — **significant** [sɪg'nɪfɪkənt] *adj* : importante — **signify** ['sɪgnəfaɪ] *vt* **-fied; -fying** : significar
sign language *n* : lenguaje *m* gestual — **signpost** ['saɪnpoːst] *n* : poste *m* indicador
silence ['saɪlənts] *n* : silencio *m* — ~ *vt* **-lenced; -lencing** : silenciar — **silent** ['saɪlənt] *adj* **1** : silencioso **2** MUM : callado **3** : mudo (dícese de películas y letras)
silhouette [ˌsɪlə'wɛt] *n* : silueta *f* — ~ *vt* **-etted; -etting be** ~**d against** : perfilarse contra
silicon ['sɪlɪkən, -ˌkɑn] *n* : silicio *m*
silk ['sɪlk] *n* : seda *f* — **silky** ['sɪlki] *adj* **silkier; -est** : sedoso
sill ['sɪl] *n* : alféizar *m* (de una ventana), umbral *m* (de una puerta)
silly ['sɪli] *adj* **sillier; -est** : tonto, estúpido
silt ['sɪlt] *n* : cieno *m*
silver ['sɪlvər] *n* **1** : plata *f* **2** → **silverware** — ~ *adj* : de plata — **silverware** ['sɪlvərˌwær] *n* : plata *f* — **silvery** ['sɪlvəri] *adj* : plateado
similar ['sɪmələr] *adj* : similar, parecido — **similarity** [ˌsɪmə'lærəti] *n, pl* **-ties** : semejanza *f*, parecido *m*
simmer ['sɪmər] *v* : hervir a fuego lento
simple ['sɪmpəl] *adj* **simpler; -plest 1** : simple **2** EASY : sencillo — **simplicity** [sɪm'plɪsəti] *n* : simplicidad *f*, sencillez *f* — **simplify** ['sɪmpləˌfaɪ] *vt* **-fied; -fying** : simplificar — **simply** ['sɪmpli] *adv* **1** : sencillamente **2** ABSOLUTELY : realmente

simulate ['sɪmjəˌleɪt] *vt* **-lated; -lating** : simular

simultaneous [ˌsaɪməl'teɪnɪəs] *adj* : simultáneo

sin ['sɪn] *n* : pecado *m* — ~ *vi* **sinned; sinning** : pecar

since ['sɪns] *adv* **1** *or* ~ **then** : desde entonces **2 long** ~ : hace mucho — ~ *conj* **1** : desde que **2** BECAUSE : ya que, como **3 it's been years** ~... : hace años que... — ~ *prep* : desde

sincere [sɪn'sɪr] *adj* **-cerer; -est** : sincero — **sincerely** *adv* : sinceramente — **sincerity** [sɪn'serəṭi] *n* : sinceridad *f*

sinful ['sɪnfəl] *adj* : pecador (dícese de las personas), pecaminoso (dícese de las acciones)

sing ['sɪŋ] *v* **sang** ['sæŋ] *or* **sung** ['sʌŋ]; **sung; singing** : cantar

singe ['sɪndʒ] *vt* **singed; singeing** : chamuscar

singer ['sɪŋər] *n* : cantante *mf*

single ['sɪŋgəl] *adj* **1** : solo, único **2** UN-MARRIED : soltero **3 every** ~ **day** : cada día, todos los días — ~ *n* **1** : soltero *m*, -ra *f* **2** *or* ~ **room** : habitación *f* individual — ~ *vt* **-gled; -gling** ~ **out 1** SELECT : escoger **2** DISTINGUISH : señalar — **single-handed** ['sɪŋgəl'hændəd] *adj* : sin ayuda, solo

singular ['sɪŋgjələr] *adj* : singular — ~ *n* : singular *m*

sinister ['sɪnəstər] *adj* : siniestro

sink ['sɪŋk] *v* **sank** ['sæŋk] *or* **sunk** ['sʌŋk]; **sunk; sinking** *vi* **1** : hundirse (en un líquido) **2** DROP : bajar, caer — *vt* **1** : hundir **2** ~ **sth into** : clavar algo en — ~ *n* **1** *or* **kitchen** ~ : fregadero *m* **2** *or* **bathroom** ~ : lavabo *m*, lavamanos *m*

sinner ['sɪnər] *n* : pecador *m*, -dora *f*

sip ['sɪp] *v* **sipped; sipping** *vt* : sorber — *vi* : beber a sorbos — ~ *n* : sorbo *m*

siphon ['saɪfən] *n* : sifón *m* — ~ *vt* : sacar con sifón

sir ['sər] *n* **1** (*in titles*) : sir *m* **2** (*as a form of address*) : señor *m* **3 Dear Sir** : Estimado señor

siren ['saɪrən] *n* : sirena *f*

sirloin ['sərˌlɔɪn] *n* : solomillo *m*

sissy ['sɪsi] *n*, *pl* **-sies** : mariquita *f fam*

sister ['sɪstər] *n* : hermana *f* — **sister-in-law** ['sɪstərˌɪnˌlɔ] *n*, *pl* **sisters-in-law** : cuñada *f*

sit ['sɪt] *v* **sat** ['sæt]; **sitting** *vi* **1** *or* ~ **down** : sentarse **2** LIE : estar (ubicado) **3** MEET : estar en sesión **4** *or* ~ **up** : incorporarse — *vt* : sentar

site ['saɪt] *n* **1** : sitio *m*, lugar *m* **2** LOT : solar *m*

sitting room → **living room**

sitter ['sɪtər] → **baby-sitter**

situated ['sɪtʃuˌeɪṭəd] *adj* : ubicado, situado — **situation** [ˌsɪtʃu'eɪʃən] *n* : situación *f*

six ['sɪks] *adj* : seis — ~ *n* : seis *m* — **six hundred** *adj* : seiscientos — ~ *n* : seiscientos *m* — **sixteen** [sɪks'tiːn] *adj* : dieciséis — ~ *n* : dieciséis *m* — **sixteenth** [sɪks'tiːnθ] *adj* : decimosexto — ~ *n* **1** : decimosexto *m*, -ta *f* (en una serie) **2** : dieciseisavo *m*, dieciseisava parte *f* — **sixth** ['sɪksθ, 'sɪkst] *adj* : sexto — ~ *n* **1** : sexto *m*, -ta *f* (en una serie) **2** : sexto *m* (en matemáticas) — **sixtieth** ['sɪkstiˌɪθ] *adj* : sexagésimo — ~ *n* **1** : sexagésimo *m*, -ma *f* (en una serie) **2** : sesentavo *m* (en matemáticas) — **sixty** ['sɪksti] *adj* : sesenta — ~ *n*, *pl* **-ties** : sesenta *m*

size ['saɪz] *n* **1** : tamaño *m*, talla *f* (de ropa), número *m* (de zapatos) **2** EX-TENT : magnitud *f* — ~ *vt* **sized; sizing** ~ **up** : evaluar — **sizable** *or* **sizeable** ['saɪzəbəl] *adj* : considerable

sizzle ['sɪzəl] *vi* **-zled; -zling** : chisporrotear

skate¹ ['skeɪt] *n* : raya *f* (pez)

skate² *n* : patín *m* — ~ *vi* **skated; skating** : patinar — **skateboard** ['skeɪtˌbord] *n* : monopatín *m* — **skater** ['skeɪtər] *n* : patinador *m*, -dora *f*

skeleton ['skelətən] *n* : esqueleto *m*

skeptic ['skeptɪk] *n* : escéptico *m*, -ca *f* — **skeptical** ['skeptɪkəl] *adj* : escéptico — **skepticism** ['skeptəˌsɪzəm] *n* : escepticismo *m*

sketch ['sketʃ] *n* **1** : esbozo *m*, bosquejo *m* **2** SKIT : sketch *m* — ~ *vt* : bosquejar — *vi* : hacer bosquejos — **sketchy** ['sketʃi] *adj* **sketchier; -est** : incompleto

skewer ['skjuːər] *n* : brocheta *f*, broqueta *f*

ski ['skiː] *n*, *pl* **skis** : esquí *m* — ~ *vi* **skied; skiing** : esquiar

skid ['skɪd] *n* : derrape *m*, patinazo *m* — ~ *vi* **skidded; skidding** : derrapar, patinar

skier ['skiːər] *n* : esquiador *m*, -dora *f*

skill ['skɪl] *n* **1** : habilidad *f*, destreza *f* **2** TECHNIQUE : técnica *f* — **skilled** ['skɪld] *adj* : hábil

skillet ['skɪlət] *n* : sartén *mf*

skillful ['skɪlfəl] *adj* : hábil, diestro

skim ['skɪm] *vt* **skimmed; skimming 1** : espumar (sopa, etc.), descremar (leche) **2** : pasar rozando (una superficie) **3** *or* **~ through** : echar un vistazo a — **~** *adj* : descremado

skimp ['skɪmp] *vi* **~ on** : escatimar — **skimpy** ['skɪmpi] *adj* **skimpier; -est 1** : exiguo, escaso **2** : brevísimo (dícese de ropa)

skin ['skɪn] *n* : piel *f* — **~** *vt* **skinned; skinning** : despellejar — **skin diving** *n* : buceo *m*, submarinismo *m* — **skinny** ['skɪni] *adj* **skinnier; -est** : flaco

skip ['skɪp] *v* **skipped; skipping** *vi* : ir brincando — *vt* OMIT : saltarse — **~** *n* : brinco *m*, salto *m*

skipper ['skɪpər] *n* : capitán *m*, -tana *f*

skirmish ['skərmɪʃ] *n* : escaramuza *f*

skirt ['skərt] *n* : falda *f* — **~** *vt* **1** BORDER : bordear **2** EVADE : eludir

skull ['skʌl] *n* : cráneo *m* (de una persona viva), calavera *f* (de un esqueleto)

skunk ['skʌŋk] *n* : mofeta *f*, zorrillo *m* *Lat*

sky ['skaɪ] *n*, *pl* **skies** : cielo *m* — **skylight** ['skaɪˌlaɪt] *n* : claraboya *f*, tragaluz *m* — **skyline** ['skaɪˌlaɪn] *n* : horizonte *m* — **skyscraper** ['skaɪˌskreɪpər] *n* : rascacielos *m*

slab ['slæb] *n* : bloque *m* (de piedra, etc.)

slack ['slæk] *adj* **1** LOOSE : flojo **2** CARELESS : descuidado — **~** *n* **1 take up the ~** : tensar (una cuerda, etc.) **2 ~s** *npl* : pantalones *mpl* — **slacken** ['slækən] *vt* : aflojar — *vi* : aflojarse

slain → slay

slam ['slæm] *n* : golpe *m*, portazo *m* (de una puerta) — **~** *v* **slammed; slamming** *vt* **1** *or* **~ down** : tirar, plantar **2** *or* **~ shut** : cerrar de golpe **3 ~ the door** : dar un portazo — *vi* **1** : cerrarse de golpe **2 ~ into** : chocar contra

slander ['slændər] *vt* : calumniar, difamar — **~** *n* : calumnia *f*, difamación *f*

slang ['slæŋ] *n* : argot *m*

slant ['slænt] *n* : inclinación *f* — **~** *vi* : inclinarse

slap ['slæp] *vt* **slapped; slapping 1** : dar una bofetada a **2 ~ s.o. on the back** : dar una palmada en la espalda a algn — **~** *n* : bofetada *f*, cachetada *f* *Lat*

slash ['slæʃ] *vt* **1** : hacer un tajo en **2** : rebajar (precios) drásticamente — **~** *n* : tajo *m*

slat ['slæt] *n* : tablilla *f*

slate ['sleɪt] *n* : pizarra *f*

slaughter ['slɔtər] *n* : matanza *f* — **~** *vt* **1** : matar (animales) **2** MASSACRE : masacrar — **slaughterhouse** ['slɔtərˌhaus] *n* : matadero *m*

slave ['sleɪv] *n* : esclavo *m*, -va *f* — **~** *vi*

slaved; slaving : trabajar como un burro — **slavery** ['sleɪvəri] *n* : esclavitud *f*

Slavic ['slɑvɪk, 'slæ-] *adj* : eslavo

slay ['sleɪ] *vt* **slew** ['slu:]; **slain** ['sleɪn]; **slaying** : asesinar

sleazy ['sli:zi] *adj* **sleazier; -est** : sórdido

sled ['slɛd] *n* : trineo *m*

sledgehammer ['slɛdʒˌhæmər] *n* : almádena *f*

sleek ['sli:k] *adj* : liso y brillante

sleep ['sli:p] *n* **1** : sueño *m* **2 go to ~** : dormirse — **~** *vi* **slept** ['slɛpt]; **sleeping** : dormir — **sleeper** ['sli:pər] *n* **be a light ~** : tener el sueño ligero — **sleepless** ['sli:pləs] *adj* **have a ~ night** : pasar la noche en blanco — **sleepwalker** ['sli:pˌwɔkər] *n* : sonámbulo *m*, -la *f* — **sleepy** ['sli:pi] *adj* **sleepier; -est 1** : somnoliento, soñoliento **2 be ~** : tener sueño

sleet ['sli:t] *n* : aguanieve *f* — **~** *vi* : caer aguanieve

sleeve ['sli:v] *n* : manga *f* — **sleeveless** ['sli:vləs] *adj* : sin mangas

sleigh ['sleɪ] *n* : trineo *m*

slender ['slɛndər] *adj* : delgado

slew ['slu:] → **slay**

slice ['slaɪs] *vt* **sliced; slicing** : cortar — **~** *n* : trozo *m*, rebanada *f* (de pan, etc.), tajada *f* (de carne)

slick ['slɪk] *adj* SLIPPERY : resbaladizo, resbaloso *Lat*

slide ['slaɪd] *v* **slid** ['slɪd]; **sliding** ['slaɪdɪŋ] *vi* : deslizarse — *vt* : deslizar — **~** *n* **1** : deslizamiento *m* **2** : tobogán *m* (para niños) **3** : diapositiva *f* (fotográfica) **4** DECLINE : descenso *m*

slier, sliest → sly

slight ['slaɪt] *adj* **1** : ligero, leve **2** SLENDER : delgado — **~** *vt* : desairar — **slightly** ['slaɪtli] *adv* : ligeramente, un poco

slim ['slɪm] *adj* **slimmer; slimmest 1** : delgado **2 a ~ chance** : escasas posibilidades *fpl* — **~** *v* **slimmed; slimming** : adelgazar

slime ['slaɪm] *n* **1** : baba *f* (de un caracol, etc.) **2** MUD : limo *m* — **slimy** ['slaɪmi] *adj* **slimier; -est** : viscoso

sling ['slɪŋ] *vt* **slung** ['slʌŋ]; **slinging 1** THROW : lanzar **2** HANG : colgar — **~** *n* **1** : honda *f* **2** : cabestrillo *m* (en medicina) — **slingshot** ['slɪŋˌʃɑt] *n* : tirachinas *m*

slink ['slɪŋk] *vi* **slunk** ['slʌŋk]; **slinking** : andar furtivamente

slip¹ ['slɪp] *v* **slipped; slipping** *vi* **1** SLIDE : resbalarse **2 let sth ~** : dejar

escapar algo **3 ~ away** : escabullirse
4 ~ up : equivocarse — *vt* **1** : deslizar
2 ~ into : ponerse (una prenda) **3 it**
slipped my mind : se me olvidó —
n **1** MISTAKE : error *m*, desliz *m* **2 ~ of**
the tongue : lapsus *m* **3** PETTICOAT
: enagua *f*

slip² *n* **~ of paper** : papelito *m*

slipper ['slɪpər] *n* : zapatilla *f*, pantufla *f*

slippery ['slɪpəri] *adj* **slipperier; -est**
: resbaladizo, resbaloso *Lat*

slit ['slɪt] *n* **1** OPENING : rendija *f* **2** CUT
: corte *m*, raja *f* — *vt* **slit; slitting**
: cortar

slither ['slɪðər] *vi* : deslizarse

sliver ['slɪvər] *n* : astilla *f*

slogan ['sloːgən] *n* : eslogan *m*

slop ['slɑp] *v* **slopped; slopping** *vt*
: derramar — *vi* : derramarse

slope ['sloːp] *vi* **sloped; sloping** : inclinarse — *n* : pendiente *f*, declive *m*

sloppy ['slɑpi] *adj* **sloppier; -est 1**
CARELESS : descuidado **2** UNKEMPT
: desaliñado

slot ['slɑt] *n* : ranura *f*

sloth ['slɔθ, 'sloːθ] *n* : pereza *f*

slouch ['slaʊtʃ] *vi* : andar con los hombros caídos (en una silla)

slovenly ['slʌvənli, 'slʌv-] *adj* : desaliñado

slow ['sloː] *adj* **1** : lento **2 be ~** : estar
atrasado (dícese de un reloj) — *adv*
→ **slowly** — **~** : retrasar, retardar
— *vi* *or* **~ down** : ir más despacio —
slowly ['sloːli] *adv* : lentamente, despacio — **slowness** ['sloːnəs] *n* : lentitud *f*

sludge ['slʌdʒ] *n* SEWAGE : aguas *fpl* negras

slug¹ ['slʌg] *n* **1** : babosa *f* (molusco) **2**
BULLET : bala *f* **3** TOKEN : ficha *f*

slug² *vt* **slugged; slugging** : pegar un
porrazo a

sluggish ['slʌgɪʃ] *adj* : lento

slum ['slʌm] *n* : barrio *m* bajo

slumber ['slʌmbər] *vi* : dormir — *n*
: sueño *m*

slump ['slʌmp] *vi* **1** DROP : bajar **2** COL-
LAPSE : dejarse caer **3 → slouch** — *n* : bajón *m*

slung → sling

slunk → slink

slur¹ ['slər] *n* ASPERSION : calumnia *f*,
difamación *f*

slur² *vt* **slurred; slurring** : arrastrar (las
palabras)

slurp ['slərp] *v* : beber haciendo ruido —
~ *n* : sorbo *m* (ruidoso)

slush ['slʌʃ] *n* : nieve *f* medio derretida

sly ['slaɪ] *adj* **slier** ['slaɪər]; **sliest**

['slaɪəst] **1** : astuto, taimado **2 on the**
~ : a escondidas

smack¹ ['smæk] *vi* **~ of** : oler a

smack² *vt* **1** : pegar una bofetada a **2**
KISS : besar **3 ~ one's lips** : relamerse — *n* : **1** SLAP : bofetada *f* **2**
KISS : beso *m* — **~** *adv* : justo, exactamente

small ['smɔl] *adj* : pequeño, chico —
smallpox ['smɔl,pɑks] *n* : viruela *f*

smart ['smɑrt] *adj* **1** : listo, inteligente **2**
STYLISH : elegante — **~** *vi* STING : escocer — **smartly** ['smɑrtli] *adv* : ele-
gantemente

smash ['smæʃ] *n* **1** BLOW : golpe *m* **2**
COLLISION : choque *m* **3** BANG, CRASH
: estrépito *m* — **~** *vt* **1** BREAK
: romper **2** DESTROY : aplastar — *vi* **1**
SHATTER : hacerse pedazos **2 ~ into**
: estrellarse contra

smattering ['smætərɪŋ] *n* : nociones *fpl*

smear ['smɪr] *n* : mancha *f* — **~** *vt* **1**
: embadurnar (de pinta, etc.), untar (de
aceite, etc.) **2** SMUDGE : manchar

smell ['smɛl] *v* **smelled** *or* **smelt**
['smɛlt]; **smelling** : oler — **~** *n* **1**
: (sentido *m* del) olfato *m* **2** ODOR
: olor *m* — **smelly** ['smɛli] *adj* **smelli-**
er; -est : maloliente

smelt ['smɛlt] *vt* : fundir

smile ['smaɪl] *vi* **smiled; smiling** : sonreír — **~** *n* : sonrisa *f*

smirk ['smərk] *vi* : sonreír con suficiencia — **~** *n* : sonrisa *f* satisfecha

smitten ['smɪtən] *adj* **be ~ with** : estar
enamorado de

smith ['smɪθ] → **blacksmith**

smock ['smɑk] *n* : blusón *m*, bata *f*

smog ['smɑg, 'smɔg] *n* : smog *m*

smoke ['smoːk] *n* : humo *m* — **~** *v*
smoked; smoking *vi* **1** : humear
(dícese de fuegos, etc.) **2** : fumar
(dícese de personas) — *vt* **1** : ahumar
(carne, etc.) **2** : fumar (cigarrillos) —
smoker ['smoːkər] *n* : fumador *m*,
-dora *f* — **smokestack** ['smoːk,stæk] *n*
: chimenea *f* — **smoky** ['smoːki] *adj*
smokier; -est 1 : lleno de humo **2 : a**
humo (dícese de sabores, etc.)

smolder ['smoːldər] *vi* : arder (sin llama)

smooth ['smuːð] *adj* **1** : liso (dícese de
superficies), suave (dícese de
movimientos), tranquilo (dícese del
mar) **2** : sin grumos (dícese de salsas,
etc.) — **~** *vt* : alisar — **smoothly**
['smuːðli] *adv* : suavemente —
smoothness ['smuːðnəs] *n* : suavidad *f*

smother ['smʌðər] *vt* : asfixiar (a algn),
sofocar (llamas, etc.)

smudge ['smʌdʒ] *v* **smudged; smudg-**

ing *vt* : emborronar — *vi* : correrse —
〜 *n* : mancha *f*, borrón *m*

smug ['smʌg] *adj* **smugger; smuggest**
: suficiente

smuggle ['smʌgəl] *vt* **-gled; -gling**
: pasar de contrabando — **smuggler**
['smʌgələr] *n* : contrabandista *mf*

snack ['snæk] *n* : refrigerio *m*, tentempié *m fam*

snag ['snæg] *n* : problema *m* — *v*
snagged; snagging *vt* : enganchar —
vi : engancharse

snail ['sneɪl] *n* : caracol *m*

snake ['sneɪk] *n* : culebra *f*, serpiente *f*

snap ['snæp] *v* **snapped; snapping** *vi* 1
BREAK : romperse 2 : intentar morder
(dícese de un perro, etc.) 3 〜 **at** : contestar bruscamente a — *vt* 1 BREAK
: romper 2 〜 **one's fingers**
: chasquear los dedos 3 〜 **open/shut**
: abrir/cerrar de golpe — 〜 *n* 1
: chasquido *m* 2 FASTENER : broche *m*
(de presión) 3 **be a** 〜 : ser facilísimo
— **snappy** ['snæpi] *adj* **snappier; -est**
1 FAST : rápido 2 STYLISH : elegante —
snapshot ['snæpˌʃɑt] *n* : instantánea *f*

snare ['snær] *n* : trampa *f* — 〜 *vt*
snared; snaring : atrapar

snarl¹ ['snɑrl] *vi* TANGLE : enmarañar,
enredar — 〜 *n* : enredo *m*, maraña *f*

snarl² *vi* GROWL : gruñir — 〜 *n* : gruñido *m*

snatch ['snætʃ] *vt* : arrebatar

sneak ['sni:k] *vi* : ir a hurtadillas — *vt*
: hacer furtivamente — 〜 *n* : soplón
m, -plona *f fam* — **sneakers** ['sni:kərz]
npl : tenis *mpl*, zapatillas *fpl* —
sneaky ['sni:ki] *adj* **sneakier; -est**
: solapada

sneer ['snɪr] *vi* : sonreír con desprecio
— 〜 *n* : sonrisa *f* de desprecio

sneeze ['sni:z] *vi* **sneezed; sneezing**
: estornudar — 〜 *n* : estornudo *m*

snide ['snaɪd] *adj* : sarcástico

sniff ['snɪf] *vi* : oler — *vt* 1 : oler 2
→ **sniffle** — 〜 *n* : aspiración *f* por la
nariz — **sniffle** ['snɪfəl] *vi* **-fled; -fling**
: sorberse la nariz — **sniffles** ['snɪfəlz]
npl **have the** 〜 : estar resfriado

snip ['snɪp] *n* : tijeretada *f* — 〜 *vt*
snipped; snipping : cortar (con tijeras)

snivel ['snɪvəl] *vi* **-veled** *or* **-velled;
-veling** *or* **-velling** : lloriquear

snob ['snɑb] *n* : esnob *mf* — **snobbish**
['snɑbɪʃ] *adj* : esnob

snoop ['snu:p] *vi* : husmear — 〜 *n* : fisgón *m*, -gona *f*

snooze ['snu:z] *vi* **snoozed; snoozing**
: dormitar — 〜 *n* : siestecita *f*, siesti-
ta *f*

snore ['snor] *vi* **snored; snoring** : roncar — 〜 *n* : ronquido *m*

snort ['snɔrt] *vi* : bufar — 〜 *n* : bufido
m

snout ['snaʊt] *n* : hocico *m*, morro *m*

snow ['sno:] *n* : nieve *f* — *vi* : nevar
— **snowfall** ['sno:ˌfɔl] *n* : nevada *f* —
snowflake ['sno:ˌfleɪk] *n* : copo *m* de
nieve — **snowman** ['sno:ˌmæn] *n*
: muñeco *m* de nieve — **snowplow**
['sno:ˌplaʊ] *n* : quitanieves *m* — **snow-
shoe** ['sno:ˌʃu:] *n* : raqueta *f* (para
nieve) — **snowstorm** ['sno:ˌstɔrm] *n*
: tormenta *f* de nieve — **snowy** ['sno:i]
adj **snowier; -est** 1 a 〜 **day** : un día
nevoso 2 〜 **mountains** : montañas
fpl nevadas

snub ['snʌb] *vt* **snubbed; snubbing**
: desairar — 〜 *n* : desaire *m*

snuff ['snʌf] *vt or* 〜 **out** : apagar

snug ['snʌg] *adj* **snugger; snuggest**
1 COMFY : cómodo 2 TIGHT : ajustado — **snug-
gle** ['snʌgəl] *vi* **-gled; -gling** : acurrucarse

so ['so:] *adv* 1 LIKEWISE : también 2
THUS : así 3 THEREFORE : por lo tanto 4
or 〜 **much** : tanto 5 *or* 〜 **very** : tan
6 **and** 〜 **on** : etcétera 7 **I think** 〜
: creo que sí 8 **I told you** 〜 : te lo dije
— *conj* 1 THEREFORE : así que 2 *or*
〜 **that** : para que 3 〜 **what?** : ¿y
qué? — *adj* TRUE : cierto — 〜
pron or 〜 : más o menos

soak ['so:k] *vi* : estar en remojo — *vt* 1
: poner en remojo 2 〜 **up** : absorber
— 〜 *n* : remojo *m*

soap ['so:p] *n* : jabón *m* — *vt or* 〜
up : enjabonar — **soapy** ['so:pi]
soapier; -est *adj* : jabonoso

soar ['sor] *vi* 1 : planear 2 SKYROCKET
: dispararse

sob ['sɑb] *vi* **sobbed; sobbing** : sollozar — 〜 *n* : sollozo *m*

sober ['so:bər] *adj* 1 : sobrio 2 SERIOUS
: serio — **sobriety** [sə'braɪəṭi, so-] *n* 1
: sobriedad *f* 2 SERIOUSNESS : seriedad
f

so-called ['so:'kɔld] *adj* : supuesto, presunto

soccer ['sɑkər] *n* : futbol *m*, fútbol *m*

social ['so:ʃəl] *adj* : social — *n* 1 : reunión *f* social — **sociable** ['so:ʃəbəl]
adj : sociable — **socialism** ['so:ʃə-
ˌlɪzəm] *n* : socialismo *m* — **socialist**
['so:ʃəlɪst] *n* : socialista *mf* — *adj*
: socialista — **socialize** ['so:ʃəˌlaɪz] *v*
-ized; -izing *vt* : socializar — *vi* 〜
with : alternar con — **society** [sə-
'saɪəṭi] *n, pl* **-eties** : sociedad *f* — **sociology** [ˌso:si'ɑlədʒi] *n* : sociología *f*

sock[1] ['sɑk] n, pl **socks** or **sox** ['sɑks] : calcetín m

sock[2] vt : pegar, golpear — **~** n PUNCH : puñetazo m

socket ['sɑkət] n 1 or **electric ~** : enchufe m, toma f de corriente 2 or **eye ~** : órbita f, cuenca f 3 : glena f (de una articulación)

soda ['so:də] n 1 or **~ pop** : refresco m, gaseosa f 2 or **~ water** : soda f

sodium ['so:diəm] n : sodio m

sofa ['so:fə] n : sofá m

soft ['sɔft] adj 1 : blando 2 SMOOTH : suave — **softball** ['sɔft,bɔl] n : softbol m — **soft drink** n : refresco m — **soften** ['sɔfən] vt 1 : ablandar 2 EASE, SMOOTH : suavizar — vi 1 : ablandarse 2 EASE : suavizarse — **softly** ['sɔftli] adv : suavemente — **software** ['sɔft,wær] n : software m

soggy ['sɑgi] adj **soggier; -est** : empapado

soil ['sɔɪl] vt : ensuciar — **~** n DIRT : tierra f

solace ['sɑləs] n : consuelo m

solar ['so:lər] adj : solar

sold → **sell**

solder ['sɑdər, 'sɔ-] n : soldadura f — **~** vt : soldar

soldier ['so:ldʒər] n : soldado mf

sole[1] ['so:l] n : lenguado m (pez)

sole[2] n : planta f (del pie), suela f (de un zapato)

sole[3] adj : único — **solely** ['so:li] adv : únicamente, sólo

solemn ['sɑləm] adj : solemne — **solemnity** [sə'lɛmnəţi] n, pl **-ties** : solemnidad f

solicit [sə'lɪsət] vt : solicitar

solid ['sɑləd] adj 1 : sólido 2 UNBROKEN : continuo 3 **~ gold** : oro m macizo 4 **two ~ hours** : dos horas seguidas — **~** n : sólido m — **solidarity** [,sɑlə'dærəţi] n : solidaridad f — **solidify** [sə'lɪdə,faɪ] v **-fied; -fying** vt : solidificar — vi : solidificarse — **solidity** [sə'lɪdəţi] n, pl **-ties** : solidez f

solitary ['sɑlə,tɛri] adj : solitario — **solitude** ['sɑlə,tu:d, -,tju:d] n : soledad f

solo ['so:lo:] n, pl **solos** : solo m — **soloist** ['so:loɪst] n : solista mf

solution [sə'lu:ʃən] n : solución f — **soluble** ['sɑljəbəl] adj : soluble — **solve** ['sɑlv] vt **solved; solving** : resolver — **solvent** ['sɑlvənt] n : solvente m

somber ['sɑmbər] adj : sombrío

some ['sʌm] adj 1 (of unspecified identity) : un 2 (of an unspecified amount) : algo de, un poco de 3 (of an unspecified number) : unos 4 CERTAIN : algunos 5 **that was ~ game!** : ¡fue un partidazo! — **~** pron 1 SEVERAL : algunos, unos 2 PART : un poco, algo — **~** adv — **twenty people** : unas veinte personas — **somebody** ['sʌmbədi, -,bɑdi] pron : alguien — **someday** ['sʌm,deɪ] adv : algún día — **somehow** ['sʌm,haʊ] adv 1 : de algún modo 2 **~ or other** : de alguna manera u otra — **someone** ['sʌm,wʌn] pron : alguien

somersault ['sʌmər,sɔlt] n : voltereta f, salto m mortal

something ['sʌmθɪŋ] pron 1 : algo 2 **~ else** : otra cosa — **sometime** ['sʌm,taɪm] adv 1 : algún día, en algún momento 2 **~ next month** : (durante) el mes que viene — **sometimes** ['sʌm,taɪmz] adv : a veces — **somewhat** ['sʌm,hwʌt, -,hwɑt] adv : algo — **somewhere** ['sʌm,hwɛr] adv 1 : en alguna parte, en algún lado 2 **~ around** : alrededor de 3 **~ else → elsewhere**

son ['sʌn] n : hijo m

song ['sɔŋ] n : canción f

son–in–law ['sʌnɪn,lɔ] n, pl **sons–in–law** : yerno m

sonnet ['sɑnət] n : soneto m

soon ['su:n] adv 1 : pronto 2 SHORTLY : dentro de poco 3 **as ~ as** : en cuanto 4 **as ~ as possible** : lo más pronto posible 5 **~ after** : poco después 6 **~er or later** : tarde o temprano 7 **the ~er the better** : cuanto antes mejor

soot ['sʊt, 'su:t, 'sʌt] n : hollín m

soothe ['su:ð] vt **soothed; soothing** 1 CALM : calmar 2 RELIEVE : aliviar

sop ['sɑp] vt **sopped; sopping ~ up** : absorber

sophistication [sə,fɪstə'keɪʃən] n : sofisticación f — **sophisticated** [sə'fɪstə,keɪţəd] adj : sofisticado

sophomore ['sɑf,mor, 'sɑfə,mor] n : estudiante mf de segundo año

soprano [sə'præ,no:] n, pl **-nos** : soprano mf

sorcerer ['sɔrsərər] n : hechicero m, brujo m — **sorcery** ['sɔrsəri] n : hechicería f, brujería f

sordid ['sɔrdɪd] adj : sórdido

sore ['sor] adj **sorer; sorest** 1 : dolorido 2 ANGRY : enfadado 3 **~ throat** : dolor m de garganta 4 **I have a ~ throat** : me duele la garganta — **~** n : llaga f — **sorely** ['sorli] adv : muchísimo — **soreness** ['sornəs] n : dolor m

sorrow ['sɑr,o:] n : pesar m, pena f — **sorry** ['sɑri] adj **sorrier; -est** 1 PITIFUL : lamentable 2 **feel ~ for** : compadecer 3 **I'm ~** : lo siento

sort ['sɔrt] *n* **1** : tipo *m*, clase *f* **2 a ~ of** : una especie de — **~** *vt* : clasificar — **sort of** *adv* **1** SOMEWHAT : algo **2** MORE OR LESS : más o menos

SOS [,ɛs,o;'es] *n* : SOS *m*

so-so ['so;'so:] *adj & adv* : así así *fam*

soufflé [su:'fleɪ] *n* : suflé *m*

sought → **seek**

soul ['so:l] *n* : alma *f*

sound[1] ['saʊnd] *adj* **1** HEALTHY : sano **2** FIRM : sólido **3** SENSIBLE : lógico **4 a ~ sleep** : un sueño profundo **5 safe and ~** : sano y salvo

sound[2] *n* — *vt* : hacer sonar, tocar (una trompeta, etc.) — *vi* **1** : sonar **2** SEEM : parecer

sound[3] *n* CHANNEL : brazo *m* de mar — **~** *vt* **1** : sondar (en navegación) **2 or ~ out** : sondear

soundly ['saʊndli] *adv* **1** SOLIDLY : sólidamente **2** DEEPLY : profundamente

soundproof ['saʊnd,pru:f] *adj* : insonorizado

soup ['su:p] *n* : sopa *f*

sour ['saʊər] *adj* **1** : agrio **2 ~ milk** : leche *f* cortada — **~** *vt* : agriar

source ['sɔrs] *n* : fuente *f*, origen *m*

south ['saʊθ] *adv* : al sur — **~** *adj* : (del) sur — **~** *n* : sur *m* — **South African** *adj* : sudafricano — **South American** *adj* : sudamericano — **southeast** [saʊθ'i:st] *adv* : hacia el sureste — **~** *adj* : (del) sureste — **~** *n* : sureste *m*, sudeste *m* — **southeastern** [saʊθ'i:stərn] *adj* → **southeast** — **southerly** ['sʌðərli] *adv & adj* : del sur — **southern** ['sʌðərn] *adj* : del sur, meridional — **southwest** [saʊθ'west] *adv* : hacia el suroeste — **~** *adj* : (del) suroeste — **~** *n* : suroeste *m*, sudoeste *m* — **southwestern** [saʊθ'westərn] *adj* → **southwest**

souvenir [,su:və'nɪr, 'su:və,-] *n* : recuerdo *m*

sovereign ['savərən] *n* : soberano *m*, -na *f* — *adj* : soberano — **sovereignty** ['savərənti] *n, pl* **-ties** : soberanía *f*

Soviet ['so:vi,ɛt, 'sɑ-, -viət] *adj* : soviético

sow[1] ['saʊ] *n* : cerda *f*

sow[2] ['so:] *vt* **sowed; sown** ['so:n] *or* **sowed; sowing** : sembrar

sox → **sock**

soybean ['sɔɪ,bi:n] *n* : soya *f*, soja *f*

spa ['spɑ] *n* : balneario *m*

space ['speɪs] *n* **1** : espacio *m* **2** ROOM, SPOT : sitio *m*, lugar *m* — **~** *vt* **spaced; spacing** : espaciar — **spaceship** ['speɪs,ʃɪp] *n* : nave *f* espacial — **space shuttle** *n* : transbor-

dador *m* espacial — **spacious** ['speɪʃəs] *adj* : espacioso, amplio

spade[1] ['speɪd] *n* SHOVEL : pala *f*

spade[2] *n* : pica *f* (naipe)

spaghetti [spə'gɛti] *n* : espaguetis *mpl*

span ['spæn] *n* **1** PERIOD : espacio *m* **2** : luz *f* (entre dos soportes) — **~** *vt* **spanned; spanning** **1** : abarcar (un período) **2** CROSS : extenderse sobre

Spaniard ['spænjərd] *n* : español *m*, -ñola *f*

spaniel ['spænjəl] *n* : spaniel *m*

Spanish ['spænɪʃ] *adj* : español — **~** *n* : español *m* (idioma)

spank ['spæŋk] *vt* : dar palmadas a (en las nalgas)

spar ['spɑr] *vi* **sparred; sparring** : entrenarse (en boxeo)

spare ['spær] *vt* **spared; sparing** **1** PARDON : perdonar **2** SAVE : ahorrar **3 can you ~ a dollar?** : ¿me das un dólar? **4 I can't ~ the time** : no tengo tiempo **5 ~ no expense** : no reparar en gastos **6 to ~** : de sobra — **~** *adj* **1** : de repuesto **2** EXCESS : de más **3** LEAN : delgado — **~** *n or* **~ part** : repuesto *m* — **spare time** *n* : tiempo *m* libre — **sparing** ['spærɪŋ] *adj* : parco, económico

spark ['spɑrk] *n* : chispa *f* — **~** *vi* : chispear, echar chispas — *vt* : despertar (interés), provocar (crítica) — **sparkle** ['spɑrkəl] *vi* **-kled; -kling** : destellar, centellear — **~** *n* : destello *m*, centelleo *m* — **spark plug** *n* : bujía *f*

sparrow ['spæro:] *n* : gorrión *m*

sparse ['spɑrs] *adj* **sparser; -est** : escaso

spasm ['spæzəm] *n* : espasmo *m*

spat[1] → **spit**

spat[2] *n* QUARREL : disputa *f*, pelea *f*

spatter ['spætər] *vt* : salpicar

spawn ['spɔn] *vi* : desovar — *vt* : engendrar, producir — **~** *n* : hueva *f*

speak ['spi:k] *v* **spoke** ['spo:k]; **spoken** ['spo:kən]; **speaking** *vi* **1** : hablar **2 ~ out against** : denunciar **3 ~ up** : hablar más alto **4 ~ up for** : defender — *vt* **1** : decir **2** : hablar (un idioma) — **speaker** ['spi:kər] *n* **1** ORATOR : orador *m*, -dora *f* **2** : hablante *mpf* (de un idioma) **3** LOUDSPEAKER : altavoz *m*

spear ['spɪr] *n* : lanza *f* — **spearhead** ['spɪr,hɛd] *n* : punta *f* de lanza — **~** *vt* : encabezar — **spearmint** ['spɪr,mɪnt] *n* : menta *f* verde

special ['spɛʃəl] *adj* : especial — **specialist** ['spɛʃəlɪst] *n* : especialista *mf* — **specialization** [,spɛʃələ'zeɪʃən] *n* : especialización *f* — **specialize** ['spɛʃə-

,laɪz/ *vi* **-ized; -izing** : especializarse
— **specially** *adv* : especialmente —
specialty /'speʃəlᶦti/ *n, pl* **-ties** : especialidad *f*
species /'spiː,ʃiːz, -,siːz/ *ns & pl* : especie
f
specify /'spesə,faɪ/ *vt* **-fied; -fying** : especificar — **specific** [sprɪ'sɪfɪk] *adj*
: específico — **specifically** [sprɪ'sɪfɪkli]
adv 1 : específicamente 2 EXPLICITLY
: expresamente — **specification**
[,spesəfə'keɪʃən] *n* : especificación *f*
specimen /'spesəmən/ *n* : espécimen *m*
speck /'spek/ *n* 1 SPOT : mancha *f* 2 BIT
: mota *f* — **speckled** /'spekəld/ *adj*
: moteado
spectacle /'spektɪkəl/ *n* 1 : espectáculo
m 2 **~s** *npl* GLASSES : gafas *fpl*, lentes
fpl, anteojos *mpl* — **spectacular**
[spek'tækjələr] *adj* : espectacular —
spectator /'spek,teɪtər/ *n* : espectador
m, -dora *f*
specter *or* **spectre** /'spektər/ *n* : espectro *m*
spectrum /'spektrəm/ *n, pl* **-tra** [-trə] *or*
-trums 1 : espectro *m* 2 RANGE : gama *f*
speculation [,spekjə'leɪʃən] *n* : especulación *f*
speech /'spiːtʃ/ *n* 1 : habla *f* 2 ADDRESS
: discurso *m* — **speechless** /'spiːtʃləs/
adj : mudo
speed /'spiːd/ *n* 1 : rapidez *f* 2 VELOCITY
: velocidad *f* — **~** *v* **sped** /'sped/ *or*
speeded; speeding *vi* 1 : conducir a
exceso de velocidad 2 **~ off** : irse a
toda velocidad 3 **~ up** : acelerarse —
vt or **~ up** : acelerar — **speed limit** *n*
: velocidad *f* máxima — **speedome-
ter** /sprɪ'dɑmətər/ *n* : velocímetro *m* —
speedy /'spiːdi/ *adj* **speedier, -est**
: rápido
spell[1] /'spel/ *vt* 1 : escribir (las letras de)
2 *or* **~ out** : deletrear 3 MEAN : significar
spell[2] *n* ENCHANTMENT : hechizo *m*
spell[3] *n* : período *m* (de tiempo)
spellbound /'spel,baʊnd/ *adj* : embelesado
spelling /'spelɪŋ/ *n* : ortografía *f*
spend /'spend/ *vt* **spent** /'spent/; **spend-
ing** 1 : gastar (dinero) 2 : pasar (las
vacaciones, etc.) 3 **~ time on** : dedicar tiempo a
sperm /'spərm/ *n, pl* **sperm** *or* **sperms**
: esperma *mf*
spew /'spjuː/ *vt* : vomitar, arrojar (lava,
etc.)
sphere /'sfɪr/ *n* : esfera *f* — **spherical**
/'sfɪrɪkəl, 'sfer-/ *adj* : esférico

spice /'spaɪs/ *n* : especia *f* — **~** *vt*
spiced; spicing : condimentar, sazonar — **spicy** /'spaɪsi/ *adj* **spicier; -est**
: picante
spider /'spaɪdər/ *n* : araña *f*
spigot /'spɪgət, -kət/ *n* : grifo *m* Spain,
llave *f* Lat
spike /'spaɪk/ *n* 1 : clavo *m* (grande) 2
POINT : punta *f* — **spiky** /'spaɪki/ *adj*
: puntiagudo
spill /'spɪl/ *vt* : derramar — *vi* : derramarse
spin /'spɪn/ *v* **spun** /'spʌn/; **spinning** *vi*
: girar — *vt* 1 : hilar (lana, etc.) 2
TWIRL : hacer girar — **~** *n* 1 : vuelta *f*,
giro *m* 2 **go for a ~** : dar una vuelta
(en auto)
spinach /'spɪnɪtʃ/ *n* : espinacas *fpl*
spinal cord /'spaɪnəl/ *n* : médula *f* espinal
spindle /'spɪndəl/ *n* : huso *m* (para hilar)
— **spindly** /'spɪndli/ *adj* : larguirucho
fam
spine /'spaɪn/ *n* 1 : columna *f* vertebral 2
QUILL : púa *f* 3 THORN : espina *f* 4
: lomo *m* (de un libro)
spinster /'spɪnstər/ *n* : soltera *f*
spiral /'spaɪrəl/ *adj* : de espiral, en espiral — **~** *n* : espiral *f* — *vi* **-raled** *or*
-ralled; -raling *or* **-ralling** : ir en espiral
spire /'spaɪr/ *n* : aguja *f*
spirit /'spɪrət/ *n* 1 : espíritu *m* 2 **in good
~s** : animado 3 **~s** *npl* : licores *mpl*
— **spirited** /'spɪrətəd/ *adj* : animado —
spiritual /'spɪrɪtʃuəl, -tʃəl/ *adj* : espiritual — **spirituality** [,spɪrɪtʃu'æləᶦti] *n, pl*
-ties : espiritualidad *f*
spit[1] /'spɪt/ *n* ROTISSERIE : asador *m*
spit[2] *v* **spit** *or* **spat** /'spæt/; **spitting**
: escupir — *n* SALIVA : saliva *f*
spite /'spaɪt/ *n* 1 : rencor *m* 2 **in ~ of** : a
pesar de — **~** *vt* **spited; spiting** : fastidiar — **spiteful** /'spaɪtfəl/ *adj* : rencoroso
spittle /'spɪtəl/ *n* : saliva *f*
splash /'splæʃ/ *vt* : salpicar — *vi* 1
: salpicar 2 *or* **~ about** : chapotear —
~ *n* 1 : salpicadura *f* 2 : mancha *f* (de
color, etc.)
splatter /'splætər/ → **spatter**
spleen /'spliːn/ *n* : bazo *m* (órgano)
splendor /'splendər/ *n* : esplendor *m* —
splendid /'splendəd/ *adj* : espléndido
splint /'splɪnt/ *n* : tablilla *f*
splinter /'splɪntər/ *n* : astilla *f* — *vi*
: astillarse
split /'splɪt/ *v* **split; splitting** *vt* 1 : partir
2 BURST : reventar 3 *or* **~ up** : dividir
— *vi* 1 : partirse, rajarse 2 *or* **~ up**

: dividirse — ~ *n* **1** CRACK : rajadura *f* **2** *or* ~ **seam** : descosido *m* **3** DIVISION : división *f*

splurge ['splərdʒ] *vi* **splurged; splurging** : derrochar dinero

spoil ['spɔɪl] *vt* **spoiled** *or* **spoilt** ['spɔɪlt]; **spoiling 1** RUIN : estropear **2** PAMPER : consentir, mimar — **spoils** *npl* : botín *m*

spoke¹ ['spo:k] → **speak**

spoke² *n* : rayo *m* (de una rueda)

spoken → **speak**

spokesman ['spo:ksmən] *n, pl* **-men** [-mən, -ˌmen] : portavoz *mf* — **spokeswoman** ['spo:ksˌwʊmən] *n, pl* **-women** [-ˌwɪmən] : portavoz *f*

sponge ['spʌndʒ] *n* : esponja *f* — ~ *vt* **sponged; sponging** : limpiar con una esponja — **spongy** ['spʌndʒi] *adj* **spongier; -est** : esponjoso

sponsor ['spantsər] *n* : patrocinador *m*, -dora *f* — ~ *vt* : patrocinar — **sponsorship** ['spantsərˌʃɪp] *n* : patrocinio *m*

spontaneity [ˌspantəˈni:əti, -ˈneɪ-] *n* : espontaneidad *f* — **spontaneous** [spanˈteɪniəs] *adj* : espontáneo

spooky ['spu:ki] *adj* **spookier; -est** : espeluznante

spool ['spu:l] *n* : carrete *m*

spoon ['spu:n] *n* : cuchara *f* — **spoonful** ['spu:nˌfʊl] *n* : cucharada *f*

sporadic [spəˈrædɪk] *adj* : esporádico

spore ['spor] *n* : espora *f*

sport ['sport] *n* **1** : deporte *m* **2 be a good** ~ : tener espíritu deportivo — **sportsman** ['sportsmən] *n, pl* **-men** [-mən, -ˌmen] : deportista *m* — **sportswoman** ['sportsˌwʊmən] *n, pl* **-women** [-ˌwɪmən] : deportista *f* — **sporty** ['sporti] *adj* **sportier; -est** : deportivo

spot ['spat] *n* **1** : mancha *f* **2** DOT : punto *m* **3** PLACE : lugar *m*, sitio *m* **4 in a tight** ~ : en apuros **5 on the** ~ INSTANTLY : en ese mismo momento — ~ *vt* **spotted; spotting 1** STAIN : manchar **2** DETECT, NOTICE : ver, descubrir — **spotless** ['spatləs] *adj* : impecable — **spotlight** ['spatˌlaɪt] *n* **1** : foco *m*, reflector *m* **2 be in the** ~ : ser el centro de atención — **spotty** ['spati] *adj* **spottier; -est** : irregular

spouse ['spaʊs] *n* : cónyuge *mf*

spout ['spaʊt] *vi* : salir a chorros — ~ *n* **1** : pico *m* (de una jarra, etc.) **2** STREAM : chorro *m*

sprain ['spreɪn] *n* : esguince *m* — ~ *vt* : sufrir un esguince en

sprawl ['sprɔl] *vi* **1** : repantigarse (en un sillón, etc.) **2** EXTEND : extenderse — ~ *n* : extensión *f*

spray¹ ['spreɪ] *n* BOUQUET : ramillete *m*

spray² *n* **1** MIST : rocío *m* **2** *or* **aerosol** ~ : spray *m* **3** *or* ~ **bottle** : atomizador *m* — ~ *vt* : rociar (una superficie), pulverizar (un líquido)

spread ['spred] *v* **spread; spreading** *vt* **1** : propagar, difundir **2** *or* ~ **out** : extender **3** : untar (con mantequilla, etc.) — *vi* **1** : propagarse, difundirse **2** *or* ~ **out** : extenderse — ~ *n* **1** : propagación *f*, difusión *f* **2** PASTE : pasta *f* (para untar) — **spreadsheet** ['spredˌʃi:t] *n* : hoja *f* de cálculo

spree ['spri] *n* **go on a** ~ : ir de juerga *fam*

sprig ['sprɪg] *n* : ramito *m*

sprightly ['spraɪtli] *adj* **sprightlier; -est** : vivo

spring ['sprɪŋ] *v* **sprang** ['spræŋ] *or* **sprung** ['sprʌŋ]; **sprung; springing** *vi* **1** : saltar **2** ~ **from** : surgir de **3** ~ **up** : surgir — *vt* **1** ACTIVATE : accionar **2** ~ **a leak** : hacer agua **3** ~ **sth on s.o.** : sorprender a algn con algo — ~ *n* **1** : manantial *m* (de aguas) **2** : primavera *f* (estación) **3** LEAP : salto *m* **4** RESILIENCE : elasticidad *f* **5** : resorte *m* (mecanismo) **6** *or* **bedspring** : muelle *m* — **springboard** ['sprɪŋˌbord] *n* : trampolín *m* — **springtime** ['sprɪŋˌtaɪm] *n* : primavera *f* — **springy** ['sprɪŋi] *adj* **springier; -est** : mullido

sprinkle ['sprɪŋkəl] *vt* **-kled; -kling 1** : salpicar, rociar **2** DUST : espolvorear — ~ *n* : llovizna *f* — **sprinkler** ['sprɪŋkələr] *n* : aspersor *m*

sprint ['sprɪnt] *vi* **1** : correr **2** : esprintar (en deportes) — ~ *n* : esprint *m* (en deportes)

sprout ['spraʊt] *vi* : brotar — ~ *n* : brote *m*

spruce¹ ['spru:s] *vt* **spruced; sprucing** ~ **up** : arreglar

spruce² *n* : picea *f* (árbol)

spry ['spraɪ] *adj* **sprier** *or* **spryer** ['spraɪər]; **spriest** *or* **spryest** ['spraɪəst] : ágil, activo

spun → **spin**

spur ['spər] *n* **1** : espuela *f* **2** STIMULUS : acicate *m* **3 on the** ~ **of the moment** : sin pensarlo — ~ *vt* **spurred; spurring** *or* ~ **on 1** : espolear (un caballo) **2** MOTIVATE : motivar

spurn ['spərn] *vt* : desdeñar, rechazar

spurt¹ ['spərt] *vi* : salir a chorros — ~ *n* : chorro *m*

spurt² *n* **1** : arranque *m* (de energía, etc.) **2 work in** ~**s** : trabajar por rachas

spy ['spaɪ] v **spied; spying** vt : ver, divisar — vi **~ on s.o.** : espiar a algn — **~** n : espía mf

squabble ['skwɑbəl] n : riña f, pelea f — **~** vi **-bled; -bling** : reñir, pelearse

squad ['skwɑd] n : pelotón m (militar), brigada f (de policías)

squadron ['skwɑdrən] n : escuadrón m (de soldados), escuadra f (de aviones o naves)

squalid ['skwɑlɪd] adj : miserable

squall ['skwɔl] n : turbión m

squalor ['skwɑlər] n : miseria f

squander ['skwɑndər] vt : derrochar (dinero, etc.), desperdiciar (oportunidades, etc.)

square ['skwær] n 1 : cuadrado m 2 : plaza f (de una ciudad) — **~** adj **squarer; -est** 1 : cuadrado 2 HONEST : justo 3 EVEN : en paz 4 **a ~ meal** : una comida decente — **~** vt **squared; squaring** 1 : elevar al cuadrado (un número) 2 : saldar (una cuenta) — **square root** n : raíz f cuadrada

squash¹ ['skwɑʃ, 'skwɔʃ] vt 1 : aplastar 2 : acallar (protestas, etc.) — **~** n : squash m (deporte)

squash² n, pl **squashes** or **squash** : calabaza f (vegetal)

squat ['skwɑt] vi **squatted; squatting** 1 or **~ down** : ponerse en cuclillas 2 : ocupar un lugar sin derecho — **~** adj **squatter; squattest** : achaparrado — **squatter** n

squawk ['skwɔk] n : graznido m — **~** vi : graznar

squeak ['skwiːk] vi 1 : chillar 2 CREAK : chirriar — **~** n 1 : chillido m 2 CREAK : chirrido m — **squeaky** ['skwiːki] adj **squeakier; -est** : chirriante

squeal ['skwiːl] vi 1 : chillar (dícese de personas, etc.), chirriar (dícese de frenos, etc.) 2 PROTEST : quejarse — **~** n 1 : chillido m (de una persona), chirrido m (de frenos, etc.)

squeamish ['skwiːmɪʃ] adj : impresionable, delicado

squeeze ['skwiːz] vt **squeezed; squeezing** 1 : apretar 2 : exprimir (frutas, etc.) 3 : extraer (jugo, etc.) — **~** n : apretón m

squid ['skwɪd] n, pl **squid** or **squids** : calamar m

squint ['skwɪnt] vi : entrecerrar los ojos — **~** n : estrabismo m

squirm ['skwərm] vi : retorcerse

squirrel ['skwərəl] n : ardilla f

squirt ['skwərt] vt : lanzar un chorro de — vi : salir a chorros — **~** n : chorrito m

stab ['stæb] n 1 : puñalada f 2 **~ of pain** : pinchazo m 3 **take a ~ at** : intentar — **~** vt **stabbed; stabbing** 1 KNIFE : apuñalar 2 STICK : clavar

stable ['steɪbəl] n 1 : establo m (para ganado) 2 or **horse ~** : caballeriza f — **~** adj **-bler; -blest** : estable — **stability** [stəˈbɪləṭi] n, pl **-ties** : estabilidad f — **stabilize** ['steɪbəˌlaɪz] vt **-lized; -lizing** : estabilizar

stack ['stæk] n : montón m, pila f — **~** vt : amontonar, apilar

stadium ['steɪdiəm] n, pl **-dia** or **-diums** : estadio m

staff ['stæfs, stævz] n, pl **staffs** or **staves** ['stævz, 'steɪvz] 1 : bastón m 2 pl **staffs** PERSONNEL : personal m 3 pl **staffs** : pentagrama m (en música) — **~** ['stæf] vt : proveer de personal

stag ['stæg] n, pl **stags** or **stag** : ciervo m, venado m — **~** adj : sólo para hombres — adv **go ~** : ir solo

stage ['steɪdʒ] n 1 : escenario m (de un teatro) 2 PHASE : etapa f 3 **the ~** : el teatro — **~** vt **staged; staging** 1 : poner en escena 2 ARRANGE : montar — **stagecoach** ['steɪdʒˌkoʊtʃ] n : diligencia f

stagger ['stægər] vi : tambalearse — vt 1 : escalonar (turnos, etc.) 2 **be ~ed by** : quedarse estupefacto por — **~** n : tambaleo m — **staggering** ['stægərɪŋ] adj : asombroso

stagnant ['stægnənt] adj : estancado — **stagnate** ['stægˌneɪt] vi **-nated; -nating** : estancarse

stain ['steɪn] vt 1 : manchar 2 : teñir (madera) — **~** n 1 : mancha f 2 DYE : tinte m, tintura f — **stainless steel** ['steɪnləs-] n : acero m inoxidable

stair ['stær] n 1 STEP : escalón m, peldaño m 2 **~s** npl : escalera(s) f(pl) — **staircase** ['stærˌkeɪs] n : escalera(s) f(pl) — **stairway** ['stærˌweɪ] n : escalera(s) f(pl)

stake ['steɪk] n 1 POST : estaca f 2 BET : apuesta f 3 INTEREST : intereses mpl 4 **be at ~** : estar en juego — **~** vt **staked; staking** 1 : estacar 2 BET : jugarse 3 **~ a claim to** : reclamar

stale ['steɪl] adj **staler; stalest** 1 : duro (dícese del pan) 2 OLD : viejo 3 STUFFY : viciado

stalk¹ ['stɔk] n : tallo m (de una planta)

stalk² vt : acechar — vi or **~ off** : irse con altivez

stall¹ ['stɔl] n 1 : compartimiento m (de un establo) 2 STAND : puesto m — **~** vt : parar (un motor) — vi : pararse

stall² *vt* DELAY : entretener — *vi* : andar con rodeos

stallion ['stæljən] *n* : caballo *m* semental

stalwart ['stɔlwərt] *adj* **1** STRONG : fornido **2** ~ **supporter** : partidario *m* leal

stamina ['stæmənə] *n* : resistencia *f*

stammer ['stæmər] *vi* : tartamudear — ~ *n* : tartamudeo *m*

stamp ['stæmp] *n* **1** SEAL : sello *m* **2** DIE : cuño *m* **3** *or* **postage** ~ : sello *m*, estampilla *f Lat*, timbre *m Lat* — ~ *vt* **1** : franquear (una carta) **2** IMPRINT : sellar **3** MINT : acuñar **4** ~ **one's foot** : dar una patada (en el suelo)

stampede [stæm'piːd] *n* : estampida *f* — ~ *vi* -**peded**; -**peding** : salir en estampida

stance ['stænts] *n* : postura *f*

stand ['stænd] *v* **stood** ['stʊd]; **standing** *vi* **1** : estar de pie, estar parado *Lat* **2** BE : estar **3** CONTINUE : seguir vigente **4** LIE, REST : reposar **5** ~ **aside** *or* ~ **back** : apartarse **6** ~ **out** : sobresalir **7** *or* ~ **up** : ponerse de pie, pararse *Lat* — *vt* **1** PLACE : poner, colocar **2** ENDURE : soportar **3** ~ **a chance** : tener una posibilidad — **stand by** *vt* **1** : mantener (una promesa, etc.) **2** SUPPORT : apoyar — **stand for** *vt* **1** MEAN : significar **2** PERMIT : permitir — **stand up** *vi* **1** ~ **for** : defender **2** ~ **up to** : resistir a — ~ *n* **1** RESISTANCE : resistencia *f* **2** STALL : puesto *m* **3** BASE : base *f* **4** POSITION : posición *f* **5** ~**s** *npl* : tribuna *f*

standard ['stændərd] *n* **1** : norma *f* **2** BANNER : estandarte *m* **3** CRITERION : criterio *m* **4** ~ **of living** : nivel *m* de vida — ~ *adj* : estándar — **standardize** ['stændər,daɪz] *vt* -**ized**; -**izing** : estandarizar

standing ['stændɪŋ] *n* **1** RANK : posición *f* **2** DURATION : duración *f*

standpoint ['stænd,pɔɪnt] *n* : punto *m* de vista

standstill ['stænd,stɪl] *n* **1** **be at a** ~ : estar paralizado **2** **come to a** ~ : pararse

stank → **stink**

stanza ['stænzə] *n* : estrofa *f*

staple¹ ['steɪpəl] *n* : producto *m* principal — ~ *adj* : principal, básico

staple² *n* : grapa *f* (para papeles) — ~ *vt* -**pled**; -**pling** : grapar, engrapar *Lat* — **stapler** ['steɪplər] *n* : grapadora *f*, engrapadora *f Lat*

star ['stɑr] *n* : estrella *f* — ~ *v* **starred**; **starring** *vt* FEATURE : estar protagonizado por — *vi* ~ **in** : protagonizar

starboard ['stɑrbərd] *n* : estribor *m*

starch ['stɑrtʃ] *vt* : almidonar — ~ *n* **1** : almidón *m* **2** : fécula *f* (comida)

stardom ['stɑrdəm] *n* : estrellato *m*

stare ['stær] *vi* **stared**; **staring** : mirar fijamente — ~ *n* : mirada *f* fija

starfish ['stɑr,fɪʃ] *n* : estrella *f* de mar

stark ['stɑrk] *adj* **1** PLAIN : austero **2** HARSH : severo, duro **3** SHARP : marcado — ~ *adv* **1** : completamente **2** ~ **naked** : en cueros (vivos)

starlight ['stɑr,laɪt] *n* : luz *f* de las estrellas

starling ['stɑrlɪŋ] *n* : estornino *m*

starry ['stɑri] *adj* **starrier**; -**est** : estrellado

start ['stɑrt] *vi* **1** : empezar, comenzar **2** SET OUT : salir **3** JUMP : sobresaltarse **4** *or* ~ **up** : arrancar — *vt* **1** : empezar, comenzar **2** CAUSE : provocar **3** *or* ~ **up** ESTABLISH : montar **4** *or* ~ **up** : arrancar (un motor, etc.) — ~ *n* **1** : principio *m* **2** **get an early** ~ : salir temprano **3** **give s.o. a** ~ : asustar a algn — **starter** ['stɑrtər] *n* : motor *m* de arranque (de un vehículo)

startle ['stɑrtəl] *vt* -**tled**; -**tling** : asustar

starve ['stɑrv] *v* **starved**; **starving** *vi* : morirse de hambre — *vt* : privar de comida — **starvation** [stɑr'veɪʃən] *n* : inanición *f*, hambre *f*

stash ['stæʃ] *vt* : esconder

state ['steɪt] *n* **1** : estado *m* **2** **the States** : los Estados Unidos — ~ *vt* **stated**; **stating 1** SAY : decir **2** REPORT : exponer — **stately** ['steɪtli] *adj* **statelier**; -**est** : majestuoso — **statement** ['steɪtmənt] *n* **1** : declaración *f* **2** *or* **bank** ~ : estado *m* de cuenta — **statesman** ['steɪtsmən] *n*, *pl* -**men** [-mən, -ˌmɛn] : estadista *mf*

static ['stætɪk] *adj* : estático — ~ *n* : estática *f*

station ['steɪʃən] *n* **1** : estación *f* (de trenes, etc.) **2** RANK : condición *f* (social) **3** : canal *m* (de televisión), emisora *f* (de radio) **4** → **fire station**, **police station** — *vt* : apostar, estacionar — **stationary** ['steɪʃəˌnɛri] *adj* : estacionario

stationery ['steɪʃəˌnɛri] *n* : papel *m* y sobres *mpl* (para cartas)

station wagon *n* : camioneta *f* (familiar)

statistic [stə'tɪstɪk] *n* : estadística *f* — **statistical** [stə'tɪstɪkəl] *adj* : estadístico

statue ['stætʃuː] *n* : estatua *f*

stature ['stætʃər] *n* : estatura *f*, talla *f*

status ['steɪtəs, 'stæ-] *n* **1** : situación *f* **2** *or* **social** ~ : estatus *m* **3** **marital** ~ : estado *m* civil

statute ['stæˌtʃuːt] *n* : estatuto *m*

staunch ['stɔntʃ] *adj* : leal

stave ['steɪv] *vt* **staved** *or* **stove** ['stoːv];
staving 1 ~ in : romper **2 ~ off**
: evitar

staves → staff

stay¹ ['steɪ] *vi* **1** REMAIN : quedarse, permanecer **2** LODGE : alojarse **3 ~**
awake : mantenerse despierto **4 ~ in**
: quedarse en casa — *vt* — : suspender
(una ejecución, etc.) — *~ n* **1** : estancia *f*, estadía *f* *Lat* **2** SUSPENSION
: suspensión *f*

stay² *n* SUPPORT : soporte *m*

stead ['sted] *n* **1 in s.o.'s ~** : en lugar
de algn **2 stand s.o. in good ~** : ser
muy útil a algn — **steadfast** ['sted-
ˌfæst] *adj* **1** FIRM : firme **2** LOYAL : leal,
fiel — **steadily** ['stedəli] *adv* **1** : progresivamente **2** INCESSANTLY : sin
parar **3** FIXEDLY : fijamente — **steady**
['stedi] *adj* **steadier; -est 1** FIRM, SURE
: firme, seguro **2** FIXED : fijo **3** DE-
PENDABLE : responsable **4** CONSTANT
: constante — *vt* **steadied; steady-
ing 1** : mantener firme **2** : calmar (los
nervios)

steak ['steɪk] *n* : bistec *m*, filete *m*

steal ['stiːl] *v* **stole** ['stoːl]; **stolen**
['stoːlən]; **stealing** *vt* : robar — *vi* **1**
: robar **2 ~ away** : escabullirse

stealth ['stelθ] *n* : sigilo *m* — **stealthy**
['stelθi] *adj* **stealthier; -est** : furtivo,
sigiloso

steam ['stiːm] *n* **1** : vapor *m* **2 let off ~**
: desahogarse — *~ vi* : echar vapor —
vt **1** : cocer al vapor **2 ~ up** : empañar
— **steam engine** : motor *m* de vapor
— **steamship** ['stiːmˌʃɪp] *n* : (barco *m*
de) vapor *m* — **steamy** ['stiːmi] *adj*
steamier; -est 1 : lleno de vapor **2**
PASSIONATE : tórrido

steel ['stiːl] *n* : acero *m* — *~ vt ~* oneself : armarse de valor — *~ adj* : de
acero

steep¹ ['stiːp] *adj* **1** : empinado **2** CON-
SIDERABLE : considerable **3** : muy alto
(dícese de precios)

steep² *vt* : dejar (té, etc.) en infusión

steeple ['stiːpəl] *n* : aguja *f*, campanario
m

steer¹ ['stɪr] *n* : buey *m*

steer² *vt* : dirigir (un auto, etc.), pilotear
(un barco) — **steering wheel** *n*
: volante *m*

stem¹ ['stem] *n* : tallo *m* (de una planta),
pie *m* (de una copa) — *~ vi ~* from
: provenir de

stem² *vt* **stemmed; stemming** : contener, detener

stench ['stentʃ] *n* : hedor *m*, mal olor *m*

stencil ['stentsəl] *n* : plantilla *f* (para
marcar)

step ['step] *n* **1** : paso *m* **2** RUNG, STAIR
: escalón *m* **3 ~ by ~** : paso por paso
4 take ~s : tomar medidas **5 watch**
your ~ : mira por dónde caminas —
~ vi **stepped; stepping 1** : dar un
paso **2 ~ back** : retroceder **3 ~ down**
RESIGN : retirarse **4 ~ in** : intervenir **5**
~ out : salir (por un momento) **6 ~**
this way : pase por aquí — **step up** *vt*
INCREASE : aumentar

stepbrother ['stepˌbrʌðər] *n* : hermanastro *m* — **stepdaughter** ['stepˌdɔtər] *n*
: hijastra *f* — **stepfather** ['stepˌfɑðər,
-fɑ-] *n* : padrastro *m*

stepladder ['stepˌlædər] *n* : escalera *f* de
tijera

stepmother ['stepˌmʌðər] *n* : madrastra *f*
— **stepsister** ['stepˌsɪstər] *n* : hermanastra *f* — **stepson** ['stepˌsʌn] *n*
: hijastro *m*

stereo ['steriˌoː, 'stɪr-] *n*, *pl* **stereos** : estéreo *m* — *~ adj* : estéreo

stereotype ['steriˌotaɪp, 'stɪr-] *vt* **-typed;
-typing** : estereotipar — *~ n* : estereotipo *m*

sterile ['sterəl] *adj* : estéril — **sterility**
[stəˈrɪləti] *n* : esterilidad *f* — **steriliza-
tion** [ˌsterələˈzeɪʃən] *n* : esterilización *f*
— **sterilize** ['sterəˌlaɪz] *vt* **-ized; -izing**
: esterilizar

sterling ['stərlɪŋ] *adj* : excelente — **sterling silver** *n* : plata *f* de ley

stern¹ ['stərn] *adj* : severo, adusto

stern² *n* : popa *f*

stethoscope ['steθəˌskoːp] *n* : estetosco-
pio *m*

stew ['stuː, 'stjuː] *n* : estofado *m*, guiso *m*
— *~ vt* : estofar, guisar — *vi* **1** : cocer
2 FRET : preocuparse

steward ['stuːərd, 'stjuː-] *n* **1** : administrador *m*, -dora *f* **2** : auxiliar *m* de
vuelo (en un avión) **3** : camarero *m* (en
un barco) — **stewardess** ['stuːərdəs,
'stjuː-] *n* **1** : auxiliar *f* de vuelo, azafata
f (en un avión) **2** : camarera *f* (en un
barco)

stick¹ ['stɪk] *n* **1** : palo *m* **2** TWIG : ramita *f* (suelta) **3** WALKING STICK : bastón
m

stick² *v* **stuck** ['stʌk]; **sticking** *vt* **1**
: pegar **2** STAB : clavar **3** PUT : poner **4**
~ out : sacar (la lengua, etc.) — *vi* **1**
: pegarse **2** JAM : atascarse **3 ~**
around : quedarse **4 ~ out** PROTRUDE
: sobresalir **5 ~ out** SHOW : asomar **6**
~ up : sobresalir **7 ~ up for** : defender — **sticker** ['stɪkər] *n* : etiqueta *f*

adhesiva — **stickler** ['stɪklər] *n* be a ~
for : insistir mucho en — **sticky** ['stɪki]
adj **stickier; -est** : pegajoso
stiff ['stɪf] *adj* **1** RIGID : rígido, tieso **2**
STILTED : forzado **3** STRONG : fuerte **4**
DIFFICULT : difícil **5** (STIFF) : entumecido
(dícese de músculos) — **stiffen**
['stɪfən] *vt* : fortalecer, hacer más duro
— *vi* **1** HARDEN : endurecerse **2** : entumecerse (dícese de músculos) — **stiffness** ['stɪfnəs] *n* : rigidez *f*
stifle ['staɪfəl] *vt* **-fled; -fling** : sofocar
stigmatize ['stɪgmə,taɪz] *vt* **-tized;
-tizing** : estigmatizar
still ['stɪl] *adj* **1** : inmóvil **2** SILENT
: callado — *adv* **1** : todavía, aún **2**
NEVERTHELESS : de todos modos, aún
así **3** sit ~! : ¡quédate quieto! — *n*
: quietud *f*, calma *f* — **stillborn** ['stɪl-
,bɔrn] *adj* : nacido muerto — **stillness**
['stɪlnəs] *n* : calma *f*, silencio *m*
stilt ['stɪlt] *n* : zanco *m* — **stilted** ['stɪltəd]
adj : forzado
stimulate ['stɪmjə,leɪt] *vt* **-lated; -lating**
: estimular — **stimulant** ['stɪmjələnt] *n*
: estimulante *m* — **stimulation**
[,stɪmjə'leɪʃən] *n* : estimulación *f* —
stimulus ['stɪmjələs] *n, pl* **-li** [-,laɪ] : estímulo *m*
sting ['stɪŋ] *v* **stung** ['stʌŋ]; **stinging**
: picar — ~ *n* : picadura *f* — **stinger**
['stɪŋər] *n* : aguijón *m*
stingy ['stɪndʒi] *adj* **stingier; -est** : tacaño — **stinginess** ['stɪndʒinəs] *n* : ta-
cañería *f*
stink ['stɪŋk] *vi* **stank** ['stæŋk] *or* **stunk**
['stʌŋk]; **stunk; stinking** : apestar, oler
mal — ~ *n* : hedor *m*, peste *f* *fam*
stint ['stɪnt] *vi* ~ **on** : escatimar — ~ *n*
: período *m*
stipulate ['stɪpjə,leɪt] *vt* **-lated; -lating**
: estipular
stir ['stər] *v* **stirred; stirring** *vt* **1** : remover, revolver **2** MOVE : mover **3** IN-
CITE : incitar **4** *or* ~ **up** : despertar
(memorias, etc.), provocar (ira, etc.)
— *vi* : moverse, agitarse — ~ *n* COM-
MOTION : revuelo *m*
stirrup ['stərəp, 'stɪr-] *n* : estribo *m*
stitch ['stɪtʃ] *n* **1** : puntada *f* **2** PAIN : punzada *f* (en el costado) — ~ *v* : coser
stock ['stɑk] *n* **1** INVENTORY : existencias
fpl **2** SECURITIES : acciones *fpl* **3** AN-
CESTRY : linaje *m*, estirpe *f* **4** BROTH
: caldo *m* **5 out of** ~ : agotado **6 take
~ of** : evaluar — ~ *vt* : surtir, abastecer — *vi* ~ **up on** : abastecerse de —
stockbroker ['stɑk,broːkər] *n* : corredor
m, -dora *f* de bolsa
stocking ['stɑkɪŋ] *n* : media *f*

stock market *n* : bolsa *f* — **stockpile**
['stɑk,paɪl] *n* : reservas *fpl* — ~ *vt*
-piled; -piling : almacenar — **stocky**
['stɑki] *adj* **stockier; -est** : robusto,
fornido
stodgy ['stɑdʒi] *adj* **stodgier; -est 1**
DULL : pesado **2** OLD-FASHIONED : anticuado
stoic ['stoɪk] *n* : estoico *m*, -ca *f* — ~ *or*
stoical [-ɪkəl] *adj* : estoico — **stoicism** ['stoɪə,sɪzəm] *n* : estoicismo *m*
stoke ['stoːk] *vt* **stoked; stoking** : echar
carbón o leña a
stole[1] ['stoːl] → **steal**
stole[2] *n* : estola *f*
stolen → **steal**
stomach ['stʌmɪk] *n* : estómago *m* — ~
vt : aguantar, soportar — **stomachache** ['stʌmɪk,eɪk] *n* : dolor *m* de
estómago
stone ['stoːn] *n* **1** : piedra *f* **2** : hueso *m*
(de una fruta) — ~ *vt* : apedrear; ston-
ing : apedrear — **stony** ['stoːni] *adj*
stonier; -est : pedregoso **2 a ~ silence** : un silencio sepulcral
stood → **stand**
stool ['stuːl] *n* : taburete *m*
stoop ['stuːp] *vi* **1** : agacharse **2** ~ **to**
: rebajarse a — ~ *n* **have a ~** : ser
encorvado
stop ['stɑp] *v* **stopped; stopping** *vt* **1**
PLUG : tapar **2** PREVENT : impedir **3**
HALT : parar, detener **4** CEASE : dejar de
— *vi* **1** : detenerse, parar **2** CEASE
: cesar, dejar **3** ~ **by** : visitar — ~ *n*
1 : parada *f*, alto *m* **2 come to a ~**
: pararse, detenerse **3 put a ~ to**
: poner fin a — **stopgap** ['stɑp,gæp] *n*
: arreglo *m* provisorio — **stoplight**
['stɑp,laɪt] *n* : semáforo *m* — **stoppage**
['stɑpɪdʒ] *n or* **work ~** : paro *m* —
stopper ['stɑpər] *n* : tapón *m*
store ['stoːr] *vt* **stored; storing** : guardar
(comida, etc.), almacenar (datos, mercancías, etc.) — ~ *n* **1** SUPPLY : reserva *f* **2** SHOP : tienda *f* — **storage**
['stoːrɪdʒ] *n* : almacenamiento *m* —
storehouse ['stoːr,haʊs] *n* : almacén *m*
— **storekeeper** ['stoːr,kiːpər] *n* : tendero *m*, -ra *f* — **storeroom** ['stoːr,ruːm,
-,rʊm] *n* : almacén *m*
stork ['stɔrk] *n* : cigüeña *f*
storm ['stɔrm] *n* : tormenta *f*, tempestad
f — ~ *vi* **1** RAGE : ponerse furioso **2**
~ **in/out** : entrar/salir furioso — *vt*
ATTACK : asaltar — **stormy** ['stɔrmi]
adj **stormier; -est** : tormentoso
story[1] ['stoːri] *n, pl* **stories 1** TALE
: cuento *m* **2** ACCOUNT : historia *f* **3**
RUMOR : rumor *m*

story[2] *n* FLOOR : piso *m*, planta *f*
stout ['staʊt] *adj* 1 BRAVE : valiente 2 RESOLUTE : tenaz 3 STURDY : fuerte 4 FAT : corpulento
stove[1] ['stoːv] *n* 1 : estufa *f* (para calentar) 2 RANGE : cocina *f*
stove[2] → **stave**
stow ['stoː] *vt* 1 : guardar 2 LOAD : cargar — *vi* ~ **away** : viajar de polizón — **stowaway** ['stoːə,weɪ] *n* : polizón *m*
straddle ['strædəl] *vt* -**dled**; -**dling** : sentarse a horcajadas sobre
straggle ['strægəl] *vi* -**gled**; -**gling** : rezagarse, quedarse atrás — **straggler** ['strægələr] *n* : rezagado *m*, -da *f*
straight ['streɪt] *adj* 1 : recto, derecho 2 : lacio (dícese del pelo) 3 HONEST : franco 4 TIDY : arreglado — ~ *adv* 1 DIRECTLY : derecho 2 EXACTLY : justo 3 CLEARLY : con claridad 4 FRANKLY : con franqueza — **straightaway** ['streɪt,weɪ, -,weɪ] *adv* : inmediatamente — **straighten** ['streɪtən] *vt* 1 : enderezar 2 ~ **up** : arreglar — **straightforward** [streɪt'fɔrwərd] *adj* 1 FRANK : franco 2 CLEAR : claro, sencillo
strain[1] ['streɪn] *n* 1 LINEAGE : linaje *m* 2 STREAK : veta *f* 3 VARIETY : variedad *f* 4 ~**s** *npl* : acordes *mpl* (de música)
strain[2] *vt* 1 : forzar (la vista o la voz) 2 FILTER : colar 3 : tensar (relaciones, etc.) 4 ~ **a muscle** : sufrir un esguince 5 ~ **oneself** : hacerse daño — *vi* : esforzarse (por) — ~ *n* 1 STRESS : tensión *f* 2 SPRAIN : esguince *m* — **strainer** ['streɪnər] *n* : colador *m*
strait ['streɪt] *n* 1 : estrecho *m* 2 **in dire** ~**s** : en grandes apuros
strand[1] ['strænd] *vt* **be** ~**ed** : quedar(se) varado
strand[2] *n* 1 : hebra *f* 2 **a** ~ **of hair** : un pelo
strange ['streɪndʒ] *adj* **stranger; -est** 1 : extraño, raro 2 UNFAMILIAR : desconocido — **strangely** ['streɪndʒli] *adv* : de manera extraña — **strangeness** ['streɪndʒnəs] *n* 1 : rareza *f* 2 UNFAMILIARITY : lo desconocido — **stranger** ['streɪndʒər] *n* : desconocido *m*, -da *f*
strangle ['stræŋgəl] *vt* -**gled**; -**gling** : estrangular
strap ['stræp] *n* 1 : correa *f* 2 *or* **shoulder** ~ : tirante *m* — ~ *vt* **strapped; strapping** : sujetar con una correa — **strapless** ['stræpləs] *adj* : sin tirantes — **strapping** ['stræpɪŋ] *adj* : robusto, fornido
strategy ['strætədʒi] *n, pl* -**gies** : estrate-

gia *f* — **strategic** [strə'tiːdʒɪk] *adj* : estratégico
straw ['strɔ] *n* 1 : paja *f* 2 *or* **drinking** ~ : pajita *f* 3 **the last** ~ : el colmo
strawberry ['strɔ,beri] *n, pl* -**ries** : fresa *f*
stray ['streɪ] *n* : animal *m* perdido — ~ *vi* 1 : perderse, extraviarse 2 : apartarse (de un grupo, etc.) 3 DEVIATE : desviarse — ~ *adj* : perdido
streak ['striːk] *n* 1 : raya *f* 2 VEIN : veta *f* 3 ~ **of luck** : racha *f* de suerte — *vi* ~ **by** : pasar como una flecha
stream ['striːm] *n* 1 : arroyo *m*, riachuelo *m* 2 FLOW : chorro *m*, corriente *f* — ~ *vi* : correr — **streamer** ['striːmər] *n* 1 PENNANT : banderín *m* 2 : serpentina *f* (de papel) — **streamlined** ['striːm,laɪnd] *adj* 1 : aerodinámico 2 EFFICIENT : eficiente
street ['striːt] *n* : calle *f* — **streetcar** ['striːt,kɑr] *n* : tranvía *m* — **streetlight** ['striːt,laɪt] *n* : farol *m*
strength ['streŋkθ] *n* 1 : fuerza *f* 2 FORTITUDE : fortaleza *f* 3 TOUGHNESS : resistencia *f*, solidez *f* 4 INTENSITY : intensidad *f* 5 ~**s and weaknesses** : virtudes y defectos — **strengthen** ['streŋkθən] *vt* 1 : fortalecer 2 REINFORCE : reforzar 3 INTENSIFY : intensificar
strenuous ['strenjʊəs] *adj* 1 : enérgico 2 ARDUOUS : duro, riguroso
stress ['stres] *n* 1 : tensión *f* 2 EMPHASIS : énfasis *m* 3 : acento *m* (en lingüística) — ~ *vt* 1 EMPHASIZE : enfatizar 2 *or* ~ **out** : estresar — **stressful** ['stresfəl] *adj* : estresante
stretch ['stretʃ] *vt* 1 : estirar (músculos, elástico, etc.) 2 EXTEND : extender 3 ~ **the truth** : forzar la verdad — *vi* 1 : estirarse 2 EXTEND : extenderse — ~ *n* 1 : extensión *f* 2 ELASTICITY : elasticidad *f* 3 EXPANSE : tramo *m* 4 : período *m* (de tiempo) — **stretcher** ['stretʃər] *n* : camilla *f*
strew ['struː] *vt* **strewed; strewed** *or* **strewn** ['struːn]; **strewing** : esparcir (semillas, etc.), desparramar (papeles, etc.)
stricken ['strɪkən] *adj* ~ **with** : aquejado de (una enfermedad), afligido por (tristeza, etc.)
strict ['strɪkt] *adj* : estricto — **strictly** *adv* ~ **speaking** : en rigor
stride ['straɪd] *vi* **strode** ['stroːd]; **stridden** ['strɪdən]; **striding** : ir dando zancadas — ~ *n* 1 : zancada *f* 2 **make great** ~**s** : hacer grandes progresos
strident ['straɪdənt] *adj* : estridente
strife ['straɪf] *n* : conflictos *mpl*

strike ['straɪk] *v* **struck** ['strʌk]; **struck; striking** *vt* **1** HIT : golpear **2** *or* ~ **against** : chocar contra **3** *or* ~ **out** DELETE : tachar **4** : dar (la hora) **5** IMPRESS : impresionar **6** : descubrir (oro o petróleo) **7** it ~s me as... : me parece... **8** ~ **up** START : entablar — *vi* **1** : golpear **2** ATTACK : atacar **3** : declararse en huelga **4** : sobrevenir (dícese de una enfermedad, etc.) — ~ *n* **1** BLOW : golpe *m* **2** : huelga *f*, paro *m Lat* (de trabajadores) **3** ATTACK : ataque *m* — **strikebreaker** ['straɪk‚breɪkər] *n* : esquirol *mf* — **striker** ['straɪkər] *n* : huelguista *mf* — **striking** ['straɪkɪŋ] *adj* : notable, llamativo

string ['strɪŋ] *n* **1** : cordel *m* **2** : sarta *f* (de perlas, insultos, etc.), serie *f* (de eventos, etc.) **3** ~**s** *npl* : cuerdas *fpl* (en música) — ~ *vt* **strung** ['strʌŋ]; **stringing 1** : ensartar **2** *or* ~ **up** : colgar — **string bean** *n* : habichuela *f* verde

stringent ['strɪndʒənt] *adj* : estricto, severo

strip¹ ['strɪp] *v* **stripped; stripping** *vt* **1** REMOVE : quitar **2** UNDRESS : desnudar **3** ~ **s.o. of sth** : despojar a algn de algo — *vi* UNDRESS : desnudarse

strip² *n* : tira *f*

stripe ['straɪp] *n* : raya *f*, lista *f* — **striped** ['straɪpt, 'straɪpəd] *adj* : a rayas, rayado

strive ['straɪv] *vi* **strove** ['stro:v]; **striven** ['strɪvən] *or* **strived; striving 1** ~ **for** : luchar por **2** ~ **to** : esforzarse por

strode → **stride**

stroke ['stro:k] *vt* **stroked; stroking** : acariciar — ~ *n* **1** : golpe *m* **2** : derrame *m* cerebral (en medicina)

stroll ['stro:l] *vi* : pasearse — ~ *n* : paseo *m* — **stroller** ['stro:lər] *n* : cochecito *m* (para niños)

strong ['strɔŋ] *adj* : fuerte — **stronghold** ['strɔŋ‚ho:ld] *n* : bastión *m* — **strongly** ['strɔŋli] *adv* **1** DEEPLY : profundamente **2** WHOLEHEARTEDLY : totalmente **3** VIGOROUSLY : enérgicamente

strove → **strive**

struck → **strike**

structure ['strʌktʃər] *n* : estructura *f* — **structural** ['strʌktʃərəl] *adj* : estructural

struggle ['strʌgəl] *vi* **-gled; -gling 1** : forcejear **2** STRIVE : luchar — ~ *n* : lucha *f*

strum ['strʌm] *vt* **strummed; strumming** : rasguear

strung → **string**

strut ['strʌt] *vi* **strutted; strutting** : pavonearse — ~ *n* : puntal *m* (en construcción)

stub ['stʌb] *n* : colilla *f* (de un cigarrillo), cabo *m* (de un lápiz, etc.), talón *m* (de un cheque) — ~ *vt* **stubbed; stubbing** ~ **one's toe** : darse en el dedo

stubble ['stʌbəl] *n* : barba *f* de varios días

stubborn ['stʌbərn] *adj* **1** : terco, obstinado **2** PERSISTENT : tenaz

stucco ['stʌko:] *n*, *pl* **stuccoes** *or* **stuccoes** : estuco *m*

stuck → **stick** — **stuck–up** ['stʌk'ʌp] *adj* : engreído, creído *fam*

stud¹ ['stʌd] *n* : semental *m* (animal)

stud² *n* **1** NAIL, TACK : tachuela *f*, tachón *m* **2** *or* ~ **earring** : arete *m Lat*, pendiente *m Spain* **3** : montante *m* (en construcción)

student ['stu:dənt, 'stju:-] *n* : estudiante *mf*; alumno *m*, -na *f* (de un colegio) — **studio** ['stu:di‚o:, 'stju:-] *n*, *pl* **studios** : estudio *m* — **study** ['stʌdi] *n*, *pl* **studies** : estudio *m* — ~ *v* **studied; studying** : estudiar — **studious** ['stu:diəs, 'stju:-] *adj* : estudioso

stuff ['stʌf] *n* **1** : cosas *fpl* **2** MATTER, SUBSTANCE : cosa *f* **3** **know one's** ~ : ser experto — ~ *vt* **1** FILL : rellenar **2** CRAM : meter — **stuffing** ['stʌfɪŋ] *n* : relleno *m* — **stuffy** ['stʌfi] *adj* **stuffier; -est 1** STODGY : pesado, aburrido **2** : tapado (dícese de la nariz) **3** ~ **rooms** : salas *fpl* mal ventiladas

stumble ['stʌmbəl] *vi* **-bled; -bling 1** : tropezar **2** ~ **across** *or* **upon** : tropezar con

stump ['stʌmp] *n* **1** : muñón *m* (de una pierna, etc.) **2** *or* **tree** ~ : tocón *m* — ~ *vt* : dejar perplejo

stun ['stʌn] *vt* **stunned; stunning 1** : aturdir (con un golpe) **2** ASTONISH : dejar atónito

stung → **sting**

stunk → **stink**

stunning ['stʌnɪŋ] *adj* **1** : increíble, sensacional **2** STRIKING : imponente

stunt¹ ['stʌnt] *vt* : atrofiar

stunt² *n* : proeza *f* (acrobática)

stupendous [stʊ'pendəs, stju-] *adj* : estupendo

stupid ['stu:pəd, 'stju:-] *adj* **1** : estúpido **2** SILLY : tonto, bobo — **stupidity** [stʊ'pɪdəti, stju-] *n* : tontería *f*, estupidez *f*

sturdy ['stərdi] *adj* **sturdier; -est 1** : fuerte, resistente **2** ROBUST : robusto

stutter ['stʌtər] *vi* : tartamudear — ~ *n* : tartamudeo *m*

sty ['staɪ] *n* **1** *pl* **sties** PIGPEN : pocilga *f*

2 *pl* **sties** *or* **styes** : orzuelo *m* (en el ojo)
style ['staɪl] *n* **1** : estilo *m* **2** FASHION : moda *f* **3 be in ~** : estar de moda — **~** *vt* **styled; styling** : peinar (pelo), diseñar (vestidos, etc.) — **stylish** ['staɪlɪʃ] *adj* : elegante, chic — **stylist** ['staɪlɪst] *n* : estilista *mf*
suave ['swɑv] *adj* : refinado y afable
sub[1] ['sʌb] *vi* **subbed; subbing** → **substitute** — **~** *n* → **substitute**
sub[2] *n* → **submarine**
subconscious [ˌsʌb'kɑntʃəs] *adj* : subconsciente — **~** *n* : subconsciente *m*
subdivide [ˌsʌbdə'vaɪd, 'sʌbdəˌvaɪd] *vt* **-vided; -viding** : subdividir — **subdivision** ['sʌbdəˌvɪʒən] *n* : subdivisión *f*
subdue [səb'duː, -'djuː] *vt* **-dued; -duing 1** CONQUER : sojuzgar **2** CONTROL : dominar **3** SOFTEN : atenuar — **subdued** *adj* : apagado
subject ['sʌbdʒɪkt] *n* **1** : sujeto *m* **2** : súbdito *m*, -ta *f* (de un gobierno) **3** TOPIC : tema *m* — **~** *adj* **1** : sometido **2** **~ to** : sujeto a — **~** [səb'dʒɛkt] *vt* **~ to** : someter a — **subjective** [səb'dʒɛktɪv] *adj* : subjetivo
subjunctive [səb'dʒʌŋktɪv] *n* : subjuntivo *m* — **subjunctive** *adj* : subjuntivo
sublime [sə'blaɪm] *adj* : sublime
submarine ['sʌbməˌriːn, ˌsʌbmə'-] *adj* : submarino — **~** *n* : submarino *m*
submerge [səb'mərdʒ] *v* **-merged; -merging** *vt* : sumergir — *vi* : sumergirse
submit [səb'mɪt] *v* **-mitted; -mitting** *vi* **1** YIELD : rendirse **2 ~ to** : someterse a — *vt* : presentar — **submission** [səb'mɪʃən] *n* **1** : sumisión *f* **2** PRESENTATION : presentación *f* — **submissive** [səb'mɪsɪv] *adj* : sumiso
subordinate [sə'bɔrdənət] *adj* : subordinado — **~** *n* : subordinado *m*, -da *f* — **~** [sə'bɔrdənˌeɪt] *vt* **-nated; -nating** : subordinar
subpoena [sə'piːnə] *n* : citación *f*
subscribe [səb'skraɪb] *vi* **-scribed; -scribing ~ to** : suscribirse a (una revista, etc.), suscribir (una opinión, etc.) — **subscriber** [səb'skraɪbər] *n* : suscriptor *m*, -tora *f* (de una revista, etc.); abonado *m*, -da *f* (de un servicio) — **subscription** [səb'skrɪpʃən] *n* : suscripción *f*
subsequent ['sʌbsɪˌkwɛnt, -səˌkwɛnt] *adj* **1** : subsiguiente **2 ~ to** : posterior a — **subsequently** ['sʌbˌkwɛntli, -kwənt-] *adv* : posteriormente
subservient [səb'sərviənt] *adj* : servil
subside [səb'saɪd] *vi* **-sided; -siding 1**

SINK : hundirse **2** : amainar (dícese de tormentas, pasiones, etc.), remitir (dícese de fiebres, etc.)
subsidiary [səb'sɪdiˌɛri] *adj* : secundario — **~** *n, pl* **-ries** : filial *f*
subsidy ['sʌbsədi] *n, pl* **-dies** : subvención *f* — **subsidize** ['sʌbsəˌdaɪz] *vt* **-dized; -dizing** : subvencionar
subsistence [səb'sɪstəns] *n* : subsistencia *f* — **subsist** [səb'sɪst] *vi* : subsistir
substance ['sʌbstəns] *n* : sustancia *f*
substandard [ˌsʌb'stændərd] *adj* : inferior
substantial [səb'stæntʃəl] *adj* **1** CONSIDERABLE : considerable **2** STURDY : sólido **3** : sustancioso (dícese de una comida, etc.) — **substantially** [səb'stæntʃəli] *adv* : considerablemente
substitute ['sʌbstəˌtuːt, -ˌtjuːt] *n* : sustituto *m*, -ta *f* (de una persona); sucedáneo *m* (de una cosa) — **~** *vt* **-tuted; -tuting** : sustituir — **substitution** [ˌsʌbstə'tuːʃən, -'tjuː-] *n* : sustitución *f*
subterranean [ˌsʌbtə'reɪniən] *adj* : subterráneo
subtitle ['sʌbˌtaɪtəl] *n* : subtítulo *m*
subtle ['sʌtəl] *adj* **-tler; -tlest** : sutil — **subtlety** ['sʌtəlti] *n, pl* **-ties** : sutileza *f*
subtraction [səb'trækʃən] *n* : resta *f* — **subtract** [səb'trækt] *vt* : restar
suburb ['sʌˌbərb] *n* **1** : barrio *m* residencial, suburbio *m* **2 the ~s** : las afueras — **suburban** [sə'bərbən] *adj* : de las afueras (de una ciudad)
subversion [səb'vərʒən] *n* : subversión *f* — **subversive** [səb'vərsɪv] *adj* : subversivo
subway ['sʌbˌweɪ] *n* : metro *m*
succeed [sək'siːd] *vt* : suceder a — *vi* : tener éxito (dícese de personas), dar resultado (dícese de planes, etc.) — **success** [sək'sɛs] *n* : éxito *m* — **successful** [sək'sɛsfəl] *adj* : de éxito, exitoso *Lat* — **successfully** *adv* : con éxito
succession [sək'sɛʃən] *n* **1** : sucesión *f* **2 in ~** : sucesivamente, seguidos — **successive** [sək'sɛsɪv] *adj* : sucesivo — **successor** [sək'sɛsər] *n* : sucesor *m*, -sora *f*
succinct [sək'sɪŋkt, sə'sɪŋkt] *adj* : sucinto
succulent ['sʌkjələnt] *adj* : suculento
succumb [sə'kʌm] *vi* : sucumbir
such ['sʌtʃ] *adj* **1** : tal **2 ~ as** : como **3 ~ a pity!** : ¡qué lástima! — **~** *pron* **1** : tal **2 and ~** : y cosas por el estilo — **as ~** : como tal — **~** *adv* **1** VERY : muy **2 ~ a nice man!** : ¡qué hombre tan simpático! **3 ~ that** : de tal manera que

suck ['sʌk] *vt* **1** *or* ~ **on** : chupar **2** *or* ~ **up** : sorber (bebidas), aspirar (con una máquina) — **sucker** ['sʌkər] *n* **1** SHOOT : chupón *m* **2** FOOL : imbécil *mf* — **suckle** ['sʌkəl] *vt* **-led; -ling** : amamantar — **suction** ['sʌkʃən] *n* : succión *f*

sudden ['sʌdən] *adj* **1** : repentino **2 all of a** ~ : de repente — **suddenly** ['sʌdənli] *adv* : de repente

suds ['sʌdz] *npl* : espuma *f* (de jabón)

sue ['suː] *vt* **sued; suing** : demandar (por)

suede ['sweɪd] *n* : ante *m*, gamuza *f*

suet ['suːət] *n* : sebo *m*

suffer ['sʌfər] *vi* : sufrir — *vt* **1** : sufrir **2** BEAR : tolerar — **suffering** ['sʌfərɪŋ] *n* : sufrimiento *m*

suffice [sə'faɪs] *vi* **-ficed; -ficing** : bastar — **sufficient** [sə'fɪʃənt] *adj* : suficiente — **sufficiently** [sə'fɪʃəntli] *adv* : (lo) suficientemente

suffix ['sʌˌfɪks] *n* : sufijo *m*

suffocate ['sʌfəˌkeɪt] *v* **-cated; -cating** *vt* : asfixiar — *vi* : asfixiarse — **suffocation** [ˌsʌfəˈkeɪʃən] *n* : asfixia *f*

suffrage ['sʌfrɪdʒ] *n* : sufragio *m*

sugar ['ʃugər] *n* : azúcar *mf* — **sugarcane** ['ʃugərˌkeɪn] *n* : caña *f* de azúcar — **sugary** ['ʃugəri] *adj* : azucarado

suggestion [səg'dʒestʃən, sə-] *n* **1** : sugerencia *f* **2** TRACE : indicio *m* — **suggest** [səg'dʒest, sə-] *vt* **1** : sugerir **2** INDICATE : indicar

suicide ['suːəˌsaɪd] *n* **1** : suicidio *m* (acto) **2** : suicida *mf* (persona) — **suicidal** [ˌsuːə'saɪdəl] *adj* : suicida

suit ['suːt] *n* **1** LAWSUIT : pleito *m* **2** : traje *m* (ropa) **3** : palo *m* (de naipes) — ~ *vt* **1** ADAPT : adaptar **2** BEFIT : ser apropiado para **3** ~ **s.o.** : convenir a algn (dícese de fechas, etc.), quedar bien a algn (dícese de ropa) — **suitable** ['suːtəbəl] *adj* : apropiado — **suitcase** ['suːtˌkeɪs] *n* : maleta *f*, valija *f Lat*

suite ['swiːt, *for 2 also* 'suːt] *n* **1** : suite *f* (de habitaciones) **2** : juego *m* (de muebles)

suitor ['suːtər] *n* : pretendiente *m*

sulfur ['sʌlfər] *n* : azufre *m*

sulk ['sʌlk] *vi* : enfurruñarse *fam* — **sulky** ['sʌlki] *adj* **sulkier; -est** : malhumorado

sullen ['sʌlən] *adj* : hosco

sultry ['sʌltri] *adj* **sultrier; -est 1** : bochornoso **2** SENSUAL : sensual

sum ['sʌm] *n* : suma *f* — ~ *vt* **summed; summing** ~ **up** : resumir — **summarize** ['sʌməˌraɪz] *v* **-rized; -rizing** : resumir — **summary** ['sʌməri] *n, pl* **-ries** : resumen *m*

summer ['sʌmər] *n* : verano *m*

summit ['sʌmət] *n* : cumbre *f*

summon ['sʌmən] *vt* **1** : llamar (a algn), convocar (una reunión) **2** : citar (en derecho) — **summons** ['sʌmənz] *n, pl* **summonses** SUBPOENA : citación *f*

sumptuous ['sʌmptʃuəs] *adj* : suntuoso

sun ['sʌn] *n* : sol *m* — **sunbathe** ['sʌnˌbeɪð] *vi* **-bathed; -bathing** : tomar el sol — **sunbeam** ['sʌnˌbiːm] *n* : rayo *m* de sol — **sunburn** ['sʌnˌbərn] *n* : quemadura *f* de sol

Sunday ['sʌnˌdeɪ, -di] *n* : domingo *m*

sundry ['sʌndri] *adj* : varios, diversos

sunflower ['sʌnˌflaʊər] *n* : girasol *m*

sung → **sing**

sunglasses ['sʌnˌglæsəz] *npl* : gafas *fpl* de sol, lentes *mpl* de sol

sunk → **sink** — **sunken** ['sʌŋkən] *adj* : hundido

sunlight ['sʌnˌlaɪt] *n* : (luz *f* del) sol *m* — **sunny** ['sʌni] *adj* **-nier; -est** : soleado — **sunrise** ['sʌnˌraɪz] *n* : salida *f* del sol — **sunset** ['sʌnˌset] *n* : puesta *f* del sol — **sunshine** ['sʌnˌʃaɪn] *n* : sol *m*, luz *f* del sol — **suntan** ['sʌnˌtæn] *n* : bronceado *m*

super ['suːpər] *adj* : súper *fam*

superb [sʊ'pərb] *adj* : magnífico, espléndido

superficial [ˌsuːpərˈfɪʃəl] *adj* : superficial

superfluous [sʊ'pərfluəs] *adj* : superfluo

superimpose [ˌsuːpərɪm'poːz] *vt* **-posed; -posing** : sobreponer

superintendent [ˌsuːpərɪn'tendənt] *n* **1** : superintendente *mf* (de policía) **2 or building** ~ : portero *m*, -ra *f* **3** *or* **school** ~ : director *m*, -tora *f* (de un colegio)

superior [sʊ'pɪriər] *adj* : superior — ~ *n* : superior *m* — **superiority** [sʊˌpɪriˈɔːrəti] *n, pl* **-ties** : superioridad *f*

superlative [sʊ'pərlətɪv] *adj* **1** : superlativo (en gramática) **2** EXCELLENT : excepcional — ~ *n* : superlativo *m*

supermarket ['suːpərˌmɑrkət] *n* : supermercado *m*

supernatural [ˌsuːpərˈnætʃərəl] *adj* : sobrenatural

superpower ['suːpərˌpaʊər] *n* : superpotencia *f*

supersede [ˌsuːpərˈsiːd] *vt* **-seded; -seding** : reemplazar, suplantar

supersonic [ˌsuːpərˈsɑnɪk] *adj* : supersónico

superstition [ˌsuːpərˈstɪʃən] *n* : superstición *f* — **superstitious** [ˌsuːpərˈstɪʃəs] *adj* : supersticioso

supervisor ['suːpərˌvaɪzər] *n* : supervisor

supper ['sʌpər] *n* : cena *f*, comida *f*

supplant [sə'plænt] *vt* : suplantar

supple ['sʌpəl] *adj* **-pler; -plest** : flexible

supplement ['sʌpləmənt] *n* : suplemento *m* — ~ ['sʌpləment] *vt* : complementar — **supplementary** [,sʌplə'mentəri] *adj* : suplementario

supply [sə'plaɪ] *vt* **-plied; -plying 1** : suministrar **2 ~ with** : proveer de — ~ *n, pl* **-plies 1** : suministro *m*, provisión *f* **2 ~ and demand** : oferta y demanda **3 supplies** *npl* PROVISIONS : provisiones *fpl*, víveres *mpl* — **supplier** [sə'plaɪər] *n* : proveedor *m*, -dora *f*

support [sə'port] *vt* **1** BACK : apoyar **2** : mantener (una familia, etc.) **3** PROP UP : sostener — ~ *n* **1** : apoyo *m* (moral), ayuda *f* (económica) **2** PROP : soporte *m* — **supporter** [sə'portər] *n* : partidario *m*, -ria *f*

suppose [sə'poːz] *vt* **-posed; -posing 1** : suponer **2 be ~d to (do sth)** : tener que (hacer algo) — **supposedly** *adv* : supuestamente

suppress [sə'pres] *vt* **1** : reprimir **2** : suprimir (noticias, etc.) — **suppression** [sə'preʃən] *n* **1** : represión *f* **2** : supresión *f* (de noticias)

supreme [su'priːm] *adj* : supremo — **supremacy** [su'preməsi] *n, pl* **-cies** : supremacía *f*

sure ['ʃur] *adj* **surer; -est 1** : seguro **2 make ~ that** : asegurarse de que — ~ *adv* **1** OF COURSE : por supuesto, claro **2 it ~ is hot!** : ¡qué calor! — **surely** ['ʃurli] *adv* : seguramente

surfing ['sərfɪŋ] *n* : surf *m*, surfing *m*

surface ['sərfəs] *v* **-faced; -facing** *vi* : salir a la superficie — *vt* : revestir

surfeit ['sərfət] *n* : exceso *m*

surfing ['sərfɪŋ] *n* : surf *m*, surfing *m*

surge ['sərdʒ] *vi* **surged; surging 1** SWELL : hincharse **2** SWARM : moverse en tropel — ~ *n* **1** : oleaje *m* (del mar), oleada *f* (de gente) **2** INCREASE : aumento *m* (súbito)

surgeon ['sərdʒən] *n* : cirujano *m*, -na *f* — **surgery** ['sərdʒəri] *n, pl* **-geries** : cirugía *f* — **surgical** ['sərdʒɪkəl] *adj* : quirúrgico

surly ['sərli] *adj* **surlier; -est** : hosco, arisco

surmount [sər'maʊnt] *vt* : superar

surname ['sər,neɪm] *n* : apellido *m*

surpass [sər'pæs] *vt* : superar

surplus ['sər,plʌs] *n* : excedente *m*

surprise [sə'praɪz, sər-] *n* **1** : sorpresa *f* **2 take by ~** : sorprender — ~ *vt* **-prised; -prising** : sorprender — **surprising** [sə'praɪzɪŋ, sər-] *adj* : sorprendente

surrender [sə'rendər] *vt* : entregar, rendir — *vi* : rendirse — ~ *n* **1** : rendición *m* (de una ciudad, etc.), entrega *f* (de posesiones)

surrogate ['sərəgət, -,geɪt] *n* : sustituto *m*

surround [sə'raʊnd] *vt* : rodear — **surroundings** [sə'raʊndɪŋz] *npl* : ambiente *m*

surveillance [sər'veɪlənts, -'veɪljənts, -'veɪənts] *n* : vigilancia *f*

survey [sər'veɪ] *vt* **-veyed; -veying 1** : medir (un solar) **2** INSPECT : inspeccionar **3** POLL : sondear — ~ ['sər,veɪ] *n, pl* **-veys 1** INSPECTION : inspección *f* **2** : medición *f* (de un solar) **3** POLL : encuesta *f*, sondeo *m* — **surveyor** [sər'veɪər] *n* : agrimensor *m*, -sora *f*

survive [sər'vaɪv] *v* **-vived; -viving** *vi* : sobrevivir — *vt* : sobrevivir a — **survival** [sər'vaɪvəl] *n* : supervivencia *f* — **survivor** [sər'vaɪvər] *n* : superviviente *mf*

susceptible [sə'septəbəl] *adj* **~ to** : propenso a — **susceptibility** [sə,septə'bɪləti] *n, pl* **-ties** : propensión *f* (a enfermedades, etc.)

suspect ['sʌs,pekt, sə'spekt] *adj* : sospechoso — ~ ['sʌs,pekt] *n* : sospechoso *m*, -sa *f* — ~ [sə'spekt] *vt* : sospechar (algo), sospechar de (algn)

suspend [sə'spend] *vt* : suspender — **suspense** [sə'spents] *n* **1** : incertidumbre *m* **2** : suspenso *m Lat*, suspense *m Spain* (en el cine, etc.) — **suspension** [sə'spentʃən] *n* : suspensión *f*

suspicion [sə'spɪʃən] *n* : sospecha *f* — **suspicious** [sə'spɪʃəs] *adj* **1** QUESTIONABLE : sospechoso **2** DISTRUSTFUL : suspicaz

sustain [sə'steɪn] *vt* **1** : sostener **2** SUFFER : sufrir

swagger ['swægər] *vi* : pavonearse

swallow¹ ['swɑloː] *v* : tragar — ~ *n* : trago *m*

swallow² *n* : golondrina *f* (pájaro)

swam → swim

swamp ['swɑmp] *n* : pantano *m*, ciénaga *f* — ~ *vt* : inundar — **swampy** ['swɑmpi] *adj* **swampier; -est** : pantanoso, cenagoso

swan ['swɑn] *n* : cisne *f*

swap ['swɑp] *vt* **swapped; swapping 1**

: intercambiar **2** ~ **sth for sth** : cambiar algo por algo **3** ~ **sth with s.o.** : cambiar algo a algn — ~ *n* : cambio *m*

swarm ['swɔrm] *n* : enjambre *m* — ~ *vi* : enjambrar

swat ['swɑt] *vt* **swatted; swatting** : aplastar (un insecto)

sway ['sweɪ] *n* **1** : balanceo *m* **2** INFLUENCE : influjo *m* — ~ *vi* : balancearse — *vt* : influir en

swear ['swær] *v* **swore** ['swor]; **sworn** ['sworn]; **swearing** *vi* **1** : jurar **2** CURSE : decir palabrotas — *vt* : jurar — **swearword** ['swær,wərd] *n* : palabrota *f*

sweat ['swɛt] *vi* **sweat** *or* **sweated; sweating** : sudar — ~ *n* : sudor *m* — **sweater** ['swɛtər] *n* : suéter *m* — **sweatshirt** ['swɛt,ʃərt] *n* : sudadera *f* — **sweaty** ['swɛti] *adj* **sweatier; -est** : sudado

Swedish ['swiːdɪʃ] *adj* : sueco — ~ *n* : sueco *m* (idioma)

sweep ['swiːp] *v* **swept** ['swɛpt]; **sweeping** *vt* **1** : barrer **2** ~ **aside** : apartar **3** ~ **through** : extenderse por — *vi* : barrer — ~ *n* **1** : barrido *m* **2** : movimiento *m* circular (de la mano, etc.) **3** SCOPE : alcance *m* — **sweeping** ['swiːpɪŋ] *adj* **1** WIDE : amplio **2** EXTENSIVE : extenso — **sweepstakes** ['swiːp,steɪks] *ns & pl* : lotería *f*

sweet ['swiːt] *adj* **1** : dulce **2** PLEASANT : agradable — ~ *n* : dulce *m* — **sweeten** ['swiːtən] *vt* : endulzar — **sweetener** ['swiːtənər] *n* : endulzante *m* — **sweetheart** ['swiːt,hɑrt] *n* **1** : novio *m*, -via *f* **2** (*used as a form of address*) : cariño *m* — **sweetness** ['swiːtnəs] *n* : dulzura *f* — **sweet potato** *n* : batata *f*, boniato *m*

swell ['swɛl] *vi* **swelled; swelled** *or* **swollen** ['swoːlən, 'swʌl-]; **swelling 1** *or* ~ **up** : hincharse **2** INCREASE : aumentar, crecer — ~ *n* **1** : oleaje *m* (del mar) — **swelling** ['swɛlɪŋ] *n* : hinchazón *f*

sweltering ['swɛltərɪŋ] *adj* : sofocante

swept → **sweep**

swerve ['swərv] *vi* **swerved; swerving** : virar bruscamente

swift ['swɪft] *adj* : rápido — **swiftly** *adv* : rápidamente

swig ['swɪg] *n* : trago *m* — ~ *vi* **swigged; swigging** : beber a tragos

swim ['swɪm] *vi* **swam** ['swæm]; **swum** ['swʌm]; **swimming 1** : nadar **2** REEL : dar vueltas — ~ *n* **1** : baño *m* **2 go for a** ~ : ir a nadar — **swimmer** ['swɪmər] *n* : nadador *m*, -dora *f*

swindle ['swɪndəl] *vt* **-dled; -dling** : estafar, timar — ~ *n* : estafa *f*, timo *m fam*

swine ['swaɪn] *ns & pl* : cerdo *m*, -da *f*

swing ['swɪŋ] *v* **swung** ['swʌŋ]; **swinging** *vt* **1** : balancear, hacer oscilar **2** MANAGE : arreglar — *vi* **1** : balancearse, oscilar **2** SWIVEL : girar — ~ *n* **1** : vaivén *m*, balanceo *m* **2** SHIFT : cambio *m* **3** : columpio *m* (para niños) **4 in full** ~ : en pleno proceso

swipe ['swaɪp] *v* **swiped; swiping** *vt* STEAL : birlar *fam*, robar — *vi* ~ **at** : intentar pegar

swirl ['swərl] *vi* : arremolinarse — ~ *n* **1** EDDY : remolino *m* **2** SPIRAL : espiral *f*

swish ['swɪʃ] *vt* : agitar (haciendo un sonido) — *vi* **1** RUSTLE : hacer frufrú **2** ~ **by** : pasar silbando

Swiss ['swɪs] *adj* : suizo

switch ['swɪtʃ] *n* **1** WHIP : vara *f* **2** CHANGE : cambio *m* **3** : interruptor *m*, llave *f* (de la luz, etc.) — *vt* **1** CHANGE : cambiar de **2** EXCHANGE : intercambiar **3** ~ **on** : encender, prender *Lat* **4** ~ **off** : apagar — *vi* **1** : sacudir (la cola, etc.) **2** CHANGE : cambiar **3** SWAP : intercambiarse — **switchboard** ['swɪtʃ,bord] *n* : centralita *f*, conmutador *m Lat*

swivel ['swɪvəl] *vi* **-veled** *or* **-velled; -veling** *or* **-velling** : girar (sobre un pivote)

swollen → **swell**

swoon ['swuːn] *vi* : desvanecerse

swoop ['swuːp] *vi* ~ **down on** : abatirse sobre — ~ *n* : descenso *m* en picada

sword ['sord] *n* : espada *f* — **swordfish** ['sord,fɪʃ] *n* : pez *m* espada

swore, sworn → **swear**

swum → **swim**

swung → **swing**

syllable ['sɪləbəl] *n* : sílaba *f*

syllabus ['sɪləbəs] *n, pl* **-bi** [-,baɪ] *or* **-buses** : programa *m* (de estudios)

symbol ['sɪmbəl] *n* : símbolo *m* — **symbolic** [sɪm'bɑlɪk] *adj* : simbólico — **symbolism** ['sɪmbə,lɪzəm] *n* : simbolismo *m* — **symbolize** ['sɪmbə,laɪz] *vt* **-ized; -izing** : simbolizar

symmetry ['sɪmətri] *n, pl* **-tries** : simetría *f* — **symmetrical** [sə'metrɪkəl] *adj* : simétrico

sympathy ['sɪmpəθi] *n, pl* **-thies 1** COMPASSION : compasión *f* **2** UNDERSTANDING : comprensión *f* **3** CONDOLENCES : pésame *m* **4 sympathies** *npl* LOYALTY : simpatías *fpl* — **sympathize** ['sɪmpə,θaɪz] *vi* **-thized; -thizing 1** ~ **with** PITY : compadecerse de **2** ~

with UNDERSTAND : comprender —
sympathetic [ˌsɪmpˈθεt̬ɪk] *adj* **1** COM-
PASSIONATE : compasivo **2** UNDER-
STANDING : comprensivo
symphony [ˈsɪmfəni] *n, pl* **-nies** : sinfonía *f*
symposium [sɪmˈpoːziəm] *n, pl* **-sia**
[-ziə] *or* **-siums** : simposio *m*
symptom [ˈsɪmptəm] *n* : síntoma *m* —
symptomatic [ˌsɪmptəˈmæt̬ɪk] *adj*
: sintomático
synagogue [ˈsɪnəgag, -ˌgɔg] *n* : sinagoga *f*
synchronize [ˈsɪŋkrənaɪz, ˈsɪn-] *vt*
-nized; -nizing : sincronizar
syndrome [ˈsɪndroːm] *n* : síndrome *m*
synonym [ˈsɪnəˌnɪm] *n* : sinónimo *m* —

synonymous [səˈnanəməs] *adj* : sinónimo
synopsis [səˈnapsɪs] *n, pl* **-opses** [-ˌsiːz]
: sinopsis *f*
syntax [ˈsɪnˌtæks] *n* : sintaxis *f*
synthesis [ˈsɪnθəsɪs] *n, pl* **-theses** [-ˌsiːz]
: síntesis *f* — **synthesize** [ˈsɪnθəˌsaɪz] *vt*
-sized; -sizing : sintetizar — **synthetic** [sɪnˈθεt̬ɪk] *adj* : sintético
syphilis [ˈsɪfələs] *n* : sífilis *f*
Syrian [ˈsɪriən] *adj* : sirio
syringe [səˈrɪndʒ, ˈsɪrɪndʒ] *n* : jeringa *f*,
jeringuilla *f*
syrup [ˈsərəp, ˈsɪrəp] *n* : jarabe *m*
system [ˈsɪstəm] *n* **1** : sistema *m* **2** BODY
: organismo *m* **3 digestive ~** : apara-
to *m* digestivo — **systematic** [ˌsɪstə-
ˈmæt̬ɪk] *adj* : sistemático

T

t [ˈtiː] *n, pl* **t's** *or* **ts** [ˈtiːz] : t *f*, vigésima
letra del alfabeto inglés
tab [ˈtæb] *n* **1** TAG : etiqueta *f* **2** FLAP
: lengüeta *f* **3** ACCOUNT : cuenta *f* **4
keep ~s on** : vigilar
table [ˈteɪbəl] *n* **1** : mesa *f* **2** LIST : tabla *f*
3 ~ of contents : índice *m* de mate-
rias — **tablecloth** [ˈteɪbəlˌklɔθ] *n*
: mantel *m* — **tablespoon** [ˈteɪbəl-
ˌspuːn] *n* **1** : cuchara *f* grande **2** : cucharada *f* (cantidad)
tablet [ˈtæblət] *n* **1** PAD : bloc *m* **2** PILL
: pastilla *f* **3** *or* **stone ~** : lápida *f*
tabloid [ˈtæˌblɔɪd] *n* : tabloide *m*
taboo [təˈbuː, tæ-] *adj* : tabú — *n*
: tabú *m*
tacit [ˈtæsɪt] *adj* : tácito
taciturn [ˈtæsɪˌtərn] *adj* : taciturno
tack [ˈtæk] *vt* **1** : fijar con tachuelas **2 ~
on** ADD : añadir — **~** *n* **1** : tachuela *f*
2 change ~ : cambiar de rumbo
tackle [ˈtækəl] *n* **1** GEAR : aparejo *m* **2**
: placaje *m*, tacle *m Lat* (acción) — **~**
vt **-led; -ling 1** : placar, taclear *Lat* **2**
CONFRONT : abordar
tacky [ˈtæki] *adj* **tackier; -est 1** : pegajoso **2** GAUDY : de mal gusto
tact [ˈtækt] *n* : tacto *m* — **tactful**
[ˈtæktfəl] *adj* : diplomático, discreto
tactical [ˈtæktɪkəl] *adj* : táctico — **tactic**
[ˈtæktɪk] *n* : táctica *f* — **tactics** [ˈtæk-
tɪks] *ns & pl* : táctica *f*
tactless [ˈtæktləs] *adj* : indiscreto
tadpole [ˈtædˌpoːl] *n* : renacuajo *m*
tag[1] [ˈtæg] *n* LABEL : etiqueta *f* — **~** *v*
tagged; tagging *vt* : etiquetar — *vi*

~ along with s.o. : acompañar a algn
tag[2] *vt* : tocar (en varios juegos)
tail [ˈteɪl] *n* **1** : cola *f* **2 ~s** *npl* : cruz *f*
(de una moneda) — **~** *vt* FOLLOW
: seguir
tailor [ˈteɪlər] *n* : sastre *m*, -tra *f* — **~** *vt*
1 : confeccionar (ropa) **2** ADAPT : adaptar
taint [ˈteɪnt] *vt* : contaminar
take [ˈteɪk] *v* **took** [ˈtʊk]; **taken** [ˈteɪkən];
taking *vt* **1** : tomar **2** BRING : llevar **3**
REMOVE : sacar **4** BEAR : soportar,
aguantar **5** ACCEPT : aceptar **6 I ~ it
that...** : supongo que... **7 ~ a bath**
: bañarse **8 ~ a walk** : dar un paseo **9
~ back** : retirar (palabras, etc.) **10 ~
in** ALTER : achicar **11 ~ in** GRASP : entender **12 ~ in** TRICK : engañar **13 ~
off** REMOVE : quitar, quitarse (ropa) **14
~ on** : asumir (una responsabilidad,
etc.) **15 ~ out** : sacar **16 ~ over**
: tomar el poder de **17 ~ place** : tener
lugar **18 ~ up** SHORTEN : acortar **19
~ up** OCCUPY : ocupar — *vi* **1** : prender (dícese de una vacuna, etc.) **2 ~
off** : despegar (dícese de aviones, etc.)
3 ~ over : asumir el mando — **~** *n* **1**
PROCEEDS : ingresos *mpl* **2** : toma *f* (en
el cine) — **takeoff** [ˈteɪkˌɔf] *n* : despegue *m* (de un avión, etc.) —
takeover [ˈteɪkˌoːvər] *n* : toma *f* (de
poder, etc.), adquisición *f* (de una empresa)
talcum powder [ˈtælkəm] *n* : polvos *mpl*
de talco
tale [ˈteɪl] *n* : cuento *m*

talent ['tælənt] *n* : talento *m* — **talented** ['tæləntəd] *adj* : talentoso

talk ['tɔk] *vi* **1** : hablar **2** ~ **about** : hablar de **3** ~ **to/with** : hablar con — *vt* **1** SPEAK : hablar **2** ~ **over** : hablar de, discutir — ~ *n* **1** CHAT : conversación *f* **2** SPEECH : charla *f* — **talkative** ['tɔkətɪv] *adj* : hablador

tall ['tɔl] *adj* **1** : alto **2 how** ~ **are you?** : ¿cuánto mides?

tally ['tæli] *n*, *pl* **-lies** : cuenta *f* — ~ *v* **-lied; -lying** *vt* RECKON : calcular — *vi* MATCH : concordar, cuadrar

talon ['tælən] *n* : garra *f*

tambourine [,tæmbə'riːn] *n* : pandereta *f*

tame ['teɪm] *adj* **tamer; -est 1** : domesticado **2** DOCILE : manso **3** DULL : insípido, soso — ~ *vt* **tamed; taming** : domar

tamper ['tæmpər] *vi* ~ **with** : forzar (una cerradura), amañar (documentos, etc.)

tampon ['tæmpɑn] *n* : tampón *m*

tan ['tæn] *v* **tanned; tanning** *vt* : curtir (cuero) — *vi* : broncearse — ~ *n* **1** SUNTAN : bronceado *m* **2** : (color *m*) café *m* con leche

tang ['tæŋ] *n* : sabor *m* fuerte

tangent ['tændʒənt] *n* : tangente *f*

tangerine ['tændʒə,riːn, ,tændʒə'-] *n* : mandarina *f*

tangible ['tændʒəbəl] *adj* : tangible

tangle ['tæŋgəl] *v* **-gled; -gling** *vt* : enredar — *vi* : enredarse — ~ *n* : enredo *m*

tango ['tæŋgo] *n*, *pl* **-gos** : tango *m*

tank ['tæŋk] *n* **1** : tanque *m*, depósito *m* **2** : tanque *m* (militar) — **tanker** ['tæŋkər] *n* **1** : buque *m* tanque **2** *or* ~ **truck** : camión *m* cisterna

tantalizing ['tæntə,laɪzɪŋ] *adj* : tentador

tantrum ['tæntrəm] *n* **throw a** ~ : hacer un berrinche

tap[1] ['tæp] *n* FAUCET : llave *f*, grifo *m* *Spain* — ~ *vt* **tapped; tapping 1** : sacar (un líquido, etc.), sangrar (un árbol) **2** : intervenir (un teléfono)

tap[2] *vt* **tapped; tapping** STRIKE : tocar, dar un golpecito en — ~ *n* : golpecito *m*, toque *m*

tape ['teɪp] *n* : cinta *f* — ~ *vt* **taped; taping 1** : pegar con cinta **2** RECORD : grabar — **tape measure** *n* : cinta *f* métrica

taper ['teɪpər] *n* : vela *f* (larga) — ~ *vi* **1** NARROW : estrecharse **2** *or* ~ **off** : disminuir

tapestry ['tæpəstri] *n*, *pl* **-tries** : tapiz *m*

tar ['tɑr] *n* : alquitrán *m* — ~ *vt* **tarred; tarring** : alquitranar

tarantula [tə'ræntʃələ, -'ræntələ] *n* : tarántula *f*

target ['tɑrgət] *n* **1** : blanco *m* **2** GOAL : objetivo *m*

tariff ['tærɪf] *n* : tarifa *f*, arancel *m*

tarnish ['tɑrnɪʃ] *vt* **1** : deslustrar **2** : empañar (una reputación, etc.) — *vi* : deslustrarse

tart[1] ['tɑrt] *adj* SOUR : ácido, agrio

tart[2] *n* : pastel *m*

tartan ['tɑrtən] *n* : tartán *m*

task ['tæsk] *n* : tarea *f*

tassel ['tæsəl] *n* : borla *f*

taste ['teɪst] *v* **tasted; tasting** *vt* TRY : probar — *vi* **1** : saber **2** ~ **like** : saber a — ~ *n* **1** FLAVOR : gusto *m*, sabor *m* **2 have a** ~ **of** : probar **3 in good/bad** ~ : de buen/mal gusto — **tasteful** ['teɪstfəl] *adj* : de buen gusto — **tasteless** ['teɪstləs] *adj* **1** : sin sabor **2** COARSE : de mal gusto — **tasty** ['teɪsti] *adj* **tastier; -est** : sabroso

tatters ['tætər] *npl* : harapos *mpl* — **tattered** ['tætərd] *adj* : harapiento

tattle ['tætəl] *vi* **-tled; -tling** ~ **on s.o.** : acusar a algn

tattoo [tæ'tuː] *vt* : tatuar — ~ *n* : tatuaje *m*

taught → **teach**

taunt ['tɔnt] *n* : pulla *f*, burla *f* — ~ *vt* : mofarse de, burlarse de

taut ['tɔt] *adj* : tirante, tenso

tavern ['tævərn] *n* : taberna *f*

tax ['tæks] *vt* **1** : gravar **2** STRAIN : poner a prueba — ~ *n* **1** : impuesto *m* **2** BURDEN : carga *f* — **taxable** ['tæksəbəl] *adj* : imponible — **taxation** [tæk-'seɪʃən] *n* : impuestos *mpl* — **tax-exempt** ['tæksɪg'zempt, -eg-] *adj* : libre de impuestos

taxi ['tæksi] *n*, *pl* **taxis** : taxi *m* — ~ *vi* **taxied; taxiing** *or* **taxying; taxis** *or* **taxies** : rodar por la pista (dícese de un avión)

taxpayer ['tæks,peɪər] *n* : contribuyente *mf*

tea ['tiː] *n* : té *m*

teach ['tiːtʃ] *v* **taught** ['tɔt]; **teaching** *vt* : enseñar, dar clases de (una asignatura) — *vi* : dar clases — **teacher** ['tiːtʃər] *n* : profesor *m*, -sora *f*; maestro *m*, -tra *f* (de niños pequeños) — **teaching** ['tiːtʃɪŋ] *n* : enseñanza *f*

teacup ['tiː,kʌp] *n* : taza *f* de té

team ['tiːm] *n* : equipo *m* — ~ *vi* *or* ~ **up** : asociarse — **teammate** ['tiːm,meɪt] *n* : compañero *m*, -ra *f* de equipo — **teamwork** ['tiːm,wərk] *n* : trabajo *m* de equipo

teapot ['tiː,pɑt] *n* : tetera *f*

tear¹ ['tær] *v* **tore** ['tor]; **torn** ['torn]; **tearing** *vt* 1 : romper, rasgar 2 ~ **apart** : destrozar 3 ~ **down** : derribar 4 ~ **off** *or* ~ **out** : arrancar 5 ~ **up** : romper (papel, etc.) — *vi* 1 : romperse, rasgarse 2 RUSH : ir a toda velocidad — ~ *n* : desgarro *m*, rasgón *m*

tear² ['tɪr] *n* : lágrima *f* — **tearful** ['tɪrfəl] *adj* : lloroso

tease ['tiːz] *vt* **teased; teasing** 1 : tomar el pelo a, burlarse de 2 ANNOY : fastidiar

teaspoon ['tiːˌspuːn] *n* 1 : cucharita *f* 2 : cucharadita *f* (cantidad)

technical ['tɛknɪkəl] *adj* : técnico — **technicality** [ˌtɛknəˈkæləti] *n, pl* **-ties** : detalle *m* técnico — **technically** [-kli] *adv* : técnicamente — **technician** [tɛkˈnɪʃən] *n* : técnico *m*, -ca *f*

technique [tɛkˈniːk] *n* : técnica *f*

technological [ˌtɛknəˈlɑdʒɪkəl] *adj* : tecnológico — **technology** [tɛkˈnɑlədʒi] *n, pl* **-gies** : tecnología *f*

teddy bear ['tɛdi] *n* : oso *m* de peluche

tedious ['tiːdiəs] *adj* : tedioso, aburrido — **tedium** ['tiːdiəm] *n* : tedio *m*

tee ['tiː] *n* : tee *m* (en deportes)

teem ['tiːm] *vi* 1 POUR : llover a cántaros 2 be ~**ing with** : estar repleto de

teenage ['tiːnˌeɪdʒ] *or* **teenaged** [-ˌeɪdʒd] *adj* : adolescente — **teenager** ['tiːnˌeɪdʒər] *n* : adolescente *mf* — **teens** ['tiːnz] *npl* : adolescencia *f*

teepee → **tepee**

teeter ['tiːtər] *vi* : tambalearse

teeth → **tooth** — **teethe** ['tiːð] *vi* **teethed; teething** : echar los dientes

telecommunication [ˌtɛləkəˌmjuːnəˈkeɪʃən] *n* : telecomunicación *f*

telegram ['tɛləˌgræm] *n* : telegrama *m*

telegraph ['tɛləˌgræf] *n* : telégrafo *m* — ~ *v* : telegrafiar

telephone ['tɛləˌfoːn] *n* : teléfono *m* — ~ *v* **-phoned; -phoning** : llamar por teléfono

telescope ['tɛləˌskoːp] *n* : telescopio *m*

televise ['tɛləˌvaɪz] *vt* **-vised; -vising** : televisar — **television** ['tɛləˌvɪʒən] *n* : televisión *f*

tell ['tɛl] *v* **told** ['toːld]; **telling** *vt* 1 : decir 2 RELATE : contar 3 DISTINGUISH : distinguir 4 ~ **s.o. off** : regañar a algn — *vi* 1 : decir 2 KNOW : saber 3 SHOW : tener efecto 4 ~ **on s.o.** : acusar a algn — **teller** ['tɛlər] *n or* **bank** ~ : cajero *m*, -ra *f*

temp ['tɛmp] *n* : empleado *m*, -da *f* temporal

temper ['tɛmpər] *vt* MODERATE : temper-

ar — ~ *n* 1 MOOD : humor *m* 2 **have a bad** ~ : tener mal genio 3 **lose one's** ~ : perder los estribos — **temperament** ['tɛmpərmənt, -prə-, -pərə-] *n* : temperamento *m* — **temperamental** [ˌtɛmpərˈmɛntəl, -prə-, -pərə-] *adj* : temperamental — **temperate** ['tɛmpərət] *adj* 1 : moderado 2 ~ **zone** : zona *f* templada

temperature ['tɛmpərˌtʃur, -prə-, -pərə-, -tʃər] *n* 1 : temperatura *f* 2 **have a** ~ : tener fiebre

tempest ['tɛmpəst] *n* : tempestad *f*

temple ['tɛmpəl] *n* 1 : templo *m* 2 : sien *f* (en anatomía)

tempo ['tɛmˌpoː] *n, pl* **-pi** [-ˌpiː] *or* **-pos** 1 : tiempo *m* 2 PACE : ritmo *m*

temporarily [ˌtɛmpəˈrɛrəli] *adv* : temporalmente — **temporary** ['tɛmpəˌrɛri] *adj* : temporal

tempt ['tɛmpt] *vt* : tentar — **temptation** [tɛmpˈteɪʃən] *n* : tentación *f*

ten ['tɛn] *adj* : diez — ~ *n* : diez *m*

tenacity [təˈnæsəti] *n* : tenacidad *f* — **tenacious** [təˈneɪʃəs] *adj* : tenaz

tenant ['tɛnənt] *n* : inquilino *m*, -na *f*; arrendatario *m*, -ria *f*

tend¹ ['tɛnd] *vt* MIND : cuidar

tend² *vi* ~ **to** : tender a — **tendency** ['tɛndənsi] *n, pl* **-cies** : tendencia *f*

tender¹ ['tɛndər] *adj* 1 : tierno 2 PAINFUL : dolorido

tender² *vt* : presentar — ~ *n* 1 : oferta *f* 2 **legal** ~ : moneda *f* de curso legal

tenderloin ['tɛndərˌlɔɪn] *n* : lomo *f* (de cerdo o vaca)

tenderness ['tɛndərnəs] *n* : ternura *f*

tendon ['tɛndən] *n* : tendón *m*

tenet ['tɛnət] *n* : principio *m*

tennis ['tɛnəs] *n* : tenis *m*

tenor ['tɛnər] *n* : tenor *m*

tense¹ ['tɛns] *n* : tiempo *m* (de un verbo)

tense² *v* **tensed; tensing** *vt* : tensar — *vi* : tensarse — ~ *adj* **tenser; tensest** : tenso — **tension** ['tɛntʃən] *n* : tensión *f*

tent ['tɛnt] *n* : tienda *f* de campaña

tentacle ['tɛntɪkəl] *n* : tentáculo *m*

tentative ['tɛntətɪv] *adj* 1 HESITANT : vacilante 2 PROVISIONAL : provisional

tenth ['tɛnθ] *adj* : décimo — ~ *n* 1 : décimo *m*, -ma *f* (en una serie) 2 : décimo *m* (en matemáticas)

tenuous ['tɛnjuəs] *adj* : tenue, endeble

tepid ['tɛpɪd] *adj* : tibio

term ['tərm] *n* 1 WORD : término *m* 2 PERIOD : período *m* 3 **be on good** ~**s** : tener buenas relaciones 4 **in** ~**s of** : con respecto a — ~ *vt* : calificar de

terminal ['tərmənəl] *adj* : terminal — ∼ *n* **1** : terminal *m* **2** *or* **bus** ∼ : terminal *f*

terminate ['tərmə,neɪt] *v* **-nated; -nating** *vi* : terminar(se) — *vt* : poner fin a — **termination** [,tərmə'neɪʃən] *n* : terminación *f*

termite ['tər,maɪt] *n* : termita *f*

terrace ['terəs] *n* : terraza *f*

terrain [tə'reɪn] *n* : terreno *m*

terrestrial [tə'restriəl] *adj* : terrestre

terrible ['terəbəl] *adj* : espantoso, terrible — **terribly** ['terəbli] *adv* : terriblemente

terrier ['teriər] *n* : terrier *mf*

terrific [tə'rɪfɪk] *adj* **1** HUGE : tremendo **2** EXCELLENT : estupendo

terrify ['terə,faɪ] *vt* **-fied; -fying** : aterrar, aterrorizar — **terrifying** ['terə,faɪŋ] *adj* : aterrador

territory ['terə,tori] *n, pl* **-ries** : territorio *m* — **territorial** [,terə'toriəl] *adj* : territorial

terror ['terər] *n* : terror *m* — **terrorism** ['terər,ɪzəm] *n* : terrorismo *m* — **terrorist** ['terərɪst] *n* : terrorista *mf* — **terrorize** ['terər,aɪz] *vt* **-ized; -izing** : aterrorizar

terse ['tərs] *adj* **terser; tersest** : seco, lacónico

test ['test] *n* **1** TRIAL : prueba *f* **2** EXAM : examen *m*, prueba *f* **3** : análisis *m* (en medicina) — *vt* **1** TRY : probar **2** QUIZ : examinar **3** : analizar (la sangre, etc.), examinar (los ojos, etc.)

testament ['testəmənt] *n* **1** WILL : testamento *m* **2** **the Old/New Testament** : el Antiguo/Nuevo Testamento

testicle ['testɪkəl] *n* : testículo *m*

testify ['testə,faɪ] *v* **-fied; -fying** : testificar

testimony ['testə,moni] *n, pl* **-nies** : testimonio *m*

test tube *n* : probeta *f*, tubo *m* de ensayo

tetanus ['tetənəs] *n* : tétano *m*

tether ['teðər] *vt* : atar

text ['tekst] *n* : texto *m* — **textbook** ['tekst,bʊk] *n* : libro *m* de texto

textile ['tek,staɪl, 'tekstəl] *n* : textil *m*

texture ['tekstʃər] *n* : textura *f*

than ['ðæn] *conj & prep* : que, de (con cantidades)

thank ['θæŋk] *vt* **1** : agradecer, dar (las) gracias a **2** ∼ **you!** : ¡gracias! — **thankful** ['θæŋkfəl] *adj* : agradecido — **thankfully** ['θæŋkfəli] *adv* **1** : con agradecimiento **2** FORTUNATELY : gracias a Dios — **thanks** ['θæŋks] *npl* **1** : agradecimiento *m* **2** ∼! : ¡gracias!

Thanksgiving [θæŋks'gɪvɪŋ, 'θæŋks,-] *n* : día *m* de Acción de Gracias

that ['ðæt] *pron, pl* **those** ['ðoːz] **1** : ése, ésa, eso **2** (*more distant*) : aquél, aquélla, aquello **3** **is** ∼ **you?** : ¿eres tú? **4** **like** ∼ : así **5** ∼ **is...** : es decir... **6** **those who...** : los que... — ∼ *conj* : que — ∼ *adj, pl* **those 1** : ese, esa **2** (*more distant*) : aquel, aquella **3** ∼ **one** : ése, ésa — ∼ *adv* : tan

thatched ['θætʃt] *adj* : con techo de paja

thaw ['θɔ] *vt* : descongelar (alimentos), derretir (hielo) — *vi* **1** : descongelarse **2** MELT : derretirse — ∼ *n* : deshielo *m*

the [ðə, *before vowel sounds usu* ði:] *art* **1** : el, la, los, las **2** PER : por — ∼ *adv* **1** ∼ **sooner** ∼ **better** : cuanto más pronto, mejor **2 I like this one** ∼ **best** : éste es el que más me gusta

theater *or* **theatre** ['θiːətər] *n* : teatro *m* — **theatrical** [θi'ætrɪkəl] *adj* : teatral

theft ['θeft] *n* : robo *m*, hurto *m*

their ['ðer] *adj* : su, sus, de ellos, de ellas — **theirs** ['ðerz] *pron* **1** : (el) suyo, (la) suya, (los) suyos, (las) suyas **2** **some friends of** ∼ : unos amigos suyos, unos amigos de ellos

them ['ðem] *pron* **1** (*used as direct object*) : los, las **2** (*used as indirect object*) : les, se **3** (*used as object of a preposition*) : ellos, ellas

theme ['θiːm] *n* **1** : tema *m* **2** ESSAY : trabajo *m* (escrito)

themselves [ðəm'selvz, ðem-] *pron* **1** (*used reflexively*) : se **2** (*used emphatically*) : ellos mismos, ellas mismas **3** (*used after a preposition*) : sí (mismos), sí (mismas)

then ['ðen] *adv* **1** : entonces **2** NEXT : luego, después **3** BESIDES : además — ∼ *adj* : entonces

thence ['ðens, 'θents] *adv* : de ahí (en adelante)

theology [θi'alədʒi] *n, pl* **-gies** : teología *f* — **theological** [,θiə'ladʒɪkəl] *adj* : teológico

theorem ['θiːərəm, 'θirəm] *n* : teorema *m* — **theoretical** [,θiːə'retɪkəl] *adj* : teórico — **theory** ['θiːəri, 'θiri] *n, pl* **-ries** : teoría *f*

therapeutic [,θerə'pjuːtɪk] *adj* : terapéutico — **therapist** ['θerəpɪst] *n* : terapeuta *mf* — **therapy** ['θerəpi] *n, pl* **-pies** : terapia *f*

there ['ðer] *adv* **1** *or* **over** ∼ : allí, allá **2** *or* **right** ∼ : ahí **3** **in** ∼ : ahí (dentro) **4** ∼**, it's done!** : ¡listo! **5** **up/down** ∼ : ahí arriba/abajo **6**

who's ~? : ¿quién es? — ~ *pron* 1 ~ is/are : hay 2 ~ are three of us : somos tres — thereabouts *or* thereabout [,ðærə'bauts, -'baut; 'ðærə,-] *adv* or ~ : por ahí — thereafter [ðær-'æftər] *adv* : después — thereby [ðær-'baı, 'ðær,baı] *adv* : así — therefore ['ðær,for] *adv* : por lo tanto

thermal ['θərməl] *adj* : térmico

thermometer [θər'mɑmətər] *n* : termómetro *m*

thermos ['θərməs] *n* : termo *m*

thermostat ['θərmə,stæt] *n* : termostato *m*

thesaurus [θɪ'sɔrəs] *n, pl* -**sauri** [-'sɔr,aı] *or* -**sauruses** [-'sɔrəsəz] : diccionario *m* de sinónimos

these → **this**

thesis ['θi:sɪs] *n, pl* **theses** ['θi:,si:z] : tesis *f*

they ['ðeı] *pron* 1 : ellos, ellas 2 where are ~? : ¿dónde están? 3 as ~ say : como dicen — **they'd** ['ðeıd] (*contraction of* they had *or* they would) → have, would — **they'll** ['ðeıl, ðel] (*contraction of* they shall *or* they will) → shall, will — **they're** ['ðer] (*contraction of* they are) → be — **they've** ['ðeıv] (*contraction of* they have) → have

thick ['θɪk] *adj* 1 : grueso 2 DENSE : espeso 3 : a ~ accent : un acento marcado 4 it's two inches ~ : tiene dos pulgadas de grosor — ~ *n* in the ~ of : en medio de — **thicken** ['θɪkən] *vt* : espesar — *vi* : espesarse — **thicket** ['θɪkət] *n* : matorral *m* — **thickness** ['θɪknəs] *n* : grosor *m*, espesor *m*

thief ['θi:f] *n, pl* **thieves** ['θi:vz] : ladrón *m*, -drona *f*

thigh ['θaı] *n* : muslo *m*

thimble ['θɪmbəl] *n* : dedal *m*

thin ['θɪn] *adj* **thinner; -est** 1 : delgado 2 : ralo (dícese del pelo) 3 WATERY : claro, aguado 4 FINE : fino — ~ *v* **thinned; thinning** *vt* DILUTE : diluir — *vi* : ralear (dícese del pelo)

thing ['θɪŋ] *n* 1 : cosa *f* 2 for one ~ : en primer lugar 3 how are ~s? : ¿qué tal? 4 it's a good ~ that... : menos mal que... 5 the important ~ is... : lo importante es...

think ['θɪŋk] *v* **thought** ['θɔt]; **thinking** *vt* 1 : pensar 2 BELIEVE : creer 3 ~ up : idear — *vi* 1 : pensar 2 ~ about *or* ~ of CONSIDER : pensar en 3 ~ of REMEMBER : acordarse de 4 what do you ~ of it? : ¿qué te parece? — **thinker** ['θɪŋkər] *n* : pensador *m*, -dora *f*

third ['θərd] *adj* : tercero — ~ *or* third-

ly [-li] *adv* : en tercer lugar — ~ *n* 1 : tercero *m*, -ra *f* (en una serie) 2 : tercero *m* (en matemáticas) — **Third World** *n* : Tercer Mundo *m*

thirst ['θərst] *n* : sed *f* — **thirsty** ['θərsti] *adj* **thirstier; -est** 1 : sediento 2 be ~ : tener sed

thirteen [,θər'ti:n] *adj* : trece — ~ *n* : trece *m* — **thirteenth** [,θər'ti:nθ] *adj* : décimo tercero — ~ *n* 1 : décimotercero *m*, -ra *f* (en una serie) 2 : treceavo *m* (en matemáticas)

thirty ['θərti] *adj* : treinta — ~ *n, pl* **thirties** : treinta *m* — **thirtieth** ['θərtiəθ] *adj* : trigésimo — ~ *n* 1 : trigésimo *m*, -ma *f* (en una serie) 2 : treintavo *m* (en matemáticas)

this ['ðɪs] *pron, pl* **these** ['ði:z] 1 : éste, ésta, esto 2 like ~ : así — ~ *adj, pl* **these** 1 : este, esta 2 ~ one : éste, ésta 3 ~ way : por aquí — ~ *adv* ~ **big** : así de grande

thistle ['θɪsəl] *n* : cardo *m*

thong ['θɔŋ] *n* 1 : correa *f* 2 SANDAL : chancla *f*

thorn ['θɔrn] *n* : espina *f* — **thorny** ['θɔrni] *adj* : espinoso

thorough ['θəro:] *adj* 1 : meticuloso 2 COMPLETE : completo — **thoroughly** *adv* 1 : a fondo 2 COMPLETELY : completamente — **thoroughbred** ['θəro,bred] *adj* : de pura sangre — **thoroughfare** ['θəro,fær] *n* : vía *f* pública

those → **that**

though ['ðo:] *conj* : aunque — ~ *adv* 1 : sin embargo 2 as ~ : como si

thought ['θɔt] → **think** — ~ *n* 1 : pensamiento *m* 2 IDEA : idea *f* — **thoughtful** ['θɔtfəl] *adj* 1 : pensativo 2 KIND : amable — **thoughtless** ['θɔtləs] *adj* 1 CARELESS : descuidado 2 RUDE : desconsiderado

thousand ['θauzənd] *adj* : mil — ~ *n, pl* -**sands** *or* -**sand** : mil *m* — **thousandth** ['θauzənθ] *adj* : milésimo — ~ *n* 1 : milésimo *m*, -ma *f* (en una serie) 2 : milésimo *m* (en matemáticas)

thrash ['θræʃ] *vt* : dar una paliza a — *vi* *or* ~ **around** : agitarse, revolcarse

thread ['θred] *n* 1 : hilo *m* 2 : rosca *f* (de un tornillo) — ~ *vt* : enhilar (una aguja), ensartar (cuentas) — **threadbare** ['θred,bær] *adj* : raído

threat ['θret] *n* : amenaza *f* — **threaten** ['θretən] *v* : amenazar — **threatening** ['θretənɪŋ] *adj* : amenazador

three ['θri:] *adj* : tres — ~ *n* : tres *m* — **three hundred** *adj* : trescientos — ~ *n* : trescientos *m*

threshold ['θrɛʃˌhoːld, -ˌoːld] *n* : umbral *m*

threw → **throw**

thrift ['θrɪft] *n* : frugalidad *f* — **thrifty** ['θrɪfti] *adj* **thriftier; -est** : económico, frugal

thrill ['θrɪl] *vt* : emocionar — ~ *n* : emoción *f* — **thriller** ['θrɪlər] *n* : película *f* de suspenso *Spain*, película *f* de suspenso *Lat* — **thrilling** ['θrɪlɪŋ] *adj* : emocionante

thrive ['θraɪv] *vi* **throve** ['θroːv] *or* **thrived; thriven** ['θrɪvən] 1 FLOURISH : florecer 2 PROSPER : prosperar

throat ['θroːt] *n* : garganta *f*

throb ['θrɑb] *vi* **throbbed; throbbing** 1 PULSATE : palpitar 2 VIBRATE : vibrar 3 ~ **with pain** : tener un dolor punzante

throes ['θroːz] *npl* 1 PANGS : agonía *f* 2 **in the** ~ : en medio de

throne ['θroːn] *n* : trono *m*

throng ['θrɔŋ] *n* : muchedumbre *f*, multitud *f*

throttle ['θrɑtəl] *vt* **-tled; -tling** : estrangular — ~ *n* : válvula *f* reguladora

through ['θruː] *prep* 1 : por, a través de 2 BETWEEN : entre 3 BECAUSE OF : a causa de 4 DURING : durante 5 ~ **Monday** ~ **Friday** : de lunes a viernes — ~ *adv* 1 : de un lado a otro (en el espacio), de principio a fin (en el tiempo) 2 COMPLETELY : completamente — ~ *adj* 1 **be** ~ : haber terminado 2 ~ **traffic** : tráfico *m* de paso — **throughout** [θruːˈaʊt] *prep* : por todo (un lugar), a lo largo de (un período de tiempo)

throw ['θroː] *v* **threw** ['θruː]; **thrown** ['θroːn]; **throwing** *vt* 1 : tirar, lanzar 2 : proyectar (una sombra) 3 CONFUSE : desconcertar 4 ~ **a party** : dar una fiesta 5 ~ **away** *or* ~ **out** : tirar, botar *Lat* — *vi* ~ **up** VOMIT : vomitar — ~ *n* : tiro *m*, lanzamiento *m*

thrush ['θrʌʃ] *n* : tordo *m*, zorzal *m*

thrust ['θrʌst] *vt* **thrust; thrusting** 1 : empujar (bruscamente) 2 PLUNGE : clavar 3 ~ **upon** : imponer a — ~ *n* 1 : empujón *m* 2 : estocada *f* (en esgrima)

thud ['θʌd] *n* : ruido *m* sordo

thug ['θʌg] *n* : matón *m*

thumb ['θʌm] *n* : (dedo *m*) pulgar *m* — ~ *vt* ~ **through** : hojear — **thumbnail** ['θʌmˌneɪl] *n* : uña *f* del pulgar — **thumbtack** ['θʌmˌtæk] *n* : tachuela *f*, chinche *f Lat*

thump ['θʌmp] *vt* : golpear — *vi* : latir con fuerza (dícese del corazón) — ~ *n* : ruido *m* sordo

thunder ['θʌndər] *n* : truenos *mpl* — ~ *vi* : tronar — *vt* SHOUT : bramar — **thunderbolt** ['θʌndərˌboːlt] *n* : rayo *m* — **thunderous** ['θʌndərəs] *adj* : atronador — **thunderstorm** ['θʌndərˌstɔrm] *n* : tormenta *f* eléctrica

Thursday ['θərzˌdeɪ, -di] *n* : jueves *m*

thus ['ðʌs] *adv* 1 : así 2 THEREFORE : por lo tanto

thwart ['θwɔrt] *vt* : frustrar

thyme ['taɪm, 'θaɪm] *n* : tomillo *m*

thyroid ['θaɪˌrɔɪd] *n* : tiroides *mf*

tiara [tiˈærə, -ˈɑr-] *n* : diadema *f*

tic ['tɪk] *n* : tic *m* (nervioso)

tick[1] ['tɪk] *n* : garrapata *f* (insecto)

tick[2] *n* 1 : tictac *m* (sonido) 2 CHECK : marca *f* — ~ *vi* : hacer tictac — *vt* 1 *or* ~ **off** CHECK : marcar 2 ~ **off** ANNOY : fastidiar

ticket ['tɪkət] *n* 1 : pasaje *m* (de avión), billete *m Spain* (de tren, avión, etc.), boleto *m Lat* (de tren o autobús) 2 : entrada *f* (al teatro, etc.) 3 FINE : multa *f*

tickle ['tɪkəl] *v* **-led; -ling** *vt* 1 : hacer cosquillas a 2 AMUSE : divertir — *vi* : picar — ~ *n* : cosquilleo *m* — **ticklish** ['tɪkəlɪʃ] *adj* 1 : cosquilloso 2 TRICKY : delicado

tidal wave ['taɪdəl] *n* : maremoto *m*

tidbit ['tɪdˌbɪt] *n* MORSEL : golosina *f*

tide ['taɪd] *n* : marea *f* — ~ *vt* **tided; tiding** ~ **over** : ayudar a superar un apuro

tidy ['taɪdi] *adj* **-dier; -est** : ordenado, arreglado — ~ *vt* **-died; -dying** *or* ~ **up** : ordenar, arreglar

tie ['taɪ] *n* 1 : atadura *f*, cordón *m* 2 BOND : lazo *m* 3 : empate *m* (en deportes) 4 NECKTIE : corbata *f* — ~ *v* **tied; tying** *or* **tieing** *vt* 1 : atar, amarrar *Lat* 2 ~ **a knot** : hacer un nudo — *vi* : empatar (en deportes)

tier ['tɪr] *n* : nivel *m*, piso (de un pastel), grada *f* (de un estadio)

tiger ['taɪgər] *n* : tigre *m*

tight ['taɪt] *adj* 1 : apretado 2 SNUG : ajustado, ceñido 3 TAUT : tirante 4 STINGY : agarrado 5 SCARCE : escaso 6 **a** ~ **seal** : un cierre hermético 7 **a** ~ **spot** : un aprieto — ~ *adv* **closed** : bien cerrado — **tighten** ['taɪtən] *vt* 1 : apretar 2 TENSE : tensar 3 : hacer más estricto (reglas, etc.) — **tightly** ['taɪtli] *adv* : bien, fuerte — **tightrope** ['taɪtˌroːp] *n* : cuerda *f* floja — **tights** ['taɪts] *npl* : leotardo *m*, mallas *fpl*

tile ['taɪl] *n* 1 : azulejo *m*, baldosa *f* (de

piso) **2** *or* **roofing ~** : teja *f* — **~** *vt*
tiled; tiling 1 : revestir de azulejos,
embaldosar (un piso) **2** : tejar (un
techo)
till¹ ['tɪl] *prep & conj* → **until**
till² *vt* : cultivar
till³ *n* : caja *f* (registradora)
tilt ['tɪlt] *n* **1** : inclinación *f* **2 at full ~** : a
toda velocidad — **~** *vt* : inclinar — *vi*
: inclinarse
timber ['tɪmbər] *n* **1** : madera *f* (para
construcción) **2 BEAM** : viga *f*
timbre ['tæmbər, 'tɪm-] *n* : timbre *m*
time ['taɪm] *n* **1** : tiempo *m* **2 AGE** : época
f **3** : compás *m* (en música) **4 at ~s**
: a veces **5 at this ~** : en este momento **6 for the ~ being** : por el momento **7 from ~ to ~** : de vez en
cuando **8 have a good ~** : pasarlo
bien **9 many ~s** : muchas veces **10
on ~** : a tiempo **11 ~ after ~** : una
y otra vez **12 what ~ is it?** : ¿qué
hora es? — **~** *vt* **timed; timing**
: tomar el tiempo a (algn), cronometrar (una carrera, etc.) — **timeless**
['taɪmləs] *adj* : eterno — **timely** ['taɪm-
li] *adj* **-lier; -est** : oportuno — **timer**
['taɪmər] *n* : temporizador *m*, avisador
m (de cocina) — **times** ['taɪmz] *prep* **3
~ 4 is 12** : 3 por 4 son 12 — **timetable** ['taɪm,teɪbəl] *n* : horario *m*
timid ['tɪmɪd] *adj* : tímido
tin ['tɪn] *n* **1** : estaño *m* **2 CAN** : lata *f*,
bote *m* *Spain* — **tinfoil** ['tɪn,fɔɪl] *n*
: papel *m* (de) aluminio
tinge ['tɪndʒ] *vt* **tinged; tingeing** *or*
tinging ['tɪndʒɪŋ] : matizar — **~** *n* **1**
TINT : matiz *m* **2 TOUCH** : dejo *m*
tingle ['tɪŋgəl] *vi* **-gled; -gling** : sentir
(un) hormigueo — **~** *n* : hormigueo
m
tinker ['tɪŋkər] *vi* **~ with** : intentar
arreglar (con pequeños ajustes)
tinkle ['tɪŋkəl] *vi* **-kled; -kling** : tintinear
— **~** *n* : tintineo *m*
tint ['tɪnt] *n* : tinte *m* — **~** *vt* : teñir
tiny ['taɪni] *adj* **-nier; -est** : diminuto,
minúsculo
tip¹ ['tɪp] *v* **tipped; tipping** *vt* **TILT** : inclinar **2** *or* **~ over** : volcar — *vi* : inclinarse
tip² *n* **END** : punta *f*
tip³ *n* **ADVICE** : consejo *m* — **~** *vt* **~
off** : avisar
tip⁴ *vt* : dar una propina a — **~** *n* **GRA-
TUITY** : propina *f*
tipsy ['tɪpsi] *adj* **-sier; -est** : achispado
tiptoe ['tɪp,toː] *n* **on ~** : de puntillas —
~ *vi* **-toed; -toeing** : caminar de puntillas

tip–top ['tɪp,tɑp, -,tɑp] *adj* : excelente
tire¹ ['taɪr] *n* : neumático *m*, llanta *f* *Lat*
tire² *v* **tired; tiring** *vt* : cansar — *vi*
: cansarse — **tired** ['taɪrd] *adj* **1 ~ of**
: cansado de, harto de **2 ~ out** : agotado — **tireless** ['taɪrləs] *adj* : incansable — **tiresome** ['taɪrsəm] *adj* : pesado
tissue ['tɪʃuː] *n* **1** : pañuelo *m* de papel **2**
: tejido *m* (en biología)
title ['taɪtəl] *n* : título *m* — **~** *vt* **-tled;
-tling** : titular
to ['tuː] *prep* **1** : a **2 TOWARD** : hacia **3 IN
ORDER TO** : para **4 UP TO** : hasta **5 a
quarter ~ seven** : las siete menos
cuarto **6 be nice ~ them** : trátalos
bien **7 ten ~ the box** : diez por caja **8
the mate ~ this shoe** : el compañero de este zapato **9 two ~ four
years old** : entre dos y cuatro años de
edad **10 want ~ do** : querer hacer —
~ *adv* **1 come ~** : volver en sí **2 ~
and fro** : de un lado a otro
toad ['toːd] *n* : sapo *m*
toast ['toːst] *vt* **1** : tostar (pan, etc.) **2**
: brindar por (una persona) — **~** *n* **1**
: pan *m* tostado, tostadas *fpl* **2 DRINK**
: brindis *m* — **toaster** ['toːstər] *n*
: tostador *m*
tobacco [tə'bækoː] *n, pl* **-cos** : tabaco *m*
toboggan [tə'bɑgən] *n* : tobogán *m*
today [tə'deɪ] *adv* : hoy — **~** *n* : hoy *m*
toddler ['tɑdələr] *n* : niño *m* pequeño,
niña *f* pequeña (que comienza a caminar)
toe ['toː] *n* : dedo *m* (del pie) — **toenail**
['toː,neɪl] *n* : uña *f* (del pie)
together [tə'gɛðər] *adv* **1** : juntos **2 ~
with** : junto con
toil ['tɔɪl] *n* : trabajo *m* duro — **~** *vi*
: trabajar duro
toilet ['tɔɪlət] *n* **1 BATHROOM** : baño *m*,
servicio *m* **2** : inodoro *m* (instalación)
— **toilet paper** *n* : papel *m* higiénico
— **toiletries** ['tɔɪlətriːz] *npl* : artículos
mpl de tocador
token ['toːkən] *n* **1 SIGN** : muestra *f* **2 ME-
MENTO** : recuerdo *m* **3** : ficha *f* (para un
tren, etc.)
told → **tell**
tolerable ['tɑlərəbəl] *adj* : tolerable —
tolerance ['tɑlərənts] *n* : tolerancia *f* —
tolerant ['tɑlərənt] *adj* : tolerante —
tolerate ['tɑlə,reɪt] *vt* **-ated; -ating**
: tolerar
toll¹ ['toːl] *n* **1** : peaje *m* **2 death ~**
: número *m* de muertos **3 take a ~ on**
: afectar
toll² *vi* **RING** : tocar, doblar — **~** *n*
: tañido *m*

tomato [tə'meɪṭo, -'ma-] *n, pl* **-toes** : tomate *m*

tomb ['tuːm] *n* : tumba *f*, sepulcro *m* — **tombstone** ['tuːm,stoːn] *n* : lápida *f*

tome ['toːm] *n* : tomo *m*

tomorrow [tə'mɑro] *adv* : mañana — ~ *n* : mañana *m*

ton ['tʌn] *n* : tonelada *f*

tone ['toːn] *n* : tono *m* — ~ *vt* **toned; toning** *or* ~ **down** : atenuar

tongs ['tɑŋz, 'tɔŋz] *npl* : tenazas *fpl*

tongue ['tʌŋ] *n* : lengua *f*

tonic ['tɑnɪk] *n* **1** : tónico *m* **2** *or* ~ **water** : tónica *f*

tonight [tə'naɪt] *adv* : esta noche — ~ *n* : esta noche *f*

tonsil ['tɑntsəl] *n* : amígdala *f*

too ['tuː] *adv* **1** ALSO : también **2** EXCESSIVELY : demasiado

took → **take**

tool ['tuːl] *n* : herramienta *f* — **toolbox** ['tuːl,bɑks] *n* : caja *f* de herramientas

toot ['tuːt] *vt* : sonar (un claxon, etc.) — ~ *n* **1** WHISTLE : pitido *m* **2** HONK : bocinazo *m*

tooth ['tuːθ] *n, pl* **teeth** ['tiːθ] : diente *m* — **toothache** ['tuːθ,eɪk] *n* : dolor *m* de muelas — **toothbrush** ['tuːθ,brʌʃ] *n* : cepillo *m* de dientes — **toothpaste** ['tuːθ,peɪst] *n* : pasta *f* de dientes, pasta *f* dentífrica

top[1] ['tɑp] *n* **1** : parte *f* superior **2** SUMMIT : cima *f*, cumbre *f* **3** COVER : tapa *f*, cubierta *f* **4 on** ~ **of** : encima de — ~ *vt* **topped; topping 1** COVER : rematar (un edificio, etc.), bañar (un pastel, etc.) **2** SURPASS : superar **3** ~ **off** : llenar — ~ *adj* **1** : de arriba, superior **2** BEST : mejor **3 a** ~ **executive** : un alto ejecutivo

top[2] *n* : trompo *m* (juguete)

topic ['tɑpɪk] *n* : tema *m* — **topical** ['tɑpɪkəl] *adj* : de interés actual

topmost ['tɑp,moːst] *adj* : más alto

topple ['tɑpəl] *v* **-pled; -pling** *vi* : caerse — *vt* **1** OVERTURN : volcar **2** OVERTHROW : derrocar

torch ['tɔrtʃ] *n* : antorcha *f*

tore → **tear**[1]

torment ['tɔr,mɛnt] *n* : tormento *m* — ~ ['tɔr,mɛnt, 'tɔr-] *vt* : atormentar

torn → **tear**[1]

tornado [tɔr'neɪdo] *n, pl* **-does** *or* **-dos** : tornado *m*

torpedo [tɔr'piːdo] *n, pl* **-does** : torpedo *m* — ~ *vt* : torpedear

torrent ['tɔrənt] *n* : torrente *m*

torrid ['tɔrɪd] *adj* : tórrido

torso ['tɔr,soː] *n, pl* **-sos** *or* **-si** [-,siː] : torso *m*

tortilla [tɔr'tiːjə] *n* : tortilla *f*

tortoise ['tɔrṭəs] *n* : tortuga *f* (terrestre) — **tortoiseshell** ['tɔrṭəs,ʃɛl] *n* : carey *m*, concha *f*

tortuous ['tɔrtʃuəs] *adj* : tortuoso

torture ['tɔrtʃər] *n* : tortura *f* — ~ *vt* **-tured; -turing** : torturar

toss ['tɔs, 'tɑs] *vt* **1** : tirar, lanzar **2** : mezclar (una ensalada) — *vi* ~ **and turn** : dar vueltas — ~ *n* : lanzamiento *m*

tot ['tɑt] *n* : pequeño *m*, -ña *f*

total ['toːṭəl] *adj* : total — ~ *n* : total *m* — ~ *vt* **-taled** *or* **-talled; -taling** *or* **-talling 1** : ascender a **2** *or* ~ **up** : totalizar, sumar

totalitarian [toː,tælə'teriən] *adj* : totalitario

tote ['toːt] *vt* **toted; toting** : llevar

totter ['tɑṭər] *vi* : tambalearse

touch ['tʌtʃ] *vt* **1** : tocar **2** MOVE : conmover **3** AFFECT : afectar **4** ~ **up** : retocar — *vi* : tocarse — ~ *n* **1** : tacto *m* (sentido) **2** HINT : toque *m* **3** BIT : pizca *f* **4 keep in** ~ : mantenerse en contacto **5 lose one's** ~ : perder la habilidad — **touchdown** ['tʌtʃ,daun] *n* : touchdown *m* — **touchy** ['tʌtʃi] *adj* **touchier; -est 1** : delicado **2 be** ~ **about** : picarse a la mención de

tough ['tʌf] *adj* **1** : duro **2** STRONG : fuerte **3** STRICT : severo **4** DIFFICULT : difícil — **toughen** ['tʌfən] *vt* *or* ~ **up** : endurecer — *vi* : endurecerse — **toughness** ['tʌfnəs] *n* : dureza *f*

tour ['tur] *n* **1** : viaje *m* (por un país, etc.), visita *f* (a un museo, etc.) **2** : gira *f* (de un equipo, etc.) — ~ *vi* **1** TRAVEL : viajar **2** : hacer una gira (dícese de equipos, etc.) — *vt* : viajar por, recorrer — **tourist** ['turɪst, 'tər-] *n* : turista *mf*

tournament ['tərnəmənt, 'tur-] *n* : torneo *m*

tousle ['tauzəl] *vt* **-sled; -sling** : despeinar

tout ['taut] *vt* : promocionar

tow ['toː] *vt* : remolcar — ~ *n* : remolque *m*

toward ['tord, tə'word] *or* **towards** ['tordz, tə'wordz] *prep* : hacia

towel ['tauəl] *n* : toalla *f*

tower ['tauər] *n* : torre *f* — ~ *vi* ~ **over** : descollar sobre — **towering** ['tauərɪŋ] *adj* : altísimo

town ['taun] *n* **1** VILLAGE : pueblo *m* **2** CITY : ciudad *f* — **township** ['taun,ʃɪp] *n* : municipio *m*

tow truck ['toː,trʌk] *n* : grúa *f*

toxic ['tɑksɪk] *adj* : tóxico

toy ['tɔɪ] n : juguete m — ~ vi ~ **with** : juguetear con
trace ['treɪs] n 1 SIGN : rastro m, señal f 2 HINT : dejo m — ~ vt **traced; tracing** 1 : calcar (un dibujo, etc.) 2 DRAW : trazar 3 FIND : localizar
track ['træk] n 1 : pista f 2 PATH : sendero m 3 or **railroad** ~ : vía f (férrea) 4 **keep** ~ **of** : llevar la cuenta de — ~ vt TRAIL : seguir la pista de
tract[1] ['trækt] n 1 EXPANSE : extensión f 2 : tracto m (en anatomía)
tract[2] n PAMPHLET : folleto m
traction ['trækʃən] n : tracción f
tractor ['træktər] n 1 : tractor m 2 or -**trailer** : camión m (con remolque)
trade ['treɪd] n 1 PROFESSION : oficio m 2 COMMERCE : comercio m 3 INDUSTRY : industria f 4 EXCHANGE : cambio m — ~ v **traded; trading** vi : comerciar — vt ~ **sth with s.o.** : cambiar algo a algn — **trademark** ['treɪd,mɑrk] n : marca f registrada
tradition [trə'dɪʃən] n : tradición f — **traditional** [trə'dɪʃənəl] adj : tradicional
traffic ['træfɪk] n : tráfico m — ~ vi **trafficked; trafficking** ~ **in** : traficar con — **traffic light** n : semáforo m
tragedy ['trædʒədi] n, pl -**dies** : tragedia f — **tragic** ['trædʒɪk] adj : trágico
trail ['treɪl] vi 1 DRAG : arrastrar 2 LAG : rezagarse 3 ~ **off** : apagarse — vt 1 DRAG : arrastrar 2 PURSUE : seguir la pista de — ~ n 1 : rastro m, huellas fpl 2 PATH : sendero m — **trailer** ['treɪlər] n 1 : remolque m 2 : caravana f (vivienda)
train ['treɪn] n 1 : tren m 2 : cola f (de un vestido) 3 SERIES : serie f 4 ~ **of thought** : hilo m (de las ideas) — ~ vt 1 : adiestrar, entrenar (atletas, etc.) 2 AIM : apuntar — vi : prepararse, entrenarse (en deportes, etc.) — **trainer** ['treɪnər] n : entrenador m, -dora f
trait ['treɪt] n : rasgo m
traitor ['treɪtər] n : traidor m, -dora f
tramp ['træmp] vi : caminar (pesadamente) — ~ n VAGRANT : vagabundo m, -da f
trample ['træmpəl] vt -**pled; -pling** : pisotear
trampoline [,træmpə'liːn, 'træmpə,-] n : trampolín m
trance ['trænts] n : trance m
tranquillity or **tranquility** [træŋ'kwɪləti] n : tranquilidad f — **tranquil** ['træŋkwəl] adj : tranquilo — **tranquilize** ['træŋkwə,laɪz] vt -**ized; -izing** : tranquilizar — **tranquilizer** ['træŋkwə,laɪzər] n : tranquilizante m

transaction [træn'zækʃən] n : transacción f
transatlantic [,træntsət'læntɪk, ,trænz-] adj : transatlántico
transcend [træn'send] vt 1 : ir más allá de 2 OVERCOME : superar
transcribe [træn'skraɪb] vt -**scribed; -scribing** : transcribir — **transcript** ['træn,skrɪpt] n : transcripción f
transfer [træns'fər, 'trænts,fər] v -**ferred; -ferring** vt 1 : transferir (fondos, etc.) 2 : trasladar (a un empleado, etc.) — vi 1 : cambiarse (de escuelas, etc.) 2 : hacer transbordo (entre trenes, etc.) — ~ ['trænts,fər] n 1 : transferencia f (de fondos, etc.), traslado m (de una persona) 2 : boleto m (para hacer transbordo) 3 DECAL : calcomanía f
transform [trænts'fɔrm] vt : transformar — **transformation** [,trænts,fər'meɪʃən] n : transformación f
transfusion [trænts'fjuːʒən] n : transfusión f
transgression [trænts'grɛʃən, trænz-] n : transgresión f — **transgress** [trænts'grɛs, trænz-] vt : transgredir
transient ['trænʃənt, 'trænsiənt] adj : pasajero
transit ['træntsɪt, 'trænzɪt] n 1 : tránsito m 2 TRANSPORTATION : transporte m — **transition** [træn'sɪʃən, -'zɪʃ-] n : transición f — **transitive** ['træntsətɪv, 'trænzə-] adj : transitivo — **transitory** ['træntsə,tori, 'trænzə-] adj : transitorio
translate [trænts'leɪt, trænz-; 'trænts,-, 'trænz,-] vt -**lated; -lating** : traducir — **translation** [trænts'leɪʃən, trænz-] n : traducción f — **translator** [trænts'leɪtər, trænz-; 'trænts,-, 'trænz,-] n : traductor m, -tora f
translucent [trænts'luːsənt, trænz-] adj : translúcido
transmit [trænts'mɪt, trænz-] vt -**mitted; -mitting** : transmitir — **transmission** [trænts'mɪʃən, trænz-] n : transmisión f — **transmitter** [trænts'mɪtər, trænz-; 'trænts,-, 'trænz,-] n : transmisor m
transparent [trænts'pærənt, trænz-] adj : transparente — **transparency** [trænts'pærəntsi] n, pl -**cies** : transparencia f
transpire [trænts'paɪr] vi -**spired; -spiring** 1 TURN OUT : resultar 2 HAPPEN : suceder
transplant [trænts'plænt] vt : trasplantar — ~ ['trænts,plænt] n : trasplante m
transport [trænts'port, 'trænts,-] vt : transportar — ~ ['trænts,port] n : transporte m — **transportation** [,trænts,por'teɪʃən] n : transporte m
transpose [trænts'poːz] vt -**posed;**

-posing 1 : trasponer **2** : transportar (en música)

trap ['træp] *n* : trampa *f* — ~ *vt* **trapped; trapping** : atrapar — **trapdoor** ['træp,dor] *n* : trampilla *f*

trapeze [træ'piːz] *n* : trapecio *m*

trappings ['træpɪŋz] *npl* : adornos *mpl*, atavíos *mpl*

trash ['træʃ] *n* : basura *f*

trauma ['trɔmə, 'traʊ-] *n* : trauma *m* — **traumatic** [trə'mætɪk, trɔ-, traʊ-] *adj* : traumático

travel ['trævəl] *vi* **-eled** *or* **-elled; -eling** *or* **-elling 1** : viajar **2** MOVE : desplazarse — ~ *n* : viajes *mpl* — **traveler** *or* **traveller** ['trævələr] *n* : viajero *m*, -ra *f*

traverse [trə'vərs, 'træ,vərs, 'trævərs] *vt* **-versed; -versing** : atravesar

travesty ['trævəsti] *n, pl* **-ties** : parodia *f*

trawl ['trɔl] *vi* : pescar (con red de arrastre) — **trawler** ['trɔlər] *n* : barco *m* de pesca

tray ['treɪ] *n* : bandeja *f*

treachery ['trɛtʃəri] *n, pl* **-eries** : traición *f* — **treacherous** ['trɛtʃərəs] *adj* **1** : traidor **2** DANGEROUS : peligroso

tread ['trɛd] *v* **trod** ['trɑd]; **treading** *vt* **1** *or* ~ **on** : pisar **2** ~ **water** : flotar — *vi* **1** STEP : pisar **2** WALK : caminar — ~ *n* **1** STEP : paso *m* **2** : banda *f* de rodadura (de un neumático) — **treadmill** ['trɛd,mɪl] *n* : rueda *f* de andar

treason ['triːzən] *n* : traición *f* (a la patria)

treasure ['trɛʒər, 'treɪ-] *n* : tesoro *m* — ~ *vt* **-sured; -suring** : apreciar — **treasurer** ['trɛʒərər, 'treɪ-] *n* : tesorero *m*, -ra *f* — **treasury** ['trɛʒəri, 'treɪ-] *n, pl* **-suries** : erario *m*, tesoro *m*

treat ['triːt] *vt* **1** : tratar **2** CONSIDER : considerar **3** ~ **s.o. to (dinner, etc.)** : invitar a algn (a cenar, etc.) — ~ *n* **1** : gusto *m*, placer *m* **2 it's my** ~ : invito yo

treatise ['triːtɪs] *n* : tratado *m*

treatment ['triːtmənt] *n* : tratamiento *m*

treaty ['triːti] *n, pl* **-ties** : tratado *m*

treble ['trɛbəl] *adj* **1** TRIPLE : triple **2** : de tiple (en música) — ~ *vt* **-bled; -bling** : triplicar — **treble clef** : clave *f* de sol

tree ['triː] *n* : árbol *m*

trek ['trɛk] *vi* **trekked; trekking** : viajar (con dificultad) — ~ *n* : viaje *m* difícil

trellis ['trɛlɪs] *n* : enrejado *m*

tremble ['trɛmbəl] *vi* **-bled; -bling** : temblar

tremendous [trɪ'mɛndəs] *adj* : tremendo

tremor ['trɛmər] *n* : temblor *m*

trench ['trɛntʃ] *n* **1** : zanja *f* **2** : trinchera *f* (militar)

trend ['trɛnd] *n* **1** : tendencia *f* **2** FASHION : moda *f* — **trendy** ['trɛndi] *adj* **trendier; -est** : de moda

trepidation [,trɛpə'deɪʃən] *n* : inquietud *f*

trespass ['trɛspəs, -,pæs] *vi* : entrar ilegalmente (en propiedad ajena)

trial ['traɪəl] *n* **1** : juicio *m*, proceso *m* **2** TEST : prueba *f* **3** ORDEAL : dura prueba *f* — ~ *adj* : de prueba

triangle ['traɪ,æŋgəl] *n* : triángulo *m* — **triangular** [traɪ'æŋgjələr] *adj* : triangular

tribe ['traɪb] *n* : tribu *f* — **tribal** ['traɪbəl] *adj* : tribal

tribulation [,trɪbjə'leɪʃən] *n* : tribulación *f*

tribunal [traɪ'bjuːnəl, trɪ-] *n* : tribunal *m*

tribute ['trɪbjuːt] *n* : tributo *m* — **tributary** ['trɪbjə,tɛri] *n, pl* **-taries** : afluente *m*

trick ['trɪk] *n* **1** : trampa *f* **2** PRANK : broma *f* **3** KNACK, FEAT : truco *m* **4** : baza *f* (en naipes) — ~ *vt* : engañar — **trickery** ['trɪkəri] *n* : engaño *m*

trickle ['trɪkəl] *vi* **-led; -ling** : gotear — ~ *n* : goteo *m*

tricky ['trɪki] *adj* **trickier; -est 1** SLY : astuto, taimado **2** DIFFICULT : difícil

tricycle ['traɪsəkəl, -,sɪkəl] *n* : triciclo *m*

trifle ['traɪfəl] *n* **1** TRIVIALITY : nimiedad *f* **2 a** ~ : un poco — ~ *vi* **-fled; -fling** ~ **with** : jugar con — **trifling** ['traɪflɪŋ] *adj* : insignificante

trigger ['trɪgər] *n* : gatillo *m* — ~ *vt* : causar, provocar

trill ['trɪl] *n* : trino *m* — ~ *vi* : trinar

trillion ['trɪljən] *n* : billón *m*

trilogy ['trɪlədʒi] *n, pl* **-gies** : trilogía *f*

trim ['trɪm] *vt* **trimmed; trimming 1** : recortar **2** ADORN : adornar — ~ *adj* **trimmer; trimmest 1** SLIM : esbelto **2** NEAT : arreglado — ~ *n* **1** : recorte *m* **2** DECORATION : adornos *mpl* **3 in** ~ : en buena forma — **trimming** ['trɪmɪŋ] *npl* **1** : adornos *mpl* **2** GARNISH : guarnición *f*

Trinity ['trɪnəti] *n* : Trinidad *f*

trinket ['trɪŋkət] *n* : chuchería *f*

trio ['triːoː] *n, pl* **trios** : trío *m*

trip ['trɪp] *v* **tripped; tripping** *vi* **1** : caminar (a paso ligero) **2** STUMBLE : tropezar **3** ~ **up** : equivocarse — *vt* **1** ACTIVATE : activar **2** ~ **s.o.** : hacer una zancadilla a algn **3** ~ **s.o. up** : hacer equivocar a algn — ~ *n* **1** : viaje *m* **2** STUMBLE : traspié *m*

tripe ['traɪp] *n* 1 : mondongo *m*, callos *mpl* 2 NONSENSE : tonterías *fpl*

triple ['trɪpəl] *vt* -**pled; -pling** : triplicar — ~ *n* : triple *m* — ~ *adj* : triple — **triplet** ['trɪplət] *n* : trillizo *m*, -za *f* — **triplicate** ['trɪplɪkət] *n* : triplicado *m*

tripod ['traɪˌpad] *n* : trípode *m*

trite ['traɪt] *adj* **triter; tritest** : trillado

triumph ['traɪəmpf] *n* : triunfo *m* — ~ *vi* : triunfar — **triumphal** [traɪˈʌmpfəl] *adj* : triunfal — **triumphant** [traɪˈʌmpfənt] *adj* : triunfante

trivial ['trɪviəl] *adj* : trivial — **trivia** ['trɪviə] *ns & pl* : trivialidades *fpl* — **triviality** [ˌtrɪviˈæləti] *n, pl* **-ties** : trivialidad *f*

trod, trodden → **tread**

trolley ['trali] *n, pl* -**leys** : tranvía *m*

trombone [tramˈboːn] *n* : trombón *m*

troop ['truːp] *n* 1 : escuadrón *m* (de caballería), compañía *f* (de soldados) 2 ~**s** *npl* : tropas *fpl* — ~ *vi* ~ **in/out** : entrar/salir en tropel — **trooper** ['truːpər] *n* 1 : soldado *m* 2 *or* **state** ~ : policía *mf* estatal

trophy ['troːfi] *n, pl* -**phies** : trofeo *m*

tropic ['trapɪk] *n* 1 : trópico *m* 2 **the** ~**s** : el trópico — ~ *or* **tropical** [-pɪkəl] *adj* : tropical

trot ['trat] *n* : trote *m* — ~ *vi* **trotted; trotting** : trotar

trouble ['trʌbəl] *v* -**bled; -bling** *vt* 1 WORRY : preocupar 2 BOTHER : molestar — *vi* : molestarse — ~ *n* 1 PROBLEMS : problemas *mpl* 2 EFFORT : molestia *f* 3 **be in** ~ : estar en apuros 4 **get in** ~ : meterse en problemas 5 **I had** ~ **doing it** : me costó hacerlo — **troublemaker** ['trʌbəlˌmeɪkər] *n* : alborotador *m*, -dora *f* — **troublesome** ['trʌbəlsəm] *adj* : problemático

trough ['trɔf] *n, pl* **troughs** ['trɔfs, 'trɔvz] 1 : depresión *f* 2 *or* **feeding** ~ : comedero *m* 3 *or* **drinking** ~ : bebedero *m*

troupe ['truːp] *n* : compañía *f* (de teatro)

trousers ['trauzərz] *npl* : pantalón *m*, pantalones *mpl*

trout ['traut] *n, pl* **trout** : trucha *f*

trowel ['trauəl] *n* : paleta *f* (de albañil), desplantador *m* (de jardinero)

truant ['truːənt] *n* : alumno *m*, -na *f* que falta a clase

truce ['truːs] *n* : tregua *f*

truck ['trʌk] *vt* : transportar en camión — ~ *n* 1 : camión *m* 2 CART : carro *m* — **trucker** ['trʌkər] *n* : camionero *m*, -ra *f*

trudge ['trʌdʒ] *vi* **trudged; trudging** : caminar a paso pesado

true ['truː] *adj* **truer; truest** 1 : verdadero 2 LOYAL : fiel 3 GENUINE : auténtico 4 **be** ~ : ser cierto, ser verdad

truffle ['trʌfəl] *n* : trufa *f*

truly ['truːli] *adv* : verdaderamente

trump ['trʌmp] *n* : triunfo *m* (en naipes)

trumpet ['trʌmpət] *n* : trompeta *f*

trunk ['trʌŋk] *n* 1 STEM, TORSO : tronco *m* 2 : trompa *f* (de un elefante) 3 : baúl *m* (equipaje) 4 : maletero *m* (de un auto) 5 ~**s** *npl* : traje *m* de baño (de hombre)

truss ['trʌs] *n* 1 FRAMEWORK : armazón *m* 2 : braguero *m* (en medicina)

trust ['trʌst] *n* 1 CONFIDENCE : confianza *f* 2 HOPE : esperanza *f* 3 CREDIT : crédito *m* 4 : trust *m* (en finanzas) 5 **in** ~ : en fideicomiso — ~ *vi* 1 : confiar 2 HOPE : esperar — *vt* 1 : confiar en, fiarse de (en frases negativas) 2 ~ **s.o. with sth** : confiar algo a algn — **trustee** [ˌtrʌsˈtiː] *n* : fideicomisario *m*, -ria *f* — **trustworthy** ['trʌstˌwərði] *adj* : digno de confianza

truth ['truːθ] *n, pl* **truths** ['truːðz, 'truːθs] : verdad *f* — **truthful** ['truːθfəl] *adj* : sincero, veraz

try ['traɪ] *v* **tried; trying** *vt* 1 ATTEMPT : tratar (de), intentar 2 : juzgar (un caso, etc.) 3 TEST : poner a prueba 4 *or* ~ **out** : probar 5 ~ **on** : probarse (ropa) — *vi* : hacer un esfuerzo — ~ *n, pl* **tries** : intento *m* — **trying** *adj* 1 ANNOYING : irritante, pesado 2 DIFFICULT : duro — **tryout** ['traɪˌaut] *n* : prueba *f*

tsar ['zɑr, 'tsɑr, 'sɑr] → **czar**

T-shirt ['tiːˌʃərt] *n* : camiseta *f*

tub ['tʌb] *n* 1 : cuba *f*, tina *f* 2 CONTAINER : envase *m* 3 BATHTUB : bañera *f*

tuba ['tuːbə, 'tjuː-] *n* : tuba *f*

tube ['tuːb, 'tjuːb] *n* 1 : tubo *m* 2 *or* **inner** ~ : cámara *f* 3 **the** ~ : la tele

tuberculosis [tuˌbərkjəˈloːsɪs, tjuː-] *n, pl* -**loses** [-ˌsiːz] : tuberculosis *f*

tubing ['tuːbɪŋ, 'tjuː-] *n* : tubería *f* — **tubular** ['tuːbjələr, 'tjuː-] *adj* : tubular

tuck ['tʌk] *vt* 1 : meter 2 ~ **away** : guardar 3 ~ **in** : meter por dentro (una blusa, etc.) 4 ~ **s.o. in** : arropar a algn — ~ *n* : jareta *f*

Tuesday ['tuːzˌdeɪ, 'tjuːz-, -di] *n* : martes *m*

tuft ['tʌft] *n* : mechón *m* (de pelo), penacho *m* (de plumas)

tug ['tʌg] *vt* **tugged; tugging** *or* ~ **at** : tirar de, jalar de — ~ *n* : tirón *m*, jalón *m* — **tugboat** ['tʌgˌboːt] *n* : remolcador *m* — **tug-of-war** [ˌtʌgəˈwɔr] *n, pl* **tugs-of-war** : tira y afloja *m*

tuition [tuːˈɪʃən, tjuː-] n 1 : enseñanza f 2 or ~ **fees** : matrícula f
tulip [ˈtuːlɪp, ˈtjuː-] n : tulipán m
tumble [ˈtʌmbəl] vi **-bled; -bling** : caerse — ~ n : caída f — **tumbler** [ˈtʌmblər] : vaso m (sin pie)
tummy [ˈtʌmi] n, pl **-mies** : barriga f, panza f
tumor [ˈtuːmər ˈtjuː-] n : tumor m
tumult [ˈtuːmʌlt ˈtjuː-] n : tumulto m — **tumultuous** [tuˈmʌltʃuəs, tjuˈ-] adj : tumultuoso
tuna [ˈtuːnə ˈtjuː-] n, pl **-na** or **-nas** : atún m
tune [ˈtuːn, ˈtjuːn] n 1 MELODY : melodía f 2 SONG : tonada f **3 in ~** : afinado **out of ~** : desafinado — ~ v **tuned; tuning** vt : afinar — vi ~ **in** : sintonizar — **tuner** [ˈtuːnər, ˈtjuː-] n 1 : afinador m, -dora f (de pianos, etc.) 2 : sintonizador m (de un receptor)
tunic [ˈtuːnɪk, ˈtjuː-] n : túnica f
tunnel [ˈtʌnəl] n : túnel m — ~ vi **-neled** or **-nelled; -neling** or **-nelling** : hacer un túnel
turban [ˈtərbən] n : turbante m
turbine [ˈtərbən, -ˌbaɪn] n : turbina f
turbulent [ˈtərbjələnt] adj : turbulento — **turbulence** [ˈtərbjələnts] n : turbulencia f
turf [ˈtərf] n 1 GRASS : césped m 2 SOD : tepe m
turgid [ˈtərdʒɪd] adj : ampuloso (dícese de prosa, etc.)
turkey [ˈtərki] n, pl **-keys** : pavo m
turmoil [ˈtərˌmɔɪl] n : confusión f
turn [ˈtərn] v 1 : hacer girar (una rueda, etc.), volver (la cabeza, una página, etc.) 2 : dar la vuelta a (una esquina) 3 SPRAIN : torcer 4 ~ **down** REFUSE : rechazar 5 ~ **down** LOWER : bajar 6 ~ **in** : entregar 7 ~ **off** : cerrar (una llave), apagar (la luz, etc.) 8 ~ **on** : abrir (una llave), encender, prender Lat (la luz, etc.) 9 ~ **out** EXPEL : echar 10 ~ **out** PRODUCE : producir 11 ~ **out** → turn off 12 or ~ **over** FLIP : dar la vuelta a, voltear Lat 13 ~ **over** TRANSFER : entregar 14 ~ **s.o.'s stomach** : revolver el estómago a algn 15 ~ **sth into sth** : convertir algo en algo 16 ~ **up** RAISE : subir — vi 1 ROTATE : girar, dar vueltas 2 BECOME : ponerse 3 SOUR : agriarse 4 RESORT : recurrir 5 or ~ **around** : darse la vuelta, volverse 6 ~ **into** : convertirse en 7 ~ **left** : doblar a la izquierda 8 ~ **out** COME : acudir 9 ~ **out** RESULT : resultar 10 ~ **up** APPEAR : aparecer — ~ n 1 : vuelta f 2

CHANGE : cambio m 3 CURVE : curva f 4 **do a good** ~ : hacer un favor 5 **whose** ~ **is it?** : ¿a quién le toca?
turnip [ˈtərnəp] n : nabo m
turnout [ˈtərnˌaut] n : concurrencia f — **turnover** [ˈtərnˌoːvər] n 1 : tartaleta f (postre) 2 : volumen m (de ventas) 3 : movimiento f (de personal) — **turnpike** [ˈtərnˌpaɪk] n : carretera f de peaje — **turntable** [ˈtərnˌteɪbəl] n : plato m giratorio
turpentine [ˈtərpənˌtaɪn] n : trementina f
turquoise [ˈtərˌkɔɪz, -ˌkwɔɪz] n : turquesa f
turret [ˈtərət] n 1 : torrecilla f 2 : torreta f (de un tanque, etc.)
turtle [ˈtərtəl] n : tortuga f (marina) — **turtleneck** [ˈtərtəlˌnɛk] n : cuello m de tortuga
tusk [ˈtʌsk] n : colmillo m
tussle [ˈtʌsəl] n : pelea f — ~ vi **-sled; -sling** : pelearse
tutor [ˈtuːtər, ˈtjuː-] n : profesor m, -sora f particular — ~ vt : dar clases particulares a
tuxedo [ˌtəkˈsiːdoː] n, pl **-dos** or **-does** : esmoquin m, smoking m
TV [ˌtiːˈviː, ˈtiːˌviː] → television
twang [ˈtwæŋ] n 1 : tañido m 2 : acento m nasal (de la voz)
tweak [ˈtwiːk] vt : pellizcar — ~ n : pellizco m
tweed [ˈtwiːd] n : tweed m
tweet [ˈtwiːt] n : gorjeo m, pío m — ~ vi : piar
tweezers [ˈtwiːzərz] npl : pinzas fpl
twelve [ˈtwelv] adj : doce — ~ n : doce m — **twelfth** [ˈtwelfθ] adj : duodécimo — ~ n 1 : duodécimo m, -ma f (en una serie) 2 : doceavo m (en matemáticas)
twenty [ˈtwʌnti, ˈtwɛn-] adj : veinte — ~ n, pl **-ties** : veinte m — **twentieth** [ˈtwʌntiəθ, ˈtwɛn-] adj : vigésimo — ~ n 1 : vigésimo m, -ma f (en una serie) 2 : veinteavo m (en matemáticas)
twice [ˈtwaɪs] adv 1 : dos veces 2 ~ **as much/many as** : el doble de (algo), el doble que (algn)
twig [ˈtwɪg] n : ramita f
twilight [ˈtwaɪˌlaɪt] n : crepúsculo m
twin [ˈtwɪn] n : gemelo m, -la f; mellizo m, -za f — ~ adj : gemelo, mellizo
twine [ˈtwaɪn] n : cordel m, bramante m Spain
twinge [ˈtwɪndʒ] n : punzada f
twinkle [ˈtwɪŋkəl] vi **-kled; -kling** 1 : centellear 2 : brillar (dícese de los ojos) — ~ n : centelleo m, brillo m (de los ojos)

twirl ['twərl] *vt* : girar, dar vueltas a — *vi* : girar, dar vueltas — ~ *n* : giro *m*, vuelta *f*

twist ['twɪst] *vt* **1** : retorcer **2** TURN : girar **3** SPRAIN : torcerse **4** : tergiversar (palabras) — *vi* **1** : retorcerse **2** COIL : enrollarse **3** : serpentear (entre montañas, etc.) — ~ *n* **1** BEND : vuelta *f* **2** TURN : giro *m* **3** ~ **of lemon** : rodajita *f* de limón — **twister** ['twɪstər] → **tornado**

twitch ['twɪtʃ] *vi* : moverse (espasmódicamente) — ~ *n* **nervous** ~ : tic *m* nervioso

two ['tuː] *adj* : dos — ~ *n*, *pl* **twos** : dos *m* — **twofold** ['tuːˌfoːld] *adj* : doble — ~ ['tuːˌfoːld] *adv* : al doble — **two**

hundred *adj* : doscientos — ~ *n* : doscientos *m*

tycoon [taɪˈkuːn] *n* : magnate *mf*

tying → **tie**

type ['taɪp] *n* : tipo *m* — ~ *v* **typed; typing** : escribir a máquina — **type-written** ['taɪpˌrɪtən] *adj* : escrito a máquina — **typewriter** ['taɪpˌraɪtər] *n* : máquina *f* de escribir

typhoon [taɪˈfuːn] *n* : tifón *m*

typical ['tɪpɪkəl] *adj* : típico, característico — **typify** ['tɪpəˌfaɪ] *vt* **-fied; -fying** : tipificar

typist ['taɪpɪst] *n* : mecanógrafo *m*, -fa *f*

typography [taɪˈpɑɡrəfi] *n* : tipografía *f*

tyranny ['tɪrəni] *n*, *pl* **-nies** : tiranía *f* — **tyrant** ['taɪrənt] *n* : tirano *m*, -na *f*

tzar ['zɑr, 'tsɑr, 'sɑr] → **czar**

U

u ['juː] *n*, *pl* **u's** *or* **us** ['juːz] : u *f*, vigésima primera letra del alfabeto inglés

udder ['ʌdər] *n* : ubre *f*

UFO [ˌjuːˌeɪˈfoː, 'juːˌfoː] (*unidentified flying object*) *n*, *pl* **UFO's** *or* **UFOs** : ovni *m*, OVNI *m*

ugly ['ʌɡli] *adj* **uglier; -est** : feo — **ugliness** ['ʌɡlinəs] *n* : fealdad *f*

ulcer ['ʌlsər] *n* : úlcera *f*

ulterior [ʌlˈtɪriər] *adj* ~ **motive** : segunda intención *f*

ultimate ['ʌltəmət] *adj* **1** FINAL : final, último **2** UTMOST : máximo **3** FUNDAMENTAL : fundamental — **ultimately** ['ʌltəmətli] *adv* **1** FINALLY : por último, finalmente **2** EVENTUALLY : a la larga

ultimatum [ˌʌltəˈmeɪtəm, -ˈmɑ-] *n*, *pl* **-tums** *or* **-ta** [-ʃə] : ultimátum *m*

ultraviolet [ˌʌltrəˈvaɪələt] *adj* : ultravioleta

umbilical cord [ʌmˈbɪlɪkəl] *n* : cordón *m* umbilical

umbrella [ʌmˈbrɛlə] *n* : paraguas *m*

umpire ['ʌmˌpaɪr] *n* : árbitro *m*, -tra *f* — ~ *vt* : arbitrar

umpteenth [ˌʌmpˈtiːnθ] *adj* : enésimo

unable [ʌnˈeɪbəl] *adj* **1** : incapaz **2** **be** ~ **to** : no poder

unabridged [ˌʌnəˈbrɪdʒd] *adj* : íntegro

unacceptable [ˌʌnɪkˈsɛptəbəl] *adj* : inaceptable

unaccountable [ˌʌnəˈkaʊntəd] *adj* : inexplicable

unaccustomed [ˌʌnəˈkʌstəmd] *adj* **be** ~ **to** : no estar acostumbrado a

unadulterated [ˌʌnəˈdʌltəˌreɪtəd] *adj* : puro

unaffected [ˌʌnəˈfɛktəd] *adj* **1** : no afectado **2** NATURAL : sin afectación, natural

unafraid [ˌʌnəˈfreɪd] *adj* : sin miedo

unaided [ʌnˈeɪdəd] *adj* : sin ayuda

unanimous [juˈnænəməs] *adj* : unánime

unannounced [ˌʌnəˈnaʊnst] *adj* : sin dar aviso

unarmed [ʌnˈɑrmd] *adj* : desarmado

unassuming [ˌʌnəˈsuːmɪŋ] *adj* : modesto, sin pretensiones

unattached [ˌʌnəˈtætʃt] *adj* **1** : suelto **2** UNMARRIED : soltero

unattractive [ˌʌnəˈtræktɪv] *adj* : poco atractivo

unauthorized [ʌnˈɔθəˌraɪzd] *adj* : no autorizado

unavailable [ˌʌnəˈveɪləbəl] *adj* : no disponible

unavoidable [ˌʌnəˈvɔɪdəbəl] *adj* : inevitable

unaware [ˌʌnəˈwær] *adj* **1** : inconsciente **2** **be** ~ **of** : ignorar — **unawares** [ˌʌnəˈwærz] *adv* **catch s.o.** ~ : agarrar a algn desprevenido

unbalanced [ʌnˈbælənst] *adj* : desequilibrado

unbearable [ʌnˈbærəbəl] *adj* : inaguantable, insoportable

unbelievable [ˌʌnbəˈliːvəbəl] *adj* : increíble

unbending [ʌnˈbɛndɪŋ] *adj* : inflexible

unbiased [ʌnˈbaɪəst] *adj* : imparcial

unborn [ʌnˈbɔrn] *adj* : aún no nacido

unbreakable [ʌnˈbreɪkəbəl] *adj* : irrompible

unbridled [ʌn'braɪdəld] *adj* : desenfrenado

unbroken [ʌn'broːkən] *adj* **1** INTACT : intacto **2** CONTINUOUS : continuo

unbutton [ʌn'bʌtən] *vt* : desabrochar, desabotonar

uncalled–for [ʌn'kɔld,fɔr] *adj* : inapropiado, innecesario

uncanny [ʌn'kæni] *adj* **-nier; -est** : extraño, misterioso

unceasing [ʌn'siːsɪŋ] *adj* : incesante

unceremonious [ʌn,serə'moːniəs] *adj* **1** INFORMAL : poco ceremonioso **2** ABRUPT : brusco

uncertain [ʌn'sərtən] *adj* **1** : incierto **in no ~ terms** : de forma vehemente — **uncertainty** [ʌn'sərtənti] *n, pl* **-ties** : incertidumbre *f*

unchanged [ʌn'tʃeɪndʒd] *adj* : igual, sin alterar — **unchanging** [ʌn'tʃeɪdʒɪŋ] *adj* : inmutable

uncivilized [ʌn'sɪvə,laɪzd] *adj* : incivilizado

uncle ['ʌŋkəl] *n* : tío *m*

unclear [ʌn'klɪr] *adj* : poco claro

uncomfortable [ʌn'kʌmpfərtəbəl] *adj* **1** : incómodo **2** DISCONCERTING : inquietante, desagradable

uncommon [ʌn'kɑmən] *adj* : raro

uncompromising [ʌn'kɑmprə,maɪzɪŋ] *adj* : intransigente

unconcerned [ʌnkən'sərnd] *adj* : indiferente

unconditional [ʌnkən'dɪʃənəl] *adj* : incondicional

unconscious [ʌn'kɑntʃəs] *adj* : inconsciente

unconstitutional [ʌn,kɑnstə'tuːʃənəl, -'tjuː-] *adj* : inconstitucional

uncontrollable [ʌnkən'troːləbəl] *adj* : incontrolable

unconventional [ʌnkən'ventʃənəl] *adj* : poco convencional

uncouth [ʌn'kuːθ] *adj* : grosero

uncover [ʌn'kʌvər] *vt* **1** : destapar **2** REVEAL : descubrir

undecided [ʌndi'saɪdəd] *adj* : indeciso

undeniable [ʌndi'naɪəbəl] *adj* : innegable

under ['ʌndər] *adv* **1** : debajo **2** LESS : menos **3** *or* **~ anesthetic** : bajo los efectos de la anestesia — **~** *prep* **1** BELOW, BENEATH : debajo de, abajo de **2 ~ 20 minutes** : menos de 20 minutos **3 ~ the circumstances** : dadas las circunstancias

underage [ʌndər'eɪdʒ] *adj* : menor de edad

underclothes ['ʌndər,kloːz, -,kloːðz] → **underwear**

undercover [ʌndər'kʌvər] *adj* : secreto

undercurrent ['ʌndər,kərənt] *n* : tendencia *f* oculta

underdeveloped [ʌndərdi'veləpt] *adj* : subdesarrollado

underestimate [ʌndər'estə,meɪt] *vt* **-mated; -mating** : subestimar

underfoot [ʌndər'fut] *adv* : bajo los pies

undergo [ʌndər'goː] *vt* **-went** [-'went]; **-gone** [-'gɔn]; **-going** : sufrir, experimentar

undergraduate [ʌndər'grædʒuət] *n* : estudiante *m* universitario, estudiante *f* universitaria

underground [ʌndər'graund] *adv* **1** : bajo tierra **2 go ~** : pasar a la clandestinidad — ['ʌndər,graund] *adj* **1** : subterráneo **2** SECRET : secreto, clandestino — ['ʌndər,graund] *n* : movimiento *m* clandestino

undergrowth ['ʌndər'groːθ] *n* : maleza *f*

underhanded [ʌndər'hændəd] *adj* SLY : solapado

underline [ʌndər,laɪn] *vt* **-lined; -lining** : subrayar

underlying [ʌndər'laɪɪŋ] *adj* : subyacente

undermine [ʌndər'maɪn] *vt* **-mined; -mining** : socavar, minar

underneath [ʌndər'niːθ] *adv* : debajo, abajo — **~** *prep* : debajo de, abajo de *Lat*

underpants ['ʌndər,pænts] *npl* : calzoncillos *mpl*, calzones *mpl Lat*

underpass ['ʌndər,pæs] *n* : paso *m* inferior

underprivileged [ʌndər'prɪvlɪdʒd] *adj* : desfavorecido

underrate [ʌndər'reɪt] *vt* **-rated; -rating** : subestimar

undershirt ['ʌndər,ʃərt] *n* : camiseta *f*

understand [ʌndər'stænd] *v* **-stood** [-'stud]; **-standing** : comprender, entender — **understandable** [ʌndər'stændəbəl] *adj* : comprensible — **understanding** [ʌndər'stændɪŋ] *adj* : comprensivo, compasivo — **~** *n* **1** : comprensión *f* **2** AGREEMENT : acuerdo *m*

understatement [ʌndər'steɪtmənt] *n* **that's an ~** : decir sólo eso es quedarse corto

understudy ['ʌndər,stʌdi] *n, pl* **-dies** : sobresaliente *mf* (en el teatro)

undertake [ʌndər'teɪk] *vt* **-took** [-'tuk]; **-taken** [-'teɪkən]; **-taking** : emprender (una tarea), encargarse de (una responsabilidad) — **undertaker** ['ʌndər,teɪkər] *n* : director *m*, -tora *f* de una funeraria — **undertaking** ['ʌndər,teɪkɪŋ, ,ʌndər-] *n* : empresa *f*, tarea *f*

undertone ['ʌndər,toːn] *n* **1** : voz *f* baja **2** SUGGESTION : matiz *m*

undertow ['ʌndər,toː] *n* : resaca *f*

underwater [ˌʌndər'woʈər, -'wɑ-] *adj* : submarino — **~** *adv* : debajo (del agua)

under way [ˌʌndər'weɪ] *adv* **get ~** : ponerse en marcha

underwear ['ʌndər,wær] *n* : ropa *f* interior

underwent → **undergo**

underworld ['ʌndər,wərld] *n* **the ~** CRIMINALS : la hampa, los bajos fondos

underwriter ['ʌndər,raɪʈər, ˌʌndər'-] *n* : asegurador *m*, -dora *f*

undesirable [ˌʌndɪ'zaɪrəbəl] *adj* : indeseable

undeveloped [ˌʌndɪ'vɛləpt] *adj* : sin desarrollar

undignified [ˌʌn'dɪgnəfaɪd] *adj* : indecoroso

undisputed [ˌʌndɪ'spjuːʈəd] *adj* : indiscutible

undo [ˌʌn'duː] *vt* **-did** [-'dɪd], **-done** [-'dʌn]; **-doing 1** UNFASTEN : deshacer, desatar **2** : reparar (daños, etc.)

undoubtedly [ˌʌn'daʊʈədli] *adv* : indudablemente

undress [ˌʌn'drɛs] *vt* : desnudar — *vi* : desnudarse

undue [ˌʌn'duː, -'djuː] *adj* : indebido, excesivo

undulate ['ʌndʒə,leɪt] *vi* **-lated; -lating** : ondular

unduly [ˌʌn'duːli, -'djuː-] *adv* : excesivamente

undying [ˌʌn'daɪŋ] *adj* : eterno

unearth [ˌʌn'ərθ] *vt* : desenterrar

unearthly [ˌʌn'ərθli] *adj* **-lier; -est** : sobrenatural, de otro mundo

uneasy [ˌʌn'iːzi] *adj* **-easier; -est 1** AWKWARD : incómodo **2** WORRIED : inquieto **3** RESTLESS : agitado — **uneasily** [ˌʌn'iːzəli] *adv* : inquietamente — **uneasiness** [ˌʌn'iːzinəs] *n* : inquietud *f*

uneducated [ˌʌn'ɛdʒəˌkeɪʈəd] *adj* : inculto

unemployed [ˌʌnɪm'plɔɪd] *adj* : desempleado — **unemployment** [ˌʌnɪm-'plɔɪmənt] *n* : desempleo *m*

unerring [ˌʌn'ɛrɪŋ, -'ər-] *adj* : infalible

unethical [ˌʌn'ɛθɪkəl] *adj* : poco ético

uneven [ˌʌn'iːvən] *adj* **1** : desigual **2** : impar (dícese de un número)

unexpected [ˌʌnɪk'spɛkʈəd] *adj* : inesperado

unfailing [ˌʌn'feɪlɪŋ] *adj* **1** CONSTANT : constante **2** INEXHAUSTIBLE : inagotable

unfair [ˌʌn'fær] *adj* : injusto — **unfairly** [ˌʌn'færli] *adv* : injustamente — **unfairness** [ˌʌn'færnəs] *n* : injusticia *f*

unfaithful [ˌʌn'feɪθfəl] *adj* : infiel — **unfaithfulness** [ˌʌn'feɪθfəlnəs] *n* : infidelidad *f*

unfamiliar [ˌʌnfə'mɪljər] *adj* **1** : desconocido **2 be ~ with** : desconocer

unfasten [ˌʌn'fæsən] *vt* **1** : desabrochar (ropa, etc.) **2** UNDO : desatar (una cuerda, etc.)

unfavorable [ˌʌn'feɪvərəbəl] *adj* : desfavorable

unfeeling [ˌʌn'fiːlɪŋ] *adj* : insensible

unfinished [ˌʌn'fɪnɪʃd] *adj* : sin terminar

unfit [ˌʌn'fɪt] *adj* **1** UNSUITABLE : impropio **2** UNSUITED : no apto, incapaz

unfold [ˌʌn'foːld] *vt* **1** : desplegar, desdoblar **2** REVEAL : revelar (un plan, etc.) — *vi* **1** : extenderse, desplegarse **2** DEVELOP : desarrollarse

unforeseen [ˌʌnfor'siː] *adj* : imprevisto

unforgettable [ˌʌnfər'gɛʈəbəl] *adj* : inolvidable

unforgivable [ˌʌnfər'gɪvəbəl] *adj* : imperdonable

unfortunate [ˌʌn'fortʃənət] *adj* **1** UNLUCKY : desgraciado, desafortunado **2** INAPPROPRIATE : inoportuno — **unfortunately** [ˌʌn'fortʃənətli] *adv* : desgraciadamente

unfounded [ˌʌn'faʊndəd] *adj* : infundado

unfriendly [ˌʌn'frɛndli] *adj* **-lier; -est** : poco amistoso

unfurl [ˌʌn'fərl] *vt* : desplegar

unfurnished [ˌʌn'fərnɪʃt] *adj* : desamueblado

ungainly [ˌʌn'geɪnli] *adj* : desgarbado

ungodly [ˌʌn'gɑdli, -'gɑd-] *adj* **1** : impío **2 an ~ hour** : una hora intempestiva

ungrateful [ˌʌn'greɪtfəl] *adj* : desagradecido

unhappy [ˌʌn'hæpi] *adj* **-pier; -est 1** SAD : infeliz, triste **2** UNFORTUNATE : desafortunado — **unhappily** [ˌʌn'hæpəli] *adv* **1** SADLY : tristemente **2** UNFORTUNATELY : desgraciadamente — **unhappiness** [ˌʌn'hæpinəs] *n* : tristeza *f*

unharmed [ˌʌn'hɑrmd] *adj* : salvo, ileso

unhealthy [ˌʌn'hɛlθi] *adj* **-thier; -est 1** : malsano **2** SICKLY : enfermizo

unheard-of [ˌʌn'hərdəv] *adj* : sin precedente, insólito

unhook [ˌʌn'hʊk] *vt* : desenganchar

unhurt [ˌʌn'hərt] *adj* : ileso

unicorn ['juːnəˌkorn] *n* : unicornio *m*

unification [ˌjuːnəfə'keɪʃən] *n* : unificación *f*

uniform ['juːnəˌform] *adj* : uniforme —

~ *n* : uniforme *m* — **uniformity** [ˌjuːnəˈfɔrməti] *n, pl* **-ties** : uniformidad *f*

unify [ˈjuːnəˌfaɪ] *vt* **-fied; -fying** : unificar

unilateral [ˌjuːnəˈlætərəl] *adj* : unilateral

unimaginable [ˌʌnɪˈmædʒənəbəl] *adj* : inconcebible

unimportant [ˌʌnɪmˈpɔrtənt] *adj* : insignificante

uninhabited [ˌʌnɪnˈhæbətəd] *adj* : deshabitado, despoblado

uninjured [ˌʌnˈɪndʒərd] *adj* : ileso

unintentional [ˌʌnɪnˈtentʃənəl] *adj* : involuntario

union [ˈjuːnjən] *n* **1** : unión *f* **2** *or* **labor ~** : sindicato *m*, gremio *m* *Lat*

unique [juˈniːk] *adj* : único — **uniquely** [juˈniːkli] *adv* EXCEPTIONALLY : excepcionalmente

unison [ˈjuːnəsən, -zən] *n* **in ~** : al unísono

unit [ˈjuːnɪt] *n* **1** : unidad *f* **2** : módulo *m* (de un mobiliario)

unite [juˈnaɪt] *v* **united; uniting** *vt* : unir — *vi* : unirse — **unity** [ˈjuːnəti] *n, pl* **-ties 1** : unidad *f* **2** HARMONY : acuerdo *m*

universe [ˈjuːnəˌvərs] *n* : universo *m* — **universal** [ˌjuːnəˈvərsəl] *adj* : universal

university [ˌjuːnəˈvərsəti] *n, pl* **-ties** : universidad *f*

unjust [ˌʌnˈdʒʌst] *adj* : injusto — **unjustified** [ˌʌnˈdʒʌstəˌfaɪd] *adj* : injustificado

unkempt [ˌʌnˈkempt] *adj* **1** : descuidado, desaseado **2** : despeinado (dícese del pelo)

unkind [ˌʌnˈkaɪnd] *adj* : poco amable, cruel — **unkindness** [ˌʌnˈkaɪndnəs] *n* : falta *f* de amabilidad, crueldad *f*

unknown [ˌʌnˈnoːn] *adj* : desconocido

unlawful [ˌʌnˈlɔfəl] *adj* : ilegal

unless [ənˈles] *conj* : a menos que, a no ser que

unlike [ˌʌnˈlaɪk] *adj* : diferente — *prep* : a diferencia de — **unlikelihood** [ˌʌnˈlaɪkliˌhʊd] *n* : improbabilidad *f* — **unlikely** [ˌʌnˈlaɪkli] *adj* **-lier; -est** : improbable

unlimited [ˌʌnˈlɪmətəd] *adj* : ilimitado

unload [ˌʌnˈloːd] *v* : descargar

unlock [ˌʌnˈlɑk] *vt* : abrir (con llave)

unlucky [ˌʌnˈlʌki] *adj* **-luckier; -est 1** UNFORTUNATE : desgraciado **2** : de mala suerte (dícese de un número, etc.)

unmarried [ˌʌnˈmærid] *adj* : soltero

unmask [ˌʌnˈmæsk] *vt* : desenmascarar

unmistakable [ˌʌnmɪˈsteɪkəbəl] *adj* : inconfundible

unnatural [ˌʌnˈnætʃərəl] *adj* **1** : anormal **2** AFFECTED : afectado, forzado

unnecessary [ˌʌnˈnesəˌseri] *adj* : innecesario — **unnecessarily** [-ˌnesəˈserɪli] *adv* : innecesariamente

unnerving [ˌʌnˈnərvɪŋ] *adj* : desconcertante

unnoticed [ˌʌnˈnoːtəst] *adj* : inadvertido

unobtainable [ˌʌnəbˈteɪnəbəl] *adj* : inasequible

unobtrusive [ˌʌnəbˈstruːsɪv] *adj* : discreto

unofficial [ˌʌnəˈfɪʃəl] *adj* : no oficial

unorthodox [ˌʌnˈɔrθəˌdɑks] *adj* : poco ortodoxo

unpack [ˌʌnˈpæk] *vt* **1** : desempaquetar, desempacar *Lat* (un paquete, etc.) **2** : deshacer (una maleta) — *vi* : deshacer las maletas

unparalleled [ˌʌnˈpærəˌleld] *adj* : sin igual

unpleasant [ˌʌnˈplezənt] *adj* : desagradable

unplug [ˌʌnˈplʌg] *vt* **-plugged; -plugging** : desconectar, desenchufar

unpopular [ˌʌnˈpɑpjələr] *adj* : poco popular

unprecedented [ˌʌnˈpresəˌdentəd] *adj* : sin precedente

unpredictable [ˌʌnprɪˈdɪktəbəl] *adj* : imprevisible

unprepared [ˌʌnprɪˈpærd] *adj* **1** : no preparado **2** UNREADY : desprevenido

unqualified [ˌʌnˈkwɑləˌfaɪd] *adj* **1** : no calificado, sin título **2** COMPLETE : absoluto

unquestionable [ˌʌnˈkwestʃənəbəl] *adj* : indiscutible — **unquestioning** [ˌʌnˈkwestʃənɪŋ] *adj* : incondicional

unravel [ˌʌnˈrævəl] *v* **-eled** *or* **-elled; -eling** *or* **-elling** *vt* : desenmarañar — *vi* : deshacerse

unreal [ˌʌnˈriːl] *adj* : irreal — **unrealistic** [ˌʌnˌriːəˈlɪstɪk] *adj* : poco realista

unreasonable [ˌʌnˈriːzənəbəl] *adj* **1** : irrazonable **2** EXCESSIVE : excesivo

unrecognizable [ˌʌnˈrekəgˌnaɪzəbəl] *adj* : irreconocible

unrelated [ˌʌnrɪˈleɪtəd] *adj* : no relacionado

unrelenting [ˌʌnrɪˈlentɪŋ] *adj* : implacable

unreliable [ˌʌnrɪˈlaɪəbəl] *adj* : que no es de fiar

unrepentant [ˌʌnrɪˈpentənt] *adj* : impenitente

unrest [ˌʌnˈrest] *n* **1** : inquietud *f*, malestar *m* **2** *or* **political ~** : disturbios *mpl*

unripe [ˌʌnˈraɪp] *adj* : verde, no maduro

unrivaled *or* **unrivalled** [ʌn'raɪvəld] *adj* : incomparable, sin par

unroll [ʌn'roːl] *vt* : desenrollar — *vi* : desenrollarse

unruly [ʌn'ruːli] *adj* : indisciplinado

unsafe [ʌn'seɪf] *adj* : inseguro

unsaid [ʌn'sed] *adj* : sin decir

unsanitary [ʌn'sænəˌteri] *adj* : antihigiénico

unsatisfactory [ˌʌnˌsætəs'fæktəri] *adj* : insatisfactorio

unscathed [ʌn'skeɪðd] *adj* : ileso

unscrew [ʌn'skruː] *vt* : destornillar

unscrupulous [ʌn'skruːpjələs] *adj* : sin escrúpulos

unseemly [ʌn'siːmli] *adj* **-lier; -est** : indecoroso

unseen [ʌn'siːn] *adj* **1** : no visto **2** UN-NOTICED : inadvertido

unselfish [ʌn'selfɪʃ] *adj* : desinteresado

unsettle [ʌn'setəl] *vt* **-tled; -tling** DIS-TURB : perturbar — **unsettled** [ʌn'setəld] *adj* **1** CHANGEABLE : inestable **2** DISTURBED : agitado, inquieto **3** : variable (dícese del tiempo)

unsightly [ʌn'saɪtli] *adj* : feo

unskilled [ʌn'skɪld] *adj* : no calificado — **unskillful** [ʌn'skɪlfəl] *adj* : torpe, poco hábil

unsociable [ʌn'soːʃəbəl] *adj* : poco sociable

unsound [ʌn'saʊnd] *adj* **1** : defectuoso, erróneo **2 of ~ mind** : demente

unspeakable [ʌn'spiːkəbəl] *adj* **1** : indecible **2** TERRIBLE : atroz

unstable [ʌn'steɪbəl] *adj* : inestable

unsteady [ʌn'stedi] *adj* **1** : inestable **2** SHAKY : tembloroso

unsuccessful [ˌʌnsək'sesfəl] *adj* **1** : fracasado **2 be ~** : no tener éxito

unsuitable [ʌn'suːtəbəl] *adj* **1** : inadecuado **2** INCONVENIENT : inconveniente

unsure [ʌn'ʃʊr] *adj* : inseguro

unsuspecting [ˌʌnsə'spektɪŋ] *adj* : confiado

unsympathetic [ˌʌnˌsɪmpə'θeʈɪk] *adj* : indiferente

unthinkable [ʌn'θɪŋkəbəl] *adj* : inconcebible

untidy [ʌn'taɪdi] *adj* : desordenado (dícese de una sala, etc.), desaliñado (dícese de una persona)

untie [ʌn'taɪ] *vt* **-tied; -tying** *or* **-tieing** : desatar

until [ʌn'tɪl] *prep* : hasta — **~** *conj* : hasta que

untimely [ʌn'taɪmli] *adj* **1** PREMATURE : prematuro **2** INOPPORTUNE : inoportuno

untold [ʌn'toːld] *adj* : incalculable

untoward [ʌn'tɔrd, -'tɔːrd, -tə'wɔrd] *adj* **1** ADVERSE : adverso **2** IMPROPER : indecoroso

untroubled [ʌn'trʌbəld] *adj* **1** : tranquilo **2 be ~ by** : no estar afectado por

untrue [ʌn'truː] *adj* : falso

unused [ʌn'juːzd, *in sense 2 usually* -'juːst] *adj* **1** NEW : nuevo **2 be ~ to** : no estar acustumbrado a

unusual [ʌn'juːʒuəl] *adj* : poco común, insólito — **unusually** [ʌn'juːʒuəl, -'juːʒəli] *adv* : excepcionalmente

unveil [ʌn'veɪl] *vt* : descubrir, revelar

unwanted [ʌn'wɑntəd] *adj* : superfluo (dícese de un objeto), no deseado (dícese de un niño, etc.)

unwarranted [ʌn'wɔrəntəd] *adj* : injustificado

unwelcome [ʌn'welkəm] *adj* : inoportuno, molesto

unwell [ʌn'wel] *adj* **be ~** : sentirse mal

unwieldy [ʌn'wiːldi] *adj* : difícil de manejar

unwilling [ʌn'wɪlɪŋ] *adj* : poco dispuesto — **unwillingly** [ʌn'wɪlɪŋli] *adv* : de mala gana

unwind [ʌn'waɪnd] *v* **-wound** [-'waʊnd]; **-winding** *vt* : desenrollar — *vi* **1** : desenrollarse **2** RELAX : relajarse

unwise [ʌn'waɪz] *adj* : imprudente

unworthy [ʌn'wərði] *adj* **be ~ of** : no ser digno de

unwrap [ʌn'ræp] *vt* **-wrapped; -wrapping** : desenvolver

up ['ʌp] *adv* **1** ABOVE : arriba **2** UPWARDS : hacia arriba **3 ten miles farther ~** : diez millas más adelante **4 ~ here/there** : aquí/allí arriba **5 ~ north** : en el norte **6 ~ until** : hasta — *adj* **1** AWAKE : levantado **2** FINISHED : terminado **3 be ~ against** : enfrentarse con **4 be ~ on** : estar al corriente de **5 it's ~ to you** : depende de ti **6 prices are ~** : los precios han aumentado **7 the sun is ~** : ha salido el sol **8 what's ~?** : ¿qué pasa? — **~** *prep* **1 go ~ the river** : ir río arriba **2 go ~ the stairs** : subir la escalera **3 ~ the coast** : a lo largo de la costa — *v* **upped** ['ʌpt]; **upping; ups** *vt* : aumentar — *vi* **she ~ and left** : agarró y se fue

upbringing ['ʌpˌbrɪŋɪŋ] *n* : educación *f*

upcoming ['ʌpˌkʌmɪŋ] *adj* : próximo

update ['ʌp'deɪt] *vt* **-dated; -dating** : poner al día, actualizar — ['ʌpˌdeɪt] *n* : puesta *f* al día

upgrade ['ʌpˌgreɪd, ʌp'-] *vt* **-graded; -grading** : elevar la categoría de (un puesto, etc.), mejorar (una facilidad, etc.)

upheaval [ˌʌpˈhiːvəl] *n* : trastorno *m*

uphill [ˌʌpˈhɪl] *adv* : cuesta arriba — ~ [ˈʌpˌhɪl] *adj* **1** : en subida **2 be an ~ battle** : ser muy difícil

uphold [ˌʌpˈhoːld] *vt* **-held; -holding** : sostener, apoyar

upholstery [ˌʌpˈhoːlstəri] *n, pl* **-steries** : tapicería *f*

upkeep [ˈʌpˌkiːp] *n* : mantenimiento *m*

upon [əˈpɒn, əˈpɑn] *prep* **1** : en, sobre **2 ~ leaving** : al salir

upper [ˈʌpər] *adj* : superior — ~ *n* : parte *f* superior (del calzado, etc.)

uppercase [ˌʌpərˈkeɪs] *adj* : mayúsculo

upper class *n* : clase *f* alta

upper hand *n* : ventaja *f*, dominio *m*

uppermost [ˈʌpərˌmoːst] *adj* : más alto

upright [ˈʌpˌraɪt] *adj* **1** VERTICAL : vertical **2** ERECT : derecho **3** JUST : recto, honesto — ~ *n* : montante *m*, poste *m*

uprising [ˈʌpˌraɪzɪŋ] *n* : insurrección *f*, revuelta *f*

uproar [ˈʌpˌror] *n* COMMOTION : alboroto *m*

uproot [ˌʌpˈruːt, -ˈrʊt] *vt* : desarraigar

upset [ˌʌpˈsɛt] *vt* **-set; -setting 1** OVERTURN : volcar **2** DISTRESS : alterar, inquietar **3** DISRUPT : trastornar — ~ *adj* **1** DISTRESSED : alterado **2 have an ~ stomach** : estar mal del estómago — ~ [ˈʌpˌsɛt] *n* : trastorno *m*

upshot [ˈʌpˌʃɑt] *n* : resultado *m* final

upside down [ˌʌpˌsaɪdˈdaʊn] *adv* **1** : al revés **2 turn ~** : volver — **upside-down** [ˌʌpˌsaɪdˈdaʊn] *adj* : al revés

upstairs [ˌʌpˈstærz] *adv* : arriba — ~ [ˈʌpˌstærz, ˌʌpˈ-] *adj* : de arriba — [ˈʌpˌstærz, ˌʌpˈ-] *ns & pl* : piso *m* de arriba

upstart [ˈʌpˌstɑrt] *n* : advenedizo *m*, -za *f*

upstream [ˈʌpˈstriːm] *adv* : río arriba

upswing [ˈʌpˌswɪŋ] *n* **be on the ~** : estar mejorándose

up-to-date [ˌʌptəˈdeɪt] *adj* **1** : corriente, al día **2** MODERN : moderno

uptown [ˈʌpˈtaʊn] *adv* : hacia la parte alta de la ciudad, hacia el distrito residencial

upturn [ˈʌpˌtərn] *n* : mejora *f*, auge *m* (económico)

upward [ˈʌpwərd] *or* **upwards** [-wərdz] *adv* : hacia arriba — **upward** *adj* : ascendente, hacia arriba

uranium [jʊˈreɪniəm] *n* : uranio *m*

urban [ˈərbən] *adj* : urbano

urbane [ˌərˈbeɪn] *adj* : urbano, cortés

urge [ˈərdʒ] *vt* **urged; urging 1** PRESS : instar, exhortar **2 ~ on** : animar — ~ *n* : impulso *m*, ganas *fpl* — **ur-**

gency [ˈərdʒəntsi] *n, pl* **-cies** : urgencia *f* — **urgent** [ˈərdʒənt] *adj* **1** : urgente **2 be ~** : urgir

urine [ˈjʊrən] *n* : orina *f* — **urinate** [ˈjʊrəˌneɪt] *vi* **-nated; -nating** : orinar

urn [ˈərn] *n* : urna *f*

Uruguayan [ˌʊrəˈgwaɪən, jʊr-, -ˈgweɪ-] *adj* : uruguayo

us [ˈʌs] *pron* **1** (*as direct or indirect object*) : nos **2** (*as object of a preposition*) : nosotros, nosotras **3 both of ~** : nosotros dos **4 it's ~!** : ¡somos nosotros!

usage [ˈjuːsɪdʒ, -zɪdʒ] *n* : uso *m*

use [ˈjuːz] *v* **used** [ˈjuːzd, *the phrase* "used to" *is usually* ˈjuːstu]; **using** *vt* **1** : usar **2** CONSUME : consumir, tomar (drogas, etc.) **3 ~ up** : agotar, consumir — *vi* **1 she ~d to dance** : acostumbraba bailar **2 winters ~d to be colder** : los inviernos solían ser más fríos — ~ [ˈjuːs] *n* **1** : uso *m* **2 have no ~ for** : no necesitar **3 have the ~ of** : poder usar, tener acceso a **4 it's no ~!** : ¡es inútil! — **used** [ˈjuːzd, *in sense 2 usually* ˈjuːst] *adj* **1** SECONDHAND : usado **2 be ~ to** : estar acostumbrado a — **useful** [ˈjuːsfəl] *adj* : útil, práctico — **usefulness** [ˈjuːsfəlnəs] *n* : utilidad *f* — **useless** [ˈjuːsləs] *adj* : inútil — **user** [ˈjuːzər] *n* : usuario *m*, -ria *f*

usher [ˈʌʃər] *vt* **1** : acompañar, conducir **2 ~ in** : hacer entrar — ~ *n* : acomodador *m*, -dora *f*

usual [ˈjuːʒuəl] *adj* **1** : habitual, usual **2 as ~** : como de costumbre — **usually** [ˈjuːʒuəli, ˈjuːʒəli] *adv* : usualmente

usurp [jʊˈsərp, -ˈzərp] *vt* : usurpar

utensil [jʊˈtɛntsəl] *n* : utensilio *m*

uterus [ˈjuːtərəs] *n, pl* **uteri** [-ˌraɪ] : útero *m*, matriz *f*

utility [jʊˈtɪləti] *n, pl* **-ties 1** : utilidad *f* **2 or public ~** : empresa *f* de servicio público

utilize [ˈjuːtəlˌaɪz] *vt* **-lized; -lizing** : utilizar

utmost [ˈʌtˌmoːst] *adj* **1** FARTHEST : extremo **2 of the ~ importance** : de suma importancia — ~ *n* **do one's ~** : hacer todo lo posible

utopia [jʊˈtoːpiə] *n* : utopía *f* — **utopian** [jʊˈtoːpiən] *adj* : utópico

utter[1] [ˈʌtər] *adj* : absoluto, completo

utter[2] *vt* : decir, pronunciar (palabras) — **utterance** [ˈʌtərənts] *n* : declaración *f*, expresión *f*

utterly [ˈʌtərli] *adv* : completamente, totalmente

V

v ['viː] *n, pl* **v's** *or* **vs** ['viːz] : v *f*, vigésima segunda letra del alfabeto inglés

vacant ['veɪkənt] *adj* **1** AVAILABLE : libre **2** UNOCCUPIED : desocupado **3** : vacante (dícese de un puesto) **4** : ausente (dícese de una mirada) — **vacancy** ['veɪkəntsi] *n, pl* **-cies 1** : (puesto *m*) vacante *f* **2** : habitación *f* libre (en un hotel, etc.)

vacate ['veɪˌkeɪt] *vt* **-cated; -cating** : desalojar, desocupar

vacation [veɪˈkeɪʃən, və-] *n* : vacaciones *fpl*

vaccination [ˌvæksəˈneɪʃən] *n* : vacunación *f* — **vaccinate** ['væksəˌneɪt] *vt* **-nated; -nating** : vacunar — **vaccine** ['væksin, væk-] *n* : vacuna *f*

vacuum ['vækjuːm, -kjəm] *n, pl* **vacuums** *or* **vacua** : vacío *m* — ~ *vt* : pasar la aspiradora por — **vacuum cleaner** *n* : aspiradora *f*

vagina [vəˈdʒaɪnə] *n, pl* **-nae** [-niː, -naɪ] *or* **-nas** : vagina *f*

vagrant ['veɪɡrənt] *n* : vagabundo *m*, -da *f*

vague ['veɪɡ] *adj* **vaguer; -est** : vago, indistinto

vain ['veɪn] *adj* **1** CONCEITED : vanidoso **2 in** ~ : en vano

valentine ['vælənˌtaɪn] *n* : tarjeta *f* del día de San Valentín

valiant ['væljənt] *adj* : valiente, valeroso

valid ['væləd] *adj* : válido — **validate** ['vælədeɪt] *vt* **-dated; -dating** : validar — **validity** [vəˈlɪdəti, væ-] *n* : validez *f*

valley ['væli] *n, pl* **-leys** : valle *m*

valor ['vælər] *n* : valor *m*, valentía *f*

value ['vælˌjuː] *n* : valor *m* — ~ *vt* **-ued; -uing** : valorar — **valuable** ['væljuəbəl, 'væljəbəl] *adj* : valioso — **valuables** *npl* : objetos *mpl* de valor

valve ['vælv] *n* : válvula *f*

vampire ['væmˌpaɪr] *n* : vampiro *m*

van ['væn] *n* : furgoneta *f*, camioneta *f*

vandal ['vændəl] *n* : vándalo *m* — **vandalism** ['vændəlˌɪzəm] *n* : vandalismo *m* — **vandalize** ['vændəlˌaɪz] *vt* : destrozar, destruir

vane ['veɪn] *n or* **weather ~** : veleta *f*

vanguard ['vænˌɡɑrd] *n* : vanguardia *f*

vanilla [vəˈnɪlə, -ˈne-] *n* : vainilla *f*

vanish ['vænɪʃ] *vi* : desaparecer

vanity ['vænəti] *n, pl* **-ties 1** : vanidad *f* **2** *or* ~ **table** : tocador *m*

vantage point ['væntɪdʒ] *n* : posición *f* ventajosa

vapor ['veɪpər] *n* : vapor *m*

variable ['veriəbəl] *adj* : variable — ~ *n* : variable *f* — **variance** ['veriənts] *n* **at** ~ **with** : en desacuerdo con — **variant** ['veriənt] *n* : variante *f* — **variation** [ˌveriˈeɪʃən] *n* : variación *f* — **varied** ['verid] *adj* : variado — **variegated** ['veriəˌɡeɪted] *adj* : abigarrado, multicolor — **variety** [vəˈraɪəti] *n, pl* **-ties 1** : variedad *f* **2** ASSORTMENT : surtido *m* **3** SORT : clase *f* — **various** ['veriəs] *adj* : varios, diversos

varnish ['vɑrnɪʃ] *n* : barniz *f* — ~ *vt* : barnizar

vary ['veri] *v* **varied; varying** : variar

vase ['veɪs, 'veɪz, 'vɑz] *n* **1** : jarrón *m* **2** *or* **flower ~** : florero *m*

vast ['væst] *adj* : vasto, enorme — **vastness** ['væstnəs] *n* : inmensidad *f*

vat ['væt] *n* : cuba *f*

vault[1] ['vɔlt] *vi* LEAP : saltar — ~ *n* : salto *m*

vault[2] *n* **1** DOME : bóveda *f* **2** *or* **bank** ~ : cámara *f* acorazada, bóveda *f* de seguridad *Lat* **3** CRYPT : cripta *f*

VCR [ˌviːˌsiˈɑr] *n* (*videocassette recorder*) *n* : video *m*

veal ['viːl] *n* : (carne *f* de) ternera *f*

veer ['vɪr] *vi* : virar

vegetable ['vedʒtəbəl, 'vedʒətə-] *adj* : vegetal — ~ *n* **1** : vegetal *m* (planta) **2** —**s** *npl* : verduras *fpl* — **vegetarian** [ˌvedʒəˈteriən] *n* : vegetariano *mf* — **vegetation** [ˌvedʒəˈteɪʃən] *n* : vegetación *f*

vehemence ['viːəmənts] *n* : vehemencia *f* — **vehement** ['viːəmənt] *adj* : vehemente

vehicle ['viːəkəl, 'viːˌhɪkəl] *n* : vehículo *m*

veil ['veɪl] *n* : velo *m* — ~ *vt* **1** : cubrir con un velo **2** CONCEAL : velar

vein ['veɪn] *n* **1** : vena *f* **2** : veta *f* (de un mineral, etc.)

velocity [vəˈlɑsəti] *n, pl* **-ties** : velocidad *f*

velvet ['velvət] *n* : terciopelo *m* — **velvety** ['velvəti] *adj* : aterciopelado

vending machine ['vendɪŋ-] *vt* : máquina *f* expendedora

vendor ['vɛndər] *n* : vendedor *m*, -dora *f*
veneer [və'nɪr] *n* **1** : chapa *f* **2** FACADE : apariencia *f*
venerable ['vɛnərəbəl] *adj* : venerable — **venerate** ['vɛnəˌreɪt] *vt* **-ated; -ating** : venerar — **veneration** [ˌvɛnə'reɪʃən] *n* : veneración *f*
venereal [və'nɪriəl] *adj* : venéreo
venetian blind [və'niːʃən-] *n* : persiana *f* veneciana
Venezuelan [ˌvɛnə'zweɪlən, -zuˈeɪ-] *adj* : venezolano
vengeance ['vɛndʒənts] *n* **1** : venganza *f* **2 take ~ on** : vengarse de — **vengeful** ['vɛndʒfəl] *adj* : vengativo
venison ['vɛnəsən, -zən] *n* : (carne *f* de) venado *m*
venom ['vɛnəm] *n* : veneno *m* — **venomous** ['vɛnəməs] *adj* : venenoso
vent ['vɛnt] *vt* : desahogar — **~** *n* **1** *or* **air ~** : rejilla *f* de ventilación **2** OUTLET : desahogo *m* — **ventilate** ['vɛntəlˌeɪt] *vt* **-lated; -lating** : ventilar — **ventilation** [ˌvɛntəl'eɪʃən] *n* : ventilación *f* — **ventilator** ['vɛntəlˌeɪtər] *n* : ventilador *m*
ventriloquist [vɛn'trɪləˌkwɪst] *n* : ventrílocuo *m*, -cua *f*
venture ['vɛntʃər] *v* **-tured; -turing** *vt* **1** RISK : arriesgar **2** : aventurar (una opinión, etc.) — *vi* : atreverse — **~** *n* *or* **business ~** : empresa *f*
venue ['vɛnjuː] *n* : lugar *m*
Venus ['viːnəs] *n* : Venus *m*
veranda *or* **verandah** [və'rændə] *n* : veranda *f*
verb ['vərb] *n* : verbo *m* — **verbal** ['vərbəl] *adj* : verbal — **verbatim** [vər'beɪtəm] *adv* : palabra por palabra — **~** *adj* : literal — **verbose** [vər'boːs] *adj* : verboso
verdict ['vərdɪkt] *n* **1** : veredicto *m* **2** OPINION : opinión *f*
verge ['vərdʒ] *n* **1** : borde *m* **2 on the ~ of** : a punto de (hacer algo), al borde de (algo) — **~** *vi* **verged; verging on** : rayar en
verify ['vɛrəˌfaɪ] *vt* **-fied; -fying** : verificar — **verification** [ˌvɛrəfəˈkeɪʃən] *n* : verificación *f*
vermin ['vərmən] *ns & pl* : alimañas *fpl*
vermouth [vər'muːθ] *n* : vermut *m*
versatile ['vərsətəl] *adj* : versátil — **versatility** [ˌvərsəˈtɪləti] *n* : versatilidad *f*
verse ['vərs] *n* **1** LINE : verso *m* **2** POETRY : poesía *f* **3** : versículo *m* (en la Biblia) — **versed** ['vərst] *adj* **be well ~ in** : ser muy versado en
version ['vərʒən] *n* : versión *f*
versus ['vərsəs] *prep* : versus

vertebra ['vərtəbrə] *n*, *pl* **-brae** [-ˌbreɪ, -ˌbriː] *or* **-bras** : vértebra *f*
vertical ['vərtɪkəl] *adj* : vertical — **~** *n* : vertical *f*
vertigo ['vərtɪˌgoː] *n*, *pl* **-goes** *or* **-gos** : vértigo *m*
verve ['vərv] *n* : brío *m*
very ['vɛri] *adv* **1** : muy **2 at the ~ least** : por lo menos **3 the ~ same thing** : la misma cosa **4 ~ much** : mucho **5 ~ well** : muy bien — **~** *adj* **verier; -est 1** PRECISE, SAME : mismo **2** MERE : solo, mero **3 the ~ thing** : justo lo que hacía falta
vessel ['vɛsəl] *n* **1** CONTAINER : recipiente *m* **2** SHIP : nave *f*, buque *m* **3** *or* **blood ~** : vaso *m* sanguíneo
vest ['vɛst] *n* **1** : chaleco *m* **2** *Brit* UNDERSHIRT : camiseta *f*
vestibule ['vɛstəˌbjuːl] *n* : vestíbulo *m*
vestige ['vɛstɪdʒ] *n* : vestigio *m*
vet ['vɛt] *n* **1** → **veterinarian 2** → **veteran**
veteran ['vɛtərən, 'vɛtrən] *n* : veterano *m*, -na *f*
veterinarian [ˌvɛtərə'nɛriən, ˌvɛtə'nɛr-] *n* : veterinario *m*, -ria *f* — **veterinary** ['vɛtərəˌnɛri] *adj* : veterinario
veto ['viːtoː] *n*, *pl* **-toes** : veto *m* — **~** *vt* : vetar
vex ['vɛks] *vt* ANNOY : irritar
via ['vaɪə, 'viːə] *prep* : por, vía
viable ['vaɪəbəl] *adj* : viable
viaduct ['vaɪəˌdʌkt] *n* : viaducto *m*
vial ['vaɪəl] *n* : frasco *m*
vibrant ['vaɪbrənt] *adj* : vibrante — **vibrate** ['vaɪˌbreɪt] *vi* **-brated; -brating** : vibrar — **vibration** [vaɪ'breɪʃən] *n* : vibración *f*
vicar ['vɪkər] *n* : vicario *m*, -ria *f*
vicarious [vaɪ'kæriəs, vɪ-] *adj* : indirecto
vice ['vaɪs] *n* : vicio *m*
vice president *n* : vicepresidente *m*, -ta *f*
vice versa [ˌvaɪsɪ'vərsə, ˌvaɪs'vər-] *adv* : viceversa
vicinity [və'sɪnəti] *n*, *pl* **-ties 1** : inmediaciones *fpl* **2 in the ~ of** ABOUT : alrededor de
vicious ['vɪʃəs] *adj* **1** SAVAGE : feroz **2** MALICIOUS : malicioso
victim ['vɪktəm] *n* : víctima *f*
victor ['vɪktər] *n* : vencedor *m*, -dora *f*
victory ['vɪktəri] *n*, *pl* **-ries** : victoria *f* — **victorious** [vɪk'toːriəs] *adj* : victorioso
video ['vɪdiˌoː] *n* : video *m*, vídeo *m* *Spain* — **~** *adj* : de video — **videocassette** [ˌvɪdioʊkə'sɛt] *n* : videocasete *m* — **videotape** ['vɪdioʊˌteɪp] *n* : video-

cinta *f* — ~ *vt* **-taped; -taping** : videograbar

vie ['vaɪ] *vi* **vied; vying** ['vaɪɪŋ] : competir

Vietnamese [ˌviˌɛtnəˈmiːz, -ˈmiːs] *adj* : vietnamita

view ['vju:] *n* **1** : vista *f* **2** OPINION : opinión *f* **3 come into ~** : aparecer **4 in ~ of** : en vista de (que) — ~ *vt* **1** : ver **2** CONSIDER : considerar — **viewer** ['vju:ər] *n or* **television ~** : televidente *mf* — **viewpoint** ['vju:ˌpɔɪnt] *n* : punto *m* de vista

vigil ['vɪdʒəl] *n* : vela *f* — **vigilance** ['vɪdʒələnts] *n* : vigilancia *f* — **vigilant** ['vɪdʒələnt] *adj* : vigilante

vigor *or Brit* **vigour** ['vɪgər] *n* : vigor *m* — **vigorous** ['vɪgərəs] *adj* **1** : enérgico **2** ROBUST : vigoroso

Viking ['vaɪkɪŋ] *n* : vikingo *m*, -ga *f*

vile ['vaɪl] *adj* **viler; vilest 1** : vil **2** REVOLTING : asqueroso **3** TERRIBLE : horrible

villa ['vɪlə] *n* : casa *f* de campo

village ['vɪlɪdʒ] *n* : pueblo *m* (grande), aldea *f* (pequeña) — **villager** ['vɪlɪdʒər] *n* : vecino *m*, -na *f* (de un pueblo); aldeano *m*, -na *f* (de una aldea)

villain ['vɪlən] *n* : villano *m*, -na *f*

vindicate ['vɪndəˌkeɪt] *vt* **-cated; -cating 1** : vindicar **2** JUSTIFY : justificar

vindictive [vɪnˈdɪktɪv] *adj* : vengativo

vine ['vaɪn] *n* **1** : enredadera *f* **2** GRAPEVINE : vid *f*

vinegar ['vɪnɪgər] *n* : vinagre *m*

vineyard ['vɪnjərd] *n* : viña *f*, viñedo *m*

vintage ['vɪntɪdʒ] *n* **1** : cosecha *f* (de vino) **2** ERA : época *f* — ~ *adj* **1** : añejo (dícese de un vino) **2** CLASSIC : de época

vinyl ['vaɪnəl] *n* : vinilo *m*

viola [viˈoːlə] *n* : viola *f*

violate ['vaɪəˌleɪt] *vt* **-lated; -lating** : violar — **violation** [ˌvaɪəˈleɪʃən] *n* : violación *f*

violence ['vaɪlənts, 'vaɪə-] *n* : violencia *f* — **violent** ['vaɪlənt, 'vaɪə-] *adj* : violento

violet ['vaɪlət, 'vaɪə-] *n* : violeta *f* (flor), violeta *m* (color)

violin [ˌvaɪəˈlɪn] *n* : violín *m* — **violinist** [ˌvaɪəˈlɪnɪst] *n* : violinista *mf* — **violoncello** [ˌvaɪələnˈtʃeloː, ˌviː-] → **cello**

VIP [ˌviːaɪˈpiː] *n, pl* **VIPs** [-ˈpiːz] : VIP *mf*

viper ['vaɪpər] *n* : víbora *f*

virgin ['vərdʒən] *n* : virgen *mf* — ~ *adj* **1** : virgen (dícese de la lana, etc.) **2** CHASTE : virginal — **virginity** [vərˈdʒɪnəti] *n* : virginidad *f*

virile ['vɪrəl, -ˌaɪl] *adj* : viril — **virility** [vəˈrɪləti] *n* : virilidad *f*

virtual ['vərtʃəl] *adj* : virtual — **virtually** ['vərtʃʊəli, 'vərtʃəli] *adv* : prácticamente

virtue ['vərˌtʃuː] *n* **1** : virtud *f* **2 by ~ of** : en virtud de

virtuoso [ˌvərtʃuˈoːsoː, -zoː] *n, pl* **-sos** *or* **-si** [-ˌsiː, -ziː] : virtuoso *m*, -sa *f*

virtuous ['vərtʃuəs] *adj* : virtuoso

virulent ['vɪrələnt, 'vɪrjə-] *adj* : virulento

virus ['vaɪrəs] *n* : virus *m*

visa ['viːzə, -sə] *n* : visado *m*, visa *f Lat*

vis-à-vis [ˌviːzəˈviː, -sə-] *prep* : con respecto a

viscous ['vɪskəs] *adj* : viscoso

vise ['vaɪs] *n* : torno *m* de banco

visible ['vɪzəbəl] *adj* **1** : visible **2** NOTICEABLE : evidente — **visibility** [ˌvɪzəˈbɪləti] *n, pl* **-ties** : visibilidad *f*

vision ['vɪʒən] *n* **1** : visión *f* **2 have ~s of** : imaginarse — **visionary** ['vɪʒəˌneri] *adj* : visionario — ~ *n, pl* **-ries** : visionario *m*, -ria *f*

visit ['vɪzət] *vt* : visitar — *vi* **1** : hacer una visita **2 be ~ing** : estar de visita — ~ *n* : visita *f* — **visitor** ['vɪzətər] *n* **1** : visitante *mf* **2** GUEST : visita *f*

visor ['vaɪzər] *n* : visera *f*

vista ['vɪstə] *n* : vista *f*

visual ['vɪʒuəl] *adj* : visual — **visualize** ['vɪʒuˌlaɪz] *vt* **-ized; -izing** : visualizar

vital ['vaɪtəl] *adj* **1** : vital **2** CRUCIAL : esencial — **vitality** [vaɪˈtæləti] *n, pl* **-ties** : vitalidad *f*, energía *f*

vitamin ['vaɪtəmən] *n* : vitamina *f*

vivacious [vəˈveɪʃəs, vaɪ-] *adj* : vivaz, animado

vivid ['vɪvəd] *adj* : vivo (dícese de colores), vívido (dícese de sueños, etc.)

vocabulary [voːˈkæbjəˌleri] *n, pl* **-laries** : vocabulario *m*

vocal ['voːkəl] *adj* **1** : vocal **2** OUTSPOKEN : vociferante — **vocal cords** *npl* : cuerdas *fpl* vocales — **vocalist** ['voːkəlɪst] *n* : cantante *mf*, vocalista *mf*

vocation [voːˈkeɪʃən] *n* : vocación *f* — **vocational** [voːˈkeɪʃənəl] *adj* : profesional

vociferous [voːˈsɪfərəs] *adj* : vociferante, ruidoso

vodka ['vadkə] *n* : vodka *m*

vogue ['voːg] *n* **1** : moda *f*, boga *f* **2 be in ~** : estar de moda, estar en boga

voice ['vɔɪs] *n* : voz *f* — ~ *vt* **voiced; voicing** : expresar

void ['vɔɪd] *adj* **1** INVALID : nulo **2 ~ of** : falto de — ~ *n* : vacío *m* — ~ *vt* : anular

volatile ['vɑləṭəl] *adj* : volátil — **volatility** [,vɑlə'tɪləṭi] *n* : volatilidad *f*
volcano [vɑl'keɪˌno:] *n, pl* **-noes** *or* **-nos** : volcán *m* — **volcanic** [vɑl'kænɪk] *adj* : volcánico
volition [vo'lɪʃən] *n* of one's own ~. : por voluntad propia
volley ['vɑli] *n, pl* **-leys 1** : descarga *f* (de tiros) **2** : torrente *m* (de insultos, etc.) **3** : volea *f* (en deportes) — **volleyball** ['vɑliˌbɔl] *n* : voleibol *m*
volt ['vo:lt] *n* : voltio *m* — **voltage** ['vo:ltɪdʒ] *n* : voltaje *m*
voluble ['vɑljəbəl] *adj* : locuaz
volume ['vɑljəm, -ˌjuːm] *n* : volumen *m* — **voluminous** [və'luːmənəs] *adj* : voluminoso
voluntary ['vɑlənˌteri] *adj* : voluntario — **volunteer** [,vɑlən'tɪr] *n* : voluntario *m*, -ria *f* — ~ *vt* : ofrecer — *vi* ~ **to** : ofrecerse a
voluptuous [və'lʌptʃʊəs] *adj* : voluptuoso

vomit ['vɑmət] *n* : vómito *m* — ~ *v* : vomitar
voracious [vɔ'reɪʃəs, və-] *adj* : voraz
vote ['vo:t] *n* **1** : voto *m* **2** SUFFRAGE : derecho *m* al voto — ~ *vi* **voted; voting** : votar — **voter** ['vo:ṭər] *n* : votante *mf* — **voting** ['vo:ṭɪŋ] *n* : votación *f*
vouch ['vaʊtʃ] *vi* ~ **for** : responder de (algo), responder por (algn) — **voucher** ['vaʊtʃər] *n* : vale *m*
vow [vaʊ] *n* : voto *m* — ~ *vt* : jurar
vowel ['vaʊəl] *n* : vocal *m*
voyage ['vɔɪɪdʒ] *n* : viaje *m*
vulgar ['vʌlgər] *adj* **1** COMMON : ordinario **2** CRUDE : grosero, vulgar — **vulgarity** [,vʌl'gærəṭi] *n, pl* **-ties** : vulgaridad *f*
vulnerable ['vʌlnərəbəl] *adj* : vulnerable — **vulnerability** [,vʌlnərə'bɪləṭi] *n, pl* **-ties** : vulnerabilidad *f*
vulture ['vʌltʃər] *n* : buitre *m*
vying → **vie**

W

w ['dʌbəlˌjuː] *n, pl* **w's** *or* **ws** [-juːz] : w *f*, vigésima tercera letra del alfabeto inglés
wad ['wɑd] *n* : taco *m* (de papel, etc.), fajo *m* (de billetes)
waddle ['wɑdəl] *vi* **-dled; -dling** : andar como un pato
wade ['weɪd] *v* **waded; wading** *vi* : caminar por el agua — *vt or* ~ **across** : vadear
wafer ['weɪfər] *n* : barquillo *m*
waffle ['wɑfəl] *n* : gofre *m* Spain, wafle *m* Lat
waft ['wɑft, 'wæft] *vt* : llevar por el aire — *vi* : flotar
wag ['wæg] *v* **wagged; wagging** *vt* : menear — *vi* : menearse
wage ['weɪdʒ] *n or* **wages** *npl* : salario *m* — ~ *vt* **waged; waging** ~ **war** : hacer la guerra
wager ['weɪdʒər] *n* : apuesta *f* — ~ *v* : apostar
wagon ['wægən] *n* **1** CART : carrito *m* **2** → **station wagon**
waif ['weɪf] *n* : niño *m* abandonado
wail ['weɪl] *vi* : lamentarse — ~ *n* : lamento *m*
waist ['weɪst] *n* : cintura *f* — **waistline** ['weɪstˌlaɪn] *n* : cintura *f*
wait ['weɪt] *vi* : esperar — *vt* **1** AWAIT : esperar **2** ~ **tables** : servir a la mesa

— ~ *n* **1** : espera *f* **2 lie in** ~ : estar al acecho — **waiter** ['weɪṭər] *n* : camarero *m*, mozo *m* Lat — **waiting room** *n* : sala *f* de espera — **waitress** ['weɪtrəs] *n* : camarera *f*, moza *f* Lat
waive ['weɪv] *vt* **waived; waiving** : renunciar a — **waiver** ['weɪvər] *n* : renuncia *f*
wake¹ ['weɪk] *v* **woke** ['wo:k]; **woken** ['wo:kən] *or* **waked; waking** *vi or* ~ **up** : despertarse — *vt* : despertar — ~ *n* : velatorio *m* (de un difunto)
wake² *n* **1** : estela *f* (de un barco) **2 in the** ~ **of** : tras, como consecuencia de
waken ['weɪkən] *vt* : despertar — *vi* : despertarse
walk ['wɔk] *vi* **1** : caminar, andar **2** STROLL : pasear **3 too far to** ~ : demasiado lejos para ir a pie — *vt* **1** : caminar por **2** : sacar a pasear (a un perro) — ~ *n* **1** : paseo *m* **2** PATH : camino *m* **3** GAIT : andar *m* — **walker** ['wɔkər] *n* : paseante *mf* **2** HIKER : excursionista *mf* — **walking stick** *n* : bastón *m* — **walkout** ['wɔkˌaʊt] *n* STRIKE : huelga *f* — **walk out** *vi* **1** STRIKE : declararse en huelga **2** LEAVE : salir, irse **3** ~ **on** : abandonar
wall ['wɔl] *n* : muro *m* (exterior), pared *f* (interior), muralla *f* (de una ciudad)

wallet ['wɑlət] *n* : billetera *f*, cartera *f*
wallflower ['wɔl,flauər] *n* **be a ~** : comer pavo
wallop ['wɑləp] *vt* : pegar fuerte — **~** *n* : golpe *m* fuerte
wallow ['wɑlo] *vi* : revolcarse
wallpaper ['wɔl,peipər] *n* : papel *m* pintado — **~** *vt* : empapelar
walnut ['wɔl,nʌt] *n* : nuez *f*
walrus ['wɔlrəs, 'wɑl-] *n, pl* **-rus** *or* **-ruses** : morsa *f*
waltz ['wɔlts] *n* : vals *m* — **~** *vi* : valsar
wan ['wɑn] *adj* **wanner; -est** : pálido
wand ['wɑnd] *n* : varita *f* (mágica)
wander ['wɑndər] *vi* **1** : vagar, pasear **2** STRAY : divagar — *vt* : pasear por — **wanderer** ['wɑndərər] *n* : vagabundo *m*, -da *f* — **wanderlust** ['wɑndər,lʌst] *n* : pasión *f* por viajar
wane ['wein] *vi* **waned; waning** : menguar — **~** *n* **be on the ~** : estar disminuyendo
want ['wɑnt, 'wɔnt] *vt* **1** DESIRE : querer **2** NEED : necesitar **3** LACK : carecer de — **~** *n* **1** NEED : necesidad *f* **2** LACK : falta *f* **3** DESIRE : deseo *m* — **wanting** ['wɑntiŋ, 'wɔn-] *adj* **be ~** : carecer
wanton ['wɑntən, 'wɔn-] *adj* **1** LEWD : lascivo **2 ~ cruelty** : crueldad *f* despiadada
war ['wɔr] *n* : guerra *f*
ward ['wɔrd] *n* **1** : sala *f* (de un hospital, etc.) **2** : distrito *m* electoral **3** : pupilo *m*, -la *f* (de un tutor, etc.) — **~** *vt* **off** : protegerse contra — **warden** ['wɔrdən] *n* **1** : guardián *m*, -diana *f* **2** *or* **game ~** : guardabosque *mf* **3** *or* **prison ~** : alcaide *m*
wardrobe ['wɔrd,rob] *n* **1** CLOSET : armario *m* **2** CLOTHES : vestuario *m*
warehouse ['wær,haus] *n* : almacén *m*, bodega *f* Lat — **wares** ['wærz] *npl* : mercancías *fpl*
warfare ['wɔr,fær] *n* : guerra *f*
warily ['wærəli] *adv* : cautelosamente
warlike ['wær,laik] *adj* : belicoso
warm ['wɔrm] *adj* **1** : caliente **2** LUKEWARM : tibio **3** CARING : cariñoso **4** I **feel ~** : tengo calor **5 ~ clothes** : ropa *f* de abrigo — **~** *vt or* **~ up** : calentar — *vi* **1** *or* **~ up** : calentarse **2 ~ to** : tomar simpatía a (algn), entusiasmarse con (algo) — **warmblooded** ['wɔrm'blʌdəd] *adj* : de sangre caliente — **warmhearted** ['wɔrm'hɑrtəd] *adj* : cariñoso — **warmly** ['wɔrmli] *adv* **1** : calurosamente **2 dress ~** : abrigarse — **warmth** ['wɔrmpθ] *n* **1** : calor *m* **2** AFFECTION : cariño *m*, afecto *m*

warn ['wɔrn] *vt* : advertir, avisar— **warning** ['wɔrniŋ] *n* : advertencia *f*, aviso *m*
warp ['wɔrp] *vt* **1** : alabear (madera, etc.) **2** DISTORT : deformar — *vi* : alabearse
warrant ['wɔrənt] *n* **1** : autorización *f* **2 arrest ~** : orden *f* judicial — **~** *vt* : justificar — **warranty** ['wɔrənti, ,wɔrən'ti] *n, pl* **-ties** : garantía *f*
warrior ['wɔriər] *n* : guerrero *m*, -ra *f*
warship ['wɔr,ʃip] *n* : buque *m* de guerra
wart ['wɔrt] *n* : verruga *f*
wartime ['wɔr,taim] *n* : tiempo *m* de guerra
wary ['wæri] *adj* **warier; -est** : cauteloso
was → be
wash ['wɔʃ, 'wɑʃ] *vt* **1** : lavar(se) **2** CARRY : arrastrar **3 ~ away** : llevarse **4 ~ over** : bañar — *vi* **1** : lavarse — **~** *n* **1** : lavado *m* **2** LAUNDRY : ropa *f* sucia — **washable** ['wɔʃəbəl, 'wɑ-] *adj* : lavable — **washcloth** ['wɔʃ,klɔθ, 'wɑʃ-] *n* : toallita *f* (para lavarse) — **washed-out** ['wɔʃ'aut, 'wɑʃ-t-] *adj* **1** : desvaído (dícese de colores) **2** EXHAUSTED : agotado — **washer** ['wɔʃər, 'wɑ-] *n* **1 → washing machine 2** : arandela *f* (de una llave, etc.) — **washing machine** *n* : máquina *f* de lavar, lavadora *f* — **washroom** ['wɔʃ,rum, 'wɑʃ-, -,rum] *n* : servicios *mpl* (públicos), baño *m*
wasn't ['wɑzənt] *(contraction of* **was not)** **→ be**
wasp ['wɑsp] *n* : avispa *f*
waste ['weist] *v* **wasted; wasting** *vt* **1** : desperdiciar, derrochar, malgastar **2 ~ time** : perder tiempo — *vi or* **~ away** : consumirse — **~** *adj* : de desecho — **~** *n* **1** : derroche *m*, desperdicio *m* **2** RUBBISH : desechos *mpl* **3 a ~ of time** : una pérdida de tiempo — **wastebasket** ['weist,bæskət] *n* : papelera *f* — **wasteful** ['weistfəl] *adj* : derrochador — **wasteland** ['weist,lænd, -lənd] *n* : yermo *m*
watch ['wɑtʃ] *vi* **1** : mirar **2** *or* **keep ~** : velar **3 ~ out!** : ¡ten cuidado!, ¡ojo! — *vt* **1** : mirar **2** *or* **over** : vigilar, cuidar **3 ~ what you do** : ten cuidado con lo que haces — **~** *n* **1** reloj *m* **2** SURVEILLANCE : vigilancia *f* **3** LOOKOUT : guardia *mf* — **watchdog** ['wɑtʃ,dɔg] *n* : perro *m* guardián — **watchful** ['wɑtʃfəl] *adj* : vigilante — **watchman** ['wɑtʃmən] *n, pl* **-men** [-mən, -,mɛn] : vigilante *m*, guarda *m* — **watchword** ['wɑtʃ,wərd] *n* : santo *m* y seña
water ['wɔtər, 'wɑ-] *n* : agua *f* — **~** *vt* **1**

: regar (el jardín, etc.) **2 ~ down** DI-
LUTE : diluir, aguar — *vi* **1** : lagrimar
(dícese de los ojos) **2 my mouth is
~ing** : se me hace agua la boca —
watercolor ['wɔt̬ər,kʌlər, 'wa-] *n* : acuarela *f* — **watercress** ['wɔt̬ər,krɛs,
'wa-] *n* : berro *m* — **waterfall** ['wɔt̬ər-
,fɔl, 'wa-] *n* : cascada *f*, salto *m* de agua
— **water lily** *n* : nenúfar *m* — **water-
logged** ['wɔt̬ər,lɔgd, 'wɔt̬ər,lagd] *adj*
: lleno de agua, empapado — **watermelon** ['wɔt̬ər,mɛlən, 'wa-] *n* : sandía *f*
— **waterpower** ['wɔt̬ər,pauɚr, 'wa-] *n*
: energía *f* hidráulica — **waterproof**
['wɔt̬ər,pruːf, 'wa-] *adj* : impermeable
— **watershed** ['wɔt̬ər,ʃɛd, 'wa-] *n* **1**
: cuenca *f* (de un río) **2** : momento *m*
crítico — **waterskiing** ['wɔt̬ər,skiːɪŋ,
'wa-] *n* : esquí *m* acuático — **watertight** ['wɔt̬ər,taɪt, 'wa-] *adj* : hermético
— **waterway** ['wɔt̬ər,weɪ, 'wa-] *n* : vía *f*
navegable — **waterworks** ['wɔt̬ər-
,wɚks, 'wa-] *npl* : central *f* de abastecimiento de agua — **watery** ['wɔt̬əri,
'wa-] *adj* **1** : acuoso **2** DILUTED : aguado, diluido **3** WASHED-OUT : desvaído
(dícese de colores)
watt ['wat] *n* : vatio *m* — **wattage** ['wat
,ɪdʒ] *n* : vataje *m*
wave ['weɪv] *v* **waved; waving** *vi* **1**
: saludar con la mano **2** : flotar (dícese
de una bandera) — *vt* **1** SHAKE : agitar
2 CURL : ondular **3** SIGNAL : hacer
señas a (con la mano) — ~ *n* **1** : ola *f*
(de agua) **2** CURL : onda *f* **3** : onda *f* (en
física) **4** : señal *f* (con la mano) **5**
SURGE : oleada *f* — **wavelength**
['weɪv,lɛŋkθ] *n* : longitud *f* de onda
waver ['weɪvər] *vi* : vacilar
wax¹ ['wæks] *vi* : crecer (dícese de la
luna)
wax² *n* : cera *f* (para pisos, etc.) — ~ *vt*
: encerar — **waxy** ['wæksi] *adj* **waxier,
-est** : ceroso
way ['weɪ] *n* **1** : camino *m* **2** MEANS
: manera *f*, modo *m* **3 by the ~** : a
propósito, por cierto **4 by ~ of** : vía,
pasando por **5 come a long ~** : hacer
grandes progresos **6 get in the ~**
: meterse en el camino **7 get one's
own ~** : salirse uno con la suya **8
mend one's ~s** : dejar las malas cos-
tumbres **9 out of the ~** REMOTE : remoto, recóndito **10 which ~ did he
go?** : ¿por dónde fue?
we ['wiː] *pron* : nosotros, nosotras
weak ['wiːk] *adj* **1** : débil **2** DILUTED
: aguado **3 a ~ excuse** : una excusa
poco convincente — **weaken** ['wiːkən]
vt : debilitar — *vi* : debilitarse —

weakling ['wiːklɪŋ] *n* : debilucho *m*,
-cha *f* — **weakly** ['wiːkli] *adv* : débilmente — ~ *adj* **weaklier, -est** : enfermizo — **weakness** ['wiːknəs] *n* **1**
: debilidad *f* **2** FLAW : flaqueza *f*, punto
m débil
wealth ['wɛlθ] *n* : riqueza *f* — **wealthy**
['wɛlθi] *adj* **wealthier, -est** : rico
wean ['wiːn] *vt* : destetar
weapon ['wɛpən] *n* : arma *f*
wear ['wær] *v* **wore** ['wor]; **worn** ['worn];
wearing *vt* **1** : llevar (ropa, etc.),
calzar (zapatos) **2** or **~ away** : desgastar **3 ~ oneself out** : agotarse **4
~ out** : gastar — *vi* **1** LAST : durar **2
~ off** : desaparecer **3 ~ out** : gastarse — ~ *n* **1** USE : uso *m* **2** CLOTHING
: ropa *f* **3 be the worse for ~** : estar
deteriorado — **wear and tear** *n* : desgaste *m*
weary ['wɪri] *adj* **-rier; -est** : cansado
— *v* **-ried; -rying** *vt* : cansar — *vi*
: cansarse — **weariness** ['wɪrinəs] *n*
: cansancio *m* — **wearisome** ['wɪri-
səm] *adj* : cansado
weasel ['wiːzəl] *n* : comadreja *f*
weather ['wɛðər] *n* : tiempo *m* — ~ *vt*
1 WEAR : erosionar, desgastar **2** EN-
DURE, OVERCOME : superar — **weath-
er-beaten** ['wɛðər,biːtən] *adj* : curtido
— **weatherman** ['wɛðər,mæn] *n, pl*
-men [-mən, -,mɛn] : meteorólogo *m*,
-ga *f* — **weather vane** *n* : valeta *f*
weave ['wiːv] *v* **wove** ['woːv] *or*
weaved; woven ['woːvən] *or* **weaved;
weaving** *vt* **1** : tejer (tela) **2** INTERLACE
: entretejer **3 ~ one's way** : abrirse
camino — *vi* : tejer — ~ *n* : tejido *m*
— **weaver** ['wiːvər] *n* : tejedor *m*, -dora
f
web ['wɛb] *n* **1** : telaraña *f* (de araña) **2**
: membrana *f* interdigital (de aves) **3**
NETWORK : red *f*
wed ['wɛd] *v* **wedded; wedding** *vt*
: casarse con — *vi* : casarse
we'd ['wiːd] (*contraction of* **we had, we
should,** *or* **we would**) → **have, should,
would**
wedding ['wɛdɪŋ] *n* : boda *f*, casamiento
m
wedge ['wɛdʒ] *n* **1** : cuña *f* **2** PIECE : porción *f*, trozo *m* — ~ *vt* **wedged;
wedging 1** : apretar (con una cuña) **2**
CRAM : meter
Wednesday ['wɛnz,deɪ, -di] *n* : miércoles *m*
wee ['wiː] *adj* **1** : pequeñito **2 in the ~
hours** : a las altas horas
weed ['wiːd] *n* : mala hierba *f* — ~ *vt* **1**
: desherbar **2 ~ out** : eliminar

week ['wi:k] *n* : semana *f* — **weekday** ['wi:k,deɪ] *n* : día *m* laborable — **weekend** ['wi:k,ɛnd] *n* : fin *m* de semana — **weekly** ['wi:kli] *adv* : semanalmente — ~ *adj* : semanal — ~ *n, pl* **-lies** : semanario *m*

weep ['wi:p] *v* **wept** ['wɛpt]; **weeping** : llorar — **weeping willow** *n* : sauce *m* llorón — **weepy** ['wi:pi] *adj* **weepier; -est** : lloroso

weigh ['weɪ] *vt* **1** : pesar **2** CONSIDER : sopesar **3** ~ **down** : sobrecargar (con una carga), abrumar (con preocupaciones, etc.) — *vi* : pesar

weight ['weɪt] *n* **1** : peso *m* **2 gain** ~ : engordar **3 lose** ~ : adelgazar — **weighty** ['weɪti] *adj* **weightier; -est 1** HEAVY : pesado **2** IMPORTANT : importante, de peso

weird ['wɪrd] *adj* **1** : misterioso **2** STRANGE : extraño

welcome ['wɛlkəm] *vt* **-comed; -coming** : dar la bienvenida a, recibir — ~ *adj* **1** : bienvenido **2 you're** ~ : de nada — ~ *n* : bienvenida *f*, acogida *f*

weld ['wɛld] *v* : soldar

welfare ['wɛl,fær] *n* **1** WELL-BEING : bienestar *m* **2** AID : asistencia *f* social

well[1] ['wɛl] *adv* **better** ['bɛt̬ər]; **best** ['bɛst] **1** : bien **2** CONSIDERABLY : bastante **3 as** ~ : también **4 as** ~ **as** : además de — ~ *adj* : bien — ~ *interj* **1** (*used to introduce a remark*) : bueno **2** (*used to express surprise*) : ¡vaya!

well[2] *n* : pozo *m* — ~ *vi or* ~ **up** : brotar, manar

we'll ['wi:l, wɪl] (*contraction of* **we shall** *or* **we will**) → **shall, will**

well-being ['wɛl'bi:ɪŋ] *n* : bienestar *m* — **well-bred** ['wɛl'brɛd] *adj* : fino, bien educado — **well-done** ['wɛl'dʌn] *adj* **1** : bien hecho **2** : bien cocido (dícese de la carne, etc.) — **well-known** ['wɛl'noːn] *adj* : famoso, bien conocido — **well-meaning** ['wɛl'mi:nɪŋ] *adj* : bien-intencionado — **well-off** ['wɛl'ɔf] *adj* : acomodado — **well-rounded** ['wɛl'raʊndəd] *adj* : completo — **well-to-do** [,wɛltə'du:] *adj* : próspero, adinerado

Welsh ['wɛlʃ] *adj* : galés — ~ *n* **1** : galés *m* (idioma) **2 the** ~ : los galeses

went → **go**
wept → **weep**
were → **be**
we're ['wɪr, 'wər, 'wiːr] (*contraction of* **we are**) → **be**

weren't ['wərənt, 'wəmt] (*contraction of* **were not**) → **be**

west ['wɛst] *adv* : al oeste — ~ *adj* : oeste, del oeste — ~ *n* **1** : oeste *m* **2 the West** : el Oeste, el Occidente — **westerly** ['wɛstərli] *adv & adj* : del oeste — **western** ['wɛstərn] *adj* **1** : del oeste **2 Western** : occidental — **Westerner** ['wɛstərnər] *n* : habitante *mf* del oeste — **westward** ['wɛstwərd] *adv & adj* : hacia el oeste

wet ['wɛt] *adj* **wetter; wettest 1** : mojado **2** RAINY : lluvioso **3** ~ **paint** : pintura *f* fresca — ~ *vt* **wet** *or* **wetted; wetting** : mojar, humedecer

we've ['wi:v] (*contraction of* **we have**) → **have**

whack ['hwæk] *vt* : golpear fuertemente — ~ *n* : golpe *m* fuerte

whale ['hweɪl] *n, pl* **whales** *or* **whale** : ballena *f*

wharf ['hwɔrf] *n, pl* **wharves** ['hwɔrvz] : muelle *m*, embarcadero *m*

what ['hwɑt, 'hwʌt] *adj* **1** (*used in questions and exclamations*) : qué **2** WHATEVER : cualquier — ~ *pron* **1** (*used in questions*) : qué **2** (*used in indirect statements*) : lo que, que **3** ~ **does it cost?** : ¿cuánto cuesta? **4** ~ **for?** : ¿por qué? **5** ~ **if** : y si — **whatever** [hwɑt'ɛvər, 'hwʌt-] *adj* **1** : cualquier **2 there's no chance** ~ : no hay ninguna posibilidad **3 nothing** ~ : nada en absoluto — ~ *pron* **1** ANYTHING : lo que **2** (*used in questions*) : qué **3** ~ **it may be** : sea lo que sea — **whatsoever** [,hwɑtso'ɛvər, 'hwʌt-] *adj & pron* → **whatever**

wheat ['hwi:t] *n* : trigo *m*

wheedle ['hwi:dəl] *vt* **-dled; -dling** : engatusar

wheel ['hwi:l] *n* **1** : rueda *f* **2** *or* **steering** ~ : volante *m* (de automóviles, etc.), timón *m* (de barcos) — ~ *vt* : empujar (algo sobre ruedas) — *vi or* ~ **around** : darse la vuelta — **wheelbarrow** ['hwi:l,bær,o:] *n* : carretilla *f* — **wheelchair** ['hwi:l,tʃær] *n* : silla *f* de ruedas

wheeze ['hwi:z] *vi* **wheezed; wheezing** : resollar — ~ *n* : resuello *m*

when ['hwɛn] *adv* : cuándo — ~ *conj* **1** : cuando **2 the days** ~ **I clean the house** : los días (en) que limpio la casa — ~ *pron* : cuándo — **whenever** [hwɛn'ɛvər] *adv* : cuando sea — ~ *conj* **1** : cada vez que **2** ~ **you like** : cuando quieras

where ['hwɛr] *adv* **1** : dónde **2** ~ **are you going?** : ¿adónde vas? — ~ *conj*

& *pron* : donde — **whereabouts**
['ʰwerə,bauts] *adv* : (por) dónde — ~
ns & pl : paradero *m* — **wherever**
[ʰwer'evər] *adv* **1** : en cualquier parte *m*
WHERE : dónde, adónde — ~ *conj*
: dondequiera que

whet ['ʰwet] *vt* **whetted; whetting 1**
: afilar **2** ~ **the appetite** : estimular
el apetito

whether ['ʰweðər] *conj* **1** : si **2 we**
doubt ~ : dudamos
que aparezca **3** ~ **you like it or not**
: tanto si quieras como si no

which ['ʰwɪtʃ] *adj* **1** : qué, cuál **2 in** ~
case : en cuyo caso — ~ *pron* **1**
(*used in questions*) : cuál **2** (*used in*
relative clauses) : que, el (la) cual —
whichever [ʰwɪtʃ'evər] *adj* : cualquier
— ~ *pron* : el (la) que, cualquiera que

whiff ['ʰwɪf] *n* **1** PUFF : soplo *m* **2** SMELL
: olorcillo *m*

while ['ʰwaɪl] *n* **1** : rato *m* **2 be worth**
one's ~ : valer la pena **3 in a** ~
: dentro de poco — ~ *conj* **1** : mientras **2** WHEREAS : mientras que **3** AL-
THOUGH : aunque — ~ *vt* **whiled;**
whiling ~ **away the time** : matar el
tiempo

whim ['ʰwɪm] *n* : capricho *m*, antojo *m*

whimper ['ʰwɪmpər] *vi* : lloriquear— ~
n : quejido *m*

whimsical ['ʰwɪmzɪkəl] *adj* : caprichoso, fantasioso

whine ['ʰwaɪn] *vi* **whined; whining 1**
: gimotear **2** COMPLAIN : quejarse —
~ *n* : quejido *m*, gemido *m*

whip ['ʰwɪp] *v* **whipped; whipping** *vt* **1**
: azotar **2** BEAT : batir (huevos, crema,
etc.) **3** ~ **up** AROUSE : avivar, despertar — *vi* FLAP : agitarse — ~ *n* : látigo *m*

whir ['ʰwər] *vi* **whirred; whirring**
: zumbar — ~ *n* : zumbido *m*

whirl ['ʰwərl] *vi* **1** : dar vueltas, girar **2**
or ~ **about** : arremolinarse — ~ *n* **1**
: giro *m* **2** SWIRL : torbellino *m* —
whirlpool ['ʰwərl,pu:l] *n* : remolino *m*
— **whirlwind** ['ʰwərl,wɪnd] *n* : torbellino *m*

whisk ['ʰwɪsk] *vt* **1** : batir **2** ~ **away**
: llevarse — ~ *n or* **egg** ~ : batidor
m — **whisk broom** *n* : escobilla *f*

whisker ['ʰwɪskər] *n* **1** : pelo *m* (de la
barba) **2** ~**s** *npl* : bigotes *mpl* (de
animales)

whiskey *or* **whisky** ['ʰwɪski] *n, pl* **-keys**
or **-kies** : whisky *m*

whisper ['ʰwɪspər] *vi* : cuchichear,
susurrar — *vt* : susurrar — ~ *n*
: susurro *m*

whistle ['ʰwɪsəl] *v* **-tled; -tling** *vi* **1** : silbar, chiflar *Lat* **2** : pitar (dícese de un
tren, etc.) — *vt* : silbar — ~ *n* **1** : silbido *m*, chiflido *m* (sonido) **2** : silbato
m, pito *m* (instrumento)

white ['ʰwaɪt] *adj* **whiter; -est** : blanco
— ~ *n* **1** : blanco *m* (color) **2** : clara *f*
(de huevos) **3** *or* ~ **person** : blanco
m, -ca *f* — **white–collar** ['ʰwaɪt'kɑlər]
adj **1** : de oficina **2** ~ **worker** : oficinista *mf* — **whiten** ['ʰwaɪtən] *vt* : blanquear — **whiteness** ['ʰwaɪtnəs] *n*
: blancura *f* — **whitewash** ['ʰwaɪt,wɔʃ]
vt **1** : enjalbegar **2** CONCEAL : encubrir
(un escándalo, etc.) — ~ *n* **1** : jalbe-
gue *m*, lechada *f* **2** COVER–UP : encubrimiento *m*

whittle ['ʰwɪtəl] *vt* **-tled; -tling 1** : tallar
(madera) **2** *or* ~ **down** : reducir

whiz *or* **whizz** ['ʰwɪz] *vi* **whizzed;**
whizzing 1 BUZZ : zumbar **2** ~ **by**
: pasar muy rápido — ~ *or* **whizz** *n,*
pl **whizzes** : zumbido *m* — **whiz kid** *n*
: joven *m* prometedor

who ['hu:] *pron* **1** (*used in direct and in-*
direct questions) : quién **2** (*used in*
relative clauses) : que, quien — **who-**
dunit [hu:'dʌnɪt] *n* : novela *f* policíaca
— **whoever** [hu:'evər] *pron* **1** : quienquiera que, quien **2** (*used in questions*)
: quién

whole ['ho:l] *adj* **1** : entero **2** INTACT : intacto **3 a** ~ **lot** : muchísimo — ~ *n* **1**
: todo *m* **2 as a** ~ : en conjunto **3 on**
the ~ : en general — **wholehearted**
['ho:l'hɑrtəd] *adj* : sincero — **whole-**
sale ['ho:l,seɪl] *n* : venta *f* al por mayor
— ~ *adj* **1** : al por mayor **2** ~
slaughter : matanza *f* sistemática —
~ *adv* : al por mayor — **wholesaler**
['ho:l,seɪlər] *n* : mayorista *mf* — **whole-**
some ['ho:lsəm] *adj* : sano — **whole**
wheat *adj* : de trigo integral — **whol-**
ly ['ho:li] *adv* : completamente

whom ['hu:m] *pron* **1** (*used in direct*
questions) : a quién **2** (*used in indirect*
questions) : de quién, con quién, en
quién **3** (*used in relative clauses*)
: que, a quien

whooping cough *n* : tos *f* ferina

whore ['hor] *n* : puta *f*

whose ['hu:z] *adj* **1** (*used in questions*)
: de quién **2** (*used in relative clauses*)
: cuyo — ~ *pron* : de quién

why ['ʰwaɪ] *adv* : por qué — ~ *n, pl*
whys : porqué — ~ *conj* : por qué
— ~ *interj* (*used to express surprise*)
: ¡vaya!, ¡mira!

wick ['wɪk] *n* : mecha *f*

wicked ['wɪkəd] *adj* **1** : malo, malvado **2**

MISCHIEVOUS : travieso **3** TERRIBLE : terrible, horrible — **wickedness** ['wɪkədnəs] *n* : maldad *f*

wicker ['wɪkər] *n* : mimbre *m* — ~ *adj* : de mimbre

wide ['waɪd] *adj* **wider; widest 1** : ancho **2** VAST : amplio, extenso **3** *or* ~ **of the mark** : desviado — ~ *adv* **1** ~ **apart** : muy separados **2 far and** ~ : por todas partes **3** ~ **open** : abierto de par en par — **wide-awake** ['waɪdə'weɪk] *adj* : (completamente) despierto — **widely** ['waɪdli] *adv* : extensivamente — **widespread** ['waɪd'sprɛd] *adj* : extendido

widow ['wɪ,do:] *n* : viuda *f* — ~ *vt* : dejar viuda — **widower** ['wɪdowər] *n* : viudo *m*

width ['wɪdθ] *n* : ancho *m*, anchura *f*

wield ['wi:ld] *vt* **1** : usar, manejar **2** EXERT : ejercer

wiener ['wi:nər] → **frankfurter**

wife ['waɪf] *n, pl* **wives** ['waɪvz] : esposa *f*, mujer *f*

wig ['wɪg] *n* : peluca *f*

wiggle ['wɪgəl] *v* **-gled; -gling** *vt* : menear, contonear — *vi* : menearse — ~ *n* : meneo *m*

wigwam ['wɪg,wɑm] *n* : wigwam *m*

wild ['waɪld] *adj* **1** : salvaje **2** DESOLATE : agreste **3** UNRULY : desenfrenado **4** RANDOM : al azar **5** FRANTIC : frenético **6** OUTRAGEOUS : extravagante — ~ *adv* **1** → **wildly 2 run** ~ : volver al estado silvestre (dícese de las plantas), desmandarse (dícese de los niños) — **wildcat** ['waɪld,kæt] *n* : gato *m* montés — **wilderness** ['wɪldərnəs] *n* : yermo *m*, desierto *m* — **wildfire** ['waɪld,faɪr] *n* **1** : fuego *m* descontrolado **2 spread like** ~ : propagarse como un reguero de pólvora — **wildflower** ['waɪld,flaʊər] *n* : flor *f* silvestre — **wildlife** ['waɪld,laɪf] *n* : fauna *f* — **wildly** ['waɪldli] *adv* **1** FRANTICALLY : frenéticamente **2** EXTREMELY : locamente

will¹ ['wɪl] *v past* **would** ['wʊd]; *pres sing & pl* **will** *vi* WISH : querer — *v aux* **1 tomorrow we** ~ **go shopping** : mañana iremos de compras **2 he** ~ **get angry over nothing** : se pone furioso por cualquier cosa **3 I** ~ **go despite them** : iré a pesar de ellos **4 I won't do it** : no lo haré **5 that** ~ **be the mailman** : eso ha de ser el cartero **6 the couch** ~ **hold three people** : en el sofá cabrán tres personas **7 accidents** ~ **happen** : los accidentes ocurrirán **8 you** ~ **do as I say** : harás lo que digo

will² *n* **1** : voluntad *f* **2** TESTAMENT : testamento *m* **3 free** ~ : libre albedrío *m* — **willful** *or* **wilful** ['wɪlfəl] *adj* **1** OBSTINATE : terco **2** INTENTIONAL : intencionado — **willing** ['wɪlɪŋ] *adj* **1** : complaciente **2 be** ~ **to** : estar dispuesto a — **willingly** ['wɪlɪŋli] *adv* : con gusto — **willingness** ['wɪlɪŋnəs] *n* : buena voluntad *f*

willow ['wɪ,lo:] *n* : sauce *m*

willpower ['wɪl,paʊər] *n* : fuerza *f* de voluntad

wilt ['wɪlt] *vi* : marchitarse

wily ['waɪli] *adj* **wilier; -est** : artero, astuto

win ['wɪn] *v* **won** ['wʌn], **winning** *vi* : ganar — *vt* **1** : ganar, conseguir **2** ~ **over** : ganarse a — ~ *n* : triunfo *m*, victoria *f*

wince ['wɪnts] *vi* **winced; wincing** : hacer una mueca de dolor — ~ *n* : mueca *f* de dolor

winch ['wɪntʃ] *n* : torno *m*

wind¹ ['wɪnd] *n* **1** : viento *m* **2** BREATH : aliento *m* **3** FLATULENCE : flatulencia *f* **4 get** ~ **of** : enterarse de

wind² ['waɪnd] *v* **wound** ['waʊnd], **winding** *vi* : serpentear — *vt* **1** COIL : enrollar **2** ~ **a clock** : dar cuerda a un reloj

windfall ['wɪnd,fɔl] *n* : beneficio *m* imprevisto

winding ['waɪndɪŋ] *adj* : tortuoso

wind instrument *n* : instrumento *m* de viento

windmill ['wɪnd,mɪl] *n* : molino *m* de viento

window ['wɪn,do:] *n* : ventana *f* (de un edificio o una computadora), ventanilla *f* (de un vehículo), vitrina *f* (de una tienda) — **windowpane** ['wɪn,do:,peɪn] *n* : vidrio *m* — **windowsill** ['wɪn,do:,sɪl] *n* : repisa *f* de la ventana

windpipe ['wɪnd,paɪp] *n* : tráquea *f*

windshield ['wɪnd,ʃi:ld] *n* **1** : parabrisas *m* **2** ~ **wiper** : limpiaparabrisas *m*

window-shop ['wɪndo,ʃɑp] *vi* **-shopped; -shopping** : mirar las vitrinas

wind up ['waɪnd,ʌp] *vt* : terminar, concluir — *vi* : terminar, acabar — **windup** *n* : conclusión *f*

windy ['wɪndi] *adj* **windier; -est 1** : ventoso **2 it's** ~ : hace viento

wine ['waɪn] *n* : vino *m* — **wine cellar** *n* : bodega *f*

wing ['wɪŋ] *n* **1** : ala *f* **2 under s.o.'s** ~ : bajo el cargo de algn — **winged** ['wɪŋ, 'wɪŋəd] *adj* : alado

wink ['wɪŋk] *vi* : guiñar — ~ *n* **1** : guiño *m* **2 not sleep a** ~ : no pegar el ojo

winner ['wɪnər] *n* : ganador *m*, -dora *f* —

winning ['wɪnɪŋ] *adj* **1** : ganador **2** CHARMING : encantador — **winnings** ['wɪnɪŋz] *npl* : ganancias *fpl*

winter ['wɪntər] *n* : invierno *m* — ~ *adj* : invernal, de invierno — **wintergreen** ['wɪntər,gri:n] *n* : gaulteria *f* — **wintertime** ['wɪntər,taɪm] *n* : invierno *m* — **wintry** ['wɪntri] *adj* **wintrier; -est** : invernal, de invierno

wipe ['waɪp] *vt* **wiped; wiping 1** : limpiar **2 ~ away** : enjugar (lágrimas), borrar (una memoria) **3 ~ out** : aniquilar, destruir — ~ *n* : pasada *f* (con un trapo, etc.)

wire ['waɪr] *n* **1** : alambre *m* **2** : cable *m* (eléctrico o telefónico) **3** TELEGRAM : telegrama *m* — ~ *vt* **-wired; wiring 1** : instalar el cableado en (una casa, etc.) **2** BIND : atar con alambre **3** TELEGRAPH : enviar un telegrama a — **wireless** ['waɪrləs] *adj* : inalámbrico — **wiring** ['waɪrɪŋ] *n* : cableado *m* — **wiry** ['waɪri] *adj* **wirier; -est 1** : hirsuto, tieso (dícese del pelo) **2** : esbelto y musculoso (dícese del cuerpo)

wisdom ['wɪzdəm] *n* : sabiduría *f* — **wisdom tooth** *n* : muela *f* de juicio

wise ['waɪz] *adj* **wiser; wisest 1** : sabio **2** SENSIBLE : prudente — **wisecrack** ['waɪz,kræk] *n* : broma *f*, chiste *m* — **wisely** ['waɪzli] *adv* : sabiamente

wish ['wɪʃ] *vt* **1** : desear **2 ~ s.o. well** : desear lo mejor a algn — *vi* **1** : pedir (como deseo) **2 as you ~** : como quieras — ~ *n* **1** : deseo *m* **2 best ~es** : muchos recuerdos — **wishbone** ['wɪʃ,bo:n] *n* : espoleta *f* — **wishful** ['wɪʃfəl] *adj* **1** : deseoso **2 ~ thinking** : ilusiones *fpl*

wishy-washy ['wɪʃi,wɔʃi, -,wɑʃi] *adj* : insípido, soso

wisp ['wɪsp] *n* **1** : mechón *m* (de pelo) **2** : voluta *f* (de humo)

wistful ['wɪstfəl] *adj* : melancólico

wit ['wɪt] *n* **1** CLEVERNESS : ingenio *m* **2** HUMOR : agudeza *f* **3 at one's ~'s end** : desesperado **4 scared out of one's ~s** : muerto de miedo

witch ['wɪtʃ] *n* : bruja *f* — **witchcraft** ['wɪtʃ,kræft] *n* : brujería *f*, hechicería *f*

with ['wɪð, 'wɪθ] *prep* **1** : con **2 I'm going ~ you** : voy contigo **3 it varies ~ the season** : varía según la estación **4 the girl ~ red hair** : la muchacha de pelo rojo **5 ~ all his work, the business failed** : a pesar de su trabajo, el negocio fracasó

withdraw [wɪð'drɔ, wɪθ-] *v* **-drew** [-'dru:]; **-drawn** [-'drɔn]; **-drawing** *vt* : retirar — *vi* : apartarse — **withdraw-**

-al [wɪð'drɔːəl, wɪθ-] *n* **1** : retirada *f* **2** : abandono (de drogas, etc.) — **withdrawn** [wɪð'drɔn, wɪθ-] *adj* : introvertido

wither ['wɪðər] *vi* : marchitarse

withhold [wɪθ'ho:ld, wɪð-] *vt* **-held** [-'held]; **-holding** : retener (fondos), negar (permiso), etc.)

within [wɪ'ðɪn, wɪθ-] *adv* : dentro — ~ *prep* **1** : dentro de **2** (*in expressions of distance*) : a menos de **3** (*in expressions of time*) : dentro de, en menos de **4 ~ reach** : al alcance de la mano

without [wɪ'ðaʊt, wɪθ-] *adv* **do ~** : pasar sin algo — ~ *prep* : sin

withstand [wɪθ'stænd, wɪð-] *vt* **-stood** [-'stʊd]; **-standing 1** BEAR : aguantar **2** RESIST : resistir

witness ['wɪtnəs] *n* **1** : testigo *mf* **2** EVIDENCE : testimonio *m* **3 bear ~** : atestiguar — ~ *vt* **1** SEE : ser testigo de **2** : atestiguar (una firma, etc.)

witticism ['wɪtə,sɪzəm] *n* : agudeza *f*, ocurrencia *f*

witty ['wɪti] *adj* **-tier; -est** : ingenioso, ocurrente

wives → wife

wizard ['wɪzərd] *n* **1** : mago *m*, brujo *m* **2 a math ~** : un genio de matemáticas

wizened ['wɪzənd, 'wi:-] *adj* : arrugado

wobble ['wɑbəl] *vi* **-bled; -bling 1** : tambalearse **2** : temblar (dícese de la voz, etc.) — **wobbly** ['wɑbəli] *adj* : cojo

woe ['wo:] *n* **1** : aflicción *f* **2 ~s** *npl* TROUBLES : penas *fpl* — **woeful** ['wo:fəl] *adj* : triste

woke, woken → wake

wolf ['wʊlf] *n, pl* **wolves** ['wʊlvz] : lobo *m*, -ba *f* — ~ *vt or* ~ **down** : engullir

woman ['wʊmən] *n, pl* **women** ['wɪmən] : mujer *f* — **womanly** ['wʊmənli] *adj* : femenino

womb ['wu:m] *n* : útero *m*, matriz *f*

won → win

wonder ['wʌndər] *n* **1** MARVEL : maravilla *f* **2** AMAZEMENT : asombro *m* — ~ *v* : preguntarse — **wonderful** ['wʌndərfəl] *adj* : maravilloso, estupendo

won't ['wo:nt] (*contraction of* will not) → **will**

woo ['wu:] *vt* **1** COURT : cortejar **2** : buscar el apoyo de (clientes, votantes, etc.)

wood ['wʊd] *n* **1** : madera *f* (materia) **2** FIREWOOD : leña *f* **3 or ~s** *npl* FOREST : bosque *m* — ~ *adj* : de madera — **woodchuck** ['wʊd,tʃʌk] *n* : marmota *f* de América — **wooded** ['wʊdəd] *adj* : arbolado, boscoso — **wooden**

['wʊdən] *adj* : de madera — **wood-pecker** ['wʊd,pɛkər] *n* : pájaro *m* carpintero — **woodshed** ['wʊd,ʃɛd] *n* : leñera *f* — **woodwind** ['wʊd,wɪnd] *n* : instrumento *m* de viento de madera — **woodwork** ['wʊd,wərk] *n* : carpintería *f*

wool ['wʊl] *n* : lana *f* — **woolen** *or* **woollen** ['wʊlən] *adj* : de lana — ~ *n* 1 : lana *f* (tela) 2 ~s *npl* : prendas *fpl* de lana — **woolly** ['wʊli] *adj* **-lier; -est** : lanudo

word ['wərd] *n* 1 : palabra *f* 2 NEWS : noticias *fpl* 3 ~s *npl* : letra *f* (de una canción, etc.) 4 **have ~s with** : reñir con 5 **just say the ~** : no tienes que decirlo 6 **keep one's ~** : cumplir su palabra — ~ *vt* : expresar — **word processing** *n* : procesamiento *m* de textos — **word processor** *n* : procesador *m* de textos — **wordy** ['wərdi] *adj* **wordier; -est** : prolijo

wore → **wear**

work ['wərk] *n* 1 LABOR : trabajo *m* 2 EMPLOYMENT : trabajo *m*, empleo *m* 3 : obra *f* (de arte, etc.) 4 ~s *npl* FACTORY : fábrica *f* 5 ~s *npl* MECHANISM : mecanismo *m* — ~ *v* **worked** ['wərkt] *or* **wrought** ['rɔt]; **working** *vt* 1 : hacer trabajar (a una persona) 2 : manejar, operar (una máquina, etc.) — *vi* 1 : trabajar 2 FUNCTION : funcionar 3 : surtir efecto (dícese de una droga), resultar (dícese de una idea, etc.) — **worked up** *adj* : nervioso — **worker** ['wərkər] *n* : trabajador *m*, -dora *f*; obrero *m*, -ra *f* — **working** ['wərkɪŋ] *adj* 1 : que trabaja (dícese de personas), de trabajo (dícese de la ropa, etc.) 2 **be in ~ order** : funcionar bien — **working class** *n* : clase *f* obrera — **workingman** ['wərkɪŋ,mæn] *n, pl* **-men** [-mən, -,mɛn] : obrero *m* — **workman** ['wərkmən] *n, pl* **-men** [-mən, -,mɛn] 1 : obrero *m* 2 ARTISAN : artesano *m* — **workmanship** ['wərkmən,ʃɪp] *n* : artesanía *f*, destreza *f* — **workout** ['wərk,aʊt] *n* : ejercicios *mpl* (físicos) — **work out** *vt* 1 DEVELOP : elaborar 2 SOLVE : resolver — *vi* 1 TURN OUT : resultar 2 SUCCEED : lograr, salir bien 3 EXERCISE : hacer ejercicio — **workshop** ['wərk,ʃɑp] *n* : taller *m* — **work up** *vt* 1 EXCITE : ponerse como loco 2 GENERATE : desarrollar

world ['wərld] *n* : mundo *m* 2 **think the ~ of s.o.** : tener a algn en alta estima — ~ *adj* : mundial, del mundo — **worldly** ['wərldli] *adj* : mundano —

worldwide ['wərld,waɪd] *adv* : en todo el mundo — ~ *adj* : global, mundial

worm ['wərm] *n* 1 : gusano *m*, lombriz *f* 2 ~s *npl* : lombrices *fpl* (parásitos)

worn → **wear** — **worn-out** ['worn'aʊt] *adj* 1 USED : gastado 2 TIRED : agotado

worry ['wəri] *v* **-ried; -rying** *vt* : preocupar, inquietar — *vi* : preocuparse, inquietarse — ~ *n, pl* **-ries** : preocupación *f* — **worried** ['wərid] *adj* : preocupado — **worrisome** ['wərisəm] *adj* : inquietante

worse ['wərs] *adv* (*comparative of* **bad** *or of* **ill**) : peor — ~ *adj* (*comparative of* **bad** *or of* **ill**) 1 : peor 2 **from bad to ~** : de mal en peor 3 **get ~** : empeorar — ~ *n* 1 **the ~** : el (la) peor, lo peor 2 **take a turn for the ~** : ponerse peor — **worsen** ['wərsən] *v* : empeorar

worship ['wərʃəp] *v* **-shiped** *or* **-shipped; -shiping** *or* **-shipping** *vt* : adorar — *vi* : practicar una religión — ~ *n* : adoración *f*, culto *m* — **worshiper** *or* **worshipper** ['wərʃəpər] *n* : adorador *m*, -dora *f*

worst ['wərst] *adv* (*superlative of* **ill** *or of* **bad** *or* **badly**) : peor — ~ *adj* (*superlative of* **bad** *or of* **ill**) : peor — ~ *n* **the ~** : lo peor, el (la) peor

worth ['wərθ] *n* 1 : valor *m* (monetario) 2 MERIT : mérito *m*, valía *f* 3 **ten dollars' ~ of gas** : diez dólares de gasolina — ~ *prep* 1 **it's ~ $ 10** : vale $ 10 2 **it's ~ doing** : vale la pena hacerlo — **worthless** ['wərθləs] *adj* 1 : sin valor 2 USELESS : inútil — **worthwhile** ['wərθ'hwaɪl] *adj* : que vale la pena — **worthy** ['wərði] *adj* **-thier; -est** : digno

would ['wʊd] *past of* **will** 1 **he ~ often take his children to the park** : solía llevar a sus hijos al parque 2 **~ go if I had the money** : iría yo si tuviera el dinero 3 **I ~ rather go alone** : preferiría ir sola 4 **she ~ have won if she hadn't tripped** : habría ganado si no hubiera tropezado 5 **~ you kindly help me with this?** : ¿tendría la bondad de ayudarme con esto? — **would-be** ['wʊd'bi] *adj* **a ~ poet** : un aspirante a poeta — **wouldn't** ['wʊd-'ənt] (*contraction of* **would not**) → **would**

wound¹ ['wuːnd] *n* : herida *f* — ~ *vt* : herir

wound² ['waʊnd] → **wind**

wove, woven → **weave**

wrangle ['ræŋgəl] *vi* **-gled; -gling** : reñir — ~ *n* : riña *f*, disputa *f*

wrap ['ræp] *vt* **wrapped; wrapping 1**
: envolver **2 ~ up** FINISH : dar fin a —
~ *n* **1** : prenda *f* que envuelve (como
un chal) **2** WRAPPER : envoltura *f* —
wrapper ['ræpər] *n* : envoltura *f*, envoltorio *m* — **wrapping** ['ræpɪŋ] *n*
: envoltura *f*, envoltorio *m*

wrath ['ræθ] *n* : ira *f*, cólera *f* — **wrath-
ful** ['ræθfəl] *adj* : iracundo

wreath ['riːθ] *n*, *pl* **wreaths** ['riːðz, 'riːθs]
: corona *f* (de flores, etc.)

wreck ['rɛk] *n* **1** WRECKAGE : restos *mpl*
2 RUIN : ruina *f*, desastre *m* **3 be a
nervous ~** : tener los nervios des-
trozados — **~** *vt* : destrozar (un automóvil), naufragar (un barco) —
wreckage ['rɛkɪdʒ] *n* : restos *mpl* (de
un buque naufragado, etc.), ruinas *fpl*
(de un edificio)

wren ['rɛn] *n* : chochín *m*

wrench ['rɛntʃ] *vt* **1** PULL : arrancar (de
un tirón) **2** SPRAIN, TWIST : torcerse —
~ *n* **1** TUG : tirón *m*, jalón *m* **2** SPRAIN
: torcedura *f* **3** *or* **monkey ~** : llave *f*
inglesa

wrestle ['rɛsəl] *vi* **-tled; -tling** : luchar
— **wrestler** ['rɛslər] *n* : luchador *m*,
-dora *f* — **wrestling** ['rɛslɪŋ] *n* : lucha
f

wretch ['rɛtʃ] *n* : desgraciado *m*, -da *f* —
wretched ['rɛtʃəd] *adj* **1** : miserable **2
~ weather** : tiempo *m* espantoso

wriggle ['rɪgəl] *vi* **-gled; -gling** : retorcerse, menearse

wring ['rɪŋ] *vt* **wrung** ['rʌŋ]; **wringing 1**
or **~ out** : escurrir (el lavado, etc.) **2**

TWIST : retorcer **3** EXTRACT : arrancar
(información, etc.)

wrinkle ['rɪŋkəl] *n* : arruga *f* — **~** *v*
-kled; -kling *vt* : arrugar — *vi* : arrugarse

wrist ['rɪst] *n* : muñeca *f* — **wristwatch**
['rɪst,wɑtʃ] *n* : reloj *m* de pulsera

writ ['rɪt] *n* : orden *f* (judicial)

write ['raɪt] *v* **wrote** ['roːt]; **written**
['rɪtən]; **writing** : escribir — **write
down** *vt* : apuntar, anotar — **write off**
vt CANCEL : cancelar — **writer** ['raɪtər]
n : escritor *m*, -tora *f*

writhe ['raɪð] *vi* **writhed; writhing** : retorcerse

writing ['raɪtɪŋ] *n* : escritura *f*

wrong ['rɔŋ] *n* **1** INJUSTICE : injusticia *f*,
mal *m* **2** : agravio *m* (en derecho) **3 be
in the ~** : haber hecho mal — **~** *adj*
wronger ['rɔŋər]; **wrongest** ['rɔŋəst] **1**
: malo **2** UNSUITABLE : inadecuado, inapropiado **3** INCORRECT : incorrecto,
equivocado **4 be ~** : no tener razón
— **~** *adv* : mal, incorrectamente —
~ *vt* **wronged; wronging** : ofender,
ser injusto con — **wrongful** ['rɔŋfəl]
adj **1** UNJUST : injusto **2** UNLAWFUL
: ilegal — **wrongly** ['rɔŋli] *adv* **1** UN-
JUSTLY : injustamente **2** INCORRECTLY
: mal

wrote → write

wrought iron ['rɔt] *n* : hierro *m* forjado

wrung → wring

wry ['raɪ] *adj* **wrier** ['raɪər]; **wriest**
['raɪəst] : irónico, sardónico (dícese del
humor)

XYZ

x *n*, *pl* **x's** *or* **xs** ['ɛksəz] : x *f*, vigésima
cuarta letra del alfabeto inglés

xenophobia [ˌzɛnəˈfoːbiə, ˌziː-] *n* : xenofobia *f*

Xmas ['krɪsməs] *n* : Navidad *f*

X ray ['ɛks,reɪ] *n* **1** : rayo *m* X **2** *or* **~
photograph** : radiografía *f* — **x–ray**
vt : radiografiar

xylophone ['zaɪləˌfoːn] *n* : xilófono *m*

y ['waɪ] *n*, *pl* **y's** *or* **ys** ['waɪz] : y *f*,
vigésima quinta letra del alfabeto in-
glés

yacht ['jɑt] *n* : yate *m*

yam ['jæm] *n* **1** : ñame *m* **2** SWEET POTA-
TO : batata *f*, boniato *m*

yank ['jæŋk] *vt* : tirar de, jalar *Lat* — **~**
n : tirón *m*, jalón *m* *Lat*

Yankee ['jæŋki] *n* : yanqui *mf*

yap ['jæp] *vi* **yapped; yapping** : ladrar
— **~** *n* : ladrido *m*

yard ['jɑrd] *n* **1** : yarda *f* (medida) **2**
COURTYARD : patio *m* **3** : jardín *m* (de
una casa) — **yardstick** ['jɑrd,stɪk] *n* **1**
: vara *f* (de medir) **2** CRITERION : criterio *m*

yarn ['jɑrn] *n* **1** : hilado *m* **2** TALE : historia *f*, cuento *m*

yawn ['jɔn] *vi* : bostezar — **~** *n* : bostezo *m*

year ['jɪr] *n* **1** : año *m* **2 she's ten ~s
old** : tiene diez años **3 I haven't seen
them in ~s** : hace siglos que no los
veo — **yearbook** ['jɪr,bʊk] *n* : anuario
m — **yearling** ['jɪrlɪŋ, 'jɛrlən] *n* : animal *m* menor de dos años — **yearly**
['jɪrli] *adv* **1** : anualmente **2 three**

times ~ : tres veces al año — **~** *adj*
: anual

yearn ['jərn] *vi* : anhelar — **yearning**
['jərnɪŋ] *n* : anhelo *m*, ansia *f*

yeast ['ji:st] *n* : levadura *f*

yell ['jel] *vi* : gritar, chillar — *vt* : gritar
— **~** *n* : grito *m*, chillido *m*

yellow ['jelo] *adj* : amarillo — **~** *n*
: amarillo *m* — **yellowish** ['jeloɪʃ] *adj*
: amarillento

yelp ['jelp] *n* : gañido *m* — *vi* : dar un
gañido

yes ['jes] *adv* **1** : sí **2 say ~** : decir que
sí — **~** *n* : sí *m*

yesterday ['jestər,deɪ, -di] *adv* : ayer —
~ *n* **1** : ayer *m* **2 the day before ~**
: anteayer

yet ['jet] *adv* **1** : aún, todavía **2 has he
come ~?** : ¿ya ha venido? **3 not ~**
: todavía no **4 ~ more problems**
: más problemas aún **5** NEVERTHELESS
: sin embargo — **~** *conj* : pero

yield ['ji:ld] *vt* **1** PRODUCE : producir **2 ~
the right of way** : ceder el paso — *vi*
: ceder — **~** *n* : rendimiento *m*, rédito *m* (en finanzas)

yoga ['jo:gə] *n* : yoga *m*

yogurt ['jo:gərt] *n* : yogur *m*, yogurt *m*

yoke ['jo:k] *n* : yugo *m*

yolk ['jo:k] *n* : yema *f* (de un huevo)

you ['ju:] *pron* **1** (*used as subject—familiar*) : tú; vos (*in some Latin American countries*); ustedes *pl*; vosotros,
vosotras *pl Spain* **2** (*used as subject—
formal*) : usted, ustedes *pl* **3** (*used as
indirect object—familiar*) : te, les *pl*
(se *before lo, la, los, las*), os *pl Spain*
4 (*used as indirect object—formal*)
: lo (*Spain sometimes* le), la; los
(*Spain sometimes* les), las *pl Spain* **5** (*used
after a preposition—familiar*) : ti; vos
(*in some Latin American countries*);
ustedes *pl*; vosotros, vosotras *pl Spain*
6 (*used after a preposition—formal*)
: usted, ustedes *pl* **7 with ~** (*familiar*) : contigo; con ustedes *pl*; con
vosotros, con vosotras *pl Spain* **8 with
~** (*formal*) : con usted, con ustedes
pl **9 ~ never know** : nunca se sabe
— **you'd** ['ju:d, 'jud] (*contraction of
you had or you would*) → **have,
would** — **you'll** ['ju:l, 'jul] (*contraction of you shall or you will*) →
shall, will

young ['jʌŋ] *adj* **younger** ['jʌŋgər];
youngest [-gəst] **1** : joven **2 my ~er
brother** : mi hermano menor **3 she is
the ~est** : es la más pequeña **4 the
~** : los jóvenes — **~** *npl* : jóvenes
mfpl (de los humanos), crías *fpl* (de

los animales) — **youngster** ['jʌŋkstər]
n : chico *m*, -ca *f*; joven *mf*

your ['jur, 'jor, jər] *adj* **1** (*familiar singular*) : tu **2** (*familiar plural*) su, vuestro *Spain* **3** (*formal*) : su **4 on ~ left**
: a la izquierda

you're ['jur, 'jor, jər, 'juər] (*contraction
of you are*) → **be**

yours ['jurz, 'jo:rz] *pron* **1** (*belonging to
one person—familiar*) : (el) tuyo, (la)
tuya, (los) tuyos, (las) tuyas **2** (*belonging to more than one person—familiar*) : (el) suyo, (la) suya, (los)
suyos, (las) suyas; (el) vuestro, (la)
vuestra, (los) vuestros, (las) vuestras
Spain **3** (*formal*) : (el) suyo, (la) suya,
(los) suyos, (las) suyas

yourself [jər'self] *pron, pl* **yourselves**
[-'selvz] **1** (*used reflexively—familiar*)
: te, se *pl*, os *pl Spain* **2** (*used reflexively—formal*) : se **3** (*used for emphasis*) : tú mismo, tú misma; usted
mismo, usted misma; ustedes mismos,
ustedes mismas *pl*; vosotros mismos,
vosotras mismas *pl Spain*

youth ['ju:θ] *n, pl* **youths** ['ju:ðz, 'ju:θs] **1**
: juventud *f* **2** BOY : joven *m* **3 today's
~** : los jóvenes de hoy — **youthful**
['ju:θfəl] *adj* **1** : juvenil, de juventud **2**
YOUNG : joven

you've ['ju:v] (*contraction of you have*)
→ **have**

yowl ['jaul] *vi* : aullar — **~** *n* : aullido *m*

yucca ['jʌkə] *n* : yuca *f*

Yugoslavian [ju:go'slaviən] *adj* : yugoslavo

yule ['ju:l] *n* CHRISTMAS : Navidad *f* —
yuletide ['ju:l,taɪd] *n* : Navidades *fpl*

z ['zi:] *n, pl* **z's** *or* **zs** : *z f*, vigésima sexta
letra del alfabeto inglés

zany ['zeɪni] *adj* **-nier; -est** : alocado,
disparatado

zeal ['zi:l] *n* : fervor *m*, celo *m* — **zealous** ['zeləs] *adj* : entusiasta

zebra ['zi:brə] *n* : cebra *f*

zenith ['zi:nəθ] *n* **1** : cenit *m* (en astronomía) **2** PEAK : apogeo *m*

zero ['zi:ro, 'ziro] *n, pl* **-ros** : cero *m*

zest ['zest] *n* **1** : gusto *m* **2** FLAVOR
: sazón *f*

zigzag ['zɪg,zæg] *n* : zigzag *m* — **~** *vi*
-zagged; -zagging : zigzaguear

zinc ['zɪŋk] *n* : cinc *m*, zinc *m*

zip ['zɪp] *v* **zipped; zipping** *vt* *or* **~ up**
: cerrar la cremallera de, cerrar el
cierre de *Lat* — *vi* SPEED : pasarse
volando — **zip code** *n* : código *m*
postal — **zipper** ['zɪpər] *n* : cremallera
f, cierre *m Lat*

zodiac ['zo:di,æk] *n* : zodíaco *m*
zone ['zo:n] *n* : zona *f*
zoo ['zu:] *n, pl* **zoos** : zoológico *m*, zoo *m* — **zoology** [zo'ɑlədʒi, zu:-] *n* : zoología *f*

zoom ['zu:m] *vi* : zumbar, ir volando — ~ *n* **1** : zumbido *m* **2** *or* ~ **lens** : zoom *m*
zucchini [zu'ki:ni] *n, pl* **-ni** *or* **-nis** : calabacín *m*, calabacita *f Lat*

Common Spanish Abbreviations

SPANISH ABBREVIATION AND EXPANSION		ENGLISH EQUIVALENT	
abr.	abril	**Apr.**	April
A.C., a.C.	antes de Cristo	**BC**	before Christ
a. de J.C.	antes de Jesucristo	**BC**	before Christ
admon., admón.	administración	—	administration
a/f	a favor	—	in favor
ago.	agosto	**Aug.**	August
Apdo.	apartado (de correos)	—	P.O. box
aprox.	aproximadamente	**approx.**	approximately
Aptdo.	apartado (de correos)		P.O. box
Arq.	arquitecto	**arch.**	architect
A.T.	Antiguo Testamento	**O.T.**	Old Testament
atte.	atentamente	—	sincerely
atto., atta.	atento, atenta	—	kind, courteous
av., avda.	avenida	**ave.**	avenue
a/v.	a vista	—	on receipt
BID	Banco Interamericano de Desarrollo	**IDB**	Interamerican Development Bank
Bo	banco	—	bank
BM	Banco Mundial	—	World Bank
c/, C/	calle	**st.**	street
C	centígrado, Celsius	**C**	centigrade, Celsius
C.	compañía	**Co.**	company
CA	corriente alterna	**AC**	alternating current
cap.	capítulo	**ch., chap.**	chapter
c/c	cuenta corriente	—	current account, checking account
c.c.	centímetros cúbicos	**cu. cm**	cubic centimeters
CC	corriente continua	**DC**	direct current
c/d	con descuento	—	with discount
Cd.	ciudad	—	city
CE	Comunidad Europea	**EC**	European Community
CEE	Comunidad Económica Europea	**EEC**	European Economic Community
cf.	confróntese	**cf.**	compare
cg.	centígramo	**cg**	centigram
CGT	Confederación General de Trabajadores *o* del Trabajo	—	confederation of workers, workers' union
CI	coeficiente intelectual *o* de inteligencia	**IQ**	intelligence quotient
Cía.	compañía	**Co.**	company
cm.	centímetro	**cm**	centimeter
Cnel.	coronel	**Col.**	colonel
col.	columna	**col.**	column
Col. *Mex*	colonia	—	residential area
Com.	comandante	**Cmdr.**	commander
comp.	compárese	**comp.**	compare
Cor.	coronel	**Col.**	colonel
C.P.	código postal	—	zip code

SPANISH ABBREVIATION AND EXPANSION		ENGLISH EQUIVALENT	
CSF, c.s.f.	coste, seguro y flete	**c.i.f.**	cost, insurance, and freight
cta.	cuenta	**ac., acct.**	account
cte.	corriente	**cur.**	current
c/u	cada uno, cada una	**ea.**	each
CV	caballo de vapor	**hp**	horsepower
D.	Don	—	—
Da., D.ª	Doña	—	—
d.C.	después de Cristo	**AD**	anno Domini (in the year of our Lord)
dcha.	derecha	—	right
d. de J.C.	después de Jesucristo	**AD**	anno Domini (in the year of our lord)
dep.	departamento	**dept.**	department
DF, D.F.	Distrito Federal	—	Federal District
dic.	diciembre	**Dec.**	December
dir.	director, directora	**dir.**	director
dir.	dirección	—	address
Dña.	Doña	—	—
do.	domingo	**Sun.**	Sunday
dpto.	departamento	**dept.**	department
Dr.	doctor	**Dr.**	doctor
Dra.	doctora	**Dr.**	doctor
dto.	descuento	—	discount
E, E.	Este, este	**E**	East, east
Ed.	editorial	—	publishing house
Ed., ed.	edición	**ed.**	edition
edif.	edificio	**bldg.**	building
edo.	estado	**st.**	state
EEUU, EE.UU.	Estados Unidos	**US, U.S.**	United States
ej.	por ejemplo	**e.g.**	for example
E.M.	esclerosis multiple	**MS**	multiple sclerosis
ene.	enero	**Jan.**	January
etc.	etcétera	**etc.**	et cetera
ext.	extensión	**ext.**	extension
F	Fahrenheit	**F**	Fahrenheit
f.a.b.	franco a bordo	**f.o.b.**	free on board
FC	ferrocarril	**RR**	railroad
feb.	febrero	**Feb.**	February
FF AA, FF.AA.	Fuerzas Armadas	—	armed forces
FMI	Fondo Monetario Internacional	**IMF**	International Monetary Fund
g.	gramo	**g., gm, gr.**	gram
G.P.	giro postal	**M.O.**	money order
gr.	gramo	**g., gm, gr**	gram
Gral.	general	**Gen.**	general
h.	hora	**hr.**	hour
Hnos.	hermanos	**Bros.**	brothers
I + D, I & D, I y D	investigación y desarrollo	**R & D**	research and development
i.e.	esto es, es decir	**i.e.**	that is
incl.	inclusive	**incl.**	inclusive, inclusively

SPANISH ABBREVIATION AND EXPANSION		ENGLISH EQUIVALENT	
Ing.	ingeniero, ingeniera	**eng.**	engineer
IPC	índice de precios al consumo	**CPI**	consumer price index
IVA	impuesto al valor agregado	**VAT**	value-added tax
izq.	izquierda	**l.**	left
juev.	jueves	**Thurs.**	Thursday
jul.	julio	**Jul.**	July
jun.	junio	**Jun.**	June
kg.	kilogramo	**kg**	kilogram
km.	kilómetro	**km**	kilometer
km/h	kilómetros por hora	**kph**	kilometers per hour
kv, kV	kilovatio	**kw, kW**	kilowatt
l.	litro	**l, lit.**	liter
Lic.	licenciado, licenciada	—	—
Ltda.	limitada	**Ltd.**	limited
lun.	lunes	**Mon.**	Monday
m	masculino	**m**	masculine
m	metro	**m**	meter
m	minuto	**m**	minute
mar.	marzo	**Mar.**	March
mart.	martes	**Tues.**	Tuesday
mg.	miligramo	**mg**	milligram
miérc.	miércoles	**Wed.**	Wednesday
min	minuto	**min.**	minute
mm.	milímetro	**mm**	millimeter
M-N, m/n	moneda nacional	—	national currency
Mons.	monseñor	**Msgr.**	monsignor
Mtra.	maestra	—	teacher
Mtro.	maestro	—	teacher
N, N.	Norte, norte	**N, no.**	North, north
n/o	nuestro	—	our
n.º	número	**no.**	number
N. de (la) R.	nota de (la) redacción	—	editor's note
NE	nordeste	**NE**	northeast
NN.UU.	Naciones Unidas	**UN**	United Nations
NO	noroeste	**NW**	northwest
nov.	noviembre	**Nov.**	November
N.T.	Nuevo Testamento	**N.T.**	New Testament
ntra., ntro.	nuestra, nuestro	—	our
NU	Naciones Unidas	**UN**	United Nations
núm.	número	**num.**	number
O, O.	Oeste, oeste	**W**	West, west
oct.	octubre	**Oct.**	October
OEA, O.E.A.	Organización de Estados Americanos	**OAS**	Organization of American States
OMS	Organización Mundial de la Salud	**WHO**	World Health Organization
ONG	organización no gubernamental	**NGO**	non-governmental organization
ONU	Organización de las Naciones Unidas	**UN**	United Nations
OTAN	Organización del Tratado del Atlántico Norte	**NATO**	North Atlantic Treaty Organization

SPANISH ABBREVIATION AND EXPANSION		ENGLISH EQUIVALENT	
p.	página	**p.**	page
P, P.	padre	**Fr.**	father
pág.	página	**pg.**	page
pat.	patente	**pat.**	patent
PCL	pantalla de cristal líquido	**LCD**	liquid crystal display
P.D.	post data	**P.S.**	postscript
p. ej.	por ejemplo	**e.g.**	for example
PNB	Producto Nacional Bruto	**GNP**	gross national product
p⁰	paseo	**Ave.**	avenue
p.p.	porte pagado	**ppd.**	postpaid
PP, p.p.	por poder, por poderes	**p.p.**	by proxy
prom.	promedio	**av., avg.**	average
ptas., pts.	pesetas		
q.e.p.d.	que en paz descanse	**R.I.P.**	may he/she rest in peace
R, R/	remite	—	sender
RAE	Real Academia Española	—	—
ref., ref.ª	referencia	**ref.**	reference
rep.	república	**rep.**	republic
r.p.m.	revoluciones por minuto	**rpm.**	revolutions per minute
rte.	remite, remitente		sender
s.	siglo	**c., cent.**	century
s/	su, sus	—	his, her, your, their
S, S.	Sur, sur	**S, so.**	South, south
S.	san, santo	**St.**	saint
S.A.	sociedad anónima	**Inc.**	incorporated (company)
sáb.	sábado	**Sat.**	Saturday
s/c	su cuenta	—	your account
SE	sudeste, sureste	**SE**	southeast
seg.	segundo, segundos	**sec.**	second, seconds
sep., sept.	septiembre	**Sept.**	September
s.e.u.o.	salvo error u omisión	—	errors and omissions excepted
Sgto.	sargento	**Sgt.**	sergeant
S.L.	sociedad limitada	**Ltd.**	limited (corporation)
S.M.	Su Majestad	**HM**	His Majesty, Her Majesty
s/n	sin número	—	no (street) number
s.n.m.	sobre el nivel de mar	**a.s.l.**	above sea level
SO	sudoeste/suroeste	**SW**	southwest
S.R.C.	se ruega contestación	**R.S.V.P.**	please reply
ss.	siguientes	—	the following ones
SS, S.S.	Su Santidad	**H.H.**	His Holiness
Sta.	santa	**St.**	Saint
Sto.	santo	**St.**	saint
t, t.	tonelada	**t., tn**	ton
TAE	tasa anual efectiva	**APR**	annual percentage rate
tb.	también	—	also
tel., Tel.	teléfono	**tel.**	telephone
Tm.	tonelada métrica	**MT**	metric ton
Tn.	tonelada	**t., tn**	ton
trad.	traducido	**tr., trans., transl.**	translated
UE	Unión Europea	**EU**	European Union
Univ.	universidad	**Univ., U.**	university

SPANISH ABBREVIATION AND EXPANSION		ENGLISH EQUIVALENT	
UPC	unidad procesadora central	**CPU**	central processing unit
Urb.	urbanización	—	residential area
v	versus	**v., vs.**	versus
v	verso	**v., ver., vs.**	verse
v.	véase	**vid.**	see
Vda.	viuda	—	widow
v.g., v.gr.	verbigracia	**e.g.**	for example
vier., viern.	viernes	**Fri.**	Friday
V.M.	Vuestra Majestad	—	Your Majesty
V^{O}B^O, V.^{O}B.^{O}	visto bueno	—	OK, approved
vol, vol.	volumen	**vol.**	volume
vra., vro.	vuestra, vuestro	—	your

Spanish Numbers

Cardinal Numbers

1	uno	28	veintiocho
2	dos	29	veintinueve
3	tres	30	treinta
4	cuatro	31	treinta y uno
5	cinco	40	cuarenta
6	seis	50	cincuenta
7	siete	60	sesenta
8	ocho	70	setenta
9	nueve	80	ochenta
10	diez	90	noventa
11	once	100	cien
12	doce	101	ciento uno
13	trece	200	doscientos
14	catorce	300	trescientos
15	quince	400	cuatrocientos
16	dieciséis	500	quinientos
17	diecisiete	600	seiscientos
18	dieciocho	700	setecientos
19	diecinueve	800	ochocientos
20	veinte	900	novecientos
21	veintiuno	1,000	mil
22	veintidós	1,001	mil uno
23	veintitrés	2,000	dos mil
24	veinticuatro	100,000	cien mil
25	veinticinco	1,000,000	un millón
26	veintiséis	1,000,000,000	mil millones
27	veintisiete	1,000,000,000,000	un billón

Ordinal Numbers

1st	primero, -ra	17th	decimoséptimo, -ma
2nd	segundo, -da	18th	decimoctavo, -va
3rd	tercero, -ra	19th	decimonoveno, -na; *or*
4th	cuarto, -ta		decimonono, -na
5th	quinto, -ta	20th	vigésimo, -ma
6th	sexto, -ta	21st	vigésimoprimero,
7th	séptimo, -ta		vigésimaprimera
8th	octavo, -ta	30th	trigésimo, -ma
9th	noveno, -na	40th	cuadragésimo, -ma
10th	décimo, -ma	50th	quincuagésimo, -ma
11th	undécimo, -ca	60th	sexagésimo, -ma
12th	duodécimo, -ma	70th	septuagésimo, -ma
13th	decimotercero, -ra	80th	octogésimo, -ma
14th	decimocuarto, -ta	90th	nonagésimo, -ma
15th	decimoquinto, -ta	100th	centésimo, -ma
16th	decimosexto, -ta	1,000th	milésimo, -ma

English Numbers

Cardinal Numbers

1	one	20	twenty
2	two	21	twenty-one
3	three	30	thirty
4	four	40	forty
5	five	50	fifty
6	six	60	sixty
7	seven	70	seventy
8	eight	80	eighty
9	nine	90	ninety
10	ten	100	one hundred
11	eleven	101	one hundred and one
12	twelve	200	two hundred
13	thirteen	1,000	one thousand
14	fourteen	1,001	one thousand and one
15	fifteen	2,000	two thousand
16	sixteen	100,000	one hundred thousand
17	seventeen	1,000,000	one million
18	eighteen	1,000,000,000	one billion
19	nineteen	1,000,000,000,000	one trillion

Ordinal Numbers

1st	first	16th	sixteenth
2nd	second	17th	seventeenth
3rd	third	18th	eighteenth
4th	fourth	19th	nineteenth
5th	fifth	20th	twentieth
6th	sixth	21st	twenty-first
7th	seventh	30th	thirtieth
8th	eighth	40th	fortieth
9th	ninth	50th	fiftieth
10th	tenth	60th	sixtieth
11th	eleventh	70th	seventieth
12th	twelfth	80th	eightieth
13th	thirteenth	90th	ninetieth
14th	fourteenth	100th	hundredth
15th	fifteenth	1,000th	thousandth